Westminster Commentaries

THE ACTS OF THE APOSTLES

The Acts of the Apostles

AN EXPOSITION BY
Richard Belward Rackham

Wipf and Stock Publishers
EUGENE, OREGON

Wipf and Stock Publishers
199 West 8th Avenue, Suite 3
Eugene, Oregon 97401

The Acts of the Apostles
An Exposition
By Rackham, Richard B.
ISBN: 1-59244-316-8
Publication date 9/9/2003
Previously published by Methuen & Co., Ltd., 1908

PREFATORY NOTE BY THE GENERAL EDITOR

THE primary object of these Commentaries is to be exegetical, to interpret the meaning of each book of the Bible in the light of modern knowledge to English readers. The Editors will not deal, except subordinately, with questions of textual criticism or philology; but taking the English text in the Revised Version as their basis, they will aim at combining a hearty acceptance of critical principles with loyalty to the Catholic Faith.

The series will be less elementary than the Cambridge Bible for Schools, less critical than the International Critical Commentary, less didactic than the Expositor's Bible; and it is hoped that it may be of use both to theological students and to the clergy, as well as to the growing number of educated laymen and laywomen who wish to read the Bible intelligently and reverently.

Each commentary will therefore have

(i) An Introduction stating the bearing of modern criticism and research upon the historical character of the book, and drawing out the contribution which the book, as a whole, makes to the body of religious truth.

(ii) A careful paraphrase of the text with notes on the more difficult passages and, if need be, excursuses on any

PREFATORY NOTE.

points of special importance either for doctrine, or ecclesiastical organization, or spiritual life.

But the books of the Bible are so varied in character that considerable latitude is needed, as to the proportion which the various parts should hold to each other. The General Editor will therefore only endeavour to secure a general uniformity in scope and character: but the exact method adopted in each case and the final responsibility for the statements made will rest with the individual contributors.

By permission of the Delegates of the Oxford University Press and of the Syndics of the Cambridge University Press the Text used in this Series of Commentaries is the Revised Version of the Holy Scriptures.

WALTER LOCK.

PREFACE

THE form of this commentary upon *The Acts of the Apostles* requires some words of explanation. Instead of breaking up the comment into disjointed notes, an attempt has been made to give a continuous interpretation which the reader can read straight on without interruption, just as he would read the book of *The Acts* itself. The aim has been simply to ascertain the meaning of the original text and to add the necessary information. Thus the commentary is practically a paraphrase of *The Acts*, in which the words of the text commented upon are distinguished by being printed in italics, and such general information or discussion as is required from time to time is inserted in the paraphrase in separate paragraphs: further illustration which the reader can leave on one side is relegated to footnotes. If, however, this method on the one hand aims at consulting the reader's convenience, on the other it is liable to err on the side of length and repetition, from which faults this commentary can hardly claim to be free. In the choice of this method, the idea was not absent that the book might not only serve the purpose of a commentary upon a text, but be in some small way a contribution to early church history.

The readers kept in view have been, in accordance with the general intention of the series, the educated English public who are not, technically speaking, 'scholars' or 'students': and this has carried with it some consequences. Thus the use of Greek has been avoided as much as possible. Again, as the aim has been simply to ascertain the meaning of the text, it has not been thought necessary to discuss or even to mention all the rejected interpretations of a passage, or to give the history of the various views. Of course it is not always possible for the commentator himself to understand the meaning of a passage or to make up his mind between rival views, and therefore discussion at times is necessary. But I would refer those readers who desire a full exegesis of the text to the exhaustive commentary upon *The Acts* which has recently issued from the pen of Professor Knowling in *The Expositor's Greek Testament* (Hodder and Stoughton, 1900) : I do not think that the merits of this work can be better described than by the word 'exhaustive.' The same reason has also led me to abstain from giving much reference to authorities. For this I may be blamed. But I do not advance any claim to originality, and students will without difficulty recognize the chief sources of the views adopted or information given. Perhaps, however, I ought to make special mention of the names of Professor Blass[1] and Professor Ramsay[2].

It will also be evident that the investigation of critical questions is beyond the scope of a work of this character. Accordingly I have not discussed the various theories as to the composition of *The Acts* which have been recently advanced in Germany or elsewhere. For my own part a careful study of the text by itself, apart from commentaries, has left upon my mind a deep impression of the unity of the book. It is true that in *The Acts* there can be detected differences of style and language, pointing to different sources or authorities which have been finally put together by the hands of some compiler. But the remarkable coincidences and similarities of diction which are to be found throughout shew that the final editor

---

[1] in particular for his commentary, published at Göttingen, 1895, and for his edition of the Acts in its 'Roman form,' Leipzic, 1896. [2] in particular for his *Church in the Roman Empire* (Hodder and Stoughton, 1893) and *Paul the Traveller and Roman Citizen* (H. and S. 1895); and also for the *Cities and Bishoprics of Phrygia* (Clarendon Press, 1895-7).

was no mere compiler but an author, who has either freely revised, or written down in his own language, the information supplied to him: the selection of incident, moreover, and the arrangement of the different parts of the book, shew that he was an author with a personality of his own which is impressed upon his work. Further, it is no less evident to me that this author must be the same as the final editor of *The Gospel according to S. Luke*: and, as will appear in the Introduction, I can find no adequate reasons for calling in question the testimony of tradition that this writer was S. Luke. Having this conviction, I have thought it sufficient—and sufficiently honest to the reader—to call attention in the commentary to the more obvious differences of style, at the same time vindicating their compatibility with the Lucan authorship, and to leave to scholars the fuller investigation of the sources of *The Acts* and its relation to the problem of the composition of the Gospels.

A few words must be added in explanation of the footnotes. Besides the ordinary use of footnotes for reference to authorities and the discussion of details, these also serve other purposes. Thus they are meant to supply the place of 'marginal references,' which can be studied by those who have the leisure. The number of such references may be thought excessive; but they are due to the conviction that the best commentary on a book of the Bible is first the book itself, and then the rest of the Bible, and I only regret that the text has not been sufficiently illustrated by references to the Old Testament. If the English reader is at times puzzled by a reference, its significance probably depends upon the original Greek. Again, many cross-references in *The Acts* (as also references to S. Luke's Gospel) which seem to be merely verbal have been given with a view to illustrate the unity and structure of the book. The footnotes on the text contain, besides the marginal notes of the Revised Version, the more important variations of reading in the Greek texts, of which the reader ought not to be left in ignorance. The rest have been added mainly for the further elucidation of the text or their own interest. These reasons also account for the frequent quotations from the Bezan text, which may provoke criticism. But, whatever may be our conclusion as to the origin of that text, the interest of many of its readings is undoubted.

In accordance with the rule of this series, the Revised Version has been adopted for the text. However much this Version may be open to criticism or have fallen short of the ideal of a version, it must be allowed to be a much closer representation of the original Greek than the Authorized Version. And in a commentary whose express aim is to ascertain for its readers as far as possible the exact meaning of a book, the first requirement is that it should supply them with a version as faithful to the original as possible.

For permission to vary, in other respects, both in form and method from the scheme of the *Oxford Commentaries*, I owe my warm thanks to the Editor and to the Publishers of the series. In addition I wish to thank the Editor, Dr Lock, most cordially and gratefully, for the patience with which he has read and corrected this commentary both in manuscript and proof. To another friend, Mr Walter Worrall, I am very deeply indebted for similar labour in reading the proofs and for much valuable criticism which I here gratefully acknowledge. Professor Ramsay has very kindly allowed me to make use of the map which he gives in his *Paul the Traveller* : this reprint has the advantage of his latest corrections, and here I express my cordial thanks. Had this commentary been suitable for a dedication, I should like to have inscribed upon its front page the names of the Rev. Charles Gore, and the Rev. R. C. Moberly, as a small acknowledgment that to their teaching is due whatever of theological truth may be found in these pages.

R. B. R.

S. Bartholomew's Day, 1901

PREFACE TO THE FOURTH EDITION

THE demand for a reprint of this Commentary gives me an opportunity of calling attention to two Contributions towards an Introduction to the New Testament which Dr Harnack has recently published and which are likely to mark an epoch in the history of the criticism of the *Acts of the Apostles*. These are *Lukas der Arzt der Verfasser des Dritten Evangeliums und der Apostelgeschichte*[1], published in 1906, and *Die Apostelgeschichte*[2] which only appeared this year. In these two essays Dr Harnack vindicates the unity of the Acts of the Apostles, both as regards style and subject; justifies tradition in ascribing its authorship to St Luke, "the beloved physician," companion of St Paul and author of the Gospel which bears his name; assigns to the book a high historical value; and pays a great tribute to St Luke's power of composition and the manner in which he has developed his subject. That subject is, to use Dr Harnack's words (p. 12)[3]: "The might of the Spirit of Jesus (at work) in the apostles, founding the early church, starting the mission to the Gentiles, carrying the Gospel from Jerusalem to Rome, and installing the Gentiles who receive it in the place of the Jews who more and more harden their hearts." This conservative conclusion is all the more striking, and will have the greater weight in Germany, since Dr Harnack started on his enquiry with no prepossession in its favour. On the contrary he seems still to hold as an axiom that "miracles do not happen." For though he admits that "signs and wonders" accompany every enthusiastic religious development, and finds some kernel of historical fact in most of the miracles recorded in the Acts, yet he holds that the account of the Ascension must

---

[1] i.e. "Luke the physician, the author of the third Gospel and of the Acts of the Apostles." An English translation of this has been published by Messrs Williams and Norgate. [2] i.e. "the Apostles' History" or "the Acts of the Apostles."
[3] This and the subsequent references refer to the *Apostelgeschichte*.

be—like the accounts of the appearances of the Risen Christ in the Gospels—legendary, while the account of Pentecost is an exaggerated doublet of what is narrated in iv 31. The chief fault which he finds in St Luke is his readiness to believe in miraculous healings (p. 18).

It is especially gratifying to learn that Dr Harnack does not find any inconsistency between the Acts and the Pauline Epistles, or between the pictures of St Paul which we derive from these sources respectively. In particular he finds no contradiction between Acts xv and Galatians ii. This will, he declares, transform whole libraries of exegesis into monuments of the history of a great error (p. 197); for this contradiction has been taken for an axiom by German criticism. He solves the difficulty found in the apostolic decree by dealing with the text. On the authority of the Western Fathers with some textual support he strikes out the words *and from things strangled*. The demand will then run that the Gentile Christians are to abstain *from idol meats, and from blood, and from fornication*, i.e. from idolatry, murder, and fornication. The moral precepts were a part of the Law no less than the ceremonial ones; hence, in conceding to the Gentile Christians freedom from the Law, it was necessary to reaffirm the Moral Law under its chief heads (pp. 188–193).

Most interesting to myself, however, is Dr Harnack's discussion of the date of the Acts. He starts in his *Apostelgeschichte* with the assumption that St Luke wrote "in the time of the Flavian Caesars," but in an excursus at the end of the essay (pp. 217–221) he gives six weighty reasons for supposing that the Acts was written at a date soon after the events recorded at the end of the book, and before the death of St Paul,—a date for which I have pleaded in this Commentary. Dr Harnack's arguments may be briefly summarized thus : (1) This date offers the simplest explanation of the way in which the book ends. (2) It explains the contradiction between Acts xx 25, 38 and the genuine information given in the Pastoral Epistles. (3) The position of the Jews both of Judaea and of the Dispersion, as described in the Acts, corresponds to their condition before A.D. 66: after that year it was quite altered. Why is St Luke silent as to what happened after A.D. 66? He notes the fulfilment of the prophecy of the famine (xi 28); but is silent about the fulfilment of the prophecy of the destruction of Jerusalem—to record which would have been very much to his purpose. (4) It is not at all certain that the destruction of Jerusalem is described in Luke xxi: for there the end of the world and the coming of the Son of Man are bound up with the destruction of the city, and we read that "this generation shall not pass away until *all* these things be fulfilled" (ver. 32). But this was not the case. Also the Christians fled to Pella, not "to the mountains" (ver. 21). (5) The earlier date makes it easier to understand why St Luke made no use of the Pauline Epistles. (6) The word "Christ" has not yet become a personal name, but stands for "the Messiah." So "Christian" is not yet used by the Christians of themselves, nor has it become a term of reproach as in 1 Peter iv 14, 16.

Against these arguments Dr Harnack only advances two as of real weight for the later date: (1) The prophecy of Luke xxi in some important points describes what actually happened at the destruction of Jerusalem. (2) There was not time before A.D. 70 for the legends of the Resurrection appearances and the Ascension to have been developed. Dr Harnack admits that the case is doubtful. He does indeed own that "it is not difficult to judge on which side the greater weight of the arguments lies"; but on the other hand he reminds us of the critical rule that "the more far-reaching the consequences of a decision, the greater must be our caution in accepting it." Therefore, he concludes (p. 221), "for the present time this must be our judgement: Luke wrote in the time of Titus [A.D. 79-81] or in the earlier years of Domitian [A.D. 81-96], but perhaps at the beginning of the sixties (*vielleicht aber schon am Anfang der sechziger Jahre*)."

R. B. RACKHAM.

St Andrew's Day, 1908.

CONTENTS

INTRODUCTION

		PAGE
Chapter I	*The Book*	
§ 1	*its history*	xiii
§ 2	*its author*	xv
§ 3	*its unity*	xvii
§ 4	*its text*	xxi
Chapter II	*The Author*	
§ 1	*his history*	xxvii
§ 2	*his character*	xxxii
Chapter III	*The Composition of the Acts*	
§ 1	*the author's aim*	xxxviii
§ 2	*his sources*	xli
§ 3	*his trustworthiness*	xliv
§ 4	*his method*	xlvii
§ 5	*the date of publication*	l
Chapter IV	*The History of the Acts*	
§ 1	*the political and social environment*	lv
§ 2	*the analysis of the history*	lxi
§ 3	*the chronology*	lxv
Chapter V	*The Theology of the Acts*	
§ 1	*the theology*	lxix
§ 2	*the soteriology*	lxxvi
§ 3	*the divine will*	lxxviii
Chapter VI	*The Church and Ministry in the Acts*	
§ 1	*general survey of the history*	lxxix
§ 2	*offices and ministries*	xc
The Analysis of the Acts		cix
Chronological Table		cxii
Addenda		cxvi

CONTENTS

THE ACTS OF THE APOSTLES

PART I THE ACTS OF PETER

		PAGE
Division I	*The beginnings of the Church at Jerusalem*	3
	ch. i	3
	ch. ii	16
	ch. iii	47
	ch. iv	55
	ch. v	64
Division II	*The extension of the Church to Antioch*	81
	ch. vi	81
	ch. vii	95
	ch. viii	110
	ch. ix	128
	ch. x	148
	ch. xi	160
Division III	*The 'passing' of Peter*	171
	ch. xii	175

PART II THE ACTS OF PAUL

Division I	*The work of Paul and Barnabas*	187
	ch. xiii	188
	ch. xiv	228
	ch. xv	243
	ch. xvi	262
Division II	*Extension of the Church in the Roman Empire* (xvi 6)	271
	ch. xvii	294
	ch. xviii	322
	ch. xix	345
Division III	*The 'passing' of Paul* (xix 21)	358
	ch. xx	370
	ch. xxi	397
	ch. xxii	419

CONTENTS

Division III *The 'passing' of Paul (continued)*

		PAGE
ch. xxiii	. . . .	431
ch. xxiv	. . . .	442
ch. xxv	. . . .	453
ch. xxvi	. . . .	465
ch. xxvii	. . . .	479
ch. xxviii	. . . .	491

Index 515

Map of the Eastern Mediterranean 514

AND THE WALL OF THE CITY HAD TWELVE FOUNDATIONS
AND ON THEM TWELVE NAMES
OF THE TWELVE APOSTLES OF THE LAMB

THOU ART PETER: AND UPON THIS ROCK I WILL BUILD MY CHURCH
HE IS A CHOSEN VESSEL UNTO ME, TO BEAR MY NAME

LUKE THE BELOVED PHYSICIAN

ABBREVIATIONS

N.B. In the commentary words of the text or their equivalent are printed in <u>italics</u>.

OT, NT = Old Testament, New Testament
  LXX   = the Septuagint Version
AV, RV = the Authorized Version, the Revised Version
  TR   = the Received Text
  WH   = Westcott and Hort's text (Camb. 1890)
  Marg = margin (of the RV)
  Gk   = Greek
  Bezan = the Bezan text (pp. xxiii–vi)

⁎ The Bezan readings are taken from Codex Bezae, or from Professor Blass' restoration of the text in his *Acta Apostolorum secundum formam quae videtur romanam*, Leipzic, 1896.

INTRODUCTION

CHAPTER I

The Book

We can hardly overestimate the importance of *The Acts of the Apostles*. After the Gospel according to S. Luke, it is the longest book in the New Testament. More than this, it is our chief authority, whether within or without the Bible, for the history of the founding of the church and its early growth. To it we owe almost all we know of the first spreading of Christianity in Syria and its arrival in Asia Minor and Europe; of the original gospel preached by the apostles; of the life and work of S. Peter, S. Stephen, and (apart from the notices in his epistles) of S. Paul. Such an authority calls for very careful study; and first we must examine the book itself.

§ 1 *Its history*

The oldest copies of our book of the Acts are contained in the oldest Greek manuscripts of the New Testament. Of these there are two which were written in the fourth century, viz. the celebrated Codex Vaticanus or B, and Codex Sinaiticus or ℵ. In B our book is found after the Gospel of S. John under the heading *PRAXEIS APOSTOLÔN* or *THE ACTS OF THE APOSTLES*: in ℵ, with the simpler title *PRAXEIS* or *ACTS*[1], it comes after S. Paul's epistles. Besides these two manuscripts, about eight other uncial MSS, written between the fifth and tenth centuries, contain the Acts—but in a more or less incomplete condition; for only two MSS (A and S) contain an entire copy. After the ninth century minuscule Greek MSS take the place of uncials, and among these have been counted about 370 copies of the Acts.

---

[1] But the fuller title occurs in the subscription of the book and is by the original hand: see Dr J. Armitage Robinson in *Euthaliana* (*Texts & Studies* III 3) p. 16.

Besides Greek manuscripts, there are manuscript versions of the scriptures, which will carry our history of the Acts still further back. For though the existing copies of the versions were written later than e.g. B and ℵ, the original versions of which they are copies may have been made earlier; and in the case of the Acts we have grounds for believing that it was translated into Syriac, Coptic, and Latin, during the course of the third century, if not before.

After B and ℵ the most important Greek MSS of the Acts are two written in the fifth century, *Codex Alexandrinus* (A) now in the British Museum, and *Codex Ephraemi* (C), a palimpsest MS at Paris: and then two MSS of the sixth century, *Codex Bezae* (D) at Cambridge, and *Codex Laudianus* (E) at Oxford. The special interest of D will appear below. The other uncial authorities are *Codex Laurensis* ii (S) at Mt Athos, of the eighth century: *Codices Mutinensis* (H) at Modena, *Angelicus* (L) at Rome, and *Porphyrianus* (P) at S. Petersburg, which date only from the ninth century: and some fragments.

The ordinary SYRIAC version is the *Peshitta*. This version was made in the fourth or fifth century and was probably a revision of earlier translations. Only slight traces however of the Acts in an earlier form have been found; but there is evidence[1] for a Syriac translation of the Acts as early as the beginning of the third century. In the sixth century a revision of the Peshitta itself was made, which received its final form in A.D. 616 from Thomas of Harkel. It is known as the Philoxenian or Harkleian Syriac, and is important for containing so many 'western readings,' on which see below, p. xxiii. The chief versions of the NT into COPTIC are the *Bohairic* of Alexandria and lower Egypt, and the *Sahidic* of upper Egypt. The *Bohairic* is probably not older than the sixth or seventh century, but the *Sahidic* may date from the fourth or even the third century; and fragments of translations into other dialects, perhaps as early or earlier, have been and are still being found. The present LATIN *Vulgate* version was made by S. Jerome between the years 383 and 405. Previous to this edition there had not been a fixed version for the whole Latin-speaking church, and the manuscripts of translations previous to the Vulgate which have come down to us differ very widely from one another. They, again, are very important for their evidence as to the 'western readings.'

The Acts was first printed in Greek in 1514 by Cardinal Ximenes for his 'Complutensian edition' of the scriptures: but it was first published in Erasmus' New Testament in 1516. In English the first printed edition was that of Tyndale, in 1525: the 'Authorized Version' was published in 1611, the 'Revised Version' in 1881.

In ascertaining the date and history of a book besides MSS and versions there is another source of information open to us, i.e. its use by other writers. And this will often carry us a good way behind our manuscripts. For instance Tertullian of Carthage and Clement of Alexandria, who both flourished about A.D. 200, quote the Acts frequently, under the titles *(the) Acts* or *(the) Acts of (the) Apostles*. Still more important is the use made of it by S. Irenaeus, the bishop of Lyons: in his work *Against the heresies*, written between 174 and 189, he quotes or summarizes whole chapters. The list of the books of the New Testament known as the *Muratorian Canon*, which was probably drawn up between 170 and 200, describes the *Acts* in its usual place. The earliest undoubted quotation from the Acts to which we can

---

[1] e.g. in the tenth canon of the Syriac *Doctrine of the Apostles* (of the early fourth century). For this and other information in this paragraph I am indebted to Mr F. C. Burkitt.

point occurs in the letter of the churches of Vienne and Lyons which was addressed to the churches of Asia and Phrygia in A.D. 177. In giving an account of the terrible persecution the churches had endured, the letter describes the martyrs as 'praying like Stephen the perfect martyr, *Lord, lay not this sin to their charge*.' But the earliest Christian writings outside the New Testament, those of the Apostolic Fathers, contain many reminiscences and echoes as it were of the language of the Acts. That we do not find more definite quotations in early times need not surprise us. Very little of the Christian literature of the first two centuries has come down to us; so there is not a large field in which to look for quotations. Further, it would take some time for a book of the character of the Acts to win its way into the Canon and become recognized as an authority. It was not always (nor even usually) copied with the Gospels, and we may infer that in the early centuries it was not very widely known. Even in the fourth century, when beginning a course of sermons upon the Acts, S. Chrysostom speaks of the book as being familiar to very few.

In S. CLEMENT's epistle, written about A.D. 95, we read *to whom God said I have found a man after my heart, David the son of Jesse* (ch. 18), a collocation which elsewhere is found only in Acts xiii 22: *more gladly giving than receiving* (2) and *especially remembering the words of the Lord Jesus which he spake* (13) remind us of Acts xx 35: with *let him give thanks to God being in a good conscience* (41) compare Acts xxiii 1: with (*Peter*) *went to his due place of glory* and (*Paul*) *went to the holy place* (5) cp. Acts i 25. S. IGNATIUS also, writing about A.D. 115, has a parallel to Judas' *going to his own place*, viz. *and each is about to go to his own place* (*Magnes.* 5). His statement that *after the resurrection* (*the Lord*) *ate with them and drank with them as being of flesh* (*Smyrn.* 3) seems based on Acts x 41. More striking evidence of familiarity with the Acts is to be found in S. POLYCARP's letter to the Philippians, written a few years after S. Ignatius' death. In this short letter we find all these phrases—*whom God raised having loosed the pains of Hades, who is coming as judge of quick and dead, remembering what the Lord said, the prophets which preached before of the coming of our Lord, if we suffer because of the name, may he give you part and lot* (cp. Acts ii 24, x 42, xx 35, vii 52, v 41, viii 21). In the account of S. Polycarp's own martyrdom A.D. 156, we read that *though he could have gone away to another place, yet he refused, saying 'the will of God be done'* (cp. Acts xxi 14). The knowledge of the events narrated in the Acts is at the base of most of the apocryphal Acts and Stories of the Apostles which were composed in great numbers in the second and third centuries.

§ 2 *Its author*

Who was the author of the Acts? To this question, so important to us, no answer is given by the book itself. Nor is any name given in its title in the Greek manuscripts before the tenth century: we simply read *THE ACTS OF THE APOSTLES*. The very first verses however tell us that the book is the continuation of a former volume. And this volume can be none other than that which is entitled *KATA LOUKAN* or (*THE GOSPEL*) *ACCORDING TO LUKE*. Both books begin with a similar preface: both are addressed to the same person, the *kratistos Theophilos* (*most excellent Theophilus*): and the style and vocabulary of both are so much alike, that we should have concluded independently that they came from the same pen. If then S. Luke was the author of the Gospel which bears his name, he also wrote the second volume or the Acts of the Apostles.

This is also the view of tradition. Certainly Clement of Alexandria, Tertullian, and Irenaeus, all speak of *LUCAS* or S. Luke as the author, as if there was no doubt upon the subject. The Muratorian Canon tells us that *the acts of all the apostles were written in one book: Luke compiled them for the most excellent Theophilus because they severally took place in his presence.*

The book of the Acts itself however contains independent evidence that S. Luke was its writer. In xvi 10 the pronoun *we* appears, and the narrative is continued in the first person to verse 17. The *we* reappears in xx 6, and the use of the first person is more or less continuous till the end of the book (xxviii 16). This shews that the writer was at these times (at least) in the company of S. Paul. Now from S. Paul's epistles we can draw up a list of his companions during or shortly after the latter period. The Epistles to the Ephesians, Colossians, Philippians, and Philemon, were written during the apostle's first imprisonment at Rome, and from them we learn that there were with him—Epaphroditus and Epaphras; Timothy, Tychicus, Aristarchus, and Mark; Jesus Justus, Luke, and Demas. The first two joined him after his arrival at Rome and so are excluded from the claim to authorship of the Acts. The next four are excluded by their mention in the Acts, Demas by his subsequent abandonment of the apostle (II Tim iv 10), and we are left with Jesus Justus and Luke. S. Paul's last epistle, the second to Timothy, written from Rome just before the close of his life, gives us some further names. Of these some are Roman Christians and recent friends of the apostle (Eubulus, Pudens, Linus, Claudia); others have appeared in the Acts (Prisca, Aquila, Erastus, and Trophimus); and we are left with Crescens, Titus, and Luke. Crescens and Jesus Justus may now be eliminated. There is no hint of their having been specially intimate with S. Paul, or in his company as early as the second journey (ch. xvi). The case is different with Titus. Titus was most intimately connected with the apostle; he was 'his own child in the faith'; and in the innermost circle of S. Paul's disciples Titus shared the first place with Timothy. There is indeed no direct evidence that he was with S. Paul during the 'we' periods of the Acts. But he was with the apostle at the council of Jerusalem (Gal ii 1), which was just before the first period; and we are led on to notice the further surprising fact that this important minister of the apostle is not once mentioned in the Acts at all. A natural inference would be that he himself was the author of the book; or if tradition is right in calling the author 'Luke,' that he and Luke are identical, and that like the Titus Justus of xviii 7, Luke's real name was Titus Lucas. Certainly the Epistle to Titus is just such an one as S. Paul might have written to S. Luke, and the identification would throw a wonderful light on the history. Tempting however or even fascinating as it is, this hypothesis must be rejected in face of the decisive evidence of II Tim iv 10 (*Titus is gone to Dalmatia; only Luke is with me*) that Titus and Luke were distinct persons. Finding then no rival claimant, we accept the voice of tradition which is unanimous in ascribing the Gospel and Acts to S. Luke: and the more readily, as there was no other reason why S. Luke should have been selected. He is otherwise practically an unknown person. We have only two brief notices of him in the NT; and these entirely agree with the hypothesis of his authorship. *Only Luke is with me* (2 Tim iv 10)—and certainly the Acts is stamped with fidelity to S. Paul. *Luke the beloved physician* (Col iv 14)—and certainly, the hint once given us, we can recognize in the Gospel and the Acts the technical language and the accurate observation of a doctor. We can then without hesitation conclude that both the Gospel and the Acts were written by S. Luke, the companion of S. Paul. And this conclusion will give us a limit for the date of the Acts. It must have been composed in the lifetime of one who had been a contemporary of S. Paul.

§ 3 *Its unity*

This conclusion however is based upon an assumption that the Acts was written as a whole by a writer who includes himself when he uses the first person 'we.' It would be seriously affected if the Acts is a compilation from various sources and writings (including a diary or journey-document, from which the 'we' passages are taken and which may or may not have been written by S. Luke's hand) which were not worked up into the Acts in its present form until well on in the second century. This is the theory of a school of critics, who spend their energy upon the work of breaking up the Acts into its original parts. The most elaborate theory is that of Dr C. Clemen. He finds four sources—a 'History of the Hellenists,' a 'History of Peter,' a 'History of Paul' with a 'Journey of Paul.' These have been put together and the result revised and re-edited by three successive editors, of whom the second was favourably disposed to the Jews, the last the reverse. The last editor left the compilation as we find it in the middle of the second century.

Now this method of compiling books was not unknown to antiquity; it prevailed especially in oriental and Jewish literature. As examples of such composite works we have in the Old Testament the Pentateuch, in apocryphal literature the Book of Enoch, among early Christian writings the Apostolical Constitutions. Again no doubt the Acts is in a sense a composite work: the author has had to make use of many different sources of information and perhaps documents; thus for instance the early chapters, or roughly speaking Part I, are marked off from the rest of the book by their strong Hebraic character. And yet on studying the Acts we find it stamped with a remarkable unity both in subject and style. The unity of idea in the composition will, we trust, appear from the commentary. The unity of style is shewn by the recurrence of the special phraseology and grammatical usages of the writer throughout the book; and they mark the 'we' passages no less than the rest of the book. In fact the various sources have been so welded or woven together into a whole, that it would be extremely hard to separate even paragraphs that at first sight may appear to be of a different character from the rest. There is a certain distinction, speaking roughly, between the two halves of the book, viz. ch. i-xii and ch. xiii-xxviii: as to this all would agree. Beyond this, however, no general agreement has been arrived at among scholars as to the different documents which are postulated as the sources of the Acts. Further, this unity takes in not only the Acts but the Gospel of S. Luke, with the scheme of which we find a distinct parallelism in the Acts[1].

We conclude, then, that there is a real unity in the Acts and that the final compiler of the Acts, whoever he was or whenever he lived, was a man of real literary power. He was not merely a compiler but an author: in fact a 'S. Luke.' But it is a maxim among philosophers that we are not 'to multiply entities beyond what is necessary.' Why then should we suppose a second S. Luke living in the second century? There certainly was a Luke (or other companion of S. Paul) who wrote the 'we' diary or journey-document in the first century—why do we require another? The introduction of this second Luke in the second century will only complicate matters, by causing (1) a conflict with the unanimous voice of tradition, (2) an unnatural and unjustifiable use of the first person, and (3) difficulties about the Gospel, which most critics would now allow to have assumed its present form by the year 80.

The theory however would be borne out, or made necessary, if our author made use of the works of Josephus, who was writing up to the year 100. Undoubtedly S. Luke and Josephus sometimes refer to the same events, and they have many words and phrases in common; some being peculiar to these two authors. A noteworthy parallel is when Josephus himself said to the people of Tiberias 'I do not refuse to die, if it is just[2].' On the other hand our two authors were almost contemporaries; they dealt with the same scenes, races, and country, and often similar situations; and they were both familiar with the Old Testament. It would be surprising if there were not some agreement. With regard to special verbal coincidences, we must remember that S. Luke, who was well read, may have read the same historians that Josephus used for his authorities[3]. Besides in matters of detail, e.g. concerning Theudas, S. Luke sometimes differs from Josephus[4]. No crucial instance has been found to prove S. Luke's use of Josephus; and we may quite as well maintain that Josephus used S. Luke, as *vice versâ*.

It is not necessary to labour the question of unity of style in the Acts, as most scholars accept it as almost self-evident. It is a matter which depends largely upon literary sense and perception, and detailed arguments about the style of a Greek composition can hardly be reproduced in a work for English readers. One or two general remarks however may be made about S. Luke's writing. His opening preface (Lk i 1-4) shews that he was master of a good

---

[1] Sir J. C. Hawkins in his *Horae Synopticae* (1899) has collected very weighty statistical evidence from the Gospel and Acts, and the we-sections in particular, as to their unity of authorship. [2] *Vita* 29; cp. S. Paul in Acts xxv 11. The sentiment itself is not so rare as to prove plagiarism. [3] As Dr Vogel suggests in his *Zur Characteristik des Lukas* etc. pp. 57-61. [4] See p. 74 and note.

Greek style. His familiarity with Greek and Greek literature is also shewn by his vocabulary. He is very fond of using rare, very often classical and poetical, words: in fact we can hardly take a single paragraph without coming across some striking or peculiar word. Thus in the Gospel and Acts there are about 750 words peculiar to S. Luke in the NT, and of these 440 occur only in the Acts[1]. In spite however of this classical learning, S. Luke's writing has a strong Hebraic or Aramaic tinge, not only when he is using Aramaic sources, but throughout. This is to be accounted for by familiarity with 'the scriptures,' i.e. the Old Testament. S. Luke is, as we should say of an English writer, very 'biblical.' There was also another influence at work which would tend to the same result, viz. the society of S. Paul. S. Paul was a Hebrew of the Hebrews, he was saturated, so to speak, with the scriptures, and his tone of conversation and thought must have been 'biblical' to a degree. The effect of S. Paul's influence on S. Luke is quite evident. The 'Gospel according to Luke' is very much what a 'Gospel according to Paul' would have been, and in Acts xiii 38-39 we have the specially Pauline doctrine of justification by faith. But the more personal and particular influence of S. Paul's conversation on S. Luke's style is seen in the list, which Dr Plummer has drawn up in his commentary on S. Luke[2], of 174 expressions which occur in S. Luke's and S. Paul's writings and nowhere else in the NT.

Points of style and vocabulary[3]

To illustrate the above statements we have as instances of Hebraic language and idea the use of *the Name* (34 times): *the Lord*, i.e. JEHOVAH, e.g. *hand* (xi 21, xiii 11), *angel, spirit, way, day* (ii 20, xvii 31)—*of the Lord: day—in, after, before* (v 36, xxi 38) *these (those) days, until this day* (ii 29, xxiii 1), *the days of, these days, days of unleavened bread* (xii 3, xx 6), *day of Pentecost* (ii 1, xx 16), *night and day* etc.: *soul* especially = person (ii 41, xxvii 37), *heart, lift up the voice* (ii 14, xiv 11), *with a loud voice* (vii 57, xxvi 24), *open the mouth* (viii 35, xviii 14), *through the mouth of* (i 16, xv 7), *by the hand of* (ii 23, xv 23), *from, in, into, through the hand (hands) of, lay on hands, on the way* (viii 36, xxv 3, xxvi 13), *way* = manner of life (twelve times), *house* = household (x 2, xviii 8: xi 14, xvi 31), *word* = subject of the word, or thing, *rise-up and, coming in and going out, before* (God), *in, from, before —the face of* (iii 13, xxv 16), *in, from—the midst of, behold : full of* (vi 5, xiii 10), *filled with* (ii 4, xiii 9 etc.), *fulfil* (cp. ii 1, xix 21: ii 28, xiv 26). Some of these occur throughout; the few references given are to parallels between the first and second divisions of the Acts (i–xii, xiii–xxiv), illustrating the unity of the book.

Out of the numerous words found only in the Acts (or Acts and Lk) it will suffice to give a few which at the same time afford evidence of the unity of the work—*language* (i 19, ii 6, 8, xxi 40, xxii 2, xxvi 14), *upper chamber* (i 13, ix 37, 39, xx 8), *which-knowest-the-heart* (i 24, xv 8), *suddenly* (ii 2, xvi 26, xxviii 6), *wind*, i.e. breath (ii 2, xvii 25), *confound* (ii 6, ix 22, xix 32, xxi 27, 31; *confusion* xix 29), *to utter* or *speak-forth* (ii 4, 14, xxvi 25), *sojourn* (ii 10, xvii 21), *mock* (ii 13, cp. xvii 32), *gladness* (ii 28, xiv 17), *foresee* (ii 31, cp. xxi 29, ii 25), *receive* (ii 41, xxiv 3 etc.), *make-strong* (iii 7, 16, xvi 5), *appoint* (iii 20, xxii 14, xxvi 16), followed *after*, i.e. *in order* (iii 24, xi 4, xviii 23), *sore-troubled* (iv 2, xvi 18), *eventide* (iv 3, xxviii 23), *builders* (iv 11, cp. vii 47, ix 31, xx 32), *public* (v 18, cp. xvi 37, xx 20), *violence*

---

[1] The numbers are taken from Dr Plummer and Prof. Blass respectively. An extreme estimate is that in Dr Thayer's *NT Lexicon*, which counts doubtful cases and gives 851 and 478. [2] In the *International Critical Commentary*. It contains an exhaustive treatment of the subject. [3] The references etc. have the Greek in view.

(v 26, xxiv 7, xxi 35, xxvii 41), *slay* (v 30, xxvi 21), *seize* (vi 12, xix 29, xxvii 15), *call-for* (vii 14, x 32, xx 17, xxiv 25), *nourished*, i.e. *brought up* (vii 20, 21, xxii 3), *time of-forty-years* (vii 23, xiii 18), *in-their-turn* lit. *having-succeeded* (vii 45, cp. xxiv 27), *thrust-out* (vii 45, xxvii 39), *young-man* (vii 58, xx 9, xxiii 17), *noon* (viii 26 marg, xxii 6), *lead-by-the-hand* (ix 8, xiii 11, xxii 11), *plot* (ix 24, xx 3, 19, xxiii 30), *went about*, i.e. *attempted* (ix 29, xix 13), *send-for* (x 5, xx 1 etc.), *talk-with* (x 27, cp. xx 11, xxiv 26), *without-gainsaying* (x 29, cp. xix 36), *doing-good* (x 38, cp. xiv 17), *expound* (xi 4, xviii 26, xxviii 23), *according to his ability* or *wealth* (xi 29, cp. xix 25), *beckoning* (xii 17, xiii 16, xix 33), *stir* (xii 18, xix 23).

Other interesting verbal parallels between the two parts are: *depart from* (i 4, xviii 1, 2), *set* (i 7, xx 28), *shall-be a witness* (i 8, xxii 15), *become* and *be it known* (i 19, ix 42, xix 17; ii 14, iv 10, xiii 38, xxviii 28), *number* or *count with* (i 26, cp. xix 19), *what meaneth this?* (ii 12, xvii 20, cp. 18), *know assuredly* or *certainly* (ii 36, xxi 34, xxii 30, cp. v 23, xvi 23, 24), *the Righteous* (iii 14, vii 52, xxii 14), *grant* (iii 14, xxv 11, 16, xxvii 24), *had-in-honour* or *precious* (v 34, xx 24), *take-heed-to yourselves* (v 35, xx 28), *beat* (v 40, xvi 37, xxii 19), *are these things so?* (vii 1, xvii 11, xxiv 9), *there came a voice* (vii 31, x 13, xix 34, ii 6), *became full-of-trembling* or *in-a-tremor*, or *all-of-a-tremble* (vii 32, xvi 29), *consent* (viii 1, xxii 20), *became full-of-fear* or *afraid* (x 4, xxii 9 AV, xxiv 25), *rushed with-one-accord* (vii 57, xix 29), *the saints* (ix 13, 32, 41, xxvi 10), *proving* (ix 22, xix 33), *an angel of God* (x 3, xxvii 23), *Christian* (xi 26, xxvi 28), *should be*, or *there-was-about-to-be* with the future infinitive, a classical idiom found only in the Acts (xi 28, xxiii 30, xxiv 15, xxvii 10).

The following are a few of the more interesting words of S. Luke which elsewhere in the NT occur only in S. Paul's writings: *apostleship* (i 25), *look-stedfastly* or *fasten-eyes-upon* (iii 4), *grant-as-a-favour* (iii 14), *set-at-nought* (iv 11), *foreordain* (iv 28), *safety* (v 23), *ordinance* (vii 53), *consent* (viii 1), *the word of the Lord* (viii 25 etc.), *make havock* (ix 21), *prove* (ix 22), *speak-* or *preach-boldly* (ix 27 etc.), *reading* (xiii 15), *course* (xiii 25), *thrust-from* (xiii 46), *ordain* or *appoint* (xiv 23), *keep-quiet* (xi 18), *decree* (xvi 4), *gain* (xvi 19), *turn-upside-down* (xvii 6), *readiness-of-mind* (xvii 11), *provoke* (xvii 16), *object-of-worship* (xvii 23), *shorn* (xviii 18), *fervent in spirit* (xviii 25), *companion-in-travel* (xix 29), *rash* (xix 36), *regular* or *lawful* (xix 39), *purchase* (xx 28), *help* (xx 35), *evangelist* (xxi 8), *walk-orderly* (xxi 24), *citizenship* (xxii 28), *live-as-a-citizen* (xxiii 1), *curse* (xxiii 12), *providence* (xxiv 2), *clemency* (xxiv 4), *void-of-offence* (xxiv 16), *indulgence* (xxiv 23), *injury* and *loss* (xxvii 10), *barbarian* and *kindness* (xxviii 2), *lodging* (xxviii 23), *salvation* (xxviii 28).

Many of the words peculiar to S. Luke are technical terms due to the wide fields of experience covered by the book. Thus there are official and military terms: *proconsul, lictor, politarch, quaternion, horsemen, spearmen* etc. Others connected with imprisonment obviously reflect the apostles' experience. Others are connected with navigation. Of these, as we should expect, chapter xxvii is full; but elsewhere in the book we have a sign of S. Luke's familiarity with the sea in these words which he alone uses: *sail-across, -away, -under, -past, -slowly, make-a-straight-course*.

There are similar signs of S. Luke's medical knowledge. Dr Hobart has written a book on the subject[1] and adduced a multitude of instances. Some of these are rather forced, but enough remains to convince us that in the Acts we follow the pen of a physician. We need only notice here that these words are peculiar to the Acts in the NT: *feet* (lit. *steps*) and *ankle bones* (iii 7), *healing* (iv 22, 30, cp. xxviii 27), *scales* (ix 18), *mist* (xiii 11), *swollen* (xxviii 6), *dysentery* (xxviii 8). *Sharp-contention* (lit. *paroxysm*) in xv 39 is also a medical term. Many of the passages about healing shew a scientific diagnosis; and a doctor's interest is to be observed in the details of iv 22, ix 33 and xix 12. In xx 9 it is carefully remarked that Eutychus was 'taken up dead,' without a positive statement that he was actually dead. In this connexion are to be observed the frequent references to the taking of *food* and its effects, e.g. ii 42, ix 19, x 10, xvi 34, cp. xx 11: as also to the effects of *fasting* (xxvii 21, 33–36).

---

[1] *The Medical Language of S. Luke*, 1882.

§ 4 *Its text*

The discovery and study of ancient manuscripts and versions since the publication of our Authorized Version (AV) in 1611 has shewn that the text of the AV varies greatly from that of the earliest authorities. This fact has been made patent to the English reader by the difference between the AV and the Revised Version (RV) published in 1881. The differences are numerous rather than important; no doctrine or historical event is affected by them, although in the Acts we lose in the new text several whole verses. But we have a natural desire to ascertain as far as possible the correct readings, i.e. the actual words written by the author. This is the aim of textual criticism; and though its attainment is still very far off, yet some very great steps have been made towards it. Thus it has been found that the whole mass of authorities,—manuscripts, versions, and quotations,—can be distributed under two or three types or 'families' of text. These families were already current in the fourth or fifth centuries, and the textual critics have to decide between their rival claims. For the reader who is not an independent critic the choice practically lies as follows.

(1) **The AV or Syrian Text.** The AV was translated from the *Received Text* (TR) of the Greek Testament, i.e. Stephanus' third edition of 1550. The first editions of the Greek Testament had been prepared from a very few and late MSS; and for Stephanus' text only a few similar authorities[1] were consulted in addition, so that the TR has no substantial claim in itself to represent the most correct form of text[2]. Making allowance however for the errors that have crept in through centuries of transcription, we find that the AV practically represents the text that was current at Constantinople and in the east about the beginning of the fifth century and which has prevailed there since. Dean Burgon stoutly maintained this to be the original form; but few critics would agree with him. The majority would accept the judgement of Dr Hort and Bp Westcott. These critics came to the conclusion that the TR represents a revision of the text made in Antioch or Syria in the fourth century; and accordingly they christened it the *Syrian Text*.

(2) **WH or the Neutral Text.** Their own edition of the NT published in 1881 (WH) represents the extreme of divergence from the AV and the highwater mark of criticism. Its characteristic is the great weight assigned to the famous *Codex Vaticanus* or B. This is indeed our most valuable and ancient MS: it was probably written at the beginning of the fourth century; and WH practically give us its text. This they assert to be a *neutral* text, lying between the divergences made in different directions and therefore going back as close as possible to the autographs of the apostolic writers. It would perhaps be safer to describe it with Dr Salmon[3] as giving us the text as revised by the scholars of Alexandria in the second and third centuries.

---

[1] They included however D; but not much weight was assigned to it. [2] The claim to be the *received text* was first made in the Elzevir edition of 1633. [3] In his *Textual Criticism of the NT* (Murray, 1897).

(3) **The RV or Eclectic Text.** For those who are not prepared to assign such overwhelming authority to B, a middle course is offered by the text of the Revised Version. This, without identifying itself with any 'family,' contains all those modifications of the Received Text which are required by the mass of ancient authorities and which would be accepted by the majority of critics, apart from that school which still adheres to the TR.

Comparison of the AV and RV texts

It may be useful to have a summary of the changes in the RV due to the adoption of a different text. This list does not profess to be exhaustive, and only those passages are noted where the change can be detected by the English reader. The classification is according to the differences in the Greek, and an asterisk marks the more interesting or important places. The changes can be divided into (i) omissions, (ii) additions, (iii) alterations.

i. *Omissions.* (A) Most striking is the disappearance of a number of clauses, sentences, or even whole texts, such as in vii 37, ix 5–6, x 6, 32, xv 24, xviii 21, xxi 22, 25, xxii 9, xxiii 9, xxiv 26; some however are retained in the margin, e.g. viii 37, xv 34, xx 15, xxiv 6–8, xxviii 16, 29.   (B) Some omissions slightly affect the sense or detail of the narrative, most often by simply making it more brief. See i 14, ii 23, 30*, 31, 47*, iii 6, iv 24, v 16, 24, 28, 32, 41, vii 32, x 11, 12, 30*, xiii 42*, xv 17–8*, 23*, xvi 6*, xvii 26*, xviii 17, xix 9, xx 24*, xxiii 30, xxiv 23. In the sacred name, *Jesus* is omitted in iii 26, ix 29, xix 10; *Christ* in xv 11, xvi 31, xix 4, xx 21 (marg).   (C) A number of explanatory words or phrases appear to have gradually been inserted in the original text with a view of making the meaning clearer or the style smoother. These accordingly have disappeared in the RV, with the effect of making the narrative more graphic and vigorous. Such are e.g. connecting particles—ii 42, iii 22, viii 33, xiii 46, xviii 15, xx 28, 29, 34, xxiv 16: *said* or *saying*—ii 38, v 9, 25, ix 5, xix 2, xxv 22, xxvi 28, 29: pronouns—i 16, iii 13, v 5, 18, 32, 41, vii 31, 43, xi 9, 13, xii 9, xiii 19, 40, xiv 13, xv 36, xvii 18, xviii 20, xix 3, 12, xx 32, xxiv 20: the substitution of the noun for pronoun—ix 19, 26, x 23, xi 25, xii 20, xviii 1, xxiii 30, 34, xxviii 30: the addition of a name—xx 32, xxiii 11, xxvi 7. For the omission of explanatory phrases generally see ii 7, iii 11, 22, iv 8, vii 11, 30, 36, 37, 48, ix 12, x 1, 21, xi 22, 28, xiii 42, 45, xiv 8, xvii 5, xix 35, xx 25, xxi 8, xxii 20, 26, 30, xxiv 15, 22, xxv 7, 16, xxvi 3, 14, 30, xxvii 41. For epithets omitted see i 19, v 37, vi 3, 13, viii 18 marg, xix 29, xx 19: for adverbs etc., ii 33, 41, iv 17, v 23, ix 18, xiv 28, xxiii 15: *certain* xiii 1, xvi 1, xix 9, xxiii 12: *this* i 16, xvi 36, xx 29: *verily* v 23, ix 4, xxii 3: articles viii 12, xvi 6, xxii 18, xxiii 30: cp. ii 22, xxiv 20, xxvii 12.

ii. The *additions* in the RV are relatively few, and (A) in the main of a minute character—the insertion of a particle, article, or preposition, which makes the passage more exact or vivid. For such see xi 21, xvi 16*, xix 29, xx 11, 32, xxvi 4, xxviii 28; xiii 31; xxvii 2; xvi 7, xx 5, xxiv 18; and in 15 places *also*, *both*, or *even*.   (B) Some however are real additions to the sense as in iv 25, 27, vii 18, viii 10, xiii 6*, xvi 7*, xvii 13, xviii 7*, xix 40, xx 1, 4*, xxiii 9*, xxiv 14, 24, xxv 6*, 18, xxvi 16*; cp. iv 33 marg. But like iii 3, xxiv 24 (*Jesus*), xxvi 25 (*Paul*) and like the pronouns in ii 38, 40, vii 22, xix 15, xx 23, xxiv 13, several of these are akin to the explanatory additions excluded in i (C).

iii. *Alterations* are more numerous.   (A) The order of the words is altered, as in i 13*, ii 47 and iii 1*, iii 20*, 21, iv 25*, v 22, viii 28, x 12, xiii 19*, xviii 26*, xxi 11, xxvi 7, xxviii 17.   (B) A different word is used in i 15, 25, ii 1, iii 20*, 21, v 33, 34, vi 8*, vii 16, 17, viii 8, ix 20*, x 14, 16, xi 20*, xiii 19*, 23*, xv 33*, 37, xvi 13*, 32, xvii 14*, xviii 5*, xix 16*, xx 1, 7*, xxi 34, xxiv 1, xxvi 15, xxvii 14*, 34, 39: different prepositions in i 17, v 15, 23, vii 35, ix 3, x 17, xx 13, xxiv 21, xxviii 9, and xii 25* margin: different conjunctions in xv 2, xvii 14, xxiv 16, xxv 11, xxviii 9, vi 3 margin. The very common interchange of *God* and *Lord* (in the Greek θc̄, κc̄) is found in viii 22, x 33, xv 40 and the margin of xiii 44, xx 28, 32; xvi 10, xvii 27, xxi 20 and the margin of xvi 32: see also ix 20, x 48, xviii 25, xxii 16. (*C*) The same word is used but with an alteration—in number ii 23, ix 31*, xxiii 20*; ix 12, xviii 15, xxiii 6*, xxiv 5, xxv 2*: case iv 6, xiii 14*, xvii 30, xix 27*, xx 24*, xxi 20, xxvii 2: gender ix 8; xxiv 18; xiii 25*, xvii 23*: and degree xxiv 10. So in the same verb there is a difference—of voice xi 12*, xvi 13*: mood ix 38*, xxi 24 (infinite verb xviii 21, xix 1, xxv 25): tense v 39, vii 35, xvi 17, xxiii 13, xxv 13*, xxvi 24: and person x 24 marg, xi 11*, xvi 13*, xviii 3*, 19, xix 13*, xxvii 19*, xxviii 1*. A difference in the compounded preposition is found —in verbs iii 24, xiii 26, xiv 14, xv 22, 30, xvi 39, xvii 26*, xix 12, 33*, xxi 4, xxiv 9, 11, xxviii 16, and the margin of xvii 30*, xx 5*, xxi 25*: and nouns xv 2*, 7*, xxiv 2*, 12, xxv 15. Lastly there are changes in the pronouns in i 8, 26, ix 25*; v 39, ix 38, x 42, xiii 33*; v 32 margin: interchange of the first and second persons in iii 25, xiv 17, xv 7, xvi 17, xxviii 25* and xiii 26, xix 37: pronoun for name in x 7, xii 13, xxiv 23, xxviii 17.

Comparison of RV and WH

i. WH side with the AV against the RV in one place xi 20, which however is marked for special discussion; and in iii 25, xiii 46, xviii 3 they admit the AV reading (rejected by RV) into their margin.

ii. In 18 places new readings of WH are admitted into the margin of RV, viz. in iv 1, vi 3, viii 18, x 24, 36, xi 23, xii 25, xv 24, xvii 30, xx 4, 5, 21, 32, xxi 25, xxvii 37, 39, xxviii 1, 13.

iii. Besides these WH have a number of readings which are not given in the RV or AV; but they are not of a significant character as will be seen from this list. (*A*) ii 44 omit *were* [together] *and*, vii 38 read *you* for *us*, x 19 *two* for *three*, 45 *who* for *as many as*, xi 3 *he went in...did eat* for *Thou wentest in...didst eat*; and omit in x 19 *unto him*, xiii 19 *And*, xxiii 10 an *and*, xxvi 26 *also*. In these places WH have the RV reading as an alternative in the margin. (*B*) In the following they reject altogether the RV and AV readings—vii 43 read *Rompha*, xviii 7 *Titius* [Justus], xix 39 *further* for *about other matters*; add in ii 33 *both* [see], ix 15 *both* [the Gentiles], xvi 9 *and* [beseeching]; omit in i 7 *And*, ii 7 *all*, xii 21 *and* [sat], xix 8 *the things*. (*C*) WH also admit a number of marginal or alternative readings which are not mentioned in the RV or AV, e.g. v 33 add *to him*, viii 27 omit *who* [had come], x 19 omit the number (*two* or *three*), xix 24 omit *silver*, 34 repeat *Great is Artemis of the Ephesians*, xx 13 [going] *to* for *before*, 15 *in the evening for the next day*, xxiii 7 *fell upon* (them) for *arose*, xxiv 26 omit [given] *him*, xxv 19 *evil charge of such things* for *charge of such evil things*, xxvii 27 [that a land] *was resounding* for *drawing near*. One of their alternative readings however has been admitted into the RV margin in xxiii 28.

(4) **The Bezan Text.** There still remains a family or type of text which of late years has been attracting very great attention, and the question of its origin and value is the chief problem of the textual criticism of to-day. Among the authorities consulted for Stephanus' edition of 1550 was an early Greek MS of the Gospels and Acts, written in the sixth century, which had found its way from a monastery in Lyons (as is supposed) into the hands of the scholar and reformer Theodore Beza. From Beza it passed on to the University Library at Cambridge, where it now rests. It is known as *Codex Bezae* or D, and has attained a world-wide reputation. For it was found that this codex was distinguished by an extraordinary number of variations from the ordinary text. At first this peculiarity only served to stamp the codex as worthless and to give it a bad name. But as time advanced, considerable support for these variations was discovered in other authorities, viz. in versions, especially the Harkleian Syriac and the early Latin versions previous to the Vulgate (p. xiv), in patristic quotations, and in a few Greek MSS. These discoveries indeed meant nothing less than the discovery of a definite type of text,

to which the name of *Western* was given by Griesbach. This text was current in very early days and widely spread, so that 'Western' is rather a question-begging title. The text was current in the east as well as the west; and WH in their *Introduction* (p. 548) speak of 'its rapid and wide propagation...in the centuries following the death of the apostles' as 'the most striking phenomenon of textual history.' Though a striking phenomenon, however, no scholar seriously entertained a claim for originality on behalf of the Western text. In the first two centuries, when our books of the New Testament were only gradually winning their way to recognition as 'scriptures,' naturally the same importance was not attached to the preservation of the exact text as in later times. This was held to be a sufficient reason to account for the appearance and widespread growth of the Western readings; besides, the Western authorities exhibit great variation among themselves, and very many of their additions bear the character of the explanatory interpolations which are a common feature in the history of ancient texts.

In connexion with the Acts however the question of the Western text assumes new proportions. For it is in this book that the variations and additions of Codex Bezae are most striking and abundant. And for these readings—in addition to the witnesses already mentioned—special support has been found in some later Latin texts[1], in quotations in Irenaeus, Cyprian, and Augustine, and in three Greek MSS, viz. E, 137 a minuscule of the eleventh century at Milan, and 58 a twelfth-century MS at Oxford. The evidence has been collected and marshalled by Dr Blass, one of the leading classical scholars of Germany, who has published the resultant text, which he calls the *Roman Text*[2]. More than this, in his commentary on the Acts published in 1895 he startled the world by maintaining that this Roman text came from the hand of S. Luke. It was a first edition or rather a rough copy of the work, written at Rome; and our text is really a revision of this or a second edition, carefully revised and sent to Theophilus. This theory was not, strictly speaking, original[3]; but it was the learning of Dr Blass and the authorities which he adduced which at once brought the problem to the front. Dr Blass' view has not as yet found general acceptance, but it has called serious attention once more to these Bezan readings. Whether they come from the hand of S. Luke or no, many of these readings bear the stamp of truth and may mark a genuine tradition, like Jn viii 1-11, or Lk xxii 43-44. Among them are to be found most of the whole verses or sentences of the AV which have been omitted in the RV (p. xxii); and in any case they are a valuable aid in explaining the text. This must be the

---

[1] e.g. a Latin Bible at Stockholm called Gigas, a palimpsest of Fleury, and some MSS of versions made in Bohemia and Provence. Herr Aug. Pott was the first to call attention to the Oxford (Gk) MS in his *Der abendländische Text der Apostelgesch.* (1900). [2] in his *Acta Apostolorum secundum formam quae videtur Romanam*, 1896. The introductions to this and to his commentary contain a list of his authorities with his arguments. [3] Leclerc, a Dutch scholar, at the beginning of the 18th century first suggested the idea of two editions of the Acts. Bornemann in 1848 maintained the originality of Codex Bezae.

excuse for the frequent reference in this commentary to the *Bezan text*, as we prefer to call it, both *Roman* and *Western* being names which beg the question of its origin.

Dr Blass' theory must be left to the discussion and decision of scholars, but there are these points to be considered which strongly make for its acceptance in a modified form.

(i) No doubt many of the Bezan readings are obviously later interpolations or additions. But we have not got (in spite of Dr Blass' edition) the original form of the Bezan text. We have only one Greek MS of a thoroughgoing Bezan type, and that not older than the sixth century: and its text like that in other MSS would have been subject to the ordinary causes of textual corruption. Indeed, if the origin of the text was a rough copy or copies, there could hardly have been much fixity of form about it, and the opportunity for corruption would have been proportionally great.

(ii) This problem is specially connected with S. Luke's writings, and of them chiefly with his second and later work. For the most important variations in his Gospel occur at its end. There the Bezan text has two famous passages regarded by WH as interpolations but authentic, viz. xxii 43-44 and xxiii 34. On the other hand it omits (which is itself a usual sign of originality) a number of passages, viz. in xxii 19, xxiv 3, 6, 12, 36, 40, 51, 52; and the last two of these closely affect the connexion of the Acts with the Gospel. Now we may fairly ask why should there be this special connexion with S. Luke? and in particular with his later work? Further, we notice that the additions are written in a very definite Lucan style, which is one of the strongest arguments for their originality. If they were the work of an interpolator, he must have been a very careful student of S. Luke and impregnated with his style and vocabulary.

(iii) The hand of an interpolator generally betrays itself by some anachronism, some inconsistency with the original work, or by some tendency, some special doctrine or theory which he desires to emphasize. Such work is not proof against the keen eye of the modern critic: the pseudo-Ignatian Epistles and the Apostolic Constitutions are classical examples of the detection of the work of a compiler. But in all the wealth of detail added to the Acts, no instance of anachronism or inconsistency has been proved. Similarly no special tendency has been detected. There is no utterance upon doctrines which became the subjects of later controversy[1]; nor is there an increase of the miraculous element, a common mark of an interpolator. On the other hand it is hard to conjecture a reason for the insertion of many details, e.g. the mention of the seven steps leading up to Herod's prison (xii 10), that S. Paul taught from the fifth to the tenth hour (xix 9), and that Demetrius' company ran out into the street (xix 28). The only explanation seems to be that they were features in the scene which impressed themselves on the memory of an eye-witness.

(iv) When we read the two texts, the RV and Blass' edition of 'the

---

[1] There is indeed an obvious emphasis on the work of the Holy Spirit; see e.g. xi 7, xv 7, 29, 32, xix 1, xx 3, xxvi 1. But this is itself a Lucan characteristic.

Roman text,' side by side, we get a strong impression that we are obtaining an insight into the work of composition. We can, so to speak, see the author at work on the revision of his first copy. He is anxious to polish the style, to make the narrative more concise, the sentences more terse. Possibly he is pressed by the exigencies of space and the limitations of his parchment. Hence he cuts out repetitions, prunes his language, and omits superfluous details. This impression is confirmed when we notice that the changes are most numerous in passages which call for editorial skill. They are less frequent where he is carefully following his authorities, as in the earlier chapters; or in scenes and speeches which he has carefully elaborated. They occur most in editorial passages, summaries of work done, and the connecting links between the different scenes. In fact they abound in the middle of the book, in chapters xiii–xx, where S. Luke has the very difficult task of describing S. Paul's missionary work and of compressing into a few verses the work of months.

(v) The additions by no means occur, as in the case of ordinary interpolations, where some roughness or ambiguity invites the touch of the copyist. In some places it is true that to cut out the Bezan reading would leave a kind of hiatus (as in xxiv 6–8), which suggests the smoothing hand of an interpolator: but such cases may equally well be due to the author's oversight of the effect of his revision. Apart from these places, however, there still remains an unevenness or want of clearness in many passages of the revised text (or second edition). Such passages are v 12–14, 38–9, vii 2–4, viii 7, x 36, xii 25, xiv 1–4, xv 33 and 40, xvi 19–20, xvii 8–9, xviii 18–21, xx 3–5, xxvii 9–12; and they make us feel that even in the RV or WH we have not yet got the author's final revision of his work. Such a reflection will give us the necessary modification of Dr Blass' theory. We are not to conceive of S. Luke as deliberately publishing two editions, like a modern writer. A book like the Acts cannot be written offhand in one autograph. The author first writes a draft and then revises it. In this case there must have been several drafts, or 'attempts' (Lk i 1), of the different parts of the Acts written at various times and in various stages, before the whole could have reached the final form in which it was sent to Theophilus. Some of the earlier drafts or rough copies may have been made public. S. Luke may have allowed the Roman Christians to make and circulate copies. It is also possible that some of the documents he used may have been in circulation, and these would give rise to differences of reading: this may in part account for many of the Western variations elsewhere in the NT. There are other possibilities which may be taken into consideration. In the uncertainty of the future outlook S. Luke may have issued the Acts prematurely before giving it the final touches. Or what is more likely, the persecution or even S. Luke's death may have cut short the work of revision, so that the Acts never did appear in a fixed and final form. By some such suppositions as these it is quite possible to accept the RV or WH as the most authoritative form of the text of the Acts, without denying the authenticity and importance of a great number of the Bezan readings.

CHAPTER II

The Author—S. Luke

§ 1 *His history*

Our information about S. Luke is practically confined to what we can glean from the pages of the New Testament itself. (*A*) At the end of the Ep. to the Colossians (iv 14), written from Rome about the year 60, S. Paul writes *Luke the beloved physician and Demas salute you*. In his letter sent to Philemon at the same time he writes *Mark, Aristarchus, Demas, Luke, my fellow workers [salute you]*. In his last letter, written shortly before his death in A.D. 64 or 65, he tells Timothy *Only Luke is with me* (2 Tim iv 11). (*B*) Besides these references there are the '*we*' passages in the Acts. In xi 27-8 the Bezan text runs thus: *There came down from Jerusalem prophets to Antioch and there was much rejoicing: and when we were gathered together, one of them named Agabus etc.* In xiv 22 the apostles instruct the disciples at Antioch in Pisidia *that through many tribulations we must enter into the kingdom of God*. No doubt this may be a general statement, but it sounds like a personal recollection. In xvi 10 the writer makes a definite appearance at Troas, when after S. Paul's vision *we sought to go forth into Macedonia*. Apparently he was left at Philippi, for after verse 17 the *we* does not reappear until the last journey to Jerusalem. Then the brethren who had gone on from Corinth *were waiting for us at Troas, and we sailed away* from Philippi etc. (**xx 5, 6**). The writer then remains in S. Paul's company till the end of the Acts. It is important however to notice that the use of the third person instead of the first does not necessarily imply the absence of the writer. For, although he was with S. Paul during the latter part of the Acts, the first person is only used in the accounts of the journeys, xx 5-xxi 18 and xxvii 1-xxviii 16, and in the latter passage the third person occurs frequently. Similarly at Philippi the third person is used on occasions when it is very probable that the writer was present e.g. in xvi 40. And it is most unlikely, as will appear below, that S. Luke joined the apostolic company for the first time at Troas. (*C*) Lastly, we have S. Luke's account of his motives for writing at the beginning of his Gospel (Lk i 1-4): *it seemed good to me also, having traced the course of all things accurately from the first, to write unto thee in order, most excellent Theophilus*.

From these notices we first gather that S. Luke was a Gentile, for in the Ep. to the Colossians Luke and Demas are distinguished from Aristarchus, Mark, and Jesus Justus,—*who are of the circumcision*. This is borne out by his name *LOUKAS* or *LUCAS*, an instance of the contraction very common in the Grecized population of the Roman empire. In the Acts we have similar contractions—*Silas* for *Silvanus*, *Theudas* for *Theodotus* or *Theodorus*, *Parmenas* for *Parmenides*, *Apollos* for *Apollonius* or *Apollodorus*. *Lucas* no doubt stands for *Lucanus*, which was a Roman name. It does not follow that he was a Roman by birth. The use of Roman names was very widespread. The Acts is full of them, e.g. *Pontius Pilatus, Cornelius, Titus Justus, Aquila, Priscilla, Crispus, Caius, Secundus, Claudius* (Lysias), *Felix, Tertullus, Porcius Festus, Julius, Publius.* Of these Felix we know was a Greek, Crispus and Aquila were Jews. Even Palestinian Jews adopted Latin surnames; and among Jews we find (Joseph) *Justus,* (John) *Marcus, Niger, Lucius, Paulus, Silvanus,* and *Rufus*[1]. Among non-Romans a Roman name was commonly the sign of a freedman: for a slave, when set free, adopted his master's name. But it may denote the possession of Roman citizenship acquired by other methods. Like Paulus and Silvanus S. Luke may have been a Roman citizen. His character however bears a Greek stamp. This is shewn by his ready pen, his versatility, and not least by his interest in the sea. At the same time his ready assimilation of the Jewish and Christian theology and his familiarity with the scriptures point to Semitic or eastern affinities. These characteristics however would be accounted for by an early conversion, which seems to be implied by Acts xi 28 (Bezan) and his own preface.

We are definitely told that S. Luke was a doctor by profession. This indeed we might have conjectured from the evidence of his writings, which has been summarized above (p. xx). Among the Romans this profession was not held in high repute: in a wealthy Roman house the part of family doctor was played by a slave or freedman; and such was Antonius Musa, the physician of Augustus. But it was otherwise among the Greeks. With them indeed the study of medicine ranked with that of philosophy; and there were medical schools at the universities, as at Alexandria where the great Galen was a student sixty years later. On another side the art of healing was closely associated with religion, and in Asia Minor the worship of Asklepios the god of healing was widely spread. At the time of the Acts there was a flourishing school of medicine attached to the temple of Men Karou near Laodicea, and the names of its presidents are found on coins[2]. This connexion however involved another which was not so creditable, viz. with magic and sorcery. In this rival science S. Luke was evidently much interested, to judge from the numerous pictures of its professors which he gives in the Acts, e.g. of Simon Magus, Elymas Barjesus, the 'Python,' the sons of Sceva, and the Ephesian exorcists.

His professional career and training would have made S. Luke a traveller, and the fact is evident from his familiarity with Galatia and the coasts of the Aegean. It is also clear that he had received a good classical education, as we should call it. He was well read in the Greek authors. This we can conclude from his language and style. But his own words in his preface are the best evidence of his literary power. We should not then go far wrong in concluding that he had studied at some university. Alexandria is probably excluded by the absence of any allusion to the city. On the other hand S. Luke

---

[1] And in the epistles *Junias* or *Junia, Lucius* (Rom xvi 7, 21), *Jesus Justus* (Col iv 11). [2] Ramsay *Cities and bishoprics of Phrygia* p. 52. Laodicea was not far from Colossae and S. Luke was apparently known to the Colossian church (Col iv 14). Both cities lie on the road from the west to Antioch in Pisidia.

seems quite at home in the Agora of Athens, and he has a thorough grasp of the Athenian character. Failing Athens, there is still another university which he may have visited, and that is Tarsus, the third on the list.

If it is legitimate to draw inferences from the selections which S. Luke gives from the apostolic preaching and from his choice of material in Gospel and Acts, we may restore his spiritual history, which would be a typical one for those early times. This is of course a matter of conjecture only; but it does not seem too strained to recognize in the author of the Acts an affectionate, joyous and pious nature which was deeply impressed with the evidence of the goodness of God, seen in the bounty of nature, *giving rains and fruitful seasons, filling men's hearts with food and gladness*; and such an one may have chosen his calling from a desire to *go about doing good*. A philosophical education would have taught him the truths which S. Paul assumes in addressing the Athenians, viz. the unity and omnipresence of the Divine Nature, together with the conviction that *the Lord of heaven and earth dwelleth not in temples made with hands*. But it could not reveal the Divine Person: and accordingly he was left *to feel after God, if haply he might find him*. In this darkness Judaism with its faith in the one God and its divine revelation in the scriptures seemed to shine with a clear light. Like many others our author was attracted and became one of *the devout* or *God-worshipping* adherents of the synagogue. But neither his yearnings for fellowship nor for joy were satisfied: Gentile converts remained very much in the outer court, shut out by the great barrier of circumcision; and instead of bringing joy and peace, the Law only increased the burden on the conscience. It was, then, at this stage that perhaps in some synagogue there fell on S. Luke's ears the glad news of the remission of sins, and he was baptized into the name of Jesus Christ.

The data, which we have collected above, are all we have to guide us in the discovery of S. Luke's origin. Eusebius indeed, writing about A.D. 330, tells us that he was *by race of those from Antioch*, and S. Jerome somewhat later writes decisively *Lucas medicus Antiochensis* (*Luke a physician of Antioch*). Antioch does in fact occupy an important position in the history, and there may be some patriotic feeling in the distinction of Nicolas among the Seven as a *proselyte of Antioch*. But the position of Antioch springs as much out of the history as that of Corinth, Ephesus, and Rome, and we find no local allusions or picturesque details. We should hardly have concluded that S. Luke had ever been at Antioch, but for the very important evidence of the Bezan reading in xi 28 which says *when we were gathered together*. The mention of *much rejoicing* in the immediate context gives the passage a very genuine and Lucan ring, and so we gather that S. Luke was present in the church at Antioch about the year 42.

This does not however necessarily imply that he was a citizen of Antioch or of Syrian race, as Jerome says; and Professor Ramsay, impressed by the Greek characteristics of S. Luke, agrees with Renan in the conviction that he was a native of Philippi. This would not be inconsistent with Eusebius' description, which would be satisfied by supposing Luke to have descended from one of the old Macedonian and aristocratic families of Antioch. Dr Ramsay bases his theory on S. Luke's first appearance at Troas, with his eagerness in directing S. Paul's steps towards Macedonia, the vividness of the narrative of events at Philippi, the civic pride shewn in calling Philippi *the first city of that part*—a title to which its claim was at least doubtful—and lastly his close and continuous connexion with the church at Philippi. This theory is very plausible. On the other hand it is extremely unlikely that S. Luke met S. Paul for the first time at Troas; it is most unlikely that a new convert, or at least a new companion, should have had so much influence on the apostolic deliberations, and within a few days should be like them addressing the women (xvi 13). S. Luke acts as one who had been a Christian, and intimate with S. Paul, for a long time. It is more probable that he had been one of the company before they reached Troas; that at Troas, as at Perga (xiii 13), there had been some hesitation and divided counsels; and if S. Luke by his pleading drove home the call of the vision and carried the day, that recollection was sufficient to prompt the words *we sought to go forth into Macedonia*[1].

In support of his contention Dr Ramsay appeals to 'the facts'—'they that have eyes to see them know[2].' Certainly the impression given by the narrative is strong, but there is an earlier scene where similar reasoning would demonstrate S. Luke's presence. Nowhere does S. Luke display more accurate local and geographical knowledge than in his account of the first missionary journey in South Galatia, where the political conditions in the first century were subject to constant change. He thoroughly understands the religious situation at Lystra, Derbe, and Iconium; and at Antioch of Pisidia we have one of the most vivid pictures in the Acts. It is the scene chosen for the typical sermon in the synagogue; and we almost feel that we are reading the words of one who was in the congregation, who noticed Paul and Barnabas coming in, and watched the rulers of the synagogue sending a message to them, and saw Paul standing up and beckoning with his hands; who heard the words of the apostle, and was himself deeply moved by the proclamation of the forgiveness of sins; who shared in the excitement of the congregation as they dispersed after service, and of the enormous crowd which came to the synagogue the next sabbath day; and who, when persecution had arisen and Paul and Barnabas were driven out, knew that the disciples were still *filled with joy and the holy Spirit*—a characteristic Lucan observation. But for the previous notice (in the Bezan text) of S. Luke's presence in the church of the Syrian Antioch, we might almost feel convinced that S. Luke was among that crowd of *devout proselytes* who followed Paul and Barnabas home from the synagogue and thenceforward *continued in the grace of God.*

But without going so far as this, the supposition that S. Luke came from this Antioch and was a companion of S. Paul on his first journey in Galatia would fall in with many of our facts. Tradition would still be true in calling

---

[1] See p. 278.   [2] See his *Paul the Traveller etc.*, pp. 200-10, 389-90.

him an *Antiochene*, though a mistake had crept in as to the Antioch in question. This personal connexion may have been one cause which helped to guide the apostles' steps from Perga to Antioch in Pisidia on their first journey. S. Paul mentions another cause of his preaching there: it was through sickness, *because of an infirmity of the flesh*, that he first preached to the Galatians[1]. And this statement reminds us that S. Luke was a physician. Antioch was not unsuitable for the study of medicine, which as we have seen flourished in Asia Minor, especially near Laodicea, which was not so very far from Antioch[2]. Antioch was also favourable for travel, it lay on the highway between the Aegean Sea and Tarsus. Again, if he was a citizen of Antioch, patriotism on S. Luke's part may account for his reticence as to the unhappy defection of the Galatian churches from the gospel of S. Paul. Finally, Dr Ramsay has himself given us the key to the settlement of the rival claims of Philippi and Antioch. The descendants of the original Macedonian conquerors and settlers formed the aristocracy in the new Greek kingdoms which grew up out of Alexander's conquests in the East. If S. Luke sprang from one of these families who had come from Philippi, it would account for his return to and affection for that city. And in this connexion we may notice that the Acts is full of evidence of aristocratic sympathies and leanings on the part of the writer[3].

Now, if a native of the Pisidian Antioch, S. Luke may have been at once of Macedonian or Greek blood, a Roman citizen, and an adherent of the Jewish monotheism. This would have given him the cosmopolitan sympathies required for the Acts; and his aristocratic descent, with the comfortable income of a physician, would have made him a useful and not unequal companion of S. Paul.

We can now draw a better, though still conjectural, sketch of S. Luke's early history. We can suppose that after much travel in the study and practice of medicine he paid a visit to Tarsus and its famous university. Here he met and was converted by S. Paul; and when Barnabas came from Antioch and took back Saul with him about the year 42 (xi 25-6), S. Luke accompanied them, and by the use of the first person in xi 28 (Bezan) has left a silent note of his entry into the church. It is just at this point that we have most light thrown upon the internal condition of the church at Antioch (xi 20-30)[4]. It is not at all unreasonable to suppose that S. Luke accompanied the apostles on their first journey in A.D. 46-7 (xiii–xiv), which will account for the graphic and accurate narrative and the *we* in xvi 22. At some point in the second journey he joined Paul again. Possibly he may have been left in charge of the church

---

[1] Gal iv 13. As will be seen below we have no hesitation in identifying the Galatian churches with those founded in the first journey. [2] It is interesting in this connexion to learn that at Adada, a town which S. Paul probably passed through on his way to Antioch, there has been found the tombstone of a young man of good family who had chosen the study of medicine but died at Alexandria, apparently in its pursuit (Dr Sterrett *Wolfe Expedition etc.* inscr. no. 408). [3] For this see p. 292 and notice that his book is dedicated to the *most excellent* Theophilus. [4] See the commentary on the passage (pp. 167-9).

at Antioch in Pisidia, and there been picked up again by S. Paul, like Timothy (xvi 1-3), in A.D. 49; for South Galatia is the starting point of the second journey, and S. Luke appears soon after they have left that country (verse 10). Apparently he was left behind in charge of the church at Philippi (verse 40); but that would not preclude his having rejoined S. Paul at, or paid visits to, Athens, Corinth, and Ephesus. If, as is very likely, Luke is *the brother, whose praise in the gospel is spread through all the churches*, of 2 Cor viii 18, he was sent by S. Paul on a mission to Corinth in 54. And the *praise in the gospel* may be a sign that one of his chief occupations at Philippi was that of collecting materials for the 'Gospel according to Luke.' The next spring (of 55) we know for certain that he joined the apostle at Philippi on his last journey up to Jerusalem: no doubt he was one of *the messengers of the churches* (2 Cor viii 23) in charge of their alms for the church at Jerusalem. From this point his history will best be followed in the narrative itself.

§ 2 *His character*

If we cannot ascertain many facts about S. Luke's life, it is comparatively easy to draw a sketch of his character from his work. Tradition tells us that he was a painter, and this expresses the truth that S. Luke was an artist by nature. The Acts alone is sufficient to shew that he had an artist's eye, an artist's ideas and imagination, and an artist's power of expression, the power of delineating a character or a scene in a few vigorous lines or even words. The scientific training of the physician shews itself in the faculty of acute observation and accurate description. His Greek nature is seen in the versatility which makes him at home in such varied scenes and situations. These qualities however bear rather upon the character of the book, and will be considered below. Here we are more interested in the man.

S. Luke is the typical disciple, or rather Christian disciple. 'By this shall all men know that ye are my disciples, if ye have love one to another.' Love was the basis of S. Luke's character, and that love which shews itself in a gentle and affectionate nature. He was *the beloved physician*. The first attribute of such affection is self-forgetfulness, and this is shewn in S. Luke's modesty or entire self-effacement. Though he could say of this history '*cuius pars magna fui*,' yet there is not a word about his own work, his 'praise in the gospel,' his services to S. Paul, not even a hint of S. Paul's affection for him. And when he cannot help betraying his presence, he does it simply by writing *we* (and not *I*).

The gentleness comes out in his interest in women. The position of women varied then as now. At Jerusalem of course they were kept very much in the background. In Macedonia, and still more in Asia Minor, women moved about in society, even in public life, very much as they do now. Agreeable to this is the influence of women at Antioch in Pisidia (xiii 50[1]),

---

[1] Cf. xvi 1-3 with II Tim i 5. This makes S. Luke's silence about Thecla all the more remarkable. See below, pp. 226-7.

Thessalonica, and Beroea (xvii 4, 12). But everywhere alike S. Luke is mindful of the part played by women: he does not forget their position in the church (i 14 *the women*, xxi 9 *prophetesses*) or among the converts (viii 12, xvi 13, xvii 4, 12, 34), their share in persecution (viii 3, ix 2, xxii 4) and church life (xxi 5). And we have a number of names and characters of all classes: Mary the mother of Jesus, Dorcas and Mary the mother of John Mark, Sapphira and Priscilla (two wives who alike seem to have taken the predominant part), Drusilla and Bernice both of royal blood, Lydia of the well-to-do *bourgeoisie* of Philippi and Damaris a lady of Athens, while even the maidservant Rhoda (xii 13) is not left out. The influence of women seems to have been a special mark of the Philippian church, with which S. Luke was so closely associated,—Lydia the purple-seller gave it a home; later on we find it distracted by the rivalries of two ladies, Euodias and Syntyche; and thus, when S. Luke writes that at the river side *we sat down and talked with the women who had come together*, we feel that he is describing a congenial scene (xvi 13-15, 16, 40 and Phil iv 2-3).

The character of a 'disciple' finds expression in faithful devotion to a 'master'; and S. Luke had found a master. This was S. Paul, and the enthusiasm and devotion which he evoked in S. Luke can be gauged by the enthusiasm which the history still arouses in us. The great example of S. Luke's dramatic sense is the first introduction of the chief actor as *a young man named Saul*, and of his dramatic skill the way in which he draws out the retribution that fell upon Saul for his *consenting to Stephen's death* (vii 58-viii 1). His personal feelings can be detected in his evident sympathy with the sorrow of the Ephesian elders *who fell on Paul's neck and kissed him*; and the relief of an anxious watcher, when on nearing Rome he saw Paul *thank God and take courage* (xx 37, xxviii 15). S. Irenaeus rightly describes S. Luke as S. Paul's 'inseparable fellow-worker'; and he received an ample reward for his devotion in the last testimony of the apostle—*only Luke is with me.*

Corresponding to S. Luke's affectionate nature, the characteristic of church life which attracted him and which he delights to portray is 'brotherly love' or 'love of the brethren.' The church is a brotherhood and acts as such. The description of the early church at Jerusalem represents no doubt S. Luke's personal ideal, when all the brethren *were of one heart and soul*, and the spiritual community was reflected in an external community of goods. He notes the joy and strength which comes from the common fellowship and from the assembling together of the brethren[1]; and there is a special word for their mutual encouragement and comfort, viz. *paraclesis* or *exhortation*. So Barnabas came to Antioch and *exhorted* the brethren, with great effect: Judas and Silas did the same: S. Paul also possessed this power of encouraging in a high degree[2]. The brotherly spirit of the church found its chief outward manifestation in hospitality. This is exemplified in the journey

---

[1] i 14, ii 1, iv 23, vi 2, ix 26-30, xi 26, xii 5, 12.   [2] xi 23, xv 32, xiv 22, xvi 40.

of the delegates to the council, brought on their way by one church and gladly received by the other (xv 3-4): in a similar journey of S. Paul, marked by affectionate intercourse and leave-takings and ending in a glad reception at Jerusalem (xx 6-xxi 17): and again in the refreshment of S. Paul by his friends at Sidon, the hospitality at Puteoli, and the courtesy of the Roman Christians in coming forty miles to meet him, a mark of brotherhood which put new life into his heart (xxvii 3, xxviii 14-15).

The brotherly love of the church is thrown into greater relief by the opposite spirit. In recording the failures in the church, it is obvious that the most heinous sin in S. Luke's eyes is covetousness or the love of money. And this apparently not so much from ascetic principles, but because covetousness denotes self-seeking, and it is self-interest which divides brother from brother and so breaks up the unity and effectiveness of the body. The first recorded sin in the church, which met with so severe a condemnation, was keeping back part of the price (v 1-11). Supposed unfair distribution was at the bottom of the first murmuring (vi 1). The fatal sin of making spiritual position an instrument of temporal gain is once for all denounced in the case of Simon Magus (viii 20). Again, the interests of selfish gain are no less an obstacle to the church from without, as is seen in the opposition of Barjesus, of the owners of the soothsaying girl of Philippi, and the silversmiths of Ephesus (xiii 6-11, xvi 19, xix 25-7). The remedy against covetousness is to call nothing *one's own* but to have all things *common*, with a corresponding simplicity of life. '*Silver and gold have I none*' says S. Peter, and S. Paul echoes his words (iii 6, xx 33-4).

Besides covetousness there was another source of weakness in the church, viz. the innate tendency to division. This served to bring out another aspect and office of S. Luke's brotherly love. As a physician by profession, so he was a healer and a peacemaker by nature. The unity of the church is to him a fundamental truth. In fact he has been severely accused of writing his history for the purpose of inventing a unity which did not exist. According to the Tübingen critics the followers of S. Peter and S. Paul were irreconcilably divided, and the aim of S. Luke was to gloze over and conceal this division. Now it is true that, as we read S. Luke's calm narrative, we feel little of the heat of controversy; although we know for certain that such there was from the impassioned language of S. Paul's epistles; and certainly others might have written the history in very different terms. It is however to be emphatically noted that with all his desire for unity S. Luke did not conceal unwelcome facts. The murmuring in the church, the reluctance of the brotherhood to receive a new brother, the Pharisaic spirit which criticized the chief apostle and which would have excluded the Gentiles, the *no small dissension and questioning* which arose in the church on the matter of circumcision— all these are duly recorded[1]. Most painful of all was the *sharp contention* which arose between the two great apostles and fellow-workers, Paul and

---

[1] vi 1, ix 26, xi 2-3, xv 2.

Barnabas; yet no hint is given of a reconciliation, which we are left to infer from the letters of S. Paul[1]. But while narrating these facts, S. Luke saw and recorded another series of facts which made for unity: the self-sacrifice and brotherly conduct of individuals like Barnabas (iv 36-7, ix 27), the unanimity of the great leaders at the council (ch. xv), and the friendly reception of S. Paul by the rulers of the church in Jerusalem (xxi 17-25).

Further, S. Luke had the historical insight which, as he looked back, shewed him how all things, even evils, had been made to 'work together for good to them that love God.' Hence throughout the Acts we breathe in an atmosphere of thankful and even joyful optimism. All ended well. The sin of Ananias against the common life served to consolidate the church. The first murmuring led to the appointment of the Seven. The martyrdom of S. Stephen with the consequent persecution started the Christian evangelists on a career of uninterrupted progress. It led to the first bursting of the confines of Jerusalem; it won for the church its greatest missionary, S. Paul; and it was followed by a deeper and more edifying peace (ix 31). Again, Herod's persecution was the occasion of a signal deliverance, and *the word of God* all the more *grew and multiplied* (xii 24). The controversy about circumcision resulted in a great increase of joy and deepening of the brotherly feeling in the church (xv 31-2). The separation from S. Barnabas may have left S. Paul freer for the great extension of the church towards the west, in any case it left his apostleship to stand out more unmistakeably; and all the sufferings, bonds, and imprisonments of S. Paul himself ended in bringing him to Rome, where for two years he was able *to preach the kingdom of God and teach the things concerning the Lord Jesus Christ with all boldness, none forbidding him*. And this is the joyful conclusion of the whole history.

It would however be a very inadequate account of S. Luke's affection and devotion to suppose it limited to man: it must have had its basis in the love of God. We have alluded to his sense of the omnipresence and bounty of God in nature; and what further attracted him to S. Paul was the apostle's personal devotion to the Lord Jesus. Throughout the Acts we feel that the presence and activity of the risen Lord is a living reality to the writer[2], and in the words which he puts into S. Paul's mouth we can hear himself speaking—*I am ready not to be bound only, but also to die at Jerusalem for the name of the Lord Jesus* (xxi 14). The divine presence was realized by S. Luke far more as an internal, than an external, presence. It was a communion in spirit. And as S. Luke's character may be best described by S. Paul's list of the fruits of the Spirit, so he was intensely conscious of the actual indwelling of the Holy Spirit. But of this more will be said below.

This communion with God finds its exercise and manifestation in prayer, which accordingly has a great place in S. Luke's history. Four prayers are recorded, in i 24, iv 24-30, vii 59-60, and xxi 14: and besides the frequent

---

[1] xv 37-9, Col iv 10, II Tim iv 11.   [2] Cp. vii 55, ix 4, 10, xiv 3, xvi 7, xviii 5, xxii 17, xxiii 11.

allusions to the practice¹, we notice that on the most critical occasions the divine interventions and revelations come in answer to prayer, e.g. the baptism of S. Paul, his 'separation' and his mission to the Gentiles, the reception of Cornelius by S. Peter, and the deliverances both of S. Peter and of S. Paul². Of prayer, praise is the chiefest element, and this also is stamped on the book. The immediate effect of the Spirit is to make men utter *the mighty works of God*, and *magnify him*: praise is the normal attitude of the Christian life: after persecution, controversy, or success, alike they *glorify God*: at midnight in the jail at Philippi S. Paul *sang hymns* unto God, and during the shipwreck and on reaching Roman territory he *gave thanks*³. With good reason, then, we can picture S. Luke as one wont to 'speak in psalms and hymns and spiritual songs, singing and making melody with his heart to the Lord': one of those best of all evangelists

> with whom the melodies abide
> of the everlasting chime:
> who carry music in their heart
> through dusky lane and wrangling mart,
> plying their daily task with busier feet,
> because their secret souls a holy strain repeat⁴.

For S. Luke's character is to be briefly comprehended in the word *joy* — joy which is the fruit of the Spirit. It was the joyousness in the church which attracted S. Luke. Not so much the teaching or the theology or the organization, but the new life of the church. This fascinated him: the joy and gladness which came from the revelation of the grace of God, the gift of the forgiveness of sins, the indwelling of the Spirit, and the life of brotherhood. The early Christians lived in a state of *exultation* or *gladness* (ii 46, xi 27 Bezan); and joy was the natural outcome of Christian work and intercourse, as of the mission of Barnabas to Antioch, the news of Paul and Barnabas' success, and the reception of the apostolic letter⁵. Even persecution was a joy, for the Twelve *departed from the council rejoicing that they were counted worthy to suffer dishonour for the Name*; and at Antioch in Pisidia after the expulsion of the apostles the disciples were yet *filled with joy and with the Holy Ghost*⁶. These words give the secret. In those days the gospel was indeed 'good tidings of great joy' (Lk ii 10), and it brought a rich gift—of the Holy Spirit. So when Philip preached in Samaria, *there was much joy in that city*; and the eunuch after he had been baptized *went on his way rejoicing*. When S. Paul turned to the Gentiles at Antioch in Pisidia, *they rejoiced and glorified the word of God*; and the jailor at Philippi after his baptism likewise *rejoiced greatly with all his house, having believed in God*⁷.

---

[1] See i 14, 24, ii 42, iii 1, iv 24–31, vi 4, 6, vii 59, 60, viii 15, 24, ix 11, 40, x 2, 4, 9, 30, xi 5, xii 5, 12, xiii 2–3, xiv 23, xvi 25, xx 36, xxi 5, xxii 17, xxiv 11, xxvii 24, xxviii 8. [2] ix 11, xiii 2, xxii 17 : x 2, 9, 30, xi 5 : xii 5, 12 : xvi 25, cp. xxvii 24. [3] ii 4, 11, x 46 : ii 47 : iv 24, xi 18, xiii 48, xxi 20 : xvi 25, xxvii 35, xxviii 15. [4] Eph v 19, and *The Christian Year* for S. Matthew's Day. [5] xi 23, xv 3, 31. [6] v 41, xiii 52. [7] viii 8, 39, xiii 48, xvi 34.

CHAPTER III

The Composition of the Acts

§ 1 S. Luke's aim

To enquire into S. Luke's aim in writing the Acts is at the same time to ask What is the meaning of the book? and what are its leading ideas? The Acts then may be regarded as:

(1) **A record of the Truth.** It is a second volume, and at the beginning of the first (the Gospel) S. Luke like a modern writer announces his motive in a preface (Lk i 1–4). This was that *Theophilus might know the certainty concerning the things wherein he had been instructed*. His aim, then, was to convey accurate information; in other words he was impelled by the historical instinct, i.e. the desire to preserve the remembrance of great deeds. At first, in their expectation of an immediate return of their Lord, the Christians needed no history. But as years went by, the end had not come. The first generation of disciples was passing away, and the foundation of the church was becoming a thing of the past. Accordingly, before he leaves the world, S. Luke is anxious to leave behind him a written record of *the matters which had been fulfilled among them*. And no doubt some of the incidents and a great deal of the detail in the Acts are simply due to the personal reminiscences and the recording instinct of the writer. There was a further motive. In the oral tradition in which Christians were *instructed* or *catechized* some accounts of the beginnings of the church must have found a place. At any rate various written attempts at gospel and church history were already in circulation, though, as it would seem, not of a high class. There was, then, great need for a *certain* or *accurate narrative*, and this S. Luke sets himself *to draw up*. Once more, the dedication to *Theophilus* is a hint that S. Luke is addressing the general reading public. The Acts, like the Gospel, is a catholic book, addressed to all men whether Roman or Greek, Christian or Jew. Of Theophilus we know nothing, but we recognize in him this catholic character: he had been instructed in the Christian faith, his name is Greek, and the complimentary epithet *most excellent* may mark a Roman official or nobleman. We may even go further. For it is possible that, like John Bunyan in *Pilgrim's Progress*, S. Luke is really addressing—not an individual but—the Christian as such, under the guise of *Theophilus* or *Lover of God*.

(2) **The gospel of the Spirit.** The great things which S. Luke wants to record are the *deeds and doctrines of Jesus* (i 1). This is the subject of the Gospel and Acts alike. But there is a difference. In the Acts Jesus is no longer present in the flesh, but works through his Spirit. The Acts is really the completion of the Gospel. Having written the Gospel, S. Luke must needs go on to the Acts, for the Lord's work is made effectual in the

world by the Spirit; and the Acts may be called 'the Gospel of the Holy Ghost.' It begins with the baptism of the church by the Spirit. It was the *gift of the Holy Ghost* (ii 38) which joined men to the Lord, and which the apostles offered to the world; and the history shews how it was extended (typically) to all men, e.g. the Samaritans, the Gentile Cornelius, and the disciples of John[1]. It is the mark of the Christian to be full of the Holy Spirit: *as Jesus was anointed with the Holy Ghost and with power*, so were the apostles and evangelists[2]. The Holy Spirit was the guide in the external action and advance of the church—he directed Philip, and sent Peter to baptize Cornelius; he ordered the separation of Paul and Barnabas, and guided S. Paul's steps[3]. Likewise within, he guided the church 'into all the truth'; he spoke in the utterances of her councils, and was the source of ministerial authority[4]. The Acts in fact is a history of 'the new dispensation'; and that is why it lacks a definite conclusion. These twenty-eight chapters are but *the beginning* (i 1, xi 15): we are still living under the dispensation of the Spirit.

(3) **The history of the Church.** *The Spirit of Jesus* (xvi 7) acts through a human society—the church, which is 'the body of Christ.' As Christ is a king, this society is also a kingdom—*the kingdom of God*[5]. The Acts contains the story of the establishment of *the kingdom* (xx 25) or the first stage in the growth of the body: in modern phrase it is a history of the church from A.D. 30 to 60. In this history there are two sides to be studied: its external and internal history. (A) Externally, the church spreads from Jerusalem to Rome, from the religious centre of the world to its secular capital. We watch it growing like a grain of mustard. First it absorbs Samaria, all Judaea and Galilee, with Caesarea; then it reaches Antioch. From Antioch, which serves as a second mother city, it rapidly spreads through one province after another—Galatia, Macedonia, Achaia, Asia—till in Ephesus it finds a third resting place. From Ephesus it leaps across the sea to Rome. (B) Internally, we witness its expansion from a Jewish sect into a catholic church. From the doctrine of Jesus as the Jewish Messiah we are led on to the full conception of Jesus as the Son of God. The church bursts the swaddling clothes of the Law with its Jewish rites, and steadily grows up 'to the stature of the fulness of Christ' (Eph iv 13). Corresponding to this growth there is a continuous widening of its borders: it starts with Jews, to whom are added Grecian Jews and proselytes; then it takes in Samaritans and the outer circle of adherents of the synagogue; then with a wide embrace it draws in the Gentiles, both Greeks and barbarians, until finally at Rome Christianity stands as the religion for all the world.

Such a history, like the growth of a highly diversified organism, will be marked by a richness of complexity, both in the church's relations with the

---

[1] ch viii 17, x 44, xix 6.   [2] vi 3, vii 55, xi 24: x 38.   [3] viii 29, 39: x 19-20, xi 12: xiii 2: xvi 6-10, xix 1 (Bezan), 21, cp. xx 23, xxi 11.   [4] xv 28: xx 28.   [5] xvii 7, Lk xxiii 2: Acts i 3, xxviii 31.

world without and in its own inner development. Consequently the historian has in his mind no doubt several subsidiary purposes in writing, some of which have been unfairly exalted to the first place. Thus:

A (i) In the external growth of the church the great factor to be considered was the State or the Roman Empire. What if it should place Christianity under its ban, prohibit its growth, and forbid its practice? The only result would be resistance and war to the death. At the time when S. Luke was writing the attitude of the Roman government was still uncertain. Hence S. Luke is anxious to vindicate the legal status of Christianity. He describes carefully the various cases of conflict with the state authorities, and in particular he shews how S. Paul in all his trials before Roman governors was acquitted of any disloyalty. To make this clear is at least one reason for the great prolixity and repetition in the concluding chapters. In them Paul stands for Christianity; and the Acts is really a 'Defence of the Church' addressed to the imperial authorities, the first of the long series of 'apologies.'

(ii) The Jews, however, were in fact the first, as they were the most bitter, persecutors of the church, and the Acts might be an *apologia* to them. S. Luke would prove that Jesus is the Messiah by the most cogent evidence of facts, viz. by the actual establishment of the Messianic kingdom in the world. But by A.D. 60 the centre of Christianity had already shifted from Judaea to Rome; and the tone in which S. Luke writes of the Jews, the way in which he unmasks their mad and unreasonable hatred against S. Paul, shews that this was a very secondary motive.

(iii) From the point of view of the world at large, there was a more serious enemy than Judaism, and that was false religion or superstition. The general population of the empire (the public for whom S. Luke chiefly wrote) was in bondage to superstitions and spiritual deceits; and to set them free, it was necessary to vindicate Christianity as the Truth against all rival religions and spiritual powers. Accordingly the Acts is the history of a succession of victories of the Truth over Falsehood—over false spiritualism, sorcerers and exorcists, both Jewish and Gentile, divination at Philippi and magic at Ephesus; over idolatry, whether that of simple country folk as in Lycaonia and Malta or the elaborate worship of Artemis at Ephesus; and lastly over false philosophy at Athens.

B (i) The obstacles to the church from within, however, were really more dangerous. First there was the moral danger. In one aspect the history of the church is a history of a decline from the first love; and the entry of sin into, and its lodgement within, the church must have been a problem to perplex the early Christians. S. Luke's answer is to give a faithful record of what happened, and so to meet the danger. For the history is at the same time the history of the conviction of sin; and the judgements of Ananias, of Simon Magus, and of others, are warnings for all time. On the other hand the picture of the original church life with its brotherhood and unselfishness will ever keep before the church her high ideal.

(ii) The greatest menace to the unity of the church is the tendency to division or the self-will (*heresy*) innate in man. Natural differences of mind and character, if accentuated by a zeal which may not be according to knowledge, lead to external schism. And in the first thirty years of her life the church was brought face to face with that peril in an acute form. Her very growth brought up the question of *respect of persons* or privilege in the church: are all men equal before God? or has the Jew any advantage? In practical life the question meant—must the Gentile be circumcised and keep the Law? There could hardly have been a subject of greater difference of opinion: Catholic and Protestant do not stand wider apart than did Jew and Gentile. The history will shew that the difference did reach the verge of division. But it was S. Luke's happy task to shew how the unity of the church was preserved. The Tübingen critics indeed maintained that this was the main object of S. Luke's writing, and that in carrying it out he has grossly perverted the truth (p. xxxiv). Instead of S. Luke they took for their main authority on early church history the so-called Clementine writings of the second century; and these writings, which emanated from sects of Judaic Christians, were prompted by a virulent hatred of S. Paul. But the Tübingen views have fallen out of favour. The truthfulness of S. Luke is vindicated elsewhere; and we may add that, as he was neither a leader nor a Jew, it was not likely that he should fully realize the intensity of feeling among the Jews on the subject. The truth of his facts has been vindicated by history itself. No trace remained of any such actual schism in the church as they supposed: in tradition S. Peter and S. Paul have always stood side by side as brother martyrs and brother princes of the church. S. Luke wrote when the struggle of opinion was rapidly dying out, and his quiet retrospect affords to the church a lesson and a guide for the right treatment of controversy.

(iii) To moral weakness and schism, for the sake of completeness, we may add the danger of error. This again S. Luke has met by his careful summaries of 'the gospel' in the speeches, by his treatment of imperfect forms of Christianity, as e.g. at Ephesus, and by the warnings uttered by S. Paul to the Ephesian elders.

(4) **The acts of the Apostles.** The first thirty years of church life was a vast subject to take in hand, but S. Luke understood the true principle of dealing with it. The history should be neither a dry collection of facts like an Anglo-Saxon chronicle, nor, like the reconstructions of some modern critics, something altogether ideal. The secret is found in personality. The Holy Spirit, working in the church, works through individuals; and so the history of the church becomes *the acts of the Apostles*. These are not the acts of certain individuals, but of 'the apostles' and of individual apostles only as apostles; for, as we shall see in chapter VI, *the apostles* are the foundation of the church[1]. Nor are they the complete acts of any one apostle, but only those in which he contributed to the life of the whole and which received the sanction

---

[1] See i 2, 26, ii 42–3, iv 33–7, v 2, 12, 18, 29, vi 6, viii 1, 14, 18, ix 27.

of his fellows. The successive phases of church thought and activity which history has to record find their best expression in some leader or representative; and so the history of the Acts is composed of chapters from the lives (or, as the Greeks expressed it, *acts*) of Peter and Stephen, Philip and Apollos, Barnabas and Paul. Similarly, subsidiary currents of life and thought are also represented in individuals, such as John Mark, Cornelius, Sergius Paulus, Aquila and Priscilla, and others.

In history of this character the personal predilections of the writer cannot be concealed, and in the Acts S. Paul is the dominating figure. S. Peter of course is his equal, but in extent and interest his acts are outweighed by those of S. Paul. This presentation of S. Paul is a great confirmation of S. Luke's historical insight. We may feel sure that among his contemporaries S. Paul did not hold so large a place in respect of the other apostles. All who came in contact with him must indeed have been stirred by his powerful personality. But there were large tracts of the church where Paul was unknown, large tracts where he was not understood, and in the eyes of the ordinary churchman the Twelve, and especially Peter, James, and John, held the first place. S. Luke, however, belonged to the group of Pauline disciples: to them S. Paul was equal even to S. Peter; and the place assigned to the apostle, under the influence of the personal devotion of our author, has been justified by the course of history.

To this we must add that the acts of the Apostles afford the best commentary on the meaning of the church. A true history of the church could not be complete without an account of its constitution and organization. But the church is a living body, and physiological processes are not subject to mechanical definition. Accordingly, like its external history, the church's internal constitution must be learnt from pictures of life; and as the church began with the Twelve, so the laws of her life are to be studied in the account of their actions, such as the ordination of the Seven, the laying on of hands upon the Samaritans, the judgement of Ananias and Sapphira, and the holding of the council at Jerusalem. Similarly the creed of the church is to be looked for in the witness of the apostles, which is enshrined in their speeches.

§ 2 *His sources of information*

For the second part of the Acts, ch. xiii-xxviii, S. Luke had the best possible sources of information. During a great part of this time he was *an eyewitness and a minister* (Lk i 2) of the chief actor, S. Paul; and S. Paul could have communicated to him nearly all that he has related. But in this capacity S. Luke was frequently an eyewitness of the events also, and therefore his own authority. The accounts of Philippi in ch. xvi, and of the two voyages in xx-xxi and xxvii-xxviii, might be leaves out of his diary. In the interval, when the use of the first person disappears (xvii 1-xx 4), he may have been at S. Paul's side from time to time; and he may have visited Thessalonica, Corinth, and Ephesus. In any case he was in close connexion with members of the apostolic company who could have given him all the information he required, e.g. Silas, Timothy of Lystra, Titus, Erastus of Corinth, Aristarchus of Thessalonica, Sopater of Beroea, Tychicus and Trophimus of Ephesus. The history of the earlier journey of ch. xiii-xiv also reads as if it came from an eyewitness. This may have been, as has been suggested (p. xxx f.), S. Luke himself; if not, there was at least Timothy, not to speak of Barnabas and Paul, to give information. S. Mark, with whom S. Luke must have become intimate later on at Rome or elsewhere, could have told him about Cyprus (xiii 1-12). For the council (xv-xvi 4) there was no lack of authorities. Besides Paul and Barnabas, there was the Antiochene deputation, of which Titus—as possibly Luke himself—was an important member (Gal ii 3).

The case is somewhat different with the first part of the Acts (i-xii), because the events for the most part occurred before S. Luke had appeared upon the scene. But still, as he tells us in his preface, he had access to *eyewitnesses and ministers of the word*. He had unrivalled opportunities for collecting information. At one time his home was in the church at Antioch, and there he could have gathered the traditions of that church: cp. xi 19-30, xii 25-xiii 3, xiv 26-xv 2, xv 22-40. There also he would have been in communication with the prophets and teachers of xiii 1, with Barnabas of Cyprus, Symeon Niger and Lucius of Cyrene (iv 36-7, ix 26-30, xi 20), Manaen, Herod's foster-brother—with whom we associate S. Luke's notices of the Herodian family (xii 20-3, xxv 13, cp. Lk xxiii 7-12)—and Saul or Paul. S. Paul was the original authority for ix 1-30 (as in xxii 3-21 and xxvi); he also took a leading part in the persecution and trial of S. Stephen (vi 8-viii 3). Later on, if not before, S. Luke visited Jerusalem itself; and if his stay in the city was short, he spent two years at Caesarea. This explains the specially full and detailed account of the origin of the church there (viii 40, ix 31-xi 18). At Caesarea moreover he was the guest of one of 'the Seven,' S. Philip the evangelist, as afterwards for a short time of Mnason. Both of these were *original disciples* (xxi 8, 16). From Philip would naturally be derived vi 1-7 and viii 4-40; and with S. Paul he would be an additional authority for the intervening persecution (vi 8-viii 3). Possibly he was also an actor in the conversion of Cornelius, and it may be he who tells the story (x-xi 18). John Mark we have already mentioned: he was no doubt present in his mother's house when Peter told the story of his deliverance from prison, and the vivid and graphic narrative of xii 1-19 is in all probability taken down from his lips.

There is now left only chapters i-v,—the history of *the beginning*. We have already enumerated some *eyewitnesses* from the beginning—e.g. Barnabas, Mnason, Philip, Mark. Besides these there were the Twelve themselves, most prominent among whom were S. Peter and S. John, with S. James the Lord's brother. Of these S. Luke met S. James at Jerusalem, and S. Peter (as we can hardly doubt) at Rome, perhaps also at Antioch (Gal ii 11). But S. Luke himself speaks of another source of information, viz. written documents (Lk i 1). The problem of these early chapters is in fact the same as that of the Gospel itself. S. Luke speaks somewhat in a tone of depreciation of these written documents, and he would no doubt have preferred to rely mainly upon what was their authority also, viz. oral tradition. Very soon, we imagine, the account of what Jesus had said and done—that in which the disciples and new believers were *instructed*—assumed a more or less fixed form or tradition. As has been hinted (p. xxxvii), it is most probable that to such a fixed form would be added some accounts of the Ascension, of the Day of Pentecost, and of the life of the early church as illustrated by some typical events, such as a miracle, a conflict with the Sanhedrin, and a judgement on unfaithful Christians. Now whatever did actually happen, S. Luke had, during his stay in Palestine, the best opportunity for making himself master of this oral tradition in whatever form it had assumed by A.D. 55; and this tradition must be considered as the basis of the early chapters. In forming the oral tradition, or at least in drawing up these brief typical accounts, S. Peter must have been the chief authority. But S. Peter was not learned and there was another disciple, one of the first three, who had much greater qualifications. This was S. John, about whom the history is very reticent, more than we should have expected and could wish. His activity may have taken this form; and if he had a large hand in drawing up these early histories, it would account for the silence about himself (as with S. Luke in the Acts). Certainly there are many phrases and turns which seem to suggest his hand.

To take a few instances—*the Father* which occurs in Acts i 4, 7, ii 33 is of course the familiar Johannine title: *names* (i 15) is used for *persons* in Rev iii 4, xi 13, cp. xxi 14: with *pricked* (ii 37) cp. Jn xix 34. The account of the miracle in iii is very similar to those in Jn v and ix; thus cp. *lame from his mother's womb* (2) with Jn ix 1: the *wondering* (12, 10, 11) with Jn v 20, 28, vii 21: the *glorifying* of Jesus (13) is a favourite Johannine thought, cp. Jn ii 11, vii 39, xii 41, xiii 32 etc.: with the *recognition* (10) cp. Jn ix 8: with *the Holy and Righteous* (14) Jn vi 69, (xvii 11, 25) I Jn ii 1, 20: with *blot out* (19) Rev iii 5, vii 17: the *sending* of the Son (26) is a favourite expression in S. John, iii 17 etc.: with iv 4 cp. Jn vi 10: John was acquainted with *the high-priestly family* (iv 6) Jn xviii 15: the thought of being *unlearned* (iv 13) occurs in Jn vii 15, 49: *seeing and hearing* (20) is S. John's summary for the reception of the revelation, Jn iii 32 etc., I Jn i 1: with iv 22 cp. Jn v 5: with *their own* (iv 23) Jn i 11: *Solomon's Porch* (v 12) is mentioned in Jn x 23: and v 13 may be a kindred statement to Jn (iii 2) vii 13, (48) xii 42 etc.: *the Life* (v 20) is a favourite idea of S. John, and cp. *the words of eternal life* in Jn vi 68: *for the Name* (v 41) cp. III Jn 7: *pleasing* (vi 2) cp. Jn viii 29, I Jn iii 22.

There remains the question of the speeches in the Acts. In classical literature, so far from feeling bound to reproduce the speakers' words, a writer looked upon the speeches as his great opportunity of expressing his own views as to what might or ought to have been said. Are we then to look upon the speeches in the Acts as S. Luke's own compositions or as genuine reports of what was said? For undeniably on a first reading they seem very much alike and they bear unmistakeable signs of S. Luke's pen. In reply, we first notice (1) that they are all exactly suitable to the occasion and are distinctly coloured by the particular and local circumstances. Next (2) as the commentary will shew, we can without difficulty detect the characteristics of the individual speaker: for instance, this is true especially of the speeches at the council; and again it is easy to distinguish S. Peter's, S. Stephen's, and S. Paul's speeches. Now some at least of these last S. Luke must have heard himself, and he may have taken notes. For the short speeches which we have, and which could be spoken in a very few minutes, can only be summaries of what was actually said. They are in fact notes (whether taken by S. Luke or by others) which S. Luke afterwards wrote out in proper form and this will account for their Lucan style and composition.

For the Petrine speeches the oral tradition may again help us. In the catechetical instruction of the disciples, besides the record of deeds and miracles, there was needed some formal summary of the gospel, an authoritative type of doctrinal teaching. This 'teaching' would be best given in the form of discourse, as in the Gospels: and the discourses would naturally be those of S. Peter. Thus S. Peter's declaration of the gospel to the Jews would be the first form of the Apostles' Creed. Indeed it is striking how there recurs throughout the Acts the same form of statement about the Crucifixion and Resurrection: this we find not only in S. Peter (ii 22-4, 32-3, iii 13-5, 26, iv 10, v 30-2, x 37-43) but in S. Luke's Gospel (xxiv 45-8), and in S. Paul (Acts xiii 27-31, cp. 1 Cor. xv 3-4 *which I also received by tradition*), and we may add in our own Apostles' Creed[1]. In a similar way S. Stephen's speech may have been committed to memory (at least on the Hellenist side of the church) as a standard interpretation of the Old Testament history. But we know that S. Paul heard it, and it probably made a deep impression on his memory. He may have been S. Luke's source in this case.

§ 3 *His trustworthiness*

S. Luke's sources may be excellent, but can we rely on his use of them? is he trustworthy? Now S. Luke was quite aware of the need of accuracy for a historian: the last chapters are mainly occupied with the attempts of the Roman authorities to find out some *certain* or *exact* information about S. Paul[2]. Further, it was the uncertainty of the other written documents which moved him to write; and he claims to have written (1) with *accuracy*, and (2) *in order*[3]. And our verdict must be that the claim is justified. To give an illustration, S. Luke is well aware of the importance of fixed dates and the need of connecting his chronology with the history of the world[4]. Accordingly in the second part of the Acts he gives regular notes of time, which when combined with the date of the succession of Felix by Festus (xxiv 27) will make a complete system. But in the first part of the Acts such notes are entirely absent: instead we have indefinite phrases like *in these days, (after) certain days*. For (as in the case of the Gospel) the original Jewish eyewitnesses or writers were indifferent to such exactness of time; and in later years S. Luke, while unable to correct the deficiency, faithfully resisted the temptation to make conjectures of his own.

---

[1] With this reason for the fixed form of the early speeches, it is important to notice that in the speeches there is little variation between the two recensions of the Acts. [2] xxi 34, xxii 30, xxv 26. [3] Lk i 1-4. [4] See Lk iii 1, 23: Lk ii 2, Acts xi 28.

We shall be abundantly satisfied as to S. Luke's historical accuracy, if we reflect on the extraordinary test to which it was put, i.e. the variety of scene and circumstance with which he had to deal. The ground covered reached from Jerusalem to Rome, taking in Syria, Asia Minor, Greece, and Italy. In that field were comprised all manner of populations, civilizations, administrations—Jewish and oriental life, western civilization, great capitals like Antioch and Ephesus, Roman colonies, independent towns, Greek cities, 'barbarian' country districts. The history covers a period of 30 years which witnessed in many parts great political changes. Provinces like Cyprus and Achaia were being exchanged between the emperor and the senate: parts of Asia Minor, e.g. Pisidia and Lycaonia, were undergoing a process of annexation and latinization: Judaea itself was now a Roman province under a procurator, now an independent state under a Herodian king. Yet in all this intricacy of political arrangement S. Luke is never found tripping. Instances of supposed mistake or anachronism have indeed been alleged and laid to his charge: but after examination (as will be pointed out in the commentary) we are fairly entitled at least to answer that they have not yet been proved. On the other hand S. Luke is equally at home with the Sanhedrin and its parties, the priests and temple guard, and the Herodian princes at Jerusalem, with the proconsuls of Cyprus and Achaia, the *rulers of the synagogue* and *first men* of Antioch in Pisidia, the *priest of Zeus* at Lystra, the *praetors, lictors* and *jailor* of Philippi, the *politarchs* of Thessalonica, the *Areopagus* of Athens, the *Asiarchs* with the *people, assembly* and *secretary* of Ephesus, the *centurions, tribune* and *procurator* of Judaea, the *first man* of Malta and the *captain of the camp* at Rome. Such accuracy would have been almost impossible for a writer compiling the history fifty years later. In some cases where his statements had been impugned S. Luke has been signally vindicated by the discovery of inscriptions, as in the case of the politarchs of Thessalonica and the proconsul of Cyprus. Historical research is also throwing fresh light on the *captain of the camp* at Rome, and the *Italic* and *Augustan cohorts* at Caesarea[1]. This holds out good hope that further study or discovery will remove what difficulties and uncertainties still remain. This hope is indeed receiving a remarkable fulfilment at this moment. The one great stumbling-block in S. Luke has been the *enrolment* or *census* of Quirinius[2]: and great authorities like Mommsen and Schürer have pronounced him guilty of error. But recent discoveries in the papyri of Egypt seem likely to clear up the difficulty by giving fuller information about the imperial census[3].

Historical accuracy goes with the faculty of exact or careful observation. Such a faculty may be looked for as a natural result of a medical training; and that S. Luke possessed it we may consider to be proved by the narrative of the voyage and shipwreck in chapter xxvii. This was most

---

[1] xxviii 16: x 1, xxvii 1.   [2] v 37, Lk ii 1.   [3] See Prof. Ramsay's *Was Christ born at Bethlehem?* (Hodder and Stoughton, 1898).

carefully examined by an expert, Mr James Smith[1]. He concluded that S. Luke was quite free from mistakes such as a landsman might easily make; and from his accurate description Mr Smith was able to trace the course of the voyage and to identify the scene of the wreck.

To these two qualities we must add a third—moral honesty or fidelity to truth. We began with an example of this in S. Luke's refusal to conjecture dates. We have also seen his faithfulness in his unfaltering record of shortcomings in the church—discontent, division, sin (p. **xxxiv**). This extends even to his master: he makes no effort to conceal or gloze over the unhappy 'paroxysm' or sharp contention between S. Paul and S. Barnabas. Then we have faithfulness in style. When the scene is in the Jewish church at Jerusalem the narrative is thoroughly Hebraic: elsewhere, in the west or in a governor's court, the style tends to lose this Hebraic character. The last chapters (xxii–xxviii) afford an illustration: for in S. Paul's two great speeches, which describe his past life, there is a remarkable return to the phraseology and ideas of the early chapters, especially of chapter ix[2]. This however is but an element in a wider fidelity, i.e. in describing the situation or state of ideas generally. Just as in the historical setting, so there are no anachronisms in the thought. We have an exact reflection of the mind of the apostles before Pentecost, of the ideas and conditions of the church at Jerusalem before the persecution broke out, and of the relation of parties in the church before the question about circumcision had died away; and without the church, of the attitude—(1) of the Jewish rulers towards the Nazarenes, and of the Jewish parties among themselves before the fall of Jerusalem in A.D. 70; and (2) of the Roman government, and the Gentiles generally, towards Christianity before the outbreak of persecution in A.D. 64 and the growth of popular odium in the decade between 60 and 70. Such a representation, so true to life, it would have been hard to paint after A.D. 70.

S. Luke's success in these points is largely due to his artistic power and his truly human character. First, he has got the sympathetic insight which can thoroughly enter into the feelings of different parties—such as Pharisees and Sadducees, Hebraists and Hellenists; different classes of society—Jews and Greeks, the populace and better classes, local magistrates, Roman officials, Herodian princes; different interests—Pharisaic rabbis and Sadducean priests, Ephesian silversmiths and Jewish sorcerers, Roman aristocrats and Greek citizens; differences of culture—Athenian philosophers and rustic Lycaonians; different professions—soldiers and sailors. Then this appreciativeness is made effective by a gift of style. By a few vigorous touches he can make a scene live before us—whether a scene in the Temple, or a service in a synagogue, or a riot at Ephesus, or S. Paul in the marketplace at Athens or before Agrippa at Caesarea or on board ship in a wreck. In a few words he

---

[1] in his *Voyage and Shipwreck of S. Paul*, 1848.   [2] Besides the very close agreement with ix 3–9, notice in ch. xxii *Jesus of Nazareth, the God of our fathers, the Righteous One, thou shalt be a witness, seen and heard, call upon his Name*; in xxvi *the Name, the saints*.

can draw a character. In the Acts we come across 110 names, besides many other persons or groups whose names are not given, and of these how extraordinarily their individuality is preserved. We have given some instances of women (p. xxxiii): among the men we have Peter and John, James and Paul; the rabbi Gamaliel and Ananias the high priest; Barnabas and Ananias; Stephen and Philip; Simon the 'magus' and Barjesus the false prophet; Cornelius and Julius; Agabus and Apollos; Herod Agrippa I and Agrippa II; John Mark and Timothy; Sergius Paulus and Gallio; the jailor of Philippi and Publius of Malta; Demetrius and the town-clerk of Ephesus; Claudius Lysias and Tertullus; Felix and Festus. Finally, S. Luke has demonstrated his artistic skill by welding this complex variety of persons and places, times and seasons, characters and circumstances, into one whole—a whole in which no tendency or side issue dominates: and a whole so complete, that we entirely forget the variety, we are unconscious of the personality of the author and his method: our attention is simply riveted on the growth of the church and on the personalities of S. Peter and S. Paul; and without any jar or break from the small beginning at Jerusalem we are led on step by step with increasing interest and enthusiasm to the great climax of Paul at Rome.

§ 4 *His method*

A. As the work of an artistic writer the Acts must be constructed on some definite plan and method. The architecture (so to speak) of the history will appear more clearly in its analysis: but there is a characteristic of the scheme which calls for special note, that is its parallelism.

(1) First, there is a general parallel between the first and second books, i.e. the Gospel and the Acts. After a prefatory sentence, both alike begin with an introductory period of waiting and preparation, which is more or less in private (Lk i–ii = Acts i). Then comes a baptism of the Spirit (Lk iii = Acts ii), followed by a period of active work and ministry. This is concluded by a 'passion' or period of suffering, which in each volume occupies a seemingly disproportionate space. The analogy here will appear more convincing as we follow the later chapters in the commentary, but the main outline stands out clear. After early anticipations (Lk ix 51 = Acts xix 21) and a detailed journey up to Jerusalem (Lk xvii 11–xix 48 = Acts xx–xxi 17) with 'last words' of the sufferer (Lk xx–xxi = Acts xx 17–38), we have the 'passion' proper (Lk xxii–iii = Acts xxi 17–xxviii). And then in each case the book ends with a period of victorious but quiet preparation for a further advance, or another volume.

(2) The Acts itself obviously falls into two divisions—Part I ch. i–xi, Part II ch. xiii–xxviii; and between these parts there is a similar parallelism. Each opens with a special manifestation of the Holy Spirit (ii 1–4 = xiii 1–3). A period of work and preaching, persecution and opposition, follows (ii 14–xi = xiii 4–xix). And each ends with a 'passion' or rather a 'passing' of the chief actor, who in each case passes through suffering to a state of deliverance (xii = xx–xxviii). These actors are S. Peter and S. Paul, and the two parts

might well be headed: I *ACTS OF PETER*, II *ACTS OF PAUL*. Further, there is a most striking parallel between the history of these two apostles individually. Whatever Peter does, Paul does, and (we might add) more also. The two apostles are represented as a pair of athletes, wrestling on behalf of the church: they are like the two prophets Elijah and Elisha, and the two witnesses in Rev xi. The parallelism extends even to verbal details, and we must dwell on this in order to be convinced that S. Luke was conscious of it[1].

Like Simon Peter, Saul after his conversion receives a new name. Peter is baptized by the Spirit, Paul separated (ii 1-4, xiii 1-3). Peter is thought to be drunken, Paul to be mad: and both made a solemn *forth-speaking* (ii 13, 14—xxvi 24, 25). In ch. ii and ch. xiii we have their 'gospel' for the Jews. Both heal a lame man which brings them into trouble (iii 1 f.—xiv 8 f.). Peter says *Silver and gold have I none*, Paul coveted *no man's silver or gold* (iii 6—xx 33). Both are arrested in the Temple and brought before the Sanhedrin (iv 1 f., v 25 f.— xxi 27 f., xxiii). Both were inspired by, *filled with, the Holy Ghost* (iv 8—xiii 9). But Peter was found to be *unlearned*, Paul the opposite (iv 13—xxvi 24). The sin of Ananias and Sapphira is analogous to the practice of curious arts at Ephesus, and in each case *fear fell upon all* (v 5, 11—xix 17). *By the hands* of both apostles *signs and wonders are done* (ii 43, iv 30, v 12—xiv 3): at two epochs in an almost superstitious manner by *Peter's shadow* and *Paul's skin* (v 15-16— xix 11-12); their success incurs the *jealousy* of the Jews (v 17—xiii 45). Gamaliel's policy resembles that of Gallio (v 34-39—xviii 14-17): a beating follows in each case; Paul himself shares the glory of being beaten elsewhere (xvi 22—v 40). Gamaliel instances Theudas and Judas, Lysias thinks of the Egyptian Jew (xxii 38). Peter ordains *the Seven*, Paul *presbyters* (vi 6—xiv 23). By the laying on of hands Peter and John give the gift of the Holy Ghost, Paul does likewise (viii 17-8— xix 6: for the speaking with tongues cp. x 46—xix 6). Peter denounced Simon Magus, as Paul Barjesus (viii 20 f.—xiii 9 f.). Peter heals Aeneas when *lying on* a *bed* of palsy, Paul heals Publius' father who was *lying sick* with dysentery: Peter *presented* Dorcas *alive* again; so Eutychus also was brought up *alive* (ix 32-41— xxviii 8, xx 9-12). Peter's first Gentile convert bears a Latin name, Cornelius: Sergius Paulus was Paul's first Gentile hearer. Cornelius was a centurion at Caesarea: so at Caesarea Paul is given into the charge of another centurion, Julius. Before his mission to Cornelius Peter is hungry (x 10—ix 9, 19), falls into an *ecstacy* (x 10—xxii 17) at *midday*, sees a *vision*, hears a *voice* from heaven three times: and the story is told three times (x 9-16, 28, xi 5-10). Compare the thrice-told story of S. Paul's conversion at midday with the voice which likewise came from heaven three times (ix 1-9, xxii 6 f., xxvi 12 f.): Ananias and Cornelius also see visions (ix 10—x 3): cp. also the vision before the mission to Macedonia (xvi 6-10). Cornelius offers Peter worship, as the Lycaonians to Paul (x 25—xiv 13, cp. the Maltese in xxviii 6): for like the jailor at Philippi (xvi 29) Cornelius fell at Peter's feet. Both apostles are called to task by those *of the circumcision* (xi 3—xv 1-5); Peter makes a defence, Paul several. Peter was arrested by Agrippa I: Paul made a defence before Agrippa II. Peter was put in prison at Jerusalem, Paul and Silas at Philippi; and both parties were *delivered* (xii 11—xxvi 17) miraculously (xii—xvi). With the appearance of *the angel* in xii 7 cp. xxvii 23: for the prayer followed by earthquake in xvi 25-26 cp. iv 24-31. Notice the details: *chains* (xii 6—xxvi 29 etc.), *light* (xii 7—xxii 11 etc.), *mad* (xii 15—xxvi 24), *beckoning with the hand* (xii 17—xiii 16, xxi 40). In the end the apostles go to the houses of Mary and Lydia respectively, and *depart* to another place (xii 17—xvi 40).

This parallelism is a weapon in the hands of those critics who impugn S. Luke's honesty. It is obvious, they say, that he has the deliberate intention

---

[1] Some of these instances which may appear strained in the case of the two apostles are added with a view of emphasizing the literary parallel between the two parts of the book.

of magnifying his favourite apostle into a position of equality with S. Peter. But, we can answer, the coincidences occur in the narrative in a most natural way: nothing could appear less artificial. Besides, had S. Luke had such a deliberate intention he could have done much more. We notice indeed that the balance seems to be on S. Paul's side: thus Paul has several visions of the Lord himself, Peter none (after the intercourse of ch. i); Paul works miracles greater in number and effect; and again the 'passing' of Paul altogether outweighs that of Peter in its length. And yet S. Peter seems to hold the first place. The relation of the two is very much that of Elijah and Elisha. In Part I S. Peter occupies the leading position among the apostles; nor does S. Luke mention later on—what would have been very much to his purpose and what actually did make S. Paul equal to S. Peter—the compact made at the time of the council by which Paul was accepted as the apostle of the uncircumcision, as Peter was the apostle of the circumcision. This compact indeed points to the true explanation. The parallelism arises out of the facts; for each of them was chosen by God for an especial work and an especial apostolate. Besides, we find the parallelism outside of the Acts; thus both apostles write Epistles to the churches of Asia Minor. Both alike worked in Jerusalem, Caesarea, and Antioch; and tradition unites them also in cities which we specially associate with the name of S. Paul—viz. Corinth and Rome.

There is a deeper explanation, which is to be found in the similarity of all Christian experience. If we had the lives of other apostles, we should find very similar histories—of prayer and preaching, of wonders and persecution: the special parallelism between S. Peter and S. Paul is due to the special positions they occupied in the apostolate. This experience is exemplified above all in the Son of Man himself; and his apostles and servants must follow in the path he trod. The same Spirit is at work in all, and he works by the same laws. Two such laws lie on the surface: (1) the law of work—which follows the course of preparation, baptism by the Spirit, work, opposition, victory; and (2) the law of victory—that success is won through suffering. This similarity of experience S. Luke observed, and it is with the idea of tracing out these laws of Christian life that he forms his plan.

This might be expressed otherwise by saying that S. Luke has a symbolical mind, in which he greatly resembles S. John. This means that his mind was open to see the underlying significance of the events and facts of life and history. Such minds are ready to perceive similarities or parallels; and a law had already been discovered by the son of Sirach. He found that 'all things are double one against another' (Ecclus xlii 24). Certainly the method of conveying emphasis by repetition prevails throughout the Bible. The Lord's life itself is full of such repetitions. Hence, as in the old kingdom there had been two prophets and as S. John saw in the Revelation two witnesses, so in the Acts the new kingdom is built up by two apostles.

B. Besides this love of parallelism we notice a definite method of composition, which if understood will obviate a criticism. At first sight as a church history the Acts is very disappointing, because it is so incomplete. There are such great gaps: not a word, for instance, about the church in Egypt, or in the further East, or even about the founding of the church in Rome. There is also so much we want to know about the church's constitution and worship, and on so many points S. Luke keeps a tantalizing silence. But the feeling of disappointment is really due to want of ability to appreciate S. Luke's historical method. As he knew that the secret of history lies in personality, so he knew that the true way of writing history is not to compile bare records but to draw living pictures. Accordingly instead of writing a dictionary of historical names and ecclesiastical usages, he gives us a succession of vivid pictures which present to us a living church. Thus we have pictures—of the preaching in the Temple (ii, iii), of the apostles before the Sanhedrin (iv, v), of the internal discipline of the church (v), of the working of signs (iii, ix, xiv), of the election and ordination of church officers (vi), of a martyrdom (vii fin.), of apostolic laying on of hands, and of the work of a Christian prophet (viii). We assist at a proconsul's court (xiii), a sabbath service in the synagogue (xiii), a city riot (xix), a meeting for Christian worship (xx 7-12) and so forth. This method really gives us all we want. For these scenes are intended for typical pictures. Having once filled in the details in one picture, S. Luke does not repeat them elsewhere: we must take them for granted. Thus we have no doubt that vi 1-6 is meant for a typical ordination, viii 14-17 for a typical apostolic confirmation of the newly baptized, xv 5-29 for a typical Christian 'council,' and xx 7-12 for a typical Christian service. In the same way we have a typical sermon to the Jews (xiii), a typical address to philosophers (xvii), a typical appeal to the unenlightened heathen (xiv), and a typical defence before a Roman governor (xxiv).

§ 5 *The date of publication*

We have already found one limit for the date of the Acts, viz. it was written in the life-time of S. Luke. Can we fix it more precisely? An ordinary reader, finding that the book ends without any mention of the result of the appeal to Caesar and that it leaves Paul working at Rome for two years in a kind of 'free custody,' would naturally conclude that the author had written his book in those two years and come to an end because he had no further information to give. If the reader was further aware that shortly after these two years not only S. Paul but S. Peter also was put to death in a fierce outburst of persecution at Rome, and knew that the account of their deaths (which would have formed the natural close of the book) would have been of intense interest not only to their contemporaries but to all future generations of Christians, his conclusion that the Acts was written before the martyrdoms took place would become an irresistible conviction.

In support of that conclusion there are very weighty arguments.

(1) In investigating the date of a book, the first step is to look for the latest event mentioned. Now in the Acts we cannot find any allusion to

events which happened after the close of these two years (A.D. 58-60). And yet within a few years there occurred stirring events with an intimate bearing upon the history, e.g. the martyrdom of S. James in 62, the persecution at Rome in 64 with the martyrdom of S. Peter and S. Paul, and the destruction of Jerusalem and the Temple in 70. He must have been a skilful writer not to let even a hint of these things escape him.

(2) Of these events the most important in this connexion is the death of S. Paul. (*a*) It seems incredible that if S. Luke had known it, he should not have mentioned it. Had he deliberately intended not to mention it, yet it would have been difficult not to let some passing allusion escape from him. In the Gospel of course there are definite predictions of the end. And if any parallel between the Gospel and the Acts is intended, how far more complete it would have been, if the latter closed with the actual laying down of S. Paul's life. As it is, all the preliminary parts of the great process are related at great length—the journey to the place of arrest, the accusations, defences, adjournments at Jerusalem, and the voyage to Rome,—the reader's interest and anxiety are keenly aroused, and then the narrative breaks off, without a word about the final result. Surely it is not what we should have expected from an artist like S. Luke, to arouse the reader's curiosity and then to leave it unsatisfied. This argument may be developed further. (*b*) We have reason to believe that at the end of these two years at Rome S. Paul was set free. Why has not S. Luke told us that? Surely the hearing at Rome, the witness before the emperor, the sentence of the Caesar himself, were far more important than the trials at Jerusalem before procurators and Herodian princes; and a successful issue of the appeal, a favourable decision of the emperor, would have been the best 'defence' of Christianity, if that lay within S. Luke's aim. We can only conclude that when he wrote, the issue had not yet been decided. Otherwise S. Luke is open to the very serious criticism of having committed a great error in the matter of proportion: he has elaborated the first part of the process and omitted to mention its conclusion, which would form the natural climax and conclusion of the book. (*c*) Once more, there is not a word of anticipation, which would have given such dramatic power to the narrative. And yet of the arts of composition S. Luke was a master. As it is, the journey up to Jerusalem is full of dramatic pathos, because of the shadows of the future cast before,—but that future is limited to bonds and imprisonment awaiting Paul at Jerusalem. How much more moving it would be, if the reader were reminded that Paul is on his way to death, as in the last journey of the Lord to Jerusalem in the Gospel! (*d*) To complete this argument, S. Paul's martyrdom would have greatly increased the balance of the book. The first part ends with the martyrdom of S. James. Before this there is a vivid account of the death of Stephen, in Saul's presence. In the subsequent sufferings of S. Paul the writer hints at retribution for that death,—how much clearer the law of retribution would have been made by the apostle's own death! Again, if it was at all S. Luke's aim to demonstrate the unity of the church, could he have found any fitter

conclusion or proof of brotherhood than to exhibit the two leading, and supposed rival, apostles united in death at Rome? A very forcible reply to these arguments is that S. Luke is reserving the deaths of the apostles for a third volume. But we may point out that neither Gospel nor Acts begins with persecution and crucifixion, rather they begin with life and the outpouring of the Holy Spirit. And we may still ask,—to what purpose then is the great and even disproportionate length of the narrative of what after all was only the first part of S. Paul's process in chapters xx–xxviii?

(3) Two matters of detail reinforce this argument. If S. Luke was aware that after his liberation S. Paul visited Ephesus again (as the Pastoral Epistles imply), it is not likely that he would have left Acts xx 25 and 38 as they now stand. Again, if S. Paul visited Spain as tradition alleges, to have mentioned it would have excellently fulfilled the purpose of the Acts to shew how the witness was borne 'unto the uttermost part of the earth' (i 8). And the idea was not new, it had been in S. Paul's mind as early as 54 (Rom xv 24).

(4) After the silence as to S. Paul's death, the weightiest argument is the fidelity with which the Acts presents a situation that could only have existed before 64. The attitude of Rome to the church in the Acts is evidently still undecided, not to say favourable; and S. Luke is writing a defence of Christianity with good hopes of success. But all this was dashed to the ground by the great fire of 64 and Nero's persecution. From that time the relation of the empire to the church is better painted by the Revelation. Rome is the scarlet woman drunk with the blood of the martyrs, and the emperor is the beast. It is true that the actual persecution was after a time relaxed, yet the line of defence had been quite changed. At any rate, if S. Luke wrote after that disaster, his peaceful joyful optimism would be hard to understand. No doubt the Acts itself shews how persecution leads to good; but it is hard to conceive S. Luke, with all his personal devotion to S. Paul, sitting down after his death and so calmly finishing the Acts with his preaching at Rome—*none forbidding him* (xxviii 31). Similarly on the Jewish side the continued existence of the Temple and the Jewish polity is, so to speak, taken for granted in the Acts. The last we hear of the Jewish church is that *there are myriads among the Jews who believe* (xxi 20); there is no hint that the church of Jerusalem with the successor of S. James is at the moment in exile at Pella. The destruction of the temple was also the final solution of the question which so vexed the early church as to the observance of the Law; but no hint of this divine decision is given at the time of the discussion in ch. xv. Nor is there any hint that chapters iii–v and xxi represent a scene and situation which no longer exist.

(5) Lastly there is the evidence of language. The Acts faithfully reflects, as the ideas, so the phraseology of the early church. In style it takes its place with the Gospels; and the reference to *the words of the Lord Jesus* (xx 35) points to a time when they were in process of formation. What is more decisive is the fact that among his authorities S. Luke makes no use of S. Paul's Epistles, the earliest of which was written in 49. While he had

access to the living apostle, there was no need of his letters. But some references, at least to explain apparent inconsistencies, must have been inevitable in the years after his death. If the Epistles were already in circulation and S. Luke was holding a copy of Galatians in his hand, he must have been more explicit as to ix 19–30 and xv. We may go further: the Acts in itself suggests living intercourse with the apostle. For in the later chapters there is much resemblance in style to the Pastoral Epistles.

These arguments are sufficiently obvious and their weight is fully admitted by critics. Professor Harnack, for instance, is so impressed by the joyful and optimistic tone of the Acts as to maintain that, if written after 64, it must have been written after a considerable interval; he also finds no evidence of the use of the Pauline Epistles. Dr Ramsay also argues "that the plan of the Acts has been obscured by the want of the proper climax and conclusion[1]." But we have had to labour the point, because nevertheless these and the majority of critics, even of those who accept the Lucan authorship, agree in putting the date much later, about A.D. 80: thus Dr Sanday puts it between 75 and 80. This is based upon one argument which is considered strong enough to upset all the rest; and it is this. The Acts was written after the Gospel; but the Gospel was written after 70, because the differences between S. Lukes and the other Gospels in the form of our Lord's prophecy of the destruction of Jerusalem shew that it had already taken place. The differences are these. S. Luke omits the warning *let him that readeth understand*, and for the words *When therefore ye see the abomination of desolation, which was spoken of by Daniel the prophet, standing in the holy place* substitutes *But when ye see Jerusalem compassed with armies, then know that her desolation is at hand* (Mt xxiv 15, Lk xxi 20). In verse 24 he adds particulars: *And they shall fall by the edge of the sword and shall be led captive into all the nations: and Jerusalem shall be trodden down of the Gentiles, until the times of the Gentiles be fulfilled.* Then he continues *And there shall be signs etc.*, omitting the note of time in S. Matthew (xxiv 29) *But immediately after the tribulation of those days.* Again in Lk xix 43 we have another detailed prophecy: *For the days shall come upon thee, when thine enemies shall cast up a bank about thee and compass thee round and keep thee in on every side, and shall dash thee to the ground and thy children within thee, and they shall not leave in thee one stone upon another.*

Now there are several considerations to rob this argument of its force. In any case it is certain that the Lord predicted, and the Christians expected, the overthrow of Jerusalem. We need only quote a striking phrase of S. Paul in I Thess ii 16, *to fill up their sins alway: but the wrath is come upon them to the uttermost.* These words were written at least as early as 49, and there are echoes of them in the Lucan passage (Lk xxi 22–23). Then S. Luke was writing for Gentile readers at Rome, and the note of warning had no application to

---

[1] *Paul the Traveller etc.* p. 23. Harnack's judgement is given in his *Chronologie der altchr. Literatur* i pp. 246–50; Dr Sanday's in his *Inspiration* pp. 278–9.

them. Nor would they have understood the enigmatical words *abomination of desolation*; so he translates them into ordinary language. This process we see at work in S. Mark's Gospel also, for he omits the mention of Daniel and for *the holy place* writes *where he ought not*[1]. Moreover the detailed language which S. Luke uses is nothing more than would be implied in the destruction of a city. Least of all was that experience new to the city of Jerusalem. Twice within the preceding century, or century and a half, had Jerusalem been taken, with great slaughter and misery and desecration of the holy place. But these disasters were far eclipsed by the way in which, under Antiochus Epiphanes, the Gentiles had trodden the temple under foot; and some centuries before that Nebuchadnezzar had destroyed and burnt the whole city. So in fact S. Luke had no lack of precedents for his language in the Old Testament, where in reference to Jerusalem we can find parallels for nearly all of his details[2]. After all, besides the general phrases, there is no detail specially characteristic of the fall of Jerusalem in particular. In the history of Josephus there are many incidents to which S. Luke could have referred: for instance, the burning of the temple. But it is indeed striking that S. Luke should have omitted all mention of the holy place in his prophecy[3]. Lastly, if he wrote even ten years after the destruction of the city, in spite of the omission of the *immediately* (which S. Mark also omits) the difficulty of the conjunctions *And...and* remains. For we still read *And there shall be signs...and then shall they see the Son of Man coming* (vv. 25, 27).

There is a similar argument used against the earlier date, of about A.D. 60, viz. that it does not allow sufficient time for the written 'attempts' at gospel narratives to which S. Luke alludes in his preface. But a whole generation is allowed; and there are sufficient writings dating from that period to show that Christian literature had already attained to maturity. For the Epistles to the Thessalonians, Corinthians, Galatians, and Romans, were all written between about 49 and 54. S. James' Epistle was written before 62; and if S. Peter was martyred in 64 we must add at least his First Epistle. It is admitted also that the Gospels of S. Matthew and S. Mark were written before the destruction of Jerusalem in 70 (and on that depended the point of the preceding argument). But if there was a considerable interval between these Gospels and his own, S. Luke would have probably seen them, and then he could hardly have used the somewhat depreciatory language of his preface.

We see, then, nothing in these arguments to invalidate the natural inference that the Acts was written during S. Paul's two years' imprisonment. And we may go a step further. It has been noticed already that the Acts

---

[1] Mk xiii 14: S. Mark may represent the original form, and then S. Matthew's would be as much an Hebraic version as S. Luke's a Gentile one. [2] For the *sword* cp. Jer xx 4; *captivity* Dt xxviii 64, 1 K viii 46; *treading* Isai v 5, lxiii 18, Dan viii 13, Zech xii 3, 1 Mac iv 60; *bank* Isai xxix 3, xxxvii 33, Jer vi 6, Ezek iv 2; *dashing* Ps cxxxvii 9, Hos xiii 16. S. Matthew is not without details: he speaks of one stone not being left upon another. [3] This argument is also against the use of Josephus by S. Luke (above p. xviii).

shews signs of want of finish, as if it had not received its author's final revision. May we not conjecture that that final revision was interrupted or prevented by this very outburst of persecution in 64, by the martyrdom of S. Paul and possibly of S. Luke himself? Professor Ramsay has come to a similar conclusion. To quote his words again: "We shall argue," he says, "that the plan of *Acts* has been obscured by the want of the proper climax and conclusion, which would have made it clear, and also that the author did not live to put the final touches to his second book....If the work was left incomplete, the reason, perhaps, lay in the author's martyrdom under Domitian." This conclusion we may readily adopt for our own, only substituting for *Domitian—Nero*[1]. (See pp. viii a-viii c for Dr Harnack's position.)

CHAPTER IV

The History of the Acts

§ 1 *The political and social environment*

(A) **Rome.** It is hard for us to realize to what an extent Rome was the centre of the world in the age when the Acts was written. In the middle ages long after its old empire was gone, the Christian poet and philosopher Dante saw in it a divine creation; and certainly the Roman empire was one of the greatest factors in the preparation for the gospel and instruments in its propagation.

More almost than Paris to France and London to England was Rome to all the countries which bordered on the Mediterranean Sea. And those countries formed the whole civilized world, if we omit the alien and rival empire of the east. This world Rome had made one; and to all intents and purposes the civilized world was the Roman Empire or the Kingdom of Rome. This political unity brought (1) peace—the famous *Pax Romana*: (2) unity of civilization—that Graeco-Roman civilization which at our epoch was rapidly assimilating Asia Minor and the eastern provinces, as also the more barbarous frontiers on the north: and (3) unity of language and law with freedom of intercourse and communication. (4) More than this, it gave rise to a sense of unity and brotherhood. It seemed to realize the ideal of philosophers, when the human race should form one society, one kingdom, one brotherhood; and of this unity the Roman citizenship was the crown, it was the entrance into the inheritance.

At the centre of this kingdom sat the city of Rome—a city powerful and populous and splendid. Like the centre of gravity, it attracted the whole empire: thither ran all roads and all lines of commerce; thither flocked leaders of society and fashion, seekers after fortune and pleasure, philosophers and the setters forth of new doctrines. Rome was also the pivot upon which turned the whole military and civil administration of the empire. Her hands

---

[1] *Paul the Traveller etc.* p. 23. Nero first persecuted the Christians in 64, and died in 68: Domitian was emperor 81-96.

grasped the reins which controlled the movements of the legions by which she had won and kept this great inheritance. She sent forth the governors or officials who worked the machinery in the provinces; and to her, as the final court of appeal, resorted all unsatisfied litigants. Rome, then, was indeed the mistress of the world. And now at her head was no longer an aristocracy or democracy, but a single ruler: one head, one absolute king, sitting as it were in the place of God. No wonder that the provincials deified the city and her ruler[1]; that the worship of the emperor became universal, and formed the chief bond of unity in the empire; and that the emperor's own head was turned, and like the mad Caligula he believed himself divine.

Nor did the Christians escape the contagion of this influence. This great kingdom of Rome with its citizenship and emperor took the place of the commonwealth of Israel as the pattern of the new kingdom of God—the kingdom which was one and universal, whose citizenship was heavenly, whose capital was the Jerusalem which is above, and whose king was the Lord Jesus Christ[2]. In the richness of the thought and language of the Epistle to the Ephesians we may find a sign that S. Paul's imagination was deeply stirred, when he witnessed the pomp of Rome, of the city and its imperial system. S. Luke also must have felt some patriotic admiration, for these imperial ideas lie at the basis of the Acts. To S. Luke the Roman takes the place of the Jewish citizenship: Rome, and not Jerusalem, is the capital of the world: and the world is the empire—the eastern kingdoms are out of his horizon[3]. The Acts indeed describes the growth of a new and spiritual kingdom[4]; but the city of Rome is the goal even of this kingdom. In fact, we shall only understand the Acts when we see in it the history of the advance of the church from Jerusalem to Rome, or, to be more exact, of the apostle Paul to Rome. Paul the Jewish Pharisee preaching the gospel of the kingdom of Jesus at Rome—that is the climax. Later, when this great power had become the adversary of the church, the impression it made on the Christian imagination is vividly portrayed in the Revelation. There it has become the type of the world power, of Antichrist. In the 17th and 18th chapters, we are almost drawn within the fascination of the spell cast over the world by the glorious city, the lady of the nations, clothed in scarlet and purple, who is seated on the seven hills; while the beast who carries her, and who also sits on the throne of this world and is worshipped and overcomes the saints, is the power of the empire personified in the emperor.

There are four departments where the church in the Acts comes into contact with the Roman system, and they were all making for unity.

(1) *The government.* The empire was divided into provinces, which very nearly corresponded with modern or at least mediaeval kingdoms, and each of these was under a Roman governor. If appointed (as all had been originally)

---

[1] Cp. xxv 26 and commentary. [2] xvii 7: the Greek words for *king* and *kingdom* are those used for *emperor* and *empire.* [3] They are only mentioned in a Jewish enumeration (ii 9). Cp. xi 28, xvii 6, xix 27, xxiv 5. [4] xvi 37, xxii 25: i 3, 6, xxviii 31.

by the senate, he was a *Proconsul*; if by the emperor he was a *Prefect*, or in an inferior province a *Procurator*. But, however appointed, he was under the immediate control of the Caesar or Augustus[1]. The governor then, together with his suite of Roman 'companions' (*comites*) who formed his court (*comitatus*) in both senses of the term[2], was the centre of Roman influence in the province and the chief bond of connexion with Rome. He was also the supreme authority, from whom an appeal lay only to the emperor, and his judicial action was directed everywhere alike by Roman law and customs[3]. In the Acts we come across two proconsuls, Gallio and Sergius Paulus, and two procurators, Felix and Festus[4].

(2) *The army* was the foundation of the Roman power. It was composed of legions, subdivided into cohorts and centuries under tribunes and centurions respectively. The legions were by no means recruited from Latin races only; the barbarians of the north, for instance, were beginning to contribute a large element to the army: but wherever the legions went they took with them the Roman discipline. In the times of the Roman Peace, the main bulk of the legions was stationed on the frontiers, along the Rhine, the Danube, and the Euphrates; and their own militia sufficed for the inner provinces. But a turbulent country like Judaea required a permanent garrison. Five cohorts were stationed at Caesarea, and one at Jerusalem in the tower of Antonia overlooking the temple. With both of these forces we are brought into contact; but the particular *Augustan* and *Italian cohorts* mentioned have not yet been identified. The influence of the army chiefly made itself felt through the centurions, who were officers of great power in the provinces. The characters of those whom we meet with in the Gospels and Acts, e.g. Cornelius and Julius, give a very high testimony to the Roman service[5].

(3) *The Roman colonies* were almost more important than the army in keeping a hold on the provinces. They were often composed of veteran soldiers, and so formed regular garrisons. But these cities possessed the Roman citizenship and their constitutions were modelled on that of Rome; and so they served as centres of latinization, and by their citizenship as it were brought Rome into the provinces. S. Paul's work in the colonies would be a preparation for work in Rome, and among such were Antioch of Pisidia, Troas, Philippi, and Corinth, although S. Luke uses the name of Philippi only.

(4) Military needs gave rise to the *Roman roads*, which were made by the soldiers. These famous roads ran throughout the empire and, like the iron railroads of to-day, formed the main arteries of civilization. As they all converged on Rome, they were a great factor in the centralization and unity of the whole. They made communication at once easy and rapid: so much so, that until railways were laid down, never was travelling in Europe so frequent and easy as in the days of the Roman empire. Of this facility of intercourse we have ample evidence in the Acts.

---

[1] xxv 25, in a Bezan authority. [2] xxv 12, xiii 7. [3] xxv 10–12: xxii 25, xxv 16. [4] xiii 7, xviii 12, xxiii 24, xxiv 27. [5] Cp. x 1, xxi 32 f., xxiii 23 f., xxvii 1, 42, xxviii 16. The soldiers of xii 4 were Jewish, of Herod's army.

It is easy, then, to see what a help the empire was to the missionary work of the church. For instance, it enabled S. Paul to pass freely from one country to another and to keep up regular correspondence with his churches: his Roman citizenship gave him everywhere the same privileges and a recognized status; the Roman governors and their law protected him against the fanatical persecution of his own nation and popular violence: the Roman roads were the guiding lines of his missionary enterprises, and they led him at last to Rome itself.

The provinces which form the scene of the Acts are these. (1) We begin in SYRIA. As this was the frontier province on the east, touching the powerful empire of the Parthians, it was one of the most important commands in the empire. In wealth and prosperity it almost ranked next to Egypt. Certainly its capital Antioch was the third city in the empire. Dependent on the prefect of Syria were (i) CILICIA, which was practically separated from the west by Mt Taurus and so was included in the east, and (ii) JUDAEA. This difficult country was at one time (A.D. 41–44) independent, under a Jewish king Herod Agrippa I, but for the rest of our period it was under a governor of the second class, a procurator. This official was subject to the higher authority of the prefect of Syria, but he was appointed directly by the emperor and was often one of his freedmen. (2) Crossing Mt Taurus by the Cilician gates, we come to GALATIA. This province was in the course of formation. The central part of Asia Minor west of Cappadocia had been split up into a variety of territories and nationalities. There were Galatia proper, the part of Phrygia outside of the province of Asia, Pisidia, Lycaonia, the tetrarchy of Iconium, and the territory of the king of Commagene. The first century witnessed the consolidation of these various elements into one province, which took its name from its chief district, Galatia or the land of the Gauls. At the time of the apostles' mission this process of organization was still going on. (3) The roads to the west led through Galatia into ASIA. This province comprised the western coast of Asia Minor, taking in Mysia, Lydia and Caria, and behind them the greater part of Phrygia. It was full of prosperous and wealthy towns, among them being the seats of 'the seven churches of Asia.' Indeed Asia with its capital Ephesus was almost a rival of Syria and Antioch. Asia and Africa were the two most important senatorial appointments, which were always given to senators of consular rank. (4) Taking the land route to Rome, we should cross from Troas to join the Egnatian way at Philippi. This road leads across the province of MACEDONIA, which bordered on Dalmatia or Illyricum and included Thessaly. This was Rome's first province beyond the Adriatic, and more than any of the eastern provinces Macedonia retained its national feeling. To break this feeling the Romans had divided it into four districts, with separate jurisdictions; and it was of one of these districts that Philippi claimed to be the capital. Thessalonica was the capital of the whole province. (5) Taking the sea route to Rome from Ephesus, we should cross the Aegean sea to Greece and take ship again the other side of the isthmus of Corinth. Greece formed the province of ACHAIA, and the flourishing colony of Corinth was its capital. Athens, out of respect for her ancient glories, had been left by the Romans a free city; and at one time, as a compliment to Greek art, Nero gave freedom to the whole of Achaia. Besides that there had been some political unsettlement, for the province had been the subject of exchange between the emperor and senate more than once. Apart from its art and its traditions Greece was not an important government. (6) One province has been omitted, which we should have passed if sailing direct from Syria to Italy, viz. the island of CYPRUS. This too had been exchanged between the emperor and senate, and so like Achaia gives an opportunity of testing S. Luke's accuracy. Cut off by the sea, Cyprus did not occupy an important place in the life of the empire; but Jews formed a very large element in the population, and it became one of the early cradles of Christianity.

(B) Judaism. Over against Rome stood another capital of the world—and no unworthy rival—Jerusalem. The city itself was by no means ignoble: it was wealthy and splendid, and its chief glory was its famous temple rebuilt on a magnificent scale by Herod the Great. Pliny calls Jerusalem "by far the most glorious city of the east." But Jerusalem owed its greatness to another cause. It was the holy city. As opposed to Rome the world power, the city of the king of this world, Jerusalem represented the spiritual power; it was the city of the Great King, and its people were the People of God. The Jewish race was then, as now, widely scattered—certainly all over the eastern half of the empire. But wherever Jews were to be found, they were sharply separated off from the rest of the world, or *the Gentiles* (*nations*) as they called them. With Romans and Greeks the Jews formed a third 'nation' in the empire. They were, again as to-day, numerous, wealthy, and influential; but also hated, with a universal hatred which they cordially reciprocated. And one of the first obstacles the church had to overcome was this mutual hatred and contempt between Jew and Gentile[1]. All these Jews looked to Jerusalem as their mother city with an intense loyalty; thither they all sent temple tribute and offerings; thither they flocked at the great feasts, and every Jew at least once in his lifetime hoped to make the pilgrimage[2].

Thus as a capital Jerusalem could not help being a rival of Rome, and Judaea was the centre of an intense anti-Roman feeling. To every Jew the idea of subjection to the yoke of the Gentiles was intolerable; it was wholly contradictory to their choice and election by God. They were convinced that God would speedily send the Messiah to break the hated yoke and to subdue the kingdoms of the world beneath the feet of Israel. Extremists taught that to pay tribute to the Gentile was contrary to the law of God, and that rebellion was a religious duty. With such a fanatical faith Judaea was growing more and more restless, and the restlessness was increased by Roman misgovernment. The Jewish authorities, the Sadducean high-priests, tried to stem the tide: but rebellion became more and more the popular creed, preached and acted

---

[1] Cp. e.g. x 28, xi 3. [2] Cp. ii 5–11, (viii 27), xx 16, xxi 27, xxiv 11, 17, xxviii 21.

upon by the faction of Zealots, until at last the flame burst out in the Jewish war of 66; and the end was the destruction of Jerusalem and the burning of the temple in 70. This was after our period, but we can trace clear signs of the growing turbulence of the fanatical party[1].

Outside Palestine 'the Dispersion' (as they were called) of the Jews formed a great element in the preparation for the preaching of the gospel among the Gentiles. The Jewish colonies and synagogues in the foreign cities gave the apostles at once a home, a starting-place for preaching, and a pattern of organization. The Jewish communities, recognized by the law as self-governing societies, with their own officers and discipline and courts, formed the model for the Christian communities: similarly the worship of the synagogue, which was distinct from the service of the temple, was the trunk on which was grafted the public worship of the church: and again the sense of brotherhood among the Jews, which was a great reality, paved the way for the Christian 'love of the brethren' and hospitality[2].

But the greatest service which the Dispersion rendered was to act as the stepping-stone by which the church crossed over from Judaism to the Gentiles; just as in fact the synagogues of the Dispersion already provided for the apostles a Gentile congregation[3]. Notwithstanding racial hatred and prejudice, great numbers of the Gentiles, in their craving for spiritual satisfaction, were attracted by the pure monotheism of the Jews and attached themselves to the synagogue. Some were circumcised and became regular proselytes. Others, declining that crucial step, became adherents under varying degrees of compliance with the Jewish law. These formed the class of *the devout* or *God-fearing* (often called *the Greeks*), which we find in every synagogue[4]. Among a far wider circle must have spread at least some knowledge of the Jewish scriptures and the Jewish faith in one God.

(C) Hellenism. Between these two antagonistic forces of Romanism and Judaism stood a third factor, viz. Greek culture or Hellenism. The Greeks were no longer a political power or a nationality like the Jews and Romans. But they had conquered the world by their language and literature, their art and philosophy. Their very masters, the Romans, proved ready disciples; and the resulting Graeco-Roman civilization was the great unifying force which went hand in hand with the conquering legions. The east had already been Hellenized by the Macedonian conquests: Rome came in to put her seal on the process and to give it the necessary stability. Thus Greek became the recognized language of good society, and 'a Greek' was synonymous with an educated person. From this point of view the world was divided into two classes 'Greeks' and 'Barbarians[5],' just as to a Jew all men were either Jews or Gentiles. This Hellenism, then, filled the part of mediator between the Jews and Romans; on the one hand it prepared Gentile minds for the religious

---

[1] v 26-8, 36-7, xxi 30, 38, xxii 22, xxiii 12.   [2] xxii 5, xxviii 21 : xvi 15, xvii 7, xviii 3, xxi 8, 16, xxviii 14.   [3] xiii 5, 14, xiv 1, xvii 1-2, 10, 17, xviii 4, 19, 26, xix 8.   [4] vi 5, viii 27, x 1-2, xi 20: xiii 16, 43, 50, xiv 1, xvi 14, xvii 4, 12, 17, xviii 4, 7.   [5] xxviii 2; cp. xiv 11: also Rom i 14, Col iii 11.

ideas of the Jews, on the other it had a great effect in softening Jewish fanaticism. The mass of the Jews of the Dispersion spoke the Greek language and used Greek translations of the scriptures. Their Hebrew brethren of Palestine called them, not without a tone of contempt, *Grecians* (*Hellenists*)[1]. For these Hellenists were not proof against the subtle influence of a more cosmopolitan experience and a broader education. They became impregnated with Greek ideas. The Alexandrian Jews were the most liberalized; and the school of Philo devoted themselves with enthusiasm to the study of the Greek classics and philosophy, and attempted the reconciliation of Plato with Moses.

In their turn it was the Christian Hellenists who were the mediators between the church and the world. As soon as the gospel reaches them we find a sudden expansion of ideas and widening of the horizon: Stephen, Philip, and the men of Cyprus and Cyrene[2], were Hellenists. Apollos was a Jew of Alexandria. Paul himself, though a Hebrew of the Hebrews, was a citizen of Tarsus. So in the Gentile cities it was the two classes of 'Grecian' Jews and 'devout' Greeks which formed the seed-plot of the church. Hellenism had thus done almost as great a work as Rome in educating the world for Christianity. It had provided a common language and rendered unnecessary a gift of strange tongues. It had provided a common culture and a common intellectual atmosphere. Paul, for instance, could speak freely at Jerusalem or in Asia Minor, at Ephesus or at Corinth, at Athens or at Rome, and everywhere be understood. But Hellenism had rendered the greatest service in the sphere of religion. Greek criticism and philosophy had undermined the old pagan beliefs and religions. Superstition dies hard, and the empire (as we see in the Acts) was full of all manner of worships and sorceries and mysteries, but as far as thinking men were concerned the old idolatry was dead. The elementary principles of natural religion had been thought out—the spirituality of the divine nature, the unity and beneficence of God, the brotherhood of man. But that was all, and religious minds were now athirst for some positive revelation. This the apostles were commissioned to give; and, finding ready to hand the first principles, they make them their starting-point. At least so we find S. Stephen doing at Jerusalem, and S. Paul at Lystra and Athens. Accordingly we have now to trace the fortunes of this fourth power, new-born into the world,—Christianity. This will best be done in a brief analysis of the history of its beginnings.

§ 2 *Analysis of the history*

The Acts obviously falls at once into two Parts, viz. chapters i-xii and xiii-xxviii: and each of these parts may be divided into three Divisions. From the personal or apostolic point of view we may call the parts—I **Acts of Peter**: II **Acts of Paul**. In analysing their contents a double line of growth is to be traced. Externally, Part I records the extension of the church from Jerusalem to Antioch; Part II from Antioch to Rome. Internally, in Part I the church, which starts as a purely Jewish body, expands to the point

---

[1] vi 1, xi 20 marg.   [2] vi 1 f., xi 20.

of admitting Greeks: in Part II we pass from the ratification of this admission to the full development of Gentile churches. So we can give the parts other titles—I The church of Jerusalem or The church of the circumcision: II The church of the Empire or The church of the uncircumcision.

Part I The acts of Peter

Division i (i–v) relates the baptism and establishment of the church at Jerusalem. (1) Chapter i is preparatory: i 1–5 or 1–14 is really introductory to the whole volume. For before the Holy Spirit can be poured forth, (*a*) the Lord must ascend to heaven in order to receive the power of bestowing him, (*b*) and the church must be prepared to receive the gift by prayer and the completion of its outward form, i.e. the filling up of the apostolate. (2) The descent of the Spirit at Pentecost is the baptism of the church, and the presence of his power is manifested at once—in the preaching and conversions without, and in the new life of the faithful within. After this (3) the church is consolidated through opposition from without and temptation from within. The opposition is aroused by the working of the Spirit in miraculous signs, and the Christian answer is prayer: the common life which is the result of the presence of the Spirit within is the occasion for the sin of covetousness, which is compensated for by the self-sacrifice of others. Jesus is preached to the Jews as their Lord and Messiah, their Prince and Saviour; and the final result is joy and progress (v 41–42).

Division ii (vi–xi 26) begins the history of the expansion of the church. It opens with mention of *Hellenists* and ends with *Greeks* at Antioch. The immediate cause of expansion was a persecution, which was itself brought on by the action of a vigorous personality; and the division accordingly falls into two sections, which describe his acts and their manifold consequences. (1) *The acts of Stephen.* The ordination of the Seven (including a proselyte of Antioch) leads to the ministry of Stephen. Stephen's deeper teaching about the law precipitates a conflict with the Jews. His death and the consequent persecution bring Saul on the stage. (2) *The things that arose about Stephen.* (2a) *The acts of Philip.* Philip's preaching of the Christ to schismatic Samaritans is sanctioned by the apostles and the Holy Spirit; he also baptizes an Ethiopian proselyte—an eunuch and a child of Ham. The church is planted in Samaria and reaches Caesarea the Roman capital of Palestine. (2b) *The acts of Saul.* There are disciples already at Damascus, and on his way thither Saul the persecutor is converted. This conversion is pregnant for the future: but for the present he is sent away to Tarsus. Meanwhile the presence of a new force in the church is seen in his preaching Jesus as the Son of God. (2c) *The acts of Peter.* These ought to begin a new section, but the next section keeps up the connexion with Stephen's death (xi 19). Peace returns after the persecution, the total result of which was the spreading of the church throughout Judaea, Galilee, and Samaria. After an apostolic visitation as far as Joppa, Peter formally opens the door of the church to a Gentile adherent of the synagogue, Cornelius, and so establishes the church at

Caesarea. He preached Jesus to Cornelius as the Lord and Judge of all, and the source of forgiveness for everyone that believeth. At Jerusalem are heard the first sounds of human reluctance, but the baptism of Cornelius is ratified by the Spirit and accepted by the church. (2d) *The acts of the Hellenists.* The church reaches Phenicia, Cyprus, and Antioch. Here the Lord Jesus is preached directly to 'the Greeks,' i.e. probably Gentile adherents of the synagogue. This advance is sanctioned by the church in Jerusalem through its delegate Barnabas. Barnabas also brings back Saul on to the stage of the history. The whole advance of this division is summed up in the title given at Antioch to the disciples, hitherto known as 'Nazareans' or 'Galileans,' viz. 'the Christians.'

Division iii (xi 27–xii) closes Part I and at the same time is transitional. The centre of interest passes from Jerusalem to Antioch, and the rôle of chief actor from Peter to Paul. The church at Jerusalem is weakened by famine and persecution. Peter, the last of the Twelve to remain, leaves the city, after a miraculous deliverance from death which is a type of resurrection. The place of Peter and the Twelve is taken by James the Lord's brother and the presbyters. The death of Herod Agrippa, which is a divine judgement, is followed by renewed growth of the word of God. The mission of Barnabas and Saul from Antioch is the connecting link with Part II.

Part II   The acts of Paul

We now turn westwards, and the political interest lies in the steady advance through the provinces to Rome, and the occasions on which the apostles are brought in contact with the Roman authorities: also in the attitude towards Christianity of the various classes and interests in the empire. When the principle of the admission of Greeks has been fully established, the theological interest centres on the relation of Christianity to its various rivals in religion. The usual division into the three missionary journeys of S. Paul is very misleading. However convenient it may be geographically,—but the convenience is very much open to question,—it certainly does not fall in with S. Luke's scheme and marks of division, which are somewhat as follows.

Division i (xiii–xvi 5). The new start is from Antioch and it begins in xiii 1–3 with a special manifestation of the Spirit, by which S. Paul is separated for his work as an apostle. Henceforward he steps into the place of Peter, and the new departure is marked by the change of name from Saul to Paul. These verses are really the introduction to the whole of Part II: and the remainder of division i comprises two sections. First (1) *the work of Paul and Barnabas.* It begins with Paul's first appearance before a Roman governor, and a conviction of a false prophet Barjesus. At Antioch in Pisidia Paul delivers to the Jews his gospel of Jesus as Saviour: when they reject it, he turns to the Gentiles, i.e. to those who are quite independent of the synagogue. This is the first absolute break with Judaism, and it brings persecution from the Jews, but the Lord confirms the apostles' action by signs and wonders. As a result we have Paul's gospel for the Gentiles, i.e. the 'barbarian' Gentiles, at Lystra;

and the definite organization of Gentile churches, in this case 'the churches of Galatia.' Thus the door of faith is opened to the Gentiles. (2) The reception of the Gentiles on equal terms arouses protest and opposition in the church, but it is solemnly ratified by the church at Jerusalem and the Holy Ghost. This gives occasion for a statement of the views of Peter and James; and the letter which conveyed the result of the council at Jerusalem is joyfully accepted by the churches of Antioch, Syria, Cilicia, and Galatia. In response S. Paul shews his loyalty to the council and even circumcises Timothy.

Division ii (xvi 6–xix 20). The principle of Gentile churches being fully established, there follows the advance of the church from Antioch to Ephesus, or the foundation of the churches of Macedonia, Achaia, and Asia. (1) *Macedonia*. After preparatory leading by the Holy Spirit, Paul comes to Philippi, and the character of the new epoch is marked by his assertion of his Roman citizenship. At Philippi the evangelists are accused of teaching Jewish customs, at Thessalonica of treason against Caesar. (2) *Achaia*. At Athens Paul is charged with breaking the city's law by the introduction of strange deities: in reply he gives his gospel for the educated Gentiles and Greek philosophers. At Corinth is forged the first definite link with Rome through the meeting with Aquila and Priscilla; on the other hand there is a second breach with the synagogue. At Corinth, for the first time since leaving Antioch, Paul settles down for prolonged work and his action is sanctioned by an appearance of the Lord. (3) *Asia*. After 18 months at Corinth Paul is indicted in the proconsul's court for teaching an 'unlawful religion': he leaves Corinth and touches at Ephesus, whither he shortly returns for permanent work. Meanwhile *the acts of Apollos* bring out the relation of the church to imperfect forms of Christianity, such as 'the way' of John the Baptist. On Paul's return a special outpouring of the Holy Spirit is the divine preface to the work at Ephesus, which succeeds to Antioch as the third metropolis or mother city of Christianity. A breach with the Jews leads to the organization of an independent church with a body of presbyters, and in two years the gospel spreads through the whole province. The presence of the Spirit vindicates itself by a conviction of superstitious practices without and a purification of the church within: and the victories of the church at Ephesus mark the climax of its advance. In the next division the personal element predominates. For

Division iii (xix 21–xxviii) concludes the book with the 'passing' of Paul. With S. Paul the headquarters of Christianity moves on from Ephesus to Rome, and the main subject is the *Apologia* or *Defence of Paul*,—that is, in effect, of Christianity. (1) First, on the fulfilment of his work, his face is directed by the Spirit Romewards. (*a*) The work at Ephesus is cut short by a conflict with the pagan worship of Artemis; the Christians are for the first time accused of impiety towards the goddess, i.e. the later charge of 'atheism.' (*b*) After finishing his work in Macedonia and Achaia, Paul goes up to Jerusalem, thence to make a new start for Rome. On his way he makes a defence of his apostolate to the church of Ephesus, which contains at the same time his 'last words' and his gospel for the Christians. (2) At Jerusalem Paul is arrested and his process begins. (a) First the unity and brotherhood of the church is vindicated in his reception by James. Then the riot in the temple calls forth his defence to the Jewish people. Failing to disarm their hostility, Paul dissociates himself from Judaism by claiming his Roman citizenship. This strong action, with his line of defence in the Sanhedrin, is approved by a consolatory vision of the Lord. Then his cause is taken out of the hands of the Jews, and the apostle himself 'delivered into the hands of the Romans. (b) At Caesarea the Jews indict him in the Roman court, and Paul makes his defence to the procurator. There is a private preaching to Felix; then, failing to obtain justice even from a juster judge, Festus, Paul appeals to the supreme court, to the Caesar at Rome. His final defence, 'before kings and governors and the people of Israel,' is answered by the third declaration of his innocence on the part of the Romans. (3) The journey to Rome proves to be a 'going down into the deep': but S. Paul is brought out of it by a great deliverance. An interval of quiet rest at Malta follows. Next spring, the season of resurrection, the voyage is resumed; Paul reaches Puteoli, is welcomed by the Roman Christians, and enters the city of Rome. At Rome the lesson of the past history is summed up in a final rejection of the gospel by the Jews with the consequent turning to the Gentiles. Then the whole book ends with two years' quiet work: though a prisoner, Paul exercises his apostolate in the capital of the kingdom of Caesar by preaching the gospel of the kingdom of Jesus to all men alike 'without any hindrance.'

For convenience of reference the analysis is given in tabular form at the end of the Introduction, pp. cix-xi.

§ 3 *The chronology*

We have already noticed that in the earlier part of the Acts there are no fixed chronological data. To the early Christians, expecting the immediate return of their Lord, chronology was supremely unimportant; and there was no Luke among them. So by his time uncertainty had crept in. Indeed we may doubt whether S. Luke himself knew the date of the crucifixion; otherwise we are left to wonder why he did not give us the date of the great Pentecost in ch. ii, to correspond with his date for the baptism of Jesus in the Gospel (Lk iii 1).

In the second part, however, he gives several definite notes of time: e.g. xi 26 *a whole year*, xviii 11 *a year and six months*, xix 8 *three months*, 10 *two years*, xx 6 *the days of unleavened bread* (cp. xii 3), 16 *the day of Pentecost*, 31 *three years*. There is a regular diary of the journey marked in xx 6, 14, 15, xxi 1, 4, 7; and of the early proceedings in Paul's case in xxi 27, xxii 30, xxiii 11, 12, xxiv 1, 11, 27 (*two years*), xxv 1, 6. Finally, we have xxvii 9 *the Fast*, 27, xxviii 7, 11 *three months*, 12-14, 17, 30 *two whole years*. These notes enable us to construct a more or less certain chronological scheme for the latter part of S. Paul's work, viz. from ch. xv (or even xiii) to xxviii. With the aid of two data given us by the apostle in the Epistle to the

Galatians[1], we can carry our scheme back to his conversion and the martyrdom of S. Stephen, and so include within it ch. vi–ix. What we want, however, is to connect this scheme with secular chronology, or to find out the dates of the years after Christ. Now among all the points of contact between the Acts and profane history, there is only one fact of whose date we are certain; that is the death of Herod Agrippa in A.D. 44. And unfortunately S. Luke has left us without any definite links of time between chapter xii, where that event is recorded, and the chapters which follow and precede it.

There is indeed an event whose date, if ascertained, would at once fit on the chronology of the Acts to that of secular history. That date was perfectly familiar to S. Luke, but unfortunately he has omitted to specify it. It is the date of the succession of Felix by Festus as procurator of Judaea (xxiv 27, xxv 1). Arguing in the main from the supposed requirements of Jewish history as recorded by Josephus, Wieseler fixed it at A.D. 60; and this date has been adopted by Bp Lightfoot and the majority of English scholars. Little attention was paid to the fact that we had the information already given us. Eusebius had put the date down in his Chronicle, which gives *the second year of Nero*. The Chronicle, however, was not compiled until the fourth century, and it has only come down to us in Armenian and Latin translations; and so its evidence was disregarded. But quite recently Professor Harnack has argued strongly in its favour. He accepts its date for Festus' arrival at Caesarea, viz. 56, and on this basis has drawn up a chronology of the Acts. His scheme, however, appears to make most of the events fall a year or two too early; and Mr Turner, who has since examined the whole subject with the greatest care, selects the year 58 for Festus' appointment[2].

Mr Turner, however, has himself given a hint for a solution, which will enable us to accept the Eusebian date and at the same time to advance the chronology by the required year. By acute calculations he claims to have made the discovery that Eusebius reckons the first regnal year of an emperor from the September next after his actual accession. The second year of Nero, who succeeded Claudius in Oct. 54, would then be Sept. 56–Sept. 57, and so we can take 57 for the date of Festus' arrival[3].

From this date, A.D. 57, for xxiv 27–xxv 1, we can work forward as follows. Ch. xxv–xxvi fall in the summer of 57, the voyage (xxvii–xxviii 6) in the autumn; the stay at Malta lasted from Nov. 57 to March 58; the party arrived at Rome in the spring of 58, and the two years at Rome extended from the spring of 58 to the spring of 60, when the Acts closes. Eusebius puts S. Paul's martyrdom in 68, which will allow eight years for the labours subsequent to his liberation, which are implied by the Pastoral Epistles. But

---

[1] i 18 *three years*, ii 1 *fourteen years*: but there is an uncertainty as to whether these dates are mutually inclusive or exclusive. [2] In Hastings' *Dictionary of the Bible*: art. CHRONOLOGY. [3] Mr Turner's theory leads to the somewhat strange result that Nero must have reigned 11 months before his first regnal year began. But it is quite easy to imagine that by some difference in reckoning the regnal years, Eusebius should be just a year out.

though Bp Lightfoot accepted this date, there are reasons (also traditional) for supposing that here Eusebius made a mistake. He has in fact put the Fire of Rome in that year. But the date of the fire was 64; and if S. Paul was put to death in the same year as the fire, i.e. in the persecution which ensued upon it (as is implied by Eusebius' reckoning), then S. Paul was martyred in 64, and an interval of four years is left after his liberation for the Pastoral Epistles.

Working backwards from 57, the last journey to Jerusalem (xx 6-xxi 26) falls between Easter and Pentecost of 55, and the riot in the temple (xxi 27 foll.) happened immediately after Pentecost. Winter 54-55 was spent at Corinth, the summer of 54 in Macedonia (xx 2-3), and S. Paul left Ephesus about Pentecost 54 (xix 21-xx 1). Accordingly he arrived at Ephesus about the autumn of 51 (xix 1, 8, 10); and in the spring of that year he left Corinth (xviii 12-21). This fixes his first arrival at Corinth to the autumn of 49 (xviii 1, 11). The summer of that year was occupied in the first visit to Macedonia and Achaia (xvi 6-xvii), and the preceding spring and winter 48-49 were spent in Galatia, Cilicia, and Syria (xv 36-xvi 5). If Paul and Silas left Antioch in the late summer of 48, the council at Jerusalem would have been in the same year, probably about Pentecost, and the disputation had raged at Antioch during the preceding winter 47-48 (xv 1-35). Allowing 18 months for the first missionary journey, if Paul and Barnabas returned to Antioch at the close of the sailing season of 47, then they started at the opening of the sailing season, i.e. in the spring, of 46 (xiii-xiv). We have now got back to chapter xii and Herod's death in 44. The mission of Paul and Barnabas to Jerusalem probably took place in the intervening year 45 (xii 25); and the visit of the prophets to Antioch, which is closely connected with Herod's persecution, was paid in 43, the year before his death (xi 27). Then the *whole year* of xi 26 will be 42-43, and Barnabas fetched Saul from Tarsus in 42. From Galatians ii 1 we learn that Paul's visit to Jerusalem in ix 26-30 took place 14 years before the council of 48, viz. in 34. This was *three years after* or *in the third year after* (Gal i 18) his conversion, which therefore fell in 32 (ix 1-19). This year will also be the date of Stephen's death and the persecution, or vi 8-vii; and Philip's work in ch. viii will fall in 33. As S. Luke generally writes *in order*, the baptism of Cornelius (ix 31-xi 18) probably followed Paul's visit of 34, but very soon after, so as to fall within *the days of the beginning* (xv 2). Allowing some interval for the ministry of the Seven (vi 7), we may put their appointment in 31 (vi 1-6). Taking 29 for the date of the crucifixion and therefore of the first Pentecost (i-ii), we have left two years 29-31 for ch. iii-v.

This chronology will agree very well with our other data[1].

Thus (1) it appears that Aretas king of Arabia (2 Cor xi 32) could hardly have been in possession of Damascus before 33-34. According to this scheme

---

[1] For authorities and fuller information I would refer to the article on CHRONOLOGY in Hastings' *Dict. of the Bible*.

S. Paul was 'let down in a basket by the wall' in 34 (ix 25): in the preceding interval 32–34 he had visited Arabia (Gal i 17).

(2) It is supposed from the order of events in Josephus that the famine under Claudius (xi 23) could not have taken place before 46. We place it in 45. Josephus gives no dates at all, and there is nothing to prevent our supposing it to have been due to the failure of the harvests of 44 and 45. S. Luke closely connects it with the death of Herod in 44.

(3) We know the names of the proconsuls of Cyprus for the years 51 and 52: as Sergius Paulus is not one of these, he must have been proconsul either after 52 or before 51. In this scheme he was in Cyprus in the year 46.

(4) Orosius, a late historian, assigns the expulsion of the Jews from Rome by Claudius (xviii 2) to his ninth year, viz. 49[1]. We make Paul arrive at Corinth in the autumn of 49 and then he could quite well have found Aquila and Priscilla *lately come from Italy*.

(5) Gallio's brother Seneca was in banishment before 49; and it is not likely that, while Seneca was in disgrace, his brother should have been treated with honour. Seneca was recalled in 49. Acts xviii 12 seems to imply that Gallio was a new governor, and according to our plan he would have arrived at Corinth at the beginning of 51 or the end of 50.

(6) Paul speaking in 55 says to Felix *thou hast been of many years a judge unto this nation*: as Felix was appointed to Judaea in 52 this only gives three years which are hardly *many*. But according to Tacitus[2] Felix had previously been in command of Samaria, while Cumanus was procurator of Judaea.

(7) In 62 Nero married Poppaea, a Jewish proselyte. It is, then, not very likely that he would have acted fairly to S. Paul in 62. Besides, in 60 (our date for his liberation) Seneca and Burrhus still had influence.

Prof. Ramsay has made an ingenious calculation which would fix 57 for the final journey up to Jerusalem. He calculates that the apostolic party left Philippi on a Friday, and therefore the passover that year must have fallen on a Thursday (xx 6). Now this was the case in 57, but not in 55, 56, 58, 59[3] Mr Turner has examined his argument and comes to the conclusion that it is not convincing, but that it leaves a certain presumption against the year 55. However, considering the general uncertainties of chronology due to the possibility of mistakes, intercalations etc., and considering the uncertainty of many points about the passover in particular, such an argument is too minute to carry conviction or seriously disturb a scheme which otherwise satisfies the requirements. The greatest objection to Prof. Ramsay's theory is that there are points in the journey where our diary fails us; thus for instance at the outset, we do not know for certain that the party left Philippi the next day after the passover.

An objection which may be made to our scheme is that it allows only

---

[1] Claudius acceded Jan. 41. His actual ninth year was from Jan. 49 to Jan. 50: according to Mr Turner, in Eusebius' reckoning it would be Sept. 49 to Sept. 50.
[2] *Ann.* xii 54.   [3] *Paul the Traveller* pp. 259–60.

three years, 29–32, for the development of the church at Jerusalem as recorded in ch. i–vii, and that this time is not sufficient. By reckoning the 14 years of Gal ii 1 as inclusive of the 3 years of Gal i 18, we might advance S. Paul's conversion to 34 and thus get two more years; but we do not really want them. In fact three years seems the outside limit of time required. For (1) such a long period of quiet development as five years would have been almost impossible. It is incredible that the church could have been growing for such a time without a conflict with the Jewish authorities. After the crucifixion of Jesus, how could they have allowed Peter to go on preaching in the temple and using such language as is recorded in ii 23, iii 15? The arrest of iv 1–3 must have followed speedily. Moreover the language of the priests in v 28 shews that at the later arrest the crucifixion was still a recent event. A second time the apostles were threatened and admonished. But they did not obey (v 29, 42), and we cannot imagine that the high-priests would for long have tamely submitted to such defiance. Further (2) the rapid growth of the church elsewhere shews how short a time was needed for the development at Jerusalem. S. Paul had only stayed for 18 months at Corinth, and the church there had only been founded about four or five years, when he wrote I and II Corinthians. At Ephesus his work, which resulted in the spreading of the word all over Asia, did not exceed three years. But there is a better illustration. Our Lord's active ministry only lasted for little more than one full year, or on the outside reckoning two years.

The results of the scheme are arranged in tabular form at the end of the Introduction, pp. cxii–xv, and there the references to current events will make further explanations unnecessary.

CHAPTER V

The Theology of the Acts

In the Acts we find the religion of Jesus Christ as originally set forth in the teaching of the apostles. This consisted of: (A) A bearing witness to, or proclamation of, certain facts, viz. the death and resurrection of Jesus and the gift of the Holy Spirit. This message was *the Word*, and it will be found to correspond very much to our Apostles' Creed. (B) A practical appeal for conduct which should result from these facts: and in this appeal is contained the apostles' account of salvation and of the Christian life.

§ 1 (A) *The theology*

The word of God in the main part consisted of the enumeration of the facts about our Lord which are contained in the Apostles' Creed[1]. But the remaining articles of the creed can also be gathered from this book.

---

[1] The chief passages are ii 22–4, 32–3, iii 13–5, 18, iv 10, v 30–2, x 36–43, xiii 27–31.

(i) **I believe in God the Father Almighty, Maker of heaven and earth.**

The Jews already possessed the doctrine of the one God, so now it is proclaimed to the Gentiles—the educated at Athens, the uneducated at Lystra[1]. What the Jews needed was a more spiritual conception of the divine nature and a less material one of the divine kingdom (vii 48-50). That we are the offspring of God is taught at Athens (xvii 28): but the doctrine of his Fatherhood is one of the inner mysteries of the brotherhood. The name of *the Father* occurs only in i 4, 7, and ii 33[2]. To the Gentiles God (the FATHER) is presented as *Maker of heaven and earth*[3]: to the Jews he is the God of the Old Testament—*the God of our fathers, of the people Israel*, and *of the glory* or the 'shekinah,' the divine dwelling place[4].

(ii) **And in Jesus Christ his only Son our Lord.**

The apostles preached '*Jesus*'[5] both to Jews and Gentiles. To the former they vindicated his claim to be the Messiah or *Christ*, and therefore *Lord*[6]; their message to the latter was that this Christ was anointed to be *Lord of all*[7]. To the Christian he was generally *the Lord*, or *the Lord Jesus* or *our Lord Jesus Christ*. S. Paul reached the climax when he *proclaimed Jesus that he is the Son of God* (ix 20).

The facts of the crucifixion and resurrection are the core of the gospel. The crucial event was the resurrection, and to bear witness to this was the special function of an apostle[8]. For *suffered*, see i 3, iii 18, xvii 3, xxvi 23: *under Pontius Pilate* iii 13, xiii 28: *was crucified* ii 23, iv 10, v 30, x 39, xiii 29: *dead* ii 23, iii 15, v 30, vii 52, x 39, xiii 28, xxv 19: *and buried* xiii 29, cp. ii 29, xiii 36: *he descended into hell* (*hades*) ii 31: *rose again the third day* x 40. Ch. i narrates the Lord's ascension, which was his exaltation, his being *taken up* (i 11, 22) or *exalted* (ii 33, v 31) by *the right hand of God* (ii 33, v 31). At that right hand he is now *sitting* (ii 34) or *standing* (vii 55-6). And *thence he shall come* again (i 11, iii 20-1) *to judge the quick and the dead* (x 42). This last doctrine, as one of the elementary principles of religion, is declared chiefly to Gentile hearers, e.g. in x 42, xvii 31, xxiv 24-5.

(iii) **I believe in the Holy Ghost.**

The Acts may be described as the gospel of the Holy Spirit, as will be shewn below (p. lxxiv). It begins with his descent, and is a record of his work. This work is manifested in *the Church*. The Spirit acts through men who form a society—a brotherhood or kingdom. And when this society is baptized with the Spirit at Pentecost, then at once it shews signs of a divine vitality.

The church is *holy* as composed of *the holy*[9], i.e. those who by the gift of the Spirit have been *consecrated*[10] to God. The great controversy of the Acts arose out of the vindication of the *catholic* character of the church, viz. that it

---

[1] xvii 22-31: xiv 15-7. [2] Cp. Lk x 21-2. [3] xiv 15, xvii 24: cp. iv 24, vii 50. [4] iii 13, xxii 14, xxiv 14: xiii 17: vii 2. [5] viii 35, xvii 3, 18, xix 13. [6] ii 36, iii 20, v 42, viii 5, ix 22, xvii 3, xviii 5, xxvi 23. [7] x 36: cp. ii 36. [8] i 22, ii 24, 32, iii 15 (26), iv 10, v 30-2, x 40-1, xiii 30-3, xvii 3, 18, 31, xxii 15, xxv 19, xxvi 8, 23: cp. I Cor ix 1, xv 3-8. [9] or *saints* ix 13, 32, 41, xxvi 10. [10] i.e. *made holy* or *sacred* xx 32, xxvi 18.

is open to all men, to Jew and Gentile alike, without respect of persons[1]; and the history shews the gradual translation of this ideal into fact. The church is 'apostolic' also, as founded by the apostles and cleaving stedfastly to their teaching (ii 42), its very history being comprised under *the acts of the apostles*. Lastly it forms a *communion of saints* : there is one common life of the whole body, in which each member has a common share in the privileges of the inheritance of God, and which is manifested externally in the common sharing of their worldly goods[2].

The entrance to the church was through baptism[3]. This baptism was for *the forgiveness of sins* (ii 38): and the offer of forgiveness with the accompanying gift of the Holy Spirit was the 'gospel,' or 'good tidings of great joy,' brought to men through the work of Christ[4].

The resurrection—from the dead, of dead men, both of just and unjust, is the natural consequence of the resurrection of Jesus, the representative Son of Man[5]. As being closely connected with the doctrine of the judgement to come it was preached mostly to Gentiles. Among the Jews, being already held by the Pharisees, it was mainly preached in opposition to the scepticism of the Sadducees[6]. The belief in *eternal life* (xiii 46-8) flowed, not necessarily from the doctrine of the resurrection, but from the character of the life already communicated to and enjoyed by the church (v 20): for this life is that of the Spirit, divine and therefore eternal. But the Christians still walk by hope[7], because the promise, i.e. the ideal, is not yet fully realized. They still wait for the return of the Lord, who will bring in the restoration of all things or 'the world to come' (iii 20-1).

It is evident from the Acts that the fundamental doctrines of the Christian faith—of the Trinity, the Incarnation, the Atonement—were not taught by the apostles dogmatically; they were rather contained implicitly in their teaching. This forms another point of resemblance to our Apostles' Creed. The reason is fairly obvious. Life comes before thought; action before reflection upon it. The church had first to live upon the doctrines before she preached them; to manifest and verify them in her living experience, before she attempted to analyse and define them.

Thus the doctrine of the Trinity, of the three Persons in one God, is nowhere asserted in the Acts in plain terms; but it is implied throughout, and without it the mutual relations of the FATHER, of the SON, and of the SPIRIT, would be inexplicable.

For (1) the three Persons are often mentioned as cooperating in the same act : in many more places the names are found in close proximity, as if they were inseparable. An instance occurs in the opening paragraph (i 4) where

---

[1] ii 21, x 43: xviii 5, 10, xx 21, xxvi 19-23 : x 34. [2] ii 42: xx 32, ii 44-5, iv 32. [3] ii 38, 41, viii 12-3, 38, ix 18, x 47-8, xvi 15, 33, xviii 8, xix 5, xxii 16. [4] v 31, x 43, xiii 38, xxvi 18. [5] iv 2, xvii 18, 32, xxiv 15, 21. [6] i.e. the resurrection of men apart from that of Jesus: cp. iv 2, xxiii 6-8, xxvi 8. [7] xxiii 6, xxiv 15, xxvi 6-7, xxviii 20.

Jesus says *Wait for the promise of the Father which ye heard from me.* The other instances are found for the most part in S. Peter's speeches[1]; but also in those of S. Paul, and in the narrative[2].

(2) The same functions are indifferently assigned to different Persons. Thus (*A*) the FATHER and the SON alike *pour out the Holy Spirit* (ii 17–33), *choose* (i 2–xiii 17), *appoint* (xxii 14–xxvi 16) and *give commandment to—the apostles* (i 2–xiii 47), and *deliver* (vii 10–xxvi 17, xii 11) by their presence (vii 9–xviii 10, cp. xiv 27). Other instances will be given below. Each of these Persons is alike *the* LORD: and this causes ambiguity as to the parallels. We have, for instance, *the grace* (xiv 26–xv 40, xx 24–32, xi 23–xv 11, xiv 3–xiii 43), *word* (viii 14–25, xiii 46–49, xiii 5–xv 36, xiii 7–xix 10, vi 7–xix 20), *way* (xviii 25–26), and *will* (xxi 14–xxii 14)—both *of God* and *of the Lord*: compare also *giving signs* (xiv 3–xv 12, cp. ii 19), and *turning to* (ix 35, xi 21–xxvi 20). In many of these cases it is undoubtedly Christ who is referred to as *the Lord*: but the very fact of the ambiguity is itself the strongest argument. Most striking of all, *the Spirit of the Lord* (v 9, viii 39) is *the Spirit of Jesus* (xvi 7). (*B*) Both the FATHER and the SPIRIT *spake through the prophets* (i 16–iv 25, iii 21–xxviii 25, ii 17–xxi 11), *call to work* (xiii 2–xvi 10, cp. ii 39), *set* or *appoint* (i 7–xx 28). A lie *to the Holy Ghost* is a lie *unto God* (v 3, 4): at one time S. Peter speaks of *tempting the Spirit of the Lord*, at another of *tempting God* (v 9, xv 10). (*C*) Between the conversion of S. Paul and the baptism of Cornelius there is a remarkable parallelism: one is distinctly the work of *the Lord* (Jesus), the other of *the Spirit*. So the SON as well as the SPIRIT is *holy* (iii 14, iv 27, 30, cp. also Lk i 49): and the word *promise* is used of both (i 4, ii 33–xiii 32). Baptism is generally *in the name of Jesus Christ*, but it is also *in the Holy Ghost* (i 5, xi 16); and this sacrament is the great occasion for the cooperation of these two Persons (ii 38, xix 5–6, cp. ix 17). A similar coordination is found in vii 51–52 and ix 31. (*D*) *Sending* and *witnessing* are predicated of all three Persons in turn. See xv 8–xx 23–v 32, cp. xiv 3: x 36–ix 17–x 20, cp. xii 11, xxii 21, xxvi 17.

(3) Functions that are unmistakeably divine are ascribed to the SON and the SPIRIT, as we shall see. But at the same time the unity of God remains unquestioned, as an axiom.

The doctrine of the Incarnation is similarly implicit. No doubt the apostles themselves did not fully realize at the first all that was intellectually contained in their attitude towards their Lord. But they lived by their faith in him, and it is easy to trace the gradual unfolding to their conscious understanding of what that faith meant.

At first Jesus is the apostles' master—*the Lord Jesus* (i 6, 21). At Pentecost S. Peter proclaims him as *Jesus of Nazareth*, the *man approved of God* and *his holy one*: he (as a true Adam) has been anointed to be the head of the human race, i.e. *the Christ, the Lord* and Conqueror, who sits on the throne

---

[1] i 7–8, ii 33, 38–9, iv 8–10, 30–1, v 30–2, x 38, 46–8, xi 17, xv 8–11. [2] xx 23–4, 28: vii 55, xi 23–4, xvi 6–10, xxviii 23–5.

of David¹. In the next sermon he is *the Servant of the Lord, holy* and *righteous*, i.e. the fulfiller of the law²: *the Prince of life* and *Saviour*, i.e. the giver and restorer of life both bodily and spiritual, or a greater Joshua³: the *Prophet* like unto Moses, i.e. the revealer of God's will⁴: and the *Seed of Abraham*, the source of blessing and the father of the new Israel⁵. Before the Sanhedrin Peter declares Jesus to be *the Stone*, the foundation of God's temple or the Jewish polity, now exalted to be its crown or *the Head of the corner*, i.e. head of the renovated temple or church of God (iv 11). S. Stephen adds, by the way of figure, the title of *Redeemer* or *Deliverer*, the office of *Ruler and Judge*, and the position of *Mediator*⁶. He also declares the perfect humanity of the *SON of MAN*: to which the complement is given (whether by Philip first or Saul) in the climax of the *SON of GOD*⁷. This name however had been already implied in the name of the FATHER in i 4, 7, ii 33. S. Philip sees in Jesus *the Lamb* led to the slaughter (viii 32). S. Paul, in his first sermon, finds in *Jesus* the fulfilment of *the Promise*—as, later on, he is *the Hope—of Israel*; and by inference gives him, as the true David, the supreme title of *King*⁸. The whole revelation is summed up, in the last verse of the Acts, in the name of *the Lord Jesus Christ*.

Some of the functions of the SON mentioned above are divine. But it is the position of Jesus which cannot otherwise be explained without blasphemy. For he is at the right hand of God, in the divine *glory* or 'shekinah,' and receives prayer (vii 56, 59, 60). To the Jews the revelation of God was summed up in *the Name*, i.e. the divine name of JHVH which might not be uttered⁹: but in the Acts *the Name* is always that of Jesus Christ; the Christians *call upon his name* (as upon that of JHVH), and his name is borne by them¹⁰.

The church is the kingdom of God, but it is Jesus who restores it and is its king¹¹; and in appointing Paul to be an apostle, his choice is identical with that of *the God of our fathers*¹². If God is *Lord of heaven and earth*, Jesus is also *Lord of all*: and if God *giveth life to all*, Jesus is the *Prince of life*—he is the *Living* one¹³. But what exceeds all, he bestows the divine Spirit; and this *Spirit of the* LORD is his own spirit, *the Spirit of Jesus*. Instances have already been quoted of the way in which Jesus imperceptibly, as it were, glides into the place of the LORD (JEHOVAH) of the Old Testament¹⁴. The crucial passage of course is xx 28, where we read of *the church of God which he purchased with his own blood*. We may possibly translate *with blood which is his very own*. But taken plainly as it stands, unless we are to make S. Paul speak of the blood of the FATHER—which is an impossible thought,—the passage must mean that Christ is God.

In this connexion we must notice that there is one point where the

---

¹ ii 22, 27: 31, 36: cp. Lk i 32. ² iii 13, 14; iv 27, 30; vii 52, xxii 14. *Holy* here is a different word from that in ii 27. ³ iii 15, v 31; i 6, iv 9, 12, v 31, ix 34, xiii 23. ⁴ iii 22, vii 37. ⁵ iii 25–6: xiii 17, 26. S. Paul speaks of the *Seed of David* xiii 23, Rom i 3, cp. Acts ii 30. ⁶ vii 35, 27, 38. ⁷ vii 56, viii 37 AV, ix 20. ⁸ xiii 23, 32, xxviii 20: xiii 22. ⁹ See Lk i 49, xi 2. ¹⁰ v 42: ix 14, 21, xxii 16 (ii 21): ix 15 (xv 17). ¹¹ i 6, iii 20–1, xvii 7. ¹² xxvi 16—xxii 14. ¹³ xvii 25—x 36: xiv 15—i 3. ¹⁴ See especially ii 33—17, i 24—iv 29, xviii 10.

coincidence of the Acts and the Apostles' Creed fails. The Acts is silent as to the article *Who was conceived by the Holy Ghost, born of the Virgin Mary*. But the Acts is only a second volume, and the first began with the explicit narrative of the facts of the miraculous conception (Lk i–ii). The reason for the silence in the Acts is the same as for the silence in the subsequent chapters of the Gospel. The Jews had to learn the meaning of the person of Jesus from his own revelation of himself in his words and works. To have begun with proclaiming the story of his miraculous birth would have created prejudice and hindered the reception of that revelation. Similarly in the Acts, both Jews and Gentiles had first to learn in the experience of the life of the church *what Jesus had done and said* (i 1). Only when they had learnt that, was it time to go on and ask Who was he? and whence came he? Accordingly the preaching of the gospel by the apostles began with the Lord's baptism, with which their own experience had begun[1]. For in fact the apostles could not bear personal witness of the miraculous conception in the same way that they could of the crucifixion and resurrection. They knew that he was the Son of God, and for the present it sufficed to declare that *God had raised him up*[2]. We may notice however that Mary is called *the mother of Jesus*, and Jesus was of the seed of Abraham and David; but there is no allusion to a human father[3].

The doctrine of the Atonement is also implicit. No theory or explanation is given, but we have the fact that through the death and resurrection of Christ there has been won for men *forgiveness of sins* and *peace* with God[4]. The necessity that the Christ should suffer is also asserted; and the law likewise holds for his followers[5]. S. Stephen implies that he is the great redeemer, like Moses who delivered Israel out of Egypt: S. Paul teaches that he purchased or acquired the church with his own blood[6]. But the early church did not require a new theory. The doctrine of atonement by vicarious suffering, however it may be explained, was enunciated in the Old Testament, especially in the great prophecy of Isaiah liii. And the apostles made its teaching their own, when Peter called Jesus *the Servant of the* LORD, and when Philip declared him to be the *sheep led to the slaughter* and the *lamb dumb before his shearer*[7]. The disciples however had no wish to theorize on the past. They were content to receive the forgiveness of their sins, and their minds were occupied with the present work of Jesus. This work is represented by

The doctrine of the Holy Spirit. The Acts is the gospel of the SPIRIT. It contains almost as distinct a manifestation of the SPIRIT, as the Gospel does of the SON. There is a new revelation of the HOLY GHOST alike (1) in his own person, (2) in his relation to man, and (3) in his relation to the divine nature.

(1) The reason is clear, for the Spirit is the intermediary between God and man. God is Spirit; and it is only in the Holy Spirit that man can hold

---

[1] i 22, x 37, xiii 24, Mk i 1.   [2] iii 26, xiii 23.   [3] i 14, iii 25, xiii 23.
[4] ii 38, xiii 38 : x 36.   [5] iii 18, xvii 3, xxvi 23: ix 16, xiv 22.   [6] vii 35: xx 28.   [7] iii 13, 26, iv 27, 30; viii 32.

§ 1 THE DOCTRINE OF GOD lxxv

communion with him[1], just as it is in his Spirit that Jesus is present in and works amongst men. We might almost say that the Holy Ghost is God (or rather, God in Christ) working in the world. But we are saved from Sabellianism (the idea that the SON and the SPIRIT are only names for different aspects of God) by the distinct assertions of the Spirit's personality. He speaks with an emphatic first person: 'go with the men, for *I* have sent them,' 'separate *for me* Barnabas and Saul[2].' He is not only given by the FATHER and poured out by the SON, he also *comes* and *falls* upon man as of his own will[3].

(2) The 'gospel' of the Acts is the gift of the Spirit, or his new relation to man. In the OT he had acted on or through man as an external force. The Gospel deals with his relation to Jesus the Son of Man. In the Acts he is given to man and dwells in man, as his very life. So close is the communion that at times (as in S. Paul's Epistles) we do not know whether to write *spirit* with a big or little S[4]. The human spirit is absorbed into the divine. The gift of the Spirit, then, makes the Christian. The Christian is one filled with the Spirit[5]. But this normal indwelling does not exclude special inspirations[6], nor special gifts or manifestations of the Spirit, such as the working of signs, speaking with tongues, and prophecy[7]. As there is but one Spirit, so all who receive the gift are made one body, the church; and the reception of the Spirit effects or completes admission into the church[8]. The essential fruit of his presence is unity and fellowship[9]; individualism is the contradictory of the true spiritual condition. And so the church is the great sphere of the Spirit's activity. The Acts is the history of his work in the church; and it is to be noticed that there is no allusion to any action of the Spirit outside the church. By his descent at Pentecost he fills the church with life and power[10]. He starts it on its living course; and he acts as its guide, manifesting himself at every critical moment and initiating every new departure[11]. As the Paraclete he nurtures the church; as the Spirit of truth he guides it into the truth[12]. In the OT his great work had been speaking by the mouth of the prophets; so now he inspires the apostles and prophets of the new covenant[13]. And lastly, as the giver of spiritual gifts and the source of inspiration, his special care and charge is the ministry of the church: he, as God, appoints the bishops to tend the church of God[14].

(3) This revelation of the work of the Spirit proves him divine. Equally with the SON and the FATHER we find the SPIRIT directing the church[15]; and as in the Gospel blasphemy against the Spirit is the most heinous sin, so in the Acts tempting the Spirit is equivalent to a lie against God[16]. The relation

---

[1] vii 55. [2] x 19–20, xiii 2: cp. viii 29, 39, xi 12, xiii 4, xvi 6–7. [3] i 8, xix 6: viii 16, x 44, xi 15. [4] as in vi 10, xviii 25, xix 21. [5] ii 4, ix 17, xiii 52: vi 3, 5, vii 55, xi 24. [6] iv 8, 31, xiii 9. [7] *Powers* cp. i 8, vi 8: *tongues* ii 4, x 46, xix 6: *prophecy* xi 28, xx 23, xxi 4, 11. [8] viii 15–9, ix 17, x 44–8, xv 8, xix 2–6. [9] See ii 1, xv 25 and 28. [10] i 8, iv 33 and v 32, vi 5 and 8, x 38: the Spirit really is the *Great Power of God* (viii 10). [11] See ii 4, iv 8, vi 3, 5, viii 15, 29, 39, ix 17, x 19, xiii 2, xv 28, xvi 6-7 (xix 1 Bezan), xix 21, xx 22. [12] ix 31: xv 28. [13] i 16, iv 25, xxviii 25: cp. vii 51-2. [14] xx 28: cp. the laying on of hands in vi 6, xiii 3. [15] x 20, xiii 2. [16] Lk xii 10, Acts v 3, 4, 9.

between the three Persons of the Blessed Trinity is also clear. *The SPIRIT proceedeth from the FATHER and the SON.* He is the promise and the gift of the Father. Jesus the Son of Man is first anointed by the FATHER with the Spirit and power. But having thus received the Spirit in his human nature, as soon as he is exalted to the FATHER'S right hand and glorified, Jesus the Son of God pours forth the Spirit upon the church[1].

§ 2 (B) *The soteriology*

The practical appeal of the apostles is the best commentary on the third paragraph of the Apostles' Creed. As expressed in S. Peter's first sermon, this appeal is unmistakeably clear; and we can distinguish three stages in the process of becoming a Christian. (1) *Repentance*[2]. This is the name for a change of mind in relation to God (xx 21) and to sin. True repentance necessitates a corresponding change in the outward life which shews itself in *works*, i.e. a manner of life, *worthy of repentance* (xxvi 20). Hence repentance involves, or may be described as, a *conversion* or turning of the whole being to God[3]. (2) This change finds its public expression and divine ratification in *Baptism* into the name of Jesus Christ[4]. Baptism itself has two sides. Outwardly it is the public profession of faith in Jesus made by the individual, and the church who receives him makes response in the symbolical signs of washing with water and of blessing by the laying on of hands. Inwardly it is the conveyance of a free gift and a blessing from God, viz. the forgiveness of sins and the gift of the Holy Spirit[5]. The latter gift was conveyed by the laying on of hands, which usually followed immediately upon the 'washing'; but an interval might occur, as in Samaria[6]. (3) By this gift man is brought into a new relation to God. He is made 'holy' or sanctified, i.e. he is made one of God's people and called into communion with him. He is also brought into a new relation to the rest of those who have been sanctified, i.e. he is added to the fellowship of the apostles[7]. In other words, baptism is the entrance into *the Church*. And henceforth the life of the baptized is life in the church. For the church is *a way* or mode of living. The way, as seen from without, is the common life of the brotherhood; to walk in it is to walk in the *ways of life*, which means *eternal life*; and so the church can be described as *this life*[8]. To be walking in the church, then, brings safety for the individual. He is in a state of salvation or *being-saved*; and the church is *the way of salvation* or *this salvation*[9]. The spiritual foundation of this new life in the individual is faith in God through Jesus Christ; so the members of the church are *the faithful* or *believers*, and the new life or salvation is also called *the faith*[10].

---

[1] x 28 : ii 33. [2] ii 38, v 31, xvii 30. [3] iii 19, xiv 15, xv 19, xxvi 20: cp. xv 3. [4] ii 38, 41, viii 12, 36–8, ix 18, x 47–8, xvi 15, 33, xviii 8, xix 3–5, xxii 16. [5] ii 37-8, ix 17–8, x 43–8, xxii 16. [6] See viii 15 f., xix 6. [7] Cp. xx 32, xxvi 18 : ii 41-2, 47, xvii 4. [8] ii 28, xiii 46, 48, v 20 : cp. xi 18, and for *walking* ix 31. [9] ii 47, cp. ii 40, xvi 31: xvi 17, xiii 26, xxviii 28. [10] vi 7, xiii 8, xiv 22, xxvi 24.

As time advanced, reflection and the experience of life brought into greater prominence the subjective side of this process, and that in three ways, in each of which we can feel the personal influence of S. Paul. (1) The faith of the believer by which he took hold of Jesus is discovered to be the crucial element in baptism; it is that which enables the gift of God to become effective in him. Hence faith is regarded as the instrument; in baptism God *cleanses the heart by faith* (xv 9, cp. xxvi 18). Similarly the word faith sums up the process of repentance: besides *Repent and turn* we have *Believe and turn* (iii 19–xi 21). S. Paul's formula also runs *Believe on the Lord Jesus Christ and thou shalt be saved* (xvi 31). Now two tenses are used in the Greek for the English *believing*—the present which describes a continuous state, and the aorist which denotes an act which takes place at a definite moment. In this case the definite moment when a man *believed* will be that of the public profession in baptism, and so S. Paul's process is the same as S. Peter's. The three stages are expressed in xxvi 18: (a) conversion or repentance, (b) forgiveness of sins, which is given through baptism, (c) the lot among the sanctified, or life in the church: and the whole is *by the faith which is in me*. This expression which emphasizes the personal element, viz. *faith in Christ Jesus*, is characteristic of S. Paul[1]. (2) Corresponding to this is the greater emphasis on what we may venture to call the subjective side on God's part, i.e. his marvellous kindness in giving such gifts so freely, in other words the *grace* of God in this redemption. To S. Paul *the word of the Lord* becomes *the word of his grace* or *the gospel of the grace of God*: and *to continue in the grace of God* corresponds to *continuing in the faith*[2]. (3) The growing experience of the new life soon shewed that baptism was but a beginning, and after it there still remained a struggle. The life of the Jews was regulated by the Law of Moses. From this the church after a struggle won its emancipation. But life cannot be lived without law, even though it be a law of liberty or a royal law. And the solution of the difficulty involved in the requirement of obedience was found by S. Paul in the doctrine of justification by faith, which he declares in xiii 39—*by him every one that believeth is justified from all things from which he could not be justified by the law of Moses*.

But these ideas were not novelties, they were implicit from the beginning; nor was their expression wholly new or confined to S. Paul. S. Peter echoes the doctrine of justification by faith when he says *We believe that we shall be saved (from the yoke of the law) through the grace of the Lord Jesus Christ*: it was S. Peter also who spoke of *cleansing by faith*. Long before this he had borne witness that it was faith in the name of Christ which had healed the lame man: and this faith he characterizes in an expression which corresponds to, and is as fundamental as, S. Paul's *faith in Jesus*—it is *the faith which is through him*[3].

---

[1] xx 21, xxiv 24, xxvi 18. [2] xiv 3, xx 24, 32: xiii 43—xiv 22. [3] xv 11, 9: iii 16: and for *faith* cp. ii 44, vi 5, xi 24.

§ 3 *The will of God*

Behind these doctrines and processes lies the ultimate problem of the relation of God and man, which is presented to us as soon as we raise the question of man's free will. The supremacy of the will of God was the foundation doctrine in the theology of the Jews; and their own selection by that will, with the absolute and irrevocable character of that choice and vocation (Rom xi 29), was their favourite and most accepted deduction. In dealing with the great scandal or stumbling-block of the cross the apostles had recourse to the same doctrine: it was the plan and will of God. This doctrine was also the basis of the Jews' reverence for the scriptures. The inspired writings revealed the will of God, the prophets unfolded his plan and purpose. The scriptures then must be fulfilled (i 16); and for the apostles it was a sufficient explanation of the crucifixion—a sufficient answer to the Jews and satisfaction to their own faith—to prove that it, with the resurrection that followed, was *according to the scriptures*[1].

Among the Greeks there was a belief in an overruling Necessity or Fate, and so S. Luke would not be unprepared for the doctrine of an overruling will of God. The divine vocation, appointment, and foreordaining held a prominent place in the teaching of the apostles; no one has expressed these ideas more forcibly than S. Paul himself[2]. And in this matter S. Luke proved a ready disciple. No writer can altogether conceal his own predilections. And so we find him using in his narrative expressions which bear a strong predestinarian sound, e.g. in xiii 48, ii 47; and cp. xxii 10. But when the Greek is accurately translated and carefully examined, it will be found impossible to build upon them any doctrine of predestination which ignores or overrules the free will of man. For the very point of the context of these passages is that man—even the chosen people, even an apostle chosen by Jesus himself,—retains the power of resisting and rejecting the call to salvation which is offered by God[3]. But when this proviso is carefully safeguarded, the doctrine that the will of God lies at the bottom of the world's history and of man's salvation remains as one great lesson of the Acts of the Apostles.

CHAPTER VI

The Church and Ministry in the Acts

The Acts is the history of the establishment of the kingdom of God (i 3, xxviii 31) or, as we generally call it, the church. And as the organization and constitution of the church is ever a matter of practical importance, the history needs careful study. The best method will be to study the historical development in its various stages.

---

[1] ii 22-3, 34, iii 18-21, iv 25-8, xiii 22, 27-9, 36. [2] i 2, 24, ix 15, xiii 17, iii 20, xxii 14, xxvi 16: ii 23, iv 28, x 41, xvii 26, 31: and cp. Rom viii 28, 29, ix 20 etc. [3] i 2, 24-5: xiii 40-1, 46, xviii 6, xxviii 25-7.

§ 1 General survey of the history

a. *Preparation* (ch. 1)

The Acts begins with the twelve apostles. The list of their names is given, and the only event recorded before Pentecost is the filling up of the vacant place. It is true there are other disciples or 120 *names*, but S. Luke's opening words make it clear that the recipients of the special commandments and promises of the Lord were *the apostles whom he had chosen*[1]. We find then (1) the twelve apostles: (2) certain bodies closely attached to them—*the women* who had seen the Risen Lord, *Mary the mother of Jesus*, and his *brethren*, among whom James had also 'seen the Lord' after his resurrection: (3) the remaining disciples, who are simply *the brethren*[2]. Among the last must have been many who had companied with the apostles since John's baptism, and who had been of the number of the Seventy. In the one event recorded the apostles consult the brethren, and all act together as one body: yet the initiative lay with the apostles, the decision was left to the divine ordering, and the result was the numbering of a new 'apostle' with the Eleven. This action is a striking vindication of the authority given by the Lord to his disciples to act as an independent church—the more striking that it happened before Pentecost.

This unique position of the twelve apostles will be quite intelligible, if we remember that the Acts is but the continuation of the Gospel of S. Luke. In the Gospel the Lord begins after John's baptism with proclaiming the near advent of the kingdom[3], and his ministry is the preparation for it. Epochs in this preparation are marked by (1) The choice of the Twelve, to whom the Lord gave the name of 'apostles.' These are always with him, and are 'the disciples' *par excellence*; they receive special instruction in private, for to them it was given to know the mysteries of the kingdom of God[4]. (2) The mission or sending of the Twelve: they receive authority to cast out devils and heal diseases, and a charge to proclaim the kingdom of God,—which are the exact features of the Lord's own ministry[5]. S. Luke also adds, and he alone, a similar mission of seventy disciples. Nothing more is heard of these seventy, but their appointment is typical of the appointment of other officers besides the Twelve; they will help to account for the appearance of apostolic powers outside the Twelve; and the Twelve and the Seventy suggest the later 'apostles and prophets[6].'

As the Lord's work developes, the position of the Twelve becomes more clearly defined. (1) A special confession of faith is won from them, and this qualifies them to hear the first, and privately uttered, prophecy of the

---

[1] i 2, cp. Lk vi 13. [2] (1) i 13, (2) verse 14—cp. Lk xxiv 33 *the eleven and they that were with them*, (3) verse 15—cp. Lk xxiv 9 *the eleven and all the rest*.
[3] Lk iv 43, vi 20, x 9, 11: cp. Mt iii 2, Mk i 15. [4] Lk vi 13-6 (Mk iii 14): viii 2: viii 9, 10 (Mk iv 10, 34). [5] ix 1-6, 10. [6] x 1-20: other analogies—with the presbyters (cp. the 70 elders of Exod xxiv 1) or the Seven—may be preferred.

passion: from S. Matthew we learn that Peter, their spokesman, was rewarded with a promise that he should be made the foundation of the church and receive the keys of the kingdom of heaven with the power of binding and loosing[1]. (2) S. Peter evidently assumes that the position of the Twelve is distinct from that of the rest, and in response the Lord characterizes it as a stewardship: with this we may connect the carrying of the keys, a steward's office[2]. (3) Some special teaching about offences and forgiveness is given to the apostles. Comparison with S. Matthew shews that this refers to the exercise of discipline in the church, and it leads to another promise of the power of binding and loosing[3]. (4) It is evident that the Twelve were looking forward to offices of high authority in the kingdom which they expected to be shortly established: the request of the sons of Zebedee is an illustration. They had indeed in a special sense left all and followed Christ, and in reply to Peter's question the Lord promises them an abundant reward. Comparison with S. Matthew again shews that in particular they were to be judges and rulers of the twelve tribes of Israel[4].

It is however the closing scenes of the passion and resurrection which give the definite seal to the authority of the Twelve. (1) The Lord specially associates them with himself in the going up to Jerusalem, and repeats to them privately the prophecy of what was to come to pass[5]. (2) The apostles alone sit down with him at the last supper[6]. (3) They accordingly receive the command to celebrate the Eucharist in his memory, with what is added by S. John—'the new commandment' of love[7]. (4) Special teaching is given as to the conduct of officers in Christ's kingdom, and enforced by the symbolic washing of feet[8]. (5) A definite legacy of the kingdom is made to them, and in his testament the Lord entrusts to them its disposition. In the kingdom their part will be to eat and drink at his table—which is the pledge of communion and shews that they are no longer servants but in the place of masters—and to sit on thrones as judges of the twelve tribes of Israel[9]. (6) The great discourses in S. John, containing the promise of the Paraclete, were spoken to the apostles; and they were the special subject of the Lord's great intercession, by which he sanctified them[10]. (7) On the morning of the resurrection the Lord calls them his 'brethren' and sends them a special message[11]. Others were with them when he appeared in the evening, but it is evident that the manifestation was directed specially to the Eleven[12]. (8) S. Matthew and S. Mark make it clear that the commission to preach the gospel and make disciples of all nations was given to the Eleven in the

---

[1] ix 18-23 (cp. xvii 5): Mt xvi 13-20.   [2] Lk xii 41-8 (cp. *the key of knowledge* xi 52).   [3] xvii 1-7, Mt xviii 1-20.   [4] Lk xix 11-28 (cp. Acts i 6), xxii 24, Mk x 35-45, ix 34-5, etc.: Lk xviii 28-30, Mt xix 27-8.   [5] Lk xviii 31-4 (cp. Mk x 32).   [6] xxii 14.   [7] xxii 19: Jn xiii 34.   [8] xxii 25-7, the apostles are contrasted with *the kings of the Gentiles and they that have authority over them*: Jn xiii 4-20, in this passage the word *apostle* occurs—the only time in S. John's Gospel.   [9] Lk xxii 28-30.   [10] Jn xiv-xvi: xvii 6-19, cp. Lk xxii 31-2.   [11] Mt xxviii 10, cp. 16: Mk xvi 7: Lk xxiv 9, 10, Jn xx 2, 17-8.   [12] Lk xxiv 33, Mk xvi 14.

first place¹. S. John gives the fullest account of their commission. (a) The Lord sent them to be his apostles, i.e. representatives, as he was the apostle of the Father. Thus they are definitely clothed with the authority which the Son of Man enjoyed on earth. This included (b) authority to remit and retain sins; and (c) the office of being shepherds and rulers of the flock².

Thus the Gospel entirely confirms the later Christian tradition which looked upon the twelve apostles as in a unique sense the founders of the church. In the Apocalypse, on the twelve foundations of the New Jerusalem corresponding to the twelve tribes, S. John saw the twelve names of the twelve apostles of the Lamb³.

b. *The church at Jerusalem* (ch. ii-v)

Accordingly, after the descent of the Holy Spirit and the establishment of the kingdom in power, the church seems embodied in the apostles. The first stage of the history is simply the record of what the Twelve said and did. Of course there were others, 'the body' or *the multitude*, but their very existence as a society is based upon the Twelve. The church is the society of those *who were cleaving to the teaching and fellowship of the apostles* (ii 42). In detail we find that the apostles (1) preach or speak the word to the outside world⁴: and (2) teach the people⁵, giving like rabbis regular instruction, and their teaching is the test of the truth. (3) They preside at the meetings of the Christian society for the breaking of bread and other purposes⁶. (4) They work signs and wonders, which appear to be a special mark of apostolic authority⁷. (5) They form a kind of college separate from the rest of the brethren: meeting both at home for consultation and special prayer, and in the temple where, like other rabbis, they have a special place of resort in Solomon's Porch⁸. (6) As presidents of the Christian assemblies, they administer the funds of the community⁹. (7) On Joseph the Levite they confer a special name, Barnabas, which probably marks the conferring of some office in the church or his official recognition as a prophet¹⁰. (8) In the case of Ananias and Sapphira we see Peter exercising discipline as judge, with proportionate effect on the whole society, which is filled with awe and here for the first time is called *the church*¹¹. (9) When the Sanhedrin determines to put down the new sect of Nazarenes, they arrest the 'apostles' as representatives of the Name and the recognized rabbis of the society¹².

---

¹ Mt xxviii 16, Mk xvi 14: Acts i 2 f. shews that Lk xxiv 44-9 was specially directed to the apostles. ² (a) Jn xx 21; cp. xvii 18, xiii 16 and 20. (b) Jn xx 23; cp. Lk v 24 with ix 1 (*authority*). (c) Jn xxi 15-7: the charge is given to Peter, but he is representative of the Twelve. ³ Rev xxi 14. Cp. Eph ii 20; Jude 17, II Pet iii 2; and the titles of the early manuals of instruction and discipline—*the Didaché of the Twelve Apostles, the Didascalia of the Apostles, the Canons of the Apostles* etc. ⁴ ii 14, 37, 41, iii 12, iv 29, 31, v 20, 42 (*evangelize*): ii 32, iii 15, iv 2, 33, v 32. ⁵ i.e. both the people of the Jews and their own, ii 42, iv 2, v 21, 25, 28, 42. ⁶ ii 42, iv 35, 37, v 2 (cp. xxii 3). ⁷ ii 43, iii 4-7, iv 10, v 12, 15-6: cp. II Cor xii 12. ⁸ (a) iv 23-31—*their own* (23) is contrasted with *the multitude* (32): (b) v 12, *the rest* of the Nazarenes hold aloof, cp. 21, 25. ⁹ iv 34-v 10, the money is laid *at their feet*. ¹⁰ iv 36. ¹¹ v 1-11, cp. viii 18-24. ¹² v 18, 28, 40.

(10) This position Peter accepts, and he claims for the Twelve a special gift of the Holy Spirit enabling them to fulfil their work[1].

Thus in the first stage the apostles are practically the church, and the repositories of all authority: it is they who 'act and teach' (i 1). But this state of things obviously could not last. (a) The Twelve by themselves would be unequal to the work; (b) in the rest of the body would rise up men of great gifts and new ideas, men who might receive divine inspirations; (c) bodies of 'Nazarenes' would spring up in cities far from Jerusalem and outside the limits of the Holy Land. Hence the remainder of the Acts is the history of (a) the devolution of apostolic authority, (b) the differentiation of function and adjustment of mutual harmony, together with (c) the preservation of the unity of the body.

c. *First expansion of the church* (ch. vi-viii)

The next stage opens with a scene which is typical of the devolution of apostolic authority. It is the appointment of officers with definite authority in the church outside of the Twelve.

(1) We start with *the multitude*—in which we already discern the beginnings of organization in the mention of *the widows* and *the younger men*[2],—and they choose the Seven. But the proposal had been submitted to them by the apostles, who also appoint the chosen candidates by laying on hands with prayer[3]. The growth of the body, however, is illustrated by the fact that in this section we read almost for the last time of the apostles acting alone[4]. (2) As the scene, so the Seven are typical. They are generally regarded as the first deacons. But their office rather seems to stand as a type of all the higher offices which subsequently appeared in the church below the apostolate[5]; and in this they correspond to the Seventy. Their office however was quite definite. They were to superintend the daily service at the common table and the distribution of alms. Prayer and the service of the word were to be reserved to the apostles. And yet the apostolic laying on of hands is not without effect in this direction also. (a) Both Stephen and Philip work signs and wonders; (b) they speak the word, proclaim the kingdom, evangelize; and (c) Philip baptizes[6]. (3) Stephen and Philip are the first examples of new ideas and independent action in the church. But this action is prompted by the Holy Spirit, and Philip is a striking type of a Christian prophet[7]. (4) Their independence, however, only brings out more clearly the differentia of apostolic authority. We note that the apostles remained in Jerusalem during the persecution; that Philip's new departure in Samaria required their sanction; and that they exercise judgement[8]. But the most significant point is that Philip's work in Samaria could be completed only by the apostles: for in spite of his prophetic gifts Philip could not

---

[1] v 32, cp. iv 8, 31.   [2] vi 1, 2 : v 6, 10.   [3] vi 2–6.   [4] viii 14: in ix 27 Barnabas brings Saul *to the apostles*.   [5] Barnabas' position at first was rather charismatic than official.   [6] (a) vi 8, viii 6, 7, 13 : (b) vi 10, vii 2 f.. viii 5, 12, 35, 40 : (c) viii 38, cp. 12, 16.   [7] vi 3, 5, 10, vii 55 : viii 26, 29, 39.
[8] viii 1 : 14 : 20–3.

convey the Holy Spirit, but—as it is now laid down as a general principle—*by the laying on of the hands of the apostles the Holy Ghost is given*[1].

d. *Extension to Antioch* (ch. ix-xii)

The problem of the next stage (which chronologically overlaps the preceding) is rather that of extension in space. (1) We begin with hearing of disciples at Damascus, among whom is a brother of some importance, Ananias[2]. Then the church is spread over *the whole of Judaea and Galilee and Samaria*; but it is still one, *the church*, and a hint as to the maintenance of unity is supplied by a visitation of S. Peter *throughout all parts*. Similarly other apostles are *throughout Judaea*[3]. But the section ends in the far more distant city of Antioch. Here grows up a body which appears almost on a level with the church of Jerusalem. Its founders shew very independent action in preaching to the Greeks; it is spoken of as *the church*; in sending alms it acts towards the church at Jerusalem as a sister, and its delegates are men of almost apostolic rank[4].

(2) This extension was largely due to individual action under divine guidance. Ananias (who may have been one of the Seventy) by special command of the Lord exercises the apostolic function of laying on of hands, that Saul *may be filled with the Holy Ghost*[5]. Besides Philip others had gone as evangelists. Such were the *men of Cyprus and Cyrene* who had founded the church at Antioch, and who marked a new departure by *speaking the word unto the Greeks also*, but their action received the divine sanction of signs and wonders[6]. More striking and more pregnant with future development is the appearance of Saul, himself a man of as great a position in the world as any of the church, and nothing less than *an apostle born out of due time*. This he was made by the vision of Jesus, which raised him to the level of the Twelve as an eye-witness of the resurrection[7]. For the time, however, the full significance of this is not realized. After an interval he preaches and teaches in Damascus, as a rabbi with his disciples. Then he disappears from view at Tarsus; but at the close of the period Barnabas brings him to Antioch, and there together, as recognized teachers, they consolidate the church[8].

(3) The new developments, however, still require apostolic sanction. Saul's position, for instance, is not fully assured until he has been brought to the apostles and received by them into fellowship[9]. Philip's work at Caesarea (as in Samaria) is followed by a visit from S. Peter. S. Peter's admission of Cornelius into the church, according to a divine revelation, gives apostolic sanction to the new preaching to the Gentiles[10]. And finally, the new departure at Antioch has to be ratified[11]. At the same time, except in the case of Peter (who did in fact take six witnesses with him), we no longer find the apostles acting by themselves alone. News of Peter's conduct

---

[1] viii 18. [2] ix 2, 10–8, xxii 12. [3] ix 31, 32; xi 1. [4] xi 20–1, 26, 29–30. [5] ix 17, cp. viii 18. [6] viii 4, xi 19–21. [7] I Cor xv 8, ix 1; Acts ix 17, xxii 14–5, xxvi 16. [8] ix 20, 22, 25; xi 26. [9] (*going in and out with them*) ix 26–8; cp. Gal i 18. [10] x–xi 18. [11] xi 22–4.

at Caesarea reaches *the apostles and the brethren that were throughout Judaea*, and *they of the circumcision* (probably holding some official position) even rebuke the apostle. The report of Antioch *came to the ears of the church which was in Jerusalem, and they sent Barnabas*, like Peter and John on a former occasion. The Antiochenes send their alms *to the presbyters* (*elders*), and Peter the news of his deliverance to *James and the brethren*[1].

(4) The last references are very significant for the history of the devolution of apostolic office. (i) We now find a body of church rulers at Jerusalem, called, after Jewish precedent, *the presbyters*. This body has taken the place of the Seven, a college which was probably broken up by the persecution. It is clear that as the ruling body it includes different classes, e.g. among them are *chief men* and *prophets*[3]: and the term *the presbyters* when it stands by itself (as in xi 30) may include apostles, who sometimes call themselves by this name[3]. These presbyters are no doubt *the brethren* of xi 1 and xii 17 (cp. xxi 18). (ii) Even more significant is the mention of James: he appears to take the place of the apostles as president of the church in Jerusalem, and later he acts as their equal in the council. He belonged indeed to one of those bodies of special dignity—*the brethren of the Lord*; he also had seen the risen Lord[4]. Thus, as it also includes the story of Saul, this stage is marked by the appearance of two who could be reckoned *apostles* in the strictest sense, although their position was only gradually recognized by the church. With S. James and S. Paul we might join S. Barnabas. At present he ranked before Saul, and being sent to Antioch as an apostolic delegate[5] he was probably sent with apostolic powers, e.g. to lay on hands.

e. *The churches of the Circumcision and of the Gentiles* (ch. xiii–xvi 4)

'The church of the circumcision' seems now fully equipped. There is a body of rulers: provision is being made for the permanent continuance of apostolic authority: and the church at Jerusalem forms a centre of unity. The problems are opened afresh by the springing up of definitely Gentile churches outside of Jewish circles—or the 'church of the uncircumcision.' This is the subject of the next stage.

(1) The start is made from Antioch; and as the church at Jerusalem arose out of the apostles, the churches of the Gentiles need the same foundation of 'apostles,' i.e. men sent by the Lord to represent him and to bear witness to him, to 'make disciples,' and to exercise his authority in the building up of the church. Accordingly at Antioch we begin with an enumeration of the heads of the church, who stand in the next rank to the apostles as *prophets and teachers*[6]. Of these two, Barnabas and Saul, have already some *primâ facie* claim to possess apostolic authority. But to make

---

[1] xi 1–2: 22–3: 30: xii 17, cp. *the brethren* in ix 30.   [2] xv 22, 32.
[3] I Pet v 1, II Jn 1, III Jn 1.   [4] i 14, I Cor ix 5, Gal i 19: I Cor xv 7.
[5] i.e. like Peter and John to Samaria. The mention of the Holy Spirit is significant (xi 24).   [6] xiii 1.

all certain, by a special divine intervention they are set apart by the laying on of hands, and henceforth they act as, and are called, *apostles*, and the Twelve recognize them as brothers[1]. In their work among the Gentiles they speak the word, evangelize, 'make disciples,' work signs and wonders, exercise the power of judgement, and on their own responsibility deliberately 'turn to the Gentiles[2].'

(2) They also make provision for the due administration of the churches in their absence, and that on the same lines as in the church of Jerusalem: they appoint a body of *presbyters* in every church. Personally attached to themselves we find *ministers*—first John Mark, later Timothy[3].

(3) How to preserve the unity of the church, is taught by the history of the relations of the two mother churches—Jerusalem and Antioch. Disputes had arisen out of a divergence of teaching, and the matter was settled by a great meeting at Jerusalem. The apostles and presbyters of that church were gathered together, and with them delegates from Antioch of similar rank, apostles and no doubt presbyters. This council is, as it were, the *Senate* or Sanhedrin of the new people,—their *high-priests and elders*[4]. The presbyters discuss, the apostles sum up the discussion, the president of the church at Jerusalem acts as chairman, the people give their consent, and the unanimity of the assembly proves the guidance of the Spirit. The decision of the council, which is practically that of the church of Jerusalem, is conveyed to *the multitude* of the church at Antioch, who joyfully accept the conclusions[5].

f. *Consolidation of the churches of the Gentiles* (ch. xvi 5–xix)

The great crisis is now past, and the next stage—which is the history of the founding of the churches of Macedonia, Achaia and Asia—only illustrates church organization incidentally. (1) It centres round the apostolate of S. Paul, which is now brought into unquestioned prominence. He acts and teaches with independent authority, exactly like S. Peter in the early church at Jerusalem. He works miracles, he breaks the bread, but above all he possesses the special apostolic power of conveying the Holy Spirit by the laying on of hands[6]. (2) The unity of discipline and order in the churches is vindicated by the treatment of Apollos and the disciples of John[7]. (3) In the ministry of the church we find (i) some who might be reckoned as 'apostolic men' (corresponding to the Seventy of the Gospel and *those who were with the apostles*[8] of the early years) such as Silas, and also Apollos—a teacher, who was ranked by some of the Corinthians as the equal of S. Paul and S. Peter[9]. Then there were Aquila and Priscilla, who instructed Apollos[10].

---

[1] xiii 2–3; xiv 4, 14: xv 12, 25. [2] See xiii 5, 32, xiv 7, 21, 25: xiv 3, 9–10: xiii 9–11: xiii 44–8. [3] xiv 23: xiii 5, xvi 3. [4] v 21, iv 23. [5] ch xv, cp. vv. 2, 4, 6: Peter, Barnabas, Paul, James are the only speakers mentioned: vv. 19, 22–3, 30–1, xvi 4. [6] Cp. especially xix 6. [7] xviii 24–xix 7, on which see commentary. [8] Cp. *all the brethren which are with me* (Gal i 2), and Acts xx 34. [9] I Cor i 12. S. Paul almost recognizes this position, cp. iii 4–iv 13 (esp. *we apostles*). [10] xviii 26. They had a church in their house.

Besides these there were a number of disciples specially attached to S. Paul—*they who were with him, they who ministered to him*,—whom he associated with himself in his work and used as delegates. Such were Timothy and Erastus, Aristarchus and Gaius, and S. Luke himself[1]. Such companions are represented in the body of the seven 'messengers' of the Gentile churches who accompanied S. Paul to Jerusalem and who correspond to the Seven of ch. vi[2]. (ii) For the normal administration of the church we find the same provision as heretofore, viz. bodies of *presbyters*[3]. (iii) Besides official ministries there is evidence that the Gentile churches were richly endowed with charismatic gifts of the Spirit, such as prophecy[4]. (iv) In the mention of Lydia, Priscilla, and Philip's daughters, there are signs of an active ministry of women[5].

This picture is abundantly confirmed by the notices in S. Paul's contemporary epistles. In the Thessalonian church there were *those who laboured and presided*, who among other works *helped the weak*[6]. In the Epistle to the Galatians we read of *him who instructs (catechizes)*[7]. The Epistles to the Corinthians afford a very rich picture. (1) There is a long discussion as to the spiritual gifts, which are thus enumerated—*the word of wisdom, the word of knowledge, faith, gifts of healings, workings of miracles, prophecy, discernings of spirits, kinds of tongues, interpretation of tongues*[8]. (2) The hierarchy of the church is also given, in which charismatic gifts are not yet clearly distinguished from official position,—*apostles, prophets, teachers, then miracles, then gifts of healings, helps, governments, kinds of tongues*[9]. (3) There is much discussion as to the authority and qualification of the apostolate[10]. (4) Much light is thrown on the position of Timothy and Titus as S. Paul's delegates, and also on that of other delegates or *apostles of the churches*[11]. (5) The house of Stephanas *set themselves to minister unto the saints*, and the Corinthians are urged to submit themselves to such, and to *everyone that helpeth in the work and laboureth*[12]. In the Epistle to the Romans (1) there is another enumeration of charismatic gifts—*prophecy, ministry, he that teacheth, he that exhorteth, he that distributeth, he that presideth, he that sheweth mercy*[13]. (2) S. Paul commends *Phoebe a deaconess of the church at Cenchreae*[14]. (3) In the list of salutations we find *fellow workers*, Prisca and Aquila, Urbanus and Timothy; women who *laboured*, Mary, Tryphaena and Tryphosa, and Persis; while Andronicus and Junias are *conspicuous among the apostles*[15]. Finally we note that each epistle is addressed to the church as a whole, and in response each church is to act as one body, in judging, exercising discipline, and so forth.

---

[1] xix 22, 29, xx 34: for the association cp. xvi 13 *we spake*, II Cor i 19, and the addresses of the Epistles. [2] xx 4 (cp. xxi 8). [3] e.g. at Ephesus xx 17. [4] Cp. xx 23, and esp. 1 Cor xii-xiv. [5] xvi 14, 40 (cp. Phil iv 2-3), xviii 2, 18, 26, xxi 9. [6] I Thess v 12-5, cp. Acts xx 35 (*labour* and *help the weak*). [7] Gal vi 6. [8] I Cor xii-xiv; xii 8-10. [9] xii 28. [10] e.g. I i-iv, esp. iv 1, 9, 15, ix 1-6, xii 28-9, xv 5-11; II x-xii, esp. xi 5, 13, 23, xii 11-3, cp. also Gal i-ii. [11] I iv 17, xvi 10-1; II vii 6-16, viii 6, 16-24, xii 17-8. [12] I xvi 15-6. [13] Rom xii 6-8. [14] xvi 1. [15] xvi 3, 9, 21; 6, 12: 7.

g. *Conclusion* (ch. xx-xxviii)

The conclusion is for the most part a narrative of S. Paul's sufferings, but it is important for our present purpose as containing his own account of his call to the apostleship[1]. The narrative also brings out the unity of the church. Thus (1) *Paul and the Seven*, the representatives of the Gentile church, are received by *James and the presbyters* of the Jewish church[2]. Again (2) Paul is received by the Roman Christians, the great and independent church of the west; and in Rome he continues to exercise his apostolate[3].

Further, one of the great texts on the ministry occurs in S. Paul's address to the Ephesian presbyters. He is taking farewell of the church of Ephesus and providing for its administration in the future. The presbyters are to rule the church as its shepherds, and it is very remarkable that S. Paul makes use of a new word *bishops*: *Take heed...to all the flock in the which the Holy Ghost appointed* (or *set*) *you bishops to tend the church of God*[4]. The solemnity of the occasion and the occurrence of the new name might almost suggest the appointment of some (or all) of the presbyters to a higher grade of office; nor is the speech itself without indications that the apostle has in view different groups of persons. But the words of the text, taken in their simple and obvious sense, plainly declare that the *presbyters* are *bishops*. *Bishop* and *presbyter* are used as synonymous terms, and it is clear that S. Paul looks upon this body of presbyter-bishops as sufficient for the local administration of the church.

The review of the Acts must be completed from the other writings of the NT in their chronological order. First, within five years of this date S. Paul writes to Ephesus from Rome and now describes the ministers of the church as *apostles, prophets, evangelists, shepherds and teachers*[5]. In the Philippians he addresses *all the saints together with (the) bishops and deacons*[6]. At Colossae Archippus had *received a ministry in the Lord*[7]. The Epistles of S. Peter and S. James cannot be very distant in time. S. Peter, also writing from Rome, calls the Lord *the Shepherd and Bishop of our souls*; and as a *fellow presbyter* he gives a charge to *the presbyters*, who fill the place of shepherds and rule the flock[8]. S. James is more explicit about *the presbyters of the church*. They visit the sick and anoint them with oil; they pray over them; and the closely connected allusion to confession and forgiveness of sins implies that they also exercised that power of discipline committed to the Twelve in John xx 23[9]. The Epistle to the Hebrews speaks of *your rulers* or *chief men*; and that is the title given to those who had first spoken the word of God to them and now were dead[10].

---

[1] xxii 6-21, xxvi 12-23. [2] xxi 18. [3] xxviii 15, 30-1. [4] xx 28. The word *bishopric* (*episcopé*) had been applied in i 20 to the office of Judas, one of the Twelve. [5] Eph iv 11, the catalogue of *charismata* of I Cor is now omitted. [6] Phil i 1. [7] *diaconia*, Col iv 17, Philem 2; cp. Acts xx 24. [8] I Pet ii 25, v 1-4. [9] Jas v 14-6; the Twelve also *anointed the sick with oil* in Mk vi 13. [10] Hebr xiii 17, 24; 7. The word is used of Judas Barsabbas and Silas in Acts xv 22: it also occurs in xiv 12, Lk xxii 26, Mt ii 6.

The Pastoral Epistles mark a later stage, not so much in years as in matter. S. Paul, in view of his speedy departure, deliberately arranges for the organization of the church, and we may sum up the position thus: (1) There is the final vindication of S. Paul's own apostolate—his office is that of *a herald and apostle and teacher of the Gentiles*[1]. (2) Timothy and Titus have now definitely, as it were, stepped into the apostle's place. Like S. Paul they teach and preach, rule and organize the church[2]. Accordingly they hold a position of authority over the presbyters, whom they appoint by laying on of hands and over whom they exercise discipline[3]. One of their functions on which S. Paul lays most stress is that of *guarding the deposit* (of faith) and *holding the pattern of sound words*. This is evidently with a view to the future, when the apostles shall have passed away; and Timothy is specially charged to provide for a succession of teachers—to commit the faith *to faithful men who will be able to teach others also*[4]. For his work Timothy had received at *the laying on of hands* a special *charisma* which was the same *Spirit* which S. Paul had received[5]. (3) The presbyters are appointed by laying on of hands: but *the presbytery* had itself taken part in the laying on of hands upon Timothy. The presbyters *preside*, and among them are different offices; thus some of them specially *labour in the word and teaching*, and those who *rule well* receive a double portion of *honour* or honorarium[6]. (4) Besides the presbyters we hear of *the bishop*, and his office of *oversight* or *bishopric*. He is spoken of as *taking care of the church of God*, as *a steward of God*, and as having a special responsibility in the matter of teaching and the preservation of the true doctrine[7]. From Titus i 5-7 and the position of *the bishop* in 1 Tim iii 1-7 it is plain that, as at Ephesus, *bishops* and *presbyters* are still identical officers. Perhaps, if *the presbyters* was a general term for the whole body of the church's hierarchy, the title of *bishop* was given to those presbyter-bishops who ruled the local church, in distinction from those ministers whose sphere of ministry was not local but universal (such as apostles and prophets), and from those whose ministry was local but did not include any special authority of government. (5) The *diaconate* now appears for the first time as a definite office[8]. Lastly (6) there is abundant information about the organization of *widows* and the conduct of women[9].

A long interval separates off the writings of S. John. In his second and third epistles he writes as *the presbyter*, and in the church to which he addresses the third epistle one Diotrephes *loveth to have the preeminence* and acts as an arbitrary ruler of the church (vv. 9-10). Whatever conclusion we may come to about the date of the Revelation, it concludes the New Testament. In the opening epistles to the seven churches, each church is represented by an *angel* or *messenger*,—a word very kindred to *apostle* or *one sent*,—and this

---

[1] I Tim i 11-6, ii 7, II i 11.   [2] Cp. e.g. I Tim i 3, iii 15, iv 6-7, 11-3, 16, vi 2, 17; II ii 14-6, iv 2: Tit i 5, ii 1, 15, iii 10-1.   [3] I Tim v 1, 17-22, Tit i 5.   [4] I Tim vi 14, 20, II i 13-4: II ii 2.   [5] I Tim iv 14, II i 6-7. [6] I Tim v 22; iv 14: v 17.   [7] I Tim iii 1-7, Tit i 7-9: the qualifications of *the bishop* much resemble those of *the slave of the Lord*, i.e. the apostolic man, II Tim ii 24-6.   [8] I Tim iii 8-13.   [9] I Tim v 1-16, iii 11.

suggests a single ruler of each several church. In heaven round the throne of God are ranged four and twenty thrones on which sit *four and twenty presbyters*, in the guise of kings and priests. The picture is probably taken from the seats of the presbytery in the local churches, but the presbyters in heaven are obviously 'apostles'—twelve for the church of the Old Jerusalem and twelve for that of the New.

After this brief survey we may sum up its leading features thus.

i The church begins in the twelve apostles, who as the accredited witnesses and representatives of the Lord, sent by him with a definite commission, are the repositories of all doctrine and authority in the church. At the same time, on the principle of the unity of the church, the church generally acts as one body. The apostles and other officers are members of the one body.

ii From the beginning the apostolic ministry is supplemented by (1) the rich outpouring of charismatic gifts from the Spirit—of which the most conspicuous was prophecy,—and by (2) groups marked by special privilege, e.g. *the brethren of the Lord, the women* who had seen the risen Lord, *those who had companied with the apostles from the time of John's baptism*, those brethren besides the Twelve who had seen the risen Lord.

iii As time advances, the need for a more definite official organization in view of the future makes itself felt. And first, there are unmistakeable signs that the apostolic office is to continue in the church. Besides S. Matthias, S. Paul and S. James become apostles in the strict sense. There is also S. Barnabas, and other 'apostolic men' on the borderland such as Silas.

iv Under the apostles we find from early times a definite body of church rulers or ministers. After Jewish analogy they are called *the elders (presbyters) of the church*, and such a body is found universally. It was some time before official titles became fixed; and later on S. Paul calls the presbyters in his churches *bishops*. Probably, in ordinary language the expression 'the elders of the church' would often have been used to denote the whole body of the church's higher ministers, such as apostles and prophets, pastors and teachers; and therefore for the sake of distinction the title *bishop* was confined to those elders or 'presbyter bishops' who bare rule in the local churches. As the church extended, the question of government became more and more important, and ultimately led to further restriction in the application of the word *bishop*.

v Before their departure from the world the apostles had to make provision for the continuance of apostolic oversight. There were already 'apostolic men' (iii); and then we find S. Paul definitely using Timothy and Titus as his delegates. For the same purpose the chief presbyter-bishops in the local churches were evidently very suitable persons; and for apostolic representatives the name of *bishop (overseer)* was most appropriate. Thus from such successors of the apostles—apostolic delegates and the chief rulers of the local churches—have descended our present order of 'bishops.'

vi Here and there are scattered in the Acts hints of lower ministries and services (specially attached to the apostles), which by the time of the Pastoral Epistles have been consolidated in the order of deacons.

vii Lastly, there is much evidence of the ministry of women.

§ 2 Offices and ministries

It will be convenient to group the evidence and references under each title, but before doing so certain cautions must be given.

(1) The characteristic which marked the birth of Christianity was the outpouring of the Spirit. This was exceedingly rich and abundant: like Jordan in time of harvest, it overflowed all its banks. The Spirit, then, flooded the church with an outburst of spiritual gifts, of which prophecy was most typical; and it took some time for this river of living water to work out for itself regular channels, so that the spiritual gifts should be recognized as the proper and normal endowments of Christian character and of ecclesiastical office. Naturally, at first, there could hardly be drawn a sharp line between individual spiritual gifts and official position. Further, the expectation of the immediate return of the Messiah, with the establishment of his kingdom in glory, would cause less attention to be paid to the need of the organizing a permanent ministry.

(2) Similarly in the terminology, there was an interval, so to speak, of experiments and local divergence before the question was finally settled by the survival of the fittest terms. Thus we find different meanings of *apostle*, various synonyms for *presbyters*, different titles for the twelve apostles etc.[1] Further the terms used had not as yet become technical. **Presbyter** was indeed already technical, but a presbyter was still as a rule *an elder*; an *apostle* was *one sent*, *deacons* were those who *served*, *presidents* those who *presided* etc.

(3) The final terminology was practically the creation of Christianity. It is true that, as was natural, the organization of the Christian communities was more or less modelled upon the lines already familiar to them in their old national life. There were *bishops* (*episcopoi*) among the Greeks, and *presbyters* among the Jews. But *apostle* and *deacon* are certainly new terms: *bishops* also were officials so rarely found, and of so little importance, among the Greeks that the title as well as the office was practically a new creation. *Presbyter* is the only term which remains to mark the continuity of the church under the Old and the New Covenants.

Apostles

The Lord himself bestowed this title upon the Twelve, and by so doing he marked them out as his representatives. The word is similar in meaning to *angel*, but is found only once in the Greek OT[2]. In the NT it occurs chiefly in the writings of S. Paul and S. Luke, elsewhere only eleven times. In the Acts it is most frequent in the early chapters; it ceases altogether after xvi 4.

---

[1] Compare the variety of terms in use to-day for a clergyman: priest, pastor, minister, rector, vicar, incumbent, curate, clergyman, clerk in holy orders etc.
[2] I Kings xiv 6.

§ 2 OFFICES

In the strictest sense—viz. that which prevailed in Christian tradition, and is already established in the New Testament (in the Revelation, II Peter and Jude, and Ephesians[1])—the apostles were the twelve founders, or rather foundations, of the church. This they were in virtue of two qualifications.

(1) The distinctive work of the Twelve in the early chapters is to bear witness to the resurrection[2]. This they were enabled to do in virtue of having seen the Risen Lord with their own eyes. This, then, was the first essential for an apostle; when S. Paul wrote I Corinthians it was plainly accepted as such, and the appearances to S. Paul and to S. James were the charter of their apostolate[3]. Other disciples however shared this privilege,—indeed more than five hundred had seen him—and to such in one or two places S. Paul seems to give the name of *apostle*[4]. But what these other witnesses lacked was

(2) The definite apostolic commission from the Lord. How this commission was conveyed before the day of Pentecost, and how the history after Pentecost illustrated its content, has been fully shewn. In this aspect the apostles were the rulers of the church, and this function of their apostolate could be continued in the church. A hint of this is given at the outset by the appointment of S. Matthias to Judas' vacant place. The office of *apostle* included implicitly all the offices which were subsequently evolved out of it; and it is noticeable that in the Acts it is called an *apostolate, episcopate* and *diaconate*[5]: while in various places of the NT apostles speak of themselves as *witnesses, prophets, teachers, presbyters, heralds* (i.e. *preachers*), *deacons, ministers, ministers-at-the-altar, servants* (i.e. *slaves*) *of Jesus Christ*[6]: they *evangelize, prophesy, speak with tongues*, they have *knowledge, revelations, gifts of healing*, they *help*, etc.[7] These various 'parts and duties' were by degrees communicated to others; but one gift was reserved as the special 'differentia' of apostolic authority: *through the laying on of the apostles' hands the Holy Ghost is given*[8].

But the term *apostle* was used of others than the Twelve, and its uses may be distinguished thus.

(1) It denotes the Twelve. This is the general use in the NT outside of S. Paul. S. Luke uses it in a wider sense only twice[9], and the rest of the writers of the NT only three times out of 11, and of these passages one applies

---

[1] Rev xviii 20, xxi 14, Jude 17, II Pet iii 2 : Eph ii 20, iii 5. [2] See the references given on p. lxx note 8, and add xxvi 16. [3] I Cor ix 1, xv 7, 8. [4] In I Cor xv 7 *all the apostles* seem to be a larger body than *the twelve* of verse 5 : perhaps this explains Andronicus and Junias, who *were in Christ before* S. Paul, being *conspicuous among the apostles* (Rom xvi 7). [5] i 20, 25, xx 24. [6] Cp. e.g. Rev i 2, 9, xix 10, xxii 9: I Tim ii 7, II i 11: I Pet v 1, II, III Jn 1 : II Cor vi 4, Eph iii 7, Col i 25 : Acts xxvi 16, Lk i 2, I Cor iv 1: Rom xv 16 : Rom i 1, Jas i 1, II Pet i 1, Rev i 1. [7] Cp. e.g. v 42 ; ii 17, Rev x 11 ; Acts ii 4, I Cor xiv 18, II Cor xii 1 : Acts xx 35. [8] viii 18, xix 6. In I Cor ix S. Paul speaks of the *right* (*authority*) of an apostle to be supported by the church (cp. I Thess ii 6): in II Cor xii 12 he speaks of *signs and wonders and powers* as the credentials (*signs*) of an apostle. [9] Acts xiv 4, 14 (of Barnabas and Paul).

it to Christ and another uses it in the general sense of *one sent*[1]. S. Paul claims the title for himself also in this strict sense,—i.e. as being on a level with the Twelve,—when he speaks of himself as *an apostle of Jesus Christ*, or *the apostle of the Gentiles*: and he gives the title in the same sense to S. James. S. Luke extends the term to include both S. Barnabas and S. Paul.

(2) In 1 Cor iv 9 S. Paul uses the term in the plural and his argument seems to rank Apollos with himself. Then in 2 Cor x–xiii we have the great controversy about certain teachers who claimed to be *apostles of Christ*, and questioned S. Paul's apostolate. S. Paul calls them *false apostles*, and now distinguishes the Twelve as *the very chiefest apostles*. In Rev ii 2 we find (false) teachers claiming to be *apostles*. This use of the term for teachers of high authority other than the Twelve is reflected in the *Didaché*, where *apostles* and *prophets* are two very similar orders of wandering teachers, of chief authority in the church[2].

(3) Lastly, the word is used in its literal sense of *messenger*, i.e. for delegates of the church. The brethren sent to Corinth from Macedonia in the matter of the collection were *apostles of the churches*. Epaphroditus, who brought the contribution of the Philippians to S. Paul at Rome, was their *apostle*[3]. This is the sense in which it came into use among the Jews later on, after the final expulsion of the Jews from Jerusalem in the second century. Their 'apostles' were the messengers who collected the half shekel which every Jew continued to pay to the central national authority in Palestine.

The consideration of the apostolate raises a further question as to rank and office among the Twelve themselves. As S. Peter was called *the rock* on which the church was to be built, so in the early chapters of our book he certainly acts with a prominence and independence which might imply that he had some superior authority as head of the apostles. But further consideration shews that this was not the case. It is the teaching and fellowship *of the apostles*, and not of S. Peter, which is the test of the church. It is by the hands *of the apostles*, and not of Peter only, that signs are wrought and the Holy Spirit is given. The apostles form a college, they *are* and act *all together* (v 12): but every college must have its chairman and spokesman, and it is in that capacity that S. Peter acts. In ii 14 we are told explicitly that *Peter* stood up *together with the Eleven*; and his hearers answered *Peter and the rest of the apostles* (verse 37). So in iv 19 *Peter and John*, and in v 29 *Peter and the apostles*, made their defence before the Sanhedrin[4]. Further, the power of the whole apostolic college over individual apostles is shewn in viii 14 where *the apostles who were in Jerusalem sent Peter and John* on a mission to Samaria. Again in xi 1 S. Peter's action at Caesarea is even called in question by *them that were of the circumcision*, i.e. some of *the apostles*

---

[1] Heb iii 1, Jn xiii 16: the third instance is Rev ii 2.   [2] Another use of the term by S. Paul in I Cor xv 8, Rom xvi 6 has been noticed above, p. xci.
[3] II Cor viii 23, Phil ii 25.   [4] A comparison of Acts ix 27 and Gal i 18–9 shews that S. Peter's action is valid as representing *the apostles*.

and the brethren that were in Judaea. So whatever authority Peter assumes in taking the lead is representative authority.

It is true that S. Paul seems to assign a preeminence to S. Peter. He implies that *the apostleship of the circumcision* had been entrusted to S. Peter: he went up to Jerusalem *to visit*—not the Twelve but—*Cephas*[1]: in 1 Cor ix 5 he writes as if S. Peter had a special position—*the rest of the apostles and the brethren of the Lord and Cephas*. But if this is urged as a proof of Peter's single headship of the church, it proves too much. For the whole point of S. Paul's argument is that he had been entrusted with the same apostleship among the Gentiles which Peter held among the Circumcision; if the argument implies headship, the conclusion will be that there are—not one but—two heads of the church of equal rank. Paul claims to be not a whit behind 'the very chiefest apostles,' and his claim is supported by the history of the Acts. We cannot fail to see that Paul occupies in the second part precisely the same position that Peter holds in the first part[2]. All that Peter does he does, and more also. He acts with the same authority and independence; we might even say greater, for among the Gentiles there is no college of eleven fellow apostles to act as a restraint upon his action.

Nor is this all. As the history advances, Peter's position in Jerusalem seems to recede, and, in proportion, another personality comes into view. This is S. James. As the eldest of the 'brethren of the Lord,' and favoured by a special appearance of his risen 'brother,' he enjoyed great honour in the church. Soon we find him acting as president of the local church at Jerusalem (xii 17); and in that capacity at the great meeting of the Christian Ecclesia in ch. xv he acts as chairman, giving his decision after S. Peter and S. Paul have spoken. Further, his extreme piety and asceticism won for him an immense personal authority in the Jewish side of the church. The extreme partisans looked upon him as head of the church rather than Peter who was half a Pauline at heart[3]. At any rate this became the tradition among the Judaistic section subsequent to NT times. For in the Clementines, the anti-Pauline literature of the second and third centuries, James, as bishop of Jerusalem, is the *bishop of bishops* and the head of the church, to whom Peter himself is subject.

In treating of S. James we have already mentioned *the Brethren of the Lord*. To ask what the relationship actually was belongs to a commentary on the Gospels, but it is obvious that it gave them a special place of dignity in the church (which was handed on to their descendants). This is shewn by Acts i 14, 1 Cor ix 5 and the Epistle of S. Jude. *The Twelve* was a common designation of the original apostles. It occurs 22 times in the Gospels; also in 1 Cor xv 5 and Acts vi 2 (*the Eleven* in Acts ii 14, i 26). The typical character of *the Seven* (xxi 8) has already been pointed out. There is no allusion to them outside of the Acts. Accordingly we pass on to the body which generally ranked next to the apostles, viz. the

---

[1] Gal ii 8, i 18.   [2] See pp. xlviii–ix. On one occasion S. Paul *withstood Cephas to the face* (Gal ii 11).   [3] Cp. Gal ii 12.

Prophets

A prophet is one to whom the word of the Lord comes and who 'speaks it forth.' He is the subject of special inspiration; and so in the OT the prophets were the chief medium of revelation[1]. There, as in the NT, we already find two classes: (1) great inspired individuals, who are 'the prophets' *par excellence*, (2) a class of professional prophets. In this Israel and JEHOVAH were not peculiar, for prophecy was not confined to them. Jezebel had her prophets of Baal and of the Asherah, and the surrounding nations had their prophets, who were like the modern dervishes. In the Greek world also the prophet was a familiar figure[2], but he was rather the interpreter of the god than the immediate forthteller of the divine word. The staff of an Egyptian temple also included prophets; and at the commencement of the Christian era, prophets, soothsayers *et hoc genus omne* abounded in the eastern half of the empire.

Prophecy formed a great link between the Old and the New Testament. For prophecy had not ceased. As we learn from Josephus, there were prophets among the Jews, especially among the Essenes[3]. Caiaphas uttered a prophecy on one occasion[4]. The Jews expected the kingdom of the Messiah to be preceded by the return of Elijah or one of the prophets; and this expectation was answered in the ministry of the Forerunner, John the Baptist, who was the greatest, as he was the last, of the OT prophets[5]. The birth of the Christ took place in an atmosphere of prophecy. Zacharias prophesied at the birth of the Baptist; Simeon received a warning from the Holy Spirit; and Anna who spake of the infant Jesus was a prophetess[6]. Jesus himself was regarded by the people as a prophet[7].

If such was the preparation, the kingdom itself was first established in power by a great outpouring of the Spirit and consequent outburst of prophecy. Indeed one mark of the new kingdom is what we may call the new prophecy. For the gift of the Spirit was to be no longer something exceptional or extraordinary: it was to be 'poured out on all flesh,' so all should prophesy and see visions, even slaves and handmaidens (ii 17–8). Accordingly the whole church is richly endowed with spiritual and prophetic gifts. At Pentecost all spake with tongues, and the community lived in a state of ecstasy or spiritual exultation (ii 46). The discussion of the spiritual gifts in I Cor xii–xiv, with their enumeration in xii 8–10, shews that at their birth the Gentile churches also enjoyed a like endowment of the Spirit: at the public meeting there was hardly one who had not a psalm or a teaching or a revelation or a tongue or an interpretation (xiv 26). For prophecy was but

---

[1] II Pet i 21. [2] S. Paul calls Epimenides of Crete a *prophet* (Tit i 12). The 'prophet' of Apollo at Chalcedon was one of the great magistrates of the city: so was the prophet of Apollo of Branchidae in Miletus. The enumeration of the Egyptian hierarchy on the Rosetta stone begins with *The high-priests and prophets*, which is a parallel to 'apostles and prophets.' [3] Cp. *Ant.* xv 10. 5 for Menahem's prophesying. [4] Jn xi 51. [5] Mk vi 15, ix 11, Jn i 21: Lk i 76, vii 26–8. [6] Lk i 67, ii 26, 36–8. [7] Mt xxi 11, Jn vi 14, vii 40, ix 17.

the greatest of those spiritual *charismata*—speaking with tongues, seeing visions, receiving revelations, etc.,—with which it was closely allied and of which it is the type. Prediction was not the distinctive function of the prophet, though that power was sometimes given to him[1]. Prophecy rather denotes the effect of the inspiration of the Spirit, as it finds utterance in exhortation, instruction, encouragement, and consolation,—aids which are now conveyed by means of preaching. The Revelation of S. John was a prophecy; and the true spirit of prophecy was evinced in bearing witness to Jesus[2].

Prophecy, then, was confined to no class. S. Paul says *Ye all can prophesy*, just as all spoke with tongues at Pentecost[3]; and the gift of the Spirit, as recorded in the Acts (whether the occasions indicate what normally happened or no), was always followed by prophetic phenomena, even in the case of Gentiles like Cornelius[4]. Nor was it confined to men. Women prophesied; and there were women 'prophets,' such as (apparently) the daughters of Philip, who correspond to Anna and the OT prophetesses[5]. Some however would possess the gift in a higher degree than their fellows; others again would specially devote their lives to the exercise of prophecy. In either case then it would be natural to speak of such men as *Prophets*; and those who possessed the gift most abundantly, as being specially inspired by the Spirit, would rank next the apostles[6]. In the Acts we find the following instances of prophecy. Whether S. Barnabas' name is correctly interpreted as *Son of prophecy* or no, he was undoubtedly a prophet. Philip is not called a prophet, but his action was exactly like that of one of the OT prophets. Agabus and those who came down to Antioch from Jerusalem are definitely called *prophets*. Agabus appears again; and on each occasion he utters a prediction enforced by a symbolic action, which was a common method of prophetic teaching[7]. At Antioch a body of *prophets and teachers*—Barnabas, Symeon Niger, Lucius, Manaen, and Saul—presided over the church and led the public worship[8]. Two *chief men* in the church of Jerusalem, Judas Barsabbas and Silas, were also *prophets*. Lastly we hear of Philip's daughters as *prophesying*[9].

Like *apostle*, the word *prophet* acquired a double signification.

(1) The leading prophets of the first era soon won a preeminent position in Christian tradition. The Twelve themselves were no doubt prophets as well as apostles. Paul and Barnabas were prophets; so probably were Philip and Stephen (who was *full of the Holy Ghost* vi 5, vii 55), besides the others just mentioned. Such early prophets were closely associated with the apostles as founders of the church, and seemed to keep up the succession of the OT prophets. Thus we find the phrase, *the apostles and prophets*, in Eph ii 20, iii 5, Rev xviii 20, where the order of the words shews that the Christian

---

[1] xi 28, xx 23, xxi 11.   [2] Rev i 3, xix 10, I Jn iv 1-3, I Cor xii 3.
[3] I Cor xiv 31.   [4] Acts ii 4, viii 18 (*saw*), x 44-6, xix 6.   [5] ii 17-8, I Cor xi 5; Acts xxi 9, Lk ii 36; cp. the false prophetess Jezebel in Rev ii 20.
[6] I Cor xii 28, Eph iv 11.   [7] xi 27-8, xxi 10-1; for other symbolic actions cp. xiii 51, xviii 6.   [8] So in the *Didaché* the prophets offer the eucharist (x 7), 'for they are your high-priests' (xiii 3).   [9] xiii 1-3; xv 22, 32; xxi 9.

prophets are referred to[1]: later on, when Christian prophecy was passing away, or rather was changing its character, the phrase was interpreted of the OT prophets.

(2) Besides these there had arisen a class of less eminent prophets who were, so to speak, more professional. These abounded: we find them at Thessalonica, in great numbers at Corinth, and *in every city* (xx 23). Of such prophets Agabus is perhaps the type, and they correspond to the order of wandering prophets in the *Didachê*. This class gradually declined in repute; as early as A.D. 49 S. Paul has to exhort the Thessalonians not to *despise prophesying* (1 Thess v 20). This is easy to understand. As a charismatic gift, prophecy was from the nature of the case independent of regulation and official control. Accordingly it afforded a great opportunity for self-advertisement, or other forms of self-seeking[2]; and the weaker men could not always rise superior to the temptation. Again, the ecstatic utterances of the prophets, when heedless of control, caused great disorder in the public meetings of the church, and they received a sharp rebuke from S. Paul[3].

What however brought most discredit upon prophecy was its counterfeit. False prophets abounded, both of greater and lesser reputation. Such were Simon Magus and Barjesus, Theudas and the Egyptian, and in the next century Barcochba[4]. False prophets even found their way into the church, where their presence was a great danger. Claiming to speak from the Holy Ghost and so to be above criticism[5], they would lead astray the unwary[6]. Hence there was a great need of the discernment of spirits—a faculty enumerated among spiritual gifts. S. Paul and S. John both give a test of true and false prophecy—the test consisting in *the testimony of* (i.e. witness to) *Jesus*[7]. Labouring under these difficulties, it is easy to understand how 'prophecy' gradually died away in the Christian church. Men like Ignatius and Polycarp were 'prophetic'; but as a special class 'the prophets' passed away, their place being taken by teachers and preachers of special power and capacity.

Teachers

In xiii 1 we hear of *prophets and teachers*, and the connexion seems obvious. The man to whom the word of the Lord comes has the best authority to impart it to others; and thus the OT prophets had their 'schools of the prophets.' On the other hand the preacher is not always the best teacher; and beside the word of the Lord there was another subject of

---

[1] So probably in I Thess ii 15, where S. Paul is speaking of the persecution of Christians. In the Revelation the prophets are generally Christian prophets. Compare the order of the *Te Deum*: apostles, prophets, martyrs. On the other hand Lk xi 49 (before Christian prophecy) has *prophets and apostles*. [2] The *Didachê* shews how. If a prophet orders a table (i.e. an agape or feast), says in the Spirit 'give me money or something else,' or does not practise what he teaches, he is no true prophet (ch. xi). [3] I Cor xiv 26–33. [4] Cp. the false prophet of Rev xiii 11–7, xix 20, xx 10. [5] Cp. *Didachê* xi 7 'every prophet speaking in the Spirit ye shall not try nor prove.' [6] Mt vii 15, xxiv 11, 24, I Jn iv 1. [7] Rev xix 10, I Jn iv 2, II 7, I Cor xii 3.

teaching, viz. the law. Thus under the old covenant the priest's lips also 'kept knowledge' and they 'sought the law at his mouth[1].' Later, when the Law of Moses was codified and revelation enshrined in books, a new class of teachers arose, viz. students and interpreters of the written scriptures. These were the 'scribes' and 'lawyers' of the NT. The greatest of them became heads of schools with disciples. They were known as 'rabbis,' and in the popular religion held the most prominent position; for they were practically the authorities on religious doctrine and practice. When the Lord came he appeared as a new rabbi with his disciples; and the popular comment was at first *A new teaching!* The Lord accepted the position, and the disciples generally called him *Rabbi* or *Master*, i.e. Teacher[2].

When the Lord was taken away, the twelve apostles stepped into his place as it were. They became the rabbis of the new teaching or school, and were formally recognized as such by the people and their rulers[3]. Thus Christianity took over, with the prophecy of the old dispensation, its teaching also; but at the same time it made it new. The newness lay in its subject. This comprised, (1) in its forefront, the facts of the crucifixion and resurrection, together with (2) the report of all that Jesus said and did; and the cycle of teaching fixed by the apostles and handed on by oral tradition is the basis of our first three Gospels. (3) Such tradition also included the Lord's moral teaching—the new and expanded interpretation of the Commandments. (4) Besides this the apostles would have to decide practical matters of worship and observance; and their teaching on these subjects, e.g. concerning baptism and the laying on of hands, would contain the 'first principles' of church worship, ritual, and discipline[4]. (5) Lastly, there would gradually be given deeper teaching about the Lord's person—such as S. Paul alludes to[5] and such as is found in S. John's Gospel[6].

It is obvious that much of this teaching could be devolved on others; and also that the church would need more teachers than the Twelve. So we can trace the growth of a class of teachers. First, the apostolic function is exercised by Paul and Barnabas, who *teach* (xi 26, xv 35, xxviii 31): S. Paul calls himself *the teacher (rabbi) of the Gentiles*, as the Twelve were the rabbis of the circumcision. Then in xiii 1 we hear of the five *prophets and teachers* at Antioch[7]. In xv 1 certain who came down from Jerusalem *taught*; and so did Apollos (xviii 25). Outside of the Acts *the teachers* appear more definitely as a class. In I Cor xii 28 they rank next to prophets. Later, in Eph iv 11 they are in the fourth rank together with *shepherds*. This shews, as we learn from elsewhere, that those who taught had a definite position among the presbyters: the presbyters who *labour in teaching* are worthy of double honour, and capacity to teach is required of the *bishop (episcopus)*[8].

The necessity of preserving the right teaching was obvious. At first

---

[1] Mal ii 7.   [2] Mk i 27: cp. e.g. Jn iii 2, xiii 13.   [3] See above, p. lxxxi.
[4] Cp. Acts xv 1, xxi 21: Heb vi 1–2.   [5] I Cor ii 6–16, cp. Hebr v 11–4.
[6] and also in the synoptists, as in Mt xi 27 and parallels.   [7] So Jezebel the false prophetess *taught*, Rev ii 20.   [8] I Tim v 17, ii 2, Titus i 9.

the apostles were the only authorized teachers, and their teaching was the test of the church's faith (ii 43). As the office was more and more delegated to others, divergences of teaching would arise, of which xv 1 gives an instance. We also hear of false teachers[1], as well as of false apostles and false prophets. This explains the important place held by teaching in the functions of the presbyterate; and the true teaching was to be preserved by handing down the tradition in an authorized succession—*the things which thou hast heard from me, the same commit thou to faithful men who shall be able to teach others also* (II Tim ii 2).

There was however a great deal of teaching to be done which did not require teachers of such high authority; and in later times the work of our schoolmasters and sunday-school teachers was performed by a class of 'catechists.' This word does not occur in the NT; but when S. Paul speaks of *him that instructs* in Gal vi 6, and S. Luke of Theophilus' *instruction*, they are using the corresponding verb and so giving indications of the beginnings of such a class. These must have been early; for oral teaching in the elements of the faith, if less interesting, was most necessary for the new converts. Indeed, before the Gospels had been written, the knowledge of what they contain must have been preserved and handed down, in the main, by such oral instruction or *catechizing*[2].

Evangelists

In the apostolic 'speaking of the word,' besides the bearing witness to the resurrection in particular, besides the teaching and exhorting of the faithful, there was also the more general duty of *evangelizing*[3] those without, i.e. proclaiming to men the 'gospel' or glad news of the kingdom of God, or (what was equivalent) of Jesus, or of 'the word[4].' This work was shared by others, first by Philip and the Hellenists who reached Antioch, then by Paul and Barnabas[5]. For, to use modern expressions, this evangelizing was the great mission work of the church. Those who excelled as missionaries were known as *evangelists*, like Philip *the evangelist*[6]; and, as the sphere of mission work expanded so rapidly, those who had a special vocation for it tended to form a class like our modern missionaries. Thus in Eph iv 11 S. Paul ranks *evangelists* next after *apostles* and *prophets*, and before the *shepherds and teachers* who tended the local churches. The apostles were the great missionaries, and the work of the missionary required apostolic authority, for it involved the founding of churches: so, when S. Paul is (as it were) handing on his office to Timothy, he bids him *do the work of an evangelist*[7]. We may see another such evangelist in Epaphras who brought the gospel to Colossae[8]. Eusebius has a chapter on the important work done

---

[1] II Pet ii 1, cp. Acts xx 30. [2] The important part which such 'catechists' may have played in the formation of the Synoptic Gospels has been vigorously put before us by the Rev. A. Wright—primarily in his *Composition of the Four Gospels* (Macmillan 1890). [3] v 42, viii 25. [4] Cp. Lk viii 1, xvi 16, Acts viii 12: v 42, viii 35, xi 20: viii 4, xv 35. [5] viii 4, 12, 35, 40, xi 20: xiii 32, xiv 7, 15, 21, xv 35. [6] xxi 8. [7] II Tim iv 5. [8] Col i 7.

by 'the evangelists' after the times of the apostles[1]. In the NT however the terminology of *evangelist, evangelize* etc. is almost confined to S. Luke and S. Paul.

Chief men

Judas Barsabbas and Silas are called *chief* or *leading men among the brethren* (xv 22). They were in fact prophets (ver. 32), and evidently persons of consequence in the church of Jerusalem. But the use of the word in the Epistle to the Hebrews (xiii 7, 17, 24) for the authorities of their church, or *those that have the rule* over them (as it is translated), shews that the word is not a mere complimentary title. It would seem to have been a competitor with the word *presbyter* for the designation of the rulers of the church—especially, we may suppose, in churches among the Jews (e.g. at Jerusalem), where it distinguished the Christian rulers from the Jewish presbyters. This brings us to the

Presbyters (Elders),

—a subject of very practical importance; for this is the office or, to speak strictly, designation which has become permanent in the church,—the word *presbyter* being the same as our *priest*.

The association of authority with age seems part of man's natural constitution. In the history of most nations we find authority originally resting with the aged. The Romans were governed by their *Senate* of *seniores* or *elders*; Greek cities had their *Gerousia* or council of *gerontes* (*old men*). As time advanced such bodies either lost their political power, or the titles *elder* and *old* became merely technical terms. But the terms remained. And at the time of the Acts in many Greek cities the members of the *gerousia* were also called *presbyters* (*elders*)[2]. In Egypt *presbyters* seem to have been the chief village authorities, like our modern churchwardens; and in the papyri from which this fact has been learnt, there is mention of *presbyters* in the college of priests attached to the temple of the god Soknopaeus in the Fayyûm[3].

Among the Jews however this conception or principle of authority had especial vitality. We find it throughout the OT. There are *elders* (*presbyters*) of villages, of towns, of tribes, and of the whole people of Israel. The institution finds its typical representation in the council of Seventy Elders, who were appointed by Moses and filled with the Spirit[4]. In the NT the system is still in full vigour. The chief seat of authority for the whole nation is the Sanhedrin or *Presbytery*[5], where sat together *the high-priests and presbyters of the people*. In the towns there were local bodies of *presbyters*[6] who administered the local affairs, and acted as magistrates, with authority over the

---

[1] *E. H.* III 37.   [2] e.g. at Ephesus, Chios, Cos, Philadelphia, and Sinope, as we learn from inscriptions.   [3] *Berlin Papyri* vol. i, nos. 16, 387, 392, 433: cp. Deissmann *Neue Bibelstudien* pp. 60-2. An inscription (*CIG* 4717) may confirm the existence of such presbyter-priests elsewhere.   [4] Exod xxiv 1-11, Num xi 16-30.   [5] Lk xxii 66, Acts xxii 5: it is also called the *Gerousia* in v 21.   [6] Lk vii 3.

synagogue also : for among them were included the *archisynagôgos* and *the rulers*, and they sat in ' the chief seats in the synagogue,' and exercised religious discipline. The same organization prevailed among the Jewish communities of the Dispersion ; though according to Schürer the word *presbyter* was not used among them as an official title till late[1]. With such a system prevailing in the Jewish nation and communities, which were the birthplaces of the Christian societies, it was natural that the latter should almost insensibly develope a similar organization. For this indeed the Lord himself had set a precedent, when besides the Twelve he appointed *other Seventy also*, after the pattern of the old covenant.

Accordingly (1) we soon find, in xi 30, a body of *presbyters* at Jerusalem. In chapter xv we have *the church and the apostles and the presbyters*, or *the apostles and the presbyters with the whole church* (vv. 4, 22). The assembly there described in part corresponds to the Jewish Sanhedrin or Presbytery— *the apostles and the presbyters were gathered together*, as elsewhere among the Jews *the high-priests and the presbyters* of the people[2]. Very likely the use of the term *presbyters* was avoided by the Christians before the decisive break with Judaism (in ch. vii-viii) in order to prevent confusion with *the presbyters of the people* who sat in the Sanhedrin. In xxi 18 the Christian presbyters are associated with S. James[3], who in his epistle speaks of them as *the presbyters of the church*.

(2) Secondly, the local churches outside of Jerusalem were, like the local Jewish communities, governed by presbyters. Paul and Barnabas established them throughout Galatia, and no doubt universally, since we find them also at Ephesus[4]. The references to presbyters in the other NT books have already been given. S. Peter gives them a charge, S. James mentions an important detail of their work, the Pastoral Epistles deal with the office most fully, S. John calls himself *the presbyter*, and lastly we have the picture of the *four and twenty presbyters* in the Revelation.

In drawing some conclusions as to the office of the presbyters we must remember the ambiguity attaching to the term. It was still used in its primary sense of elder men[5]; it denoted Jewish as well as Christian rulers ; and it is used of themselves by the apostles, e.g. S. Peter and S. John.

(1) In the earliest days—to judge from Jewish usage—*the presbyters* was probably a general term, which denoted not so much a particular order of officers as the whole body of church rulers. Among the Jews the presbyters (elders) of a village and the presbyters of the Sanhedrin must have been officers of a very different standing ; so among the Christian presbyters were probably included prophets, teachers, shepherds, presidents, 'helps,' and

---

[1] *Jewish People etc.* Index, p. 39.   [2] Cp. iv 5, 8, 23, vi 12 : xxiii 14.
[3] Hence the presbyters are probably *the brethren* of xii 17. With James and the presbyters of the church contrast the high-priest Ananias and the presbyters of the Jews (xxiv 1, xxv 15).   [4] xiv 23, xx 17.   [5] Hence arises some ambiguity, e.g. in I Tim v 1. Also among the Jews, *the elders* stands for *the ancients* in the expression *the tradition of the elders*.

'governments¹.' The composition of the church at Jerusalem is summed up thus—*the apostles and the presbyters and the church*: and among *the presbyters* were included 'chief men who were also prophets.' Indeed, a body consisting of apostles and presbyters together might be called 'the presbyters'; as is shewn in the Revelation, where the twenty-four presbyters are the chief representatives of the church or apostles. When S. Paul enumerates the hierarchy of the church, neither in I Corinthians nor in Ephesians does he mention presbyters,—no doubt because it was the general term which stood for all the *prophets, teachers,* and *pastors* alike. In the Pastoral Epistles there seem to be different classes or grades among the presbyters: there are those who preside, and those who teach; some receive more 'honour' than others; and if *episcopus* is not simply a convertible term with *presbyter*, then the *bishops* will be another class among the presbyters. In this connexion it is not without significance that we do not hear of *a presbyter* (in the singular) until we get to the Pastoral Epistles; similarly, while there are words for the office of apostle, episcopus, and deacon², there is no mention of the presbyterate.

(2) Later—and the Pastoral Epistles represent the transitional period—the general word was specialized and confined to a definite class,—though not absolutely, as long after NT times we find bishops calling themselves 'presbyters.' This came about, we suppose, in some such way as this. On the one hand the president of the college of local presbyters became the apostolic delegate, i.e. to him were committed the special apostolic powers of government; his position therefore became much more distinct and the title of *episcopus* was confined to him. On the other hand, as the requirements of such ministries as the 'serving of tables' increased, the deacon became, like the 'bishop' with whom he was closely associated, an officer with a very definite position. Between these two, the body of presbyters would tend to become more uniform; and this process would take place more rapidly as the special charismatic gifts became rarer, and different functions fell to the lot of the same individual. The final result was the emergence of one definite 'order' (to use a technical term) of *Presbyters* or *Priests*³.

(3) The Presbyters, then, were in NT times the body of local church rulers under the apostles. Accordingly the apostles associate them with themselves in general church government, summoning them to their deliberations, for instance about the matter of the Gentiles in chapter xv. As church rulers they administer the finances⁴. S. Paul in his farewell to the Ephesian presbyters says that they were appointed to tend or rule the church, i.e. as

---

¹ but not 'ministers' such as deacons. There is an analogy in modern usage. Our present order of *Priests* includes pastors, missionaries (both home and foreign), teachers in schools and colleges, officials such as deans and archdeacons, members of collegiate bodies such as canons and fellows, members of religious orders, etc. ² viz. *apostolé, episcopé, diaconia.* ³ The problem to be accounted for is really not the origin of the order of *bishops*, but of the order of *priests*. ⁴ xi 30, xxi 18.

shepherds, and he leaves them in charge of the church as its watchmen and stewards. In the Pastoral Epistles we find that they teach, and preside,—which probably means at the agapê and eucharist. Further, they share the spiritual powers of the apostles. The presbytery joined S. Paul in the laying on of hands upon S. Timothy: and from S. James we have already learnt (p. lxxxvii) of other spiritual functions—praying over and anointing the sick, and exercising the ministry of reconciliation.

(4) They were definitely appointed to their office by apostles, e.g. Paul and Barnabas, or by 'apostolic men' like Timothy and Titus[1]. The method was by laying on of hands, by which on all analogy the Spirit was conveyed. In this they answered to the Seventy of the old covenant who received the Spirit which was in Moses[2].

In conclusion, while speaking of the presbyters as rulers of the church, we must remember to qualify this by the wholly new principle of authority and rule in the Christian church laid down by the Lord (e.g. in Lk xxii 25–7): he who is chief shall be as he who serves, and the Christian ruler is the shepherd who *tends* his flock. Nowhere in the NT is the usual Greek word for *ruler*[3] used of Christian officers.

Episcopi (Bishops)

Episcopus, visitor or *overseer*, is a title even more important than *presbyter*; for it is the same word as our *bishop*, and over it have raged great battles of controversy. Avoiding controversy we shall simply try to suggest what may be gathered from the NT itself, where the word only occurs five times in all. We may say at once that it has not yet acquired the definite sense which it holds in the letters of Ignatius (c. A.D. 115) and which it still holds to-day, viz. of a single ruler of a diocese. From Acts xx 28, Titus i 6–7, and comparison with I Timothy iii 2 f., we should conclude that *episcopus* was simply a synonym for *presbyter*, and that the two offices were identical. As long, however, as 'the presbyters' was used in a general sense for the whole body of the higher ministers of the church, the *episcopi* would denote the more definite class of local church rulers, or 'presbyter-bishops' (as we may call them).

The term first appears in the Greek churches, viz. in those of Ephesus, Philippi, and Crete; and it has been supposed to have been borrowed, together with the office, from contemporary Greek institutions. But *episcopi* are found in the Syrian (or Egyptian) *Didachê*; and though there were *episcopi* among the officials in Greek cities, their office was neither widespread nor significant enough to account for the Christian use of the term[4]. The word really came

---

[1] Acts xiv 23, Titus i 5.   [2] I Tim v 22: cp. I Tim iv 14, II i 6, Acts vi 8, viii 17 etc.: Num xi 25 (cp. xxvii 18, Deut xxxiv 9).   [3] *archon*; among the Jewish presbyters were *archontes* and *archisynagôgi*.   [4] Two inscriptions tell us that there were some officials of this name in the Athenian confederacy in the 5th century B.C. but no information is given about them beyond the mention of their name. At Rhodes in inscriptions of B.C. 49 and 50 *episcopi* appear as magistrates of the

into the church through the Greek version of the OT, though there were no special officers of this name in the old history to suggest its adoption.

The new use of the word, then, was a Christian creation, although the underlying idea was Jewish and derived from the OT. The idea of the visitation of God was deeply implanted in the Jewish mind, i.e. the idea of God coming to man, inspecting him and searching him out. Such a visitation involved on the one hand judgement, for God will convict and punish what was wrong. On the other hand to the righteous it brought comfort and strength. By visiting his clients a powerful patron shews his interest in and care for them, and by staying with them he assures them of his protection. So the *visitor* passes into the *overseer*; and therefore visitation is connected with the offices both of judge and shepherd. It was in this latter sense that the Jews expected and longed for the visitation of God—for God was their *Episcopus*[1]. Now the joy of the gospel was that God had visited his people: the coming of the Christ was 'the time of visitation[2].' This meant judgement for the unbelieving Jews, but for the believing joy and comfort; for in visiting them God came to abide with them. First he separated them out from the goats to be his flock, and henceforth he would preside over them as their shepherd—for Christ is *the shepherd and bishop of our souls* (I Pet ii 25).

Naturally the term would also be given to one who visited or presided as the representative of God. In the Greek OT the term is applied to various overseers or officers, none however of any striking significance[3]. But there was one text which would make a great impression on Christian teachers, viz. Isaiah lx 17 *I will make thy officers* (Gk *archontes*) *peace and thine exactors* (Gk *episcopi*) *righteousness*. Further, when it was seen that Ps cix referred to Judas, it was found that his office was called an *episcopê* or *bishopric* (Acts i 20).

Now when S. Paul was taking his farewell of the Ephesian church and had to make provision for the future he calls the presbyters *episcopi* (*bishops*). Hitherto he had been their *episcopus*, visiting them and exercising the oversight; now he commits this office to the presbyters. We feel very much tempted to imagine that at this solemn scene he actually conferred upon them, or some of them, a new privilege or gift of the Holy Spirit: but while this idea can only remain in the region of conjecture, there is no necessity to suppose that because these presbyters are *episcopi* (i.e. presbyter-bishops) and sufficient for the oversight of the church, therefore all presbyters everywhere were in the same position. Again, the Epistle to the Philippians (i 1) shews that the same provision had been made at Philippi; and S. Peter,

---

city in the third rank, after generals (*stratēgi* Acts xvi 22), and treasurers. An *episcopus* is also mentioned in a list of the officials of a temple of Apollo at Camirus in Rhodes. [1] Job xx 29 (LXX), Wisdom i 6. [2] Lk i 68, 78, vii 16: cp. Acts xv 14: Lk xix 44. [3] Eleazar had *oversight* of the tabernacle (Num iv 16): other *overseers* were connected with the temple, II Kings xi 18, II Chr xxxiv 12, 17, Neh xi 9, 14, 22. On the military side we have *overseers of the host* in Num xxxi 14, II K xi 15. Judges ix 28 completes the list.

writing shortly after, calls the Lord *the shepherd and bishop of souls*[1], which implies an office of great dignity in those who were 'shepherds and bishops' under him.

Lastly, we have the Pastoral Epistles. Here we must remember that the work of Timothy and Titus was to leave their churches fully equipped for the future—to commit the teaching *to faithful men able to teach others also*. In Crete Titus was to appoint presbyters in every city, and after some general qualifications S. Paul continues *For the episcopus must be*—and then follow qualifications, among which faithfulness in a divine stewardship and in the preservation of the right teaching is prominent. In I Timothy the apostle speaks again of the *episcopê* as a 'noble' work, and of the qualification of *the episcopus* (in the singular): here too it appears that the work of the episcopus is *to take care of the church of God*. If then *the presbyters* was the general title for church officers, it is quite possible that *the episcopus* was the one among them selected to preside and act as the chief ruler of the church. As Timothy and Titus represented S. Paul, so *the episcopus* was to represent them, and to fulfil their office in their respective churches. Thus he too would be an 'apostolic man'; and the *episcopi* as a class would be ranked with those men of eminence in the early church whom we found exercising apostolic authority besides the Twelve. Like them they would be successors of the apostles; and if this is a fair representation of what happened, it is easy to understand how from such ancestry was developed the 'order' of diocesan bishops as it is found fully established in the second century.

Attendants: they that minister (serve)

It is noticeable that the word *deacon* (*servant* or *minister*) does not occur in the Acts[2]; but there are several traces of subordinate *ministries* or *services* which we will briefly collect.

In v 6 and 10 appears a body of *the young men* or *younger men* who bury Ananias and Sapphira. The words[3] are interesting and illustrate the use of *the elder men* (*presbyters*) with which they stand in contrast[4]. If 'the presbyters' stand for the body of church rulers, 'the younger men' would denote the body of church servants. The phrase is not confined to young men in our sense of the term; it rather stands for men in the prime of life as distinguished from the definitely elder men.

Elsewhere (p. 86, on vi 1-6) we shew reasons for supposing that the Seven were appointed to an office which was considerably more important than that of deacons. In fact the 'daily ministration' (vi 1) implies the previous

---

[1] It is interesting to note that Christ is called *apostle, high-priest, episcopus, deacon, minister-at-the-altar* (*leitourgos*)—but never *presbyter*. He was in fact still *a younger man* at the time of his crucifixion—and is so represented in early Christian art. [2] except in the Bezan text of vi 1. [3] Two different (though similar) words are used in the Greek. [4] e.g. in I Tim v 1, I Pet v 5.

existence of a class of ministers to serve the apostles in the distribution of food and drink at the agapê and eucharist.

On their first journey Barnabas and Paul take John Mark as their *attendant*. This word had not high associations. It is the Greek word for the *chazzan* or sacristan of the synagogue, who hands the scriptures, executes the judgements of the synagogue court, and so forth[1]; it is also used for the servants and officials of the high-priests and Sanhedrin who arrested Jesus and the apostles[2]. The word reminds us that the Christian synagogues must have required some such functionaries at an early date. John Mark however was an attendant on the apostles, rather than on the church; and one service which he rendered may have been to baptize[3].

On his second journey S. Paul took Timothy with him (xvi 1-3); and we find him usually surrounded by a company *who minister unto (serve) him*, like Timothy and Erastus[4]. Of such ministers we hear much in the Epistles, and they are typified for us in the company of the Seven in the final journey to Jerusalem[5]. Such were no doubt personal attendants on the apostle like S. Mark: but we see signs of a wider service. Thus the Seven were chosen by the churches of the Gentiles to convey their alms to Jerusalem. Again S. Paul often employed them as his delegates and lieutenants; and this association with the apostle would win for them an important status in the church; just as in later times deacons presumed to place themselves before presbyters, and the chief (or arch-) deacon became the special ruler of the clergy. Some of them, e.g. Timothy and Titus, were left by S. Paul with a definite commission of apostolic authority.

We are not surprised, then, to find that by the decade 60-70 these various ministries have given rise to an order of *deacons*, whose qualifications are laid down by S. Paul in I Timothy iii 8-13. As these ministers were in the first place attendants on the apostles, so we find the *deacons* closely associated with *bishops*—first in Phil i 1 (cp. I Tim iii 1, 8), and afterwards in the *Didachê*[6] and church history.

Elsewhere we hear of Phoebe *a deaconess of the church at Cenchreae*: at Corinth the household of Stephanas *addicted themselves to the ministry* (Gk *diaconia*) *of the saints*: and in S. Paul's last letter he asks Timothy to bring Mark *for he is profitable for the ministry* (Gk *diaconia*)—he may at last fulfil the office of a minister which he surrendered in Pamphylia[7].

The use of *deacon* for an official was the creation of Christianity. The word means *servant*, denoting a higher status than *slave* (*doulos*). In the Gospels it was used (1) of service at table,—as of the servants at Cana in Galilee, of Peter's wife's mother, and of Martha[8]: (2) from supplying with

---

[1] Lk iv 20, Mt v 25. [2] Cp. e.g. Mt xxvi 58, Jn vii 32, 45-6, xviii 12, 18, 22: Acts v 22, 26. [3] for apparently the apostles did not usually baptize themselves, see page 33. [4] xix 22: cp. xx 34, Gal i 2. [5] xx 4. [6] e.g. c. xv: 'Elect for yourselves bishops and deacons.' [7] Rom xvi 1: I Cor xvi 15: II Tim iv 11. [8] Jn ii 5, 9, Lk iv 39, Jn xii 2: cp. Lk xii 37, xvii 8, xxii 26-7.

food and drink, it came to include supplying with necessaries of life generally,—so certain women ministered to the Lord of their substance[1]: (3) then it denoted personal service—the Lord speaks of *my servant*, and we have *your servant, servant of God, of Christ, of the church*[2]. These ministries in the Gospels and Acts correspond exactly to the functions of the later deacons. (1) They were primarily 'ministers of meats and drinks' as S. Ignatius[3] phrases it: they served the table and the bishop by distributing the food at the agapê, and also at the eucharist. (2) They also served the bishop in the administration of the alms, distributing them to the poor and needy. (3) They were generally the officers of the bishop. As such their office grew greatly in importance, and the inferior forms of attendance or service were left to lower officials, to subdeacons, doorkeepers, and acolytes.

The Women: Widows: Virgins

It would take us too far afield to discuss the ministry of women in the church, but we may put together the notices in the Acts.

(1) In i 14, next to the apostles are grouped *the women and Mary the mother of Jesus*. These women were they who had ministered to the Lord and had seen him risen. In fact they were the first 'witnesses' and 'evangelists.' Hence they held a special place of honour in the church.

(2) As early as vi 1 we hear of *widows* in the church, and a body of widows is also found at Joppa in ix 39. This organization was mainly for purposes of relief; but in return for support the widows served the church by their prayers and in other offices. This system had its origin among the Jews; but in the church the organization of widows—especially for purposes of good works—developed rapidly and is the subject of careful regulation in I Tim v 3-16. Anna is the type of the widow devoted to prayer; and Dorcas of Joppa of the Christian woman devoted to good works[4]. As *the widows* specially lamented the latter, she may have had some connexion with them—perhaps, while not needing support, she ranked as a 'widow.'

(3) In the missionary work of S. Paul women play a great part. (*a*) Lydia was a kind of mother to the church of Philippi[5]; and in founding that church other women laboured with the apostles[6]. (*b*) Priscilla or Prisca, the wife of Aquila, was another great worker. S. Paul, who puts Prisca first, calls them together his 'fellow-workers': they had a 'church in their house,' and they instructed Apollos in the way of the Lord. (*c*) The First Epistle to the Corinthians illustrates the position of women in the Gentile churches. They prayed and prophesied, even in church: but this practice S. Paul strongly

---

[1] Lk viii 3, Mt xxvii 55.   [2] Jn xii 26: Mt xx 26, xxiii 11: Rom xiii 4, II Cor vi 4: II Cor xi 23: Rom xvi 1. As the deacons waited on the bishops, so the apostles were the deacons of the Lord: the Lord himself was the deacon of the Father; and in him Ignatius finds the type of the diaconate (*Magn.* 6); cp. Mt xx 28, Rom xv 8.   [3] *Trall.* 2.   [4] Lk ii 36-7: Acts ix 36.
[5] *Mother of the synagogue* was a complimentary title in vogue among the Jews.
[6] xvi 14, 15, 40: Phil iv 2, 3.

forbade¹. At Cenchreae there was a *deaconess of the church, Phoebe*: and in writing from Corinth to Rome S. Paul mentions the names of many women, some of whom *laboured in the Lord*².

(4) On the way up to Jerusalem, we meet the four daughters of Philip the evangelist, who were *virgins and did prophesy*. Of women prophets we have already spoken (p. xcv); and now *virgin* appears to denote a definite state of life. In pagan religions there was a recognized place for 'virgins' among the ministers of the gods: but virginity had not received any special honour among the Jews. It was otherwise in the church. In the Gospels we find the parable of 'the ten virgins'; and Mary of Bethany figures as a type of virginity. As early as A.D. 54 the question of celibacy for the sake of similar 'attendance upon the Lord' had been the subject of much discussion at Corinth, and in his first epistle to that church S. Paul lays down regulations especially *concerning the virgins*³.

[*Priest*]

We have found the parallels to the prophets, presbyters, and rabbis, of the old ecclesia in the new. But there is one term which in the Acts is only used of the Jewish rulers,—viz. *priest* (Gk *hiereus*). Here we must distinguish, as in the other cases, between (1) the ordinary *priests* (vi 7) who did not hold a prominent place in the life of the nation, and (2) *the high-priest*, the head of the nation, or—when grouped with his fellows—*the high-priests*. Of the correspondence in reality in the Christian church there was no doubt, for in xiii 2 S. Luke applies to Christian prophets the word which was used of the sacerdotal service in the temple; and S. Paul similarly describes himself as a priest offering at the altar (*leitourgos*)⁴. In the Revelation the four and twenty presbyters are both kings and priests⁵: and when we compare the *priests and prophets* of the OT and the *high-priests and presbyters* of the Jews in the NT with the *apostles and prophets, apostles and presbyters*, of the church, there can be no doubt that the apostles are the priests (or high-priests) of the new ecclesia⁶. The absence of the name is not hard to explain. (1) There was the danger of confusion with the Jewish priests and high-priests, as also with the pagan priests in the cities of the Gentiles. (2) The popular ideas of priesthood were associated with the slaying of animals. But the Christian sacrifice was no longer the slaying of animals, and 'the priesthood was changed': as the church had a new altar, so the priesthood likewise was new⁷. (3) There is a deeper reason. Christ united in himself the supreme

---

¹ In I Tim ii 11-5 S. Paul has again to check the evident desire of women to speak in church and be teachers. Cp. the false prophetess Jezebel who also taught (Rev ii 20).   ² Rom xvi 6, 12. *Labouring* is a special mark of ministers of the church, Acts xx 35, I Thess v 12, I Tim v 17.   ³ I Cor vii 25-40. See p. 490.   ⁴ Rom xv 15-6.   ⁵ Rev iv 4: cp. i 6, v 10. ⁶ All Christians are priests, but that does not exclude a special order of priests: they can all prophesy, they all know all things (I Jn ii 21, 27 etc.), but this does not exclude special prophets and teachers.   ⁷ Heb vii 12, xiii 10.

embodiments of authority. He was High-Priest and King. Now, great as is the emphasis laid on *the kingdom* in the Acts, the title of *king* is never applied to the apostles: they are rather the princes of the church. For the same reason they are not called high-priests. As members of the Lord's body and representatives of his authority, they share his **royalty and priesthood**; but it is only at the end that they will be manifested, sitting on their thrones and clothed in white, as kings and priests.

THE ACTS OF THE APOSTLES

i 1–5 Preface

I THE ACTS OF PETER

THE CHURCH OF THE CIRCUMCISION AND PROGRESS FROM JERUSALEM TO ANTIOCH

1 *The baptism and establishment of the church at Jerusalem*

(1) The preparation

i 6–11	the ascension of the Lord
12–14	the waiting disciples
15–26	the filling up of the apostolate

(2) The baptism of the church at Pentecost

ii 1–13	the descent of the HOLY SPIRIT
14–40	the preaching of Peter
41–47	the church 'of the beginning'

(3) The consolidation of the church at Jerusalem

iii 1–iv 4	the sign of healing and Peter's sermon, followed by the arrest
iv 5–22	Peter and John before the Sanhedrin
23–31	the prayer of the church and confirmation of the apostles
32–37	the common life of the church: Joseph Barnabas
v 1–11	the entrance of sin: Ananias and Sapphira
12–16	signs and wonders, followed by
17–42	the arrest and trial of the Twelve

II *The extension of the church to Antioch and admission of the Gentiles*

(1) The acts of Stephen and the first persecution

vi 1–7	the ordination of the Seven
8–15	the ministry and arrest of Stephen
vii 1–60	his defence and martyrdom
viii 1–3	the consequent persecution

(2) The things that arose about Stephen

(a) The acts of Philip

4–13	his preaching in Samaria
14–25	its confirmation by the apostles with the gift of the Spirit, and their conviction of Simon Magus
26–40	the baptism of the eunuch and arrival at Caesarea

(b) The acts of Saul

ix 1–9	his apprehension by the Lord
10–19	his baptism
20–25	his preaching to the Jews at Damascus
26–30	his reception by the apostles at Jerusalem

ANALYSIS

	(c)	The act of Peter in opening the door to the first Gentile
31–43		the peace of the church and preparatory signs
x 1–22		the preparation of Cornelius and of Peter
23–48		Peter at Caesarea, and his gospel for the Gentiles: the descent of the Spirit and baptism of Cornelius
xi 1–18		Peter's defence to the church at Jerusalem
	(d)	The acts of the Hellenists
19–26		the foundation of the church at Antioch; and preaching to the Greeks, which is confirmed by Barnabas

III *The passing of Peter and transition from Jerusalem to Antioch*

27–30	the mission from Jerusalem to Antioch
xii 1–17	the second persecution, and the deliverance of Peter
18–24	the judgment of Herod, and peace
25	the mission of Barnabas and Saul from Antioch to Jerusalem

II THE ACTS OF PAUL

THE CHURCH OF THE UNCIRCUMCISION AND PROGRESS FROM ANTIOCH TO ROME

I *The work of Paul and Barnabas and its ratification by the church*

xiii 1–3 (1) The HOLY SPIRIT separates Paul and Barnabas

(2) The work of Paul and Barnabas in opening the door to the Gentiles and founding the churches of Galatia

4–12	Cyprus		Sergius Paulus and Barjesus
13–52	Galatia	Antioch of Pisidia	Paul's gospel for the Jews, and turning to the Gentiles
xiv 1–7		Iconium and	the work confirmed by miracles
8–18		Lystra	Paul's gospel for the Gentiles, and his stoning
19–28			return and organization of the churches

(3) The confirmation of Gentile liberty by the whole church

xv 1–5	the controversy at Antioch and Jerusalem
6–29	the council at Jerusalem, and its letter
30–35	its acceptance at Antioch and peace
36–xvi 4	its acceptance in Syria, Cilicia, and Galatia

II *Extension of the church in the Roman empire: the churches of Macedonia, Achaia, and Asia*

xvi 5–10		The divine call to new work		
11–18	(1)	Macedonia	Philippi	the women and the 'pytho'
19–40				imprisonment and Roman citizenship
xvii 1–9			Thessalonica	hostile Jews
10–15			Beroea	friendly Jews
16–34	(2)	Achaia	Athens	Paul and philosophy
xviii 1–4			Corinth	a link with Rome
5–11				breach with Jews and vision of the Lord
12–23	(3)	Asia		Paul before Gallio: he touches at Asia
24–28			Ephesus	the acts of Apollos
xix 1–7				Paul and John's disciples
8–10				the breach with the synagogue and spread of the church
11–19				Jewish magic and Christian repentance
20				the triumph of the word

ANALYSIS

III *The passing of Paul and his defence of the gospel*

(1) The fulfilment of his work and journey to Jerusalem

21–22	the Spirit directs him Romewards
23–41	the riot at Ephesus: Paul and the worship of Artemis
xx 1–3	a year in Macedonia and Achaia: the start for Jerusalem
4–16	from Philippi to Miletus: the raising of Eutychus
17–38	Paul's defence to the church of Asia
xxi 1–14	from Miletus to Caesarea

(2) Paul the prisoner and his process

15–26 (*a*) Paul and the church at Jerusalem

(*b*) Paul and the Jews at Jerusalem

27–40	the riot in the temple and arrest
xxii 1–22	Paul's defence to the Jewish people, and
23–29	claim of Roman citizenship
30–xxiii 10	his trial before the Sanhedrin, and
xxiii 11	consolatory vision
12–35	the conspiracy of the Jews and delivery of Paul to the governor

(*c*) Paul and the Romans at Caesarea

xxiv 1–23	Paul's defence to the Romans, and
24–27	his preaching to Felix
xxv 1–12	the trial before Festus, and appeal to Caesar
13–27	the visit of Agrippa, and
xxvi	Paul's defence to the world

(3) Paul and Rome

xxvii 1–8	(*a*)	the journey towards Italy
9–xxviii 6		the shipwreck and deliverance
xxviii 6–10		the winter at Malta
11–15	(*b*)	the voyage to Italy and reception by the Roman Christians
16		Paul's entry into Rome
17–28		his appeal to the Jews and turning to the Gentiles
30–31	Epilogue	Paul preaching the kingdom at Rome

CHRONOLOGY OF

(Rome)	(Palestine)	(The Jews)
[14] TIBERIUS emperor	[26] PONTIUS PILATUS procurator of Judaea Joseph Caiaphas high priest	
		35 Pilate causes slaughter of Samaritans at Gerizim and is sent to Rome by Vitellius prefect of Syria Herod Antipas is defeated by Aretas king of Arabia
	36 MARCELLUS procurator Jonathan, son of Annas, high priest	36–37 Vitellius at Jerusalem, treats the Jews with favour
37 March 18 CALIGULA emperor	37 MARULLUS procurator Theophilus, son of Annas, high priest	37 Herod Antipas is banished to Gaul and succeeded by Herod Agrippa I 38 Persecution of the Jews at Alexandria Philo's embassy to Caligula 39 Caligula orders his image to be set up in the temple: great consternation among the Jews
41 Jan CLAUDIUS emperor	41 HEROD AGRIPPA I king of Judaea Simon Cantheras Matthias, son of Annas, and two others high priests 44 CUSPIUS FADUS procurator	41–44 Golden times for the Jews under Agrippa

THE ACTS

(Jerusalem)	The Church	(S. Paul)
29 *Passover*: The Crucifixion		
Pentecost: Descent of the Spirit		
29–32 Growth of the church in Jerusalem (i–v)		
32 Martyrdom of S. Stephen and persecution		32 Conversion of Saul who retires to Arabia
Scattering of the church in Jerusalem		
	Philip preaches in Samaria	
Peter and John visit Samaria		
	and the Shephelah	
	Hellenists preach in Phenicia and Cyprus	
Peace and recovery of the church at Jerusalem		34 Saul preaches at Damascus
34 Saul at Jerusalem		visits Jerusalem
		retires to Tarsus
	Hellenists reach Antioch and preach to Greeks	
	Peter visits Caesarea and baptizes Cornelius	
	Barnabas sent to the church at Antioch	
41 Agrippa unfavourable to the church		42 Barnabas fetches Saul from Tarsus to Antioch
The apostles leave Jerusalem		42–43 One year's work at Antioch
	43 Prophets go down from Jerusalem to Antioch	
44 *Easter*: Herod beheads James and imprisons Peter		
Peter leaves Jerusalem		
James, the Lord's brother, head of the church		Collection made at Antioch for the church at Jerusalem and sent by Barnabas and Saul
Herod's death restores peace to the church		

CHRONOLOGY OF

(Rome)	(Palestine)	(The Jews)
	TIBERIUS ALEXANDER procurator Ananias, son of Nedebaios, high priest	45 Helena queen of Adiabene visits Jerusalem Famine in Judaea, Helena's great generosity Alexander executes the sons of Judas of Galilee (v 37)
49 Seneca recalled from banishment Expulsion of the Jews from Rome	48 VENTIDIUS CUMANUS procurator	Conflicts with Roman authority under Ventidius Cumanus Herod Agrippa II made king of Chalcis Collisions between Jews and Samaritans lead to fall of Ventidius Cumanus
54 Oct. NERO emperor	52 ANTONIUS FELIX procurator	Felix marries Agrippa's sister Drusilla Felix suppresses the brigands Assassination of Jonathan, son of Annas, and growth of the Sicarii The Egyptian Jew (xxi 38)
55 Nero murders Britannicus his brother Pallas (Felix' brother) loses his influence	57 PORCIUS FESTUS procurator	Riots between Jews and Gentiles at Caesarea cause recall of Felix
59 Nero murders his mother Agrippina		c. 59 Ismael, Joseph Kabi, Ananus son of –70 Annas, and others, high priests
62 Death of Burrhus Nero marries Poppaea a Jewish proselyte	61 ALBINUS procurator 62 GESSIUS FLORUS procurator	
64 Great fire of Rome and persecution of Christians 65 Conspiracy of Piso and death of Seneca		
68 June 9: Death of Nero		66 Outbreak of Jewish war 70 Destruction of Jerusalem

THE ACTS

(Jerusalem)	The Church	(S. Paul)
45 Barnabas and Saul at Jerusalem		
		46 *spring*: Paul and Barnabas start for their first journey, visit Cyprus and Galatia, return to Antioch in
		47 *autumn*: Disputes about circumcision; (? Peter at Antioch;) delegates sent to Jerusalem
48 Council at Jerusalem		
		48 *autumn*: Paul and Silas leave Antioch, visit Cilicia and Galatia,
		49 Macedonia and Achaia, reach Corinth by winter
		(*I II Thessalonians*)
		50 Paul at Corinth
		51 *spring*: Paul leaves Corinth, visits Jerusalem and Antioch (? *Galatians*), traverses Galatia, and
51 Paul's fourth visit to Jerusalem		
	Apollos at Ephesus and Corinth	
		autumn: comes to Ephesus
		52–53 Paul at Ephesus
		54 *spring*: (*I Corinthians*) Riot at Ephesus; Paul leaves the city
		summer: in Macedonia (? *Galatians*) (*II Corinthians*)
		winter: at Corinth (*Romans*)
55 *Pentecost*: Paul comes to Jerusalem		55 *Easter*: Paul sails from Philippi for Jerusalem
His arrest and despatch to Caesarea		
55–57 Paul in custody at Caesarea (? *Epistle of James*)		
57 Paul is tried by Festus and appeals to Caesar, and		
late summer: is sent to Rome		57 *autumn*: the shipwreck
		57–58 *winter*: at Malta
		58 *spring*: arrival at Rome
		58–60 Paul in free custody at Rome (*Philippians*) (*Ephesians, Colossians, Philemon*)
		60 Paul liberated
61 In the interval between Festus' death and the arrival of Albinus Ananus son of Annas causes the death of S. James		Missionary journeys
		(*S. Luke's Gospel* and *Acts*) (*Pastoral Epistles*)
(*S. Mark's Gospel*) (*S. Matthew's Gospel*)		64 Martyrdom of S. Paul (*I Peter*) Martyrdom of S. Peter
		(? *Epistle to the Hebrews*)
68 Flight of the church of Jerusalem to Pella		

ADDENDA

Page lvii (2). It should have been made clear that the garrison of Judaea was drawn, not from the legions, but from the auxiliary forces, which were to some extent raised locally (Mommsen in *Hermes* xix (1884) p. 217).

p. 170. The Latin form of *Christian*, the reappearance of the term in Festus' court at Caesarea (xxvi 28), and the quasi-official epithet of *most excellent* given to the Theophilus to whom the Acts is dedicated,—these data incline many scholars to look to the circle of Latin officials at Antioch for the origin of the name of CHRISTIAN.

p. 302 note ². Mr Worrall has informed me that the quotation in the commentary is taken from the description of the city of Eurycômis, at the opening of a Greek novel 'Concerning Hysmine and Hysminia,' which was written by a certain Eumathius or Eustathius (in Didot's *Erotici Scriptores*). Very little is known of this Eumathius, except that he wrote at a late date—'not later than the twelfth century' (*Dict. Classic. Biography*). Hence the words were *not* 'spoken of Athens by an ancient writer'—unless indeed Eumathius borrowed his sentence from a classical author. The same must be said of a quotation from Petronius, which is often met with in comments on Acts xvii 16, to the effect that [at Athens] one could sooner find a god than a man: in the original there is no reference to Athens.

p. 357. To the names given on this page should be added that of Philip the apostle, who—according to Polycrates of Ephesus (quoted by Eusebius, *H. E.* iii 31, v 24)—was buried at Hierapolis, together with two of his daughters; a third daughter being buried at Ephesus. There may however be some confusion here with Philip the evangelist.

THE ACTS OF THE APOSTLES

PART I
(Ch. 1-12)

THE ACTS OF PETER

THE CHURCH OF THE CIRCUMCISION
AND
PROGRESS FROM JERUSALEM TO ANTIOCH

DIVISION 1

(= Ch. 1-5)

THE BAPTISM AND ESTABLISHMENT OF THE CHURCH AT JERUSALEM

From c. A.D. *29 to 32, Tiberius being emperor of Rome, Pontius Pilate governor of Judaea, Herod Antipas tetrarch of Galilee and Joseph Caiaphas high priest.*

SECTION I (= Ch. 1)

The Preparation

Introductory

1 [1]THE former treatise I made, O Theophilus, concerning
2 all that Jesus began both to do and to teach, [2]until the day in which he was received up, after that he had given commandment through the Holy Ghost unto the apostles whom he
3 had chosen: to whom he also shewed himself alive after his passion by many proofs, appearing unto them by the space of forty days, and speaking the things concerning the kingdom

---

[1] Gk *The first word*: cp. Lk i 1-4. [2] The starting point is not mentioned and some Bezan texts read here *in the day when he chose the apostles through the Holy Ghost and commanded them to preach the gospel, to whom etc.* In verse 5 also some read—*but ye shall baptize with the Holy Ghost whom ye are also about to receive.*

4 of God: and, ¹being assembled together with them, he charged them not to depart from Jerusalem, but to wait for the promise of the Father, which, *said he*, ye heard from me:
5 for John indeed baptized with water; but ye shall be baptized with the Holy Ghost not many days hence.

1   S. Luke begins his second *Word*, as he had begun *the first*, with a long prefatory sentence. This sums up the conclusion of the Gospel and gives the three keynotes of the treatise to follow. (1) The subject of the Acts is the same as that of the Gospel, viz. the words and deeds of JESUS. For the Gospel was only the beginning: it contained what *Jesus began to do and to teach* up to his ascension. This word *began*, which is frequent in the first three gospels and is still characteristic of the Acts², teaches us that the work of the church now to be described is still the work of the
2 Lord, although he has now been *taken up* into heaven. Before his ascension however he had (2) *given commandment to the Apostles*, who were to represent him and *whom he had chosen* for that purpose out of the larger circle of disciples as recorded in the Gospel³. The commandment was, as the Bezan text adds, *to preach the gospel*⁴; and the Acts is the history of the fulfilment of their commission. Once more (3) this commandment was given *through the Holy Ghost*, which is another keynote of the Acts. The Lord had himself been 'anointed with the Spirit,' and all he did and taught in the gospel was in that 'power' (x 38). On the evening of the resurrection when giving his charge to the apostles he had breathed on them and said 'Receive ye the Holy Ghost,' and henceforth all his work in the church through the apostles is to be in the same power.
3   For fulfilling the command the apostles needed special preparation. (1) They had to bear witness of the resurrection and so needed full assurance for themselves. Accordingly *during an interval of forty days* he *appeared* or rendered himself visible unto them⁵ on several occasions, and proved himself to be *living* by *incontestable evidence*, e.g. such as that afforded by touch and by eating⁶. (2) They had to establish *the kingdom of God*, and therefore needed instruction concerning it. Of the instruction which the Lord gave the Gospels afford us specimens, though but fragmentary⁷. From them we learn that it included (*a*) a summary of the gospel, viz. the death and resurrection of the Christ and forgiveness of sins through his name, which gospel was the key to

---

¹ Marg *eating with them*.   ² See especially i 22, x 37: cp. ii 4, viii 35, xi 15, xviii 26.   ³ Lk vi 13: cp. Jn vi 70, xv 16.   ⁴ x 42. The command is recorded in the Gospels—Mt xxviii 19, 20, Mk xvi 15, Jn xx 21 and Lk xxiv 47 which is almost a summary of the Acts.   ⁵ The Gk is a rare word, specially appropriate to heavenly appearances: cp. xxvi 19, Lk i 22, xxiv 23, II Cor xii 1.
⁶ The Gk word (*signs*) is technical for this kind of *proof*: cp. Lk xxiv 39, 43, I Jn i 1.   ⁷ Cp. Mt xxviii 18-20. Mk xvi 15-18, Lk xxiv 44-49, Jn xx 21-23.

the true interpretation of the Old Testament: (b) a command to preach this gospel to all the world and to make disciples, 'baptizing' and 'teaching' them: (c) a commission to represent the Lord as he had represented the Father, and this representation carried with it the power to forgive and retain sins. (3) For their difficult work the apostles needed a personal equipment. As the Lord had been baptized with the Spirit and power, so they needed a baptism to make them new men full of strength, and to enable them to represent the Lord with authority.

4 With a special view to this last need the Lord appeared to the apostles. The occasion may have been some solemn meal to which S. Peter may allude in x 41: for the Greek word for *being assembled together* (a very rare one) may be taken, as by S. Chrysostom and the margin, as *while eating with them*. On this occasion then the Lord gave them a definite *charge to wait* at Jerusalem *for the promise of the FATHER*, i.e. the Holy SPIRIT[1]. This promise the Lord had plainly given for the first time in his discourses at the last supper as recorded by S. John. S. John however does not use the word *promise*, which belongs to S. Paul's vocabulary. But the title *the FATHER* is very Johannine, and its occurrence here and in verse 7 is a sign of the genuineness of the narrative[2], just as the sudden change from indirect to direct speech (*said he* is not in the Greek) is characteristic of the dramatic style of S. Luke. The
5 Lord himself explains the promise as *baptism in the Holy Spirit*. The preparation for the gospel had been a baptism of repentance[3]. This had been preached by John the Baptist, and some at least of the apostles had received that baptism. But *John* had only *baptized with water*, and the true baptism is 'of water and the Spirit' (Jn iii 5). Such baptism had hitherto been impossible, for 'the Spirit was not yet, because Jesus was not yet glorified' (Jn vii 39), i.e. he had not yet ascended to heaven and in his glorified humanity received that gift for men.

§ 1 *The Ascension*

The ascension of the Lord is a connecting link between the Gospel and the Acts, and so it occurs in both. It is the end of the Lord's 'sojourning' on earth: it is also the immediate preparation for the descent of the Holy Ghost. The two cardinal events however are the resurrection and the gift of the Spirit at Pentecost: and the ascension holds an intermediate position. There was not much reference to it in the early apostolic teaching, and apparently it did not at first mark such a break as it does to us now. The apostles did not know but that the Lord might shew himself again at any moment, as he did in fact to S. Stephen, to S. Paul and S. John: and in I Cor xv 5-8

---

[1] ii 33, Lk xxiv 49.   [2] Elsewhere in the Acts it only occurs once, ii 33.
[3] Cp. x 37, xiii 24. For John's work see Mt iii, Mk i 2-11, Lk iii 1-22, Jn i 19-36: and for references to it in the Acts see i 22, x 37, xi 16, xiii 24-5, xviii 24-xix 7.

S. Paul enumerates the appearances after the resurrection without allusion to the ascension. The 'great forty days,' which preceded the ascension, occupy a similar intermediate position, and this may account for the scantiness of our information concerning them. It is clear that the apostles waited in Jerusalem until the 8th day after Easter, when the Lord appeared to them the second time (Jn xx 26). Then they went to Galilee where they saw him for the third time (Jn xxi 14). At some other appearance in Galilee the Lord must have directed the Eleven once more to return to Jerusalem. For the scene of his exaltation on the cross—his own city—must be the scene of his exaltation in glory; and 'the law must go forth out of Zion and the word of the Lord from Jerusalem' (Isai ii 3). In Jerusalem he met them once more—perhaps in the same upper chamber which was the scene of the last supper. And then, after a farewell discourse, the Good Shepherd 'led them out' of the city across Cedron to the mount of Olives (as seven weeks before he had led them by the same path to Gethsemane) and there was parted from them in the manner now to be related.

The other accounts of the ascension are given in Mk xvi 19 and Lk xxiv 50-53; we must also bear in mind the kindred scene of the transfiguration in Mt xvii 1-8, Mk ix 2-8, Lk ix 28-36 together with the ascension of Elijah in the OT (II Kings ii).

6 They therefore, when they were come together, asked him, saying, Lord, dost thou at this time restore the kingdom to
7 Israel? And he said unto them, ¹ It is not for you to know times or seasons, which the Father hath ²set within his own
8 authority. But ye shall receive power, when the Holy Ghost is come upon you: and ye shall be my witnesses both in Jerusalem, and in all Judæa and Samaria, and unto the
9 uttermost part of the earth. And when he had said these things, as they were looking, he was taken up; and a cloud
10 received him out of their sight. And while they were looking stedfastly into heaven as he went, behold, two men stood by
11 them in white apparel; which also said, Ye men of Galilee, why stand ye looking into heaven? this Jesus, which was received up from you into heaven, shall so come in like
12 manner as ye beheld him going into heaven. Then returned they unto Jerusalem from the mount called Olivet, which is nigh unto Jerusalem, a sabbath day's journey off.

6 The apostles' question shews how much they need the enlightenment of the Spirit. Still, in spite of the lesson of the crucifixion,

---

¹ Bezan *No one can know*—a Johannine phrase. ² Marg *appointed by*.

they retain the old Jewish idea of the Messianic 'kingdom of God' as a glorious empire of Israel: and now after the resurrection they are still more confident than when on the journey up to Jerusalem they had thought that it was 'immediately to appear' (Lk xix 11). Their expectation was indeed to be realized, but in a very different way to what they expected; the Acts ends with the establishment of the kingdom even at Rome, but at the cost of the rejection of the old Israel. They now ask if the time has come for the *restoration to Israel* of *the kingdom*, which God in his original purpose had destined for Israel and which he had promised throughout the OT. The glorious promises in the prophets shewed that the 'restoration' of this kingdom would be the consummation of the present world, in fact the 'restoration of all things[1].' This restoration is nothing else than the manifestation of the glory of the Messiah, so the apostles really are repeating a question which they had asked before[2]— 'when shall be thy coming and the end of the world?'

There was among the Jews much curiosity as to the time of 'the age to come[3]': just as at a later time a similar curiosity vexed the Christians at Thessalonica. But the Lord once for all rebukes such curiosity or impatience, *It is not for you to know times or seasons.* To the view of the FATHER of all things lay open the whole plan of creation, the *times* or critical moments of its history and the *seasons* or epochs of its orderly development: but these he had *set*, i.e. *reserved, within his own authority.* The translation of the margin *which he hath appointed by his own authority*[4] makes them equally lie within his sole jurisdiction. The time of the final hour had not even been revealed to the SON in his humanity. Authority had been given him to execute the judgement (Jn v 27) but not to know the time. And as he had come into the world not to satisfy curiosity but to give life: so he was sending his apostles not to utter predictions but to proclaim the gospel of salvation. For this work they needed divine assistance or *power*, which they would receive *when the Holy Ghost came upon them.* The gospel itself was simply the message of what Jesus had done. The apostles had simply to bear witness to what they had heard and seen, and in particular to the crucifixion and resurrection of the Lord. So the Lord gives the definition of the apostolate which lies at the root of the Acts of the Apostles. The 'apostles' are simply '*witnesses* of Jesus[5]'; and as the resurrection was the crucial fact which proved the divine sonship of Jesus, an 'apostle' is in particular one who can bear witness that with his own eyes he has seen the risen Jesus. This is stated again and again—i 22, ii 32, iii 15, v 32,

---

[1] iii 21: cp. Mt xvii 11, Mk ix 12. [2] Mt xxiv 3, Mk xiii 4. [3] This is evident from the contemporary apocalyptic literature, e.g. *Apoc. Baruch* xlviii 2 f. Cp. I Thess v 1 foll., II ii. [4] So in xx 28, which is rather S. Paul's use of the word: cp. I Cor xii 18, 28, I Th v 9. S. Luke usually means *set*; cp. v 4, xix 21, Lk i 66, ix 44, xxi 44. Cp. Judith ii 2. [5] So the Lord's own work was *to bear witness to the truth* (Jn xviii 37).

x 39, 41, xiii 31, xxii 15, xxvi 16—and it becomes a criterion of an 'apostle' to ask, Has he '*seen* Jesus our Lord' (I Cor ix 1)? In further defining the sphere of the witness the Lord sums up the external history of the Acts: it is (1) to begin 'from *Jerusalem*' ch. ii-vii, (2) to pass to *all Judaea and Samaria*, viii-ix 31,—at present the extreme limit of the narrow Jewish ideas of the disciples: (3) but the bounds of Jewish narrowness are to be burst one after another until the church is planted at Rome, and the capital of the empire where (to quote Irenaeus' words) 'all meet from every quarter' will represent *the uttermost part of the earth*, x–xxviii[1].

9 When the Lord *had said this*, as we learn from the Gospel, he lifted up his hands in blessing and so was parted from them. *He was taken up* from the earth in his 'bodily form' (Lk iii 22) in the *sight* of their eyes until a bright *cloud* intervened and concealed him as at the transfiguration. In the language of the creed he was raised up to 'the right hand of the FATHER.' As God is spirit, this is of course a metaphor. But the reality cannot be represented to us otherwise. What is signified is that the manhood of Jesus was exalted to heaven or glorified. A foretaste of this had been given at the transfiguration. But now, having died and risen again, the SON returns to the glory which he had with the FATHER before the world was (Jn xvii 5): he reassumes all those glories of deity of which he had emptied himself at the incarnation, and in this glorification the human nature which he then assumed has now a part. What are the conditions of a human body, glorified and united with deity, it is impossible for us in our present state to conceive or imagine. In the Old Testament the incomprehensibleness of the divine nature was typified by a cloud which hid JEHOVAH from human view: so now the human body of Jesus is concealed by the same cloud which is the cloud of the Shekinah or divine glory. He is now 'in glory[2].'

10 The apostles *gaze intently*[3] into space. But as the women at the tomb were recalled from groping among the dead (Lk xxiv 5) so were the apostles from star-gazing. As then, so now, *two men clothed in white*—in such a form do angels appear—address them:

11 *Men of Galilee*—as if to remind them of their lowly origin[4]—*why stand ye looking into heaven?* As with the women, so reflection would suffice to shew the apostles their line of duty, for their work lay on earth. Nevertheless the angels have a 'gospel' to console them. The restoration of the kingdom will take place, the Messiah will come again: and though the circumstances will be very different, for he will come on the clouds of heaven with all the angels and the glory of the FATHER, yet he will come *in like manner*, i.e. in his

---

[1] Cp. Lk xxiv 47. Prof. Knowling (in the *Expositors' Gk Test.*) points out that in the *Psalms of Solomon* (viii 16) Pompey is described as *he that is from the uttermost part of the earth*. [2] vii 55-6, xxii 11, 1 Tim iii 16: cp. vii 2 *God of the glory*. [3] This word is characteristic of S. Luke; cp. iii 4, 12, vi 15, vii 55, x 4, xi 6, xiii 9, xiv 9, xxiii 1. [4] Jn i 46, vii 41, 52.

human nature. He who will come is *this* same *Jesus who is now*
12 *taken up from you.* Fortified by this gospel, the apostles *return to Jerusalem*, even 'with great joy[1].'

The note about the *sabbath day's journey* implies a Jewish source, the expression would be strange to Gentile ears at Rome. But there would be a reason for its use if the ascension happened on a sabbath day, which is the inference drawn by S. Chrysostom: and certainly the sabbath would have been the most appropriate day for the Lord to have *entered into his rest* (Hebr iv 10). If the forty days were reckoned exclusively they would bring us to a Saturday. The observance of Ascension Day on a Thursday cannot be traced back earlier than the 4th century, and the day was probably obtained by counting forty days after Easter. Forty was the Jewish round number.

§ 2 *The waiting disciples*

S. Luke now gives us the first of his pictures of church life at Jerusalem. But it is anticipating to speak of 'the church': we shall not meet with the word till v 11 (or possibly ii 47). At present we have as in the time of the Lord's ministry (1) a more or less unorganized body or *multitude* of disciples who are known as *the brethren* (verse 15). Their number amounted to *about 120*[2], that is the number of the brethren at Jerusalem, for there must have been many more in Galilee, where the Lord had appeared to over 500. The mention of *names* seems almost to imply some register or roll.

(2) In this body a group stands out prominent and distinct from '*the rest*' (Lk xxiv 9, 33). They are *the Eleven*, and S. Luke marks their importance by giving their names, though in fact only three will recur again. The list agrees with that in his Gospel—except that *John* is now next to *Peter*, as he will appear in the history[3]. Thomas is also coupled with Philip: they both were brought into prominence at the passion and resurrection. The Eleven are the nucleus of the community, and they have as their rendezvous or headquarters *the upper chamber*. The Jews used the upper parts of their houses for purposes of meditation and retirement; so S. Peter went upon the housetop to pray at Joppa (x 9, cp. xx 8). This upper chamber was no doubt the scene of the last supper[4] and of the gatherings after the resurrection. It may have been in the house of Mary the mother of Mark (xii 12): and it holds an important place as the cradle of the church in Jerusalem.

Besides the Eleven there are other groups—first (3) *the women and Mary the mother of Jesus*. A company of women had followed the Lord and his disciples and contributed to their support in the days of his Galilean ministry. Among them were included Mary Magdalene,

---

[1] Lk xxiv 52: cp. Jn xvi 22. [2] i.e. ten times twelve: cp. the 144,000 of Rev vii. [3] iii 1: cp Lk xxii 8, Jn xx 2. [4] Though a different Greek word is used in the Gospels.

another Mary, Salome, Joanna, Susanna, and others. They had come up on the last journey to Jerusalem, and some of them had won the great reward of receiving the first tidings of his resurrection and of being the first witnesses of the risen Lord. It was this privilege, and the addition of *the mother of Jesus*, which won for them this high place in the church, which was so contrary to oriental custom. Next to them came (4) a group, honoured because of their blood-relationship to the Lord, his *brethren*. One of these, James, will come into great prominence in the history of the church of Jerusalem.

Among '*the rest*' must have been some who *had companied with the apostles since the baptism of John*, such as Joseph Barsabbas, Matthias, and many of the Seventy; personal friends of the Lord as Lazarus, Martha and Mary; disciples such as the 'goodman of the house' (Mk xiv 14): Cleopas, John Mark and his mother Mary: Mnason of Cyprus (xxi 16). We may probably add Joseph Barnabas and Silas, and possibly Simon of Cyrene, Joseph of Arimathaea and Nicodemus. In the Gospel of S. Luke we find the same groups —the body of disciples (vi 13), the women (viii 2, 3) and the Twelve (vi 14, xxiv 9, 10, 33). Their life is now described.

13 And when they were come in, they went up into the upper chamber, where they were abiding; both Peter and John and James and Andrew, Philip and Thomas, Bartholomew and Matthew, James *the son* of Alphæus, and Simon the
14 Zealot, and Judas *the son* of James. These all with one accord continued stedfastly in prayer, with the women, and Mary the mother of Jesus, and with his brethren.

There is as yet little sign of organization. There is no mention of teaching or breaking of bread, but only of their unanimity. They were all *together* (verse 15). But strictly speaking this description in vv. 13-4 only applies to the Eleven and the associated groups. Their life was one of *abiding* or expectant waiting; its characteristic was *cleaving stedfastly* to the Lord and one another in constant *prayer*[1]. Such prayer included regular attendance at the temple worship, but no doubt the upper chamber was still a centre for reunions among themselves. The dominant element of the prayer was praise (Lk xxiv 53).

§ 3 *The filling up of 'the Twelve'*

The one incident of this interval which S. Luke has elected to record stamps at once the fundamental position of the apostolate, i.e. of 'the Twelve.' Upon the foundations of the new Jerusalem are the twelve names of the twelve apostles of the Lamb (Rev xxi 14), and as the foundations are now to be laid the place of the name that has been erased must be filled. The fate of Judas resembles the fate of

---
[1] This close adhesion is a regular mark of church life: cp. ii 42, 46, vi 4, viii 13.

Ahithophel in II Sam xvii 23, and the substitution of Matthias in his room is parallel to the substitution of the house of Zadok for the house of Eli (I Sam ii 30-35, I Kings ii 35) and of Eliakim for Shebna the treasurer in Isai xxii 15-25. For similar contrasts compare among the prophets Samson and Samuel, among the kings Saul and David.

15 And in these days Peter stood up in the midst of the brethren, and said (and there was a multitude of ¹persons
16 *gathered* together, about a hundred and twenty), Brethren, it was needful that the scripture should be fulfilled, which the Holy Ghost spake before by the mouth of David con-
17 cerning Judas, who was guide to them that took Jesus. For he was numbered among us, and received his ²portion in this
18 ministry. (Now this man obtained a field with the reward of his iniquity; and falling headlong, he burst asunder in the
19 midst, and all his bowels gushed out. And it became known to all the dwellers at Jerusalem; insomuch that in their language that field was called Akeldama, that is, The field of
20 blood.) For it is written in the book of Psalms,
    ³Let his habitation be made desolate,
    And let no man dwell therein:
and,
    His ⁴office let another take.
21 Of the men therefore which have companied with us all the time that the Lord Jesus went in and went out among us,
22 beginning from the baptism of John, unto the day that he was received up from us, of these must one become a witness with us of his resurrection.
23 And they put forward two, Joseph called Barsabbas, who
24 was surnamed Justus, and Matthias. And they prayed, and said, Thou, Lord, which knowest the hearts of all men, shew
25 of these two the one whom thou hast chosen, to take the place in this ⁵ministry and apostleship, from which Judas fell
26 away, that he might go to his own place. And they gave lots for them; and the lot fell upon Matthias; and he was numbered with the eleven apostles.

18 Into a narrative which evidently comes from an Hebraic source S. Luke has inserted a note of his own (vv. 18-9)⁶. It was the

¹ Gk *names*. ² Gk *lot (clēros)*. ³ Pss lxix 25 and cix 8. ⁴ Gk *episcopē*, AV *bishoprick*. ⁵ Gk *diaconia*. ⁶ For a similar note see Lk vii 29-30.

tradition which he had found current about the years 55 to 57 in the church at Jerusalem as to the fate of Judas: and this tradition was the popular Jewish explanation of a local name *Akeldama*. S. Matthew (xxvii 3-10) gives another and somewhat different tradition: and indeed there seems to have been a third account of Judas' end handed down in the church by Papias bishop of Hierapolis[1]. All accounts agree in the fact of a terrible end. S. Matthew makes this follow immediately upon the crime. But this is probably due to a foreshortening in the retrospect. S. Luke's narrative plainly implies some interval, at least enough to have bought the field. When S. Peter speaks of Judas' 'own place,' he does not necessarily refer to Gehenna. He makes no allusion to Judas' fate where we might have expected it, e.g. before the Sanhedrin. Nor do we hear of any awe falling upon those that heard of it, as after the deaths of Ananias and Sapphira. Accordingly we conclude that Judas did satisfy his covetousness by *the purchase of an estate* (verse 18) with the 30 pieces of silver, and that at some subsequent time he committed suicide on his property by hanging himself or casting himself down a precipice. Both methods are reconciled in the version which S. Augustine quotes: *he hanged himself and falling headlong on his face* (through the rope breaking) *he burst asunder in the midst*. This was enough to make the ground polluted or accursed: it was set apart by the authorities as a burying ground for aliens and got the name of *Field of Blood*.

15 In filling up the vacant place of Judas the Eleven do not as we might have expected use the method of cooptation, but notwithstanding their distinct position seek the cooperation of the whole body of *brethren*. *S. Peter* takes the initiative, and in his address we perceive
16 the result of the Lord's having 'opened their mind to understand the scriptures': S. Peter now understands 'what had been written in the Psalms concerning him' (Lk xxiv 44-5). In the Psalms among the sorrows of the persecuted righteous is the treachery of his most intimate friend: and *the scripture must be fulfilled*. This then explained the problem which had baffled the apostles: how could *Judas* have played the part of traitor—one whom the Lord himself
17 had chosen and had *numbered among themselves*, i.e. the Twelve, to whom he had allotted, as his *portion, this service* of the *apostle-*
20 *ship*? It was part of the divine plan. But Judas must also suffer the fate of the traitor, and S. Peter probably read the whole passage of judgement in the Messianic psalm (lxix 22-28), out of which S. Luke selected verse 25 because of the allusion to the *habitation* or 'field.' But a passage in another psalm (cix 8) implies that the traitor's *office*—in the Greek, his *overseership* or *episcopate*—is not
21 to remain vacant. As the scripture must be fulfilled, this is
22 equivalent to a command. Accordingly the apostolic college must be filled up by the appointment of a new apostle. An apostle is 'a witness of Jesus' (i 8), i.e. (1) *a witness of his resurrection*, but also

---

[1] See Gebhardt and Harnack *Patr. Apost.* (ed. minor) p. 73.

(2) of all he said and did, i.e. of his ministry which *began from the baptism of John.*

23 The case of Judas was a warning to the apostles to distrust their human judgement, and so the final decision is left to God. But first, out of those who were qualified the brethren select *two*, whom *they put forward* or *set forth* in the midst of the assembly. These two were *Matthias* and *Joseph*, distinguished by a surname *Barsabbas*[1] from the numerous other Josephs, such as Joseph Barnabas, Joseph of Arimathaea: Joseph Barsabbas also rejoiced in a Latin surname —*Justus* or *the Righteous*, a name which betokened faithful observance of the law[2], and so was also given by the Jews to 24 James the Lord's brother. Then to ascertain the divine choice (1) *they prayed*. This is the first recorded public prayer of the church. S. Peter was no doubt their spokesman, and he uses the same attribute of God as he does in xv 8—*knowing the heart*[3]. The prayer is addressed either to God the Father as in iv 24; or to 'the Lord,' viz. Jesus, to whom they had been accustomed to appeal in every difficulty and of whose presence (though unseen) they were fully conscious. They were convinced that he had already *chosen* one to fill this place of ministry, as he had originally chosen the 25 Twelve: and they ask him to make the appointment by shewing his choice. *Judas had transgressed* or *stepped aside* from his *place of ministry to go to the place which was his own.* It is generally supposed that by this place S. Peter means Gehenna: and certainly Clement, Ignatius, and Polycarp speak of 'the place' of glory or punishment hereafter[4]. But that use was probably taken from this passage interpreted in the light of Judas' fate. In the Scriptures 'place' is generally used of position in this world, and 'his own' stands for 'home' in Jn xix 29. However whether it were Gehenna or the old worldly life, Judas' *place* was his deliberate choice and his proper home in harmony with his character. The prayer of the disciples shews us the true aim of prayer. They did not pray to alter or direct the choice of the Lord, but that they might know 26 his will. To learn that they then (2) *cast lots.* The choice of him who reads the heart, as in the case of David (I Sam xvi), shewed that 'the Lord seeth not as man seeth': *the lot fell* not upon 'the Just' but *upon Matthias*, who was therefore formally *reckoned among and with 'the Eleven,'* i.e. he was now an '*Apostle.*'

The extreme fidelity of this record is proved not only by its Hebraic character but by the circumstances. (1) There is the absence of organization. Only passive verbs are used, *must be made, was reckoned*: for Matthias was appointed neither by the apostles nor by the church, but directly by the Lord. It was entirely his doing;

---

[1] There is uncertainty as to the meaning of the name and its derivation. *Bar* means *son*. If the word is a patronymic—*son of Sabba*—Joseph might be a brother of Judas Barsabbas of xv 22. [2] Cp. Lk i 6. [3] Cp. Jerem xi 20, xvii 10, xx 12. [4] Clem. *ad Cor.* 5, Ign. *ad Magn.* 5, Polyc. *ad Phil.* 9. Cp. Num xxiv 5 (of Balaam).

and we have a picture of the disciples acting just as in the old gospel days, the only difference being that the Lord's presence is invisible to the eye. (2) Similarly there is no mention of laying on of hands or the gift of the Holy Spirit, for 'the Spirit was not yet.' (3) The method of casting lots adopted for learning the Lord's will is thoroughly in the spirit of the OT. This primitive method disappears after Pentecost; henceforth the apostles are guided not by external signs but by the indwelling Spirit. The word *lot* (*cléros*) however was retained in its OT usage to denote the ministry, and in the word *clergy* remains with us to this day. It denoted (*a*) those on whom the lot of God's choice had fallen, and (*b*) those who were God's lot or portion, and both senses ran into one.

This incident concludes the preparation for the descent of the Holy Ghost. The Lord, the bestower of the Spirit, is prepared by the glorification of his human nature: the church, which is to receive the Spirit, is prepared (*a*) inwardly by the spirit of prayer. (*b*) organically by the completion of the apostolate.

SECTION II (= Ch. 2)

The Baptism of the Church at Pentecost

In the Gospel, after the preparation in the first chapter, we come to the birth of the Lord, who was 'conceived of the Holy Ghost, born of the Virgin Mary.' So in the 2nd chapter of the Acts we seem to read the fulfilment of a prophecy similar to that made to the Virgin, *The Holy Ghost shall come upon thee and the power of the Most High shall overshadow thee*, and the day of Pentecost is commonly spoken of as the birthday of the church. But this is not quite accurate. We read of the working of the Spirit before Pentecost—in the first chapter of S. Luke's Gospel, and in the Old Testament. On Easter Day the Lord had breathed on the apostles and said *Receive ye the Holy Ghost*. Similarly the church was already in existence when the Lord laid the foundations by choosing the Twelve: it existed in the Old Testament, for the people of Israel were 'the church of God' (vii 38): it existed indeed before the foundation of the world in the mind of God. What then does Pentecost represent? What change is effected by the outpouring of the Spirit?

The change lies in the relation of the Holy Spirit to the human spirit. This relation was made quite new. Previously the Holy Spirit had acted on men from without, like an external force; as the prophet Ezekiel describes it, 'the hand of the Lord was upon me.' But now the Holy Spirit acts from within. He is in man (Jn xiv 17). Before Pentecost his manifestations had been transient and exceptional: now his presence in man's heart is an 'abiding' one and regular. This change had become possible because the Holy Spirit is 'the Spirit of Jesus' (xvi 7). It was the union of the divine and human natures in the person of Jesus Christ which first made it possible for the divine Spirit to dwell in a human personality. When the Word was made flesh, the Holy Ghost became the Spirit of the man Jesus; and now that Jesus was glorified the Spirit of Jesus was become the Spirit of consummated humanity, and through the channel of that humanity he could be poured out upon the brethren of Jesus. This new presence of the Spirit has also a corresponding effect on human society. Being the Spirit of the Son of Man, the church which his indwelling creates is a universal church: no longer the church of a small select race but the church of humanity.

On earth then the day of Pentecost marks the beginning of this new relation. It is the beginning of the new spiritual life of the church—its second birth. And the characteristic of this life is Power. A transformation takes place, the apostles are new men, all fear of the Jews is gone. Peter, but now afraid of a servant girl, stands up boldly before all the people. The apostles' tongues are loosed and three thousand are converted. The work of the church begins. Now in the Gospel the Lord's ministry began after his baptism when he was 'anointed with the Holy Ghost and with power' (x 38): and accordingly here we have not the birth, but the second birth, the baptism of the church. So the Lord himself had spoken of it as the baptism in the Spirit (i 5).

When the Lord was baptized, there came a voice from heaven and the appearance of a dove; so the baptism of the church is attended by similar extraordinary phenomena—an appearance of fire, a noise from heaven, and an unusual 'voice' from the disciples. The disciples themselves, and much more the world, needed some external evidence to assure them that the baptism of the Spirit had taken place. This would save them from becoming the prey of imagination or self-deceit. They needed (to quote the Catechism) 'an outward visible sign' as a pledge 'of the inward and spiritual grace given.' And so we find that at other times special manifestations are recorded, where there is special need of assurance as to the baptism of the Spirit, as in the case of the Samaritans (viii), Gentiles (x), John's disciples (xix). On this occasion however there is every reason why we should expect miraculous symptoms. This Pentecost witnessed the introduction into the world of a new order of life—the life of the divine Spirit in humanity. This spiritual life is not contrary to nature, but it is above nature—certainly above the 'nature' of the fleshly life (Jn iii 6). And just as the union of the divine and human natures in the incarnation was marked by a unique or miraculous birth, so we should expect the new birth of the Spirit to be unique. Every new beginning in thought or life is inevitably accompanied by disturbance. There is the struggle with the old, and the re-adjustment to the new, environment. So the coming of the Spirit is followed by irregular and abnormal phenomena. Like Jordan, the full and plenteous flood of the Spirit 'overflows all its banks' (Josh iii 15). At first the old worn-out vessels of humanity cannot contain it: and there is a flood of strange and novel spiritual experiences. But when it has worn for itself a deep channel in the church, when the laws of the new spiritual life are learnt and understood, then some of the irregular phenomena disappear, others become normal, and what was thought to be miraculous is found to be a natural endowment of the Christian life.

These miraculous phenomena however are not merely external signs of some unusual occurrence. There is in them a definite correspondence with the reality they signify, that is, they have a definite symbolical meaning. The prophetic writings of the OT were largely marked by the use of symbolical imagery, as in the passage of Joel which S. Peter here quotes. Now very similar in style to the OT are some of these early narratives in the Acts which evidently come from the hand of some Christian prophet: and in interpreting the phenomena they record we must be guided by the laws of prophecy. To help us we have the accounts of divine epiphanies in the OT such as those at the burning bush (Exod iii 2, 3) and Sinai (ib. xix 18-20, xxiv 17, etc.), to Elijah (1 Kings xix 11, 12) and Ezekiel (Ez i 4, etc.).

§ 1 *The descent of the Spirit*

2 And when the day of Pentecost [1]was now come, they were
2 all together in one place. And suddenly there came from heaven a sound as of the rushing of a mighty [2]wind, and it
3 filled all the house where they were sitting. And there appeared unto them tongues [3]parting asunder, like as of fire ;
4 and it sat upon each one of them. And they were all filled with the Holy Spirit, and began to speak with other tongues, as the Spirit gave them utterance.

5 Now there were dwelling at Jerusalem Jews, devout men,
6 from every nation under heaven. And when this sound was heard, the multitude came together, and were confounded, because that every man heard them speaking in his own
7 language. And they were all amazed and marvelled, saying,
8 Behold, are not all these which speak Galilæans ? And how hear we, every man in our own language, wherein we were
9 born ? Parthians and Medes and Elamites, and the dwellers in Mesopotamia, in Judæa and Cappadocia, in Pontus and
10 Asia, in Phrygia and Pamphylia, in Egypt and the parts of Libya about Cyrene, and sojourners from Rome, both Jews
11 and proselytes, Cretans and Arabians, we do hear them
12 speaking in our tongues the mighty works of God. And

---

[1] Gk *was being fulfilled* (as in Lk ix 51).   [2] Gk *breath*.   [3] Marg *parting among them* or *distributing themselves*.

they were all amazed, and were perplexed, saying one to
13 another, What meaneth this? But others mocking said, They
are filled with new wine.

1 *The day of Pentecost was now being fulfilled*, i.e. it had begun but
was not yet past. This day was one of the three great festivals
when the law required the attendance of all Israel at the temple,
and Jerusalem would be thronged with pilgrims. As the Passover fell
rather early for the navigation season, Jews from the west especially
would prefer to make their pilgrimage at the time of Pentecost,
as we shall find S. Paul doing later on. Pentecost was also called
the Feast of Weeks, because it fell seven (i.e. a week of) weeks after
the Passover. To be exact, it was the fiftieth (Greek *pentecoste*) day
after the offering of the sheaf of the firstfruits of the harvest during
the feast of unleavened bread. And as its characteristic ceremony
was the offering of the first two loaves—the firstfruits—of the new
corn, it marked the close of harvest. The disciples no doubt attended
the temple soon after dawn for the morning sacrifices and the
offering of the firstfruits, and then in a body *all together* assembled
at their own *house, where they were sitting*, i.e. which was their
headquarters, probably the house with the 'upper chamber[1].' This
gathering would be for prayer and worship. For the rest of the
Jews would be engaged in similar exercises in the other synagogues of
Jerusalem: and on sabbath and festival days, till such services were
over, they abstained from eating and drinking, not breaking their
2 fast till the fourth hour, about 10 a.m., or even noon. While the
brethren were thus engaged, they *suddenly* heard a great sound
coming down from above. It was like the *echoing noise* of a *wind
blowing violently*. It sounded through *the whole house*, for the
hundred and twenty must have occupied more than one chamber;
3 and it was accompanied by an appearance of *fire*. The fire was in
the form of *tongues* which *distributed themselves*[2] over the company,
4 a tongue *settling upon* the head of *each one*. That moment *they were
filled*, and so baptized, *with the Holy Spirit*, and the immediate
result was that they *began to speak*. They praised and glorified God
with other tongues, i.e. in utterances different from their ordinary
speech—utterances enthusiastic and ecstatic, of a novel eloquence
exceeding their usual form of speech. For in fact these *utterances*—
and a stately word is used in the Greek—were the direct inspiration
of the Spirit.
6   These phenomena manifesting themselves in a body of 120 must
have attracted attention, and a crowd of inhabitants and pilgrims
soon collected. Possibly under the influence of the Spirit—for while
the appearance and sound may have been but momentary, the speaking
continued—the apostolic body made their way to the temple and

---

[1] Cp. i 13, xviii 11 Gk, Lk xxiv 49 Gk.   [2] That this is the meaning is shewn
by ii 45, Lk xxii 17, Mt xxvii 35 where the word recurs. *Cloven* tongues would have
required a different tense, as in Lk xi 17, xii 52.

R. A.

prepared to address the concourse there in Solomon's porch. Oriental cities were familiar enough with phenomena of ecstasy and fanaticism, yet the multitude of the Jews were perplexed and even *thrown into confusion*. The more so that in the utterances of the disciples many
13 strangers recognized words of their own languages. Some found it the easiest solution to put it down to intoxication. This charge gave
14 the fitting opportunity: to answer it the Twelve, as the representatives of the whole body, stood forward, and *Peter* acting as their spokesman under the inspiration of the Holy Spirit *made utterance*[1].

The symbolic teaching of the narrative is very clear. The word *being fulfilled* which S. Luke had used in his Gospel (ix 51) of 'the days of the Lord's being received up,' and which does not occur again in the NT, may remind us that this descent is the true fulfilment of those days of the Lord's ascension. It is also the fulfilment of the pentecostal offering of the firstfruits, for on this day were gathered the firstfruits of the harvest of the world. On Pentecost the Jews also celebrated the giving of the law on Sinai; so also on this day God gave the new law, writing it in the heart by his Spirit (Hebr viii 10). In the scene itself we find illustrated that unity with diversity, which is the mark of the Spirit's operation: 'there are diversities of gifts but the same Spirit—who divideth to each one severally as he will' (I Cor xii 4, 11). They are *all together—in one place*: the sounds fill *the whole house*, the fire sits upon the head of *each one*: the tongues *distribute themselves* to each individual, but the many utterances make one *sound* or *voice* (verse 6). The various phenomena are familiar to us already from the divine epiphanies of the OT. The most striking likeness is found in the strong wind, fire, and voice of Elijah's vision[2]. The Spirit is like the wind, hence his coming is *sudden*; for 'the wind bloweth where it listeth, and thou hearest the voice thereof, but knowest not whence it cometh and whither it goeth' (Jn iii 8). The apostles however knew that the Spirit came down *out of heaven*. The wind really was a *breath*[3]; for the Spirit is the breath of life, which giveth life and understanding. This breath is '*mighty* in operation': it is *borne* from on high, and as at the creation its *moving* is the beginning of life[4]. *Fire* is always a sign of the divine presence. So it was at the burning bush, and throughout the OT. Pagan writers also recognized the symbolism, as when Virgil describes the portent which appeared to Aeneas[5]:

> Between us while Iulus stands
> 'Mid weeping eyes and clasping hands,
> Lo! from the summit of his head
> A lambent flame was seen to spread,
> Sport with his locks in harmless play,
> And grazing round his temples stray.

---
[1] The word is the same as in ver. 4: cp. iv 8. [2] I K xix 11–13: for the earthquake, see iv 31. [3] That is the word in the Greek which occurs in Gen ii 7, Job xxxii 8, xxxiii 4. [4] See Gen i 2, I Pet i 13, II i 17. [5] *Aen.* II 682–4 (Conington's trans.).

Fire purifies by consuming the evil[1]. It shews the burning zeal of love. Here however it is rather the light of divine inspiration. For it appears in the form of *tongues* and its effect is speech. The apostles speak *with other tongues*: for this voice of the Spirit speaking in humanity is something new: it is the new 'law or word of the Lord going forth from Jerusalem': the apostles 'sing a new song[2].' But this new speech is to continue and be the constant language of the church, for the apostles only *begin to speak*. It will also heal the division caused by the confusion of tongues at Babel. The voice of the Spirit is intelligible to *every nation under heaven*, i.e. to the true *Jews*, the spiritual Israel in each nation. His presence brings them *together* and will once more make 'the whole earth of one language and one speech,' and unite into one church 'the families of the sons of Noah—of whom the nations were divided in the earth[3].' The parallel in the Acts to the list of the nations in Genesis x and to the confusion of tongues in Genesis xi is most obvious.

The speaking with tongues (ii 4)

Apart from the symbolism however we have to investigate the literal meaning of the *speaking with other tongues*. This was in truth only a beginning, for 'speaking with tongues' or 'glossolaly' continued long in the church, and it ranked among the *charismata* or spiritual gifts (I Cor xii 10, 30). In the Acts we shall meet with two more instances of it (x 46, xix 6), but the gift was so abundant and disturbing in the church at Corinth that S. Paul devotes a long section of his first epistle to the Corinthians (ch. xii-xiv) to its consideration. Both in the epistle and the Acts glossolaly is closely connected with prophecy[4]; for both are utterances under the influence of the Spirit. The distinction is this—prophecy is a speaking to men for their edification, glossolaly was addressed to God directly. The subject of the 'tongues' was 'the great works of God[5],' and it was in fact a glorifying of God which might be in psalm or hymn, in prayer or thanksgiving. But there was a further distinction. Glossolaly was in the main unintelligible—not always, for the speaker sometimes edified himself, and the utterances in the spirit (whether of God or of evil) which S. Paul quotes in I Cor xii 3, viz. *Jesus is Lord* or *Jesus is anathema*, may be specimens of 'tongues.' But glossolaly was emphatically a speaking *in the spirit* as distinct from speaking *with the intelligence*, and to be understood by others the tongue had to be interpreted. In one way it might chiefly edify others, but chiefly the unbelievers, that is as being an evident sign of a divine presence within.

From this description we may gather that speaking with tongues was a kind of ecstatic or even hysterical utterance, such as is often found to accompany religious revivals or excitement. If the mind

---

[1] Isai xxxiii 14, Hebr xii 29: cp. Num xvi 35. [2] Isai ii 4, Jer xxxi 33: Ps xcvi 1 etc. [3] Gen xi 1, x 32. [4] In vv. 17, 18 S. Peter says *they shall prophesy*. [5] verse 11, and x 46.

loses control over the nerves which produce the voice, the connexion between speech and the rational faculties is severed. Such severance may be a permanent physical disorder as in the case of lunatics: it may be a temporary dislocation due to some great mental blow or excitement. But it may be due to a higher cause. Besides our intellectual faculties we have a spiritual nature. This is the seat of our personality and the medium of communion with the divine nature. And it is easy to imagine that the 'power' of the divine Spirit may manifest itself in us in phenomena which seem abnormal in comparison with our ordinary activities. The individual may be in 'ecstasy,' i.e. entirely absorbed in his spiritual being or in spiritual things, so as to be for practical purposes 'out of the body' and 'in the spirit[1].' Sometimes the spiritual energy may manifest itself in ecstatic speech or utterance—and that is what we understand by 'speaking with tongues.' The use of such external manifestations by the Spirit may be regarded as a condescension to human ideas. For the idea of 'possession' by spirits, whether good or bad, was carried to its extreme length in the ancient world, and to such possession were ascribed the phenomena of ecstasy and so forth. In fact madness and insanity were regarded with awe as forms of divine inspiration, and our word 'enthusiasm' still bears witness to the external excitement which the divine presence was supposed to produce. Plato himself seems to accept the possibility of divine revelations apart from the reason, when, speaking of the popular belief that the liver was the seat of divination, he writes[2]: 'herein is a proof that God has given the art of divination not to the wisdom but to the foolishness of man. No man, when in his wits, attains prophetic truth and inspiration: but when he receives the inspired word, either his intelligence is enthralled in sleep, or he is demented by some distemper or possession."

We notice that, though S. Paul 'spoke with tongues more than all' the Corinthians, he does not set a high value on the gift of glossolaly. He ranks it last of the *charismata*, and apparently among *childish things*[3]. For (1) it did not edify others. Rather (2) it tended to cause disorder in the church. (3) The fact that glossolaly lay in the spiritual, and not in the rational, sphere opened the door to dangerous confusion. Its phenomena might be counterfeited either by evil spirits, to whose operation the early Christians ascribed the miracles of paganism; or by religious impostors and charlatans, of which the world was then full. Again it might be hard at times to distinguish them from similar symptoms due to physical causes —such as madness, or even intoxication[4]. The church very soon realized the necessity of 'discerning the spirits,' and this applied to 'the tongues' as well as to prophecy. Hence we are not surprised to find that in some quarters it began to be looked upon with disfavour.

---

[1] See x 10, xxii 17, II Cor xii 2, Rev i 10, iv 2.   [2] (whether ironically or no) *Timaeus* 71 a (Jowett's trans.).   [3] I Cor xiv 18-20.   [4] (*a*) xxvi 24 (*b*) ii 13: cp. Eph v 18-9 where being *filled with the Spirit* is contrasted with being *drunken with wine*.

Some of the Corinthians would have forbidden it: and S. Paul has to exhort the Thessalonians not to 'quench the Spirit[1].' S. Paul himself does not assign to the charisma a high place; and as the new spiritual life of the church becomes normal and regular, the speaking with tongues gradually drops off and dies away.

This account, however, of the phenomena which took place at Pentecost is not the one which is usually accepted. It is commonly supposed that the apostles actually talked in different languages and so were able to be understood by the crowd of different nationalities, and this is the *prima facie* impression given by the narrative, especially by verses 6 to 8. If this was the case, then it was certainly a unique event, suitable for a unique occasion, and it did not occur again. But the impression is probably due to the symbolic and prophetic character of the narrative, as it works out the correspondence to Genesis x, xi: for there are several points which imply the opposite. (1) In the Greek the *other tongues* would denote not so much foreign languages as a different kind of utterance, and that would be the meaning of the *new tongues* of Mk xvi 17. Similarly S. Paul speaks of *the tongues*—i.e. speech, not languages—*of men and angels* (1 Cor xiii 1): and the usual term for glossolaly is simply *speaking with tongues*. The same word for *other* recurs in verse 40, where it does not mean foreign words. (2) There is no trace of the apostles' having possessed such a gift permanently. S. Paul and Barnabas certainly did not understand the Lycaonian dialect. But as a matter of fact the universal prevalence of Greek made the gift almost unnecessary. (3) The utterances were addressed not to the crowd but to God. They were glorifying God, not preaching the gospel: that was reserved for S. Peter. (4) In any case the utterances were ecstatic, and not in the form of continuous discourse: the effect produced on the hearers was perplexity and amazement. One class of hearers concluded that the disciples were drunken, which certainly does not suggest intelligible speech. (5) The phenomenon at the baptism of Cornelius was exactly the same as now (x 46, xi 15): but on that occasion there is no hint of or need for foreign languages. (6) The catalogue of nationalities is obviously meant to represent *every nation under heaven*, but though there would have been no doubt pilgrims among Peter's audience, they are here described as *dwellers at Jerusalem*, and certainly S. Peter assumes that they were familiar with recent events in Jerusalem. But in this case they would have understood for the most part either Greek or the Aramaic vernacular. S. Peter proceeds to address them in one of these languages and they are able to understand him.

We conclude then that the narrative taken as a whole does not require us to suppose that the speaking with tongues at Pentecost was different in essence from the ordinary glossolaly, described in the Epistle to the Corinthians. At the same time verses 8 and 11 require that some of the utterances should, as was natural, have been clothed in foreign words.

---

[1] See I Thess v 19-21, I Cor xii 10, xiv 39, I Jn iv 1-6.

The Dispersion (ii 9–11)

The catalogue of vv. 9–11 is meant to represent *every nation under heaven*, that is to say *Jews*, the true servants of God, from every nation. It is copied by S. Luke from his written authority. S. Luke would not have been likely to omit Galatia, Macedonia or Achaia; and the geography is not that of the Romans or the Greeks. It is really a description of the Jewish Dispersion written by a Jew, and the remarkable omission of Syria would suggest a Jew writing at Antioch. The Dispersion was the name for the thousands, possibly even millions, of Jews scattered throughout the world outside the Holy Land. It was, as it still is, a striking characteristic of the Jewish race. Strabo writing in the first century says[1] that 'the Jews had already penetrated into every city, and that it would not be easy to find a place in the world where this race had not arrived and taken possession.'

Parthia, Media and *Elam* denote the countries east of the Roman empire. Here would be found the remains of the ten tribes and of the Babylonian captivity. The Jews in Babylonia were so numerous and important as to form a special school of theology of their own. From the subjects of the Parthian empire we pass to *the dwellers* in the empire of Rome. Between the two empires lay the debatable ground of *Mesopotamia*. Here Jewish influence and proselytism were very active, and the royal family of Adiabene on the upper Tigris had become converts to the Jewish faith. Crossing the Euphrates we come to Syria and Antioch. In Syria the Jews formed a larger percentage of the population than elsewhere, and there was a most numerous community of Jews in Antioch who possessed the full rights of citizenship. Instead of mentioning Syria[2] however the writer passes by it on the one hand to *Judaea* proper or Palestine, on the other to Asia Minor. Here we pass through *Cappadocia* to *Pontus* on the northern coast and then to the province of *Asia* on the western coast. Turning inland, through *Phrygia* we come to the southern coast in *Pamphylia* where was Myra the port for Egypt. The Jews of Asia, especially of Ephesus, were wealthy and important, and we shall meet them again at Jerusalem (xxi 27). The journeys of S. Paul will introduce us to the Jewish settlements in southern Galatia and Phrygia. Antiochus the Great had transplanted thither 2000 Jewish families to strengthen his hold on the country. But the baths and wines of Phrygia had had a deteriorating influence on their character, and the strict rabbis spoke of them as separated from their brethren[3]. They certainly had made themselves at home in their adopted country, for inscriptions shew that in Phrygia, Galatia and Pontus Jewish families had attained to high positions of affluence and official dignity[4].

From Myra in Pamphylia we sail across to Egypt, passing Cyprus

---

[1] In Joseph. *Ant.* xiv 7. 2. [2] The omission was felt to be strange in early times, and for *Judaea* was substituted *Armenia* (Tertullian) or *Syria* (Jerome). [3] Neubauer *Géogr. du Talmud* p. 315. [4] See Ramsay *Cities and Bishoprics of Phrygia* ch. xv.

on the way. In Cyprus there was a large Jewish colony. In the revolt in Trajan's reign the Cypriote Jews rose and were said to have massacred 240,000 of their Gentile fellow-citizens[1]. Jews from Cyprus were among the earliest converts, and had a great share in the work of spreading the gospel: but their chief glory was Joseph Barnabas, 'a Levite, a man of Cyprus by race[2].' The Jews in *Egypt* were perhaps the most important element of the Dispersion: they numbered a million according to Philo, and their quarter covered nearly two of the five divisions of the city of Alexandria. Their importance however lay in their theology rather than in their number. Alexandria was the home of that school of liberal Platonic Judaism which formed a halfway house between Hellenism and Judaism, and of which the great representative was Philo, himself a contemporary of the early part of our history. In the years 37 and 38 the Alexandrian Jews suffered a terrible persecution at the hands of their Gentile fellow-citizens; and Philo was one of the embassy they sent to appeal to Caligula. We recognize the characteristics of Alexandrine Judaism in the eloquence and learning of Apollos, but, unless Stephen was also trained in the learning of Egypt, this is the only appearance of Alexandrian wisdom in the Acts[3]. Journeying to the west along the coast of Africa or *Libya* we come to *Cyrene*. Here a hundred years ago, in Sulla's time, the Jews had already formed a fourth class among the citizens. They possessed, or shared, a synagogue at Jerusalem, and like the men of Cyprus were of note 'in the gospel.' Simon who carried the cross, some of the early evangelists, and Lucius the prophet of Antioch, were Cyrenians[4].

From Cyrene ships crossed the Mediterranean to Italy. At *Rome* there was a large Jewish settlement. If this was not so large numerically as at Antioch or Alexandria, the deficiency in numbers was made up for by zeal in proselytizing; and by their intrigues and religious influence the Jews acquired an extraordinary influence even in the highest circles of Rome. When Pompey had taken Jerusalem in 63 B.C. he brought great numbers of Jewish captives to Rome, who as they were gradually set free formed the nucleus of the colony. It rapidly increased, and soon the Jews attracted the notice of politicians like Cicero, and literary men such as Horace, Martial and Juvenal. Jewish beggars, proselytes, and superstitions were a favourite butt of the satirists. The demonstration they made round Caesar's catafalque in the forum was the first sign of their appearance as a factor in politics. To keep them down Tiberius deported some thousands to Sardinia. Under Claudius tumults among the Jews, probably occasioned by the preaching of 'the Christ,' led to further repressive action, and the emperor banished all the Jews from Rome. These Jews were proud of their citizenship and so *the visitors* from Rome are called *Romans*, whether *Jews* by race or *proselytes*, though this division probably refers to the whole catalogue.

Rome and Cyrene represented at present the western limit of the

[1] Dio Cassius LXVIII 32. [2] xxi 16, xi 19, 20, iv 36. [3] xviii 24-28: cp. vi 9. [4] Lk xxiii 26, Acts xi 20, xiii 1.

Dispersion, and to complete the list the writer adds *Cretans and Arabians*. Crete stands for 'the isles' of the Old Testament, and for Jewish influence there we can refer to the epistle to Titus (i 5, 10). Arabia—whither S. Paul retired after his conversion (Gal i 17)—is the country east and south of Palestine, and the attitude of the Arabians, as of the Bedouin of to-day, was always a serious question for the Jews. As their relations have a bearing on the chronology of the Acts we may note that at this period Aretas king of Petra had consolidated a kingdom, and later on he acquired Damascus (II Cor xi 32). Herod Antipas, tetrarch of Galilee, married his daughter, and when Herod rejected her in favour of Herodias his brother's wife, a quarrel naturally ensued. Aretas defeated Herod in battle, and the appeals to Rome resulted in Herod's downfall. But apart from the Jews Arabia had been attracting the attention of the Roman public, when S. Luke was writing: Augustus had sent an expedition under Gallus to obtain a footing in the country, and it had met with a fatal reverse. But at some later period, before A.D. 70, a Roman force destroyed Aden[1].

§ 2 *The preaching of Peter*

To this crowd, representative of the whole Jewish race, S. Peter *made utterance*. The word *foreknowledge* at once gives a stamp of authenticity to the speech, for it is used in the first epistle of S. Peter (i 2, cp. verse 20) and nowhere else in the NT. This suggests a clue which can be followed up. In the same epistle recur the expressions *call upon* God (i 17), *rejoice* (i 6, 8, iv 13), the *flesh* of the Christ (iv 1), *the right hand of God* (iii 22), *exalt* (v 6), *the house*—of God's people (ii 5, iv 17). The following ideas are also strongly marked—that the Christ is Lord (iii 15, cp. verse 6), his rejection by his own (ii 4, 7), his ascension and sitting at the Right Hand (iii 22), the promised gift of the Spirit (i 12, iv 14), the prophecy of the glories after the sufferings (i 11, 12), salvation through baptism (iii 21), the present age as 'the last days' (i 5, 20). Apart from marks of Petrine authorship, however, the contents of the speech shew its early character. It was the apostles' first duty to bear witness to facts, i.e. the facts of the Lord's life culminating in the resurrection. And this speech is just such a summary of facts, and represents the apostolic 'preaching' long before any gospels or epistles were written. But though a proclamation of facts rather than an exposition of doctrine, we find in it the elements of the Apostles' Creed: the Father, Son, and Spirit (32–3): Jesus is man (22) but also Lord (36), and he bestows the divine Spirit: the Spirit being poured upon the disciples makes them a divine fellowship: the offer is made of remission of sins which is conveyed through baptism.

The Holy Spirit is the great subject of the sermon, just as he is the foundation of Christianity. The boldness with which S. Peter accuses the Jews of the murder of their Christ testifies to the power of the Spirit within. What argument or proof he uses consists in an

---

[1] Mommsen *Roman Provinces* II pp. 290–4.

appeal to the Scriptures, in which the Spirit of Christ bore witness beforehand (I Pet i 11). And his personal appeal was to the heart or conscience of his hearers, which was convicted by the Spirit speaking within him (Jn xvi 8).

The sermon falls into three parts, each beginning with a personal address and ending with a 'scripture,' and the practical conclusion follows after an interval. The change of address further illustrates the growing spiritual tie. Part I (vv. 14-21) starts with the incident which occasioned the speech. S. Peter, a despised Galilean (verse 7), addresses the crowd of verse 5 as Jews, *Men of Judaea and all ye that dwell at Jerusalem*, and answers the charge of drunkenness: if 'they are drunken,' it is not with wine but with the Spirit. II (vv. 22-28). To prepare for the explanation of this phenomenon, he unfolds the work of Jesus. This is 'the word of the gospel,' addressed to them as God's chosen people of whom he himself is one—*Men of Israel*; and the first word *Jesus* tells us that it is 'the testimony of Jesus' (Rev xix 10), i.e. the witness to his life, crucifixion, and resurrection. III (vv. 29-36). The meaning of the resurrection is now interpreted, as the fact is confirmed by an appeal to prophecy. It is the resurrection which affords the explanation of the present outpouring of the Holy Spirit, while in turn this gift proves that Jesus is indeed himself the longed-for 'promise of Israel'—the Messiah and Lord. This gift offered them a common spiritual brotherhood, and S. Peter had called his hearers *Brethren*. Now, IV (vv. 37-40), he drives home the practical appeal which this faith makes to the individual, which is for repentance and baptism. On repentance forgiveness of sins and the same gift of the Spirit will be conveyed to all, without any limitation. But a note of warning as to the consequences of refusal concludes.

With this sermon we must compare S. Peter's other sermons—to the Jewish people (iii 12-26) and to the Gentiles (x 34-43), and S Paul's sermon to the Jews in xiii 16-41.

14 But Peter, standing up with the eleven, lifted up his voice, and spake forth unto them, *saying*,

Ye men of Judaea, and all ye that dwell at Jerusalem, be
15 this known unto you, and give ear unto my words. For these are not drunken, as ye suppose; seeing it is *but* the third
16 hour of the day; but this is that which hath been spoken by the prophet Joel;
17   ¹And it shall be in the last days, saith God,
    I will pour forth of my Spirit upon all flesh:
    And your sons and your daughters shall prophesy,
    And your young men shall see visions,
    And your old men shall dream dreams:

---
¹ Joel ii 28-32; for ver. 21 cp. Rom x 13.

18   Yea and on my servants and on my handmaidens in those days
Will I pour forth of my Spirit; and they shall prophesy.
19   And I will shew wonders in the heaven above,
And signs on the earth beneath;
Blood, and fire, and vapour of smoke:
20   The sun shall be turned into darkness,
And the moon into blood,
Before the day of the Lord come,
That great and notable *day*:
21   And it shall be, that whosoever shall call on the name of the Lord shall be saved.

22 Ye men of Israel, hear these words: Jesus of Nazareth, a man approved of God unto you by [1]mighty works and wonders and signs, which God did by him in the midst of you, 23 even as ye yourselves know; him, being delivered up by the determinate counsel and foreknowledge of God, ye by the 24 hand of lawless men did crucify and slay: whom God raised up, having loosed the pangs of death: because it was not 25 possible that he should be holden of it. For David saith concerning him,

[2]I beheld the Lord always before my face;
For he is on my right hand, that I should not be moved:
26   Therefore my heart was glad, and my tongue rejoiced;
Moreover my flesh also [3]shall dwell in hope:
27   Because thou wilt not leave my soul in Hades,
Neither wilt thou give thy Holy One to see corruption.
28   Thou madest known unto me the ways of life;
Thou shalt make me full of gladness with thy countenance.

29 Brethren, I may say unto you freely of the patriarch David, that he both died and was buried, and his tomb is with us 30 unto this day. Being therefore a prophet, and knowing that God had [4]sworn with an oath to him, that of the fruit of his 31 loins [5]he would set *one* upon his throne; he foreseeing *this*

---

[1] Gk *powers*.   [2] Ps xvi 8–11: Acts xiii 35.   [3] Literally *shall pitch its tent upon hope*.   [4] Ps cxxxii 11, II Sam vii 12.   [5] AV and Bezan *according to the flesh he would raise up (the) Christ to sit* (or *and set him*) *upon*.

spake of the resurrection of the Christ, that neither was he
32 left in Hades, nor did his flesh see corruption. This Jesus
33 did God raise up, whereof we all are witnesses. Being
therefore by the right hand of God exalted, and having
received of the Father the promise of the Holy Ghost, he
34 hath poured forth this¹, which ye see and hear. For David
ascended not into the heavens: but he saith himself,

²The Lord said unto my Lord, Sit thou on my right hand,
35 Till I make thine enemies the footstool of thy feet.
36 Let all the house of Israel therefore know assuredly, that
God hath made him both Lord and Christ, this Jesus whom
ye crucified.
37 Now when they heard *this*, they were pricked in their heart,
and said unto Peter and the rest of the apostles, Brethren,
38 what shall we do? And Peter *said* unto them, Repent ye,
and be baptized every one of you in the name of Jesus Christ
unto the remission of your sins; and ye shall receive the gift
39 of the Holy Ghost. For to you is the promise, and to your
children, and to all that are afar off, *even* as many as the
40 Lord our God shall call unto him. And with many other
words he testified, and exhorted them, saying, Save yourselves
from this crooked generation.

14   S. Peter speaks *together with the Eleven*, i.e. *the rest of the apostles* (verse 37), as their spokesman, and his elaborate opening after the style of the OT marks the solemnity of the occasion.
15   I. The apostolic company *are not drunken*, for *it is but the third hour of the day*, about 9 a.m., when no Jew on a festival day would have as yet broken his fast³. But this is the fulfilment of a
16 prophecy of *Joel*. A plague of locusts had been devastating the land of Judah, and seeing in them a type of the divine judgements on his people, Joel prophesies that God will remove them, and
17 then he adds that 'afterward' God will *pour out his Spirit on all flesh*, which will cause his servants to *prophesy*—the prediction now
19 fulfilled in the speaking with tongues. Further this outpouring will
20 be accompanied by '*wonders in the heavens and in the earth*,' which shall usher in '*the great and* terrible *day of the Lord*,' i.e. of the Lord's appearance in the final judgement and restoration of all things. For 'afterward' S. Peter substitutes *in the last days*. The Christian era is itself 'the last days,' or 'the last hour,' and 'at the

---
¹ Bezan adds *gift*.   ² Ps cx 1: Mt xxii 44, Mk xii 36, Hebr i 13.
³ See p. 17.

end of the times,' because it is the final dispensation. It begins with the first coming of the Messiah and will only end when he returns in glory, to consummate all things and bring in 'the world to come.' This idea is common to all the apostolic writers[1]. But more than this, at the first the apostles were expecting that the time before the return would be 'short.' This had been their belief before the crucifixion; the Lord had made no specific mention of delay, and the indications which he had let drop had not been taken to heart. The disciples had just seen him depart into heaven, and now that the Holy Spirit was outpoured, they were convinced that the Lord's glorious return was at hand[2]. And so S. Peter no doubt was even now looking for those portents which were to herald that consummation. The portents were in part fulfilled at the destruction of Jerusalem 40 years later, but the lapse of time caused a gradual change in the expectation of the Christians which we can trace in S. Paul's epistles.

22 II. *Jesus of Nazareth*—that was the name by which the Lord was known to the Jews, and S. Peter speaks to his hearers as those who *themselves knew* him. Many of them must have witnessed his miracles; many must have been among the crowd which seven weeks ago had cried out 'Crucify him.' As in x 38, S. Peter makes use of the evidential force of the Lord's miracles—the *powers*, i.e. works demonstrating power, which are also *wonders* above the ordinary working of nature and *signs* conveying spiritual and symbolic instruction. The Lord himself had repeatedly appealed to 'the works' as the FATHER's witness to him. They shewed that God had approved or set him forth[3] as his appointed one. So far

23 the Jews could admit the argument (Jn iii 2), but then there came the crucifixion. This was the stumblingblock or scandal. How could the appointed Messiah be put to a malefactor's death? The cross absolutely confuted the claim of Jesus of Nazareth. S. Peter has a threefold reply. (1) Jesus was *delivered up by the determinate counsel and foreknowledge of God*. It was the will of God. According to the divine plan, as it had already been disclosed in the scriptures, 'the Christ must suffer these things and so enter into his glory.' Jesus was 'he who had been ordained, i.e. *determined* by God,' as the Christ (x 42); in this determination the delivery up to death had its part, and so 'he had been *foreknown*' unto God as the Lamb slain 'before the foundation of the world[4].' (2) But this foreknowledge of God did not relieve the human agents from their guilt. The Son of man went 'as it had been determined of him': but the Jews had put him to death. They had delivered him to Pilate and the Romans, and so by *lawless men*, that is men without the law of Moses[5], they had actually crucified him, and

---

[1] See Jas v 3, I Pet i 5, 20, I Jn ii 18: Heb i 1: I Tim iv 1, II iii 1.   [2] I Cor vii 29, I Th iv 15: Lk xix 11: Jas v 9, Rev iii 11, 20, xxii 6, 20. For the indications see Lk xx 12, xxi 24.   [3] I Cor iv 9, II Th ii 4.   [4] I Pet i 2, 20, Rev xiii 8.
[5] Cp. Rom ii 12-14, I Cor ix 21.

24 were now responsible for the murder of their Messiah. (3) But his death was not the end. Through these sufferings the Christ entered into his glory. *God raised him* from the dead; and this, the crowning 'power,' was the crowning proof of his Messiahship. It shewed that he *could not be held of death* and therefore fulfilled
28 the prophecy of David. Accordingly Jesus must be (*a*) the living one to whom God hath *made known the ways of* eternal *life*; and
27 (*b*) *the holy one* of God, separate from sinners and the consequences of sin[1].
24 S. Peter's words contain a hint of further consequences. In raising him *God loosed the travail pangs of death*. We are to conceive of Hades as travailing with the millions of dead souls in her womb. When Jesus—the first-begotten of the dead—was brought forth from the tomb, the travail pangs were loosed and now the way is open for others to follow. The expression is taken from Ps xviii 4, where the word which the Greek translators rendered *travail pangs* is really *cords* (of death). The Hebrew gives a more natural but less picturesque sense: and at the same time *to loose the pangs* was quite a correct expression in Greek.
29 III. The prophecy of David carries much with it and must be fully interpreted. S. Peter's ardour and affection are kindled: he speaks to his *brethren* and *with boldness*. It was quite clear that *David—the patriarch*, i.e. the head of the royal family[2]—*was dead*
30 *and buried*, as *his tomb* was to be seen[3]. But David was fully recognized as *a prophet*, and as such he must here be speaking in the person of one of his descendants to whom God had promised *his throne*. The promise had been primarily spoken of Solomon, but the addition of 'for ever'[4] shewed that it was also given to a greater
31 seed of David, i.e. the Messiah. According to this prophecy then the Messiah was not to be *left* or *forsaken*[5] in Hades, nor was even
32 *his flesh* to be left there. And it was fulfilled when *God raised this Jesus* whom the apostles had seen after his resurrection in the flesh.
33 But Jesus of Nazareth was no longer present or to be seen among the Jews in bodily form: and the answer to this difficulty brings Peter back to the present manifestation at Pentecost. The resurrection was only the first step: for as *God* with a mighty hand had brought the children of Israel through the Red Sea and 'exalted them out of Egypt' (xiii 17), so with the same *right hand* or almighty power had he now *exalted* Jesus to heaven. There Jesus as man had *received* the gift of *the Holy Spirit*. He had been anointed with the Spirit at his baptism for the work of the Messiah (x 38): now, the work completed, he receives the gift not for himself but for men. As the crown of the glorified humanity of Jesus, this gift was the consummation of the divine promises made to

---

[1] Cp. (*a*) Rev i 18, Jn xiv 6, etc.: (*b*) Hebr vii 26, Acts iii 14. [2] Cp. I Chron ix 9, xxiv 31, xxvii 22, etc., where *patriarch* is used in the LXX for *heads of houses*. [3] Nehem iii 16. [4] In II Sam vii 13; cp. Lk i 32. [5] The same word as in Mt xxvii 46.

the human race through the history of the old covenant. Accordingly the Messiah was now pouring forth this culminating *promise*
34 upon his brother men, as S. Peter's hearers could witness. Like the resurrection, the fact of the ascension required confirmation out of the scripture. So S. Peter quotes the critical passage of the 110th Psalm which the Lord had himself used. From this it appears that the Messiah is also LORD. The exaltation into heaven and the anointing with the Spirit would of themselves have demonstrated his lordship or sovereignty over the human race (x 36) and *the house of*
36 *Israel*. With perfect *certainty* then Israel, the peculiar household or family of God, may fearlessly *recognize this crucified Jesus* not only as the *Christ* but as their *Lord* and Master.
37 IV. By this 'word of God, sharper than any two-edged sword,' *the heart* or conscience of the multitude was pierced or *pricked* (Jn xix 34). This is a rare word, used by the Greek translators for *broken in heart* in Ps cix 16, which well denotes the compunction accompanying the conviction of the Holy Spirit (Jn xvi 8), the first step in repentance. Convinced of their guilt, they ask the apostles as *brothers, What shall we do?* And in reply S. Peter lays down the conditions which the reception of the gospel demands on
38 part of the individual. They are (1) *repent*; and (2) *be baptized*. So will be obtained (a) *forgiveness of sins*, and (b) *the gift of the Spirit*. This preaching is very similar to that of John the Baptist. He too warned a 'generation of vipers' to flee from wrath and seek salvation: he was asked 'What shall we do?' and in answer preached 'a baptism of repentance for the remission of sins.' But there was a great difference between the two baptisms, which will be brought out clearly in xix 1-7. One was the shadow; the other the substance. One was with water only; the other with water and the Holy Ghost. (1) The baptism itself was no longer simply a sign of repentance: it was now a public confession of faith *in the name of Jesus Christ*, i.e. that Jesus is the Christ of God. (2) There is now on God's side *the gift of the Holy Spirit*. This was *the free gift* of God, won for us by the work of Jesus Christ (Jn iv 10); and it was the characteristic of the new Messianic
39 kingdom (Jn vii 39). For it was *the promise* or fulfilment of God's covenant with Israel. This covenant was one of promise on God's part and involved continuous expectation or looking forward on man's part. The promise had at first been of material blessings, e.g. the land of Canaan, but as these were obtained and yet the ideal was not attained, the content of the promise grew deeper and more spiritual until it became the promise of the presence of God himself in his Spirit[1]. This indwelling presence was promised to S. Peter's hearers and the Jewish race, and further even *to all those afar off*, i.e. all whom it shall please *the Lord to call to himself*. *Those afar off* are really the Gentiles[2]; so here at the very beginning

---

[1] See e.g. Isai xxxii 15, xliv 3, Jerem xxxi 31-4, Ezek xxxvi 25-7, xxxvii 14, Joel ii 28-9, Zech xii 10   [2] xxii 21, Eph ii 13, 17.

is a proclamation of the universal character of the gospel which had been already foreshadowed in the words of Joel *upon all flesh* and *whosoever shall call* (vv. 17, 21). The subsequent history however shews how slow the apostles were to realize the practical results of this universal call, and we must beware of reading into these early utterances the full experience of later years. S. Peter no doubt was thinking mainly of the Jews of the Dispersion, 'the children of God scattered' far off among the Gentiles[1]: and the Gentiles whom the Lord should call S. Peter would as yet expect to come in through the gate of Judaism as proselytes (verse 11).

40 This sermon did not exhaust the *testifying* of the apostle, and the other references to such fulfilment of the apostolic function may suggest some of the *other words* or subjects of his present witness[2]. One of them was evidently the need of *salvation*. This implied (1) The guilt and danger of the Jews: the present *generation* by their crucifixion of the Messiah had shewn that they still retained their *crooked* and perverse character of old, not 'walking in the straight ways' of obedience to the Lord[3]. (2) A doctrine of future judgement: as we shall see (x 42), Jesus as Christ and Lord had also received the office of Judge.

§ 3 *The church of the beginning*

41 They then that received his word were baptized: and there were added *unto them* in that day about three thousand
42 souls. And they [4]continued stedfastly in the apostles' teaching and fellowship, in the breaking of [5]bread and the prayers.
43 And fear came upon every soul: and many wonders and
44 signs were done by the apostles. And all that believed [6]were
45 together, [6]and had all things common; and they sold their possessions and goods, and parted them to all, according as
46 any man had need. And day by day, continuing stedfastly with one accord in the temple, and breaking bread at home, they did take their food with gladness and singleness of heart,
47 praising God, and having favour with all the people. And the Lord added [7]to them day by day those that were being saved.

The *then* in verse 41 is the word with which S. Luke usually sums up the result of a preceding passage as a new point of departure: so this

---

[1] Cp. vv. 5, 14, I Pet i 1: Jn xi 52.   [2] Cp. viii 25, x 42: iii 15, iv 33, v 31-2, x 39, 41, xiii 31.   [3] Cp. Deut xxxii 5, Lk ix 41, Phil ii 15: Acts xiii 10.
[4] Gk *were continuing*.   [5] Gk *the bread*: Bezan has *the fellowship of the breaking of the bread*.   [6] B omits *were* and *and*.   [7] *To them* in the Gk is *together*. AV has *added to the church......Now Peter and John went up together*. Codex Bezae has *together in the church*.

verse need not necessarily describe what followed immediately upon S. Peter's speech, and we are released from speculations as to how the sudden baptism of so many persons could have been effected[1]. *That day* according to regular biblical usage may stand for 'that period,' i.e. the first epoch in the life of the church, when it was altogether prosperous and the numbers rose rapidly from 120 to 3000—that is, in Jerusalem alone, not counting any pilgrims who may have returned home and carried the seeds of the gospel with them. And S. Luke proceeds to give us his first picture of the church, though we are not certain whether the term 'church' has as yet come into common use. With this we must compare the companion picture in iv 32-35, or to be more accurate iv 23-v 16. Here we have described (*A*) the entrance into the society : (*B*) the conditions of membership : (*C*) its outward appearance before the world : and (*D*) its daily life.

A (verse 41). The entrance into the society was through *Baptism*[2]. Baptism was 'a washing of the body with pure water' which symbolized a simultaneous washing of the soul or forgiveness of sins. Hence there were necessary conditions : (1) previous repentance and confession of sin (Mt iii 6); and (2) as forgiveness was through the blood of Christ, confession of faith '*in the name of Jesus Christ.*' From verse 38, x 48, and xix 5[3], we should naturally infer that these words were actually the formula used in baptizing. On the other hand the Lord, in Mt xxviii 19, commanded the disciples to baptize '*into the name of the Father and of the Son and of the Holy Ghost.*' The apparent discrepancy was noticed by the Fathers and various solutions were proposed. A simple explanation is to suppose that '*in the name of Jesus Christ*' had been the original formula, which was afterwards superseded by the name of the Father, Son and Spirit; and that the final editor of S. Matthew's Gospel, writing about A.D. 60-70, in giving a summary of the Lord's commands, had used the formula familiar to him from its universal use in the church. On the other hand there is no difficulty in the use of the threefold name from the first. The Lord had spoken of Father, Son and Spirit[4]; and indeed we might almost say that for a Jew to confess Jesus as Lord and Christ was to implicitly confess his faith in the same Trinity. viii 37 (margin) and xxii 16 suggest a better solution, viz. that '*in the name of Jesus Christ*' refers to the confession of faith in Jesus made by the baptized and not to the form used by the baptizer. In the *Didaché* we find the same language as in the NT. In ch. 7 it explicitly enjoins baptism in the threefold

---

[1] The Greek however may be translated *They then (i.e. the hearers) received his word and were baptized,* as in i 6, v 41, viii 25. The translation in the text is like viii 4, xi 19. For this *then* cp. also ix 31, xiii 4, xv 3, 30, xvi 5, xvii 12, xxiii 22, 31, xxvi 3, 9. [2] Cp. viii 12-3, 36-8, ix 18, x 47-8, xvi 15, 33, xviii 8, xix 3-6. [3] Cp. Rom vi 3. [4] In the synoptists, 'the Son' occurs in Mt xi 27, Mk xiii 32, Lk x 21-2. In commenting on 'the implicit reference to the Threefold Name' in I Pet i 2, Dr Hort says ' How such an idea could arise in the mind of S. Paul or any other apostle without sanction from a word of the Lord, it is difficult to imagine: and this consideration is a sufficient answer to the doubts which have, by no means unnaturally, been raised ' as to Mt xxviii 19.

name: in ch. 9 it speaks of 'those who were baptized in the name of the Lord.'

To baptism there was attached the gift of the Holy Spirit[1]. This gift was essential: it was not however identical with baptism. This is clear from the cases of Cornelius, the Samaritans and John's disciples[2]. The last two instances shew that the gift was conveyed by the laying on of hands. Such laying on of hands was confined to the apostles (viii 18), but not so the administration of baptism. Indeed from S. Peter's words in x 48 and S. Paul's practice (I Cor i 14-17) it would seem that the apostles did not usually baptize with their own hands but left it to some minister, such as John Mark (xiii 5). In so doing they were following their Lord's example (Jn iv 2). Not much preparation or instruction was necessary in the case of Jews: to join the apostles simply meant the addition of another article to their creed, viz. 'Jesus is the Christ, the Son of God.' But we are surprised at the rapidity with which baptism was given in the case of a Gentile like the Philippian jailor, or even a proselyte like the Ethiopian eunuch[3].

B (verse 42). Baptism *added* or *joined* men—S. Luke does not say to whom, but the next verse shews us—to the apostles, as representing the church. Membership in this society meant a continuous effort: it was a *persevering adherence*, both (*a*) to persons and (*b*) to duties, especially prayer[4]. Here S. Luke gives the four essentials which must not be abandoned: and they fall into two pairs, dealing with (*a*) organization and (*b*) worship.

(1) *The Teaching of the Apostles.* At once we begin with the principle of authority; membership means fellowship with the apostles. The church is apostolic because it cleaves to the apostles and through fellowship with them it has fellowship with the Father and his Son Jesus Christ[5]. The basis on which the authority rests is the Teaching or Doctrine. The apostles had been the disciples of the Lord and the witnesses of his resurrection, hence they were best qualified to be the teachers of the new body. But they had been definitely appointed Teachers by the Lord in Mt xxviii 19, and the office was included in that of witness and apostle.

The prominence of teaching among the Jews was due to their possession of written scriptures. The scriptures contained their law and rule of life, social and civil as well as religious, and so their interpretation was a matter of supreme importance. Learned students of the law became rabbis or teachers, who expounded the scriptures and taught publicly; they were surrounded by classes of disciples and formed different schools of interpretation. The Christian society first appeared as such a school. The Lord was a great teacher or rabbi who taught with authority. He was the Master surrounded by his disciples[6]. And when he was taken away the apostles took his place as teachers. They taught publicly, having a place of teaching in the

---
[1] See i 5, ii 38, ix 17-8.   [2] x 44-8, viii 14-19, xix 1-6.   [3] xvi 33, viii 38.
[4] (*a*) viii 13, x 7, Mk iii 9: (*b*) i 14, vi 4, Rom xii 12, Col iv 2.   Cp. p. 10.
[5] I Jn i 8.   [6] Jn iii 2, xiii 13.

temple, and were recognized as rabbis, although they taught in an untechnical manner. As with their master, their work also was 'both to do and to teach': and teaching and preaching go side by side as the normal work of the church—both to those without and those within[1]. The believers underwent a regular course of instruction which became known as the *catechesis*. Later on a prolonged *catechesis* became a necessary qualification for baptism, and the candidates were known as *catechumens* or 'those under instruction.' All this instruction called for a number of teachers and catechists of more or less authority, and so there grew up a definite order of teachers in the church (Introd. chapter VI).

At the first however the apostles were the teachers. The subject of the Teaching was *the things concerning the Lord Jesus Christ* (xxviii 31), of which the apostles were the witnesses and interpreters. As yet there was no written gospel, and all depended upon the lips of the apostles for full and authoritative information. The Teaching then comprised the facts of our Lord's life, his doctrine and teaching: *the things concerning the kingdom of God* (i 3) which resulted from his Messiahship: the new understanding of the OT scriptures, which he had given them (Lk xxiv 45): and the moral demand upon men which his Messiahship made[2].

The Teaching, as was the custom among the Jews, was conveyed by word of mouth and continual repetition. So it would tend to assume a fixed *type* or *form of sound words*. This when handed down as a *good deposit* from one generation to another became a *tradition* or matter handed down[3]. But such traditions would soon be written down, and so we practically possess the great bulk of the apostolic teaching about the Lord's life in the first three Gospels, especially in the triple tradition, i.e. that part which is common to all the three. In the speeches of the Acts we have summaries of what we should call their creed: and in the epistles again large portions of dogmatic and other teaching are embedded, almost as it were incidentally[4].

(2) Adhering to the apostolic teaching, the believers adhered to *the Communion or Fellowship*[5], i.e. not only to the fellowship of the apostles, but also to *The Fellowship*. On the social instincts of man all civil and political life depends. But fellowship is no less a necessity in the regions of thought and faith. Greek philosophers had their schools, and the empire was honeycombed with religious societies and guilds. Israel itself was a great religious fellowship: and in it were found

---

[1] See i 1, ii 42, iv 2, 18, v 21, 25, 28, 42, xi 26, xv 35, xviii 11, xx 20, xxviii 31: cp. xv 1, xxi 21. For the *catechizing* see xviii 25 (xxi 21, 24), Lk i 4, Rom ii 18, I Cor xiv 19, Gal vi 6.   [2] The elementary principles of this teaching are given in Hebrews vi 1-3. They are *repentance and faith*—the fundamental relation to God: *baptism and laying on of hands*—sacramental incorporation into the body of Christ: *resurrection and the judgement to come*, or moral responsibility.   [3] Rom vi 17, II Tim i 13, 14: cf. I Cor xi 2, 23, xv 1-3, Gal i 9, II Th ii 15, iii 6, II Tim ii 2.   [4] See especially I Cor xi 23-25, xv 1-8.   [5] The Greek κοινωνία and Latin *communio* are the same as the English *fellowship*. They are derived from the Greek κοινός, Lat. *communis* (i.e. *common*).

societies still more closely knit, such as the 'sects' of the Pharisees and Sadducees or the 'brotherhoods' of the Essenes and Therapeutae. And now Christianity is revealed as a fellowship: rather it is The Fellowship—'the communion of the saints.'

This Fellowship was begun by our Lord, when he called the apostles to leave all and follow him. So they formed a fellowship, living a common life and sharing a common purse. When the Lord was taken up, the common life continued: and the most characteristic words in the early chapters of the Acts are *all, with one accord, together*[1]. The great effect of the resurrection had been to transform this fellowship of disciples into an actual brotherhood (Jn xx 17). The Jews indeed had a strong sense of their brotherhood of race, and in this the early believers had a share. But when the tie of blood was broken by persecution and unbelief, the Christian society became 'the brotherhood[2].'

The Fellowship is, spiritually, *the fellowship of*, i.e. a real vital unity with, *the Son of God Jesus Christ*. This unity is effected through the Spirit, so it becomes *the fellowship of the Holy Ghost*. And where the Son and Spirit are, there is the Father, so it is *fellowship with the Father*. Christians then are *fellow partakers of the divine nature*: therefore they have fellowship one with another. S. John also puts it conversely: through fellowship with the apostles we come to fellowship with the Father. And the fellowship is attained through (*a*) *cleansing by the blood of Jesus his Son*; (*b*) profession of *the common faith* or revelation of the word of life; and (*c*) actual *fellowship of the body and blood of Christ* through the sacrament of Holy Fellowship[3]. Doctrinally, it may be represented as the unity of the church, which is expounded dogmatically by S. Paul, symbolically by S. John, and historically by S. Luke in the Acts[4]. Morally, the fellowship was a unity of heart and soul, or of love, the bond of the new brotherhood[5].

The marks of the church which follow are the chief outward manifestations of this inner unity, and they may be briefly summed up as—a common life, with common eating (whether of bodily or spiritual food) and common worship: common work[6] and suffering[7] for the common faith: and a common sharing of the goods of this life. As this last makes the greatest impression on the outside world, it is carefully reported, not only here but more fully below in iv 32—v 11.

(3) *The Breaking of the Bread* or the sacrament of Holy Communion has always been recognized as the central means and test of fellowship with the church. And because of its practical importance for all time, it needs a closer enquiry. (*a*) The human race has

---

[1] See Lk viii 1-3, Jn xii 6, xiii 29, Acts i 12-14, ii 41-47, iv 32-5, etc. *All* occurs in i 14, ii 1, 4, 32, 44-5, iv 31, 33, v 12: *with one accord* i 14, ii 46, iv 24, v 12, viii 6, xv 25: *together* i 15, ii 1, 44, 47. [2] xxii 5, xxviii 21: ii 29, 37, iii 17, vii 2, ix 17, xxii 1, xxiii 1, xxviii 17: *the brethren* for the Christians exclusively begins ix 30. [3] See I Cor i 9, II Cor xiii 13, I Jn i 1-3: II Pet i 4: (*a*) I Jn i 7: (*b*) Tit i 4: (*c*) I Cor x 16. [4] I Cor x 17, xii, Eph iv; Jn xix 23-4, xxi 11—and dogmatically also xv 1-6, xvii. [5] iv 32, Jn xiii 34-5. [6] Phil i 5: II Cor viii 23. [7] Phil iii 10: II Cor i 7: Hebr x 33, I Pet iv 13.

always looked upon eating as a solemn action, and eating together as a sign of fellowship. Especially this was (and is) the case among the Semites. To eat bread or salt with another, even a deadly enemy, created a bond which could not be violated; on the other hand Jews might not eat with Gentiles who were out of the covenant[1]. Hence a common meal became not only an emblem but a seal of fellowship. And universally friendship and goodwill are manifested in giving banquets and invitations to dinner. In societies and guilds the common festival meal was a central and essential feature, and the form of this has lasted till to-day. In some cities like Sparta, or religious societies like the Essenes among the Jews, a public common meal was the daily rule. Such a meal, besides being a sign of fellowship, also served to maintain it, for the poorer brethren thus found sustenance provided for them, and common feasts became a recognized channel of 'charity.'

(b) The solemnity of eating no doubt was due to its connexion with life. The same connexion imparted to it a religious character. Life came from the gods, and was preserved by communion with them. And as with men, so fellowship with the gods was realized by eating together with them, i.e. in a sacrificial meal. Upon this subject great light has been thrown by the comparative study of religions. The authorities[2] tell us that, while in later times the god was conceived of as sharing the sacrificial meal with the worshippers, the original idea was far more striking: it would seem that the flesh of the victim was thought to be the flesh of the god, and the worshippers renewed their life by feeding upon their god. Whether this were so or no, we certainly find in the origins of religion a close connexion between sacrifice and the eating of flesh meat. It is probable that the former gave rise to the latter, and that for a long time a sacrifice was the only occasion on which an animal was slain and eaten. Even in the days of the Acts, the meat which was sold in butchers' shops had not infrequently been slain in sacrifice: and this caused one of the earliest 'cases of conscience' in the church, that about 'meats offered to idols[3].' But besides the feasting upon victims, there were other sacrificial meals. Thus the partaking of bread at a solemn feast renewed communion with the deities who presided over the harvest. The famous Eleusinian mysteries culminated in a meal in which the eating of cakes formed the bond of communion between the initiated, and prepared them for the final vision of the sheaf of wheat which was an epiphany of the corn goddess Demeter herself[4]. We can then see how the common meals of guilds and societies were in themselves acts of worship. The meal formed the central rite of religion because it established communion (i) between the worshippers, (ii) between the worshippers and their deity.

---

[1] x 28, xi 3, Gal ii 12. For eating or eating together, see Gen xviii 5–8, xxxi 54, Judges xiii 15 f, I Sam xx 18, 24–7, II iii 20, I K i 9, xiii 8 foll. [2] See Jevons' *Introduction to the History of Religion* (ch. xii), Robertson Smith's *Religion of the Semites*, Frazer's *Golden Bough*. [3] I Cor viii 10, x 25–8. [4] See Jevons ch. xxiv.

In the OT it is true that nowhere is this idea of finding communion with God in a common meal explicitly stated or taught. Eating however is closely connected with sacrifice[1]. Peace-offerings ended with a feast upon the victim, and the priests ate the remains of the guilt- and trespass-offerings: sacrifices are called 'the bread of God[2]': and besides animal victims, meal-offerings, shewbread, and firstfruits were offered to God and eaten by the priests. On the other side the ordinary meals of the Jews bore a religious character, as was shewn by the practice of blessing God or giving him thanks over the food, i.e. of saying grace. The Jews' bread was baked in cakes and divided for distribution by breaking[3], and apparently the head of the house would begin the meal by solemnly breaking bread and giving thanks over it; and so the term *breaking of bread* came to denote this commencement of a meal with blessing.

In the life of our Lord and his disciples the meal was no less part of their religious life. (*a*) Eating together formed the bond of union between them[4], and the Lord would begin their daily meal by breaking bread and giving thanks in the manner described in the feeding of the 5000[5]. No doubt it was his familiar grace or *breaking of bread* which revealed him to the eyes of the two disciples at Emmaus; and at the sea of Tiberias he first 'taketh the bread and giveth them[6].' The Twelve naturally continued their common meal after the Lord was taken away from them, and this no doubt accounted for their being together when he appeared to them on the evening of Easter Day[7]. After Pentecost we find the whole society daily breaking bread together (verse 46); and the meal must have held a central place in their life[8]. It was the bond of fellowship: it gave opportunity for common worship and mutual instruction and exhortation: it provided sustenance for the poorer members of the society, e.g. the widows. As the numbers and poverty of the society increased, this *daily ministration* or *serving of tables* became a serious and overwhelming business, as we shall learn from chapter vi. Later, when the church had spread abroad, to hold such a reunion daily became a practical impossibility: and the common meal became specialized. It was called an *Agapé* or *Love*-feast. This word denoted the double aim—the cultivation of brotherly love and the exercise of 'charity.' The latter tended to predominate, and to give an agape became a recognized form of benevolence on the part of a wealthy brother. At the same time the religious character was not lost sight of. The agape was frequently held in church: grace was pronounced by one of the clergy: and the singing of psalms and hymns had its place. This observance of Christian life attracted the interest of the

---

[1] Cp. e.g. Gen xxxi 54, Exod xviii 21, xxxii 6, I Sam ix 12–3, xiv 34–5, xvi 2, xx 6, 29, Ps cvi 28. In Acts x 13 S. Peter is told to *sacrifice and eat*: cp. I Cor x. 18–21.
[2] Levit iii 11, xxi 6, 8, 17, 21–2, xxii 25.   [3] See J. Lightfoot on this passage; and cp. Jn vi 12, *the broken pieces*.   [4] See x 41 and i 4 marg: Mk xiv 18.   [5] Mt xiv 19 and xv 36 with the parallels.   [6] Lk xxiv 30, 35, Jn xxi 13.   [7] Lk xxiv 41–2.   [8] S. Luke gives great attention to the thought of bodily nourishment (more than his medical training would account for): the references are (i 4), ii 42, 46, vi 2, ix 19, x 9–16, 41, xi 3, xiv 17, xvi 34, xx 7, 11, xxvii 33–6.

outside world. Naturally it was open to abuse, and this even in the earliest days, when there was disorder, selfishness, and drunkenness at the Corinthian agape[1]. Accordingly it became one of the earliest subjects of church legislation, and in the 4th century there was a strong tendency towards its suppression. The practice did gradually die out, but it was still necessary for the Trullan Council of A.D. 692 to forbid an agape to be held in a church.

(b) Turning to the second circle of ideas, we find that the Lord as it were consecrated the association of divine worship and communion with a sacred meal. He made a feast the central rite of his church as the memorial of his sacrifice of himself; and at the same time transformed the meal into the deepest mystery. For the food and drink were to be his own body and blood, and so by feeding upon him the worshipper was to attain to communion with God. In the OT the greatest sacrificial meal was the feast of the Passover. For it was the memorial of the redemption from Egypt, and at the paschal supper a lamb was eaten whole by every family of Israel. It is also to be noted that a lamb formed the daily sacrifice, offered every evening and morning in the temple. Now at the beginning of his ministry the Lord was announced by the Baptist as the Lamb of God. At the Passover which was its turning point he had spoken of eating the flesh and drinking the blood of the Son of Man. Then at his last paschal supper, the night he was betrayed, the Lord took the bread, and after blessing it (perhaps with the usual benediction) he said *Take, eat: this is my body.* Afterwards he distributed the cup with similar words, *This is my blood of the new covenant.* So he ratified the new covenant; and when he added *This do in remembrance of me,* he instituted a new feast to be (i) his perpetual memory, and (ii) the means of union with himself and so with God. This feast is the Eucharist, the Christian service of divine worship and communion.

The question arises—What relation had this feast to the daily common meal? How, and how often, was it to be celebrated? If the words in S. Paul 'This do, *as oft as ye drink*[2]' may mean—not every time that thirst is quenched but—as often as ye eat and drink together as a society, we may understand that the apostles interpreted the Lord's command by making the daily common meal or *breaking of bread* a repetition of the Last Supper. This meal then would include both elements, (a) Agape and (b) Eucharist: and the Agape symbolized

---

[1] I Cor xi 17–34. Among the many references to the agape Tertullian's picture is the most vigorous. In contrast to heathen religious orgies he describes it thus (*apolog.* 39): 'Before (the brethren) take their seats, prayer to God forms the first course: hunger is the measure of their food, modesty places the limit on their cups. They feast as men who remember that even at night God is to be worshipped: they talk as those who know that the Lord is listening. After the washing of hands and lighting of the lamps, according to their several ability out of the scripture or their own heart they provoke one another to singing the praises of God. Here is the test of their drinking! As it began so the feast ends with prayer.' [2] I Cor xi 25, the *it* is not in the Greek.

and cemented the fellowship with one another which was created by their common communion with the Lord in the Eucharist. Later, when it was found impossible to meet together daily, this Breaking of Bread was celebrated at least once a week and it formed the great act of worship on the Lord's Day (xx 7).

If the Christian Breaking of Bread followed the precedents of the Last Supper, which was a paschal meal, it would begin with 'grace,' i.e. a blessing of a cup and the breaking of bread. Hands were washed—a relic of which still remains in the washing of the priest's hands in the liturgies. The offertory in the liturgies also reminds us that originally the brethren used to bring their contributions to the common meal[1]. At the Jewish feast, the head of the table then explained at length the meaning of the feast and recited the mighty acts of the LORD in the redemption of Israel: in the new covenant this would be the place for the apostles' teaching and exhortation. At intervals also psalms and hymns were sung[2],—the natural expression of Christian joy (verse 46). Then at the end of the meal came the crowning mystery. The presiding apostle gave thanks to God over the offerings of bread and wine for his redemption of the world by the crucifixion and resurrection of his Son, and then following the example of the Master took 'the loaf,' i.e. one of the paschal cakes, and blessed it, and brake it for distribution; then the cup likewise; and so the brethren partook of the body and blood of the Lord. As the whole meal was an act of worship, so this action of offering and feeding was sacrificial[3]; and thus the Eucharist formed the church's daily sacrifice and took the place of the daily offering of the lamb in the temple, while the drinking of the cup was a daily renewal of the covenant.

Our conclusion then is that the *Breaking of Bread* is the term for a solemn religious meal. This may be (i) an Agape alone, or (ii) the Eucharist alone, or (iii) as at the first the Agape followed by the Eucharist: which is meant on a particular occasion we must ascertain from the context. This conclusion seems to be confirmed by the references in the Acts and I Corinthians xi.

From the epistle it is clear that the Corinthians came together for the Eucharist. It is also clear that their evening meal or agape preceded it, and both together made 'the Lord's Supper[4].' Abuses had crept in—controversy, selfishness, greediness and even intemperance. The Eucharist was profaned by drunkenness[5]. S. Paul did not however abolish the Agape. But he directed them to wait for one another, i.e. for the solemn grace; they were not to come hungry and look upon the meal as the satisfaction of their bodily appetite but to treat it as an act of worship; and then he unfolded the true meaning of the mystery

---

[1] Cp. I Cor xi 21–2. [2] Mt xxvi 30. [3] Cp. Hebr. xiii 10. In I Cor x 18 S. Paul contrasts *the table of the Lord* with *the table of devils*. S. Augustine defines a 'sacrifice' (*de Civit.* x 5. 6) as 'everything that is done in order that we may by a holy fellowship inhere in God. See Bp Gore's *Romans* II p. 241. [4] I Cor xi 20: *dinner* is the better modern equivalent of the Greek δεῖπνον. [5] We find Jewish rabbis contemplating the possibility of drunkenness at the paschal supper. This may lessen our surprise if not our horror.

in the Eucharist. The apostle's deliberate language about its profanation (*shall be guilty of the body and blood of the Lord*), and the penalty of death which had ensued, marked for ever the clearest distinction, a distinction in kind, between the eatings of the Eucharist and of the Agape.

The celebration at Troas described in Acts xx 7-13 occurred a year or two after the epistle had been written, and we find that the Breaking of Bread is now the distinctive worship of the first day of the week. The Agape and Eucharist appear still to be together. The brethren meet in the evening to *break bread*, i.e. for their common meal or agape. At this S. Paul discourses at great length. The fall of Eutychus interrupted the ceremony, and when S. Paul had returned from raising him, it was time to *break the bread*, i.e. of the Eucharist[1]. After this S. Paul discoursed again till morning dawned.

Lastly in the account of the shipwreck (xxvii 33-36) we are told how before dawn S. Paul *took bread and gave thanks to God before all and brake it and began to eat*. This is evidently not *the bread* of the Eucharist. It is incredible that S. Paul would have celebrated the crowning Christian mystery in the presence of so many unbaptized soldiers and sailors and in the distressing circumstances of the tempest. The words describe the solemn grace with which the apostle, following the Lord's example, usually *began to eat*[2].

Soon after these events—and no doubt in consequence of abuses such as had occurred at Corinth—the Agape and Eucharist were dissociated. The Eucharist was postponed till the hours of the early morning[3], while the Agape remained as the evening meal. Of this separation we have evidence in the letters of Pliny governor of Bithynia, writing about the year 110. This custom became all but universal. There were however exceptions. Thus early in the 5th century the custom of having the Eucharist in the evening after an agape was still maintained in Egypt, outside of Alexandria, on Saturdays[4]: and in the rest of Africa the same custom was observed on one day in the year, viz. on Maundy Thursday, as an exact commemoration of the original institution.

(4) As the fellowship was of the apostles but extended to the whole church, so *the Prayers* included the breaking of the bread and more also. At first the Christians of Jerusalem continued to frequent the temple for prayer and worship both public and private[5]. But just as Jerusalem was full of synagogues in addition to the temple, so the

---

[1] But see below on the passage for another interpretation. [2] The *food* which S. Paul took in ix 19 was probably religious food. The first meal after his fast and baptism was, we can safely imagine, the *breaking of the bread*. So the common *table* which Paul and Silas shared with the jailor after his baptism in xvi 34 was no doubt treated by them as a religious meal, when they would have *broken the bread* in thanksgiving for the jailor's conversion and their own deliverance. [3] For such postponement the service at Troas would set a precedent. We must remember that in the Jewish reckoning, which was followed by the early church, the day began with sunset: evening came before morning. [4] Socrates *Eccl. Hist.* v 22.
[5] verse 46, iii 1, xxi 23-6, xxii 17. For synagogues see vi 9, James ii 2.

Christians would meet for prayer and worship '*at home,*' i.e. in 'synagogues' of their own. There are several references to such domestic prayer, as in i 24, iv 23 f, xii 12; and the expression *the Prayers* almost implies that there were regular hours of prayer, corresponding perhaps to the Jewish synagogue prayers, but we have no information on the subject[1].

C (vv. 43-45). Having given us the essential constitution of the church, S. Luke passes to the impression made on the world without—both by (1) the apostolic body, and (2) the whole church.

(1) The startling phenomena which marked the outpouring of the Holy Spirit and the events which followed it, like those at the beginning of the Gospel, spread a feeling of *awe* and amazement over the people[2]. This feeling was maintained by the *Wonders and signs* which *the apostles* began to work. These miracles served the same purpose as those of the Lord. As his works had borne witness to him, so the works of the apostles were signs of divine approval and the credentials of their apostolate[3]. The first miracle is just going to be described for us in iii 1-10; other instances occur in ix 32-43; and v 12-16 gives a picture of miraculous energy. Probably striking miracles or *powers* such as those just quoted[4] were rare, and the *wonders and signs* mainly denote the beneficial effects upon the souls and bodies of others which resulted from the spiritual force and energy of the apostles (iv 33). At first this wonder-working power was confined to the hands of the apostles; but after the laying on of hands in vi 6, we find it exercised both by S. Stephen and S. Philip[5]. S. Paul enjoyed a rich endowment of it. Later on, like the 'speaking with tongues' the 'working of miracles' took its place among the customary spiritual gifts (*charismata*) of the church.

(2) The 'wonder and sign' which created the greatest impression was no doubt the *Common* life of the whole church or the community of goods[6]. This was however not a compulsory division of property on communistic principles, but a voluntary following of the example and teaching of the Lord. Jesus and the Twelve had lived a common life and shared a common purse; and the communion at Jerusalem was the continuation of that life. Again the Lord never laid down a law that all must have equal shares; but he had taught that wealth was a loan from God of which we are stewards; that we should love our neighbour as ourselves; that poverty is in itself a happy condition, and it is more blessed to give than to receive (xx 35). So the Christian communism was not a matter of law but sprang inevitably out of 'brotherly love.' As is explained in iv 32, *they were of one heart and soul*, hence they

---

[1] For other cities see xiii 3, xiv 23, xvi 16, xx 7, 36, xxi 5.   [2] Lk i 65, ii 18 (the *wonder* comes in Acts iii 10-12).   [3] ii 22, II Cor xii 12 : xiv 3, Mk xvi 20, Hebr ii 4.   [4] It is noticeable that the word *powers* is not used here, nor in v 12, of the apostles, as it was of our Lord in ii 22. It occurs only twice besides—of S. Philip viii 13, and S. Paul xix 11.   [5] vi 8, viii 7, 13. For S. Paul see I Cor xii 10, 28.   [6] In iv 32-35 there is the same connexion with (divine) power and grace. Compare the impression made at Ephesus by the sacrifice of the books (xix 19).

did not look upon their possessions as *their own* but as *common* or equally at the service of their brethren in need. And so *they had all things common.* Neither the idea nor the practice was in fact new. The Greeks had perceived that this was the true ideal of friendship, as is shewn by their proverb—'Common are the possessions of friends.' Plato had sketched an ideal state founded on this principle, while among the Jews the Essenes had already carried it into practice. What was new was the enthusiasm and the true spirit of love and self-sacrifice of the Christian 'communists.'

Their success depended first on the local unity—*they were all together*: and then on the unselfishness of individuals. Many of the brethren must have come from the ranks of the poor, and the preaching of the gospel prevented the apostles from practising their trades[1]. Hence the charge 'go sell all that thou hast and give to the poor' must have been urgent on the wealthier converts. Accordingly many *sold their possessions* (lands and property) *and goods* (furniture and valuables). The money realized was given to the apostles, and through them distribution was made—not to effect an equality but—for the relief of want, *as every man had need*. This distribution involved a *daily ministration*, and in this ministration no small part must have been occupied by the provision of the common meal or *serving the table*. For both kinds of ministration the apostles would certainly have needed *ministers*[2]. That the selling of property was quite voluntary is clear from the special commendation bestowed upon Joseph Barnabas for so doing, and from the words of S. Peter to Ananias, which shew that, as long as the individual retained them, both the property and its price were entirely 'his own.' Besides we shall come across examples of private property; there was e.g. 'the house of Mary the mother of Mark[3].'

As the church rapidly expanded and they could no longer be 'all together,' the community of goods passed away. Indeed it had never been more than a local institution. And at Jerusalem the ultimate result was not an economical success. This was probably due to the want of the necessary complement of an organization of labour. The expectation of the Lord's immediate return diverted the attention of the church from the need of provision for the future; and many years later S. Paul found it necessary to insist on the duty of working[4]. Jerusalem itself, like other pilgrimage centres, was noted for its poverty. This the church shared, and in addition it underwent the spoiling of its goods in persecution, so that the apostles had to ask S. Paul 'to remember the poor[5].' For the principle of community remained[6], and the selling of possessions was succeeded by the sending of alms from one church to another. So Antioch sent relief to Jerusalem in 45, and later S. Paul brought a contribution[7] from the Gentile churches.

---

[1] Cp. vi 2. [2] i.e. *deacons*, vi 1–6. [3] xii 12: cp. also Jn xix 27, Hebr x 34. Simon Magus had not given up his money on his baptism (viii 20). [4] II Thess iii 10, Eph iv 28: cp. *Didache* 12. [5] viii 1–3: cp. Hebr x 34, Gal ii 10. [6] II Cor viii 14. [7] He calls it a *communion* or *fellowship*, Rom xvi 26.

D (vv. 45–47). S. Luke concludes with a picture of the *Daily* life of the believers. They were *persevering* in *daily* attendance at *the temple* as a body (*with one accord*) for public worship. The apostles also, as we have seen, preached and taught in the temple, where they had a regular rendezvous in Solomon's Porch, where Jesus also 'had walked[1].' But besides the temple they had their own places of meeting or 'synagogues,' such as the upper chamber and Mary's house[2]. Here, *at home*, they gathered together every evening for the *breaking of bread*. This service of Agape and Eucharist was the centre of their life, as the Greek shews; for the single finite verb in this sentence is *they partook of their food*, both bodily and spiritual. This they did *with gladness and singleness of heart*: the meal was a real eucharist or sacrifice of thanksgiving. But these words are the keynotes of the whole Christian life—(1) joy, and (2) singleness of purpose, or sincerity of character. These represent the true relation to God and man: (1) the joy manifests itself in *praising God*[3], and (2) the singleness of heart, shewing itself in the unselfishness of their common life, wins *favour with all the people*. The community at first enjoyed great popularity; and its ideal life *daily* attracted new adherents. But the real source of increase was *the Lord*[4]. The unity of the church is strikingly illustrated by S. Luke's expression, which is literally *added to the same* or *together*[5]. Those who were added (verse 41) are *those that were being saved*. There is no reference here to predestination. The AV *which should be saved* is a simple mistranslation. The expression simply means the Lord 'guided them into the way of salvation.' The church is the way of life; those who are walking therein are in a state of present safety; and if they persevere it will bring them to a future and eternal safety or salvation.

In S. Luke's writing a summary of progress like this marks the conclusion of a chapter, here of the first chapter of the church's life—her baptism and vigorous childhood. This corresponds to the beginning of the Gospel. Like her Lord, the church 'waxes strong,' and is 'in favour with God and man[6].' How the clouds of trouble and opposition were first to darken the sky, the next chapter will shew.

SECTION III (= Ch. 3-5)

The Consolidation of the Church at Jerusalem

The 'beginning of travail pains': persecution without, peril within

The growth of this new society with its public appearance in the temple could not fail to attract the attention of the authorities, and

---

[1] See iv 1, v 12, 20–1, Jn x 23. [2] i 13, xii 12. For other 'churches in houses' see xviii 7, I Cor xvi 19, Rom xvi 5, Col iv 15, Philem 2. *At home* may be translated *from house to house* (AV) or *in every house*: see xiv 23, xv 36. [3] Cp. Lk xxiv 52–3. [4] Cp. I Cor iii 6. [5] See note on text (p. 31). [6] Lk i 80, ii 52.

the subject of this section is the conflict which ensued. The government of Jerusalem at this time was in the hands of an aristocracy. Since A.D. 6 Judaea had been a Roman province under a procurator—at present Pontius Pilate: but the internal affairs of the Jews were left very much to their own authorities. These were (1) the High-priest, and (2) the *Senate*. This senate or council was called the Sanhedrin, and consisted of about 70 members drawn from three classes—(*a*) *rulers*, (*b*) *elders* or *presbyters*, and (*c*) *scribes*. These classes represented (*a*) the actual holders of office and of political power, (*b*) the leading men of influence, owing their position to their blood or wealth or religious dignity, and (*c*) the chief rabbis or teachers of the law. The high-priest—at this time Joseph Caiaphas—was president of the Sanhedrin; and he and his party (*they that were with him*) practically formed the first class. These were *the high-priests*[1], i.e. not only those who had been deposed from the office of high-priest which they had once held, but also their relatives—*as many as were of the high-priestly race*. For at this time the high-priesthood was practically confined to a few aristocratic families. Chief amongst these was the family of Annas or Ananus. Annas himself had been high-priest from A.D. 6 to 15, and five of his sons also enjoyed the priesthood[2], and Joseph Caiaphas was his son-in-law. This accounts for the leading position assigned to Annas both in the Gospels and the Acts[3]: he was popularly known as 'the high-priest.'

This hierarchical aristocracy was Sadducean in theology. In fact *the high-priest and they that were with him* practically formed t*h*e sect *of the Sadducees* (v 17). This 'sect' represented the rationalistic and sceptical tendency among the Jews: they denied the resurrection and the existence of angels and spirits. But in fact their religious views were entirely subordinated to their worldly policy. This policy is summed up in their cynical admission: *If we let him thus alone, all men will believe on him; and the Romans will come and take away both our place and our nation* (Jn xi 48). The one aim of the high-priests was to maintain ascendency in the nation. This was endangered by the restlessness of the people, which might provoke the Romans to extreme measures. Accordingly 'the rulers' were the steady opponents of national fanaticism and religious enthusiasm. This of course made them unpopular, and we find their action constantly thwarted by *fear of the people*[4]. And when at last all powers of control were exhausted and the people rushed into rebellion the aristocratic party collapsed and their leaders were assassinated[5].

Over against the Sadducees stood the Pharisees; and in xxiii 6–10 we have a graphic picture of the bitter hatred which divided the two sects. If the Sadducees had secured for themselves the positions of

---

[1] Translated in the RV *chief priests*, but the word is the same as *high-priest*. For references see iv 5, 6, v 17, 21.   [2] viz., Eleazar c. 16–17, Jonathan 36–37, Theophilus 37, Matthias c. 41, and Ananus 62.   [3] iv 6, Lk iii 2, Jn xviii 13.   [4] iv 21, v 26 and in the Gospels Mt xxi 26, xxvi 5 etc.   [5] Three high-priests (two of them sons of Annas), Jonathan, Ananus and Ananias, thus met their end.

authority, the Pharisees formed the majority of the 'presbyters' and 'scribes' in the Sanhedrin, and they made up for the want of political power by their greater numbers and enormous popularity. For they were the religious and national party: the 'teachers of Israel' like Nicodemus and *doctors of the law* like Gamaliel, *had in honour of all the people*, were Pharisees. Among them there were different schools. Some were full of religious enthusiasm and longing for the consolation of Israel, but deprecated violence and the appeal to arms—quiet and religious spirits, the nursery ground for Christianity, among whom we might reckon Nicodemus and Joseph of Arimathaea[1]. Wealthy and influential Pharisees no doubt felt the force of political exigencies as much as the Sadducees—such a one was Josephus the historian. Others again were religious zealots like Saul the Pharisee. In their zeal for righteousness they exacted every jot and tittle of the law till it became a yoke too heavy to be borne (xv 10). But the Pharisees as a whole by their narrowminded dogmatism and rigorism were crushing out the spirit of true religion; and by their uncompromising hatred of the Gentiles, their boasting in the law, and their unswerving but misguided faith in Israel's destiny, were fostering in the mass of the people that fanatic spirit which was to bring the nation to ruin.

The relation of parties is so accurately portrayed in these chapters as to form a strong proof of their contemporary origin. The Sadducean aristocracy had ignored the Lord until the enthusiasm he aroused in the people threatened to precipitate a crisis. Even then they were held back by fear of the people. And it was only by the aid of treachery and by cajoling the mob for the moment that they secured his crucifixion. And now a few weeks later history seems repeating itself. The disciples of Jesus enjoy the favour of the people; they teach publicly that Jesus is the Messiah and they boldly accuse the rulers of having crucified him. There was no little danger that a tumult might arise and the people demand his blood at their hands. Filled with alarm for themselves, and jealousy of new and rival rabbis, they arrest the apostles, but by surprise and without violence, and for fear of the people they are compelled to let them go[2]. Between high-priests and people the Pharisees hold the balance and are masters of the situation. This party was at first favourably impressed with the religious fervour of the new 'sect'; many Pharisees were found among them; and in any case they were secretly delighted to have the aid of the new teachers in vigorously asserting the doctrine of the resurrection as against the Sadducees[3]. Accordingly, as represented by their great rabbi Gamaliel, the Pharisees are inclined to hedge. It was only when they had discovered that the faith in Jesus was as little compatible with Pharisaic legalism as with Sadducean scepticism, that any serious opposition could be made to the church's growth. How that momentous discovery was made will be related in the section

---

[1] And the contemporary author of the Jewish book called *The Assumption of Moses*. [2] See iii 17, iv 10, v 28: iv 2, v 17: iv 21, v 26. [3] See xv 5: iv 2, xxiii 6—10.

which follows this. Meanwhile the first collision with the high-priests was brought on by a scene in the temple.

With regard to the exact site and size of *the Temple* there still remains uncertainty, but there is no doubt as to its general plan. In B.C. 20 Herod the Great had begun to rebuild the temple on a scale of great magnificence and it was not finished yet. On the eastern hill of Jerusalem—separated from Mount Zion or the Upper City on the west by the deep cleft of the Tyropoeon, and from the Mount of Olives on the east by the far deeper valley of Cedron—stood the vast enclosure called by the Jews the 'Mountain of the House.' This overlooked Ophel or the quarter of the city on the southern slopes of the hill, but in its turn was commanded by the great tower of Antonia which adjoined the temple on the north. This *Castle*[1] stood on a rocky eminence and was occupied by a Roman garrison. Beyond it on the north the still rising ground was covered by the suburb of Bezetha or Newtown. The massive foundations of the temple were built up from the adjacent valleys, and this gave the walls an enormous height on the outside[2]. When the worshipper *went up*[3] from the southern or western city, on passing through the gates he found himself in a vast court, a square of 600 or probably even 1000 feet. This was the Court of the Gentiles. It was surrounded by cloisters or porticoes formed by double rows of pillars. The cloisters on the northern and western sides were connected with Antonia by a flight of *stairs*[4]. Those on the east were known as *Solomon's Porch*[5], i.e. *Portico*, because they rested on Solomon's foundations. The Royal Porch on the southern side was unique: four rows of massive pillars, 162 in number, with their lofty ceilings formed a building as long and lofty as York Minster. In this Court of the Gentiles stood the tables of the money-changers and cattle on sale for sacrifice[6], for it was but the outer court. *The Temple* or *Holy Place*[7] was situated in its northern part, on a platform formed by the rising ground and approached by a flight of 14 steps. Round it was erected a barrier containing at intervals marble tablets which forbade strangers to go further on pain of death[8]. Along the top of the steps ran another wall, which afforded entrance through nine gateways or *doors*[9]. Four of these were on the south side, and four on the north. The ninth, which was in the eastern wall, was particularly splendid. It was covered with bronze and must have been the *Beautiful Gateway* of iii 2, 10, though the name has not been met with elsewhere. Through it the worshipper passed into the Court of the Women, which was a square of 135 cubits. The court had this name because women might come so far and no farther; and in it they had a special place in balconies supported on

---

[1] xxi 34 etc. [2] Cp. Mt iv 5–6. [3] iii 1, Lk xviii 10. [4] xxi 35–40. [5] iii 11, v 12, Jn x 23. [6] Jn ii 14, Mt xxi 12. [7] The *Hieron*, iii 2, 3, 8, xxi 28–30, xxiv 6. *Hieron* is also used for the whole Mountain of the House as in iii 1, v 20, Jn ii 14 etc., so its meaning is sometimes ambiguous. [8] xxi 28–30. One of these tablets was discovered by M. Clermont Ganneau in 1871 and is now in Constantinople. [9] iii 2, xxi 30.

pillars. These pillars formed a cloister all round the court as in the Court of the Gentiles; and against them were placed chests for offerings, from which the court was also known as the *Treasury*[1] Further in each corner of the court was a chamber: that in the southeast corner was allotted to the Nazirites for the performance of the ceremonies at the completion of their vow[2]. West of the Court of the Women, and separated from it by a wall, was the most sacred part, the Courts of Israel and of the Priests. The wall was pierced by the Gate of Nicanor, and ascending its fourteen steps we are brought face to face with what we should call the Temple—the House itself[3], standing in the Court of the Priests. A lofty porch faces us in which we can see a great vine of gold[4]. Between us and the House we see the Altar of Burnt-offering, a huge mass of unhewn stone 15 feet high and 48 feet square, on which the fire is kept perpetually burning. The House, the Altar with all the appliances for sacrifice, and the various chambers round the outer walls, filled the Court of the Priests, and left only a narrow space for the Court of Israel inside the Gate of Nicanor. But Israelites only came so far when they had sacrifices: the usual place for worshippers was the Court of the Women. And this court was thronged at the time of the daily sacrifices and the burning of incense, i.e. at early morning and at *the ninth hour* (3 p.m.), *the hour of prayer*[5]. It was at the latter service that the following incident occurred.

§ 1 *The sign of healing*

3 Now Peter and John were going up into the temple[6] at
2 the hour of prayer, *being* the ninth *hour*. And a certain man that was lame from his mother's womb was carried, whom they laid daily at the door of the temple which is called Beautiful, to ask alms of them that entered into the temple;
3 who seeing Peter and John about to go into the temple, asked
4 to receive an alms. And Peter, fastening his eyes upon him,
5 with John, said, Look on us. And he gave heed unto them,
6 expecting to receive something from them. But Peter said, Silver and gold have I none; but what I have, that give I thee. In the name of Jesus Christ of Nazareth, walk.
7 And he took him by the right hand, and raised him up: and immediately his feet and his ankle-bones received strength.
8 And leaping up, he stood, and began to walk; and he entered

---

[1] Mk xii 41, Jn viii 20. [2] xxi 26-7. [3] The *Naos* or shrine, Lk i 9, 21, Jn ii 19-21, Mt xxvii 40, 51. It is the word used by the Lord for the temple of his body. Cp. Acts xvii 24, xix 24. [4] Jn xv 1. [5] Cp. Lk i 8-23. [6] The Bezan text inserts *in the afternoon*. In this passage it varies from our text very much in form and may represent an earlier draft.

with them into the temple, walking, and leaping, and praising
9 God. And all the people saw him walking and praising God:
10 and they took knowledge of him, that it was he which sat for alms at the Beautiful Gate of the temple: and they were filled with wonder and amazement at that which had happened unto him.

With this miracle we should compare the similar healing by S. Paul at Lystra in xiv 8-18: also the miracles of the Lord at Jerusalem in Jn v and ix.

1 As in i 13, Lk xxii 8, and Jn xx 2, *John* is closely connected with Peter: at the time of ch. xv he ranks with Peter and James the Lord's brother as a '*pillar apostle*[1].' But he does not appear again in the Acts after this scene. Very likely he is the original source of information for most of this narrative, at least down to
2 iv 22. *The lame man* was over forty years old (iv 22) and must have witnessed our Lord's teaching in the temple. But he had to wait for his healing. Apparently the apostles fell in with him as he *was being carried* to his post just before service-time, as beggars still haunt church doors in southern countries. When healed he
8 *entered with them* into the Court of the Women to give thanks to God in the public worship; and the sacrifice over, when the apostles went out again into the outer court, he still kept with them, even *keeping hold* of them. What was S. Peter's motive we cannot say. He may have been prompted simply by compassion: he may have perceived in the man that *faith to be made whole* which was evinced by his gratitude and devotion afterwards[2]: or he may have desired to attract the attention of the people and by a *sign* of 'making sound' teach the power of *the Name of Jesus Christ of Nazareth* in making sound the whole man, body, soul
9 and spirit. In any case this result was attained. In the inner court at the hour of prayer, by his evident devotion and also by his *leaping* and delight in the new-found use of his legs, the man had
10 attracted notice and *the people recognized him*. Then when service
11 was over in the outer court they *ran together* and formed a great throng (a common incident of temple life, xxi 30) gazing in wonder at the apostles. They seized the opportunity and from their position in Solomon's Porch preached to the multitude.

S. Peter's gospel for the Jews

S. Peter preaches the same gospel as in his first 'word,' but this is more especially the gospel for the *men of Israel*, and two new points are developed: (i) that suggested by the occasion, the present power of the name of Jesus Christ, and (ii) the special hope of Israel, the doctrine of the Messianic kingdom. These points correspond with the

---

[1] Gal ii 9.   [2] verse 16, xiv 9.

two parts into which the sermon falls after the introductory address—(I) the gospel message, (II) the practical appeal.

(i) The name of a person or thing sums up to us all that we know about him or it. So to the Jews 'the Name of God' was the sum of the revelation of God, and the Name of the LORD became an equivalent for 'the LORD[1].' With the deepening of their conceptions of the divine nature, their reverence for God had increased to such an extent that they shrank from calling him by name and spoke of 'the Name' instead. As a practical result the actual name of the LORD in Hebrew has been lost. Similarly *the Name of Jesus Christ* would signify all that was contained in the revelation of God in Jesus Christ. Thus in his Name was preached repentance and forgiveness of sins: in his Name Peter raises up the lame man, and works miracles[2]. The use of this phrase then shews the early and Hebraic character of the narrative. It also shews that in speaking of the Name of Jesus the apostles are unconsciously as it were placing Jesus of Nazareth in the position of 'the LORD' (JEHOVAH) of the Jews.

The sermon is marked by its Christology or the unfolding of the different names of the Lord—*Servant of Jehovah, Holy and Righteous, Prince of life, the Christ of God, the Prophet, Seed of Abraham* (and, as below, *the Stone*): but the special power of the Name demonstrated by the miracle is the gift of *soundness* or salvation. Perfect soundness of spirit and body is equivalent to life (verse 15). And the one contention of S. Peter's sermon is that salvation is the gift of Jesus Christ: 'thou shalt call his name JESUS, for it is he that shall save his people from their sins' (Mt i 21). To receive the gift of salvation however requires a receptive faculty in man or *faith*, which is thus proclaimed at the beginning of the history.

(ii) Besides the scandal of the cross, there was another difficulty which would present itself to a Jewish audience. If Jesus is the Messiah and risen from the dead, where is he now? why is he not 'manifesting himself to the world' and 'establishing his kingdom'? The worshippers in the temple would include especially those Jews who were 'looking for the consolation of Israel' and 'the redemption of Jerusalem'; and like the later scoffers of II Pet iii 4 they might have well wondered—'where is the promise of his [kingdom][3]?' In his first sermon S. Peter had explained the Lord's absence by the necessity for the outpouring of the Spirit: now he answers the difficulty about the Messianic kingdom by unfolding its true nature.

A comparison with S. Peter's first epistle shews the Petrine character of the sermon. There we have the same thoughts—of the future inheritance kept for us which is a 'salvation' (i 3–5); of the function of prophecy dealing in particular with 'seasons' (i 11); of the Lord now in heaven while the Spirit is 'sent' from heaven (iii 22, i 12); of faith as bringing salvation and strength, and as being 'through him' (i 5, v 9, i 21). S. Peter has already identified

---
[1] Cp. Levit xxiv 11–16.   [2] x 43, Lk xxiv 47; Acts ix 34.   [3] See i 6, Jn xiv 22; Lk ii 25, 38, xix 38.

R. A.

Jesus as the Servant in Acts ii 22-25: among the epistles his alone uses the verb *suffer* of Christ, and that four times (ii 21, 23, iii 18, iv 1), and it speaks of him as suffering 'the righteous for the unrighteous' (iii 18). The words *murderer* and *turn* also recur in Acts ii 25, iv 15. There are also traces of S. John's language and thought, on which see Introduction ch. iii § 2.

11 And as he held Peter and John, all the people ran together unto them in the porch that is called Solomon's,
12 greatly wondering. And when Peter saw it, he answered unto the people,

Ye men of Israel, why marvel ye at this man? or why fasten ye your eyes on us, as though by our own power or godliness
13 we had made him to walk? ¹The God of Abraham, and of Isaac, and of Jacob, the God of our fathers, hath glorified his ²Servant Jesus; whom ye delivered up, and denied before the face of Pilate, when he had determined to release him.
14 But ³ye denied the Holy and Righteous One, and asked for a
15 murderer to be granted unto you, and killed the ⁴Prince of life; whom God raised from the dead; ⁵whereof we are
16 witnesses. And by faith in his name hath his name made this man strong, whom ye behold and know: yea, the faith which is through him hath given him this perfect soundness in the presence of you all.
17 And now, brethren, I wot that in ignorance ye did it, as
18 did also your rulers. But the things which God foreshewed by the mouth of all the prophets, that his Christ should
19 suffer, he thus fulfilled. Repent ye therefore, and turn again, that your sins may be blotted out, that so there may come
20 seasons of refreshing from the presence of the Lord; and that he may send the Christ ⁶who hath been appointed for
21 you, *even* Jesus: whom the heaven must receive until the times of restoration of all things, whereof God spake by the mouth of his holy prophets which have been since the world
22 began. Moses indeed said, ⁷'A prophet shall the Lord God raise up unto you from among your brethren, ⁸like unto me;

---

¹ Exod iii 6.   ² AV has *son*, and in verse 26: in iv 27, 30 *child*. See below p. 61.   ³ Bezan *ye were heavy upon*.   ⁴ Marg *Author*.   ⁵ Marg *of whom*.   ⁶ AV reads *who hath been preached before*.   ⁷ Deut xviii 15, 19: Acts vii 37.   ⁸ Marg *as he raised up me*.

to him shall ye hearken in all things whatsoever he shall
23 speak unto you. And it shall be, that every soul, which
shall not hearken to that prophet, [1]shall be utterly destroyed
24 from among the people. Yea and all the prophets from
Samuel and them that followed after, as many as have spoken,
25 they also told of these days. Ye are the sons of the prophets,
and of the covenant which God made with your fathers,
saying unto Abraham, [2]And in thy seed shall all the families
26 of the earth be blessed. Unto you first God, having raised
up his Servant, sent him to bless you, in turning away every
one of you from your iniquities.

12   I. The miracle, S. Peter says, had not been wrought by any *power of their own*, either inherent in themselves—such as Simon Magus claimed to possess[3],—or won by their own merits and *piety*[4].
13 It was wrought by *God* to the glory of *Jesus* of Nazareth, in whose name the lame man had been healed. As he is going to speak of a new redemption and a new covenant, S. Peter begins with that Name by which God had revealed himself to Moses (verse 22). This *God of their fathers* then *had glorified Jesus*: (1) by the evidence of power in this 'sign,' but more than this—as S. Peter is going to shew—(2) by raising him from the dead[5].

The sign had shewn that Jesus was the author of salvation; he is then the *Servant* of Jehovah, portrayed in the famous passages of Isaiah—xlii 1-9, xlix 1-13, lii 13-liii 12. For this Servant was to raise up the tribes of Jacob and restore the preserved of Israel (verse 21); to be God's salvation unto the ends of the earth (iv 10-12); to justify many by bearing their iniquities (verse 26); and so to be a covenant for the people (vv. 22-26)[6]. All this however was to be effected through suffering. The Servant is the man of sorrows and pours out his soul unto death. *The Christ must suffer*, and this part of the prophecy the Jews had themselves fulfilled, when they *gave up* Jesus to be judged[7].

14   With the same courage as before S. Peter now accuses the people. They as well as the rulers were guilty, and the reason leads to the next Name of Jesus. For free choice had been offered to the people between Jesus and the robber Barabbas: but they had *denied* (and we may fancy that his own denial was in his mind) *the Holy and Righteous*. This name is chosen to emphasize the guilt of the Jews: *ye denied* the innocent *and petitioned for the present of a murderer!* The name describes a character blameless

---
[1] Gen xvii 14.   [2] Gen xxii 18: Gal iii 8, 16, Lk i 55.   [3] viii 10.
[4] Cp. *Assumption of Moses* xii 7 'Not for any *virtue* or *strength* of mine but in his compassion and longsuffering was he pleased to call me.'   [5] Cp. S. John's doctrine of glory, which includes the cross, Jn vii 39, xii 28, xiii 31-2, xvii 1-5.
[6] Isai xlix 6: liii 11: xlii 6, xlix 8.   [7] A Bezan addition.

in relation both to God and man[1], but more is contained in it. (1) Holiness signifies special consecration to the service of God. Israel was his holy nation, but had not been faithful in his service. In the place of Israel Christ was '*the holy one* of God,' the true 'consecrated servant of Jehovah' (iv 27, 30): and his divine sonship was declared by his spirit of holiness[2]. (2) Righteousness signifies the fulfilment of the law of God. Here again Israel, and all men besides, had fallen short: all were transgressors and unrighteous. But Christ obeyed the will of God to the uttermost and so was *the righteous one*[3].

15 As Holy and Righteous Jesus must also be 'the Living one[4].' The Jews killed him. But it was not possible to put the Life to death (ii 24): and by his resurrection Jesus won his third Name, *the Prince of Life*. The word *Prince* or *Author* (1) means *he who goes first* or *Leader*; and Jesus was the first to rise, he was 'the first begotten of the dead': in truth he is 'the Beginning' of all things[5]. (2) The Leader is generally the *Captain* or *Prince*, which is the ordinary meaning of the Greek word in the OT[6]; and Christ by his victory over death was declared to be the Prince of Life, the victorious Captain who 'brought to nought him that had the power of death' and who 'brought life and immortality to light[7].' Both these ideas occur in the Hebrews. There Jesus is both 'the author (i.e. beginner) and finisher of our faith,' and also 'the captain of salvation[8].' There too, as here, the Principate is closely associated with, or rather made perfect and complete by, his sufferings.

16 And now S. Peter shews that his power over life is a present reality. For it is *his name*, i.e. Jesus revealed as the Lord's Servant and Prince, Holy and Righteous, which has given this man *strength* and *perfect soundness*. In iv 9 and 12 Peter says that the man *had been saved*: 'salvation' is literally the state of safety or soundness, and in our diseased and imperfect condition to be restored to soundness is 'life.' The Name however will only heal those who accept it and its claim, in other words those who have *faith in the name*. Receptivity on man's part, which is faith, is a condition of all spiritual activity. And here we have faith (1) on the man's part, which enabled the Name to strengthen him, (2) on Peter's part, which enabled him to give the soundness. But again this wonder-working faith itself comes from the Name, it is made possible *through him*, i.e. Jesus.

17 II. S. Peter has meanwhile been removing the offence of the cross. (1) It was the deed of the Jews; (2) Jesus was perfectly

---

[1] Mk vi 20, Lk i 75 : cp. Jn viii 46.   [2] Exod xix 6 : Mk i 24, Lk i 35, Jn vi 69, Rom i 4.   [3] Lk i 6: Isai liii 11, I Pet iii 18, I Jn ii 1. It is evident that holiness and righteousness are preeminently divine attributes; cp. Jn xvii 11 and 25: Ps xcix 9 and cxix 137: Isai vi 3 and Dan ix 7: I Pet i 15 and I Jn i 9.   [4] Rev i 18: Lk xxiv 5.   [5] Rev i 5, Col i 18: Rev iii 14, xxii 13, Col i 15.   [6] e.g. Num xiii 3, xiv 4, xvi 2. Joshua was the great type of the Lord in this aspect: cp. the vision of the *Captain of the host of the Lord* in Josh v 13-5.   [7] Hebr ii 14: II Tim i 10.   [8] Hebr ii 10, xii 2.

innocent; (3) he had conquered death, and the suffering was but
18 the gate to the true Messiahship—viz. a Lordship of Life; (4) it
was the will of God foreshadowed in the suffering Servant of Isaiah.
His main object however is to win his hearers, and having accused
them of the murder of the Prince of Life, he makes excuse for them.
They did it *in ignorance*. This excuse (which S. Peter could not
plead for his own denial) was also an excuse for God's mercy[1].
19 *Therefore* he urges them (1) to *repent* of their guilt, and (2) to *turn*
to Jesus (as he had done after his denial[2]), i.e. to own his Name.
This would secure (1) present forgiveness of *their sins*, which would
be *wiped out* like writing from off a parchment or old scores off a
bill[3], and (2) ultimately the realization of the Messiah's kingdom.

This brings us to the answer to the difficulty of the Jews—why
is not Jesus restoring the kingdom to Israel? Like the apostles
(i 6) they wanted to know the *times* and *seasons* of the restoration.
S. Peter's answer is that the delay was due to themselves, for an
essential condition of the restoration was their own repentance.
This idea was familiar to his hearers, for the rabbis taught that 'if
all Israel together repented for a single day, redemption through
the Messiah would come[4].' *Repent therefore*, says S. Peter also,
and he defines (1) the *seasons* or epoch which will ensue and (2) *the
times* or the moment of the final manifestation of the kingdom.
For the apostle has already learnt to distinguish between a present
realization and a final and glorious establishment of the kingdom.
Such writings as the Book of Enoch and the more or less contemporary Psalms of Solomon, Apocalypse of Baruch and Assumption
of Moses give abundant illustration of the longing of the Jews for
the Messianic kingdom and their conceptions of it. These writings
find a reflection in this passage which gives the Christian adapta-
tion of their leading ideas. (1) The word *refreshing* was used by
the Greek translators in Ps lxvi 12 for *the wealthy place* into which
Israel was brought after passing through fire and water, and so it
takes us back in thought to the Exodus. As Israel then groaned
under the tyranny of Pharaoh, so were the Jews now groaning under
the yoke of Rome. It was the 'seasons of the Gentiles' (Lk xxi 24)
and the Jews longed for a second Exodus. They wanted *seasons
of refreshing* or of *recreation*, for that is the better meaning, as in
Ps xxxix 13 where the word again occurs. In fact Israel wanted
'the regeneration' (Mt xix 28), to be made once more a people.
21 (2) The Exodus was completed by the entrance upon Israel's
inheritance of Canaan. The loss of that inheritance in the Captivity had deeply impressed upon the Jews the idea of *Restoration*.
Restoration became the necessary fulfilment of their recreation,
and as the Exodus had been the work of Moses, the restoration was
assigned to Elijah. As interpreted by the prophets, e.g. Malachi iv 6,

---

[1] 1 Tim i 13.   [2] Lk xxii 32.   [3] Ps li 9, Isai xliii 25, xliv 22, Col ii 14, Rev iii 5.   [4] So *Assumption of Moses* i 18 'until the day of repentance in the visitation wherewith the Lord shall visit them in the consummation of the end of the days.'

the restoration was a moral one, and in that sense John the Baptist had fulfilled Elijah's office[1]. But the idea had received a wider expansion. The restoration which would follow the recreation of Israel had become *the restoration of all things*, both of the world of men and of nature. So S. Paul taught that the recovery of Israel would be the salvation of the world: and that the creation also would share in the liberty of the glory of the children of God[2]. The restoration then was the fulfilment of Isaiah's prophecy of a new heaven and new earth[3]. But apart from this literal prediction, all *the holy prophets which have been since the world began*, i.e. the whole OT from Genesis iii 15 to Malachi iv 6, had looked forward to
20 a restoration. And *the times* for this restoration would come when Jesus, as a second Elijah, returned from heaven.
21   Without dwelling on the future glory, S. Peter returns to the present delay. Besides the Jews' impenitence, it was due to the fact that meanwhile *the heaven must receive Jesus*. The reason why S. Peter had shewn in ii 33-4. It was that he might send the Holy Spirit; and through that gift, although the Messiah was now in heaven, his reign had already begun on earth. For
22 before the restoration of all things must come the restoration of man. 'The righteousness' which is to 'dwell in the new heavens and earth' must be made ready[4], and that by man's deliverance from his iniquities (verse 26). This is the work of *these days*, or, we might call it, the first Messianic age. And it means the creation of a new covenant and a new Israel. Of this new covenant Jesus is the mediator. For he is the *Prophet like unto Moses*. It was Moses who 'dedicated' the covenant between God and Israel: and now Jesus is a second Moses[5]. To understand the significance of this we must realize the extravagant heights to which the pious imagination of Israel had exalted their founder. 'God designed and devised me,' he is made to say in his Assumption (i 14), 'and he prepared me before the foundation of the world that I should be the mediator of his covenant': and to compare any man with
23 him would have sounded to a Jew like blasphemy. The conclusion of the prophecy, which is taken from another place (Gen xvii 14), shews that the idea of the covenant is at the bottom of S. Peter's mind : it is the punishment of the man who breaks the covenant of circumcision. *Moses* himself had spoken of a new *prophet* who was
24 to be the spokesman of God to man. But *all the prophets from Samuel* (generally reckoned as the first of 'the prophets,' xiii 20) had announced *these days* of the new covenant as well as the days of the final Messianic consummation[6].

---

[1] In Malachi the Gk for *turn* is *restore*.   [2] Rom viii 19-22, xi 11-2.
[3] Isai lxv 17, lxvi 22, II Pet iii 13, Rev xxi 21.   [4] Mal iv 6, II Pet iii 13.
[5] Exod xxiv 3-8. The comparison between Christ and Moses is fully drawn out in Hebrews iii 1-6 : cp. ix 18-20, xii 24. The same is found in S. John, Jn i 17, Rev xv 2, 3 : cp. also the position Moses holds in Stephen's speech. For Jesus as Prophet, cp. Lk vii 16, xxiv 19, etc.   [6] Cp. Jer xxxi 31-34, Ezek xxxvii 26, Hebr viii 6-13. The Greek is literally *all from Samuel and from those which followed after*, a slight irregularity which occurs also in Lk xxiv 27.

25 Carried away by his enthusiasm the apostle makes a personal appeal to his hearers to believe *the prophets* and to accept *the covenant*—of which they are *sons* and heirs. *You...To you* he repeats without any conjunction¹. 'You are the seed of *Abraham*, yours therefore is the covenant, which was first made with Abraham but which was only the promise and pledge of this new covenant.' It was almost wrong however to speak of this as a covenant: it was a *blessing*, and the blessing was to extend to *all nations*, though to
26 the Jews *first*². And God had fulfilled this promise in *raising up*³ *his Servant* JESUS (verse 13)—the true *Seed* of Abraham, the second Moses. He had *sent* him once in his earthly life, and he would send him again (verse 20). And as in his earthly life he went about doing good (x 38), so now at the Father's right hand (verse 21) the Servant was exercising his ministry of spiritual *blessing*. In heaven he was making intercession for transgressors, and on earth *turning them from their iniquities*. For in his Name the lame are made sound, sins are forgiven, and—as S. Peter completes the ministry of the Servant in his epistle—'by his stripes we are healed⁴.' The apostle is prevented from further instruction as to how this blessing is conveyed by a sudden interruption.

The arrest

4 And as they spake unto the people, the ⁵priests and the captain of the temple and the Sadducees came upon them,
2 being sore troubled because they taught the people, and
3 proclaimed in Jesus the resurrection from the dead. And they laid hands on them, and put them in ward unto the
4 morrow: for it was now eventide. But many of them that heard the word believed; and the number of the men came to be about five thousand.

1 The concourse of people would soon attract the attention of the high-priests and provoke their alarm. It was just such gatherings as these which led to tumults and collisions with the Romans, and certainly S. Peter had used inflammatory language (iii 15, 17,
2 cp. v 28). They were also *very much annoyed* (xvi 18) (1) at the presumption of the apostles in *teaching the people* like recognized rabbis (verse 13); and (2) being *Sadducees*, at the doctrine taught, viz. *the resurrection from the dead*. In the sermon as recorded

---

¹ Though as this asyndeton occurs in several speeches it may be a Lucan characteristic. For the pronouns cp. ii 39. ² The universal character of the promise S. Peter had already learnt from the prophecy of Joel, cp. ii 17 (*all flesh*), 21, 39. For *the Jew first* see Rom i 16, ii 9, xv 8. S. Peter quotes the promise famous from S. Paul's argument in Galatians iii 15–18. ³ Not here limited to the raising from the dead: cp. verse 22, xiii 33, Rom ix 17. ⁴ I Pet ii 24–5. In verse 26 S. Peter returns to the prophecy of the Servant; cp. Isai liii 11–2.
⁵ Marg with B reads *high-priests*.

no mention had been made in fact of our resurrection : but it was
3 contained implicitly *in* that of *Jesus* (xvii 18). Besides this *it was
now evening*—the evening sacrifice (iii 1) would have lasted till
about 4 p.m.—and time for the guard of Levites and priests to
shut the temple gates. Accordingly the authorities suddenly
intervened and arrested the apostles as disturbers of the public
peace. All precautions had been taken. The arrest was made by
the captain of the temple in person : he was an officer of high rank,
probably identical with the Sagan of the Talmud who ranked next
the high-priest. He was also supported by a strong body of the
Sadducean high-priestly faction, very possibly by Caiaphas himself
or Annas. With this arrest we should contrast that of S. Paul in
4 xxi 27-36. Here the people were favourable to the apostles and
many believed, i.e. declared their faith in or acceptance of the Name
by joining the apostolic fellowship. These conversions brought *the
number* of that society up to *about 5000*, the same number that
were fed in the wilderness (Jn vi 10). The second mention of a
number marks the close of a period, but it is the last time that
'the people are numbered.'

§ 2 *Before the Sanhedrin*

S. Luke gives a full account of the proceedings in the Sanhedrin,
as he does of S. Paul's trials before the Romans, in order to place
before the world the true relation of Christianity to 'the law.' The
scene is very dramatic. S. Luke is very likely repeating the account
of an eye-witness who would fully realize its significance, S. John[1].
Only a few weeks ago the Lord himself had been arraigned before this
tribunal, and now in accordance with his prophecy (Mk xiii 9) his
disciples are to stand at the same bar—first Peter and John, then
the Twelve, then S. Stephen and after a long interval S. Paul : see
v 21-40, vi 12-vii 58, xxiii 1-10.

5 And it came to pass on the morrow, that their rulers and
6 elders and scribes were gathered together in Jerusalem ; and
Annas the high priest *was there*, and Caiaphas, and [2]John,
and Alexander, and as many as were of the kindred of the
7 high priest. And when they had set them in the midst, they
inquired, By what power, or in what name, have ye done this ?
8 Then Peter, filled with the Holy Ghost, said unto them,
9 Ye rulers of the people, and elders[3], if we this day are
examined concerning a good deed done to an impotent man,
10 [4]by what means this man [5]is made whole ; be it known unto

---

[1] With verse 6 cp. Jn xviii 13 *Annas first*: 7 Jn ix 15, 19, 26 : 10 Jn v 6, 9 *whole*:
13 *behold* is Johannine, and cp. Jn vii 15 : 16 Jn xi 47 : 19 Jn xii 43 : 20 Jn iii 11,
32 : 22 Jn v 5. For vv. 15-17 see on page 69.   [2] Bezan has *Jonathan*.
[3] AV and Bezan add *of Israel*.   [4] Marg *in whom*.   [5] Gk *hath been saved*.

you all, and to all the people of Israel, that in the name of
Jesus Christ of Nazareth, whom ye crucified, whom God
raised from the dead, *even* in ¹him doth this man stand here
11 before you whole. He is ²the stone which was set at nought
of you the builders, which was made the head of the corner.
12 And in none other is there salvation : for neither is there any
other name under heaven, that is given among men, wherein
we must be saved.
13 Now when they beheld the boldness of Peter and John,
and had perceived that they were unlearned and ³ignorant
men, they marvelled ; and they took knowledge of them, that
14 they had been with Jesus. And seeing the man which was
healed standing with them, they could say nothing against it.
15 But when they had commanded them to go aside out of the
16 council, they conferred among themselves, saying, What shall
we do to these men? for that indeed a notable ⁴miracle hath
been wrought through them, is manifest to all that dwell in
17 Jerusalem; and we cannot deny it. But that it spread no
further among the people, let us threaten them, that they
18 speak henceforth to no man in this name. ⁵And they called
them, and charged them not to speak at all nor teach in the
19 name of Jesus. But Peter and John answered and said unto
them, Whether it be right in the sight of God to hearken
20 unto you rather than unto God, judge ye : for we cannot but
21 speak the things which we saw and heard. And they, when
they had further threatened them, let them go, finding nothing
how they might punish them, because of the people; for all
22 men glorified God for that which was done. For the man
was more than forty years old, on whom this ⁴miracle of
healing was wrought.

5 When morning came the Sanhedrin met *in Jerusalem*. This
word stands in antithesis to Nazareth (verse 10). But there is a
further touch of irony as in verse 27: in 'the holy city' they were
gathered together against 'the holy and righteous one' and his
followers. The senate-house was probably outside the temple
and so in the city : Josephus says that it adjoined the temple
6 wall on the west. The *high-priestly families* met in full force,

---

¹ Marg *this (name).*   ² Ps cxviii 22, I Pet ii 7.   ³ Gk *idiōtae.*   ⁴ Gk *sign.*
⁵ Bezan *And*] *when they had (all) consented to this opinion [they called* (cp. Lk xxiii 51).

for it was their quarrel with the apostles. S. John who was an acquaintance of Caiaphas (Jn xviii 15) would know the names of the leaders. *Alexander* however is not mentioned elsewhere, nor is *John*[1]. Probably the Bezan text is right in reading *Jonathan*, who would be the son of Annas. The court sat in a semicircle, and the three front rows were occupied by 'the disciples
7 of the learned men.' *In the midst* of the arc S. Peter and S. John are now *set*, and with them the lame man, as chief witness (vv. 10, 14). There was no definite charge; it was a preliminary enquiry as in xxv 26. As the supreme religious as well as civil tribunal the Sanhedrin *enquire, By what power or name*[2] the *good deed*[3] had been wrought. In the same way a deputation of the Sanhedrin had enquired of the Lord 'by what authority' he had cleansed the temple[4].
8 The Lord however had promised to give his disciples 'a mouth and wisdom'; and so S. Peter now received a special *inspiration of the Holy Spirit*, and 'witnessed a good (and bold, verse 13) con-
9 fession.' *The man has been saved*, or *made whole, by the name*
10 *of Jesus Christ of Nazareth*, i.e. the power contained in the revelation of Jesus of Nazareth as the Messiah, and in that revelation the apostle unfolds yet another name. First he who had once flinched before a maid-servant of the high-priest now accuses the priests and rulers of having *crucified* their Messiah, using (as in v 30) a word of special indignity. But *God raised him from*
11 *the dead*, and by that proved him to be *the Stone*—both (*a*) foundation-stone and (*b*) corner-stone—of God's temple. The Jews were familiar with the idea of Israel as 'the house of God[5]'; they called themselves 'the temple of the Lord.' The rulers of their polity would be *the builders*; but the chief *stone* was the Messiah or Christ. This stone had been laid (*a*) for a foundation in Zion by God[6], but the rulers had *set it at nought*, and cast it out. God however had lifted it up from the rubbish heap where it had been cast, that is from the grave, and made it (*b*) *the head of the corner*[7]. The corner is the critical part of a building—(1) structurally, because here the side walls meet; and (2) in warfare, because it is the vantage point of defence, and here the battlements often rise into a tower. Strength then should be the mark of the corner, and this is typified most of all in *the head of the corner*, or the stone or tower which crowns the battlements. We can understand then the metaphorical use of 'corner' for 'prince' in the OT[8]. And now Jesus is made head of the corner. (1) As the foundation-

---

[1] It is conjectured (*Encycl. Biblica*, 1 p. 171) that Alexander was the Greek name for Eleazar, son of Annas, high-priest between A.D. 15–18. Felix procured the assassination of Jonathan about 50–52. [2] Cp. iii 12, 16. [3] A Lucan word: cp. x 38, Lk xxii 25. [4] Lk xx 1, 2. [5] So S. Peter, ii 36, I Pet ii 5, iv 17: Jerem vii 4. [6] Isai xxviii 16, quoted by S. Peter I Pet ii 6, and S. Paul, Rom ix 33. Cp. also Zech iii 9, iv 7. [7] Ps cxviii 22, quoted by the Lord in Mt xxi 42, Mk xii 10–11, Lk xx 17. [8] e.g. Num xxiv 17, Judges xx 2, Isai xix 13. Cp. also RV margin of II Chr xxvi 15, Zeph i 16, iii 6.

stone his Messiahship had been lying hid in God's foreknowledge, but now it had been made manifest to the world; it was raised from the lowest layer to the top. (2) As corner-stone he binds the two walls of Jews and Gentiles into the one building of the
12 Christian church[1]. (3) As corner tower or battlement he is a defence, and this building is the house of salvation. This is evident from Ps cxviii which S. Peter is quoting, where the preceding words declare that 'the Lord is become my salvation.' This interpretation of the psalm is sanctioned by the Lord's own use of it. In this corner-stone, then, is true safety or *the salvation* to be found; and the variety of terms employed in this passage shews its completeness —*to make strong* and *give perfect wholeness, save* and *make healthy, cure, heal*[2].
13 (1) The effect produced upon the Sanhedrin was *astonishment*: first at the *boldness of Peter and John* in thus accusing them; then at their use of scripture, when it was obvious that (a) they had not been trained in the technical learning of the rabbinical schools. This is the meaning of *unlearned*; and in this sense the Lord himself had never learnt[3]. Nor (b) had they any professional status. They were *ignorant*: the Greek word is '*idiots*,' and an '*idiot*' was a private person who possessed no official position or special ability. So in I Cor xiv 16 the word is used for an ordinary member of the congregation. It had been adopted into Hebrew, and gradually the idea of ignorance began to cling to it. (2) At the same time *they recognized that they had been of Jesus' company*. We are surprised that this fact was not known to the Sanhedrin from the first. The word however denotes personal recognition[4]: and a Bezan text has *some of them recognized*. Hitherto the Sadducean rulers had been indifferent to the doings and the persons of the followers of the enthusiastic prophet of Nazareth. Now however they recognized Peter and John as having been in the immediate company of Jesus in the temple in that last week, or even as present in the high-priest's house on that last night[5]. They were then the ringleaders of the sect. John himself was known to Caiaphas, but it was an acquaintanceship which the high-priest might find it convenient to forget at this juncture.
14 (3) The fact however of the miracle was incontrovertible: and it had aroused such enthusiasm among *the people* (verse 21) that they could do nothing. When the Lord answered them by a reference to John the Baptist, they had not dared to impugn the
18 popular verdict; so now they simply forbade the apostles *to speak or teach in the name of Jesus*. In the Lord's time, those who confessed him had been excommunicated or put out of the synagogue by the Pharisees, the religious leaders and rulers of the synagogue[6]. Now

---

[1] This is the thought developed by S. Paul in Eph ii 14–22.   [2] iii 16, iv 9, 10, 14, 22. The last three words occur in the case of the impotent man, Jn v 1–13.   [3] Jn vii 15.   [4] Lk xxiv 16, 31.   [5] Cp. Jn xviii 15–27, Lk xxii 56 *with him.*   [6] Jn ix 22, xii 42.

public profession of the name of Jesus is made illegal by the Jewish
19 government. The apostles however were not afraid of men, and
together they made a determined reply in which we can hear an
21 echo of S. John's voice[1]. The Sanhedrin retorted with *further
threats* and *dismissed* them.

The assembly, prayer, and confirmation of the apostles

S. Peter and S. John went straight to the rest of the Twelve,
assembled no doubt in the upper chamber and praying for them[2].
That *their own company* was the Twelve seems clear from verses 29
and 31: it was the office of the apostles, as distinct from the multitude
(verse 32), *to speak the word*. As speaking the word was now definitely
declared illegal, the apostles had to decide upon their future policy.
For themselves there was no alternative—they 'must obey God.' But
the threats they commit to God in prayer; for indeed in this action
they *recognized his working* (Bezan). In the same manner Hezekiah
had gone up to the house of the Lord and laid the blasphemous letter
and threats of Sennacherib before the Lord[3]. The apostles indeed
needed an answer from God. It was their first collision with 'the law,'
and they had decided to disobey their rulers and thus apparently break
the fifth commandment, about which their Master had been so firm[4].
The answer came, and the divine sanction was given in a most decisive manner.

The prayer, like the former one in i 24–5, was probably spoken by
the mouth of S. Peter. Jesus is *the Servant*: for his anointing cp.
x 38; for the foreordaining by God's counsel ii 23; the hand of the
Lord I Pet v 6; nations and peoples I Pet ii 9; 'Master' II Pet ii 1;
'of a truth' x 34.

23 And being let go, they came to their own company, and
reported all that the chief priests and the elders had said
24 unto them. And they, when they heard it[5], lifted up their
voice to God with one accord, and said,

'O Lord, [6]thou that didst make the heaven and the earth
25 and the sea, and all that in them is: who by the Holy Ghost,
by the mouth of our father David thy servant, didst say,

'Why did the Gentiles rage,
And the peoples imagine vain things?
26 The kings of the earth set themselves in array,
And the rulers were gathered together,
Against the Lord, and against his [9]Anointed:

---
[1] Jn iii 11, 32 etc., I Jn i 3. [2] i 13, xii 12. [3] II K xix 14–19.
[4] Mt xv 1-6, cp. Acts xxiii 5. [5] Bezan adds *and perceived the working of God.*
[6] Gk *Master.* [7] Marg *thou art he that did make.* Cp. Exod xx 11, Ps cxlvi 6,
etc., Acts xiv 15. [8] Ps ii 1-2. [9] Gk *Christ.*

27 for of a truth in this city against thy holy ¹Servant Jesus, whom thou didst anoint, both Herod and Pontius Pilate, with the Gentiles and the peoples of Israel, were gathered
28 together, to do whatsoever thy hand and thy counsel fore-
29 ordained to come to pass. And now, Lord, look upon their threatenings: and grant unto thy servants to speak thy
30 word with all boldness, while thou stretchest forth thy hand to heal; and that signs and wonders may be done through the name of thy holy ¹Servant Jesus.
31 And when they had prayed, the place was shaken wherein they were gathered together; and they were all filled with the Holy Ghost, and they spake the word of God with boldness².

24 The apostles pray to God (1)—like Hezekiah in face of his enemies—as Creator of the world, and so Lord of all the earth and its kingdoms³; and (2) as their own *Master*, whose will they must obey
27 being his *servants*⁴ (verse 29). The present gathering together of the Sanhedrin against the Name of Jesus is a repetition of the *gathering together* of *the rulers* against *Jesus* himself. As Jesus had been anointed as the *Messiah* with the Holy Spirit (x 38), that assembly had been a conspiracy *against the Lord and his Anointed*, and was in truth that conspiracy pictured in the second psalm⁵. The psalm shewed the vanity of their attempt. *Of a truth* it had been allowed,
28 because in reality they were only carrying out *what had been foreordained by the counsel and hand* of the Lord, i.e. his will and power⁶. The Hand of the Lord was a recognized Hebrew metaphor for the divine power, when actively manifested as in the deliverance
29 of his people or the working of signs⁷. Now in the present conspiracy the apostolic prayer is simply that the will of God may
30 be fulfilled by their *speaking of the word*, while he '·confirms the word' with his hand, i.e. 'with signs following' to glorify *the name of Jesus*.
31 Over against the gathering together of the Sanhedrin here was the *gathering together* of a new Sanhedrin—the apostles; and on which the divine approval rested was soon made manifest. The answer to the apostles' prayer was almost a second Pentecost. There was (1) an outward sign—an earthquake. This was generally recognized as a sign of divine working, and is the only one of the four signs in the epiphany to Elijah which had not occurred at

---

¹ AV *child*: cp. iii 13 n. ² Bezan adds *to everyone who willed to believe*.
³ II K xix 15, 19, Ps ii 8, 10, Rev. xi 15. ⁴ *Master* and *servant*, o. *slave*, are correlative I Pet ii 18, I Tim vi 1-2. *Master* is used of God in Lk ii 29 (the Nunc Dimittis), Rev vi 10: of Christ in II Pet ii 1, Jude 4. ⁵ The psalm is also quoted in xiii 33 and Hebr i 5, v 5. ⁶ Cp. *Apoc. Baruch* liv 13 ' with thy *counsel* thou dost govern all the creatures which thy right *hand* has created.'
⁷ Cp. (*a*) ii 33, Exod iii 20, xiii 3, xv 6, etc., (*b*) verse 30, xi 21, xiii 11.

Pentecost[1]. Now it was a sign of (2) an inward inspiration by *the Holy Spirit*. And then in the strength of that power the Twelve continued their work of *speaking the word*.

§ 3 *The common life of the church and the entrance of sin*

Between the two trials in the Sanhedrin S. Luke gives us a second picture of the church modelled upon the same outlines as the first in ii 42-47. (1) *The prayers* we have just had (vv. 23-31): (2) *the fellowship* and common life follows in iv 32-v 11 : (3) *the signs and wonders* in v 12-16. The enlargement of the picture is due to the new features of opposition from without and sin within. The story how sin entered into the church is now to be told. First we have as it were an 'earthly paradise,'—the garden of Eden (Gen ii 4-25).

The community of goods

32 And the multitude of them that believed were of one heart and soul[2]: and not one *of them* said that aught of the things which he possessed was his own; but they had all
33 things common. And with great power gave the apostles their witness of the resurrection of the Lord Jesus: and great
34 grace was upon them all. For neither was there among them any that lacked: for as many as were possessors of lands or houses sold them, and brought the prices of the things that
35 were sold, and laid them at the apostles' feet: and distribution was made unto each, according as any one had need.

32 While the apostles taught and preached, the common life of *the body of believers* continued, being based on their spiritual unity; even the word '*own*' was discarded. The apostolic 'word' of
33 verse 31 is defined as *the witness of the resurrection*. This the apostles *gave back*, as if it were a debt they owed to men[3], *with great power*. The power was given (1) by this common life of the community, which was the best proof of their preaching: and also (2) by the inspiration of the Spirit, the source of 'demonstration and power' in preaching[4]. But *great grace* or favour was indeed *upon them all*. In i 47 it was the favour of the people: here it is
34 that of God. For it was only divine grace which enabled the wealthier individuals to overcome selfishness and make the community of goods a reality by selling their private property. *The prices* were laid *at the feet of the apostles* as the presiding teachers or rabbis of the society[5]. And by this unselfishness for a time the problem of poverty was solved: *there was none that lacked*.

---

[1] I K xix 11, 12: cp. below, xvi 26, and Mt xxvii 51, xxviii 2. [2] Bezan adds *and there was no distinction among them*. [3] Rom i 14. [4] verse 31, I Cor ii 4. [5] xxii 3.

That the selling was entirely voluntary, and the effect of grace, is shewn by two typical actions. These in S. Luke's artistic composition form a companion pair of pictures like the two assemblies above.

Joseph Barnabas

36 And Joseph, who by the apostles was surnamed ¹Barnabas (which is, being interpreted, Son of ²exhortation), a Levite, 37 a man of Cyprus by race, having a field, sold it, and brought the money, and laid it at the apostles' feet.

The type of correspondence with the divine grace is shewn in one who will become a prominent figure in the church. In fact in the calendar of the English church he is entitled an 'apostle,' and he is the only saint (besides S. Paul and the Evangelists) outside the Twelve who is honoured with a red letter day. He was *Joseph*, by birth a Cypriote, by blood an Israelite of the tribe of Levi. He had connexions with Jerusalem, for John Mark was his cousin. We might almost infer from I Cor ix 4–6 that like S. Paul he was unmarried; and he was apparently well to do. Theoretically priests and Levites might not have any inheritance in Israel, for 'the Lord was their portion,' but in practice the rule was not observed³. So Joseph had *an estate* which he now *sold*. He possessed however a truer wealth. He had great spiritual gifts, and this is shewn in the *surname* which was given him *by the apostles*, and by which he is generally known, viz. *Barnabas*. From what has been said about the importance of 'the name' among the Jews (p. 49) we see that the giving of a name was a significant action. In this case it probably marked the definite admission to an office, the authoritative reception or recognition of Barnabas as a prophet or teacher in the society.

The interpretation of the name itself however is not easy. *Bar* means *son* and *Nabas* may be connected with the Hebrew *Nebi* (*prophet*), or the Aramaic *Nevahah* (*refreshment*). Deissmann thinks it is a Hebrew form of *Barnebous* (*son of Nebo*), a name which has been found in a Syrian inscription⁴. The difficulty, which occurs with several of the names in the Acts, is really due to our ignorance of the vernacular; and we must fall back upon S. Luke, our best authority, who interprets it as *son of paraclesis*. Paraclesis was a spiritual gift, closely akin to but distinct from prophecy and teaching. Its meaning is shewn by the work of the Holy Spirit who is the Paraclete. A paraclete is one whom we 'call to our side' to help us by his advocacy or otherwise. And so paraclesis denotes the spiritual help which Christians render to one another. At one time it may take the form of *exhortation*, at another of comfort or *consolation*. The best equivalent, which will cover both elements, is *encouragement*. In this power

---

¹ For Barnabas see ix 27, xi 22–30, xii 25–xv 39, I Cor ix 6, Gal ii 1, 13, Col iv 10.
² AV and marg *consolation*. Gk *paraclēsis*.   ³ Num xviii 20–24, Jerem xxxii 7–15.
⁴ *Bibelstudien* pp. 175–8, *Neue Bibelstudien* pp. 15–7.

of help S. Barnabas excelled, and we find him exercising it at Antioch together with the kindred gifts of prophecy and teaching[1]. Thus the words of our collect truly describe the character of Joseph Barnabas—'O God who didst endue thy holy apostle Barnabas with singular gifts of the Holy Ghost.'

Ananias and Sapphira

On the other hand there were those who failed of the grace of God. Like the individual, the growing church has many painful discoveries to make: first the hatred of the world; then—and far more painful—the appearance of sin within, the discovery that as into Eden, so into the kingdom of the Messiah, sin could find an entrance[2]. The disciples had indeed been prepared, as for the former by the persecution of the Christ, so for the latter by the treachery of Judas. But it was a discovery clean contrary to man's natural ideas; and against this experience of the kingdom of God spiritually minded men in all ages have risen in revolt. From the Montanists and Novatians of the early church to the Puritans of to-day, attempts have continually been made to found new and 'pure' churches. Against such attempts S. Luke bears witness once for all by recording facts: and from this point of view the history of the Acts is a history of the growth of tares among the wheat—first hypocrisy; then murmuring (vi); dissension (xv); and sharp contention (xv 39).

The first seed of bitterness is most important. So familiar are we with 'spots and wrinkles' in the church that we can with difficulty realize the significance of this, the first sin in and against the community. It corresponds to the entrance of the serpent into Eden with the fall of Eve in the OT: and the first fall from the ideal must have staggered the apostles and the multitude. Its enormity is marked by the punishment which fell upon Ananias, the same which had been meted out to Achan, him who first troubled Israel at the entrance into the Holy Land[3]. The gravity of the offence is not to be measured by the quantity of money or the words of the lie. The sin really was not the particular deceit, but the state of heart—hypocrisy and unreality. And if sin and Satan are to find a lodgement in the church, then the ways of God will require some justification to the perplexed believer, his holiness some vindication. And so the death of Ananias was a signal proof that though hypocrisy and impurity cannot be kept out of the church, the law of holiness remains inexorable; there can be no compromise with God's righteousness.

5 But a certain man named [4]Ananias, with Sapphira his wife, 2 sold a possession, and kept back *part* of the price, his wife also being privy to it, and brought a certain part, and laid it

---

[1] xi 23, 26, xiii 1. The Jews were already familiar with paraclesis—cf. xiii 15.
[2] Dante symbolizes this by making the serpent find its way even into the mount of Purgatory (*Purgat.* c. viii).   [3] Gen iii 1-19, Josh vii.   [4] Or *Hananias* (WH).

3 at the apostles' feet. But Peter said, Ananias, why hath Satan filled thy heart to lie to the Holy Ghost, and to keep
4 back *part* of the price of the land? Whiles it remained, did it not remain thine own? and after it was sold, was it not in thy power? How is it that thou hast ¹conceived this thing in thy heart? thou hast not lied unto men, but unto God.
5 And Ananias hearing these words fell down and gave up the
6 ghost: and great fear came upon all that heard it. And the ²young men arose and wrapped him round, and they carried him out and buried him.
7 And it was about the space of three hours after, when his
8 wife, not knowing what was done, came in. And Peter answered unto her, Tell me whether ye sold the land for so
9 much. And she said, Yea, for so much. But Peter *said* unto her, How is it that ye have agreed together to tempt the Spirit of the Lord? behold, the feet of them which have buried thy husband are at the door, and they shall carry thee
10 out. And she fell down immediately at his feet, and gave up the ghost: and the young men came in and found her dead, and they carried her out and buried her by her husband.
11 And great fear came upon the whole church, and upon all that heard these things.

1 The selling of property was quite voluntary; but it had some reward of praise among the brethren, and there must have been some moral compulsion. Accordingly one *Ananias sold a piece*
2 *of ground*, and at the meeting of the church *brought part of the price* and *laid it at the feet of the* presiding *apostles*, when an
3 unexpected catastrophe occurred. Like Judas, Ananias was covetous: and just as greed of gain lay at the bottom of most of the sins and failures in the Acts—the sin of Simon Magus, the opposition of Elymas, of the Philippian 'masters' and the Ephesian silversmiths, the shortcomings of the Ephesian converts and the injustice of Felix³—so Ananias *kept back part of the price*. This had been the sin of Achan; as also of Gehazi, for it is the sin of *purloining* against which S. Paul warns servants⁴. But though 'love of money' was the root of the sin, it was another sin which constituted the capital offence, viz. the *lying*. Ananias was 'making a lie⁵.' He desired the praise of the community for the sacrifice of his goods, and at the same time to enjoy the money: he was making the best

---

¹ Gk *put* or *set*.   ² Gk *younger*.   ³ viii 18–24, xiii 8, xvi 19, xix 27, xix 19, xxiv 26.   ⁴ Cp. Titus ii 10: Josh vii 1, 21, II Kings v 20–27, I Tim vi 10.
⁵ Rev xxi 27, xxii 15: I Jn i 6 etc.

of both worlds. This is 'the lie' which is opposed to 'the truth.' It is (1) that hypocrisy or wilful unreality which our Lord so sternly denounced in the Pharisees; (2) the double-mindedness which is the exact opposite of that singleness of heart or truth of purpose which is the first essential for the life, as of the community, so of the individual Christian[1]; and (3) sin against the Holy Ghost who is the Spirit of truth. For Ananias lied (*a*) *against the Holy Ghost* in his own heart and conscience; and (*b*) to the church[2], acting a lie, which carried with it the lie spoken by Sapphira in verse 8. But the lie to the church was *not to men but to God*, i.e. to the Holy Spirit in the church. In either case Ananias was *tempting the Spirit of the Lord*, both (1) individually, 'provoking the Lord,' trying how far the Spirit would abide with and overlook the double heart[3]; and (2) corporately, testing the extent and reality of the Spirit's knowledge in the church.

But the temptation only served as a testimony to the divine nature of the Spirit. *To tempt the Spirit of the Lord* is *to tempt God; to lie to the Spirit* is *to lie to God*[4]. And in the power of the Spirit[5] S. Peter convicted Ananias of sin. There was indeed no denunciation, only an interrogation[6] — but one which 4 unmasks the true character of sin. The origin of sin is in *the heart*; it is 'the thought of the heart[7].' In Hebrew psychology the heart, the centre of life, corresponds most to our will or purpose. The heart of man is not however an absolutely independent and self-determining agent. It is open to influence from without; or to use another figure, like a 'house empty, swept and garnished,' it can and will be occupied by a spirit — either the Spirit of God or the spirit of evil. Those outside the sphere of the Spirit are in 'the power of Satan.' When men sin wilfully it is because in the place of the Holy Spirit *the heart is filled with Satan*, or speaking impersonally, 'guile and villainy.' This is both S. Luke's and S. John's explanation of the sin of Judas[8]. But this does not free man from his personal responsibility. He is responsible for keeping his heart. *Why didst thou put this in thy heart*, suffer Satan to enter thy heart? asks S. Peter. As yet the entrance of Satan has not destroyed the individual personality, for — *thou didst lie*. And the personal responsibility is shewn by the deliberate consent of the will: Ananias and his wife had *agreed together* (verse 9, cp. verse 2).

5 When the Lord gave the apostles the power of forgiving sins, that of retaining them necessarily accompanied it: with the power of loosing goes that of binding. And the apostles did not shrink from their responsibility. Thus S. Paul used his 'authority for

---

[1] ii 46: cp. Jas i 8. [2] There is a different case in the Greek: accusative in verse 3, dative in verse 4. [3] Gen vi 3 marg, I Cor x 9. [4] Cp. verses 3 and 4; 9 and xv 10, I Cor x 9. [5] Cp. Lk ii 26; Acts iv 8, xiii 9. [6] As in the conviction of Adam and Eve in Eden (Gen iii 9, 11, 13). [7] Mt xv 18-20, Mk vii 9-23. [8] xxvi 18: xiii 10: Lk xxii 3, Jn xiii 2, 27.

casting down' when he struck Elymas with blindness and excommunicated the offender against the Corinthian church. Peter exercised the same authority in the judgement of Simon Magus[1]. Here however no sentence was uttered. Ananias suddenly fell down dead. It was the immediate result of his conviction by the Holy Spirit in his own conscience. This sudden judgement
6 struck awe into the whole assembly. And without delay Ananias was *wrapped round* in grave-clothes, *carried out* of the city and laid in some tomb in the rocks. A development of organization seems to be implied in the mention of the *younger men*, apparently a body of men devoted to such offices as burying. Some such 'ministers' the community must have needed. A slightly different word however is used in verse 10: and 'younger men' was the usual term for adults as distinct from the specifically 'elder men[2].' Thus the word, if it is to be pressed, may imply the
7 existence of a body of elders or presbyters. *After an interval of three hours* Sapphira *came in* and the same scene was repeated. This time however Sapphira uttered the lie in word, and S. Peter in
10 answer foretold her fate. The rapidity of the burials and the apparent absence of enquiry suggest difficulties to our minds. But it is to be remembered that, just as in the account of Pentecost, our 'prophetic' authority[3] is not concerned to supply us with the social details which interest the modern antiquarian. His interest is entirely confined to the prophetic elements in the history.
11   It was natural that this great 'sign' of the divine conviction of sin should fill with *great awe all who heard of it*[4]; but it had a special effect on *the whole church*. In the Revised text the word *church* occurs here for the first time[5], and this is an indication that, like the persecution from without, this judgement within had a great effect in the consolidation of the church as an organization. And this effect was greatly confirmed by other *wonders and signs*, which formed one of the marks of the church (ii 43). The judgement was followed by an epoch of spiritual activity taking this outward form, which corresponds to similar periods in the Lord's ministry (Mk vi 53-56) and the work of S. Paul (xix 11-12).

§ 4 *Signs and wonders, and the apostolic college*

12   And by the hands of the apostles were many signs and wonders wrought among the people; and they were all with
13 one accord in Solomon's porch. But of the rest durst no man join himself to them: howbeit the people magnified

---

[1] Jn xx 23: Mt xviii 18, II Cor xiii 10: I Cor v 3-5: Acts xiii 9-11, viii 20-23.
[2] Cp Lk xxii 26. Also I Pet v 1 and 5, I Tim v 1, Tit ii 2 and 6. Both words *younger* and *elder* hover between the natural and technical senses: cp. Judith vii 23.
[3] The narrative here is very Hebraic in character.   [4] As at the beginning of the Gospel, Lk i 65: cp. Acts xix 17.   [5] But AV and Bezan text have it in ii 47.

14 them; ¹and believers were the more added to the Lord,
15 multitudes both of men and women; insomuch that they even carried out the sick into the streets, and laid them on beds and couches, that, as Peter came by, at the least his
16 shadow might overshadow some one of them². And there also came together the multitude from the cities round about ³Jerusalem, bringing sick folk, and them that were vexed with unclean spirits: and they were healed every one.

12   The *working of signs* is still confined to *the hands of the apostles*. And S. Luke inserts a note (for from *and they were all* to *men and women* in verse 14 is obviously a parenthesis) on the result of these signs. (1) Great emphasis was given to the position of the Twelve. We find them occupying, like a body or college of authoritative teachers, a definite station in *Solomon's porch*, where they teach daily in the morning in spite of the Sanhedrin's prohibition³.
13 (*a*) In the church *none of the rest*, after the punishment of Ananias, *dared join himself* to the body of the apostles, i.e. venture to usurp their authority or encroach upon their functions. The fate of Ananias conveyed the same warning as that of Uzzah⁴. But (*b*) among *the people* of the Jews their repute was greatly *magnified*.
14 (2) A further result followed in the continued *addition* to the church of *great numbers of men and women—believing the Lord*⁵. The effect on the rulers of the Jews will be seen later on. Many think that they are *the rest* here mentioned, and that the meaning is that for fear of their fellows (as in Jn xii 42) none of the upper classes dared openly join the Christian body. But conversion is spoken of afterwards in verse 14⁶: and it would be a strange use of the term *the rest* to apply it to the few as opposed to the many, to superiors as opposed to inferiors. It is nowhere used in the NT in such a way, while in his Gospel S. Luke has already used it markedly of the rest of the Christian body as distinct from the apostles⁷.
15   We now return to the general effect of the miraculous activity of the apostles, in which S. Peter is seen to be most conspicuous. It made a deep impression on the people, who are generally attracted by the marvellous, especially where there is the profit of healing also. So it was in our Lord's ministry, so it is to-day. The

---

¹ Marg *and there were the more added (to them), believing on the Lord*.   ² Bezan adds *for they were delivered from every infirmity that each one had*: and with AV in 16 *to [Jerusalem*.   ³ Cp. iv 18, v 21, 42, Lk xxi 37–8.   ⁴ II Sam vi 6–10.
⁵ The RV text *were added to the Lord* teaches that the church is his body, but the phrase is unusual—in ii 47 it was the Lord who added. The order of the Greek, the need of an object for the participle *believing*, and xviii 8 (cp. Judith xiv 10) are in favour of the margin.   ⁶ *Join* is used of being added to a body, but not as a synonym for being converted: cp. viii 29, ix 26, x 28, xvii 34.   ⁷ Lk xxiv 9, cp. viii 10: and for contemptuous use Lk xviii 9, 11.

people thronged the apostles, sought to derive benefit even from S. Peter's *shadow*. This savours to us of superstition. But miracles are 'signs,' and the best signs for the instruction of the simple-minded; and by this, and similar instances in the case of the Lord (*the hem of his garment*) and S. Paul (*cloths from his skin*[1]), the lesson is taught that spiritual influence can be conveyed through material things. The instances however are few and the appeal has the least permanent effect. The people throng the streets, but do not come into the church; and in time of persecution they fall away, or join the adversary and cry 'Crucify[2].'

16 Meanwhile as the fame of Peter spread even in the country districts a popular movement seemed imminent and this once more aroused the rulers.

The second arrest and trial before the Sanhedrin

This encounter with the Sanhedrin is very similar to the preceding one described in iv 1–21, and at first sight a critic might imagine that it is only a different relation of the same events. The recurrence however is quite natural, and affords another instance of the emphasis given by repetition which is found so often in the Bible. Further there are differences in this second account which point to the greater intensity of opposition. A new motive is mentioned; the unanimity of the Sadducees is more marked and the feeling of the Sanhedrin more violent; the arrest is more formal and public; all the apostles are imprisoned, and this time punishment is inflicted. For the first time notice is taken of the attitude of the Pharisees, and their policy is enunciated by Gamaliel. We must remember that Nicodemus and Joseph of Arimathaea who were disciples of a sort were also senators, and they may have reported to the church Gamaliel's speech. But what happens at a meeting of a body so large as the Sanhedrin is not easily kept private. Lastly, we have a divine intervention in favour of the apostles, with which compare xii 1–19.

17 But the high priest rose up, and all they that were with him (which is the [3]sect of the Sadducees), and they were
18 filled with jealousy, and laid hands on the apostles, and put
19 them in public ward[4]. But [5]an angel of the Lord by night opened the prison doors, and brought them out, and said,
20 Go ye, and stand and speak in the temple to the people all
21 the words of this Life. And when they heard *this*, they entered into the temple about daybreak, and taught.

But the high priest came, and they that were with him,[4]

---

[1] Mk vi 56, Lk viii 44 : Acts xix 12. [2] vi 12, Lk xxiii 21. [3] Gk *heresy*.
[4] Bezan adds *and each one went home* (Jn vii 53) : and in 21 *and they rose up early* [*and called.* [5] Or *the angel of the Lord* (AV).

G

and called the council together, and all the senate of the children of Israel, and sent to the prison-house to have them 22 brought. But the officers that came found them not in the 23 prison ; and they returned, and told, saying, The prison-house we found shut in all safety, and the keepers standing at the doors : but when we had opened, we found no man within. 24 Now when ¹the captain of the temple and the chief priests heard these words, they were much perplexed concerning 25 them whereunto this would grow. And there came one and told them, Behold, the men whom ye put in the prison are in 26 the temple standing and teaching the people. Then went the captain with the officers, and brought them, *but* without violence ; for they feared the people, lest they should be 27 stoned. And when they had brought them, they set them 28 before the council. And the high priest asked them, saying, ²We straitly charged you not to teach in this name : and behold, ye have filled Jerusalem with your teaching, and 29 intend to bring this man's blood upon us. But Peter and the apostles answered and said, ³We must obey God rather 30 than men. The God of our fathers raised up Jesus, whom ye 31 slew, hanging him on a tree. Him did God exalt with his ⁴right hand *to be* a Prince and a Saviour, for to give repentance 32 to Israel, and remission of sins. And we are ⁵witnesses of these ⁶things ; ⁷and *so is* the Holy Ghost, whom God hath 33 given to them that obey him. But they, when they heard this, were cut to the heart, and ⁸were minded to slay them.

34 But there stood up one in the council, a Pharisee, named Gamaliel, a doctor of the law, had in honour of all the people, 35 and commanded to put the men forth a little while. And he said unto them, Ye men of Israel, take heed to yourselves 36 as touching these men, what ye are about to do. For before these days rose up Theudas, giving himself out to be ⁹some-

---

¹ AV reads *the high Priest and the captain of the Temple and the chief Priests*, literally *the priest and the captain...and the high-priests*. ² Literally *With charging we charged you*—a Hebraism. ³ Some Bezan texts have *Whom must we obey, God or men? And he said, God*. ⁴ Bezan *glory* (Lk xxiv 26). ⁵ So WH with אAD : Bezan and AV have *his witnesses*, Marg with B and WH mg *witnesses in him*. ⁶ Literally *sayings*—a Hebraism (Jn vi 63). ⁷ Marg with B reads *and God hath given the Holy Ghost to them that obey him*. ⁸ i.e. *intended* (verse 28) : AV and Bezan *took counsel*. ⁹ Bezan *some great one* (viii 9).

body; to whom a number of men, about four hundred, joined themselves: who was slain; and all, as many as
37 obeyed him, were dispersed, and came to nought. After this man rose up Judas of Galilee in the days of the enrolment, and drew away *some of the* people after him: he also perished; and all, as many as obeyed him, were scattered
38 abroad. And now I say unto you, Refrain from these men, and let them alone[1]: for if this counsel or this work be of men,
39 it will be overthrown: but if it is of God, ye will not be able to overthrow them; lest haply ye be found even to be fighting
40 against God. And to him they agreed: and when they had called the apostles unto them, they beat them and charged them not to speak in the name of Jesus, and let them go.
41 They therefore departed from the presence of the council, rejoicing that they were counted worthy to suffer dishonour
42 for the Name. And every day, in the temple and at home, they ceased not to teach and to [2]preach Jesus *as* the Christ.

17 The whole high-priestly faction, which from the religious point of view constituted the *party of the Sadducees*, were now *filled with jealousy*. The Greek word is *zeal*, and there is a good zeal or jealousy for God, which was a marked feature of the Jewish character. But this was a zeal against man based not on religious but on selfish grounds, a real jealousy of the influence of rival teachers[3]. The apostles had moreover disobeyed the commands of the Sanhedrin. And the Sadducean party were apprehensive of a popular movement which would endanger their own political position. This
18 moved them to *rise up* and take decided action. The apostles were probably arrested in Solomon's porch in the evening as in iv 3.
19 *But* in the night *the angel of the* LORD *released them*. How? we ask, and who is *the angel of the* LORD? For that is probably the right translation[4], as this angel corresponds to 'the Angel of the LORD,' i.e. JEHOVAH, in the OT. In the Acts he appears five times[5]. First (1) here; then (2) Stephen speaks of him; (3) he guides Philip; (4) he liberates Peter from prison; and (5) smites Herod. In the Gospel, the angel of the Lord appeared to Zachariah and named himself 'Gabriel who stands before God': Gabriel announced the birth

---

[1] Bezan adds *and defile not your hands*: and after *overthrow them* in 39 *neither ye nor kings nor despots. Refrain therefore from these men [lest* etc.   [2] Gk *evangelize, tell the good news (gospel) of.*   [3] Cp. (*a*) Rom x 2, II Cor xi 2: (*b*) Acts xiii 45.   [4] As in AV. RV has *an angel*. But we have here a Hebraism: as *the day* (ii 20), *voice* (vii 31), *Spirit* (viii 39), *hand* (xi 21), *glory* (Lk ii 9), *law* (ii 23), *power* (v 17), *name* (xiii 35)—so we have *the angel* or *messenger—of the* LORD. In x 3, xxvii 23 we have *of God* and should translate *an angel*.   [5] v 19, vii 30-8, viii 26, xii 7-10, 23. Cp. Lk i 11-38, ii 9: Mt i 20-4, ii 13, 19, xxviii 2.

of the Lord to Mary: and again the angel of the Lord 'came upon the shepherds. In S. Matthew the angel appears to Joseph in a dream three times, and at the end of the Gospel descends from heaven and rolls away the stone from the tomb. Now the word *angel* simply means *messenger*. And in the OT we can distinguish three uses of this expression : (*a*) The Angel of JEHOVAH is really a manifestation of JEHOVAH himself, and so is a foreshadowing of the doctrine of the Incarnation and of the WORD of God. (*b*) The angel is a messenger of JEHOVAH, other than the WORD, acting as his instrument or interpreter: this messenger appears in the later books, e.g. Ezekiel, Daniel and Zechariah, and in Daniel he is called Gabriel[1]. (*c*) The messenger is often an impersonal agent of the divine working; that is, the angel of the Lord is a Hebrew description of what we should call the action of divine providence; whether in punishing, as when the angel smites Israel, and again Sennacherib's army, with pestilence, or in delivering, as when the angel stops the mouths of the lions from hurting Daniel[2]. In the Acts we find the same uses. S. Stephen is speaking of a theophany (*a*)[3]. The angel who liberates Peter appears as a messenger in human form (*b*). The angel who smites Herod is simply the messenger of death : there is no appearance (*c*). Two passages remain. The guidance of Philip seems to imply an inward intuition rather than an external vision[4]. In this passage we note the bareness of the statement, very different from the circumstantial account of the deliverance of Peter. Nor does any stress seem to be laid upon the incident : neither the apostles nor Gamaliel allude to it, and yet the indisputable appearance of an angel should have had some weight with the Sanhedrin. So we may take it in the third sense, i.e. as the Hebraic expression for some divine intervention, the manner of which is not defined. It may have been connivance on the part of an officer, or the help of a friend[5].

20 However liberated, the apostles in obedience to the divine injunction continued their work of *speaking the words of this Life*, i.e. the gospel of the Prince of Life (iii 15), without any reserva-
21 tion for fear of man (*all the words*). In the morning as usual they *entered the temple just before dawn*. At the same time *the*
22 *Sanhedrin assembled* in their senate-house. *The captain of the temple* took his seat as Sagan or vice-president (p. 56), but great perplexity was caused when his subordinates announced to him
25 that the apostles were not in the prison. On the further report that they were *in the temple* he went and arrested them in person : but so great was their popularity that it was done *without* any roughness or *violence*—a treatment very different from that meted
28 out to S. Paul in xxi 30-36. This time there was a direct charge against the apostles : (1) They had disobeyed the command of the Sanhedrin given in iv 18. (2) They had been inciting the people to rise against the Sanhedrin and exact vengeance for the *blood* of

---

[1] Dan viii 16, ix 21: cp. Lk i 19.   [2] II Sam xxiv 16, II K xix 35 : Dan vi 22, Ps xxxiv 7.   [3] See below p. 101.   [4] Cp. viii 26 and 29, 39.
[5] When angels appear, however, they take the form of men; cp. i 10.

Jesus[1]. This referred to their candid and continual witness that
29 the rulers had crucified the Lord. Peter's answer was to ask the
high-priest whether they *must obey God or man?* The Lord had
used a similar dilemma in defence of his authority. This conflict
between the two laws of obedience has been familiar at all times.
The most classical example is in Sophocles, when Antigone says to
Creon who had forbidden her brother's burial[2]:

> Nor did I deem thy edicts strong enough,
> That thou, a mortal man, should'st overpass
> The unwritten laws of God that know not change.

30 Now through *Jesus* they had received the command of *the God of
their fathers*, which was that they should bear witness to himself[3].
And the witness S. Peter once more summarizes: (1) The Suffering—and again he charges his judges with the guilt of the Messiah's
blood: as before he had said *crucified*, so now he adds the igno-
31 minious detail of the cursed *tree*[4]. (2) The Exaltation, which is
summed up in the titles of *Prince* and *Saviour*, the names un-
32 folded in his second sermon[5]. (3) The gift of the Spirit and the
Mission of the church. S. Peter claims that the *Holy Spirit* (who
was *given* at Pentecost) is in the church and so bears *witness*;
and this witness of the church is coordinate with that of the
apostles, in whom the Spirit speaks also[6].

33 This 'boldness' filled the Sanhedrin (or at least the high-priest's
faction) with fury. The words went through their hearts like a
saw[7], and they were likely to have anticipated the conclusion of
S. Stephen's trial and 'defiled their hands' by a summary condem-
34 nation and stoning of the apostles. From such illegal action they
were saved by Gamaliel. *Gamaliel* was one of the most celebrated
of the rabbis or *teachers of the law*. He enjoyed the title of
Rabban, and appears in the traditional list of the successive 'heads
of the schools.' His *honour among the people* is testified by the
saying—'Since Rabban Gamaliel the elder died, there has been
no more reverence for the law: and purity and abstinence died out
at the same time[8].' Among Gamaliel's pupils was 'Saul the
Pharisee,' and his zeal for God and for the traditions of the fathers
bears witness to the 'strict manner' of Gamaliel's school[9]. As an
honest and religious student Gamaliel[10] was evidently impressed by
the signs of divine favour upon the Christians: but it is difficult to
exclude the suggestions of policy. Gamaliel was *a Pharisee* and
would sit as the leader of the Pharisees, and they could not possibly
let the Sadducees secure a bloody triumph over a popular 'sect,'

---

[1] For *the blood* cp. Mt xxvii 25: also xxvii 4. [2] *Antigone* 453-6 (Plumptre's trans.): cp. also Susanna 23, I Macc ii 22. [3] i 8, and p. 7. [4] xiii 29, I Pet ii 24: Gal iii 13. [5] (a) iii 15: (b) iii 16, iv 10, 12. [6] See Jn xv 26, 27; and for the Holy Spirit in the church, v 3–4, xv 28. [7] Literally *they were sawn through*: so in vii 54. Cp. the *piercing* power of the word of God in Hebr iv 12. [8] Quoted in Schürer *Jewish people in the time of Jesus Christ*, II 1, p. 364. [9] xxii 3, xxvi 5, Gal i 14. Possibly S. Paul was present in the Sanhedrin as a 'disciple of the learned' (p. 58) or a senator (p. 125). [10] Like Nicodemus in Jn iii 1.

which was full of religious zeal and seemed likely to prove a useful
35 ally (iv 3). Accordingly Gamaliel advocated an opportunist policy.
His meaning is quite obvious, though in our text from *for if this
counsel* down to *overthrow them* must be treated as a parenthesis.
38 In either case whether this movement was *from God or from men*
his advice was '*Leave it alone.*'

36   The case of *Theudas*, which Gamaliel instances, causes some difficulty. Josephus[1] tells the story of a Theudas who claimed to be a prophet and led a great multitude to the river Jordan, having promised that (like Elijah and Joshua) he would divide the river before them. Cuspius Fadus however, the Roman procurator, sent after him a squadron of horse, who slew many and made others prisoners. Theudas himself was captured and beheaded. Now Cuspius Fadus was not made procurator till the death of Herod Agrippa in A D. 44, at least 30 years later than the date assigned to him by Gamaliel, and indeed ten years later than Gamaliel's speech itself. Some critics assume that S. Luke has borrowed from Josephus and argue that this discrepancy proves the former to be an untrustworthy authority. It is obvious however that S. Luke is using some Aramaic document or oral tradition, which carries back his evidence to a much earlier period. And apart from this, on simple historical grounds it is quite possible to suppose that Josephus was as capable of making a mistake as S. Luke[2]. But in all probability both are right. There were many similar disturbances throughout this period, as Josephus himself testifies. Theudas is a contracted form, which may stand for a number of names—Theodotus, Theodosius, Theodorus, etc., so it is quite possible that different persons are referred to: and there is nothing in verse 36 beyond the name to identify the movement with that recorded by Josephus[3].

37   About *Judas* there is no difficulty. When Archelaus was deposed and Judaea made a Roman province in A.D. 6, Augustus sent 'Quirinius, the governor of Syria' (Lk ii 2) to draw up the *enrolment* or *census* of Judaea, i.e. the register of the population and their property for purposes of taxation[4]. On this occasion

---

[1] *Ant.* xx 5. 1.   [2] In his *Antiquities* Josephus corrects many mistakes which he had made in his earlier work on the *Jewish War*. In Acts xxi 38 S. Luke gives a more moderate and therefore more credible estimate of the followers of the Egyptian, viz. 4000 against Josephus' 30000.   [3] For *was slain* in 36 the Bezan text has *was dispersed*, without mentioning Theudas' death; and Eusebius in quoting this passage omits the words. This points to a different ending from the summary execution in Josephus. Prof. Blass has suggested a new solution. It is known that Christians have added to Josephus' accounts of John the Baptist and our Lord; and it is possible that a Christian hand, wishing to confirm the Acts, has inserted the words *Theudas by name* in Josephus' text. Josephus' account would run quite well without the name.   [4] The census in Lk ii 2 refers to a preceding enrolment by the same Quirinius, which has caused difficulty to the historians. The discussion does not fall within our province. But recent discoveries have thrown great light on the question, as Prof. Ramsay has shewn in his book *Was Christ born at Bethlehem?*

Judas of Gamala, a city reckoned to Galilee, rose in revolt. He taught as a doctrine that the Jews could have no earthly lords in the place of the LORD; hence all acts of lordship exercised by the Romans ought to be resisted to the death. To this movement Josephus ascribes the origin of the *Zealots*. The fanatical spirit was common among the Jews, but from this time the fanatics are reckoned as a definite party, by the side of the Pharisees, Sadducees and Essenes. The name of Zealot, in Aramaic 'Cananaean,' declared their zeal for God and the law, and they were chiefly responsible for the final outbreak and catastrophe. One of the apostles, Simon (i 13), had come from this sect.

40 As the Pharisees took up this attitude, the Sadducees were obliged to acquiesce. But for their disobedience the apostles received the usual Jewish penalty of 'forty stripes save one' and
41 then were *dismissed*, with further warnings. Thus the apostles for the first time suffered *for the Name* of Jesus, and S. Peter first began to learn by experience the doctrine he was so emphatically to preach to others[1]. More painful than the bodily suffering was the *shame*. But they remembered the Lord's beatitude and '*rejoiced*
42 and were exceedingly glad[2],' and in spite of the Sanhedrin continued their daily work as usual, both *in the temple* and *at home*, i.e. in their own meetings. This work was that of (1) *teaching* or regular instruction, and (2) *evangelizing* or public proclamation of the *gospel of the Christ*, that is, *of Jesus*[3].

The Church (v 11)

This summary of progress closes the first chapter in the history of the church. It has been a time of peace and prosperity. This peace was secured by the favour of the people and the neutrality of the Pharisees which checked the threatened persecution of the Sadducees: and it lasted long enough to enable the society to develope its own common life. The threats from without and peril from within only served to consolidate the community: and such consolidation was absolutely necessary before any real advance could be made from the centre. The picture given in iv 23–v 16 shews the progress that has been made in organization. The apostolic authority has become more clear and defined: and above all the body of believers definitely emerges at the end as *the Church*. The first appearance of this vital word suggests that we should pause and try to estimate the meaning of the term.

When the apostles began their witness, they had no consciousness that they were beginning to build up a new church in distinction from the old church or theocracy of Israel. Israel was 'the people of God,' and the apostles had no doubt that the kingdom of God which the Christ had come to establish was the old kingdom of Israel—only

---

[1] Jn xv 21: I Pet ii 20–1, iii 14, 17, iv 1, 12–19, v 1, 10.   [2] Mt v 10–12, Lk vi 22–3.   [3] Cp. Lk xx 1: Nahum i 15, Isai lii 7, Lk ii 10.

restored and glorified (i 6). But the restoration of the Messianic kingdom was delayed by the unaccountable hardness of heart and unbelief of the rulers and people of Israel, which left the small company of disciples to realize the kingdom by themselves as a mere nucleus.

To the Jews this nucleus appeared as a new sect. Among the Jews there were already several different schools both of thought and practice, such as the Pharisees and Sadducees, the Herodians and Zealots, and the Essenes. These were known by the name of *heresies* or *sects*[1]. For *haeresis* means *choice*, and stands for a deliberate choice or adoption of some particular tenets of faith or habits of life. The new 'heresy' was conspicuous, not only for its belief in Jesus as the Messiah, but also, like the sect of the Essenes, for its common life. Hence the Jews would speak of it as '*this way*[2].' The metaphor of the path or road of life is very common in the OT: we meet it in quotations in the Acts, in ii 28 and xiii 10. There was a contemporary popular manual which described *The Two Ways*, viz. the way of life and the way of death. In the NT we read of *the way of salvation, of peace, of truth, of righteousness*: and on the other hand there is *the way of Balaam* and *of Cain*[3]. Our Lord had called himself '*the Way*,' and so it was natural that those who were following in the footsteps of his life should also call their society or body *the Way*[4].

This way they claimed to be *the way of the* LORD (xviii 25): and so this new body is created by and for the revelation of a Name, the divine Name. The Israel of old had been separated from the world by the Name of JEHOVAH. They were the people who called upon the Name of the LORD and upon whom his Name was called[5]. But the divine Name which the new sect bears is *the Name* of the Lord Jesus Christ[6]. Into this Name they are baptized; in it they live and speak and work; for it they suffer[7]. Accordingly by 'this Name' they are known. They are the people 'who call upon the name of the Lord Jesus'; and 'upon whom his name is called[8].' And when at last a distinctive name had to be invented for the new body, it was taken from this Name, and they were called the CHRISTIANS[9]. The Jews however could not recognize a name which implied the truth of this faith. The Christ was 'to come out of Bethlehem': but Jesus was 'of Nazareth,' and out of Nazareth no good thing could come. So they called his disciples in contempt Nazarenes or Galileans[10].

Within the main divisions of Pharisees or Sadducees, the great rabbis had each his school of disciples: and to all outward appearance Christ with his apostles was a new rabbi with his disciples. They called him *Rabbi* (*Master*), and they were known to one another as

---

[1] v 17, xv 5, xxvi 5: xxiv 5, 14, xxviii 22.   [2] xxii 4, xxiv 14.   [3] xvi 17, Lk i 79, II Pet ii 2, 21: II Pet ii 15, Jude 11.   [4] Jn xiv 6: Acts ix 2, xix 9, 23, xxiv 22.   [5] ii 21, xv 17.   [6] ix 15. Cp. p. 49.   [7] ii 38, viii 16, x 48, xix 5: iii 16, iv 17, 30, v 28, 40, iii 6, ix 27, xvi 18: v 41, ix 16, xv 26, xxi 13.   [8] ix 14, 21, xxii 16, I Cor i 2: Jas ii 7.   [9] xi 26.   [10] Jn vii 41-2, i 46: Acts ii 22, iii 6, iv 10, vi 14: xxiv 5.

'the disciples.' After his departure the apostles had stepped into his place as the rabbis of the school, but both they and their company continued to be alike disciples of the Lord, or *the Disciples*. Only once do we hear of an apostle's disciples, in ix 25. As new generations grew up who had not known the Master in the flesh, the name of disciple gradually dropped out of daily use. Thus we do not find it in the epistles. But S. Luke uses the actual language of the period of which he writes, and *the Disciples* is a usual term for the Christians, occurring 30 times.

In relation to themselves the Christians were brothers. After his resurrection the Lord had called the apostles his brothers: and the descent of the Holy Ghost at Pentecost, filling each one with the same life and same Spirit, made the society into a real family or 'brotherhood¹.' The Christians were *the Brothers*: the individual Christian was e.g. 'Quartus the brother.' This title soon became universal and supplanted that of disciple: it is still heard in the 'dearly beloved brethren' of our own services. This was not however something entirely new, either in idea or in title. The Jews called themselves 'the brothers.' And when distinction from the Jews was desirable, other terms were needed. In the Acts we are watching the trial as it were of various suggestions—*the (being) saved, the believers, the faithful, those who call upon the Name, the saints*. However appropriate these might be in meaning, for common or technical use a particular and personal name is more useful, and so the name taken from 'the Name' secured a final and complete triumph, viz. *the Christians*.

A similar history is to be traced in the naming of the society as a corporate whole. At first a separate name was not needed. But as it gradually became evident that the new society was not going to coincide with the old commonwealth of Israel, various terms became current, e.g. *the Way, this Life, the Faith, this Salvation*². The Lord had constantly spoken of *the Kingdom*, but the common use of this name would have caused perilous confusion with 'the kingdom' of Caesar. A more distinctive term was wanted, and there was another name which the Lord himself had used in two crucial utterances, viz. *Ecclesia* or *Church*: this name won its way—and that speedily—into universal acceptance.

The word *Ecclesia* was already associated with Israel. In the OT the children of Israel were the people of the LORD and 'the People' was their title in relation to God. But when they were assembled together for public acts of worship or judgement or deliberation they formed a special presentation of the people of the LORD as one body. For such an assembly two words were used in the OT, *'ēdhāh* (RV *congregation*) and *qāhāl* (RV *assembly*)³. Both

---

¹ Jn xx 17, Mt xxviii 10 : I Pet ii 17, v 9.   ² ix 2 etc., v 20, vi 7, xiii 26.
³ The RV is not quite consistent in these translations. The mention of the assembly of the people begins after the institution of the Passover in Exodus and practically occurs in two parts only of the OT, viz. the Hexateuch and Chronicles Ezra Nehemiah. Of the two terms *'edhah* is found 151 times, *qahal* 123. *'Edhah*

words were general in their meaning and often used in exactly the same sense, but a distinction can be traced. '*Edhah* could denote all the Israelites as a society, but *qahal* was rather confined to the actual assembly of the people, and so we have the phrase—'the assembly of the congregation[1].' When the OT books were translated into Greek the distinction was emphasized. There was a Greek word *synagôgé* used for any gathering together. This was largely employed by the translators, and especially for the assembly of the people—always for *'edhah*, often for *qahal*. But there was another Greek word which had acquired a very definite technical meaning. *Ecclesia* had originally denoted any meeting of people summoned or 'called out' from their homes by the sound of a trumpet or otherwise. In Greek cities it generally denoted the assembly of all the citizens as distinguished from the aristocratic Boulê or Senate. In the typical democracy of Athens the Ecclesia was the ruling body in the state. This ecclesia however was not a fortuitous collection of the men in the street. It was confined to the duly enfranchised citizens, and so in respect of the whole population of Athens with its strangers, slaves, etc., the ecclesia itself was a somewhat aristocratic and exclusive body. Its meetings were conducted with due formalities and solemnities, and it had its own president, committee, and secretaries. The famous history of Athens brought the title of Ecclesia into great repute, and established it as the general term for a democratic assembly. (In ch. xix we shall come across this Greek usage in the account of the meeting of the *ecclesia* of Ephesus.) Finding this word with its technical meaning, the Greek translators of the OT employed it to distinguish the senses of 'assembly[2].' They used *ecclesia* for *qahal* only, and as a rule only for the most solemn religious assemblies, as those at Mt Sinai, at Mt Ebal and Mt Gerizim, at the Dedication of the Temple, Hezekiah's and Josiah's Passovers. Hence it became natural to look upon Israel as *the Ecclesia* or *Church of the LORD*[3]. But Israel was also *the Synagogue of the LORD*[4], a title which occurs in a very striking passage where we should have expected ecclesia. In Psalm lxxiii 2, the prayer runs 'Remember thy synagogue which thou hast purchased and redeemed of old': and it is significant that when S. Paul quotes it (in xx 28) he substitutes ecclesia for synagogue[5].

---

occurs in the Hexateuch 124 times, but only in the priestly document and not in Deuteronomy at all. *Qahal* is found in these books 34 times, including 11 times in Deuteronomy; in Chronicles Ezra Nehemiah 43 times. [1] In Exod xii 6.
[2] *Synagogue* occurs 204 times, *ecclesia* (the root of which is probably kindred to that of *qahal*) only 79 times. In Levit viii 3 the Greek runs *make-an-assembly-of the synagogue*. [3] Deut xxiii 1, 2, Micah ii 5, I Chr xxviii 8. [4] Num xvii 3, xx 4, xxvii 17 etc. [5] The subject is carefully examined by Dr Hort in his *Christian Ecclesia* pp. 3-15. But when he says (p. 13) that the OT use of these words is 'almost wholly historical, not ideal or doctrinal,' he seems to underestimate what he calls on p. 8 their 'religious use.' In the Apocrypha, which intervene between the LXX and the NT, we find both words: *synagogue* 19 times, *ecclesia* 22. And it is clear that *synagogue* is used in the more general sense, and so of rival assemblies e.g. of Korah, of the Gentiles etc. *Ecclesia* is confined to Israel, and is particularly used of meetings of the people for deliberative (Judith vi 21, vii 29), judicial (Ecclus xxiii 24, xxxviii 33), and religious purposes (Ecclus l 13, 20).

For the Jewish usage in New Testament times, our chief authority is the NT itself, where we can hardly escape Christian influence. We gather that the special name for Israel as God's holy nation was, as of old, *the People*. But there are signs that the Jews were still accustomed to think of themselves as both 'the Synagogue' and 'the Ecclesia of the LORD.' S. Stephen spoke to them of *the Ecclesia in the wilderness*[1]: Caiaphas prophesied of the *gathering-together into one [synagogue]* of the scattered children of God (Jn xi 52). The general use of synagogue however was overshadowed by a new meaning it had acquired. Synagogue—and not ecclesia—was used for the assembling of the people for worship in foreign cities, or at home outside of the temple; and from the meeting the name was transferred to the building itself. Hence the familiar and constant meaning of synagogue in the NT. In the Gospels the Lord seems to have made seldom use of either term: and instead of *the People* his constant phrase was *the Kingdom*. But in two utterances, in special reference to the future society, he called it *Ecclesia*: *upon this rock I will build my church*; *if he refuse to hear them, tell it unto the church*[2]. Later when the apostles discovered the need for a distinctive name for the new Israel of God, they naturally followed the Lord's precedent and spoke of it as the Ecclesia or Church. If synagogue was the more usual Jewish term, it was very natural that the hostility of the Jews should confirm the Christians in their preference for ecclesia: over against the synagogue of the Jews stood the Christian ecclesia. The Christians indeed, as we see from James ii 2, continued to call their places of meeting in Jerusalem synagogues: but the body which met there was the ecclesia (Jas v 14): and synagogue was used only for the faithless assembly of the Jews—'the synagogue of Satan[3].' What further decided the balance in favour of ecclesia was the fact that it was a thoroughly Greek word and familiar to the Gentile world in which the church made its chief progress.

Among the Christians themselves the word *Ecclesia* acquired various meanings, which will be best illustrated by its history in the Acts. *The (whole) church* first appears in v 11 and it stands as the obvious antitype of *the* (OT) *church in the wilderness*. The disciples soon spread beyond the walls of Jerusalem, and then the brethren in Jerusalem are still *the church* (but that part of it) *which was in Jerusalem* (viii 1, xi 22). Similarly the Christians of a wider area together form *the church—throughout all Judaea and Galilee and Samaria* (ix 31). Going further afield, we hear of *the church that was at Antioch* (xiii 1). The assembly there is called *the church* absolutely in xi 26; and so locally to the people of a city their assembly is to them always

---

[1] vii 38: cp. I Macc ii 56, Caleb bore witness *in the ecclesia*. [2] Mt xvi 18, xviii 17. [3] Rev ii 9, iii 9. The Gospels of Mt and Mk coming from Jewish hands often speak of *their synagogues*, viz, the Jews', as distinct from those of the Christians. But S. Luke the Gentile always (with one exception) writes *the synagogues*: the Gentile Christians had churches, not synagogues.

'the church,' as e.g. at Jerusalem (viii 3, xii 1, 5, xviii 22) and Ephesus (xx 17). But such local assemblies are only limbs of the one body: the oneness of which is strikingly shewn in the xvth chapter, where *the church* in one verse (3) means the Christians of Antioch, in the next those of Jerusalem. The growth then of local bodies—each being *the church* in its own locality—soon led to the use of the plural *the churches*. This first occurs in xv 41 and xvi 5, in reference to the churches of Syria, Cilicia, and Galatia[1]. But this phrase did not for a moment clash with the truth that these churches were the local members of the one church, which was *the church of God* (xx 28). The many synagogues of the Jews did not destroy their belief in the one synagogue of Israel which was the people of God[2]. If there were many local churches, there was only one church in one place: we read of 'the churches of Syria and Cilicia,' not of 'the churches of Antioch.' The last quotation comes from S. Paul's speech to the Ephesian elders, and it must have been the more easy for the Ephesians to grasp the doctrine of the church, because of their familiarity with another 'church,' viz. the Ecclesia of the Ephesians.

S. Luke's usage of 'ecclesia' corresponds with that of his master S. Paul. In S. Paul's epistles we have: (1) *The Church of God*: the whole church, standing over against Jews and Gentiles. 'Jews and Greeks and the church of God[3]'—that is the division at Corinth. (2) Then there is the local church: and each local body is still *the church of God* or *the church* in its district—*which is at Corinth*, etc. In this sense we have 'the churches' e.g. of Galatia, of Asia, 'all the churches,' 'no church.' (3) The word is also used in its original sense to denote the assembly of Christians gathered together, e.g. at Corinth[4]. Hence we have the phrase *en ecclesiā* exactly corresponding to our *in church*, and the phrase in Acts xiv 23, *kat' ecclesian*, may be parallel to the *at home* of ii 46 and mean *at* (the public meeting in) *church*. 'The church in so and so's house' probably includes both the second and third meanings. Lastly, (4) like the Jewish synagogue, the Christian assembly gave its name to the actual building: of this we may find an instance in I Cor xi 22. So *ecclesia* has become *église, chiesa, iglesia*. But philologically the reverse process happened in Teutonic languages, and the building (*kuriakon, the Lord's house*) gave its name to the body which met in it, *kirche, kirk, church*.

---

[1] Not, as in AV, in ix 31.   [2] In the OT there is only one Ecclesia of God. The plural is found only twice and then it refers to meetings for worship (Ps xxvi 12, lxviii 26).   [3] I Cor x 32.   [4] See I Cor xiv throughout and cp. Acts xi 26, xiv 27, xv 22.

DIVISION II
(= Ch. 6—11. 26)

THE EXTENSION OF THE CHURCH TO ANTIOCH AND ADMISSION OF THE GENTILES

From A.D. 31 *to* 42, *under the emperors—Tiberius, Caligula* (37–41), *Claudius* (41): *procurators of Judaea—Pontius Pilate, Marcellus* (36), *Marullus* (37–41): *Herod Agrippa king of Judaea from* 41: *the high-priests being Joseph Caiaphas, Jonathan* (36) *and Theophilus* (37) *sons of Annas, Simon Cantheras* (41).

SECTION I (= Ch. 6—8. 3)
The Acts of Stephen and the first Persecution

We now enter upon a new epoch of continuous development which will lead us without a pause to xi 26, i.e. from Hebrew disciples at Jerusalem to Greek Christians at Antioch. S. Luke fixes upon the first step in that progress. It was a shortcoming in the church, which however was overruled for good and gives occasion for a picture of the first apostolic ordination. It is evident that some interval of time separates chapters v and vi. A great growth has taken place within the church. The Hellenists now form an important element among the disciples; there is a proselyte from Antioch; and we shall soon hear of men of Cyprus and Cyrene, and of disciples at Damascus. There is also an organized body of 'widows' : and the daily ministration has assumed such proportions as to require a new development of the machinery. To meet the need the church creates an office or ministry. Precedent for this was to be found in the appointment of the seventy elders by Moses, and of the Seventy by the Lord[1].

§ 1 *The ordination of the Seven*

6 Now in these days, when the number of the disciples was multiplying, there arose a murmuring of the [2]Grecian Jews against the Hebrews, because their widows were neglected in

---

[1] Num xi 16–25 : Lk x 1. See also Exod xviii 13–26, Deut i 9–15. [2] Gk *Hellenists*. A Bezan text continues *because in the daily ministration the widows of the Hellenists were neglected by the ministers (deacons) of the Hebrews*.

2 the daily ¹ministration. And the twelve called the multitude
of the disciples unto them, and said, It is not ²fit that we
3 should forsake the word of God, and ¹serve tables. ³Look ye
out therefore, brethren, from among you seven men of good
report, full of the Spirit and of wisdom, whom we may
4 appoint over this business. But we will continue stedfastly
5 in prayer, and in the ¹ministry of the word. And the saying
pleased the whole multitude: and they chose Stephen, a man
full of faith and of the Holy Spirit, and Philip, and Prochorus,
and Nicanor, and Timon, and Parmenas, and Nicolas a
6 proselyte of Antioch: ⁴whom they set before the apostles:
and when they had prayed, they laid their hands on them.
7 And the word of God increased; and the number of the
disciples multiplied in Jerusalem exceedingly; and a great
company of the priests were obedient to the faith.

1   Where no provision for the poor and aged was made by the
state, their support was one of the most pressing duties of a religious
body. Among the poor in oriental countries the case of *widows*,
left without any legal protector, was particularly hard. The Jews
had a fund for the relief of widows and orphans, and the church
could not but provide for her own⁵. In return for their support
the widows, like Anna the prophetess⁶, devoted themselves to prayer
and good works. Such widows formed a recognized body; their
names were entered on a roll; and S. Paul in writing to Timothy
devotes a whole chapter to their organization. Already at
Jerusalem there is a body of widows in the church and a little
later we shall find them at Joppa (ix 41).

Their support was a matter of *the daily ministration* or, to be
consistent in translation, *the daily service*⁷. This service we must
connect not only with the distribution of iv 35 but with the daily
meal of ii 46, and *the serving of tables* in verse 2 must include the
literal task of serving the common table, distributing the provisions.
As the Christians had so *multiplied*, it must have been difficult to
secure absolute fairness. In any case practical experience in
almsgiving shews that with the best intentions it is not possible to
avoid complaint. The early Christians were not exempt from the
limitations of human nature, and accordingly *there arose a murmuring*. This is the second instance of infirmity in the church, but it

---
¹ Cognate words in the Greek; either *ministry* and *minister*, or *service* and *serve*.
² Gk *pleasing*.   ³ Bezan has *What is it then, brethren? Look ye out.* Marg
with ℵB has *but* for *therefore*.   ⁴ Bezan *these were set*.   ⁵ II Macc iii 10:
1 Tim v 8.   ⁶ Lk ii 36–8.   ⁷ The Greek *diaconos, diaconein, diaconia* = the
Latin *minister, ministrare, ministratio*, and correspond to the English *servant, serve,
service*, though these last are connected with the Latin *servus (slave)*.

is to be overruled for good, in the same way as the murmuring of the Israelites over the manna in Numbers xi.

The murmuring had a natural source in the general jealousy between *the Hebrews*, or Jews born and bred in the Holy Land, and *the Grecian Jews* or *Hellenists*, i.e. Greek-speaking Jews of foreign origin, such as have been described in ii 5–11. The Hebrew distributors were accused of *passing over* the widows of the Hellenists.

2 The real objects of the murmuring were the apostles; for though no doubt they had subordinates to help in the actual distribution, with them lay the responsibility. *The Twelve* accordingly summoned a meeting of the church. *The multitude of the disciples* does not denote (as does the word used in verse 7 and i 15) a mere crowd: it stands for the whole body as distinct from its officials. Thus it is used of councils, of the citizens of Iconium and Ephesus, and of the general body of Jews or Christians[1]. To the assembled church the apostles make a proposal. Hitherto all authority and office had been concentrated in their hands, but they found it impossible to combine the *service of tables* with the *service of the word*, i.e. the practical work of organization with the spiritual work of preaching and teaching (v 42). The latter, with *prayer* (ii 42, i 14), was the special duty of the apostles and it was not God's *pleasure*[2] that they

3 should neglect it. Accordingly they propose that the former *business* should be entrusted to a new body of officers: and in the creation of such a body begins the differentiation of function in the organism of the church. For the candidates three conditions are stipulated. (1) They must be of good character and that certified by public *testimony*: this condition was always essential to any promotion in the church[3]. (2) They are to be *seven* in number: the limitation is like that of the apostles to twelve; and seven was a sacred and obvious number among the Jews, not to speak of the precedent of the Seventy[4]. (3) There must be some special capacity for the work. (*a*) All church work is really spiritual, so they must be *full of the Spirit*. (*b*) The union of compassion and sympathy with justice and impartiality necessary for organized almsgiving requires a special gift of tact, so they must also be *full of wisdom*. As S. Chrysostom puts it 'it needed great *philosophy* to bear the complaints of the widows.'

5 *The whole multitude* selected the Seven and the list of their names is given, as of the apostles in i 13. They are all Greek. This shews that they were chosen in the Hellenist interest. But it does not follow that they were all Hellenists themselves; for Greek names were common among the Jews, and among the apostles we have a Philip and an Andrew. The seventh however was *a proselyte*,

---

[1] xv 12, xxiii 7, Lk xxiii 1: xiv 4, xix 9: xxv 24, iv 32, xv 30. [2] See note on text, and Jn viii 29. I Jn iii 22. The Bezan text makes it *pleasing to us*: in verse 5 we have *pleasing the multitude*. [3] Cp. xxii 12, I Tim iii 7, v 10, Titus i 6. [4] Among the Roman magistrates titles derived from their number are frequent: e.g. *IIviri, IIIviri, IVviri*.

i.e. not a Jew at all. Proselytes indeed were circumcised and thus joined to the people of God, but this is the first extension of the church outside the literal seed of Abraham. The mention of his home *Antioch* betrays a special interest on the part of the writer and is a forecast of the future. Of *Stephen* and *Philip* we shall hear more, but of the rest nothing is known except their names, for it is a mere conjecture that *Nicolas* was founder of the sect of Nicolaitans[1]. In this the Seven resemble the Twelve. For only three of the apostles find any record beyond that of their names in 'the Acts of the Apostles.' The Seven now chosen are, like Joseph and Matthias in i 23, *set before the apostles*; and they ordain them to their office by *laying on of their hands* with *prayer*.

S. Luke evidently means us to take this first instance as a typical picture of apostolic ordination, and we should compare the briefer notices in xiii 3, xiv 23. In the process we must distinguish (*a*) the *election* from (*b*) the *ordination* proper—both together constituting (*c*) the *appointment*. (*a*) The method of election illustrates the constitution of the church. As yet the only authority which we have come across has been that of the Twelve: now however there appears to be another seat of authority, viz. 'the whole multitude.' The apostles like all rulers are liable to criticism; but 'they make answer for themselves' to the multitude; S. Chrysostom comments 'so ought it to be now also.' As rulers they summon the church; but they lay their proposal before it and the meeting gives its consent. Though themselves the best judges of character[2] they leave the selection of the Seven to the multitude, and its choice is justified by the event. (*c*) The apostles say *we will appoint* (verse 3): but the contrasted and emphatic *we* in the next verse shews that in verse 3 they are speaking as representatives of the whole church by which the appointment is made. (*b*) Still there remains a part peculiar to the apostles, viz. what we now call the ordination, the ceremony by which is conferred the necessary spiritual authority or 'character.' The multitude present the Seven to the apostles, and the latter (reserving the right to refuse an unworthy candidate) ordain them by prayer and by laying on of hands. The whole church, then, appoints: the multitude elect and present: the gift of the Spirit required for office in the church is conferred by the apostles, who themselves had received the gift from above.

The *ordination* comprises two elements, (*a*) *prayer* accompanied with (*b*) a *symbolical action*. In this it is akin to the whole worship and action of the church, but especially to the two sacraments of Holy Baptism and Holy Eucharist. Ordination partakes of the sacramental character because with the laying on of hands is conveyed an inward spiritual grace. The gift of the Spirit is indeed not expressly mentioned, and before ordination they were 'full of the Spirit.' But (1) that endowment they shared with the whole Christian body. Entrance to the church was sealed by the gift of the Spirit[3]: but this

---

[1] Rev ii 6, 15; but the name is probably symbolical. [2] S. Peter reads the hearts of Ananias and Sapphira in v 1-11. [3] ii 38: cp. viii 17, x 44, xix 6.

initial gift did not preclude further gifts of the Spirit—as we see in the case of the apostles themselves, if we compare iv 31 with ii 4. (2) S. Paul definitely connects the bestowal of a *charisma* or spiritual gift with his laying on of hands upon Timothy[1]: indeed we may assume that some spiritual gift always accompanied apostolic laying on of hands. (3) Certainly in the case of S. Stephen and S. Philip the history shews a great increase of spiritual power after their ordination. This is evident, not only from their preaching, but from the working of wonders, which had hitherto been restricted to the Twelve[2].

It has however been contended that laying on of hands was simply the formal sign of appointment to an office: thus new members of the Sanhedrin were admitted with laying on of hands, by which no gift of the Spirit was supposed to be conveyed. In answer we must first ask why was *Laying on of hands* adopted for such a sign? What did it symbolize? In the OT (1) laying on of hands was the usual form of blessing. (2) In the sacrifice of a sin-offering the offerer first laid his hands upon the victim: and when the Levites were consecrated to the service of God, the children of Israel laid hands upon them. Lastly (3) when Moses appointed Joshua to be his successor, he laid hands upon him[3]. In the NT the Lord laid on hands when he blessed little children, and frequently in healing. After him the apostles laid on hands in healing, confirming, and ordaining[4]. In all these cases the laying on of hands symbolizes the establishment of a vital connexion between two persons through which some gift or power abiding in the one flows into the other. This is most obvious in cases of healing and blessing. In the case of the sin-offering, the Israelite by the laying on of his hands conveyed his guilt into the victim. The Levites were accepted by God in lieu of the firstborn; and when the children of Israel laid hands on them, they gave them a share, we might almost say, in their own personality, so that the Levites could truly represent them. Similarly in an appointment one who holds the office conveys to the candidate the power and authority in virtue of which he exercises it. Thus Moses was to 'put of his own honour upon' Joshua; and 'Joshua was full of the spirit of wisdom because Moses had laid his hands upon him[5].' But in the Christian church the power and authority by which ministry is exercised is that of the Holy Ghost: the gift of the Spirit, then, is conveyed by the laying on of the apostles' hands. For as yet the apostles being the sole officers were the only possessors of the *charisma* necessary for ruling, and only by their hands could it be conveyed to others[6].

---

[1] II Tim i 6, I iv 14. [2] Cp. vi 8, viii 6, 7 with v 12. [3] (1) Gen xlviii 14 etc.: (2) Lev i 4 etc.; Num viii 10: (3) Num xxvii 23. [4] Mk x 16: Mk i 41 etc.: Acts v 12, xxviii 8 (iii 7, ix 41): viii 17, xix 6: vi 6. [5] Num xxvii 20, Deut xxxiv 9. [6] Cp. viii 14–16. S. Chrysostom's comment is 'See how the writer avoids all superfluity. He does not say how—but simply *they were ordained with prayer.* For this is ordination. The hand of man is laid on, but all is the work of God, and it is his hand which touches the head of the candidate, if he is rightly ordained.'

Another question arises, *To what office were they ordained?* The almost universal tradition of the church, going back at least as far as Irenaeus[1], sees in them the first Deacons. Were they then 'deacons'? It is really too early in the history to put the question in such a definite shape, and so far as a definite answer can be given we should be inclined to say that they certainly were not deacons in the subsequent technical sense. For (1) they are never called 'deacons,' indeed the word does not occur in the Acts at all[2]: their official title is 'the Seven' (xxi 8). (2) They were identified with deacons no doubt because of the 'service of tables,' a service which in its turn also reacted upon the conception of the deacon's duties. But it would give an inadequate idea of the Seven to limit their work to this serving of tables. There were probably 'ministers' under them who assisted in the actual distribution and waiting at table: such ministers (*deacons*) are mentioned as already in existence by a Bezan text. The Seven were appointed 'over this business,' i.e. they were to superintend and bear the responsibility in the place of the apostles. Accordingly they rank next the apostles. Stephen and Philip become leading figures in the church, and after their ordination they are also conspicuous in the ministry of the word. In chapter viii we find Philip doing the work of an 'evangelist,' and that is his official title when he reappears later in the history (xxi 8). (3) The work of the Seven was of but short duration: it was broken off by the death of Stephen and the subsequent persecution. After that we hear no more of their office. In their place we meet with presbyters, who seem to be their successors. They even succeed to them in their special 'service of tables' or almsgiving (xi 30). In the Gentile churches in Galatia, and at Ephesus, S. Paul appoints presbyters; deacons we hear of nowhere; and it would be strange if the apostles in creating the first new office in the church were to pass over the presbyterate and appoint a diaconate.

These considerations lead to the conclusion that, as S. Chrysostom says, the Seven were 'neither presbyters nor deacons.' Their office was unique: i.e. unique in the same sense as was the apostolate. Indications of this are given by their title of 'the Seven,' corresponding to 'the Twelve,' and by the full record of their names in vi 5. Their relation to the Twelve would be like that of 'the Seventy'; and like the Seventy they have a type in the seventy elders appointed to assist Moses in the rule of Israel. But though unique, the Seven, like the Twelve, had successors. At first all the future orders of church ministers were embodied in the apostolic college, from which body they were derived by differentiation. The first order differentiated is that of the Seven. So we may look upon them as containing implicitly the remaining orders. Though neither a presbyterate nor diaconate, they include both offices and are the ancestors of both presbyters and deacons.

7   The ordination of the Seven was followed by a period of

---

[1] But see S. Chrysostom below. He is quoted and approved by the Trullan Council of A.D. 692 (canon 16).   [2] Except in a Bezan text at this passage.

progress[1]. For it restored harmony and set the apostles free for greater devotion to the service of the word. The seed of *the word* grew and had a rich *increase*. The kingdom spread in inward power like the leaven in the meal, and externally like the mustard tree. *The number of the disciples* reached its highest point before the disaster that was to come. Among them was *a great crowd of the priests*. This is not surprising. For on the one hand adherence to the new faith did not interfere with the performance of their duties in the temple; on the other there was a great gulf between the ordinary priests and the class of ruling and wealthy 'high-priests.' The latter acted towards their brethren like tyrants: some of them went so far as forcibly to rob them of their tithes[2]. So when a large body of the priests joined the apostles, it would have the effect, politically, of a very practical protest against their Sadducean rulers: it had something of the effect of a political demonstration: and we notice that S. Luke uses a word (*obey*) which would indicate a transference of allegiance[3].

The numbers and outward results, however, were not the most important consequence. That was the activity of S. Stephen, which was started by this ordination and was to end in dissipating (for the moment) these results and threatening the very existence of the church. The church was thus to begin to realize the law of the cross, viz. that death must precede new life, and destruction of the old the reconstruction of a greater temple.

§ 2 *The ministry and arrest of S. Stephen*

Almost as soon as S. Stephen appears upon the stage his career is cut short. But its vital importance for the history is obvious from the pages of the Acts. His speech is the longest in the book; it is as long as the three sermons of S. Paul put together. S. Stephen also, and not an apostle, had the glory of being the first to lay down his life 'for the Name.' Again his preaching caused a revolution in the attitude of the Jews to the church and his death was the signal for the first persecution. And yet S. Stephen was 'a new man,' not apparently one of the original body, but a Hellenist. But in this fact lies the whole secret. As soon as the church reaches the broader field of Hellenism, then struggle and advance begin. With the wider experience and broader training of a Hellenist Stephen was able to look on 'the faith' (verse 7) in its wider bearings, in its relation to the world at large. So he perceived, and evidently was the first to perceive clearly, the incidental and temporary character of the Mosaic law with the temple and all its worship. This

---

[1] The language taken from Exodus i 7 (Acts vii 17) reminds us of the progress of Israel in Egypt. Cp. also Lk viii 5-8, xiii 19-21. [2] Such at least was the conduct of the Ananias of Josephus *Ant.* xx 9. 2. [3] The idea of obedience is especially characteristic of S. Peter (I Pet i 2, 14, 22). But they were obedient not so much to the apostles as to *the faith*, a Pauline idea: cp. Rom i 5 *obedience of faith*, vi 17.

was the fruitful germ of doctrine which S. Paul was afterwards to carry out to its full logical and far-reaching consequence, viz. the perfect equality of Jew and Gentile in the church of God. This it was which aroused first against S. Stephen the hostility of his fellow Hellenists, and afterwards against S. Paul not merely the implacable hatred of his fellow countrymen, but bitter opposition among his fellow churchmen.

S. Stephen then is the connecting link between S. Peter and S. Paul—a link indispensable to the chain. Stephen, and not Gamaliel, was the real master of S. Paul. And the main significance of these two chapters is summed up at their close in the dramatic mention of *a young man named Saul.* In S. Stephen we see how little necessary connexion there is between length of time and greatness of work. He is the type of the man who 'being made perfect in a little while, fulfils long years' (Wisdom iv 13). His career was abruptly cut short; its external results were nothing or worse than nothing. And yet in the account of his work and words is written the history of the second chapter of the church's life, which is the turning point of the Acts. For 'the work' of Stephen lasts on till chapter xii (see xi 19), and then it is taken up by his greater pupil and successor—Paul.

Of Stephen's personal history we know nothing beyond what is here recorded. He was a Hellenist, that is a Greek-speaking Jew from abroad: his name is Greek and means *Crown.* The scene of the disputation, *the Synagogue of the Libertines, Cyrenians, and Alexandrians,* ought to give some clue to his origin. His speech savours of Alexandrine culture, and it is to be noticed that the word *wisdom* occurs four times in these two chapters and nowhere else in the Acts. Wisdom was the characteristic of the Jewish theologians of Alexandria and it was introduced into the church at Corinth by the Alexandrian Apollos. It might however be pointed out that men of Cyrene were notable in the early church (p. 23). And a third alternative remains: he may have been a Libertine. A *libertine* was a (Roman) *freedman;* and as the community of Jews at Rome had its origin in the thousands of Jewish captives taken to Rome by Pompey and afterwards set at liberty, the Libertines here would specially denote the Roman Jews. S. Stephen then, if a Libertine, may have been among the *sojourners from Rome* of ii 10: but see below on verse 9. Unlike the Twelve, but like S. Paul, Stephen was a man of learning: his speech shews that he was instructed in the wisdom of the rabbis as well as of the Alexandrians. Once more, if we contrast his address to the Sanhedrin *Brethren and fathers* with S. Peter's *Rulers of the people and elders,* we might suppose that he was a man of some position. In this he would again resemble S. Paul.

8 And Stephen, full of [1]grace and power, wrought great
9 wonders and signs among the people. But there arose certain of them that were of the synagogue called *the synagogue* of the Libertines, and of the Cyrenians, and of the

---

[1] AV reads *faith.*

VI 8-9   DISPUTES IN THE SYNAGOGUE

Alexandrians, and of them of Cilicia [1]and Asia, disputing
10 with Stephen. And they were not able to withstand the
11 wisdom and the Spirit by which he spake[2]. Then they
suborned men, which said, We have heard him speak blas-
12 phemous words against Moses, and *against* God. And they
stirred up the people, and the elders, and the scribes, and
came upon him, and seized him, and brought him into the
13 council, and set up false witnesses, which said, This man
ceaseth not to speak words against this holy place, and the
14 law : for we have heard him say, that this Jesus of Nazareth
shall destroy this place, and shall change the customs which
15 Moses delivered unto us. And all that sat in the council,
fastening their eyes on him, saw his face as it had been the
face of an angel[3].

8   Verse 8 describes S. Stephen's ministry, which was like that of
the apostles and included preaching and the working of signs. After
his ordination he was *full of grace and power* (see verse 3). From
Lk iv 22 we should gather that the *grace* was upon his lips, and
refers to *the wisdom with which he spake*. *Power* was the direct
consequence of the gift of *the Spirit*, and had been a special characteristic of the apostles[4]: now it shewed itself in Stephen's *speaking*
and also in *great wonders and signs*, which he *wrought among the
common people*[5]. But there was another sphere of his ministry
revealed by the sudden climax now to be described.

9   This work was *disputing* in *the synagogue* with his fellow
Hellenists, and it marks a new era both in manner and place. From
preaching in the temple we come to arguing in the synagogues.
Argument in the synagogue—that was to be the great labour of
S. Paul in the future. But the synagogue had been the scene of
the teaching of a greater than either. The Lord's ministry in
Galilee had begun in a synagogue[6]. Even in Jerusalem itself the
Jews needed besides the temple, the place of sacrifice, buildings for
reading of the scriptures and prayer, instruction and exhortation.
The Jewish tradition that there were 480 synagogues in the city is
no doubt a Jewish fable. But there must have been many synagogues,
with regular and distinct congregations of their own. The synagogue
to which S. Stephen belonged was one belonging to Hellenists ; its
name was '*of the Libertines, Cyrenians, and Alexandrians.*' It is
surprising to find these numerous and influential bodies of Hellenists

---

[1] Some MSS (AD) omit *and Asia*.   [2] Bezan adds *because they were convicted
by him with all boldness. Therefore not being able to face* (xxvii 15) *the truth* [they
suborned*.   [3] Bezan adds *standing in the midst of them*.   [4] See i 8, iv 33.
[5] and which no doubt won him 'favour,' ii 47, iv 33.   [6] Cp. Mk i 21-8, Lk iv
16-30.

sharing in one synagogue[1]: but probably they possessed other synagogues besides, and this represented a peculiar combination. It is again surprising to find the Libertines forming one in this trio. For as has been said they represented chiefly Jews from Rome. An early and not improbable conjecture was to read *Libystine*, viz. of Libya; for Libya (ii 10) was adjacent to Cyrene and Alexandria. Later on, however, the discussions attracted outsiders, chiefly other Hellenists from Cilicia and Asia, i.e. the Roman province of Asia in the west of Asia Minor. Jews from Asia we shall meet again in Jerusalem (xxi 27); and among the Jews from Cilicia was an ardent and extreme Pharisee, who it may be conjectured was the leading spirit in the actions now to be narrated. He was that 'young man named Saul' (vii 58).

The ministry of Stephen then stirred up the opposition of the Hellenists: they *rose up* (v 17). As the Christian Hellenist first saw the full meaning of the faith, so the unbelieving Hellenists were the first to realize the doctrinal significance and logical outcome of Stephen's teaching. On either side it was the Hellenist Jews
10 who possessed the deepest insight. But his opponents were no match for Stephen in argument. He was '*full of the Spirit*,' and had the Lord's promise of a mouth and *wisdom* (Lk xxi 15). And on the other side, as the Sanhedrin in ch. iv 14–16 could not gainsay the facts, so now the Hellenists could not but agree with the principles on which Stephen based his argument. For these principles, such as the spiritual character of religion, the Hellenists with their wider knowledge of the world had learnt to appreciate far more than the Jews at home confined within the narrow limits of Palestine. Baffled in argument they had recourse to the device of defeated but obstinate disputants—viz. an appeal to popular prejudice. It was Stephen's conclusions which they *resisted*, and they knew well that in the ears of the common people his 'liberal views' would sound
11 like rank blasphemy. Accordingly they instigated men to spread among *the people* and among the Pharisees (for, taking away 'the rulers,' *the elders and scribes* stand for the Pharisaic party) the news that Stephen was *speaking blasphemy against Moses and God*. This was the fatal charge. Hitherto the disciples had been popular with the people and tolerated by the Pharisees, but to breathe a suspicion of disloyalty to Moses was to blast their popularity at once. Moses to the Jews summed up all their worship and polity. S. Peter himself had appealed to Moses, and his contention had been
12 that Jesus was a second Moses. *The people* then and the Pharisees were *greatly stirred*, and under cover of the excitement the Hellenists seized an opportunity of suddenly arresting Stephen and *dragged* him with violence to the Sanhedrin. The loss of the people's favour has entirely changed the situation: contrast iv 1, 21, and v 26.

---

[1] The Jews formed one of the four classes of the inhabitants of Cyrene, and occupied two out of the five wards of Alexandria. The rabbis mention a 'synagogue of the Alexandrians' built at their own expense (J. Lightfoot, *ad loc.*).

13 In the Sanhedrin also a regular charge was preferred. Stephen was accused of 'blasphemy.' Blasphemy was technically to sin against God 'with a high hand,' i.e. wilfully, in such a way as to break the covenant. Such sins were—any kind of idolatry, breaking the sabbath, neglecting circumcision, cursing by the Name[1]. The penalty was death by stoning. The charge had to be substantiated by 'two or three witnesses[2]': and accordingly *false witnesses* were set up. The falseness lay not in the actual words reported, but in the intention—wresting S. Stephen's words from their context and giving them a false meaning. This is that half truth which is worse than a lie, because it cannot be flatly denied. The blasphemy of which Stephen was accused was *speaking words*—and that constantly—*against* (1) *this holy place*, i.e. the temple, to which the senate-house was adjacent, (2) *and the law*. The charge is
14 explained by the evidence of the witnesses. They quote this 'word' of Stephen's—'*This Jesus of Nazareth shall destroy this place and change the customs which Moses delivered unto us.*' That is, 'the place which God has chosen to place his name there' is to be robbed of its peculiar sanctity; and the law of Moses, contained in the Pentateuch, with its vast commentary of the 'traditions of the elders,' in other words, the whole Jewish system of civil and religious life, is to come to an end.
15 Stephen heard his own words repeated, and he could not deny them. He had no doubt declared that the law would pass away, but only in the sense of being perfectly fulfilled (Mt v 17). And now the injustice of the charge made his face flash fire[3]. But he was also '*full of the Holy Ghost*' (vii 55): he remembered that he was standing where the Lord had once stood: he realized the crisis, how much turned on the witness which he would bear, on what defence of the gospel he would make; and at the thought of the opportunity, his face glowed with enthusiasm also. The unwonted sight arrested the eyes of *all who were sitting in the council*, not only of the judges but also of the officers and disciples. Among them was one on whose memory the sight imprinted itself so as never to be forgotten. Years afterwards he learnt that it was indeed the reflection of the divine glory which made Stephen's *face* to shine *as the face of an angel*[4]. He was that Saul the Pharisee, who was then a prime mover in the charge, and to whom we probably owe this report of the scene. The momentary silence was then broken by the judicial voice of the high-priest, Caiaphas, calling upon the accused for his defence.

We seem to have been reading a repetition of the trial of the Lord. The parallel with it here is much more striking than in the hearings of the apostles. S. Stephen's was a regular trial which

---

[1] Exod xxii 20, Deut xvii 2–7: Num xv 32–6, Exod xxxi 14: Gen xvii 14: Levit xxiv 10–23.   [2] Deut xvii 6.   [3] Like that of the angel in Judges xiii 6. With the injustice cp. Naboth's experience in I K xxi 12, 13.   [4] See vii 55 and II Cor iii 18.

ended in death. Like Jesus Stephen was accused of blasphemy, and by false witnesses; even the charge ran in almost the same words—'destroy the temple.' To both the high-priest made appeal: but there the parallel ends. The Christ held his peace: the disciple made an elaborate 'apology[1].'

§ 3 *S. Stephen's defence*

At first sight S. Stephen's speech seems baffling and disappointing. There is no direct answer to the charge; and the name of Jesus Christ does not occur at all. An obvious reason is that he was cut short and his defence left incomplete. But deeper consideration will shew that it does furnish a complete reply. In fact the speech is unique. It corresponds exactly with the time, place, and audience: at the same time it is marked by a strong individuality. It stands midway between the speeches of S. Peter in chapters ii and iii and of S. Paul in chapter xiii; but though S. Stephen has points of contact with each apostle[2], his presentation of the gospel is entirely his own. As special characteristics we note at once—the use made of the OT, revealing an Alexandrine training; the criticism of materialistic religion (verse 48), betraying a Hellenist; the prominence of the ministry of angels, due to Jewish influence; the mention of 'the *church* in the wilderness'; and in Christian theology the ideas of redemption and mediation (vv. 35, 38). More personal traits are the strong irony, as e.g. in verse 25, and the fiery outburst of passion at the close (51-53) which stands almost alone in the Acts. The speech is also full of expressions which are not found elsewhere in the NT, e.g. *the God of glory, possession, sustenance, deal-subtilly, avenge, redeemer* (35), *make-a-calf, in-their-turn, stiffnecked, resist, the coming*: in the Acts *traitors* (52) and *Son of man* (56) do not occur again. We can clearly trace the influence of S. Stephen upon S. Paul[2]. But the writer of the Epistle to the Hebrews is more decidedly of Stephen's school. He makes a similarly elaborate use of the OT, and recounts the history of

---

[1] This word in its original meaning of a legal answer or defence exactly describes the speech of S. Stephen and those of S. Paul below. So Newman in his *Apologia pro vita sua*.   [2] S. PETER like Stephen goes back to the *covenant* with *Abraham* (verse 8—iii 25), lays stress on the *tomb of the patriarch* David (16—ii 29); the *ruler* corresponds to *prince* (35—iii 15), with *living* oracles cp. *prince of life* (38—iii 15); Peter too uses Moses' prophecy (37—iii 22), the words *denied, foreshewed, murderer* (35, 52—iii 14, 18: cp. 24), and the name of *the Righteous* (52—iii 14). S. PAUL follows S. Stephen in reviewing the history of Israel down to *David* (xiii 17-22). These ideas also are common to both: God punishing by giving men up to their own wills (vii 42—Rom i 24-28): God does not dwell in temples (vii 48—xvii 24): the law was ministered by angels (vii 53—Gal iii 19, 20). The germ of S. Paul's doctrine of the law is contained in S. Stephen's speech: see below, and cp. the *Righteous (just)* of vii 52 with *justify* in xiii 39. *A time of forty years*, and *fulfil*, occur in both speeches, vii 30—xiii 18 and 25. *Appeared* is specially characteristic of S. Stephen's speech (vv. 2, 26, 30, 35) and it seems to have been S. Paul's word (xiii 31, xxvi 16, I Cor xv 5-8). *Promise, oracles*, and the idea of *redemption* are common to all three (vii 17, ii 33, 39, xiii 32: vii 38, I Pet iv 11, Rom iii 2: vii 35, I Pet i 18, 1 Tim ii 6, Tit ii 14): the same words also mark the Epistle to the Hebrews (*promise* frequently, *oracles* v 12, *redemption* ix 12).

'the fathers[1].' He draws out explicitly the comparison between Moses and the Christ; and in his arguments refers to the tabernacle instead of the temple, as that 'which had been appointed' by God[2]. The revelation of God is described by him as a 'speaking' or 'talking' to men[3], and the ministry of angels is the ground of a special argument[4].

The charge against S. Stephen was (A) in general, that of treason against Moses and therefore against God, for Moses substituting a pretender Jesus of Nazareth. (B) In particular he had spoken 'blasphemy' against (1) the temple and (2) the law. In answer Stephen gives a summary of the history of the chosen people from the call of Abraham to the days of David. Of such retrospection the Jews were fond: and similar summaries are very frequent in the sacred and other contemporary books[5]. Under persecution, the Jews recalled God's past mercies in order to renew their trust and courage. In adversity, especially after the destruction of Jerusalem, they pondered on their past history to find an answer to their profound perplexity—why had God dealt thus with his chosen? The history revealed it: it was a divine judgement on the sin of Israel. The Christian apologist studied the past to find in it the purpose and plan of God working towards its fulfilment in the revelation of Jesus Christ, and to learn from it the meaning of that revelation. So S. Stephen goes back to Abraham: S. Luke, in his Gospel, still earlier—to Adam, the beginning of the human race: S. John earlier still—to 'the beginning' itself, before the world was. To such writers the 'prophecy' was the purpose of God which was as it were wrapped up in the external history and unveiled to those whose eyes were opened by the Holy Ghost. To this purpose of God hidden in the history of Israel Stephen, like S. Peter, makes appeal.

The history, when unveiled or revealed, vindicated the claims of Jesus of Nazareth. It shewed him to be (1) the Saviour, Redeemer and so Ruler of his people, verses 25, 35, 36; (2) the true Prophet and Mediator between God and his people, verses 37, 38; (3) the Righteous one, that is the Fulfiller and therefore the End of the Law. Though the name of the Christ is not once mentioned, Stephen is all the time 'preaching Jesus.' He preaches him in his types, especially in Joseph (vv. 9-16) and Moses (20-43). The scriptures contained prophecies of the Christ in word, but the lives of 'the fathers' were prophecies in deed. There is one law of righteousness, and in 'learning obedience' saints such as Joseph and Moses (and indeed Israel itself, the chosen people) had passed through experiences similar to those of the Christ and so they foreshewed his sufferings and the glories that should follow (I Pet i 11, 12). What was unique in the Lord's case was the entire submission of his will to the Father, to which the greatest saints could not attain. Argument based upon type or allegory does not commend itself to the modern mind, but in those days it was familiar

---

[1] Hebr xi.   [2] iii 1-6, xi 23-9: viii 2, 5, ix 1 etc.: cp. Acts vii 44.   [3] Hebr i 1, 2, ii 2 etc.: cp. Acts vii 6, 38, 44.   [4] Hebr i 5-ii 9: cp. also ii 2 with Acts vii 53.   [5] See e.g. Deut i-iii, Josh xxiv, Nehem ix, Judith v.

and popular. S. Stephen in any case indulges in no extravagances, and his hearers would thoroughly understand him. They would have recognized in Joseph and in Moses portraits of Jesus of Nazareth; they would have felt the irony, by which in the jealousy of Joseph's brethren and the dulness of Moses' contemporaries their own folly was laid bare[1]; and the words made them gnash their teeth.

(*A*) So far from blaspheming God S. Stephen looks up to the God of glory and bases his defence on God's true will. He traces that will in the history of Israel and shews that as it was God who sent Moses, so it is God who has raised up the new Prophet (vv. 35-7). But the main defence turns upon Moses. Quotations have already been given to illustrate the position he held in Jewish estimation (p. 54). One more will better enable us to realize the mind of Stephen's judges. In the *Assumption of Moses*[2] Joshua speaks of him as 'the sacred spirit who was worthy of the Lord, manifold and incomprehensible, the lord of the word, who was faithful in all things, God's chief prophet throughout the earth, the most perfect teacher in the world...advocate to offer prayers on the behalf [of Israel]...the great messenger (angel) who every hour day and night had his knees fixed to the earth, praying...calling to mind the covenant of the fathers and propitiating the Lord with an oath.' Now so far from blaspheming Moses, Stephen's contention is that of S. Peter—as Moses was the founder of Israel, so Jesus is a second and a greater Moses[3]. As S. Peter had shewn, Moses in his own words had declared himself to be but a figure of the prophet to come (*like unto me*). But the special addition of S. Stephen was to shew that Moses and the Christ had passed through the same experience: and that not so much in their deliverance of the people as in their rejection by their own people. If the crucifixion of Jesus was a stumblingblock to his audience, Moses their founder had been rejected by his generation. The comparison between the Jews of the present and their fathers was too obvious, and led to a scene of passion which cut short Stephen's speech. But he had already been indirectly dealing with the two specific charges.

(*B*) (1) He had been secretly undermining the doctrine of the unique sacredness of the temple[4], while he was shewing that God's chief dealings with his people—in promise, redemption, and covenant—took place before the temple existed. Again, the most sacred places happened to be outside the 'holy land.' God had appeared in Ur of the Chaldees, and at Sinai: Moses had been a sojourner in Midian: Egypt was the scene of Joseph's glory and the great deliverance of the people: the bodies of the patriarchs were buried in schismatical Samaria. But in truth it was not the temple, but the tabernacle, which God had ordained: and as soon as the temple was built, prophets

---

[1] vv. 9, 25: with 9 cp. v 17. [2] Ch. xi (Charles' trans.). In Jn vi a recorded miracle of Moses outweighs with the people an actual miracle of the Lord witnessed by their own eyes. [3] Compare *this Moses* (vv. 35, 37, 38, 40) with *this Jesus* (vi 14), *this man* (v 28). [4] vv. 2-4, 9-16, 29-34, 44-50.

began to declare the spirituality and omnipresence of God. This doctrine was brought home to the Hellenist by his close contact with heathen temples and idols, and S. Stephen here uses a name by which the deity was known among the Gentiles also—*the Highest*[1]. S. Paul proclaimed the doctrine in Athens in almost the same words: the Lord himself had prophesied its recognition—'the hour cometh when neither in this mountain nor in Jerusalem shall ye worship the Father' (Jn iv 21).

(2) The answer on the second point, the law, is less obvious[2]. But we find in S. Stephen all the germs at least of the teaching afterwards developed by S. Paul. First, the promise was given before the law. Then, when the law was given, Stephen recognizes that it was 'holy and righteous and good,' for it was *living oracles*. But the Israelites had been unable to keep it: as soon as it was given, they made a calf, and next they exchanged the divinely appointed tabernacle for a temple. There was indeed one who had fulfilled the law, the Righteous one, viz. Jesus: and S. Stephen might have gone on to declare the doctrine of justification. But at this moment his feelings overmastered him, and he drove home the inability of man to keep the law by a personal retort, 'It is not I, but you who by your murder of the Righteous have broken the law.' This was the end; and it was reserved for one of his present hearers—S. Paul—to complete his doctrine by proclaiming that *by this man everyone that believeth is justified from all things, from which ye could not be justified by the law of Moses* (xiii 39).

7 And the high priest said, Are these things so? (2) And he said,

Brethren and fathers, hearken. [3]The God of glory appeared unto our father Abraham, when he was in Meso-
3 potamia, before he dwelt in Haran, and said unto him, 'Get thee out of thy land, and from thy kindred, and come into
4 the land which I shall shew thee. Then came he out of the land of the Chaldæans, and dwelt in Haran: and from thence, when his father was dead, *God* removed him into this land,
5 wherein ye now dwell: and he gave him none inheritance in it, [5]no, not so much as to set his foot on: [6]and he promised that he would give it to him in possession, and to his seed
6 after him, when *as yet* he had no child. And God spake on this wise, [7]that his seed should sojourn in a strange land, and

---

[1] verse 48: cp. xvi 17. [2] vv. 5, 17, 38–43, 51–53. [3] Blass' edition of Bezan text has only *The God of glory appeared unto our father Abraham, and said unto him, Get thee out...shew thee. And he [removed him into this land*, etc. See Gen xi 27–xii 5. [4] Gen xii 1. [5] Deut ii 5. [6] Gen xvii 8 (xlviii 4). [7] Gen xv 13, 14.

that they should bring them into bondage, and entreat them
7 evil, four hundred years. And the nation to which they shall
be in bondage will I judge, said God: and after that shall
8 they come forth, ¹and serve me in this place. ²And he gave
him the covenant of circumcision: and so *Abraham* begat
Isaac, and circumcised him the eighth day; and Isaac *begat*
Jacob, and Jacob the twelve patriarchs.
9 And the patriarchs, ³moved with jealousy against Joseph,
10 sold him into Egypt: and ⁴God was with him, and delivered
him out of all his afflictions, ⁵and gave him favour and
wisdom before Pharaoh king of Egypt; and he made him
11 governor over Egypt and all his house. ⁶Now there came a
famine over all Egypt and Canaan, and great affliction: and
12 our fathers found no sustenance. But when Jacob heard that
there was corn in Egypt, he sent forth our fathers the first
13 time. And at the second time ⁷Joseph was made known
to his brethren; and Joseph's race became manifest unto
14 Pharaoh. ⁸And Joseph sent, and called to him Jacob his
father, and all his kindred, threescore and fifteen souls.
15 And Jacob went down into Egypt; and ⁹he died, himself,
16 and our fathers; and they were carried over unto Shechem,
and laid in the tomb ¹⁰that Abraham bought for a price in
silver of the sons of Hamor in Shechem.
17 But as the time of the promise drew nigh, which God
¹¹vouchsafed unto Abraham, ¹²the people grew and multiplied
18 in Egypt, till there arose another king over Egypt, which
19 knew not Joseph. The same dealt subtilly with our race,
and evil entreated our fathers, that they should cast out their
20 babes to the end they might not live. At which season Moses
was born, ¹³and was ¹⁴exceeding fair; and he was nourished
21 three months in his father's house: and when he was cast
out, Pharaoh's daughter took him up, and nourished him for
22 her own son. And Moses was instructed in all the wisdom

---

¹ Exod iii 12. ² Gen xvii 9-12, xxi 2-4 (Lk ii 21). ³ Gen xxxvii
11, 28. ⁴ xxxix 2, 21, 23. ⁵ xli 40-46 (Ps cv 17-23). ⁶ xli 54, xlii 2.
⁷ xlv 1-4, 16. ⁸ xlv 9, xlvi 6, 27. ⁹ xlix 33, l 13, 25, Exod xiii 19, Josh
xxiv 32. ¹⁰ Gen xxiii. ¹¹ Gk *agreed to* (Mt xiv 7), AV reads *sworn*.
¹² Exod i 7, 8: 10, 11: 15-17. ¹³ ii 2, 5, 10. ¹⁴ Gk *fair to God*—a Hebraism:
cp. Gen xxiii 6, Jonah iii 3, II Cor x 4.

of the Egyptians; and he was mighty in his words and
23 works. ¹But when he was well-nigh forty years old, it came
into his heart to visit his brethren the children of Israel.
24 And seeing one *of them* suffer wrong, he defended him, and
25 avenged him that was oppressed, smiting the Egyptian: and
he supposed that his brethren understood how that God by
his hand was giving them ²deliverance; but they understood
26 not. ³And the day following he appeared unto them as they
strove, and would have set them at one again, saying, Sirs, ye
27 are brethren; why do ye wrong one to another? But he
that did his neighbour wrong thrust him away, saying, Who
28 made thee a ruler and a judge over us? Wouldest thou kill
29 me, as thou killedst the Egyptian yesterday? And Moses fled
at this saying, and ⁴became a sojourner in the land of Midian,
30 where he begat two sons. And when forty years were
fulfilled, ⁵an angel appeared to him in the wilderness of
31 mount Sinai, in a flame of fire in a bush. And when Moses
saw it, he wondered at the sight: and as he drew near to
32 behold, there came ⁶a voice of the Lord, ⁷I am the God of
thy fathers, the God of Abraham, and of Isaac, and of Jacob.
33 And Moses trembled, and durst not behold. And the Lord
said unto him, ⁸Loose the shoes from thy feet: for the place
34 whereon thou standest is holy ground. ⁹I have surely seen
the affliction of my people which is in Egypt, and have heard
their groaning, and I am come down to deliver them: ¹⁰and
now come, I will send thee into Egypt.
35 This Moses whom they ¹¹refused, saying, Who made thee
a ruler and a judge? him hath God sent *to be* both a ruler
and a ¹²deliverer with the hand of the angel which appeared
36 to him in the bush. This man led them forth, ¹³having
wrought wonders and signs in Egypt, and in the Red sea,
37 and in the wilderness forty years. This is that Moses, which
said unto the children of Israel, ¹⁴A prophet shall God raise
38 up unto you from among your brethren, like unto me. This

---

¹ Exod ii 11, 12: Gk *when his time of forty years was being filled* (verse 30, ii 1, etc.: xiii 18).   ² Gk *salvation*.   ³ Exod ii 13–15.   ⁴ ii 22.   ⁵ Or *the angel [of the Lord* AV] Exod iii 2 foll.   ⁶ Or *the voice*.   ⁷ iii 6.
⁸ iii 5.   ⁹ iii 7, 8.   ¹⁰ iii 10.   ¹¹ Gk *denied*.   ¹² Marg *redeemer*.
¹³ Exod vii 3.   ¹⁴ Deut xviii 15 (Acts iii 22).

is he that was in the ¹church in the wilderness with the angel
which spake to him in the mount Sinai, and with our fathers:
39 who received living oracles to give unto us: to whom our
fathers would not be obedient, but thrust him from them,
40 and turned back in their hearts unto Egypt, saying unto
Aaron, ²Make us gods which shall go before us: for as for
this Moses, which led us forth out of the land of Egypt, we
41 wot not what is become of him. And they made a calf in
those days, and ³brought a sacrifice unto the idol, and
42 rejoiced in the works of their hands. But God turned, and
gave them up to serve the host of heaven; as it is written in
the book of the prophets,

⁴'Did ye offer unto me slain beasts and sacrifices
Forty years in the wilderness, O house of Israel?
43   And ye took up the tabernacle of Moloch,
And the star of the god ⁵Rephan,
The figures which ye made to worship them:
And I will carry you away beyond Babylon.

44   Our fathers had ⁶the tabernacle of the testimony in the
wilderness, even as he appointed who spake unto Moses,
⁷that he should make it according to the figure that he had
45 seen. Which also our fathers, in their turn, brought in
with ⁸Joshua when they entered on the possession of the
nations, which God thrust out before the face of our fathers,
46 unto the days of David; who found favour in the sight
of God, and asked ⁹to find a habitation for the ¹⁰God of
47 Jacob. ¹¹But Solomon built him a house. Howbeit the
48 Most High dwelleth not in *houses* made with hands; as
saith the prophet,

49   ¹²The heaven is my throne,
And the earth the footstool of my feet:
What manner of house will ye build me? saith the
  Lord:
Or what is the place of my rest?

---

¹ Gk *ecclesia*.   ² Exod xxxii 1, 4, 6.   ³ Or (AV) *offered sacrifice*
⁴ Amos v 25–7.   ⁵ Rompha B, Romphan ℵ, Rempham Bezan, Remphan AV.
⁶ Exod xxxviii 21 (Rev xv 5).   ⁷ xxv 40 (Hebr viii 5).   ⁸ Gk *Jesus*
(Hebr iv 8).   ⁹ Ps cxxxii 5 (II Sam vii 1–3).   ¹⁰ Some MSS (ℵBD) have
house.   ¹¹ I K vi 2.   ¹² Isai lxvi 1 (Mt v 34–5).

50 Did not my hand make all these things?
51 Ye ¹stiffnecked and uncircumcised in heart and ears, ye do always resist the Holy Ghost: as your fathers did, so do
52 ye. Which of the prophets did not your fathers persecute? and they killed them which shewed before of the coming of the Righteous One; of whom ye have now become betrayers
53 and murderers; ye who received the law ²as it was ordained by angels, and kept it not.

The first thing which attracts attention in the speech is the number of variations from, and additions to, the record of the Old Testament. This has caused a great deal of labour to commentators, but it need not cause us much anxiety. The five books of the law possessed a unique sacredness in the eyes of the Jews, but outside the Pentateuch there were many other writings and books in circulation, some included in 'the Prophets' and 'the Psalms,' others not. With regard to the Pentateuch itself, it is doubtful whether its text had as yet received the final fixed form in which it has come down to us: the Greek translations made during the preceding two or three hundred years shew what varieties of reading were once in existence. Again there was a mass of current interpretation and traditional filling up of the history. The almost contemporary works of Philo and Josephus, and the writings of the rabbis, are themselves great monuments of such exegesis; and they shew us that Stephen was only reproducing to his judges the learning of the day³. Indeed his general agreement with Philo deepens the suspicion that he was himself an Alexandrian.

To take the points of disagreement briefly and in order, (1)
2 Stephen makes God appear to Abraham for the first time *in the land of the Chaldaeans* (i.e. 'Ur of the Chaldees' which was sometimes reckoned by the Greeks in *Mesopotamia*). Genesis is silent about this appearance, and makes the first call, the words of which are quoted by Stephen, at Haran. Philo and Josephus however agree with Stephen, and the earlier appearance is supported
4 by Josh xxiv 2–3, Nehem ix 7. (2) Stephen—and Philo agrees—says that Terah died before Abraham left Haran. The figures given in Genesis (xi 26, 32, xii 4) would imply that Terah had yet
6 60 years to live⁴. (3) Stephen and Philo, with Genesis xv 13, give *400 years* as the time of Israel's bondage in Egypt, evidently using a round number. Exodus xii 40 is more exact and says 430 years.

---

¹ Exod xxxiii 3: Deut x 16, Jer ix 26. ² Literally *unto ordinances of angels*, i.e. *at the ordinance (appointment* verse 44) *of angels.* ³ The *Assumption of Moses* is a specimen of current literature, which S. Stephen may have himself read. Certainly in iii 11 it has a striking parallel to verse 36: 'Is not this that which Moses did then declare unto us in prophecies, who suffered many things in Egypt and the Red Sea and in the wilderness during forty years?' ⁴ The Bezan text as given by Blass, chiefly on the authority of Irenaeus, would remove both these discrepancies. See note on text.

This is the number given by S. Paul in Gal iii 17, but he makes it cover the whole period from the covenant with Abraham. This was also the reckoning of the rabbis, and of the Greek translators who in Exod xii 40 read *in Egypt and in Canaan*. Sometimes Josephus agrees, assigning 215 years to the stay in each country;
7 at other times he says simply '400 years.' (4) Stephen adds to Gen xv 13-14 *and serve me in this place*, words taken from Exod iii 12, and so understands by *the place* Palestine and not
14 Mt Sinai as is meant in Exodus. (5) He says *75 souls*: Gen xlvi 26, Exod i 5, Deut x 22 say 70, and so Josephus. But the LXX in Exodus and in some MSS in Deuteronomy have 75, reckoning in Joseph's offspring born in Egypt. Philo had observed the dis-
16 crepancy and found an allegorical explanation for it. (6) Joshua xxiv 32 tells us that Joseph was buried at Shechem: in adding his brothers—*our fathers*, i.e. Jacob's twelve sons,—Stephen is probably quoting contemporary tradition. Jerome says that their tomb was shewn at Shechem in his day, and the rabbis agree as to their bodies having been brought up out of Egypt. (7) The latter part of Stephen's statement further implies some confusion. According to Genesis (xxiii, xxxiii 19) Abraham bought a burial ground of Ephron at Hebron; and later on Jacob bought a parcel of ground at Shechem '*of the children of Hamor, Shechem's father*.' On the strength of this information, the AV in this place gratuitously translates *of the sons of Emor the father of Sychem*, though *father* is not in the Greek: the true reading is as in the RV *in Shechem*. There were many traditions and writings current in the holy land about the lives of the patriarchs, and Stephen is quoting some such autho-
22 rity. (8) The education of Moses *in all the wisdom of the Egyptians* is not mentioned in Exodus, but is reported by Philo. It was indeed an obvious conclusion, at a time when Egypt had become a centre, not only of Egyptian, but also of Greek and Jewish learning. Philo and Josephus also mention Moses' eloquence, which hardly agrees with Exodus iv 10-14. S. Stephen's phrase *mighty in his words and works* need not be more than the general description of a
23 great prophet, as in Lk xxiv 19. (9) The age of Moses at the crisis, *forty years*, was discovered by the rabbinical interpreters. Forty is the Jewish round number. The OT only states, in Exod
25 vii 7, that he was eighty at the time of the exodus. (10) The deeper motive, the desire to *give deliverance* to his people, which is important in the parallel with the Christ, is ascribed to Moses by Philo as well as by Stephen. Exodus is silent on the subject, and also puts his flight down to fear of Pharaoh rather than, as here
30 apparently, to rejection by his own people. (11) Exodus iii 1 has
42 Horeb instead of *Sinai*. (12) Nothing is said in the Pentateuch as to this worship of *the host of heaven*, i.e. sun, moon and stars: it is taken from descriptions of later Jewish idolatry found in the prophets, e.g. Jer viii 2, xix 13 etc.: cf. 2 Kings xxi 3, xxiii 5. (13) The quotation from *the book of the prophets*, i.e. the 12 minor

prophets which formed one roll, is an example of contemporary exegesis. In the original prophecy Amos asked his question as a protest against the externalism of the worship of the Israelites; he shews that God did not require sacrifices in the wilderness.
43 Then the following sentence is either a picture of the idolatry into which they had actually fallen, or more probably a prophecy of punishment, i.e. they shall carry in captivity the shrines and images of the Assyrian gods[1]. S. Stephen treats the passage as a description and reproach of Israelitish idolatry in the wilderness. He also substitutes *Babylon* for *Damascus*, just as the Greek translators had already changed the names of the gods. In the OT we read *ye have borne Siccuth your king and Chiun your images, the star of your god* (RV). These are probably Assyrian deities—one rather obscure, Sakkut, and one more familiar, the star god Kaivan or Saturn. *Siccuth* however as the RV margin shews may be taken as *tabernacles*, and so the AV and LXX have translated it. Then for *king* they have substituted the Palestinian deity *Moloch*, almost the same word in the Hebrew. The common confusion between the Hebrew letters K and R probably caused the change of *Kiun* into *Rephan* or *Romphan*, a name otherwise unknown. (14) In
52 the OT we read of but few martyrdoms of the prophets: besides the slaughter of the prophets of the LORD by Jezebel, there are the murders of Zechariah the high priest in 2 Chron xxiv 20-2 and of Urijah in Jer xxvi 23. But again current literature was not limited to the books of our Old Testament. There were many traditions as to the fates of the prophets; and the persecuting and slaying of the righteous was recognized as a feature of the history of Israel. This accusation was driven home by the Lord himself, quoting 'the wisdom of God,' which was perhaps some contemporary 'wisdom'
53 book[2]. (15) The most interesting advance upon the OT is found in the *ordinances of angels*. While the awe of the sacred Name had been deepening among the Jews (p. 49), the philosophers of Alexandria had on their side been developing the doctrine of the divine incomprehensibility, or, if we may so speak, the aloofness of God. Both alike shrank from the idea of an immediate revelation of God, and in consequence they developed the doctrine of angels. Thus (*A*) for JEHOVAH was substituted his Angel. This doctrine is indeed to be found in the OT itself. According to the OT, which S. Stephen quotes, it was *the angel of the LORD* which appeared to Moses in the bush. The angel of the LORD also appeared to Abraham, Hagar, and Jacob; and he was 'the angel of the presence' who was with the Israelites in the wilderness[3]. This angel speaks with *the voice of the LORD*, as God; and he is in fact, to use another name which had come into use, the Word of the LORD. How this doctrine had been growing we see from verse 38, whence we learn

---
[1] See Isai xlvi 1.   [2] Mt xxiii 37: Lk xi 49. Cp. also I Th ii 15, Hebr xi 37.
[3] Gen xxii 11-18, xvi 7-14, xxi 17-19, xxxi 11, xlviii 16, Exod iii 2; Isai lxiii 9. See pp. 71-2 above.

that at Sinai it was the angel who spake to Moses and gave him the law. (*B*) In its turn that revelation required mediation. As the angel of the LORD more and more filled the place of JEHOVAH, he was himself removed from men by the cloud of divine majesty, and mediators were again needed. For the giving of the law he had to employ 'ministers and stewards of his mysteries.' And following the suggestion of Deut. xxxiii 2, these ministers were identified with *the angels*: and their office in the *appointing* or *ordaining the law* was fully recognized by the Jews in the first century. We find it in Josephus; and in the NT in S. Stephen, S. Paul, and the Epistle to the Hebrews[1].

Having somewhat cleared the ground, we can the more freely follow the argument of the speech. Stephen begins with *the God of*
2 *glory*. The title is only found here[2]: it is really *the God of the glory*, i.e. the Shekinah or 'glory of the LORD'—the bright cloud of divine majesty which was as it were the pavilion of God himself. The title then denotes God in his divine being, rather than in his relation to man of which S. Peter reminded his hearers in his 'God of our fathers.' It was then the very God who *appeared to Abraham*. How he appeared, S. Stephen does not say: but the word denotes a visible appearance. Probably he would have said in the person of his Angel. *Appearing* however and *speaking* (verse 6) are the words for a divine revelation, the manner of which is less important. The revelation of God is the foundation of all religion; and S. Stephen's argument is marked by three progressive revelations or appearances, viz. of (1) the God of glory in verse 2: (2) Moses, the prophet and mediator, in verse 20: (3) the Angel of the Lord in verse 30. The last appearance was the occasion of the formation of the ecclesia (verse 38). This threefold revelation is as it were sealed by the threefold vision of S. Stephen at the close of his speech.

3   The first revelation was made in an idolatrous country. Abra-
5 ham was indeed called into Canaan. But there was no temple as yet, when God gave him (before the law) a *promise*. In sign
8 of acceptance Abraham submitted to *circumcision*, and so the promise was strengthened into a *covenant*. The promise was in the first place *the inheritance* of this land of Canaan[3]; but contrary to his expectation Abraham himself did not receive so much
6 *as a foot*[4]. For preparation is necessary on man's side. Abraham's descendants must endure the fire of adversity and the trial of waiting, for *400 years*. (As the Christ had to suffer before enter-

---

[1] Josephus *Ant.* xv 5. 3: Acts vii 53, Gal iii 19, Hebr ii 2.   [2] i.e. in the NT: in the OT cp. Ps xxix 3.   S. Paul speaks of God as *the Father of the glory*, and of Christ as *the Lord of the glory* (Eph i 17, I Cor ii 8): S. Peter adds *the Spirit of the glory* (I Pet iv 14).   [3] S. Stephen is only concerned with the literal sense as yet. In S. Peter the promise is the Holy Spirit (ii 33), in S. Paul the raising up of the Christ (xiii 32): in S. Stephen's mind the thought is probably of the new ecclesia (verse 38: cp. xx 32).   [4] Cp. Hebr xi 8-12, which also speaks of *the land of the promise*.

ing into his glory, so¹) Israel had first to be rejected and cast out of that holy land which they were to receive. This experience however finds a more vivid expression in the fortunes of an
9 individual—*Joseph*. (As Jesus was sold by Judas to the high-priests, and by them delivered up to the Gentiles, and that *for*
10 *envy*², so) his *jealous* brethren *sold Joseph into Egypt*. But there *God delivered him*³, and *made him governor over Egypt and all Pharaoh's house*, (so God raised up Jesus from the dead and exalted him to be a Prince and Saviour, and gave him to be head of the
11 church, the house of God). Joseph thus proved to be the salvation
14 of his brethren. He *called* them *into Egypt*; and there they formed the first ecclesia, or rather the germ of the ecclesia, for as yet they
15 were in the house of bondage. The patriarchs too, like another
16 patriarch—David (ii 29), *died* and were buried; and their *tomb* lay, as Stephen points out by the way, not in the holy places but in schismatical *Shechem* or Samaria. Before Israel can enter on its inheritance (or the ecclesia be manifested) a deliverance is necessary.
17 Of this deliverance Moses was the instrument, and his work and appointment must be fully understood. *In proportion as the time of the promise* (of the inheritance) *was drawing near*, the people were prospering in numbers (vi 7), but a new king brought upon
20 them affliction and persecution. At such a *season* God raised them up a saviour—*Moses was born*; (so when the fulness of the time came, when after so many oppressions the iron hand of Rome now lay upon Israel, God sent forth his Son born of a woman to deliver his people). Moses had all the qualities requisite for his task: (1) natural gifts—he *was exceeding fair*⁴, (2) education—*in all the wisdom of Egypt*, and (3) force of character—he was *mighty in words and works*; (so Jesus advanced in wisdom and stature and was mighty in deed and word). But Moses, like the other servants of the Lord, must first pass through the experience of rejection and
21 suffering. This began early. *He was cast out* at the age of *three months*, and then *brought up* in a strange house; (so Jesus after his birth was carried hastily from Bethlehem to Egypt, and he was brought up not in his own city Jerusalem but in the despised
23 Nazareth). When his *time* of preparation, *forty years long*, *was now being fulfilled*⁵, Moses *visited his brethren* to bring them *salvation*, and *appeared* unto them. (So about his thirtieth year Jesus *visited his people and revealed himself to them, appearing in the* synagogue at Nazareth to *proclaim release to the captives*; but the Nazarenes cast him out of their city, as) his brethren refused to believe in Moses: *they understood not* (25), *they thrust him away*
29 (27), *they denied him* (35)⁶. Moses therefore fled into 'a strange

---

¹ The sentences in brackets are the arguments implied but not expressed.
² Mk xv 10.   ³ *God was with him*, i.e. Joseph (verse 9), as with Jesus (x 38).
⁴ Both Philo and Josephus tell us of the beauty of Moses, but the Servant of Jehovah had no beauty that we should desire him (Isai liii 2).   ⁵ Cp. ii 1, xiii 25: Lk iii 23.   ⁶ Cp. xiii 46: iii 13.

land': *Midian*, a place particularly hateful to Israel, became his home for another *forty years*, and there he married and had sons[1].

30 But the promise of God cannot fail; and when the people are prepared by affliction, God is ready to exalt them (xiii 17). Accordingly he *appears* unto Moses. For the fulfilment of the promise demands a fuller revelation, which is summed up in the
33 giving of the law. The scene of this appearance—true *holy ground*—was again outside the holy land, *in the wilderness*.

35 Here S. Stephen breaks off the continuous narrative to present to his judges in four dramatic sentences the chief elements of the work of Moses—that is of the Christ. (1) The stone which the builders had rejected is made head of the corner. *This* rejected *Moses* is made by God *ruler and redeemer*: so he had made the crucified Jesus Lord and Christ, Prince and Saviour. Moses redeems Israel by bringing the people out of Egypt: the Christ
36 redeems by delivering from sin and death. (2) The divine appointment was confirmed by *wonders and signs*, which also formed part of the credentials of the Christ[2]. For Moses was accompanied by *the hand of the angel*, i.e. by the strength or power of the LORD[3]. By this arm of the LORD Moses had wrought the chief wonder and sign, i.e. the *bringing forth* of Israel out of Egypt through *the Red Sea*, as the same right hand had exalted Jesus
37 from the dead. (3) But this redemption was not final: Moses himself declared that his work was only preparatory to and typical
38 of that of a greater *Prophet*, whom *God would raise up*[4]. (4) For the redemption out of Egypt was only preparatory to a revelation which should make the people into an *ecclesia* or *church*. Of this revelation Moses was the *prophet*, filling a threefold position. (*a*) He was *in the ecclesia*, i.e. in the midst of the people, one in full sympathy with and a true representative of them. (*b*) He was mediator between *the angel*, i.e. God so far as he *appeared* or revealed himself, *and the fathers*[5]. (*c*) For this purpose *he received* from God *living words of God*, which he was to utter—as a prophet— to the people. So *like unto* Moses, the Christ (*a*) was the Son of man, verse 56: he took flesh and blood that he might be one with his brethren, 'in the midst of the ecclesia[6].' (*b*) He was the one mediator between God and men, himself man Christ Jesus[7]. (*c*) He received gifts for men, viz. the 'living water' or the Spirit of Life[8].
39 The parallel is made complete by what follows. The revelation in the law was *living*[9], and meant to give life, but the Israelites *would not obey* it : so now the Jews of S. Stephen's day were disobedient to the new Moses

---

[1] Exod ii 22, xviii 4.   [2] Cp. ii 22, x 38.   [3] iv 30, xi 21, xiii 11. The *hand* is the power of the Spirit with which Jesus was anointed.   [4] iii 22, 26, xiii 33.   [5] The law was *ordained by angels in the hand of a mediator* (Gal iii 19).   [6] Hebr ii 10-18.   [7] 1 Tim ii 5.   [8] Acts ii 33.   [9] Hebr iv 12. For *life* cp. Deut xxxii 47, Levit xviii 5, Rom x 5. The law is for life or death Deut xxx 15-19, Rom vii 7-23. *Oracles* are words of God Rom iii 2, 1 Pet iv 11.

This has brought us to the specific charge of blasphemy against the law. Stephen's answer is that from the first Israel had not obeyed it. He dwells on their idolatry, no doubt for the edification of and a warning to the Sadducean priests. The source of disobedience lay in obstinacy of the will: *they willed not to become obedient.* The causes of this obstinacy were (1) hankering after
40 *Egypt*, i.e. lust of worldly position; (2) lack of faith,—and as the Israelites had said of Moses on the mountain top, so the Jews now were saying *As for this* Jesus *we know not what is become of him*;
41 (3) self-will—*they rejoiced in the works of their hands*, i.e. idols: so the present generation had formed their own conceptions of what the Messiah should be and do, and refused to surrender them. The
42 punishment now would be the same as of old, when God simply *gave them up* to their own hearts' desires, their self-chosen blindness[1]. This is the doctrine of punishment by which S. Paul accounts for the depravity and blindness of the pagan world also, in the first chapter of the Romans (cp. II Thess ii 9–12).
44 From the law to the temple. At Sinai besides the law the fathers received *the tabernacle (tent) of the testimony*[2]. It was this, and not the temple, which was *appointed* by God and made
45 after a heavenly *pattern*. It was this which *Joshua* had brought into the holy land, when God gave them the promised *possession* (verse 5), expelling the former owners of the land. It was this which remained the sanctuary *till the time of David*. If JEHOVAH had required a temple, surely no fitter builder could have been found
46 than David, who *found favour* with God[3], or, as S. Paul puts it, was after God's own heart and did all his will; and yet, although David himself *asked* to build a more worthy *dwelling place for the God of Jacob*, his prayer was refused, and the king who built the temple was
47 *Solomon*, who afterwards fell away. Solomon then *built* for God the first *house*, the precursor of Herod's temple, the glory of the Jews, 'the work of their hands' in which they were rejoicing (cp. verse 41). But
48 S. Stephen reminds them that *the Most High does not dwell within* walls *made by hands*. By his recital of the divine appearances Stephen has himself shewn that God can specially manifest his presence in particular places, and therefore in a temple. But the word *dwell* denotes (as in verses 3 and 4) having a fixed and limited dwelling place. The Alexandrian philosophers had been developing the doctrine of the divine nature, and from them Stephen would have learnt that it was absurd to suppose that the Creator could

---

[1] Cp. xxviii 25–7.   [2] This is a mistranslation in the Greek Bible for *the tent of meeting*. With this passage cp. Hebr viii 2, 5, ix 1 foll. The Hebrews also agrees with Stephen in referring to Joshua, not mentioned elsewhere in the NT: cp. Hebr iv 8, xi 30–1.   [3] Cp. verse 10, ii 47, iv 33, Lk ii 40, and below xiii 22. The OT gives a different impression of the relations of Solomon and David in building the temple, but the words of the Acts certainly imply that S. Stephen took the line of argument represented above. S. Stephen is at least adding the supplement to the OT in his doctrine of verse 48, as the Lord had similarly 'fulfilled' the OT in Jn iv 21–4.

be contained by a creature, or the omnipresent Spirit be confined within four walls. But this truth had already been revealed in the scriptures. Solomon himself at the dedication of the House had declared that though it was built for the Name of the LORD, yet heaven was his dwelling place[1]. And this doctrine was driven home
49 by Isaiah, who by the title of *the prophet* is made to rank on a level with Moses (verse 37) in the authoritative revelation of the divine truth.
51   This open criticism of their most cherished glories was too much for the Sanhedrin. For a long time Stephen's bitter irony had been cutting them to the heart[2]; and now their indignation must have given rise to some demonstration, some grinding of their teeth. For Stephen in return is provoked to an outburst. He breaks off his argument for a personal home thrust, which proves to be the conclusion. *Stiffnecked*, i.e. disobedient to God like that generation of old[3], and though boasting in their circumcision (verse 8) yet in heart *uncircumcised*, i.e. with will and understanding hardened against God's revelation, *it is you* he says *who are resisting the Holy Spirit*. Then God had put his Spirit in Moses, but their fathers resisted or strove against him[4]. So now God is speaking in the new
52 ecclesia against which the Sanhedrin are striving. The Israelites of old had indeed *killed the prophets*, but *it is you* who have actually *betrayed* and *murdered* the Christ himself, 'the Prophet.' The Israelites of old had disobeyed the law: but the Sanhedrin had put to death *the Righteous one*, the one—and the only one—who
53 had fulfilled the law. By this crucial act they had proved that they were still of the same character as their ancestors, who when they had received the divine revelation at the hands of heavenly ministers yet *kept it not*. This direct attack rendered conciliation impossible, and the next utterance of Stephen under the inspiration of the Spirit brought about the catastrophe.

S. Stephen's death

The defence of Stephen resulted in his murder. (*A*) It is the second death recorded in the Christian community, and the first martyrdom, so corresponding to the death of Abel in Genesis iv 1–15[5]. Similar martyrdoms in the OT are the murder of Zechariah in the temple in 2 Chron xxiv 20–22 and the stoning of Naboth in I Kings xxi 13. (*B*) The occasion is worthily marked. S. Stephen's defence had been to trace the progressive revelations of God in history, and now they are completed by a crowning appearance of the divine glory, of which he had spoken in verse 2. The language reminds us (*a*) of Isaiah's vision[6] when he *saw his glory* (Ju xii 41) and heard the seraphim cry Holy, Holy, Holy: and also (*b*) of the baptism of the

---
[1] I K viii 27 f.   [2] Cp. v 33.   [3] verse 39 and Exod xxxiii 3, 5.   [4] Cp. Num xxvii 14, Isai lxiii 10.   [5] Cp. Lk xi 51, Hebr xi 4, xii 24.   [6] In his history S. Stephen had not reached so far, but he had spoken of Isaiah as 'the prophet,' viz. as marking an epoch in the divine revelation.

Lord at the beginning of the Gospel, when the *heavens were opened and the Spirit appeared* in visible form and a voice came from heaven[1]. Like those, this vision is marked by threefoldness: Stephen is *full of the Spirit*; he sees *the glory of God*; and *Jesus at his right hand*. (C) This brings us to the new circumstance which makes it the complete and final revelation. *Jesus is standing at the right hand of God*. It is the first appearance of Jesus in his divine glory. At the transfiguration he had appeared in glory to Peter, James and John, but on earth: now Stephen sees him in heaven. This vision, which is hereafter to be granted to S. Paul and S. John alone, is the proof of the apostolic testimony to his exaltation in ii 33, iii 21, v 31, and of Stephen's own teaching. He sees Jesus standing, i.e. as Prophet and Mediator standing between God and men (vv. 37, 38). And the unique character of the revelation is sealed by the name SON OF MAN, which in the NT occurs here alone outside of the four Gospels.

54 Now when they heard these things, they were cut to the
55 heart, and they gnashed on him with their teeth. But he, being full of the Holy Ghost, looked up stedfastly into heaven, and saw the glory of God, and Jesus standing on the right
56 hand of God, and said, Behold, I see the heavens opened, and
57 the Son of man standing on the right hand of God. But they cried out with a loud voice, and stopped their ears,
58 and rushed upon him with one accord; and they cast him out of the city, and stoned him: and the witnesses laid down their garments at the feet of a young man named Saul.
59 And they stoned Stephen, calling upon *the Lord*, and saying,
60 Lord Jesus, receive my spirit. And he kneeled down, and cried with a loud voice, Lord, lay not this sin to their charge.
8 And when he had said this, he fell asleep. And Saul was consenting unto his death.

54 Amidst the evident signs of the fury of his judges[2], Stephen
55 *looked up to heaven* for succour, and he received an answer. In the power *of the Holy Spirit* he *saw the glory of God* and *Jesus standing*
56 *on his right hand*. At once Stephen as a true 'martyr' bears witness and so adds that name—of which he had been silent in his speech—*Son of man*. Of course in describing such a vision of divine and spiritual realities human language and experience altogether fail. The *opening of the heavens* is a Jewish metaphor for insight into

---

[1] As in verse 32. See Isai vi: Lk iii 21-2. For other visions cp. I K xxii 19, Ezek i, Dan vii 9-14: Acts ix 3-9, Rev i 9-20. [2] The Greek tenses denote not a sudden outburst, but a continuous state. So in 55 *full of the Holy Ghost* does not mean a sudden inspiration as in iv 8, but Stephen's existing condition: cp. vi 3, 5, 8.

divine things[1]: and on this ground there is no difficulty when the apostles speak of Jesus as *sitting*, S. Stephen as *standing*. Both expressions are symbolical: and the Lord stands as intercessor for his people, or because he has risen to aid his 'martyr,' to welcome and receive him. Stephen's utterance indeed takes us back to the First Martyr himself, who had exclaimed in the Sanhedrin 'From henceforth shall the Son of man be seated at the right hand of the power
57 of God' (Lk xxii 69). In each case the utterance proved fatal. Stephen's judges uttered a cry of horror at the blasphemy, the high-priest no doubt rent his clothes and gave the verdict 'he hath blasphemed,' and with one mouth all condemned him to death. But their feelings were too exasperated for judicial order: the whole
58 assembly, like a tumultuous mob (xix 29), *rushed upon him*, carried him *out of the city*—as the law required[2]—and then and there *proceeded to stone him*. In this summary execution the Sanhedrin were exceeding their powers. They say explicitly in Jn xviii 31 'it is not lawful for us to put any man to death,' and in A.D. 62, when in the interval between two governors the high-priest Ananus seized the opportunity to destroy James the Lord's brother, he was deposed for it. Here it is obvious that passion had overcome their prudence; but Pilate being what he was, with his weakness of character and necessity of standing well with the Jews, they would not have had much difficulty in getting him to overlook it[3].

The death is briefly described. According to the law (Deut xvii 7) *the witnesses* must cast the first stones, so they strip off their flowing upper garments and *lay* them *at the feet of Saul*. Saul, as we have inferred, was a member of the Cilician synagogue, and had been one of the disputers with Stephen. Probably as a member of the Sanhedrin, he had heard Stephen's defence and given his vote for his death. And his own words in xxii 20, *I was standing by* or *over*, with his subsequent commission, seem to imply that he was in charge of the execution. He is called *a young man*, but that need only mean a man in the prime of life, between thirty and forty, as distinct
59 from an 'elder' man (p. 67). *Stephen* meanwhile was *calling upon* the Lord whom he had seen to *receive his spirit*. To *call upon* means to invoke in prayer, but the AV had no ground for inserting
60 *God*: the object of the prayer was the *Lord Jesus*. When the stoning had begun[4], *he knelt down* and shewed his own obedience to his Lord[5] by forgiving his murderers. When we contrast the dying prayer of the OT martyr Zechariah 'The Lord look upon it and require it,' we see that the cross had done its work.

---

[1] Cp. x 11, Lk iii 21, Rev iv 1, xix 11 etc. [2] Levit xxiv 14, Num xv 35. So, like Christ, he suffered 'without the gate,' Hebr xiii 12. Cp. Lk iv 29, Jn viii 59, x 31. [3] If the martyrdom and persecution took place in 36 or 37 as some chronologists reckon, this difficulty would disappear. Pilate had been recalled in disgrace, and Vitellius the governor of Syria who twice visited Jerusalem treated the Jews with marked favour. [4] According to Jewish tradition stoning began with casting the victim from a raised platform on to a great stone. [5] In contrast to the disobedience of the Israelites to Moses (verse 39).

Like Christ on the cross[1], Stephen prayed for them—literally *Set not this sin to them*; where *set* means either (1) set in the scales against them, or (2) set it down firm, unmovable, to their account.

8 1 Of this tragedy, though he did not throw a stone, *Saul* bore the full guilt. For he *was consenting* to it. The word denotes the consent of the will, as in Lk xi 48; and such moral consent carries with it far more responsibility than the actual doing of the deed, as Saul himself had learnt when he wrote of those who, 'knowing the ordinance of God that they which practise such things are worthy of death, not only do the same but also consent with them that practise them' (Rom i 32). S. Luke his faithful disciple records his action as briefly as possible: but the blood of Stephen was upon him, and he never forgot the scene; years later, he says 'when the blood of Stephen was shed, I was standing by and consenting and keeping the garments of them that slew him' (xxii 20). The Acts itself affords a striking illustration of the working of divine retribution. For although forgiven S. Paul bears his punishment, and we shall see him undergoing all the sufferings of S. Stephen, only increased tenfold[2].

§ 4 *The persecution*

The immediate consequence of these events was a *persecution*. The Sadducees had been hostile from the first, and now the Pharisees and the people are turned into enemies by Stephen's 'blasphemy.' Very likely the triumphant Saul led the excited crowd from the stoning to a raid upon the houses of the Nazarenes *on that* very *day*; and so the church had its first taste of that which was to be the mark of its external history for the next 300 years,—persecution. This is the first of the famous series of 'Persecutions.' It had been hard for the disciples to understand the sufferings of the Christ; it must have been no less hard for them to understand their own sufferings for righteousness' sake. As a clue to the explanation, they had, however, not only the history but the warnings of Christ, and the experience of the church of the OT as set forth in its Psalms of Persecution (lxxix, lxxx). Even many years later it seemed a 'strange thing' to them (1 Peter iv 12). We notice that the actual sufferings are not dwelt upon: no names of the martyrs are given: only incidentally do we gather a few particulars. So it was in the other early persecutions. It was reserved for later generations to describe the physical tortures and glorify the names and tombs of the martyrs. But the severity of

---

[1] Lk xxiii 34. The prayer of S. Stephen is an early testimony to that utterance of the Lord. [2] The Jews disputed with and resisted Paul in the synagogues: he was falsely accused, mobbed at Philippi and in the temple, tried before the Sanhedrin in Jerusalem, stoned at Lystra. The same accusations were made against him—of *blasphemy* (xix 37), disloyalty to *Moses* (xxi 21) the *holy place* and *customs* (xxi 28, xxiv 6, xxv 8, xxviii 17). Verbally, cp. *crying out* (xxi 28), *rushed with one accord* and *seized* (xix 29), *out of the city* (xiv 19). Further he suffered *persecution* at Antioch (xiii 50), was *dragged* (xiv 19; cp. xvii 6) *into prison* (xvi 23), and was *bound* (xxi 13, 33): cp. viii 1–3.

this *great persecution* can be measured by its result—the temporary break up of the church in Jerusalem. And it left bitter memories, as we should infer from 1 Thess ii 14–16 and Hebrews x 32–4. In the OT we may compare Jezebel's persecution of the prophets of the LORD (1 Kings xviii 4, 13, xix 2).

8 And there arose on that day a great persecution[1] against the church which was in Jerusalem; and they were all scattered abroad throughout the regions of Judæa and 2 Samaria, except the apostles. And devout men buried 3 Stephen, and made great lamentation over him. But Saul laid waste the church, entering into every house, and [2]haling men and women committed them to prison.

The Nazarenes were *all* driven from the city and *scattered abroad*. Though the word *all*, if taken literally, would be an exaggeration, yet it means that for the present *the church at Jerusalem*, which had been making such vigorous progress, was now broken up. It did not indeed cease to exist, for *the apostles* remained in Jerusalem: they could not desert their post in the time of danger. It seems strange that we do not hear of their arrest or persecution. In later times the bishops of the church were the first object of attack. Saul however does not seem to have come in contact with them. No doubt they could lie hid as after the crucifixion (Jn xx 19): but perhaps the real reason is that it was the Hellenist side of the church which had been most aggressive and therefore bore the brunt of the attack. The affair had begun in a Hellenist synagogue and the chief of those who were scattered were Hellenists (xi 20). An immediate result was that S. Stephen lacked Christian burial: but, as in the case of the Lord, there were *devout men* among the Jews who recognized his holiness and the monstrous injustice of his murder, and they *buried him* with *great lamentation*[3].

Jewish devotion to the law took another form in the case of *Saul*, the zealous Pharisee. He was the leading spirit in the persecution. In fact it could be described as his work, and he could say of himself with truth 'I persecuted the church of God.' S. Luke says he *devastated* or *laid waste the church* like a savage animal, quoting the very word of Ps lxxx 13 'the boar out of the wood doth ravage it': in his own words he 'sacked the church,' like soldiers who have stormed a city. He was almost beside himself with anger, 'being exceeding mad against them'; and like an infuriated beast he breathed out 'threatening and slaughter.' From his own subsequent references to the persecution we can form some picture of it[4]. Armed with a

---

[1] Bezan adds *and affliction*.   [2] i.e. *dragging*.   [3] *Devout* is generally used by S. Luke in connexion with the law, cp. ii 5, xxii 12, Lk ii 25. Josephus records similar conduct among the pious Jews at the murder of James by Ananus.
[4] See xxii 4, 19–20, xxvi 10–11, Gal i 13, I Cor xv 9, I Tim i 13. We must however remember that in these words we are listening to the self-accusations of a great saint.

commission from the high-priests he visited *every house* of the Nazarenes, and there made inquisition. All who would not blaspheme the Name were put in bonds and *dragged off to prison*, not only *men* but *women* also. Numbers of victims were thus obtained. These were then examined in the synagogues—the courts of first instance; and if they proved obdurate were beaten and otherwise tortured. Loss of their property was a natural consequence. Such scenes were enacted in 'all the synagogues.' But did the punishment extend to death? If the murder of Stephen was illegal, the Jews could hardly have ventured on a number of similar executions in cold blood. In any case only the Sanhedrin could have pronounced sentence of death. It is true that S. Paul speaks of his 'giving his vote when they were put to death' and says 'I persecuted unto death.' But such phrases may be generalizations from S. Stephen's case[1]. Possibly some other cases terminated fatally, and the death of a few religious fanatics would not have caused the Roman government much concern. The case of Ananias and Sapphira shews how easily in an oriental city sudden death may occur without enquiry. Whatever we may conclude, there was enough to enable S. Paul to call himself one who had been 'a blasphemer and persecutor and injurious.' If, as is likely, this persecution is 'the great conflict of sufferings of the former days' of Hebrews x 32-34, then the sufferings were mainly disgrace, imprisonment and confiscation, and they had not 'resisted unto blood' (Hebr xii 4).

SECTION II (=Ch. 8. 4—11. 26)

The things that arose about Stephen

The death of Stephen was the crucial event which started the expansion of the church. And now S. Luke is going to trace its result in four different lines which will bring us to the great work which opens in chapter xiii. The blood of the martyr was the seed of the church. And that in a very literal sense; for (1) the Christians *were scattered abroad, and went about* unto many places. The word *scatter-abroad* is derived from the word for sowing: and so they were *scattered-abroad* like seed sown, and consequently the word grew. For (2) where they went, they *evangelized* or *preached the word*. Thus as the chief strength of Judaism, both political and intellectual, lay in its Dispersion or Scattering-abroad, so the new Dispersion of the Christians formed the progressive and missionary element in the church. At first this spreading of the word was confined to the country districts of Palestine, but some prophetic spirits were ready to overleap these bounds. Such an one was Philip the Evangelist.

---

[1] Just as *the outside cities* of xxvi 11 means probably only Damascus. S. Luke mentions *slaughter* in ix 1, but it may mean only uttering threats of slaughter.

SECTION II A (= Ch. 8. 4—40)
The Acts of Philip

The first missionary work of the church was spontaneous, not undertaken under the lead or official guidance of the apostles. The Twelve remained at Jerusalem, and the place of leadership was filled by those who ranked next to them. After the death of Stephen, S. Philip is now first of the Seven, and like Stephen he now appears as (1) endowed with that wonder-working power which had hitherto been confined to the apostles; and (2) a preacher of the word, or, as he was entitled later on, an evangelist. But he has also (3) a special characteristic of his own. This chapter is thoroughly Old Testament in its spirit and language, and the evangelist acts exactly like one of the prophets of old : we could imagine that we are reading of a second Elijah or Elisha. Philip then is a Christian prophet—one of those prophets who were ranked with the apostles in the foundation of the church. Like an OT prophet he wanders about, with sudden and spontaneous movements under the immediate impulse of the Spirit. But the true inspiration of the Spirit which marks a prophet is above all seen in the daring insight which led him to begin the work of breaking through the barriers of Jewish limitation. He was thus a true predecessor of S. Paul ; and as he will hereafter (in ch. xxi) meet with the apostle in the flesh, he forms a connecting link between the two parts of the Acts—the original and the developed, the Jewish and the Catholic, church.

He made two steps forward. (1) He preached to the Samaritans. The Samaritans were not entirely an alien race; there was Israelitish blood in their veins. But when they advanced pretensions to possession of the true law and temple, a violent quarrel with the Jews was the result. The Samaritans were worse than aliens. They were heretics, schismatics, more to be hated than infidels. In the OT the bitterest enemy of Israel had been his brother Edom ; so now the Jews had no dealings with the Samaritans. (2) He baptized the Ethiopian eunuch. As an Ethiopian, the eunuch was a stranger ; and though he was an adherent of Judaism, the law was stern in excluding such as he from 'the assembly or ecclesia of the Lord' (Deut xxiii 1).

We also detect an advance in his teaching. At Samaria he preached *the kingdom of God*, and it is the first time the kingdom is mentioned since the first chapter (i 6). This doctrine of the kingship of the Christ we shall find developed by S. Paul in his gospel to the Jews (ch. xiii).

§ 1 *Philip preaches in Samaria*

The picture of the prophet is matched by the picture of a 'false prophet'[1]—Simon Magus. The whole east at this time, we are told by

---
[1] Cp. Micaiah and Zedekiah in I K xxii 22-24, Jeremiah and Hananiah in Jer xxviii.

the historian Suetonius[1], was flooded with Messianic expectations, and the expectations produced a harvest of false Christs. But apart from such special ideas, there was, in the decay and exhaustion of the old pagan religions, a greatly increased demand among men for religious teachers, to tell them something of the truth, to heal their diseases of spirit and mind as well as of body, to open up some channel of intercourse with the spiritual world, and in a word give them some knowledge of God. The class of 'prophets,' 'seers,' and 'magi,' who answered to this demand had always existed in the east, but now they were especially abundant. The developments and intermixture of Greek philosophy and oriental religion had given them most varied characters. They appeared sometimes as exorcists, healers, wonder-workers; sometimes as astrologers or spiritualists. Some really tried to fill the place of philosophers and moral teachers; others claimed to be prophets and possess a divine inspiration. A few of the class may have been great men with more or less sincerity, like Apollonius of Tyana, whose biography was put forward in a later generation to compete with the gospels. But the temptation to gain and cheat was too powerful, and the majority were nothing else than pretenders, quacks, and charlatans. Some were learned in astrology and the learning of the east, and the magi of Chaldea had an honourable reputation[2]. But the boundaries between true and false science, as between religion and superstition, had not yet been clearly marked out, and so the word *magus* had already acquired its evil associations of magic and sorcery.

As the counterfeit of the true, these false prophets were among the most dangerous enemies of Christianity; and the distinction between the true and the false, between religion and spiritualism, had to be sharply drawn once for all. The Lord had warned his disciples against false prophets and false Christs, and in the Acts we find the class convicted and judged in the persons of Simon Magus and Barjesus. Simon, as his name 'the Magus' and his position in Christian tradition shew, was in the first rank of these pretenders. By his skill in magic he had acquired quite a sovereignty over the Samaritans. His claim to be *some great one* (verse 9) was probably a Messianic pretension[3]. But he aspired still higher. Besides being a magus, he was a philosopher; and he had elaborated a hierarchy of divine emanations (i.e. successive mediators between God and man) which he called Powers. Of these Powers he professed to be himself the chief, giving himself the name of *The Great Power of God*. It is in view of such theories about Powers that the apostles assert the superiority of Christ to all such orders of being. S. Paul calls Christ 'the Power of God'; in the Acts the divine Power is generally associated with the Holy Spirit[4].

---

[1] *Vespas.* 4.   [2] Cp. the magi in Mt ii.   [3] Cp. Lk i 32 (and Acts v 36).
[4] As the word '*great*' seems hardly to require the explanation *which is called*, it has been suggested by Klostermann that it is really the transliteration of a Samaritan word which means *revealing*. So Simon would be the *Power which*

4   They therefore that were scattered abroad went about
    ¹preaching the word.
5   And Philip went down to the city of Samaria, and
6   proclaimed unto them the Christ. And the multitudes gave
    heed with one accord unto the things that were spoken by
    Philip, when they heard, and saw the signs which he did.
7   For *from* many of those which had unclean spirits, they came
    out, crying with a loud voice: and many that were palsied,
8   and that were lame, were healed. And there was ²much joy
    in that city.
9   But there was a certain man, Simon by name, which
    beforetime in the city ³used sorcery, and amazed the people
10 of Samaria, giving out that himself was some great one: to
    whom they all gave heed, from the least to the greatest,
    saying, This man is that Power of God which is called Great.
11 And they gave heed to him, because that of long time he
12 had amazed them with his ³sorceries. But when they believed
    Philip ¹preaching good tidings concerning the kingdom of
    God and the name of Jesus Christ, they were baptized, both
13 men and women. And Simon also himself believed: and
    being baptized, he ⁴continued with Philip; and beholding
    signs and great ⁵miracles wrought, he was amazed.

The Lord himself had preached to the Samaritans at Sychar (about 7 miles from Samaria) for two days, and the conversation of the Samaritan woman shewed their strong Messianic convictions⁶.
5 Now Philip goes down to their capital, the old Samaria, which had been rebuilt by Herod the Great on a magnificent scale and called after Augustus—in Greek Sebastos—Sebaste. Here like a herald *he proclaimed the Messiah*, i.e. the establishment of *the kingdom of God* (verse 12). This kingdom was neither the Jewish ecclesia nor the rival Samaritan ecclesia, but a new ecclesia which bore *the name of Jesus*, who had been anointed as its Messianic king or *Christ*.
6 Philip confirmed his words by working many *signs* of healing. The superstition of the Samaritans made them specially liable to *amazement* (vv. 9, 11, 13), or, as the AV implies, to 'being be-

---

reveals. For Powers see Rom viii 38, Eph i 21, I Pet iii 22: I Cor i 24: Acts i 8, iv 33, x 38 etc. This idea of successive gradations in the revelation of God was greatly elaborated by the Gnostics. It also lay at the bottom of Jewish angelology, such as was condemned by S. Paul in the Colossians.   ¹ Gk *evangelizing*, and so in verse 12.   ² AV and Bezan read *great*.   ³ Gk *was-a-magus* or *practised-magic*, and in verse 11 *magical doings*.   ⁴ Gk *continued-stedfastly* (i 14).   ⁵ Gk *powers*.   ⁶ Jn iv 4–42, esp. verse 25.

9 witched' by a power they could not understand[1]. Accordingly the miracles were necessary in order to overthrow the power and influence which *Simon* had acquired over them by his false miracles. Those of Philip were real, and the result was corresponding. The
6 *attention* of the whole population was won; the healings caused
12 great *joy*; the people at once *believed* that Philip's words must likewise be true, and many began to carry their belief into action
13 by *being baptized*. It is surprising that no opposition was offered by Simon. But in fact he himself was deeply impressed by the real spiritual power of Philip and by his signs which altogether eclipsed his own. *He believed*, i.e. recognized their reality; and in consequence *was baptized*, and became a disciple of[2] Philip as of a superior master. The nature of his faith was soon to be tested and laid bare.

§ 2 *The gift of the Holy Ghost and the conviction of Simon*

The new step of evangelizing the Samaritans required the sanction of the church and also the divine approval. The approval depended on the Pentecostal gift—would the Lord give to the Samaritans also of his Spirit? Again, as always, grace is dogged by sin. The great spiritual endowment is counterbalanced by a further lodgement of sin in the church, and S. Luke gives the judgement of this its second manifestation. The OT parallel to Simon is Gehazi, the prophet's servant, making money out of the baptism of Naaman in II Kings v. In S. Paul's career compare xix 19.

14 Now when the apostles which were at Jerusalem heard that Samaria had received the word of God, they sent unto
15 them Peter and John: who, when they were come down, prayed for them, that they might receive the Holy Ghost:
16 for as yet he was fallen upon none of them: only they had
17 been baptized into the name of the Lord Jesus. Then laid they their hands on them, and they received the Holy Ghost.
18 Now when Simon saw that through the laying on of the apostles' hands the ³Holy Ghost was given, he offered them
19 money, saying, Give me also this ⁴power, that on whomsoever
20 I lay my hands, he may receive the Holy Ghost. But Peter said unto him, Thy silver ⁵perish with thee, because thou hast

---

[1] Their superstition is illustrated by the event which led to the downfall of Pontius Pilate. About A.D. 35 a false prophet gave out that he would find on Mt Gerizim the sacred vessels hidden there by Moses, and an immense multitude followed him. Pilate however was beforehand and had sent some soldiers who dispersed the crowd with much slaughter. The Samaritans appealed to the proconsul of Syria, Vitellius, who sent Pilate to Rome for trial. [2] *Continued-with* is the word used in ii 42. [3] Marg with ℵB omits *Holy*. [4] Gk *authority*. [5] Gk *be with thee for* or *unto perdition*.

21 thought to obtain the gift of God with money. Thou hast
neither part nor lot in this ¹matter: for thy heart is not
22 ²right before God. Repent therefore of this thy wickedness,
and pray the Lord, if perhaps the thought of thy heart shall
23 be forgiven thee. For I see that thou ³art in the gall of
24 bitterness and in the bond of iniquity. And Simon answered
and said, ⁴'Pray ye for me to the Lord, that none of the things
which ye have spoken come upon me.

14   After an interval, perhaps when the persecution was over, news
of Philip's work reached *the apostles at Jerusalem* (verse 1). The
Samaritans had accepted the Lord Jesus as the Messiah and *had
been baptized into his name* (p. 32); but on the other hand there
had been no sign of any outpouring of the Spirit, no speaking with
tongues nor any such sign as had happened at the first Pentecost.
The apostles fully appreciated the importance of the occasion, for
they sent to Samaria the first two of their body, *Peter and John* (iii 1).
15 *They in their turn* gave their sanction to the work, for they desired
it to be completed by the gift of the Spirit. They adopted the
same mode of procedure as in the ordination of the Seven. They
17 *prayed*, and then *laid their hands on* the Samaritans. The prayer
was answered, and the Samaritans began to *receive the Holy Spirit*.
18 There must have been some external phenomena (such as speaking
with tongues) as evidence of the fact, for *Simon saw that through
the laying on of the apostles' hands the Spirit was given*⁶.
It is evident from the NT that that which makes a man a fully
equipped member of the church is the indwelling of the Holy Ghost.
This presence is not innate in man; it is a gift from God, given as
here described. But there are manifold workings of the Spirit. Even
before Christian faith the Spirit works, for S. Paul says 'no man can
say *Jesus is Lord* without the Holy Spirit⁵.' Similarly the Pentecostal
gift does not, as we have seen (p. 61), exclude further gifts afterwards;
and this is indicated in the Greek in this passage, where there is no
article and it runs *receive Holy Spirit* in verses 15, 17, 19. However
the initial gift which makes the man a full Christian is so special
and distinct, that of cases where it had not been received we read in
scripture that *the Holy Spirit was not yet*, or that *as yet he was fallen
upon none of them*⁶. On the other hand this gift does not necessarily
accompany either baptism or the act of faith by which Jesus is accepted
in the heart. This is clear from this passage and ix 17. When and
how, then, is this gift received? We learn, as the church has learnt

---

¹ Gk *word*.   ² Gk *straight*.   ³ Marg *wilt become gall* (or *a gall root*)
of bitterness and a bond of iniquity.   ⁴ Bezan has *I beseech you, pray for me to
God that none of the evils which ye have spoken of may come upon me. And he ceased
not weeping greatly*.   ⁵ I Cor xii 3.   ⁶ verse 16 and Jn vii 39. S. Chrysostom thus distinguishes this gift from that of their baptism: 'they had received the spirit of forgiveness, but not yet the spirit of signs (wonder-working).'

in the main, from this incident. The apostles supposed that the Spirit would be given in answer to prayer and the laying on of their hands. Their expectation was justified; and the church has accepted this as the normal method.

S. Luke gives us, in all, four accounts of the outpouring of the Spirit—(1) at Pentecost, on the original disciples; (2) here, on the Samaritans; (3) at Caesarea, on Cornelius and his company who were Gentiles; and (4) at Ephesus, on the disciples of John the Baptist. These are evidently meant as typical pictures. They represent each a different class of religious status; and as evidence that the Spirit is given to all classes alike, the gift is followed by external or extraordinary signs. (*a*) On two occasions the gift itself was extraordinary. The Spirit fell as it were immediately out of heaven upon the church at Pentecost, and upon Cornelius' company even before their baptism. (*b*) The other occasions were normal, and the gift was conveyed by prayer and the laying on of hands. These hands were apostolic; in the one case those of Peter and John, in the other of Paul. Nowhere in the Acts is the laying on of hands by other than apostles mentioned in this connexion; and it is evident from this incident that, although Philip was a prophet and one of the Seven, although he preached the word and baptized, yet he did not possess this power. We conclude then that, as S. Luke states it, *through the laying on of the hands of the apostles the Spirit is given.*

We are justified then in finding here the beginning of the church's rite of Confirmation. We say 'beginning' because it was inevitable that at the first some time must elapse before the establishment of fixed order. The method of the gift had to be learnt in a measure experimentally from the signs which confirmed the gift. Its regulation had to follow. Of the absence of regulation we find an illustration in the next episode. We are surprised to find the eunuch so suddenly baptized and then continuing his journey to a country where he would find no fellow Christians, no ministry, no sacraments. And we may ask—who laid hands upon him? Again, already there are Christians at Damascus (ix 2) when as yet the apostles have not left Jerusalem. Who laid hands upon them[1]? Who was to lay hands upon distant converts? This is the very problem which the apostles are now being called to face. Their first solution is to send Peter and John to Samaria. But it would be impossible for the Twelve to visit all the churches, and so another solution was found, viz. the method of delegation. Simon assumes that Peter and John can give this *authority* to others, and they do not contradict him. Later we find Paul exercising the authority, and apparently he also delegates it to Timothy in the Pastoral Epistles. The Christians at Antioch, who will soon come before us, present us with a case in point. They needed the gift of the Spirit as much as the Samaritans, but this time the apostles did

---

[1] Ananias at Damascus laid hands on Saul. He was evidently a person of note in the church, and may have been one of the Seventy as tradition alleges.

not go themselves. Instead the church at Jerusalem sent a representative, Barnabas. He appears to exercise apostolic powers, and so may have been a delegate of the Twelve for this purpose also.

This new Pentecost is followed by the conviction of sin—a true sign of the presence of the Spirit. As the generosity of Barnabas had been counterbalanced by the covetousness of Ananias and Sapphira, so was the free gift of the Spirit by the error of Simon. For Simon's sin or rather *wickedness* (verse 22) lay in his principles, the conceptions of his heart. The love of gain introduced a false principle which would have fatal consequences in action. It connected money with the exercise of spiritual authority and functions. The two spheres of the spiritual and the carnal must indeed touch; the minister of the gospel must live of the gospel. But to preserve the connexion from confusion is the more essential in proportion to the difficulty. Untold evil has ever resulted to the church from the buying and selling of spiritual office. However carefully disguised, it ultimately rests on this thought, first expressed by Simon, that *the gift of God can be acquired for money*. This idea and the consequent sin of simony (for from Simon comes the name of the sin) must receive a decisive judgement once and for all[1].

The sin was within the church, for Simon had believed and been baptized; and apparently he continued faithful to Philip. But he had neither fully understood, nor was his will wholly turned. (*a*) He had a false *thought* or intellectual conception about the laws of spiritual life. (*b*) But this thought was *of the heart*, i.e. it arose from his will or his own moral intention; and this intention, or *his heart, was not straight with God*[2]. It was distorted by selfishness. He saw the evident power of the Spirit and he coveted
19 it for his own aggrandizement. Hence he found no mental difficulty in supposing that this power could be purchased *for money*. Again, as from Ananias (v 4), we have found that sin lies 'in the heart,' i.e. the will. And as soon as it is laid bare, the moment for judgement has come. This rests with the apostles[3]. It is a striking scene—
20 the two Simons face to face, Simon Magus and Simon Peter. For the second time Peter exercises the power of binding. '*Thy money go with thee to perdition*'—the proper end for 'sons of perdition' like Judas. In spite of his baptism Simon had not really accepted
21 *the word* or doctrine of the Messiah; and *his part and lot*[4] in the
22 kingdom was taken away, until he should repent. For, although the sin was after baptism[5], yet *repentance*, i.e. a change of will and mind, of *the thought of the heart*, was still possible, and therefore *forgiveness*. S. Peter speaks doubtfully, but the doubt concerned

---

[1] No one has more fiercely denounced the sin or more completely revealed its evil consequences than Dante. See especially the *Inferno*, canto xix. 'Woe to thee, Simon Magus! woe to you, his wretched followers!' etc.   [2] The phrase is taken from Ps lxxviii 37. Simon *had gone astray having forsaken the straight way and followed the way of Balaam who loved the hire of wrong-doing* (II Pet ii 15).   [3] S. John concurs: cp. *ye* in verse 24.   [4] From Deut xii 12: cp. Col i 12. The lot is the share in the inheritance (xxvi 18).   [5] Cp. Hebr. vi 4-8.

not so much the possibility of forgiveness as of Simon's repent-
23 ance. For his heart (*a*) was full of *the bitter gall* of sin and fast
bound with *the chain of his iniquity* (a reminiscence of Isai lviii 6).
Such is the meaning of the English translation. The first expression however is taken from Deut xxix 18, where the Israelite whose heart turns away from God is among the people as 'a root that beareth gall and wormwood,' i.e. 'a root of bitterness[1].' And as the Greek is literally *thou art for* or *unto*[2], (*b*) the rendering of the RV margin is the best. S. Peter sees—and sees most truly—that Simon's sin will be a root of bitterness and gall to the church and
24 a fetter[3] of iniquity, impeding its free course. Simon instead of repenting is apparently only moved by fear. Unable to pray himself, he asks for their intercessions for his deliverance from the perdition of which they had spoken. From the Bezan text we learn that he shewed his sorrow in loud weeping[4].

Simon Magus now disappears from the Acts—but not from Christian tradition. In that he received the unenviable position of proto-heresiarch or first founder of heresy. Justin Martyr, who was himself a native of Samaria and lived about a hundred years after this, is our first informant. He tells us that Simon was a native of Gittho in Samaria, that he was almost worshipped by the Samaritans, and that he went to Rome in the reign of Claudius (A.D. 41 to 54) where the senate erected a statue to him as to a god. The last statement has received an interesting explanation. In 1574 a statue was dug up at the place Justin mentions bearing a dedication to a Sabine god, SEMONI SANCO DEO FIDIO. This is evidently what Justin saw, and being a stranger not familiar with Latin he had read it as SIMONI SANCTO DEI FILIO, i.e. TO SIMON THE HOLY SON OF GOD. Justin further and erroneously attributes to Simon the fully developed doctrines of the Gnosticism of his own day. But the words in the Acts, *Power* and *Thought*, which played a part in those systems, shew that Simon may have held the germs of gnostic doctrine. In Justin's time there were some heretics called Simonians, and they would naturally be glad to claim as their founder a famous wonder-worker of the preceding century. On the other hand the church would naturally look for a father of heresy in scripture, and so make Simon Magus, who in the Acts was the first to enunciate false doctrine, responsible for all the subsequent gall and bitterness caused by heresy. In any case his legend continued to grow. The so-called Clementine literature was written in the third century to glorify S. Peter and denounce S. Paul, and in it Simon appears as the great opponent of Peter, with whom he has public disputations at Caesarea, Tyre, Laodicea, and Antioch. In the next century legend was busy with his end. At Rome he again met, and was denounced by, S. Peter. To

---

[1] Hebr xii 15.   [2] Like *unto perdition* in verse 20.   [3] Or possibly *conspiracy*, for which the Greek word is used in Jer xi 9, as for *treason* in II K xi 14.
[4] This would be a sorrow of the world unto death; Peter's bitter weeping was of repentance unto salvation (II Cor vii 10).

maintain his reputation with the emperor and the populace, he undertook some feats of magic, and offered either to fly or to be buried alive. An experiment was made and it terminated fatally. Without committing ourselves to legend at all, it is extremely probable that Simon did not repent; but that having lost his reputation or at least his influence in Samaria, he went to Rome—the common resort of all new teachers, philosophers, and doctrinaires—and there won a body of disciples who preserved his memory and teaching, and proved to be a root of gall and bitterness to the church.

§ 3 *The conversion of the eunuch and arrival at Caesarea*

Having completed their mission and themselves also *testified*[1], the apostles return to Jerusalem; and on their way home follow up the work by preaching also *in many Samaritan villages*. Philip by direct inspiration is guided to another step forward, the baptism of the eunuch, and this concludes his special contribution to the advance of Christianity. From the Didachê we learn that wandering prophets might settle down[2]; and so S. Philip seems to have settled down to a stationary ministry at Caesarea, where he prepares the ground for the further and decisive advance in the baptism of Cornelius. In the Ethiopian eunuch are fulfilled the divine promises to the faithful eunuchs of Isai lvi 3–5 and to Ebed-melech, the Ethiopian eunuch of Zedekiah (Jer xxxviii 7–13, xxxix 16–18). There is a contrast between Simon Magus and this Ethiopian treasurer which recalls the contrast between Gehazi and the stranger Naaman who was baptized in the Jordan.

25 They therefore, when they had testified and spoken the word of the Lord, returned to Jerusalem, and ³preached the gospel to many villages of the Samaritans.
26 But ⁴an angel of the Lord spake unto Philip, saying, Arise, and go ⁵toward the south unto the way that goeth
27 down from Jerusalem unto Gaza: the same is desert. And he arose and went: and behold, a man of Ethiopia, a eunuch ⁶of great authority under Candace, queen of the Ethiopians, who was over all her treasure, who had come to Jerusalem
28 for to worship; and he was returning and sitting in his
29 chariot, and was reading the prophet Isaiah. And the Spirit said unto Philip, Go near, and join thyself to this chariot.
30 And Philip ran to him, and heard him reading Isaiah the

---

[1] The apostolic function, see pp. 7, 31.   [2] 'Every true prophet who wishes to settle among you is worthy of his food' (ch. xiii).   [3] Gk *evangelized*, so in vv. 35, 40.   [4] Or *the*.   [5] Marg *at noon*.   [6] Gk *a magnate*.

prophet, and said, Understandest thou what thou readest?
31 And he said, How can I, except some one shall guide me?
32 And he besought Philip to come up and sit with him. Now
the place of the scripture which he was reading was this,
[1]He was led as a sheep to the slaughter;
And as a lamb before his shearer is dumb,
So he openeth not his mouth:
33   In his humiliation his judgement was taken away:
His generation who shall declare?
For his life is taken from the earth.
34 And the eunuch answered Philip, and said, I pray thee, of
whom speaketh the prophet this? of himself, or of some
35 other? And Philip opened his mouth, and beginning from
36 this scripture, [2]preached unto him Jesus. And as they went
on the way, they came unto a certain water; and the eunuch
saith, Behold, *here is* water; what doth hinder me to be
38 baptized?[3] And he commanded the chariot to stand still:
and they both went down into the water, both Philip and the
39 eunuch; and he baptized him. And when they came up out
of the water, [4]the Spirit of the Lord caught away Philip;
and the eunuch saw him no more, for he went on his way
40 rejoicing. But Philip was found at Azotus: and [5]passing
through he [2]preached the gospel to all the cities, till he came
to Cæsarea.

26   The opening words and others in this paragraph remind us very
much of Elijah[6]. Like a new Elijah, then, Philip is divinely[7]
directed to *go southwards* (or *at noon*[8]) till he reaches the road
from Jerusalem to *Gaza*. Gaza was a strong fortress, two miles from
the sea, at the extreme south of Palestine. As the Egyptian traffic
passed through it, it had for a long time been a flourishing city in
spite of many reverses, such as that in the 4th century B.C. when on
his march into Egypt Alexander the Great had sacked it after two
months' siege. In B.C. 96 however the Maccabean prince Alexander

---

[1] Isai liii 7, 8.   [2] Gk *evangelized*.   [3] AV, Bezan, and 'some ancient authorities insert, wholly or in part, verse 37' (RV marg) *And Philip said, If thou believest with all thy heart, thou mayest. And he answered and said, I believe that Jesus Christ is the Son of God*.   [4] Bezan has *the Holy Spirit] fell upon the eunuch, but the angel [of the Lord caught away Philip*.   [5] Or *going about*.
[6] Elijah was guided by the angel of the LORD (I K xix 5-7, II K i 3, 15). He also *ran* (verse 30, I K xviii 46), and was *caught away by the Spirit* (verse 39, I K xviii 12, II K ii 11, 16).   [7] For the angel, see pp. 71, 72.   [8] The word occurs in xxii 6: cp. also *at noon* I K xviii 27.

had utterly destroyed it: and after this it remained *desert*. Nevertheless, under the favour of the Romans it revived, but the new city, distinguished by the name of 'maritime,' was built on the coast, leaving the old Gaza still in ruins. The direct road to Egypt would run through the old Gaza, and this is the point of the remark
27 —*this*, viz. the old city, *is desert(ed)*[1]. On his road Philip fell in with the caravan of an important official of *Ethiopia*. Ethiopia was a wide term which covered all Africa south of Egypt, including Nubia, Abyssinia, etc. Among its kingdoms that of Meroe was at this time, according to Pliny[2], governed by queens whose royal title was *Candake*. In B.C. 22 one of these queens had attacked the Roman frontier of Egypt, and now the treasurer[3] and chamberlain of another had been on a journey to Jerusalem. He was a *eunuch*, and he had 'joined himself to the Lord'; for he was a student of the scriptures, and had come up to Jerusalem as a pilgrim to some feast, probably Pentecost. Such intercourse was not new. The queen of Sheba had visited Solomon, and Zedekiah had an Ethiopian eunuch. And so to-day the Abyssinians have their church, and
28 that an imposing one, at Jerusalem. The eunuch *was reading*
29 *aloud* his Greek Bible, and Philip under a sudden divine impulse
30 *ran up* and asked if he *understood what he was reading*[4]. The
31 eunuch confessed his need of a *guide*—a very obvious metaphor for a teacher, when life is thought of as a road, and the church is called 'the way.' And *the Spirit* who was then guiding Philip is the guide of the church into all the truth (Jn xvi 13).
32 *The passage* indeed called for an interpreter. For it was the great picture of the suffering Servant of JEHOVAH in Isaiah liii, and by his enquiry the eunuch shewed his ignorance of this Servant. That he meekly submitted to death was clear from the words quoted in verse 32, but the meaning of the following verse was
33 itself obscure. There are many different interpretations of the Hebrew original, but the RV seems the best: *By oppression and judgement he was taken away* (i.e. he was cut off by an oppressive judgement); *and as for his generation, who among them considered that he was cut off out of the land of the living?* The Ethiopian however was reading the Greek version, and that seems to refer the 'taking away' to the glorification consequent upon the suffering. *When he humbled himself* (in death, Phil ii 8), *his judgement was taken away*, his condemnation reversed: *and who shall be able to declare his generation*, the new seed which he wins by his death (Ps xxii 30)? *For his life is taken away from the earth*, it has been taken up into a higher, a heavenly sphere.
35 In any case the great prophecy of the atonement was an excellent text for Philip. Starting from it he *preached the gospel of Jesus*

---

[1] This is Prof. G. A. Smith's account in *Hist. Geogr. of the Holy Land* pp. 186–7.
[2] *Hist. Nat.* vi 29.   [3] The Greek for treasure is *gaza*.   [4] There is a play upon the sound here: the Greek words for *understand* and *read* are *ginóskein* and *anaginóskein*.

unto him. S. Peter in presenting Jesus as the Servant of the LORD had referred to this prophecy chiefly in reference to the exaltation of the Servant[1], but the special mention of the *Lamb* may suggest that S. Philip rather dwelt upon what we should speak of as the doctrine of the atonement. The word *take away* is that used by S. John of 'the Lamb of God, which taketh away the sin of the world.' Philip's gospel however also included the doctrine of
36 baptism. For on reaching some water the eunuch asked if there were any *impediments* in the way of his *being baptized*. A strict Jew could have alleged two: (1) he was a Gentile, (2) he was a eunuch. But Philip knew that only faith and repentance were
38 necessary, and *he baptized him*. The RV has removed verse 37 to
37 the margin, which leaves the eunuch's question unanswered. Certainly the verse cannot remain in the text according to the best Greek MSS. But it is part of the Bezan text; and we can imagine that S. Luke, when revising his work, in his effort after conciseness and brevity drew his pen through it. The profession of faith at baptism must have been familiar enough to his Christian readers. The alternative is that it was an early interpolation. But the other accounts of baptisms were not interpolated in this way, and the appositeness and extreme simplicity of the question and answer point to their genuineness. After his experience of Simon it is natural that Philip should lay stress on *faith from the whole heart* (vv. 21, 22): and that *Jesus*, the Lamb slain but taken up from the earth, was *the Son of God* must have been the very gospel he preached to the Gentile eunuch[2].
39   The baptism over, S. Philip was immediately *caught away* by divine agency, in this case represented by *the Spirit*. The 'catching away' implies some extraordinary separation, not merely parting company[3]. The eunuch however *went on his way rejoicing*. There had been *joy* in Samaria (verse 8), but the idea of joy after separation[4] as after persecution (v 41, xiii 52) is very characteristic of S. Luke. Nothing more is known of the eunuch, nor do we hear again of Christianity in Ethiopia until the starting of a mission there by two Christian laymen in the fourth century. The eunuch, as already noticed, goes home, apparently without the gift of the Spirit: unless indeed an immediate descent, as on Cornelius, is implied in the mention of *the Spirit of the LORD*. This gives a great probability to the Bezan text which explicitly states that the Holy Spirit fell upon the eunuch and ascribes the snatching away of Philip to the same agency as before—*the angel of the LORD* (verse 26)

---

[1] Cp. iii 13, 26, I Pet ii 22-25: Jn i 29, I Jn iii 5.   [2] The chief objection is that this profession of faith anticipates S. Paul. See on ix 20: but notice the complement in the *Son of God* to the *Son of man* of vii 56. Perhaps the elimination of the text was due to the tendency to conceal the Christian mysteries.   [3] The word is used of S. Paul's being *caught up* to heaven (II Cor xii 2, 4) and forcibly *carried away* by violence (Acts xxiii 10). See also the references above about Elijah. The word *was found* also points to something exceptional.   [4] Cp. Lk xxiv 52. Contrast the Ephesian elders in xx 37.

40 However conveyed thither, *Philip was found at Azotus* the old Philistine city of Ashdod, about 20 miles north of Gaza. This he made the starting point of a new missionary tour¹, visiting and *proclaiming the gospel* in *all the cities* of the Shephelah or low coastland. These *cities* were more important than the Samaritan *villages* (verse 25), and contained a large Gentile population. Among them we may reckon Jamnia, Lydda, Joppa, and Antipatris. Last of all he would come to the most northern city, *Caesarea*. This was indeed a great centre, for it was the Roman capital of the province of Judaea.

Here Philip stopped. And here we shall find him again, twenty years later, entertaining S. Paul and S. Luke. On that occasion most likely he supplied S. Luke with the present narrative, which even among these early chapters with their Hebraic style has a distinct character of its own². S. Philip had then a house, with four daughters who like himself prophesied. So we shall hardly err in concluding that Philip had resided at Caesarea during the interval as head of the local church. His arrival and early preaching probably had some connexion with the critical event in the history of this church which is soon to be related. Meanwhile the name of Caesarea which concludes this section marks a great extension of the church. And as S. Philip must have been only one of many evangelists we shall not be surprised at the rapid growth of the church or to find Christians even before this at Damascus.

SECTION II B (= Ch. 9. 1—30)

The Acts of Saul

We now retrace our steps to another result of S. Stephen's death. S. Luke places it here, because it is the central result, which makes Stephen's death a station on the great main line of church development. It was also the immediate result: the direct answer to Stephen's prayer and the firstfruits of his blood. The chapter opens with an extraordinary manifestation of Jesus in glory, which also connects it with S. Stephen's death. This epiphany was for the purpose of apprehending (Phil iii 12), that is laying hold of, the great apostle of the second part of the Acts—S. Paul. The conversion of S. Paul brings the church into a wider sphere. For unlike the other apostles S. Paul was a man of aristocratic birth and influence, a learned scholar and theologian, a statesman and man of affairs. Possessing these special qualifications, S. Paul was the Lord's 'chosen vessel' for carrying forward the work which was the great necessity of the

---

¹ *going about*, as in verse 4, xi 19, xiii 6, xvi 6, xx 25. ² This section is specially marked by the word *evangelize* which occurs five times and in different constructions (vv. 4, 12, 25, 35, 40). The works of *prophet* and *evangelist* go hand in hand: cp. Isai xl 9, lii 7, lxi 1, Nahum i 15.

church at this stage of its growth. This work was the extension of the church to the Gentiles and its transformation from a church of Jews into a church of all men and nations. And the part S. Paul plays in it raises him to a level with S. Peter. The two apostles stand side by side as the apostle of the Circumcision and the apostle of the Gentiles (Gal ii 8).

We must then first form some idea of the new actor. S. Luke introduces him to us as 'a young man,' probably about 35 years of age[1], consenting to Stephen's death and persecuting the church. That is all S. Luke gives us, but the apostle's own words and writings[2] supply us with abundant material for filling out the portrait of Saul. For 'Saul' we must call him as yet. There were three distinct epochs in his life, and S. Luke carefully distinguishes (1) Saul the Pharisee, (2) Saul the Christian, and (3) Paul the Apostle.

To begin then with Saul the Pharisee. (i) He was born at Tarsus,—'a citizen of no mean city' he says with a ring of civic patriotism. For Tarsus was an ancient city and the capital of Cilicia: more than this, it was at this time the seat of a university and school of philosophy which came behind Athens and Alexandria alone[3]. But if by accident of birth Saul was a Hellenist, in other respects he remained a thorough Jew: he was 'a Jew of Tarsus,' 'an Israelite of the tribe of Benjamin.' His family could have settled at Tarsus only recently or temporarily, for they prided themselves on their Hebraic and Pharisaic traditions: Saul was 'a Hebrew sprung from Hebrews,' 'a Pharisee, a son of Pharisees.' He himself was educated at Jerusalem in the school of the greatest rabbi of the Pharisees, Gamaliel; and he had a married sister in the city who evidently moved in high-priestly circles[4]. These circumstances, together with the important commission entrusted to Saul by the Sanhedrin, assure us that Saul's family must have held a high place in the Jewish aristocracy. Indeed his own words 'I gave my vote,' taken strictly, imply that he himself was a member of the Sanhedrin[5]. His 'gains' (Phil iii 7) were further enhanced by the possession of the Roman citizenship[6]. In days when the *civitas* or citizenship was still hard to obtain, it was indeed a privilege, and one which carried with it very solid advantages, to be able to say *Civis Romanus sum*, 'I am a citizen of Rome,' a fellow-citizen of the Augustus. Saul was 'a Roman born,' and as Tarsus did not possess the Roman civitas, it must have been a special privilege of his own family. The citizenship might be acquired (1) by manumission: when a slave was liberated by a Roman master and became a freedman, he also became a Roman citizen. In this case Saul's father would have

---

[1] S. Paul then at his conversion would have been like Dante 'nel mezzo del cammin di nostra vita' (in the middle of the journey of our life). In the east men would hardly enter into public life till about 30. This was the age at which our Lord began his ministry, and the minimum age required for bishops and presbyters. [2] See especially ch. xxii, xxvi: II Cor xi—xii, Gal i, ii, Phil iii. [3] So Strabo informs us, *Geogr.* xiv 5. 13. [4] xxiii 16 foll. [5] xxvi 10. Professor Ramsay has also drawn attention to the evidence of wealth in Paul's family. This will be considered when we come to ch. xxi foll. [6] See xvi 37–39, xxii 25–29.

been the freedman of some Roman family. (2) By purchase: so Claudius Lysias, a Greek, had bought it for a heavy price. But S. Paul's answer to Lysias in xxii 28 and the dignity of his family exclude both these alternatives. It must then have been (3) a gift, bestowed as a mark of favour or as a reward of special service; and in those days the gift would have come from some great general or statesman, such as Pompey or Julius Caesar, Antony or Augustus. As a Roman citizen Saul must have had, in addition to his Jewish, a Roman name. And such a name was ready to hand. By a slight change *Shaúl*, in Greek *Saulos*, would become the Latin *Paulus*, a name which carried all the associations of the great and aristocratic Aemilian house or *gens*[1].

(ii) At Tarsus the Jews must have needed a knowledge of Greek, and it is unlikely that Jews of good position, and Roman citizens to boot, would have altogether denied themselves the educational advantages of the place. And so at Tarsus Saul, although he did not get his main education there, would have acquired that intimacy with Greek customs, literature, and philosophy, which is shewn by his life and letters. It was the Jewish custom to teach all boys some manual trade, and once more we can trace the influence of Tarsus, for Saul learnt its local industry of making tents out of the goats' hair which was called after Cilicia, *cilicium*. In accordance however with the strict Hebrew traditions of his family, Paul was sent to Jerusalem to be 'brought up at the feet of Gamaliel'; and there he became versed in all the learning of the rabbis, as is abundantly evidenced by his rabbinical interpretations of the scriptures of the OT. So he became 'learned[2].' But he had far more than mere learning. He possessed the originality of thought which makes a philosopher and the spiritual insight which makes a theologian. It was Saul who first grasped the drift of Stephen's teaching; who when he became a Christian was the first fully to understand the outcome of the gospel of the Christ; and who in his writings laid the foundations of Christian theology.

(iii) His character is patent from his letters and his whole history. All its varied aspects were controlled by and can be summed up in one central thought—that of Religion. One overmastering principle ruled Saul's heart and mind, and this was Faith: faith in Jehovah the God of Israel, in his promises and the destiny of Israel; faith in the unseen, to which the spiritual is the real world; faith in his own personal relation to God, his call and election. This faith shewed itself outwardly in a burning 'zeal for God,' which was the distinguishing feature of the contemporary Jews in general (xxii 3). But faith also requires a personal satisfaction, that is union with its

---

[1] The name may denote some special connexion with that family: Joseph, the Jewish historian, called himself *Flavius Josephus* after the emperors Vespasian and Titus of the Flavian gens. As a Roman citizen S. Paul must have had at least one more name, viz. a *gentile* name to shew which *gens* he or his patron belonged to, and it is singular, not to say disappointing, that we are quite ignorant of it.
[2] Jn vii 15: contrast Acts iv 13.

object or the finding of God. And there was but one means to this, viz. obedience to the will of God or Righteousness. That then was the one end and aim of Saul's life—to attain unto righteousness. As yet the divine will was known to the Jews only in the law, and righteousness meant observance of the law. To fulfil the law, to obey its letter to the utmost, the zealous Jews left no stone unturned; and their scrupulous fear of disobedience had fenced it all round with an additional burden of the traditions of the fathers. But in the matter of 'zeal for religion' Saul outstripped all his contemporaries. And in Saul as in the rest, this zeal led to (1) an intense pride of race and religion, of which we can hear an echo in the 'boasting' of Phil iii and 2 Cor xi; and (2) an intense hatred of any disloyalty to the law; hence his fanatical persecution of Stephen and the Nazarenes because of their 'blasphemy against Moses.' But (3) within Saul's own heart no real satisfaction had been won. In his epistle to the Romans he has laid bare all the inner experience by which he found the law to be unto death. For he found it to be impossible by his own efforts to attain to righteousness and fulfil the law; and the law, thus transgressed, became a stern judge, uttering the sentence of death on its transgressors. And at this moment his very excess of zeal, venting itself in the persecution of the Christians, had itself disturbed his conscience.

(iv) If this description is rather that of a restless fanatic, there is quite another side which must not be left out of sight. Saul was a born leader of men, possessing an extraordinary power of fascination over others and of arousing enthusiasm in them: and to this he may have owed in part his commission from the Sanhedrin. This power however springs from sympathy and implies strong affections. And when S. Paul became a disciple of Jesus, under the new commandment of love the affectionate side of his nature became the ruling one. In his writings he appears almost to rival S. John as an apostle of Charity[1]; and in his history, wherever he goes we find him surrounded by a band of absolutely devoted disciples and friends, his 'very children in the faith.'

§ 1 *The vision on the road to Damascus*

We now turn to the first step in the conversion or 'turning' of Saul the Pharisee into Saul the Christian; that is, the vision of the Lord on the road to Damascus. The story of the vision is fully told altogether three times in the Acts, here and in xxii 5-16, xxvi 12-18; and this indicates its crucial importance. S. Paul further alludes to it in Gal i 15-16 and 1 Tim i 12-13. We may compare the call of Samuel by name and the change of heart in Saul the son of Kish, and there are recorded the different calls of the prophets Moses and Elisha, Isaiah and Ezekiel, Jonah and Amos[2]: but this 'conversion' remains unique. Conversion such as this was a new thing in the world. Perhaps the

---

[1] Cp. e.g. I Cor xiii, Rom xiii 8-10, Col iii 14.   [2] Cp. I Sam iii 1-10, x 1-13: Exod iii: I K xix 19-21: Isai vi, Ezek i, Jonah i-iii, Amos vii 14-15.

greatest likeness to the apostle is to be found in Jeremiah[1]. For (1) he too had been predestined before birth for his office; (2) this included a special mission to the Gentiles; and (3) involved great opposition from his own people and the kings of Judah.

S. Paul himself was the authority, and the sole authority, for this narrative. It was a story he must have told again and again. Excluding the adaptations to local circumstances, both the agreements and disagreements in the accounts in the Acts are the signs of an ofttold tale. Accordingly, in one comment we will try to gather together the scattered details into one picture and harmony. This chapter like the last is still very Hebraic and similar to the OT, both in matter and style. The calls both of Saul and Ananias by name and their colloquies with the Lord continue the series of similar dialogues in the OT, only here the Lord (Jesus) takes the place of the Lord JEHOVAH. The Christians are still known by Hebrew terms—*those who call upon the Name*, and a title which appears here for the first time but was already familiar to the Jews, viz. *the saints* or *holy ones*. For a long time past among the Jews there had been those who aspired to greater devotion to the LORD and shewed their protest against the worldliness of their contemporaries by greater strictness of life; and such were known as the Pious (*Chasidim*). Both terms form part of S. Paul's vocabulary. Another mark of this chapter is the definite and common use of *the Lord* simply for the Lord Jesus. This was the regular title among Christians at the time of S. Paul's epistles. Hitherto in the Acts this use has not occurred, except possibly in one instance (ii 47).

9 But Saul, yet breathing threatening and slaughter against
2 the disciples of the Lord, went unto the high priest, and asked of him letters to Damascus unto the synagogues, that if he found any that were of the Way, whether men or
3 women, he might bring them bound to Jerusalem. And as he journeyed, it came to pass that he drew nigh unto Damascus: and suddenly there shone round about him a
4 light out of heaven: and he fell upon the earth[2], and heard a voice saying unto him, Saul, Saul, why persecutest thou me?
5 And he said, Who art thou, Lord? And he *said*, I am Jesus
6 whom thou persecutest[3]: but rise, and enter into the city,
7 and it shall be told thee what thou must do. And the men that journeyed with him stood speechless, hearing the [4]voice,
8 but beholding [5]no man. And Saul arose from the earth; and

---

[1] Jer i 4–10. [2] A Bezan text adds *with great amazement (ecstasy)*.
[3] AV and Bezan add here, or in verse 4, *it is hard for thee to kick against the pricks* (cp. **xxvi** 14). Then *And he trembling and astonished said, Lord, what dost thou will me to do? And the Lord said to him,* [*Rise* (cp. **xxii** 10). [4] Marg *sound* (ii 6).
[5] A Bezan text reads *no man*] *with whom he was talking. But he said to them, Raise me from the earth; and when they had raised him* [*and his eyes*.

when his eyes were opened, he saw nothing; and they led him by the hand, and brought him into Damascus. And he was three days without sight, and did neither eat nor drink.

1 *Saul* then, having as he thought stamped out the church in Jerusalem, but still '*being exceedingly mad* against the disciples,' still *breathing in*[1]—as we should say, an atmosphere of—*threatening and slaughter*, looked about to complete his work. It is evident that outside of Jerusalem there were at present no bodies of Christians in the holy land of any account: the church in Judaea, Samaria, and Galilee, owed its rise to the persecution itself (viii 1, ix 31). And yet we hear of a considerable body of Christians at *Damascus*. This is however readily to be accounted for, and the case of Damascus will illustrate the growth of Christianity in other *foreign cities* such as Alexandria and Rome[2]. We are familiar with Damascus in the OT as the capital of Syria. Under the Greek kings of Syria it was partially eclipsed by the glories of the new capital Antioch. But its natural advantages—its situation in the fertile plain which was watered by the golden streams of the Chrysorrhoas[3], and on the highway of traffic with the east— prevented its losing its importance; and centuries later under Mohammedan rule it regained its former position, which it still retains. To-day it is a city of 150,000 inhabitants, while Antioch has sunk into a mere village. Damascus was close to Palestine, and naturally had a large colony of Jews. There were several synagogues; all the women of the city (so Josephus informs us[4]) had fallen under Jewish influence; and in the Jewish war as many as 10000 or even 18000 Jews were massacred in Damascus. Such an important centre must have been in close communication with Jerusalem. The fame of the Lord's ministry had spread over all these parts of Syria; many of the Damascenes may have heard him, and Ananias may have been one of his disciples. Again, many Jewish pilgrims must have taken home to Damascus the news of Pentecost and the doings of the apostles[5]. The result was a similar rapid acceptance in Damascus of the new 'way' of Judaism, and the new teaching of Jesus as the Messiah. For that was as yet the simple form of Damascene Christianity; the Nazarenes had not yet separated from the synagogues, and their head, Ananias, *had a good report of all the Jews* for his piety in observance of the law (xxii 12). They appeared among the Jews as a new Way or party conspicuous for strictness of living; hence the name by which they are known—*Saints*. Damascus, then, appeared to Saul as the next 2 obvious point of attack, and he obtained *letters from the high priest*

---

[1] So the Greek (as in Josh x 40): we say *breathe out*. [2] Andronicus and Junias, who were connected with the Roman Church and *conspicuous among the apostles, were in Christ* before Saul's conversion (Rom xvi 7). They may have been missionaries at Rome, even at this time. [3] i.e. the golden-flowing. [4] *B. J.* ii 20. 2. [5] So news of Saul's commission had preceded him (verses 13, 14).

and the Sanhedrin, that is from both Sadducees and Pharisees, *to the rulers of the synagogues*, authorizing him to arrest *any whom he should find of the Way*[1] and to *bring them to Jerusalem* for punishment. The Jews had obtained from the Romans many privileges, among them the right of managing their own judicial affairs. Exact details are wanting; but this jurisdiction would be exercised in the synagogue, and the beatings of S. Paul afford evidence of its existence. Such judicial powers would not of course cover the infliction of death, while everywhere the synagogues would recognize the Sanhedrin as their supreme court of appeal.

3 The *journey* (possibly on foot) was nearly at an end. It was *mid-day*, the usual hour for rest; but Saul was eager to finish his work, and Damascus is already in sight. *Suddenly* like lightning there *flashed upon them from heaven* a dazzling *light*, far more dazzling than the blazing mid-day sun. All *fell to the ground*.

4 But in that momentary flash Saul had caught sight of a human form, whose dazzling brightness blinded his eyes. He had fallen at his feet as one dead (Rev i 17), and then *he heard a voice speaking in* his own *Hebrew tongue* and calling him by his own name with solemn reiteration, *Shaúl, Shaúl*[2]. It asked *Why art thou persecuting me?* The question was a simple one, but it contained an overwhelming revelation. In Stephen, in the hapless Nazarenes, Saul had been persecuting the Messiah himself, 'the Lord of the glory.' The voice added *It is hard for thee to kick against the pricks*. This is a common proverb, found in Greek and Latin literature as well as Hebrew; and it might seem a bathos, but that it is thoroughly in the proverbial style, familiar but incisive, of Jesus of Nazareth. And in fact it was the best description of what Saul had been doing—trying to stifle the pricks of his inmost heart or conscience, which all the time was asking, Is this righteousness of mine own really joy and peace? what if Stephen and the Nazarenes are right after all, and in possession of the true secret?

5 There was little need now to ask who was speaking, but it was all that the trembling and amazed[3] persecutor could say, *Who art thou, Lord?* For indeed could that Lord of dazzling glory be the crucified Nazarene? Yes: *I am Jesus of Nazareth whom* (for the second time) *thou art persecuting*. Once more, even in this bewildering conviction of his past life, the character of the zealous doer of works betrays itself, *What shall I* or *must I do*, i.e. to be saved[4]? There are indeed *great things* for Saul *to do* and *to be*

---

[1] See p. 76. *The way* is a mark of this section and a sign of an early date.   [2] This repetition always carries with it warning or reproach in S. Luke: *Martha Martha* (x 41), *Jerusalem Jerusalem* (xiii 34), *Simon Simon* (xxii 31). In the OT we have the double *Abraham, Moses* and *Samuel*—all direct from heaven (Gen xxii 11, Exod iii 4, I Sam iii 10). For calling by name, see Jn x 3.   [3] The *trembling* and *amazement* have disappeared from the revised text. The same emotions marked the first news of the resurrection (Mk xvi 6, 8).   [4] Like the question of the Philippian jailor, xvi 30. But it was a common thought among the Jews: cf. Lk xviii 18.

done to him, but as yet he cannot bear them. He cannot understand, his whole philosophy of religion has first to be reformed, and
6 so the command is given *Arise, and go into the city: there it shall be told thee* (by those of *the Way* which he came to stamp out)
7 *what thou must do*. This brief colloquy took but a moment. His company were already on their feet but still struck *dumb* by the sudden flash and the *sound which they heard*, but which to them
8 was inarticulate and may have been taken for thunder[1]. They lifted up the exhausted *Saul*, who on *opening his eyes* found that he was blind. And so the proud Pharisee and infuriated persecutor had to be *led by the hand into Damascus*. There he was taken to *the house of Judas* in the '*Straight Street*,' which at this day still
9 runs straight through the city from east to west. Instead of delivering his letters and commencing the inquisition, Saul remained three days in darkness, both physical and spiritual, without food or drink[2], overwhelmed at the collapse of his past life and dark as to the future. All he could do was to *pray*.

This interval will afford us space for some reflection upon this appearance. For it was a Vision (i.e. a Seeing) in the real sense of the term,—a Seeing of the Lord Jesus. Thereby God revealed to Saul his own Son[3], and that in glory, 'in the glory (the Shekinah) of the Father.' Thus like Stephen Saul also saw 'the glory of the Lord.' That in the flash of light Saul actually saw with his eyes Jesus the Lord is evident from the words of Ananias, Barnabas, and Saul himself[4]. Further, S. Paul always claimed with emphasis to have seen the Lord. The question will probably suggest itself, If Saul had been brought up in Jerusalem, must he not have met with Jesus of Nazareth? must he not have seen Christ crucified only three years back? He does in fact speak of having 'known Christ after the flesh[5].' But in any case 'if he had known Christ after the flesh, he knew him so no more.' If he had seen him then, it was not with the eyes of a disciple. And compared with this, all such sight of the Lord sank into insignificance. For this vision was (1) a sight of the Risen Lord. To have seen the risen Lord was, we remember, the unique qualification of the apostolate, for it enabled them to bear witness to the resurrection. And accordingly on this vision S. Paul bases his claim to be an apostle; it raises him to the level of the Twelve, and of James the Lord's brother to whom also the Lord had shewn himself[6]. Bestowing then such a qualification, this vision of the risen body of Jesus must be distinguished from the other appearances of the Lord with which S. Paul was so richly favoured, in dream and trance or ecstasy[7]: it was seeing him with the naked eye. It was also (2) a vision of the Glorified Lord, and so a

---

[1] As in Jn xii 29: cp. the *voice* at Pentecost like the wind (ii 2, 6). The distinction between *hearing the sound* as here and (*not*) *hearing the articulate words* (xxii 9) is marked by the use of a different case in the Greek. [2] Thus there is a fast at the crisis, as in the life of Elijah (1 K xix 8) and after the baptism of the Lord (Lk iv 2). [3] Gal i 16. [4] verse 17, xxii 14: verse 27: xxvi 16. [5] II Cor v 16. [6] I Cor ix 1, xv 5–8. See pp. 5–6. [7] Cp. xxii 17–21, xviii 9, xxiii 11; and II Cor xii 1–4.

mark of special honour. For, as has been noticed (p. 107), only four such appearances are recorded in Scripture. One was before the crucifixion, when Jesus was transfigured before Peter, James and John. The other three were after he had been taken up into glory: first to S. Stephen, then to S. Paul, and the third to S. John, which was many years later and concludes the Scripture.

Just as the reality of the vision was called in question by S. Paul's opponents, so it is to-day by certain critics. It is assumed that the literal sense of the narrative is impossible, and an easy explanation is forthcoming. Realize the uneasy conscience with unstrung nerves, the fatigue of the journey and eyes inflamed by the hot sun, add the sudden change from the blazing sand to the refreshing green of gardens, with a sudden stroke of fever, and we have quite sufficient cause for an hallucination, and therefore for 'one of the most important facts of the history of humanity[1].'

(1) A sufficient answer to such a theory is given by the plainness and simplicity of the narrative. It is extremely natural and quite matter of fact. There is none of the rhetorical embellishment which that age was so very capable of adding. The situation presented is certainly most dramatic: Saul the persecutor brought face to face with his persecuted Lord and God (Jn xx 28), and if it was the work of a literary imagination, we cannot conceive an author (least of all in those days of fading talent) thinking out a colloquy, so extraordinarily simple, and yet on the other hand so full of deep pathos, so characteristic of both the speakers, and we might add so much in harmony with the subsequent intercourse of the Lord with his disciple. To this argument must be added the effect produced, for to it S. Paul always and with truth ascribed his whole after life. We know what that was, and cause must have some adequate relation to effect. This argument we also use about the resurrection itself, and the two events stand or fall together.

(2) The discrepancies between the three narratives are alleged. But our harmony above shews that they are susceptible of an explanation. If any real contradictions are involved they must have been as patent to the compiler of the Acts as to us. In fact the variations are rather a proof of genuineness. In telling and retelling the story, while using in the main the same words, S. Paul must have sometimes varied in detail, and used a freedom relative to his environment; as in ch. xxvi, where in one sentence he sums up much subsequent revelation.

(3) A final confirmation of the narrative is given by the last words *Go into the city and it shall be told thee*, etc., in other words by its exact correspondence to the spiritual conditions of the moment. At that moment Saul could not possibly have borne any further revelation (Jn xvi 12). His mind, dazed and bewildered, could only realize this—that he had made a disastrous mistake, and that he had seen the Messiah the hope of Israel. Beyond this all was darkness. The sudden and complete transformation of Saul the Pharisee into Paul the

---

[1] This is Renan's account in *Les Apôtres*.

apostle, with which our imagination is familiar, is not the impression which the Acts would convey. This incident is but the first step in Saul's 'conversion'; to define more exactly, it is his arrest or 'apprehension,'—from another point of view, the conviction of his sin. This is followed by death, death to the old life. He is crucified with Christ, and the three days of darkness are like the three days in the tomb. But on the third day with Christ he rises from the dead in baptism ; after this he is filled with the Holy Ghost—his Pentecost ; then he is joined to the disciples and admitted to the fellowship of the common meal; and henceforth Saul the Pharisee is a new creature, Saul the Christian. In Romans vi 3–11 S. Paul describes holy baptism as a death and burial followed by a resurrection to a new life, and no doubt he is writing out of his own experience.

§ 2 *The baptism of Saul*

10 Now there was a certain disciple at Damascus, named Ananias ; and the Lord said unto him in a vision, Ananias.
11 And he said, Behold, I *am here*, Lord. And the Lord *said* unto him, Arise, and go to the street which is called Straight, and inquire in the house of Judas for one named Saul, a man
12 of Tarsus: for behold, he prayeth ; and he hath seen[1] a man named Ananias coming in, and laying his hands on him, that
13 he might receive his sight. But Ananias answered, Lord, I have heard from many of this man, how much evil he did to
14 thy saints at Jerusalem: and here he hath authority from
15 the chief priests to bind all that call upon thy name. But the Lord said unto him, Go thy way: for he is a ²chosen vessel unto me, to bear my name before the Gentiles and
16 kings, and the children of Israel: for I will shew him how many things he must suffer for my name's sake.
17 And Ananias departed, and entered into the house ; and laying his hands on him said, Brother Saul, the Lord, *even* Jesus, who appeared unto thee in the way which thou camest, hath sent me, that thou mayest receive thy sight, and be filled
18 with the Holy Ghost. And straightway there fell from his eyes as it were scales, and he received his sight ; and he arose
19 and was baptized ; and he took food and was strengthened.

10   News of Saul's mission, as well as of the havoc he had wrought at Jerusalem, had reached the Christians *at Damascus*; and *Ananias*,

---

[1] AV with B adds *in a vision*.   ² Gk *vessel of choice (election).*

I

no doubt one 'chief among the brethren[1],' was deliberating with anxiety when he had a *vision*. This vision is complementary to the one on the way to Damascus. *The Lord* (Jesus) as master of the house must, so to speak, complete the arrangements for adding Saul to
13 his household. Like the prophets of old, Moses and Samuel, Jonah and Jeremiah[2], Ananias at first shrank from facing the persecutor:
15 then the Lord revealed to him what had happened (verse 17) and the future destiny of Saul. For he was '*a vessel of choice unto me.* As the human body is the vehicle and instrument of the spirit, it is very natural to speak of it as a vessel: but the Jews probably drew the metaphor from the work of the potter, and regarded men as vessels made by the Creator. Thus Jeremiah spoke of Coniah as a despised broken vessel, and in the Maccabees the Jews are called vessels of glory. Similarly Christians are vessels of God, filled with his grace, furnishing and adorning his house[3]. And now Saul is a chosen, specially selected, vessel. (1) As the Lord (Jesus Christ) had *chosen* the Twelve to be his apostles, and Matthias to fill the vacant place, so he had *chosen* Saul for the work of an apostle. This was to *bear his name* or bear witness to him; and that primarily, though not exclusively, *before the Gentiles*, for Saul was to be the apostle of the Gentiles; and it was to reach even *kings*, not merely petty kings like Agrippa or delegates like the Roman governors,
16 but the king himself, the Caesar (xvii 7). Such bearing of the Name would necessarily also carry with it a load of *suffering*[4]. (2) But the choice was not only for office: there was a prior choice —for the sonship of God. So God had 'chosen the fathers,' i.e. Israel, to be his people, and their divine choice was the pride and fundamental doctrine of the Jews. In the NT we learn most about this divine election to sonship from S. Paul, though as a Christian doctrine it is of course common to all the apostles. The choice is of God's pure goodness; it precedes human effort, and runs back to the eternal will, even before the world began. But though it is prior to human choice, the will of God requires human correspondence, and so the eternal choice is manifested in time. It then becomes a call, which man has to answer. Thus Saul, who like Jeremiah had been 'set apart even from the womb,' who had been chosen and foreordained, is now 'called by the grace of God'— called on the road to Damascus and again through Ananias. Obedience to the call is followed by a further divine favour of justification which opens the way for the gift of sonship, and so in answer to Ananias Saul arises and is baptized[5].
17 For the interview between the two we may compare S. Paul's

---

[1] Tradition—not an early one—places him in the Seventy, and this is not at all improbable. See above, pp. 117, 129. [2] Exod iii 10 f, I Sam iii 15, Jonah i 3, Jer i 6. [3] II Cor iv 7, I Th iv 4: Jer xxii 28, I Macc ii 9: II Tim ii 20-21.
[4] The word *bear* is the same which S. John (xix 17) uses of *bearing* the cross.
[5] For *election* see i 2, 24, vi 5 (Stephen): xiii 17: (S. Paul's) xxii 14, xxvi 16 cpd with x 41. Also Rom ix 11, xi 5, Eph i 4: *calling and election* II Pet i 10, Rev xvii 14: Gal i 15, Rom viii 28-30.

account in chapter xxii. Ananias addresses the persecutor with words of forgiveness as *Brother Saul*, declares his mission from
18 *the Lord, even Jesus*, and *lays on hands*, when the *scales* fall off from Saul's eyes and sight is restored. Then he interprets the meaning of the vision (xxii 14) : (1) It was the revelation of the *will of God*. (2) This will is revealed in Christ, and so Saul had seen *the Righteous One*[1]. The occurrence of this name is one of those subtle coincidences which are the surest marks of genuineness. It is not merely that this was an early name for the Lord : it was the name which would at this stage more than any other appeal to Saul. Here was the Righteousness after which he had been striving all his life. (3) This vision and hearing of the Lord had been vouchsafed to him, because he was *to be a witness of what he had seen*, viz. the Lord in glory. In other words, as Saul would learn later on, the vision potentially constituted him an apostle[2]. Therefore *Why hesitate? Arise and be baptized*. (1) By being baptized Saul *washed away his sins*; and God in forgiving him justified him or accepted him as righteous. In baptism also, by *calling upon the name* of Jesus Christ, Saul professed his faith in Jesus as Lord. (2) Then he was *filled with the Holy Ghost* (verse 17) and so sanctified[3]. How this gift was conveyed we are not told. (*a*) It might have accompanied Ananias' laying on of hands and the recovery of sight. In that case it would have preceded baptism, as in the case of Cornelius. (*b*) Ananias may have again laid on hands after his baptism. (*c*) The Spirit may have fallen immediately from heaven, as on the apostles at the beginning. However received, the gift was probably followed by speaking with tongues and prophesying as in ii 4, x 46, and xix 6[4]. (3) By his baptism Saul was added to the church, and would therefore be admitted to the
19 common meal of the brethren, their Agape and Eucharist. At this meal he probably broke his fast; and thus *taking food*, he was *strengthened* in body, mind, and spirit.

---

[1] xxii 10 : cp. vii 52, iii 14.   [2] The words *thou shalt be a witness* are the same (in the singular) as those addressed to the Eleven in i 8.   [3] S. Paul constantly speaks of Christians as having received the gift of the Spirit at some definite moment, as in II Cor i 22, v 5, Gal iii 2. This must cover his own experience, and he would be referring in his own case to this moment. In I Cor vi 11 he describes the process thus : *ye were washed* (from your sins in the blood of Christ), *ye were sanctified* (by the gift of the Holy Ghost), *ye were justified* (accepted as righteous children by the Father).   [4] It is not necessary to suppose that the recovery of sight, baptism, and gift of the Spirit, all took place at once at this interview. The word *arise* (xxii 10) seems to imply some definite change of scene and action (cp. v 17, viii 26). Baptism required some open confession of faith in the name of Jesus (viii 37) which is intimated in *calling upon his name* (Greek aorist). In any case some witnesses would have been required for such an event as the baptism of Saul. It is quite possible then that the baptism and laying on of hands took place at some gathering of the disciples and was followed by their 'breaking of bread' together. On the other hand we have the sudden baptisms of the eunuch and the Philippian jailor.

§ 3 *Saul's preaching to the Jews and reception by the church*

After his vision and baptism the one thing which Saul needed was a space for silent reflection and communing with God. His old ideas of righteousness, of the scriptures, of the Messiah, had to be formed anew: he had to learn the true meaning of the new revelation of God and the gospel of the Christ, of his own election and the work to which he was called. So like Moses, like Elijah, like the Lord himself, he retired into the wilderness. 'Immediately,' he writes to the Galatians[1], 'I conferred not with flesh and blood: neither went I up to Jerusalem to them which were apostles before me: but I went away into Arabia and again I returned unto Damascus.' He may have gone like Elijah to the mount of God in the peninsula of Sinai[2]; but S. Paul does not appear to have been much subject to the influence of place, and any of the deserts in the neighbourhood of Damascus would be included in 'Arabia.' S. Paul continues 'Then after three years (i.e. in the third year) I went up to Jerusalem,' so that his retirement in the desert and his work at Damascus must have filled at least two full years. Subsequent history gave a new importance to this retirement. It strengthened S. Paul's contention that he had not received his gospel from human teaching; but at present all this was hid in the future. Nor did the visit to Arabia either belong to the public history of the church or contribute to S. Luke's aims; so the historian has altogether omitted it, like so much else that would be of intense interest to us, but not without leaving space for it. The words *he was strengthened* end a paragraph, and the first words of the next paragraph *And he was* may mark a new start. Elsewhere they represent the Hebrew phrase *And it came to pass*, which generally begins a narration after some interval, whether short or long[3].

What was of importance to Christian readers and the public was (1) Saul's new teaching; and we see at once the result of a new personality and of his meditations in Arabia in a new advance. For the first time in the Acts, as far as our records go (if we exclude from our text viii 37, p. 123), Jesus is proclaimed as the SON OF GOD. S. Peter had called him LORD and CHRIST, but S. Paul was the first to make explicit what was contained in the relationship of the Messiah to the FATHER. It is true that in the Gospels the Lord had called himself the SON of the FATHER in the unique sense of the only begotten[4], and this title had been treasured in the memory of some at least of the apostles, notably S. John. But though from the time of the resurrection and ascension the disciples had worshipped Jesus and acted towards him as towards the LORD (JEHOVAH), yet they were slow to adopt new

---

[1] Gal i 16 foll. [2] Cp. Gal iv 25. [3] So e.g. in Lk i 5, 59, ii 1, 6, iii 21, v 1. 12; Acts iv 5, viii 1, ix 32, xvi 16, xix 1, 23, xxviii 17. The tenses also in verse 21 (aorist and pluperfect) are those of persons looking back over a considerable interval. How the two years are to be divided between Damascus and Arabia we do not know. Verses 19-25 point to a considerable period at Damascus. [4] Lk x 22: cp. also iii 22, ix 35.

and startling terms. There is a difference between implicit faith and explicit statement: and the gradualness of development in the form of 'the teaching' is evident. So it was in the change in ordinary speech from *the Master* to *the Lord* : so in other cases of doctrine, markedly that of the catholic character of the gospel; it takes the whole of the Acts almost to make explicit what was contained in the words of S. Peter's first sermon—*pour out my Spirit upon all flesh*. (2) The new relation of Saul to the church. What would the church say to his account of himself? would the apostles forgive the persecutor, believe his story, and accept him for a teacher? The answer to this is the main subject of the following passage.

20 And he was [1]certain days with the disciples which were at Damascus. [1]And straightway in the synagogues he pro-
21 claimed Jesus, that he is the Son of God. And all that heard him were amazed, and said, Is not this he that in Jerusalem made havock of them which called on this name? and he had come hither for this intent, that he might bring them bound
22 before the chief priests. But Saul increased the more in strength[1], and confounded the Jews which dwelt at Damascus, proving that this is the Christ .
23 And when many days were fulfilled, the Jews took counsel
24 together to kill him: but their plot became known to Saul. And they watched the gates also day and night that they
25 might kill him: but his disciples took him by night, and let him down through the wall, lowering him in a basket.
26 And when he was come to Jerusalem, he assayed to join himself to the disciples: and they were all afraid of him, not
27 believing that he was a disciple. But Barnabas took him, and brought him to the apostles, and declared unto them how he had seen the Lord in the way, and that he had spoken to him, and how at Damascus he had preached boldly in the
28 name of Jesus. And he was with them going in and going out at Jerusalem, preaching boldly in the name of the Lord:
29 and he spake and disputed against the [2]Grecian Jews; but
30 they went about to kill him. And when the brethren knew it, they brought him down to Cæsarea[3], and sent him forth to Tarsus.

---

[1] Some Bezan texts have *very many days*, as below *And he entered into the synagogues of the Jews and proclaimed with all boldness Jesus, that he is the Christ,* [*the Son of God* : also in verse 22 with some other MSS *was the more strengthened*] *in the word*; and *the Christ*] *in whom God is well pleased.*   [2] Gk *Hellenists*.
[3] Some Bezan texts add *by night*.

19 On his return from Arabia Saul was received by the church at
Damascus, and made his home *with the disciples* instead of the
20 Jewish authorities. After this had been settled, he *straightway*
made public confession of his new faith *in the synagogues* by
proclaiming Jesus; i.e. he proclaimed him as a herald proclaims
21 the name of his sovereign, and this name was *the Son of God*. This
bold preaching and public recantation caused first amazement[1], then
controversy. The effect of this new force among the disciples was
22 to precipitate the disruption between '*the Jews*' and 'the church';
and in the unique mention of *his* (i.e. Saul's) *disciples* we find a sign
that the cause was a strong personal influence. It became more and
more a personal matter. Saul on his part was daily growing in the
power[2] of the Spirit, so that like Stephen he reduced his Jewish
opponents to *confusion*. With the Jews the first subject of
controversy, which preceded the question of divine worship, was
whether *Jesus is the Messiah*; and the manner in which Saul *put
23 together*[3] the scriptures was irresistible. History began to repeat itself.
24 The defeated disputants made a *plot to kill him*. It *became known
to Saul* and he hid himself. At this time the Arab kings of Petra
had won a considerable dominion on the boundary of the Roman
empire, and Damascus wavered between the two jurisdictions. To
judge from coins, it was under the Romans from about A.D. 30 to 34.
But in the latter year it may have been given back to Aretas
(Hareth), the able king of Petra who about this time inflicted a
severe defeat upon Herod Antipas. The Jews, then, secured the
good offices of Aretas' governor, and were allowed to *keep a watch at
25 the city gates* to prevent Saul's escaping. Saul, perhaps in a state of
nervous prostration, as on some subsequent occasions[4], passively ac-
quiesced in the action of *his disciples*, who *let him down in a basket
through* a window on *the wall*. The shame of this humiliating
escape seems to have affected the once proud nature of Saul more
than any of his bodily pains. Years later he singles it out as the
greatest of all his weaknesses and sufferings[5].
26 From Damascus Saul went up *to Jerusalem*. In the two years'
interval peace had been restored to the devastated church: but the
scattered Christians had hardly returned as yet; and so in Galatians i 22 S. Paul speaks of 'the churches of Judaea' rather than
'the church of Jerusalem.' Saul now looked upon them as brethren
and *attempted* to be received into their body[6]. But this was no easy
matter. *The disciples*, including the apostles, were full of *fear*
and suspicion: they had no clear proof of his sincerity. On the
other hand Saul's nature could ill brook mistrust; and there might

---

[1] Cp. the effect of the change of Saul's heart in I Sam x 11–12. [2] The word in Greek is different from the *strength* of verse 19: cp. I Cor ii 4. [3] The somewhat unusual word *proving* means literally *putting together*, and so is used for the putting together of arguments. In the (Greek) OT it is regularly used in the sense of *instruct*, as in I Cor ii 16. It recurs in xix 33 where is a similar connexion with *confounding*. [4] Cp. verse 30, xvii 14. [5] II Cor xi 31–3. For similar incidents see Josh ii 15, I Sam xix 12. [6] Cp. v 13.

have been unhappy consequences but for the work of a mediator.
27 *Barnabas* was at Jerusalem, and he was a man of authority in the church. Cyprus, his home, lay opposite Cilicia, and thus he may have had some previous acquaintance with Saul or his family. In any case he now welcomed him and heard his story. Then, true to his character of 'son of consolation,' he *took him* by the hand, formally introduced him to the apostolic college, and as a sponsor vouched for the truth of his vision. *The apostles*, who were in fact represented only by Peter and James the Lord's brother[1], received him; S. Peter even took him into his own house; and after this
28 Saul lived *with them* in regular intercourse. This intercourse, with the Hebrew expression for it—*going in and going out*[2], almost implies some recognition of an apostolate. Certainly Saul began to work in Jerusalem as at Damascus. Like an authorized preacher of the word he *spake boldly in the name of the Lord*. It is difficult however to understand why Saul had in fact so little social intercourse with his fellow-Christians, that years later he could say generally that he was 'unknown by face unto the churches of Judaea.' (1) There are some explanations ready to hand. Saul was a 'new man,' and differences of character and of antecedents remained. The disciples were still scattered, and in fact *them* in verse 28 applies to the apostles. Moreover Saul was in Jerusalem only a fortnight. (2) Probably however the real reason lay in the distinction between the Aramaic-speaking and Greek-speaking disciples, i.e. between the Hebrews and the Hellenists. That this division was far greater in ordinary life than we suppose we have been already led to suspect by the strange escape of the apostles in the persecution (p. 110), and henceforth Saul's life and activity lay on the Hellenist side of the church.
29 In this direction he now turns his face. Like Stephen he *argued with the Hellenist Jews*, probably in the very same synagogue, and already we see the retribution begin to work. The Hellenist Jews dealt to him the same measure as to Stephen: they sought an
30 opportunity *to kill him. The brethren perceived it*, and Saul let them—no doubt Barnabas in the first place—*take him down to Caesarea* and there put him on board ship for *Tarsus*. This time we know the reason why Saul yielded to their wishes, for he tells us himself in xxii 17-21. Like the other Christians Saul frequented
22 *the temple* for *prayer*: and one day, being weighed down with
17 despondency at the obstinacy of the Jews, he *fell into a trance* or
18 *ecstasy*. He again *saw* the Lord, who ordered him to *leave Jerusalem*
19 *with haste*. Saul almost excused the Jews for their unbelief: with his work as a Persecutor so fresh in their minds, how could they
21 trust him as an Evangelist? But the Lord was going to *send him*

---

[1] For these and other details see Gal i 15-24. [2] It is used of the Lord in i 21, and of the shepherd in Jn x 9; in the OT of David, I Sam xviii 16. It seems to imply that Saul had already become a shepherd or leader of the people.

forth[1] from Jerusalem to a wider field where this obstacle would not be felt, viz. *to the Gentiles far off.* This vision Saul no doubt kept
9 to himself. But when shortly afterwards the brethren wanted to *send*
30 *him forth*[1], he recognized the hand of the Lord and gladly retired for the time to his native city *Tarsus.* There he could revolve in his mind this new idea of a mission to the Gentiles, and there we leave him, working 'in the regions of Syria and Cilicia' and being prepared for the future.

This history has already brought us to a difficulty in the Acts. For the life of S. Paul we have besides S. Luke another authority, and that of the first class, viz., S. Paul himself in his own writings and speeches. Now at times, and especially in Galatians i and ii, S. Paul seems to give quite a different account from that of the Acts. This difference becomes crucial when we get to the council in the 15th chapter, but we must consider it at once. That the differences are not irreconcilable the attempted harmony may have shewn. But there are certain differences in fact and nature, which when realized will teach us that the difficulty is exactly what we should expect to occur in a true history.

(1) First, there is the difference between facts as seen from within and without, i.e. between the inner and outer history. After all it is the inner thoughts and feelings, motives and policy, of the actors which make history. But the general public can only see the external action. Until the inner working is laid bare, this outward action is capable of very different and quite erroneous explanations. These can only be set right when the diaries, letters, and secret despatches, of statesmen and others are published, and the result of such publication is full of surprises: there often seems to be a contradiction between the facts of the history as hitherto known to the public, and the real history as revealed in the minds and private deeds of the statesmen. Now this is the first difference between the Acts and S. Paul's epistles. In the epistles we have his inner history, in the Acts the history of his external action as an apostle of the church.

(2) There are differences of view between individuals. No two persons have exactly the same ideas; and the difference of mind makes a difference of vision. Men see the same facts differently. There is perhaps hardly an event in history, of which the different accounts will be found to agree exactly. Now S. Luke was an ardent disciple of S. Paul, but he had a character of his own. His own personality was by no means swallowed up in that of his master, and naturally they saw things differently. Thus we have two accounts of the council which give different impressions; and no doubt, if S. Peter and S. James had written on the subject, we should have had two more accounts, each perfectly true and yet each giving a new version of it.

(3) Again, in writings everything depends on the intention of the writer. S. Paul had a definite purpose in giving us what auto-

---

[1] The Greek words in ix 30 and xxii 21 are the same.

biographical notices he does. But S. Luke's aim in the Acts was a different one. It was to write neither S. Paul's inner history nor a complete history of his life, but the history of the church of God. Thus he omits a great deal in S. Paul's life which does not bear immediately on his purpose. He omits the visit to Arabia; he passes over in silence several years of work between ix 30 and xi 25 (c. A.D. 35 to 42); years of work at Corinth and Ephesus, and missionary tours of several months, are summed up in a paragraph or even a sentence, e.g. in xx 2; and, lastly, not a word is said about S. Paul's epistles. If we compare S. Paul's list of his sufferings in II Cor xi with the Acts, we shall get an idea of how much S. Luke has left out. Indeed, if he had attempted to record all that S. Paul said or did, he might have complained, like the Evangelist S. John, that the world would not contain the books to be written.

Now with regard to the affairs at Jerusalem, S. Paul is simply concerned with his relation to the Lord. He had had such direct visions and calls that external recognition by the other apostles was to him in his personal life of minor importance. But in this matter the point of view of the church was very different, and S. Luke was writing for the church. The ordinary churchman might not be acquainted with S. Paul's inner life and spiritual experiences: but he did require to be assured of S. Paul's position—viz. whether he was an apostle or no. In the matter of apostleship, as well as of sacraments, the inward and outward are inextricably bound together. And so S. Luke, in writing the external history, is careful to shew that S. Paul was duly baptized, filled with the Spirit, and received into the fellowship of the apostles.

To conclude, S. Luke himself[1] can have seen no contradiction or incompatibility between these different views; else he would not have inserted in the same book the different accounts of the vision at Damascus and of Saul's departure from Jerusalem. That he was also perfectly aware of his omissions will be evident, if we compare, e.g., his report of S. Paul's speech at Ephesus in xx 18-35, and especially verses 19 and 34, with his own account of the apostle's ministry there in xix 1-22.

SECTION II C (=Ch. 9. 31—11. 18)

The Acts of Peter and the opening of the door to the Gentiles

While the future apostle of the Gentiles, having received his mission, is gone to Tarsus, his work is anticipated by the apostle of the circumcision. S. Peter was chosen by God (xv 7) formally to admit the

---

[1] Or, for those who reject the Lucan authorship, the final compiler whoever he may have been.

Gentiles to the church. As the apostle to whom the keys of the church had been entrusted, he opens the door; and the first entrance of the Gentiles is the subject of this section. Hitherto the church has had to deal only with Samaritans, or proselytes like Nicolas of Antioch, or a 'stranger' in the exceptional position of the Ethiopian eunuch. Now it is brought face to face with the ordinary Gentiles of the world, uncircumcised Gentiles. It will take several chapters (x-xv) and many years before their reception on a basis of equality will be fully and frankly conceded, as at the council of A.D. 48 (ch. xv). But the baptism of Cornelius is the initial step and the decisive one. Cornelius had indeed made some steps towards Judaism, but his case was evidently crucial and typical. His baptism was the Pentecost of the Gentiles. By the gift of the Holy Spirit, in no whit short of the gift at the first Pentecost, God shewed that he was no respecter of persons, that in his sight Jew and Gentile were equal. It was, as it were, the divine announcement to the world that henceforth distinction of race in the matter of spiritual privilege is abolished. By this baptism God cleansed the hearts of the Gentiles (xv 9). It was, we might almost say, a new creation.

In the history of it, as we shall see, there are two points to be carefully distinguished: viz. (1) the relation between Jews and Gentiles in respect of simple race distinction, (2) the relation of Gentiles to the church in respect of the gospel. S. Peter (1) by his eating with Gentiles shews that the barriers of intercourse are broken down: and (2) by the baptism of Cornelius he receives them into the church. The narrative from ix 31 to xi 18 forms one whole, which evidently forms a companion picture to ix 1-30. It bears the same Hebraic complexion as the early chapters; the mention of *the saints* links it with the preceding paragraphs, and so with them it may have come from Philip; but it has none the less a character of its own[1]. The incidents narrated in ix 32-42 form the introduction to the cardinal event and bring Peter down to Joppa: while as a starting point S. Luke gives us a picture of the quiet growth of the church.

§ 1 *The peace of the church*

The Persecution of the church was followed by a *Peace*. This was the natural consequence of the conversion of the chief persecutor, Saul. But as time advanced, the Jews were to find good reasons for leaving the church alone. In the year 38 the Gentile population of Alexandria made an onslaught upon the Jewish quarter, and a terrible persecution of the Jews ensued. Next year the mad emperor Caligula, having discovered that he was a god, insisted on his image being put up in the temple at Jerusalem. This presented to the Jews a dire dilemma: to

---

[1] (a) *Saints* in ix 32, 41: cp. verse 13, xxvi 10: cp. *vessel* ix 15, x 11; (b) cp. *peace* ix 31, x 36: *alms* ix 36, x 2, 4, 31; the Hebraism *it came to pass* is a mark of this section ix 32, 37, 43, x 25: the same (Greek) word occurs six times besides. The question of the Bezan text here becomes of importance: it has some interesting additions which have all the marks of genuineness.

permit the erection of the statue was an absolute impossibility, and rebellion and war would have been the only issue. After months and months of terrible strain and suspense, they were however happily delivered by the assassination of Caligula in 41. The long Peace thus secured for the church was a period of quiet and steady growth.

31   So [1]the church throughout all Judæa and Galilee and Samaria had peace, being edified ; and, walking in the fear of the Lord and in the comfort of the Holy Ghost, was multiplied.

The 'scattering abroad' of the persecution has spread *the church over the whole* of Palestine. But this is the only time we hear of the church in *Galilee*,—the chief scene of our Lord's ministry, and a century later the headquarters of rabbinism. The growth of the church is described from within and without. (1) Internally, the church was *being edified*, that is *builded up*. The metaphor of a building or temple has already been used by S. Peter in iv 11, as it will be by S. Paul in xx 32 ; and the word *edify* is generally used in the spiritual sense. The stones had been hewn and prepared by the persecution, and now in the time of peace they are firmly built in their place. Wavering and uncertain adherents have been changed into definite and decided Christians. (2) The next clause describes the external *multiplication* of numbers, and we glide into the familiar metaphor of the way. To walk in the way the Christian needs two helps : *the fear of the Lord* drives him to keep the commandments, and the *help (paraclesis) of the Holy Ghost* enables him to do so. Like the judgement of Ananias, the persecution had taught the church the fear of the Lord (Jesus)[2]—to be near him was to be near the fire: now in the peace they were enjoying the comfort of the Paraclete.

The apostolic visitation and preparatory signs

The case of the Samaritans had shewn the need of apostolic journeys ; and now the great extension of the church was drawing the apostles away from Jerusalem. When S. Paul visited the city, he found there Peter alone of the Twelve (p. 139), and in xi 1 the apostles are *throughout Judaea*. S. Luke, then, gives a typical picture of an apostolical, or we might say episcopal, visitation *through all parts*. The incidents further illustrate the place of miracles within the Christian household. Here they come in answer to prayer, as gifts of divine favour. But they do not lose their symbolical character. The record of these two miracles at this point makes us fancy that S. Luke saw in them a double sign of the great event to which they were the preface, viz. the gift to the Gentiles of *repentance unto life* (xi 18). For they are complementary : (1) The healing of Aeneas denotes the restoration of activity; and in the parallel sign of the Lord,

---

[1] AV and Bezan have *the churches*.   [2] v 11: cp. II Cor v 11.

the healing of the palsied man at Capernaum, this is associated with the forgiveness of sins[1]. (2) The raising of Dorcas denotes the gift of life; and it shews the need of it even for the pious such as Dorcas, as for the innocent like Jairus' daughter, whom the Lord raised[2]. In Aeneas then we may see symbolized the healing of those Gentiles who are sick with sin, or *repentance*; in Dorcas the giving of *life* to those Gentiles who, though full of good works, are yet aliens from the life of God because of the ignorance that is in them (Eph iv 18)[3]. Besides the Lord's miracles, we have similar miracles of life-giving wrought by Elijah and Elisha[4]; and in S. Paul's ministry (1) the healing of Publius' father and (2) the raising of Eutychus[5].

32 And it came to pass, as Peter [6]went throughout all parts, he came down also to the saints which dwelt at Lydda.
33 And there he found a certain man named Æneas, which had
34 kept his bed eight years; for he was palsied. And Peter said unto him, Æneas, Jesus Christ healeth thee: arise, and
35 make thy bed. And straightway he arose. And all that dwelt at Lydda and in Sharon saw him, and they turned to the Lord.
36 Now there was at Joppa a certain disciple named Tabitha, which by interpretation is called [7]Dorcas: this woman was
37 full of good works and almsdeeds which she did. And it came to pass in those days, that she fell sick, and died: and when they had washed her, they laid her in an upper chamber.
38 And as Lydda was nigh unto Joppa, the disciples, hearing that Peter was there, sent two men unto him, intreating him,
39 Delay not to come on unto us. And Peter arose and went with them. And when he was come, they brought him into the upper chamber: and all the widows stood by him weeping, and shewing the coats and garments which Dorcas made,
40 while she was with them. But Peter put them all forth, and kneeled down, and prayed; and turning to the body, he said, Tabitha, arise[8]. And she opened her eyes; and when she
41 saw Peter, she sat up. And he gave her his hand, and raised her up; and calling the saints and widows, he presented her
42 alive. And it became known throughout all Joppa: and

---

[1] Lk v 17–26: Mt ix 2–8, Mk ii 3–12. [2] Lk viii 41–56: Mt ix 18–26, Mk v 22–43. [3] Cp. ix 34 and x 38: ix 36 and x 1, 38. [4] I K xvii 17–24, II iv 8–37. [5] xxviii 8, xx 7–12. [6] Or *went about* (cp. viii 40, xiii 6). [7] i.e. *Gazelle.* [8] Bezan texts add *in the name of Jesus Christ* or *our Lord J. C.*

43 many believed on the Lord. And it came to pass, that he abode many days in Joppa with one Simon a tanner.

32 *Lydda* was a large village, almost a city, on the road from Jerusalem to Joppa and 12 miles from the latter. It was at the foot of the hills of central Palestine in the fertile plain of *Sharon* (so famous for its flowers)[1], which lay between the hill country and
36 the sea. *Joppa*, the modern Jaffa, was (and is) the port of Jerusalem. To it Hiram sent the timber for the temple; and thither Jonah fled to find a ship bound for the west[2]. The Maccabees had won it in B.C. 148, and they made it into a thoroughly Jewish city: it was the only seaport which the Jews ever possessed for themselves. These two cities lay in the district evangelized by S. Philip on his way to Caesarea: and Aeneas with his thoroughly Greek name and Simon the tanner (verse 43) sound very much like his work. Joppa however was in such close connexion with Jerusalem, that, as at Damascus, there must have been disciples there almost from the beginning; and the mention of *the widows* points to a developed organization as in the mother church (vi 1).
33 If these events took place in A.D. 37, the *eight years* of Aeneas' paralysis would coincide with the years of the church's new life.
34 In working the cure S. Peter, as before in iii 1, makes it clear that it is Jesus Christ who is still *doing good and healing* (x 38) in the
35 person of his apostle[3]. The sign had a great effect on the whole of the surrounding population who consequently *turned towards the Lord*. Their attention was attracted to the church and the Messianic claim of Jesus. It is not stated that *all* believed (verse 42) or were baptized.
36 At *Joppa* at this moment there had *died a disciple, Tabitha*. Tabitha is the type of the Christian woman devoted to practical good works, as distinct from the more contemplative 'virgin' or 'widow' devoted to prayer[4]. And in the modern *Dorcas* societies she
38 appears as the patroness of such domestic charities. The expectation of *the disciples* shews their faith in the power of S. Peter (cp. v 15-16), although hitherto we have not read of an instance of the apostles fulfilling their commission to 'raise the dead' (Mt x 38). As the Macedonian invites S. Paul in xvi 9, they invite S. Peter to come and help them; and they use the words with which Balak
40 summoned Balaam (Num xxii 16). The description of the miracle closely resembles that of the raising of Jairus' daughter, but unlike
41 his Lord Peter first *kneels and prays*. He also takes Tabitha's hand after she has returned to life; to have done so before would have made him unclean. Further, like Elijah and Elisha, he wrought the

---

[1] Song of Songs ii 1.   [2] II Chron ii 16: Jonah i 3.   [3] In the Greek there is a similarity of sound: *iátai se Iēsous* would be like saying *the Healer heals thee*: cp. p. 122 note [4].   [4] See I Tim ii 10, v 10 and in the OT Proverbs xxxi 10-31. The contemplative side is represented by the prophetess Anna in Lk ii 36: cp. Mary and Martha Lk x 38-42.

42 miracle in complete solitude. News of the sign spread outside the church, and made a great impression on the whole city. *Many believed* and were added to the church.

43 To gather up the fruits of the work demanded a prolonged stay in Joppa. The lodging S. Peter chose—the house of *Simon a tanner*—is a sign of the breaking down of Jewish prejudices, and a fit preparation for the following history. For the trade of tanning, involving continual contact with the skins of unclean animals, was inevitably held unclean by the Jews. And now from Joppa we must look north to Caesarea.

§ 2 *The preparation of Cornelius*

Caesarea owed its greatness to Herod the Great. It was originally an insignificant town called 'Strato's Tower.' Augustus gave it to Herod, and Herod transformed it into a great city. First he made a superb harbour, which was a great want on that open coast, and the remains of his immense breakwaters are still to be seen. Then he rebuilt the city on a magnificent scale, and renamed it after his patron CAESAREA AUGUSTA. It was built in the Greek style with theatre, amphitheatre, and a palace for himself (xxiii 35); and it was selected by Herod as the centre for the worship of Rome and the Emperor. This cult was rapidly spreading over the provinces, and was becoming almost a test of loyalty. Accordingly, to the great scandal of the Jews, a temple with images of Augustus and of Rome stood overlooking the harbour. In the population the Gentile element naturally predominated, and the Jews were in the minority, although Herod was a Jewish king. Both races however had equal civil rights, and this proved a source of constant friction.

When the Romans took over Judaea, they made Caesarea the capital of the province and the residence of the governor or procurator. As such it also became what we should call a garrison town. According to Josephus, five cohorts and a squadron of cavalry were stationed at Caesarea. These were auxiliary troops, levied for the most part out of Syria. Nothing is told us of any other forces there; but it is quite reasonable to suppose that there would have been a nucleus of Roman soldiers in the province. Legions were not stationed in the smaller provinces, and so S. Luke is probably quite right in speaking of *the Italian cohort*, for that was the name for auxiliary cohorts raised out of Italian volunteers. One inscription shews that there was such an Italian cohort in Syria in the 2nd century, and another recently discovered in Austria proves that there was one there in A.D. 69[1]; and

---

[1] Mr Haverfield called attention to this inscription in the *Guardian* of June 10, 1896. The significant words are *OPT. COH. II. ITALIC. C. R. F..TINI RX VEXIL. SAGIT. EXER. SYRIACI*, i.e. *adjutant of the 2nd Italian cohort of Roman citizens, of the century of Faustinus, from the archery division of the army of Syria*. It is not necessary to suppose that Cornelius' cohort was part of the garrison of Caesarea: he seems to have been well known in Judaea (x 22). Or again, I do not know that the Greek prevents our supposing that he may have retired from an Italian cohort and settled at Caesarea.

it cannot be very rash to infer that there was also one in Judaea before the reign of Herod Agrippa (41–44) when this incident happened. Possibly S. Luke has not given us the name in common use: having his eye ever upon Rome, the goal of the book, he may have intentionally selected out of the full official title the epithet *Italian*.

The legion was the regiment of the Roman army, and it consisted nominally of 6000 men. Each legion was divided into ten cohorts, and again each cohort contained six centuries or 'hundreds' of men. The officer in command of a cohort was called a *tribune* or in the Greek *chiliarch*: such was Claudius Lysias of xxi 31 and xxiii 26. A century was under a *centurion* or *hekatontarch*. The centurions then would rather correspond to our non-commissioned officers; but any Roman officer would enjoy great authority and power in respect of the provincials, and easily find opportunities of amassing money. The NT however presents the centurions in a very favourable light. In an army when a soldier is religious, his religion is, or rather must be, thorough. Like other armies the Roman army was not wanting in soldiers of deep religious feeling and genuine piety. Such men would be mostly found among the centurions, men who had risen by their character, and for such soldiers of a simple and natural religion, who were 'feeling after God,' the Jewish faith of the One God must have had a great attraction. Thus at Capernaum there was a centurion, who 'loveth our nation and hath built us a synagogue' (Lk vii 5), and now at Caesarea we find another *well reported of by the whole nation of the Jews*.

This was *Cornelius*. From the name of his cohort we may conclude that he was an Italian (if not a Roman by birth), and as such he possessed the Roman citizenship. He himself bears the name of the great Roman house to which belonged the Scipios and Sulla, and must have stood in some connexion with it. Sulla himself manumitted 10,000 slaves all of whom would have taken the name of Cornelius. Our Cornelius however was evidently (1) a man of importance in Caesarea. He was well known *to the whole Jewish nation*; and he had many *close friends and kinsfolk* in Caesarea, whether we are to understand by the latter actual relations, or simply Italians, of the same nationality as himself[1]. Besides this he was (2) *a devout man and one who feared God*[2]. This is the regular description in the Acts for the outer ring of God-fearing adherents to the Jewish faith. They were not 'proselytes': 'proselytes' were circumcised and bound to keep the whole law[3]. The 'God-fearing' only accepted the creed of the One True God, made varying compliances with Jewish customs, and were admitted to a place in the synagogue. Their position is well illustrated by Cornelius. (1) He was friendly to, and *well reported of* by, *the Jews*. (2) His religion shewed itself in the forms of natural piety recognized by them,

---

[1] S. Paul speaks of the Jews as his *kinsfolk* in Rom ix 3. [2] There are two Greek words for *devout* in the Acts, one used of Jews in ii 5, viii 2, xxii 12: the other as here of Gentiles vv. 2, 7. [3] Gal v 3.

Prayer and *Almsgiving* (especially *to the People*)[1]. The subject of his constant prayer is revealed by this history, and shews that he was one of those seekers who were 'feeling after God if haply they might find him.' In this position he was not alone in Caesarea. He seems to have been the centre of a kind of church in his house. His own household, as was natural then, followed his faith[2]; his kinsfolk were in sympathy with him: and he had *those who stedfastly continued with him*. This word is used in the Acts for religious adhesion[3], and certainly one of these was a soldier like himself *devout*. Perhaps in all this we may see some effect of Philip's influence, for before this probably he had reached Caesarea and begun to evangelize. For an OT parallel we may compare the chief captain of Syria, Naaman, coming to the prophet of despised Israel, and sent to baptize himself in Jordan (II Kings v 1–19).

10 Now *there was* a certain man in Caesarea, Cornelius by
2 name, a centurion of the band called the Italian *band, a devout man, and one that feared God with all his house, who gave much alms to the people, and prayed to God alway.
3 He saw in a vision openly, as it were about the ninth hour of the day, an angel of God coming in unto him, and saying to
4 him, Cornelius. And he, fastening his eyes upon him, and being affrighted, said, What is it, Lord? And he said unto him, Thy prayers and thine alms are gone up for a memorial
5 before God. And now send men to Joppa, and fetch one
6 Simon, who is surnamed Peter: he lodgeth with one Simon a
7 tanner, whose house is by the sea side[5]. And when the angel that spake unto him was departed, he called two of his household-servants, and a devout soldier of them that waited
8 on him continually; and having rehearsed all things unto them, he sent them to Joppa.

3 According to his custom Cornelius was observing with *prayer the ninth hour*, which was the time of the evening oblation, about 3 p.m.[6] According to the AV of verse 30 he was also *fasting*: but the word is absent from the earliest MSS and there is confusion in the readings of the MSS which mention it. On this occasion he had a *vision*. He *clearly saw a man in bright apparel enter* the room and *stand before him*. Cornelius perceived that he was *an*

---

[1] For almsgiving cp. e.g. Tobit iv 8–11. If with some MSS in x 30 we add *Fasting*, we have the three duties of Mt vi 2–18. [2] Cp. xvi 32, 34, xviii 8. [3] In ii 42, viii 13. [4] Gk *cohort*. [5] AV with some Bezan texts adds *he shall tell thee what thou must do* (cp. ix 6, xi 14). [6] Cp. iii 1, I K xviii 36, Dan ix 21.

4 *angel of God*[1], and was filled with the fear which accompanies supernatural appearances. He was however reassured by the message of the angel. '*His prayers had been heard, and his alms were had in remembrance before God*' (verse 31). The Jews had rightly perceived that the real punishment to be dreaded was to be forgotten or forsaken of God[2]; and their constant prayer was 'Remember me, O God,' their anxious desire to find something to serve for a *memorial* of them before God. In particular this name of *memorial* had been given to that part of the meal offering—the handful of flour with oil and incense—which the priest burnt upon the altar and which ascended unto the Lord as a sweet savour[3]. The fragrance of the incense called Israel to remembrance before JEHOVAH, as the sweet smell of Noah's sacrifice reminded him of Noah. This offering then accompanied the daily sacrifice and putting the Lord in remembrance made the sacrifice acceptable to him. It is evident that this was a foreshadowing of the 'perpetual memory' of the sacrifice of Christ which, to use human speech, by reminding the FATHER of the oblation upon the cross makes the Christian prayer and sacrifice acceptable and efficacious. One of the Psalmists however had seen that prayer itself was a sweet savour, when he said (cxli 2) 'Let my prayer be set forth as incense before thee; the lifting up of my hands as the evening sacrifice': so in the case of Cornelius, who as a Gentile had no share in the daily offering in the temple, his prayers and alms *went up to God*[4] and served as a memorial before him. God then remembered Cornelius, but the revelation for which he prayed was not to be given directly:
5 like Saul he must be told by the church. Accordingly he is to *send*
6 *for one Simon surnamed Peter*,—an unknown Jew, *lodging* in a
7 very humble abode, the house of *a tanner*. Cornelius, however,
8 overcoming any instincts of pride, obeyed at once. He sent three messengers who at noon of the next day reached *Joppa*, a distance of 30 miles or more. While they were asking for Simon's house, another divine communication was there being made.

The preparation of Peter and vision of cleansing

The mere growth of the church of itself was forcing upon the apostles the practical problem of their relation to the Gentiles. To the Jews all Gentiles were unclean: consequently, although there were different views as to the amount of rigour in practice, *it was unlawful for a Jew to join himself or come unto one of another nation*. Jews and Gentiles were separated by a sharp barrier. For (1) in general, in

---

[1] The natural expression of a Gentile: not as heretofore *the angel of the* LORD. Cp. i 10. [2] Cp. Mt xxvii 46. [3] *Mnemosunon*. It occurs in Levit ii 2, 9, v 12, etc.: Isai lvi 5: Ecclus xxxviii 11, xlv 11 (the breastplate), 1 16 (the singing of the priests). For Noah cp. Gen viii 21. In Lk xxii 19 a different word *Anamnesis* is used for the Lord's memorial. [4] Through the ministry of angels according to the later Jewish doctrine. Raphael says to Tobit (xii 12) 'I did bring the memorial of your prayer before the Holy One.' Cp. Rev viii 3-4.

contrast to Israel, the 'peculiar people' having a definite covenant with God, the Gentiles were *common* : they had not been called into relation with God, they were 'aliens from the commonwealth of Israel and strangers from the covenants of the promise.' (2) In particular, they were all in fact *unclean* in virtue of the law of cleanliness. The Gentiles did not observe the distinction between clean and unclean meats : consequently to avoid pollution Jews abstained, not only from the use of Gentile markets and butchers, but practically from all social intercourse with Gentiles ; for there can be no real social intercourse when eating together is prohibited[1]. On the other hand, if Jews despised Gentiles as common and unclean, Gentiles retorted by ridiculing Jews for their abstinence from pork, and the separation was complete.

Thus the question of clean and unclean meats was fundamental. We can see the distinction becoming emphatic in the Captivity as in the case of Daniel[2]. It was the subject of special teaching of our Lord[3], as it now occasions a special revelation to S. Peter. For it was the first difficulty that would present itself in practice. What was a Christian Jew to do ? was he still cut off from intercourse with Gentiles by this law of uncleanness ? This question must have been pressed upon Peter by his visit to Joppa with its shipping and busy Gentile population. Joppa also must have made him think of Jonah, the prophet who had been entrusted with a message to the Gentiles and had fled to Joppa to escape from it. Was he a second Jonah shrinking from the solution of this question ? The solution he ought to have known. For the Lord had long ago settled it. When he said that *there is nothing from without the man that going into him can defile him, but the things which proceed out of the man are those which defile the man*, he 'made all meats clean[4].' But S. Peter had forgotten and was slow to understand, and a second cleansing was necessary.

9 Now on the morrow, as they were on their journey, and drew nigh unto the city, Peter went up upon the housetop 10 to pray, about the sixth hour: and he became hungry, and [5]desired to eat: but while they made ready, [6]he fell into a 11 trance ; and he beholdeth the heaven opened, and a certain vessel [7]descending, as it were a great sheet, let down by four 12 corners upon the earth : wherein were [8]all manner of fourfooted beasts and creeping things of the earth and fowls of 13 the heaven. And there came a voice to him, [9]Rise, Peter ;

---

[1] See Jn xviii 28. For *eating together*, see xi 3, Gal ii 12-14 · it was the charge brought against the Lord that he *did eat with publicans and sinners* (Lk v 30, xv 2) : cp. x 41, I Cor x 25-29. [2] Dan i 8-16 ; cp. Ezek iv 13, 14, Hos ix 3. [3] Mt xv 10-20, Mk vii 14-23. [4] Mk vii 19. [5] Gk *willed to* (AV *would have eaten*). [6] Gk *there came upon him an ecstasy.* [7] AV and Bezan texts have *descending*] *to him...bound by (knit at) the four corners and let down.* [8] Gk *all the [fourfooted.* [9] Augustine quotes thus : *Peter, all which thou seest in the vessel slay and eat... Lord, common and unclean I will not touch...What I have made holy call not unclean.*

14 kill and eat. But Peter said, Not so, Lord; for I have never
15 eaten anything that is common and unclean. And a voice
came unto him again the second time, What God hath
16 cleansed, make not thou common. And this was done thrice:
and straightway the vessel was received up into heaven.
17 Now ¹while Peter was much perplexed in himself what
the vision which he had seen might mean, behold, the men
that were sent by Cornelius, having made inquiry for Simon's
18 house, stood before the ²gate, and called and asked whether
Simon, which was surnamed Peter, were lodging there.
19 And while Peter thought on the vision, the Spirit said unto
20 him, Behold, ³three men seek thee. But arise, and get thee
down, and go with them, nothing doubting: for I have sent
21 them. And Peter went down to the men, and said, Behold,
I am he whom ye seek: what is the cause wherefore ye are
22 come? And they said, Cornelius a centurion, a righteous
man and one that feareth God, and well reported of by all
the nation of the Jews, was warned *of God* by a holy angel
to send for thee into his house, and to hear words from thee.
23 So he called them in and lodged them.

9 With all his need for light *Peter went up upon the housetop*
for his mid-day *prayer*. To pray three times a day was a Jewish
custom: 'in the evening and morning and at noonday will I pray⁴.'
The flat housetop of oriental houses was in general use for prayer
10 and meditation, as also for sleeping and recreation⁵. S. Peter
probably had not yet broken his fast, and he felt *hungry*. This
in itself may have suggested the thought of meats, and in this
11 condition *he fell into a trance* or *ecstasy* (xxii 17). He saw a *vessel*
in the shape of *a great sheet* with its *four corners* knit together and
by them *lowered upon the earth*. It came down where he was, and
12 looking into it he saw that it was full of living creatures. As he
looked he *began to notice* that they were of all kinds, both clean
13 and unclean⁶. Great then was his wonder when he heard *a voice*
14 he knew well saying *Rise, Peter; slay and eat*. In the old days
Peter had not hesitated to rebuke his Master more than once and
say 'Far be it from thee⁷,' and now with the same impulsiveness
he answers at once *Not so, Lord*. The disciples had not indeed

---

¹ Bezan *when Peter came to himself, he [was much perplexed*.   ² Or *gateway*.
³ B reads *two*: D and other mss omit the number.   ⁴ Ps lv 17. Cp. the prayers
of ii 42 (p. 38): there is no clear evidence however for the observance of the third,
sixth and ninth hours in particular among the Jews.   ⁵ II K xxiii 12, Neh
viii 16: I Sam ix 25-6, II xi 2.   ⁶ Cp. xi 5, 6.   ⁷ Cp. Mt xvi 22, Jn xiii 8.

observed all the refinements of Pharisaic tradition; they had plucked and eaten ears of corn on the Sabbath. But the law of unclean meats, which was in the Pentateuch, they had always observed. So S. Peter utters a surprised reproach 'Say not so, do not bid me to break the law!' and protests like Ezekiel[1] '*Never have I eaten anything common and unclean.*' The apostle had probably never realized the reproach to the Creator implied in this use of the word *common*. It is an inherent tendency among the few whether in culture, society, or religion, to look upon what is common to the ordinary man as 'vulgar' or 'unclean,' and this is stamped upon human language. The revelation of the new life in Christianity, whose glory was to have all things 'common,' ought to have taught the disciples better things. But the old Jewish nature was not yet dead, and at once S. Peter receives a rebuke. The enumeration of all kinds of living creatures takes us back to the first chapter of Genesis, when the Creator had pronounced all things good. The necessities of sin had indeed required a law of cleanness, but the Incarnation and Redemption of the Word of God had been a new creation. His body was the true *vessel*[2] which 'sealed up the sum
15 of' created life, and so his incarnation had *cleansed* creation. And now he, by whom all things were made, pronounces all things clean.
16 Henceforth nothing is unclean of itself[3]. To make this declaration most emphatic, it is repeated *three times*.
17 To the apostle however its meaning was as yet by no means obvious. Was this an abrogation of the law of clean and unclean meats? or was something far deeper signified? He was *perplexed*
18 and deeply *pondering on the vision*, when Cornelius' messengers knocked at the door. God was providing his own commentary on the text: it was the commentary of facts. Peter has only to obey
19 and be led by the Spirit. For it is *the Spirit* who says *I have sent them*. The words are a striking testimony to the personality of the Holy Spirit[4]. The Spirit, who is the Spirit of Jesus and who is in the apostles (Jn xiv 17), is completing the work which Jesus had
20 done or rather declaring it unto S. Peter (Jn xvi 15). So he bids Peter *go with them—nothing doubting*, i.e. without hesitation, or (as in xi 2) *without contention* or disputing: in xi 12, where S. Peter uses the same verb in its active voice, it means *making no distinction*, i.e. between Jew and Gentile. Like Cornelius S. Peter obeys
23 at once *without* any more *gainsaying*, and begins by giving hospitality to the Gentile messengers.

§ 3 *Peter and Cornelius at Caesarea*

Peter had begun to understand that the vision was a parable of men, and that by it God *had shewn to him that he was not to call any*

---

[1] Ezek iv 14. [2] Cp. ix 15. [3] Gen i 31, Rom xiv 14, I Tim iv 4, Tit i 15. The universal reach of this cleansing is forcibly brought out by the Greek, which has in verse 12 simply *all the beasts* etc. [4] See Introd. ch. v § 1. The vision comes down from the FATHER, the vessel is symbolical of the WORD, the SPIRIT prepares man's heart to respond to the revelation.

man common or unclean (verse 28). And therefore he must not shrink from any intercourse with Cornelius. The full import—that the sheet is the church¹, and to contain all races and classes without any distinction at all—will only be made clear by the events at
23 Caesarea. Meanwhile, conscious that a crisis is at hand, *on the morrow* he takes with him as witnesses *six brethren*, circumcised
24 Jews, from the church at Joppa. And at Caesarea Cornelius, equally conscious of a crisis, on the fourth day, when he expected S. Peter, summons a large company of his friends to hear him.

And on the morrow he arose and went forth with them, and certain of the brethren from Joppa accompanied him.
24 And on the morrow ²they entered into Caesarea. And Cornelius was waiting for them, having called together his
25 kinsmen and his near friends. ³And when it came to pass that Peter entered, Cornelius met him, and fell down at his
26 feet, and worshipped him. But Peter raised him up, saying,
27 'Stand up; I myself also am a man. And as he talked with
28 him, he went in, and findeth many come together: and he said unto them, Ye yourselves know how that it is an unlawful thing for a man that is a Jew to join himself or come unto one of another nation; and *yet* unto me hath God shewed that I should not call any man common or unclean:
29 wherefore also I came without gainsaying, when I was sent
30 for. I ask therefore with what intent ye sent for me. And Cornelius said, Four days ago, until this hour, I was ⁵keeping the ninth hour of prayer in my house; and behold, a man
31 stood before me in bright apparel, and saith, Cornelius, thy prayer is heard, and thine alms are had in remembrance in
32 the sight of God. Send therefore to Joppa, and call unto thee Simon, who is surnamed Peter; he lodgeth in the house
33 of Simon a tanner, by the sea side⁶. Forthwith therefore I sent to thee; and thou hast well done that thou art come. Now therefore we are all here present ⁷in the sight of God, to hear all things that have been commanded thee of the Lord.

---

¹ which is the body of Christ.   ² Marg with BD reads *he*.   ³ Bezan has *And*] *as Peter was drawing near unto Caesarea one of the servants (slaves) announced that he was come, and Cornelius sprang forth* (cp. xvi 29) *and [met him.*   ⁴ Or *Arise.* Bezan adds *What art thou doing?*   ⁵ AV reads *I was] fasting and [keeping*: some Bezan texts have *From the fourth day* (=*four days ago*) *until this (present) hour I was fasting, and at the ninth hour I was praying.*   ⁶ AV and Bezan add *who when he is come will speak unto thee.*   ⁷ Bezan *before thee.*

25   The picturesque narrative in the Bezan text explains the double entry of S. Peter in our text (verses 25 and 27), and bears all the marks of genuineness. For what scribe would have taken the trouble to add these extra details which would have appeared so trivial to the ordinary interpolator? Cornelius then had stationed a slave (probably outside the city) to keep watch for S. Peter, and when he brought news of his approach Cornelius *hurried out and met him* at the entrance of the city, and then *conversing together they entered* Cornelius' house. When he met S. Peter, Cornelius *worshipped him*, i.e. prostrated himself at his feet. Such prostrations before royal and superior personages were common in the east, as to this day[1]. But the action was closely associated with the idea of divine worship, for which this word *worship* was also used: and the doctrine of the one and jealous God would lead to corresponding jealousy in practice among the Jews and their adherents. Certainly in the Gospels in the temptation Satan makes this 'worship' the crucial test; and where such reverence was paid to the Lord, it either came from those who were not Jews, as from the Magi and Canaanitish woman, or if paid by Jews, it was a definite act of faith, as when the disciples 'worshipped him' after the resurrection[2] Moreover the idea of prostration was alien to the western mind, and the custom was not introduced into the imperial court till the reign of Diocletian. Hence the action of Cornelius is very marked. He regarded S. Peter as a heaven-sent messenger or inspired prophet, bearing the commandments of God (verse 33). But the reverence is at once rejected by S. Peter: it is not to be paid by man to man, nor by man to angels, as is shewn in the Revelation[3] where an apostle receives the same rebuke as Cornelius here.

27   S. Peter's entry into Cornelius' house was a distinct breach of
28 Jewish custom, and S. Peter first (1) makes it clear to the assembled Gentiles that he is acting consciously and deliberately. They would recognize this as a 'noble' act, and it merited Cornelius' '*well done.*'
29 Then (2), though he was aware of the circumstances, for the sake of
34 the hearers he asks Cornelius to repeat his story. (3) With this for his starting point, as guided and prepared by the Spirit, he preaches the gospel to them.

Peter's Gospel for the Gentiles

The introduction—he *opened his mouth*—marks the solemnity of the occasion[4]. The sermon falls into two parts: I. the response to the particular circumstances (34-5), II. the sermon or *word* itself (36-43), which is the same gospel as heretofore, only so presented as to appeal more particularly to the Gentiles. Hence there are new points. (1) In the Christology, (*a*) Jesus Christ is not only the 'Lord

---

[1] Cp. Mt xviii 26.   [2] Mt xxviii 17, Lk xxiv 52: cp. also Mt xiv 33, Mk xv 19, Jn ix 38.   [3] xix 10, xxii 9.   [4] Cp. ii 14: and for *opening the mouth* viii 32 35, xviii 14.

and Christ' of the Jews as in ii 36, he is now 'the *Lord of all* men.' (*b*) The fulfilment of national Messianic expectations would not be understood by the Gentiles, so he is presented not as the Christ but as *the Judge* of all men. (2) Corresponding to this in practical religion we have laid down (*a*) the catholic relation of God to the righteous in every nation alike, then at the end (*b*) a deeper view of faith on which this depends. S. Peter had spoken of faith from the beginning (iii 16), but it does not seem wholly accidental that here he uses that phrase which more correctly would be translated '*believing into* Christ,' and so expresses the true character of faith[1]. The catholic relation of God to man is declared in the introduction, which as it involves an important question of theology will be considered at once.

I. All this time S. Peter had been learning from the circumstances in which he found himself, and without a formal address his full heart finds utterance in an earnest asseveration: *Of a truth* (iv 27) *I am perceiving*, or getting a firm grasp of[2] this truth, *that God is no respecter of persons*. This doctrine had been stated in the OT, Deut x 17; but it had been limited in scope and application[3]. The expression is borrowed from the administration of justice. Human judges are tempted to respect—in the Greek to *accept* or *receive*—the persons of the rich and powerful, and to give judgement in their favour. But God respects no man; he is strictly impartial towards all. And now S. Peter perceives that this impartiality applies to spiritual relationships, and towards all men, i.e. *in every nation he that feareth God and worketh righteousness is acceptable to him*: or, as S. Paul expresses it in Romans ii 10, there shall be *glory and honour and peace to every man that worketh good, to the Jew first and also to the Greek, for there is no respect of persons with God.* S. Peter had already, but without being fully conscious of the extent of its application, declared this principle in his first sermon (ii 21) when he said *whosoever shall call on the name of the Lord shall be saved.* In this sermon (verse 43) his commentary is this—*every one that believeth on him shall receive remission of sins.*

It is obvious that this doctrine deals with the mysterious operations of divine grace, and in particular with 'works before justification.' In the sixteenth century, led away by reaction against exaggerated merit attached to good works, with minds dominated by the idea of justification by faith and by S. Paul's words, 'whatsoever is not of faith is sin,' extreme reformers denied the possibility of any righteousness before justification. This question largely depends upon the meaning of 'justification,' for the discussion of which this is hardly the place. But it will be profitable to notice what is plainly revealed to us by this history of Cornelius. It is clear that he was already working righteousness and acceptable to God, before he had con-

---

[1] It occurs also in xix 4: cp. xiv 23. [2] The Greek is an emphatic word for seizing, grasping, used in Phil iii 12, Jn i 5, Rom ix 30. [3] See Exod xxiii 6–8, Levit xix 15, Deut xvi 19 etc. S. James (ii 1) and S. Jude (16) use the word in a similar sense. Cp. also I Pet i 17, Eph vi 9, Col iii 25.

sciously 'believed in Christ.' But he was not therefore without the inspiration of the Spirit of Christ. For, as S. Augustine says (Ep. 194, 18), 'the Spirit breathes where he wills...in one way he helps before indwelling, in another by indwelling. For before he indwells he helps men to become faithful, those already faithful he helps by indwelling.' And, as we have seen, the Holy Spirit was at work in bringing about the conversion of Cornelius (verse 20). But, although acceptable to God, his righteousness was still imperfect. For it did not spring from the highest motive, viz. conscious faith in Christ, of whose work of redemption he was ignorant. It was then acceptable to God in the sense that it predisposed him for justification. Not that even thus it had any merit. The mission of the angel and of S. Peter came of God's pure mercy. The outpouring of the Spirit was a 'free gift.' Cornelius had not earned that mercy, his goodness rather was a sign that he was ready to receive it. There were many others at that moment among the Gentiles working righteousness, but only Cornelius was selected by God for this conversion. To inquire further why God chooses this particular person or that is to lose ourselves in the inscrutable mysteries of the Divine Being[1]. Further, we notice the relation between life in the church and natural goodness. The whole point of the narrative is that Cornelius had not as yet obtained the full light or eternal life, i.e. the knowledge of God. But his natural goodness had fitted him to receive 'the word,' which God of his free grace now sent him; and the climax is the descent of the Holy Spirit with the baptism of Cornelius, i.e. his reception into the church. *The word* of God S. Peter now proceeds to unfold.

34 And Peter opened his mouth, and said,

Of a truth I perceive that God is no respecter of persons:
35 but in every nation he that feareth him, and worketh right-
36 eousness, is acceptable to him. [2]The word which he sent unto the children of Israel, [3]preaching good tidings of peace
37 by Jesus Christ (he is Lord of all)—that saying ye yourselves know, which was published throughout all Judæa, beginning
38 from Galilee, after the baptism which John preached; *even* Jesus of Nazareth, how that God anointed him with the Holy Ghost and with power: who went about doing good, and healing all that were oppressed of the devil; for God was
39 with him. And we are witnesses of all things which he did both in the country of the Jews, and in Jerusalem; whom

---

[1] Cp. Dante *Paradiso* xxi 91-6. [2] RV margin and WH with ℵAB omit *which—He sent the word*: Blass omits *Lord* and, keeping the *for* in the Bezan text, reads *For the word, which he sent unto the children of Israel preaching peace by Jesus Christ, this (word) is of* (i.e. belongs to) *all.* [3] Gk *evangelizing.* Cp. Isai lii 7, Nah i 15.

40 also they slew, hanging him on a tree. Him God raised up
41 the third day, and gave him to be made manifest, not to all
the people, but unto witnesses that were chosen before of
God, *even* to us, who did eat and drink with him after he
42 rose from the dead¹. And he charged us to preach unto the
people, and to testify that this is he which is ordained of God
43 *to be* the Judge of quick and dead. To him bear all the
prophets witness, that through his name every one that
believeth on him shall receive remission of sins.

36   II. If with the RV margin we omit *which*², then S. Peter
(i) begins with a declaration of the *gospel* or *good news* to the
Gentiles. Cornelius and the God-fearing Gentiles had been longing
for a revelation of God. This revelation had now been made.
God had sent his word; and by *word* both Jews and Gentiles
would understand a divine revelation³. This revelation was made
(*a*) primarily *to the children of Israel*: but (*b*) it was a *good message
of peace*, viz. of reconciliation with God, to the Gentiles also:
because (*c*) it was effected *through Jesus Christ*, who is *Lord of all
men*, and who is the Peace-maker. For 'he is our peace who
made both one,' viz. both God and man, as also Jew and Gentile;
and 'he came and preached peace to them that were far off and
peace to them that were nigh⁴.'
37   (ii) *The story* how the revelation had been made and peace won
was indeed known to Cornelius, for the fame of what the Lord had
done had spread *throughout all Palestine*⁵; and it was summed up in
38 a name—*Jesus of Nazareth*. In the work of Jesus there were four
stages. (1) It *began after John's baptism*. This baptism taught
all, both Jew and Gentile alike, the need of repentance on man's
part; but the baptism of Jesus by John was his *anointing* to be the
Christ, *with the Holy Ghost and with power*. (2) The ministry in
Galilee was one of *doing good and healing*. This would appeal to
the Gentiles, and at the same time it served as a parable to teach
them the nature of the kingdom of Jesus and the meaning of *all
39 that he did*. (3) This work ended in the crucifixion, over which
S. Peter passes briefly, for the Gentiles had not been guilty in the

---

¹ Bezan adds *and conversed with him forty days*.   ² And then the central statement *he is Lord of all* will not be in a parenthesis. If we retain *which*, the *word* will be the object of *ye know*, and in apposition to *saying*: *Ye know the word* (*logos*) *which...viz. the saying* (*rhêma*) *which was published* (or *the thing which happened*). The AV uses *word* in both verses 36 and 37. But in 37 the Greek *rhêma* stands for the Hebrew *dâbhâr*, which as often means the matter of the saying as the saying itself. So Lk ii 15 is literally *the saying which had come to pass*. The best English equivalent is *story* or *history*: which from signifying the relation of events etc. have come to signify the events themselves.   ³ Cp. Ps cvii 20, cxlvii 15–8.   ⁴ Eph ii 11–22 is the best commentary on this passage.
⁵ *Judaea* is used in its wider sense including Galilee and Samaria.

same literal sense as the Jews. And he wanted rather to dwell on
(4) the good tidings of the resurrection. This brought him to the
40 office of himself and the apostles: viz. the bearing of *witness*.
This witness applied to the whole ministry (as in i 22) but was
of crucial importance in the matter of the resurrection; for, after
he had risen, the Lord no longer appeared openly *to all the people*.
41 Their witness was sealed by their *eating and drinking with him*. This
was a proof not only of the reality of the risen body, but also of
his fellowship with the apostles. And by the same means S. Peter
was to testify his fellowship with Cornelius and the Gentiles (xi 3).
42   (iii) Then follows the practical result. The apostles had received
a *charge*. (1) They were to *proclaim* Jesus *to the people* of the Jews
as Lord and Messiah, and that by bearing witness of what he did
and of his resurrection. (2) But their witness extended to a
further point, viz. his *ordination by God to be Judge*. This was an
office which would belong to the Messiah as king, but it rested on
deeper grounds. S. John[1] tells us that the Lord received authority
to execute judgement because he is the Son of Man. This office
then rested on his humanity, and it involved a universal relation
to all men alike, Jew and Gentile. To the Jews this doctrine had
been hinted at in ii 39, iii 25-6. Now to the Gentiles S. Peter (as
S. Paul in xvii 31) declares it explicitly: and, as the judgement
reaches to the *dead* as well as the *living*, it carries with it the
43 resurrection of the dead. (3) For the individual the work of Jesus
Christ or *his name* had won *forgiveness of sins*. This was the great
need of the Gentiles, and needed all the more in view of judgement
to come. To *receive* the gift the individual had to surrender
himself unto, or rather *into*, Jesus Christ by an act of *faith*. As
faith is a property of the will common to all human nature, so is
forgiveness open to *every man* whether Jew or Gentile. This doctrine
is also a matter for *witness*; and now the apostle appeals to *the
prophets*, viz. the scriptures of the OT, which have their indispensable
place in the divine plan of revelation, for Gentiles as well as
for Jews.

S. Peter was only *at the beginning* of his gospel (xi 15),—he had
as yet said nothing of baptism and the gift of the Holy Spirit,—
when the testimony of the apostles and prophets received a divine
confirmation by the sudden descent of the Holy Ghost.

The descent of the Holy Ghost

44   While Peter yet spake these words, the Holy Ghost fell
45 on all them which heard the word. And they of the circumcision
which believed were amazed, as many as came with
Peter, because that on the Gentiles also was poured out the
46 gift of the Holy Ghost. For they heard them speak with

---
[1] Jn v 27.

47 tongues, and magnify God. Then answered Peter, Can any man forbid the water, that these should not be baptized,
48 which have received the Holy Ghost as well as we? And he commanded them to be baptized in the name of Jesus Christ. Then prayed they him to tarry certain days.

44 To the *amazement* of Peter's company of circumcised Jews, upon these *Gentiles*—uncircumcised and unclean—*the Holy Spirit*
45 *was poured out*[1], immediately from heaven. The fact was proved
46 by the external manifestation[2]: for Cornelius' party had begun *to speak with tongues and magnify God*. These were the same phenomena which had occurred *at the beginning*'(xi 15) at the first Pentecost; and the inference was that the inward *gift* was also exactly *the same* as that which had then been given to the apostles and the brethren. So then the great event to which the divine hand had been guiding was the Pentecost of the Gentiles.
47 This was evident to S. Peter, and it was the answer to all doubts. It *reminded him of the saying of the Lord* that they should be *baptized with the Holy Ghost*, and he saw that the promise was for all. But the Lord had said '*except a man be born of water and the Spirit*[3],' and the water was still lacking. First, however, he asks the six brethren if they have any *impediment*[4] to allege. This there could hardly be, for God had accepted them; by the gift of his Holy Spirit he had borne witness to them (xv 8) and himself become
48 their sponsor. Then S. Peter *commanded them to be baptized*[5]: and on profession of faith *in Jesus Christ* they were baptized, and so God cleansed and washed their hearts by faith (xv 9), and they were admitted into the church, the way of salvation (xi 14).

The Holy Spirit fell upon Cornelius' company before their baptism. This is a striking reversal of the usual church order. It proves that God is free, and that his grace is not confined to any channels. But it is one of those unique exceptions which 'prove the rule.' Though he had received the Spirit, Cornelius was afterwards baptized; so also Saul, though he had seen the Lord face to face, had been afterwards baptized. These instances shew the necessity of baptism, and testify to the divine will that order should prevail in God's household the church and in its administration of grace.

To gather up the fruits of this Pentecost S. Peter *stayed* at Caesarea *some time*, and no doubt enjoyed the cooperation of S. Philip. If he stayed with Cornelius he would have been making public declaration of his new principles. But the baptism of Cornelius was sufficient in itself to attract the attention of the disciples and so to lead to its ratification by the church.

---

[1] Cp. ii 17, 33. [2] Cp. viii 18. [3] Jn iii 5. [4] Cp. viii 36. [5] This then was the *command of the Lord*, verse 33. The baptism was evidently performed by some other person than the apostle, some *minister*, see p. 33.

§ 4 *Peter's defence to the church and the ratification of his action*

News of what had happened would quickly spread *throughout Palestine*, where the other *apostles* would likewise be engaged in the work of visitation; and S. Peter's action came as a surprise or scandal to many. It gave rise to the first signs of division among the brethren. For the fourth time S. Luke directs our attention to the spread of human infirmity within the church. We have had murmuring, covetousness, and simony, and now we come to *contention* or party spirit, the testing of the church's internal unity.

(1) The word *contended* in verse 2 signifies that they were *divided* in opinion[1]. Such division was almost inevitable. While in the church there were many Hellenists who, following S. Stephen, would be quick to perceive the transitory character of the law, there were on the other hand many Pharisees and a large company of priests[2]. These would naturally be zealous for the law; the idea of the conversion of the Gentiles was new to them; if a Gentile could be saved, it could only be by his being circumcised and so becoming a Jew[3]. The development of more liberal views would arouse alarm and provoke a more dogmatic insistence on these points. The more determined spirits would gradually form a definite party; and their watchword would be 'circumcision'—already in this narrative we read of *them of the circumcision*. To such disciples S. Peter's violation of the law of uncleanness must have been a grievous scandal.

(2) The way in which the 'contention' was met illustrates the methods of authority in the church. Hitherto the government had rested with the apostles. There had been murmuring against them, but they took the initiative in the consequent action. They decided on the matter of the Samaritans (viii 14). But now, as soon as conscience is touched, brethren do not hesitate to make a charge, even against S. Peter himself. In reply the apostle does not dismiss the charge with an assertion of his own authority, or with a dogmatic decision; nor does he refer the matter to his fellow-apostles alone. Instead, he makes a defence to the church; he narrates what had happened, and trusts for his vindication to the divine will revealed in the facts. From this we may infer that in an important question like the admission of the Gentiles, while the divine will guides, and the apostle interprets and acts upon its indications, it is well that the apostle's interpretation should be submitted to, and obtain the consent of, the church. It is significant that instead of *the apostles* simply, we have in verse 1 *the apostles and the brethren*; and after this in verse 22 *the church*, in ch xv *the apostles and the presbyters*.

11 Now the apostles and the brethren that were in Judæa heard that the Gentiles also had received the word of God.

---
[1] In x 20 the same verb is translated *doubting*. [2] xv 5, vi 7. [3] xxi 20: xi 18: xv 1.

2 ¹And when Peter was come up to Jerusalem, they that were
3 of the circumcision contended with him, saying, Thou wentest
4 in to men uncircumcised, and didst eat with them. But
Peter began, and expounded *the matter* unto them in order,
saying,

5   I was in the city of Joppa praying : and in a ²trance I saw
a vision, a certain vessel descending, as it were a great sheet
let down from heaven by four corners ; and it came even
6 unto me : upon the which when I had fastened mine eyes,
I considered, and saw the fourfooted beasts of the earth and
wild beasts and creeping things and fowls of the heaven.
7 And I heard also a voice saying unto me, Rise, Peter ; kill
8 and eat. But I said, Not so, Lord : for nothing common or
9 unclean hath ever entered into my mouth. But a voice
answered the second time out of heaven, What God hath
10 cleansed, make not thou common. And this was done thrice :
11 and all were drawn up again into heaven. And behold,
forthwith three men stood before the house in which we were,
12 having been sent from Cæsarea unto me. And the Spirit
bade me go with them, ³making no distinction. And these
six brethren also accompanied me ; and we entered into the
13 man's house : and he told us how he had seen the angel
standing in his house, and saying, Send to Joppa, and fetch
14 Simon, whose surname is Peter ; who shall speak unto thee
words, whereby thou shalt be saved, thou and all thy house.
15 And as I began to speak, the Holy Ghost fell on them, even
16 as on us at the beginning. And I remembered the word of
the Lord, how that he said, ⁴John indeed baptized with water ;
17 but ye shall be baptized with the Holy Ghost. If then God
gave unto them the like gift as *he did* also unto us, when we
believed on the Lord Jesus Christ, who was I, that I could
withstand God⁵ ?
18   And when they heard these things, they held their peace,

---

¹ Bezan runs *Peter then after some time would* (i.e. *willed to*) *go to Jerusalem, and he called to him the brethren and confirmed them and, making also a long discourse, went forth* <and passed> *through the country places teaching them. Now when he came to Jerusalem and announced to them the grace of God, the brethren* [*that were of the circumcision contended.*]   ² Gk ecstasy.   ³ AV reads *nothing doubting.*   ⁴ i 5.   ⁵ Bezan adds *that he should not give the Holy Spirit to them that had believed on him ?*

and glorified God, saying, Then to the Gentiles also hath God granted repentance unto life.

2 The Bezan text gives a more detailed account of S. Peter's movements. It is quite clear that he expected some criticism, not to say opposition, for he took up the *six brethren* with him as
3 witnesses (verse 12). The charge brought against him was not, as we might have expected, that he had baptized Cornelius but that he had *entered* his house and *eaten with* him. The Jews were accustomed to baptize Gentile proselytes, while, as we have seen, the first practical difficulty which would present itself would arise from the law of cleanness, and this law S. Peter had undoubtedly broken. It is an instance of the way in which in great controversies the question generally turns upon some practical detail
4 rather than upon the great principles at stake. The apostle's defence consisted of a recitation of the facts: and they were
18 unanswerable. His critics had nothing to say, and *they glorified God* because he had *granted even to the Gentiles repentance unto life*. The form of statement testifies to some surprise, but it is a fitting conclusion to a narrative, which had begun with the restoration of Dorcas to life.

There is still a difficulty to face. Twelve or fourteen years later (ch. xv) there is an influential party in the church of Jerusalem still insisting on the necessity of circumcision; and in the discussion which ensues S. Peter does indeed appeal to this event as deciding the question, but he alludes to it as to something almost forgotten, whereas it ought to have prevented the discussion arising at all. Again, S. Peter then appears as the 'apostle of the circumcision.' Apparently he has not followed up his work among the Gentiles. On one occasion even, at Antioch, his action was quite inconsistent with that at Caesarea; for, after eating with the Gentile Christians, he separated himself from them. Deeper reflection will however shew that the history is true to human nature. Human nature is very slow to grasp new principles and realize their consequences. The Gospel itself is to us a story of almost inconceivable slowness on the part of the disciples in understanding the Lord's words and actions. And the slowness remained: it is still characteristic of the Acts. There too the apostles and disciples are slow to understand the action of the Spirit. 'O foolish men and slow of heart to believe'—that is the character of the disciples in each book. Certainly S. Peter had not realized that the Lord had cleansed all meats. And if Peter required a divine vision to open his eyes, it is not surprising that it should take some years for the hidden principle to be fully understood and accepted by the Jewish church. Nor is this slowness peculiar to the apostolic age. It is almost more inconceivable how in the seventeenth century a good protestant English captain could be praying and reading the Bible on deck, while beneath the hatches he was carrying a cargo of negro slaves to work on American plantations. Nor must the church of to-day throw stones. In foreign missions it is still difficult in practice to recognize the equality of the converting and converted races : while in America where there are practically two churches, one for the coloured and one for the white people, it is hard to believe that the principle that God is no respecter of persons has been fully realized as yet.

Again, the incident may have passed without a deep effect on the Jewish mind of the church of Jerusalem because of its unique character. It was a special manifestation of God's mercy to certain persons—not without precedent in the OT, e.g. in the cleansing of Naaman, but not one to be actively followed up. It was only when the activity of S. Paul had worked out the consequences,—consequences which would in their turn affect the life and conduct of Jewish Christians—that the whole question blazed out afresh. Then in the light of the subsequent history S. Peter saw the full significance of this particular event at Caesarea. Its narration is, moreover, a great testimony to the honesty and trustworthiness of S. Luke. Devoted as he is to S. Paul and to the great work of the conversion of the Gentiles, which he ascribes to that apostle, yet looking back years afterwards when S. Paul's principles had won a complete victory, he nevertheless gives the palm, the glory of the first admission of the Gentiles, to the apostle of the circumcision. And that not grudgingly, but with the fullest emphasis and detail. Indeed from a literary point of view, in regard to language, details, and circumstances, the admission of Cornelius by S. Peter is the companion picture to the conversion of Saul which precedes it. There is indeed one difference which has a bearing upon theology, viz. upon the relation of the Persons in the Blessed Trinity. The one was the direct work of the Lord (Jesus), the other of the Holy Ghost: both of whom are linked together in the intermediate verse ix 31[1]. The difference might be expressed otherwise: the one was effected through external voice and vision, the other through inward spiritual impulse.

SECTION II D (= Ch. 11. 19-26)
The Acts of the Hellenists
and foundation of the church at Antioch

S. Luke once more returns to the death of Stephen, that is, to those Hellenists who *were scattered abroad* in viii 4 ; and the work of Barnabas here corresponds to that of Philip in ch. viii, both together flanking the central narratives about Saul and S. Peter. S. Luke retraces

---

[1] e.g. cp. x 19, 20 (xi 12) *I [the Spirit] have sent them* with ix 11, 17 *the Lord hath sent me, even Jesus.* Compare also the double visions to Peter and Cornelius, Saul and Ananias: the similar dialogue: the answer to the *prayers* of Cornelius and of Saul (ix 11, x 30): the baptism of both, who are filled with the Spirit (ix 17-8, x 44-8): the crisis at midday (ix 3, xxvi 13, and x 9): the word *vessel* (ix 15, x 11) etc.

his steps because this is the main line of connexion with the future work. And in these few verses four important points are brought out. (1) The church of Antioch is founded—the second mother city or metropolis of the church, from which issued the great missionary movement in the Roman empire. (2) For Antioch itself was the scene of the first preaching to the Gentiles on a considerable scale, and this preaching receives the sanction of the church of Jerusalem. (3) Saul is brought back into the history. (4) The church for the first time attracts the notice of the Graeco-Roman world.

19 They therefore that were scattered abroad upon the tribulation that arose about Stephen ¹travelled as far as Phœnicia, and Cyprus, and Antioch, speaking the word to
20 none save only to Jews. But there were some of them, men of Cyprus and Cyrene, who, when they were come to Antioch, spake unto the ²Greeks also, ³preaching the Lord Jesus.
21 And the hand of the Lord was with them: and a great number that believed turned unto the Lord.
22 And the report concerning them came to the ears of the church which was in Jerusalem: and they sent forth Barnabas
23 as far as Antioch: who, when he was come, and had seen the grace of God, was glad; and he exhorted them all, ⁴that with
24 purpose of heart they would cleave unto the Lord: for he was a good man, and full of the Holy Ghost and of faith:
25 and much people was added unto the Lord. ⁵And he went
26 forth to Tarsus to seek for Saul: and when he had found him, he brought him unto Antioch. And it came to pass, that even for a whole year they were gathered together ⁶with the church, and taught much people; and that the disciples were called Christians first in Antioch.

19 The geographical course of *the word* is clear. From Jerusalem it ran to the port of Caesarea; then following the track of coasting vessels, it went northwards along *Phenicia*, touching at Ptolemais, Tyre, and Sidon, in which cities we find bodies of disciples twenty years later⁷. From these ports some of the evangelists sailed westwards, and the first land sighted was *Cyprus*, which had already

---

¹ Or *went about*.　² Gk *Hellenas*, with ℵAD (and Bezan authorities): AV and WH read *Grecians* (*Hellenistas*) with B and the majority of MSS: ℵ originally had *evangelistas*.　³ Gk *evangelizing*.　⁴ WH with B read *in the Lord*, and RV marg translates *that they would cleave unto the purpose of their heart in the Lord*.　⁵ Bezan has *And*] *when he heard that Saul was in Tarsus he went forth seeking him, and when he met with him he exhorted him to come to Antioch: and they, when they were come,* [*were gathered together.*　⁶ Gk *in*.　⁷ xxi 4, 7, xxvii 3.

furnished disciples[1]. Others however kept to the coasting route, and after passing the important cities of Berytus, Byblus, Aradus and Laodicea, came to Seleucia, the port of Antioch, and so to *Antioch* itself, which lay fifteen miles inland. And so the church reached Antioch, and thus early displayed its tendency to follow the highways of civilization and seek the densest centres of population.

Antioch was the capital of the east. After Rome and Alexandria it ranked as the third city in the empire. And this position it maintained in the church. It became distinguished for its school of theology and of the interpretation of scripture; its bishop ranked as one of the four great patriarchs; and it was honoured with an illustrious roll of martyrs and saints, pre-eminent among whom were S. Ignatius and S. John Chrysostom. The city was beautifully situated on the river Orontes where it forces its way through the mountains; and the beauty of the site was matched by the beauty of the city. Towards this Herod the Great had made no little contribution, when he paved and lined with colonnades the main street, which ran right through the city like the Straight Street at Damascus. The mass of the population was Syrian; the society and culture was Greek; while the Roman governor of Syria, with his court and bureaucracy, secured the official predominance of the Latins. Side by side with these the Jews added a fourth, and not insignificant, element to the city. Antioch had been founded by Seleucus Nicator about B.C. 300, and he planted in it a number of Jews, giving them equal citizen rights with the Macedonians and Greeks. As at Alexandria, the Jews formed almost a separate community under a governor of their own; they had attained to a great degree of prosperity; and were specially noted for the number of proselytes they had won to Judaism[2]. The aspiration after a higher life to which this testifies was no doubt due to reaction against the prevailing moral atmosphere. The one occupation of the Antiochenes was pleasure-seeking; and stimulated by the luxurious beauty of the scenery, the mixed population, and the voluptuous character of the oriental worships, such pleasure-seeking led to disastrous moral results. The famous sanctuary of Daphne, which lay five miles from the city and was the favourite resort of the citizens, had an evil name. When the satirist Juvenal wants to sum up in one line the moral degradation of Rome, the most scornful reproach he can find is that 'the Syrian Orontes has flowed into the Tiber[3].' Such a city was a field white for the harvest, 'gasping like a thirsty land' for a renovating and life-giving gospel; and the large fringe of Gentile adherents which hung round the synagogue offered the Christian evangelist a golden opportunity.

20 At Antioch *some of* the evangelists made a new departure. They were *men of Cyprus and Cyrene*,—countries which figured largely in the origins of Christianity,—and as such they were Hellenists, Greek-speaking Jews, like Stephen and Philip. Among them no

---

[1] e.g. Barnabas (iv 36), Mnason (xxi 16).   [2] Josephus *B. J.* vii 3. 3.
[3] *Sat.* iii 62.

doubt were Simon Niger (i.e. 'the black') and Lucius of Cyrene[1]. Hitherto they had *spoken to Jews only*, but now in the great Greek city of Antioch they *preached the gospel of the Lord Jesus to the Greeks also*. It is curious that at this word, which is the pivot of the whole narrative, our best manuscripts should differ, some reading *Greeks*, others *Grecians* (i.e. *Hellenists*). In spite however of the great authority of Dr Hort, who still adheres to the Vatican MS B and reads *Grecians*, the history itself leaves in us no doubt that the right reading is *Greeks*. The word had already been spoken to Hellenists, the church contained a large body of Hellenists, the evangelists themselves were Hellenists; and so there would be little point in the remark that they preached—*even* to the Hellenists. The reason for the confusion is obvious. The condition of the relations between Jews and Gentiles which prevailed at that moment quickly passed away; and after two or three hundred years the distinction between *Greek* (*Hellen*) and *Grecian* (*Hellenist*) was as little understood as it is by the ordinary reader of to-day.

It is however very necessary for us to obtain a clear idea of the distinction, if we are to understand the history of the Acts as a whole, and in particular the relation of this preaching to Greeks at Antioch on the one hand to S. Peter's work at Caesarea, on the other to the work of S. Paul and S. Barnabas on their first journey. How does this preaching mark an advance, and yet not anticipate the turning of S. Paul to the Gentiles, which was obviously a new thing (xiii 46)? The truth is that the simple division into Jew and Gentile is far too simple for the facts. Without counting circumcised proselytes, who may be reckoned to the Jews, we can distinguish at least four classes. Among the Jews there were (1) Jews proper or Hebrews, (2) Greek-speaking Jews or Hellenists; and among the Gentiles there were (3) 'God-fearing' adherents of the synagogue, (4) the mass of heathen without any relation to Judaism. By the thorough Jew both these classes (3) and (4), being without circumcision, were summed up under the somewhat scornful name of *the Gentiles* (literally *nations*). But Hellenist Christians, like S. Paul and these evangelists, were broad-minded enough to appreciate the wide difference between the two classes, and they made a distinction: by *Gentiles* generally they meant the latter (4), while to the former (3) they gave the name of *Greeks*[2]. And this word occurs here for the first time in the Acts.

The preaching at Antioch we suppose was to the third class of the God-fearing Greeks, whom we know to have been very numerous at Antioch. This was, then, a new departure; for in Jerusalem this

---

[1] xiii 1: where we should have expected also to find the name of *Nicolas of Antioch* (vi 5).   [2] Of course S. Paul as a Roman citizen would also speak of civilized men in general as *Greeks*. But that there is some ground for the distinction between *Greeks* and *Gentiles*, on the lips of a Hellenist Jew, will be seen if we compare e.g. the *Gentiles* in xiii 46, 48, xiv 2, 5, 27, xv 3, with the *Greeks* in the synagogue (xiv 1). Also in xvii 4, xviii 4, xxi 28 (and probably xvii 12) *Greeks* is used of the *God-fearing* class. At Ephesus (xix 10, 17, xx 21) it is used in the wider sense.

class was very small, if not almost non-existent, while in Phenicia and Cyprus the evangelists had preached to Jews only. Cornelius and his friends were of this class, and we have seen what an extraordinary event intercourse with them had appeared to S. Peter and the Hebrew Christians. Whether this preaching at Antioch actually preceded S. Peter's mission we do not know. S. Luke does indeed go back to S. Stephen's death, but his general aim was to write 'in order' (Lk i 3), and in any case the baptism of Cornelius was the first public act of authority in opening the door of the church. On the other hand this preaching did not anticipate S. Paul's advance. For when he 'turned to the Gentiles,' they were Gentiles of the last class, and he spoke to them directly, not through the synagogue.

What was the result at Antioch S. Luke now tells us, and his language must be read with care. To the English reader it may sound like a succession of the general phrases of piety. But the words have a definite meaning, and they describe a great development and change which was taking place in the church at Antioch. For this church was to become the great Hellenist or 'Greek' church, holding a position half-way between the Hebrew church of Jerusalem and the Gentile churches founded by S. Paul[1].

21 This new step of the evangelists received (1) the divine sanction, which was shewn in signs and wonders—for that is the meaning of *the hand of the Lord*[2]. They had also (2) the sanction of success, for *a great number who had believed*[3] *turned to the Lord*. They had *believed* that what they had heard, *the good news about the Lord Jesus*, was true; and consequently their minds and wills were *turned* to the church, they were 'giving heed[4].' It is not stated in the text that the turning included baptism. It would have been a bold step for the evangelists to have baptized them on their own responsibility, as S. Peter's hesitation at Caesarea has shewn[5]. The converts themselves may have shrunk from the definite act of self-identification with the church, a body of alien Jews, which involved cutting themselves off from their old life. It was one thing to believe with the mind and to give attention, another to act. On the other hand 'turning' was generally followed by baptism[6], and S. Philip had baptized the Samaritans. But even if baptized this *great number* remained in an anomalous position. (1) There was the gift of the Holy Ghost. Had they received it, or were they still in the position of the Samaritans of viii 16? (2) There was their relation to the Jewish believers. They were uncircumcised. Were they then still unclean? would their fellow-Christians enter their

---

[1] It was in Antioch that the great disputation about circumcision arose (xv 1).
[2] Cp. iv 30, xiii 11: also what happened at Samaria, viii 6-7. The exact phrase occurs in Lk i 66. [3] The omission of the article in the Greek with AV, Bezan, and later MSS, would make an easier reading—*a great number believed and turned*. [4] Cp. viii 6, 10, 11, xvi 14. The phrase occurred in ix 35. *Turn* is the word used for the Gentiles turning to the true God (xiv 15, xv 3, 19, xxvi 18, 20, I Thess i 9). [5] x 47; cp. viii 36 (*hinder*). [6] Cp. xvi 14-5.

houses and eat with them¹? Must they be circumcised as well as baptized, or are the Jewish Christians to receive them as they are? 22 Some decision must be made, and it rested obviously with the apostles and the mother church. There is no suggestion of any appeal, but *the report* of these developments and the ambiguous position of this great body² reached *Jerusalem*, and *the church* there felt bound to take some cognizance : as in the matters of Samaria and Cornelius, it had either to bind or to loose. No dogmatic decision about preaching to the Greeks was made; but they—viz. (to judge by analogy with xv 22) the apostles and presbyters with the whole church—*sent forth* a delegate, evidently with full powers. The choice of delegate for this mission was a proof of the brotherly feeling and conciliatory spirit of the elder church. For he was *Barnabas*, himself a Cypriote like some of the evangelists. And 24 Barnabas (1) was in character *a good*, i.e. kindly, *man*; his power of conciliation had been proved in his introduction of Saul to the Twelve. Also, (2) like Stephen³, he was fully endowed with *faith* and the gifts of *the Spirit*—in particular that of 'paraclêsis.' When we further compare the words of ix 17 *be filled with the Holy Ghost*, the condition of being *full of the Holy Ghost* seems to be specified here in view of the gift of the Spirit by the laying on of hands⁴.
23 On his arrival S. Barnabas (1) was convinced of the divine sanction from the evident signs which he *saw of the grace of God* in the wonders wrought and the fervour of faith; and this filled him with *joy*: cp. viii 8, 39. (2) His decision was to accept the situation. In this he was not acting without the Spirit's guidance, for he was exercising his spiritual gift of 'paraclêsis' or exhortation. He accepted the Greeks, and pleaded for unity; for *he exhorted them all*, both Jews and Greeks, *to cleave to the Lord with the purpose of their heart*. The Greek word for *purpose* is literally *setting forth*; metaphorically it denotes the setting forth in the mind or purpose; and S. Paul uses it for the divine purpose⁵. Thus the general idea is of purpose as set forth or testified by outward action. The word for *cleave to* is translated *continue* in xiii 43, and the phrase there, *continue in the grace of God*,—which contains the idea of waiting for further divine response—throws light on this passage. S. Barnabas then exhorts the Antiochene Christians to continue in their present state of grace and liberty: only they must carry out their spiritual *purpose*—the Greeks, by receiving baptism

---

¹ x 28, xi 3. This is the very question which did cause difficulty at Antioch later on (Gal ii 12). ² The report was (we note) *about them*. ³ vi 5.
⁴ viii 18. The case of Samaria must be carefully compared, as giving the key to what happened at Antioch. Having given a typical picture, S. Luke does not repeat himself. ⁵ xxvii 13 : Rom viii 28, ix 11, Eph i 11, iii 11. This word *prothesis* was used in the Greek Bible (and so in Mt xii 4, Lk vi 4, Hebr ix 2) for the loaves of the shewbread, i.e. *the loaves of the setting forth*. Thus, like the word *memorial* in x 1, *purpose* has associations with Jewish ritual. So to this day the title *prothesis* is given to the 'setting forth' of the bread and wine in the Greek liturgy, and it is also the name of the sacristy where this takes place.

or the laying on of hands (as was needed), the Jews by accepting the Greeks as their brothers : and so *cleaving to the Lord*, they would be one—for he (and not the law or circumcision) is the source of unity—and might look for further signs of his favour[1]. That this exhortation of S. Barnabas was one of conciliation is shewn by the subsequent condition of the church at Antioch. The Greeks were not circumcised : and yet the Jewish Christians lived and ate with them—in fact the whole church lived 'as the Gentiles do.' (This we learn from xv 1, and from Gal ii 11-14.)

24 The immediate result was a great advance. *Much people* (or *a great crowd*) *was added to the Lord*. These were probably new converts in addition to the *great number* of verse 21 who had now been definitely joined to the fellowship of the apostles (ii 42, 47).

25 This addition must have made a great demand upon the church's ministerial resources, but S. Barnabas was equal to the occasion. He knew of one exactly suited for this development of church work—a Hebrew yet full of Roman sympathies, intimate with Greek thought, and familiar with the neighbourhood. This was *Saul*. Hearing that he was still at *Tarsus*, Barnabas went thither,

26 and after some reluctance on Saul's part[2], *brought him to Antioch*, about the year 42. Here, together with other prophets and teachers (xiii 1), they exercised their ministry *for a whole year*[3]. In this interval (1) *they were gathered together in the church*. This is the ordinary phrase for the assembling for worship ; but here no doubt it refers to verses 20 and 23, and describes the work of gathering together Jews and Greeks into one body in the church[4]. (2) *They taught a great crowd*. This mass of new Greek converts, although coming for the most part (we suppose) from adherents of the synagogue, required a great deal of systematic teaching after their acceptance of the first preaching of the gospel.

This systematic organization of the church had a further effect. It attracted the notice of the Antiochene public. The pleasure-loving city was noted for its epigrams and witty nicknames, and they soon coined a name for this new body. Its watchword was *the Christ—CHRISTOS*. That was a title not very intelligible to the outsider, but it was very like another word—*chréstos*, which meant a good worthy fellow. So with an intentional confusion they

---

[1] These phrases *turned to, added to, cleave to the Lord* are signs of the identity of the Lord with the church as his body. Cp. *in the church*, verse 26 ; and verse 24 with ii 47. The interpretation given above is better expressed by the reading of the RV margin. [2] This we infer from the *exhortation* of the Bezan text. [3] This is the first of the series of spaces of time by which S. Luke marks S. Paul's ministry. The others are 18 months at Corinth (xviii 11) : two years at Ephesus, Caesarea, Rome (xix 10, xxiv 27, xxviii 30). [4] So Jn xi 52. *Synaxis*, the *gathering together*, became the usual word for 'service' : cp. iv 31 and xx 7, 8. The word is somewhat characteristic of Antioch, xiv 27 and xv 30. There is no mention of the synagogue at Antioch, and we may suspect that the Antiochenes were the first Christians to possess a proper ecclesia or church of their own. The English versions have no right to translate *with the church*: the Greek is *in*.

dubbed the followers of the Christ *the CHRESTIANOI* or *the worthy folk*. For it seems most likely from the evidence of early MSS and inscriptions[1], and the passage in Suetonius about one *Chrestus* who disturbed the Jews at Rome, that this was the original form of 'Christian.' In Agrippa's mouth (xxvi 28) the word has a ring of contempt; and if, like 'Nazarene,' it was a term of reproach, we can understand why the disciples were slow to adopt a title in which they would otherwise have naturally gloried. In S. Peter's first Epistle (iv 16) it still appears as the name current without, rather than within, the church. In *Christian*, as in the inscription on the Cross, we may see figured the universal character of Christianity. The word is Greek, the idea Hebrew, and the form Latin[2]. But this is an afterthought; at the time the populace of Antioch simply coined a Greek name out of a Greek word *chrestus* or *christus*. This significant word *CHRISTIANS* comes last in the sentence, and is evidently meant to close not merely a sentence but a whole chapter in church history: just as the following words *Now in these days* are the formula for a new beginning, as in i 15, vi 1, Lk i 5, ii 1.

---

[1] In both of these there is always confusion between E, EI, I. Thus codex ℵ has here *chrēstianous*, B and D *chreistianous*. [2] i.e. the termination *-anus*: but *-ianos* was also a Greek form. See p. cxvi.

DIVISION III

(= Ch. 11. 27—12)

THE PASSING OF PETER AND TRANSITION FROM JERUSALEM TO ANTIOCH

In the year 44, when Herod Agrippa died and Judaea was made a Roman province, under the procurator Cuspius Fadus: Claudius being emperor (A.D. 41-54).

The scene is now changing *from Jerusalem to Antioch* (verse 27), as the rôle of chief actor from S. Peter to S. Paul. We are passing from Part I to Part II. And this division which brings together Saul and Peter, Antioch and Jerusalem, marks the transition. As the subject of the division is the removal of the apostle to another place, it concludes the *ACTS OF PETER*, and may be entitled *THE PASSING OF PETER*, or, as that was brought about through suffering, *THE PASSION OF PETER*. S. Luke, however, by his use of the formula *Now in these days*, rather regards it as the introduction to the *ACTS OF PAUL*. There is also a new and most interesting feature, which is the appearance of the writer himself in verse 27 (i.e. according to the Bezan text). S. Luke, then, was at this time a member of the church at Antioch,—was he one of the 'great number' or the 'much people' of xi 21, 24?—and that is why he is able to give a picture, so accurate and so full of tact, of the growth of the Greek church at Antioch. We miss indeed local touches, such as he gives at Philippi: but this loss may be compensated for by the notices of persons. These matters, however, rather belong to the Introduction, where see ch. ii § 1.

§ 1 *The prophetic mission from Jerusalem to Antioch*

There does not appear to have been a community of goods at Antioch as at Jerusalem, but this section shews that there was the same spirit. (1) We learn that the 'common' feeling should bind together not only the individuals in the local community, but also the different communities however widely separated, for all are *brothers* (verse 29). This is the first instance of a public collection in one church for another and it originates in the spontaneous liberality of the disciples. S. Paul followed up the precedent by making a collection among his Gentile churches for the brethren at Jerusalem which is of some importance in the history: see xxiv 17, Rom xv 25-26, I Cor xvi 1, II Cor viii-ix[1]. (2) We notice in particular the friendly

---

[1] Cp. II Cor viii 14.

relations of the church of Antioch to Jerusalem. The church at Jerusalem was poor (p. 42), the more so after the persecution, and a famine gave their comparatively richer brethren at Antioch an opportunity of shewing their gratitude for S. Barnabas' mission. They send him back, as it were, with interest.

The famine was first intimated by *a prophet*. We have already had prophetic action and utterances; but this is the first mention of *prophets*, as in verse 30 of *presbyters* (i.e. *elders*). The position of these orders is discussed in the Introduction (ch. vi § 2).

27 Now in these days there came down prophets from
28 Jerusalem unto Antioch.¹ And there stood up one of them named Agabus, and signified by the Spirit that there should be a great famine over all the world: which came to pass in
29 the days of Claudius. And the disciples, every man according to his ability, determined to send ²relief unto the brethren
30 that dwelt in Judæa: which also they did, sending it to the elders by the hand of Barnabas and Saul.

27 The date of *these days* is not given. From the narrative we may put it in the year 43 or 44; and the visit of the *prophets* may have been due to the threatening attitude or actual hostility of Agrippa towards the church at Jerusalem. Exhortation or encouragement being the chief function of prophets, their arrival
28 caused *great gladness* or *exultation* at Antioch³. There was some special gathering of the church, perhaps for the paschal festival; and when *we were collected together* (S. Luke himself being present), *one of* the prophets *named Agabus* received a revelation and prophesied⁴. In this case the prophecy was a prediction. It was *signified*, that is illustrated by a *sign* or symbolical action, such as when several years later the same Agabus bound his hands and feet with Paul's girdle (xxi 11). This action was entirely after the manner of the prophets of old, of whose signs the OT record is full. We read for instance of Ahijah tearing Jeroboam's cloak into twelve pieces, Zedekiah the false prophet making horns of iron, and Jeremiah breaking a potter's vessel⁵. The prediction was of *a famine, which did come to pass in* the reign *of Claudius* (A.D. 41-54)⁶. The famine was to be *over all the world*, i.e. the civilized (in the Greek *inhabited*) world of the Roman empire. In Roman

---

¹ Bezan adds *And there was much gladness. And when we were collected together, one of them named Agabus spake [and signified]*. ² Gk *for ministry or service* (*diakonia*). ³ The addition in the Bezan text is very Lucan. The *gladness* (ii 46, xvi 34, Lk i 14, 44) gives the note of joy, otherwise omitted at Antioch: the epithet *much* is used as in viii 8 *much joy*. *Collected together* occurs in the active xxviii 3: and it is read in Mt xvii 22 (RV margin). Most likely it expresses the collecting together after evangelistic work in the neighbourhood. ⁴ I Cor xiv 26-30 helps us to picture the scene. ⁵ I K xi 30, xxii 11, Jer xix 10. ⁶ This is a note of S. Luke (not of Agabus) writing probably in the next reign.

historians there are notices of some distress caused at Rome by famine more than once in Claudius' reign, but there is no mention of a universal famine, and *all the world* is probably to be taken as one of the exaggerated expressions which are found here and there in the Acts. From the Acts itself we should not gather that the famine extended as far as Antioch. On the other hand S. Luke is confirmed by Josephus, who gives an account of a severe famine
29 in Palestine in the interval between the years 44 and 48. The Christians at Antioch at once *determined to minister* to their Jewish brethren. They raised a sum, each contributing *in proportion to his means*[1], and then sent it by two delegates of high
30 position in the church, none other than *Barnabas and Saul*, who delivered it *to the presbyters* at Jerusalem. The phrase *which also* (or *actually*) *they did* serves a real purpose in the literary composition of the section. It marks the sending as a distinct act which took place later on when the famine actually came, viz. after the events of xii 1-24, and S. Luke thus gives a hint that he is anticipating xii 25.

§ 2 *The second persecution. The imprisonment and deliverance of Peter*

About that season, viz. of the visit of the prophets to Antioch or the interval between that visit and the return of Barnabas and Saul to Jerusalem, for the third[2] time persecution fell on the church. It had been persecuted by the Sadducean high-priests: then by the Pharisees and the people. There remained one more party among the Jews—the Herodians. And now *Herod* himself, *the king, thrust out his hands*[3] and struck a blow at the church. This Herod, commonly known as Agrippa I, was grandson of Herod the Great and had been brought up at Rome in intimate relations with the imperial family. He had become a great friend of the young Caligula; and while this friendship brought him in danger of his life under Tiberius, it made his fortune at the accession of Caligula. For Caligula gave him with the title of 'king' the tetrarchy of Philip (Lk iii 1), and shortly afterwards the territory of Herod Antipas, viz. Galilee and Peraea. But the death of Caligula was still more profitable to Agrippa than his friendship in life. For Agrippa was instrumental in getting the senate to accept Claudius as his successor; and the grateful emperor added to Agrippa's kingdom Judaea and Samaria. Agrippa had hitherto remained at Rome, where he had been notorious chiefly for his prodigality and extravagance. Now he returned to his kingdom of Judaea, and there, in order to gain the favour of the Jews, he displayed the greatest assiduity in the observance of the law and the exhibition of external righteousness. Having been baffled in his more ambitious political projects by the prefect of Syria, Herod found another outlet for a display of patriotism in an attack on 'the Nazarenes,' who during

---
[1] S. Paul's principle in I Cor xvi 2. [2] but second, in the technical sense of 'persecution' unto death. [3] Lk xxi 12.

the trouble of the Jews under Caligula had been enjoying a time of peace.

This persecution was not general: as in the usual course of subsequent persecutions, it was directed first against *certain of the church*, i.e. its leaders—in this case S. James and S. Peter, and, comparing verse 17, we may infer that they were the only members of the Twelve remaining in Jerusalem. S. James, the son of Zebedee, with his younger brother John and S. Peter, held a leading place in the Lord's company of disciples: together they formed 'the first three[1].' Since the resurrection John had been coming more to the front (cp. i 13, iii 1), and here James is distinguished as *the brother of John*—the apostle still living and famous in the church when the Acts was written[2]. This is the only place, outside of the list of the Twelve, where he is mentioned in the Acts. His individual work had apparently no special influence on the side of the history which it was S. Luke's aim to emphasize; and the manner of his death is barely indicated. We are struck with the brief notice given to an event which in our eyes would be so important—the martyrdom of an apostle. It is of a piece with the silence about the details of Stephen's persecution, and about the deaths of the other apostles; and reflects the true instincts of the early church. In days of ardent faith and also of expectation of the Lord's speedy return, death sank into its true place as simply a change of condition: at the worst it was but a falling asleep (vii 60). For an apostle indeed it was a birthday, an entrance into true life and return to companionship with the Master. Accordingly instead of dwelling with morbid interest on the painful details of the martyrs' sufferings, the church pressed forward to reap with joy the harvest of their blood. S. Luke may single out S. James for mention because (1) he was the first of the apostles (as far as we know) to pass away: and (2) his death led up to the following history of Peter's deliverance. (3) The removal of James would also obviate confusion with the other James—the 'James' known to the church at large—who was the Lord's brother[3]. (4) Lastly, S. Luke may have wished the church to mark the fulfilment of the promise to the son of Zebedee which probably was already current, as it has found a place in the Gospels of S. Matthew and S. Mark[4].

S. Peter's imprisonment on the other hand was important because it took him—the last of the Twelve remaining there—away from Jerusalem. But there seems no special call for such a wealth of detail in contrast to the brief sentence about James. S. Luke no doubt relates it because he had received a vivid account which was too precious to be lost. S. Peter must have been the sole authority for the greater part of the story: and S. Luke may have received it from John Mark, very much as the latter heard it from the lips of S. Peter in his mother's house. The story also served as a lesson to the church of

---

[1] They alone were present at the raising of Jairus' daughter, the transfiguration, and the agony in Gethsemane. [2] In the Gospels (Mt Mk) it is *John the brother of James*. In Acts i 13, however, John comes first. [3] The James of xii 17 xv 13, xxi 18: cp. Gal ii 9, 12. [4] Mt xx 20-28, Mk x 35-45.

the power of prayer, a parable of hope in the face of obstacles, and a type of resurrection. Lastly, in the sequel, the judgement on Herod, we have a signal instance of divine retribution. Besides the direct parallel to Herod's trial of Jesus, the details and language very much recall S. Peter's own failures in the Gospel[1], in Gethsemane and in the high-priest's house. Thus S. Peter also suffered retribution like S. Paul; and with this deliverance from imprisonment we should compare that of S. Paul and Silas at Philippi (xvi 23-34).

12 Now about that time Herod the king put forth his hands
2 to afflict certain of the church. And he killed James the
3 brother of John with the sword. And when he saw that [2]it pleased the Jews, he [3]proceeded to seize Peter also. And
4 *those* were the days of unleavened bread. And when he had taken him, he put him in prison, and delivered him to four quaternions of soldiers to guard him; intending after the Passover to bring him forth to the people.
5 Peter therefore was kept in the prison: but prayer was
6 made earnestly of the church unto God for him. And when Herod was about to bring him forth, the same night Peter was sleeping between two soldiers, bound with two chains:
7 and guards before the door kept the prison. And behold, [4]an angel of the Lord [5]stood by him, and a light shined in the cell: and he smote Peter on the side, and awoke him, saying, Rise up quickly. And his chains fell off from his
8 hands. And the angel said unto him, Gird thyself, and bind on thy sandals. And he did so. And he saith unto him,
9 Cast thy garment about thee, and follow me. And he went out, and followed; and he wist not that it was true which
10 was done by the angel, but thought he saw a vision. And when they were past the first and the second ward, they came unto the iron gate that leadeth into the city; which

---

[1] Thus vv. 5-9 call to mind the scene in Gethsemane—the *prayer*, its *earnestness*, the *sleeping* of Peter and appearance of the *angel*, the *smiting* (as of Malchus) and the *rising up*. S. Peter was the authority for the narrative, and the verbal coincidences shew at least what was in his mind. With *the iron gate* of verse 10 cp. a similar obstacle, the stone at the sepulchre (Mk xvi 3-4): and on the *evening* of the resurrection the disciples believed not *for joy* (Lk xxiv 41: contrast their sleeping *for sorrow* at Gethsemane xxii 45). 13-16 call up the picture of Peter *standing without at the door* of the high-priest (Jn xviii 16): there too was a *maid* who kept the door, *recognition by the voice*, and *confident affirmation*. [2] Bezan has *his attack upon the faithful*. [3] Gk added *to take* (a Hebraism). Or *the angel* (AV). [5] AV *came upon*, as in Lk ii 9.

opened to them of its own accord: and they went out[1], and passed on through one street; and straightway the angel
11 departed from him. And when Peter was come to himself, he said, Now I know of a truth, that the Lord hath sent forth his angel and delivered me out of the hand of Herod, and
12 from all the expectation of the people of the Jews. And when he had considered *the thing*, he came to the house of Mary the mother of John whose surname was Mark; where
13 many were gathered together and were praying. And when he knocked at the door of the gate, a maid came to answer,
14 named Rhoda. And when she knew Peter's voice, she opened not the gate for joy, but ran in, and told that Peter stood
15 before the gate. And they said unto her, Thou art mad. But she confidently affirmed that it was even so. And they
16 said, [2]It is his angel. But Peter continued knocking: and when they had opened, they saw him, and were amazed.
17 But he, beckoning unto them with the hand to hold their peace, [3]declared unto them how the Lord had brought him forth out of the prison. And he said, Tell these things unto James, and to the brethren. And he departed, and went to another place.
18   Now as soon as it was day, there was no small stir among
19 the soldiers, what was become of Peter. And when Herod had sought for him, and found him not, he examined the guards, and commanded that they should be put to death. And he went down from Judæa to Cæsarea, and tarried there.

1   From Herod's death we can date S. Peter's imprisonment at Easter, A.D. 44. The *affliction* (or persecution, vii 6) had begun previously. According to a tradition reported by Clement of Alexandria, it arose in a way similar to that about Stephen. Some
2 one brought an accusation against S. *James*. This time, however, the charge was made in the king's court, and the penalty was not the legal one of stoning, but the civil and political mode of beheading: S. James was *killed with the sword*, like John the Baptist. The charge, then, was one of disloyalty rather than of breaking the Law. King Agrippa would have been as jealous of the preaching of the kingdom of the Messiah, as his grandfather had been at the news of the birth of the King of the Jews.

---

[1] Bezan adds *and descended the seven steps*.   [2] Bezan inserts *Perhaps*.
[3] Bezan inserts *went in and*.

Whether others beside Peter are included in the *certain of the church* we do not know. Five years later S. Paul wrote that the Jews 'both killed the Lord Jesus and the prophets and drave out us¹': and besides the persecution about Stephen there is no other
3 occasion to which we can refer this 'killing of the prophets.' The Nazarenes had never regained the popularity which they lost through Stephen's preaching; and the death of James was very *pleasing²* *to the Jews. Seeing* this, Herod determined to strike a decisive blow at the church by slaying its ringleader³—Peter. Like the Lord, Peter was arrested at *the Passover*; but the scrupulous Herod would not pollute *the* eight *days of unleavened bread*
4 by the shedding of blood, and Peter was *kept in prison*, i.e. the royal prison in the city. This was his third imprisonment, and possibly the recollection of a former deliverance caused special precautions to be taken⁴. Peter was confined in the inmost ward, and *four quaternions* guarded him—one for each watch. Of the four men in each quaternion, two were in the cell itself, each one chained to the prisoner, and the others kept watch at the doors of the outer and inner walls.
5 This was a heavy blow to fall upon *the church* at its *Easter* (AV), and the holy days were spent in *earnest prayer* for Peter's deliverance. The Greek word for *earnest* is literally *stretched out*, but it denotes not the extent of the prayer in time (*unceasing*, AV), but its intensity, i.e. intent-ness in quality. All the spiritual faculties were intent and taut. Such had been the character of the Lord's prayer in Gethsemane, when he 'prayed more earnestly⁵.'
6 The prayer was answered⁶. On the eve of the day fixed for his public execution, when he was to be sacrificed⁷ to the people, *on that night⁸ Peter was sleeping* quietly, *chained* to the *two soldiers*, his sandals and cloak laid aside and his girdle unloosed. The time seemed to have come 'when another should gird him and carry him
7 whither he would not,' and so he would return to his Master⁹. But the end was not yet. He felt a blow on his *side* and *waking* found
8 *the cell* full of *light*, and a man bidding him dress himself and follow, while at the same time *the chains fell off* his wrists. It was *the angel of the Lord* who had *come upon him* suddenly as upon the shepherds in the field, and the light was not a mere substitute for a
9 lantern, but the glory of the Lord¹⁰. Peter obeyed, thinking it was

---

¹ I Thess ii 15. As has been suggested the *prophets* of xi 27 may have been 'driven out' by Herod. ² vi 5 (Gk). ³ xxiv 5. ⁴ iv 3, v 18: v 18–25.
⁵ Lk xxii 44. This *earnestness* was also the mark of Jewish worship (Acts xxvi 7) and Christian love (I Pet i 22, iv 8). ⁶ As had been the earlier prayer of the church in iv 24–31. ⁷ B has a reading which is not so simple as the RV *bring forth*: it is rather *bring to*, i.e. the people, and is the word used by S. Peter of Christ *bringing* us *to* God (I iii 18). It occurs in xvi 20 of *presenting* to magistrates.
⁸ The solemn phrase 'the same night' recalls 'the same night in which (the Lord) was betrayed' (I Cor xi 23); but this was a week later, at the end of the feast.
⁹ See Keble's poem for S. Peter's Day in *The Christian Year*. He seems to read the apostle's thoughts. ¹⁰ Lk ii 9.

10 all *a vision*, and they passed out through the doors. The last great *iron gate* which opened on the city must have seemed an insuperable obstacle. But as the women on the way to the Lord's tomb had wondered *Who shall roll us away the stone from the tomb?* and then found it removed[1], so this door *opened of its own accord*, and *they went down the seven steps* into the street. The seven steps are just one of those unimportant details in the picture, which even at the most exciting crises strike the eye and fix themselves in the
11 memory[2]. When the angel left him and S. *Peter came to himself*, he perceived it was all actual *fact*[3]: and that it was a true passover or deliverance for him[4]. But he had quickly to decide on his course of action. In a few hours the soldiers would discover his
12 escape and start in pursuit. So he made his way *to the house of Mary the mother of John Mark.*

This introduces us to another Mary, another of those women whose praise was in the early church[5]. The *gate*, i.e. the gateway into the courtyard, and the *maid* or portress, indicate the residence of a well-to-do family[6]. The house being spacious had become a kind of centre in the church; there was a 'church in Mary's house[7].' Mary was a widow, and of note in the church. She was related to Barnabas. Peter calls her son John 'my son[8]'; his voice is well known to the portress; and when released from prison, it is to Mary's house that he turns his steps. At the moment that house was full of disciples engaged in *prayer* for him. It is an early instance of the Christian custom of spending the whole night in watching and prayer[9]. The *gathering* was however informal and none of the official leaders of the church were present (verse 17).
13 When they heard Peter's *knocking*, *Rhoda* crossed the courtyard to
14 answer; but when she *ran* back with the news that *Peter stood before the gate*, like the disciples on the resurrection day unable to believe
15 *for joy* (Lk xxiv 41), they concluded that *it is his angel*. This verse, with the Lord's sanction in Mat xviii 10, is generally appealed to for proof of the doctrine of guardian angels. The idea of an accompanying angel is found almost at the beginning of the Bible[10]; but the earliest idea was rather—*God was with him*[11], and the

---

[1] Mk xvi 3-4. [2] The *steps* come from the Bezan text. The narrative is full of those accurate terms which testify to personal acquaintance with the scene: *the cell, the first and second ward, the door, the iron gate, the seven steps, the quaternions, the two chains.* [3] With *of a truth* cp. x 34, iv 27. [4] The Lord *brought him out* (verse 17), as he *brought out* Israel from Egypt (xiii 17). For deliverance by the angel cp. Ps xxxiv 7, Dan iii 28, vi 22. [5] The other Marys were the mother of Jesus, Mary wife of Cleopas, mother of James and Joses, Mary of Bethany and Mary of Magdala. [6] There was a *gate* and *portress* in the high-priest's house (Jn xviii 16). Barnabas a relative of the family had been a man of means. [7] It has been conjectured that this house was the scene of the Last Supper; cp. Edersheim *Life etc. of the Messiah* II p. 485. This would naturally follow upon the identification of the *young man* of Mk xiv 51-2 with John Mark. [8] I Pet v 13. [9] After the example of the Lord: so at Troas (xx 7-12, which see). [10] Gen xlviii 16, Exod xiv 19, xxiii 20, xxxii 34, xxxiii 2 etc. [11] Acts vii 9, Gen xlvi 4, xxi 22, xxvi 24, 28, xxviii 15, Exod xxxiii 3, 14 etc.

accompanying angel is the angel of JEHOVAH or his WORD (see above, pp. 71–2). However, in the last two or three centuries before Christ the doctrine of angels had been greatly developed. The Jewish apocryphal literature is full of information and speculation about angels, which speculations were destined to prove a source of trouble to the church in the later apostolic age[1]. In Daniel's *Michael your prince, the prince of Persia* etc. we find guardian angels of nations[2]. Tobit v 21, *a good angel shall go with him*, seems to be the first definite allusion to the guardian angel of an individual: and this verse in the Acts shews that the belief had become current among the Jews[3] in the apostolic age. The passage in Tobit however and those in Talmudic literature[4] speak of angels, one or more, sent by God from time to time rather than of a particular angel assigned to each person at birth. Here the parallel between *his angel* and *the Lord's angel* in verse 11 may imply that the angel was some spiritual representative of S. Peter—perhaps, as we should say, 'his ghost.'

16 But whatever their belief about it, Mary's company were soon to be convinced that it was Peter himself; and when, for fear of attracting
17 notice, he had secured silence by *beckoning with his hand*, he told them what had happened, almost in the very words which we now read, and which were then drunk in by the eager ears of John Mark. S. Peter had to leave the city at once, so he only sent a message to *James and the brethren*, and *departed*. Very
18 soon *the soldiers* discovered his escape—to their consternation, for according to Roman custom they were responsible for their prisoners
19 with their lives[5]. Herod instituted a *search* for Peter in the city; and when it proved fruitless, he held a court-martial and the guards were executed. This done and the feast over, not without a feeling of chagrin, he left Jerusalem for his palace at *Caesarea*.

What *the other place* was to which S. Peter went S. Luke has not told us[6]. It is very tantalizing, but all we can say is that it was some place outside Herod's jurisdiction. It may have been Antioch; S. Peter certainly did visit that city at some time[7], and its tradition claims him for its first bishop. The Roman Catholic commentators generally conclude that Rome is meant. Certainly it is impossible to doubt the universal tradition that S. Peter did visit Rome and was martyred there. Tradition further is in favour of a visit in Claudius' reign. On the other hand S. Paul's Epistle to the Romans, written in 54, at first sight implies that no apostle had as yet visited the city; but the language of the epistle is quite capable of another interpretation. Another serious argument against a visit to Rome is that the whole tenor of the history is against S. Peter's having risen to the conception of a mission to Rome at this early date. He was apparently

---

[1] Coloss ii 18.   [2] Dan x 21, xii 1: x 20.   [3] excepting, that is, the Sadducees.
[4] See Weber's *Jüdische Theologie*, p. 172.   [5] xvi 27, xxvii 42.   [6] The silence may point to the early character of this narrative. In its first form the name of the place may have been withheld to keep it secret from the authorities. For *place* cp. i 25, Judas' *own place*.   [7] Gal ii 11.

unknown to the Jews of Rome in 58 (xxviii 22); and from the evidence of chapter xv he does not seem to have followed up the work among the Gentiles. At that date also (A.D. 48) he was back in Jerusalem. There is however a means of reconciling these objections with a Roman visit. As London now, so Rome then was the best of all hiding places, and what S. Peter wanted was to remain hidden for a while. It would not have been safe for him to do any more public work in the neighbourhood of Palestine; for the local governor, whether a dependent prince or even the Roman prefect of Syria, might have given him up to Herod for the sake of cultivating friendly relations[1]. Certainly the Jewish authorities of the synagogues would have been only too anxious to do so. It is, then, very likely that Peter took ship at Joppa and made his way to Rome. There he would avoid the Jewish synagogue and live in retirement. This retirement need not have been of more than brief duration; for almost on his footsteps must have followed the news of Agrippa's death.

Wherever he went, with S. Peter the last of the Twelve left Jerusalem[2]. Indeed it seems surprising to us that with their charge to evangelize the world they had stayed so long (cp. viii 1). But very likely the tradition which speaks of our Lord's having commanded them to stay in Jerusalem for twelve years is based on some truth. For whether they were conscious of it or no, they had to lay the foundations for the new Jerusalem: they had, that is, to fix the outlines of the teaching or 'the form of sound words,' and of the oral tradition which is the basis of the Gospels, and also to determine the elementary principles of church order and worship. To do this required common agreement and consent, which could only be secured by continuous fellowship and residence at the centre of affairs. Now however sufficient time had elapsed, and when Peter leaves the city *James*, the Lord's brother, is already in the position (which we find him holding later on) of president—or to use the later term, bishop—of the church at Jerusalem[3]; and no doubt *the brethren* are the college of his assistant presbyters, recently mentioned for the first time[4]. S. James may have acted as president even while the Twelve were in Jerusalem. Long ago they had found it difficult to combine the work of serving tables with the ministry. And as the church grew, the calls upon them for missionary work, and for the supervision and visitation of other churches, must have been rendering it more and more difficult for them to attend to matters of local administration and government. In the early days, accordingly, they had appointed the Seven[5]. That body was broken up by the persecution, and then the Twelve, as far as we can judge, found it necessary to replace them by a more permanent body

---

[1] Cp. Pilate and Herod Antipas, Lk xxiii 12: also Acts xxiv 27, xxv 13-22.
[2] This we conclude from the expression in verse 17. But if John (Gal ii 9) or others had remained, this would not have interfered with the position of James as explained below. [3] Cp. xv 19, xxi 18, Gal i 19, ii 9, 12. [4] xi 30: cp. xv 4, 6, 22, xxi 18, Jas v 14. [5] vi 1-6.

with a more definite authority, and such a body we now find in James and the presbyters.

§ 3 *The judgement of Herod*

It had been a 'day of visitation' for the church. James was slain: but sorrow had been turned into joy by the deliverance—almost a resurrection—of S. Peter. And now 'the judgement which had begun at the house of God[1]' is going to pass over to the adversaries, and the first part of the Acts will close with a 'day of the Lord,' a scene of judgement. The angel of the Lord who had delivered Peter was now to smite Herod the persecutor. He had 'smitten' Peter[2], and we see that the same divine visitation may be for life or for death. Herod Agrippa is the NT antitype of Pharaoh and Sennacherib, the oppressor smitten by the angel of the Lord[3].

20 Now he was highly displeased with them of Tyre and Sidon: and they came with one accord[4] to him, and, [5]having made Blastus the king's chamberlain their friend, they asked for peace, because their country was fed from the king's
21 country. And upon a set day Herod arrayed himself in royal apparel, and sat on the [6]throne, and made an oration unto
22 them. And[7] the people shouted, *saying*, The voice of a god,
23 and not of a man. And immediately an angel of the Lord smote him, because he gave not God the glory: and he [8]was eaten of worms, and gave up the ghost.

20 There had been a quarrel between *Herod* and the cities of *Tyre and Sidon*. Jealousies and disputes between subject cities and dependencies of the empire were not uncommon. Only ten years before there had been a quarrel between Sidon and Damascus as to their mutual boundary. In the present case Herod had the key of the situation in his hand. As in king Solomon's days centuries before[9], the Phenician cities still depended largely on the cornfields of Galilee for their food. Herod now cut off the supplies, which brought the Phenicians to his feet. They sent an embassy to Caesarea to *sue for peace*, i.e. reconciliation. They had chosen a favourable moment, when Agrippa was celebrating with great magnificence a festival at Caesarea in thanksgiving for the safe return of the emperor Claudius from his expedition against Britain. They had also secured the interest of *the king's chamberlain*; in plain words they had *bribed* him. The king granted them a public audience and

---

[1] I Pet ii 12, iv 17.   [2] verse 7 (and 23): cp. II Cor ii 16.   [3] Exod xii 29, II K xix 35: cp. Holofernes and Heliodorus in the Apocrypha.   [4] Bezan adds *from both cities*.   [5] Gk *having persuaded B*.   [6] Gk *bēma*.   [7] Bezan adds *when he was reconciled to the Tyrians*.   [8] Bezan reads *came down from the throne and was eaten of worms while still living and so [gave up*.   [9] I K v 9-11, ix 11-13.

21 fixed the second day of the festival. Herod was determined to make an impression upon them ; and *on the appointed day*, being as vain as he was superstitious, he arrayed himself in a robe made entirely of silver, and surrounded by a body of courtiers and flatterers *took his seat on the béma, or throne*[1], in the theatre. There *he made a public oration* to the ambassadors, and declared that he was re-
22 conciled. The crowd who packed the theatre, dazzled by the splendour of the scene and the brilliance of the royal apparel, with flatterers to lead them, began to applaud the orator with loud shouts—*It is God's voice, not man's.* This did not mean much : orientals were quite accustomed to the deification of their monarchs, and the worship of the Augustus was spreading throughout the
23 empire. Nevertheless Herod was quite carried away by the specious flattery. But at that moment, as he sat on the throne, violent pains seized him ; he had to be carried to the palace and there on the fifth day he died of a loathsome disease. Then was laid bare the hollowness of human flattery. The Judaism by which Herod curried favour with the Jews had made him detested by his Gentile soldiers and subjects. His death was the signal for a public riot in Caesarea, and the populace manifested their joy by heaping insults upon his name and his children.

The supplementary details have been added from Josephus, who gives a circumstantial account of Herod's death[2]. He also notices Herod's impiety ; and adds that the pains attacked him at the sight of an owl sitting on one of the ropes of the awning of the theatre, for the superstitious king had been taught to look upon that bird as the harbinger of his fate. But it is S. Luke who gives us the true cause. Herod was *smitten* by *the angel of the Lord* ; and this is the regular OT phrase for declaring that the event was a divine judgement, whatever the physical cause may have been[3].

§ 4 *The peace of the church and mission of Barnabas and Saul*

On Herod's death Palestine was again made into a Roman province. And the Roman power secured peace, not only for Tyre and Sidon, but also for the church. The peace was a time of growth. The blood of James proved to be rich seed, like that of Stephen, and its shedding was followed by the same harvest, to be gathered in the subsequent peace ; the church *grew and multiplied* (as in vi 7, cp. vii 17). By a note like this S. Luke as usual marks the close of a chapter : and he passes on to the incident of the peace which was most fruitful for the future. This was the mission of *Barnabas and Saul to Jerusalem*, which carried into effect the resolution made by the Christians of Antioch in xi 29.

---

[1] The *béma* was properly a tribune, which also served for the seat of judgement etc. (xxv 6, Jn xix 13).   [2] In *Ant.* xix 8. 2.   [3] II Sam xxiv 16, II K xix 35 : see p. 72.

24   But the word of God grew and multiplied.
25   And Barnabas and Saul¹ returned ²from Jerusalem, when they had fulfilled their ³ministration, taking with them John whose surname was Mark.

The famine did not occur till after the death of Herod. No doubt it was the premonitory symptoms which had made the Phenicians so anxious for peace. But Josephus will not allow us to date the full severity of the famine until 45. In this year, then, *Barnabas and Saul* brought the alms from Antioch. This Christian *service* was not indeed unique. About this time there had come to Jerusalem a royal proselyte, and a very profitable convert for the Jews,—Helena, queen of Adiabene. When the famine fell upon Jerusalem, she distinguished herself greatly by her contributions and successful efforts in obtaining provisions⁴.

According to the evidence of the best MSS S. Luke says that *Barnabas and Saul returned to Jerusalem*: and this is the natural expression, seeing that Jerusalem is still the centre of the history, and it was from Jerusalem that Saul had been sent to Tarsus and Barnabas to Antioch⁵. Their visit was uneventful: S. Paul does not think it necessary to mention it in his retrospect in Gal i–ii. There were none of the Twelve at Jerusalem: so Paul had no intercourse with them, and he and Barnabas *fulfilled their ministry* by delivering their alms *to the presbyters*. Then they went back to Antioch; but they took back in exchange some living gold—they *took with them John Mark*. Barnabas was related to John, and the two delegates may have stayed in Mary's house. John was closely attached to S. Peter, but S. Peter having departed, he was ready to join his cousin and Saul. These two had no doubt already in their minds the idea of further missionary enterprise, and for such work John had very serviceable gifts⁶. He had a good knowledge of Greek together with the faculty of composition. Moreover he was thoroughly acquainted with the teaching of Peter and the oral traditions of the church of Jerusalem. With a view to giving such help, like most Jews who travelled in the Graeco-Roman world, he adopted a Roman name—*Marcus*, a very common 'praenomen' or as we should say now 'Christian name.' The use of the aorist tense in the Greek here (instead of the present tense of verse 12), as in the case of Joseph Barnabas in iv 36 (p. 63), is a probable sign that he received the name now. So then the company left Jerusalem and with them we also take our farewell.

The reading and interpretation of this passage have been confused through want of perception of S. Luke's style and plan. S. Luke is very fond of using participles. He expresses the fact of main importance by a finite verb and then adds to it other facts in participles,

---

¹ Some Bezan texts add *who is surnamed Paul*.   ² Marg, with the best MSS ℵB and other authorities, gives *to Jerusalem*.   ³ Or *service* (xi 29).   ⁴ Joseph. *Ant.* xx 2. 5.   ⁵ ix 30, xi 22: cp. viii 25, xiii 13.   ⁶ S. Paul in later years found Mark *useful for ministering (service)*, II Tim iv 11. According to tradition he acted as S. Peter's interpreter at Rome, and in this way wrote his Gospel.

which must be taken in order. Accordingly the correct translation here would be *they returned to Jerusalem and fulfilled their ministry and took with them John*. Not having observed this habit of his style, and puzzled by the return to Jerusalem, when they had just come from and were going back to Antioch, some scribes thought S. Luke meant *when they had fulfilled their ministry they returned*, and therefore changed *to* into *from—Jerusalem*. And the mistake has lasted on to the RV[1].

---

[1] For S. Luke's fondness for participles (which vary the monotony of the style) see xiv 14, 19, 21, xv 40, xvi 27, xviii 18, etc. In such passages the participles have to be taken in the order of their sequence. Participles which follow a finite verb either (*a*) define or explain the action thereby signified, in which case they are generally present participles (sometimes aorist); or (*b*) denote a subsequent action and then they are aorists. This seems to be the general rule: for the few exceptions can easily be accounted for (vii 45, x 24, 33, xv 40, xxvi 10). Decisive examples are xvi 6, xxii 24, xxiii 34–5, xxiv 22, xxv 13 (vii 36). The use of the participles in connexion with the verb *return* confirms this; several times an accompanying aorist participle denotes an action preceding the return, but in that case it is always found before the verb.

Verse 25 then will be an editorial note of S. Luke's in his characteristic style, and it marks the close of Part I, at the same time (like similar notes) forming the transition to the following part. It may be objected that S. Luke in that case does not mention their return to Antioch; but it is his way to leave obvious inferences to the reader: cp. xv 33 and 40 (Silas' staying at Antioch).

PART II
(Ch. 13-28)

THE ACTS OF PAUL

THE CHURCH OF THE UNCIRCUMCISION
AND
PROGRESS FROM ANTIOCH TO ROME

THE ACTS OF PAUL

CHAPTER xiii opens the second part of the Acts. S. Luke indeed seems to make Part II begin at xi 27. For the emphatic word *CHRISTIANS* would make a good end for Part I; and there is no new (literary) start like the formula of xi 27, *Now in these days*, until we get to xix 21 or xxi 15. But in any case chapter xii would only be an introduction; for it stands in the same relation to xiii–xxviii as chapter i to ii–xi. Like the second chapter, the thirteenth is a real beginning. And the difference in the new part is obvious. (1) Throughout—except in a very small section (xviii 24–28), and in chapter xv, where S. Peter reappears but not in the same pre-eminence as before—the leading figure is S. Paul. And the change is marked by the change of name: *Saul who is also called Paul*[1]. (2) This change is significant of the change of scene. For the work now lies in the Roman empire outside of the Holy Land, and for the most part among Gentiles. (3) The starting-point, both locally and spiritually, is Antioch. Antioch takes the place of Jerusalem as the metropolis or mother city of the church.

---

[1] This note occurs in the Bezan texts at different points: some begin *Paul* in xii 25, and have it in xiii 1, 2. This shews that the change took place at this epoch but that we cannot assign to it a definite moment.

DIVISION I

(= Ch. 13-16. 5)

THE WORK OF PAUL AND BARNABAS AND ITS RATIFICATION BY THE CHURCH

In the years 46 to 48 after Christ, Claudius being emperor of Rome.

Introductory (= Ch. 13. 1-3)

The Holy Ghost separates Barnabas and Saul for the work

The position of *the church at Antioch* is shewn by the significant paragraph xiii 1-3, which marks it as the starting-point. The former history began with an enumeration of the Twelve and their occupation in prayer: a great outpouring of the Spirit ensued, and this was the beginning of active work. So at Antioch we have the names of the rulers of the church, and their service of the Lord; and then a direct inspiration of the Holy Ghost leads to the new work of Barnabas and Saul. Thus S. Luke indirectly establishes the right of the brethren at Antioch to be considered a true 'ecclesia,' and as such to initiate a new departure. His words are literally *Now there were at Antioch in that which was the church*[1]; and in his narrative we recognize the ecclesia at Antioch as possessing all the marks of the church of God. (1) The mission to them of the apostolic delegate S. Barnabas, and his sanction of their proceedings, had proved their stedfast adherence to *the teaching of the apostles.* (2) Their *fellowship* with the apostolic church they had just demonstrated in a very practical manner by sharing their goods

---

[1] Cp. v 17 *that which was the sect of the Sadducees,* xiv 13 (Bezan) *that which was Zeus Before-the-city,* xxviii 17 *they that were first of the Jews.*

with them in the famine. (3) Perseverance in *the breaking of bread and the prayers* is implied in the liturgical notice of xiii 2. Indeed, as there was no Jewish temple at Antioch, nor is there any mention of the synagogues, we may conjecture that Antioch witnessed some of the earliest developments of independent Christian worship. The frequent notices of the *gathering together* at Antioch, if they cannot be pressed too much in this direction, at least shew that the church had (4) the note of unity. As we learn from the Ep. to the Galatians, the Jews and Greeks lived side by side as one body[1]. In addition we observe that the church was organized as a corporate body. At its head, corresponding to the Twelve at Jerusalem, there was a body of *prophets and teachers* whom we might call the Five. At the same time we trace in the notices of the church a certain independence or democratic feeling. In speaking of its action S. Luke uses the indefinite *they*: *they* determined to send relief, *they* sent Barnabas and Saul as their delegates, *they* determined that Paul and Barnabas should go up to Jerusalem: *the brethren* sent back Judas and Silas in peace, and commended Paul and Silas to the grace of God. The body of the church, technically called *the multitude*[2], possessed a real activity and authority: Paul and Barnabas gave an account of their work to *the church*; the letter of the council of Jerusalem was delivered to *the multitude*[3]. The comparative independence of the church of Antioch in relation to the mother church is seen alike in its sending of alms and in this new departure. This freedom of spirit was no doubt due to the composition of the Antiochene church. For, as we have already seen[4], its members were in the main either Hellenist Jews or God-fearing Greeks: and, as the Hellenist or Greek church, Antioch was the connecting link between the Hebrew church of Jerusalem and the churches of the Gentiles whose foundation is now to be recorded.

13 Now there were at Antioch, in the church that was *there*, prophets and teachers, Barnabas, and Symeon that was called Niger, and Lucius of Cyrene, and Manaen the foster-
2 brother of Herod the tetrarch, and Saul. And as they ministered to the Lord, and fasted, the Holy Ghost said, Separate me Barnabas and Saul for the work whereunto I
3 have called them. Then, when they had fasted and prayed[5] and laid their hands on them, they sent them away.

The office of *prophets and teachers* is discussed elsewhere[6]. Here the Greek may intimate that Barnabas, Symeon and Lucius were

---

[1] For the notes of the church see pp. 33-43; and for references compare (1) xi 22-4 and ii 42: (2) xi 29-30, xii 25 and ii 44-5, iv 32-35: (3) xiii 2, xi 26, 27, xiv 27, xv 30 and pp. 35-41: (4) Gal ii 11-13 and pp. 41-2.   [2] In ordinary Greek we find the same technical use of *the multitude*, Deissmann *Neue Bibelstudien* p. 59.
[3] Cp. xi 29, 30, xv 2: xv 33, 40 and xiv 26: xiv 26, xv 30.   [4] xi 20 and pp. 166-7.   [5] Bezan adds *all (of them)*.   [6] Introd. ch. vi § 2.

prophets, Manaen and Saul teachers. But it is simpler to consider them as one body of rulers, who both prophesied and taught—the rabbis of the Christian society[1]. Among the Five *Barnabas*, as we should have expected from xi 22, holds the first place, *Saul* as yet the last. Of the other three, as of most of the Twelve and the Seven, we know nothing but their names. *Lucius of Cyrene* was evidently one of the original evangelists of xi 20, and to him we may join *Symeon*, whose surname *the Black* suggests an African origin. *Manaen*, i.e. Menahem, is interesting as an instance of the power of Christianity to touch the highest ranks. He had been *the foster-brother of Herod* Antipas *the tetrarch* of Galilee. This term seems to have been a court title of honour like 'the friend of the king' in the OT[2]. Manaen may have been a son of Menahem the influential Essene of the days of Herod the Great. If so our prophet Manaen was the son of a prophet. For, according to Josephus[3], when Herod the Great was yet a boy, Menahem had assured him that he would be king; and when the prediction was fulfilled, Menahem became a special object of Herod's favour. The mention of Herod here is one of those touches which betray the author's hand. In his Gospel S. Luke appears to be very well acquainted with or interested in the doings of the Herodian family, and no doubt his information came from Manaen[4].

This body presided over the church's worship: *they were ministering*, i.e. offering service, *to the Lord and fasting*. The Greek word used for public worship or *service* is *leitourgia* (*liturgy*), which has an important history. Originally among the Greeks it denoted a service rendered to the state by an individual, such as fitting out a ship of war or providing a public entertainment. Then (1) the Greek translators of the Bible adopted it for the service of God in the temple. In so doing they were, it seems[5], only following the language of their country. For in Egypt it was already used in this sacred sense. From the OT this one naturally passed into the NT. Thus S. Luke calls Zacharias' priestly service in the temple his *leitourgia*, and it is the regular word in the Ep. to the Hebrews for the work of the priests. S. Paul writes to the Philippians of 'the sacrifice and *service* of their faith'; and in one very sacrificial passage he represents himself as the *servant* (*leitourgos*) of Christ, offering up the Gentiles in sacrifice to God. (2) But S. Paul also uses it of the general service of God outside of the special sacrificial or liturgical sense; for instance he calls the magistrates the *servants* (*leitourgoi*) of God, very much as we speak of 'cabinet ministers.' (3) And we also find in the NT the original meaning of *leitourgia*, viz. the service of man. S. Paul speaks of contributions of money as the *service*, or as we

---

[1] Barnabas and Saul were prophets, and they also taught (ix 26). Cp. Eph iv 11 where *pastors and teachers* form one class: so also in I Tim v 17 *presbyters and teachers*. [2] So Deissmann *Bibelstudien* p. 179. Cp. I Chron xxvii 33.
[3] *Ant.* xv 10. 5. [4] The connexion of S. Luke and the Herodian family is well drawn out in a sermon in Archdeacon Wilson's *Things New and Old* (1900).
[5] From the evidence of papyri etc., collected by Deissmann *Bibelstudien* pp. 137-8.

might say 'offering,' rendered to him by the brethren[1]. This double usage contains in itself the great lesson that the true service of God is the service of man and *vice versâ*. But in the NT the primary signification, which now colours the two other meanings, is that of the service or worship of God. And that is the sense in S. Luke's mind here: they were offering priestly service to God, and in such service the first element would be the breaking of bread and the prayers. To this day the common name among Greek Christians for the service of Holy Communion is *the Liturgy (the Service)*. This service was performed at Antioch by the prophets and teachers; and the Didachê shews us how the celebration passed into the hands of 'the bishops (*episcopi*, i.e. presbyter-bishops) and deacons.' 'Elect for yourselves,' it says[2], 'bishops and deacons...for they also perform for you the service (*liturgy*) of the prophets and teachers.'

With the service is associated *fasting*. There was only one fast, the day of atonement, appointed in the Law. But it had become the practice for pious Jews to fast twice a week; and it was natural that those who became Christians should continue the habit. That this actually happened we see in the Didachê[3], only the days of fasting were changed from Monday and Thursday to Wednesday and Friday. *The Fast* (of the atonement) is mentioned in xxvii 9; S. Paul was 'in fastings oft,' whether voluntary or involuntary[4]; and here fasting appears as a normal observance in the life of the church. In verse 3 and xiv 23 it is especially connected with the laying on of hands in ordination. Fasting, then, was not a specially Christian practice. It was really part of the asceticism which was so highly esteemed and inculcated in all the oriental religions: we might almost call it a practice of natural religion in the east. But herein lay its danger. It might (and did) very easily lead to doctrinal error, viz. the belief that matter in itself was evil, and also to spiritual pride, together with false ideas about merit and good works. Consequently there is but little emphasis laid on fasting in the NT. In some places in the AV where *fasting* was joined with prayer it seems to have been an interpolation and has disappeared from the text in the RV[5]. The Lord fasted for forty days absolutely, but after that does not appear to have observed the weekly fasts. In the parable of the Pharisee and the Publican he makes it one of the Pharisee's boasts: 'I fast twice in the week.' On the other hand in the Sermon on the Mount he deals with fasting as a normal religious practice[6]. He did not legislate about it; but if we look for particulars, the mention of 'the days when the bridegroom shall be taken away' would indicate the time of fasting, viz. Good Friday and the Great Saturday[7]. This would correspond to the one great annual fast of the old law. And in fact the fasting on the anniversary of the

---

[1] The references are (1) Lk i 23, Hebr viii 6, ix 21, x 11, Phil ii 17, Rom xv 16. (2) Rom xiii 6. (3) Phil ii 25-30, II Cor ix 12, Rom xv 27. [2] xv 1: cp. x 7. [3] viii 1. [4] II Cor vi 5, xi 27. [5] Mt xvii 21, Mk ix 29, Acts x 30, I Cor vii 5. [6] Mt iv 2; Mk ii 18; Lk xviii 12; Mt vi 16. [7] Mt ix 15, Mk ii 20, Lk v 35.

XIII 3   BARNABAS AND SAUL ARE SEPARATED   191

Lord's death and burial is no doubt the *raison d'être* (apart from the natural suggestions of self-discipline) and the origin of Christian fasting. These days were kept as strict fasts from the beginning. And the fasting in our present text may have been at that season.

At this paschal season, then, in the spring of A.D. 46 *the Holy Spirit* ordered *Barnabas and Saul* to be *set apart*. The form of expression here, as in the tenth chapter and elsewhere, is a strong testimony to the personality of the Holy Spirit and to his divine nature[1]. The Holy Spirit was to be the guide of the church; and it is just at the critical points in the road that we find him making his guidance most manifest[2]. The manifestation was very frequently given through prophecy[3], and the words here recorded were probably uttered by one of the five prophets at a solemn meeting of the church. (This in turn throws light on the ordination of Timothy, which was in accordance with preceding prophetic utterances[4].) The word of command *Set apart* or *Separate*, like the word *service*, already bore many sacred associations. It was used in the Greek Bible for the consecration of the first-born, of the Levites, and of Aaron and his sons,—in the last case, particularly for the separation of the wave offering which was symbolical of their own separation unto God: similarly the first of the dough was set apart for an offering to the Lord. In Isaiah those who bear the vessels of the Lord are bidden to 'be separate': and the son of Sirach compares David to the fat separated for God from the peace offering[5] Here were a number of types of dedication now to find a fresh fulfilment in the setting apart of Barnabas and Saul; and that they were in S. Paul's mind at least is shewn by his words when he calls himself *set apart for the gospel of God*[6]. Similarly the Greek word here for *call*, besides its ordinary use, had been applied to the divine call—both of Israel and the individual[7].

The command was emphatic[8], and the church obeyed. Either at the end of the season of *fasting*, or after a special fast[9], there was a special service when *after prayer hands were laid* upon Barnabas and Saul. By this action the church set them apart, committed them to the grace of God, and so *dismissed them*. Besides an ordination, it was a farewell service. The question arises—who did this? The Holy Spirit was the real consecrator, but who were his human instruments? The only antecedent to the pronouns in verse 3 are the *prophets and teachers* of verse 1; and so they uttered the prayer and laid on hands. By thus assigning the whole action to the Five, S. Luke emphasizes the parallel between them and the Twelve at Jerusalem. But no doubt (as

---

[1] See x 19-20 and Introd. ch. v § 1. viii 29, x 19-21, xiii 2, 4, xvi 6 (xix 21). and xxi 11. So S. Peter (I i 11, II i 21). [2] Jn xvi 13, and compare Acts ii 4, [3] Cp. ii 17, viii 29, 39, xix 6, xx 23 [4] I Tim i 18 and iv 14. [5] Exod xiii 12, Num viii 11, Exod xxix 24-6-7; Num xv 20: Isai lii 11; Ecclus xlvii 2. In Exod xix 12, 23, it is used for the setting apart of Mt Sinai and of the people for the reception of the law. [6] Rom i 1 and Gal i 15. [7] Exod iii 18, v 3: Joel ii 32 (Acts ii 39). [8] A strengthening particle is added to the imperative as elsewhere in the NT only in I Cor vi 20: but cp. Lk ii 15, Acts xv 36 (Gk). [9] As may be indicated by the Greek tenses.

xv 40 suggests) the whole church took part in the service and dismissal, as in the ordination of the Seven at Jerusalem[1].

Another question is—what was the significance of the act? By laying on of hands was conferred some office or some blessing and spiritual gift (p. 85). The solemnity of the circumstances—the command of the Spirit, the fasting, the prayer, the public ceremony—goes to shew that something, and something of no slight importance, was thereby conveyed to Barnabas and Saul. What was it? Barnabas and Saul were already prophets and teachers, nothing remained for them but the apostolate. After this setting apart (and not before) they are called 'apostles[2],' and in their work they exercise apostolic functions,—they preach the word and work signs, they lay on hands and organize churches. S. Paul (as we shall see) now appears in the church as a second Peter. Moreover S. Paul regarded his 'separation' as no temporary but a permanent condition. We conclude then that this was the ordination of Barnabas and Saul to the apostolate. It was not so much that the church at Antioch was consciously consecrating them to a defined office; rather they were consecrated to a work which would be recognized as the work of apostles and in which they would act with apostolic authority, holding a position corresponding to that of the Twelve.

Against this view there lie two obvious objections. (1) 'How could the church at Antioch convey what it did not possess—apostolic authority?' (2) On the other hand it is said 'S. Paul did not require ordination: he received his apostolate *neither from nor through men* but straight from the Lord.' The way to an answer will be cleared by distinguishing between the functions of an apostle. (*a*) There was the unique function of bearing witness to the resurrection of the Lord. This was the special privilege of the Twelve (shared by S. James the Lord's brother), and it obviously could not be handed down to others by laying on of hands. It had however been given to S. Paul and that directly by our Lord himself, for Saul's vision of the risen Jesus on the road to Damascus in itself had qualified him to be *an apostle of Jesus Christ*. (*b*) But the apostles were also *apostles of the church*; they were the chief rulers of the church. That office and authority could, and had to be, handed down; and the tangible evidence of its transmission was given by the laying on of hands. This apostolate may have been conferred on Barnabas and Saul at Antioch, and so we must consider the two objections to this view. (1) It might be supposed that some of the rulers at Antioch already possessed apostolic authority; for the recent mention of James at Jerusalem and the mission of Barnabas shew that this authority was now being delegated. But as hands were laid upon Barnabas himself, we must conclude that the prophets did not lay on hands as delegates of the Twelve. The whole occurrence however was extraordinary and exceptional. The immediate action of

---

[1] As the *all* in the Bezan text indicates—unless indeed it means that *all* the Five, including Barnabas and Saul, fasted and prayed, while the remaining three laid on hands.   [2] xiv 4, 14.

the Spirit corresponded to that at Pentecost: as then the first 'apostles,' the Twelve, were empowered by a descent of the Spirit direct from heaven, so now Barnabas and Saul are separated to be 'apostles' on an equal footing by an interposition of the Spirit no less direct[1]. That this was S. Luke's view is shewn by the striking words by which in verse 4 he interprets their dismissal—*so they, being sent forth by the Holy Ghost.* (2) Those who dispute the necessity of any ordination by the church fail to see the correspondence between the eternal will of God and its revelation in time and the visible world. God had 'separated Paul from his mother's womb,' and yet there came a definite moment in time when he said 'Separate me Paul.' In his eternal will the Lord had 'chosen' Saul to be his 'vessel,' yet there came the definite moment when the Christ was revealed to him and he received the call. Even when the revelation had been given, he had still to be baptized three days later in accordance with the divine order of grace. Similarly he had received at Jerusalem a mission from the Lord (xxii 21), but he had to wait some years before he could carry it out. So now, though he had been separated for an apostle long ago, the moment came, in accordance with the same divine order, for the choice to be made known to the church by the laying on of hands. For it was not for himself alone. As has been shewn before, the rest of the brethren would need some sign or proof of the validity of S. Paul's apostolate, viz. that he was not only an apostle of Jesus Christ but also an apostle of the church. And we know that subsequently S. Paul's apostolate was actually called in question, which would not have been possible, had it been perfectly normal and regular. There still remains S. Paul's own protest in Gal i-ii that he was not made an apostle by man. In considering this, we must remember S. Paul's unique position. He was an apostle in a third sense, which made him preeminent among the apostles. He had a special mission from God to be an *apostle of the Gentiles*, and to hold a position corresponding to that of S. Peter. This could not be conveyed by the laying on of hands. It was the special divine will, and the revelation of that will to S. Paul had been so convincing that by the side of it the external ordination would in his own spirit and mind hold a secondary place. And as his contention was that he was independent of the Twelve in his mission, so the fact that he had been ordained not by their hands but irregularly, by specially inspired prophets, was so to speak of advantage to him: it enabled him to say with truth that he had not been made an apostle by man.

---

[1] The Twelve had received a previous mission or appointment from the Lord (Jn xx 21): and so had S. Paul (Acts xxii 21).

SECTION I (= Ch. 13. 4—14)

The work of S. Paul and S. Barnabas

The work to which Barnabas and Saul were called was evidently a great step forward. But it is not clear at first sight wherein the novelty consisted. (1) Missionary work was not new in the church Nor was (2) travelling to the west. Jewish settlements, great in numbers and influence, extended as far west as Rome, and there was lively intercourse between them and Jerusalem. Again (3) preaching to the Gentiles was not new. Cornelius had been baptized, and large numbers of Greeks converted at Antioch. (4) To us 'the work' is important as the First Missionary Journey of S. Paul. But the division of these later chapters into three Missionary Journeys, though convenient for memory, is not the scheme in the mind of the author. We must then, to solve the difficulty, study S. Luke's selection of incidents. We have (1) the scene at Paphos before the Roman governor: (2) at Antioch Paul's sermon to the Jews and 'the turning to the Gentiles': (3) at Iconium and Lystra signs and miracles, and direct preaching to the Gentiles: (4) on the return, organization of the churches on an independent basis. At Antioch the work done is summed up as (*a*) what God had done with them, (*b*) the opening of a door of faith to the Gentiles. Then follows in chap. xv the solemn ratification of the work by the whole church: and lastly Paul's separation from Barnabas.

From this it is clear that 'the work' was (A) *the conversion of the Gentiles.* Hitherto Gentiles had indeed been admitted to the church; but they had come in through the synagogue as God-fearing Greeks. Now S. Paul turns to the Gentiles directly, and out of them builds up organized churches, which are catholic churches—founded, that is, not on Jewish privilege but on the universal relation of man to God. This was the great mission of S. Paul—the foundation of 'the churches of the Gentiles' (Rom xvi 4).

(B) But the validity of the foundation depends on the authority of the founder, and these chapters also contain the proof from facts of *S. Paul's apostolate.* They begin with his extraordinary ordination by the Holy Ghost, and in the following history we shall recognize all 'the signs of an apostle'—the power of binding and of working miracles, the laying on of hands and foundation of churches. His gospel is identical with the apostolic doctrine as declared by S. Peter; and his work is accepted by the church at Jerusalem. Finally, even the painful separation from S. Barnabas serves a purpose. Saul began in subordination to Barnabas, but at the end he stands forth alone and independent as the 'apostle of the Gentiles.'

The scene of the work—'the churches of Galatia'

We shall obtain a much clearer grasp of the history of the Acts when we have realized that the churches founded in this journey were *the churches of Galatia*. This statement indeed has not yet been generally accepted in England. The opposition to it is largely owing to the great influence of Bishop Lightfoot, who maintained the older view, and therefore a careful consideration of the matter is necessary. The facts are briefly these.

About 278 B.C. a great wave of Celtic invaders poured into southern Europe, and a host of these Gauls (*Galli* or *Galatae*) crossed over the sea into Asia Minor. Here for fifty years they roamed and plundered at will. Then Attalus king of Pergamum succeeded in confining them to a tract of country which from them received the name of GALATIA. The land was in the northern part of the great central plateau, and there the Galatians lived in three clans or cantons, which were grouped round the cities of Ancyra, Tavium, and Pessinus. They continued to form the chief fighting element in Asia Minor, but in B.C. 189 were subdued by the arms of Rome. Subsequently, during the Roman civil wars in the first century before Christ, one of their princes, Amyntas, acquired a large dominion, which by the favour of Augustus he was allowed to retain with the title of king. This 'kingdom of Galatia' comprised, besides Galatia proper, a part of Phrygia, Lycaonia, Isauria, Pisidia, Pamphylia and Western Cilicia. On the death of Amyntas in B.C. 25 it passed into the hands of the Romans. Pamphylia was separated and made a province by itself. The administration of the other districts was subject to fluctuation. At the time of our journey (A.D. 46–47), Western Cilicia with part of Lycaonia belonged to the kingdom of Antiochus of Commagene: the remainder composed the Roman province of Galatia. It is true that in the formal title of the governor the various districts were all enumerated: he was 'Propraetor of the province of Galatia, Pisidia, Phrygia, Lycaonia, etc.' But in ordinary Roman conversation the province would be known as 'Galatia,' just as Mysia, Lydia, and Caria, were included in the one province of 'Asia.'

The mountains of the Taurus range in Pisidia, Isauria, and Western Cilicia, were infested with brigands. It was in fighting with them that Amyntas had lost his life; and it required the power of Rome to cope with them. Augustus accordingly made the towns of Antioch and Lystra into Roman colonies and garrisoned them with veteran soldiers, while later Claudius did something in the way of strengthening Iconium and Derbe. These four cities all lay in the district just north of the Taurus range, but south of Galatia proper, from which they were separated by a great desert called the *Axylon* or *Woodless*. They were of different nationalities and under different political conditions. But they had one point in common; they all belonged to the province of Galatia. In virtue of this their citizens—whether Phrygian or Lycaonian, Jewish or Greek, by birth—were all *Galatians*. Similarly, Trophimus who was of Ephesus was an *Asian*, and Aristarchus of Thessalonica a *Macedonian*[1]. The cities of Philippi, Thessalonica, and Beroea, were all in the province of Macedonia, and when S. Paul thinks of these churches together, he calls them *the churches of Macedonia* and their members *Macedonians*. Similarly, no doubt, when he wanted to speak of the churches of Antioch and Iconium, Lystra and Derbe, as one body, he would call them *the churches of Galatia*, and when he wrote to them in common he would address his readers as *Galatians*.

After about 300 years the old grouping of the provinces was given up. The emperors ceased to try and unite heterogeneous nationalities under the fictitious unity of a single province. Among others the province of Galatia was broken up. The name Galatia was confined to the northern part, Galatia proper; and its wider meaning was forgotten. When this had come about, it naturally made readers suppose that S. Paul's epistle was written to the Celts of North Galatia. It is only by the exacter study of modern times that the wider and Roman use of the term has been fully brought to light, and that has brought with it the illuminating inference that in the NT by *the churches of Galatia* are meant the churches of Antioch and the other towns of South Galatia.

According to the old view they were the churches of Ancyra, Tavium, and Pessinus; but this involves almost insuperable difficulties. (1) The Acts professes to contain a record of S. Paul's work. His work culminates in the foundation of the church in three great Roman provinces, viz. Macedonia, Achaia, Asia, and this foundation is narrated at length (in ch. xvi-xx). But from his epistles we learn that S. Paul also planted the church in a fourth province, viz. Galatia. He visited the Galatians at least twice; he wrote to them, and the letter we possess shews such an intimate acquaintance with them as could only be the result of close intercourse: in his eyes the churches of Galatia rank with those of Macedonia, Achaia and Asia. And yet, on the old theory, the Acts omits all mention of S. Paul's work in Galatia, and beyond a possible hint it contains no allusion to Galatia whatever. (2) From the other side, the silence of the epistles would be no less remarkable. S. Paul wrote letters to churches in Macedonia, Achaia and Asia, and these letters give a vivid picture of his personal relations with, and affection for, those churches. They correspond to the record in the Acts of his work at Philippi and Thessalonica, at Corinth and Ephesus. But in the Acts we find also two chapters devoted to an account of work at Antioch and Iconium, Lystra and Derbe. S. Paul founds churches there. His foundation cost no less labour, and he cannot have felt less interest in, or less affection for, their members, than in the case of the other churches. And yet, on the old theory, except in a letter to Timothy written at the end of his life, there is no reference to these churches in his writings. The churches are founded, and revisited; but we hear nothing more of them until he writes his

---

[1] xx 4, xix 29.

last letter. (3) In his travels as recorded in the Acts there are two points, we might say two only, when S. Paul could have visited North Galatia. They occur at these words: (*a*) xvi 6, *they passed through the Phrygian and Galatian region*, and (*b*) xix 1, *Paul having passed through the upper country came to Ephesus*. If these words describe visits to Galatia proper, then in the first case (*a*) on his way to the west S. Paul made an enormous détour to the north and east and did a work which in proportion to that in Macedonia, Achaia, and Asia, must have been a matter of some months; in the second case (*b*) on his return to Ephesus he chose a road which took him one or two hundred miles out of his way. S. Paul did achieve extraordinary results and covered in his journeys an enormous area of country, but it must have been hard to find time and strength for this extension of his labours.

On the other hand, if we accept the proposed identification all becomes clear. Chapters xiii and xiv then describe the foundation of the churches of Galatia. These churches also lay on the high road between the Syrian Antioch and the west; and on two occasions afterwards S. Paul would naturally pass through them, on his way to Troas (xvi 6) and to Ephesus (xix 1). The agreement between the Acts and Epistles becomes clear. In both alike, four great provinces, Galatia and Macedonia, Achaia and Asia, fill an almost equal part in S. Paul's work[1]. And if in intensity of feeling and vigour of expression the Epistle to the Galatians exceeds all the others, the reason is clear: in bitterness of spirit S. Paul is contemplating the defection of his first-begotten churches, which he loved with the love of a parent for his eldest son[2].

The acceptance of the theory will have another valuable result. We shall be able to refer to the Epistle to the Galatians for additional information to illustrate and interpret chapters xiii and xiv. In these chapters themselves we find such local accuracy and such graphic pictures (e.g. the scenes in the synagogue at Antioch and before the temple of Zeus at Lystra), that we are driven to conclude that they come from the report of one present—not so much from the apostles themselves, as from an on-looker. There is no reason why S. Luke himself might not have been such a witness. He does not always exclusively enumerate S. Paul's companions, and as a rule the subordinates in a journey would be hardly less numerous than the apostles. John Mark would have had less compunction in returning to Jerusalem if he had left behind another attendant with the apostles, and the expressions of verses 13–14 imply the presence of others. It is

---

[1] In the Acts Galatia xiii 13–xiv 23, Macedonia xvi 11–xvii 14, Achaia xvii 15–xviii 17, Asia xix 1–40.   [2] See Gal iv 19. This unhappy relation between S. Paul and the Galatians may account for a difficulty which remains, viz. why does not S. Luke use the word *Galatia*? He shrinks, as it were, from reminding his readers that these were the Galatians. Or, if he was a native of Antioch in Pisidia, perhaps he did not altogether acquiesce in the Roman grouping and willingly accept the ruder Lycaonians as fellow-countrymen. It would be a trait of provincial patriotism, like the civic patriotism which Prof. Ramsay finds in the description of Philippi as the *first* city. See Introd. ch. ii § 1.

L.

indeed tempting to picture S. Luke as one of the Gentiles who heard and received the word with joy in the synagogue at Antioch; but on this see the Introduction, ch. ii § 1. Failing S. Luke, however, there would be no lack of informants. Timothy was a native of Lystra, and S. Paul himself appeals to his recollection of the events at Antioch, Iconium and Lystra[1]. Besides Timothy there was Titus. After this journey he appears in close company with Paul and Barnabas, and S. Paul writes of him to the Galatians as if they knew him well[2]: we may readily imagine that he was a Galatian. The Bezan text in this chapter has many interesting variations which bear high marks of originality. We can almost follow S. Luke in the process of correcting and revising the original accounts given to him, or possibly his own contemporary notes.

§ 1 *Cyprus. Paul and Barjesus before Sergius Paulus*

4 After the service of verse 3,—at which, as S. Luke reminds us, Barnabas and Saul received their commission, if through the hand of man, yet none the less directly from *the Holy Ghost*,—the two apostles and their company go down to *Seleucia* the port of Antioch and *sail away to Cyprus*. There was a large Jewish population in Cyprus (p. 23), and as the country of Barnabas and other evangelists it was an obvious starting-point for the mission. The work in Cyprus however had no special interest from S. Luke's point of view, as it was confined to the synagogues. But it ended in a striking scene which he depicts as giving the keynote of the new advance. The true religion appears and confutes the false in the presence of the Roman world: Saul emerges as Paul, and as a second Peter binds a second Simon Magus (cp. viii 18–24).

4 So they, being sent forth by the Holy Ghost, went down
5 to Seleucia; and from thence they sailed to Cyprus. And when they were at Salamis, they proclaimed the word of God in the synagogues of the Jews: and they had also John as their attendant.
6 And when they had gone ³through the whole island unto Paphos, they found a certain ⁴sorcerer, a false prophet, a
7 Jew, whose name was ⁵Bar-Jesus; which was with the proconsul, Sergius Paulus, a man of understanding. The same called unto him Barnabas and Saul, and sought to
8 hear the word of God. But ⁵Elymas the sorcerer (for so is his name by interpretation) withstood them, seeking to turn

---

[1] II Tim iii 11.   [2] Gal ii 3. In the *Acts of Paul and Thecla* he is mentioned as having gone on to Iconium to prepare a lodging for the apostle. [3] Or *about*.   [4] Gk *magus*.   [5] The readings are various, e.g. *Bariesou* (א), *-iesous* (B), *-iesoun* (A). Bezan texts have *Bariesouan* or *-am*, *Bariesuban*: the Syriac *Barschumo*. For *Elymas* Bezan has *Etoimas*.

9 aside the proconsul from the faith¹. But Saul, who is also
  called Paul, filled with the Holy Ghost, fastened his eyes on
10 him, and said, O full of all guile and all villany, thou son of
  the devil, thou enemy of all righteousness, wilt thou not cease
11 to ²pervert ³the right ways of the Lord? And now, behold,
  the hand of the Lord is upon thee, and thou shalt be blind,
  not seeing the sun for a season. And immediately there fell
  on him a mist and a darkness; and he went about seeking
12 some to lead him by the hand. Then the proconsul, when he
  saw what was done, ⁴believed, being astonished at the teaching
  of the Lord.

5   The apostles *preached in the synagogues*, and from this we
incidentally learn another fact. They had an *attendant* with them,
John Mark. *Attendant* is a different word from *minister* or *servant*
(deacon). In the Gospels it is used for the servants of the priests
who were sent to arrest the Lord, and for the *chazzan* of the
synagogue who handed him the roll. This official acted as con-
stable and would correspond to our verger or sexton⁵. It is most
unlikely that the apostles required personal service; indeed S. Paul's
hands 'ministered to those who were with him⁶.' But we have
observed⁷ that it was not the custom of the apostles—neither of
Peter nor Paul—to baptize with their own hands. So baptism
might well be a service for the attendant. And we notice that
John is mentioned in connexion with the preaching in the synagogues, on which we might expect some baptisms to follow.

6   The apostles worked their way through the chief towns and
synagogues of the island until they reached *Paphos* at its western
extremity. Paphos was the capital, and it had an evil reputation
for its temple and worship of Aphrodite (Venus), the most popular
deity of the Cypriotes. Their mission must have caused some stir,
for at Paphos they attracted the notice of two typical personalities.
(1) The first was *a Jew, Barjesus,* known to the Greeks as *Elymas*⁸.

---
¹ Bezan adds *for he was listening to them very gladly.*   ² Or *turn aside.*   ³ Hosea
xiv 9.   ⁴ Bezan has *marvelled and believed God.*   ⁵ Jn vii 32, 45, xviii 3, Acts v 22:
Lk iv 20, Mt v 25. See Introd. ch. vi § 2.   ⁶ xx 34. But the OT prophets were
generally accompanied by ministers or attendants, such as Gehazi; see I K xix 3,
21, II K iv 12.   ⁷ See p. 33.   ⁸ As in the case of Barnabas, there is difficulty about the name. Here it is increased by the confusion in the reading of the
name. If *Jesus* was in the original text, we can imagine scribes gradually altering
the sacred name; but perhaps the original was a more exact transliteration of
Joshua. *Barjesus* itself is a patronymic, *son of Jesus*, and he would have had a
proper name of his own. (a) This may have been *Elymas* which is very like an
Arabic word in the Koran for (?) *wise* (whence the modern *ulema*), and the Greeks
may have translated it, rightly or wrongly, as *magus.* (b) *Elymas* may be meant
for the translation of the original Hebrew which is not given. But *Elymas* is not
a Greek word: and the Bezan *Etoimas,* which resembles the Greek word for *ready,*
may be the truer reading. If we were better acquainted with the Cyprian dialect,
the difficulty might not be insuperable.

Perhaps he heard the apostles in the synagogue, and at once detected a rival power. For he was one of that class of religious professors or impostors of whom Simon Magus is the typical representative[1]. S. Luke describes Barjesus as (a) *a magus* or '*wise man*,' i.e. versed in oriental lore, astrology etc.: and (b) *a false prophet*, i.e. he made some claims to divine inspiration. In this character we may trace the influence of his Jewish origin; and certainly the Jews contributed their full share of these false professors. There were Jewish exorcists at Ephesus; and another Jewish magus of Cyprus was in the suite of Felix[2]. Our magus Elymas was likewise *with* (2) *the proconsul Sergius Paulus*: and he is the second type. In the division of the provinces between Augustus and the senate Cyprus had fallen to the former, and was therefore governed by a *legate* or *propraetor*. Subsequently Augustus effected an exchange and Cyprus became one of the senatorial provinces which were ruled by *proconsuls*. This is the very word used by S. Luke, and his accuracy is further confirmed by the discovery in recent times[3] of an inscription dated *in the proconsulship of...Paulus*. Pliny mentions a Sergius Paulus who had a scientific turn of mind and was interested in natural history. The characteristic which S. Luke noted in this Paulus was also *insight* or *understanding*, but in human affairs. This would account for his patronage of Barjesus. Among the Roman aristocracy were many who, wearied with scepticism, were asking in all seriousness Pilate's question *What is truth?* Again, it was the fashion for a nobleman to have a philosopher attached to his household, like a domestic chaplain. And so it is not surprising that on coming to Cyprus Sergius Paulus should have been impressed by the supernatural claims of Elymas and have given him a place in his household or court, that is the body of friends, officials, and subordinates, who accompanied a governor to his province and formed his suite[4].

In the Greek world it was the custom for philosophers, rhetoricians, or religious propagandists, to travel about from city to city and give public orations. By this means they often secured permanent professorships. So when Sergius Paulus heard of Barnabas and Saul, he took them for similar professors, and having an interest in these matters[5] he *summoned* them to give a declamation before his court[6]. He was curious to learn their 'philosophy.' The apostles complied; and soon they began to arrest the serious attention of Paulus, who had never heard doctrine like this. *Elymas* saw at once the incompatibility of his own *word* and that of the apostles; and fearing lest his influence over

---

[1] See pp. 112-3.   [2] Josephus *Ant.* xx 7. 2.   [3] By General Cesnola. The most recent description of the stone is given by Mr Hogarth in his *Devia Cypria* p. 114.   [4] In Latin his *comitatus*, from *comites* (*companions*).   [5] Thus he was the opposite of Gallio, who cared for none of these matters—oriental faiths and practices.   [6] The scene would be similar (though on a smaller scale) to that described in detail in xxv 23-xxvi.

the proconsul should be undermined, began to dispute. No doubt he denied the statements of the apostles, and gave a very different version of the life of Jesus and the Messianic hopes of the Jews. The moment was critical. It was the first presentation of *the word of God* to the Roman world: and naturally it was not easy for Sergius Paulus to detect the vital distinction between the true prophets and the false[1]. Once and for all that distinction, and the separation of Christianity from all trafficking in spiritualism,
9 must be demonstrated. This was clear to *Saul*. He grasped the situation, and under a sudden inspiration *of the Spirit*[2], he stepped
10 forward. He *fixed his eyes* on Elymas with a piercing look, and laid bare his true character. His pretended wisdom was all *guile and villainy*: he was no son of a saviour (Jesus), but a *son of the devil*: instead of being a prophet of God, he was *an enemy of all righteousness*. His spiritualism was not subservient to the attainment of righteousness, nay, it was fatal to real morality. For in his attempt *to turn aside the proconsul* as he had others, he was really *turning aside* and making crooked *the ways of the Lord* which are *straight*. The work of the gospel was to make the crooked straight. This had been the mission and preaching of John the Baptist[3]; and in the straightforwardness, sincerity, and simplicity, of Christianity lay its chief appeal to 'men of understanding.' In this lay the significance of the apostle's quotation from Hosea: 'Who is wise and he shall understand these things? prudent and he shall know them? for *the ways of the LORD are right (straight)*, and the just shall walk in them.' Conscious and wilful perversion of, or resistance to, the truth was the sin of false prophets like Elymas and Simon Magus: the sin against the Holy Ghost is of this character[4]; and the only hope of remedy is in stern punishment which, when it has had time to work its work, in
11 due *season*[5] may bring to repentance. Accordingly Saul invokes upon him *the hand of the Lord*, which is mighty to destroy as well as to heal[6]. Blindness was an obvious 'sign' for punishment, as spiritual blindness is the natural result of wilful shutting of the eyes to the truth[7]. The effect of this judgement of Elymas was electrical. None dared give the wretched man a hand[8]. *The*
12 *proconsul* himself was filled with *amazement* and *believed*. He recognized in the act the presence of divine power, and that Saul was the true prophet: *he believed God*.

It is commonly supposed that when he *believed* Sergius Paulus

---

[1] It was hard enough for the Christians themselves. The false prophet resembled the true in all external signs: cp. II Cor xi 14–5, II Thess ii 9, I Jn iv 1–6, Rev xiii 14. [2] Like S. Peter in iv 8. [3] Lk i 76, iii 4. [4] Mt xii 31-2, Mk iii 28–30, Lk xii 10. [5] Cp. Lk iv 13. [6] Exod ix 3, I Sam v 6-7, Heb x 31, I Pet v 6; see p. 61. [7] Spiritual blindness was the punishment of the unbelieving Jews (xxviii 26-7). We cannot forget that Saul himself had been punished with physical blindness, which resulted in the opening of the eyes of his heart. [8] Another note of an eye-witness: the graphic imperfect in the Greek shews us Barjesus groping about in the court.

became a Christian. It seems incredible that at this date a Roman proconsul could have been converted[1]. Of course it was not impossible to the power of God, any more than the blinding of Elymas. But it would have made a great stir in the church and in the world, of which some echo must have reached us. For one thing it would have been almost impossible for Paulus to continue in his office, which involved official patronage of idolatrous worship. But there are no signs in the narrative of anything extraordinary having taken place. It was quite possible to believe, like Simon Magus[2], in the reality of the divine power, without being converted in heart. S. Luke does not add *and was baptized*, but only *being astonished at the teaching of the Lord*. In the Gospel this phrase is the regular description for the attitude of the multitudes towards the Lord, an attitude very different from discipleship. At the sight of the judgement on Elymas Paulus would rather have been filled with fear[3], and he would have thought it safer to leave these dangerous questions and prophetic rivalries alone. In any case he had no more dealings with the apostles, who leave Cyprus, instead of seizing the great opportunity which a real conversion of the governor would have given them.

The real importance of the incident, however, does not turn upon the question of an individual conversion. (1) It is the first appearance of Christianity before the Roman aristocracy and authorities; and so it is the first step in the new stage of the progress of the gospel, which will lead on to the appearance of Paul before the emperor himself. And when Christianity does appear before the Roman world it is with dramatic effect, with a striking conviction of false religion. (2) The effect upon the apostles themselves must have been no less. They also were no less *astonished*. The success of their first utterance of the word in the court of a proconsul must have vastly enlarged their hopes and widened their horizon. The deepest impression no doubt was made on the mind of Saul. He was a Roman citizen, a privilege he had not fully valued hitherto because of his Jewish pride. Still the picture of the mighty empire of Rome, one and universal, may have already impressed his imagination. And now that 'the teaching of the Lord' was breaking down his Jewish pride, and his kinsmen the Jews were rejecting 'the word of the Lord,' his thoughts and aspirations must have been turned more and more to his other fellow-citizens, the Romans and their Gentile subjects. He had a call to stand before Gentiles and kings; and the sight of the amazement of Sergius Paulus may have fired his imagination to rise to the idea of the conversion of the empire—even of Rome itself, the centre of the world,—to Christ. (3) This, indeed, is in the far future; but a change of environment in the history of the apostles dates from this time, and it is typified by a change of name—*Saul who is also*

---

[1] Agrippa's irony in xxvi 28 shews how impossible the idea seemed to the aristocracy ten or twelve years later. [2] viii 13. Cp. also Judith xiv 10 where Achior also *believed God* in this sense. [3] Like Felix, xxiv 25.

called Paul. Saul's Jewish name drops out of use, and its place is taken by his Gentile name, which by a coincidence was that of the governor himself[1]. In the court of Sergius Paulus, Paul had stood as a Roman citizen. Henceforth his work lies in the Roman world, he travels as a Roman and a citizen of the empire, and he bears a Roman name. (4) The scene also marks a change in Saul's relation to the church. Saul's sudden vigour brings him to the front; and in the missionary work which ensues his Roman citizenship and his power of speech[2] tend to make him the prominent member of the party. We began with *Barnabas and Saul*, now we read of *Paul and his company*, and so it will remain, except at Jerusalem[3]. This incident effected the transition without any friction or jealousy. For the blinding of Elymas demonstrated that S. Paul possessed the power of binding, and that the hand of the Lord was with him.

§ 2 GALATIA. *Journey to the Pisidian Antioch*

13 Now Paul and his company set sail from Paphos, and came to Perga in Pamphylia: and John departed from them
14 and returned to Jerusalem. But they, passing through from Perga, came [4]to Antioch of Pisidia; and they went into the synagogue on the sabbath day, and sat down.

S. Paul generally accepted a scene before the authorities as bringing his work in a city to an end: perhaps Sergius Paulus himself (like the magistrates at Philippi at a later date), awed by the judgement on Elymas, requested them to leave his jurisdiction. Accordingly the apostles crossed the sea to Perga in Asia Minor, but there an unfortunate division of counsels occurred. *John* Mark declined to go further *and returned* from Perga *to Jerusalem*. Our first impression would be that S. Mark shrank from an advance into a new country at such a distance from home. But Asia Minor was by no means a *terra incognita*, full of terrors, to the Jews. And John Mark had come prepared for missionary work. Further, if it had been a case of simple cowardice, it is not likely that S. Luke would have recorded it. The case would be otherwise, if it had been a matter of policy. Now it is significant that he returned to Jerusalem, and that here and in verse 5 he is still called by his Hebrew name of John, not as later Mark. S. Paul himself looked upon the return as an act of 'apostasy'—he would not 'go to the work,'—and that would account for his severity towards S. Mark in ch. xv, which otherwise would be

---

[1] If there is anything more than a coincidence between the two names, the connexion (if any) may help to explain the appearance of the apostles in Paulus' court. Those who suppose that Saul adopted the name in compliment to his first convert only shew their own (and not S. Paul's) want of taste.   [2] xiv 12: in dignity S. Barnabas, as the elder, still holds the first place.   [3] xv 12, 25.
[4] The best MSS have *to Antioch, the Pisidian* (*Antioch*): the received text reads *to Antioch of Pisidia* (=AV *in Pisidia*).

so inexplicable : it was not a personal matter, but one of principle. We conclude then that John Mark was unable to keep pace with the rapid expansion of S. Paul's views of work in the Gentile world.

Perga was an important city, the capital of *Pamphylia*; it was not however the apostles' aim, for they did not preach there but went on a hundred miles further, across the Taurus mountains, to *the Pisidian Antioch*. Nor does Antioch seem to have been their immediate aim According to S. Paul's definite statement to the Galatians, he only preached there by accident, in consequence of an attack of illness[1]. Antioch (as we shall see) offered many advantages for the preaching of the gospel : but there were in its neighbourhood many other towns, quite as favourable and more important, such as Apamea. Nor does there seem to have been any commercial route which would have naturally led them from Perga to Antioch—the mountains and the brigands formed a barrier to frequent intercourse. We are left then entirely to conjecture as to the plans of the apostles. (1) The old idea was that they found Perga deserted, its population having migrated up to the hills for the hot months. But, as Professor Ramsay has shewn, this nomadic habit was introduced by the Turks and would have been unknown to a Greek city. (2) Professor Ramsay's own theory is much more plausible. At Perga S. Paul had an attack of malarial fever which prostrated him. The remedy was to move at once to higher ground. Now a hundred miles inland stood the city of Antioch, which in itself, as a Roman colony, offered to S. Paul an attractive sphere of work. Thither accordingly the apostles went. It is surprising, indeed, to find a traveller prostrated with fever making a difficult journey of a hundred miles. But a really serious objection lies in S. Paul's own words : *Ye know that because of an infirmity of the flesh I preached unto you the first time.* The most natural interpretation of these words is that it was at Antioch that he was visited by this 'stake in his flesh' and so stopped in his journey. Certainly the infirmity was with him at Antioch, for it was a temptation to the Galatians to despise and reject the sufferer. (3) If S. Luke was a native of Antioch and in the company of the apostles, his knowledge of the country and civic patriotism would have sufficed to guide them thither. But both the premises being conjectural, this is not to be pressed. (4) For there is still left a very probable explanation. The manifestation of the hand of the Lord at Paphos and the impression made upon the proconsul gave (we may suppose) a new impetus to S. Paul's missionary aspirations. In particular it turned his eyes to the west. There they would have fallen first upon the important province of Asia, with its flourishing capital Ephesus, the seat of the proconsul and the greatest city in Asia Minor. At Ephesus there was an influential Jewish colony. Ephesus also was half-way to Rome; and yet, being on the coast, it had much more direct communication with Jerusalem itself than any of the inland towns.

---

[1] Gal iv 13–4.

So we conjecture that the apostles were now turning their steps towards Ephesus. Rome we know was S. Paul's aim long before the divine will enabled him to reach it, and it may have been the same with Ephesus[1]. This sudden expansion of their plans was too much for the conservative John Mark and he returned to Jerusalem. The apostles however persevered. The great road from the east to Ephesus ran through the interior of Asia Minor; and accordingly they sailed to Perga, and then crossed the Taurus to Antioch, where they would strike the great highway from Antioch in Syria. But as so often happened with S. Paul's plans, the divine will had ruled otherwise[2], and they were stopped.

Antioch was really a Phrygian city, situated in the south-eastern corner of Phrygia, which bordered on Pisidia. Hence its proper name was ANTIOCHIA AD PISIDIAM, *Antioch which borders on Pisidia*, though colloquially it may have been called simply *the Pisidian Antioch*[3], to distinguish it from other Antiochs, e.g. the Syrian. This district is separated from the rest of Phrygia by the lofty range of the Sultan Dagh (on a southern spur of which the city stood); it was therefore assigned to the province of Galatia, and called the Galatian Phrygia[4]. The Sultan Dagh had another effect. It lay right across the direct line of communication between east and west. To avoid it the great road from Ephesus made a détour to the north between Apamea, 60 miles west of Antioch, and Laodicea, 60 miles to its east. At Laodicea it branched into two: one road went straight on through Cappadocia to the northern Euphrates, the other turned south to Iconium and then ran south-east to the Cilician gates, by which it crossed the Taurus to Tarsus, and so on to Antioch in Syria. Now a short cut might be made by going south of the Sultan Dagh—from Apamea to Antioch and from Antioch on to Iconium. This route was at this epoch being opened up by the latinization of the district north of Mount Taurus—a process which was being actively pushed forward with a view to checking the brigands in the mountains. Of this work Antioch formed the centre. Augustus had made it a Roman colony (whence it also enjoyed the name of CAESAREA) and planted a number of veteran soldiers there. We must realize then that when S. Paul entered it, Antioch was (1) a Roman city, as much as, for instance, Philippi. Like Philippi it had a Latin constitution and Latin magistrates, its official language was Latin, and in the population there was a Latin, and that the dominating, element.

---

[1] Cp. xix 21 and xxviii 16. Ephesus certainly was his aim in his second journey, xvi 6. We should have expected them to go thither by sea. Possibly there was no ship at Perga, and, if it was late in the season, the north-westerly winds would be blowing: cp. xxvii 4-8.   [2] As in the instances quoted in the preceding note, and the Bezan text in xix 1.   [3] Prof. Ramsay is our chief authority in these matters. It is admitted that the name 'Pisidian Antioch' is not found outside of the Acts. But as suggested above it may be a local touch, the popular name. xiv 24 shews that our author knew that Antioch was not in Pisidia.   [4] This is inferred from the name in xvi 6 *the Phrygian and Galatian region*.

Many of the inscriptions found here are in Latin, and bear the names of soldiers and other Roman citizens. From them we also learn that the city was an object of much imperial attention. A Drusus (? the father of Tiberius) and Cn. Domitius Ahenobarbus, the father of Nero, both accepted the office of *duumvir*[1], and distinguished Romans were among the city's patrons[2]. (2) In appearance, however, the city would present the ordinary features of Hellenic civilization, with its agora and theatre, its temples and porticoes. Roman influence added an amphitheatre for gladiatorial shows and an aqueduct, and their ruins are still standing. (3) There was also a Jewish colony. Antioch like many other cities, including its namesake of Syria, had been founded about 300 B.C. by Seleucus Nicator the Macedonian king of Syria and named after his wife; and to attach Asia Minor to Syria, Antiochus the Great transplanted thither 2000 families of Jews. These were the origin of the Jewish element in Phrygia, which attained to great influence, as is evident from our narrative; cp. xiii 50, xiv 4–5[3]. If we remember in the last place (4) the Phrygian substratum, we shall see that Antioch was one of those cities which reflected the cosmopolitan character of the empire, and were the best seed-plots for the cosmopolitan or catholic religion of the gospel.

Paul however had not meant to preach here; but about the time of his arrival he was attacked by *an infirmity of the flesh*. It is tempting to suppose that this *stake in the flesh*, as he elsewhere calls it[4], was ophthalmia. S. Paul would then carry about a life-long memorial[5] of his conversion. This weakness would also account for his not recognizing the high-priest in the Sanhedrin; and give great point to his otherwise strange expression for the devotion of the Galatians—*if possible ye would have plucked out your eyes and given them to me*[6]. On the other hand ophthalmia is supposed to be inconsistent with the power of his look, his *fastening his eyes* upon people. This phrase is however an expression of S. Luke's, who does not confine it to S. Paul[7]; and a weakness of vision would rather intensify the eagerness of the look. Epilepsy and malarial fever have been suggested. But of this only are we certain, that the infirmity was something which made S. Paul contemptible to look upon,—*ye did not despise nor reject me*, he says to the Galatians,—and to such personal contempt S. Paul was by no means insensible[8]. His loss however was the Galatians' gain. Being unable to proceed, the apostles *on the sabbath day went into the synagogue and sat down*.

---

[1] This we learn from the inscriptions of their deputies, Sp. Pescennius and P. Anicius Maximus. Domitius died about A.D. 40. [2] e.g. Cn. Pompeius Collega, prefect of Galatia in Vespasian's time. [3] And also from inscriptions of the empire. For the inscriptions see J. R. S. Sterrett, *Epigraphical Journey in Asia Minor* vol. II, nos. 92-154. [4] II Cor xii 7. [5] Or *stigmata* (Gal vi 17). [6] xxiii 5: Gal iv 15. [7] S. Luke uses it 12 times altogether: elsewhere in the NT it occurs in one passage only (II Cor iii 7, 13). Out of the ten instances in the Acts, it is only used of S. Paul three times. [8] Cp. II Cor x 1, 10-11, I ii 1.

The Synagogue at Antioch

In so doing the apostles followed the custom of the Lord, and this scene is a companion picture to the memorable service in the synagogue at Nazareth described in the Gospel of S. Luke (iv 16-30). It also introduces us to a community of the Jews of the Dispersion (p. 22). The Romans recognized the Jews as a 'nation,' and allowed them great liberty. Accordingly in the Gentile cities we find them organized in separate communities with a jurisdiction and magistrates of their own. These magistrates were known as the *Rulers* or *Elders* (*presbyters*), and they were the ruling body in religious matters also: to the Jew there was no division between religious and secular, all his life was covered by 'the Law.' For the management of public worship, however, there was added to this body of rulers a special official—the *Archisynagogos* or *Ruler of the synagogue*[1]. His office was to preside over the public service, and in particular to arrange it, that was to provide for the reading, praying, and preaching. For there were no definite ministers attached to the synagogue, nor were these functions confined to a special class. Any Israelite of good standing, though preferably a priest, might pray, preach, or read; and the selection lay with the ruler of the synagogue. In the case of preaching ability was required, and only a priest could pronounce the blessing. The arrangements of the building were simple. At one end was the ark containing the books of the Law; a veil hung before it, and also lamps. At the same end were ranged, facing the people, the 'first seats' appropriated to the ruler and other dignities. In the centre was a raised platform, on which stood a lectern for reading and a seat for the preacher. The men and women were probably separated—how, exactly, we do not know. Among the congregation in the foreign cities would be found a large number of Gentiles—some circumcised proselytes, but the majority simply adherents of the 'God-fearing' class, or 'Greeks[2].' The service on the Sabbath day[3] consisted of three parts: (1) The recitation of the Shema—a kind of creed composed out of Deut vi 4-9, xi 13-21, Num xv 37-41,—Prayer, Eulogies or Benedictions, to which the people responded *Amen*, and, if a priest was present, the Blessing. (2) Then followed the reading of the Scriptures[4]: first of *the law*, i.e. the five Books of Moses, then of *the prophets*, which included the historical books. The Law was divided into lessons forming a three years' course. In Palestine seven persons took part in its reading, the attendant (*chazzan*) handed the roll, and a *methurgeman* interpreted the Hebrew into the current Aramaic. In the synagogues of the Dispersion, it is most likely that the Greek Bible (the Septuagint) was

---

[1] Mk v 35-8, Lk viii 49, xiii 14, Acts xviii 8. At Antioch (and Iconium according to the Bezan text) there seems to have been more than one *archisynagogos*; so also at Capernaum (Mk v 22). Perhaps the plural denotes the *archisynagogos* with the body of ruling *presbyters*. [2] vv. 16, 26: cp. vv. 43, 44; and p. 166.
[3] There were also services on Mondays and Thursdays. [4] vv. 15, 27, xv 21, Lk iv 17-20.

generally read instead of the Hebrew. (3) At the end came an exposition or *exhortation* by some competent person, which might be followed by discussion. The preacher sat and 'taught' the people, for that was the technical phrase. This, then, was 'the teaching in the synagogues' which formed so large a part in the Lord's ministry; and now we have a picture of what must have usually taken place when S. Paul entered a synagogue of the Dispersion[1].

15 And after the reading of the law and the prophets the rulers of the synagogue sent unto them, saying, Brethren, if ye have any word of [2]exhortation for the people, say on.

It would soon have become known in the Jewish quarter, where Barnabas and Paul had found a lodging, that the new comers were teachers or rabbis. Accordingly, whether there had been previous communication or no, *after the reading, the rulers sent* the attendant to invite them to teach or exhort the people. Of the two *Paul* was the most learned and eloquent (xiv 12), so he *rose* from his place and took his seat on the platform[3]. Then, having first *beckoned with his hand*[4], to call for their closest attention, he began.

S. Paul's Gospel to the Jews

We have heard the preaching of S. Peter at Jerusalem[5]; and now S. Luke is going to give a representation of S. Paul's teaching, or, as he liked to call it, 'his gospel[6]'; and here 'to the Jew first,' though even here 'to the Gentile also.' This sermon is obviously but a summary of the long address which the apostle actually delivered; in its present form, like the other sermons in the Acts, it bears the signs of compression, and in its final composition S. Luke's hand is evident. In its matter also it closely resembles the other sermons. And yet in these few verses there are unmistakable marks of the characteristic thought and phraseology of S. Paul, as will be pointed out below. Further, there is in particular such a constant agreement with the Epistle to the Galatians as can hardly be accidental. This will appear from the references given below.

The sermon falls into three parts: I (vv. 17-25) the introduction; II (26-37) the gospel; III (38-41) the practical appeal. I. Like S. Stephen S. Paul begins by giving a survey of the history of Israel. At the same time his originality and independence of mind is obvious. To S. Stephen the history gives the doctrine of the Messiah, contained in types: to S. Paul it is the actual preparation for the Messiah's

---

[1] The above is chiefly gathered from Edersheim *Life and Times of the Messiah* bk. II, ch. x (and Schürer's *History of the Jewish People*) which see for a full account of all that is known about the synagogue service at this time. [2] Gk *paraclēsis*: Bezan has *wisdom or paraclēsis*. [3] So, perhaps, we can reconcile our Lord's sitting and Paul's rising. [4] Cp. xxi 40, xix 33, xii 17. [5] To Jews ii 14-39, iii 12-26: to Gentiles (at Caesarea) x 34-43: to the church, xi 5-17. [6] To Jews xiii 16-41: to Gentiles xiv 15-17, xvii 22-31: to the church xx 18-35.

coming. With S. Stephen the great prototype is Moses the mediator: with S. Paul it is David the king. II. The gospel which S. Paul 'preached to the Galatians the first time¹' is the same as S. Peter's —a proclamation of the facts of the crucifixion and resurrection. The presentation of the facts is varied; thus mention of the burial is added. There is also an advance in the Christology. Jesus is *Saviour* (verse 23)² and *King*. But beyond this he is *the Son* of God. And sonship, —of Israel, of the Christ, of the believers,—is the thought which runs throughout. III. The moral is the same—the offer of forgiveness of sins. Only here again there is a new application in the form which has ever since been specially associated with S. Paul, viz. the doctrine of justification by faith. Lastly the apostle concludes with the warning of judgement.

16 And Paul stood up, and beckoning with the hand said,
17 Men of Israel, and ye that fear God, hearken. The God of this people Israel chose our fathers, and exalted the people when they sojourned in the land of Egypt, and with a high
18 arm led he them forth out of it. And for about the time of
19 forty years ³suffered he their manners in the wilderness. And when he had destroyed seven nations in the land of Canaan, he ⁴gave *them* their land for an inheritance, ⁵for about four
20 hundred and fifty years: and after these things he gave *them*
21 judges until Samuel the prophet. And afterward they asked for a king: and God gave unto them Saul the son of Kish, a man of the tribe of Benjamin, for the space of forty years.
22 And when he had removed him, he raised up David to be their king; to whom also he bare witness, and said, ⁶I have found David the son of Jesse, ⁷a man after my heart, who
23 shall do all my ⁸will. Of this man's seed hath God according
24 to promise ⁹brought unto Israel a Saviour, Jesus; when John had first preached ¹⁰before his ¹¹coming the baptism of re-
25 pentance to all the people of Israel. And as John was fulfilling his course, he said, ¹²What suppose ye that I am? I am not *he*. But behold, there cometh one after me, the shoes of whose feet I am not worthy to unloose.

---

¹ Gal iv 13, i 6–9.   ² This we have had before in S. Peter's preaching, especially in his second sermon.   ³ Gk *etropophorésen*: so ℵBD. But AC and other authorities have *etrophophorésen*, *bare them as a nursing father* (Deut i 31).
⁴ AV *divided their land to them by lot*.   ⁵ AV *and after that he gave unto them judges about the space of four hundred and fifty years, until Samuel the prophet*.
⁶ Ps lxxxix 20.   ⁷ I Sam xiii 14.   ⁸ Gk *wills*.   ⁹ AV reads *raised* (Judg iii 9, 15).   ¹⁰ Gk *before the face of*—a Hebraism.   ¹¹ Gk *entering in* (*eisodus*).   ¹² AV reads *Whom*.

26 Brethren, children of the stock of Abraham, and those among you that fear God, to ¹us is the word of this
27 salvation sent forth. For they that dwell in Jerusalem, and their rulers, because they knew ²him not, nor the voices of the prophets which are read every sabbath, fulfilled *them* by
28 condemning *him*. And though they found no cause of death *in him*, yet asked they of Pilate that he should be slain.
29 And when they had ³fulfilled all things that were written of him, they took him down from the tree, and laid him in a
30 tomb. But God raised him from the dead: and he was
31 seen for many days of them that came up with him from Galilee to Jerusalem, who are now his witnesses unto the
32 people. And we ⁴bring you good tidings of the promise
33 made unto the fathers, how that God hath fulfilled the same unto ⁵our children, in that he raised up Jesus; as also it is written in the ⁶second psalm, Thou art my Son, this day have
34 I begotten thee. And as concerning that he raised him up from the dead, now no more to return to corruption, he hath spoken on this wise, ⁷I will give you ⁸the holy and sure
35 *blessings* of David. Because he saith also in another *psalm*,
36 ⁹Thou wilt not give thy Holy One to see corruption. For David, after he had ¹⁰in his own generation served the counsel of God, fell on sleep, and was laid unto his fathers, and saw
37 corruption: but he whom God raised up saw no corruption.
38 Be it known unto you therefore, brethren, that through
39 this man is proclaimed unto you remission of sins¹¹: and ¹²by him every one that believeth is justified from all things, from
40 which ye could not be justified by the law of Moses. Beware

---

¹ AV reads *you*. ² Or *this* (*word*). Bezan readings here differ very much. D has *because they understood not the scriptures of the prophets*: and after *sabbath* Blass restores the text thus—*rejected him. And though they found no cause of death in him, they condemned him and delivered him to Pilate to be put to death: and they were accomplishing all things that were written of him, and they asked Pilate to crucify him...and when they had obtained their request they again asked to take him down from the tree, and they took him down* [*and laid him in a tomb.* ³ Or *accomplished*. ⁴ Gk *evangelize*. ⁵ AV reads *us their children*. ⁶ D and some fathers have *first*, according to a numbering of the Psalms of which there are traces in early authorities. Ps ii 7 (Heb i 5, v 5). Bezan completes the quotation *ask of me and I will give thee the Gentiles for thine inheritance and the ends of the earth for thy possession*. ⁷ Isai lv 3. ⁸ Gk *the holy* (*things*) *of David, the sure* (*things*). ⁹ Ps xvi 10 (Acts ii 27). ¹⁰ Marg *served his own generation by the counsel of God, fell on sleep* or *served his own generation, fell on sleep by the counsel of God*. ¹¹ Bezan adds *and repentance*. ¹² Gk *in*.

therefore, lest that come upon *you*, which is spoken in the prophets;

41 ¹Behold, ye despisers, and wonder, and perish;
For I work a work in your days,
A work which ye shall in no wise believe, if one declare it unto you².

16 S. Paul addresses both the Jews, under the covenant name of *Israel*³, and the *God-fearing* Gentiles, among whom were some of the leading ladies in the city (verse 50).

17 I. In his review of the history (*A*) S. Paul begins at the very beginning, the choice of Israel by God. In his eternal will and purpose *God chose Israel*, when as yet Israel was not, as he had chosen Paul, and as he had fore-ordained the Christ before the foundation of the world⁴. Then we pass to the fulfilment of this will in time. First (*B*) the creation of Israel. *In Egypt he exalted the people*, i.e. he raised them up out of nothingness to be a people, or more particularly, as Isaiah expresses it, to be his sons. So he also exalted David, one chosen out of the people, and after that his own Son⁵. Being in the house of bondage Israel had to be redeemed⁶, so *he brought them out* of it and saved them: cp. verse 23. (*C*) After

18 the deliverance of the Exodus the people needed education; so as a father God first taught his sons in their youth *in the wilderness for*

19 *forty years*; and then, when they came of age, *he gave them an inheritance* of their own, a gift which involved the dispersion or rejection of other *nations* who had never attained to sonship. S. Paul says, according to the reading of the best MSS, that in the wilderness God *suffered their manners*, i.e. as a father he put up with their childish wilfulness and waywardness. The change of only one letter however would give us (as is read in some MSS) *bare them as a nursing father*. This word is found in Deut i 31⁷, and is very tempting. But the first reading is to be preferred. S. Paul wants to emphasize the patience of God, and the divine patience is the burden both of Stephen's history and of Deuteronomy

20 itself⁸. In the next verse the weight of the MSS, this time unquestionable, has caused an alteration from the AV by which the *450 years*—evidently a round number—there assigned to the period of the Judges, are now given to the time (reckoned presumably from the promise to Abraham⁹) up to the Judges. This again falls in with S. Paul's argument, as the Epistle to the Galatians explains: he wishes incidentally to call attention to the long interval between

---

¹ Hab i 5. ² Bezan adds *and they* (or *he*) *became silent*. ³ Cp. the *Israel of God* in Gal vi 16. ⁴ Paul, ix 15, cp. xxii 14: the Christ, Lk xxiii 35, ix 35 (RV); cp. Acts iii 20 etc. The church is also chosen, Eph i 4: and cp. I Cor i 27–8. ⁵ For *exalt* in this sense see Exod vi 7, Gen xlviii 19: and also Isai i 2, Ps lxxxix 19, Acts ii 33. ⁶ For the idea of redemption see Gal i 4, iii 13, iv 5. ⁷ and also in II Macc vii 27. ⁸ The *Assumption of Moses* dwells on the patience of Moses: 'he suffered many things' (p. 99 note⁸). ⁹ when God *chose the fathers*.

the promise and 'the law which came after¹.' (*D*) In Canaan we have the preparation of Israel for the Messiah 'under guardians and stewards until the term appointed of the father²'—first *judges*, 21 then a *prophet*³, then a *king*. In the mention of *Saul, the son of Kish, a man of the tribe of Benjamin* the voice of Saul of Tarsus, himself a man of the tribe of Benjamin, is unmistakable. But the allusion serves to teach the doctrine that God can reject those 22 whom he has chosen, if they fail to respond. And so *when he had removed* Saul⁴, *he raised up* in his place *David the son of Jesse*;—to specify his tribe was unnecessary, for he had the inward spirit of response, he was *a man after God's own heart*. (*E*) In David we have the climax of the tuition of the people, and he was the best 'tutor' to bring them to the Messiah⁵. For (1) he was *raised up* by God himself, as was Moses⁶. (2) He was raised up *to be king*; and though David was also a prophet⁷, the office of king surpasses all other offices. (3) God himself *bore him witness*⁸, as he did to his own son Jesus when he said 'This is my beloved son in whom I am well pleased'; and the witness was that what David did was in 23 fulfilment of the divine *will*. (4) The *promise* given long ago to Abraham was renewed to David, and confined to *his seed*. It now ran thus: 'I will set up thy seed after thee, which shall proceed out of thy bowels, and I will establish his kingdom⁹.' It is the fulfilment of this promise which S. Paul has come to announce, and he 24 passes to it. But (*F*) the OT preparation is not even now complete. There is needed the immediate preparation—the forerunner to announce the arrival, and (as it were) to open the door for *the entrance*¹⁰, of the Messiah. This was *John* the Baptist, the greatest of the prophets; and also the last, for 'the law and the prophets were until John.' His special work was to *preach repentance*, and 25 to bear personal witness to the Christ. And in so doing *he was fulfilling*, not only his own *course* or office, but the whole history of the OT. 'The fulness of the time had come¹¹.'

In this summary of the history of Israel, brief as it is, we can unmistakably recognize the mind of S. Paul. (1) He passes over in silence the giving of the law, which was to the Jews the greatest epoch

---

¹ Gal iii 17. There S. Paul gives 430 years from the promise to the law, which only leaves 20 years for the wanderings in the wilderness. ² Gal iv 2.
³ S. Peter had also recognized Samuel as introducing the prophetic era (iii 24).
⁴ The reverse happened to Saul of Tarsus: God called him to himself. The *forty years* of Saul's reign are not given in the OT; it is a part of current lore, found in Josephus. ⁵ Gal iii 24. ⁶ iii 22, vii 37: the Messiah was also *raised up*, see below. ⁷ ii 30. ⁸ The witness is taken from Ps lxxxix 20, I Sam xiii 14 and Isai xliv 28 (LXX). The last clause reminds us of 'Paul an apostle *through the will of God*' (Gal i 1). ⁹ II Sam vii 12–6; cp. Ps lxxxix 29, 36, Acts ii 30. The *seed* is also prominent in Galatians. There (iii 16) Abraham's seed is the Christ. ¹⁰ The entrance (*eisodus*) is the opposite of the *exodus* (verse 17). S. Paul uses the word of himself in I Th i 9, ii 1. ¹¹ Gal iv 4; cp. Acts xiv 26, xix 21 (*fulfil*). S. Paul was fond of the metaphor of the race-course for the work of the ministry or of life: *I have finished the course* (II Tim iv 7: cp. Gal v 7, ii 2 *running*).

in their history. Nor does he use the word 'covenant'—concerning which the Jews had fallen into such error, supposing that God was himself inextricably bound to them by it. Instead of these he speaks of the *promise* in verses 23 and 32; and the distinction between the law and the promise is one of the ground arguments in Galatians[1]. (2) The unbelief of the Jews was the problem which vexed the early Christians and not least S. Paul himself[2]. Here he shews the freedom of God to *reject* those who do not obey in the instance of Saul, mentioned here alone in the NT. That the same principle applies to the Gentiles as well as to the Jews is shewn by the destruction of the seven nations of Canaan. In Galatians the antithesis between choice and rejection is illustrated by the two sons of Hagar and Sarah[3]. (3) The history of Israel is represented as the growth and education of a *son*: first brought out of Egypt[4]; then exhibiting the waywardness of youth in the wilderness; entering at last upon his inheritance, but still kept in a state of pupilage under guardians and stewards. So he speaks of the Jews as the *sons of the stock of Abraham*, while the Christians are the true *children of the fathers* (verses 26 and 33): the Messiah also is *the Son of God*, as S. Paul had preached at Damascus[5]. This exactly corresponds with the doctrine of Galatians, where the Israelites are the children of God, and to redeem them God has sent forth his Son, and the result is that we have received the adoption of sons[6]. (4) In this education—although the word does not occur till verse 43[7]—the work of God was entirely one of *grace*. He chose, he endured as a father, he gave judges, he gave Saul, he raised up David and he brought a saviour Jesus. So again he raised Jesus from the dead, and fulfilled his own promise[8]. Similarly in Galatians 'God sent forth his Son,' and 'sent forth the Spirit of his Son'; and the Son 'gave himself for our sins.' (5) Instead of Moses, *David* is the great type of the Christ. Elsewhere S. Paul describes the Lord as 'born of the seed of David[9].' In part this was to dissociate the mind of the Jew from the inalienable privileges which he believed to belong to the literal seed of Abraham and from the supreme importance which he attached to the law which was given through Moses[10]. But the chief reason is that David was *king*. S. Paul had realized that the

---

[1] Gal iii 15–29. A comparison of verse 27 (*the prophets*) here and xv 21 (*Moses*) may indicate the different points of view. [2] See Rom ix–xi and below on ch. xxviii. [3] Gal iv 22–v 1. Below (verses 27–8) the same lesson is suggested by the names of *Jerusalem* and *Pilate*. [4] *Out of Egypt did I call my son* (Mt ii 15). [5] ix 20. Stephen had spoken of *the Son of Man*, and Philip had taught of *the Son of God* (in the AV and Bezan texts of viii 37): otherwise in the Acts S. Paul alone calls Christ *the Son*. [6] The word *son* occurs 13 times and *child* 4 times in Galatians. The actual expression *sons of Abraham* in iii 6. Cp. i 16, ii 20, iv 4, 6: iii 23–iv 7, iv 21–v 1. [7] and again in xiv 3, 26. [8] Cp. the repeated *will give* (34, 35) and *gave* (20, 21). [9] Rom i 3: cp. also II Tim ii 8, Jn vii 42, Lk i 27, 32, 69, ii 4, 11. For *Abraham's seed* see Rom ix 7–9, iv 13–22, Jn viii 33, Lk iii 8. On the *seed* of Abraham S. Paul builds an important argument in Gal iii 16. [10] In Gal iii 19 S. Paul speaks of the *mediator* without mentioning the name of Moses.

inheritance (verse 19) was to be a kingdom[1]. Of course this idea was not peculiar to him: the Lord had spoken of 'the kingdom' and called himself a king[2]. But it was S. Paul who fastened on the idea, and that no doubt because of the deep impression made upon him by the great Roman kingdom or empire. He saw in Christ the true king or emperor. And so in fact the words 'king' and 'kingdom' are associated in the Acts with the work of S. Paul[3], or rather (we may say) with work among the Gentiles,—Philip had preached the kingdom at Samaria[4], Paul and Barnabas founded the kingdom in Galatia, Paul proclaimed the kingdom at Rome.

It is also interesting to note how the teaching of the OT history is summed up in the names S. Paul quotes. It is the preparation of Israel, God's chosen people. The stages in the divine education are represented by Abraham their father, Moses the lawgiver, Samuel the prophet, David the king, John the preacher (or herald): and all lead up to JESUS the Saviour. On the other hand the names of Canaan and Saul, of Jerusalem and Pilate, declare the possibility of rejection.

26   II. S. Paul has now come to the gospel or *good tidings* (verse 32). He betrays his emotion[5] by addressing the Jews as his *Brothers* and kinsmen, *sons of the stock of Abraham*. But he does not forget the Gentiles (the *God-fearing*), and identifying himself with both exclaims *To us is the word* (i.e. the message and revelation) *of this salvation sent forth*[6]. It was the same message with which S. Peter had opened the gospel to Cornelius[7], only in S. Paul's mind salvation is the predominant idea: the gospel is *this salva-*
27 *tion*[8], Jesus *the Saviour* (verse 23). The message is brought to the Antiochenes, because (*for*) it had been rejected in Jerusalem. This brings the apostle to the most difficult part of his message, and the difficulty is reflected in the broken and uncertain character of the text[9]. For (1) in the forefront of the gospel, S. Paul, like S. Peter at Jerusalem, had 'to set forth Christ crucified[10]'; and this was 'to the Jews a scandal and to the Gentiles foolishness[11].' (2) That *the dwellers in Jerusalem*, God's own city, *and their rulers*, the guardians and interpreters of the law, should have crucified the Messiah seemed a monstrous assertion. Such madness would have been far worse than the disobedience of Saul (verse 22): and their action created a presumption against the truth of the preacher's good tidings. In answer, and to excuse

---

[1] So in Gal v 21 the *inheritance* is *the kingdom of God*. For the *inheritance* cp. also Gal iii 29 (*according to promise*), iv 1-7.   [2] Cp. especially Mt xxv 34.
[3] Cp. verse 21, xiv 22, xix 8, xx 25, xxviii 23, 31 all connected with S. Paul.
[4] viii 12.   [5] S. Paul's message is almost as moving as that of the Lord in the synagogue at Nazareth—*To-day is this scripture fulfilled in your ears* (Lk iv 21).
[6] In Gal iv 4, 6 God *sent forth* his Son and the Spirit.   [7] x 36.   [8] Cp. v 20 *the words of this life*: cp. also xxviii 28.   [9] Thus to make verse 27 clear the RV supplies *them* and *him* which are not in the Greek: also in the Greek it is *the voices* which are *read*. The uncertainty may be owing to compression on S. Luke's part, and then the Bezan text will represent stages in the process.   [10] Gal iii 1.
[11] I Cor i 23, cp. Gal vi 12-4.

the people of Jerusalem, S. Paul uses the same arguments as S. Peter. (1) They had done it *in ignorance*: for 'had they known, they would not have crucified the Lord of glory[1].' (2) Their action had really *fulfilled the voices of the prophets*[2]. The crucifixion of the Christ was part of God's eternal counsel: more, it was the full
29 and final *accomplishment*[3] of the scriptures. When Jesus died upon the cross, the law came to an end too: for having fulfilled it, he 'redeemed us from the curse of the law[4].' (3) Though, by being hanged upon *the tree*, he had 'been made a curse,' it was 'for us[5]':
28 in himself he was innocent, entirely separate from sin, as the rulers themselves admitted; they had *found no cause of death in him*.
29 When they had taken him down, *they laid him in a tomb*. S. Peter had enlarged upon David's burial[6], but the burial of the Lord had not yet formed part of the apostles' witness. It was however an integral part of S. Paul's gospel, which was 'that Christ died for our sins according to the scriptures, and that he was buried, and that he hath been raised on the third day according to the scriptures[7].' The reason was the same for which Peter had cited David's burial. It proved the reality of the death and therefore of the resurrection from the dead. Had the end of the Christ been like that of Enoch or Elijah, or had he been taken up from the cross into heaven, there would have been no proof that he had really
31 died. But Christ had been buried, and (4) his resurrection was the last and glorious vindication of his crucifixion. This is the *good*
32 *tidings*[8] which takes away the offence of the cross and brings the preacher back to *the promise*.
30 The cardinal fact of the resurrection requires proof and ex-
31 planation. For proof S. Paul appealed in verse 31 to the witness of the apostles. S. Peter had spoken as one who had seen to Jews who had crucified; S. Paul is speaking to Jews who had not crucified, and not wishing to complicate matters by referring to his own vision of the Lord, he simply refers to the undoubted *witnesses* at Jerusalem. His part is now that of an *evangelist*,
32 and as such he has to interpret the fact. For this resurrection of Jesus was as great a surprise to the Jews as the crucifixion. Their Messianic hopes had never taken such a form as that.
33 And yet *God* had thus *completely fulfilled* these hopes, or *the promise made to the fathers*,—and the fulfilment was offered *to the* true spiritual *children* of God and the fathers, whether of the seed of Abraham or no[9],—*by the raising up of Jesus*. This raising up was

---

[1] I Cor ii 8, Acts iii 17. It was S. Paul's excuse for himself (I Tim i 13).
[2] Gal v 14 and vi 2 shew how the law is *fulfilled*, viz. by the exact opposite of the rulers' conduct—love.   [3] Jn xix 30 *It is accomplished*.   [4] Gal iii 13.
[5] Gal iii 13.   [6] ii 29: cp. the burial of the patriarchs, vii 16.   [7] I Cor xv 3–4.
[8] *Evangelize* occurs five times in Galatians, *evangel* (*gospel*) seven times.   [9] The reading of the text *our children* can hardly be right: the AV has *us their children* which is very like a correction, and would also exclude the Gentiles. Gal iv 28 and iii 7 help to explain it. S. Paul probably meant the 'children of the promise,' 'those of faith who are the real sons of Abraham.' Perhaps the original reading

in fact twofold[1]: (1) He was raised up, like Moses and David, in his incarnation and birth. (2) He was raised up from the dead. But what was *the promise* itself—that is, the true inheritance of which the old had been a figure (verse 19)? When we compare S. Peter's interpretation of 'the promise of the Father,' and S. Paul's teaching of the Galatians 'that we might receive the promise of the Spirit[2],' there can be little doubt that by the promise S. Paul also understood the gift of the Holy Spirit, who is 'the Spirit of Jesus.' Else the doctrine of the Holy Spirit, which is fundamental in S. Paul's gospel, would be lacking here. But, though the apostle does not develope this doctrine now, it will be found to have an intimate connexion with both the raisings-up of Jesus. (1) In his birth Jesus was raised up as the Son of God. This is declared in that great utterance of the Father, here quoted for the first time, *Thou art my SON, this day have I begotten thee.* This was the meaning of the Baptist's witness (verse 25): it had been the preaching of S. Paul (ix 20). But when Jesus was 'brought into the world' it was as 'firstborn,' to be 'the firstborn among many brethren[3].' He introduced into the world a new sonship, the sonship of God. That sonship is the fulfilment of Israel's destiny and our inheritance; and that sonship, as the Epistle to the Galatians teaches, is made over to us by the gift of the SPIRIT[4]. (2) Again this gift is only made possible by the resurrection. For if the gift is given through Jesus the Son of Man[5], if it is the gift of his own Spirit, it depends on his continued and eternal life. Accordingly, the apostle proceeds to prove from the scriptures that *having been raised from the dead* Jesus possesses an incorruptible life, and that death hath no more dominion over him. The promise to David, as recorded in Isaiah, ran 'I will make an everlasting covenant with you, even the sure mercies of David,' or, as the Greek Bible had it, *the holy things of David, the sure things.* And the security signified is explained by the words of the original promise in 2 Sam vii 16, 'Thy kingdom shall be made sure for ever,' that is, it was an eternal covenant[6]. And this interpretation is confirmed by another passage which asserts the incorruptibility of God's *Holy One.* This passage had already been used by S. Peter[7], and S. Paul follows him. *David* had done all God's will (verse 22) by *serving his own generation,* and then, *in accordance with the counsel of God, he fell asleep* and was buried

---

was simply *to the children,* which the copyists did not understand and tried to correct. The Greek word here, *child,* is different from that for *son.* Cp. S. Peter in ii 39. [1] The double sense of the word *raise up* is no difficulty. The ideas of course run into one another; and another Greek word is used in the same double sense in this sermon (RV *raise up, raise* in vv. 22, 30). For the former sense compare iii 22, 26: vii (18) 37. [2] i 4, ii 33: Gal iii 14. [3] Heb i 6; Rom viii 29 —cp. verse 17 *fellow-heirs with Christ.* [4] Gal iv 5–6: see the whole passage from iii 23. [5] ii 33. [6] Isai lv 3, cp. Ps lxxxix 4, 29, 36 *thy seed will I establish for ever.* The Greek word for *sure* is the same as for *faithful.* [7] ii 25–31.

and his body decayed away¹. The promise then could not apply to
37 David, but only to the Christ, who, by the same *counsel of God, saw no corruption* in the tomb, and being raised out of it dieth no more, but, sitting at God's right hand, *serves* all generations.
38   III.   That service S. Paul now makes *known* unto his hearers. With an affectionate yearning for his *brothers*, he makes his *proclamation*². It is (1) the offer of *forgiveness of sins through this man*, viz. through his death and 'faith in his blood.' The condition of repentance has already been intimated in the mention (in verse 24)
39 of John's baptism of repentance. But (2) something more is needed. Forgiveness relates to the past, but the present and future life remains. And as the Lord delayed his coming, and as selfishness and covetousness, murmuring and division, were making their appearance in the church, the need of walking in newness of life was being felt more and more. The divine gift which is the answer to this need is contained in S. Paul's offer of *justification*. In this matter the controversies of centuries have darkened counsel, and the meaning of the offer here will be best interpreted out of S. Paul's personal experience. His life had been one single and continued search after righteousness. Of this we have seen signs in his vision of *the Righteous One* and his denunciation of Barjesus as the *enemy of all righteousness*³. This righteousness involved two requirements: first, the blotting out of past unrighteousness, or the forgiveness of sins, which is the being accepted by God as righteous; secondly, the being made actually righteous, so as to walk in righteousness, and that with no fictitious but a real righteousness—no mere external compliance with a law could suffice, nothing less than a 'righteousness of God.' In his epistles S. Paul generally uses 'justification' in the former or 'forensic' sense of being acquitted and accounted innocent. But such acquittal is only in view of an actual righteousness hereafter to be attained. Thus the two aspects are really inseparable, and we find them both in this passage. S. Paul had been striving to realize the life of righteousness by a strict compliance with *the law of Moses*, but attainment by such means was *impossible*. Instead of attainment, his failure had only brought him under the condemnation or 'curse' of the law. Then he had found the secret, which he now reveals to his hearers. The sentence of condemnation had been done away and he had been justified by Christ: righteousness had been brought within his reach, and he was made just, in Christ. For the life of righteousness is a life *in Christ*, viz. a life lived in actual vital union with the life of the risen Lord: and this can be attained through faith, which is the spiritual effort of incorporation into the life of Christ. As such a spiritual energy, faith is possible to every man, and so the offer of righteousness is catholic: *in him every one that believeth is justified.* Here

---

¹ The balance of the sentence is in favour of the second marginal rendering, as is also ii 23. Cp. xx 27.   ² This word seems characteristic of S. Paul's manner: cp. xiii 5, xv 36, xvi 17, 21, xvii 3, 13, 23, xxvi 23.   ³ xxii 14: xiii 10.

then is at least the germ of the famous doctrine of Justification by Faith, of which the epistles to the Romans and the Galatians are the text-books. In the latter our text is thus paraphrased: *knowing that a man is not justified by the works of the law, save through faith in Jesus Christ, even we believed on Christ Jesus, that we might be justified by faith in Christ and not by works of the law.* And this is the interpretation of the *in him* here: *that life which I now live in the flesh I live in faith, the faith which is in the Son of God*[1].

40 The offer made, there was left to his hearers the choice between acceptance and rejection. Rejection was possible on the part of both Jew and Gentile[2]. So S. Paul ends with a note of warning, which implies the doctrine of judgement to come. He speaks with care, using the very words of scripture. Habakkuk had warned the Jews
41 of his day of *a work* of judgement which God was preparing for them, viz. the Babylonian invasion. But they would not *believe*, they despised the warning and consequently were utterly destroyed. S. Paul likewise knew that a day of the Lord was being prepared for the unbelieving Jews. Three years later he writes to the Thessalonians that 'the wrath of God is come upon them to the uttermost[3].' And it came in the utter destruction of Jerusalem. But the truth of judgement is universal and the warning applied to his Gentile hearers also, as in fact in the Hebrew original instead of *despisers* stands *ye among the nations*. With these words S. Paul stopped. According to the dramatic addition in the Bezan text *he became silent*. And so ended the greatest sermon that was ever preached in the synagogue of Antioch.

The turning to the Gentiles

The effect of the sermon was proportionate. It led to the crisis of 'the work.' The Jews rejected the offer: the Gentiles accepted it. Accordingly God rejects the Jews, and the apostles turn to the Gentiles. And in this crisis at Antioch were fulfilled at last so many prophecies of the OT[4], so many parables of the Gospel[5], and the direct command of the Lord[6]. This was the first and typical 'turning'; but it was to be followed by similar incidents, attended with more bitter feeling, at Corinth and Ephesus[7].

42 [8]And as they went out, they besought that these words
43 might be spoken to them [9]the next sabbath. Now when the

---

[1] Gal ii 16: ii 20. The epistle is full of similar passages. The doctrine is the same as here: we are forgiven *through Christ*; justified *in Christ*, i.e. by union with him, which starts from faith and is consummated in sacraments (e.g. baptism, Gal iii 27). In S. Peter's teaching we find the same two elements (x 43 and xv 10–1).   [2] Cp. vv. 19, 27, 28.   [3] I Th ii 16.   [4] e.g. Isai xlii 6, xlv 22, xlix 6: lxv 1–2.   [5] e.g. of the two sons, and the wicked husbandmen (Mt xxi 28–43).   [6] Mt xxviii 19, Mk xvi 15, Acts i 2, 8.   [7] xviii 6, xix 9.
[8] AV reads *And when the Jews were gone out of the synagogue, the Gentiles besought* [or *As they were going out of the synagogue of the Jews, the Gentiles besought*].
[9] AV margin *in the week between*.

synagogue broke up, many of the Jews and of the devout proselytes followed Paul and Barnabas¹: who, speaking to them, urged them to continue in the grace of God².

44 And the next sabbath almost the whole city was gathered
45 together ³to hear the word of ⁴God. But when the Jews saw the multitudes, they were filled with jealousy, and contradicted the things which were spoken by Paul, ⁵and blasphemed.
46 And Paul and Barnabas spake out boldly, and said, It was necessary that the word of God should first be spoken to you. Seeing ye thrust it from you, and judge yourselves unworthy
47 of eternal life, lo, we turn to the Gentiles. For so hath the Lord commanded us, *saying*,

> I have set thee for a light of the Gentiles,
> That thou shouldest be for salvation unto the uttermost part of the earth.

48 And as the Gentiles heard this, they were glad, and ⁶glorified the word of ⁴God: and as many as were ordained to eternal life believed.
49 And the word of the Lord was spread abroad throughout
50 all the region. But the Jews urged on the devout women of honourable estate, and the ⁷chief men of the city, and stirred up ⁸a persecution against Paul and Barnabas, and cast them
51 out of their borders. But they shook off the dust of their
52 feet against them, and came unto Iconium. And the disciples were filled with joy and with the Holy Ghost.

42 After the sermon the preacher might be questioned and a discussion follow. But it is evident from the RV text, which is quite certain, that the apostles did not stay for this. Paul, we remember, was suffering from an infirmity, the sermon must have been a great effort, and *they went out* of the synagogue at once. A favourable impression however had been made on the Jews, who *requested* them to preach on *the same subject the next sabbath*⁹.
43 Then, *when the congregation dispersed, many* of them, both *Jews* and *proselytes* of the *devout* or 'God-fearing' class, made their way

---

¹ Bezan adds *asking to be baptized*. ² Bezan adds *And it came to pass that the word of God was spread through the whole city*. ³ Bezan has *to hear*] Paul. *And when he had preached for a long time about the Lord and* [*the Jews*. ⁴ Or with some MSS *the Lord*, and so in verse 48. ⁵ AV and Bezan *contradicting and blaspheming*. ⁶ Bezan *received*. ⁷ Gk *first*. ⁸ Bezan adds *great affliction and* [*persecution*. ⁹ The Greek may be translated *in the intervening week*, which would mean at the Monday and Thursday services.

to the apostles' lodgings and asked for further instruction. This the apostles gave, and they *were persuading them*[1] *to continue in the grace of God*. *Grace* is S. Paul's favourite word for describing the special gift of God to us in our redemption and justification. We have already had it in the sense of *favour*, whether human or divine; but here it occurs for the first time[2] in the special Pauline sense, corresponding to his words in verses 38-9. The idea of expectation is also contained in the word for *continue*[3]. S. Paul asks them to correspond to the measure of faith they have already received—viz. to hold it fast and fulfil all its requirements, e.g. in being baptized (as is suggested by the Bezan text), and to expect further divine favour in answer to their stedfastness.

44   The apostles no doubt freely spoke at home to the 'devout' Greeks as well as to the Jews; their report soon *spread all over the city*, and *next sabbath* the synagogue was packed. *The whole city almost* was there, and the congregation must have contained numbers of Gentiles who had no association with Judaism at all —Latins and Greeks and Phrygians. They had come *to hear the word of God* or (as the Bezan text with striking fidelity to human nature expresses it) *to hear Paul*. It was the new preacher which attracted them. As before, *Paul* was the speaker, and he spoke *at great length about the Lord*: he preached
45   Christ unto them, and with evident effect[4]. At the sight of this eager crowd the Jews, however favourably disposed before, were now filled *with jealousy*[5]; and (like Elymas) *they began to contradict Paul*. Debate was thus started, and the Jews even *blasphemed* or cursed Christ; no doubt they contended that 'everyone that hangeth on a tree is accursed[6].' In the presence of the Gentile congregation, as of the proconsul at Paphos, the situation was
46   critical. The gospel was at stake. And the apostles saw that the moment had come when they must choose between Jews or Gentiles. Accordingly they summoned up all their courage and spoke out the *plain* truth. Paul was the spokesman, but Barnabas fully concurred. The apostles had preached to the Jews first, because of the order of God's election—'to the Jew first, and also to the Greek.' But the Jews by their own action *were thrusting away*[7] the offer of *eternal life*[8]; they were, the speaker adds with some irony, passing judgement on themselves[9]. The apostles therefore now *turn to the*

---

[1] S. Paul possessed great powers of *persuasion*: cp. xviii 4, xix 8, 26, xxvi 28, xxviii 23. It was made a matter of reproach against him, and that in Galatia as well as elsewhere (Gal i 10, II Cor v 11).   [2] Cp. xiv 3: also xx 24, 32. S. Peter also uses it in xv 11; and his first epistle is marked by the word.   [3] As in xi 23.   [4] Gal iii 1, and below.   [5] Cp. v 17.   [6] Gal iii 13. For the *blasphemy* see vi 11, xxvi 11; cp. I Cor xii 3.   [7] The same word as in Rom xi 1, 2: God did not *cast off* his people, they cast themselves off.   [8] The thought of *eternal life* was familiar to the Jews: see Mt xix 16 and parallels. But its use is specially characteristic of S. John. It corresponds to *salvation* in verse 47: cp. verse 26 and v 20.   [9] The metaphor of *judging* accords with the forensic idea contained in *justifying* (verse 39).

Gentiles. Henceforth in Antioch they would cease to attend the synagogue and would address themselves to the Gentile population
47 directly. For this apostasy—for so the Jews would regard it— they had *a command of the Lord*[1]. For in Isaiah God had declared that his servant was to restore not only the tribes of Israel, but the Gentiles also: he was to be the *light* and the *salvation* of the whole world[2]. Evidently the apostles regarded themselves as one with the servant: his mission is continued in theirs. These words
48 must have roused the Jews to fury, but the Gentiles *heard* them with *joy*, and their feelings found vent in utterances[3]. The synagogue became a scene of excitement, which must have been something like the original speaking with tongues. Afterwards those whose wills as well as emotions were touched, *believed* and were baptized, and so became *disciples* (verse 52). Thus the ways of the divine wisdom were justified.

Those who believed are described by S. Luke as those who *were ordained to eternal life*. These words have been wrested to teach the doctrine of predestination in a rigorous sense which they do not necessarily bear. In the first place S. Luke is thinking, not so much of individuals, as of classes—Jews and Gentiles; and again among the latter, those who believed and those who did not. Secondly, his phrase contains a double idea according as it is looked at from the divine or human side. (1) The Greek word translated *ordain* means properly 'to set in order'; and its primary use was for ordering or marshalling troops in line of battle, and so stationing them at a post. So the centurion of Lk vii 8 was *one marshalled under authority*; *the powers that be are stationed at their post by God* (Rom xiii 1). Now, as the Jews at Corinth 'set themselves in array[4]' against the apostles, so from the human point of view these Galatians *had marshalled themselves* on the side of, or rather with a view to capture, *eternal life*. (2) But it is the general who marshals the troops, and in this case the general is God. As he had chosen Israel, and fore-ordained Paul and the Twelve for the apostolate, so he had marshalled these Galatians in order to attain eternal life, and to that end had guided the course of history. Thus we are brought back to the ultimate ground of the divine will (Introd. ch. v § 3). It was the will of God that the Galatians should be saved. But this will, with all the guiding of circumstances and the prevenient grace given, did not take away the power of man to reject, as is shewn by the disobedient Jews who had also received the call to eternal life. Even with regard to these same Galatians Paul himself is perplexed a few years later. They had deserted from him and were ranged on the

---

[1] Cp. i 2.   [2] Cp. the Nunc Dimittis: *thy salvation—a light to lighten the Gentiles.* Also Jn iv 42 *Saviour of the world*, viii 12 *Light of the world*: and for the idea of preaching to the Gentiles, vii 35.   [3] Cp. the *magnifying God* in x 46, ii 11.   [4] xviii 6.

other side[1]. They were falling back in their course: 'Ye were running well, who did hinder you[2]?'

At present however they 'were running well.' From S. Paul's own words to them we learn that they received the gospel with extraordinary enthusiasm, that they lived in a state of 'bliss.' Their personal gratitude and devotion to S. Paul knew no bounds; they received him as an angel of God, even as Christ Jesus himself; they did not despise his pitiable infirmity; they would have dug out 49 their own eyes if they could have given them to him[3]. And so the turning to the Gentiles was followed by a period of successful work, in which a real church of the Gentiles was founded at Antioch; and S. Luke marks it, as an epoch, by one of those sentences with which from time to time he describes the church's growth. *The word spread throughout the whole region also*, i.e. the whole country district which was dependent upon Antioch, or that part of Phrygia which was in the province of Galatia, *the Phrygian and Galatian region* of xvi 6.

50 The rapid growth of this new society, and the loss of so many of their adherents, must have increased the jealousy of *the Jews*, who shared the jealousy of the Sadducean priesthood at Jerusalem. At bottom there was no doubt 'zeal for God,' but it was one of those cases in which religious devotion coincided with selfish interests. It was selfish exclusiveness and the pride of privilege which prevented the Jews' accepting the Gentiles as their fellow heirs in the divine promises. This 'religious' zeal roused them to active opposition and *persecution of the apostles*. As a Jew, Paul was subject to the jurisdiction of the synagogue, whether he attended it or no; and so at Antioch he probably received one of his five beatings, or 'forty stripes save one[4],' at the hands of the Jews. But this was little to arrest the progress of the gospel. To do that they had to *stir up* the city authorities—*the First* (*men*) *of the city*, i.e. the Duumviri and the First Ten[5]. In this they succeeded through the influence of the numerous *ladies of the aristocracy*[6] who were attached to the synagogue. The apostles probably were formally accused of causing public disturbances, imprisoned, and after various sufferings[7] *banished from* 51 *the region or territory of the city*. As they crossed its *border*, in accordance with the Lord's command[8] *they shook off from their feet the very dust* of the inhospitable city, for a testimony *against them*, i.e. as an act of repudiation. We are reminded how once Stephen had been cast out of the gates of Jerusalem and Saul

---

[1] Gal i 6 *remove* has a technical military sense.   [2] Gal v 7: cp. iv 10, 20.
[3] Gal iv 4–5.   [4] II Cor xi 24.   [5] The First Ten were a board of magistrates in the Greek cities of the east. In Roman colonies in Italy the name had been given to the ten who ranked first on the roll of the senate. Cp. Marquardt *Röm. Staatsverwaltung* vol. I p. 213–4.   [6] The word *honourable* frequently occurs in the inscriptions found at Antioch.   [7] For the extent of the sufferings see II Tim iii 11 *persecutions, sufferings, what things befell me at Antioch, at Iconium, at Lystra—what persecutions I endured!*   [8] Mt x 14, Lk ix 5.

had raised up a persecution against the Nazarenes. As before[1], however, the effect of the persecution was the contrary to what the persecutors intended. In spite of the departure of the apostles, 52 who were apparently the main objects of the persecution, *the disciples continued to be filled with joy and the Holy Ghost*. Joy generally followed upon the first reception of the gospel: such we had in verse 48. But as S. Paul taught the Galatians, joy, the true and deepest joy, is the fruit of the Spirit[2]; and the mention of the Spirit here adds what was lacking in the sermon.

§ 3 *Work among the Gentiles and signs*

The critical event of the journey is now past, and S. Luke records the divine approval of the turning to the Gentiles and the divine confirmation of S. Paul's apostolate[3]. This was witnessed by—(1) The successful result: the building up of Gentile churches, compacted with the mortar of persecution and with S. Paul's teaching, of which we have two fragments—his appeal to the unconverted (verses 15–17), and his edification of the converted (verse 22). (2) Signs and wonders, which are a leading feature in this chapter. At Paphos in the judgement of Elymas we saw the 'authority' given to the apostle 'to cast down.' Now we see his authority 'to build up[4],' shewn in (i) *signs and wonders* at Iconium, (ii) a 'power' or miracle at Lystra, and sealed by (iii) a personal deliverance vouchsafed to himself.

(i) The *signs and wonders* denote those external phenomena which are manifestations of the spiritual life of the church—a life itself supernatural. Probably, as has been suggested above (pp. 15–6, 41), these signs in large part describe phenomena of the Christian life, which from their long continuance have ceased to be regarded as extraordinary or abnormal. Among such phenomena we may class the conversion of the wicked and reformation of character, the casting out of evil passions, the healing of the sick (when evidently due to faith and prayer), special personal illuminations and mercies, etc. At the beginning these phenomena formed a regular and unfailing mark of church life: and their freshness and abundance made a deeper impression than now. They contributed largely to the exuberant joy which marks the early stages of the gospel. The churches were full of 'gifts of healing, workings of powers, prophecy, tongues,' etc. These gifts indicated the presence of the Spirit: they were 'distributions of the Holy Ghost[5].' They were by no means confined to the apostles, but they were enjoyed by the apostles to an exceptional degree, insomuch that they became almost the credentials of an

---

[1] Cp. iv 31 following after 21, v 42 after 41, ix 31 after viii 1–3, xii 24 after 1–3. [2] For joy see viii 8, 39, after persecution v 41, through the Spirit Gal v 24. The three ideas are brought together in I Thess i 6 *in much affliction with joy of the Holy Ghost*. Cp. also Gal iii 3, the Galatians *began in the Spirit*. [3] xi 23: cp. xiv 27, xv 12. [4] II Cor xiii 10. [5] Heb ii 4. The classical passage on the 'gifts' is I Cor xii–xiv: see esp. xii 4–11.

apostle, the sign of the Spirit within[1]. Wherever S. Paul went he was accompanied by these 'signs of an apostle,' he moved in an atmosphere of spiritual activities—at Jerusalem and throughout Galatia, at Philippi and Thessalonica, at Corinth and Ephesus[2]. This abundance of spiritual gifts no doubt exercised a great and steady influence on the outside world : it was a *sign* of the presence of a divine power. But that it was a customary accompaniment of Christianity is shewn by the general effect. There was no sudden stir or excitement caused in the other cities as by the miracle at Lystra[3]. Rather, men expected this kind of power from religious professors and teachers, and there was no lack of effort to supply the demand on the part of the contemporary prophets, exorcists, diviners, and the like[4]. It was their reality and truth which distinguished the Christian signs.

(ii) In this manifestation of spiritual power there stand out prominently some unique *powers* which were in themselves extraordinary, and therefore signs of a special divine power—what we should now call 'miracles.' Such were the miracle at Lystra and the similar 'power' wrought by S. Peter at Jerusalem, the raising of Dorcas and the raising of Eutychus[5]. That they were extraordinary to the apostles' usual work is shewn by the interest of the narrator himself, who, like a scientific witness, reports the details 'lame from his mother's womb,' 'over 40 years old,' etc. In these miracles we are chiefly to consider their effect. (1) They attracted attention. Both in Jerusalem, where the people were entirely absorbed in the revelation already made to them in the Old Testament, and at Lystra, among a somewhat rude country folk who had had no grounding in the Jewish faith of the one God, but were dominated by the conceptions of primitive natural religion, it must have been hard for the word of the Lord to find entrance. The miracle then opened the door for the gospel. (2) At the same time it served as a sermon. It was a parable of the truth, and, as deeds teach better than words, it was the best exponent to an uneducated people of the meaning of a new religion brought by strangers. Some of these 'powers' were wrought within the area of the church, irrespective of their effect upon those without. In this case they must be regarded as the divine response to faith and prayer : but even here we must not forget their work in deepening the faith, and enlightening the understanding, of the faithful. If such unique miracles ceased to appear in the church, it is not hard to assign a reason. Later on the effect was produced in other ways. The spread of Christianity made faith as it were at home in the world; it restored it to its place as a natural faculty which did not need an abnormal

---

[1] II Cor xii 12 : Rom xv 18-9. For the Twelve cp. Acts ii 43, v 12 : then the power passes to the Seven, Stephen vi 8, Philip viii 6-7 (and to the evangelists of Antioch? xi 21) : then to 'the apostles' Paul and Barnabas xiv 3. [2] See Gal iii 5 : Acts xvi 18 : I Thess i 5 : I Cor ii 4, II xii 12 : Rom xv 18-9 : Acts xix 11-7 : xx 7-12 : xxviii 2-8. [3] At Philippi the stir was not because of the exorcism but the interference with gain. [4] Cp. II Thess ii 9. [5] xiv 8-10, iii 1-10—in relation to the world without : ix 36-42, xx 7-12—in relation to the church.

event to give it birth. The environment, i.e. the mind of the world, has also changed. An abnormal event to-day would not arouse real faith. It would either be denied, or, if believed, it would probably only minister to curiosity and superstition.

(iii) Personal deliverances are a sign of divine favour to the individual or rather to the church for whose profit the individual exists. They come in answer to earnest prayer and strong faith. Thus Peter and the Eleven were delivered from prison, and Peter again from an imminent death. S. Paul was raised from a certain death at Lystra, and freed from prison at Philippi; he was saved from shipwreck, and towards the end of his career 'delivered from the lion's mouth[1].' Such personal mercies are not peculiar to any age. All Christians, like S. Paul, have learnt to set their hope on 'God which raiseth the dead, who delivered us and we trust will also still deliver us[2].'

Work at Iconium and persecution

On leaving Antioch the apostles would take the new Roman road, —'the imperial road'—which connected the colonies of Antioch and Lystra. Thirty-five miles would bring them to Misthia; here if they took the branch road to the left, after 50 miles they would reach Iconium. *Iconium* was a Phrygian city on the border of Lycaonia, a dull flat country which lay between the range of Taurus and the desert of the Axylon. With Lycaonia Iconium was associated both geographically and politically. Thus it had once been the head of an independent tetrarchy of 14 Lycaonian towns. This like other territories had fallen into the hands of Amyntas the Galatian king, and at his death passed to the Romans. The inhabitants of Iconium however would pride themselves on their Phrygian blood, and S. Luke betrays his accuracy— not to say actual acquaintance with the town—by carefully distinguishing it from Lycaonia (verse 6). Compared with the colony of Antioch, Iconium was quite a native town. The names on its inscriptions are generally Phrygian, and their Greek is very bad. But its position on the great trade route between east and west gave it a great advantage. It had already a very ancient history, and it was soon to eclipse its more modern rival Antioch. About this very time the emperor Claudius had been taking some steps to consolidate or compliment the city, and its name was changed to CLAUDICONIUM. In the later empire, when the province of Galatia was divided, Iconium became the capital of Lycaonia and the seat of the proconsul. Still later the Seljuk Turks seized it and made it the capital of their empire. The church at Iconium had a corresponding history. Several Christian inscriptions have been found at Iconium, none at Antioch. A council of Iconium in the 3rd century has an important place in the history of the church. But the city was indebted for its reputation among the mass of church people chiefly to the virgin Thecla.

---

[1] v 19, xii 5–17: xiv 20, xvi 25–30: xxviii 1, II Tim iv 17.   [2] II Cor i 9–10.

The story of Thecla is contained in the *Acts of Paul and Thecla*[1] and runs as follows. Thecla belonged to one of the chief families in Iconium, and when S. Paul visited the city she overheard his preaching from a window. She was very soon inspired with a personal devotion to the apostle and with a determination to remain a virgin. Unfortunately she had been affianced to an aristocratic youth named Thamyris; and when she refused to marry him, Thamyris with her mother's help caused both Paul and Thecla to be brought before the magistrates. Paul was scourged and expelled from the city, Thecla condemned to be burnt in the theatre. A fall of rain saved her, and she followed after Paul to Antioch. On reaching Antioch she fell in with Alexander, the high-priest of Galatia, who had come to celebrate a festival and exhibit games in the amphitheatre. Alexander made advances to her in the public street, but Thecla made a vigorous resistance, and even tore the image of Caesar on his diadem. Such an offence was high treason, and the proconsul condemned her to be thrown to the wild beasts in the amphitheatre. But when the moment came, she excited the pity of a great lady, Tryphaena. Tryphaena had been queen of Pontus; she was also a connexion of the emperor Claudius; and so she was powerful enough to secure the deliverance of Thecla. Once more Thecla found out Paul; she also converted Tryphaena; and then retired to Seleucia on the coast of Cilicia. Here she lived as a virgin, preached the word, and died in a good old age. Her fame soon spread far and wide; bishops and fathers wrote sermons in her honour. She became the type of a virgin saint, and received the title of 'the first martyr' among women.

This story, according to Tertullian, was 'put together' by a presbyter of Asia 'out of love for S. Paul.' The presbyter was deposed from his office for his forgery, and the Acts of Paul and Thecla as they now stand are mainly a glorification of virginity. Thecla is the heroine and Paul, in spite of the presbyter's love, holds the second place. The story however was not pure invention on the presbyter's part. Tertullian says he 'compiled' it. And Professor Ramsay has pointed out a number of local and historical touches which could only occur in an almost contemporary writing. On this ground, and because of the universal tradition of the east, we must believe that there is some foundation of fact. Thecla then would be a real person, and we may believe that she became devoted to S. Paul, and that her devotion brought them both into conflict with the authorities; that interference with family life was one of the causes of the persecution at Iconium; that Thecla visited Antioch and was brought before the governor and in some way bore witness to the faith; that she owed her deliverance to queen Tryphaena; and that ultimately she settled and died at

---

[1] Mr F. C. Conybeare has published a translation of these Acts from the Armenian in his *Armenian Monuments of Early Christianity*. This form of the Acts is free from many extravagances and errors which occur in the Greek version and probably is closest to the original work of the presbyter. It is followed here.

Seleucia. But the chief interest for us in her story lies in the light it throws upon the period and scene of our Acts.

Thus we notice—(1) The extraordinary personal devotion which S. Paul inspired. This helps us to understand the speedy growth of churches in the cities he visited and the enthusiasm that his personal followers and fellow workers, such as Timothy, Titus, and Luke, felt for him. To these Acts we are indebted for a description of the apostle's personal appearance: he was *one of moderate height, scanty hair, bow-legged, with large eyes, meeting eyebrows and rather a long nose*[1]. But his power lay in his expression: he was *full of grace and pity; now he looked like a man, now he had the face of an angel.* (2) The picture of missionary work and life. Titus is sent on to prepare a lodging at Iconium, and describes Paul's appearance to his host Onesiphorus. Onesiphorus goes to meet him, and when S. Paul comes to the house, *there was great joy and bending of knees and breaking of bread and word of God about temperance and the resurrection.* Paul preached at great length *in the midst of the church in Onesiphorus' house,* and Thecla *saw many women going in.* '*All the women and young people go in to him,*' Thamyris declares, and he goes himself to watch *the men going in and coming out.* (3) In this mention of women we have almost the freedom of modern times. Similarly in the proconsul's court they loudly protest against Thecla's condemnation, and they openly exhibit their sympathy in the amphitheatre. The influence of Tryphaena is very great; Thecla herself preaches the word. Such liberty for women would hardly have been possible in a Syrian town or in Greece. But it entirely agrees with what we learn from inscriptions of the position of women at this time in Asia Minor, especially in this part; and also what we learn from the Acts of the part played by women in the furtherance of Christianity. (4) The story also explains the unpopularity of Christianity. Paul was accused, not of being a Christian, but of disturbing family life. Pagan life was so bound up with idolatrous customs that conversion to Christianity must have meant much social inconvenience, if not an entire break with the old society[2]. But more even than idolatry, the terribly low standard of morals which prevailed in the matter of purity, both in theory and practice, must have made the cleavage sharp and penetrating. The account in Thecla's Acts of Paul's preaching of virginity is no doubt exaggerated and almost heretical, although indeed in his teaching of the church the apostle did lay great stress on the spiritual advantage of the single life[3]. But the simple preaching of Christian truth on this matter was sufficient to cause conflict in a state of society where purity in the Christian sense was an unrecognized ideal. The gospel, then, incurred the hatred of the world because it interfered not only with Jewish privilege and Gentile gain but also with family life and social customs.

---

[1] From the Syriac and Armenian: the latter however has *curly hair* and *blue eyes.* The Greek has *small in stature, baldheaded,* and adds *well made.* [2] There was e.g. the difficulty about meat, in the market and 'dining out' (I Cor viii, x 25-30). [3] I Cor vii 25-40.

With the scene thus made familiar by the Acts of Paul and Thecla, and with the help of the Bezan text, which is here unusually good and reliable, we can reconstruct the course of events at Iconium. S. Luke's narrative is very condensed, and the gap in our text between verses 2 and 3 is evident.

14 And it came to pass in Iconium, that they entered together into the synagogue of the Jews, and so spake, that a great multitude both of Jews and of Greeks believed.
2 ¹But the Jews that were disobedient stirred up the souls of the Gentiles, and made them evil affected against the brethren.
3 Long time therefore they tarried *there* speaking boldly in the Lord, which bare witness unto the word of his grace,
4 granting signs and wonders to be done by their hands. But the multitude of the city was divided; and part held with
5 the Jews, and part with the apostles². And when there was made an onset both of the Gentiles and of the Jews with their rulers, to entreat them shamefully, and to stone them,
6 they became aware of it, and fled unto the cities of Lycaonia,
7 Lystra and Derbe, and the ³region round about: and there they ⁴preached the gospel.

1 At Iconium there was a colony of Jews with a synagogue. In spite of the separation at Antioch, the apostles according to their custom made a fresh start in a new city, and *in the same way went into the synagogue*⁵. Here they had better success, for *a great multitude of the Jews* as well as of the *Greeks* or God-fearing
2 Gentiles *believed*. The authorities of the Jews however, *the archisynagogos* (ruler-of-the-synagogue) *and the rulers* or presbyters, were not convinced⁶, and they excited *persecution against*

---

¹ Bezan has *But the archisynagogi and the rulers (of the synagogue) brought persecution upon them, against the just, and made the souls of the Gentiles evil affected against the brethren. But the Lord quickly gave peace.*   ² Bezan adds *cleaving to them because of the word of God.* A Bezan authority continues *And again the Jews with the Gentiles stirred up persecution a second time, and they stoned them and cast them out of the city, and they fled and came to Lycaonia to a certain city which is called* [Lystra.   ³ Bezan adds *whole*.   ⁴ Gk *were evangelizing*. Bezan adds *And the whole multitude was stirred at the teaching. But Paul and Barnabas tarried in Lystra.*   ⁵ The words for *together* are better translated *in the same way* (i.e. as at Antioch). Cp. Lk vi 23, 26, xvii 30. For S. Paul's custom see Acts xvii 2 (Lk iv 16, xxii 39).   ⁶ In the NT the classical word for *disobey* imperceptibly passes into the meaning of *disbelieve*. To disbelieve the Messiah was to disobey God. Cp. Rom x 22 (Isai lxv 2) *a disobedient and gainsaying people* and Lk i 17 *the disobedient in*(to) *the wisdom of the just*.

the just[1]. This they effected by poisoning the minds of *the Gentiles outside the synagogue*[2] against the Christians. The story of Thecla suggests a means, and perhaps the apostles were brought before the magistrates on some charge of interference with family life. The magistrates however must have seen at once that there was no legal case against them; and by a sentence of acquittal or in some other way *the Lord gave peace*. After persecution we have again a peace
3 which is a period of progress. If there had been a public vindication in the law-courts, it must have given Paul and Barnabas a great opportunity. *Therefore* they worked *for a long time* without hindrance. The persecution probably involved a separation from the synagogue, and the apostles taught the Gentiles openly, teaching the whole gospel without flinching (xiii 46). Their *boldness* or confidence rested *upon the Lord* Jesus, and he *testified* his approval of the gospel they taught, viz. of the offer of *his grace* to all, by working *signs and wonders through their hands*. This also placed
4 them on a level with the other apostles[3]. The apostolic preaching affected the whole *city* and created a schism. The citizens were *divided* into two parties, one *held with the Jews*, the other *clave to*
5 *the apostles*. Legal proceedings having failed, the only resource left for the Jews was illegal violence. *The Jews* then and their party in the city, *with* the complicity of *the magistrates*, plotted to bring about a public riot and attack on the apostles which might end
6 in their stoning. But at the first signs of violence, the suspicions of the apostles were aroused: they *made their escape*, and in accordance with the Lord's directions[4] left the city. They fled into
7 *Lycaonia*. This was mainly a country district, and the flight of the apostles thither was the commencement of an active evangelization which had great effect—*the whole population was stirred at the teaching*. As Barnabas and Paul could not speak Lycaonian or Phrygian, and the Bezan text says expressly that *they abode in Lystra*, we must suppose that the evangelization of the country was the work of disciples who accompanied them from Iconium, or even Antioch.

The miracle at Lystra and the gospel for the 'barbarians'

The sixth and seventh verses cover the whole period of work in Lycaonia up to its conclusion in verse 21. But S. Luke stops to

---

[1] The Bezan text may represent an original (1) *the archisynagogos and the rulers* (i.e. the presbyters), or (2) *the archisynagogoi* (*the rulers of the synagogue* being an interpretation). The term used for the Christian party—*the just*, like *the holy*, *the devout*, and the Hebrew *Chasidim*—would be a sign of the early character of the narrative. But it may mean *in the matter of legal proceedings*, or be a corruption for *before the magistrates* (Ramsay). [2] See p. 166 for the distinction here between *Greeks* and *Gentiles*. [3] See iv 29-30, ii 43, v 12: Paul and Barnabas are called *apostles* for the first time in verse 4. Mk xvi 20 shews that *the Lord is Christ*, and also what was the object of the signs: cp. Heb ii 4. [4] Mt x 23. In Stephen's case the *onset* (the same word is used) did end in a *stoning*. For the *shameful treatment* or personal violence see I Thess ii 2, II Cor xii 10, Lk xviii 32, (Acts xxvii 10, 21).

narrate a striking incident at Lystra, which helps to explain the great stirring up of the population and success of the work, and brings out the special power of S. Paul.

The apostles found an opening in the two cities of Lycaonia because of the Roman influence there and then at work. Together with Antioch *Lystra* had been made a Roman colony by Augustus[1]; and the new 'imperial road' connected the two cities together. But Lystra was a much smaller town; and being very much isolated in the barbarian country of Lycaonia, its Latin colonists must have looked to Antioch for sympathy and support. Hence this dedication, which has been discovered at Antioch, explains itself: *The most brilliant colony of the Lystrians honours with this statue of Concord her sister the most brilliant colony of the Antiochenes.* The site of Lystra was unknown till Professor Sterrett identified it in 1885 by means of its inscriptions: he deciphered fourteen in all, half of which were Latin and half Greek.

There was no synagogue at Lystra, and therefore only a few Jews. But among them was a pious Jewess Eunice who had married a Greek. He was apparently a man of some position and well known in south Galatia (xvi 3); but now he was dead, and Eunice lived with her mother Lois, her chief care being the education of her son Timothy. She had taught him the scriptures from his infancy, but he had never been circumcised. With this family S. Paul formed an intimate acquaintance; and we may conjecture that when they first visited Lystra the apostles found hospitality in their house[2]. As there was no synagogue S. Paul may have taught at home, or talked in the market-place with those who would, or lectured in some porch or school[3]. Probably at Lystra there was a nearer approach to modern out-of-door preaching than hitherto. But the apostles found the somewhat dull and slow country folk of Lycaonia hard to reach, until the Lord opened a door to them[4] by granting a 'power' to be wrought by S. Paul. S. Peter had wrought a similar miracle at Jerusalem (iii 1–10), and a corresponding result followed at Lystra. It also gives us an opportunity of hearing how S. Paul would begin to preach to the Gentiles.

8 And at Lystra there sat a certain man, impotent in his feet, a cripple from his mother's womb, who never had
9 walked[5]. The same heard Paul speaking: who, fastening his eyes upon him, and seeing that he had faith to be *made
10 whole, said with a loud voice, 'Stand upright on thy feet.
11 And he leaped up and walked. And when the multitudes

---

[1] It received the name of COLONIA JULIA FELIX GEMINA LUSTRA. Cp. Sterrett *Wolf Expedition* vol. I, no. 242. [2] Cp. xvi 1–3, II Tim i 5, iii 10, 15. [3] Cp. xvii 17, xix 9. There seem to have been public disputations with the Jews, see below p. 234 n.[1]. [4] Cp. verse 3, xvi 14, I Cor xvi 9 etc. [5] A Bezan text adds *being in the fear of God*. [6] Gk *saved*. [7] Bezan has *I say unto thee, in the name of the Lord Jesus Christ, [stand upright on thy feet] and walk. And immediately at once [he leaped up.*

saw what Paul had done, they lifted up their voice, saying in the speech of Lycaonia, The gods are come down to us in the
12 likeness of men. And they called Barnabas, ¹Jupiter; and
13 Paul, ²Mercury, because he was the chief speaker. And ³the priest of ¹Jupiter whose *temple* was before the city, brought oxen and garlands unto the gates, and would have done sacrifice with the multitudes.
14 But when the apostles, Barnabas and Paul, heard of it, they rent their garments, and sprang forth among the multi-
15 tude, crying out and saying, Sirs, why do ye these things? We also are men of like ⁴passions with you, and bring you good tidings, that ye should turn from these vain things unto the living God, who made the heaven and the earth and the sea,
16 and all that in them is: who in the generations gone by
17 suffered all the nations to walk in their own ways. And yet he left not himself without witness, in that he did good, and gave you from heaven rains and fruitful seasons, filling your
18 hearts with food and gladness. And with these sayings scarce restrained they the multitudes from doing sacrifice unto them⁵.

8 Among the beggars of Lystra was a poor cripple, *lame from birth*, who had his station for begging, perhaps at the entrance of some temple in the market-place⁶. And the scene which follows occurred on a market day, or more likely on the day of some great religious festival, for the city was full of *crowds* of people. According to one MS this cripple had heard of the God of the Jews, for he was *in the fear of God*, that is, one of the 'God-fearing.' This would enable him the more readily to understand and believe
9 S. Paul's doctrine. One day as S. Paul was *speaking* or talking with the people the cripple *was listening* with gladness⁷. The apostle was speaking of being saved through faith in Jesus, and the dawning faith which shewed itself in the lame man's face caught S. Paul's attention and won his pity. He looked at him with *a searching glance*, and *saw* as it were *the faith* within which would enable him *to be saved*. The thought possibly flashed across him that an act of bodily salvation would be the best

---

¹ Gk *Zeus*. ² Gk *Hermes*. ³ Bezan *the priests of (him who was*—p. 187 note) *Zeus Before-the-city*. ⁴ Marg *nature*. ⁵ Some MSS add *but that they should go away each to his home*. ⁶ But see note ⁵, p. 232. ⁷ As we may add with a Bezan text. The tense of the verb in Greek may denote a habit, *he used to listen*, i.e. he heard S. Paul often. A various reading is *he listened*, the simple fact.

10 explanation to his hearers of his doctrine of spiritual salvation¹, and so he cried *with a loud voice* to the lame man to get up, and he
11 at once did so. *The crowds* of Lycaonians were struck with amazement, and their cry of wonder reveals the primitive state of their religious ideas. They were as yet untouched by the civilized scepticism of society; and the idea of appearances and visits of *the gods* was quite natural to them as to a genuine pagan peasantry. They concluded at once that Paul and Barnabas were
12 their gods, visiting them in human form. Barnabas, the elder and more reserved, was evidently the supreme deity and special guardian of their city, *Zeus*; Paul the spokesman, the younger and more eloquent, exactly filled the part of *Hermes* the messenger of the gods². In their excitement they dropped the foreign Greek (if indeed many of them could speak it) and spoke *in Lycaonian*; and consequently the apostles returned home in ignorance of their
13 novel reputation. The temple of the city's patron god lay outside its walls. It was probably on the site of an aboriginal sanctuary; and now that its deity was identified with the Greek Zeus, for distinction's sake he was called *Zeus Before-the-city*. His *priest* would be one of the chief personages in Lystra. News was quickly brought to him of the divine epiphany, and he was equal to the occasion. Sacrifice must be done. So with his attendant ministers and in solemn procession he *brought bulls*, duly decked with festal *garlands*³, *to the gates* of the temple, i.e. the great gateway which led into the temple area. Here, before the abode of the gods and in the midst of *the crowds, he purposed to offer*
14 *the sacrifice*. But there was a sudden interruption. The supposed gods—whom some rumour had reached at last—were seen to issue from the city gates; *they tore their clothes in two* as at the spectacle of some awful act of sacrilege⁴; and *leaping into the midst of the multitude*, with loud *cries* they tried to stop the proceedings⁵.

---

¹ Salvation was the lesson of S. Peter's miracle (p. 49). It was an idea familiar to the Gentiles; cp. xvi 17, and in the same chapter vv. 30-1.   ² The commentators quote Ovid's story of the visit of Jupiter and Mercury to the two Phrygian peasants, Baucis and Philemon. But the idea was not peculiar to Phrygia, it is a relic of primitive religion. In his *Golden Bough* (2nd ed. II, p. 237) Mr Frazer shews that *strangers* were regarded as embodied spirits: 'The Greeks were quite familiar with the idea that a passing stranger may be a god. Homer says that the gods in the likeness of foreigners roam up and down cities.' *Hermes* was the messenger, Gk *angel*, of the gods. Thus in a very literal sense the Lycaonians 'received S. Paul as an angel of God' (Gal iv 14, cp. i 8). Jupiter and Mercury were the two Latin deities identified with the Greek *Zeus* and *Hermes*. The Phrygian names of the native gods of Lystra we do not know.   ³ On a coin of Lystra is a figure of a priest leading two oxen.   ⁴ Like the high-priest in Mt xxvi 65. The symbolism was familiar among Gentiles as well as Jews: see note on xvi 22.   ⁵ There is some uncertainty as to the scene of the intended sacrifice. The Greek word for *gate* in v. 13 is *pylōn*. *Pylōn* is used of the gateway or porch of a house (xii 13), but here it is in the plural and may well apply to the gateways or 'pylons' which formed the entrances into the precincts of a temple. A different word is used for city gates (ix 24, xvi 13). The apostles would hardly have been lodging in a house with more than one *pylōn*, and the narrow streets of an eastern

15 The apostles were horror-struck at an action which, far more than Cornelius' prostration before S. Peter, infringed the divine prerogative of worship. But we notice their great tact. They address the people with politeness—*Sirs*; and instead of rebuking them, they appeal to their reason and conscience—'*Why are you doing these things?* For, as all your senses as well as our own words assure you, *we are men of the same nature*, exactly like yourselves[1].' At the same time S. Paul insinuates the gospel, and it is instructive to study his method. (i) He begins with the simplest, but the fundamental, truth of religion : the doctrine of the one God and Creator—'I believe in God...Maker of heaven and earth.' (ii) He uses the method of accommodation. He starts with a doctrine they would readily accept—creation by God; he appeals to that evidence which would be most obvious to country folk—the witness of nature; and he makes use of their present state of feeling—the gladness and joy of a festival. S. Paul then (1) explains who he and his companion are—not gods but *evangelists*, i.e. *messengers bringing news*, and that *good news*, of *the living*, i.e. the true and real, *God*, who is the *maker of heaven and earth*. The gods of the Lycaonians, their Zeus and Hermes, with all their paraphernalia of temples and sacrifices, were *vanities*, i.e. no-gods, no-things; they had no real existence. This was the Hebrew doctrine about the gods of the heathen[2], to which in Christian times succeeded the view that they were devils. Accordingly the apostles' mission was—not at once to subvert all their religious ideas but simply—to *turn* their allegiance from one to the other[3].

16 They preached first a living Person. (2) At once, however, an objection must have occurred—Why then has he left us all this time in ignorance of himself? This is indeed a problem of the world's history, of universal interest, which Paul, like ourselves to-day, had then to face. He addressed himself to it fully when speaking to the Athenians and writing to the Romans[4]. But the present moment was no time for discussion, nor were the Lycaonians apt for philosophy. So S. Paul contents himself with the assertion that it was God's plan. For some reason *he had permitted all*

17 *the nations to* follow their own desires until now. (3) But this was not the full answer. The ignorance was in part the nations' own fault. For *he had not left himself without a witness*,

---

town would hardly lend themselves for a dignified sacrifice. It will indeed simplify matters very much if we suppose that the lame man had been at the gate of the temple of Zeus, and that the crowds were assembled there on the occasion of some great religious festival. The priest would then have been on the spot, and the bulls and garlands all ready. Instead of sacrificing within the area as usual, the priest brought them to the gates, the scene of the miracle, where the crowds were still collected. The words of S. Paul in verse 17 run almost like a quotation from some joyful hymn sung at the festival. [1] The meaning of *passions* in English has become narrowed since the AV translation. Cp. Jas v 17. [2] Deut xxxii 21, I Sam xii 21, Jer xiv 22 : cp. Ps cxv 4–8, cxxxv 15–8. [3] Cp. xxvi 18, I Thess i 9. [4] Cp. xvii 30, Rom i 18–32, ii 14–6.

and that witness was nature. In his argument from nature, in the Epistle to the Romans, the apostle finds in creation itself the lesson of the everlasting power and divinity of God; he assumes an analogy between the things that are made and the things invisible; and in the case of man he points to the law written in the heart and the witness of conscience. But with the Lycaonians he appeals to simple evidence which country people would recognize, the simplest form of the argument from design, viz. the succession of *seasons, rains* and harvests, which prove the *bounty* of God, who brings 'food out of the earth, and wine that maketh glad the heart of man and oil to make his face to shine and bread that strengtheneth man's heart.' It was in fact this form of the bounty of God which gave birth to religious festivals. For they began when men met together and in *feasting and gladness* expressed their gratitude for the fruits of the earth, for harvest or for vintage.

§ 4 *The stoning of Paul, and the fulfilment of the work*

The miracle at Lystra was followed by the active evangelization of Lycaonia, already summarized in verse 7. Then it was suddenly cut short by a tragic occurrence. The fickleness of the Galatians (Gal i 6) has been quoted as a sign of their Celtic blood, but no fickleness could exceed that of the inhabitants of Lystra. And the apostasy of the heathen populace is a foretaste of the subsequent defection of the Galatian Christians. After this S. Luke only pauses to shew us 'the fulfilment of the work' (verse 26) in (1) the organization of the Christian disciples into churches, and (2) the report of the work delivered to the church at Antioch.

19 'But there came Jews thither from Antioch and Iconium: and having persuaded the multitudes, they stoned Paul, and dragged him out of the city, supposing that he was dead.
20 But as the disciples stood round about him[2], he rose up, and entered into the city: and on the morrow he went forth with Barnabas to Derbe.
21 And when they had preached the gospel to that city, and had made many disciples, they returned to Lystra, and to
22 Iconium, and to Antioch, confirming the souls of the disciples, exhorting them to continue in the faith, and that through many tribulations we must enter into the kingdom of God.
23 And when they had appointed for them [3]elders in every

---

[1] Bezan authorities give *But*] *while they were tarrying and teaching there came certain Jews from Iconium and Antioch; and as they were disputing publicly they persuaded the multitudes to withdraw from them, saying that nothing which they say is true but all false, and they stirred up the multitudes and* [*stoned.* [2] A Bezan text adds *at evening.* [3] Gk *presbyters.*

church, and had prayed with ¹fasting, they commended them
24 to the Lord, on whom they had believed. And they passed
25 through Pisidia, and came to Pamphylia. And when they
had spoken the word in Perga, they went down to Attalia²;
26 and thence they sailed to Antioch, from whence they had
been committed to the grace of God for the work which they
had fulfilled.
27 And when they were come, and had gathered the church
together, they rehearsed all things that God had done with
them, and how that he had opened a door of faith unto
28 the Gentiles. And they tarried no little time with the
disciples.

19 News of the work at Lystra must have soon reached *Antioch
and Iconium*, and some Jewish emissaries arrived who began to
argue with the apostles in public and deny their statements. The
citizens no doubt were somewhat sore and ashamed of themselves
and so the Jews would have less difficulty in *persuading* them that
these men were really false prophets or sorcerers. Full of indignation at having been duped, *the crowds* were easily incited at one
of these public disputations to take up stones and throw them at
the one who had done the mischief, the talker, the Hermes. Or
perhaps it was the Jews who, having obtained the connivance of the
people, took upon themselves to punish the apostle for his 'blasphemy': for stoning was the Jewish form of punishment. In any
case, whether it were the Jews or the populace, such taking of the
law into their own hands might lead to difficulties with the government, especially if it was known that Paul was a Roman citizen, and
so they *dragged* what they thought to be the *dead* body of the
20 apostle *out of the city*³. Then *the disciples*, among whom we can
picture Barnabas, Eunice, and Timothy, came and *stood round*. But
while they may have been thinking of his burial, it being now
evening, *he rose up and entered the city*. *Next day*, without any
attempt to obtain legal redress or compensation, but as usual
yielding to violence⁴, S. Paul *with* the assistance of *Barnabas* went
on *to Derbe*—a distance of thirty miles. S. Paul had now suffered
retribution in kind for the death of S. Stephen, but he 'obtained
mercy.' S. Luke's careful language avoids any statement that the
apostle had been killed or that anything miraculous happened; but
the narrative (the supposed death followed by a long journey the
next day) gives the impression of an extraordinary recovery—a
restoration which resembled a resurrection from the dead.

---

¹ Gk *fastings*. ² Bezan adds *preaching the gospel to them*. ³ In the Greek
the Jews is strictly the subject of the verbs. ⁴ See Mt v 39–42 and x 23.

21   Roman influence just now was strong at Derbe as at Lystra; like Iconium, it had received a name from the emperor, CLAUDIODERBE. It was however but a small town, and the apostles' work was easier and more complete. It might almost be said that *they evangelized the* whole *town,* certainly they *made many disciples,* among whom we may reckon 'Gaius of Derbe,' (xx 4).

The travelling season must have now been drawing to a close and the apostles had to decide on their movements. Derbe was on the high road from Iconium to the Cilician gates and only 160 miles from Tarsus. But it was very necessary to revisit the churches they had founded, the more so that they were now suffering persecution. Accordingly they retraced their steps *to Lystra, Iconium and Antioch.* From the former cities they had been driven by illegal violence and Paul as a Roman citizen could return with confidence. In Antioch new magistrates had probably come into office.

22   On their return visit the apostles did two things. (1) They *confirmed the disciples,* literally *made them stand firm upon, established them upon*—that is, upon the Lord. This sure standing depended on (*a*) *abiding in the faith*—whereunto they had attained by the grace of God, therein to continue[1]: (*b*) a right understanding of persecution—persecution was, as the apostles had shewn in their own persons, the necessary *entrance,* the strait and narrow gate, *into the kingdom of God.* It was a moral law of God's kingdom—*we must.* In this *we must* we seem to hear the very words of S. Paul as they sank deep into the heart of some listener. *The kingdom of God* takes us back also to the first preaching of the gospel in Antioch[2]. It is the inheritance there offered, into which some of them have now entered. Lastly, the whole work of *confirming* reminds us of the Epistle to the Galatians. The churches of Galatia were particularly lacking in stability. In the Acts twice, if not three times, out of the four times[3] in which the word *confirm* occurs it is in relation to these churches. They soon, as the epistle tells us, removed to another gospel, and did not stand in that liberty wherewith Christ had made them free; they shunned persecution, and instead of abiding in faith they sought to be justified by the works of the law[4].

23   (2) As a kingdom the church required organization: especially these Gentile communities which were now to be left independent of the synagogue and without the apostles. What would they do when the apostles were gone? This is the question that had presented itself at Jerusalem also; and S. Paul answers it in the same way. S. Luke once for all shews us S. Paul's custom: it was to give his churches a body of presbyters[5]. *They appointed presbyters for each*

---

[1] Cp. xi 23, xiii 43: cp. *obey the faith* vi 7.   [2] p. 214: cp. also Gal v 21.
[3] xiv 22, xv 32, 41, xviii 23. The compound form *establish-upon* is rare: it does not occur in the NT out of the Acts. It is akin to S. Peter's '*stedfast* in the faith' (I Pet v 9): cp. xvi 5.   [4] See Gal i 6, v 1, vi 12, iii 2 etc.   [5] Cp. xx 17, 28.

church[1]. The word for appointment originally denoted *election by shew of hands*; but the special meaning had long been lost, and the word might be used of (*a*) a popular election, as by the churches, or (*b*) of a monarchic appointment, as by God[2]. The idea of election thus ceased to be essential, and ultimately in ecclesiastical Greek the word was appropriated to 'ordination' in the technical sense. Thus for the method here we have only analogy to go upon, but S. Luke has already given us three typical pictures of election and ordination in the cases of Matthias, the Seven, and Paul and Barnabas[3]. To judge from these analogies, in each city the presbyters were chosen by 'the multitude,' i.e. the body of brethren, and then presented to the apostles, who retained the power of refusal (I Tim v 22). The presentation was made at a public service, which had been preceded by a fast, and then with prayer the apostles laid on hands[4]. At Antioch in Syria (xiii 3) the ordination service had also been a service of farewell. So here when they had laid on hands, the apostles *commended* the presbyters and the whole church *to the Lord*[5]—the true Ruler of *the kingdom*, the object of *the faith* in which they were to continue, the foundation on whom they were to stand *firm*. Among the affectionate and enthusiastic Galatians, the scenes at these services no doubt anticipated the farewell at Miletus described in xx 17–38.

24 The return journey to the Pisidian Antioch need only have
25 taken a few days, and thence the apostles recrossed the mountains of *Pisidia* to *Perga*, where they now preached, utilizing the time left before the close of the sailing season. Then finding a ship at *Attalia*, the port of Perga, they returned to *Antioch* after an
26 absence of about eighteen months. *The grace of God, to which they had been delivered* (xiii 3), had enabled them *to fulfil the work*[6] to which the Spirit had called them; and as 'apostles of the
27 church' they had to give an account of their mission. There was an assembly of the whole church, and Paul and Barnabas there recounted all that had happened, which clearly shewed that it was God who had been working *with them*[7]; and declared the result— *God had opened to the Gentiles a door of faith*[8], viz. he admitted them into his kingdom through the door, not of circumcision and the law as heretofore, but of faith in Jesus. This is the complement to the expression of the Jerusalem church in xi 18—*God*

---

[1] Cp. Titus i 5, and Acts xv 21, 36 for the Greek. But like *at home* in ii 46 the words might mean *at church*, viz. at a meeting of the ecclesia when the ordination took place. That there was an ordination in each city and not at Antioch only is indicated by the plural, *fasts*. [2] (*a*) II Cor viii 19, (*b*) Acts x 41. [3] i 23–6, vi 1–6, xiii 1–3. [4] That hands were laid on seems an inevitable conclusion from xiii 3, cp. vi 6. Space would not allow S. Luke to specify all the details on each occasion. Indeed the laying on of hands was so frequent a ceremony in the religious life of the Jews, that the burden of proof lies on those who would deny it. [5] Cp. xiii 3, xiv 26, xv 40 and xx 32. [6] Cp. xiii 25, xix 21 (Gk). [7] Cp. vii 9, x 38, xi 21, xv 4. The special reference is to the signs and wonders; cp. xv 12, where a different preposition (*through* them) is used. [8] A favourite metaphor with S. Paul, cp. I Cor xvi 9, II Cor ii 12, Col iv 3; and ver. 22 above

hath granted them repentance unto life. Repentance and faith are united by S. Paul himself in xx 21. The church of Antioch
28 accepted the result, no doubt with joy: Saul and Barnabas were received back into close fellowship *with the disciples*, and they stayed at Antioch *a considerable time* which proved to be eventful. For indeed as yet 'the work' was not finished.

SECTION II (= Ch. 15—16. 5)

Confirmation of Gentile liberty by the whole church

In the fifteenth chapter we come to a great crisis in the history of the whole church. We have witnessed the entrance into the church of, first, selfishness, then murmuring, then simony: and now we come to religious controversy. There had been some preliminary symptoms in chapter xi (p. 160); but it was only by this time that differences of opinion had so developed as to threaten the church with actual schism or rending into two. S. Luke wrote some years after the event, when peace had been long established, and yet even in his tranquil style there are evident signs of the severity of the struggle. But the storm was weathered, and the schism averted. The method by which it was averted should be carefully studied in every age. For this was the first of the long series of controversies which have torn the church, and the cleavage of opinion was no less sharp than that which has since divided Catholic and Protestant, Anglican and Papist, Puritan and Churchman[1]. The particular subject of debate—circumcision—had only a temporary significance, but the principles involved were fundamental and perpetual.

For the right understanding of such a crisis we want to know not merely the external history of the events as they were known to the church at large, but the inner or secret history of the motives and policy of the chief actors. Of such history we are fortunate in possessing a valuable document in the account given by S. Paul himself to the churches of Galatia (Gal ii 1-10). This document is invaluable for its revelation of feeling, but it occasions a difficulty. S. Paul's account of his visit to Jerusalem presents at first sight such a very different aspect from that given in this chapter of the Acts that many have denied the identity of the visits. Professor Ramsay, for instance, maintains that in Gal ii 1-10 S. Paul is speaking of the visit recorded

---

[1] If this seems exaggerated, we can only point to the language of S. Paul, specially in Galatians and II Corinthians. Thus he speaks of the propagandists of circumcision as teaching *a wholly different gospel* or rather *no gospel at all*, and as *annulling* the work of Christ (Gal i 6-9, v 2-12). He calls some of their leaders *false brethren, false apostles, ministers of Satan*. This is the language of an inspired apostle, and must refer to something more fundamental than a mere variety of ritual or custom.

in Acts xi 30 and xii 25. This identification however is all but impossible. The whole course of the history is against it. The visit of Acts xi 30 is much too early for that in the epistle. The baptism of Cornelius was more recent (cp. xv 7): James, the presbyters, and the circumcision party, had only just appeared upon the scene (xii 17, xi 30, 2). 'Saul,' as he was then called, was still subordinate to Barnabas, and his own mind had hardly reached the stage of development depicted in the epistle. Indeed the history of the 'work' of Paul and Barnabas as narrated in chapters xiii and xiv, with its decisive turning to the Gentiles and its revelation that God had opened a door of faith to them, would come singularly out of place,—or rather would be entirely without point—*after* Gal ii 1-10.

(1) One argument against the identification adopted here is that there will then be no mention in Gal i-ii of Paul's second visit. But those chapters do not profess to be a complete autobiography of S. Paul. His aim in the epistle is to shew that his apostolic authority was not derived from other apostles. Hence he gives an exhaustive account only of his intercourse with the Twelve. (i) When he went up to Jerusalem after his conversion he saw S. Peter and S. James. (ii) On his second visit with the alms from Antioch, as the narrative in the Acts shews us, in all probability none of the Twelve were at Jerusalem: nothing of importance happened, and so S. Paul does not mention this visit. (iii) The third visit was on occasion of the present council—a public and historical event known to and affecting the whole church. It was also known that S. Paul had played a leading part in the controversy: and apparently the Galatians had received a version of what had happened which was very unfavourable to himself and his gospel. Hence the apostle has to vindicate himself, very much like J. H. Newman in writing his *Apologia pro vita sua*[1].

(2) Here we find the answer to the main objection to our identification, viz. the apparent discrepancy between the two accounts. The reason for such discrepancy has indeed already been discussed above, p. 140. It lies in the difference between the external and internal history. S. Luke writes an account of what the church saw and heard, he puts on record the public deliberations of the council, and copies its resolution and the encyclical they issued. S. Paul reveals to us his own motives and emotions, and the private consultations of the leaders and his relations to them. Again, we have to consider the aim of each writer, and the public he is addressing. S. Luke is writing for the whole church and he simply wants to inform them of the main result. S. Paul is writing to particular persons and concerning particular points, viz. the questions of his own apostleship and of Titus' circumcision. He is also apparently endeavouring to correct misrepresentation or false reports which had reached the Galatians: such, for instance, as is suggested by the Bezan text, that he had gone up to be judged by the Twelve. Naturally, then, the accounts of S. Luke and S. Paul

---

[1] (i) Acts ix 26-30, Gal i 18-20; (ii) Acts xi 30, xii 25; (iii) Acts xv, Gal ii 1-10.

differ. But they correspond exactly to the characters of the writers and their different relations to the council. They are not contradictory but supplementary, as is seen by the ease with which they can be fitted into one another. There is no inconsistency, but an immense addition to our information; and to have a perfect understanding of the crisis all that is wanting is similar insight into the minds of S. Peter and S. James.

The subject of the controversy was the relation of Jew and Gentile within the church. This question has been before us almost from the beginning of the book, and as it received its final answer (so far as the Acts is concerned) at this council, it will be well to review the whole matter even at the cost of some repetition. Wherever the Jews went in the Gentile world, their presence gave rise to two conflicting tendencies. On the one hand the Jew possessed the knowledge of the one true God; and amidst the universal corruption, idolatry, and superstition of the ancient world, this saving knowledge exercised a powerful attraction. The synagogues of the Jews became the centre of a large body of seekers after truth—whether actually circumcised 'proselytes' or simply 'God-fearing' Gentiles. On the other hand this knowledge was enshrined in a law which imposed upon the Jews a number of distinctive customs and observances, and these separated them off from the rest of mankind and made a real coalescence impossible. Four characteristics in particular struck the Gentile— the absence of all images or emblems of the deity from Jewish worship, the observance of the sabbath, abstinence from unclean meat and especially swine's flesh, and circumcision. This last was sufficient in itself to prevent the world from adopting Judaism. But the law of uncleanness caused the Jew on his side to look upon the Gentiles with contempt as unclean, and put an effectual bar on any real fellowship. The Gentiles in their turn readily paid back Jewish exclusiveness with an ample interest of ridicule and hatred. This double relation to the Gentiles divided the Jews themselves into two schools. On the one side there were those who, with some consciousness of the brotherhood of common humanity, were striving to remove barriers, and to present the Jewish faith to the world in its most spiritual and philosophic aspect. Such were the Hellenists of Alexandria. On the other side the salvation of the Gentiles was inconceivable to the genuine Hebrew; and this was the attitude of mind which prevailed in Judaea. There the 'Hebrews of the Hebrews' were growing more and more rigid: instead of lowering they were raising the fence round the Law, and trying to make the barrier between Jew and Gentile absolutely impassable.

Into this world of Jews and Gentiles the church was born, and the same problems were presented to her: what was to be her relation to the world outside? was she to remain Jewish or, dropping the distinctive marks of the Law, become Catholic? And again, how were the Gentiles to be received? must they, to become Christians, first become Jews? As she worked out the answer, we find in the church the same tendencies to divergence as in Judaism,—viz. one side tending to liberalism, the other to rigour. The idea of the necessity of the Law for Christians seems to us almost inconceivable. But we must remember that Christianity began in Judaism. All the early disciples were Jews, bred up in the observance of the Law, and they naturally continued to observe it, as did S. Paul himself. These matters of abstinence from unclean meat, observance of the sabbath, circumcision etc., had become almost second nature to them. The Lord himself had not directly taught the abolition of the Law: rather he had said that not one jot or one tittle was to pass away. He had indeed come into conflict with the authorities as a transgressor: but what he had transgressed was not the Law but the traditions of the elders. In fact he left the church to deduce the passing away of the Law from the principles which he had laid down, and the whole history shews how 'slow of heart' the disciples were to understand. But this question of the Law is not merely a matter of antiquarian study. It was the temporary form of a problem which man will always have to face in this world. While he is in the body he cannot live without some law, nor can he worship without some form; as long as the church is in the world, spirit and matter, law and gospel, are inextricably bound together and cannot be divorced. Puritans by their sabbath-keeping, Catholics by their use of the sacraments, all Christians by their common habits of prayer and worship, are separated from the world as Jews were by their circumcision. In obedience to the ten commandments and the doctrines of the faith Christians are all under law. The problem present to the church at all times is to find the practical balance between the two principles of liberty and obedience, and the two conflicting claims of the inward and the outward. And it was just this problem which was now presented to the church at Jerusalem.

We have seen the development of the situation step by step. First the Twelve appoint to office in the church a circumcised proselyte —Nicolas of Antioch: then the preaching of Stephen foreshadows the changing of the customs: then Philip baptizes the Samaritans, who were schismatics, although they were circumcised and had a version of the Law, and also an Ethiopian eunuch, excluded from the covenant not merely by his race but by his condition: then Peter admits Cornelius and a party of God-fearing Gentiles, at the same time that evangelists at Antioch are preaching to Greeks: lastly, when S. Paul and S. Barnabas turn to the Gentiles, the process of expansion is complete.

The inevitable effect of such a progress however was the development of parties within the church. The expansion was mainly on the Hellenist side of the church, and its successive leaders were Stephen, Philip, the Cyprian and Cyrenian evangelists, S. Barnabas and S. Paul. But this advance provoked alarm and reaction. The church at Jerusalem was Hebraic in feeling; it was composed mostly, if not entirely, of 'Hebrews[1],' who had by no means lost their Jewish

---

[1] The persecution of viii 1-3 dispersed the Hellenist element in it (vi i).

patriotism; its type was S. James, the Lord's brother, who for his rigorous piety and observance of the law won even from the Jews the title of 'the Just.' Thus, while the Hellenists were continually widening the entrance to the church, those whose faith in the law was unshaken were being consolidated into a definite party. When S. Peter baptized Cornelius we hear of *them of the circumcision*: now we find many of the sect of the Pharisees among the believers; several years later the thousands of Jewish Christians are *zealous for the law*[1]. This growing self-consciousness of the Judaic spirit in the church corresponded with, and was a symptom of, the same tendency in Judaism itself. The Jews were getting more and more irreconcilable towards the Gentile world, until their invincible fanaticism brought on the fatal catastrophe.

At this time then we find two definite parties in the church—the Greek or Gentile party, represented by the church of Antioch and headed by S. Paul and S. Barnabas; and the Hebraic party, strongest in the church at Jerusalem and typified in S. James. Perhaps it is misleading to speak of 'parties'; we ought rather to appreciate more carefully the situation in the church. For (1) the leaders and representatives of the different states of mind, e.g. S. Paul and S. James, would have been the first to disown the action of the extremists. (2) It was these who exaggerated their principles until they had formed definite parties, animated by party spirit. On the one side there were the Judaizers who insisted on circumcision and the law, and accordingly hated Paul. On the other side some of the Gentiles who protested against Judaic legalism pushed the doctrine of Christian liberty to an excess of licentiousness; these corresponded to the Antinomians of a later date[2]. Between these two parties however lay (3) the great mass of the brethren, with, of course, sympathies on this side or that, but on the whole undecided, subject to surrounding influences, and waiting to be guided by the Holy Spirit in the course of events. Of this great party of the 'moderates' S. Peter stands as the representative.

And the moment has now come for the guidance of the Spirit; for the questions which press for an answer can no longer be put off. They must be distinguished clearly as follows: first (A) the doctrinal question, Can a Gentile be saved? This all admit. But how? (1) Must he be circumcised and keep the law? And, if the Gentile need not be circumcised, (2) is circumcision still obligatory for the Jew? (B) The practical point of discipline. Assuming that circumcision is not necessary for the Gentiles, what is to be their position? (1) Can Jewish Christians associate with them freely, without defilement? that is, is the church to be one body? Or (2) are the Gentile Christians to remain in an inferior position, like the 'God-fearing' in the synagogue? that is, are there to be two standards of higher and lower merit or only one Christian life?

---

[1] xi 2, xv 5, xxi 20.   [2] The existence of such a class, and on no small scale, is testified by the pages of the NT.

The circumcision party saw the logical consequences of surrendering the first point (A 1), so they boldly laid down the dogmatic position, *Except ye be circumcised ye cannot be saved*,—in other words circumcision is necessary to salvation. If this be true, it ought to be made known to the brethren in these new churches of the uncircumcised, and so a propaganda was set on foot, no doubt in all sincerity and earnestness. *Certain* of them accordingly *came down* to Antioch. But there they met S. Barnabas and S. Paul, and these apostles had learnt that the church must be catholic, open to all, and that there must be but one Christian life and one Christian body. A struggle was inevitable, and ch. xv is the record of the decisive engagement and of the victory of the truth.

§ 1 *The controversy at Antioch and the deputation to Jerusalem*

15 And certain men[1] came down from Judæa and taught the brethren, *saying*, Except ye be circumcised[2] after the
2 custom of Moses, ye cannot be saved. And when Paul and Barnabas had no small dissension and ³questioning with them⁴, *the brethren* appointed that Paul and Barnabas, and certain other of them, should go up to Jerusalem unto the apostles and ⁵elders about this question.
3 They therefore, being brought on their way by the church, passed through both Phœnicia and Samaria, declaring the conversion of the Gentiles: and they caused great joy unto
4 all the brethren. And when they were come to Jerusalem, they were received⁶ of the church and the apostles and the elders, and they rehearsed all things that God had done with
5 them. But ⁷there rose up certain of the sect of the Pharisees who believed, saying, It is needful to circumcise them, and to charge them to keep the law of Moses.

1 The Bezan text, as in chapters xiii-xiv, is again very instructive. From it we learn that the visitors to Antioch were *of the sect of the Pharisees*. With great delicacy S. Luke withholds their names⁸.

---

[1] Bezan texts add *of those who had believed of the sect of the Pharisees*. [2] Bezan adds *and walk* [*after*. [3] AV reads *disputation*. [4] Bezan runs *for Paul said that they should so abide even as they had believed* (I Cor vii 20), *vehemently affirming it. But they that had come from Jerusalem charged them, Paul and Barnabas and certain others, to go up to the apostles and presbyters at Jerusalem in order to be judged before them*. [5] Gk *presbyters* as elsewhere. [6] Bezan adds *with great* (*honour*). [7] Bezan *they that had charged them to go up to the presbyters rose up,* [*saying*. [8] As S. Paul in other cases; cp. e.g. Gal i 7, v 10, II Cor x 7.

They seem to have alleged some commission from the church at Jerusalem[1], but they certainly had no apostolic authority for the doctrine which *they began to teach*, viz. that *Except ye be circumcised* [and walk] *after the custom of Moses, ye cannot be saved*—a very different doctrine from S. Paul's, 'Believe on the Lord Jesus and thou shalt be saved' (xvi 31). The keeping of the Law added in the Bezan text was the natural consequence of circumcision[2], as is apparent from verse 5. This doctrine came like a bombshell into the church of Antioch where the majority of brethren were uncircumcised and they and their Jewish brothers were living side by side in peace. It was indeed a 'root of bitterness' (viii 23). It *troubled them*, i.e. cast them into confusion, and *subverted their souls*, i.e. upset all their principles of faith and life[3]. The immediate effect would be to divide the church into two classes[4]; and at the moment *there was a great dissension*—the word used in Greek for civil strife or sedition[5]. For resistance was offered to such division. *Paul and Barnabas* called in *question* the doctrine itself. S. Paul (according to the Bezan text) maintained that *each should remain in the state in which he was when he believed*—the principle which he reaffirmed when dealing with the subject of marriage at Corinth[6]. And this after his wont he *affirmed vehemently*, so there was a deadlock.

The obvious solution was an appeal to the mother church at Jerusalem, and accordingly *they appointed that Paul and Barnabas and certain other of them should go up to Jerusalem unto the apostles*[7] *and presbyters about this question*. The indefinite *they* (p. 188) must be taken as *the brethren* (RV). So the church at Antioch sent up an embassy to the church at Jerusalem. That was the visible outcome. But that a good deal more lay under the surface is shewn by S. Paul's words *I went up in accordance with a revelation*[8]. And the Bezan text helps to reconcile the two statements. Apparently the Pharisaic teachers *charged Paul and the other leaders to go up to Jerusalem to be judged before the apostles and presbyters*. Put in this way, S. Paul naturally would not yield to the proposal. If he was quite confident that he had received his gospel from the Lord direct, it was not a matter to be submitted to human judgement. And if Christ had made him his apostle, the apostles at Jerusalem were now his peers, and not his judges[9]. But the Lord appeared to him in a vision and reassured or commanded him; and accordingly he consented to go up to Jerusalem with the rest of the

---

[1] verse 24: cp. Barnabas (xi 22), the prophets (xi 27), Judas and Silas (xv 22).
[2] Gal v 3.   [3] verse 24. For *trouble* cp. Jn xii 27, xiii 21, Gal i 7, v 10. The Greek word for *subvert* means literally *to turn one's furniture upside down*, and so *to dismantle*. The opposite process is indicated in the *prepare* of Lk i 17, vii 27. Another compound of the same verb occurs below in xxi 15.   [4] As in Gal ii 12.
[5] Cp. xix 40 (*riot*), Lk xxiii 25 (*insurrection*).   [6] 1 Cor vii 18-24.   [7] Since his departure from the city in A.D. 44 (xii 17, p. 180), S. Peter has returned: S. John is with him; and S. James now is reckoned as an 'apostle.'   [8] Gal ii 2.
[9] Cp. the argument of Gal i-ii, esp. i 1, 11-2, 15-7.

party as a delegate or 'apostle' of the church of Antioch. S. Luke was very possibly among the *certain others*. We know that Titus was. Titus, one of S. Paul's most faithful disciples, was a Gentile and uncircumcised, and S. Paul took him up deliberately. This shewed the spirit of the deputation. And that it represented the real mind of the Antiochene church was shewn by its honourable
3 dismissal. The whole church *brought* the apostles *on their way*[1], probably escorting them as far as Seleucia, the port of Antioch. The like sympathy was shewn by the churches of *Phoenicia and Samaria* which they passed through—Tyre, Sidon, and Ptolemais, Caesarea and Samaria (Sebaste). These received the news of the turning of the apostles to *the Gentiles*, and *the turning* or *conversion of* the latter to God, with *great* and *universal joy*[2]. The journey almost assumed the character of a demonstration; and so S. Paul
4 and S. Barnabas *arrived at Jerusalem* with all the weight of the northern churches at their back.

At Jerusalem, as 'apostles of the church' of Antioch, they had an honourable *reception* at a meeting of *the church*, assembled in due order—the whole body and its officers. Then S. Barnabas and S. Paul formally *announced what God had done with them*[3]: their 'work' in the journey and its result in the conversion of the Gentiles with the manifest approval of God. But the experience of S. Peter (xi 1-3)
5 was to be repeated. The Pharisaic teachers *who had charged them to come up to the presbyters*[4] had themselves also returned from Antioch, and now they *rose up* out of their place and said *It is necessary to circumcise them and charge them to keep the law of Moses*. The gauntlet was now thrown down; and S. Paul was ready to take it up. Possibly he did at that moment make a statement of his gospel, in accordance with Gal ii 2 *I laid before them the gospel which I preach among the Gentiles*. But in any case the matter was too important to be settled at once. There must be an interval for deliberation and discussion, and so the meeting broke up. How the interval was spent we are told in the second chapter of the Epistle to the Galatians, to which accordingly we now turn.

Gal 2 3 The interval was a stormy one. There was a sharp sting in the demand of the Pharisaic party that 'they should be circumcised': it had a personal reference—in the 'they' was included one of the deputation, *Titus*. Great must have been the indignation of the strict party, when they discovered that Paul had 'privily brought into' their midst an uncircumcised *Greek*, and on his circumcision they insisted. On his side S. Paul resisted the demand with equal strenuousness. It was indeed a home thrust: but not merely his own liberty, the liberty of the Gentile churches was at stake. In
4 making the demand these Pharisaic teachers had revealed their true

---

[1] Cp. the *bringing on the way* at Miletus xx 38, Tyre xxi 5; and the *meeting* at Appii Forum xxviii 15. [2] Again the note of *joy* after conversion, cp. p. 223. [3] The *with them* (cp. xiv 27) is explained by (*a*) verse 12 *by them*, and (*b*) vii 9, xi 21 etc., he was *with them*. [4] This is following the Bezan text.

Gal 2 4 character—they were *false brethren*, still Jews at heart *who had privily come into* the church, like the spies into the holy land, *to spy out* the Gentiles' *liberty in Christ Jesus, and bring them back into complete bondage* under the Law. Yield to such he could not. And yet, on the other hand, there was not only the hopelessness of the issue otherwise, there was the still small voice of charity—'give no offence to the church of God neither *to Jew* nor to Greek,' 'if meat make my brother to offend, I will eat no meat while the world standeth'; and he might be scandalizing not merely the extremists, but the whole church at Jerusalem. According to his own teaching both 'circumcision and uncircumcision were alike nothing.' Hence, though it might appear to the Gentiles as a betrayal of their cause, though it would lay him open hereafter to a charge of inconsistency, yet for the peace of the church he became 'to the Jews as a Jew,' and circumcised Titus. What a struggle it cost him is evident from this Epistle, where in going over the scene again his emotion makes havoc of the grammar and prevents his actually stating the fact of Titus' circumcision. But there was no need to state it. The Galatians knew it perfectly well, as they also knew of Timothy's circumcision (xvi 3), and the charges of inconsistency brought against the apostle. What was vital for S. Paul was to make clear that Titus was circumcised, *not under compulsion*, but out of voluntary
5 self-sacrifice; as an act not of *submission to the false brethren*, but of charity towards the weaker brethren[1].
6 But submission brings victory. This particular 'scandal' removed, S. Paul was the better able to discuss his gospel *privately with those of repute*, with *James and Cephas and John*. They— like S. Peter himself in the past, like S. Barnabas, like the church at
7 Antioch[2]—could not resist the teaching of facts. *They perceived the grace* of God *given to* S. Paul, and that God had evidently *entrusted* to him a work among the Gentiles, in which he was destined to hold a position similar to that which S. Peter had held in the church of Jerusalem. The fervour, the spirit, the genius of S. Paul, backed by the charity of which he had just given so signal a proof, were
9 irresistible. The three *gave to him and Barnabas the right hands of fellowship*, and, as it were, divided the mission field. Where the Gentiles predominated, that was to be the province of Paul and
10 Barnabas; where the Jews, that of the other apostles. *Only* there was one condition. Jerusalem suffered from poverty and the Jewish poor received alms from the Jews of the Dispersion. *The* Christian *poor* were cut off from this supply, and accordingly the apostles plead that the Gentile churches should *remember* their poorer brethren at

---

[1] It is only fair to the reader to add that, as the fact of the circumcision of Titus is not stated in Galatians, so many commentators consider that Titus was *not* circumcised. The account given above however seems to the writer to be the only adequate explanation of the emotion evident in the style of the Greek of Gal ii 3-5 (and in particular of the *but that* or *and that* of verse 4). But of this each reader must form his own judgement.   [2] xi 17, 23.

Jerusalem—this would be a practical bond of union, and would 'make both (sides of the church) one (Eph ii 14).' This request, as we shall see, S. Paul fulfilled, loyally and *with zeal*, even at the cost of much labour and danger to himself. This agreement between the leaders practically settled the question. As happens with the deliberations of large bodies and meetings, the resolutions adopted are as a rule those prepared beforehand by the leaders. This was the case at Jerusalem then, and so there was no need for S. Paul to say more to the Galatians about the council itself. What happened there they knew already; in fact they had received the letter of the council, containing its resolutions. What they had not heard of was the private conference of S. Paul with the three and their entire unanimity[1].

§ 2 *The Council at Jerusalem*

We now come to a narrative which bears strong testimony to the fidelity of S. Luke. This is indeed incidentally confirmed by the relation of S. Paul to S. Barnabas: at Jerusalem, and in official records, Barnabas stands first (verses 12 and 25), but where S. Luke narrates, or gives his version of the record, he slips into the usual *Paul and Barnabas* (verse 22: cp. 2 and 35). But the chief evidence is afforded by the speeches. These are of course only brief notes of what was actually said, written out afterwards by S. Luke; and yet in these few verses the characteristic attitudes and phraseology of the speakers unconsciously assert themselves.

Thus S. Peter's impulsive and generous character is seen in the eager question and honest confession of verses 10 and 11: his language minutely recalls that of his speech, as also of the general narrative, in chapters x–xi[2]: and there are, besides, some striking coincidences with his words elsewhere. He had, for instance, asked Ananias and Sapphira *why they had tempted the Spirit of the Lord*, and he alone applies to God the attribute of *knowing-the-heart*[3]. At the same time, just as we find his first epistle reflecting the ideas and phrases of the Epistle to the Romans, so here it is evident that S. Peter, true to his impressionable character, has been much influenced by intercourse with

---

[1] We can now see how remarkably the account in Galatians dovetails in with the Acts. There is (1) Gal ii 1–2 a the going up to Jerusalem: (2) Acts xv 4–5 the public reception: [?Gal ii 2 b, at which S. Paul states his gospel:] (3) Gal ii 3–5 the affair of Titus' circumcision: (4) Gal ii 6–10, with 2 c, the private conferences of the apostles: (4) Acts xv 6 and foll. the meeting of the council and decision.
[2] Going through the speech here—cp. *ye know* x 28, 37, *at the beginning* x 37, xi (4) 15, *Peter opened his mouth* x 34, *into my mouth* xi 8, *the word...preaching good tidings* x 36, *every one that believeth* x 43, *the prophets bear witness* x 43 (22), *received the Holy Ghost* x 47, *even as we*, *even as unto us* x 47, xi 17, *making no distinction* xi 12 (x 20), *cleansed* x 15 (28), xi 9. [3] v 9: i 24. The compound epithet *knowing-the-heart* has not yet been found in classical literature or the LXX. For *heart* cp. also v 3–4, viii 21–2. *Through the mouth of* is found only in S. Peter's speeches i 16, iii 18, 21, iv 25. *Cleansing by faith* (in its position in the sentence as well as thought) corresponds to *cleansing all meats* Mk vii 19 (which represents the Petrine tradition). For *chosen* cp. i 24 and *beginning* i 22.

S. Paul. In his faith in salvation from the burden of the law by grace we almost hear S. Paul himself[1]: *purifying by faith* is only another form of *justifying by faith*: and besides the doctrine, the phraseology also bears distinct traces of S. Paul's language[2].

When we come to S. James' speech almost his first word stamps it as thoroughly Hebraic in thought and expression. He calls S. Peter by his Hebrew name (*Simon*), and in its Hebrew form *Symeon*. His phrases—*God did visit, a people, for his name, from the beginning of the world, turn to God, generations of old*—recall the Hebraic canticles and narratives at the beginning of the Gospel[3]. He uses the same word as S. Peter, *of-old* (i.e. *of-the-beginning*)[4]: only with S. Peter the beginning is that of the gospel, with S. James it is still apparently 'Moses.' So in contrast to S. Paul he speaks of the reading of the Law in the Jewish synagogues as a witness to God, parallel almost to the Gentiles' faith in Christ. Further than this, there is not much in this short speech to mark a distinct individuality. But it contains some coincidences with his other speech in the Acts[5], and one or two unusual words[6].

The letter affords a third test of genuineness. Here the construction of the first sentence corresponds so exactly to the period with which S. Luke begins his Gospel, that many conclude that this letter is likewise his composition. But the existence of the original letter must have been a check to inventiveness on S. Luke's part, nor would he have lacked opportunities of copying it. Besides, such official communications had probably assumed an almost stereotyped form. Another explanation of the resemblance is quite possible. If S. Luke accompanied S. Paul to Jerusalem, being a good Greek scholar, he may have been employed by the apostles as their scribe[7]. In its

---

[1] Cp. xiii 38-9, Gal ii 15-6. [2] e.g. *the gospel* (verse 7, I Pet iv 17) occurs in S. Paul's writings 60 times, elsewhere only 16 times: S. Luke only uses it here and when quoting S. Paul xx 24. *Neck* in a metaphorical sense only occurs Rom xvi 4. *Be able*, i.e. *have strength* (10), is used in Gal v 6, vi 15 of circumcision not *availing*. The view of the law as a *yoke* is found in Gal v 1. The thought of *God bearing witness* is Pauline, cp. xiii 22, xiv 3, Rom i 9, II Cor i 23, Phil i 8, I Thess ii 5, 10. *Grace* has occurred before, but now it is used in S. Paul's special sense, cp. xiii 43, xiv 3, 26, xv 40, xviii 27, xx 24, 32. For *purifying by faith* cp. xiv 27 *door of faith*: *chosen* ix 15, xiii 17. [3] Cp. Lk i 16, 17, 31, 48, 49, 50, 68 (vii 16), 70 (Acts iii 21), 77, 78. [4] vv. 21 and 7. [5] xxi 20-5. In both he speaks of *Moses*, of *judging*, and of *writing*: the last word occurs only in these places. Among the epistles the word *visit* and the phrase *the name which is called upon you* are found in S. James alone (i 27, ii 7). In the epistle also he speaks of the (Christian) *synagogue* (ii 2). [6] e.g. *trouble, pollutions*, not elsewhere in the NT. *The words of the prophets* is a unique phrase. But to use uncommon words is a habit of S. Luke's. There is besides a little similarity with S. Paul's speeches; cp. *the voices of the prophets...read every sabbath day* xiii 27, *turn unto the living God* xiv 15, *the words of the Lord Jesus* xx 35. S. Paul also (with S. Luke) alone uses the personal object of *proclaim* (viii 5, ix 20, xix 13). [7] The occurrence of words and phrases peculiar to the letter, such as *subvert, by word of mouth, these necessary things, it shall be well with you*, agrees with S. Luke's habit. Besides these the compound word translated *keep* (verse 29) occurs elsewhere only in Lk ii 51 (but there in a different sense). Verse 22, in which S. Luke summarizes part of the letter, may serve as an example of his use of his documentary authorities. Notice

matter the letter faithfully reflects the situation. As regards the style, *laying no burden upon you* is a distinct echo of S. Peter's words in verse 10[1]; and there is also some resemblance to the Epistle to the Galatians, in which letter we may expect to find verbal reminiscences of the struggle[2].

The narrative before us presents a typical picture of the church in consultation. We may refer to the other 'assemblies' for illustration[3]: but to this chapter the church will always turn for guidance in its conciliar action. Its relation to church councils will be considered below (p. 266), but the best guide is carefully to follow our text.

6   The first words of S. Luke at once introduce the question of the composition of councils. He says *the apostles and the presbyters were gathered together*. The letter runs in their name alone (according to our text). In ch. xxi *James and the presbyters* (alone) assembled to receive S. Paul and his fellow delegates. The term *the multitude* (12) might be used of such a limited assembly, as it is of the Sanhedrin in xxiii 7. And if only apostles and presbyters were now present, the assembly would have been as it were the Sanhedrin of the Christian ecclesia. On the other hand, the language of verse 12 naturally implies a large number. The word *multitude* was an almost technical term for the whole body of church members, corresponding to its secular use for the body of enfranchised citizens (p. 188). In verse 22 the consent of *the whole church* is asserted, and must have been obtained in some way. And in verse 6 some Bezan texts definitely assert the presence of *the multitude*[4]. To judge then from former precedents we may conclude that *the apostles* (to whom are now joined *the presbyters*) *met together to see about the matter*, for the discussion and decision of the matter rested with them. But they *called to themselves* or *summoned the multitude* (vi 2), because though the initiative rested with the apostles, the consent of *the whole church* was required. The council was then a real 'ecclesia,' an assembly of the whole church[5] in due order, i.e. of (*a*) apostles, (*b*) presbyters, and (*c*) the multitude.

---

the change to *Paul and Barnabas*, the addition of *with the whole church* (which may point to a mention of *the brethren* in the original address, as in the AV), and the description of Judas and Silas which is omitted in the letter itself in accordance with modesty.   [1] *Give commandment* (ver. 24) is not found elsewhere in S. Luke, but it is used five times by S. Mark (Peter).   [2] *Trouble* is used of the same kind of teachers in Gal i 7, v 10: *subvert* is similar to *unsettle* Gal v 12. S. Paul there also speaks of *bearing burdens* (vi 2, v 10, vi 5: cp. also Rev ii 3), and of Christ *delivering up* himself (ii 20: here verse 26). We may add that while *Greeting* is the ordinary commencement of a Greek letter, it is only used by James (i 1) among the epistles of the NT.   [3] e.g. in i 15-26, iv 23-31, vi 2-6, xi 2-18, xxi 18-25 and at Antioch xiii 1-3, xiv 27, xv 30-2.   [4] Irenaeus in his account of the council (c. *Haer.* III 4) speaks of *the whole church* (*universa ecclesia*) as having met together. The Bezan addition was not likely to have been made in later times when the church was growing more monarchic and oligarchic.   [5] As at Antioch xiv 27 *the ecclesia*, xv 30 *the multitude*. The multitude is the body of the ecclesia, of which of course the apostles and presbyters form a part. In verse 4 a similar meeting of the ecclesia is described.

We may picture the scene thus. At the upper end of 'the upper room' of i 13, or of some Christian 'synagogue,' sat the apostles and presbyters facing the multitude. In the centre of the semicircle was the chair of James, the president of the church of Jerusalem; on his right were sitting S. Peter and S. John, on his left S. Barnabas and S. Paul with the other delegates from Antioch.

6 And the apostles and the elders[1] were gathered together
7 to ²consider of this matter. And when there had been much ³questioning, Peter rose up⁴, and said unto them,

Brethren, ye know how that ⁵a good while ago God made choice among you, that by my mouth the Gentiles should
8 hear the word of the gospel, and believe. And God, which knoweth the heart, bare them witness, giving them the Holy
9 Ghost, even as he did unto us; and he made no distinction
10 between us and them, cleansing their hearts by faith. Now therefore why tempt ye God, that ye should put a yoke upon the neck of the disciples, which neither our fathers nor we
11 were able to bear? But we believe ⁶that we shall be saved through the grace of the Lord Jesus, in like manner as they.
12 And⁷ all the multitude kept silence; and they hearkened unto Barnabas and Paul rehearsing what signs and wonders
13 God had wrought among the Gentiles ⁸by them. And after they had held their peace, James answered, saying,
14 Brethren, hearken unto me: Symeon hath rehearsed how first God did visit the Gentiles, to take out of them a people
15 for his name. And to this agree the words of the prophets; as it is written,
16 ⁹After these things I will return,
And I will build again the tabernacle of David, which is fallen;
And I will build again the ruins thereof,
And I will set it up:
17 That the residue of men may seek after the Lord,
And all the Gentiles, upon whom my name is called,

---

[1] Some Bezan texts add *with the multitude.* ² Gk *see concerning.* ³ AV reads *disputing* as in verse 2. ⁴ Bezan adds *in the (Holy) Spirit.* ⁵ Gk *from days of old* (verse 21) or *of the beginning* (xxi 16). ⁶ Gk *to be saved.* ⁷ Bezan inserts *when the presbyters had consented* (Lk xxiii 51) *to the things which had been said by Peter.* ⁸ Gk *through.* ⁹ Amos ix 11-12.

18   Saith the Lord, ¹who maketh these things known from the beginning of the world.
19 Wherefore my judgement is, that we trouble not them which
20 from among the Gentiles turn to God; but that we ²write unto them, that they abstain from the pollutions of idols, and from fornication, ³and from what is strangled, and from
21 blood³. For Moses from generations of old hath in every city them that ⁴preach him, being read in the synagogues every sabbath.
22   Then it seemed good to the apostles and the elders, with the whole church, to choose men out of their company, and send them to Antioch with Paul and Barnabas; *namely*, Judas called Barsabbas, and Silas, chief men among the
23 brethren: and they wrote ⁵*thus* by them, *The apostles ⁶and the elder brethren unto the brethren which are of the Gentiles*
24 *in Antioch and Syria and Cilicia, greeting: Forasmuch as we have heard that certain ⁷which went out from us have troubled you with words, subverting your souls⁸; to whom*
25 *we gave no commandment; it seemed good unto us, having come to one accord, to choose out men and send them unto*
26 *you with our beloved Barnabas and Paul, men that have ⁹hazarded their ¹⁰lives for the name of our Lord Jesus Christ.*
27 *We have sent therefore Judas and Silas, who themselves also*
28 *shall tell you the same things by word of mouth. For it seemed good to the Holy Ghost, and to us, to lay upon you*
29 *no greater burden than these necessary things; that ye abstain from things sacrificed to idols, and from blood, and ¹¹from things strangled, and from fornication¹¹; from*

---

¹ Marg *who doeth these things which were known*. AV with the later MSS reads *who doeth all these things. Known unto God are all his works from the beginning of the world*. Bezan *who doeth these things. Known from the beginning of the world to the Lord is his work*. Cp. Isai xlv 21.   ² Marg *enjoin them*.   ³ Bezan omits *and from what is strangled*; and after *blood* adds *and whatsoever things they would not be done to them, not to do unto others*: cp. verse 29.   ⁴ Gk *proclaim*.
⁵ Bezan reads *a letter after this manner*: and so AV adds.   ⁶ AV with later MSS reads *and elders and brethren*: from Bezan authorities Blass reads *The apostles and presbyters*, omitting *brethren*. Perhaps the original ran *The brethren, the apostles and the presbyters, to the brethren*.   ⁷ Marg with אB omits *which went out*.
⁸ AV with some Bezan texts adds *saying Ye must be circumcised and keep the law*.
⁹ Gk *delivered up*: Bezan adds *unto every temptation* (Lk iv 13).   ¹⁰ Or *souls* (verse 24).   ¹¹ Bezan and early Fathers omit *and from things strangled*; and add after *fornication*] *and what things ye would not be done to yourselves, do not to others*.

which if ye keep yourselves, it shall be well with you[1]. *Fare ye well.*

7 The meeting was not unlike other human synods and parliaments. There was *much discussion* (RV) conducted no doubt with *disputation* (AV) and vehemence: the Hebraic party was in the majority and Barnabas and Paul would have difficulty in obtaining a hearing. When, however, the feelings of the assembly had found some relief in free utterance, the time came for the apostles to intervene and to win the church to the acceptance of the understanding upon which they had privately agreed. *Peter* first caused silence by an appeal to the unquestionable fact that the Holy Ghost had been given to *the Gentiles* in the persons of Cornelius and his friends. Of this fact S. Peter, enlightened by the same Spirit, now reminds his hearers who had not realized its significance (see p. 163), and in so doing he stirs their conscience—*Ye know*, he begins. Like S. Paul, he was a chosen vessel, for *in the days of the beginning*, that is, in the early days of the church[2], he had been *chosen* to preach *the gospel* to Cornelius' party (and so he
8 had anticipated S. Paul). These Gentiles had received the word,
9 and God had received them. By so doing God had declared that *the distinction* between Jew and Gentile was now done away. For in his sight distinction between men did not depend upon external differences of birth and race, or upon accidental cleanness or uncleanness, but on the purity of the heart. And then *God*, who alone can *know the heart*, had *borne witness* that the hearts of the Gentiles, Cornelius' party, were clean *by giving them the Holy Spirit. By the faith* which he had first inspired he had himself *cleansed their hearts.* This divine cleansing had been effected when they
10 were as yet uncircumcised. Accordingly to declare *now* that circumcision was necessary and to insist on the observance of the law was *to tempt God.* As Ananias and Sapphira had tempted the Spirit of the Lord by doubting his power to read their hearts, so now the circumcision party were tempting God if they called in question his power to cleanse the heart of the uncircumcised by his Spirit. To deny the reality of the cleansing of Cornelius would be to sin like the Pharisees, who had blasphemed against the Holy Spirit by ascribing the miracles of Christ to an unclean spirit[3]. The apostle concludes with an *argumentum ad hominem*[4]. This law which they wished to impose upon the Gentiles, the Jews themselves had been unable to keep. Even the apostles in their own personal experience had found it to be *a yoke* of slavery[5], and
11 they themselves could only hope to find *salvation in the very same way as these Gentiles*—viz. by taking up the light and easy

---

[1] Bezan adds *going on in the Holy Ghost.* [2] Cp. pp. 1, 13, 157. The baptism of John was the *beginning* of the gospel, the baptism at Pentecost the beginning of the church. [3] Mk iii 29–30. [4] Like S. Paul in Gal vi 13.
[5] Gal v 1.

yoke of Christ, or accepting by faith *the grace* or free gift *of the Lord Jesus*. This doctrine S. Peter had declared long ago, 'through faith in his name hath his name made this man strong'...'and in none other is there salvation¹'; he now repeats it as a matter of personal experience, just as S. Paul testifies in Gal ii 15–6: '*We*, being Jews by nature and not sinners of the Gentiles, yet knowing that a man is not justified by the works of the law, save through faith in Jesus Christ, *even we* believed on Christ Jesus.'

12 The fact quoted by S. Peter could not be gainsaid. *The presbyters expressed their acquiescence*, and *the whole assembly kept silence²*. This gave an opportunity for *Barnabas and Paul* to drive home S. Peter's argument by further evidence. Besides Cornelius, other Gentiles had received the word without circumcision and by *signs and wonders* God had declared his acceptance of them.

13 It only remained now for the chairman to sum up the debate by suggesting the practical decision, or in modern language, proposing a resolution. Accordingly in *answer* to the universal expectation *James* rose up. Everything turned upon his utterance. S. James commanded the veneration of all, and hardly needed to
14 ask for a *hearing*. As James the Just, he represented in particular the ideal of the Hebraic party, and if anyone was to win them to the acceptance of the Gentiles, it would be he. And now S. James completes S. Peter's argument by adding the proof (essential to the Jew) from scripture that it was the purpose of *God to take from the*
15 *Gentiles a people for his name³*. S. James' proof is the more remarkable in that its argument turns upon the Greek translation, which differs from the Hebrew. The Hebrew original was rather conducive to Jewish pride; it concluded thus—*that they* (the Jews) *may possess the remnant of Edom and all the nations which are*
16 *called by my name, saith the Lord*. According to the Greek Bible the whole passage runs as follows⁴. The prophet Amos is contemplating the ruin of Israel. The kingdom, called after its divinely appointed king⁵ *the Tabernacle of David, is fallen* and *in ruins*. But God had sworn to David that he would set up his throne, and that in Zion would be his own resting-place, for ever⁶. Accordingly the prophet prophesied that the fallen tabernacle *shall be raised up again*, in order that in it, i.e. in the new Messianic
17 kingdom, God might dwell for ever. But if this Tabernacle be the dwelling-place of God, all who *seek after him* will seek him there, and it will become the centre and means of union for the whole race of men, both Jew and Gentile. For *all the Gentiles* belonged to God who was the Creator and Lord of all things: in the Hebrew idiom *his name was called upon them⁷*. The time would come when they would turn and seek after their Lord, and then they would flow unto this Tabernacle, the new kingdom or ecclesia of God. Simi-

---
¹ Acts iii 16, iv 10–12, cp. x 43.   ² Cp. xi 18.   ³ Cp. I Pet ii 9–10.
⁴ The translators read *Adam* (= *man*) for *Edom* and gave a different sense to *possess*.
⁵ Cp. xiii 22.   ⁶ Ps cxxxii 14.   ⁷ Jas ii 7 margin.

larly Isaiah had prophesied that when the mountain of the Lord's house should have been exalted, i.e. by the divine presence, all nations should flow unto it[1]. Completing his quotation from Amos with another from Isaiah, S. James shews that this call of the Gentiles was part of God's eternal purpose. It had been known to him before the world was, *from eternity*. He had kept it hidden from past generations except in prophetic intimations, but now he is *making it known* to men[2].

19 Having thus completed the argument S. James proceeds to the practical conclusion. He uses a strong word *I judge*, and although, strictly speaking, his proposal was neither a *sentence* (AV) nor a *judgement* (RV), yet it was the decision[3]. For he alone was able to carry the Hebraic majority with him. But because of that majority the decision had to be in the form of a compromise. S. James confines himself to the practical question before them. The Gentile converts were *not to be disquieted*[4] by the requirement

20 of circumcision. But to facilitate intercourse with their Jewish brethren they should be *charged*[5] *to abstain from* certain Gentile practices which were the chief causes of offence to the Jews[6]. Such a concession out of charity on the Gentiles' part was entirely in accord

21 with the principles of S. Paul himself. On the other hand the Hebrew party ought to be satisfied, for nothing had been suggested about 'apostasy from Moses' (xxi 21) on the part of the Jewish Christians. Wherever there were Jews, *Moses*, i.e. the Law, would continue to be read and *proclaimed every sabbath day* as heretofore. Moses, so to speak, would suffer no loss, in failing to obtain the allegiance of those who never had been his.

The epistle of S. James shews that his chief characteristic was

22 wisdom—wisdom practical and peaceable[7]. And that is exactly the character of this Eirenicon. It was at once adopted by the assembly and that *unanimously* (verse 25). *The apostles and the presbyters* probably uttered their judgements or votes in turn, and the multitude, *the whole church*, expressed their assent by acclamation. The Lord had promised his own presence where two or three were gathered together to bind or to loose, and also the presence of his Spirit to be the guide of the church, when the ways appeared to

---

[1] Isai ii 2, Micah iv 1. Cp. Rev xxi 3 and 24, 26. [2] Isai xlv 21. This quotation gives the sense of the words in Amos, *as in the days of old*, which S. James had omitted. The Bezan and AV give the same sense with a different emphasis. For the thought, cp. S. Paul in Rom xvi 25, Eph iii 9. S. James had quoted *the prophets*; and his treatment of their words illustrates the freedom of interpretation in those days. [3] It was really S. James' own personal opinion or vote (*sententia*—the proper meaning of the AV *sentence*), important because he was chairman. The *I* is emphatic in the Greek. The word *judge* is used of (1) an opinion in iv 19, xiii 46, xvi 15, xxvi 8; (2) a determination in iii 13, xx 16, xxv 25, xxvii 1: cp. xvi 4 *the decrees which had been determined*. [4] So Dr Field (*Notes on Translation of the NT*) translates, comparing I Sam xxviii 15. [5] The Greek word may be translated either *write* or *enjoin*. [6] On these see below p. 264. [7] Jas i 5, iii 13–8.

diverge¹. Accordingly in this unanimous decision they recognized the mind of the Holy Spirit (verse 28); for oneness of heart and mind was a special sign of his working². The result had to be made known to the church at Antioch, so they passed a second resolution; they decided to send two delegates or 'apostles of the church' to Antioch, bearing a letter³.

The choice of delegates shewed the wisdom and brotherly mind of the church. They were chosen *out of* the ruling body of apostles and presbyters, being *chief men among the brethren*⁴; and they were more than presbyters, they were *also prophets* (verse 32). One of them was a Hebrew—*Judas Barsabbas*, perhaps brother of the Joseph Barsabbas who had been put forward for the vacant apostolate (i 23). The other was evidently a Hellenist. For he possessed a Latin name—*Silas* is short for *Silvanus*⁵—and the Roman citizenship (xvi 37). His sympathies are shewn by his subsequent attachment to S. Paul, which however did not interrupt a close intimacy with S. Peter⁶. As a bond of unity, he was a worthy successor of Barnabas.

23 A letter conveyed by messengers or 'apostles' was a familiar method of communication among the Jews. Thus the 2nd Book of Maccabees opens with a letter announcing the purification of the temple, from *The brethren, the Jews who are in Jerusalem and in the land of Judaea, to the brethren, the Jews who are in Egypt*⁷. Formally, the letter formed the credentials of the delegates. But it also contained the decision of the council, and its composition was not an easy matter. The apostles had a delicate task. They had to avoid giving offence either to Jewish or to Gentile Christians. On the one hand, any declaration that circumcision and the law were abrogated would rouse the Hebrew party: on the other, some burdens had to be laid on the Gentile converts⁸. But they surmounted the difficulty, and the letter is a masterpiece of tact and delicacy. They avoided the enunciation of dogmatic principles which might be distorted and misused by either party, and confined themselves to the practical points of present conduct.

The letter is not addressed to the Gentile brethren universally, but only to those of *Antioch and Syria and Cilicia*, in other words

---

¹ Mt xviii 18-20 (xxviii 20): Jn xvi 13. Cp. also S. Paul's claim in I Cor ii 16, vii 40.   ² Cp. ii 1, iv 24 and 31: ii 46, v 12.   ³ Both these resolutions are expressed by the Greek verb *it seemed good* to them (vv. 25, 28), or *they thought good* (xxvi 9, cp. verse 34 marg). From this verb is derived the noun *dogma*; and *dogma* is the Greek word for both the *decrees* of this council (xvi 4) and the *orders* of Caesar (Lk ii 1, cp. Acts xvii 7).   ⁴ In Heb xiii 7, 17, 24 the word is translated *they that bear the rule (over you).* See Introd. ch. vi § 2.   ⁵ I Thess i 1, II i 1, II Cor i 19.   ⁶ I Pet v 12.   ⁷ Cp. the letters in II Chron xxx 1, Jer xxix 1, 25: also II Chron xxi 12, xxxii 17.   ⁸ The *Didachê* (vi 2-3) illustrates the *burden* laid upon them. *If thou canst bear the whole yoke of the Lord, thou shalt be perfect, but if thou canst not, do what thou canst. Now about eating, bear what thou canst, but from meat sacrificed to idols be exceedingly on thy guard, for it is the worship of dead gods.*

24 of the province of Syria[1]. *The apostles and the presbyters* (1) disown the conduct of the Pharisaic teachers which had begun the dispute (verse 1). This disowning however, while it is itself indirect—*to whom we gave no commandment*,—contains implicitly the doctrine
25 that circumcision is not necessary to salvation. (2) The main subject of the letter is the accrediting of *Judas and Silas*, who are
27 *to announce the same things*, still left undefined, *by word of mouth*. To prepare their way (*a*) mention is made of the *unanimity* of the church at Jerusalem, and (*b*) the church of Antioch is conciliated
26 by high praise of their delegates *Barnabas and Paul* for *having delivered up their lives to all manner of peril for the name of our Lord Jesus Christ*[2]. (3) Last of all, almost as in a postscript,
28 comes the chief point of the letter—*the burden*. To facilitate obedience the apostles first claim that their decision is the mind of *the Holy Spirit*, and then they make four demands on the
29 disciples which are indispensable. They are *to abstain from* four things, viz. *meats* that had been *sacrificed to idols*, flesh with *the blood* in it, the flesh of *strangled* animals, and *from fornication*. The ground of the necessity is not stated, but the last clause suggests the profitable motive—*ye shall fare well*. To say the least, such abstinence would promote peaceful relations with the Jewish brethren, and the self-discipline would be good for their own spiritual life. For in the concluding words added in the Bezan text, *going on in the Holy Spirit*[3], lies the essence of the whole matter. That too is S. Paul's conclusion in his epistle to the Galatians. Neither circumcision nor uncircumcision is anything, but life in the Spirit: 'walk in the Spirit[4].'

§ 3 *Peace restored at Antioch*

They had yet to wait to see how the church of Antioch would receive the letter; and when it accepted the decision joyfully, peace was restored to the church. Thus the council proved an effectual method of settling the controversy; and, like persecution from without, strife within was also followed by a peace[5].

30 So they, when they were dismissed, came down to Antioch[6]; and having gathered the multitude together, they delivered

---

[1] *Cilicia* was at this time closely attached to Syria and seems to have been under the same Roman Prefect: see Marquardt *Röm. Staatsverwaltung* I p. 387. [2] As he had delivered up himself to death for them (Gal ii 20, cp. II Cor iv 11). The word translated *hazard* is literally *give up* or *hand over to*. The addition in the Bezan text tells us to what—*to temptation*, e.g. trial in danger. Cp. Lk iv 31, xxii 28, Acts xx 19, Gal iv 14. But to protect them against temptation they had been *delivered up* by the church to the grace of God (xiv 26). [3] The Greek word for *going on* (translated by Irenaeus *walking*) is the middle or passive participle of the verb *to bear* (Heb i 3). This expression is connected with the work of the Spirit in ii 4, II Pet i 21. It also occurs in xxvii 15, 17: I Pet i 13, II i 17, 18: Heb vi 1, being variously translated *press on, be driven, brought, moved*. [4] Gal v 16–26, cp. iii 2–3. [5] Cp. ix 31, xii 24 [6] Bezan adds *in a few days*.

31 the epistle. And when they had read it, they rejoiced for
32 the ¹consolation. And Judas and Silas, being themselves
also prophets², exhorted the brethren with many words, and
33 confirmed them. And after they had spent some time *there*,
they were dismissed ³in peace from the brethren unto ⁴those
that had sent them forth.⁵
35   But Paul and Barnabas tarried in Antioch, teaching and
⁶preaching the word of the Lord, with many others also.

30   On the arrival of the delegates at Antioch there was a public
assembly of the church, in fact another council, only at Antioch the
emphasis is on *the multitude*. Judas and Silas publicly *delivered*
31 *their letter to* the authorities, and it was *read* aloud. It caused
at once an outburst of *joy*. The verdict so to speak was in their
favour—this was a great *consolation*, and even the demand for
abstinence at the end would appear only in the light of an
32 *exhortation*⁷. Then it was the turn for *Judas and Silas* to
announce the same things *by word of mouth* (verse 27), and their explanation of the meaning of the letter passed into a *long prophetic
exhortation*. There was a repetition of the scene in xi 27-28
(p. 172): there was prophecy and exultation. The exhortation
of Judas and Silas was no doubt in the main an earnest appeal
for unity and mutual charity; and so they *established* the church,
made it firm and compact after its recent shaking and division⁸.
33 A service preceded their return to Jerusalem, at which the church
of Antioch solemnly bade them farewell. '*Peace* be with you'
was the Jewish formula for goodbye; but in this word here S. Luke
rather intimates that they returned *with peace*⁹, having won peace
[34] for the church. As a matter of fact Silas found the atmosphere of
Antioch so congenial, or S. Paul's personality so attractive, that he
35 stayed on at Antioch¹⁰. A time of peace was then a time of progress,
and there followed an outburst of renewed apostolic activity on the
part of *Paul and Barnabas*: they *taught* those within the church
and *preached the gospel* to those without. Their efforts were
seconded by similar work on the part of *many others also*, of less
distinguished position in the church¹¹.

---

¹ Marg *exhortation*, Gk *paraclēsis*; and in verse 32 *exhorted=used paraclēsis*,
marg *comforted*.   ² Bezan adds *full of the Holy Ghost*.   ³ Gk *with*.
⁴ AV reads *the apostles*.   ⁵ AV and Bezan insert verse 34 *But it seemed good
unto Silas to abide there*, and Bezan continues *and Judas went alone*.   ⁶ Gk
evangelizing.   ⁷ In *paraclēsis* the meanings of consolation and exhortation
run into one another and can hardly be separated.   ⁸ Cp. xiv 22.   ⁹ Cp.
I Macc xii 52, xvi 10.   ¹⁰ It is probable that Silas was not Judas' sole companion.
¹¹ This is parallel to the *teaching and evangelizing* of the Twelve in v 42. The
word for *others* marks a distinction (cp. the *also*): it might denote preachers of the
opposite (Hebraic) school. In Gal i 6 S. Paul uses it of 'quite a different' gospel.
With the interpretation adopted above we may cp. *the rest* of v 13.

In a sense, however, the struggle was not yet over. In fact this council, in its history, very much resembled that of Nicaea. That great council met in 325 after the first outbreak of Arianism, and almost unanimously adopted the creed which excluded Arianism from the faith. But this was only the beginning of the struggle. After the council the controversy grew more intense, the church was nearly torn in two, and only after fifty years of fighting was the Nicene Creed generally accepted as the faith of the church. So now after this council the circumcision party renewed their efforts with greater zeal. S. Luke, however, is right in speaking of *peace*, because the struggle changed its character. The extreme party in its fanaticism became almost a separate 'sect' of 'Judaizers'; and their work was transformed into a personal attack on S. Paul. They recognized that 'the apostle of the Gentiles' was the great champion of Gentile liberty; and accordingly they dogged his steps, they disputed his teaching, they denied his apostolate. They sent emissaries even into his own Gentile churches to steal his converts away from him, and in many places they succeeded in stirring up scenes of strife such as had occurred at Antioch, and this with most disastrous effect in the churches of Galatia, which almost apostatized from S. Paul's gospel. We learn these facts chiefly from the letters of the third missionary journey—to the Galatians, Corinthians, and Romans. This last however, written in 54, marks the turn of the tide. It was S. Paul's great vindication of his gospel; after that, we only find some last flames as it were flashing up in the Ep. to the Philippians, and the dying embers of the controversy in the Pastoral Epistles. But in attacking S. Paul the Judaizers were not alone. If they were zealous against Paul because of circumcision, the unbelieving Jews who did not even accept Jesus as the Messiah must have been infuriated at his preaching to the Gentiles. Accordingly, as we shall see, they pursued him with a relentless hatred. This controversy with the Jews altogether eclipsed in magnitude that with the Judaizers; and of the latter S. Luke tells us no more. Indeed he had no reason to break silence. The controversy was personally most painful to S. Paul; but in the council at Jerusalem the church had definitely decided against the Judaizing party and the truth must prevail. The rapid growth of the Gentile churches of itself caused the controversy to die out, and there was no need to rake up the embers[1].

Even at Antioch the question was reopened. In Gal ii 11-14, after recounting this visit to Jerusalem, S. Paul passes on to an incident at Antioch in which S. Peter figures. When this happened he does not say. It must have been before the separation from Barnabas immediately to be related in this chapter of the Acts[2]. And there is

---

[1] This is perhaps a reason why S. Luke does not speak of the *Galatians* by name in ch. xiii-xiv, and why he passes so curtly over S. Paul's subsequent visits. Better silence than a narrative which could only be painful. [2] It could hardly have been at the visit of xviii 22-3. We do not know that Barnabas was then at Antioch and about that time the Epistle to the Galatians was being written.

much to support the view that it took place even before the council[1]. But on the whole the internal evidence shews that in the Epistle S. Paul is keeping to the chronological order and that the incident happened in this interval between the council and the breach with S. Barnabas. The question at issue was one which would present itself after that which had been decided at the council and form the logical conclusion of the whole matter; it deals with the conduct of the Hebrew Christians about which nothing was said in the apostolic letter[2]. If then the incident happened at this moment, we may find a hint of further division or controversy in the *others* of verse 35, as has been suggested in the note above; and it will be easier to understand the separation from Barnabas.

Gal 2 11 Shortly after the council, then, *Cephas* (i.e. Peter) himself *came* down *to Antioch*. When he came, like the other Jews in the Antiochene church, *he ate with the Gentiles* and *lived as a Gentile*,
12 so far disregarding the Law. Then *certain of the circumcision* party *came from* Jerusalem, bearing commendatory letters from *James*. S. Paul does not say that they reopened the controversy, but they lived strictly as Jews. This made the Jews in the Antiochene church uncomfortable. Even S. Peter *was afraid* of them, i.e. of their censure and of causing them scandal; and thoroughly in accordance with his character *he began to draw*
13 *back and separate himself* from the Gentile brethren. With such an example *the rest of the Jews* did the same, and *even Barnabas was carried away*. There was no dogmatic teaching as in xv 1, only a preaching by action, but action utterly inconsistent *with the truth of the gospel* and in fact—what S. Paul calls it—'acting' (or *dissimulation*). Once more there was a crisis, and the recently won liberty of the church was threatened. But S. Paul was equal
14 to the emergency. By his inconsistent action Peter was already self-*condemned*, and the only thing to do was to point out the inconsistency. It would be painful to Peter,—painful also to Paul himself,—but the cause of the gospel called for courage. Therefore at a public meeting of the church Paul rose up and *resisted* Peter *to the face*, and *before all* asked '*If thou being a Jew livest as do the Gentiles, and not as do the Jews, how compellest thou the Gentiles to live as do the Jews?*' S. Peter we know would take the rebuke with all generosity, and S. Paul once again saved the church. It was thus made clear that Jewish Christians might freely mingle with their Gentile brethren and live as do the Gentiles, and so far they also were free from the Law.

---

[1] Thus (*a*) the *certain from James* in Gal ii 12 would be the *certain who came down from Jerusalem* in Acts xv 1. (*b*) It is very likely that S. Peter may have visited Antioch between ch. xii and xv. He must have been there early, if there is any foundation for the tradition which makes him the first bishop of Antioch. See p. 179. (*c*) The separation of Jews from Gentiles as described in Galatians would correspond to the *division* or *faction* of xv 2. [2] That is, with questions *A* 2 and *B* on p. 242.

§ 4 *The separation of Barnabas and Paul*

Victory now secured, S. Paul is again free for mission work; but his stay at Antioch ended in an unhappy incident which left him alone. This S. Luke narrates because it falls in with his plan, which is to shew S. Paul standing out at the end of this period in single and unquestioned preeminence as 'the apostle of the Gentiles,' corresponding to S. Peter at Jerusalem (see p. 186). The narrative also confirms S. Luke's honesty. He does not hide the human shortcomings through which this result was brought about. His pen has faithfully recorded the various sins which made their appearance in the church, and now he has to tell of a *sharp contention* between his favourite apostles.

36 And after some days Paul said unto Barnabas, Let us return now and visit the brethren in every city wherein we proclaimed the word of the Lord, *and see* how they fare.
37 And Barnabas was minded to take with them John also, who
38 was called Mark. But Paul thought not good to take with them him who withdrew from them from Pamphylia, and
39 went not with them to the work. And there arose a [1]sharp contention, so that they parted asunder one from the other, and Barnabas took Mark with him, and sailed away unto
40 Cyprus; but Paul chose Silas, and went forth, being com-
41 mended by the brethren to the grace of the Lord. And he went through Syria and Cilicia, confirming the churches[2].

36 It was probably the autumn of 48; and S. Paul's missionary spirit felt an ardent longing to *turn again* to the work[3], as his affectionate heart yearned to *visit* the converts they had made on
37 their first journey[4]. So he made an appeal to *Barnabas*. *Barnabas* was ready, but his *plan* included the addition to their company of *John Mark*, who was now at Antioch[5]. The *also*, as in xiii 5, may imply another 'attendant'—possibly Luke himself whom we shall
38 find in the company later on. *Paul*, however, had not forgotten Mark's *desertion of them* at Perga, for so it appeared to him still; and *to take him with them* was *not right*[6]. John Mark was 'not worthy,' having once taken back his hand from the plough. S. Paul was not yet convinced of his full sympathy with *the work*, and perhaps in the recent difficulty at Antioch John also had been carried away on
39 the Hebrew side together with Barnabas. So there arose a *sharp*

---

[1] Or *provocation*, Gk *paroxysm*. [2] Bezan adds *delivering the commandments of the (apostles and) presbyters*. [3] The same strong hortative particle (RV *now*) is used as in xiii 2. [4] For similar yearnings cp. 1 Thess ii 17, iii 10: Rom i 11, xv 23. [5] If S. Peter had come down to Antioch this summer, as suggested, S. Mark may have accompanied him. [6] The original Greek is much more emphatic than the English: *Paul thought right* (or *demanded*) *in regard of him who had withdrawn...work—not to take with them such an one.*

contention or *provocation* between the apostles. Neither would give way, and consequently they were *parted asunder*[1]. They divided the field, and *Barnabas taking with him Mark sailed out of Seleucia to Cyprus*, his native country. In the place of Barnabas *Paul chose Silas* for his fellow-worker. As a Roman citizen (p. 255) Silas was admirably suited for work in the Roman empire, but in comparison with Barnabas he would, though himself also a prophet, decidedly stand second to S. Paul[2]. On whichever side the fault lay, S. Paul had not forfeited the confidence of *the brethren* at Antioch, who, as before, in a solemn service *delivered him up to the grace of the Lord* (Jesus). Barnabas having gone to Cyprus, Paul turned towards South Galatia. But the road first ran *through Syria and Cilicia*. Here he visited the various churches and *confirmed them*, i.e. (as in verse 32) settled them again after the recent dissension which, as we learn from the apostolic letter, had spread over all these parts.

So the two champions were separated. They never worked together again, and S. Barnabas disappears from the Acts. It seems inexpressibly sad : the more so when we remember that S. Paul owed to S. Barnabas his very introduction both to the church and to his special work[3]. No one probably felt it more than S. Paul himself. It was an occasion when he felt he had to give up all for Christ, and suffer the loss of all 'gains,' even of friendship (Phil iii 7–8). The quarrel was indeed made up afterwards. In the first Epistle to the Corinthians, S. Paul speaks of Barnabas as of one mind with himself[4]; and at the last, even Mark had won his entire confidence[5]. But the smart remained in his conscience, and no doubt the apostle was writing out of his own bitter experience and with a pang of sorrow for his own shortcoming, when in the same epistle he says 'Love...is not provoked[6].' There are indeed two *provocations*. One is 'unto love and good works"[7]; the other tends to separation. In this case the latter provocation was overruled for good, and led to the former result—the increase of good works. Two missionary parties started instead of one, and new workers were taken into the field.

§ 5 *Galatia. Circumcision of Timothy and loyalty to the council*

Of this visit to Galatia, S. Luke notices only two points, which serve to make thoroughly clear S. Paul's position in the recent controversy. (1) After winning for the Gentiles freedom from circumcision, he yet circumcises Timothy. This shews that S. Paul was no fanatical

---

[1] A strong word : elsewhere in NT only in Rev vi 14. [2] Thus the plural *they* first occurs in xvi 4. It was the action of S. Paul which required to be recorded in xv 40–xvi 3. [3] ix 27, xi 25–6. [4] I Cor ix 6. Renan in his *S. Paul* has some very sympathetic remarks on S. Barnabas at this parting. [5] II Tim iv 11, Col iv 10. [6] I Cor xiii 5. [7] Heb x 24. There is yet another good *provocation*, viz. at the sight of evil (Acts xvii 16). Similarly God *is provoked* by sin, Deut xxix 28, Jer xxxii 37 (Gk).

opponent of circumcision in itself. Circumcision and uncircumcision were alike nothing in themselves; they only received a value when related to the law of charity. To remove offence, or to pave the way for preaching the gospel, the apostle was ready to circumcise. So *he circumcised Timothy because of the Jews that were in those parts.* (2) S. Paul was thoroughly loyal to the council, although he may have thought its decision too much of a compromise. For, though the letter was only addressed to the Syrian church, he yet voluntarily *delivered the decrees* to the churches of Galatia for them also *to keep.* There are however signs in the narrative that the controversy had already begun to pass over the border from Syria into Galatia.

16 And[1] he came also to Derbe and to Lystra: and behold, a certain disciple was there, named Timothy, the son of [2]a Jewess which believed; but his father was a Greek. 2 The same was well reported of by the brethren that were at 3 Lystra and Iconium. Him would Paul have to go forth with him; and he took and circumcised him because of the Jews that were in those parts: for they all knew that his father was a Greek.

4 And as they went on their way through the cities, [3]they delivered them the decrees for to keep, which had been ordained of the apostles and elders that were at Jerusalem.

5 So the churches were strengthened in the faith, and increased in number daily.

1 The interest of the narrative is still confined to Paul's action (*he*). Continuing his journey from Tarsus in Cilicia and crossing the Taurus range by the Cilician gates, he would come first *to Derbe* and then *to Lystra*. Here he doubtless lodged with Eunice (p. 230), 2 and would hear of the good work done since his departure by her son *Timothy* in the church *at Lystra and Iconium*. The place of John Mark had not been filled up. It is extremely likely that S. Luke was with them, but a second 'minister' was needed. S. Paul 3 had been greatly drawn towards Timothy, and now he *wished*[4] to take him *with him*. His wish was confirmed by the Spirit. Like S. Paul and S. Barnabas, Timothy was called to the work by the Spirit, for there were some prophetic utterances 'which went before' (either now or even at Antioch) and marked him out[5]. Accordingly, there was another ordination. First *the testimony of the brethren*

---

[1] Bezan adds *when he had gone through these nations.* [2] Some texts add *a widow.* [3] Bezan has *they] proclaimed to them with all boldness the Lord Jesus Christ, at the same time delivering (to them) also the commandments [of the apostles.* [4] There are two different Greek words for *he willed* in xv 37, xvi 3 (RV *was minded, would*). One refers to plan or purpose, the other to inclination or desire. *Barnabas' plan was to...Paul had a great wish to...* [5] I Tim i 18, cp. iv 14.

at *Lystra and Iconium* to his good character was obtained: this was always an essential requisite for ordination. Then he was set apart with laying on of hands by S. Paul and the presbyters of the church, whereby he received a 'charisma' or spiritual gift, defined as 'the Spirit of power and love and discipline.' This fact of Timothy's ordination we learn from S. Paul's own letters to him[1]. S. Luke does not mention it; for the purposes of the history his circumcision was more important. Timothy was uncircumcised, and this was well known to *the Jews in those parts* and would cause scandal. Further, as the missionaries would generally lodge in the Jewish quarters of the cities they visited and begin work in the synagogues, the presence of the uncircumcised Timothy would be an impediment, like that of Titus at Jerusalem (p. 245). Accordingly, on grounds of expediency as well as of charity, Paul *took and circumcised him*. This circumcision would be notorious in Galatia, and when the Judaizers arrived they soon laid hold of it. 'Why, this apostle of Gentile liberty himself preaches circumcision!' 'he is indeed a mere man-pleaser, utterly without principle!' And when S. Paul in his letter to the Galatians enters so fully into the question of Titus' circumcision, he is at the same time defending his action in Timothy's case also[2].

4   The circumcision of Timothy itself is a sign that the discussion about circumcision and the law had begun to shew itself in Galatia also, and in consequence Paul and Silas, who now act as representing the church of Jerusalem, gave the Galatians the *apostolic* letter, and charged them *to keep* its requirements. The Epistle to the Galatians confirms this. For from it we learn that already S. Paul had been obliged to teach expressly against two threatening tendencies. (1) On the one side, warning them against teachers of the law and circumcision, he said—'if any man should come and preach a different gospel from that they had received, let him be anathema.' (2) On the other side there were Gentiles who were exaggerating their freedom from the law into freedom from all moral restraint. Such, he warned the Galatians, 'should not inherit the kingdom of God[3].' This double teaching is reflected in the Bezan text. (1) *They preached the Lord Jesus Christ with all boldness:* (2) *they gave them the commandments of the apostles and elders.*

5   This is the last mention of the letter, and it forms the close to the history of the council. Further, as the council was the ratification of S. Paul's work in ch. xiii–xiv, and of his position as an apostle in the church, this paragraph is the real conclusion of the chapter of the history which began in xiii 1. And to mark this S. Luke here adds one of those sentences of his which sum up the past work and give a picture of the progress of the church. The final result

---

[1] I Tim iv 14, II i 6–7. It is assumed above that the ordination took place now. It may of course have happened later.   [2] Gal v 11, i 10 and ii 3–5.
[3] Gal i 9, v 21, *to keep* occurs in Gal vi 13.

of the controversy after all was: (1) A great confirmation of the faith of the church; the council was the scene of a victory of the 'faith in the Lord Jesus' and that *faith* made the church *strong*[1]. (2) A great increase of numbers. The sentence recalls the early chapters of the history. *The churches*—of Jerusalem, of Syria, and of Galatia—*were being strengthened in* or *by the faith*, like the lame man in the temple (iii 16; cp. vi 7), *and were abounding in number* (iv 4, vi 7) *daily* (ii 47). The conclusion of the whole matter is exactly parallel to that which had followed upon Stephen's martyrdom and the subsequent events: cp. ix 31, which forms the conclusion of vi 1–ix 30.

The four necessary things (xv 28)

It is now time to examine the meaning of the four demands of the letter. The first three concern eating. It was the matter of food which was the chief ground of separation between the Jews and Gentiles[2]. The 'bread of the Gentiles' was unclean: and it was a mark of piety in a Jew rigorously to abstain from it, like Ezekiel, Daniel, and Tobit[3]. It was unclean in these respects. (i) The Gentiles ate *meat sacrificed to idols*. Eating flesh-meat probably had its origin in the feast upon an animal slain in sacrifice, and still in the apostles' days much of the meat eaten had been so slain. This connexion with the idol of course 'polluted[4]' the meat: and the eating of such meat by the Gentiles had an intimate effect upon the daily life of the Jews in their midst. Jews were obliged to have their own butchers, and it was perilous for them to accept Gentile hospitality. This pollution touched the Christian conscience also; and S. Paul had to discuss the question for the Corinthian church, as he does in I Cor viii–x. (ii) The Gentiles ate *the blood*. This the Jews were strictly forbidden to do, and that for a reason likewise coming down from primitive religion,—the life was supposed to be in the blood. This idea was consecrated in the Law of Moses, which declared that 'the life is in the blood[5].' The blood then had to be all poured out; and therefore (iii) in this prohibition was included that of meat killed by *strangling*,—which the Gentiles esteemed a great delicacy.

Then we are startled to find joined with these purely ceremonial matters a fundamental moral command, (iv) abstinence from *fornication*. In consequence of this difficulty some commentators interpret this *fornication* to mean marriage within the prohibited degrees as given in the 18th chapter of Leviticus. This is possible, for incest is covered by the word in I Cor **v** 1, but the limitation is unnecessary.

---

[1] For *the faith* see xiv 27, xv 9, 11: and for the *firmness* needed after disturbance and subverting xv 32, 41. The phrase corresponds to S. Peter's *stedfast in the faith* (I Pet v 9). [2] xi 3 (p. 150), Gal ii 12. [3] Ezek iv 13–4, Daniel i 8, Tobit i 10–1. [4] The word used by S. James in xv 20 *pollutions of idols* is peculiar in the NT. But the pollution is connected with eating, cp. Dan i 8, Mal i 7, 12, Ecclus xl 29. [5] Cp. Gen ix 4, Lev iii 17, vii 26, xvii 10–4, xix 26, Deut xii 16, 23–5, xv 23.

For there are some ways of considering the precepts which will diminish our surprise.

(1) Like the meats sacrificed to idols, this matter was closely connected with idolatry. The practice of immorality formed an essential part of the worship of many deities. To prostitute oneself was, at some religious centres, an act of worship. Attached to great temples were large bands of prostitutes who were 'sacred,' and 'slaves of the god (*hierodouloi*)'; and such temples were the scenes of incredible corruption, 'sanctified' by religion. Hence the close association of eating idol-meats and fornication which we find elsewhere in the NT, as in I Cor x 7 and 8, Rev ii 14-20[1]. To prohibit idol-meats and fornication is to say *Flee from idolatry*. And this interpretation is confirmed by S. James' speech, which places fornication next after the idol-meats.

(2) Again, the sharp distinction between the moral and ceremonial law had not been as yet clearly drawn, not even in Jewish ethics. This we can see in the law itself, where moral and ceremonial precepts stand side by side; and in practice the Jews regarded them as on a level—to eat an idol-meat would probably have been esteemed a greater sin than to commit fornication. There being then no recognized distinction *per se* between the moral and the ceremonial commands of the law, it might appear that the Gentiles, when freed from the yoke of the law, were freed from the former as much as the latter, and they would be left to the moral law of nature, the law written on the heart, interpreted and expanded by the moral teaching of Christ as handed down by the apostles. Now it was just in this matter of purity that the Gentile conscience fell short in its moral standard. Even in the law of the Jews, although they themselves had a high standard in the matter, it was nowhere actually forbidden to commit fornication[2]. But among the Gentiles this form of impurity was not looked upon as a sin at all: it was, as we have just seen, an act often consecrated by religion as part of divine worship. Hence the Christian teachers found it necessary to give very dogmatic teaching on this point from the first, as we can see from the epistles[3]. And therefore it is not at all surprising that the apostles, while making a kind of concordat between the Gentile Christians and their Jewish brethren, should make an express pronouncement upon a subject where the Gentile standard differed so widely from that of the Jews—and how much more from the moral law of the Christ.

Further, the question of purity, like that of eating, did closely

---

[1] Cp. also the contiguity of fornication and idolatry in Gal v 19, Eph v 5, Col iii 5. In the OT, adultery and fornication are constant metaphors for the desertion of JEHOVAH and the worship of idols.   [2] Cp. Deut xxiii 17-8. If there is no actual prohibition of fornication in the law, the reason is the same as that for the toleration of polygamy etc. in the OT. The strict Christian law of purity is based upon the new creation of our human nature in Christ, and the sanctification of our bodies by the indwelling of the Spirit. For this law then the foundation had first to be laid in the incarnation.   [3] Cp. e.g. I Thess iv 1-8, Gal v 19-21, I Cor v 1-9, vi 9-19, Eph v 3-14, I Pet ii 11, Rev xxi 8, xxii 15.

affect family life and social intercourse (p. 227). Accordingly, taking the commands as a whole, we may view them in either of two ways. (A) They deal with two important social questions—Eating (i, ii and iii); and Purity (iv, this latter being a new precept which completes the law). Or (B) according to the order of S. James, they deal with two fundamental points of contact between Jew and Gentile—Idolatry (i and iv); and Eating (ii and iii, two commands which practically are one, the prohibition of blood).

Nothing is said about meats which were pronounced unclean by the Law of Moses. For these regulations are based on an earlier law, the covenant of Noah (Gen ix 4), and the prohibition of the blood which it contains is a part of primitive religion. And yet the apostles are following the precedent of the Law of Moses. For according to Levit xvii 8-16 the precept about the blood was to be taught to the stranger sojourning in Israel. And if we compare the whole passage we shall find a striking correspondence with the apostolic rules. For there we find in the same order the apostolic precepts (1) about sacrificing flesh-meat, Lev xvii 1-7, (2) about eating the blood, verses 8-16, (3) about marriage, ch. xviii.

(C) There is yet another view possible. The Bezan text, which is that of the early Fathers, certainly illustrates the absence of the dividing line between the moral and the ceremonial. It omits *things strangled*, which is included in the *blood*, and adds another moral precept, *what ye would not have done to you, do not to others*. This is the negative form of 'the golden rule,' and as a summary of the second table it had long been current among the Jews[1]. It formed part of their instructions to Gentile disciples, for we find it at the beginning of the *Didaché*. If this be the original form of the apostolic letter, the prohibitions will then form a summary of elementary morality, needed by Gentile converts who had not been grounded in the law. For it contains four elementary rules—of worship (*eat no idol-meats*); of regulation of the appetite (*eat no blood*); of purity (*do not commit fornication*); and of duty to one's neighbour (*do not to others as you would not be done by*). Cf. Dr Harnack's view on p. viii b.

The first council of the church (xv–xvi 5)

As the history of the council is now closed, we may consider its bearing upon the conciliar action of the church. In the council we see the church exercising the power of binding and loosing, that is of saying what burdens are to be borne, what loosed; and the power of the keys, that is of laying down the conditions of entrance and membership in the church. These are legislative powers, and they were conferred upon the church by Christ himself. He also promised that its decisions should be ratified in heaven, for when assembled together the church enjoys his presence, and it can then claim the promised

---

[1] It occurs in Tobit iv 15. The quotation from the *Didaché* given on p. 255 shows how the rules of eating were mixed up with moral precepts in the Jewish mind.

guidance of the Holy Spirit[1]. Here, then, on the occasion of the first recorded exercise of this power by the church as a whole, it is important to study (A) the object, (B) the method, (C) the decrees, and (D) the policy, of this council.

A. The council was not summoned arbitrarily to utter definitions or enlarge the faith. It was occasioned by a particular emergency, and its aim was to restore peace to the church. In fact, doctrine in the narrower sense of the term was not the subject of its discussions. The 'teaching' or 'the faith[2]' had been learnt by the apostles from the Lord directly, or through the inspiration of his Spirit; and it was this 'teaching of the apostles' which was the test of church membership. The apostles therefore would be the authorities to decide as to what was contained in this original 'deposit' of the faith. Then from the apostles this teaching was handed down by tradition, as we learn from the Pastoral Epistles[3]: *Hold the pattern of sound words which thou hast heard from me: the things which thou hast heard from me among many witnesses the same commit thou to faithful men, who shall be able to teach others also.* S. Paul indeed had not received his gospel from the Twelve, but he claimed to have received it direct from the Lord, and therefore when he came up to Jerusalem he did not submit it to the council, but conferred privately with the leading apostles about it. It is true that the Pharisaic teachers put the matter in a doctrinal form, alleging that *circumcision is necessary to salvation*. But the apostles persisted in treating it as a practical question concerning the amount of burden to be laid upon the Gentile brethren at the moment. Thus a practical difficulty of serious magnitude was the occasion, and its solution the aim, of the council and its legislation[4].

B. It has often been denied that this is to be reckoned as a 'council' of the church. Some dislike the scriptural precedent it gives for conciliar action and authority. Others exclude it because it does not satisfy later canonical requirements as to the composition, procedure, summoning etc. of councils. It is too informal. But for that very reason it is a real council. For in truth a council or synod of the church is simply the church 'meeting together' and so expressing its mind. It was to the church that Christ gave the authority to legislate: his presence is secured by the assembling together: and unanimity is the surest sign that the decision is the mind of the Spirit. Of course, as numbers increased, it soon became impossible for all the brethren to meet together. Yet an assembly of 'the whole church' is always possible. On this occasion the church of

---

[1] See Mt xviii 15-20, xvi 18-9; Jn xx 22-3; Jn xiv 26, xvi 13, Acts xv 28.
[2] ii 42: vi 7.   [3] Cp. II Tim i 13-4, ii 2, I vi 20.   [4] This council then can hardly be considered as forming an absolute precedent for the decision of a matter affecting the creed, e.g. the question of Arianism and heresies affecting the incarnation. It may be said that the letter asserted the doctrine that circumcision is not necessary to salvation. It did so *implicitly* but not *explicitly*,—no more than it asserted the doctrine that the 'four necessary things' were necessary to salvation.

Antioch was represented by delegates, and so by the method of representation the whole church can still be gathered together.

In the procedure also we recognize the church acting as a whole in due order. In all great societies, however democratic in their constitution, the practical administration of affairs must fall into the hands of a smaller or selected assembly, such as the Greek *Boulé* and the Roman *Senate*, the Jewish *Sanhedrin* and the modern *Parliament*. Similarly in these bodies the initiative and control centres in a small committee of the leaders, whether magistrates, or high-priests, or cabinet ministers. So in the church we find the same three elements: (1) the multitude, (2) the 'senate' of apostles and presbyters, (3) the apostles. Only there is this difference. The two smaller bodies possess, besides their authority of personal influence, a definite commission received from above—by the apostles from the Lord directly, by the presbyters from the apostles through laying on of hands. Now in the council we see the three elements cooperating in their due order. (1) The 'senate' of apostles and presbyters is summoned (verse 6): it is mainly their business as the responsible authorities to discuss the matter, and they give their opinions or votes (verses 22, and 12 Bezan): the letter of the council runs in their name. (2) But in this senate the apostles take the leading part. They sum up the discussion at the end, and their speeches, which are alone recorded, decide the voice of the assembly. Further, we learn from S. Paul that they had previously discussed with him in private the more doctrinal side of the matter, his gospel, and come to an agreement thereupon. (3) The popular element is not wanting, viz. 'the multitude' of so to speak enfranchised citizens of the church. They are present (see p. 249), and their consent is emphatically expressed (verse 22): without it the mind of the whole church would not have been expressed. There was still (4) a further body to consider, the church of Antioch, which represents distant churches who must have a voice in the decision if it is to be the mind of the universal church. This church was represented by delegates; and besides this, the decision was sent to it in the form of a letter for its acceptance. The brethren of Antioch accepted it with joy. What would have happened if they had refused we are not told.

An interesting parallel to the whole is to be found in II Chronicles ch. xxx. The occasion was Hezekiah's great Passover. (a) *The king had taken counsel and* (b) *his princes and* (c) *all the congregation* (*ecclesia*) *in Jerusalem to keep the Passover...and the matter pleased* (cp. Acts vi 5) *the king and all the congregation; so they established a decree to make proclamation throughout* (d) *all Israel...So the posts went with the letters from the king and his princes* (vv. 2-6). Some received the letters, others scorned them and did not obey. At the feast itself *the whole congregation* (*ecclesia*) *took counsel to keep other seven days* (ver. 23).

Such being the council in its composition and procedure, viz. the whole church acting in due order, it is obvious that details as to summoning, presidency, etc., are of minor importance. They would naturally vary according to the ideas and customs of the age. Thus at Jerusalem S. James presided, evidently because he was the president of the church where the council met. He occupied his own 'chair.'

C. The actual decrees of the council (1) concern, as we have seen, not doctrine—except implicitly, as is of course inevitable,—but matters of practical discipline. But even for such disciplinary rules the guidance of the Holy Spirit is needed and claimed. (2) In form they are not expressed as canons or laws; but in accordance with the customs of the time they are sent in a letter and are also to be published by word of mouth. (3) They are in part local, to meet the local circumstances and heal the local dispute in the church of Syria; and in part temporary, in the sense that when the conditions that occasioned them disappear, they disappear likewise. (One rule which deals with a moral question is of course of perpetual validity.) This character of the precepts explains the conduct of S. Paul at Corinth. There he discusses the whole question of idol-meats on independent grounds without any reference to the letter. For the letter did not run as far as Corinth; and the conditions of the church there were quite different from those at Antioch. But where the conditions remained the same, as in the churches of Syria, they continued to be observed (xxi 25). The later history of the rules tells the same story. (i) The question of idol-meats became a test question between Christianity and paganism, and therefore abstinence was observed until idolatry passed away and with it the prohibition *ipso facto*. (ii, iii) Abstinence from blood is observed to this day in the east, but in the west, after a temporary survival, it died away. (iv) The decree against fornication, as part of the eternal moral law, will never pass away.

D. The decision itself seems open to criticism. It resembles a compromise, and seems to shirk the direct question. It implicitly denied the necessity of circumcision for salvation, yet it did not openly assert the liberty of the Gentiles. It did neither the one thing nor the other. Criticism on this ground however is but superficial. The letter is really a model how to deal with burning questions which do not immediately affect the primary deposit of the faith with which the apostles were entrusted. Such questions, arising out of matters of ritual or discipline, constantly recur in the history of the church, and the best method of solving them is by way of compromise, avoiding dogmatic decisions. This method is generally open to the charge of being illogical, but ultimately it is seen to have been true to the logic of facts. On this occasion there were two parties in the church, diametrically opposed to each other on a particular point. A dogmatic decision would probably have excluded one, but the apostles wished to retain both. So a *modus vivendi* had to be found; each must give up something—they must live and let live; a *via media*, in fact, which pleases neither party, but is successful in the end.

For the apostles were justified in the event. The real decision lay with the church. The council indeed was the church in assembly.

But the church is also a living and growing body; and its very life will decide the question at issue. The council frames an expedient to enable the church to go on living, and then in the life and growth of the church the doctrinal problem will be solved: *solvitur ambulando*, or rather *vivendo*. This is what happened. The burning question was the relation of Jew and Gentile in the church of God. The council did not commit itself to any doctrinal assertions about the law or circumcision, but found a compromise to enable Jew and Gentile to go on living side by side. And the whole problem was soon settled by history itself. The rapid development of Gentile churches caused Jewish ideas and scruples to fall into the background. And at last in the year 70 the destruction of Jerusalem cut away the ground of Judaism not only within the church but without. This great judgement of God, then, we may regard as his final ratification of the council. *Wisdom was justified of her children*[1].

To sum up our conclusions:

(1) The legislative power of the church was called into action by a practical difficulty affecting the peace of the church.

(2) The church assembled together in due order propounds a present practical solution; and as the decision possessed the mark of unanimity, we can be absolutely confident that it was the mind of the Spirit.

(3) The church accepts the solution loyally and lives by it.

(4) God gives his final judgement in history.

---

[1] Renan (*S. Paul* ch. iii) very tersely expresses the wisdom of the apostles: *Ils virent que le seul moyen d'échapper aux grandes questions est de ne pas les résoudre, de prendre des moyens termes qui ne contentent personne, de laisser les problèmes s'user et mourir faute de raison d'être.*

DIVISION II

(= Ch. 16. 6—19. 20)

EXTENSION OF THE CHURCH IN THE ROMAN EMPIRE AND FOUNDATION OF THE CHURCHES OF MACEDONIA, ACHAIA, AND ASIA

From the year 49 to 54,—Claudius (who died Oct. 54) being emperor of Rome, Ventidius Cumanus (48–52) and Felix (52) being procurators of Judaea, and Ananias son of Nedebaios high priest.

It is quite evident that the paragraph xvi 6–10 begins a new division in the Acts. Grammatically the paragraph begins with verse 5. That verse, after S. Luke's style, is a summary of the past which forms the starting point for the future. Indeed even in the preceding passage, xv 36 to xvi 4 (which is a piece of editorial joining), the mind of the writer is divided between the past and the future. It is the preparation for the future and yet looks back to the council. In verse 5 however is reached the limit of S. Paul's original plan, which was 'to revisit the brethren,' and verses 6 to 10 record what was most clearly a divine call to a new work, corresponding to the call in xiii 1–3. This new work begins in Macedonia[1]. As has been already pointed out, it is a mistake to divide S. Paul's work by missionary journeys[2], and from this time Antioch ceases to be his centre. When the brethren there commended him to the grace of God (xv 40), he took his farewell. Henceforth he 'had no certain dwelling place,' and his headquarters changed with the work. To Antioch succeeded Corinth, to Corinth Ephesus. S. Luke's notes of time mark the successive resting places : at first he was with the assembly of the church at Antioch for one year : then he 'sat' at Corinth for eighteen months : then at Ephesus for two years[3]. The visit to Jerusalem and Antioch, which is summed up in one sentence in xviii 22–3, was but an episode in his ministry at Ephesus. Subsequently to that visit, the true conclusion of the whole period is given in the summary note of progress in xix 20; the next verse (21) gives unmistakeably the beginning of the end.

What then is the subject of this division? (1) Having related the internal struggles and development of the church S. Luke now turns to

---

[1] Cp. verse 10 '*go forth* unto Macedonia' with the *sending forth* by the Spirit in xiii 2, 4: cp. xv 38, 40 (*went forth*). [2] The word *journey*, although convenient, is hardly the best expression for a ministry which included long residences of months or even years. *Campaign* would be a better word. The word used by S. Paul and S. Luke is *the work*. [3] xi 26, xviii 11, xix 10.

its external progress. His subject is the rapid extension of Christianity among the Gentiles, especially in three great provinces of the empire, MACEDONIA, ACHAIA, and ASIA; and he describes the firm establishment of the church in their capitals, Thessalonica, Corinth, and Ephesus[1]. Here we have to be on our guard against the influence of modern ideas of geography. The crisis of the work was not, as is popularly supposed, the crossing over from Asia into Europe. The Macedonian did not say 'Come over into Europe,' but 'into Macedonia.' These three great provinces embraced respectively the northern, western and eastern coasts of the Aegean Sea, and they were all members of one great Roman empire, and all enjoyed one great Hellenic civilization. Indeed the Asiatic coast of the Aegean Sea, that is the western part of Asia Minor, was at this period the theatre of the greatest Greek and Graeco-Roman activity; and for a division between the east and the west we must look to the mountains of Taurus rather than to the Bosporus and Dardanelles. To the Romans Syria was the first province of 'the east.'

(2) The foundation of the churches of Macedonia, Achaia, and Asia was the work of S. Paul, and it was his greatest achievement. Ch. xvi 11–xix 19 is really the record of his life's work. It filled a period of five years from 49 to 54; and in the composition of the book it corresponds to the ministry of the Lord in the Gospel (Lk iv 16 to xvii 10 or xviii 30)[2] and of S. Peter in the church of Jerusalem in the first part of the Acts (ii 14–xi 26). This period may be looked upon as that of S. Paul's life-work for another reason. The churches of these provinces gave occasion for those works of his by which he has influenced the whole world, viz. his letters. To them were addressed the *Epistles to the Thessalonians* and *Philippians, to the Corinthians, to the Ephesians* and *Colossians*; the *Epistle to the Galatians* was also written within these years, and at their close that to the *Romans*.

S. Luke has written the history in his usual manner. Out of the multitude of stirring events which must have filled these five years he has selected a few typical pictures. And it is not hard to see the motives which guided the selection. He wanted to illustrate especially (1) the relation of the church to the various secular authorities, and (2) the relation of the faith to the false religions which occupied the field. And (3) in so doing he is able to record the offer made by Christianity to the world. Thus (1) we see S. Paul before the 'duoviri' of a Roman colony, and the 'politarchs' of a provincial and free capital; before the areopagus of Athens which had the prestige of a central religious tribunal in Hellenism, and the supreme secular authority of a Roman proconsul. (2) The true faith has to meet the hatred of the old faith of Judaism and the criticism of philosophers at philosophy's true home and birthplace, the indifference of the cultured circles of Rome

---

[1] xvi 9–10: xviii 12; xix 10. xvii 1: xviii 1: xviii 19, xix 1. [2] The same difficulty as to the exact line of division occurs in the Acts as in the Gospel. The actual work in these provinces goes on for a year after the beginning of the end (in xix 21), and up to xx 3. This makes up a total of six years.

and the superstitions of the populace: it inflicts decisive defeats on its most serious rival, false spiritualism or magic, whether of a Gentile 'python' or of Jewish 'exorcists.' (3) In contrast to all these rivals we have S. Paul's gospel of salvation for the individual, given to the jailor at Philippi: his gospel of the Messiah, fulfilling the aspirations of the Jews, at Thessalonica; his gospel of the revelation of the true God, presented to the philosophic public of Athens.

Incidentally, also, we obtain many interesting glimpses into the inner life of the church. Each of these provincial churches is gratified by the record of one or two of its early converts whose names it will love to cherish—at Philippi there is Lydia, at Thessalonica Jason, at Athens Dionysius and Damaris, at Corinth Titus Justus and Crispus, and at Ephesus Priscilla and Aquila: many other names are also mentioned. Like the Lord, his apostle moves about surrounded by a band of disciples and 'ministers.' Such were Sopater of Beroea, Aristarchus and Secundus of Thessalonica and Gaius of Derbe, Timothy from Galatia and Tychicus and Trophimus from Ephesus; among them were also Erastus and S. Luke himself: and the work they did is abundantly illustrated in the Epistles. The missionaries found their lodging at Philippi in the house of Lydia, with Jason at Thessalonica, and with Priscilla and Aquila at Corinth as no doubt at Ephesus also. In the house of Titus Justus at Corinth and the school of Tyrannus at Ephesus we see the first 'churches,' the parents of the future basilicas. There is also the record of baptisms, of laying on of hands, and of gifts of the Spirit; there are visions of the Lord with signs and miracles. Lastly, from S. Paul's vow and the shaving of his head at Cenchreae, with his anxiety to be at Jerusalem for 'the feast,' we learn that he conformed outwardly to Jewish life and customs.

The authority for this history is of the first class. For the author himself was an actor in the opening scenes. They begin with the first undoubted 'we' passage; and the presence of S. Luke will account for the somewhat disproportionate space allotted to Philippi. From the disappearance of the 'we,' we gather that S. Luke was left behind at Philippi; but that does not exclude his presence with S. Paul at intervals during the five following years. Communication across the Aegean Sea was easy and frequent. In any case he enjoyed intercourse with first-class witnesses, such as the members of S. Paul's company enumerated above. And beyond all this the letters of S. Paul himself are invaluable as documents which enable us both to test S. Luke's narrative and to fill out its scanty framework

Introductory (= Ch. 16. 6—10)

The divine call to the work

The close of the first division (xvi 4) leaves Paul, Silas, Timothy, and possibly S. Luke, at the Pisidian Antioch at the end of their return visit to the cities of South Galatia. Their further course was under the direct guidance of the divine will. By a series of divine prohibitions, they were driven across Asia Minor to its north-west extremity, not knowing whither they were going. But the Holy Ghost knew, for he was calling them to Macedonia; and so this second 'work' of the apostle, like the first (xiii 1-3), is due to the direct action of the Spirit.

The appreciation of this divine call is much obscured by the idea which has been so prevalent that in the single clause *they went through the Phrygian and Galatian region* is contained S. Paul's first visit to (North) Galatia, and the founding of the Galatian churches. The meaning of the 'churches of Galatia' has already been discussed (pp. 195-7). Here we need only reflect on what the old North-Galatian theory would mean. It would mean that on leaving Antioch, the missionaries were prevented from preaching in Asia, and so turned first north through Phrygia and then back again eastwards for one or two hundred miles into North Galatia. And yet the aim of this détour was not Galatia, for S. Paul assures us that only through sickness did he preach there: it must have been some goal further east, Pontus or Cappadocia. However that may be, it was now (on this supposition) that the apostle founded the churches of Galatia, a work which would take at the least several weeks, if not months. Then they retraced their steps westward and arrived *over against Mysia*. Now (1) an omission of a work on this scale would be certainly unprecedented. For it was a work, the record of which would have fallen well within S. Luke's scope, viz. the addition of another great Roman province to the kingdom of Christ. But (2) S. Luke's own language is against the old view. His words give the impression of a single and direct journey—from South Galatia in the south-east to Troas in the north-west. To keep them in this direction they were prevented by the Spirit from preaching either on the right hand or the left, in Bithynia or in Asia: and yet, on the old theory, a great exception was made in favour of the province of Galatia. In particular (3), if our interpretation of S. Luke's use of the participles is correct (see p. 184), the RV is hardly right in translating *having been forbidden*: the prohibition came after the journey through the Galatian region; the order is *they passed through...and were forbidden*. (4) Why does not S. Luke write 'Galatia' like *Asia, Bithynia*, and *Macedonia*? Instead he writes *the Phrygian and Galatian region*, a phrase which would naturally make us think of a 'region'—not a 'province'—which in some sense could be called both Phrygian and Galatian, and that description certainly would not apply to North Galatia. It would however correctly describe that part of Phrygia which was reckoned to Galatia politically, and this was the district in which the Pisidian Antioch was situated : it would in fact be identical with *the region* mentioned in xiii 49. There seems then to be no reason for the gratuitous insertion here of the evangelization of Galatia. And S. Luke's words simply state that after leaving Derbe and Lystra the apostolic company pursued their journey through South Galatia until they reached the border of Asia.

6 And they went through ¹the region of Phrygia and Galatia, ²having been forbidden of the Holy ³Ghost to
7 speak the word in Asia; and when they were come over against Mysia, they assayed to go into Bithynia; and the
8 Spirit ⁴of Jesus suffered them not; and passing by Mysia,
9 they came down to Troas. And a vision appeared to Paul in the night; There was a man of Macedonia standing, beseeching him, and saying, Come over into Macedonia, and
10 help us. ⁵And when he had seen the vision, straightway we sought to go forth into Macedonia, concluding that God had called us for to preach the gospel unto them.

6 When they had *passed through the region* of the city of the Pisidian Antioch, Paul and Silas would be on the border of the province of Asia, which was only about 15 or 20 miles distant from Antioch. This rich and flourishing province, if it had not already been in S. Paul's mind (pp. 204-5), would now at any rate seem the obvious field for work. From Antioch to Ephesus there were two routes. The usual road led first to Apamea, the most important city in Phrygia, 60 miles south-west of Antioch; there it joined the great high road from the east, which next ran down the Lycus valley past Colossae and Laodicea to the Maeander, then along the Maeander to the coast. But from Metropolis, a station on the road to Apamea, a track ran along the higher ground in almost a straight line of about 180 to 200 miles to Ephesus⁶. This route S. Paul seems to have taken on a later occasion (xix 1); and so now probably, in the spring of A.D. 49, the missionaries made their way from Antioch to Metropolis. But what is obvious to man is

---

¹ Gk *the Phrygian and Galatian region*. ² Translate with AV *and were forbidden* (literally *prevented*). ³ Or *Spirit*. ⁴ AV with later MSS omits *of Jesus*. ⁵ Bezan has *When] therefore he arose, he related the vision to us and we perceived [that God had called us for to preach the gospel unto] those in [Macedonia*.
⁶ For this statement Prof. Ramsay is the authority. See his *Church in Roman Empire* p. 94, *Paul the Traveller* p. 265.

not always the choice of God, and S. Paul's plans were overruled. He was to reach Ephesus—but not this way. As 'Asia' was now the great centre of Hellenism, it seemed as if the apostle needed a preliminary training in pure Greek life, just as Ephesus itself with its cosmopolitan elements was a preparation for Rome. Accordingly *the Holy Spirit prevented them from speaking the word to anyone* 7 *while they were in Asia.* The only course, then, was to go to another province. North of Asia and Galatia lay Bithynia. This province contained a number of flourishing cities which offered a rich harvest for the gospel,—Prusa, Nicaea, Nicomedeia, Chalcedon, and Heracleia. Accordingly towards *Bithynia* they turned their steps, crossing Phrygia either to Dorylaeum 100 miles north, or more probably to Cotiaeum 80 or 90 miles north-west: for at Cotiaeum they would have reached a point *over against Mysia*,—which was the geographical term for the north-western part of the province of Asia. But the harvest of Bithynia was not for S. Paul to reap. It was apparently reserved for S. Peter; for his first epistle, written about fifteen years later, was addressed (among others) to the Christians in Bithynia. At the beginning of the next century these had grown so numerous that the worship of idols was falling into neglect, as we learn from a letter of the Roman governor Pliny. At present however *the Spirit of Jesus forbade* the missionaries to cross the frontier. They made an earnest endeavour; but the prohibition was emphatic, and to persevere would be to tempt the 8 Spirit. The only course left open was to turn west. So they *passed through Mysia*—without preaching[1], for they were still in Asia. Whatever road they took would bring them *down to Troas* on the coast, about 200 miles from Cotiaeum as the crow flies. For Troas was the natural terminus for travellers through Mysia. It was its chief port, and lay on one of the main routes to Rome. Here the traveller from the east took ship for Philippi: at Philippi he joined the Egnatian way, which ran straight across Macedonia and Illyricum to Dyrrhachium: from Dyrrhachium he crossed the Adriatic to Brindisium, and thence the road led him across Italy in almost a straight line to Rome.

Troas would have been attractive to S. Paul in any case. It was a busy city and a Roman colony. It had been faithful to Rome in her Asiatic wars, but the neighbouring site of ancient Troy and the legend which made the Romans descendants of the Trojans through Aeneas were more effective in winning privileges for Troas. The city itself—for the whole district was called Troas or the Troad—was not ancient. It had been founded by the successors of Alexander, and called after him ALEXANDREIA TROAS. Then Rome raised it to the rank of a colony, and from Augustus it received its full name of COLONIA AUGUSTA ALEXANDREIA TROAS. It was the special object of imperial favour because the Julian family boasted

---

[1] This is the meaning of the word which is accurately translated *passing by* (omitting): cp. Mk vi 48, Lk xi 42, xv 29.

their descent from Iulus the son of Aeneas, and it was reported in Rome that Julius Caesar had thoughts of transferring the capital from Rome to a new Ilium in the Troad—a plan which would have
9 anticipated the work of Constantine by three centuries. In after years S. Paul preached in Troas, but now on their arrival the travellers had to take counsel as to their further course. There was not much choice: being forbidden to preach in Asia and Bithynia, they must either go on across the sea or return home. But at the critical moment the divine guidance was ready. Macedonia must have been much in S. Paul's mind and *at night* he dreamt of it. He saw *a Macedonian*—such his words proved him to be—who *stood* in front of him and eagerly *entreated him*: '*Cross over into Mace-*
10 *donia and help us*.' In the morning the apostle *related the vision* to the rest of the party. The divine suggestion required a corresponding exercise of judgement on their side. They *concluded* that it was a divine message: '*God has called us to evangelize them*.' It was a call similar to the earlier one at Antioch[1]. At once they *sought* for means to obey. They went down to the harbour and found a ship sailing *on the morrow* (Bezan).

In this paragraph, as in xiii 1-3, the divine leading is unmistakeable, and in it S. Luke sees the cooperation of all three Persons of the Blessed Trinity—the SPIRIT, the SON, and GOD the FATHER (verses 6, 7, 10). The direction is given in a negative manner. In other hindrances S. Paul sometimes saw the work of Satan[2]: here it is God who prevents. How the prohibitions were manifested we are not told. The action of the Holy Ghost is generally associated with prophecy: two of the company were prophets, and the warnings of xxi 11 and xx 23 may suggest an analogy. The guidance of the Lord Jesus seems to have been afforded to S. Paul in visions or 'revelations of the Lord,' such as are recorded in xviii 9-10 and xxii 17-8[3]. Lastly, the hand of God is seen in the overruling of external events and circumstances by the divine providence. Thus in this paragraph are grouped together the various forms of divine intervention which have occurred at previous crises. The chain of events which led to the baptism of Cornelius was ordained of God: the Lord converted Saul by appearing to him face to face: the Holy Ghost called Barnabas and Saul 'to the work[4].' *The Spirit of Jesus* (which is the correct reading in verse 7) marks an important point in theology. After the resurrection the Christ was become altogether spiritual: henceforth his action upon, and revelations to, men take place through his Spirit. Even what seem to be visions of bodies take place in the sphere of spirit. When he sees the Lord S. Paul does not know whether he is in the body or out of the body: he is in a state of *ecstasy*, i.e. literally a standing-out-of the body[5]. Hence we can

---

[1] The word for *call* is the same as in xiii 2.   [2] I Thess ii 18.   [3] Cp. ix 10, II Cor xii 1-9.   [4] x 2-4: ix 5: xiii 2.   [5] Cp. II Cor xii 2, 3: Acts xxii 17.

understand that S. Paul might speak of the Lord appearing to him in a vision as 'the Spirit of Jesus.'

This paragraph is remarkable for another reason. In verse 10 S. Luke suddenly discloses himself in the word *we*[1]. The natural inference is that here at Troas he met or joined the party for the first time. Further thought however shews that this inference is by no means inevitable, and we rather conclude that he had for long been a member of the party[2]. Several times already we have had occasion to suspect the presence of S. Luke. And now the decided way in which he identifies himself with the work of the apostolic band is almost convincing—*we sought to go forth, God hath called us, we spake unto the women, she cried after us saying These men*[3] etc. This is hardly the language of a new comer, or a new worker,— certainly not of a recent convert. S. Luke's modesty is sufficient to account for previous silence about himself, and it is not hard to find a reason for his breaking the silence now. It is evident, as we shall see presently, that he had a very intimate connexion with the church at Philippi, and now that we are coming to the founding of that church, S. Luke 'the evangelist,' sharing the joy of S. Paul in spiritual fatherhood, is anxious to let the Philippians know the share he had in their foundation. Yet even here his modesty receives a new proof. He does not mention his name, —the Philippians knew that,—he simply lets his pen slip from *they* into *we*. Possibly there may be a simpler explanation. The situation at Troas somewhat resembles that at Perga, when John Mark turned back (xiii 13). And if there is any emphasis on the word *concluding*[4], it may point to some discussion, if not division of counsels. The direct form of speech *God hath called us* reads as the quotation of an actual utterance. The voice of S. Luke may have decided the balance. In any case it was a momentous decision, and as the writer goes over the scene, the recollection of the anxious feelings and of the victory he helped to win is too much for him and almost unconsciously he writes *we sought.*

SECTION I (= Ch. 16. 11—17. 15)

MACEDONIA

11 The new enterprise began with good omens. The missionaries had a good passage. On the first day *they had a straight run to* the isle of *Samothrace* where they anchored for the night, *and the next day to Neapolis*, and so accomplished in two days the run of 125 miles, which on a return voyage took five days. Neapolis was the port of Philippi which lay ten miles inland, and thither the party 12 took their way. *And thence to Philippi* S. Luke writes, as if

---

[1] For the first time in our text. The Bezan text had it in xi 27. [2] So S. Irenaeus quotes: *we came to Troas*. [3] vv. 10, 13, 17. [4] It occurred in ix 22.

copying from a diary, and then—what is quite unique for him—adds a description of the town. It was (1) *first of the district*, (2) *a city of Macedonia*, (3) *a colony*.

So S. Paul entered *Macedonia*. Though akin to the Greeks, the Macedonians were a distinct race. They were a simple, rough, hardy people, who in the glorious time of Greek history had been looked upon by the Athenians as almost barbarians. But their time was to come. First, under their king Philip (B.C. 360–336), they shattered the power of the Greeks. Then, under his son Alexander the Great (B.C. 336–323), they conquered the Persian Empire. So it was the Macedonians who established in the east the Greek civilization and the Greek monarchies, which reached as far as India. The royal houses of Syria and Egypt, and the aristocracy of Alexandria and Antioch, were Macedonian in blood and origin. The great cities of Asia Minor and Syria bear Macedonian names: and in following the history of the Acts this connexion of Macedonia with the east must be borne in mind. In spite of their prosperity, the Macedonians at home did not lose their hardy character. Of all the countries east of the Adriatic they offered the most stubborn resistance to the rising power of Rome. But after three obstinate wars (215–168) they were conquered; in 147 Macedonia became the first province of Rome beyond the Adriatic; and the more completely to destroy the national spirit of independence, the Romans broke up the country into four *districts*, each under a separate jurisdiction. This stubborn national character can still be recognized in the Acts and Epistles. In the cities of Macedonia we find the people the important factor. With the more simple faith of a hardy rustic race—very different from the *blasé* indifference of an Athens or a Corinth,—they are hard to win and easily prejudiced against a new religion, and from each city S. Paul is driven away by a popular tumult. But on the other side, when won their national sturdiness displays itself in their intense fidelity and affectionateness. To none of his converts was S. Paul bound with closer bonds than to the disciples of Thessalonica and Philippi. Macedonian independence also asserted itself in the comparative freedom allowed to their women. So in the Acts in each city, at Philippi, Thessalonica and Beroea, we find mention of the God-fearing women[1]; and certainly in the church at Philippi the women Lydia, Euodia and Syntyche, stand in a very prominent position.

§ 1 *The entrance into Philippi*

In the First District of Macedonia on the borders of Thrace lay the city of *Philippi*. The surrounding mountains were once rich in gold, and they had been worked from an early date by Greek settlers. But the savage Thracians had always proved troublesome neighbours. To hold these in check Philip of Macedon founded a new city on a

---

[1] xvi 13, xvii 4, 12, cp. the Pisidian Antioch xiii 50. It may be also significant that the title *brethren* rather than *disciples* is used of the Macedonian Christians.

strong site, which he called, after himself, Philippi. After two more centuries of working, however, the mines had become exhausted, when a great event of history gave Philippi a new notoriety. Its citadel was built on a steep hill between the mountains and a marshy lake, and so it commanded the road which formed the only communication by land between the east and the west. This defile was the place where, during the Roman civil wars, in B.C. 42, the armies of the republicans Brutus and Cassius and of the triumvirs Antony and Octavian, advancing from east and west respectively, met together, and where the decisive battle was fought. In gratitude for their victory the triumvirs made Philippi a Roman colony and settled it with soldiers. Seventeen years later, when Octavian, the future Augustus, defeated Antony at Actium, Philippi received another settlement of veteran soldiers. Thus COLONIA AUGUSTA JULIA PHILIPPI VICTRIX was a thoroughly Latin town when S. Paul entered it, and its citizens were *Romans* (verse 21). In keeping with this both the tone and language of the inscriptions found on the now deserted site are Latin. Most interesting of these is an *album* (i.e. roll) of a *Collegium Cultorum Silvani* or *Society of the Worshippers of Silvanus*, one of the primitive Latin deities. For it was just as such another society or collegium that the new Christian body would present itself to the citizens—with this difference, that the new collegium was *illicit*, that is, it had not yet received sanction from the authorities. Besides the worship of the Latin deities, e.g. Silvanus, Diana, Minerva, and of course of the emperor[1], we find devotion paid to the Thracian Liber and also to a Phrygian deity, Men. There was some kinship of race between the Thracians and Phrygians and the same nature-worship prevailed among both. Thus a connexion between Philippi and Asia Minor already existed, and in the Acts a hint is given of another channel of communication, viz. the purple trade with Lydia. The Jews however had not been attracted to Philippi. There were some women, 'infected with the Jewish superstition' (as the classic writers would phrase it), but there was no synagogue. This combines with the other evidence to shew that Philippi was not a very important city[2], and it makes the prominence of Philippi in the Acts more remarkable. For (1) much more space is allotted to Philippi than to the far greater city Thessalonica, the capital of the province; more indeed than to Athens or Corinth. (2) As there was no synagogue at Philippi, it would have been much more in accordance with S. Paul's custom to have gone on straight to Thessalonica. He passed by Amphipolis and Apollonia (xvii 1-2), why not Philippi? (3) It is the only city which S. Luke describes, and the description itself has puzzled commentators. For in fact Amphipolis, and not Philippi, had been *the first city of the district*. But we are not acquainted with all the administrative changes of antiquity and very likely when Philippi was made a colony it was given precedence over Amphipolis. At any rate it may have claimed

---

[1] At Troas has been found the inscription of a Philippian who was priest of the divine Augustus. [2] Compared e.g. with Beroea, where the Jews had a synagogue.

precedence[1]. This perhaps suggests the explanation. The description of the city betrays some civic patriotism. The writer is anxious (a) to vindicate the claim of Philippi as against Amphipolis, (b) to make it clear that Philippi was in *Macedonia* not Thrace, (c) to remind his readers that it was a *colony*. Of the five colonies[2] we visit in the Acts Philippi is the only one which is called by that name. The Philippians were evidently proud of their city—*we are Romans* they say (verse 21) —and perhaps it is not by mere accident that in the Acts the word *city* occurs more often in connexion with Philippi than with any other city except Jerusalem, while in his Epistle to the Philippians S. Paul twice refers to the true 'citizenship' of Christians[3]. Besides interest in the city, the narrative reveals personal acquaintance with it on the part of the writer. This is shewn by its vivid touches, like the evidently local expression in verse 13 *to river*[4], which resembles the English *to town*.

On the ground of this evident connexion some critics, notably Professor Ramsay[5], have concluded that S. Luke was a native of Philippi. But this conclusion is not really necessary. Prof. Ramsay lays great stress on S. Luke's Greek characteristics; but in fact Philippi was a Macedonian and Latin city rather than Greek. S. Luke, as we have found reasons for believing, had been chiefly associated with the east, and certainly from the text here it appears that on his arrival at Philippi, he had no personal friends in the city, nor intimate knowledge of the locality: they were taken in by a stranger (verse 15), and they guessed rather than knew of a *proseucha* at the river side. From this time however Philippi was S. Luke's home for a long period, till A.D. 55 (xx 6). A residence there of six years would sufficiently account for his catching the *genius loci*; and if S. Luke played a prominent part in the evangelization of the Philippians, and was left in charge of their church, his strong affection would soon identify him with the civic patriotism of his brethren[6]. If however we still feel that a closer relationship is wanted, it is rather to be looked for in the existence (of which Prof. Ramsay has reminded us[7]) of Macedonian families in the Hellenistic cities of the east. Philippi may have been the home of S. Luke's ancestors, and this would have made him eager for the evangelization of Macedonia, and for beginning at Philippi.

11 Setting sail therefore[8] from Troas, we made a straight course to Samothrace, and the day following to Neapolis;

---

[1] This then makes unnecessary the very plausible conjecture that the original reading was *of the first district*: it would be tame compared with our text. The word *district* was rare in this territorial sense, but it has now been met with in Egyptian papyri. In the east *First* was a complimentary title conferred upon cities, but the custom does not seem to have prevailed in Europe, so we cannot translate a '*first*' *city of the district*.   [2] i.e. Pisidian Antioch, Lystra, Troas, Corinth, Philippi.   [3] *City* occurs 4 times, in vv. 12, 20, 39. Cp. Phil i 27, iii 20. For an instance of civic patriotism on S. Paul's part cp. xxi 39 *Tarsus—no mean city*. [4] That is the literal translation of the Greek for *by a riverside*.   [5] *Paul the Traveller etc.* pp. 200-10.   [6] Notice *this city* in verse 12 as if that passage was written at Philippi.   [7] *Paul etc.* pp. 389-90.   [8] Bezan adds *on the morrow*.

12 and from thence to Philippi, which is ¹a city of Macedonia, the first of the district, a *Roman* colony: and we were in this city tarrying certain days.
13 And on the sabbath day we went forth without the ²gate by a river side, ³where we supposed there was a place of prayer; and we sat down, and spake unto the women which
14 were come together. And a certain woman named Lydia, a seller of purple, of the city of Thyatira, one that worshipped God, heard us: whose heart the Lord opened, to give heed
15 unto the things which were spoken by Paul. And when she was baptized, and her household, she besought us, saying, If ye have judged me to be faithful to the Lord, come into my house, and abide *there*. And she constrained us.

12 The travellers evidently arrived early in the week. As there was no Jewish quarter, they *stayed* at some inn and waited for the sabbath. Where there was no synagogue, the Jews generally preferred to say their prayers by the waterside, whether of sea or river, for this afforded opportunity for their ablutions⁴. A mile west of the town the river Gangites flowed across the plain and on its bank there was a simple enclosure which served as the substitute for a synagogue for the use of those inclined to Judaism. Such a place was called a *Proseucha* or *Prayer*(-place), though the term
13 could also be used of a synagogue⁵. The travellers had noticed this enclosure and *had taken it to be a proseucha*, and thither they went *on the sabbath day*. Their conjecture proved to be correct, and they found several *women* of the God-fearing class, possibly with
14 some Jewesses among them, *assembled* for prayer. One of these women at least was of considerable position in the town. She was really a native of *Thyatira*, a city of Lydia in the province of Asia, and so she was called after her country *Lydia*. Purple dyeing was a Lydian industry which flourished especially at Thyatira⁶, where there was a guild of dyers. Their trade with the west would pass through Troas and Philippi, and at Philippi Lydia had settled as *a seller of purple*. She was evidently a widow and wealthy, but her name indicates the reverse of blue blood or aristocratic connexions. For racial names such as 'Lydus,' 'Thrax' (Lydian, Thracian), etc.

---

¹ AV *the chief city of that part of Macedonia and a Colony*, Gk *first of the district of Macedonia a city a colony*. ² AV reads *city*. ³ AV with later MSS reads *where prayer was wont to be made*. ⁴ Cp. xxi 5 and Ezra viii 15, 21. Josephus (*Ant.* xiv 10. 23) quotes a decree of Halicarnassus allowing the Jews *to make their prayers* (Gk *proseuchas*) *on the sea-shore according to the custom of their fathers*; and 200 years after Christ Tertullian still mentions *orationes litorales* (*prayers on the shore*) as a characteristic of the Jews. ⁵ As in Juvenal (III 296) *in qua te quaero proseucha?* ⁶ Later, when the Apocalypse was written, we find Thyatira the seat of one of the seven churches of Asia.

were usually borne by slaves; so even Lydia may have been a freed woman. It must have been a godsend to the little company to have secured a preacher, but the missionaries preferred to *sit and talk* with them. They all talked apparently, but Lydia *was listening*[1] with the keenest interest to *Paul.* His words went home, because the way was prepared by the divine grace, as at the Pisidian Antioch: only instead of the military metaphor, here S. Luke uses that of the door[2]. *The Lord opened* the door of *her heart to give heed,* just as after his resurrection he had opened the mind of the disciples to
15 understand the scriptures (Lk xxiv 45). The gospel of S. Paul included baptism; Lydia therefore *was baptized*[3], perhaps that very day, and with her all *her household.* This happened also in the case of the jailor, and of Crispus at Corinth, and Cornelius at Caesarea. It was due to the great power of the parent or head of the house over his family or household. This authority was a relic of the patriarchal stage of early civilization, and from this we can see that the 'patria potestas' was still a living reality not only at Rome but throughout the ancient world. Almost as a matter of course the father set the religion for his 'family' of children and servants[4].

S. Luke then adds one of those touches which give such vividness and interest to the history. It gives us a glimpse into home life, and has a companion picture in the Gospel—in the house of Martha and Mary at Bethany. Lydia invited the missionaries to *stay* with her, 'seeing (she said) that *ye have judged me to be a true believer in the Lord*' (verse 1) by admitting me to baptism. For the sake of the freedom of the gospel S. Paul was very reluctant either to lay himself under obligation to his converts or to expose himself to the charge of interested motives; but Lydia was urgent. *She constrained* them, as the disciples at Emmaus had constrained the Lord (Lk xxiv 29). So she proved herself indeed a woman 'who used hospitality to strangers,' and in taking them in she 'entertained angels unawares[5].' Her house became the home of the four missionaries and the first 'church' in Philippi (verse 40). When Paul and Silas went on to Thessalonica, it continued to be S. Luke's home; and when pecuniary help was sent to Paul, no doubt it came mainly out of Lydia's wealth. Lydia is one of the striking women who were, so to speak, the nursing mothers of the infant church (Isai xlix 23). Like Dorcas she was a woman devoted to good works, like Eunice she entertained the apostle, like Mary the mother of John Mark she had a church in her house, like Priscilla she 'laboured with the apostle in the gospel.' Indeed many are inclined to identify her with the 'true yokefellow' of Phil iv 3.

---

[1] Like the lame man at Lystra xiv 9.   [2] xiii 48: for 'the door' cp. xiv 27.
[3] So at Samaria (viii 6, 12) *baptism* had followed upon *giving heed.*   [4] No doubt some families that were baptized contained infants, and so these passages have been used as an argument for infant baptism. But that practice rests on surer foundations.   [5] 1 Tim v 10, Hebr xiii 2.

The 'python' and expulsion from Philippi

S. Luke tells us nothing of the work at Philippi. From allusions in the following verses we gather that the *proseucha* continued to be its centre, and that the evangelists became well known in the city. They were recognized as Jews and as on a mission from the God of the Jews. The burden of their message was salvation; but to accept it involved a change of life, and so the conversions that were made caused some considerable disturbance in social and civic life. To this picture we can add colour from the Epistle to the Philippians. An air of joy and thankfulness pervades that epistle, and for one reason S. Paul's work here must have been exceptionally happy: it was almost the only place where he was free from the deadly hostility of his fellow-countrymen. The characteristic of this church was work. Timothy laboured as a son with a father, and no doubt Silas and S. Luke did likewise. The new converts proved from the first zealous fellow-workers in the gospel: among the labourers were Clement and Epaphroditus. Women also were prominent in the evangelistic work: two ladies, Euodia and Syntyche, with others, 'wrestled together' with S. Paul[1] As in the churches of Galatia (xiv 23) a body of rulers was formed, consisting, in this case, of two classes or orders—presbyters, here called *bishops* (*episcopi*) i.e. overseers of the church, and *deacons* or ministers of the church. Of this body it would be natural to suppose that S. Luke acted as president when left behind by the apostle[2].

Of all this work of building up S. Luke says nothing: he passes straight on to the incident which led to their expulsion from Philippi. This is to be carefully noted as the first conflict of Christianity, apart from Judaism, with the heathen world. (1) We learn that the cause of hostility was not the faith in itself but the interference with gain caused by righteousness. (2) We learn 'the way of salvation' which is held out to the Gentiles: cp. ii 38. (3) We find a lesson in S. Paul's behaviour. While prepared to suffer personal injustice, he claims his civil rights and privileges; but he also yields to the powers that be (Rom xiii 1-7), that is, so long as it is possible to follow the Lord's directions—'when they persecute you in one city flee into another' (Mat x 23). For illustration of this paragraph we may compare (*a*) the demoniacs in the Gospel, especially Lk iv 41, viii 26-39, and the exorcists at Ephesus, Acts xix 13-16 : (*b*) the riot at Ephesus, xix 23-41 : and (*c*) the deliverance of S. Peter from prison, xii 6-17, and in the OT of Jeremiah (Jer xxxviii 7-13).

16 And it came to pass, as we were going to the place of prayer, that a certain maid having [3]a spirit of divination met us, which brought her masters much gain by soothsaying.

---

[1] Cp. Phil ii 19-22: iv 3 and ii 25: iv 2-3. [2] Phil i 1: this is the earliest appearance of the title *episcopi* and of *deacons* (as an order). [3] Gk *a spirit, a python.*

17 The same following after Paul and us cried out, saying,
These men are ¹servants of the Most High God, which
18 proclaim unto you the way of salvation. And this she did
for many days. But Paul, being sore troubled, turned and
said to the spirit, I charge thee in the name of Jesus Christ
to come out of her. And it came out that very hour.
19   But when her masters saw that the hope of their gain was
²gone, they laid hold on Paul and Silas, and dragged them
20 into the marketplace before the rulers, and when they had
brought them unto the ³magistrates, they said, These men,
21 being Jews, do exceedingly trouble our city, and set forth
customs which it is not lawful for us to receive, or to observe,
22 being Romans. ⁴And the multitude rose up together against
them: and the magistrates rent their garments off them, and
23 commanded to beat them with rods. And when they had
laid many stripes upon them, they cast them into prison,
24 charging the jailor to keep them safely: who, having received
such a charge, cast them into the inner prison, and made
their feet fast in the stocks.
25   But about midnight Paul and Silas were praying and
singing hymns unto God, and the prisoners were listening to
26 them; and suddenly there was a great earthquake, so that
the foundations of the prison-house were shaken: and immediately all the doors were opened; and every one's bands
27 were loosed. And the jailor being roused out of sleep, and
seeing the prison doors open, drew his sword, and was about
to kill himself, supposing that the prisoners had escaped.
28 But Paul cried with a loud voice, saying, Do thyself no
29 harm: for we are all here. And he called for lights, and
sprang in, and, trembling for fear, fell down ⁵before Paul and
30 Silas, and brought them out, ⁶and said, Sirs, what must I do
31 to be saved? And they said, Believe on the Lord Jesus⁷,
32 and thou shalt be saved, thou and thy house. And they
spake the word of ⁸the Lord unto him, with all that were in

---

¹ Gk *slaves*.   ² Gk *come out*.   ³ Gk *stratēgi* (=marg *praetors*).
⁴ Bezan has *And*] *a great multitude rose up together against them, crying out: then* [*the magistrates*.   ⁵ Bezan has *at the feet of* [*Paul*.   ⁶ Bezan reads *and*] *when he had secured the rest he came to them and* [*said*.   ⁷ AV with later MSS adds *Christ*.   ⁸ Marg *God* (ℵB).

33 his house. And he took them the same hour of the night, and washed their stripes; and was baptized, he and all his,
34 immediately. And he brought them up into his house, and set ¹meat before them, and rejoiced greatly, with all his house, having believed in God.
35 But when it was day, ²the magistrates sent the ³serjeants,
36 saying, ⁴Let those men go. And the jailor reported the words to Paul, *saying*, The magistrates have sent to let you go:
37 now therefore come forth, and go in peace. But Paul said unto them, They have beaten us publicly, uncondemned, men that are Romans, and have cast us into prison; and do they now cast us out privily? nay verily; but let them come them-
38 selves and bring us out. And the serjeants reported these words unto the magistrates: and they feared, when they heard
39 that they were Romans; ⁵and they came and besought them; and when they had brought them out, they asked
40 them to go away from the city. And they went out of the prison, and entered into *the house of* Lydia: and when they had seen the brethren, ⁶they comforted them, and departed.

16 Philippi was not exempt from superstition and attempts to trade upon the spiritual cravings of man. A well-known figure in the city was a young *slave girl*, seemingly a ventriloquist, who was credited with a power of divination⁷. She belonged to some *masters*⁸, possibly a corporation of priests, who made a good *business* out of her *fortune-telling*. This slave girl is a contrast to the well-to-do Lydia; and, like the maidservant who troubled Peter in Caiaphas' palace, she was

---

¹ Gk *a table*. ² Bezan reads *the magistrates*] *assembled together at the market-place and remembering the earthquake which had happened were afraid and* [*sent*. ³ Gk *lictors*. ⁴ Bezan reads *Let those men*] *whom ye received yesterday go. And the jailor went in and* [*reported*. ⁵ Bezan reads *and they came*] *with many friends into the prison and besought them to come forth, saying 'we did not know concerning your affairs that ye are just men,' and they brought them out and besought them saying 'go forth from this city, lest again they make a tumult against us crying out against you.'* ⁶ Bezan reads *they*] *related what things the Lord had done for them and* [*comforted* (marg *exhorted*) *them*. ⁷ The right reading is, as RV margin, *having a spirit, a python* (not as AV *a spirit of Python*). Now *a python* may be in apposition to *a spirit* or to *a slave girl*. Python was the name of a great dragon at Delphi slain by Apollo, who accordingly received the title of *Pythius*. Hence probably arose the connexion of the name with divination. According to Plutarch—and he is supported by other authorities (see Wetstein on this place)—in his time a ventriloquist was called a *python*. This will throw light on the present incident: the girl was probably a ventriloquist. Ventriloquism like insanity was closely associated with spiritual agency, and ascribed to the possession of a spirit. In the Greek OT the Hebrew for *having a familiar spirit* is generally translated by *ventriloquist*, e.g. in I Sam xxviii 3–9, Lev xix 31 etc. ⁸ The Greek word for *Lord, Master, Sir* (verse 30), is the same.

to be the involuntary cause of much evil to S. Paul¹. For she had formed a habit of intercepting the missionary party *on their way to* 17 *the proseucha*, and then, *following close behind them, she kept crying out* loudly *These men are slaves of the Most High God, who proclaim unto you the way of salvation.* The evil spirits in the Gospel (as at Ephesus, xix 15) appear to have had a more than human insight into the Lord's personality, but in this girl's conduct there need not be anything that is impatient of a natural explanation. A belief in one supreme deity and the desire for salvation were widespread. Several of the gods were worshipped under the name of *Saviour*, and *God Most High* is found in inscriptions. The latter was the term used by the demoniac in the Gospel, and to judge from its use in scripture, it would seem to have been the usual Gentile title for the God of the Jews². Further, there were in the ancient world various classes of persons who had consecrated themselves to the service of some deity, for a special purpose or a special time, or who were under his special inspiration. Such persons were regarded as belonging to the god as much as the ordinary slaves who were temple property. The slave girl, then, had taken Paul and Silas for two such inspired *slaves of God*; and she shewed the impression they 18 made on herself in this excited fashion. It was very inconvenient to them personally: but it was more *vexing*³ for the gospel's sake. The Lord's example had shewn that the gospel was to be propagated neither by the testimony of evil spirits, nor by the methods of excitement. *Paul* at last was forced to *bid the spirit go out from her*. The maiden returned to her right mind, but at the same time lost her power of ventriloquism, and so with the spirit *there went* 19 *out* also *the hope of* further *business* or gain.

Her owners, thus robbed of their profit, determined on revenge; nor was it difficult to find an opportunity. Besides the general unpopularity of the Jews, the preaching of the Most High God must have been stealing converts from the votaries of Silvanus, Liber, and Men (p. 280). Accordingly on a court-day, when *the magistrates* were holding their sessions in the town-hall in *the marketplace* (p. 309), *they seized hold of Paul and Silas, dragged them* thither 20 and formally *presented them*⁴ *to the duumvirs*. After the pattern of the consuls at Rome, the chief magistrates of a Roman colony were two in number and their official title was 'duoviri' i.e. 'the two-men⁵.'

¹ Lk xxii 56 and parallels. Rhoda (xii 13) makes a third *slave girl*. They had their place in the gospel as well as the rich. ² Cp. Lk viii 28, Mk v 7. Dr Plummer in his commentary on S. Luke quotes Gen xiv 20, 22, Num xxiv 16, Isai xiv 14, Micah vi 6, Daniel iii 26, iv 24, 32, v 18, 21 etc. It is nowhere used of God by Christians or Jews in the NT. ³ The Greek word is the same as in iv 2.
⁴ See xii 6 (p. 177 note⁷) and Lk xxiii 14: for the *dragging* cp. viii 3. All the authorities (*rulers*) of the city were assembled, but the owners present their indictment to the proper chief magistrates, the *duoviri*. ⁵ The RV gives *praetors* in the margin. But the duumvirs of colonies did not enjoy that proud Roman title; at least not now, if they had done so in earlier times. *Stratēgos* was the Greek term for other Roman titles besides *praetor*. See Mr Haverfield in *Journal of Theol. Studies*, vol. I pp. 434-5.

The charge preferred was that *these Jews were causing great dis-*
21 *turbances in the city by proclaiming customs which it was unlawful for Romans to observe.* In other words they were introducing an 'unlawful religion' (*religio illicita*). Judaism indeed, from which the accusers did not distinguish Christianity, was a 'lawful religion[1].' But the missionaries were evidently proselytizing; and it was one thing for a Jew to live as a Jew and another for a Roman citizen to adopt Jewish customs. These customs interfered, for instance, with service in the army and with the various ceremonies connected with the public state worship. Without inculcating specifically Jewish customs, S. Paul certainly turned away his converts from idols, and therefore from the worship of Rome and the Augustus. It was in these last words *being Romans* that the sting lay. The rumour
22 of disloyalty to the sacred name of *Roman* was enough *to rouse up* the mob of '*Romans*' in the market-place as one man; the hint of treason would cast magistrates and all alike into a panic. There was then no time for legal proceedings; prompt measures had to be taken, and to satisfy the people as well as themselves *the duumvirs gave orders* for them to be *stripped* naked[2] and *beaten* by the lictors on the spot[3]. In the panic and tumult it would have been useless to plead their citizenship, and Paul and Silas bowed their backs to
23 the rods. After a severe beating they were sent *to prison. The jailor* received a special *charge* to keep them in all *security* as dangerous political prisoners. He was no mere turn-key, but the governor of the prison,—probably of the rank of a centurion, like Cornelius at Caesarea, of whose history there is much to remind us here. The prison probably stood on the side of, and was partially excavated out of, the steep hill on which the citadel was built, with
24 the jailor's house above it (verse 34); *the inner prison* at least would have been most likely a cell excavated in the rock. Into this cell the jailor now thrust his prisoners, just as they were, with their blood-stained backs unwashed; and he took the additional precaution of *securing their feet in the stocks.*

---

[1] Judaism is called a *religio licita* in Tertull. *Apolog.* 21. We do not know the actual regulations of the Roman law in relation to *lawful* or *unlawful religions*. Probably only a religion which proselytized would come within the scope of the law. The case is different with the societies or *collegia*. By a Lex Julia definite sanction from the state was required for such associations: otherwise they were *illicita* or illegal. Some exceptions however were tolerated. See E. G. Hardy *Christianity and the Roman Government* § ix (Longmans 1894). [2] The stripping in public would be an additional insult which the apostles as orientals would feel keenly. S. Paul in writing to the Thessalonians specially mentions the *shameful* treatment they had received at Philippi (I Thess ii 2). Prof. Ramsay (*Paul etc.* p. 219) thinks that the praetors tore their own garments in horror at the blasphemy against the majesty of Rome, like the apostles at Lystra (xiv 14) and Caiaphas at the Lord's trial (Mt xxvi 65). But this would have required either the middle voice, or a different preposition (διά for περί), in the Greek. II Macc iv 38 is strongly in favour of the usual interpretation. The rest of the account above is much indebted to the Professor. [3] The lictors were the attendants on Roman magistrates and beat criminals with the rods or *fasces* which they carried. This is one of the three *beatings with rods* of II Cor xii 25.

25 *At midnight*, after all this, the rest of *the prisoners* were astonished to hear *Paul and Silas praying aloud and singing hymns to God, and they listened* eagerly. Night was a usual time for Christian worship, as we shall see at Troas (**xx** 7), and perhaps these midnight 'lauds' represent the apostle's customary practice¹.
26 *Suddenly* there was felt the shock of *an earthquake*. It is not likely that Paul and Silas had asked for such a special intervention, but we may look upon it as a sign of divine favour in answer to prayer, like the earthquake which followed the prayer of the Twelve in iv 31². It was a *great* shock, for *the foundations of the* whole building *were shaken*, the wooden bolts which held *the doors* were flung back out of their sockets, and *the fetters* by which the prisoners were chained to the walls were *loosened* in their holes. These effects are quite intelligible if the prison was in great part excavated in the rock as we have suggested³. It was an excellent opportunity for escape, but the prisoners themselves were for the moment panic-stricken, and S. Paul, who first realized the situation,
27 would have restrained them⁴. *The jailor* too, awakened by the same shock, came down with all haste from his private house; for as jailor he was responsible for his prisoners with his life⁵. When he caught sight of *the doors* all flung *open*, he concluded that the prisoners were escaped; in a sudden access of despair *he drew his sword, and was on the point of committing suicide*, when he was
28 arrested by *a loud cry*. If he was standing at the outer door, his movements must have been visible from the dark interior, and S. Paul perceiving his intent cried out to reassure him '*we are all here, every one*.' The loud cry out of the dark and the sudden recall from the brink of death, following close upon the shock of the
29 earthquake, completed the overthrow of the jailor's nerves. *He called* to his servants *to bring lights* and himself *sprang into* the prison; there *shaking for fear* he first *fell down* as an act of
30 reverence or worship⁶ at the feet of *Paul and Silas*, and then *brought them out* into the courtyard. He had now regained sufficient self-possession *to secure the rest of the prisoners*, and then returning to Paul and Silas asked *Sirs⁷, what must I do to be saved?* Paul and Silas were well known at Philippi as 'slaves of the Most High God,' and they had openly proclaimed 'a way of salvation.' Only within the last twenty-four hours they had been cruelly and shamefully treated on the very ground of their religion, and now there could be but one conclusion. The Most High God had avenged his servants: they were no impostors but true messengers of God⁸. The jailor himself may have been, like

---

¹ Ps cxix 62. ² We may see a reminiscence of the earthquake in II Thess ii 2 (*shaken*): cp. also Acts xvii 13 (*stirring up=shaking*). ³ Otherwise so great a shock would have caused the building to fall. ⁴ So verse 28 implies. He exercised a similar restraint in xxvii 30–2. ⁵ Cp. xii 19, xxvii 42. ⁶ Like Cornelius before Peter, x 25. ⁷ See p. 286 note ⁵. ⁸ For other sudden revulsions of feeling cp. xxviii 6 and xiv 19.

Cornelius, a seeker after salvation; at any rate he would be terrified at the harsh treatment he had meted out to the 'slaves of the Most High' and earnestly crave to be delivered from the divine vengeance. No wonder then that he asked how he could be saved
31 The answer was ready, *Believe on the Lord Jesus*[1]. This was S. Peter's message to Cornelius: like that, it would need explana-
32 tion, nor would Paul and Silas lose any opportunity. Accordingly, tired, sore, unwashed as they were, *they spake to the jailor and all his establishment* of warders, slaves, and family, who had gathered round, the same *word of God*[2]. That word embraced the sending of Jesus to be the Christ, his life of good works, his crucifixion and resurrection, the promise of forgiveness and of the gift of the Spirit to all who should repent and be baptized. Their audience received
33 the word; nothing hindered them from being baptized, and the whole company went to the prison well or fountain. Then at last the jailor recollected the condition of Paul and Silas, and first *he washed* their bodies, and then they gave *him and all his* the water
34 of *baptism*, the 'washing of regeneration and renewing of the Holy Ghost'[3].' After this the jailor *took them up to his own* (i.e. the governor's) *lodgings and spread a table before them*. Paul and Silas needed food, but recollecting the religious significance of the common meal (pp. 36–40) we have little doubt that they and the new converts partook of the food in the first place as a sign of fellowship in the new faith: in other words it was a 'table of the Lord,' an agape and eucharist, and so the completion of their communion with the church[4]. Such a sudden salvation and successful sequel was followed by more than joy—by *exultation*, which pervaded *the whole house*.
35 *In the morning the lictors* came with a not very courteous order to the jailor to *dismiss*[5] *those men*. The reason is not far to seek. The magistrates had felt the shock of the earthquake; like the jailor they also had connected it with the two prisoners and were alarmed. This the Bezan text states for us explicitly. Now
37 however S. Paul's time had come. One of the most valued privileges of the Roman citizenship was immunity from corporal chastisement. According to Cicero 'to fetter a Roman citizen was a crime, to scourge him a scandal, to slay him—parricide!' The actual legal exemptions are difficult to ascertain, but a Porcian law expressly forbade the scourging of a Roman citizen. Under the republic an arbitrary governor like Verres might not scruple even to beat to death a Greek who possessed the citizenship in spite of his

---

[1] The Jewish title of the *Christ* would not have been very intelligible to the jailor and is omitted here by the best mss. [2] x 43, xi 14: x 36. [3] Titus iii 5. The analogy of ix 17–9, x 44–8, xix 2–6 would lead us to infer that there was also laying on of hands with the gift of the Holy Spirit. The emphatic word for *all* seems to shew that the whole establishment, and not merely the jailor's wife and children, were baptized. [4] Cp. ix 19. [5] The Greek word is used of the liberation of Barabbas (Lk xxiii 25); and also of the dismissals of the missionaries by the church (e.g. xiii 3), and the Lord's servant in the *Nunc dimittis*.

cries *Civis Romanus sum*: even then Cicero, with some rhetorical exaggeration, could declare that 'in the most distant lands, even among barbarians, that cry has often brought succour and safety.' The emperors however were very careful to maintain the dignity of the citizenship; about this very time Claudius deprived the city of Rhodes of its freedom for having crucified some citizens of Rome. And now Paul and Silas *who were Romans* had been *publicly beaten*, and that *without a hearing*[1]. The utter illegality of the whole of the proceedings was a great aggravation of the offence. The magistrates had put themselves in the wrong and S. Paul would give them a lesson. He would vindicate justice for its own sake; and also secure protection for his brethren at Philippi from similar illegalities in the future. Accordingly Paul and Silas
38 refused to leave the prison. The news that they had beaten
39 *Romans* threw the duumvirs into another panic, and *they came* in person with a large escort of notables *and entreated* Paul and Silas *to come out*. Their plea was ignorance: *they did not know that they were righteous men*, that is—either just and innocent in the eye of the law, or righteous and true servants of the God[2]. When the prisoners had come out of the prison, they then *asked them to leave the city*. They pleaded inability to protect them in case another tumult should arise and the populace should mob them. S. Paul's custom was to yield to the inevitable: there was no good in continuing work in the face of excited popular feeling. So he
40 complied with the request. First however *they went to the house of Lydia*; there they found *the brethren* already assembled and *they told what the Lord had done for them*. S. Luke himself was among them, we have little doubt, and so he would have heard their story and written it down on his memory or on some tablets; and thus have been preserved for us what are probably some actual words of S. Paul[3]. Then after the needful *encouragement* of the brethren, Paul and Silas left the city. They took Timothy with them, but Luke they left behind in charge of the young church.

Thus ended S. Paul's first work at Philippi. As the firstfruits of Macedonia[4], the church there must have been specially dear to him. Unlike the Galatians the Philippians never fell away from him; and his letter to them, written eight or ten years later, is full of affection;

[1] S. Luke used a word *uncondemned* which does not seem to have been a Roman legal phrase. He probably means by it *unheard* (Lat. *indictâ causâ*), for even if condemned the scourging would have been illegal. Paul and Silas had had no opportunity of making their defence, which was contrary to Roman custom (xxv 16). As Paul's companion at Rome, we should have expected S. Luke to be thoroughly familiar with the procedure and phraseology of the Roman law-courts: and probably fuller information would explain the term. [2] The same word occurs in the Bezan text of xiv 2. The additions are from the Bezan text, see p. 286. [3] The scene is similar to that in Mary's house (xii 16-7) where S. Mark filled the part here ascribed to S. Luke. One question may occur to us—why does not S. Luke tell us the jailor's name, as he mentions e.g. Dionysius and Damaris at Athens? Could he have been Epaphroditus? [4] Cp. Phil i 5-6, iv 15 *the beginning*.

its characteristic word is 'joy.' Perhaps the continuous presence of S. Luke had something to do with this fidelity. S. Paul gave the Philippian church a very practical proof of his affection. He allowed it, and it alone, the privilege of ministering to his wants. Four times they sent him a gift of money : twice to Thessalonica, once to Corinth, and once to Rome. The last contribution was sent by the hands of Epaphroditus to S. Paul when in prison, and the Epistle to the Philippians is his grateful acknowledgment of the gift[1]. The epistle contains a very sharp warning against Jews or Judaizers and on the other hand a rebuke of antinomian tendencies[2]. But the chief danger of the church came from divisions within, arising out of personal jealousies and social or spiritual pride, such as the rivalry between Euodia and Syntyche[3]. From without, the Philippians, as the Thessalonians also, had suffered much persecution at the hands of their pagan fellow-citizens[4].

§ 2 *Thessalonica and Beroea*

1   From Philippi the missionaries took the Egnatian way which ran *through Amphipolis and Apollonia* to Thessalonica. They may have preached in the former cities, but their mention (like xvi 11-12) seems to be copied from some diary, possibly kept by Timothy, which marked the evangelists' resting places for the night. So after three stages of an average thirty miles, they reached *Thessalonica*. This city was their goal because (1) it contained a colony of *Jews* with a *synagogue*, and (2) it was the capital of the province.

A brief summary of the visits to Thessalonica and Beroea completes the work in the province of Macedonia ; and the absence from the narrative of vivid incidents like that at Philippi makes us feel the loss of S. Luke's company. (1) The main feature in the history is the action of the Jews. There is a brief statement of the gospel preached to them ; moreover an express contrast is drawn between the friendly Jews of Beroea and the hostile Jews of Thessalonica. (2) In another respect there is a contrast between the two cities. The history of ancient and independent Greece may be summed up in one sentence : it was the conflict between aristocracy and democracy. In no other country can the struggle be witnessed so clearly. The whole of Greece, and each city within itself, was divided into two camps of the aristocrats and the democrats, the few and the many. And now S. Luke seems to be comparing the attitude towards Christianity of the two parties, of the democracy of Thessalonica and the aristocracy of Beroea, and the comparison is much to the credit of the latter. It is evident from the Acts that S. Luke himself was quite alive to social distinctions, much more so than S. Paul[5]; and if he was

---

[1] Phil ii 25, iv 10-8.   [2] iii 2-6 and 17-21.   [3] iv 2, cp. i 27, ii 1-11.
[4] i 27-30.   [5] Cp. his frequent allusions to *the first, the noble* or *the honourable* (xiii 50, xvi 12, xvii 4, 12, xxv 2, 23, xxviii 7): nor does he forget to name any converts of distinction, e.g. Dionysius and Damaris at Athens, Crispus at Corinth

descended from an old Macedonian family, we can well understand his attitude towards these cities.

Thessalonica as capital of a province ranks with Antioch[1] and Caesarea, Corinth and Ephesus. With the last two it may also be grouped as a flourishing commercial city. It was situated on the sea at the head of the gulf of Salonica and at the edge of the plain of Macedonia, down to which ran all the valleys which penetrated the interior; to Thessalonica accordingly all the commerce of the country gravitated and from its harbour found a ready outlet. Further, by means of the Egnatian way it enjoyed direct communication with Rome. In fact after Ephesus and Corinth it was the most busy city on the coasts of the Aegean, and as such it contained—we might say of course—a Jewish quarter. Its natural advantages have preserved its position and enabled it altogether to eclipse its two rivals. For 'Saloniki' is to-day the second city of Turkey in Europe, with a population of over one hundred and fifty thousand inhabitants. Historically the town owed its rise to the Macedonians. Its original name was Therma, but Cassander, king of Macedon, refounded the city and called it after his wife, a daughter of Philip,—Thessalonica. Through the royal favour it soon outstripped the neighbouring cities, and under the Romans it was made the capital of the province and residence of the proconsul. The Romans left to the city its freedom, of which fact it makes proud mention on its coins. From these we also learn that it had the dignity of a METROPOLIS and NEOKOROS (p. 363). Thus when S. Paul visited it, Thessalonica was a 'free city,' possessing its own Macedonian constitution. This was democratic in form, and so the supreme authority rested with the *Démos* or *People* (verse 5), i.e. the assembly of all enfranchised citizens. The chief magistrates were called *Politarchs*, i.e. *City-rulers* (verses 6 and 8). This title has not been met with in classical literature, and so it was once quoted as a proof of S. Luke's inaccuracy, not to say powers of invention. In fact it proves to be exactly the reverse. The scholars who made that criticism were unaware that, at the very time they were writing, there was standing at Saloniki a Roman triumphal arch, erected probably in the first century after Christ, on which the word POLITARCH was engraved in large letters. Unfortunately the arch was destroyed in 1867, but the block containing the word was rescued and is now to be seen in the British Museum[2]. Since then it has been found in inscriptions elsewhere in Macedonia: so it would appear to be a word of specially Macedonian use.

(xvii 34, xviii 8). Cp. also his impression at the scene in the auditorium at Caesarea (xxv 23). Paul, whom we take to have been a member of the Jewish aristocracy (p. 125), like many such, made light of these distinctions. For Christ's sake he considered them loss rather than gain.   [1] Antioch without an epithet is always of course *the* Antioch of Syria.   [2] The inscription contains some names which we shall find in xx 4. It runs thus: 'the politarchs being *Sosipater* son of Cleopatra and Lucius Pontius *Secundus*, Aulus Avius Sabinus, Demetrius son of Faustus, Demetrius son of Nicopolis, Zoilus son of Parmenio also called Meniscus, *Caius* Agilleius Potitus...' (*Gk Inscriptions in Brit. Mus.* pt II no. 171).

O

The Jews and mob law at Thessalonica

17 Now when they had passed through Amphipolis and Apollonia, they came to Thessalonica, where was a synagogue
2 of the Jews: and Paul, as his custom was, went in unto them, and for three [1]sabbath days reasoned with them from
3 the scriptures, opening and alleging, that it behoved the Christ to suffer, and to rise again from the dead; and that this Jesus, whom, *said he*, I proclaim unto you, is the Christ.
4 And some of them were persuaded, and consorted with Paul and Silas; and [2]of the devout Greeks a great multitude, and of the [3]chief women not a few.
5 But the [4]Jews, being moved with jealousy, took unto them certain vile fellows of the rabble, and gathering a crowd, set the city on an uproar; and assaulting the house of Jason,
6 they sought to bring them forth to the [5]people. And when they found them not, they dragged Jason and certain brethren before the [6]rulers of the city, crying, These that have turned the world upside down are come hither also; whom Jason
7 hath received: and these all act contrary to the decrees of
8 Cæsar, saying that there is another king, *one* Jesus. And they troubled the multitude and the [6]rulers of the city, when
9 they heard these things. And when they had taken security from Jason and the rest, they let them go.

2 The travellers found hospitality in the house of a fellow-countryman[7]. His Greek name *Jason* from its resemblance to Joshua was one frequently adopted by Jews of that name[8]. On the sabbath day *Paul went into the synagogue*. His work there lasted *three weeks* (margin). The sabbath day was of course the day for the great service, but services were held during the week, and it seems to have been S. Paul's *custom* to *reason* daily[9]. This word, which makes its first appearance here[10], seems to mark a change of method on his part. *To reason* is a characteristic Greek word. Originally meaning *to converse*, it came to denote *discussion* by means of question and answer. This method of eliciting the truth was the

---

[1] Marg *weeks*. [2] Bezan has *many of the devout and of the* [*Greeks a great multitude*. [3] Gk *first*. [4] AV and Bezan add *unbelieving*. [5] Gk *dēmos*. [6] Gk *politarchs*. [7] Jason was a Jew, if he was the same Jason who was with S. Paul at Corinth when he wrote the Ep. to the Romans (Rom xvi 21). [8] Cp. Saul and Paul. [9] So at Beroea and Ephesus (ver. 11, xix 9); cp. Athens (ver. 17). For Paul's *custom* of entering the synagogue, see the scene at the Pisidian Antioch and cp. xiv 1. [10] Cp. xvii 17, xviii 4, 19, xix 8, 9, xx 7, 9.

special characteristic of Socrates; and after him the Greek philosophers developed it, until *dialectic* (or *reasoning*) became a definite branch and method of philosophy. Here of course the word is used in the more general sense of reasoning or arguing. In the synagogues of the east *teaching* was the method of instruction (p. 208), and the Christian evangelists accordingly *taught* and *preached* the word. But in the more critical atmosphere of the west dogmatic assertion was not sufficient, and S. Paul had to adopt the method of *reasoning*, in which he was an adept. The reasoning of course was Jewish; it was based on *the scriptures*. But until they recognized the Christ in them, the scriptures were a sealed book to the Jews[1]. This
3 book S. Paul now *opened* for them, by *alleging*, i.e. proving by the comparison of passages, the doctrine of the Messiah. The summary of his teaching here given agrees with the gospel he preached at Corinth, which was also based on the scriptures[2]. There were two main positions: (1) *the Christ must suffer and rise again*; (2) '*this is the Christ, this Jesus whom I proclaim unto you.*' The latter fact did not rest on the scriptures, but upon personal testimony; and the convincing testimony to the resurrection of an eye-witness could only be given by S. Paul,—and not by Silas or Timothy; hence the emphatic '*I*.' S. Luke, we notice, quotes the actual words of S. Paul. This assertion must have been constantly on his lips; and the truest description of his preaching was this: 'he preached Jesus,' whether as (*a*) a herald, or (*b*) a messenger, or (*c*) a bearer
4 of good tidings[3]. The result at Thessalonica was the *persuasion*[4] of only a few of the Jews (among whom was Aristarchus[5]), but of a great number of *the devout* or God-fearing *Greeks*, including several of *the wives* of *the first* men of the city. S. Luke varies his narrative by using a new and uncommon word for their adhesion: they *consorted with Paul and Silas*. The verb is compounded from the significant word *cléros* or *lot*, and may be taken either (1) in the middle sense—they *cast in their lot with* Paul and Silas; or (2) in the passive, which is much in accordance with S. Luke's fondness of dwelling on the preventing grace of God[6]. In this case it will mean that *they were assigned by lot*, i.e. by the divine will, to Paul; or that *they were allotted* to him, i.e. assigned to him as his lot[7].

Between verses 4 and 5 there is an interval[8]. The Epistles to the Thessalonians postulate a much longer ministry than three weeks. They also shew that the majority of converts had been converted from paganism directly. Now verse 4 deals only with the congregation of

---

[1] Rev v 1: cp. II Cor iii 14–6. For *the opening* cp. xvi 14 and Lk xxiv 45. S. Paul opened the scriptures, but to convince the Lord must first open the heart.
[2] I Cor xv 3–4: cp. also Lk xxiv 46.   [3] Cp. (*a*) ix 15, 20, I Cor i 23, xv 12, II Cor i 19, iv 5, xi 4, I Tim ii 7: (*b*) xvii 3, 18, Col i 28: (*c*) xvii 18, I Cor ix 16, Gal i 16.   [4] Cp. xiii 43 (p. 220), xviii 4, xix 8, 26.   [5] xx 4, Col iv 10.
[6] As in xiii 48, xvi 14.   [7] Cp I Cor iii 6–9. This thought is familiar to S. Paul. From I Thess ii 19–20 we learn that the Christians of Thessalonica were his *hope*, and *joy*, and *crown of glorying*.   [8] As at Iconium (xiv 2 and 3) and Philippi (xvi 15 and 16).

the synagogue; and the definite mention of the three weeks' preaching in the synagogue seems to imply a turning to the Gentiles at its end, as at the Pisidian Antioch[1]. Of the subsequent preaching to the Greeks, the beautiful letters to the Thessalonians, written within a few months of the apostle's departure, will enable us to draw a picture.

The house of Jason would form the first 'church,' and S. Paul's preaching there was 'with power and the Holy Ghost.' Consequently great numbers of the Thessalonians 'turned from idols to serve the living and true God[2].' The growth of the church was accompanied with the usual joy and exultation, and also with prophetic phenomena and visible manifestations of the Holy Spirit. A great personal affection grew up between S. Paul and his converts: he was tender to them as a nurse, or as a father with his children[3]. As at Philippi, the converts became evangelists also; the news of the gospel was spread through the whole of Macedonia and along the lines of the city's commerce, so that the echo of their faith reached to Achaia[4]. From S. Paul's allusions to his teaching and 'the traditions' which he had handed on to them we gather that: (1) There was very definite teaching about the *parousia* (*presence*), i.e. the return of the Lord, and this was accompanied by further apocalyptic doctrine. It is quite clear that when at Thessalonica S. Paul, like the rest of the church, believed that the parousia was imminent, and this expectation deeply impressed the Thessalonians. They too accepted the belief and the very fervour of their faith resulted in some disorganization of social life[5]. (2) The charge brought against Paul and Silas in Acts xvii 7 proves that there had been considerable preaching of 'the kingdom of God.' The relation of this new kingdom of the church to the existing kingdom of Rome required some explanation, which because of the danger of treason had to be veiled in more or less mysterious language[6]. (3) Besides these doctrines there were moral 'traditions.' (*a*) Like other Gentiles, the Thessalonians needed very definite commandments on the subject of purity[7]. (*b*) The doctrine of the parousia together with the excitement of conversion and the manifestations of spiritual gifts gave rise to some disorder; daily work was neglected and the behaviour towards those without was somewhat contemptuous. Hence S. Paul laid down the laws of work and social duty, of orderly and 'gentlemanly' conduct. He also set them a practical example by working with his own hands for his daily bread[8]. Lastly, a body of 'labourers and presidents,' in other words of presbyters, was formed; we notice also the beginnings of discipline, and, in the 'holy kiss,' of Christian ritual[9].

There was, however, another side to this joyful work. The converts had to face persecution. There was 'much affliction,' and S. Paul taught them, as he had taught the Galatians (xiv 22), that 'we must

---

[1] Similarly at Ephesus the 3 months' reasoning in the synagogue was followed by 2 years' work outside (xix 8–10).   [2] I Thess i 5, 9.   [3] I i 6: I v 20, II ii 2: I ii 7, 11.   [4] I i 7–8.   [5] I iv 13–v 11, II i 7–10, ii 1–12.   [6] I ii 12, II i 5: II ii 4–7.   [7] I iv 2–8 (see pp. 264–6).   [8] I iv 10–2, II iii 6–15: I ii 9.   [9] I v 12–5, 27: II iii 14–5: I v 26.

be afflicted¹.' His own preaching was 'in much conflict,' and he was reduced to great straits. Twice he had to accept pecuniary help from the Philippians². The main cause of this affliction was the enmity of *the Jews*. Their motive was the usual one of *jealousy*³, and their first weapon was slander and misrepresentation. The preachers were represented as 'deceivers' and charlatans: they were 'pleasing men' and 'using words of flattery'; they were actuated by the most corrupt motives of vain-glory and greed of gain⁴. In answer, the missionaries proved their absolute disinterestedness by refusing to accept a penny from their converts. This method having failed, the Jews resorted to violence which resulted in the expulsion of Paul and Silas from the city. No wonder that when he writes his epistle the apostle suddenly gives way to an outburst of righteous wrath against 'the Jews⁵.'

5   In the absence of any legal ground for indicting Paul and Silas, the only method was to adopt the tactics practised at Philippi and stir up the populace. This was not a hard matter. The centre of life in a Greek city was the Agora or Market-place, and there would generally be found in it a crowd of idlers⁶ ready for any excitement or mischief. So numerous was this class that they had a name; they were the *agoraioi* or *market-men*. Out of these the Jews selected for their *confederates*⁷ those who were specially conspicuous for moral obliquity, and our sober historian can hardly contain his disgust at these *lewd fellows of the baser sort* (AV), or *vile fellows of the rabble* (RV). With their aid it was easy to *set the city in an uproar*, and when a sufficient mob was collected the Jews led them to *the house of Jason*. They burst in and *searched for Paul and Silas to carry them before* the ecclesia or assembly of *the People* 6 (*Démos*). Paul and Silas, however, could not be found and in their place the mob *dragged Jason and some* other Christians *to the politarchs*. It was a repetition of the scene at Philippi. On their way the Jews and their accomplices kept *shouting out* the cause of the tumult : '*The men who have turned the world upside down have come hither also and Jason has harboured them*⁸.' The charge was of course an exaggeration, but it is evidence of the stir which Christianity was making. The Jews would have heard of the disturbances in Palestine and in the towns of Galatia : what had happened at Philippi would be known in Macedonia, and news of recent tumults among the Jews in Rome caused by 'one Chrestus' may have reached Thessalonica. The formal accusation was brought 7 against *all* the Christians alike—*they are acting in defiance of the decrees of Caesar, saying that there is another emperor*⁹, *one Jesus*.

---

¹ I i 6, iii 4.   ² I ii 2: Phil iv 16.   ³ Acts xvii 5; cp. v 17, xiii 45.
⁴ I Thess ii 3–10.   ⁵ I iii 14–6.   ⁶ The Thessalonian converts themselves were somewhat disinclined to work (II Thess iii 10).   ⁷ *Took unto them* implies rather close relations, cp. xviii 26, Mt xvi 22, Rom xiv 1, 3, xv 7, Philem 17.   ⁸ There may be a suggestion of secret harbouring in *received*; cp. Jas ii 25.   ⁹ *Basileus*, the Greek for *king*, was the title used for the Roman emperor. The charge brought against the Lord was that he *said that he is Christ a king*, or *the king* (Lk xxiii 2).

8 The suggestion of treason *cast into a panic* both the politarchs and
the crowd who were witnessing the disturbance. There was, however,
9 no immediate danger, and the magistrates were most anxious to put
an end to the tumult, so they postponed the case to another day
when they could give it a fuller and more impartial hearing. At
the same time there was no evidence of any wrong-doing on the
part of *Jason and the rest*; it was clear that they were not the
ringleaders of the body accused; and so the politarchs did not put
them in prison, but *dismissed them* after they had first given *bail*
for their appearance when called up for trial[1].

10 *At once the brethren* took care to put *Paul and Silas* out of
reach; under cover of darkness they *sent them away to Beroea*.
Once more we find S. Paul a passive agent[2]. This may have been
because he was much discouraged by what had happened; but more
likely the thought of the trouble in store for Jason and the brethren
whom they were leaving behind made both Silas and himself loath
to depart. Certainly their departure was followed by a persecution
of the Christians at the hands of their fellow-citizens, a persecution
as severe as that which had befallen the Jewish Christians at
Jerusalem[3]. This caused S. Paul the greatest anxiety during the
following months. He longed to return and strengthen them. But
Satan hindered him once and twice[4]. Prof. Ramsay thinks that
Jason had given security that the apostle would not return to
the city. This would indeed have been a 'device of Satan';
but such security we can hardly suppose that Jason would have
given. S. Paul's language rather suggests definite obstacles which
prevented his starting on a visit to them, and nothing seems so
likely as visitations of his peculiar malady which he recognized as
'the messenger of Satan[5].'

The nobility of the Beroeans and expulsion of S. Paul from Macedonia

Beroea was forty miles from Thessalonica, in another district of
Macedonia. The city was beautifully situated at the edge of the
mountains where they rose from the plain which stretched away for
25 miles to the sea. Beyond the mountains lay Illyricum, and when
S. Paul writes to the Romans (xv 19) of his having preached 'as far

---

[1] At first sight the Greek expression for *had taken security* seems to stand for the Latin *satis accipientes* or *satis dato*. This however was the term for depositing security that the sentence of the court would be obeyed, and not for giving bail in our sense. But the Thessalonians being 'free' would not be under Roman law, and the interpretation of the *security* given above is supported by an interesting parallel in a letter published among the *Oxyrhynchus Papyri* (II. no. 294) by Messrs Grenfell and Hunt. The letter is dated from Alexandria A.D. 22. In his absence from home Sarapion's house had been 'searched,' and he was going to appeal to the Prefect. Meantime two of the officials implicated were in prison till the session—'unless indeed they persuade the chief usher *to give security* for them until the session.'   [2] As in ix 25, 30 and see below vv. 14–5.
[3] I Thess ii 14, iii 1–5, II i 6.   [4] I ii 18.   [5] Cp. II Cor ii 11, xii 7.

as Illyricum,' Beroea may have been in his mind. Beroea was a city of some importance. It was a meeting-place of 'the confederation of the Macedonians'; like Thessalonica it was honoured with the title of NEOKOROS; and it had a colony of Jews with a synagogue. It is still a flourishing town and retains its ancient name—Verria. Livy calls Pella, Edessa, and Beroea a trio of 'noble towns[1].' Now it is to be noticed that the characteristic of the Beroean Jews which struck S. Luke was their *nobility*[2]. He is speaking indeed of the Jews, but they would have caught the spirit of the city in which they lived. Moreover several of the women converts were *of honourable estate*, i.e. of aristocratic families. It is also remarkable that the one Beroean convert whose name we know is the only disciple distinguished by his father's name,—an addition which was, so to speak, the mark of a gentleman: he was *Sopater (son) of Pyrrhus* (xx 4). As an ancient Macedonian city, Beroea no doubt prided itself on the pure blood of its citizens, and S. Luke contrasts the gentlemanly behaviour of the better sort with the noisy democracy of Thessalonica.

10 And the brethren immediately sent away Paul and Silas by night unto Beroea: who when they were come thither
11 went into the synagogue of the Jews. Now these were more noble than those in Thessalonica, in that they received the word with all readiness of mind, examining the scriptures
12 daily, whether these things were so[3]. Many of them therefore believed[4]; also of the Greek women of honourable estate, and of men, not a few.
13 But when the Jews of Thessalonica had knowledge that the word of God was proclaimed of Paul at Beroea also, they came thither likewise, stirring up and troubling the multi-
14 tudes[5]. And then immediately the brethren sent forth Paul to go *as far as to the sea: and Silas and Timothy abode
15 there still. But they that conducted Paul brought him as far as Athens[7]: and receiving a commandment unto Silas and Timothy that they should come to him with all speed, they departed.

10 At Beroea again without delay *Paul and Silas went away*[8] *into the synagogue*. Here they were surprised by a unique reception.

---

[1] *Hist.* XLV 30. [2] It is the same word as in Lk xix 12, I Cor i 26. [3] Bezan adds *as Paul announces*. [4] Bezan adds *but some disbelieved*. [5] Bezan adds *without ceasing* (viii 24), and has other variations in the passage. [6] AV with later MSS reads *as it were to the sea*. [7] Bezan adds *but he passed by* (xvi 8) *Thessaly, for he was prevented from proclaiming the word to them*. [8] The form of the tense in Greek (which appears again in *departed* in verse 15) is unusual. Can it be an echo of Beroean refinement?

11 The Jews received S. Paul's message *with readiness* and zeal. Instead of refusing to listen out of pride and prejudice, *daily* in the synagogue they *examined* his arguments and the passages he
12 quoted out of *the scriptures*. Consequently *many of them believed* and several also of the notables of the town, both men and women.
13 Even those who disbelieved did not manifest any opposition. This was left for *the Jews of Thessalonica*. Like the Jews of Iconium and the Pisidian Antioch (xiv 19), they too followed up S. Paul and practised the same tactics as at Thessalonica. They excited the common people, *the crowds*, and by so doing they caused quite
14 'an earthquake[1]' in the quiet and 'noble' country town. The wisest policy for the Christians was to remove the cause of irritation for the time, and they *sent forth Paul to go as far as to* (or *towards*) *the sea*. This expression is somewhat obscure. It (1) seems to mean that they sent him forth to journey on foot until he reached the sea-coast, where at Methone or Pydna he would find a ship bound for Athens: the word *send forth* was used in ix 30, where the brethren took Paul down from Jerusalem to Caesarea and there, putting him on board ship, *sent him forth* to Tarsus. (2) If we press the words *to* or *towards* (*the sea*), perhaps a large body of disciples, for the sake of protection or of compliment, escorted him a certain distance until he was on the direct road *for the sea*, and then left him to a smaller escort. (3) Geographical considerations will probably solve the difficulty. Between Macedonia and Thessaly lay a great barrier in the huge mass of Mt Olympus; and the mountain forced the road from one country into the other to run along the coast. Hence, even if S. Paul had intended to go to Greece on foot, he would have been obliged to go *as far as to-the-sea*, i.e. the sea-coast, before he could join the road. And this is probably what happened. A large party of Beroean Christians accompanied the apostle as far as the coast: then instead of taking ship, as might have been expected by his adversaries, he turned to the right into Thessaly with a smaller escort, while the rest of the brethren returned to Beroea. This view is borne out by the AV reading *as it were*, which suggests the idea of giving pursuers the slip. The Bezan text also definitely implies that S. Paul traversed *Thessaly* on foot; but he *passed it by*, i.e. he did not preach there, being *prevented* by some hindrance or divine intimation (as in xvi
15 6–10). In any case, whether they took ship at Methone or after crossing Thessaly, or did the whole distance on foot, his escort did not leave the apostle till they had reached *Athens*.

The whole narrative points to great depression or weakness on S. Paul's part. Silas and Timothy remained at Beroea to guide the church through the crisis, but Paul was not able or not allowed to travel alone: some of the brethren *conducted him*. Very likely this was one of the moments when he desired to return to Thessalonica

---

[1] *Stirring up* is literally *shaking* as by an earthquake.

(instead of going on to a strange place), but Satan hindered him. Then, according to the Bezan text, he was *prevented* from preaching in Thessaly. Lastly, at Athens he could not endure to be left alone, but sent a *command to Silas and Timothy* to join him *as soon as possible*. All this points to some extreme depression, such as that portrayed in II Cor i 8–9 or ii 12–13, which was the result of similar violence at Ephesus, or to a visitation of his 'stake in the flesh,' the 'messenger of Satan.'

So S. Paul was driven out of Macedonia, but he had done his work. He had founded the churches of Macedonia[1].

SECTION II (=Ch. 17. 16—18. 11)

ACHAIA

When S. Paul crossed the border into Thessaly, or (if he went by sea) when he landed at the Piraeus, the port of Athens, he set foot upon a new province, that of ACHAIA. This province very nearly coincided with the present kingdom of Greece. Greece had been made Roman territory in B.C. 146; and from the Achaean League, the strongest power among its rival and struggling confederations and cities, it received the name of Achaia. Achaia however was not made a province by itself. It was added to Macedonia, and so the close connexion between those two countries was kept up, as we find indicated by the language of I Thess i 7–8[2]. In B.C. 27, when the provinces were divided between Augustus and the Senate, Achaia was separated from Macedonia and given to the latter body, who therefore appointed the proconsul. Corinth was selected as the seat of government and became the capital of the province. In A.D. 15, however, in consequence of complaints of over-taxation Tiberius again united Achaia to Macedonia; and this régime lasted till A.D. 44, when Claudius restored it to the Senate and the rule of a proconsul of its own. It was five years after this date, in the autumn of A.D. 49, when S. Paul entered Athens.

§ 1 *Paul at Athens*

Paul at Athens, Paul the Jew of Tarsus in the city of Pericles and Demosthenes, of Sophocles and Euripides, of Socrates and Plato—that is a situation to which our pen cannot attempt to do justice. Nor is it less difficult adequately to estimate the place of Athens in the Roman Empire. For at this date Athens was still the intellectual and artistic capital of the world. It was also a religious capital, for it was the stronghold of the Greek mythology, which was generally accepted as the most authentic account of the gods and their history.

---

[1] For a full and interesting account of these churches, see Lightfoot's *Biblical Essays* no. vi. [2] Cp. also Acts xix 21, Rom xv 26.

The famous history of the democracy of the Athenians will never be forgotten; but their political importance had now long been a thing of the past. When the Romans began to interfere in the affairs of the east, Athens had the misfortune of invariably being on the wrong side. Nevertheless, out of respect for her past glories, the Romans left to her citizens their freedom. Athens, then, was 'a free city'; though at this time its Demos or People, unlike those of the busy cities of Thessalonica and Ephesus, had lost even the semblance of authority, and the municipal administration had reverted to the ancient and aristocratic court of the Areopagus. It was to its art and literature and philosophy that the city owed its greatness. Athens had been the home of the greatest artists and poets, writers and orators, of the world; and it possessed the masterpieces of the greatest sculptors and architects. The city itself was still clothed in its mantle of external glory and beauty; its streets and buildings were crowded with statues and exquisite works of art; and the greedy hands of the Romans which had spoiled so many cities of their treasures had as yet refrained from touching Athens. The philosophy of Athens was even more celebrated than its art. In Athens, Socrates, Plato and Aristotle had lived and taught: in Athens their successors had elaborated the different systems which now divided the thinking world. So Athens was at once the chief birthplace and the natural home of philosophy. Every one of the schools had its head-quarters there; and among its sacred spots pilgrims visited the Academy of Plato and the Lyceum of Aristotle, the Porch of Zeno the Stoic and the Garden of Epicurus. Once more, and in the main through her art, Athens had become the religious centre of Hellenism. Her citizens indeed had always been noted for their 'religious' character and the solemnity and multiplicity of their festivals. But it was her poets that had given to the local sanctuaries a world-wide reputation, and the hands of her artists that had filled her streets and temples with images of the gods. To judge from the reports of antiquity, Athens must have been 'full of idols' and altars and temples to an extent which it is difficult for us to realize[1]. An ancient writer[2] could speak of the city as being 'the whole of it one altar, one sacrifice and votive offering to the gods.' This 'religious' reputation, together with the antiquarian spirit that succeeded to the epoch of originality, made the Athenians zealous in maintaining their observances. And this would be a factor in the revival of the Areopagus, a sacrosanct tribunal which had its origin in the days of gods and heroes and which from its jurisdiction in matters of religion served as a kind of 'sanhedrin,' or religious court of appeal, for Hellenism.

As Hellenic civilization spread, it carried with it the fame and attraction of Athens. The Macedonian conquests brought the east under her spell; and when the Romans came from the west, they

---

[1] For references see Wetstein on this passage; also Pausanias' *Attica*.
[2] Quoted by Wetstein from Xenophon; but I have been unable to verify the quotation. But see p. cxvi.

were themselves conquered by the art and literature of the Greeks, and Athens led her captors captive. After this the education of the Roman aristocrat could not be considered complete without a course of study at Athens. Accordingly Athens became the university of the empire, and her streets were crowded with students and young men who lived and amused themselves, studied or did not study, very much as do the undergraduates of Oxford to-day. The city became also a place of pilgrimage; and the princes and royal families of Asia Minor, Syria, and Egypt, vied with the Roman aristocracy in adding new ornaments to the city or in bestowing favours upon its citizens. Even the Jews were not proof against the universal attraction. Herod the Great shewed his phil-hellenic sympathies in numerous dedications or offerings; and the Jewish philosopher Philo was full of enthusiasm for the birthplace of Platonism[1]. At an earlier date also we are surprised to find the Athenians honouring John Hyrcanus 'high-priest and ethnarch of the Jews' with a golden crown and a brazen statue in the theatre[2]

The chief interest of our Athens however lay in its philosophy; for philosophy supplied the place of serious religion for the educated citizens of the empire. It had been growing more and more impossible for a cultivated man to have any serious faith in the popular stories of the gods or in the efficacy of the old ritual forms. In their place the true Greek had found satisfaction in the love of beauty and the pursuit after knowledge for their own sakes. But the genuine Hellenic spirit was dying out under the pressure of Roman and oriental influences. The religious easterns wanted something spiritual —food for their souls; the serious westerns wanted something practical—help and guidance in facing the practical difficulties of life. To meet these new demands there had been on the one hand a great development of mysteries and the mystic worships of the east, on the other a change in the character and aims of philosophy itself. The philosophers had turned their attention away from the investigation of truth in itself, and from metaphysical discussions as to the meaning of existence, to the practical application of moral philosophy. The primary interest of the Stoics and Epicureans was practical and ethical, and their aim the attainment of the 'end' of man—the blessed life. These two were the only philosophies which at this time possessed any vitality. They offered men a guide of life and a moral creed, and so they were a living force in the world. The other schools, who maintained their devotion to theoretical speculation—the Academics, Peripatetics, and Sceptics,—had no practical influence and were purely 'academic.'

It was the *Epicurean and Stoic philosophers* who encountered S. Paul. This is not the place to summarize their doctrines: it is sufficient to point out that they represented two great types of thought and character which always will divide men. Thus (1) in

---

[1] See art. ATHENS in Hastings *Dict. of the Bible*. [2] See Josephus *B. J.* i 21. 11, *Ant.* xiv 8. 5. This Hyrcanus was high-priest from 63 to 40 B.C.

ethics the Stoics were on the side of the ideal. Duty, law, and virtue, were their favourite conceptions; virtue for its own sake their doctrine; and their 'end' the condition of the wise man who, having risen superior to all the circumstances of life and to human passions, is 'self-sufficient'—'a king,' or rather 'a god,' in himself. The Epicureans on the other hand adopted the common-sense standard of the world; an enlightened prudence with practical experience of life was their guide; and their 'end' was pleasure. Such a theory was of course open to great perversion and misunderstanding. But it would be a gross injustice to Epicurus to say that he aimed simply at the gratification of sensual desires. His ideal was not so much pleasure as happiness, which he found in freedom from the distractions of life and in which the enlightened pleasures of the mind and of social intercourse form the chief ingredients. In fact Epicureanism is most fairly described as the ancient representative of modern utilitarianism.

(2) In regard to religion, the Epicureans believed in the gods; but to satisfy their own conception of blessedness, the gods were banished to a distant celestial sphere of bliss altogether removed from the disturbances of this life and the cares of providence. So this world was left to itself; and their view of it was very much that of modern materialism. In fact they held the atomic theory of modern science, although of course in a crude form. Their theory carried with it the denial of life after death. Like everything else, the human soul was composed of material atoms which, in themselves indestructible, were dissipated at death, so that personal existence came to an end. But neither theories of the universe nor physical science were in themselves attractive to the Epicureans. They only studied these subjects as weapons of criticism for the sake of deliverance from popular superstitions and the fear of death. *Tantum religio potuit suadere malorum*—that was the guise in which religion presented itself to the eyes of the great Epicurean poet Lucretius[1]; and the attitude of these philosophers towards worship was simply that of emancipated men of culture. The Stoics on the contrary had a strong belief in God and in spirit. But even their faith will not stand a thorough examination. They believed that throughout the universe there was a pervading spirit, a universal reason, a creative word of God—the *anima mundi*. And of this spirit the human spirit was a part. Our souls therefore share its immortality, although at intervals cosmic conflagrations will occur, when all the universe, including all human spirits, will be reabsorbed into the fire of the divine spirit. Such a creed is pure pantheism; and the Stoics were no less materialists than the Epicureans, for after all their 'spirit' was itself but refined matter, or as S. Chrysostom bluntly puts it 'their god is a body[2].' Still, apart from their logical and scientific theories, the Stoics were possessed by a real religious fervour. To this Deity they addressed the language of personal worship and fervent devotion; and by their doctrine of predestination they made up for the absence of the divine intervention in daily

---

[1] *de Rer. Nat.* I 101. [2] *Hom. on the Acts* xxxviii. 1.

human life. For all things proceeded according to the law and will of this universal reason, and therefore man could have faith that he was under the protection of the divine providence.

(3) Once more, the same difference underlay their respective doctrines of human society. The Epicureans attached a great value to friendship, but as one of the greatest pleasures of life and as an essential factor in man's highest happiness. The Stoics treated it dogmatically and on *a priori* grounds. As each human soul was a fragment of the pervading spirit,—the *anima mundi*, which was God,— all men were brothers. And so from the side of philosophy they were breaking down the barriers between city and city, and race and race, which so hopelessly divided the ancient world. In fact they had anticipated Christianity in rising to the conception of the world as one great 'city of God.'

To sum up—the Stoic was the idealist; the Epicurean the utilitarian. The Stoic was the stern dogmatist, the unflinching man of duty; the Epicurean the practical common-sense man of the world, the philosopher who could make the best out of circumstances. The Stoic was deeply interested in the doctrine of God and the soul: the Epicurean indulged in the dilettante scepticism of the man of culture. To stretch a comparison—the Epicureans were the Sadducees, the Stoics the Pharisees of Hellenism. The Stoic held fast to the law; the ideal of the Epicurean was lawlessness, in the sense, that is to say, of freedom from arbitrary restrictions.

It is obvious on which side Christian sympathy would lie. For Stoicism—and only Stoicism—could make any claim to be a religion, and as such it served the nobler Romans. In the dying republic it was the religion of Cato, the noblest Roman of them all, and under the empire it was the creed which inspired those who ventured to make any open stand for righteousness—Seneca and Barea Soranus and Thrasea Paetus and Helvidius Priscus. This strong religious element really came from the east. It was drawn from the Semitic blood in the veins of its founders, for Zeno was a native of Cyprus and Chrysippus came from Cilicia. There was then a slight kinship of blood. Stoicism and Christianity were distant cousins, many times removed. This relationship was also seconded by some striking resemblances to Christianity in Stoic doctrine and phraseology. Christian teachers could lay hold, for example, of the doctrines of the universal presence of God and the divine predestination, of the city of God and brotherhood of man, and of the ideal of the wise man; and so it was easy for S. Paul to use its language and become 'a Stoic to Stoics[1].' Stoic philosophy, then, was an element in the divine preparation for

---

[1] The comparison between Christianity and Stoicism has been drawn out most completely by Bp Lightfoot in the essay on *Paul and Seneca* in his *Philippians*. Here we need only add that the Stoics had also a doctrine of 'joy' following upon virtuous activity which resembles S. Luke's joy after conversion. An account of Stoicism and Epicureanism is contained in all histories of philosophy: perhaps that in Prof. J. B. Mayor's *Sketch of Ancient Philosophy* will suffice the ordinary reader.

the gospel. It had been preparing a moral ground for Christianity. Yet there was a great deal wanting. If the Stoics resembled the Pharisees, they also fell into the sins of Pharisaism. Stoicism was the nurse of pride and rigidity. It was not a religion for the vulgar; from them the philosopher stood apart in self-sufficing and contemptuous exclusiveness. But even the philosopher found the 'wise man' an impracticable ideal. For after all they had not found God. Their God was but Nature, and what they needed was the gospel of a human personality.

And now Paul stands face to face with philosophy. The contrast between the Christian Jew and the Greek philosophers is striking, but not so sharp as we have been in the habit of thinking. S. Paul was by no means unfitted for the encounter. He was familiar with the life of Greek cities, and must have frequently met with philosophers before. He himself was a native of Tarsus, which ranked as a university-town next after Athens and Alexandria. Cilicia was also a great nursery ground for Stoics; besides Chrysippus other heads of the school, and the poet Aratus, were Cilicians by birth. S. Paul's own writings shew that he had studied Stoicism; he was at least acquainted with its leading doctrines and had read some of its authors[1]. Above all he had the sympathy of kindred character, for in his stern Pharisaism, his eager pursuit after righteousness and a life according to law, he had been a Jewish Stoic.

Now however S. Paul faces philosophy in its own home. He had been brought up in the religious capital of the world: he was to end his days in its political capital: and now in the midst of his life's work he proclaims the gospel in its intellectual capital. But to the brilliant exterior of that capital, there was but little correspondence in the reality within. The real greatness of Athens had long since departed, and the city was a body without a soul. Even in regard to race, the blood of the old Athenians must have been sadly diluted by the fluctuations of its history and the invasions of foreigners. The Athenians of S. Paul's day were a degenerate people who lived upon the glories of their past and by flattering their masters. In a few bitter words S. Luke gave us his opinion of the mob of Thessalonians: in a sentence no less severe he expresses the contempt of a serious Christian for the frivolous populace of Athens. They *spent their time in nothing else than hearing or saying something 'newer'*: i.e. their one aim in life was to satisfy their vanity by the display of originality, and their curiosity by the hearing of some novelty. Athens indeed, as the place of resort for students and the *jeunesse dorée*, still stood first in the empire, but the real progress of thought was being carried on elsewhere —at Alexandria and Tarsus and Rome. Of the philosophers at Athens at this moment not one is known to us by name. Similarly in the world of art, while Athens continued to find her boast in the masterpieces of the past, the living force of art was occupied in clothing the cities of

---

[1] Cp. Lightfoot's essay, and the quotation from Aratus in S. Paul's speech.

the east with a robe of Grecian beauty, and in civilizing the wild and distant north with the more rugged arts and architecture of Rome. Nor was there any more reality in Athenian religion: the outward forms of worship were diligently maintained but out of an antiquarian and conservative spirit, not wholly disinterested, and the religious cravings of the soul had to find solace elsewhere. Even at Athens the foreign mysteries of Thrace and Phrygia, the gods of Egypt and Tyre, had obtained a firm footing; and among them the LORD of the Jews had his synagogue. When S. Paul called the Athenians *very religious*, he was using a word with a double meaning—and not unintentionally. We cannot find a better summary of the real condition of Athens than in the severe sentence of Dr Hort¹: 'the professed study of truth had withered into the idlest of all imaginable frivolities.'

Paul in the Agora of Athens

16 Now while Paul waited for them at Athens, his spirit was
17 provoked within him, as he beheld the city full of idols. So he reasoned in the synagogue with the Jews and the devout persons, and in the ²marketplace every day with them that
18 met with him. And certain also of the Epicurean and Stoic philosophers encountered him. And some said, What would this babbler say? other some, He seemeth to be a setter forth of strange gods: because he ³preached Jesus and the ⁴resurrection.
19 And⁵ they took hold of him, and brought him ⁶unto ⁷the Areopagus, saying, May we know what this new teaching is,
20 which is spoken by thee? For thou bringest certain strange things to our ears: we would know therefore what these things
21 mean. (Now all the Athenians and the strangers sojourning there ⁸spent their time in nothing else, but either to tell or to hear some ⁹new thing.)

16 When the Beroean escort left *Paul* alone *at Athens*, being in a state of depression, he intended to *wait* for Silas and Timothy before commencing work (p. 301). Silas, it would appear from xviii 5, did not arrive from Macedonia until S. Paul had gone on to Corinth. Timothy however, as we learn from I Thess iii 1-2, did rejoin him at Athens; but the news he brought about Thessalonica made S. Paul so anxious that he sent Timothy back again in order to be reassured as to their faith, and perhaps was only prevented from going himself by the 'hindrance of Satan (ii 18).'

¹ *Hulsean Lectures*, p. 63.   ² Gk *agora*.   ³ Gk *evangelized*.   ⁴ Gk *anastasis*.   ⁵ Bezan adds *after some days*.   ⁶ Marg *before*.   ⁷ Marg *the hill of Mars*. AV has *Areopagus*, and in marg *Or Mars' hill: It was the highest court in Athens*.   ⁸ Marg *had leisure for nothing else*.   ⁹ Gk *more new*.

Meanwhile, like many another visitor, Paul wandered about the city and *looked at*[1] the sights. The sights which S. Paul would want to see, and which he would *observe* carefully, we could tell beforehand: they were *the objects of* the city's *worship*—its temples, altars, and statues. But these beautiful works of art only *provoked*[2] or embittered *his spirit*: he was filled with a divine jealousy or indignation, for *the city was full of idols*. And the character of the people corresponded. He soon discovered that the Athenians 22 were *very religious*. Very likely he was a *spectator* of some of the solemn religious ceremonies for which the Athenians were notorious. But wherever he went, *in everything* he found the stamp of their *superstition*. The epithet in which S. Paul sums up the Athenian character, *religious* or *superstitious*, means literally *god-fearing*[3]. So it may be applied to any 'religion,' as e.g. to Judaism itself (xxv 19), and in itself it is ambiguous. That is to say, whether it is to be taken as a compliment, *very religious*, or the reverse, *somewhat superstitious*, whether it expresses devotion or superstition, depends on the *fear of God* according as it is either a filial awe or an unreasoning dread. S. Paul no doubt left it to the Athenian conscience to decide his meaning. But of this character of their 23 worship he had come across a signal instance. On his arrival, as he went up the road from the Piraeus to Athens, his eye fell on *an altar* by the road-side on which was cut the dedication *TO (THE) UNKNOWN GOD*[4]. Other ancient authorities[5] testify to the existence at Athens of 'altars of the unknown gods'; and this expression may cover an altar with the dedication in the singular 'to an unknown god.' Such altars had no doubt been erected from time to time on the occasion of some calamity when the pious Athenians were unable to discover the deity whose hand was afflicting them[6]. But whatever their origin or the exact form of their inscriptions, these altars afforded an excellent parable of pagan religion. To the pagans every action of life, every spot of ground was under the control of some supernatural agency; and in accordance with these ideas they admitted into their pantheon not only such strange divinities as diseases, but also mental conceptions, virtues, and emotions. In this process of deifying as it were the whole of nature, the Athenians had outstripped all competitors, and by this dedication they added the completing touch to their religion: for fear lest any deity had been left out they at once

---

[1] The verb translated *behold, perceive*, in vv. 16, 22 (*observe* in ver. 23 is a compound of the same verb) is that used of a sightseer, and also of a religious ambassador, one sent to consult an oracle or to represent the state at some religious festival.   [2] The verb corresponding to the substantive *sharp-contention* in xv 39 (p. 266).   [3] The Greek words used here for *god* and *fear* are different from those for the *God-fearing* Gentiles, and bear a less favourable sense: the Greek for *god* (the same as for *gods* ver. 18) has become our *demon*. For the comparative see Blass *Grammar of NT Gk* § 44. 3.   [4] There is no article in the Greek and we can supply either *AN* or *THE*.   [5] e.g. Pausanias, Philostratus, Lucian, and S. Jerome.   [6] So the story told of Epimenides at Athens by Diogenes Laertius suggests.

took in the whole of heaven by worshipping the 'unknown' god or gods. It was indeed a 'catholic' paganism. Besides S. Paul there is another witness to this all-embracing piety of the Athenians. Pausanias, who was the Greek 'Murray' or 'Baedeker,' visited Athens a hundred years after this, and he tells us: 'The Athenians have in the agora...an altar of MERCY. To this deity, of all the gods the most useful to the life of man and its vicissitudes, the Athenians alone of all the Greeks assign honours. For as they pay more regard to philanthropy than other men, so they exhibit more piety to the gods. For they have also altars to SHAME and RUMOUR and ENERGY[1].'
This extreme 'religiousness' however only stirred up S. Paul to
17 utterance. In the bitterness of his spirit (Ezek iii 14), he could no longer keep silence, and he *began to reason* both in the *synagogue* and in the *agora*.

Marketplace conveys a very inadequate idea of the Greek *agora*[2]. The agora was an open space in the centre of the city which served as the focus of the civic life. Around it were grouped the public buildings of the city—the temples of its patron gods, its senate-house, town-hall and law-courts. Besides these there were *stoas* or *porticoes*, i.e. *porches* or colonnades, which were used for exchanges or places of concourse; and the rest of the circuit would be filled up with shops. Within this square beat the heart of the city. All the morning the agora was the scene of market, and crowded with country-people, buyers and sellers, merchants and business men. Hither also repaired all who had civic business, the magistrates and civic functionaries. Business over, it became the resort of the idle, the gossips and the newsmongers, whether loungers of fashionable society or lazy 'fellows of the rabble.' Being the resort of the citizens, we should also find in the agora those who wanted an audience, whether philosophers and travelling rhetoricians, or charlatans and quacks. Such teachers or declaimers, if they came to stay, would take up their station in some porch and there gather round them a body of disciples. Of the agoras of Greece most famous was that of Athens. At this time among its sights were to be counted the Senate-house, the Temple of Zeus Eleutherius (the god of freedom), the Stoa Basilica (royal porch), where the Archon Basileus held his sessions and where the court of the Areopagus frequently met, a gymnasium built by Ptolemy Philadelphus king of Egypt, a porch built by an Attalus king of Pergamum, and, more famous than all, the ancient Painted Porch[3], so called because it was adorned with frescoes by Polygnotus. This celebrated porch had been the scene of the labours of Zeno of Citium, and from it his disciples received the name of Stoics.

In this agora Socrates used to practise his dialectic. He would arrest the passers-by and by a rigorous cross-examination try to destroy their superficial self-confidence and to arouse in them some desire for better things. And now, 450 years later, a second Socrates is seen *daily* to '*reason in the marketplace.*' This was

[1] *Attica* 17. [2] Cp. the *agora* at Philippi xvi 19, and the *agoraioi* at Thessalonica xvii 5 f. [3] Stoa Poikilê.

S. Paul. He would not lack hearers, for his teaching would fully
18 satisfy the Athenian desire for *something new* or *strange*. Among
others *some of the philosophers, both Stoics and Epicureans, crossed
swords with him*; they had some argument together. S. Paul *was
preaching the gospel of Jesus and the resurrection* : the gospel of
Jesus sent by God, of Jesus crucified and risen, and by his resurrection giving the pledge of salvation, offering to man the forgiveness
of sins and the gift of the Spirit. But such a gospel was quite
unintelligible to the Athenians : in their self-complacent culture
and wisdom of this world they did not want any gospel. *Some*,
and among them the Epicureans, thought it simple 'folly' (I Cor
i 23) and put down S. Paul for a *seedpicker*. This was current
Attic slang for the idler in the agora, who like a bird picking up
seeds made his living on what scraps and droppings he could pick
up. Such a man was a fitting type for a *babbler*, the literary idler
who picked up scraps of knowledge from others and tried to win
a reputation by parading his pickings without having been able
to digest them himself. *Others*, and more especially the Stoics,
took it more seriously. S. Paul was obviously a religious enthusiast, and they took him for the 'slave' of some *gods* whose
cult he was trying to propagate (xvi 17, p. 287). Their names
seemed to be *Jesus and Anastasis* (the *Resurrection*)[1]; and
certainly strange and *outlandish* was S. Paul's *contribution*[2] to
the pantheon of Athens. This view of his teaching put matters
on another footing. The gods and religions of antiquity were
extraordinarily tolerant to one another except in one place, viz.
in their respective homes. Each city had its own tutelary deities
and their worship was intimately bound up with the welfare of
the state. To omit their sacred rites, or to introduce strange and
foreign worships, might imperil the state; for this was treason to its
gods. Hence the introduction of a new cult or deity was a public
matter, and fell under the cognizance of the most august authority
in the state, without whose consent it was not allowed. At Rome
this body was the Senate, at Athens the Areopagus. Socrates
himself had been condemned to death on this very charge, viz. that
'he deemed the gods of the city to be no gods and introduced new
deities.' Since Socrates' days indeed all manner of mysteries and
strange gods had found a footing in Athens. Because they were
tolerant in their turn, they did not interfere with the city's worship
or steal away her citizens from attendance at her ceremonies. But
it was just this which made the difference in the case of Christianity.
The God whom S. Paul 'set forth' was a jealous God, and the
apostle was trying with intense zeal to turn away his hearers from the

---

[1] The quotation from Pausanias above, and the condition of the pagan mind therein indicated, would shew how possible the mistake would be. There was a famous temple to *Victory* on the Acropolis; why should not *Resurrection* be a *goddess* likewise? We notice it was *Anastasis—the resurrection*, not *Staurôsis—the crucifixion*. [2] or what he *brought to* Athens (verse 20).

other 'vain gods.' Such proselytism called for investigation by the authorities. Accordingly one day, when 'the agora was full,' *they laid hands upon* Paul, i.e. quietly arrested him, *and led him into* the Stoa Basilica where *the Areopagus* was sitting, to give a formal account of his *new teaching*. The court of refined and polished Athenians was very different from the rough provincial magistrates of Philippi, and the philosophers who presented Paul to their cognizance very different from the mob of Thessalonians; this we can see at once in the very polite and civil phrases in which the demand was couched.

A different conception of the scene has prevailed in England. It is supposed that the crowd in the agora in its eagerness to hear S. Paul's doctrine and prompted by some sudden suggestion, carried him up to the top of the hill of Areopagus—which lay to the south of the agora. This would be a more convenient place for a public exposition, which S. Paul then gave in answer to their request. Certainly this is the popular view in England, which has been greatly encouraged by the AV rendering of *Mars' hill* in verse 22—the corrective in the margin, *or court of the Areopagites*, having escaped notice. To this view however there is one great objection, viz. that though the hill was the ancient meeting-place of the court of the Areopagus, there is no evidence that it was used for such a public and popular address as this view supposes. Indeed there was not room on the summit for a large gathering. Accordingly, if S. Paul's speech was delivered there, it would have been as a legal defence before the court of the Areopagus. That this was its character (whatever was the scene of its delivery) seems clear from the language of S. Luke. There is the bringing of S. Paul into court, or his presentation, as in xvi 19, (xvii 6), xviii 12[1]: the opening of the case as in vii 1: the defence: the adjournment (verse 32) as in xxiv 22: and S. Paul's departure from the court, literally *from the midst of them* (iv 7, xxiii 10). It is true that the language on both sides, of the Athenians and of S. Paul, does not read like that of accusation and defence. But apart from the politeness of the Greek mode of expression, the doctrine of S. Paul was too novel for a definite charge to be laid against him. The Athenians were in fact in the same difficulty as Festus, who found himself quite unable to 'signify to the emperor the charges brought against the apostle'; and this was a preliminary examination, like that before Agrippa, to see if he should be 'committed for trial.' If this was the case, it is more natural to suppose that the examination took place in the Stoa Basilica, when the Archon Basileus was holding a court. The Basilica would be filled with a crowd of spectators and philosophers, and S. Paul, as in the audience chamber at Caesarea, seized the opportunity of making his defence a public declaration of the gospel, which left the Athenians more puzzled than before[2].

---

[1] *Brought-unto* in ver. 19 is used of the presentation of the Lord before Pilate (Lk xxiii 1). [2] There is a parallel in the examination before the Sanhedrin in xxii 30–xxiii 1, and a still more remarkable one in that before Festus and Agrippa. See xxv 23–xxvi 2.

S. Paul, then, *stood in the midst of the Areopagus* and began his reply. The word *stood* arrests our attention, and makes us realize the dramatic situation. As Peter stood and proclaimed the gospel to the bewildered Jews (ii 14), so Paul stands and preaches to the astonished Greeks. There is no exact parallel in the OT: but there we have the contrast between Moses and the wisdom of Egypt, between Daniel and the wisdom of the Chaldeans[1].

S. Paul's gospel for the Greeks

This defence is thoroughly Pauline in manner and method. S. Paul shews his usual tact by conciliating his audience with as great a compliment as he can truthfully pay[2]. He seizes some local circumstance for a text, and lays himself open to the influence of his surroundings[3]. He makes himself all things to all men, speaking to Greeks as a Greek and as a philosopher to philosophers. Where he can, he employs the doctrines now of the Stoics, now of the Epicureans. Similarly in regard to method,—on the negative side, when criticizing popular idolatry, he uses arguments that had been common-places in philosophic Greek thought since the days of Xenophanes in the sixth century B.C. In more recent times such criticism had been largely employed by Hellenistic Jews on behalf of the Jewish faith in the one God; and so we find S. Paul clearly echoing the Hellenistic teaching of S. Stephen in vii 48–50. On the positive side, he does not advance doctrines that were distinctively Jewish, such as that of the Messiah, nor again such as might prove a stumbling-block, as that of the crucifixion[4], but he first lays down the fundamental principles of natural theology: the doctrines of God as (*a*) the Creator of the world and (*b*) its Ruler and Preserver, (*c*) omnipresent and immanent. And for each of these doctrines he could find support in some one or other of the schools of philosophy. This foundation laid, he passes on to the doctrine of judgement, which also is almost a part of natural religion, for the natural conscience of man speaks to him of judgement. And only then, when he has stirred the conscience and aroused a sense of danger, does he introduce a specially Christian message.

The speech has an interest apart from the personality of its author. It is a typical sermon to the Gentiles. In the Acts the gospel for the Gentiles is contained in S. Peter's sermon to Cornelius, the practical Roman centurion, and in S. Paul's words to the 'barbarians' of Lycaonia and his defence here to the cultivated Greeks[5]. The message to the individual is 'believe on the Lord Jesus and thou shalt be saved' (faith): with warnings about 'righteousness and temperance and the judgement to come' (repentance)[6]. From these we see that to the Gentiles the announcement of judgement was the starting-point of

---

[1] Exod vii 11-2, 22, viii 7, 18-9: Dan i 20, ii 27-8 etc. [2] Cp. xxiv 10, xxvi 2-3. [3] e.g. in touching upon the origin of man (see on ver. 26), the tribunal of God (in contrast to the tribunal of the Areopagus, ver. 31) etc. [4] I Cor i 23. [5] x 34-43; xiv 15-7; xvii 22-31. The defence before Festus and Agrippa was addressed to all the world, Jews as well as Gentiles. [6] xvi 31 (the jailor of Philippi): xxiv 25 (Felix).

the apostles' gospel, but only when they had first won their hearts by shewing the goodness and love of God whether in nature (Paul) or in the gift of his Son (Peter)[1]. In this speech however we are, most unmistakeably, listening to the voice of S. Paul. The lesson of the judgement is what he preached to both Jews and Greeks[2]—*repentance* and *faith.* He cannot restrain himself from speaking of *faith,* though the word is used in a general sense (*assurance* RV). The *righteousness* of the judgement brings up the problem of the times of man's ignorance, which was in his mind at Lystra and when writing to the Romans[3]. Lastly, as in Rom i 4 the resurrection of Jesus declares his divine sonship, so here it declares his appointment to be judge. Peter had left judgement simply to God's will: Paul associates it with the resurrection[4]. *The offspring of God* in verse 29 is the prelude to the doctrine of our 'adoption' into the sonship of God[5].

The speech is also important as a vindication of Christian philosophy. The lesson of S. Paul at Athens is not—as it might be superficially interpreted—the refutation of the claim of learning or philosophy to have any part or lot in the gospel. It is the refutation not of wisdom but of the wisdom of this world. We have seen how poor a wisdom was to be found at Athens: there was no Socrates to be found there then, no Plato, no Aristotle, but in their place degenerate philosophers, whose eyes were blinded by their own self-conceit so that they could not see the wisdom of God. But there is a true wisdom, a 'wisdom among the perfect'—strong meat for grown-up men, which, when his disciples are able to bear it, S. Paul will set before them in his Epistles to the Ephesians and Colossians. Here he answers false philosophy not by obscurantism but by declaring the true philosophy of God and the world. To quote Dr Hort, 'it was the solemn unfolding of the gospel as the sanction and the fulfilment of knowledge in the metropolis of the human search after truth[6].' And in so doing Paul shares with S. John the glory of being an ancestor of the long line of Christian philosophers and theologians.

The analysis of the speech is quite simple. I. Introductory. S. Paul answers the enquiry of the Areopagus and declares himself a messenger of God. II. The main subject. He unfolds the Divine Nature: there is one God—the Creator, and Ruler of the world; he is everywhere present, and he is the Parent of men. This doctrine convicts paganism of error (and therefore of sin). III. The practical appeal. God has now sent a message to men to repent of sin and so to escape the punishment of sin in the day of judgement which he has appointed.

22   And Paul stood in the midst of [7] the Areopagus, and said, Ye men of Athens, in all things I perceive that ye are

---

[1] Cp. xiv 17 (the bounty of God), xvii 25–9 (the parentage of God); x 36–8 (*good tidings, doing good*).   [2] xx 21. The same doctrine had been declared by S. Peter in another form in x 43.   [3] xiv 16, Rom i 18–ii 16.   [4] Both use the same word *appoint* (x 42, xvii 31, Rom i 4).   [5] Rom viii 14–6, Gal iv 6.   [6] *Hulsean Lectures* p. 63.   [7] AV *Mars' hill,* and in marg *Or, court of the Areopagites.*

23 ¹somewhat superstitious. For as I passed along, and observed
the objects of your worship, I found also an altar with this
inscription, TO ²AN UNKNOWN GOD. ³What therefore ye
worship in ignorance, ³this set I forth unto you.
24 The God that made the world and all things therein, he,
being Lord of heaven and earth, dwelleth not in ⁴temples
25 made with hands; neither is he ⁵served by men's hands, as
though he needed anything, seeing he himself giveth to all
26 life, and breath, and all things; and he made of one⁶ every
nation of men for to dwell on all the face of the earth, having
determined *their* ⁷appointed seasons, and the ⁸bounds of their
27 habitation; that they should seek God, if haply they might
feel after him, and find him, though he is not far from each
28 one of us: for in him we live, and move, and ⁹have our being;
as certain even of your own poets have said, For we are also
29 his offspring. Being then the offspring of God, we ought not
to think that ¹⁰the Godhead is like unto gold, or silver, or
stone, graven by art and device of man.
30 The times of ignorance therefore God overlooked; but
now he ¹¹commandeth men that they should all everywhere
31 repent: inasmuch as he hath appointed a day, in the which
he will judge ¹²the world in righteousness ¹³by the man whom
he hath ordained; whereof he hath given ¹⁴assurance unto all
men, in that he hath raised him from the dead.

22 I. S. Paul opens his lips with the classical words *Ye men of
Athens* so familiar to readers of Thucydides and Demosthenes; and
then according to both AV and RV begins with a rebuke. This
is indeed gently administered (RV), but it would still be quite
contrary to the custom of orators and the tact of S. Paul. Hence
it is better to translate *very religious*. This was perfectly true, for
the word can well be applied to the maintenance of external religious
forms. The Athenians would accept it as a compliment, though as
the orator proceeded they would perceive that in his eyes it was a
23 very doubtful compliment. The text which S. Paul makes use of

---

¹ Or *very religious* (marg *somewhat religious*): AV *too superstitious*.   ² Marg
THE.   ³ AV and later MSS read *Whom...him*.   ⁴ Marg *sanctuaries*.   ⁵ AV
worshipped.   ⁶ AV, later MSS and Bezan add *blood*.   ⁷ AV and Bezan read
before-appointed.   ⁸ Literally *setting-of-bounds*.   ⁹ *have our being*] Gk *are*:
Bezan adds *every day*.   ¹⁰ Marg *that which is divine*.   ¹¹ Marg with אB
reads *declareth to men*.   ¹² Gk *the inhabited (earth)*.   ¹³ Gk *in the* (or *a*)
man: Bezan adds *Jesus*.   ¹⁴ Gk *faith*: AV marg *he hath offered faith*.

likewise bore an ambiguous meaning. The inscription TO THE UN-KNOWN GOD may be taken as expressing the very essence of superstition. To a stern Christian philosopher it is the 'confession at once of a bastard philosophy and of a bastard religion[1].' But S. Paul took it in a kindlier sense. It shewed that the Athenians, with all the complacent self-conceit and self-confidence of their philosophy and religiousness, did recognize the possibility of some depths in heaven which their knowledge had not fathomed, some divine power to which *worship* was due. Of such a Divine Power or Nature, i.e. *Godhead* (verse 29) hitherto unrevealed, S. Paul now professes himself to be the messenger or *setter-forth* (verse 18).

24   II. This Divine Power is a personal God; and the apostle proceeds to unfold his relation (1) to the universe and (2) to men. (1) *God made the world.* The definite doctrine of creation was characteristic of Judaism; S. Paul, in fact, is using words of Isaiah[2]. By its assertion, to which the Stoics would have assented in a sense, he quietly sets aside the Epicurean theory of the universe. They denied creation, holding that matter was eternal,—for 'out of nothing nothing can come,'—and that our world was the result of a chance collision of atoms. The doctrine of creation by God, however, leads to logical conclusions affecting paganism generally: it is fatal to two pagan ideas respecting divine worship, viz. (*a*) that
25 God *dwelleth in temples*[3] and (*b*) that he *is served* or *worshipped* (AV) by human offerings, i.e. fed by the fat of sacrifices and pleased by the smell of incense. For, *being Lord* or master[4] and owner of all things, (*a*) how can he be confined within four walls? (*b*) how can he *need anything more*? Such ideas had been clearly refuted in the OT—(*a*) in Isai lxvi 1-2, and (*b*) in Ps l 8-12. S. Stephen also had addressed the first argument to the Jews[5]: for even to them the doctrine was a matter of difficulty—'what then (they would ask) about the temple at Jerusalem?' The answer is best given in the words of S. Chrysostom—'did not God dwell in the temple at Jerusalem? Nay verily; but he worked therein[6].' Walls *built by hands* cannot confine the deity, but they can be the scene of special manifestations of his presence: so likewise the service offered by *human hands* can be acceptable if accompanied by the service of the heart. Such an answer, indeed, might have been given by an enlightened Gentile, and as he spoke S. Paul would carry with him the cordial agreement of the philosophers. In pressing the second argument, he is almost using the language of the Epicureans, who taught that the divine nature is self-sufficing and 'needs nothing from us' (*nihil indiga nostri*)[7]. But then at once he gives a turn to his sentence which converts it into a rebuke. Because it is self-

---

[1] Dr Hort, *Hulsean Lectures* p. 64.   [2] Isai xlii 5: cp. also Acts iv 24, xiv 15.
[3] S. Paul uses, very correctly, the word for the inner temple or shrine.   [4] So the word is translated in xvi 16.   [5] vii 47-50.   [6] *Hom. on Acts* xxxviii 2. The word *dwell* in ver. 24 implies a fixed and permanent habitation: cp. vii 2, 4, 48.
[7] Lucretius ii 650.

sufficing, the divine nature is not therefore separate from and indifferent to us. On the contrary God is the continual *source of life and breath to all*; he gives (nay more, he is[1]) *all things to all*. In saying this, S. Paul declares that God is not only (*a*) Creator, but also (*b*) Preserver, of the world.

26 (2) The universe includes man, and to the human race S. Paul now passes. As (*a*) Creator, God *made man*. This statement tacitly rebukes Athenian pride. Unlike the rest of Greece, the population of Athens had been stationary from time immemorial, so the Athenians prided themselves on being 'autochthonous' (i.e. indigenous), and the common people believed that their first fathers had literally 'sprung from the soil.' The further assertion however that *God made of one* (man or blood) *every race of man* was a serious blow at Greek pride in general. Very much like the Jews in this respect, the Greeks divided the world into two kinds of men—Greeks and Barbarians,— and the latter were of no account. Hence it was necessary for S. Paul to preach to Greeks as well as to Jews the doctrine of catholicity, and this is marked by the characteristic recurrence of the word *all*[2]. For this teaching, indeed, the way had been prepared by the Stoics, who had taught the brotherhood of man and that all men alike are citizens of the one great city of Zeus. Again, as the Stoics agreed with S. Paul in the doctrine of creation, so they would also accept the further doctrine of (*b*) the divine providence and predestination. This doctrine also S. Paul now proceeds to apply to man. As God is the Preserver of the world, so is he the Governor of man. Having made man, he did not leave him alone. The successive stages or *seasons* of the development of mankind had followed one another in accordance with his *command*[3] or will: the present distribution of the different races, Greek and Roman, Jew and Barbarian, with the balance of power and variety of privilege, was also in accordance with his *appointment*[4]. And both together, i.e. the whole history of mankind, had been *ordained* by God for an end. The end of man's creation was that he should 'replenish *the whole earth*' (Gen i 28):

27 the end of his education in history, that men should *seek after God in the hope that possibly they might feel after him and find him*. Here S. Paul himself adopts the refinement of the Greek style of speech. For by using a form of the hypothetical sentence which indicates a somewhat dubious hope, he avoids the direct and unpleasant assertion that men—the Athenians included—had signally failed in their search after God. Instead of consciously realizing his presence, as by touch of hand[5], they had groped about, like men in the dark, without success; *and yet* there was no excuse for their failure, because God was *close to* man, even to *every single individual*, whether Greek or Barbarian.

---

[1] Cp. e.g. I Cor xv 28, Eph iv 6. [2] It occurs 9 times in the Greek, in vv. 22, 24, 25 (2), 26 (2), 30 (2), 31. [3] Cp. xiii 48. The word was used of God in x 33 (*commanded*). [4] For the divine *appointment* or *setting* cp. i 7. [5] Cp. Lk xxiv 39, I Jn i 1 (*handle*).

28   This conclusion follows from the divine nature—God as God is omnipresent: and so the apostle is led on to the doctrine of (c) our dwelling in God with all that it involves. If God is the giver of life and breath and all things, *in him we* literally *live and move and are*. The continued existence of our physical life, the exercise of our faculties, and—what is alone true being or life—our self-conscious existence with all its intellectual and spiritual activity, all these so depend upon God that we can be said to be *in him*. This doctrine was also that of the Stoics, though they would have rather spoken of God being in us: it represents the truth contained in their pantheism, however crudely and materially it was conceived. Accordingly, to support his argument S. Paul quotes *some of their own* authorities, e.g. the Cilician Stoic, Aratus. But as he had rebuked
29 the Epicureans, so now he shews the defects of Stoicism. Out of their own mouth he shews that pantheism is only one half of the truth: God universally immanent in nature is not identical with nature, but a Being independent of nature and the source of all its life. The very words of the poet[1], *we are his offspring*, declare the true relation of God to man. As giver of our life, he is the Parent of man[2]. The parentage of God—that is the conclusion of natural theology. Further, this belief has a practical effect; it destroys a third error—which is the fundamental error—of pagan religion. The doctrine of creation, as the apostle has already shewn, uproots the pagan ideas concerning temples and sacrifices; the doctrine of the divine parentage uproots idolatry itself. That we are, in our human nature, *the offspring of God*, declares the true anthropomorphism, viz. that we are made in the image of God: and the philosophers again would have heartily concurred with the speaker as he convicted the false anthropomorphism of idolatry. It is derogatory to our dignity, nay contrary to filial *duty, to imagine* that *the Divine Nature* or *Godhead*, which is the source of all our life, spiritual as well as bodily, could have any resemblance to material images, which can bear nothing beyond the *impress*[3] *of man's thought and hand*.

III. Hitherto the Areopagus had heard nothing exactly startling or *strange* (verse 20). But now S. Paul is come to the difficult

---

[1] Very similar words occur in the *Hymn* of Cleanthes, a kind of Stoic creed, or confession of faith, in verse. Another line out of Aratus would have illustrated well S. Paul's teaching of the divine omnipresence: 'Full of Zeus are all the streets, and exchanges of men: full of him the sea and all its havens.'   [2] The word *parent* is the correlative of *offspring*, and denotes the natural relation of God to man. Christianity makes a further offer to man of an adoption into a closer relationship—that of *son* to *father*. This relationship springs out of the presence of the Spirit of God in our hearts; and the gift of the Spirit is conveyed to us in Holy Baptism, which is therefore our adoption into sonship (Gal iv 5-6). The Jews were the natural *offspring of Abraham* (xiii 26): all men are the natural *offspring of God*, as S. Luke shews in tracing the genealogy of our Lord back to *God* (Lk iii 38).
[3] The Greek word (translated *graven by*) is that used for 'the *mark* of the beast' in Rev xiv 16, 17 etc. It was the form stamped by man upon the gold etc. to which *the Godhead* was likened.

part of his task, to the introduction of the gospel; and for the reception of the gospel a conviction of sin is the necessary preliminary. He has to tell his audience that the ideas and forms of pagan worship are not harmless matters of speculation or useful errors of the common people, to be tolerated and condoned by the educated, but actually culpable and involving guilt in the eyes of God. But he still proceeds with all delicacy and gentleness.

30 As S. Peter had excused the Jews, so S. Paul excuses the Athenians on the ground of ignorance: they had been *worshipping in ignorance* (verse 23). But this *ignorance* itself suggests a difficulty, which the Greeks could raise at once. If God is creator and parent, how is it that he left man in ignorance of himself? how can he have ordained such countless ages of almost universal ignorance? and what of the past generations? This problem had vexed the apostle himself; and he now finds an answer in three lines of thought. (1) The first anticipates the modern idea of evolution. There were definite *times of ignorance* which had their place in *the appointed seasons* of the divine education of the world, just as in the life of man there is a 'time of ignorance' in childhood. God, then, 'permitted[1]' them; and man, if unable to read the whole plan of God, must be content to know that it is his will. (2) Where God had not revealed himself in the law, there guilt was not imputed; and so the apostle conceives of God as *overlooking* or 'passing over[2]' the times of ignorance. (3) But this does not relieve man of all responsibility; for God had not left himself 'without witness[3],' whether in nature or in the heart of man—the law written in his conscience. Man is responsible for reading this witness; and for failure he incurs guilt and is liable to judgement, as his own conscience bears witness[4]. The question of the times past is a matter of speculation: S. Paul's concern and ours is with the present and ourselves. And *now* God has taken away from men the plea of ignorance by a definite revelation of himself, a *message* or even *command*[5].

This delivery of a message proves that God is a living Person, as against the impersonal, pantheistic conceptions of the philosophers; and also that all men stand in a personal relation to him. To God all men owe faith and obedience; and therefore the message is that *all men*—for 'all have sinned and fall short of the glory of God[6]'—should *repent* of their idolatry. And the
31 apostle adds an imperative reason for repentance. God has *appointed a day in which he is about to judge the world*. There is another aspect of the divine character involved in the former revelations. (*a*) Creation itself, as it is, involves a day of judgement, when God's purpose shall be fulfilled and order restored to the universe. This *day* was eternally appointed in the divine will, and has its place in the *appointed seasons*. S. Paul's words indeed,

---
[1] xiv 16.   [2] Rom iii 25.   [3] Acts xiv 16.   [4] Rom ii 15.   [5] See the variant reading.   [6] Rom iii 23.

as also his contemporary letters to the Thessalonians, shew that at that time he was expecting it to be imminent. (*b*) But it is the world of man, *the inhabited earth*, which most calls for a day of judgement. If God is Parent of man, he is also Judge. His *righteousness* must be vindicated, and the standard of the judgement is *righteousness*. This again raises difficulties: (*a*) How can the God who 'dwelleth not in temples' reveal himself as Judge and appear upon the tribunal? (*b*) How can God who must be untouched by human ignorance and weakness judge man *in righteousness*[1]? The answer is—he will judge *in* (the person of) *a man whom he ordained*, and whose appearance therefore is the true end of the appointed seasons and the world's history (verse 26). So (*a*) God will be revealed in one who is the Son of God; (*b*) and the judge, being at the same time Son of Man, will be able justly to measure the allowance for human infirmity[2]. The mention of the *man*, as of the *day*, brings the fact of judgement within the conditions of time and space, and therefore makes it subject to the demand for evidence. Now proof of the judgement and of the appointment of the Judge God has given—and that in the *resurrection* of Jesus Christ *from the dead*; which being a fact of a catholic character—he rose as 'man'—affects *all men* alike, as men. In it God has given (1) *assurance* of his office; by his resurrection Jesus was 'declared to be the Son of God[3]' and therefore to possess the authority and power for judgement: (2) *assurance* of the general *resurrection of the dead*, so that all men can be judged in their bodies[4]; for Christ is the Son of Man and the firstfruits of our race: (3) by it also, if they could have understood, God *afforded* to all men *faith* in Jesus which is the assurance of salvation.

Thus S. Paul preached unto the Athenians 'Jesus and the Resurrection.' But at the mention of the *resurrection of the dead* (verse 32) they would hear no more.

The judgement of the Athenians

32 Now when they heard of the resurrection of the dead, some mocked; but others said, We will hear thee concerning
33 this yet again. Thus Paul went out from among them.
34 But certain men clave unto him, and believed: among whom also was Dionysius the Areopagite, [5]and a woman named Damaris, and others with them.

32 There was a division of opinion. *Some* saw in the affair only a matter of ridicule and *began to mock* (ii 13). There were indeed

---

[1] Cp. Job ix 32-3 *For he is not a man, as I am, that I should answer him, that we should come together in judgement. There is no daysman betwixt us.* [2] Cp. Jn v 27. [3] Rom i 4, where the Gk for *declare* is the same as for *ordain* here. [4] II Cor v 10. [5] Instead of *and a woman named Damaris* Bezan has *of honourable estate* (verse 12).

marvellous stories in pagan mythology; but to speak in sober earnest of a dead man rising again to life was a sign of madness (xxvi 24), of some mental delusion. *Others* however were in favour of an adjournment, and this apparently was the formal decision of the court¹. *Paul* then left the Areopagus *thus*—that is, having caused a division. Wherever the message is delivered, it divides for life or for death: and if S. Paul stood at the bar, his presence there in itself brought a judgement upon his judges². As usual his earnestness had made a deep impression on some, who *attached themselves to him and became believers*. One of them was indeed a member of the court³, an *Areopagite*, named *Dionysius*. There was also an aristocratic lady named *Damaris, and others* of a humbler station *together with them*, perhaps their households and other dependants. Tradition calls Dionysius the first bishop of Athens, and no doubt his name was well known in the churches of Achaia. But a greater fame was in store for him. As an Athenian and an Areopagite, his name seemed to an Egyptian⁴ author of the 5th or 6th century to be a very suitable one to be put at the head of a number of writings on mystic theology. These writings exercised a great influence on the church; and when they reached France in the ninth century, it was probably their popularity which led to a further confusion of the Areopagite with another Dionysius, a martyr of Paris and patron saint of France, familiarly known as S. Denys.

To return to the first century, the result of S. Paul's work at Athens was but small. Intellectual pride and the superficial culture of a spoilt population could not make a good ground for the seed of the gospel. At Athens S. Paul tried the wisdom of the world and found it wanting; and when he went on to Corinth, he determined not to try excellency of speech or the persuasive words of wisdom, but to preach—what he had not proclaimed in the Areopagus—Christ crucified⁵. His disappointment at the failure of the former method to touch the frivolous Athenians no doubt kindled the fire with which he denounces the wisdom of the world in his first epistle to the Corinthians⁶.

Whether further proceedings took place we are not told, but with a careful writer like S. Luke the words *yet again* (verse 32) must have some meaning. In any case S. Paul shortly afterwards went on to Corinth. The word for *departed* in xviii 1 is rare in the Acts and is used in the following verse for a forcible expulsion of the Jews from Rome⁷. Accordingly, we have some grounds for the conjecture that Paul *departed from Athens* in obedience to an order of the Areopagus.

---

¹ The difference in the tenses suggests this. ² Cp. xxviii 24, xvii 12 (Bezan): II Cor ii 15–6. Cp. the result of his appearance before the Sanhedrin in xxiii 7.
³ Like Joseph of Arimathea who was a member of the Sanhedrin, he was *a councillor* (Lk xxiii 50). ⁴ Or Syrian (?). On him see Inge *Christian Mysticism* p. 104 f.
⁵ I Cor ii 1–5. ⁶ I Cor i 17–iii: cp. viii 1–2. ⁷ It is in the passive voice. The Bezan text reads *withdrew* which contains the idea of retreat or retirement.

§ 2 *The church at Corinth*

From Athens Paul naturally passed on *to Corinth*, only fifty miles distant and the capital of Achaia. But great was the change, not to be measured by the number of miles. It was like passing from Oxford to London. For Corinth was a flourishing commercial city with a cosmopolitan population, where S. Paul would feel more at home, so much so indeed that at Corinth for the first time since A.D. 44 he *sat down* (verse 11) for a period of settled work. The note of time, *a year and six months*, is a sign that he had made the city his head-quarters[1]. The vision of the Lord shews that, as the entry into Macedonia, so the settlement at Corinth was undertaken in accordance with the divine direction. And the summary, with which S. Luke concludes the paragraph, marks the close of a period in the history.

Corinth had perhaps the largest population of any city which S. Paul had as yet visited, with the exception of the Syrian Antioch. The old Corinth of Greek history had been entirely destroyed by the Roman general Mummius in B.C. 146. But a hundred years later Julius Caesar founded the city anew as a Roman colony and gave it the name of COLONIA LAUS JULIA CORINTHUS. It became the seat of the proconsul, and was thoroughly Roman in constitution and loyalty. The geographical position of the city soon restored it to more than its old prosperity. By its citadel on the lofty summit of Acrocorinthus, 1800 feet high, Corinth had in old days commanded the land entrance into the Peloponnese, while its ports of Cenchreae on the gulf of Aegina and Lechaeum on the gulf of Lepanto gave it complete control over the traffic across the isthmus of Corinth. It was this traffic which now proved the source of the new colony's prosperity. For this was the most direct and quickest route to Rome from Asia, viz. to cross the Aegean from Ephesus to Cenchreae and then crossing the isthmus take ship for Brindisi. Besides, by hauling their ships over the isthmus[2] mariners escaped the dangers of rounding Cape Malea. This proximity to Italy would in itself have been an attraction for S. Paul; and, as we shall see, Corinth marks a definite stage in his course to Rome. Further, the population of Corinth presented a very favourable soil for Christianity: not only from its cosmopolitan character, but from the consequent spiritual need. In antiquity Corinth enjoyed an evil notoriety. As the traveller approached the city, one of the sights which met his eye by the road-side was the tomb of a celebrated courtesan, Lais; and the very name of the city had added another word to the vocabulary of immorality. The immorality was even consecrated by religion: for the temple of Aphroditê Pandêmos on Acrocorinthus possessed, after the oriental fashion, a thousand 'hieroduli' or consecrated prostitutes. Great then was the need for a purifying gospel; and by the grace of the Lord through the ministry of the apostle many were to be delivered out of the corruption which is in the world through

---

[1] The last note of time was in xi 26.   [2] It was reserved to modern times to cut a canal through the isthmus. Nero began the work without finishing it.

lust: 'and such were some of you,' S. Paul writes in I Cor vi 11, 'but ye were washed, but ye were sanctified, but ye were justified.' Indeed that epistle throughout bears marks of the moral atmosphere with which the converts had to contend[1].

This quotation reminds us of the abundance of our authorities for this period. We have two important Epistles to the Corinthians, the first of which throws more light than any other epistle on the organization and daily life of an early Christian church. Besides this, the Epistles to the Thessalonians and to the Romans were written at Corinth. Yet to the record of the active life into which these letters give us a glimpse S. Luke assigns but seventeen verses; and of eighteen names connected with Corinth, he mentions but three. This is a useful warning against the unreasonableness of drawing arguments from silence on S. Luke's part. He seems to have been less interested in Corinth than in Macedonia and Ephesus: possibly, because the Corinthian church, like the churches of Galatia, did not prove very faithful to S. Paul. The brief account he does give clearly illustrates his principles of selection. He (1) mentions the meeting with Aquila and Priscilla—evidently because of the connexion with Rome: the word *Rome* occurs here for the first time[2]. (2) The decided breach with the Jews and 'going to the Gentiles,' as at Antioch in Pisidia (xiii 45–47), shews that the Corinthian church was distinctly a Gentile church. (3) The vision of the Lord gives divine sanction to the founding of the church—one of the greatest fruits of S. Paul's apostolate. This vision closes the period of work in Macedonia and Achaia, which the vision at Troas had inaugurated. But at the end of the sojourn at Corinth S. Luke adds (4) the affair before Gallio which is the second occasion on which S. Paul is brought into contact with the Roman government in the person of a proconsul.

18 [3]After these things he departed from Athens, and came
2 to Corinth. And he found a certain Jew named Aquila, a man of Pontus by race, lately come from Italy, with his wife Priscilla[4], because Claudius had commanded all the Jews to
3 depart from Rome: and he came unto them; and because he was of the same trade, he abode with them, and [5]they
4 wrought; for by their trade they were tentmakers. And he reasoned in the synagogue every sabbath, and [6]persuaded Jews and Greeks.

---

[1] Ch. v, vi 9–20, vii 2, 5, 9, x 8, xv 33–4.   [2] But *Romans* in ii 10.   [3] Bezan has *And he withdrew [from*.   [4] The Bezan text, as restored by Blass, continues *and saluted them. Now they had come from Rome because Claudius had commanded all the Jews to depart (from Rome); and they dwelt (settled) in Achaia. Now Paul was known to Aquila, (? and) because he was of the same race and trade, and he abode with them and wrought. And entering into the synagogue he reasoned every sabbath day, inserting the name of the Lord Jesus; and he was persuading not only Jews but also Greeks.*   [5] So אB: AV with majority of MSS reads *he wrought*.   [6] Gk *was persuading* or *sought-to-persuade* (RV marg).

5   But when Silas and Timothy came down from Macedonia,
    Paul was constrained ¹by the word, testifying to the Jews
6   that Jesus was the Christ. And when² they opposed them-
    selves, and blasphemed, he shook out his raiment, and said
    unto them, Your blood *be* upon your own heads; I am clean:
7   from henceforth I will go unto the Gentiles. And he ³departed
    thence, and went into the house of a certain man named
    ⁴Titus Justus, one that worshipped God, whose house joined
8   hard to the synagogue. And Crispus, the ruler of the syna-
    gogue, believed in the Lord with all his house; and many
    of the Corinthians hearing believed, and were baptized⁵.
9   And the Lord said unto Paul in the night by a vision,
10 Be not afraid, but speak, and hold not thy peace: for I am
    with thee, and no man shall set on thee to harm thee: for
11 I have much people in this city. And he ⁶dwelt *there* a year
    and six months, teaching the word of God among them.

1   When Paul left Athens, Silas and Timothy had not yet arrived:
    the cessation of navigation for the winter probably delayed them.
2   So Paul entered Corinth alone. There he turned to the Jewish
    quarter and had the good fortune *to find Aquila with his wife
    Priscilla*, who had *just come from Italy*. The apostle may have
    had some previous acquaintance with Aquila, but here at any rate
    begins that close intimacy with Priscilla and Aquila which has left
    its mark on the NT. They were his hosts at Corinth and shared
    his work at Ephesus, where they also 'laid down their necks' for
    him. Aquila illustrates the migratory character of much of the life
    under the empire. He was a native of *Pontus*⁷, but had settled at
    Rome. Banished from Rome, we meet him at Corinth. From
    Corinth Aquila and Priscilla pass on to Ephesus; later, we find them
    at Rome; our latest notice leaves them at Ephesus⁸. It may have
    been at Rome that Aquila won his wife Prisca or (in the more familiar
    diminutive form) Priscilla⁹. Both names indeed are Roman; and
    both have been found in the cemetery of the Acilian gens, so that
    they may have been freedmen of that family. Of the two Priscilla
    was the predominant personality: in four places out of the six

---

¹ AV with later mss reads *was pressed*] *in spirit*.   ² Bezan inserts *there was much speaking and interpretation of the scriptures, and*: one text continues *some of the Jews opposed themselves and blasphemed: then Paul [shook out*.   ³ Gk *crossed over*: Bezan adds *from Aquila*.   ⁴ AV and some early authorities omit Titus: BD read *Titius*.   ⁵ Bezan adds *believing on God through the name of the Lord Jesus Christ*.   ⁶ Gk *sat*.   ⁷ In the second century there was another Jew of Pontus named Aquila who made a new Greek translation of the OT.   ⁸ See xviii 2, 18, 26; I Cor xvi 19; Rom xvi 3–5: II Tim iv 19.   ⁹ S. Paul uses the more formal, S. Luke the more familiar name.

where the couple are mentioned her name comes first. She probably took the leading part in evangelistic work; and therefore is to be classed with Lydia and the other notable women who 'laboured for the gospel.' It has indeed been suggested[1]—and the suggestion is most interesting and probable—that Priscilla was a Roman lady, of higher rank than Aquila. But whether Roman or Jewess, she shared her husband's exile. For they had that additional bond of sympathy with S. Paul; they too were exiles from their home. Ever since Pompey had brought a contingent of Jewish prisoners to Rome in B.C. 61, the Jewish settlement, which had rapidly grown in numbers and importance, had formed a turbulent element in the city, very distasteful to the authorities. Tiberius had deported 4000 Roman Jews to Sardinia in the hope that the malaria might destroy them. And now, about A.D. 49, *Claudius* had issued an edict banishing the Jews from the city altogether. Suetonius[2] tells us the reason; it was because 'the Jews were in a state of constant tumult at the instigation of one Chrestus.' These words no doubt refer to disturbances which ensued upon the preaching of the Christ at Rome similar to those in other Jewish quarters, in Galatia and in Macedonia. A ready inference to be drawn is that Aquila and Priscilla were Christians already[3]. This would greatly have increased the joy of S. Paul's greeting: he would have not only found a Christian home but established a link with the church in Rome.

3 Aquila's business was *tentmaking*, which would afford an additional reason for living together. For this was the *trade* which S. Paul himself had been taught (p. 126); and as at Thessalonica (p. 296), so at Corinth, to avoid any appearance of interested motives, *he worked* for his living with his own hands[4].

4 While thus occupied in the week, *every sabbath day* he went to *the synagogue* and *began to reason*—*trying to persuade* both elements of the congregation, *Jews* and 'God-fearing' *Greeks*. The marginal rendering of the Greek imperfect tense is made almost certain by the next verse. For the apostle does not seem to have made much impression: he had indeed *inserted the name of the Lord Jesus* (Bezan),—he could hardly have done otherwise,—but we know that he was hardly himself. His anxiety about the Macedonians, his failure at Athens, and the continued separation from Silas and Timothy, depressed his spirits. His bodily strength too was overwrought: if he had recently had a visitation of his 'stake in the flesh,' it would have left him weak. In any case his first appearance in the congregation was 'with bodily weakness and fear and much trembling[5].' Some converts however were made, and in the absence

---

[1] by Dr Plumptre, who is supported by Dr Hort in his lectures on the *Romans and Ephesians* pp. 12–4. [2] in his life of *Claudius* c. 25: for *Chrestus* see pp. 169–70. [3] Certainly there is no mention in the Acts of their *believing* and *being baptized* as we should otherwise have expected. [4] I Cor ix 12, 15, II xiii 13. [5] I Cor ii 3. See also below. He writes to the Corinthians as if they were familiar with his stake in the flesh.

of Timothy Paul baptized them with his own hands. Among these were Gaius and the household of Stephanas, the latter being the first converts of all—' the firstfruits of Achaia¹.' The name of Stephanas is a shortened form—most likely of Stephanêphoros (*crown-bearer*), and it must have reminded S. Paul of Stephen the firstfruits of the martyrs.

5   An entirely new complexion however was to be given to the work at Corinth by the arrival of *Silas and Timothy from Macedonia* as soon as the advent of spring had reopened navigation. Their presence was a personal comfort to the apostle. The good news Timothy brought from the Thessalonians filled him with joy and induced him to write them a reply at once (I Thessalonians). They also brought with them an offering of money from Philippi, which set the apostle free for the moment from the necessity of manual labour, and enabled him to give all his time to the work². Consequently *Paul was constrained by the word*: he surrendered himself to the constraint of the word, i.e. the necessity to preach the gospel. The AV gives (though probably not the right reading) the right sense—he was *pressed in spirit*. Like the Lord himself, he felt a pressure on his spirit, either (1) from without, as of the 'hand of the Lord' strong upon him driving him to preach (Ezek iii 14); or (2) from within, of the word pressing against the walls of his heart in a struggle for utterance. The force which was exerting the pressure, or *constraining* him, was really the love of Christ³; and its effect was seen in a change of method. Instead of *reasoning*, he now *testified*⁴; he once more made proof of his apostolate, in testifying to his own personal experience in his vision of the risen Lord, which had proved that *the Messiah was* none other than this *Jesus* (xvii 3). This brought matters to a crisis.

6   The Jews now definitely *ranged themselves in hostile array* against S. Paul⁵. They denied his witness. They *blasphemed* Christ, and exclaimed ANATHEMA IESUS⁶. Out of this deadlock there was only one issue—separation, as at the Pisidian Antioch. Only here the scene was more startling. S. Paul as it were excommunicated them: he *shook out his lap*, as if he were shaking out their lot from the kingdom of God⁷. What that meant his words shew. They were rejecting Christ like the Jews who crucified him at Jerusalem,

---

¹ I Cor i 14-6; xvi 15. *Gaius* is probably the same as S. Paul's host on his second visit (Rom xvi 23). As it was *the house*(hold) *of Stephanas* which was *the firstfruits of Achaia* and baptized by S. Paul, it would seem that Stephanas was a Christian already: his case may have been like that of Aquila and Priscilla. But the mention of converts made at Athens (Acts xvii 34) still makes a difficulty. Probably, as a free city, Athens was not reckoned in Achaia.   ² Cp. (*a*) II Cor i 19, I, II Thess i 1: (*b*) I Thess iii 6-10: (*c*) II Cor xi 9, Phil iv 15.   ³ Cp. I Cor ix 16: Lk xii 50: II Cor v 14 (Phil i 23). The word is rather a favourite one with S. Luke, cp. Lk iv 38 (Acts xxviii 8), viii 37, 45, xix 43, xxii 63.   ⁴ A special word for the apostolic witness: cp. ii 40, viii 25, xx 21, 24, xxiii 11, xxviii 23.   ⁵ Cp. xiii 48 (p. 221).   ⁶ Cp. I Cor xii 3 (and xvi 22), and Acts xiii 45 p. 220.   ⁷ Cp. Neh v 13. In xiii 51 the shaking off the dust of the city was a symbol of separation; but that was from the city as a whole.

and *their blood*—their consequent exclusion from the eternal life (xiii 46)—*was upon their own heads*[1]. Paul's conscience was clear; he was innocent; his hands were *clean* from the stain of their blood. This excommunication on S. Paul's part was no doubt his answer to the sentence of excommunication which they had already passed upon him. Thus, once more, he *goes to the Gentiles*[2]; and among them his work at Corinth henceforth lay.

7 The apostle now assembled his 'ecclesia' in the house of a 'Godfearing' Gentile, named *Titus Justus*. The surname *Justus* was common among the Jews[3], but in the case of a Gentile it points to a Latin origin. *His house was next to* the synagogue, perhaps on the opposite side of the street, for Paul *crossed over* thither[4]. His action was stamped with the divine approval[5]. (1) There was the
8 sanction of success. Even *the ruler of the synagogue, Crispus*, threw in his lot with S. Paul, and to mark the occasion the apostle made an exception to his usual custom and baptized him with his own hands[6]. The Gentile Corinthians attended in large numbers, and many *heard, believed*, and *were baptized*[7].

9 (2) There was the sanction of the divine presence working with him and so confirming his apostolate. The knowledge of this was vouchsafed in an especial manner. S. Paul was still 'in fear and trembling.' For, on the one hand, the defection of Crispus must have exasperated the Jews, and the contiguity of Justus' house was a continual aggravation[8]. S. Paul was even in danger of his life from their menaces and plots, and he asks for the prayers of the Thessalonians that 'he may be delivered from unreasonable and evil men[9].' On the other hand, the Greek congregation in the house of Justus were another source of depression. They wanted wisdom and eloquence. But as they were 'babes,' the apostle could not feed them with the strong meat of the Christian wisdom; nor—after his experience at Athens—would he try to satisfy them with the rhetorical displays with which the contemporary rhetoricians tickled the ears of their audiences[10]. Besides this, the Greeks laid great stress on a good presence and personal beauty; and S. Paul had to realize that in their eyes 'his bodily presence was weak and his speech of no account,' that he was 'rude in speech[11].' At this crisis then, when the erection of the church was at stake, for the

---

[1] Mt xxvii 25, Josh ii 19, II Sam i 16. [2] For the distinction between Godfearing *Greeks* (ver. 4) and *Gentiles* pure and simple (ver. 6) see p. 166. [3] Cp. Joseph Justus (i 23), Jesus Justus (Col iv 11). [4] *Joined hard*, taken strictly, implies a party wall, in which case the expression *crossed over* is hardly applicable. So perhaps the Bezan text is right in suggesting that he changed his residence from Aquila's house to that of Titus Justus. [5] Cp. xi 21. [6] I Cor i 14.
[7] They 'were washed from their sins, sanctified, and justified in the name of the Lord Jesus Christ and in the Spirit of our God'—this implies baptism and laying on of hands (I Cor vi 11). The Greek tenses here shew that it was a process continually going on. For the attendance of outsiders see I Cor xiv 23. [8] We are surprised at the use of Justus' house, considering S. Paul's usual tact. Perhaps he had no choice in the matter. [9] II Thess iii 2; cp. I ii 14–6. [10] Cp. I Cor ii 1–5. [11] II Cor x 10, xi 6.

master builder¹ was giving way, *the Lord* Jesus himself intervened. *In a vision* he took away S. Paul's *fear* and assured him of his own presence—to protect him, like Jeremiah, against his own countrymen; to encourage him, like Joshua, in his attack on the citadels of paganism². But the significance of the vision reached beyond the
10 personal encouragement of the apostle. (i) The divine presence was the sanction of S. Paul's apostolate. At no place hardly was this more called in question in after years than at Corinth: and the record of the vision is S. Luke's answer to all attacks. *The Lord* shewed by his words that the divine presence *was with* S. Paul as with Joseph and Moses³: God had sanctioned this work as that of the evangelists at Antioch and that of S. Paul and S. Barnabas in their first journey⁴. (ii) The church at Corinth enjoyed an unusual immunity from persecution: *the Lord* was their shield, so that none could *do* them *evil*⁵. (iii) The church also flourished exceedingly in numbers. Again the reason is contained in the Lord's words: he *had much people* belonging to him in the city⁶. This confirms S. Luke's emphasis upon the prevenient choice of God⁷; but it did not do away with the need of human cooperation. The sheep must be gathered by a shepherd, and the harvest by reapers. So *because* the Lord had much people, therefore the apostle was *not to be silent*, but to *speak* all the more. (iv) The Corinthian church is vindicated as a true 'ecclesia' or *people* of the Lord. The Greek word is not that for a mere crowd or numbers; it is the title of Israel the People of God. The Lord had in this city *a numerous* or *great People*, a new Israel⁸.
11 This divine consolation gave new life to S. Paul⁹. His preaching was now 'with demonstration,' not of rhetoric, but 'of the Spirit and of power.' It was accompanied with 'the signs and wonders' which were 'the credentials of an apostle¹⁰.' In obedience to the divine vision and in order to gather in the abundant harvest S. Paul determined to *sit*, i.e. settle, at Corinth and make it his headquarters, in fact a new Antioch or metropolis for the church in the west. His stay was indeed cut short by the attacks of his enemies, but not until he had spent *eighteen months* at Corinth. And his work there was very much like what it had been at Antioch¹¹. Instead of having to seek out converts and proclaim the gospel abroad, his main occupation was rather to *teach* or instruct the great number of somewhat undisciplined and unruly Corinthians who were flocking into the church. This sentence of S. Luke, which

---

¹ I Cor iii 10. ² Jer i 8, Josh i 5–6. ³ vii 9, 38: cp. also x 38.
⁴ xi 21, xiv 27, xv 4. ⁵ A word for persecution, vii 6: cp. xiv 2. ⁶ Cp. Jn x 16 *other sheep I have which are not of this fold*: cp. also Jn iv 35, Mt ix 37–8.
⁷ Cp. xiii 48, xvi 14, xvii 4. ⁸ Gal vi 1, cp. II Cor vi 16, Acts xv 14. Except in quotations and Tit ii 14 (and Rom xi 1 of the Jews), S. Paul does not use this word *people* in his epistles. In his speeches in the Acts he uses it (of the Jews) xiii 17, 24, 31, xix 4, xxvi 17, 23, xxviii 17: in quotations, xxiii 5, xxviii 26, 27.
⁹ We must not forget that Silas and Timothy took part in the preaching (II Cor i 19).
¹⁰ I Cor ii 4: II xii 12, Rom xv 18–9. ¹¹ Cp. xi 26, xv 35.

ends with *the word of God*[1], evidently marks the close of a chapter in the history, viz. the foundation of the churches of Macedonia and Achaia[2].

According to his wont S. Luke passes over this period of steady organization in silence. But the Epistles to the Corinthians afford so much information that here we can only summarize a few points. As in Macedonia, the church spread all over the province: there were saints 'in the whole of Achaia': a church was established at Cenchreae in which a deaconess—Phoebe—ministered[3]. In Corinth itself the gospel met with an exceptionally ready response. The number of converts was very large and they received the word with extraordinary enthusiasm. There was a great display, or we might say outburst, of spiritual gifts, of prophecy and speaking with tongues. The church was an organism whose intense vitality found expression in a variety of highly diversified ministries: there were apostles, prophets, teachers, miracle-workers, healers, helps, 'governments,' speakers with tongues. The excess of enthusiasm gave rise to actual disorder in the assemblies of the brethren[4]. This almost too exuberant growth of the vine of the church was partly due no doubt to immunity from the pruning and chastening hand of persecution. The attitude of the Roman governor helped to secure this freedom; but the unusual experience was in the main, as S. Luke has shewn us, the fruit of the protecting presence of the Lord. In part also the disorder may have been due to the democratic spirit of the Corinthians and the want of a more formal and definitely organized ministry. In the long list of ministries we hear nothing of a college of presbyters or 'episcopi' at Corinth, as at Ephesus and Philippi. In his first epistle to the Corinthians the apostle associates Sosthenes with himself. Sosthenes then must have been preeminent in some respects[5]. Perhaps he held a place analogous to that of 'Crispus the ruler of the synagogue' among the Jews, and of S. Luke in the church at Philippi: he may have been the leading overseer or president or presbyter of the church. The mass of converts came from the middle or lower classes, but there were some 'wise' and 'noble after the flesh': e.g. Crispus the ruler of the synagogue, and Erastus the treasurer of the city. Among the well-to-do we must also class Stephanas and Gaius, who were able to exercise hospitality on a large scale, and a lady, Chloe, who had a 'household' of servants. Besides these we know the names of Fortunatus, Achaicus, Tertius (who acted as S. Paul's amanuensis in writing the Epistle to the Romans) and Quartus. From these names we see that the Latin element was strong in the church[6].

---

[1] *The word of God* (or *the Lord*) forms a similar close in iv 31, xv 35. *The word was the seed sown* (Lk viii 11); for its growth cp. Acts vi 7, xii 24, xix 20.
[2] See p. 301 for the close connexion between these two provinces. [3] II Cor i 1: Rom xvi 1. [4] I Cor xii–xiv. [5] The apostle, we notice, associates with himself neither Aquila and Priscilla (xvi 19) nor Apollos (xvi 12). [6] Cp. I Cor i 26: i 11, 14, xvi 15–7, Rom xvi 22–3.

§ 3 *From Achaia to Asia* (= Ch. 18. 12—23)

After the eighteen months' interval S. Luke narrates the incident which practically concluded S. Paul's work at Corinth. Hence though it occurred at Corinth, it falls logically under the next chapter of work, viz. that in the province of Asia, which will occupy us till xix 20[1]. This overlapping corresponds to the actual conditions of life. For the usual voyage across the Aegean was from Corinth to Ephesus; and there was the closest intercourse between the two cities, as the history of their churches will shew. The event now to be related concerned the proconsul of Achaia, and so both at the beginning and at the end of his sojourn at Corinth the apostle is brought into contact with Rome.

Paul and Gallio

S. Luke marks a new period by giving a chronological note *Now Gallio being proconsul of Achaia*. It is his first and almost his only reference to secular chronology[2]. But it does not help us much. We can only say that Gallio could hardly have been proconsul before 49, for previously to that year his brother Seneca had been out of favour at the imperial court. Incidentally, however, it affords an illustration of S. Luke's accuracy. In A.D. 15, Achaia, which (as we have seen on p. 301) had previously been a senatorial province under a proconsul, was united by Tiberius to the imperial province of Macedonia, which was under a *legate* or *propraetor*. But in A.D. 44 Claudius restored it to the senate, and therefore S. Luke is right in calling its governor a *proconsul*[3].

Gallio, the second proconsul before whom S. Paul stood[4], was a remarkable man. He came of a Spanish family which had won for itself a distinguished place in Roman letters and society. M. Annaeus Seneca, his father, was a well-known rhetorician; Seneca the Stoic and tutor of Nero was his brother, and the poet Lucan his nephew. His own name was originally M. Annaeus Novatus, but having been adopted by Lucius Junius Gallio he became Lucius Junius Annaeus Gallio. He had attained the highest office in the state, the consulship. But he was best known for his amiable character,—'sweet Gallio' Statius calls him, and Seneca speaks of him as one who could not be loved enough[5]. Such was the governor before whom the Jews indicted S. Paul. In their hatred of Rome and their repudiation of Gentile jurisdiction (in theory), a Roman governor was the last person to whom the Jews should have appealed for a decision concerning the things of God. But hatred knows no logic, and other methods having failed, they appeal unto the power of Caesar.

---

[1] The Gallio incident immediately preceded, or led up to, S. Paul's first visit to Ephesus (ver. 19). In the same way the conclusion of his work at Ephesus (xix 20-41) falls into the following division.   [2] Cp. xxiv 27. There is nothing corresponding to Lk iii 1 in the Acts.   [3] Cp. the similar case of Cyprus xiii 7 (p. 200).
[4] The first was Sergius Paulus (xiii 7). Festus and Felix (xxiv-v) were procurators.
[5] Statius *Silv.* II vii 32; Seneca *Nat. Quaest.* IV praef. 10.

12 But when Gallio was proconsul of Achaia, the Jews with one accord rose up¹ against Paul, and brought him before
13 the ²judgement-seat, saying, This man persuadeth men to
14 worship God contrary to the law. But when Paul was about to open his mouth, Gallio said unto the Jews, If indeed it were a matter of wrong or of wicked villany, O ye Jews,
15 reason would that I should bear with you: but if they are questions about ³words and names and your own law, look to it yourselves; I am not minded to be a judge of these
16 matters. And he drave them from the judgement-seat.
17 And ⁴they all laid hold on Sosthenes, the ruler of the synagogue, and beat him before the ²judgement-seat. ⁵And Gallio cared for none of these things.

12 It would not be easy to convince the Roman governor of S. Paul's guilt; so the Jews devised a plan, viz. to impress or overawe him by a sudden *insurrection*⁶ (AV) or rising of the whole Jewish quarter. Accordingly on some 'court day,' when the proconsul was sitting on his *béma* or seat of judgement in the basilica in the forum or agora, and was there occupied in the administration of justice, the Jews in a body tumultuously dragged
13 Paul before him and formally accused him of *persuading men to worship God contrary to the law*. A similar charge had been brought against him at Philippi (xvi 21) but had fallen through, and it seems strange that the Jews did not adopt the more fatal charge of treason as at Thessalonica. S. Paul may have been more careful in his preaching of 'the kingdom' at Corinth. But the more likely explanation is that the Jews were dealing not with the provincial magistrates of a 'free city,' but with a Roman proconsul, and their own relations with Rome were becoming so strained that charges of disloyalty might recoil on their own heads. So they fell back upon the religious charge. *To worship God* appears (from the Acts) to have been the technical phrase for being an adherent of Judaism. But Judaism was a 'lawful religion' and it was not forbidden them to win adherents. The legal sanction of their religion did not indeed directly cover proselytism among Roman citizens, and the government retained its general power of restraint; but in practice there was little interference with the extension of Judaism⁷. Accordingly the Jews had to prove that S. Paul was a heretic. He was not a true Jew and was making converts *contrary*

---

¹ Bezan continues *having spoken together amongst themselves [against Paul and] laying hands on him [they brought him before the judgement seat] crying out and [saying*. ² Gk *béma*. ³ Gk *a word*. ⁴ AV reads *all the Greeks*.
⁵ Some Bezan texts have *Then Gallio feigned that he did not see*. ⁶ The Greek word for *rose-up* is very emphatic. ⁷ See note ¹ on p. 288.

to *(their) law* which was the form of their 'religion' recognized by the state. This their spokesman *Sosthenes*, who had succeeded Crispus as *ruler of the synagogue*, endeavoured to prove. But it was too
14 much for Gallio's patience. Without waiting for Paul to make any defence, he had settled the matter. '*O ye Jews*¹,' he exclaimed with impatience, for he could not *endure* them any longer. The matters of which his court was cognizant were either cases *of wrong* i.e. injury done to others, or *of wicked villany*² i.e. such vicious practices as were a public scandal or caused danger to the state by their violation of the elementary laws of morality. Concerning such matters *it would have been reasonable*, nay his plain duty, to
15 give them a patient hearing. But this was a question concerning oriental religions and heresies about which a Roman knew little and cared less. For such matters Rome had left to the Jews a jurisdiction of their own, and it was their business. '*See to it yourselves*³. *I have no intention of being a judge of these*
16 *matters.*' With these words Gallio ordered the lictors to clear the court of the mob of Jews. The rebuff of the hated Jews was
17 too good an opportunity for the Gentiles to lose. And *all* the Greek bystanders *seized Sosthenes and gave him a beating* on the spot. Gallio, thinking that the Jews richly deserved it for their unjustifiable accusation, connived at this violence, affecting not to perceive it.

The result was at once encouraging and disappointing. It was encouraging; because the supreme tribunal had practically given a decision in favour of Christianity, and Paul could now rely on the solid justice of Rome for protection from the Jews and immunity in his work. But it was also disappointing. The refusal of Gallio to interfere may seem at first sight to be a model for the attitude of the secular government towards religious questions. But there is a distinction between impartiality and indifference, between judging and *caring*. Hence the disappointment. On the judgement-seat sat Gallio, a noble specimen of the Roman aristocracy; at the bar stood Paul, one of the greatest religious teachers of the world, —and nothing happened. For *Gallio cared nothing for these matters*. These words may indeed have their proper application to Gallio's connivance at the beating of Sosthenes⁴, but they also read very much like S. Luke's sober judgement on the judge. And whether we consider his attitude as the outcome of impartiality or indifference, it caused him to lose a great opportunity.

The journey to Asia viâ Jerusalem and Galatia

S. Paul vindicated his freedom by *remaining* at Corinth *some time longer*, but the affair before the proconsul was as usual the signal for departure to a new field of work. First, however, as if to recover

---

¹ A different address from the polite *Men of Athens* etc. ² Cp. xiii 10.
³ This was a Roman phrase. Cp. Mt xxvii 4, 24. ⁴ As is suggested by the Bezan reading.

strength for a new advance and to maintain the unity of the churches in the east and the west, he pays a visit to Jerusalem and Antioch. When at Corinth Rome was already in S. Paul's thoughts (Rom i 13). But there was an important position behind him, which a good general and strategist could not afford to neglect. This was the province of Asia. The divine prohibition to preach there (xvi 6) was now apparently removed; and when S. Paul landed, for the first time, at *Ephesus*, its capital, his favourable reception confirmed the previous longings of his own heart. So now we pass from Achaia to Asia; and all the time and travelling which intervened between the first landing at Ephesus and the apostle's return thither is summed up by S. Luke in one of his long and characteristic sentences[1].

Brief as this section is, it contains a detail which cannot be altogether without significance. *At Cenchreae Paul cut his hair, for he had a vow*[2]. (1) This fact shews that in ordinary life S. Paul conformed to the law as a Jew. In place of 'the law' we might indeed have written 'the customary observances of contemporary religion.' For cutting the hair was a primitive ceremony of widespread observance. Sailors shaved their heads after deliverance from shipwreck, mourners shaved after a death, pilgrims did not cut their hair till their pilgrimage was over. But there was a special connexion between the cutting of the hair and the taking of vows. Vows were constantly being taken to obtain, or to express gratitude for, deliverance from danger and trouble; and the beginning and the end of the period of a vow were marked by the shaving of the head. The custom of taking vows found a place in the Jewish law, where the vow of the Nazirite is expressly legislated for. And now S. Paul takes a vow, and this quite spontaneously. His motive herein was not, we presume, to avoid giving scandal to his fellow-countrymen or for the sake of charity, because the ceremony was entirely voluntary. With this action we may join the other hints in the Acts of compliance with the law, e.g. the visits to Jerusalem to keep the feast of Pentecost, the mention of the Passover at Philippi and of the Fast, i.e. the Day of Atonement, at Fair Havens, and the Nazirite vow at Jerusalem; and hence we may conclude that S. Paul normally observed the law[3]. Accordingly we must remember to balance his vehement assertion of the principle of liberty in the Epistles to the Galatians and Romans with his own practice of obedience to the law, when no principle was at stake. To the Jews he 'was a Jew and under the law[4].'

(2) This notice will also afford us a clue to S. Paul's journey, e.g. it will explain his refusal to stay at Ephesus. When a Jew took upon himself the vow of a Nazirite, at the end of the time of his separation

---

[1] i.e. in the Greek: cp. xvi 6-7. According to the Bezan text of xix 1 S. Paul is driven to Ephesus the second time by the Holy Spirit almost against his will.
[2] Grammatically the words *having shorn...a vow* may apply to Aquila. But the mention of this detail would then be so purposeless that this alternative cannot be seriously entertained.   [3] Cp. xx 16; xx 6; xxvii 9; xxi 26.   [4] Cp. I Cor viii 9-13, ix 19-23, x 23-33.

—usually thirty days—he offered a certain sacrifice at the temple, shaved his head, and burnt the hair in the fire of the sacrifice[1]. If he was in a foreign land at the expiration of the vow the head might still be shaved and the hair kept till he reached Jerusalem. This may have been the condition of S. Paul; but we notice that the Greek word is *cutting* (not *shaving*[2]), and this may denote the cutting short of the hair at the beginning of the period of the vow, preparatory to letting it grow for 30 days. In either case a visit to Jerusalem would have been necessary. Now S. Paul was anxious to make such a visit. He had however reason already to apprehend danger at Jerusalem[3], and Ephesus might be a temptation to turn aside. Therefore, to place himself under a necessity, he took this vow. The ceremony at Jerusalem which attended the completion of the vow may well account for the suggestion made to him by James and the presbyters on the occasion of his next and last visit.

18 And Paul, having tarried after this yet many days, took his leave of the brethren, and sailed thence for Syria, and with him Priscilla and Aquila; having shorn his head in
19 Cenchreæ: for he had a vow. And [4]they came to Ephesus, and [5]he left them there: but he himself entered into the
20 synagogue, and reasoned with the Jews. And when they
21 asked him to abide a longer time, he consented not; [6]but taking his leave of them, and saying, I will return again unto
22 you, if God will, he set sail from Ephesus. And when he had landed at Cæsarea, he went up and saluted the church, and
23 went down to Antioch. And having spent some time *there*, he departed, and went through the region of Galatia and Phrygia in order, stablishing all the disciples.

18 S. Paul probably took a passage in a pilgrim ship bound *for Syria*, taking pilgrims for the feast of Pentecost. He had no doubt companions, but only *Priscilla and Aquila* are mentioned—to explain their appearance at Ephesus in the next section. From *Cenchreae*,
19 the port of Corinth, the vessel crossed the Aegean *to Ephesus*. There it stopped to enable the pilgrims to join in the worship of the synagogue on the sabbath day; and so S. Paul was at last enabled to carry out the original intention with which he and Silas had started upon their journey from the Pisidian Antioch in A.D. 49 (xvi 6).

---

[1] Numbers vi. [2] As in xxi 24; for the distinction cp. 1 Cor xi 6. [3] Cp. *if God will* in verse 21, and xxi 14. [4] AV and Bezan read *he came*.
[5] Bezan inserts *on the following sabbath*, some texts omitting *he left them there, but*.
[6] AV and Bezan read *but*] *bade them farewell, saying I must by all means keep this feast that cometh in Jerusalem but* [*I will return again to you if God will*]: some Bezan texts continue *but Aquila he left in Ephesus and he himself set sail and came to* [*Caesarea*.

In *the synagogue* he *reasoned* with *the Jews*. The Jews at Ephesus formed an important body. Josephus gives us several decrees of Roman governors and of the Ephesian People guaranteeing to them the free observance of their national customs. They had close intercourse not only with the Jews at Corinth (verses 27-8) but with Jerusalem itself (xxi 27). For at Ephesus were put on board the contributions of the Asian Jews towards the temple, which formed no small element in its revenue, and indeed proved too tempting a prey for many a governor of Asia. Hence it was impossible for the Ephesian Jews not to have heard of Christianity, and having now in their midst 'a ringleader of the sect,' they were, like the Jews at
20 Rome (xxviii 22), anxious for further information. S. Paul however, as we have seen, was under a necessity to visit Jerusalem;
21 so after a courteous *farewell* with a promise to *return* he sailed
22 to *Caesarea*, *went up* to Jerusalem[1], paid his respects to *the church* in an official call upon its rulers, fulfilled his vow[2], and *went down*
23 *to Antioch*. After some interval *he went forth* from Antioch—for the third and the last time[3]. Antioch is not mentioned again. He was anxious to visit the churches of Galatia, so he took the land route for Asia as on the previous occasion. He passed through Tarsus and the Cilician gates, and once more visited the churches of Galatia *in order*—Derbe, Lystra, Iconium, and Antioch. And as he went he *stablished all the disciples*. Under that simple phrase a world of meaning may lie hid which we should never have conjectured but for the Epistle to the Galatians.

The Epistle to the Galatians

The word *stablishing*, as was pointed out on a former occasion (xiv 22, p. 236), implies a need of being confirmed or established; and S. Luke's brevity may have a deeper motive than mere conciseness of narration, viz. the desire to pass over what could only arouse painful recollections. For this brings us to the question—when was the Epistle to the Galatians written? It must have been written within a few years of this time—but when? There seem to be two possibilities. (A) It was written from Antioch or some other place just before the visit to Galatia here mentioned. This view was held by Renan, and has been very powerfully advocated by Prof. Ramsay. (B) It may

---

[1] Jerusalem is not mentioned in the text. But *going up* is the regular pilgrim word, cp. Lk ii 42, Jn vii 8; and in this neighbourhood *the church* could only be that of Jerusalem. This phrase then and the omission of 'Jerusalem,' together with *came* to Caesarea and *went* up to Jerusalem and down to Antioch, may afford a slight indication that this sentence was penned at Caesarea. [2] A similar ceremony is recorded in xxi 18-9; and a detailed picture of this journey can be restored from the account of the next visit, just as verse 23 is a summary of a journey through S. Galatia, such as has already been described more fully in xv 41–xvi 5. [3] This is usually marked as the beginning of the 'third missionary journey.' But it is obvious that there is no new beginning here. The new work begins with Paul's arrival at Ephesus, whether we reckon it from xix 1 or xviii 19. This time S. Paul starts alone—at least we are not told of any fellow missionary on a level with Barnabas or Silas. The last mention of Silas was in xviii 5.

have been written towards the end of, or shortly after, the stay at Ephesus to which we are coming. Either supposition will fall in excellently with the course of the history, and we cannot profess to decide between them. The case for each must be fairly stated and the choice left to the judgement of the reader.

(A) In the former case, the reconstruction of the history will be something of this sort. We must return to the council at Jerusalem in A.D. 48, three years ago[1]. Though the council had come to an unanimous decision, the Pharisaic or Judaizing party was by no means satisfied, and they started a propaganda to teach the necessity of circumcision in the new Gentile churches. This meant undoing the work of S. Paul, and their chief weapon was an attack upon his apostolate. The Lord, they declared, had appointed the Twelve as his apostles, and with them rested the apostolic authority. S. Paul was a newcomer, who had not gone in and out with the other disciples[2], had not seen the risen Lord (except in an ecstatic vision which depended solely on his own assertion), and finally had received no apostolic commission from the Twelve: his gospel therefore was without authority. On the other hand the Judaizing emissaries took care to fortify themselves with commendatory letters from Jerusalem, and then invaded S. Paul's churches. They would reach Galatia first, soon after S. Paul and Silas had started on the long journey which led them to Macedonia and Achaia. Amongst these emissaries there seems to have been a leader who stood out above the rest in a very preeminent position, whether this was owing to the power of his personal influence or to some high office in the church[3]. This 'false apostle' had complete success in Galatia. First he caused alarm and consternation[4]. Then he convinced them of the truth of his teaching. The gospel of S. Paul, of justification by faith and of liberty in the Spirit, was a lofty one and hard to grasp; and the simple Galatians found it easier to believe in a gospel of salvation by works, by circumcision and the law, by the observance of days and months, seasons and years. And so 'very quickly' after his departure they 'deserted' S. Paul and went over to this rival evangelist[5], and S. Paul could only account for it by a kind of witchcraft—'O foolish Galatians,' he exclaims, 'who hath bewitched you[6]?'

Meanwhile S. Paul had returned from Achaia to Jerusalem, where he made but a short stay. The increasing noise made by his work, with the consequent hostility of the Jews, was already making Jerusalem a place of danger for him. Of his intercourse with the church we can however restore one detail. The apostles spoke to him of his promise to 'remember the poor' (pp. 246–7). In his extreme desire to avoid all appearance of interested motives, he had, on his first visit to the cities of Macedonia and Achaia, not only worked with his own hands but refused to ask for a penny for any purpose at all. Therefore he had returned to Jerusalem without an offering for the poor. It was

---

[1] See p. 258. [2] Cp. i 21–2. [3] Gal v 10, i 8–9. His position may have depended upon a close relation of kinship to the Lord, cp. II Cor x 7, xi 23.
[4] i 7, v 10 (*trouble*). [5] i 6. [6] iii 1.

now time for him to redeem his promise. It would indeed be difficult for him to ask; yet on the other hand a contribution from the Gentile churches to the Christian poor of Jerusalem would form a great bond of love and would cement the unity of the Jewish and Gentile churches. Hence the collection of alms for Jerusalem formed an important feature in the 'third journey.'

From Jerusalem S. Paul went down to Antioch, and then (if not before) news of the Galatian defection reached him. He was stung to the quick by their infidelity to himself and his apostolate: but he also realized the seriousness of the crisis and the need of confuting this Christian Pharisaism. At once he wrote off a fiery letter (our present epistle) to the Galatians; and then followed up the letter by a visit in person. He crossed Cilicia and the Taurus and once more appeared in Galatia. That was enough. The force of his personality again proved irresistible, and the presence of their first father in Christ won back the allegiance of the Galatians. According to S. Luke he *confirmed*—set upright and made firm in their original faith—*all the disciples*. The Judaizing emissaries had however the start of him. They had gone on, and were soon to sow seeds of faction and discord in other churches, notably that of Corinth. If we are justified in following the Bezan text of xix 1, the state of affairs in Galatia was so serious that S. Paul for the moment thought of giving up his journey to Ephesus and wished to return to Jerusalem to have the matter authoritatively settled. But his own private plan was again overruled, and the Holy Spirit who before had prevented his preaching in Asia now bade him go on thither.

(B) On the other hand there is much to make us think the epistle of a later date. In style and matter it is very closely associated with the Second Epistle to the Corinthians and the Ep. to the Romans. In particular the same teacher who had troubled the Galatians seems to have caused similar confusion at Corinth; but he could not have arrived there till the end of S. Paul's stay at Ephesus or later. With that epoch the Ep. to the Galatians will fit in very well. But we had better wait till we reach that time for a fuller exposition of this view[1], and for the present content ourselves with pointing out a serious objection to the earlier date. There is no allusion to an impending visit to Galatia in the epistle. And yet the apostle must surely have warned them of his intention, if we may judge from his other epistles[2]. As it stands, he seems to be taking a final farewell of them.

According to this second view, what has been said above about the collection for the poor still holds good, and also the account of the general attitude of the Judaizers. But we must suppose that when S. Paul visited Galatia at this time, the emissaries had not yet arrived and the defection of the churches had not taken place. S. Paul, then, when he had confirmed the disciples and traversed the region of Galatia and Phrygia, would have been brought once more to the frontier of Asia; and here we may pause to survey the new province.

---

[1] See p. 360. [2] Cp. I Cor iv 18-21, II xii 14, Rom i 10: contrast Gal vi 17.

SECTION III (= Ch. 18. 24—19. 20)
ASIA and Ephesus

Ephesus was a more populous, wealthy and important city than Corinth; and similarly its province 'Asia' far surpassed in these respects the provinces of Galatia, Macedonia, and Achaia. This province roughly coincided with the western part of Asia Minor. It was the first part of the continent of Asia with which the Romans had come in contact, and they knew it as 'Asia'; as their knowledge and dominion extended further east and new provinces were added to the empire, the original province still retained the name of 'Asia,' and hence arose a double and confusing use of the term for both province and continent. Here, as in the text of the Acts, Asia is used in the former sense. This western coastland of Asia Minor is so favoured by nature in its climate, soil, and position, that it can hardly help being wealthy and prosperous even under oppressive governments and in time of war,—from which drawbacks it has seldom been free. In very early times the Greeks discovered its value and studded the coast with colonies. Then it was conquered by the Persians and became subject to an oriental despotism, but subsequently most of the cities on the coast, with the aid of Athens, secured their independence. When Greece was entirely freed from the Persian yoke by Alexander the Great, 'Asia' became the theatre of continual wars among his successors, until it fell into the hands of the Romans who made it into a province about 130 B.C. It then had to suffer from the exactions of Roman governors and from the invasion of Mithridates: but now it had enjoyed for a full century the 'peace of Rome'; the strong hand of the emperor checked the oppression and greed of the proconsuls; and under the imperial government the province had reached the climax of its prosperity. It was covered with flourishing and opulent cities, whose ruins testify to a vigorous life and are mines of information about the Roman empire. Such were Ephesus, Smyrna, Pergamum, Thyatira, Sardis, Philadelphia, Laodicea (the seven churches of Asia), with Colossae, Hierapolis, Apamea, and many others. No wonder then that Asia was one of the richest jewels of the empire. 'Asia' and 'Africa' ranked together as the two most important and wealthy of the senatorial provinces. The civilization of the province was thoroughly Greek. The coast had for so long been colonized and possessed by the Greeks that there the native races had lost all significance, while the interior also was dominated by Greek influence and ideas. When poverty and desolation fell on Greece proper, the centre of Hellenic life and civilization was shifted across the Aegean to the Hellas of Asia Minor; and thence—through the political influence first of the Macedonians, then of the Romans,—Hellenism had been extending its sway over the distant countries of the east.

Of this province *Ephesus* was the not unworthy capital. The city indeed had not had a very brilliant history. It was originally a colony of Athens, but in the flourishing times of Greek history it had held quite a second place. In the later Macedonian and Roman times, however, it came to the front and was now at the height of its prosperity. This advance was mainly due to natural and physical causes. Ephesus was situated near the entrance to the valley of the Maeander and this valley was the easiest and most frequented trade route into the interior. The point of departure had formerly been Miletus, the port at the mouth of the river, which accordingly stood first among the Greek cities. But the alluvial deposits of the river had gradually blocked up the harbour of Miletus, and the traffic had to find another outlet. This it did by leaving the Maeander and crossing over a spur of Mt Pactyas to Ephesus, which city had accordingly risen to wealth and prosperity.

Smyrna however occupied an equally favourable position at the mouth of the Hermus valley, and the wealth of Asia is chiefly shewn by the number of cities which ran Ephesus close in an eager rivalry. The competition was decided in favour of Ephesus by the Romans, who made it the capital of the province and the centre of their administration. They had indeed left the Ephesians their freedom, and Ephesus was a 'free city.' But it was selected for the residence of the proconsul, and in his court the majesty of Rome was amply displayed. For the proconsul of Asia was a very great personage; his office was confined to magistrates of the highest rank, viz. those who had held the consulship at Rome; and, like the proconsul of Africa, he enjoyed the privilege of being attended by twelve lictors instead of the usual six. There was then a close political connexion between Rome and Ephesus; and a slight hint of this may be found in our narrative in the occurrence of the Latin words *sudaria, semicinctia,* and the name of *Scaeva* (xix 12 and 14).

A preponderating local attraction combined with the Roman connexion to give Ephesus the supremacy. This was a religious attraction. Within a short distance of the city stood the famous *Temple of Artemis*. The worship of Artemis must be considered more in detail below. It is enough now to notice that here the native aboriginal element avenged itself on the domination of Greek ideas. For the temple was on the site of a primitive sanctuary and the worship was a survival of the primitive worship of nature. Adopted by the Greeks, and identified with the Greek goddess Artemis (as she in turn with the Latin Diana), the aboriginal goddess had acquired a world-wide reputation; and her magnificent temple, raised by Greek art, had become not only a most popular place of pilgrimage but one of the wonders of the world. The goddess had an enormous establishment of hundreds or thousands of priests and other ministers, who constituted a powerful hierarchy. And the Ephesians, conscious of the wealth which the goddess brought to their city, added their grateful and official support to her worship. Thus at Ephesus we have an instance of an established religion, still flourishing and possessing a real power and vitality,—we might almost say a pagan 'established church.' Unfortunately Artemis exercised other influences over the city which were the reverse of blessings. We do not know whether, like some oriental goddesses and like Aphroditê at Paphos and Corinth, she gave public and religious sanction to immorality and prostitution. But it is certain that she gave countenance to the growth of superstition and the cultivation of magic. The *curious arts* of all kinds so flourished at Ephesus, that 'magic' became one of the 'specialities' of the city: certain forms of incantation were known as 'Ephesian letters.' Thus at Ephesus Hellenic culture and philosophy had made a most disastrous union with oriental superstition.

We can now understand the important position which Asia and Ephesus held in the progress of the gospel. In itself Ephesus was a field most attractive to S. Paul and full of promise for the gospel. It was a busy and populous city; and like such places of concourse, great was its need of salvation. It was also thoroughly cosmopolitan; the might of Rome and Greek civilization, barbarian superstition and the Jewish faith, here dwelt side by side: and being a commercial, administrative, and religious centre, the city was also an admirable centre for the propagation of the gospel. Travellers between east and west, the merchants and pilgrims from all parts, the Roman officials, and the inhabitants of the province who flocked to the capital for their annual festivals or for judicial and other business, made the city a microcosm.

Beyond these general advantages of a great centre, there was one special characteristic of Ephesus which struck the observer, and that was power and *magnificence* (or *greatness*). There was the power of Rome fully represented in the proconsular court; the power of the 'great' goddess in her temple and its hierarchy; the power of Greek art and civilization in the splendour of the temple which was a wonder of the world: and, lastly, the power of the spiritual 'powers of darkness' in all the 'curious arts' of Ephesian science[1]. In this respect, almost more than its cosmopolitan character, Ephesus was a copy of Rome: and we see why it eclipsed not only Corinth but even Antioch in the progress of the gospel. It was the stepping-stone to Rome; because it reflected in itself the 'power of darkness,' the kingdom or 'course of this world,' which had its capital in Rome[2]. That this was the main impression which Ephesus made on S. Luke can be seen in the very words of the narrative[3]. But more than in the words we can see it in his thoughts. The underlying idea of this chapter is the establishment of 'the church' (xx 17) in power. Over against all these powers is raised up another power, which prevails over them, that is the power of the kingdom of God (verse 8). And the development of that power as recorded in the Acts here reaches its highest point.

---

[1] Eph ii 2, vi 12.   [2] Col i 13, Eph ii 2.   [3] See xviii 24 *mighty*, 28 *powerfully confute*, xix 8 *with great power* (Bezan), 11 *no common powers*, 16 *mastered*, *prevailed*, 17 *was magnified*, 20 *mightily...prevailed*, 27 *great goddess, magnificence* (or *majesty*), 28, 34, 35 *great*.

The victory of the church is shewn: (1) In the person of her champion, the apostle, who now is at the climax of his activity. He conveys the gift of the Holy Ghost; and even from his body there issues miraculous power. He is the friend of Asiarchs, and is matched like a gladiator in the arena with the great goddess herself. (2) In her own self-realization. In this chapter we feel the power of the church, more than the personality of the apostle. The church appears once more as *the way*, i.e. the way of truth; and the great contest with Ephesus was to be fought in the arena of truth. With its false religion, false science, false spiritualism, Ephesus was to be the source of the greatest danger to the church, viz. of danger to the faith from within. Warnings against false teachers are a prominent element in S. Paul's charge to the Ephesian presbyters. The burden of the Epistles to Timothy, which were written to him at Ephesus, is 'Guard the faith.' Subsequently Ephesus became the home of S. John, and the false teaching which was threatening the church afforded the occasion for the final and supreme vindication of the truth in his Gospel. We are not then surprised to find that this relation of the church to the truth dominates S. Luke's narrative at this point. First we see the church realizing itself both (1) against imperfect forms of the truth, e.g. the baptism of John, and (2) in independence of the parent faith of Judaism. Then it prevails over (3) false spiritualism without, and (4) false profession within. Lastly (5) the whole power of heathenism, summed up in the person of the great goddess, enters the lists against the church's apostle, but achieves nothing beyond present confusion and uproar.

§ 1 *The church and the baptism of John*

The next paragraph in the Acts (verses 24-28) at first sight seems very isolated, a stray disconnected fragment, like an erratic block deposited in some valley by a glacier. Apollos suddenly appears and disappears. It may be that S. Luke, being acquainted with the First Epistle to the Corinthians, for the sake of its readers here explains the source of Apollos' Christianity. But when we look on to the following paragraph (xix 1-7), the difficulty disappears. Here is evidently a pair of companion pictures[1]. They both deal with the relation of Christianity to imperfect or immature forms of the faith, as exhibited in (1) a teacher and (2) disciples; and in each case the rudimentary stage of development which they have reached is the same—*the baptism of John*. We are surprised to find disciples of S. John the Baptist more than twenty years after he had been superseded by the Messiah. But his preaching represented a great movement in Judaism, besides being the preparation for the Messiah. The apostles indeed had fully realized the close connexion between the two; to them the gospel began with the baptism of John[2]. But this was by no means recognized by the Jews or by the majority of John's disciples. To

---

[1] like the pictures of Barnabas and Ananias (iv 36–v 11), Peter and Herod (xii 6–23), Thessalonica and Beroea (xvii 1-15).   [2] Cp. i 5, 22, x 37, xiii 24–5.

them he appeared as a prophet, preaching a revival of righteousness His preaching had great success and, we might say, caused a widespread religious revival among the people. Enormous numbers flocked to him and testified their repentance and desire for righteousness by receiving baptism. The Baptist himself was aware that his office was to point out the Messiah. But even after the baptism of Jesus, he continued to make disciples[1]; and at times his own faith wavered[2]. Of his more immediate disciples, besides those who passed on to Jesus, some who had come from distant lands may have returned home before his death and before the ministry of the Christ had begun. Others may have remained doubtful whether Jesus were really 'he that should come' or no. Others again may have accepted Jesus as the Messiah, but from lack of intercourse with the Twelve and the church at Jerusalem they had remained in ignorance of 'the baptism of the Spirit' at Pentecost and the new life of the church: their spiritual status would have been very much that of the Samaritans in ch. viii before the coming of Peter and John and the gift of the Holy Spirit. To this last class we may ascribe both Apollos and the twelve disciples at Ephesus.

The acts of Apollos

Apollos, or *Apollonius* as his name should be in full, is an interesting figure for several reasons. (1) He was *a Jew of Alexandria*. Besides the occurrence of the word *Alexandrian* in vi 9, xxvii 6, xxviii 11—and the possibility that S. Stephen was an Alexandrine Hellenist,—this is the sole reference in the Acts to Alexandria, whose church was to become so famous as the head-quarters of Christian philosophy. Philo the Alexandrine Jew introduced Platonism into Judaism: the Alexandrine fathers introduced it into Christianity. And here we meet with Apollos who was no doubt of Philo's school. (2) He had the Alexandrian characteristics. On the one hand he was *eloquent*. The word may mean *learned* (RV), and indeed it includes learning and study; for he was a philosopher and 'wisdom' his strong point. But with the Greeks wisdom was usually understood to carry with it the ability to set it forth with eloquence and grace. On the other hand he was *powerful*[3] *in the scriptures*: as a loyal Jew he devoted his learning and eloquence to the exposition of scripture.

(3) What is more interesting to us, Apollos illustrates the gradual growth of the Christian faith in the individual. He had (a) received *the baptism of John*, (b) *been instructed in the way of the Lord*, and he (c) *knew the things concerning Jesus*. This represents the stage reached either by those who themselves had been disciples of Jesus, or brought very near to him, but had returned to a distant home before Pentecost or for some other reason had not maintained communications with the apostolic church; or by those who had been instructed by such disciples. Of these two classes there must have

---

[1] Jn iv 1. [2] Lk vii 18-23. [3] or *mighty*: Moses in virtue of his Egyptian education was *mighty in his words and works* (vii 22). Cp. I Cor i 26.

been considerable numbers at centres like Alexandria, Ephesus, and Rome; for news of what had happened in Judaea must have spread far and wide. Put otherwise, they would represent those who had a Gospel and a Gospel only. *The baptism of John* was the preparation for the new kingdom: *the way of the Lord* was the new way of righteousness as set forth by the Lord in the Sermon on the Mount and other discourses: *the things concerning Jesus* were the main facts of his life—baptism, ministry, crucifixion, resurrection. What was wanting was *the baptism of the Spirit* (xix 6) and *the things concerning the kingdom of God* (xix 8), which together make up *the more accurate way of God* (xviii 26),—or in other words the 'Acts of the Apostles[1].' Apollos belonged to the second class of these disciples: *he had been instructed*. His knowledge was *accurate*[2],—a word which makes us strongly suspect that he had come across some documents, a written gospel or rather one of the original sources of our present Gospels. This supposition would explain his position exactly, and is maintained by Professor Blass[3]. On the other hand it is asserted[4] that the word *instruction* is only used of oral teaching[5]. In this case we must suppose him to have been instructed by some teacher of the first class. This teacher must have been of great authority, able to communicate accurate knowledge corresponding to the contents of one of our Gospels, but no further. This seems to us surprising. But it may well represent the condition of Christianity in Alexandria. News of events in Judaea, and documents, when they began to be written, would reach Egypt as soon as anywhere; and there must already have been there bodies of Christians in various stages. But there is not a single allusion in the Acts to a church at Alexandria, and probably no apostle or evangelist with apostolic authority had as yet visited the city and organized the various bodies into a church.

The perfecting, then, which Apollos needed he was to find at Ephesus; and the part he played in the synagogue reminds us very much of S. Stephen in the Alexandrian synagogue at Jerusalem (vi 9). Like Stephen he was preparing the way for Paul.

24 Now a certain Jew named [6]Apollos, an Alexandrian by race, a [7]learned man, came to Ephesus; and he was mighty
25 in the scriptures. This man had been [8]instructed in the way of the Lord; and being fervent in spirit, he spake and taught

---

[1] In the 'first principles' of Hebrews vi 2 we find another picture of an elementary stage of Christianity. [2] or *exact*, vv. 25, 26. The word occurs at the beginning of S. Luke's Gospel (i 4). It is to be noted that both in S. Luke's preface and here we find the same words *exactly, instruct, begin*. The experience of Theophilus and that of Apollos were perhaps very similar. [3] in his *Philology of the Gospels* pp. 29 foll. [4] by Mr Wright in *Expository Times*, 1897-8, pp. 8 foll., 437 foll. [5] i.e. *catéchésis*: the verb occurs in Lk i 4, Acts xxi 21, 24, Rom ii 18, I Cor xiv 19, Gal vi 6. [6] Cod Bezae has *Apollonius*. [7] Marg and AV *eloquent*. [8] Gk *catechized*: Bezan adds *in his country*.

[1]carefully the things concerning Jesus, knowing only the
26 baptism of John : and he began to speak boldly in the
synagogue. But when Priscilla and Aquila heard him, they
took him unto them, and expounded unto him the way of
27 God more [1]carefully. [2]And when he was minded to pass over
into Achaia, the brethren encouraged him, and wrote to the
disciples to receive him : and when he was come, he [3]helped
28 them much which had believed through grace: for he
powerfully confuted the Jews, *and that* publicly, [4]shewing by
the scriptures that Jesus was the Christ.

24 *Apollos came to Ephesus* after S. Paul had gone on to Jerusalem.
25 Being full of enthusiasm, or in the picturesque phrase of the
original *boiling in (his) spirit*[5], and also a teacher or rabbi of
26 ability, like S. Paul *he began to speak boldly in the synagogue.* He
preached no doubt the need of righteousness and of repentance,
and also that Jesus was the Messiah. But here he stopped short—
upon the further question of the bearing of the deeds and words of
Jesus upon our present life, he was silent. At Ephesus there had
as yet been no division between the synagogue and ecclesia; and
Priscilla and Aquila, who were in the congregation, must have
heard him with joyful surprise. But they perceived at once what
was lacking—the doctrine of the Spirit and the church; and inviting
Apollos to their house, *they put before him more exactly the way of
God*, i.e. the new life of the Spirit in the church. Apollos readily
accepted the fuller teaching, and to judge from the following section
(xix 5-6) must have been baptized into the name of Jesus and
received the Holy Spirit by the laying on of hands. If so, we have to
ask—of whose hands ? for Apollos had left Ephesus before the return
of S. Paul. The apostle however may have, as it is not unreasonable
to suppose, provided for some apostolic delegate to act during his
absence, such as Silas or Timothy: in any case at Corinth, with its
hierarchy of spiritual gifts and ministries, there could hardly have
been lacking some representative of the first order of 'apostles[6].'
27 In the congregation of the synagogue there were present also
some other Christians. These were Corinthians on a visit to
Ephesus; and when they heard Apollos' eloquence, they too were
delighted. He was just the teacher they wanted at Corinth—a man
'with excellency of speech and of wisdom,' able to give a 'demonstration' of oratory[7]. Besides this, they seem to have been in special

---
[1] Gk *accurately* or *exactly*: AV *diligently, perfectly*.   [2] Bezan has *And
there were certain Corinthians sojourning in Ephesus, and when they heard him they
besought him to cross over with them to their country. And when he had consented,
the Ephesians wrote to the disciples in Corinth that they should receive the man.
And when he had journeyed to Achaia he helped them much in the churches, [for he
powerfully.*   [3] Marg *helped much through* [Gk *the*] *grace them which had believed.*
[4] Bezan inserts *reasoning and.*   [5] Rom xii 11.   [6] I Cor xii 28.   [7] I Cor ii 1-5.

need of a champion in the controversy with the Jews. Accordingly they invited him to return with them to *Achaia*. Apollos gave a cordial assent; but being reluctant to take such a step on his own responsibility, the Ephesian Christians, chief among whom were Priscilla and Aquila, gave him the needed sanction by *writing* to the Corinthian church a commendatory letter[1]. Apollos' arrival at Corinth brought the requisite aid to *the believers*, i.e. the Christians: *through the grace* given unto him[2], manifest especially in 'the word of wisdom and the word of knowledge,' he brought them a great addition of force. In some 'school' (p. 351) or place of resort Apollos gave *public* disputations or 'demonstrations,' in which he argued against the Jews *that Jesus was the Messiah*, and his 'power in *the scriptures*' gave him a decided victory. S. Luke uses very strong words, far stronger than those he uses of S. Paul's preaching. Apollos *vehemently*[3] and *utterly confuted the Jews*. Accordingly he became a great power in the church, almost a second apostle: 'Paul planted, Apollos watered.' Unfortunately the difference between their respective gifts and methods lent a handle to the spirit of party which was beginning to manifest itself in the church at Corinth. Some of the disciples formed themselves into a definite section and styled themselves 'of Apollos.' When however his popularity had become dangerous to the cause of Christian unity, Apollos withdrew to Ephesus, where we find him two or three years later, and unwilling to return to Corinth even at S. Paul's request[4].

The twelve disciples of John

Apollos was a teacher; the twelve men now to be considered were *disciples*; and as both parties *knew only the baptism of John*, we might suppose that the twelve were Apollos' disciples. But in that case we should expect them as well as Apollos to have received instruction from Priscilla and Aquila. It is quite possible that in a large city like Ephesus bodies of Jews—and (the church being yet unorganized) of Christians too—might exist apart and in isolation, meeting in the great congregation in the synagogue on the sabbath day but otherwise unknown to one another. Of such a character was this body of John the Baptist's disciples, who had besides like Apollos some connexions with Christianity. How they were made perfect is best told by the narrative itself; and the proper commentary is to be found in the parallel case of the Samaritans in ch. viii, which should be carefully

---

[1] This account is mainly from the Bezan text, which says correctly *the Ephesians*: as yet the Christians at Ephesus were not organized into a body. With his great gifts Apollos seems to have united that of modesty: cp. I Cor xvi 12. This enabled S. Paul to speak of him so freely in I Cor iii 4-8, iv 6 etc. [2] This interpretation (of the margin) is supported by S. Paul's familiar phrase *the grace given unto me* (I Cor iii 10, xv 10, II i 12 etc.): the *believing through grace* of the text is supported by the similar expressions in xiii 48, xvi 14 etc. [3] Lk xxiii 10.
[4] I Cor xvi 12 and cp. generally I Cor ii-iv. Also cp. Clement *ad Cor*. ch. 54.

studied, as also the other special descents of the Holy Ghost, in ii 1-4, and x 44-8. This descent is, as it were, the Pentecost of the church at Ephesus.

19 ¹And it came to pass, that, while Apollos was at Corinth, Paul having passed through the upper country came to 2 Ephesus, and found certain disciples : and he said unto them, Did ye receive the Holy Ghost when ye believed? And they *said* unto him, Nay, we did not so much as hear ²whether 3 the Holy Ghost was *given*. And he said, Into what then were ye baptized? And they said, Into John's baptism. 4 And Paul said, John baptized with the baptism of repentance, saying unto the people, that they should believe on him 5 which should come after him, that is, on Jesus. And when they heard this, they were baptized into the name of the 6 Lord Jesus³. And when Paul had laid his hands upon them, the Holy Ghost ⁴came on them ; and they ⁵spake with 7 tongues, and prophesied. And they were in all about twelve men.

1 We left S. Paul on the borders of Galatia and Asia (p. 336). As in the former journey he had been forbidden to enter Asia by the Spirit, so now (according to the Bezan text) the Spirit, again over-ruling the apostle's own plans, bids him return to the province. Accordingly *he came* down *to Ephesus through the upper country*, that is he took the direct route from Metropolis along the higher ground which has been discovered by Prof. Ramsay (p. 275). The high road ran down the valley of the Lycus past Colossae and Laodicea; but S. Paul writes to the Colossians that the Christians of this valley had not seen his face in the flesh⁶. He would have arrived at Ephesus in the late summer of A.D. 51 and after the departure of Apollos ; and no doubt he took up his abode with Priscilla and Aquila. Shortly after his arrival he came across⁷ these twelve men who professed to be *disciples*. S. Paul took their baptism for granted (verse 3), but something aroused his 2 suspicions. The gift of the Holy Spirit has a double manifestation in the life of the Christian. His fruits—of love, joy, peace, etc.— are seen in the character; and he is the source of spiritual gifts,

---

¹ Bezan has *Now when Paul was wishing* (or *willing*, as in xviii 21) *after his own (private) counsel to go to Jerusalem, the Spirit bade him return into Asia. And he [passed through.* ² The Greek is simply *whether (the) Holy Spirit is*: Bezan reads *whether any are receiving the Holy Spirit.* ³ Bezan adds *for the forgiveness of sins.* ⁴ Bezan *straightway fell.* ⁵ A Bezan authority has *spake with] other tongues and had knowledge in themselves so that they interpreted them to themselves; but some also [prophesied.* ⁶ Col ii 1. ⁷ Op. the *finding* of Aquila in xviii 2.

especially that of spiritual understanding. Now in some of these gifts or fruits these twelve disciples must have been deficient. Possibly after the example of the Baptist they were living the life of rigid ascetics, severe and gloomy, without Christian joy[1]: or again they may have failed to understand S. Paul's spiritual teaching. In any case S. Paul was induced to ask *Did ye receive the Holy Spirit when ye believed?* The AV *Have ye received...since ye believed?* is very misleading. The meaning of the Greek tenses is unmistakeable. They describe neither a gradual process nor a reception at some interval after believing, but a definite gift at a definite moment: '*Did ye receive...when ye believed* (that is, when ye professed your belief in baptism)?' That S. Paul did refer to the moment of baptism is proved by his next question. But the twelve disciples *did not even hear*—they were not informed at the time of their baptism—*that the Holy Ghost is* given. The meaning of the Greek *is* is fixed by S. John's phrase[2]—*for the Holy Ghost was not yet* (i.e. given); and it is rightly paraphrased in the Bezan text *whether any are receiving the Holy Spirit*. For the disciples must have known that there was a Holy Spirit; the Spirit of the LORD is frequently spoken of in the OT[3], and their master John had himself prophesied

3 of a baptism in the Spirit. Having received such an answer, S. Paul goes on to enquire into their baptism, and finds that they had only been baptized with *John's baptism* of water. This *baptism of*

4 *repentance* was a necessary preparation (xiii 24); but it was only a preparation for, as also a profession of *faith in, the coming* Messiah whose baptism was to be with water and the Spirit. The need of supplementing the baptism of water with that of the Spirit had been laid down by the Lord at the beginning of the Acts (i 5).

5 The twelve disciples were then *baptized* again with water, but *into*

6 *the name of the Lord Jesus* for the forgiveness of sins[4], *and Paul laid on his hands and the Holy Spirit came upon them.* Their baptism with the Spirit was manifested by visible phenomena, viz.

7 *speaking with tongues and prophesying*—the same that had happened 'at the beginning,' at the first Pentecost (pp. 19–21).

This descent of the Holy Spirit, proved by external evidence which could not be gainsaid, is S. Luke's final proof of the necessity of the baptism of the Spirit for all Christians of whatever religious status. The disciples of Jesus (whose experience had been the same as that of these twelve), the Samaritans who had been baptized into the name of Jesus, the unbaptized Gentiles, and the disciples of John the Baptist, all alike needed and received this completion of Christian life. This completion is here given at a definite moment in a sacrament, viz. of baptism accompanied with laying-on of hands; and it is a coincidence

---

[1] Cp. Lk vii 33. They may have been practising their asceticism on wrong grounds, e.g. abstaining from flesh-meat as evil in itself; cp. I Tim iv 1–5.
[2] Jn vii 39.   [3] e.g. in Gen i 2, Ps li 11, Isai lxiii 14.   [4] This addition from the Bezan text would imply that John's baptism did not convey forgiveness; hence the repetition of the baptism of water.

to be noted that in the Epistle to the Ephesians[1] the 'one baptism' is enumerated among the foundations of the unity of the church.

§ 2 *The establishment of the church in power*

After this long introduction, we may at last turn to S. Paul's actual work at Ephesus, which now takes the place of Corinth as his head-quarters. To this work are assigned but thirteen verses (8-20), but these are richly supplemented by other authorities. We have—a vivid account from an eye-witness of the riot which concluded S. Paul's sojourn at Ephesus (verses 23-41): S. Paul's farewell address to the presbyters of the Ephesian church (xx 18-35): the first Epistle to the Corinthians which was written at Ephesus, and the Epistle addressed a few years later to the Ephesians[2]. This last however, being in all probability a circular letter addressed to the churches of Asia, does not give much detail about Ephesus in particular. Then we have to ask who was S. Luke's authority for this account? For this section (and in it we now include xviii 24-xix 7) is strongly marked by a return to the Hebraic character of the early chapters; and this distinguishes it from the following narrative of the riot (verses 21-41), which must therefore be ascribed to a different source[3]. The Hebraism is seen in the style and phrases and ideas[4]: *the way* and *the name* return into prominence[5], and we also notice the attention paid to numbers[6]. S. John, who may have been one of S. Luke's authorities for the early chapters[7], did indeed spend the later years of his life at Ephesus: but his residence there was subsequent to the composition of the Acts. Besides we notice certain distinct features in the style[8], which point to a source different from those for the early chapters; and indeed who were so likely and able to have given information as Priscilla and Aquila the Jew? We recognize however Lucan characteristics, including for instance the use of uncommon words[9]; and there

---

[1] iv 5: cp. Col ii 12. [2] To these we may add, as authorities for the history of the Ephesian church,—the Epistles to Timothy; the Revelation of S. John, especially ii 1-7, and the Epistles and Gospel of S. John. But, dating from a later period, they fall out of our reach. [3] Possibly Aristarchus (ver. 29). [4] e.g. verse 1 (and 10) *it came to pass*, verses 10, 17 *all the dwellers in* (i 19, ii 9, 14, ix 32, 35 etc.), verse 4 *the people*, verse 11 *through the hands of* (v 12), verse 14 *doing this* (iv 7), verse 17 *this became known* (i 19, ii 14, iv 10, 16 etc.), *fear fell upon* (Lk i 12, Acts v 11 and x 44), *magnify* (Lk i 46, 58, Acts ii 11, v 13, x 46), verse 19 *count* (i 26 *numbered* i.e. *counted among*), verse 20 *the word grew* (vi 7, vii 17, xii 24). [5] Cp. xviii 25, 26, xix 9, 23: xix 5, 13, 17. [6] e.g. verse 7 *twelve*, 14 *seven*, 19 *fifty thousand*. The coincidence with the twelve (vi 2), seven (vi 3) and the five in xiii 1 is curious. Add also verse 8 *three months*, 10 *two years*. [7] See p. xliii. [8] e.g. the Holy Spirit here *came*, before he *fell* (x 44) or *was poured out* (ii 33) or *given* (viii 18): here we have *evil spirits*, before *unclean* (v 16, viii 7) and a different word is used for their *going out*: *powers* is used for the *signs and wonders* of v 12: the perfect tense is used for *believers* (xviii 27, xix 18), before the aorist (iv 32, xi 17). [9] Thus verse 9 *be hardened, speak evil*, verse 12 *carry-away, handkerchiefs, aprons, depart from*, verse 13 *exorcist, name, adjure*, 16 *master*, 18 *confess, deeds* (i.e. *practices*), 19 *curious, bring-together*, occur here only in the Acts.

are coincidences with S. Paul and the later chapters[1]. Therefore in any case S. Luke has revised his authority, and perhaps the lapse into a more Hebraic style may be intentional; he would call our attention to the parallel between the history of the beginnings of the church at Ephesus and of the church at Jerusalem.

Brief as the account is, S. Luke, with his usual skill, by a few salient touches makes the significant features of the work out before us. This work is the establishment of the church; just as the doctrine of the church is the main subject both of S. Paul's charge to the presbyters and of his epistle to the Ephesians. The church is presented to us (A) ideally, and (B) historically.

A. Viewed from without as a society, the church is *the kingdom of God*[2]. Over against the Roman empire, which is the kingdom of the world, and the proud ecclesia of the city of Ephesus, over against God's old ecclesia of the Jewish synagogue and the imposing ecclesiastical establishment which centred round the temple of Artemis, S. Paul establishes the kingdom of God, the true *ecclesia* (xx 17). Viewed from within, the church is *the way*[3]. It is the way of truth and life, straight and narrow, as opposed to the crooked and manifold paths of superstition, of curious arts and Ephesian lore. The unity of the church within is seen in its inclusion of *both Jews and Greeks*, and this corresponds to its universal claim—over *all* the world[4].

B. The actual growth of the church at Ephesus affords us a typical example, from which we may draw a picture of the beginnings of the church in other great cities, such as Rome and Alexandria. There is the sowing of the seed in divers ways and manners, and its growth in various plots or groups. There are first the Jews generally, who have heard something of the new way and desire to hear more. Then Priscilla and Aquila settle at Ephesus and gather disciples round them, forming a church in their house. Then Apollos arrives knowing only the baptism of John, and among his audience we find Christians from Corinth. Lastly there is a band of twelve disciples of the Baptist. The only common tie between all these is the Jewish synagogue which they all frequent. And in that synagogue what a variety of doctrines the congregation must have listened to! First S. Paul

---

[1] Thus *prophesy* occurs xxi 9 (in ii 17–8 only in a quotation from OT): verse 7 is in form exactly like xxvii 37: *before* is characteristic of the early chapters and *before the multitude* (verse 9) occurs vi 5, but *before all* (verse 19) only in xxvii 35; *no common* (verse 11) occurs xxviii 2; another tense of the verb for *strolling* (verse 13) in xxviii 13. *Take in hand* or *attempt* (verse 13) is Lucan (Lk i 1, Acts ix 29). Other words are also Pauline. Notice especially *both Jews and Greeks* (vv. 10, 17) which recurs in xx 21, also in xiv 1, xviii 4, and is characteristic of Romans and I Cor. *Name* (verse 13) which is Lucan (Lk vi 13–4) occurs 8 times in Ephesians, twice in I Cor, elsewhere only in Rom xv 20 (II Tim ii 10); *declare* (verse 18) is characteristic of the later chapters and is Pauline. *Deed* occurs Lk xxiii 51, Col iii 9. Cp. also for *separate* (verse 9) xiii 2 and Gal i 15. [2] This title has not occurred since xiv 22 and only returns at Rome at the end of the book (xxviii 23, 31). [3] This title is especially characteristic of the Ephesian section, occurring 4 times— xviii 25, 26, xix 9, 23. Excluding xvi 17, it only occurs 4 times elsewhere—ix 2, xxii 4, xxiv 14, 22. [4] See vv. 10, 17 *all* the dwellers in Asia and Ephesus.

appears one sabbath day and reasons. Then an eloquent Alexandrian preaches boldly, but a somewhat different gospel. Lastly S. Paul returns and argues with all his powers of personal persuasion.

This arrival of S. Paul is the climax : as an apostle he possesses the due authority to build up the varied elements or isolated edifices into one church or temple of God (Eph ii 19-22). But for such a building, there must be an independent and self-supporting foundation. For this reason a separation from the synagogue is indispensable. Therefore the real work at Ephesus begins with such a separation, as at the Pisidian Antioch (xiii 44-8), Corinth (xviii 6-7), and Rome (xxviii 23-8).

8 And he entered into the synagogue, and spake boldly[1] for the space of three months, reasoning and persuading *as to*
9 the things concerning the kingdom of God. But when some were hardened and disobedient, speaking evil of the Way before the multitude[2], he departed from them, and separated the disciples, reasoning daily in the school of Tyrannus[3].
10 And this continued for the space of two years ; so that all they which dwelt in Asia heard the word of the Lord, both Jews and Greeks.

In the synagogue, after Apollos' powerful demonstrations of the Messiahship of Jesus, S. Paul was able to advance further and declare what followed upon this, viz. the royal dignity and the kingdom of Jesus or *the kingdom of God*,—in other words *the church of God which he had purchased with his own blood*[4]. From the Epistle we can gather some of the ideas which were the ground-work of his preaching. The church was—the body of the Messiah, drawing all its life from Christ its head : the bride, made one flesh with Christ the bridegroom : the fulness of the Christ, viz. that in which his divine fulness finds expression in the world of time : the new temple built upon the foundations of the Old and the New Testaments. Of this temple Jesus Christ was the chief corner-stone, and as such he bound both Jews and Greeks into one. But the church was specially the promised inheritance of the Jews which the apostle urged them to rise up and occupy[5]. At the same time he did not shrink from declaring to them *the whole counsel of God*, the truth—so unpalatable to the Jews—of the catholicity of the church, that the Gentiles were fellow-heirs with the Jews, fellow-members of the body, fellow-partakers of the promise in Christ Jesus[6]; a doctrine which S. Paul illustrated in practice by testifying to Jew and Greek alike[7].

---

[1] Bezan adds *with great power.*   [2] Bezan adds *of the Gentiles.*   [3] Bezan adds *from the fifth to the tenth hour.*   [4] xx 28.   [5] Eph i 22-3, iv 4-16: v 23-32: i 23, iv 10: ii 19-22 and Acts xx 32.   [6] xx 27: Eph iii 1-12.
[7] xx 21, xix 10, 17.

S. Paul's reasoning had greater effect on the Ephesian Jews than on any others of the Dispersion (except the Beroeans). For he preached in the synagogue *for three months*[1] and the opposition was confined to a party (*some*) among them. Hitherto S. Luke has given the reason for belief; here he gives that for unbelief. He traces it back not to divine predestination, but to moral causes, to the heart. They *stiffened* their necks and refused to enter through the low gate into the way of truth; they *hardened* their hearts and refused to *obey* the claims of the kingdom[2], and this disobedience is unbelief. Failing to carry the whole synagogue with them, they were unable to procure S. Paul's punishment or excommunication and had to confine themselves to the weapons of controversy. The synagogue at Ephesus would be a large one and S. Paul's preaching would attract large congregations from the Gentiles as well as the Jews; at the Pisidian Antioch the whole city had assembled. Before these great audiences[3] S. Paul's opponents *spoke evil of the way*. The word is that used for the *reviling* of the most sacred relationships—of parents and of God[4]. This evil-speaking was therefore equivalent to the blasphemy at Antioch and Corinth[5], and S. Paul felt justified in making a separation. There does not seem to have been a scene of violence as at Antioch or Corinth[6]; the apostle simply *withdrew* and *separated the disciples*, dividing them from the Jews as a shepherd separates the sheep from the goats[7].

This 'separation' of the disciples, like that of Paul and Barnabas[8], was itself a divine call of the church to the work. And as in responding to the call Paul and Barnabas had realized their apostolate, so now by a similar response the church at Ephesus realized its own self-conscious existence as an independent ecclesia of God. S. Paul was of course the centre of unity in the church and with him were a band of *ministers* and *fellow-travellers*—*they that were with him*[9]. Among these we find Timothy and Erastus, Gaius and Aristarchus (two Thessalonians), Titus also and two Ephesians, Tychicus and Trophimus[10]. Moreover Priscilla and Aquila were at Ephesus, and Apollos was soon to return[11]. But the church would soon need a more definite and permanent government; and accordingly S. Paul, under the guidance of the

---

[1] At Antioch he left the synagogue on the second sabbath, at Thessalonica after 3 weeks. [2] Cp. vii 51: Hebr iii 8–15 (Ps xcv 8). The *hardening* may be of heart or neck. S. Paul assigns the same cause for unbelief at Rome (xxviii 27). [3] *The multitude* ($\pi\lambda\hat{\eta}\theta$ος) denotes neither a mere crowd ($\check{ο}\chi$λος) nor the assembly of the citizens of Ephesus ($\delta\hat{\eta}\mu$ος). Corresponding to its use for the body of the church, it would well denote the congregation of a church or synagogue. [4] (a) Exod xxi 17, Prov xx 20, Ezek xxii 7, Mt xv 4, Mk vii 10: (b) I Sam iii 13, cp. Exod xxii 28. [5] xiii 45, xviii 6. [6] But xx 26, which recalls xviii 6, may point to such a scene. [7] Mt xxv 32. The idea of the shepherd is almost confined to the Ephesian part of S. Paul's writings (Acts xx 28, Eph iv 11). To the Jews the *withdrawal* was an *apostacy* (xxi 21). [8] xiii 2, cp. Gal i 15. [9] xx 34: Gal i 2. [10] vv. 22, 29: II Cor vii 6–15 etc.: Acts xx 4. [11] Cp. I Cor xvi 12, 19. Among the converts we can reckon Epaenetus *the firstfruits of Asia*, possibly like Aquila a Roman Jew (Rom xvi 5), and Onesiphorus (II Tim i 16). Later on we have Hymenaeus and Alexander, Phygelus and Hermogenes (I Tim i 20, II i 15); but these proved faithless to the church.

Holy Ghost, appointed a body of *presbyters*, to whom he also gave the Greek title of *bishops* (Gk *episcopoi*), to be the 'pastors' of the church[1].

Besides rulers the church also needed a home of its own. It would find 'an upper room' for worship in the house of Priscilla and Aquila; but this would hardly suffice for public preaching on a large scale. Accordingly S. Paul took a step further, and *taught publicly* (xx 20), *reasoning daily in the school of Tyrannus*. Such a *school* or lecture-room we should expect to find in some gymnasium. In the out-of-door life of the ancient world, among the most important features of a city were its places of public resort. For this purpose western and Roman cities had their 'baths,' Greek and eastern cities their 'gymnasia.' These gymnasia, whose original purpose had been simply the exercise of the body in athletic sports, had long since become places of general recreation. Besides running and wrestling grounds, they included gardens, walks, and colonnades, together with a number of halls and semicircular 'exedrae.' These buildings were made use of by grammarians, poets, and philosophers, for giving lectures and recitations. To listen to such 'displays' was a favourite way of killing time, and so the word for leisure, *scholé* (*school*), came to be applied to the lecture itself, and from the lecture it passed on to the place of delivery and to the class who attended. Ephesus had no less than five gymnasia[2], and possibly in one of these was *the school* which had been built by, or was the scene of the labours of, *Tyrannus*[3]. By some arrangement—which in this case would have implied the permission of the 'gymnasiarch[4]'—S. Paul obtained the use of it; and he reasoned there every day *from the fifth to the tenth hour*, i.e. from just before midday till the end of the afternoon. That would be the time when the serious work of the day was over and the citizens would frequent the places of recreation.

The early morning hours were thus left free to S. Paul for his own daily task. For as at Thessalonica and Corinth, so at Ephesus he worked with his hands, only in this case not so much to earn his living as to set an example to the church, for by his labours he was able to help others also[5]. Then besides the public disputing in the school of Tyrannus, there was his private ministry—in the church and in pastoral visitation. He taught from house to house and admonished the disciples individually. His main theme was *repentance towards God and faith towards our Lord Jesus Christ*[6]. This he testified *both to Jews and Greeks*. But in addition he had to teach the Gentiles the elements of monotheism and of spiritual religion, e.g. the doctrine *that they be no gods which are made with hands*. Such a doctrine obviously would affect the worship of Artemis, but the apostle was careful to avoid giving unnecessary provocation by any blasphemy or evil speaking against the goddess[7].

---

[1] xx 28. [2] according to E. Falkener *Ephesus* (1862). [3] The omission of the AV *one* from our text shews that Tyrannus was some well-known person or that the school was a public building known as *the school of Tyrannus*. [4] i.e. the magistrate in charge of the gymnasia. We know that some of the Asiarchs were friendly to S. Paul. [5] xx 34–5. [6] xx 20–1. [7] xix 26, 37: cp. xiv 15, xvii 29.

To this ministry Ephesus made a great response: crowds apparently attended first the synagogue, then the school of Tyrannus. 'A great door was opened[1]': and S. Paul continued his work *for two years*, or, if we add the three months in the synagogue and the shorter time at the end, considerably over two years,—in Jewish reckoning *a three-years'-space*[2]. As a result the news of the gospel spread not only throughout the city but over the whole province. The provincials who flocked to Ephesus for legal or commercial business, for the worship of Artemis and the magnificent festivals and spectacles, carried *the word of the Lord* home with them. On the part of the church also there was an active propaganda[3]. It is very probable that S. Paul revisited Corinth in this period, and his words *among whom I went about* in xx 25 may cover visits to cities in Asia. In any case there was no lack of evangelists like Epaphras, who carried the word into the valley of the Lycus, where grew up the flourishing churches of Laodicea, with its 'church in Nymphas' house'; of Hierapolis; and of Colossae, with Archippus for its minister and its 'church in the house of Philemon,' himself a friend of the apostle[4]. At the end of the period we find a church at Troas[5]; and now no doubt were laid the foundations at least of the remainder of the 'seven churches of Asia,' viz. Smyrna, Pergamum, Thyatira, Sardis, Philadelphia. So great was the effect that *almost throughout all Asia this Paul turned away much people* from the worship of idols and therefore of Artemis (verse 26). In Ephesus itself a great number of the professors of the curious arts, like the priests at Jerusalem (vi 7), became obedient to the faith. The repute of S. Paul reached the highest circles of society, and among his friends he counted some of the Asiarchs. His own disciples loved him with a passionate devotion[6].

There was however another side to the picture. S. Paul's service of the Lord was accompanied *with tears and with trials*. For success inevitably arouses opposition. Unpopular as they were, the Jews had no opportunity of influencing either the government or the people, and their hostility vented itself in plots[7]. But the progress of the faith must have affected many vested interests, both religious and secular, and so have roused up 'many adversaries.' S. Paul could speak of himself as 'dying daily': on one occasion he 'fought with wild beasts': and Priscilla and Aquila had an opportunity of laying down their necks for his sake[9]. At last the pent-up hostility burst out in a sudden explosion which drove S. Paul from the city. But the success of the preaching brought in its train temptations which were far more perilous than open opposition, and with these the church has to deal before the final crisis.

---

[1] I Cor xvi 9. [2] xx 31. [3] as in Galatia (xiv 6-7, p. 229), Macedonia (I Thess i 8), Achaia (II Cor i 1). [4] Cp. Col i 7, iv 12; 15-17, Philemon 1-2, 23. [5] xx 5-12, II Cor ii 12. [6] xix 31; xx 37-8. [7] xx 19. [8] This is probably a metaphor (as in II Tim iv 17). It is almost impossible to suppose that S. Paul was literally exposed to the wild beasts in the amphitheatre. [9] I Cor xvi 9; xv 31, 32: Rom xvi 4.

§ 3 *Jewish and Christian 'magic' and the church*

Nothing has been said as yet of a most important element in S. Paul's success—viz. his miraculous power. Everywhere indeed he has been attended by miracles, but at Ephesus we seem to reach a climax in this matter also. For (1) *God wrought* some *exceptional powers by his hands*; and these indicated, in the eyes of the Ephesians, (2) a permanent power residing in him[1]. This idea gave rise to superstitious practices: cloths[2] which had touched *his skin* were *carried away* and applied, with apparent efficacy, *to the sick*. This feature forms a parallel to the similar outburst of miraculous activity at Jerusalem described in v 12–16. There S. Peter's shadow now possesses the virtue now ascribed to S. Paul's skin: we notice however that for the *signs and wonders* wrought by the apostles in Jerusalem the writer here substitutes the stronger word *powers*. In each case, both at Jerusalem and Ephesus, we have an instance of the divine condescension or accommodation: to a superstitious people a superstitious appeal is allowed[3]. But there is a further explanation, of special application to Ephesus. The manifestation of divine power was needed to convict the false power—'the power and signs and lying wonders with all the deceit of unrighteousness[4]'—which had kept the Ephesians in bondage. *Powers* had been wrought at Samaria by Philip and evil spirits cast out, and for the same reason —to deliver the Samaritans from the spiritual tyranny of Simon Magus, who called himself 'the Great Power of God.' In many respects there is a noticeable parallelism between Ephesus and Samaria[5].

But the manifestation of divine power precipitated the conflict with evil. (1) Without the church, it roused up in competition the most dangerous rival of Christianity—false spiritualism. Barjesus, the 'magus' of Paphos, had resisted the word; but Simon Magus had desired to employ the power of the Spirit for his own purposes, and now the spiritualists of Ephesus boldly made the same experiment. In exorcisms and similar magic the virtue lay in the formula or incantation used, and the 'Ephesian letters' were such incantations. The success of these formulas depended upon the 'name which was named' in them; and now the Ephesian professors had discovered a new and potent name, the name which S. Paul used with such effect in his powers. But their use of it was taking the name in vain, and its majesty as well as its superiority over all other names must be vindicated[6].

(2) Within the church, the power wielded by S. Paul proved too attractive. The sun of prosperity draws up a plentiful crop of weeds

---

[1] as in the Lord (Lk viii 46).   [2] They were *napkins*, for wiping off sweat, and *half-cinctures* or *aprons*, which were worn by working men.   [3] See above pp. 68–9.
[4] II Thes ii 9–10.   [5] Besides the *great powers* (viii 13) and *unclean spirits* (7), we have *proclaiming* (5), *the kingdom of God* (12) and *baptism into the name of the Lord Jesus* (16)—phrases which occur in xix 13, 8, 5.   [6] Cp. Eph i 21. The verb *to name* (ver. 13) occurs 3 times in Ephesians: elsewhere in NT only 6 times. For the *Name* cp. Eph v 20, Col iii 17.

together with the good wheat. At Jerusalem disciples, like Ananias and Sapphira, had been drawn to the church who had not put off their covetousness, as later on Pharisees who had not put off their Pharisaism: at Samaria Simon Magus had believed and been baptized, and yet was hoping to purchase the right to give the Holy Spirit. And now at Ephesus numbers had joined the church who had not realized the entire moral change demanded of them, viz. to 'put away the old man of their former manner of life, and be renewed in the spirit of their mind.' They had not ceased 'to have fellowship with the unfruitful works of darkness¹,' but secretly retained their *curious arts* and practices. To save the church from a definite lowering of the spiritual life and moral standard, a reformation was needed, a real repentance —to be exhibited in deed, like that preached by John the Baptist to the Jews.

11 And God wrought ²special ³miracles by the hands of
12 Paul: insomuch that unto the sick were carried away from his body ⁴handkerchiefs or aprons, and the diseases departed from them, and the evil spirits went out.
13 But certain also of the strolling Jews, exorcists, ⁵took upon them to name over them which had the evil spirits the name of the Lord Jesus, saying, I adjure you by Jesus whom
14 Paul preacheth. ⁶And there were seven sons of one Sceva,
15 a Jew, a ⁷chief priest, which did this. And the evil spirit answered and said unto them, Jesus I ⁸know, and Paul I
16 know; but who are ye? And the man in whom the evil spirit was leaped on them, and mastered ⁹both of them, and prevailed against them, so that they fled out of that house naked and wounded.
17 And this became known to all, both Jews and Greeks, that dwelt at Ephesus; and fear fell upon them all, and the
18 name of the Lord Jesus was magnified. Many also of them that had believed came, confessing, and declaring their deeds.
19 And not a few of them that practised ¹⁰curious arts brought their books together, and burned them in the sight of all:

---

¹ Eph iv 22–4: v 11.   ² or *no common* (xxviii 2).   ³ Gk *powers*.
⁴ Gk *sudaria* or *semicinctia* (Latin words).   ⁵ Gk *took in hand* (Lk i 1), i.e. *attempt*.   ⁶ Bezan has *Amongst whom also the sons of one Sceva a priest wished to do the same, (who) were accustomed to exorcise such persons. And entering into (the house of) the possessed they began to invoke over him the name, saying We charge thee by Jesus whom Paul preacheth to come forth.* Then [*the evil spirit.*   ⁷ Gk *high-priest*.   ⁸ Marg *recognise*.   ⁹ AV reads simply *them*.   ¹⁰ i.e. *magical* (marg).

and they counted the price of them, and found it fifty thousand pieces of silver.

20   So mightily grew the word of the Lord and prevailed.

13   The Jews had become greatly addicted to the study of magic. Around the name of Solomon clustered great traditions of magical powers, and the Jewish Kabbala was to become the type of this lore. Barjesus of Paphos was a Jew, and Simon Magus a Samaritan. Exorcism however or the casting out of spirits was a recognized practice, much as the practice of medicine to-day. In Palestine 'the sons of the Pharisees' cast out devils[1], and 'exorcists' came to
14   form a regular class in the Christian church. So now at Ephesus we find some *travelling*[2] *Jewish exorcists.* Among them were some of high rank, *the sons of a Jewish priest.* Our text says a *high priest*, which would denote a member of the high-priestly families at Jerusalem; but perhaps there is some confusion, and *Sceva* may have been a priest who was also a ruler of the synagogue[3]. The distinction between the right and wrong exorcism lay in the faith of the exorcist. The sons of Sceva, without any faith in the Lord[4], thought they would make trial of the formula which S. Paul used 'IN THE NAME OF JESUS.' Two of them[5] uttered it over a demoniac.
15   But their exorcism had an unexpected effect. Like the evil spirits in the Gospel, this spirit *knew*, i.e. recognized the power of, *Jesus*; he also *knew Paul*[6], i.e. the demoniac had probably met or heard the
16   apostle, and was quite aware that the sons of Sceva had no part with him. As if infuriated at the deception practised on him, he *leaped upon them, and overpowering them both,* used such violence that they *made their escape* with difficulty.
17   This 'judgement' became notorious throughout the city, and it had the same effect as the judgement of Ananias and Sapphira[7]. It caused universal *awe* and *reverence* for *the name of the LORD JESUS.* In the church it even brought about a reformation. The evident presence of the Spirit of power convicted the conscience of
18   sin and brought to repentance. (1) *Many who had believed began to come* forward and *confess openly*[8] to the church, or to the church authorities, the evil *practices* which they had not abandoned. (2) But the final test of repentance is amendment[9], and of this

---

[1] Lk xi 19, Mt xii 27.   [2] i.e. *going round* or *about*, from place to place, very much like S. Paul himself.   [3] Some Bezan authorities have *ruler* instead of *priest*.   [4] Cp. Mt xvii 16–20, Mk ix 28–9.   [5] This we gather from the better reading in verse 16 *both of them.*   [6] Two different Greek words are here used for *know.* The one (*Paul I know*) is a general term, which does not suggest the source or nature of the knowledge: the other (*Jesus I know*) implies that the knowledge has been gained by personal experience. Similar combinations occur in xv 7 and 8, xix 25 and 35, xx 18 and 34.   [7] v 11: cp. Lk i 65.   [8] The word denotes confession with the lips: for such confession see Mt iii 6, Jas v 16, I Jn i 9.   [9] Cp. xxvi 20, Lk iii 8. The candidate for baptism in early days had to abjure many professions and callings (such as these curious arts), which was in itself a great test of repentance.

19 there was a signal proof. *Not a few* of the *professors of curious arts*[1] *now collected the books* (parchments, rolls etc.) which contained their magical formulas and Ephesian letters, and *burnt them* publicly (*before all*) in a great bonfire. It must have made a deep impression on the city, like 'the bonfire of vanities' which resulted from Savonarola's preaching at Florence. It was equivalent to a public recantation, for the custom of burning sacrilegious works was not unknown in those days[2]. What was still more impressive was the value of the sacrifice, which afforded a proof of their sincerity. These books, containing such efficacious secrets, were very valuable; and some who were interested *added up their prices*. The sum came to 50000 *drachmas*[3] or about £1700, which from the greater purchasing power of money in those days really represents a much greater value.

20 This bonfire was the crowning victory of the church over its greatest enemy—evil within; and S. Luke concludes with one of his summaries. The sentence is stamped with the characteristic of the work at Ephesus, viz. *might* or *power*[4]. *Thus*, in such decisive victories[5], the kingdom of God was established in power; and *the word of the Lord*, manifested *with might, continued to grow and to prevail* over all adversaries—visible and invisible.

This victory also concludes the history of aggressive work in the Acts: as the next verse tells us—*these things* (i.e. this work) *were fulfilled*. The fulfilment at Ephesus answers to the beginning of the church at Jerusalem; and so is made manifest the unity which underlies the church's life and growth. The church is the same Way and founded on the power of the same Name. Again we have, as at the beginning, the baptism of John (i 5), followed by that of the Holy Ghost (ii 1-4) manifested in speaking with tongues and prophecy (ii 5-13): an outburst of miraculous energy (ii 43, v 12-16): a decisive judgement on hypocrites within (v 1-11) and without (viii 18-24): a consequent exhibition of repentance (ii 37-43) and of self-abnegation in the matter of money and possessions (ii 44, iv 32-35). In its organization the church is built upon the foundation of the apostles—at Jerusalem S. Peter and the Twelve, at Ephesus S. Paul. In conveying the gift of the Spirit, in his miraculous power, and in his victory over the church's adversaries, Paul is a second Peter; and verse 20 represents the climax of his work also. The result is commensurate. In the first centuries Ephesus, as a centre of the church,

---

[1] *Curious* (from the Vulgate *curiosa*) exactly represents the Greek word. These magicians were *busied about, inquisitive into*, the secrets of nature. They were, like the alchemists, ancestors of our chemists and scientists. [2] Dr Field in his *Notes on translation of NT* gives instances. [3] The (piece of) *silver* was the drachma, which corresponded to the Latin *denarius* or *penny* and was = 8d. or 9d. [4] The phrase translated *mightily* occurs here only in the Acts. The substantive is used in Eph vi 10 together with two other ideas characteristic of this section: *be made powerful* (xviii 24, xix 11) *in the might* (ver. 20) *of his strength* (corresponding to *prevail*, vv. 16, 20): so too in Eph i 19. [5] Very different from the manner in which the apostle went out from the Areopagus, xvii 33 (*thus*).

eclipses Antioch. At Ephesus S. John, the last of the Twelve, fixed his abode, bequeathed his Gospel to the church, and died. With Ephesus and Asia are associated most of the great names of early church history, S. Polycarp and S. Irenaeus, Papias of Hierapolis, Polycrates of Ephesus, and Melito of Sardis[1]. 'Asia' was indeed the heart of the church, the scene of its greatest activity. This is also evident from the growth of heresies, which fully justified the apostolic warnings and anticipations. The names of Cerinthus of Ephesus, Marcion of Pontus, and Montanus of Phrygia, have given Asia an unhappy notoriety. But if the exuberance of error dims the glory, it is the sign of the vitality, of a church. In later centuries political and natural causes brought about a decline. The silting up of its harbour destroyed the prosperity of Ephesus. Asia declined with the decay of the empire, and the invasion of Mohammedanism overwhelmed its churches. To-day the port of Ephesus is a marsh, and its site is marked by a few ruins: 'its candlestick has been removed out of its place.' A small village still exists in the neighbourhood of the once famous temple of Artemis; but the temple itself fell into ruins, was covered with rubbish, and utterly lost, until its remains were discovered and excavated in the year 1869 by an English architect, Mr J. T. Woods[2].

---

[1] See also p. cxvi.
[2] See his *Discoveries at Ephesus*, 1877.

DIVISION III
(= Ch. 19. 21—28)

THE PASSING OF PAUL AND HIS DEFENCE OF THE GOSPEL

From A.D. 54 *to* A.D. 60—*Nero being emperor of Rome (from Oct.* 54): *Antonius Felix* (52-57) *and Porcius Festus* (57-60) *being procurators of Judaea; Ananias son of Nedebaios and Ishmael son of Phabi* (c. 58) *high-priests.*

Now when these things were fulfilled—these solemn words[1] shew that here we enter upon the last division of the Acts. After the riot at Ephesus there follows the narrative of the final journey to Jerusalem, and though there was an interval of a year between the two, there is no break in the narrative. From the point of view of the Acts the departure from Ephesus was the beginning of the journey, and therefore the beginning of the end.

(1) This division may be headed *THE PASSING* or *PASSION OF PAUL*. Not that it will actually contain his death, but it is the record of all the steps which led up to it—the conclusion of his active ministry: his farewells to the brethren: his *apologia pro vitâ suâ* to the church, the Jews, and the Romans: his arrest, trials, and despatch to Rome.

(2) This ending of the Acts forms a striking parallel to the ending of the Gospel. There the passion of the Lord with all its immediate preparation is related in great detail; so here the 'passion' of Paul is on a scale altogether disproportionate to the rest of the book. The Acts however does not end in fact with S. Paul's death, but with a condition of renewed life; similarly at the end of Part I the 'passion' of S. Peter had ended with a deliverance. Thus in each case there is a parallel to the resurrection in the Gospel. Again the preparatory stages are alike distinctly marked in the structure of each book. In the Gospel of S. Luke (*a*) the first intimation of the end occurs in ix 51, just after the transfiguration which formed the climax in the Lord's ministry,—*now it came to pass when the days of his being received up were being fulfilled:* (*b*) the journey to Judaea begins in xvii 11: and (*c*) in xviii 31 the actual going up to Jerusalem. Similarly in the Acts (*a*) the period of active work is fulfilled in the climax at Ephesus: (*b*) the journey to Judaea begins in xx 6: and (*c*) the going up to the city in xxi 15. There is yet another beginning in the Gospel, viz. of the passion proper (Lk xxii 1), and to this we may find a parallel in Acts xxvii 1.

---

[1] Cp. Mt xxvi 1: Lk ix 51, Acts ii 1.

(3) The book ends at Rome, and this division begins with *Rome*. That word is the keynote. Rome now takes the place of Ephesus and henceforward is the real centre and subject of the narrative. It had indeed long been S. Paul's goal (verse 21), and now we are to read how he attained it. The purpose of S. Paul, which coincided with the will of God, was achieved; but, as in other cases, the means by which he was brought to Rome were far different from what he had wished or arranged. Thus we have presented to us a typical instance of the divine overruling of human plans, but to the achievement of one and the same end.

SECTION I (= Ch. 19. 21--21. 14)

The fulfilment of S. Paul's work and his journey to Jerusalem

§ 1 *The apostle's plan*

No small part of the 'tears and trials which befell' S. Paul at Ephesus (xx 19) was due to his 'daily anxiety for all the churches' (II Cor xi 28), and especially for the church at Corinth. The development of that church had been almost too rapid; and S. Paul soon heard from visitors such as 'those of Chloe's household,' and from Stephanas and Apollos himself, of the growth of division and disorder amongst the brethren[1]. This gave rise to much correspondence with the Corinthians both by messenger and by letter. It is possible that the apostle himself paid a visit to Corinth during his two years' sojourn at Ephesus[2]. But the difficult question of investigating the history of this correspondence belongs to a commentary on the epistles. For us it is sufficient to know that about Easter[3] in this last year of S. Paul's residence at Ephesus (A.D. 54) he sent to Corinth a letter which is our 'I Corinthians.' At its conclusion (xvi 5-9) he tells them his plans: *I will come unto you when I shall have passed through Macedonia: for I do pass through Macedonia: but with you it may be that I shall abide, or even winter, that ye may set me forward on my journey whithersoever I go...But I will tarry at Ephesus until Pentecost; for a great door and effectual is opened unto me and there are many adversaries.* There was a great deal of uncertainty as to S. Paul's plans at this critical time, and from a later epistle (II Corinthians) we learn that at one moment he had intended to go straight from Ephesus to Corinth by sea[4]. But whether that was the original or a subsequent plan, the first letter exactly agrees with the situation and plans of the apostle as here described in the Acts, although the letter was not actually sent till after the departure of Timothy recorded in Acts xix 22.

---

[1] I Cor i–iv, vi 7-8, xi 17-9, xii–xiv: see i 11, xvi 17, 12. [2] as seems to be implied in II Cor ii 1, xii 14, 21, xiii 1-2. But these passages are not decisive. [3] I Cor v 8. [4] II Cor i 15 foll.

There were also other churches which were causing S. Paul anxiety, and this brings us back to the question of the Epistle to the Galatians. For we have now arrived at the alternative date for that epistle. The reconstruction according to the earlier date has been given above on pages 334-6. If we accept the other theory, the history will be somewhat as follows. When S. Paul passed through South Galatia in A.D. 51 (xviii 23, xix 1), the Galatians were still faithful to him. It was only at the end of his residence in Ephesus, when he was still *staying in Asia*[1] after writing I Corinthians (xix 22), that news reached him of the defection of the Galatian churches. In reply, either while still at Ephesus or after his departure, he wrote the Epistle to the Galatians. Both the state of the controversy as represented in the epistle and its style induce us to put it after I Corinthians, while in both points it closely agrees with II Corinthians, especially the concluding chapters. On such grounds we should place it in the interval between the two; and this would agree with S. Paul's own condition. From II Corinthians we learn that when he left Ephesus the apostle was suffering from extreme spiritual depression[2]. The news from Galatia would help to account for this, as also for 'the anxiety for the churches which pressed upon him daily' (II Cor xi 28), and the anxiety reacted in turn on the style of S. Paul's reply to the Galatians. Then there are coincidences in details. As S. Paul had only two years before *stablished all the disciples* of Galatia (xviii 23), their defection was indeed 'quick' or sudden (Gal i 6). *All the brethren who are with me* (i 2) exactly describes the company of ministers whom S. Paul had round him at Ephesus[3]. The picture of the working of the Spirit in Gal iii 5, where the verbs are in the present tense, exactly describes the apostle's miraculous activity in Acts xix 11-12. We may find other reminiscences of Ephesian life, e.g. in the reference to witchcraft (iii 1)[4]. Lastly, there is no hint of a forthcoming visit to Galatia. Rather the apostle seems to be taking farewell. For indeed he is on his way to Corinth and has further plans in view; he is on the point of leaving Asia and going to the west, so 'from henceforth let no man trouble me[5].' Such considerations as these incline us to place the Epistle to the Galatians in this interval chronologically; the theological situation in Galatia however would not be different from that required for the earlier date.

In any case we have been anticipating, for both epistles (Galatians and II Corinthians) would only date from or after *the stay in Asia* which followed after S. Paul had formed the definite plan of verse 21.

21   'Now after these things were ended, Paul'purposed in the
    [8]spirit, when he had passed through Macedonia and Achaia,

---

[1] Perhaps the state of the Galatian churches was one of the causes of the delay. [2] Cp. e.g. II Cor i 8-11, ii 12-3.   [3] Cp. xix 22, 29, xx 34 (*they that were with me*).   [4] Perhaps the mutilation of Gal v 12 was suggested by the eunuch priests, the Megabyzi, of Artemis.   [5] Gal vi 17.   [6] Gk *Now when these things were fulfilled.*   [7] Gk *set* (i 7).   [8] or *Spirit.*

to go to Jerusalem, saying, After I have been there, I must 22 ¹also see Rome. And having sent into Macedonia two of them that ministered unto him, Timothy and Erastus, he himself stayed in Asia for a while.

It seemed to S. Paul that *these* victories of the word (verses 15-20) had *fulfilled* his ministry at Ephesus. The idea of fulness or fulfilling is characteristic of the Epistle to the Ephesians, and it implies a reference to the divine will. By this will a definite work there had been assigned to S. Paul, which (like John the Baptist) he had so far fulfilled²; and indeed the work was 'fully done' (Rev iii 2). The work of S. Paul was that of a missionary and evangelist, rather than of a settled and abiding teacher. Now he had by this time evangelized the provinces of Galatia, of Macedonia, Achaia, and Asia, so that 'from Jerusalem and round about even to Illyricum'—the province bordering Macedonia on the west—'he had fulfilled the gospel of Christ,' and therefore 'had no more any place in these regions³.' Accordingly he looked westwards. His view extended even to Spain⁴. But first there lay on the way the great city which had so long been the goal of all his ambitions—Rome⁵. Now therefore at last *Paul set* firmly *in his spirit* that he *must see even Rome*. Elsewhere S. Luke speaks of 'setting in the *heart*⁶'; here he may be using *spirit* intentionally because of the ambiguity of the word. 'Spirit' may denote either the human or the divine spirit: but in the case of the true Christian we need not be careful to distinguish, for his spirit is governed by the Spirit of God which dwells in him. So with S. Paul, the Holy Spirit had always prompted each advance in his career; and now this critical decision is not taken without his inspiration⁷. There was a necessity laid upon him—'*I must* see Rome.' The will of God was prospering him (Rom i 10), blowing with a fair wind upon the sail of S. Paul's desires: and it was his conviction of the divine guidance which now kept the apostle so firm in his purpose. For first he had to visit *Macedonia and Achaia*, in order to confirm the disciples and to finish the collection of alms for the church at Jerusalem. Then he must *go to Jerusalem* to deliver the alms. Then at last, starting from the birthplace of the church with the sympathy and prayers of the brethren, he could embark on his new enterprise.

We notice that the apostle says *see* Rome, and in his Epistle to the Romans his modesty is most striking. He hopes to bring them some spiritual gift, but he apologizes for seeming to imply that they needed any admonition. He speaks of his visit as only a temporary sojourn on his way to Spain⁸. His words do not at all convey the impression that he is coming to found or organize a church. On the contrary the church at Rome was already so important that he thought it best to

---

¹ or *even*. ² Cp. Eph i 10, 23, iii 19, iv 10, 13, v 18: II Tim iv 7, Acts xiii 25, xiv 26. ³ Rom xv 19, 23. ⁴ Rom xv 24-8, cp. I Cor xvi 6.
⁵ Rom i 10, 13, xv 22. ⁶ Lk i 66, Acts v 4: cp. i 7. ⁷ Cp. xiii 2, xvi 6, xix 1 (Bezan): xx 22, xxi 13-4. ⁸ Rom i 11-2, xv 14, 24, 28.

address 'to the Romans' his greatest theological writing, the public exposition of his gospel. If with these facts we couple the stress which he lays in the epistle upon his principle of not preaching the gospel on other men's foundations[1], we cannot help feeling that some apostle—and he could be none other than S. Peter—had already visited and worked in the city. If it was about this time that S. Peter paid such a visit to Rome, he would probably have passed through Corinth on his way and so unintentionally have given rise to the party 'of Cephas' in the Corinthian church. The tradition of that church, as well as of those of Antioch and Rome, certainly claimed S. Peter as a co-founder with S. Paul[2].

To return to the latter apostle. To prepare his way, he now *sent on to Macedonia two of* his 'deacons' or *ministers, Timothy and Erastus.* From Macedonia they were to go on to Corinth[3], of which city Erastus was the treasurer[4]. S. Paul himself *stayed in Asia,* either to seize some opportunity for work (an 'open door') or to withstand some of 'the many adversaries' of the church.

§ 2 *The riot at Ephesus*

S. Paul's stay however was cut short by one of those 'perils in the city' which chequered his career. The peril came neither from the government nor from the Jews, but from 'the Gentiles.' It was a popular riot, and on a scale which cast the riots at Thessalonica and Philippi into the shade. Ephesus was nominally a democracy; and the city was swept by a sudden frenzy, which all but resulted in one of those legal travesties of justice which so often blot the history of democracies. This frenzy was caused, not by the plotting of the Jews as at Thessalonica, but as at Philippi by interference with the vested interests of a class. It was not the doctrines of Christianity which aroused the hostility of the Gentiles. Criticism of idolatry they were accustomed to from the lips of their own philosophers or of Hellenistic Jews[5]. Moreover their first attitude to S. Paul was generally favourable. It was when his preaching affected personal gain or interfered with customs of trade that opposition began. The significant word *gain* or *business* marks both the narratives, at Philippi and at Ephesus[6]. The ostensible cause of the riot was indeed religious zeal—though with the instigators this was only a cloak—which served to increase the danger. When devotion to religion coincides with self-interest, then the fury of fanaticism is resistless.

Fully to appreciate the incident, a more detailed account of the constitution of Ephesus is required. At Ephesus there met together four authorities. (1) There was the supreme authority of Rome, represented by the *proconsul.* For judicial purposes the provinces

[1] xv 20-1, cp. II Cor x 13-6. [2] See pp. 179-80 for a possible visit of S. Peter to Rome still earlier than this. [3] I Cor iv 17, xvi 10. [4] i.e. if he is the same Erastus as in Rom xvi 23 : cp. II Tim iv 20. [5] such as the Ephesian Jew who about this time wrote the *Letters of Heracleitus.* [6] It is the same word in the Greek : xvi 16 (*gain*), xix 24, 25 (*business*). Cp. with this section xvi 16-23.

were divided into shires (*conventus*), each with its assize town. In the province of Asia Ephesus was the chief assize town; and accordingly *court-days were kept* there (verse 38), when justice was administered by the proconsul. (2) The city itself like Athens was 'free,' and retained its Greek constitution which was democratic in form. There was a Senate or Boulê, to which power gravitated in imperial times. But nominally Ephesus was still governed by the *Dêmos* or *People* (verse 30) assembled in their *Ecclésia* or *Assembly*. An ecclesia was held three times a month, and these meetings were the *regular* or *ordinary assemblies* (verse 32): but an 'extraordinary assembly' could be convened as on the present occasion. Where, as in cities of the empire, the powers of such an ecclesia were limited to purely domestic and formal matters, the substantial authority would fall into the hands of its secretary—the official who summoned and *dismissed* the assembly (verse 41), prepared the agenda, kept the minutes and acted as chairman. Thus the secretary of the ecclesia or *townclerk* (verse 35) would naturally be one of the magnates of the city; and this we find to have been the case from the inscriptions, in which the secretary often appears as holding also the highest offices, such as the Asiarchate.

(3) The *Asiarchate* was a provincial office. There was a provincial organization, which was greatly fostered by the emperors. Each province had a 'Common (Council),' composed of delegates from the chief cities, for the management of common provincial business. In this business the chief element was the supervision of the provincial worship of the emperor, a cult which furnished, besides a test of loyalty, a bond of unity for the empire. A temple and altar to Rome and the emperor were erected in some city, which thereupon was designated NEÔCOROS or *Sacristan*[1] (literally, *temple-sweeper*), i.e. of the imperial temple; and the common worship of the province was celebrated there with games and festivals. The president of the common council acted as high-priest and presided over the festivities and games, which were given at his expense. In return he enjoyed the title of 'Ruler of the province,'—Asiarch, Galatarch, Lyciarch etc., as the case might be—and he would rank as first of all the provincials. *The Asiarchs* of verse 31, then, were such high-priests and the chief representatives of the aristocracy and plutocracy of Asia. There is a difficulty in the use of the plural, for as a rule there was only one Ruler for a province. It has been suggested that the Ruler retained the designation as an honorary title after his period of office. But a better explanation is to be found in the exceptional prosperity of Asia. It contained several wealthy cities which were rivals of Ephesus and, like it, had temples of the Augustus. Probably the high-priests of these temples also were called Asiarchs, and all these together formed a kind of college. At the present juncture this college seems to have been assembled at Ephesus, probably for the purpose of celebrating the great festival of 'the Common (Council) of Asia,' which occurred every fifth year.

---

[1] verse 35: Thessalonica and Beroea were also *Neôcoroi*. Mr E. G. Hardy has given an account of the 'Provincial Concilia' in the *Eng. Hist. Review*, April, 1890.

And we may make the further supposition that its celebration was made to coincide with the Artemisia, the chief annual festival of Ephesus, which was kept in March or April.

(4) The festival of the Artemisia was celebrated in honour of Artemis. She was, as we have seen, the (patron) goddess of the city[1]; and Ephesus was *Sacristan* not only of the temples of the emperors but also of the temple *of Artemis*[2]. Mr Woods' excavations of this temple and the numerous inscriptions there discovered have given a revelation of this worship which entirely corroborates the life-like picture in the Acts. The goddess, as has been said (p. 338), was really one of the primitive nature deities. And though identified by the Greeks with Artemis and by the Latins with Diana, she was no beautiful huntress goddess. Her image in the upper part had been carved into the shape of a woman covered with paps to represent the fertility of nature; but the lower part retained its original form. It was in fact nothing else than a block of wood, so ancient that tradition held it for one of the sacred images reputed to have '*fallen from heaven*' (verse 35). Her adoption by the Greeks however increased, if not the beauty, yet the repute of the goddess. She became an object of adoration throughout *the whole* Graeco-Roman *world* (verse 27): and her festivals were styled 'ecumenical.' Her distinctive attribute was greatness[3]: 'GREAT ARTEMIS' was her usual invocation and title[4]: in some inscriptions she is called the MOST GREAT GODDESS[5]. The month in which her chief festival, the Artemisia, occurred was called after her Artemisiôn, and later on by a decree of the city was entirely consecrated to her[6]. Her temple, built in the beautiful Ionic style, was one of the wonders of the world: it was one of the great cathedrals (so to speak) of paganism. According to Mr Woods it was 418 feet long by 239 feet broad, viz. the platform of the temple with its peristyle of 100 columns, each 56 feet high. The relics of the temple now in the British Museum, and in particular a sculptured drum which was the base of one of the columns, testify to the size and *magnificence* (verse 27) of the building. The claim to magnificence was also warranted by the splendid works of art with which it was adorned; while behind the cell of the goddess was deposited a vast amount of treasure, for it was the safest bank in Asia. This use to which the temples were generally put explains the charge of *temple-robbing* in verse 37. The temple was some distance from the city; and it stood in an ample precinct which possessed the

---

[1] Cp. Xenophon Ephes. *Eph.* i 11 *I swear to thee by our country's goddess, Great Artemis of the Ephesians.* [2] This use of *Neôcoros* (in reference to Artemis), which used to puzzle scholars, has been verified by inscriptions. [3] *Greatness*, i.e. *magnificence* or *majesty* (verse 27), is a divine attribute. Simon Magus called himself *Great*. Cp. Lk i 32 (*he shall be great*): Lk ix 43, II Pet i 16, 17: Heb i 3, viii 1, Jude 25: and *to magnify* verse 17, Lk i 46, Phil i 20. [4] The same invocation is found in other cities e.g. GREAT ARTEMIS, GREAT APOLLO. Cp. *Encycl. Biblica* art. DIANA, which sums up our information about the goddess. [5] Cp. the MOST HIGH GOD of xvi 17, also found in inscriptions. [6] This decree, now in the British Museum, mentions the decline of the worship of Artemis, and so furnishes a parallel to the Acts: see Hicks *Gk Inscriptions in Brit. Mus.* III no. 482.

right of asylum or sanctuary. For her worship Artemis enjoyed the services of an army of priests, eunuch priests, virgin priestesses, temple-wardens, 'theologians[1],' choristers, vergers, tire-women, and 'acrobats.' For the maintenance of this regal establishment the goddess possessed a sufficient revenue from her ample estates. Within the temple was stored her 'plate,' viz. her images, shrines, and sacred utensils, of gold and silver, which on great festivals were carried to the city and back in a magnificent procession.

It is obvious that the trade of the city would largely flourish upon this worship of Artemis and the concourse of pilgrims which it attracted. There would, for instance, be a demand among the pilgrims for memorials of the goddess to carry home with them; and grateful worshippers would want thank-offerings to dedicate in her temple. The form these took was that of *shrines*. The *shrine* was properly the inner cell in which stood the image of the deity. Then it was applied to technical representations of the same, figures of the goddess standing in a niche. Such shrines, like reliquaries in the middle ages, were carried in the festival processions and formed a conspicuous adornment[2]. Small copies of *silver* or potter's work were sold to the public; and specimens of them are to be seen in our museums[3]. The demand for these gave rise to a flourishing manufacture of *silver shrines* at Ephesus. At its head stood one *Demetrius*, who organized the trade or supplied the capital (verse 24). This industry was now seriously affected by S. Paul's preaching; and the depreciation of trade brought about a crisis, *a great stir* or uproar (xii 18). Of this we have here a most vivid account derived from an eye-witness. It is marked by some difficulties in the Greek, which may be due to Ephesian usage.

23 And about that time there arose no small stir concerning
24 the Way. For a certain man named Demetrius, a silversmith, which made silver shrines of ⁴Diana, brought no little ⁵business
25 unto the craftsmen; whom he gathered together, with the workmen of like occupation, and said, ⁶Sirs, ye know that by
26 this business we have our wealth. And ye see and hear, that not alone at Ephesus, but almost throughout all Asia, this Paul hath persuaded and turned away much people, saying
27 that they be no gods, which are made with hands: and not only is there danger that this our ⁷trade come into disrepute; but also that the temple of the great goddess Diana be made

---

[1] For this title see Deissmann *Neue Bibelstudien* p. 58.   [2] S. Ignatius is alluding to these processions when he calls the Christian Ephesians *god-bearers and shrine-bearers* (Eph i 9).   [3] No *silver* specimen has been found, but that is a fact which hardly calls for explanation. *Silver* is omitted from the text by Codex B.
[4] Gk *Artemis*, and so throughout.   [5] or *gain* (AV).   [6] Bezan has *Fellow-craftsmen*.   [7] Gk part, *share*.

of no account, and ¹that she should even be deposed from
her ²magnificence, whom all Asia and the world worshippeth.
28 And when they heard this, they were filled with wrath³, and
cried out, saying, 'Great *is* Diana of the Ephesians.
29   And the city was filled with the confusion: and they
rushed with one accord into the theatre, having seized Gaius
and Aristarchus, men of Macedonia, Paul's companions in
30 travel. And when Paul was minded to enter in unto the
31 people, the disciples suffered him not. And certain also of
the ⁵chief officers of Asia, being his friends, sent unto him,
and besought him not to ⁶adventure himself into the theatre.
32 Some therefore cried one thing, and some another: for the
⁷assembly was in confusion; and the more part knew not
33 wherefore they were come together. ⁸And they brought
Alexander out of the multitude, the Jews putting him forward.
And Alexander beckoned with the hand, and would have
34 made a defence unto the people. But when they perceived
that he was a Jew, all with one voice about the space of two
hours cried out, ⁹Great *is* Diana of the Ephesians.
35   And when the townclerk had quieted the multitude, he
saith, Ye men of Ephesus, what man is there who knoweth
not how that the city of the Ephesians is ¹⁰temple-keeper of the
great ¹¹Diana, and of the *image* which fell down from ¹²Jupiter?
36 Seeing then that these things cannot be gainsaid, ye ought
37 to be quiet, and to do nothing rash. For ye have brought
hither these men, which are neither robbers of temples nor
38 blasphemers of our goddess. If therefore Demetrius, and
the craftsmen that are with him, have a matter against any
man, ¹³the courts are open, and there are proconsuls: let
39 them accuse one another. But if ye seek any thing ¹⁴about
other matters, it shall be settled in the ¹⁵regular assembly.
40 For indeed we are in danger to be accused concerning this
day's riot, there being no cause *for it*: and as touching it we

---

¹ AV and later mss read *her magnificence should be destroyed.*   ² Properly, '*great*'*-ness.*   ³ Bezan adds *and ran into the street.*   ⁴ Bezan reads *Great Artemis of the Ephesians!* and so in verse 34.   ⁵ Gk *Asiarchs.*   ⁶ Gk *give himself.*   ⁷ Gk *ecclésia* and in vv. 39, 41.   ⁸ Marg *And some of the multitude instructed Alexander.*   ⁹ B repeats this clause.   ¹⁰ Gk *neócoros (sacristan).*   ¹¹ AV inserts *goddess.*   ¹² Marg *heaven* (Gk *Zeus*).   ¹³ Marg *court days are kept.*   ¹⁴ B and Bezan read *further* for *about other matters.*   ¹⁵ AV marg *ordinary.*

41 shall not be able to give account of this concourse. And when he had thus spoken, he dismissed the assembly.

24 Trades and handicrafts were as fully organized in the Greek cities of 'Asia' as in medieval Europe, and *Demetrius* was no doubt
25 warden of the guild of the silver shrine makers. He now summoned a meeting of his guild, together with the associated and dependent *workmen*[1], and put the situation before them. He had chosen his time well, for the Artemisian festival, when the city was thronged with visitors, was the great harvest for the shrine makers and any fall in the demand would be felt at once. Demetrius cynically avowed his true motive. The worship of Artemis was *their wealth*,
26 and the depression from which they were suffering was due to *this Paul* with his doctrine that gods *made with hands*—these silver images, not to speak of the heaven-fallen image itself—*were no*
27 *gods*[2]. This doctrine was a real *danger* to them and likely to bring *their part* in the religion, i.e. their trade, *to a disreputable* end[3]. Having thus appealed to their self-interest, the orator provided a decent pretext for action from the danger to their religion. For the same logic must apply to *Great Artemis* herself; her *temple will be reckoned for nothing*, and the goddess herself *be stripped of her*
28 *magnificence*[4]. This skilful combination of religious devotion and patriotism with their own interests *filled* the guildsmen *with fury*, and *they ran out into the street, vociferating* the city's watchword
29 *GREAT IS ARTEMIS OF THE EPHESIANS*[5]. The appearance of such a body in the crowded agora of an excitable Greek city could have but one result—a riot, and *the confusion* spread through the whole *city*. The instigators passed round the word 'to the theatre.' The theatre of Ephesus was an immense excavation in the hillside which could contain over 24000 persons and was frequently used as a meeting-place for the ecclesia[6]. Thither accordingly the citizens *rushed as one man* to hold an 'extraordinary assembly.' The craftsmen would want some prey, as it were, for the People; and falling in with two of *Paul's* company, *Gaius* and *Aristarchus* who were *Macedonians*, they *dragged them to the*
30 *theatre*[7]. They had not attacked S. Paul's own lodging, but news

---

[1] The Greek distinguishes the higher *craftsmen* or *artisans* from the inferior *workmen* or *labourers*.   [2] Cp. xiv 15 and p. 233.   [3] The Greek word is only found here. It denotes *refutation*, and what is refuted or exposed falls into disrepute.
[4] The construction of the Greek here in the best text is rather difficult. The verb means *to put down*, thence *destroy* (xiii 19); and the literal translation will be either *be destroyed in respect of somewhat of her majesty*, or *be put down (from) her majesty*. But the word also means *to diminish* and is e.g. the medical term for reducing superfluous flesh. This seems the likeliest sense here—the goddess was in danger of being smitten with leanness (Isai x 16) in the reduction of the pomp of her services. A medical phrase would come naturally from S. Luke's pen.   [5] The omission of one of two consecutive Etas (E) in the text would give the Bezan reading: in the one case we have a profession of faith, in the other the usual invocation.
[6] Another estimate puts the number at 56,000. The outline of the theatre can still be traced.   [7] The words *rushed with one accord* occurred in vii 57, and remind us of S. Stephen's fate.

soon reached him and *his mind* was at once made up to *appear before the people* and make his defence to the ecclesia. He knew what it was to face a furious mob; he had already 'fought with wild beasts' at Ephesus: but he was always ready to follow the example of the Lord in *giving himself* up[1]. However, as on former occasions[2], *the disciples* intervened and stopped him. Further, a
31 message had come even from *some of the Asiarchs*, who had had *friendly* intercourse with him. Well aware not only of the peril from the mob but of S. Paul's courage, *they begged him not to* come *to the theatre*.
32 There meanwhile *the assembly was in a* wild *confusion*: *the majority knew not* why an ecclesia had been convened, and there was a babel of conflicting cries. In front of them, perhaps on the stage, were Demetrius and his guildsmen with Gaius and Aristarchus in their hands, whom they apparently wished to prosecute;
33 but in the confusion no formal steps could be taken. At last however an orator struggled out *of the throng* and got on to the 'pulpit' to address the people[3]. He had been *put forward by the Jews*. For the tumult was as dangerous to the Jews as to the Christians. The Jews were notorious for their fanaticism against idolatry, and they might easily become the victims of the champions of Artemis. The scenes of Jew-baiting and pillaging which had disgraced Alexandria in Caligula's reign might be repeated at Ephesus. One of the prisoners, Aristarchus, was himself a Jew by race. Their main hope lay in diverting the wrath of the assembly upon the Christians. Accordingly *Alexander* their spokesman got up,
34 and *by waving his hand* endeavoured to secure a hearing. But as soon as the people *saw that he was a* god-hating *Jew*, the spark was as it were thrown into the gunpowder. One cry *GREAT IS ARTEMIS OF THE EPHESIANS* burst from their lips and for two hours the whole ecclesia did nothing else than vociferate
35 the same profession of faith. At last, when they were somewhat exhausted, *the secretary of the ecclesia* succeeded in *quieting* them and made a speech. It was a thoroughly Greek speech, like that of Demetrius, admirably suited for the occasion.

He first soothed their vanity by an appeal to the world-wide fame of Ephesus as *sacristan of Artemis and of her heaven-fallen*
36 *image*. Their position was so *unquestionable* that it could not be

---

[1] This is the literal meaning of the phrase translated *adventure himself*: S. Paul uses the expression of the Lord in Gal i 4, I Tim ii 6, Tit ii 14.   [2] ix 25, 30, xvii 10, 14.   [3] The Greek again is difficult. The word in the RV text means literally *put together* and is used in the Bible for *instruct* (LXX), *prove* (Acts ix 22), or *conclude* (xvi 10). The margin adopts the first sense: *some of* (i.e. a party in) *the throng instructed Alexander*, i.e. as to his action or argument. The simplest interpretation is that given in the text, if the Greek can bear it. Alexander may have been the copper-smith who did S. Paul much evil (II Tim iv 14). From the sudden way in which his name is introduced we should gather that he was a person well known either in the city or to the church. Contrast the silence of the Jewish crowd in xxi 40, xxii 2.

endangered by a few strangers, and the frenzied alarm or panic of the Ephesians was uncalled for, not to say undignified. In fact they had been betrayed into an exhibition of conduct the very reverse of the standard of a Greek gentleman, viz. acting *rashly* or
37 *precipitately*, without dignity or deliberation. *For these men*, Gaius and Aristarchus, who had been dragged before the ecclesia, were perfectly innocent—(so fully recognized was the good character of the Christians[1]). It was true that *'temple-robbery'* (which was extended to include other acts of sacrilege) and 'impiety' (which covered *blasphemy* or insulting language towards the goddess) were indictable offences, and liable to public prosecution[2]; but these Christians had
38 been guilty of neither. If there was any charge against them, it was a matter which concerned *Demetrius and his guildsmen*, and they
39 should sue them in the *proconsul's court*. But if the citizens demanded *further enquiry into the matter*[3], it should be conducted, and the difficulty *solved, in the ordinary* meetings of the *ecclesia*.
40 But in fact, he added, *we* as citizens of Ephesus *are in danger* of being called to account. The Romans were exceedingly jealous of any gathering or association which might have a political bearing; and a tumultuous assembly like this, a concourse not of a few guildsmen but of all the citizens, might arouse suspicion and bring on the city a *prosecution for sedition*; and if accused, the Ephesians had no defence to offer, for there was no *reason* for this tumultuous *concourse*, which in the Roman courts might be distorted into a
41 conspiracy[4] The speech had the desired effect; the secretary pronounced the formula of *dismissal*, and the uproar was at an end.

In ver. 38 he had spoken with some sarcasm; *court days*—you are surely aware—*are kept, and there are* (such persons as) *proconsuls*. But if this happened in the year 55 there would be a reason for speaking of *proconsuls* generally rather than of *the proconsul*. For towards the end of 54 the proconsul of Asia, M. Junius Silanus, was poisoned by two of his subordinates at the instigation of Agrippina, and his successor had not yet arrived. The absence of a proconsul would also account for the inaction on the part of the Roman authorities, during a riot which lasted so many hours and involved the whole city.

To enable us to realize the scene in the theatre and the danger of S. Paul, there has fortunately come down to us an account by an

---

[1] They observed S. Paul's directions, e.g. Col iv 5.   [2] An Ephesian decree gives a list of such cognizable offences in the matter of religion. Another decree made interference with the Jewish contributions to the temple at Jerusalem an act of *temple-robbery* (*hierosulia*). By a strange irony, the robbing of temples was a charge brought against the Jews: and not without ground (Rom ii 22).   [3] This seems the better reading.   [4] Again, as in vv. 27 and 33, the Greek reading and construction are not very certain, but the general sense is clear. A literal translation would be *we are in danger of being accused of sedition for to-day* (or *concerning to-day's sedition*), *there being no cause for it, in which matter* (or *which being the case*) *we shall be unable to give account for this concourse*. The word *concourse* is used for the *conspiracy* of the Jews in xxiii 13: the corresponding verb occurs in Mt xvii 22 (marg).

eye-witness of a similar scene in the Stadium of Smyrna. It happened just a hundred years later, and ended in the martyrdom of the bishop of Smyrna, S. Polycarp. Polycarp had been arrested and was brought to the Stadium, where the people had been assembled for some shows. Then arose 'such a tumult that no man's voice could be so much as heard. But as Polycarp entered, a voice came to him from heaven, *Be strong, Polycarp, and play the man.*' Then followed the examination before the proconsul, the result of which was that he 'sent his herald to proclaim three times in the midst of the Stadium *Polycarp hath confessed himself to be a Christian.* Then the whole multitude both of Gentiles and Jews cried out with ungovernable wrath and with a loud shout *This is the teacher of Asia, the father of the Christians, the puller down of our gods, who teacheth numbers not to sacrifice nor worship.* Saying these things they shouted aloud and asked the Asiarch Philip to let a lion loose upon Polycarp. But he said that it was not lawful for him, since he had brought the sports to a close. Then they thought fit to shout out with one accord that Polycarp should be burned alive.' Their voices prevailed and Polycarp was forthwith burned[1].

S. Paul indeed escaped with his life. But coming on the top of all his anxieties about Corinth, and probably Galatia too, the catastrophe cast him into a terrible depression. After building up by two years' hard toil a flourishing church and finding 'a great door opened,' he now saw as it were a great tidal wave suddenly rise up and sweep away his labour. Not indeed that the church was destroyed, but his own hopes of further progress for the present were shattered, and he left Ephesus in great dejection: *we would not have you ignorant, brethren, concerning our affliction which befell us in Asia, that we were weighed down exceedingly, beyond our power, insomuch that we despaired even of life: yea, we ourselves have had the answer of death within ourselves* (II Cor i 8–9).

A year in Macedonia and Achaia

20 And after the uproar was ceased, Paul having sent for the disciples and exhorted them, took leave of them, and
2 departed for to go into Macedonia. And when he had gone through those parts, and had given them much exhortation, he came into ²Greece.

After this uproar the obvious course for the apostle was to leave the city at once. Priscilla and Aquila also left Ephesus and returned to Rome, where we find them a year later. S. Paul writes that they had 'laid down their necks' for him; if their devotion was displayed on this occasion, then it is likely that they too were leaving Ephesus at the same time[3]. For *when the uproar had ceased* Paul summoned a

---
[1] These extracts are from Bp Lightfoot's translation of the *Letter of the Smyrnaeans*. They also illustrate the Asiarchate, and the 'fighting with beasts.'
[2] Gk *Hellas*.   [3] Rom xvi 3–5.

meeting of the church, probably at his lodging in their house, and after *bidding farewell*, he *departed for Macedonia*. This was his goodbye to the body of *the disciples*, for when he passed by a year later he only saw the clergy. The note of farewell[1] marks the whole journey to Jerusalem, which begins now,—at least from S. Luke's point of view; for all that now happened in Macedonia and Achaia, covering a period of nearly twelve months, he sums up in a single sentence. We however cannot pass over it so quickly, for the history is reflected in one of S. Paul's most 'weighty and powerful letters[2],' the Second Epistle to the Corinthians.

This epistle more than any other is a revelation of S. Paul's own heart: it is his spiritual autobiography and *apologia pro vitâ suâ*. It seems to have been written from time to time, like a diary; and certainly it gives the key to his present movements. If he had had any thought of going to Corinth direct from Ephesus, his plans were frustrated by the riot[3]; and he went on to Troas, the port for Macedonia (i 8–ii 12). Here, where on his first visit he had not been permitted to preach (p. 277), he now found 'a door opened.' But his extreme dejection prevented his entering in. He was longing for the return of Titus, who had been sent on a mission to Corinth, and who would bring back word how they had received his first epistle about which he was very anxious. As Titus did not come, he went on to Philippi (ii 12–13). Here Titus came at last, and the good news he brought was like a resurrection from the dead to the apostle (vii 5–16). Out of the fulness of his heart he wrote II Cor i–vii. There was however a matter in which the Corinthians had not shewn much zeal before Titus, viz. the collection for Jerusalem. S. Paul had to write chapters viii and ix and send another mission to Corinth— Titus again, with 'the brother whose praise is in the gospel through all the churches,' i.e. very likely S. Luke, and another brother 'many times proved earnest in many things[4].' Then a sudden change occurs. Before this mission started, fresh news seems to have reached the apostle of some new and very bitter personal attacks upon himself and his apostolic authority. It is evident—we might say, certain—that in the interval after Titus had left Corinth, the same Judaizing leader who had troubled the Galatians had arrived at Corinth and stolen away the heart of that church also, that very wilful child of the apostle and fickle bride of Christ[5]. The news of this provoked the very sharp outburst of passionate rebuke and self-vindication—but at the same time wonderful self-revelation—with which the epistle concludes (x–xiii). These chapters were perhaps written at Thessalonica after S. Paul had been rejoined by Timothy (i 1); and the whole epistle dispatched thence, by the hands of Titus and the brethren.

The whole summer and early autumn were spent in Macedonia. S. Paul *went through those parts*, i.e. he visited Philippi, Thessalonica,

---

[1] Cp. vv. 7, 25, xxi 6.   [2] II Cor x 10.   [3] But see II Cor i 23.
[4] II Cor viii 17, 18, 22.   [5] I Cor iv 15, II xi 2, 3.

Beroea, and perhaps went to other cities further west, if we are to press his words in Rom xv 19 *even unto Illyricum*. All this time a matter of business was engrossing S. Paul's attention, and that was the collection of alms for the poor Christians of Jerusalem. This work he had gladly undertaken (pp. 246-7), for such an offering would not only be a proof of, but would serve to cement, the unity between the Gentile and Jewish churches. But its prosecution was a delicate matter. In Galatia the apostle had instituted a Sunday 'offertory,' and he had enjoined the same by letter on the Corinthians. They were indeed ready in profession 'a year ago,' before he left Ephesus; but their performance had not quite corresponded, and, as we have just said, S. Paul had to send some brothers from Macedonia to stir them up. On the other hand the poorer churches of Macedonia had exhibited great generosity[1]. To avoid any appearance of interested motives, the funds were to be entrusted to delegates of the churches for conveyance to Jerusalem[2]. But the apostle was anxious that the delegates should accompany himself, as the alms would greatly affect his own relation to the church of Jerusalem; and accordingly the delivery of the contribution was a reason for his own persistence on his journey.

Of all this S. Luke says nothing, and he only specifies one characteristic of this summer's work: there was *much exhortation*—literally *he exhorted* (or *encouraged*) *with much discourse* (or *word*). As S. Paul's bodily presence is now to be withdrawn from these churches, his *word*, which is to live after him and continue his work, becomes more important. And this journey is the record of his 'last words[3]' as far as concerns the Acts; just as at Corinth (as we shall presently learn) he is going to utter his 'last word' in another sense.

On the approach of winter S. Paul, with Timothy and others, *passed into Greece*[4]. He came to Corinth; and there, in accordance with his original plan (I Cor xvi 6), he spent the greater part of the *three winter months*, lodging in the house of Gaius, probably that early convert baptized by his own hands[5].

The appearance of the apostle, who came with the severity as well as the gentleness of the Christ speaking in him and with the authority which the Lord had given him[6], no doubt dissipated once more all opposition and restored peace. It was his final victory over the Judaizers, and in the measure of calm and peace now attained[7] he

---

[1] I Cor xvi 1-2: II viii 10, 17-23, ix 3-5: II viii 1-5.   [2] Rom xii 17, II Cor viii 21: I xvi 3, II viii 19, 23: Rom xv 26, 31.   [3] Cp. xx 7, 11, 18-35.   [4] Here, instead of the usual Roman title *Achaia*, S. Luke uses the old Greek name of *Hellas*, which does not occur elsewhere in the Acts. He may be quoting his authority; but as the passage is a summary it would be his own composition, and the choice of the word may be intentional. The year was one of bitter memories; and S. Luke, feeling still sore at the treatment the apostle received, cannot bring himself to write down *Corinth* or *Achaia*. A similar reason has been suggested (p. 197 n.[2]) for S. Luke's avoidance of the terms *Galatia* and *Galatians*. *Corinth* and *Corinthian* occur in the Acts, as was inevitable; but only 3 times altogether, while *Ephesus* is found 8 times, *Ephesian* 5 times.   [5] See Rom xvi 23, I Cor i 14.   [6] II Cor xiii 3, 10.   [7] This is shewn by the general tone of the Epistle to the Romans.

was able to sum up the result of the controversy in a measured treatise. This is our Epistle to the Romans, which was now written; and thus, as at Ephesus S. Paul fulfilled his 'work,' and at Rome his 'course,' so at Corinth he fulfilled his 'word' or doctrine. For this epistle is unique not merely among the writings of the apostle, but in the NT itself. It is the document which first revealed to the world the real meaning of faith and of the righteousness of faith. As we generally identify S. John with love, and S. Peter (though less markedly) with hope, so the Ep. to the Romans marks out S. Paul as the apostle of faith. Unlike the letters to the Galatians and Corinthians, written in the heat of sudden emotion and to meet special emergencies, the letter to the Romans is a doctrinal treatise, written with deliberate and careful argument. It was the exposition and vindication of his doctrine of justification by faith; and being meant for the whole church, the apostle addressed it to that particular church which could best stand for the whole. This was a church too with which he had had no personal dealings and which had therefore stood aloof from the controversy. And it was the church of the capital of the empire—Rome—from which the truth might radiate into all parts of the world, and which was itself the goal of his ambitions, and therefore worthy to receive the fullest expression of his faith. There is little doubt that the epistle was written at this time, by the hand of Tertius, and despatched to Rome by the hands of Phoebe the deaconess of Cenchreae, with the further view of preparing S. Paul's own way thither. This done, the apostle himself must follow. So having finished his work at Corinth, he starts on that journey to Jerusalem after which 'he must see Rome.'

§ 3 *The journey to Jerusalem*

The journey will occupy us till xxi 17; and, like the voyage to Rome, is narrated with great richness of detail. The reasons for this are not far to seek. (1) The accurate marking of the different stages in the journey gives the impression of a traveller's diary[1], and even without the use of the first person would indicate the presence of S. Luke. (2) We recognize the hand of an artist in the satisfaction of a literary want. In great histories, at the critical moments we often find the tension relieved, and at the same time the pathos deepened, by a detailed narrative of some of the ordinary events of life which preceded or led up to the crisis[2]. (3) The remarkable correspondence, in the structure of the book, with the last journey of our Lord up to Jerusalem in the Gospel makes it clear that the emphasis on detail is intentional.

In two points the parallel was very exact. (i) S. Luke makes S. Paul's journey his farewell to those parts, and the disciples knew it to be so. Hence the long discourses and last words, the prayers and tears, the farewells and the 'being torn away from one another';

---

[1] Cp. xvi 11-2, xvii 1 (pp. 279, 292).   [2] Cp. David's flight from Jerusalem in II Sam xv-xvi, and Sennacherib's march in Isai x 28-32.

for they were to see his face no more. (ii) Besides the pathos, there was the actual danger. It was a critical moment in S. Paul's work. He had written calmly to the Romans, as if the heat of the battle with the Judaizing Christians was over: but there remained the Jews. And the more S. Paul's gospel prevailed in the church, the fiercer burned the hatred of the Jews against the apostle. Besides this, in Judaea itself the national feeling of the Jews against the Romans and all Gentiles was growing more and more exasperated, so that for S. Paul to return thither at this moment was indeed to put his head in the lion's mouth. S. Paul himself was apprehensive of danger, and asked for the earnest prayers of the Roman church for his deliverance from the 'disobedient' in Judaea[1]. The danger was obvious to the Gentile Christians, and they used all their efforts to stop the journey. *In every city*—in Corinth, Thessalonica, Philippi, and Troas (xx 23), at Tyre and Caesarea—Christian prophets announced bonds and afflictions awaiting him at Jerusalem.

The apostle however was *bound in the Spirit*. He had a deep conviction that through Jerusalem lay the road to Rome, even though it led through the gate of affliction[2]; and he was confident that the Lord could preserve him, if it was his will[3]. This conviction came from the Spirit, and if the prophecies of danger were also inspired by the Spirit, S. Paul saw in them only a testing of his courage and perseverance. Finally, any hesitation was brushed aside by the business of the collection, which the apostle was anxious to deliver in person at Jerusalem. Accordingly, when the delegates chosen by the churches to carry their alms were now assembled at Corinth,—viz. those of Macedonia *Aristarchus and Secundus*, and of Galatia *Gaius and Timothy*,—as soon as navigation reopened after the *three* winter *months*, S. Paul took his passage in a ship bound *for Syria*. It was, we may suppose, as on the former occasion (p. 333), a pilgrim ship, and apparently the pilgrims were bound for the Passover festival. The ship would first cross to Ephesus, and there S. Paul would be joined by the delegates of Asia *Tychicus and Trophimus*[4]. But once more his plan was overruled.

From Corinth to Troas

3 And when he had spent three months *there*, and a plot was laid against him by the Jews, ⁵as he was about to set sail for Syria, he determined to return through Macedonia. 4 And there accompanied him ⁶as far as Asia Sopater of Berœa, *the son* of Pyrrhus; and of the Thessalonians, Aristarchus

---

[1] Rom xv 30–1. [2] Cp. xiv 22. [3] xxiii 11. [4] Nothing is said of any Corinthian delegates. Either the church was not ready after all, or perhaps, in reaction from former mistrust, gave their alms into the hands of the apostle.
[5] Bezan reads *he wished to set sail for Syria, but the Spirit bade him return through Macedonia. Therefore when he was about to go forth* [*there accompanied*].
[6] Marg with ℵB omits *as far as Asia*.

and Secundus; and Gaius of Derbe, and Timothy; and ¹of
5 Asia, Tychicus and Trophimus. But these ²had gone before,
6 and were waiting for us at Troas. And we sailed away from
Philippi after the days of unleavened bread, and came unto
them to Troas in five days; where we tarried seven days.

3   S. Paul had formed his intention *of embarking* at Cenchreae, when
he discovered *a plot of the Jews*. After their discomfiture in the
proconsul's court (p. 331), the Jews at Corinth, like those of Ephesus
(verse 19), had recourse to a plot; and their plot was no doubt to
murder Paul at sea³. The apostle accordingly changed his plan,
and *determined to return through Macedonia*⁴. He let the delegates
go on to Ephesus with the treasure, in order to give information to
Tychicus and Trophimus, and appointed Troas as the rendezvous
4 where they were all to meet him. He himself, taking with him *Sopater
of Beroea*, retraced his steps to Macedonia. Sopater *accompanied him*
as a personal friend and not as a delegate of the churches, for
apparently he only went *as far as Asia*, i.e. to Troas, and then
returned home, his place being taken by another, as we shall
see⁵.

This is a probable account of what happened, but there may be
other solutions. The fact is that the language of verses 4 and 5 is
rather ambiguous: it is a passage which was probably left without
the author's final revision. The difficulty arises from the enumeration of the names in verse 4, and their insertion is due to S. Luke's
artistic sense. From the historian's point of view the detailed
movements of the various delegates were not of any consequence: it
is sufficient to know that the party was finally made up at Troas. What
S. Luke wanted was to give us a picture of Paul and his company
to form a companion picture to the Seven of ch. vi 5⁶. Both bodies
were occupied with the 'serving of tables': and thus, as the church
of Jerusalem, so the churches of the Gentiles had their Seven.
These Seven included the most faithful and intimate disciples of
the apostle. There was Timothy; also Aristarchus, who shared his
imprisonment and voyage to Rome; Tychicus, who was also with
him at Rome and was despatched thence on an important mission⁷.
Lastly, as we shall see, S. Luke had his place among them.

---

¹ Gk *Asians*, Bezan has *Ephesians*.   ² Marg with ℵAB has *came* (i.e. to Troas) *and were waiting*.   ³ Cp. xxiii 12.   ⁴ S. Luke's phrase (literally *he became of judgement*) is an unusual one: besides Philemon 14, the word *judgement* occurs in the Epistles to the Corinthians I i 10, vii 25, 40, II viii 10. It may point to the direction of the Holy Spirit, as in the Bezan text.   ⁵ For Sopater see p. 299. The words *as far as Asia* were perhaps omitted, because they seemed inconsistent with the presence of Trophimus and Aristarchus at Jerusalem (xxi 29, xxvii 2). But they need only apply to Sopater, as does the verb which is in the singular: *and Sopater accompanied* (literally *followed close with*) *Paul*.   ⁶ The Seven are in S. Luke's mind during this part of the narrative: cp. xxi 8.   ⁷ For Aristarchus see xix 29, xx 4, xxvii 2, Col iv 10, Philm 24: for Tychicus Eph vi 21, Col iv 7, Tit iii 12, II Tim iv 12.

6   The change of plan and choice of the longer route through Macedonia had made it impossible for S. Paul to reach Jerusalem in time for the Passover. The next festival, at which he now aimed, was Pentecost, fifty days later. This respite, then, gave him time to stop in Macedonia and keep Easter with the faithful church of *Philippi*. This observance of *the days of unleavened bread* must be noted as a comment on the meaning of his denunciation of the Galatians for 'observing days and months and seasons and years[1].' For there was no Jewish element to speak of in the Philippian church, and so this passover cannot have been observed as a concession to Jewish custom. It was in fact the Christian Easter. At Philippi Paul had the further comfort of the companionship of S. Luke, who now joined him to remain at his side till the end of the book. For once more the *we* appears. It ceased last at Philippi (xvi 16), which city had probably been S. Luke's head-quarters ever since. But, as has been shewn, this would not prevent his having been in S. Paul's company in the interval. Indeed, as he may have been sent on a mission to Corinth (p. 371), it is quite possible that he too started with S. Paul from Corinth. For a reason can be given for the resumption of the *we* at this particular point. In this delicate and modest way[2] S. Luke lets us know—what must have been a great glory to him—that he was one of S. Paul's Seven; for at Troas he took the place of Sopater, who went no further.

When the eight days (or octave) of the Paschal festival were over, on a Tuesday, S. Paul with Sopater and Luke *sailed out from* Neapolis, the port of *Philippi*. He was retracing the line of his first visit to Macedonia[3]; and the winds which were favourable to his coming would now be in his face, so that, instead of two days at sea as before, only *on the fifth day* did they arrive *at Troas*; consequently they just missed the service of the first day of the week,
5   i.e. the first Sunday after Easter. At Troas they found the rest of the party already *arrived* from Ephesus *and waiting*[4]; and
6   S. Paul *stayed a week*, possibly in the house of Carpus[5]. It may have been that there was no ship sailing; more probably S. Paul wanted to make his farewell to the church at their assembly on the Sunday (i.e. on Saturday evening), and the interval would be some compensation for his hurry on his last visit (p. 371). The service of that Sunday (the second after Easter) was stamped upon S. Luke's memory by an incident so remarkable that he proceeds to relate it in detail.

The Sunday service and raising of Eutychus at Troas

This history of S. Paul's farewells affords us many glimpses into the internal life of the Christian society, and enables us to form a picture of the Gentile churches corresponding to that which we can

---

[1] Gal iv 10.   [2] See p. 273, Introd. p. xxxii.   [3] xvi 11-2.   [4] This agrees with the reading of the margin—*came*: but it is not inconsistent with their *having gone on*, i.e. from Corinth to Ephesus, and so to Troas.   [5] II Tim iv 13.

draw of the church at Jerusalem from the summaries in chapters ii and iv. There is also another point to be observed. We have noticed how careful S. Luke was to shew at Antioch all the marks which constitute a true 'church' (pp. 187–8). Similarly, this paragraph completes the claim of the church of Asia to be a 'church' (verse 17). In xix 1–10 and xx 18–35 is evidence of adherence to the teaching of the apostles: the sacrifice of property in xix 19 was an illustration of the relation of the community to worldly goods: in xix 11–16 and xx 9–12 signs and wonders are wrought by apostolic hands: and lastly, here we find continuance in the breaking of bread and the prayers, as in ii 42. At Antioch the breaking of bread had not been specified but it was included in the 'liturgy' of xiii 2.

In this section, then, we come to a picture of a Christian service drawn by one who was present. It is therefore invaluable for the study of the origins of Christian worship; and without trenching upon the special province of liturgiology, we may here briefly notice the following points:

(1) In the preceding verses we had an incidental notice of the observance of Easter[1]. Here there is unmistakeable evidence of the observance of Sunday or *the first day of the week*. Saturday, the seventh day, was the Jewish sabbath, but in the church the first day of the week has taken its place, because on the first day the Lord rose from the dead. We have an earlier allusion a year before this, in I Cor xvi 1; but Jn xx 26 seems to shew that the observance dates from the very beginning[2].

(2) The day was observed, not by any Judaic or sabbatical prohibitions, but by the *gathering-together* of the Christians for worship. The Greek word is a general one for any gathering, but as the chief gatherings of the Christians were for worship, the *gathering-together* or *synaxis* became the technical word for a service, as it is to this day in the east[3].

(3) We must however get rid of our modern ideas of observing Sunday by 'gatherings' at 11 a.m. and 7 p.m. The early Christian gathering-together was on Saturday evening. For the Jewish reckoning was 'evening and morning'; their day was from sunset to sunset. On Saturday, then, at 6 p.m. (at this time of the year), the sabbath ended, and the first day of the week began; and the Christians, who would follow the Jewish reckoning, began the first day with an assembly for worship. This mode of calculation must be remembered in following the diary of the journey

(4) They met together *to break bread*. Christian worship began in a common meal—the Agapê followed by the Eucharist, which was the repetition of the original Last Supper. This has been sufficiently dwelt upon above (pp. 35–40). Here we will only add that Saturday evening,

---

[1] verse 6: cp. xii 3, Lk xxii 1, I Cor v 7–8.   [2] A later reference is Rev i 10.
[3] For *gathering together* see iv 31, xi 26, xiv 27, xv 6, 30, I Cor v 4 and p. 169. A paper by Rev. J. R. Milne on *Primitive Christianity and Sunday Observance* (Goose, Norwich, 1900) throws much light on early Christian worship.

after the close of the sabbath, was generally celebrated among the Jews by a festive meal or banquet[1]: and such a meal would naturally lend itself to the specially Christian observance. We may conclude then that the Christians at Troas met after sunset and had their evening meal or Agapê, and this was prolonged to midnight. Then an interruption occurred, and afterwards S. Paul broke *the bread*[2], viz. of the Eucharist, and this service lasted till dawn. Another view however may be suggested, if we observe S. Luke's language and allow due weight to his usual accuracy. There is no mention of eating before midnight; but after S. Paul had broken *the bread* of the Eucharist, S. Luke adds *and eaten*. The word *eat* may denote merely *tasting*, such as would be applicable to the Eucharist; but it is elsewhere used by S. Luke for satisfying hunger in eating[3], and we may not unreasonably infer that by its use here he alludes to the Agapê, which would in that case have followed the Eucharist. We know that at an early period the Eucharist and Agapê were separated and their order reversed. Now a year ago S. Paul had heard at Ephesus of the disorders which occurred at the Eucharist in Corinth, which arose from its coming after the Agapê. He wrote that he would set these matters in order when he came[4]; and one of his 'orders' may have been the transposition of the Eucharist and Agapê[5].

(5) Besides the breaking of bread, the service contained other elements, particularly the 'ministry of the word,' which was on this occasion very much prolonged. The word which S. Luke uses, *discoursing* (= *reasoning*), is that used of S. Paul's work in the synagogue and may include conversation (as also *talked* in verse 11); but *the word* (verse 7) would most naturally denote continuous discourse (such as that in 18-35). The precedent for this would be not only the Jewish practice in the synagogue, but also the discourses of the Lord at the Last Supper. On the same analogies we may also add prayer and the singing of psalms, together with reading of the scriptures.

(6) The service at Troas was very much prolonged, even until dawn; and so it is the first recorded instance of the all-night watchings, or vigils, which were so characteristic of early Christianity. The suitability of night for worship was indeed an idea older than Christianity: 'at midnight I will rise to give thanks to thee' said the Psalmist (cxix 62), and we found Paul and Silas singing at midnight (xvi 25). But Christians had special reasons for the choice of night. The two events which Christian worship commemorated, the Last Supper and the Resurrection of the Lord, occurred in the night hours. There was also a practical reason. There was of course no public observance of

---

[1] Cp. the supper in Jn xii 1-8. [2] verse 11: in verse 7 it is simply *break bread*, which is indefinite and may be said of any meal, see p. 37. [3] x 10, xxiii 14, Lk xiv 24. [4] See I Cor xi 20-34. [5] This is only a conjecture, and may be built on too slight a foundation. In any case this scene at Troas does not bear upon the practice of receiving Holy Communion fasting from midnight. For then Sunday began at sunset on Saturday, and the first food taken after that would be the first food eaten on the Sunday.

Sunday and business went on as usual. Many of the Christians were occupied in trade : many more were actually slaves and these certainly would not be able to devote many hours in the daytime to attendance at Christian worship. The service at Troas may also account for the custom of devoting the whole night to this exercise; for the prolonging of the Agapê, of the reading, preaching and singing, postponed the Eucharist, the natural close of the service, till the hours of dawn, the most fitting time for the commemoration of the resurrection[1]. We can take a step further. Human infirmity would assert itself, and insist on a break in this prolonged effort of devotion; and thus we should have two services—the Agapê in the evening: the Eucharist at the dawn. This separation we find had already taken place in Bithynia in the days of Pliny (c. A.D. 110), and following the Roman reckoning he speaks of the morning service first: the Christians meet before dawn, he says, to sing hymns to Christ as to God and to bind themselves by a solemn oath (*sacramentum*) not to commit crime; then, after separating, they come together again to partake of food. In Jerusalem however it would appear, from an account which a lady has left of her pilgrimage thither in the fourth century, that a vigil was observed every Saturday night, during which the bishop read the narrative of the resurrection[2]. And at certain seasons, pre-eminently at Easter, an all-night vigil was observed universally in Christendom.

(7) The place of the gathering together was still a private house, but in that part of it which was most removed from interruption, and therefore usually set apart by the Jews for devotion, viz. an upper room. The room at Troas was in *the third story*. So the Last Supper was celebrated in an upper room, Dorcas was laid out in one, and S. Peter went up on the house-top to pray[3].

(8) We learn incidentally that there were *many lamps* (verse 8)— more apparently than were needed for purposes of light. It was, we know, the custom of the Jews as well as of the Gentiles to celebrate their festivals with illuminations, and in particular the Jew marked the commencement of the sabbath by hanging a lamp in his window— a practice which became notorious among the Gentiles, as we can see from the lines of the satirist Persius[4]. Here the Christians seem to be following their example; certainly the symbolical use of lights prevailed in the church from very early times[5].

S. Luke, however, does not describe the meeting at Troas for the

---

[1] If the transposition of Eucharist and Agapê had already taken place, as was suggested above in (4), then in this sentence for 'Agapê' we should have to substitute 'the preparation for the Eucharist.'   [2] *Peregrinatio Silviae*, in Duchesne's *Origines du Culte Chrétien*, p. 493. This vigil however may have begun only at cock-crow.   [3] Lk xxii 12, Acts i 13, ix 37, x 9. See p. 9. Among other early Christian 'churches' we may reckon the houses of Titius Justus at Corinth, of Priscilla and Aquila at Rome, of Nymphas at Laodicea, and of Philemon at Colossae.   [4] v 180–184.   [5] This symbolical use of light was recognized in the lamp in the temple; and taken from that we have the seven candlesticks of Rev i 12 (op. iv 5). Silvia tells us of the 'huge glass candle(stick)s,' the 'numerous torches' and 'infinite luminaries' used in the churches and services at Jerusalem (Duchesne *Origines* p. 473).

purpose of satisfying liturgical curiosity; but because it was the occasion of a remarkable 'power,' which not only is parallel to the raising of Dorcas in ix 36–41, but also places S. Paul in the first rank of the workers of signs,—with Elijah and Elisha in the Old Testament, S. Peter in the New, and with our Lord himself[1].

7 And upon the first day of the week, when we were gathered together to break bread, Paul discoursed with them, ²intending to depart on the morrow; and prolonged
8 his speech until midnight. And there were many ³lights in
9 the upper chamber, where we were gathered together. And there sat in the window a certain young man named Eutychus, borne down with deep sleep; and as Paul discoursed yet longer, being borne down by his sleep he fell down from the
10 third story, and was taken up dead. And Paul went down, and fell on him, and embracing him said, Make ye no ado,
11 for his life is in him. And when he was gone up, and had broken the bread, and eaten, and had talked with them a
12 long while, even till break of day, so he departed. And⁴ they brought the lad alive, and were not a little comforted.

9 *A lad* (verse 12) *Eutychus was sitting on the window* sill, for with the *many lamps* it was very hot. *Paul's discourse* also was very long, for he was taking his farewell and preaching his last sermon. He was still speaking at *midnight* when a cry arose. Eutychus had struggled hard⁵, but *sleep* at last overcame him and he *fell down* to the ground outside. The congregation rushed down and picked him up *dead*. At once there was a great cry of lament-
10 ation, for apparently he was much beloved (verse 12). *Paul*, however, having also *come down*, lay upon the lad and *embraced him*, after the example of Elijah and Elisha. Then arising, he bade them cease from their *ado* or mourning⁶, for the lad was alive.
11 They obeyed and returned to the upper chamber and to their worship Paul consecrated the eucharist, a fitting thanksgiving for a restoration from death to life. After they had partaken, and the formal service was over, Paul *talked* to them at great length—for they were his last words,—until they were forced to disperse by *dawn*, for that
12 day he must start. Meanwhile his friends had taken Eutychus

---

¹ Cp. I K xvii 17–24, II iv 32–7: Lk vii 11–5 (a young man), viii 49–56 (a damsel). ² Gk *being about to* as in verse 3: so verse 13, and 38. ³ Gk *lamps*. ⁴ Bezan adds *as they were taking farewell*. ⁵ The tenses in the Greek exactly paint the continuous struggle and the moment of defeat. For the *deep sleep* (Bezan *heavy*) cp. Lk ix 32, Mk xiv 40. ⁶ From the account of Jairus' daughter this seems the meaning of *the ado* (Mk v 38–9). The noun is used for the *uproar* in verse 1. Cp. also the Lord's words *She is not dead but sleepeth*.

home, and now, just as S. Paul and the congregation were saying goodbye, *they brought him* back *alive*, safe and sound[1]. This greatly *encouraged* and cheered the whole congregation—not merely because of the restoration of Eutychus, but also for its confirmation of S. Paul's apostolic power. *Thus* S. Paul *went forth*, viz. once more a victor, only this time over the greatest enemy—death[2]. It was a good omen for the future.

From Troas to Miletus

13 But we, [3]going before to the ship, set sail for Assos, there intending to take in Paul: for so had he appointed, intending
14 himself to [4]go by land. And when he met us at Assos, we
15 took him in, and came to Mitylene. And sailing from thence, we came the following day over against Chios; and [5]the next day we touched at Samos; and[6] the day after we came to
16 Miletus. For Paul had determined to sail past Ephesus, that [7]he might not have to spend time in Asia; for he was hastening, if it were possible for him, to be at Jerusalem the day of Pentecost.

13   The mention of *the ship* in verses 13 and 38 (contrasted with *a ship* in xxi 2) and the fact that they coasted along, stopping (longer than for the night) only where S. Paul wished, viz. at Miletus, would almost indicate that they had chartered a coasting vessel at Troas, or even Philippi, to take them as far as Lycia. They were not a small party. They were also in a hurry, and it would have been a difficult matter to find passages in a coasting vessel which did not
16   stop at Ephesus. The hurry was due to S. Paul's anxiety *to be at Jerusalem for Pentecost*, which now left them about 30 days—by no means too much, considering the uncertainties of ancient navigation. For this reason S. Paul had decided not to touch at *Ephesus*: the affairs of the church there would be sure to cause him *to spend time*, and he might be detained by some untoward event, or collision with his adversaries[8]. For it was just a year after the riot, and S. Paul was one who could not be hid.
13   S. Paul however did not himself go on board at Troas. The long discourse, lasting through the night, the farewell, and the raising of Eutychus, had been a strain. Like Elijah, he wanted to be alone for a time: like the Lord himself, he wanted to send away even his disciples[9]. Accordingly he first sent off his company by sea,

---

[1] This is a suggested explanation of the text with the help of the Bezan reading. Cp. Hebr xiii 20.   [2] For *thus* (so) cp. xix 20 and p. 356.   [3] Some good mss have *going-to* (for *-before*) as in verse 5.   [4] Literally *go afoot* (AV).   [5] B reads *in the evening*.   [6] Marg with AV and Bezan adds *having tarried* (the night) *at Trogyllium*.   [7] Bezan reads *that no detention* (=*possession*, vii 45) *might happen to him*.   [8] The Bezan reading makes this reason clear.   [9] Mk vi 45.

while he would *go by land to Assos*. This would save the large détour due to the promontory of Lectum; but there was still left a good day's journey of twenty miles, though the Greek word does not compel us to suppose that the apostle necessarily went on foot. The ship was to sail round the promontory and *take him up at Assos*. The disciples possibly demurred to his going alone, for S. Luke uses a strong word for *appointed*, elsewhere translated *com-*
14 *mand*[1]. The ship seems to have reached Assos first; and when S. Paul arrived *they took him on board* and coasted *to Miletus* in three days, stopping for the nights at *Mitylene*, a point *opposite Chios*, and
15 *Trogyllium*. From Chios *they had crossed over*[2] the more open sea *to Samos*; but, hoping to get to Miletus that night, they did not stop there. However, when they reached *Trogyllium* the promontory opposite Samos, the wind fell, or it was too late to go on; so they anchored for the night, and next morning, i.e. Wednesday (or Thursday)[3], went on to *Miletus*.
17 The favourable run gave them time to rest for the Sabbath and Sunday (the third after Easter). But S. Paul had another reason for stopping at Miletus. He had passed by Ephesus intentionally, but he was very anxious to see the church in the persons of its rulers[4] and give them a last charge. Miletus was about 30 miles from Ephesus[5]. *From Miletus*, then, the apostle *sent a summons to the presbyters of the church* of Ephesus; and they obeyed with alacrity and came not only from Ephesus, but from other cities as well[6]. They arrived at Miletus in time for the gathering together (synaxis) on the first day of the week, i.e. on Saturday evening. No doubt, as at Troas, the watching was prolonged till Sunday's dawn, for S. Paul had much to say. During the course of the night he uttered this last charge which follows; then, after the meeting had broken up on Sunday morning, they solemnly escorted him to the ship.

§ 4 *Farewell charge to the Ephesian presbyters and S. Paul's defence to the church*

This address possesses unusual interest. (1) It is the only specimen in the Acts of a sermon addressed to the church. We have had three

---

[1] Cp. vii 44, xviii 2, xxiii 31, xxiv 23, Lk iii 13, xvii 9, 10. There is no mention of the Trojan Christians escorting him, as in verse 38, xxi 5. The whole sentence is rather remarkable: the repetition of *intending* and the imperfect tense (*was meeting*) almost imply that the plan was not fully carried out. Paul may have been picked up at an earlier point; or they may have spent a night at Assos, Paul not reaching it till the next day. The run from Assos to Mitylene was about 30 miles. [2] The Greek word is the usual one for *touching at* a port: but to judge from the Bezan and AV text they do not appear to have stopped at the town of Samos, which was on the south side of the island. [3] according to whether they spent a night at Assos or not. [4] So S. Ignatius saw 'all the Ephesian church in the person of Onesimus its bishop' with his fellow-delegates. [5] See p. 338 for the relation of the two cities. [6] Cp. verse 25. So S. Irenaeus infers—*who came from Ephesus and the other neighbouring cities* (con. *Haer.* III 14. 2). They may have been assembled at Ephesus for some festival or common business, like the Asiarchs (p. 363).

sermons of S. Paul's: to the Jews at Antioch and to the Gentiles—both educated at Athens, and uneducated at Lystra. We shall have three speeches: to the Jews of Jerusalem, to Felix the Roman governor, to Agrippa and the world at large. Here, in the centre, stands S. Paul's charge to the church. The three sermons present the gospel aggressively; the three speeches present it apologetically; the charge combines both aspects, together with a third element of personal affection. For there were three strains of thought running in S. Paul's mind. (i) He was speaking his last words or farewell. And so, in the parallel with the Gospel, this corresponds to the Lord's last discourse on the eve of the passion in S. Luke xxi (Mt xxiv–xxv). Like the Lord, the apostle speaks of things to come, sufferings for himself and perils for the church; and the same words of warning recur, *Take heed* and *Watch*[1]. (ii) As S. Paul had been so fiercely attacked, he vindicates his past ministry and makes his *apologia* or defence to the church. Like Samuel, he testifies to his own integrity: like Moses, he reviews his ministry[2]. (iii) The review of his past preaching, and the charge to the church to cleave to the truth after his departure, are alike motives for a final setting forth of the gospel.

(2) S. Paul however was not going to leave the church orphaned. There are stewards in the household and shepherds in the flock: as the province of Asia had its Asiarchs, so the kingdom of God has its rulers. Accordingly, as the Lord's last words had been spoken to the Twelve, so S. Paul's are now addressed to the presbyters. He is giving, as it were, a pastoral or episcopal charge; and this charge is in brief the pastoral manual of the NT, the earliest and pattern *Priest to the Temple* or *Pastor in Parochia*.

(3) The chief office of the presbyters would be to guard the truth. The truth is the foundation of the church, and its vindication was the characteristic of the work of the church at Ephesus (p. 348): knowledge of 'the way' depends upon the teaching of 'the truth.' Thus the doctrinal interest is in the foreground in this address, and indeed one famous verse (28), in spite of the uncertainty as to the reading, is one of the clearest assertions in the NT of the doctrine of the atonement, and implies as its background the doctrines of the Holy Trinity and of the divinity of our Lord.

At first sight there appears to be some repetition in the charge. Further, S. Paul appears to be addressing different audiences: first the church at large, then after verse 28 the presbyters alone. It is possible that S. Luke has joined together the notes of two farewell addresses: and in the final form of the speech, as in the case of the other sermons, the work of his hand is unmistakeable[3]. And yet there are many reasons

---

[1] verse 28 and Lk xxi 34 (the same word): 31 and Lk xxi 36. We may note also that though S. John xiii–vii was not yet written, there is great correspondence in *tone* with those discourses. [2] Cp. I Sam xii, Deut i–iii. [3] This is more obvious in the Greek than in the English: e.g. *temptations, bonds, take heed to yourselves* are Lucan in their form. There is also the use of unusual words, emphasis on pronouns, and asyndeton, which are marks of his style.

which convince us that we have here a faithful report of what was uttered on this occasion. (1) There is a real advance in thought, as will be seen below. (2) The speech reflects the circumstances of the moment—the atmosphere of prophetic excitement and the anticipations of evil to come[1]. (3) It is full of Pauline characteristics, both in word and thought: e.g. his bold egotism, his self-vindication and the appeal to his own example; his commission received from the Lord and his anxiety to 'fulfil his course'; his gospel of faith and grace, with its catholic character, for Jew and Gentile alike; his boldness, especially in face of the Jews, and the labouring with his own hands[2]. (4) The local colouring is in remarkable accord with the picture of his ministry at Ephesus[3]. There are also special affinities with the Epistles to the Asian churches, viz. to the Ephesians and Colossians. In them we find the same insistence on the plan of God, on the church as being his building and kingdom, on the institution of a pastoral ministry for the edification of the body, and on the wealth of the Christian inheritance. (5) There is a great resemblance in style to the Pastoral Epistles, especially the letters to Timothy[4]. These were written to Timothy when in charge of the church of Ephesus, and they exhibit a picture of the same organization of presbyter-bishops under an apostolic 'man of God.' They also contain similar anticipations of the development of error. This resemblance confirms the genuineness of both the epistles and the speech. In both we can detect a hand which is not quite that of S. Paul. This hand must be that of S. Luke, who wrote the speech and probably acted as amanuensis for the letters. (6) Even in its written form the speech retains signs of its dramatic delivery. *Ye yourselves*, S. Paul exclaims, adding his emphatic *I*: *and now behold* he says twice: he testifies *on this very day*: he lifts up *these very hands* which laboured: he declares that they *will see his face no more*—a conviction faithfully reported, although perhaps literally falsified in the event. He begins smoothly; but as his spirit is stirred, his style becomes

---

[1] Cp. xxi 4, 10–4. [2] These words occur in the Acts in S. Paul's mouth or in close connexion with him—*plots* (ix 24, xx 3, xxiii 30), *house to house* (viii 3), *faith in* (the Lord Jesus, xxiv 24, xxvi 18), *and now behold* (xiii 11), bound *in the spirit* (xix 21), *afflictions* (xiv 22), *course* (xiii 25), *I am pure* (xviii 6), *the counsel of God* (xiii 36), *appointed* (*set*, xix 21), *perverse* (xiii 8, 10), *the word of his grace* (xiv 3). Also with verse 18 cp. I Th i 5, 9 etc.; *serving the Lord* Rom xii 11; *humble-mindedness* Col ii 18, *tears* II Cor ii 4, *profitable* I Cor x 23 etc., *Jews and Greeks* Rom i 16 etc., *accomplish my course* Phil iii 12, II Tim iv 7, *ministry which I received* Col iv 17, Rom i 5, Eph iii 7, Col i 23, 25, I Tim i 12 etc., *from the Lord* Gal i 12, I Cor xi 23; *see my face* Col ii 1, *admonish* Rom xv 14, Col i 28, iii 16, *covet* Rom vii 7, *these hands ministered* I Cor iv 12, I Th ii 9, II iii 8, *labouring* I Th v 12 and I Tim v 17, *help the weak* I Th v 14 and I Cor xii 28, *remember* Gal ii 10, Eph ii 11, Col iv 18, II Tim ii 8. [3] The two words for *know* vv. 18, 34 occur xix 15; for *plots* see xix 33, xx 3, *publicly and from house to house* xix 9, xx 7–12, *Jews and Greeks* xviii 4, xix 10, 17, *bound in spirit to go to Jerusalem* xix 21, with verse 24 cp. xix 30, *preaching the kingdom* xix 8, with *ecclesia of God* cp. xix 32, with vv. 20, 27 cp. xix 8, *silver* xix 19. The references to Eph and Col will be given in the paraphrase. With vv. 26, 34 cp. xviii 6, 3. [4] These words occur in, or are characteristic of, the Pastoral Epistles: *testify, course, pure, take heed, presbyter* and *bishop, acquire* (I Tim iii 13), *apparel.*

broken, and his feelings find vent in short sentences without any connecting particles. In these last sentences we hear the very words which came from his lips. S. Luke was present and, alive to the seriousness of the outlook[1], took the notes which are here written out for us. The apostle, as at Troas, spoke at great length; and for the sake of emphasis he repeats his fundamental thoughts. First he addresses himself to the whole congregation at the synaxis, or rather to the whole church of Asia as represented in its officers: then at a later point he turns suddenly and directly to the presbyters who surrounded him and gives his final charge to them personally[2].

The analysis of the speech is not easy, because of the various aspects in which it may be considered, the many strains of thought in S. Paul's mind. It falls at once into two parts at verse 28 according to the audience in view—the church at large (18-27) and the presbyters (28-35). Again, there is a further division in the second part at verse 32: so that there are really three divisions, of which the dominant ideas are I (18-27) *vindication*, II (28-31) *charge*, III (32-35) *farewell*. But each of these ideas also runs throughout the whole and in relation to different spheres, viz.—*a* (18-27) the world at large, *b* (28-31) the church, *c* (32-35) the life of the individual. Thus there is I. S. Paul's *defence* (*a*) to the world—he has paid his debt to Jew and Greek, (*b*) to the church—he has fulfilled his ministry, (*c*) in respect of his personal sincerity—this he has proved by his simplicity of life. II. His *charge* (*a*) to all the Christians and the world—to repent and believe, (*b*) to the presbyters—to be faithful in their ministry, (*c*) and to lead lives of self-denial and self-devotion. III. His *farewell*: (*a*) he foretells his own departure, (*b*) he gives the church a warning in view of the future, (*c*) he commends them personally to the grace of the Lord.

A few words must be said on the special aspect of the speech as a pastoral charge. (1) The officers addressed are *the presbyters of the church*. Though their ministry is locally confined to Ephesus or Asia, the flock they tend is a part of the one church of God. (2) They are *the elders*, i.e. the 'senate' of the church. They are, then, rulers; and their title indicates the natural ground of authority. In history we generally find the 'senate' to have been the original or most ancient governing body. Age however enjoyed special honour among the Jews, with whom the rulers were always 'the elders,' whether of city or family, tribe or nation. So by the use of this expression S. Luke vindicates the churches of the Gentiles: like the church at Jerusalem (xi 30), the church of Asia has also its senate of *presbyters*. By calling them the presbyters of 'the church' S. Luke also distinguishes them from the presbyters of 'the Ephesians.' For besides the Boulê or Council at Ephesus, there was a *Gerousia* or

---

[1] We may note here how the verb *being-about-to*, which occurs in vv. 3, 7, 13 (twice), 38, gives to the whole chapter the tone of looking forward to the immediate future. [2] See Dr Bernard on the Pastoral Epistles (*Camb. Gk Test. for Schools*) p. lxxi.

Senate, composed of 'old men' (*gerontes*) or 'elders' (*presbyters*). The functions of this Gerousia are not quite clear, but it was closely connected with the temple of Artemis: it seems to have acted as guardian of the temple revenues and also of the large sums deposited or banked in the temple[1]. This gives particular point to S. Paul's mention of silver and gold in verse 33. (3) A special title was however needed to distinguish the rulers of the Christian ecclesia alike from the 'presbyters' of the synagogue and the 'priests' of Artemis. And so S. Paul calls them *episcopi* or *overseers*. This is a Greek word and in some places was a Greek official title; but the Greek 'episcopi' were not important or numerous enough to cause any confusion with the Christian use of the term. In the numerous staff and variety of ministers attached to the temple of Artemis no 'episcopi' are to be found. Subsequently in the church the use of the term was limited to those higher officers who exercised 'oversight' over the presbyters themselves, i.e. to those who held a position analogous to that of Timothy at Ephesus and Titus at Crete[2]. (4) Their office is of divine appointment. In accordance with the other typical pictures in the Acts, they had no doubt been chosen by the multitude, and set apart by the laying on of the apostle's hands; but the inner and real meaning of such ordination was that, as in the case of Paul and Barnabas themselves, *the Holy Ghost had appointed* or *set them* (in the church) by his own choice and for his work[3]. (5) Their function is indicated by their title: they were to exercise oversight. S. Paul further defines the oversight to be that of a shepherd—*to tend the church*. Thus these presbyters correspond to the *pastors and teachers* of Eph iv 11: indeed the ideas of oversight and tending generally go together, as when S. Peter says *Tend the flock, exercising the oversight thereof*, and when he calls the Lord *the shepherd and bishop of our souls*[4]. This association is derived from the OT where rulers (such as kings) are called shepherds, and the word *tend* has become a synonym for *rule*. The original idea of pastoral oversight however was not lost. Thus the Lord's charge to S. Peter was *Tend my sheep, Feed my sheep*; and in the Revelation he both tends the nations with an iron rod, and tends the redeemed, leading them to living waters[5]. The tending is further defined in the charge which follows verse 28: (*a*) The shepherd protects the flock against the wolf, and that by *watching* against false doctrine: that is, the *episcopus* is a teacher, and guardian of the faith. (*b*) The shepherd leads the flock, i.e. he teaches them by his example, by 'going before them': and so the presbyter has an active ministry of *helping the weak*—and this at the cost of self-sacrifice, even as the Good Shepherd laid down his life for the sheep.

---

[1] On this gerousia see Hicks in *Gk Inscriptions of the B. Mus.* vol. III pp. 74–8.
[2] Cp. I Tim v 17-25, Titus i 5-9. For fuller discussion of this office see Introd. ch. vi § 2.   [3] verse 28: the verb in the middle voice is used of divine appointment, as in i 7, I Cor xii 18, 28. Cp. xiii 2 (middle voice also).   [4] Cp. I Pet v 2 (אBD however omit *exercising oversight*), ii 25.   [5] Ezek xxxiv 1-16, Zech xi, Mt ii 6 etc.: Jn xxi 16-7: Rev ii 27, xii 5, vii 17.

But, besides giving specific directions, the whole speech is indirectly a charge to the presbyters. For it holds up before them the example of their own pastor—'Be ye imitators of me as I am of Christ.' From him they learnt (1) The pastor's intention. His ministry is received from the Lord; and therefore his one spring of action is obedience. His one ambition is to fulfil the work given him to do. For himself he covets nothing, he has no self-interest. (2) The pastor's work: (*a*) in relation to the world—to preach the gospel, (*b*) to the church—to tend, i.e. to teach and help, (*c*) to himself—to renounce all covetous desires and devote himself to the service of the weak. This threefold division of work corresponds to the differentiation of function among the officers of the church, which we find already taking place. The work of the evangelist, of declaring the gospel to the nations with authority, was primarily that of the apostle or the one 'sent' with authority. The more domestic work of shepherding the church fell into the hands of the presbyters. The administration of help in the material form of alms was the special business of the deacons[1]. Thus we may see outlined in the speech the three orders of ministry which have always characterized the church of Christ—of Bishops, Priests, and Deacons. And the teaching of the charge is most aptly summed up in the words of the Anglican Ordinal, in which the bishop reminds the candidates for the priesthood of the weighty office to which they are called—'to be messengers, watchmen, and stewards of the Lord: to teach and to premonish, to feed and provide for the Lord's family; to seek for Christ's sheep that are dispersed abroad, and for his children, who are in the midst of this naughty world, that they may be saved through Christ for ever.'

17 And from Miletus he sent to Ephesus, and called to him
18 the [2]elders of the church. And when they were come to him,[3]
he said unto them,

Ye yourselves know,[4] from the first day that I set foot in
19 Asia,[5] after what manner I was with you all the time, serving
the Lord with all lowliness of mind, and with tears, and with
20 trials which befell me by the plots of the Jews: how that
I [6]shrank not from declaring unto you anything that was
profitable, and teaching you publicly, and from house to
21 house, testifying both to Jews and to Greeks repentance
toward God, and faith [7]toward our Lord Jesus [8]Christ.
22 And now, behold, I go bound in the spirit unto Jerusalem,

---

[1] In his epistles to the Asian churches S. Paul calls himself (*a*) *apostle* Eph i 1, (*b*) *the aged* (= elder) Philm 9, (*c*) *deacon* Eph iii 7, Col i 23-5.   [2] Gk *presbyters*.
[3] Bezan adds *while they were together*, and [4] *brethren*, and [5] *for about three years or even more*.   [6] or *kept back nothing that was profitable* (AV) *that I should not declare it unto you* (verse 27).   [7] Bezan *through*.   [8] Marg with B omits *Christ*.

23 not knowing the things that shall befall me there : save that the Holy Ghost testifieth unto me in every city, saying that
24 bonds and afflictions abide me. ¹But I hold not my life of any account, as dear unto myself, ²so that I may accomplish my course³, and the ministry⁴ which I received from the Lord
25 Jesus, to testify the gospel of the grace of God. And now, behold, I know that ye all, among whom I went about
26 preaching the kingdom⁵, shall see my face no more. ⁶Wherefore I testify unto you this day, that I am pure from the
27 blood of all men. For I shrank not from declaring unto you the whole counsel of God.

28 Take heed unto yourselves, and to all the flock, in the which the Holy Ghost hath made you ⁷bishops, to feed the church ⁸of God, which he ⁹purchased with his own blood.
29 I know that after my departing ¹⁰grievous wolves shall enter
30 in among you, not sparing the flock; and from among your own selves shall men arise, speaking perverse things, to draw
31 away the disciples after them. Wherefore watch ye, remembering that by the space of three years I ceased not to admonish every one night and day with tears.

32 And now I commend you to ¹¹God, and to the word of his grace, which is able to build *you* up, and to give *you* the
33 inheritance among all them that are sanctified. I coveted no
34 man's silver, or gold, or apparel. Ye yourselves know that these hands ministered unto my necessities, and to them that
35 were with me. In all things I gave you an example, how that so labouring ye ought to help the weak, and to remember the words of the Lord Jesus, how he himself said, It is more blessed to give than to receive.

36 And when he had thus spoken, he kneeled down, and
37 prayed with them all. ¹²And they all wept sore, and fell on
38 Paul's neck, and kissed him, sorrowing most of all for the

---

¹ AV and Bezan read *But none of these things move me* (lit. *I make account of none of these things*), *neither count I my life dear unto me*. ² Marg *in comparison of accomplishing my course*. ³ AV adds *with joy* (Col i 11). ⁴ Bezan adds *of the word*. ⁵ AV adds *of God*, Bezan *of Jesus*. ⁶ Bezan reads *Unto this present day therefore am I pure from the blood of all men*. ⁷ or *overseers*, Gk *episcopoi*. ⁸ אB read *of God*, ACDE (and RV marg) *of the Lord*, many later MSS *of the Lord and God*. ⁹ Gk *acquired*, Bezan adds *for himself*. ¹⁰ literally *heavy*. ¹¹ Marg with B reads *the Lord*. ¹² Gk *And there arose a great lamentation of all*.

word which he had spoken, that they should behold his face no more. And they brought him on his way unto the ship.

18 I. Like Demetrius and the townclerk, S. Paul in addressing an Ephesian audience appeals to their knowledge[1]. But indeed S. Paul's general principle of self-defence lay in commending himself to the conscience of men[2]; accordingly *knowing* is a key-note of the speech[3]. *You*, presbyters, *know* my life *from the first day that I set foot in* the province of *Asia*. He had landed at Ephesus in the spring of 51, just four years ago; but his actual ministry had begun in the autumn of 51 and ended in the spring of 54. This period, as it exceeded two years, could, according to Jewish usage, be reckoned as *a three-years'-space*[4]. His life had been that of *a*
19 *slave of the Lord*[5]—the name which S. Paul adopts almost as a formal title at the head of his epistles. This service had three marks[6]: (1) *Humblemindedness*—S. Paul was lowly in his bodily presence, of which he was keenly sensitive; but the lowliness of his outward appearance was, so to speak, balanced by humility of mind within, after the pattern of the Christ[7]. (2) *Tears*—of sorrow for those who will not be saved and of anxiety for the Christians (verse 31). the Second Epistle to the Corinthians was written 'with many tears[8].' (3) *Trials* or *temptations*[9]—from without, especially from *the Jews*; verse 26 points to a state of exasperation on their part similar to that at Corinth, and in both cities they had had recourse to *plots*.
20 The chief work of 'the servant of the Lord' was to bear witness to him. S. Paul's testimony at Ephesus bore the same character as elsewhere. Its special mark was its openness or fulness, and its
21 'boldness' or plainness of speech[10]. He had *testified both to Jews and to Greeks*; both *publicly* in the school of Tyrannus and *from house to house*, viz. at the private gatherings of the Christians[11]. And in his utterances *he had not shrunk from declaring the whole counsel of God*. The different constructions of this word *shrink* in verses 20 and 27 mark a variation in the meaning. (1) He did not cloak or *keep back* (AV) any part of the gospel. In Christianity there is no system of esoteric doctrine: there is one truth for all alike. But such simplicity was quite contrary to the religious ideas of the

---

[1] xix 25, 35. [2] II Cor iv 2. [3] There are in the Greek three different words for *know*: (a) verse 18, (b) vv. 22, 25, 29, (c) verse 34. (a) is used in xix 25, (c) in xix 35, (a) and (c) in xix 15. [4] verse 31: cp. xviii 19, xix 1, 10. S. Paul had in fact *first set foot in* the province of *Asia* in the spring of 49 (xvi 6). [5] as opposed to Artemis; cp. xvi 17, p. 287: the phrase occurs Rom xii 11, Col iii 24. [6] or 'stigmata' Gal vi 17. [7] Cp. II Cor x 1, 10, vii 6: for the humble mind of Christ see Phil ii 1-8: the word *humblemindedness* occurs in Eph iv 2, Col ii 18, 23, iii 12. [8] II Cor ii 4; cp. Phil iii 18, Ps cxix 136. [9] Cp. xv 26 (Bezan): Lk xxii 28. [10] Cp. xiii 46, xiv 3, xviii 26, xix 8, xxvi 26, xxviii 31, Eph vi 19, 20. [11] This is the meaning rather than house to house visitation, which however would be covered by verse 31. The phrase, with the noun in the singular, is translated *at home* in ii 46: the plural noun here may shew that they had more than one place of meeting.

Ephesians. Mysteries, open only to the initiated, abounded at that period; and, as elsewhere, secrecy and esotericism were important elements in Ephesian superstition. Such ideas of special doctrines, of a wisdom or knowledge known only to the enlightened few, who are the 'elect,' the 'spiritual,' the 'knowing ones,' were soon to invade the church. They were a symptom of gnosticism, that 'spirit of error' which found a very fruitful soil in Asia and quickly beset Christianity; already in his Epistle to the Colossians S. Paul has to combat its incipient traces. In opposition to such tendencies he had taught the full gospel to all. This fulness of course excludes neither the gradual method in teaching—S. Paul himself had 'fed' the Corinthians at first 'with milk'—nor the possibility of varying grades of spiritual insight and knowledge. It does mean that nothing that is *expedient* or necessary to salvation is to be kept back, viz. no part of the *gospel of the grace of God*, which S. Paul sums up in the teaching of *repentance* and *faith*.

27 (2) Sometimes teachers have another motive for keeping back the truth, viz. the fear of causing offence. The special temptation of S. Paul was the fear of offending and alienating the Jews by preaching the equal share of the Gentiles in the privileges of the church. But he was not one to shrink back (Heb x 29); and he *declared* to all, to Jew and Greek alike, *the whole counsel of God*, i.e. the catholic appeal of the gospel. This is marked by the recurrence of the word *all*,—four times in verses 25-27 (also in 18, 19, 35). This doctrine was, as he writes later to the Ephesians, the great mystery of God, now revealed to men and made known chiefly through 'the dispensation committed to him,' viz. that 'the Gentiles are fellow-heirs, and fellow-members, and fellow-partakers in Christ Jesus[1].'

22 S. Paul now passes on to vindicate his present purpose and
23 sincerity. On his way *to Jerusalem, in every city* Christian prophets were *testifying* to *bonds and afflictions awaiting him*[2]. The emphatic word *testify* is that used for the apostolic testimony to the gospel; and these prophets spoke under the inspiration of the Holy Ghost. But the circumstances illustrate the true character of inspiration and Christian prophecy. They did not specify further than to speak of *bonds*—and S. Paul, who was a greater prophet than all, had received no special illumination: *he knew not* the particulars of *what was to
25 befall him*. He did indeed *know* or, as we should say, he had a conviction (which, if we are to trust the construction of his later history from the Pastoral Epistles was not literally correct) that
29 *they should see his face no more*[3]. He also *knew*, with the insight characteristic of the OT prophets, that evil times were in store for

---

[1] Eph iii 1-12. [2] Cp. xxi 4, 11. For the *binding* and *bonds* cp. Eph iii 1, iv 1, Col iv 4, 18, Philm 10, 13: for *afflictions* Eph iii 13, Col i 24. [3] Cp. Col ii 1. But S. Paul is thinking, not so much of a literal glimpse with the eye, as of the constant beholding of his face in a regular ministry. The prophecy is true in this sense that his practical work was over.

the church. Further, S. Paul appeared to be acting in contradiction to these warnings of the Spirit. Such conduct—or even self-will, as it might appear,—required explanation. S. Paul's reason was that
22 already, at that very moment, he stood before them *bound*, i.e. in the bonds of the Lord's service. For he felt a deep conviction *in his spirit*, which he could not dissociate from the action of the divine
24 Spirit (xix 21), that the road to Jerusalem was part of *the course* which God had given him to run[1]. To reach the goal of that course was his one ambition, and in comparison with that *he took no account of his life* in the body; he reckoned it *of no value*, as utterly cheap[2] The course on which he had entered was *the ministry*, or *service, which he had received from the Lord Jesus*. The Lord had committed to him a special dispensation or revelation of the grace of God[3], which he had to administer; and as the servant of the Lord he was running in a double capacity. (1) He ran as an evangelist or bearer of good news[4], viz. *the good news of the grace of God*. By this grace or free gift of God men are to be saved, and not by works of the law; and again, through the divine grace, this salvation was offered to every man, Jew and Gentile. The offer itself was one of wonderful bounty; it was the unsearchable riches of Christ which S. Paul had to preach among the Gentiles[5]. (2) He
25 ran as a herald through the nations, *proclaiming the kingdom of God*. This course then he would *accomplish to the end*,—first by reconciling at Jerusalem the Jewish and Gentile disciples in the church; and then, as he had already *passed through* Macedonia, Achaia and Asia, by so passing on to Rome and uttering his proclamation there. But the apostle recollects that the proclamation had not been altogether successful. Jews had rejected it, Gentiles had
26 declined it; and the messenger has to protest his innocency. *He was pure from their blood*. If they were rejected from eternal life because of their rejection of the gospel, he was guiltless. For the preacher is only responsible for the faithful and acceptable setting
27 forth of *the counsel of God*[6]. And as S. Paul reviews his past career, his conscience tells him that he had *declared* it in its completeness. The plan or counsel of God's will is one of the ruling thoughts in the Epistle to the Ephesians[7]; and the special dispensation which the apostle there claims to have received is the teaching of that truth of the catholicity of the gospel, by which the fulness of God's counsel is most richly set forth.

We notice that *to testify the gospel* is coordinated with *preaching the kingdom*. The gospel involves a kingdom. Repentance is the

---

[1] Cp. xiii 25, Phil iii 10-4, II Tim iv 7. [2] This is the meaning of the reading of the best MSS, which we must accept. The Greek however is difficult. The AV reading, which gives the best sense, looks like a later correction; yet it is quite possible, as has been strongly argued by Dr Field (*Notes on trans. of the NT*), that a line fell out in an early copy, which if restored would give us the AV sense.
[3] Cp. Eph iii 2, 7, Col i 23, 25, I Tim i 12. [4] Isai lii 7, Nahum i 15, Rom x 15.
[5] Cp. Eph ii 8, i 7, iii 8 etc. [6] Cp. Ezekiel iii 16-21, xxxiii 1-9. [7] Cp. Eph i 11.

entrance to a society, and faith is the principle of life in it. This kingdom had been proclaimed by S. Paul at Ephesus (xix 8), and the doctrine of the church is one of the great subjects of the Epistle to the Ephesians. So here also the idea of the church is presented in rich variety. It is the kingdom and ecclesia of God, the flock which is God's peculiar possession, and the inheritance of the saints[1].

II. Having fulfilled his part, the responsibility now rests with 28 the presbyters; and S. Paul warns them to *take heed* to themselves[2] in a sentence pregnant with teaching. Thus, from it we learn (1) that this *ecclesia* of Ephesus is *the church of God*. S. Paul has in mind the words of Psalm lxxiv 1-2: *O God, why doth thine anger smoke against the sheep of thy pasture? Remember thy congregation (synagogue), which thou hast purchased of old, which thou hast redeemed to be the tribe of thine inheritance.* So the new ecclesia of the Christ has succeeded to the synagogue of old: it is the true Israel[3]. And as God had redeemed the Israel of old to be his peculiar people or inheritance among all the peoples of the earth, so now he has *purchased* or *gotten for himself* the church to be his own possession[4]. (2) God had redeemed the former Israel by a double deliverance—first from the destroying angel by the blood of the paschal lamb, then from the Egyptian oppressors by the passage of the Red Sea. So the new Israel had been won *by the blood*[5] of Christ shed upon the cross, and by his having been 'brought again from the dead with the blood of the eternal covenant' (Heb xiii 20) in the resurrection. In the first part of the Acts the crucifixion as a fact was an essential element of the apostolic testimony; here the underlying doctrine is asserted, i.e. the doctrine of the atonement. By the blood of Christ God purchased the church. We must not however press the metaphor contained in the word *purchase*, and ask to whom was the price paid. Indeed the idea of buying is not necessarily contained in the Greek word, which denotes 'acquiring' or 'getting for one's own.' God, then, *got the church for his own* by not sparing the life of his Son. For *the blood* (as in verse 26) means the life. By the life of his Son surrendered on the cross our sins were covered; by the life of his Son risen from the dead he raises us to newness of life. (3) But if the possession won was so great—a renewed humanity,—what must have been the cost? The blood must be more than human, it must be divine; and when S. Paul says *his own blood*, the antecedent of *his own* is God. Christ, then, whose blood was shed, is God; and yet 'the blood of God' seems an impossible expression for S. Paul to have used. In later centuries, when the theological

---

[1] See above pp. 348-9. The word *kingdom* occurs Eph v 5, Col i 13, iv 11.
[2] Cp. v 35, Lk xxi 34. [3] The word *ecclesia*, we must remember, would remind the Ephesians in the first place of the ecclesia of their city (xix 32, 39, 41) rather than of the ecclesia of Israel (vii 38). [4] Exod xix 5-6: Eph i 14: I Pet ii 9.
[5] *The blood* occurs in Eph i 7, ii 13, Col i 20.

expression of the doctrine of the incarnation had been thoroughly wrought out, it could be explained by the *communicatio idiomatum* (sharing of attributes), which describes in Hooker's words[1] those 'cross and circulatory speeches, wherein are attributed to God such things as belong to manhood, and to man such as properly concern the deity of Christ Jesus, the cause whereof is the association of [two] natures [divine and human] in one subject'—the one person Jesus Christ. Hence we can speak without offence of 'the mother of God,' 'the blood of God.' But as yet, in the Acts, it is early for such theological phraseology[2]. Many manuscripts solve the difficulty by substituting *the Lord* for *God*. But against them we have the two best MSS ℵ and B; the more difficult reading is generally to be preferred; and the reference to the Psalm makes it almost certain that S. Paul spoke of the church 'of God[3].' (4) The real solution is to be found in the doctrine of the Trinity, which is here implicit. This doctrine is nowhere explicitly asserted by S. Paul, perhaps it was not fully defined in his own mind; but he evidently believed in the Father, in the Lord Jesus Christ, and in the Holy Ghost; and he recognized each Person as divine, and the three Persons as inseparable in their working. Thus in verse 21 *repentance towards God* is parallel to *faith in our Lord Jesus*, and in the next sentence *the Holy Spirit witnesses*. In verse 24 we have the *ministry of the Lord Jesus* and *the grace of God*. Here we have *the church of God*, in Ephesians (v 5) *the kingdom of the Christ*. And now the work of the three Persons is described in one sentence—the church is *God's*, purchased by *the blood* of Christ, ruled by *the Holy Spirit*. With such a faith for the groundwork of his life and thinking, it is easy to see how the apostle, without any change of subject grammatically, can yet pass in thought from one person to another. He begins with GOD the FATHER, but when he says *his own*, he is now speaking of the SON. In such an interchangeableness we have reached the highwater mark of S. Paul's theology. From belief in Jesus as the Messiah, he had quickly risen to accept him as the Son of God (ix 20). Now he unmistakeably implies his equality and unity in divine prerogatives with the FATHER. So the Epistle to the Romans, written only a few months or weeks before the present moment, contains a similar passage, which speaks of Christ as being 'over all, God blessed for ever[4].'

Yet again, from the pastoral point of view, this verse is, so to speak, the charter of the Christian ministry. In this relation it

---

[1] *Eccl. Polity* v 53. 4. [2] Yet only 50 years later S. Ignatius speaks of *the blood of God* (*Eph.* i 1); so Tertullian *ad uxor.* II 3. [3] So *the Lord*, if we adopted that reading, would stand for JEHOVAH. Dr Hort admits of *God* as the genuine reading, but suspects some early corruption, e.g. that the verse ended with the word *son* which has dropped out—*by the blood of his own* (*son*). [4] Rom ix 5: cp. Phil ii 6. *His own* as applied to Christ brings out the entirety of the self-sacrifice, cp. Eph v 2; so in Rom viii 31 God spared not *his own* Son.

has already been examined above (p. 385); here we will only note that the relation of the ministry to the church is presented under that figure which differentiates the Christian from all other priesthoods and which makes the deepest impression on men's hearts. The church is God's *flock*; and as Christ is the chief shepherd[1], so the ministers he sends are shepherds or pastors: the 'treasure' committed to their charge is 'the sheep of Christ which he bought with his death and for whom he shed his blood[2].' This verse is the utterance of S. Paul's—and the only one—which corresponds to the great pastoral passages in S. John (x 1-18, xxi 15-17) and S. Peter (I v 1-4), which in their turn are the NT parallels to Psalm xxiii, Isaiah xl 10-11, Ezekiel xxxiv. Thus in the NT the figure is not frequent[3].

29 The reason for taking heed lies in the imminent peril of false teaching, coming both from without and within. (1) From without —and S. Paul keeps up the metaphor—*wolves will enter in*. The typical wolf comes, as an enemy, to destroy (Jn x 12); S. Paul is rather thinking of the wolves who will find their way into the fold in sheep's clothing, i.e. of false teachers. Such will be a *heavy* weight, or burdensome[4]: they will not *spare the flock*, for they seek their own, and will use their authority to acquire gold and
30 silver (verse 33) from the flock. (2) Other false teachers *will arise* out of the Ephesian church itself, *speaking perverse things*; that is, like Elymas they will make the straight paths of the Lord crooked and involve the disciples in 'the wiles of error[5],' and that under a profession of wisdom which will *drag away disciples* to form parties *after* their own names—and not after Christ,—as at Corinth[6]. S. Paul's anticipations were fully realized. In the Epistle to the Ephesians he combats such crooked wisdom, and the deceit which justified immorality; in that to the Colossians the false philosophy and asceticism by which the Colossians were spoiled and led captive[7]. The Pastoral Epistles represent the conflict at its height, and give us the names of some such teachers—Alexander, Hymenaeus and Philetus. Later still S. John writes at Ephesus of
31 the many 'antichrists' who have gone out 'from us[8].' The only safeguard was to *watch*[9] against the wolf from without; and to *admonish* and teach, and so make perfect, each individual within[10]. For such was the example the apostle had set them.
32 III. But 'vain is the help of man'; and therefore, as the apostle

---

[1] I Pet v 4; cp. Jn x 11, 14, I Pet ii 25, Hebr xiii 20. [2] Eph iv 11: PBk Ordinal. [3] In I Cor ix 7 S. Paul draws an illustration from shepherding. Besides this, in S. Luke we have the *little flock* of xii 32 and the appearance to the shepherds (ii 8-18): in S. Matthew four allusions ii 6, xxv 32, and (with Mk) ix 36, xxvi 31: and in the Revelation one (vii 17). [4] I Thess ii 7. II Cor xi 20 gives an example of *grievous* conduct towards the flock: 'lording' and covetousness are associated with shepherding in I Pet v 3. [5] xiii 10: Eph iv 14. [6] *drag away* occurs in xxi 1, Lk xxii 41. [7] Eph iv 14, v 6: Col ii 8, 18. [8] I Tim i 20, II ii 17: I Jn ii 18-9. [9] This supplements the *Pray* of Lk xxii 40: cp. Col iv 2, Eph vi 18. [10] Col i 28, cp. Eph iv 11-3.

had himself been commended by the church to God (xiv 26, xv 40), so he now *commends* the presbyters *to God and to the word*, i.e. the revelation, *of his grace*[1], of his goodness to man revealed in Christ Jesus. This message of the free bounty of God is the word which has the greatest effect on the heart of man, and so it is *able to build up* the church. Thus S. Paul returns to the church, but the church in its inward and subjective idea rather than in its outward aspect as kingdom and ecclesia. He now conceives of it (1) as a building[2]. Ephesus had its gorgeous temple of Artemis, but Paul had laid the foundations of a far more glorious temple, the stones of which were the converts he won. But the idea of building, in relation to the individual, is rather associated with the *building up*, or edification, of the spiritual life which the Christian enjoys in virtue of his having been built into the church; and this edification is the special work of the ministry[3]. (2) When he was thus built into the church, the Christian entered upon his *inheritance*. The call of Abraham carried with it the promise of an inheritance (vii 2–7); and after the delivery out of Egypt, Israel entered upon the promised land (vii 45). When this possession failed to give perfect satisfaction, (*a*) the Israelites began to look forward to the future for a more perfect temporal inheritance; but (*b*) spiritual minds found their inheritance either in the law—as in Deut xxxiii 3–4, a passage now in S. Paul's mind, —or in God, 'the portion of their inheritance' (Ps xvi 5). The true inheritance combines both ideas, the outward and the inward. For it is the church. Now (*a*) the church is, externally, the society of *all those who have been consecrated* to God and so made his holy people and peculiar possession, and this 'lot of the saints in light' is equivalent to 'the kingdom of the Son of his love[4].' And (*b*) within the church is contained a rich estate of spiritual privileges which the Christian inherits,—the riches of God's grace and mercy, the treasures of wisdom and knowledge, the unsearchable riches of the Christ[5]. To these must be added the treasures of hope. For no more than the Israel of old can the church attain its ideal in this world; and *the inheritance* will only be fully realized in the future, in 'the riches of the glory of the inheritance in the saints,' of which our present possession of the Spirit is the foretaste and the pledge[6]. The thought of riches, to which the inheritance has brought us, dominates the Epistle to the Ephesians. This may be a sign of the impression made on the apostle by the wealth and magnificence of Ephesus and the temple of Artemis, and shew that he felt the need of supplying the Ephesians with some counter-attraction.

33 They had to learn that true wealth did not consist in *silver and gold and* gorgeous *apparel*; and in this the apostle had given them
34 an object-lesson. They had seen their founder and chief priest,

---

[1] The combination of *word* and *grace* is found in Eph iv 29, Col iv 6. [2] So in Eph ii 19–22: cp. I Cor iii 9. [3] Cp. Eph iv 12, 16, 29, Col ii 7. [4] Col i 12–3: cp. Eph v 5, Acts xxvi 18. [5] Eph i 7, ii 4: Col ii 2–3: Eph iii 8; cp. iii 16. [6] Eph i 18, 14: cp. Col iii 24.

their proconsul and Asiarch, working with his own hands for his livelihood (p. 351)[1].

For S. Paul has now come to the last and most delicate subject of defence: like Samuel, he appeals to the integrity of his private
35 life. This had been marked by a self-denial, which exceeded the highest demand of the ordinary standards of honesty. But in this self-restraint he had given a living *example*[2], like the washing of the disciples' feet by the Lord. And this lesson was especially needed at Ephesus, where priestly office and spiritual power were viewed as the stepping-stones to worldly wealth, where many of the converts had themselves by these means gained large sums (xix 19), and where the special duty of the presbyters of the Ephesian Gerousia was to protect and manage the vast sums deposited in the temple of Artemis. In direct contradiction to such ideas the law of Christian office was service—*helping the weak*[3], whether in body (the sick), mind (the scrupulous), or spirit (the downcast and sinful). Money is to be regarded as the instrument of such help, and is needed by the Christian minister only so far as to satisfy his own bodily *necessities*, and to enable him *to help* others. For these purposes he should even *labour* hard with his hands, as the apostle directs in his epistle[4]. Since those days the mind of the church has changed, and the clergy are now forbidden to follow secular employments—with equal apostolic sanction: for 'it is not good for us to serve tables, we will give ourselves to prayer and the ministry of the word' (vi 2, 4). But the spirit of ministry remains unaltered; and, in conclusion, the apostle declares its underlying principle. He had in his life renewed the example, he now quotes *the words, of the Lord Jesus—Blessed is it to be a giver rather than a receiver*. The presbyters would *remember* not only how the apostle had held his own life *cheap* (verse 29), but how the Good Shepherd had shed *his own blood* for the flock (verse 28). This beatitude is one of the sayings of the Lord which were current in the early church beside those preserved in the Gospels. Some of them have come down to us through various channels, and probably S. Clement of Rome is giving another form of this saying when he writes to the Corinthians that 'once they were humble-minded… more gladly giving than receiving[5].'

36 These words of the Lord were the last words of the apostle, and at once the whole assembly *knelt down* and S. Paul *prayed* aloud.
37 Then follows a picture drawn with S. Luke's inimitable command of pathos, which reveals the apostle's wonderful power in attracting personal affection and devotion. There was a *loud* sound of

---

[1] as at Thessalonica and Corinth, pp. 296, 324.   [2] The noun occurs in Jn xiii 15, the verb in Acts ix 16.   [3] This explains the meaning of *helps* in I Cor xii 28. For *the weak* cp. Rom v 6, xiv 1, I Thess v 14.   [4] Eph iv 28. The word *labour* occurs there and Col i 29. It is used of both spiritual and manual labour, cp. the *labour of love* (I Thess i 3). With S. Paul's example in verse 33, cp. the words of S. Peter in iii 6.   [5] *ad Cor.* 2.

38 sobbing or *wailing, every one* was weeping. *The saying, that they should see his face no more*, filled the presbyters with the deepest *sorrow* or grief of heart, and they embraced him, *falling on his neck* and *kissing* him earnestly[1]. Kissing was a usual form of salutation in the east, especially between master and disciple (as in the kiss of Judas), host and guest, brothers and such close relations[2]. Hence it naturally became the form of greeting between Christian brothers; and, in the ritual of divine service, the kiss of brotherly fellowship became the necessary preparation for the divine fellowship in the breaking of bread[3]. Kissing however is as often the sign of farewell, and the kiss here reminds us of other pathetic partings in the OT, e.g. those between Joseph and his dying father, Naomi and her daughters-in-law, Jonathan and David[4]. Thus, when they had taken their farewell and the day had fully dawned, the presbyters in a body *escorted* Paul *to the ship*.

§ 5 *From Miletus to Caesarea: Paul's temptation*

The conclusion of the journey brings us back to old scenes and persons, old ideas and language: we return to Phenicia[5] and Caesarea[6], to Philip[7] and Agabus[8]. The narrative affords us most interesting glimpses into the organization of the church and the action of Christian prophecy, together with fresh testimony to the great personal affection inspired by S. Paul. The main thought in the mind of the writer seems to be that of the temptation to S. Paul to break off his purpose, a temptation all the harder as it apparently arose from the direct action of the Spirit (verses 4, 11). We might in fact call this paragraph 'S. Paul's temptation': it corresponds to the temptations of Moses and of Elijah[9], and, we may add, of the Lord himself.

21 And when it came to pass that we were [10]parted from them, and had set sail, we came with a straight course unto Cos, and the next day unto Rhodes, and from thence unto
2 Patara[11]: and having found a ship crossing over unto
3 Phœnicia, we went aboard, and set sail. And when we had come in sight of Cyprus, leaving it on the left hand, we sailed unto Syria, and landed at Tyre: for there the ship was to

---

[1] There was great *wailing* at Bethlehem (Mt ii 18): cp. also the *wailing and gnashing of teeth* (Lk xiii 28 etc.). The *sorrow* is sorrow of heart (Lk ii 48, Rom ix 2, I Tim vi 10). The father *fell upon the neck of* the prodigal son (Lk xv 20).
[2] Lk xxii 47, vii 45, Exod iv 27, Gen xxix 11, xlviii 10. [3] Rom xvi 16, I Cor xvi 20, I Thess v 26, I Pet v 14. As a salutation, the kiss was also a sign of reconciliation: cp. Esau and Jacob, Joseph and his brothers (Gen xxxiii 4, xlv 15), David and Absalom (II Sam xiv 33), the father and the prodigal (Lk xv 20).
[4] Gen l 1, Ruth i 9 (14), I Sam xx 41; cp. also II Sam xix 39, I Kings xix 20.
[5] xi 19, xv 3.   [6] viii 40, ix 30, x 1–48, xii 19–23, xviii 22.   [7] vi 5, viii 5–40.
[8] xi 27–8.   [9] Cp. Num xx 7–13, I K. xix 4: Lk xxii 40–4.   [10] Gk *torn away from*.   [11] Bezan adds *and Myra*.

4 unlade her burden. And having found the disciples, we tarried there seven days: and these said to Paul through the
5 Spirit, that he should not set foot in Jerusalem. And when it came to pass that we had accomplished the days, we departed and went on our journey; and they all, with wives and children, brought us on our way, till we were out of the
6 city: and kneeling down on the beach, we prayed, and bade each other farewell; and we went on board the ship, but they returned home again.
7 And when we had finished the voyage from Tyre, we arrived at Ptolemais; and we saluted the brethren, and
8 abode with them one day. And on the morrow we¹ departed, and came unto Cæsarea: and entering into the house of Philip the evangelist, who was one of the seven, we abode with him.
9 Now this man had four daughters, virgins, which did
10 prophesy. And as we tarried there many days, there came
11 down from Judæa a certain prophet, named Agabus. And coming to us, and taking Paul's girdle, he bound his own feet and hands, and said, Thus saith the Holy Ghost, So shall the Jews at Jerusalem bind the man that owneth this girdle,
12 and shall deliver him into the hands of the Gentiles. And when we heard these things both we and they of that
13 place besought him not to go up to Jerusalem. Then Paul answered, What do ye, weeping and breaking my heart? for I am ready not to be bound only, but also to die at Jerusalem
14 for the name of the Lord Jesus. And when he would not be persuaded, we ceased, saying, The will of the Lord be done.

1   When S. Paul's party had thus been reluctantly *torn away from* the Ephesians², they had a favourable voyage or series of *straight runs* to *Cos, Rhodes*, and *Patara*. Patara was on the coast of Lycia; and Myra, fifty miles further east, was the usual starting-place for the voyage across the open sea either to Egypt or past *Cyprus*
2 *to Syria*. At Patara then, or Myra, *they found a ship* bound *for*
3 *Phenicia*. The distance was about 400 miles; and having a favourable wind, in three or four days—which included another Sunday (the fourth after Easter)—they *arrived at Tyre*. Phenicia

---
¹ AV adds *that were of Paul's company* (xiii 13).   ² This is the literal meaning of the Greek word, which occurs in Lk xxii 41: it suggests something more than a simple parting.

had been one of the earliest scenes of missionary activity outside the Holy Land; and as its churches had been planted by Hellenists, they would have been favourably inclined to S. Paul's gospel. On a memorable occasion he had passed through Phenicia and caused them great joy by the news of the conversion of the Gentiles (xv 3). At Sidon he had personal friends, and the same seems to have been
4 the case at Tyre; for the word *finding-out* seems to imply a search for some particular friends[1]. *The ship*—as we gather from verse 6—was bound for Ptolemais; but *at Tyre it was unlading* or changing *its cargo*. This gave a welcome delay, and S. Paul may have pleaded with the shipmaster for *seven days* in order to cover the 'synaxis' on the first day of the week (Saturday evening); the remarkable
5 phrase of *completing the days* points to an exact time which they might not exceed. Accordingly on the morning of the fifth Sunday after Easter another farewell took place[2]. S. Paul's party went straight from the service to the ship. When they *went forth* out of the building to resume their journey, the whole congregation—men, *women and children*—*escorted* them to the beach *outside the*
6 *city* wall. Here a final commendation took place. They *knelt and prayed* and kissed one another[3]. Then the travellers *went on board* and *continued their voyage*[4]. The scene would not have appeared so strange to the Tyrians as to us. The Jews were accustomed to practise their devotions on the sea-shore or by rivers, as we saw at Philippi (xvi 13); and such devotions would be public, like the
7 prayers of the Mohammedans to this day. The same day Paul and his party *arrived at Ptolemais*, the modern Acre. Here the Christians were perhaps not personally known to the apostle and he *saluted*
8 *them* more formally. After a day's rest and intercourse, the travellers finished on foot the forty miles which brought them *to Caesarea*, where they found hospitality *in the house of Philip*.

Philip, the second among the Seven, had been the first to evangelize Caesarea, and there we left him. And now, twenty years later, we find him settled in the city with his family. Probably he had been there ever since; if so, he would supply us with an example of the 'settling' of a wandering prophet, of which the *Didaché* speaks[5]. No doubt also, being what he was, he would preside over the church at Caesarea. S. Luke makes his identity clear by a full description of Philip, which contains an official title and a personal distinction. He was (1) *the evangelist*—and evangelists were becoming almost a recognized order[6]; (2) *one of the Seven*. Thus at the same time he is distinguished from 'Philip the apostle,

---

[1] xi 19, xv 3; xxvii 3; II Tim i 17. [2] This is described, according to S. Luke's style, in one long sentence with many participles. [3] In the Greek there is an unusual compound form of the verb for bidding farewell. [4] This, according to Dr Field (*Notes etc.*), is the correct meaning of the words translated *finishing the voyage*. [5] ch. 13. [6] *To evangelize* was the special function of the apostles. This passed on to others, who are ranked between apostles and presbyters; cp. Eph iv 11, II Tim iv 5. So perhaps *evangelist* was an experimental or temporary title for a president of a church.

9 being one of the Twelve.' An interesting note is added; its motive is probably suggested by the incident which follows, but we can also recognize the happy reminiscences of a guest. Philip *had four daughters*; and the sympathy they shewed for S. Paul, with the labour they doubtless bestowed upon him in the two years' confinement at Caesarea, made a great impression upon S. Luke. He could appreciate the services of women; and their sympathy, like that of the women of Jerusalem, received its reward in this mention[1]. They were also of note in the church, and occupied a kind of official position. S. Luke accordingly describes them, as he does their father. (1) They were *virgins*. A long while ago we heard of 'widows' as an institution in the church[2], now we read of 'virgins.' The idea of a life specially consecrated to God in virginity was by no means new. It had received the Lord's sanction; and it soon found a place in the church, for nearly two years before this S. Paul had to discuss some details of the matter in his First Epistle to the Corinthians[3]. (2) Besides this recognized status, they possessed the personal gift of *prophecy*. This again was not new. In OT times there had been women prophets, such as Miriam, Deborah, and Huldah. At the time of the Lord's birth, Anna a 'widow' was also a 'prophetess[4].' In the next century prophetesses were to play a leading part in the movement of Montanism. But S. Paul was not in favour of women speaking or teaching in the church; in fact he had forbidden it[5], and so women were not officially recognized as prophets. The daughters of Philip may have exercised their gift in the utterance of such hymns as that of the Blessed Virgin[6]. But the following verses suggest that they too uttered warnings to S. Paul, similar to the prophecies which had marked the whole course of the journey, and of which we now come to a typical instance.

10 Among the *prophets* of *Judaea* was *one named Agabus*. More than ten years ago this same Agabus had gone down to Antioch and uttered an important prediction[7]. At Antioch he had also met Saul who is now called Paul; and now, hearing of his approach to Jerusalem and aware of his danger, he goes down *to Caesarea* to prevent his coming. There, at a meeting of the church—probably the 'synaxis' on the first day of the week (the Sunday after Ascension

---

[1] Lk xxiii 27; cp. Mt xxvi 13.   [2] vi 1, ix 39.   [3] Cp. Mt xix 12, Lk x 42, and the 'ten virgins' of Mt xxv: I Cor vii 25-38.   [4] Exod xv 20, Judges iv 4, II K. xxii 14, Lk ii 36: cp. I Cor xi 5 *every woman prophesying*.   [5] I Cor xiv 34-5.   [6] Lk i 46-55: this would be a *prophecy* (i 67). Cp. the hymn of Hannah, and the words of Miriam and of Elisabeth (Lk i 42-5).   [7] xi 27-8. It seems strange to find Agabus, after his previous appearance, here introduced and named as a new character. We should have expected some such words as *Agabus the prophet*: but cp. xxvii 2 after xx 4. Possibly Agabus was not, personally, of great note in the church (like e.g. S. Barnabas) so as to be remembered after a single allusion. The construction of the sentence here is very similar to that in xi 27-8; and in both cases the emphasis falls on the office (*prophets, prophet*) rather than on the man, whose name is given as an afterthought.

Day)—the word of the Lord came unto him and bade him make a sign, like the prophets of old. Jeremiah, for instance, had once bought a linen girdle and bound his loins with it[1]; so now Agabus
11 suddenly approached Paul's company of Greek delegates, *took away Paul's girdle* from him and *bound his own hands and feet with it*. So he 'signified' (xi 28) that *the man who owns this girdle—him shall the Jews so bind in Jerusalem, and they will deliver him into the hands of the Gentiles*. After the ancient manner he declared this to be 'the word of the LORD,' only with a significant change—*Thus saith the Holy Spirit*. As elsewhere 'the Lord' Jesus, so here the
12 Holy Spirit stands in the place of JEHOVAH. This was the most decisive warning of all, and the whole congregation, *the local Christians as well as the company of Greeks, with tears entreated Paul not to go up to Jerusalem*. This entreaty on the eve of his
13 entry into Jerusalem was the keenest trial to S. Paul; it almost *broke his heart* (literally, *crushed it to pieces*). But however his affections might be tried, his resolution was firm[2]. Although it might perplex his friends and give the appearance of obstinacy,— as if he who spent his life in persuading others *would not be persuaded* himself[3],—he was convinced that it was the will of God that he should go up to Jerusalem. So he set his face like a flint and declared his readiness *even to die at Jerusalem for the name of the Lord Jesus*[4]. At this utterance his hearers perceived that this
14 was no human obstinacy but *the will of the Lord*; they too prayed that *it might be done*, and ceased from their protests.

The words '*The will of the Lord be done*,' which end the account of the journey, irresistibly call up to our mind the scene in Gethsemane, where the prayer of the Lord was '*Not my will but thine be done*.' There too his soul was sorrowful even unto death, as here S. Paul's heart was breaking. Again the words, *they shall deliver him into the hands of the Gentiles*, exactly express the critical act in the Jews' rejection of their Messiah[5]. These coincidences force us to conclude that while S. Luke is describing S. Paul's victory over the temptation to abandon his purpose, he has in his mind the last journey of the Lord to Jerusalem and his preparation for the passion which culminated in Gethsemane. This at once gives significance to a number of other coincidences in the narrative of the present journey, which by themselves would have escaped notice. Accordingly, we observe that as the Lord uttered three prophecies of his passion[6], so the Spirit three times warns S. Paul in xx 23, xxi 4 and 11. S. Paul *kneeled and prayed* (xx 36, xxi 5) like the Lord in Gethsemane. The mention of kneeling is the more remarkable, as standing was the usual attitude

---

[1] Jer xiii. [2] The *heart* in Hebrew denotes the seat of the will, rather than of the affections: cp. viii 22. [3] For S. Paul's *persuasion* see xiii 43, xvii 4, xviii 4, xix 8, 26. [4] This phrase takes us back to v 41 and xv 26. [5] Lk xviii 32, Mk x 33, Mt xx 19: cp. Lk ix 44, Mk ix 31, Mt xvii 22; Mk xiv 41, Mt xxvi 45.
[6] Lk ix 22; ix 44; xviii 31-3. Perhaps the unusual phrase, *accomplishing the days*, may be accounted for by reference to such language as that of Lk ix 51.

of prayer; perhaps the Lord's example gave rise to the Christian habit of kneeling. At Gethsemane there is also mention of a *kiss* (cp. xx 37), and the kiss was followed by *binding* (cp. xxi 11). In the near context S. Peter makes a profession of his *readiness to die* for the Lord, like S. Paul in xxi 13 (Lk xxii 33). A verbal parallel is to be found in the *being torn away* of xxi 1 (Lk xxii 41). The 'last words' of S. Paul to the Ephesians in chapter xx reminded us of the 'last words' of the Lord, whether in the upper room or on Mount Olivet. At the Last Supper the Lord spoke of *temptations* (Lk xxii 28, Acts xx 19): and the *Take heed* and *Watch* of Acts xx 28, 31 take us back to Lk xxi 34-36. The *Watch* in Acts xx 31 further supplements the *Pray* which S. Luke gives by itself in his account of Gethsemane (Lk xxii 40).

Note on the diary of the journey

Some commentators give an exact diary of the journey with the days of the week and month. But it is hardly possible to be so precise. For (1) S. Luke himself does not give enough particulars; he leaves many gaps and uncertainties. E.g. how soon after the paschal days did S. Paul start from Philippi? did he stay a night at Assos? how long did he stay at Miletus? how many days was the passage from Patara to Tyre? (2) We do not know the year; and if we did, in order to fix the right dates, we ought to know the exact date of the Passover in the year. But our knowledge about the Jewish method of astronomical reckoning is not absolutely certain, and modern authorities differ. To discuss such points fully does not fall within the scope of this commentary; but it is possible to give a relative and tentative diary of the journey, which may be useful for our purpose. And if, as we have found reason to suspect, S. Luke reckons by the weeks, and indirectly marks where each Sunday's service was held, then we shall have obtained the correct framework. The Sunday service, we must remember, began on the evening of our Saturday (p. 377).

Mon			The Passover	[or Tuesday]
Sat	Sabbath			
Sun	Easter Day		The morrow after the Sabbath (Levit xxiii 11)	
Mon			Last day of unleavened bread [or Tuesday]	
Tues			Leave Philippi	
Wed			Leave Neapolis	
Sun	i after Easter		Arrive at Troas	
			A week at Troas	
Sat	Sabbath	*erg*	Synaxis (i.e. service)	
Sun	ii after Easter	*morn*	Leave Troas	
Mon		*e*	Arrive at Mitylene	[or Assos]
Tues		*e*	Arrive off Chios	[or Mitylene]
Wed		*e*	Arrive at Trogyllium	[or Chios]
Thurs		*m*	Arrive at Miletus	[or Trogyllium]
Fri				[arrive at Miletus]
Sat	Sabbath		Arrival of presbyters	[or on Sat]
Sun	iii after Easter	*e*	Synaxis	
Mon		*m*	Leave Miletus	
		e	Arrive at Cos	
		e	Arrive at Rhodes	

Tues		*e*	Arrive at Patara
Wed		*m*	Leave Patara
Thurs			(? Leave Myra)
Sun	iv after Easter		Arrive at Tyre
			A week at Tyre
Sat	Sabbath	*e*	Synaxis
Sun	v after Easter	*m*	Leave Tyre
		e	Arrive at Ptolemais
Mon			A day at Ptolemais
Tues		*m*	Leave Ptolemais
		e	Arrive at Caesarea
			Several days at Caesarea
Thurs	Ascension Day		
Sat	Sabbath	*e*	Synaxis
Sun	S. aft. Ascension Day		
Thurs		*m*	Leave Caesarea
		e	Lodge at a certain village
Fri			Enter Jerusalem
Sat	Sabbath		Interview with James
Sun	Pentecost or Whitsunday		

SECTION II (= Ch. 21. 15—26)

Paul the prisoner and his process

The words *after these days*[1] mark the beginning of a new chapter of the history, which runs without a break to the end of the book[2]. It describes the 'bonds and afflictions' which befel S. Paul, and that on a scale and at a length which seem quite disproportionate; for the narrative from this verse to the end takes up a quarter of the whole book, from xix 21 a third. We have already seen two reasons for this.

(1) There is the personal factor. Throughout this period S. Luke was at S. Paul's side. The strain on his feelings must have been great, and as he looks back he cannot suppress the crowd of recollections which come flooding up in his memory. He remembers the kindness of their host Mnason; he went in with S. Paul to James and the elders; he was a spectator of the riot in the temple and saw Paul lifted over the soldiers' heads; he was with the apostle in the castle when his nephew brought news of the plot, and he saw the tribune kindly take the lad's hand; he was one of the crowd in the audience chamber of the palace at Caesarea and his eye was somewhat dazzled by the great pomp of king Agrippa and his sister, Berenice, and the procurator's court.

(2) S. Luke writes as an artist. He evidently intends this part of the Acts to correspond with the conclusion of his Gospel, where the

---

[1] Cp. i 15, vi 1, xi 27.   [2] although, for convenience sake, we break it into two sections.

passion of the Lord is narrated at equal length and with equal richness of detail. Nor indeed must we forget the parallel with the first part of the Acts. Paul is now filling at Jerusalem the part once played by S. Peter: like S. Peter he also addresses the Jews at a Pentecost, stands before the Sanhedrin, utters a sentence of judgement on an Ananias and a hypocrite, and like S. Peter's his career is arrested by bondage at Jerusalem. But this parallel is absorbed in the imitation of a greater than either. The history of the Lord's passion seems to be repeating itself. Like the Lord Jesus, Paul is carried before the Sanhedrin and smitten on the mouth; the multitude of the people cry out *Away with him*; his fellow-countrymen deliver him into the hands of the Gentiles; he is accused before the Roman governor, and stands before a Herod; his accusers are the same, the Sadducean high-priesthood, as also the counts of the indictment which culminate in the charge of treason against Caesar; three times he is pronounced to have done nothing worthy of death, yet he narrowly escapes a scourging, and the governor leaves him bound in order to please the Jews[1]: incidentally the trial of Jesus resulted in the renewal of friendly relations between Pilate and Herod Antipas, so likewise Paul's case enables Festus to pay a compliment to Herod Agrippa II. Finally, the close of the book leaves the apostle in a state of comparative freedom and activity: like S. Peter in ch. xii, he has experienced a deliverance—almost, we might say, a resurrection from the dead. This resemblance is not due to arbitrary invention. It is the natural working out of a law which had been enunciated by the Lord himself: 'as the master, so shall the servant be.' In the Revelation, in a symbolical picture (xi 1-12), S. John has shewn that the experience of the Lord's witnesses must be the same as that of the Lord, the Faithful Witness, himself. How much more certain this will become, when the servant is standing in the same position and on the same spot as the master. Granted the same situation, then the greater the inward likeness of the servant to his master, the greater will be the outward likeness of their experience.

(3) There is a third reason for S. Luke's prolixity, and that a practical one. These chapters are the record of S. Paul's Defence or *Apology*[2]. And the defence is 'complete' (xix 21). We have his answer both to the Jews—to the People, the Sanhedrin, and to a Jewish king—and to the Romans; or otherwise, to the Jews (xxi-xxiii), Romans (xxiv-xxv), and the world at large (xxvi). But this apology is not merely a personal matter. S. Paul is 'set for the defence of the gospel,' and these chapters contain the apology for Christianity. They form in fact the first in that series of 'apologies' which were so important an element in the Christian literature of the first centuries. And as the typical apologist Justin Martyr addressed 'apologies' both to Jews and to Romans, so this apology is written for both of these 'nations' on whose attitude to the church so much depended. In one sense the Roman

---

[1] Lk xxiii 25.   [2] xxii 1, xxv 16; cp. xxiv 10, xxv 8, xxvi 1, 2, 24.

public was the more important of the two. The Romans were lords of the world, and Christianity as a new 'religion' had to vindicate its claim to exist. Paul the defendant was himself a Roman citizen, and as a Roman citizen he appeals to the Roman emperor. The Acts itself is dedicated to a Christian who is addressed, as if he were a member of the ruling society, by the same complimentary title as the governors Felix and Festus—*most excellent*. This aspect of these chapters cannot but affect the question of the date when they were written. This has been dealt with in the Introduction (pp. l-lv); and here we need only recapitulate some of the points. The great persecution under Nero in A.D. 64 entirely altered the relation between the empire and the church. It was an open declaration of war; and after that there would have been small profit in the laborious composition of these chapters, whose peaceful tone in itself implies a situation previous to the persecution. Again, the hearing of the appeal in the emperor's court and the defence of Paul at Rome were far more important than the trials in the province before petty governors and princes like Felix, Festus, and Agrippa. Had the emperor heard the case and (as we believe) let the apostle go free, then it would have been doubtful art, as well as a waste of labour, to have devoted so much time and space to the preliminary stages of the process and not to have said a word about the final issue. The ultimate martyrdom of the apostle in A.D. 64 would of course, as has just been said, have entirely altered the whole aspect of the case.

The process of S. Paul introduces us to a side of the life and history of the church which is of the greatest importance but which is involved in the greatest difficulty, viz. its relation to secular law. For here we are brought definitely face to face with the problem of the relation of church and state, of ecclesiastical and secular courts. This problem is in the main the creation of Christianity itself. Previously there had been no distinction between civil and religious laws; all alike were laws of the state, and they had not yet been differentiated. We can see the beginnings of the divergence when S. Paul rebukes the Corinthians for going to law before unbelievers and bids them judge their causes among themselves[1]. The Lord himself, in Mt xviii 17, had recognized the independent judicial power of the church; and he also laid down the principle which should be the guide of the Christians in harmonizing the judicial action of the church with that of the state—*Render unto Caesar the things that are Caesar's and unto God the things that are God's*. The practical application of the principle, however, has always proved a difficulty; and the trials of S. Paul may serve as a commentary.

The process was a long one; but there were only three legal trials or examinations, viz. those (1) in the Sanhedrin, (2) before Felix, (3) before Festus, which last ended in the appeal to Caesar. (1) The Sanhedrin was the supreme court of the theocratic nation, and the

---

[1] I Cor vi 1–8.

apostle recognized its authority and was ready to plead before it; but it arrived at no conclusion. (2) The Jewish priests themselves indicted Paul in the procurator's court. The Jews were the 'ultramontanes' of that day in their theories as to the independence of the people of God in respect of the jurisdiction of the world, i.e. of the power of Rome; yet now, as before at Corinth, they appeal to the Roman judge. The accusation indeed concerned matters of fact and the infraction of religious privileges legally conceded to them; Paul, e.g., was accused of having caused pollution of the temple; and appeals to Rome in these matters were frequent. But the accusation also included the charge that S. Paul was a 'heretic,' viz. that he was acting 'contrary to the Jewish law'; and this must have involved a discussion of their law in the Roman courts which should have been most repugnant to them. (3) S. Paul himself recognized the Roman authority, and that as the supreme court of appeal: he appealed unto Caesar. But this was clearly a case of vindicating the liberty of the individual, and of securing for him protection against injustice. By appealing to Nero, S. Paul was not giving him the right to define the faith, 'the ministering either of God's word or of the sacraments[1].' But he did recognize the Caesar as a 'minister of God,' to whom the sword was committed for the maintenance of justice[2]. And as far as the things of this world are concerned, this power of the sword must be the final court of appeal for all causes, whether ecclesiastical or civil. For it has the control over all the externals of life and civil status, and over life itself; it can enforce obedience or at least punish disobedience; and on it depends all title to property or endowments. But with the things of this world, i.e. the things of Caesar, its jurisdiction ends. S. Paul appealed to Caesar for the decision—not of theological questions, such as whether Jesus was the Messiah, or whether there will be a resurrection of the dead,—but of facts and of conduct in relation to the administration of the state: had he broken the law? was his preaching contrary to 'the law' of the Jews, which had been recognized by the Roman government? was it subversive of order in the empire? And yet the decision of these points of law and fact would inevitably involve some theological discussion. It is impossible wholly to eliminate the religious element. Paul would certainly have to bear some witness to his gospel: and the Caesar would have to form in his own mind some idea as to the truth of Paul's preaching and give sentence accordingly[3]. The sentence might be unjust, but there was no higher court to appeal to, save that of God. The appellant, if his conscience forbade him to obey, must suffer and die, as S. Paul did in the end. That was the only vindication of his cause open to him on earth; its final vindication he must leave to the judgement-seat of Christ at the last day.

In reading S. Paul's defence we seem to have got upon different ground from that of the earlier chapters. Instead of arguing that Jesus is the Messiah, S. Paul makes his defence turn upon *the hope of Israel*

---

[1] Article xxxvii.   [2] Rom xiii 1-7, I Pet ii 13-7.   [3] Absolute impartiality—or indifference, as affected by Gallio (p. 351)—is impossible.

and *the resurrection of the dead*[1]. For in fact the circumstances have changed. To hold that Jesus was the Messiah is, in itself, a tolerated 'pious opinion' amongst the Jews—witness the myriads of believers left unmolested (xxi 20). The real crime of S. Paul was preaching to the Gentiles, and the real heresy his gospel of equality of privilege. Hence he defends himself by asserting (1) his loyalty to Israel, and (2) that his preaching was simple obedience to a divine command. This command depended upon the reality of his vision of the Lord at his conversion, and therefore upon the resurrection of Jesus. That resurrection was the primary subject of the apostolic preaching throughout the first part of the Acts: the peculiar function of an apostle was to give his personal testimony that he had seen Jesus risen from the dead, and thereby declared to be the Messiah. In S. Paul's defence the resurrection of Jesus is still the fundamental fact, but his horizon has expanded. (1) The resurrection of the Christ is intimately bound up with that of all the dead. Because Christ the firstfruits is risen, in him 'shall all men be made alive.' And so in arguing with the Jews he speaks of *the resurrection of the dead*. This doctrine was rejected by the Sadducees: but the Pharisees held it in some sense, and the apostle in making use of this common ground desires to shew them that their belief in the resurrection of the dead necessitates and rests upon that of the Christ. (2) In his belief in the resurrection he shews himself a true patriot. For the real *hope of Israel* is to be sought for, not in an earthly empire or inheritance, but in the resurrection of the dead and the world to come. (3) The resurrection of the dead is also a necessary preliminary to future judgement; and that is an elementary doctrine of religion, with which the apostles began their appeal to a Gentile audience[2]. Both to Jews and Gentiles, then, S. Paul's defence centred in the resurrection of the dead; and there was obviously no occasion for insistence on his specially characteristic doctrine of justification by faith, which nevertheless asserts itself in his last speech.

The question as to the genuineness of the speeches must be answered as before (Introd. pp. xliii–iv). It is obvious that they are summaries of speeches which must have taken much longer to deliver than the few minutes required by the written report. S. Luke, who may have been present on each occasion, probably took notes which he had subsequently to write out; one of the speeches indeed was in Aramaic and had to be translated. At the same time in each of the speeches there is a very close and natural correspondence with the circumstances of its delivery; and they bear strong marks of S. Paul's individuality. In many places no doubt they embody his actual words. This would be especially true of the accounts of his conversion, which agree very much in the actual words used: they probably give the story in the form in which S. Luke heard S. Paul tell it over and over again.

It remains to picture to ourselves the historical environment of the

---

[1] xxiii 6, xxiv 15, xxvi 6–8, xxviii 20. [2] xxiv 25, cp. x 42.

narrative. A preliminary question arises about S. Paul's external circumstances. At Ephesus and elsewhere he had laboured with his hands to support himself; now however the narrative gives the impression of his being a man of means. The Christians ask him to pay the expenses of the Nazirites; towards the Jewish aristocracy S. Paul acts as an equal: the Romans treat him with a courtesy not usually meted out to poor and insignificant prisoners. Felix expected a bribe from him. The appeal to Caesar must have been a very expensive affair; no more then than now could a poor man carry his case from court to court. The expense of the voyage and imprisonment was increased by the presence of Luke and Aristarchus. At Rome Paul lived for two years in a dwelling for which he had to pay rent. No doubt the Christians would gladly have contributed; but refusing as S. Paul did to make his gospel a burden to any church, it is most unlikely that he would have put them to the expense of an appeal in a case where his personal liberty rather than a principle of the gospel was at stake. The Philippians indeed sent a contribution to Rome, but S. Paul's letter of acknowledgment seems to imply that he had sufficient. Prof. Ramsay[1] has called attention to these points and suggests that as Paul came of a wealthy family, either they may have been reconciled to him by this time (and the action of his nephew at Jerusalem points to friendly relations) or S. Paul may have inherited property through the death of some relative. On the other hand it is precisely in the abovementioned Epistle to the Philippians, written subsequently to this time, that S. Paul declares he had 'suffered the loss of all things.' But there is a way out of the difficulty. We may imagine that S. Luke was fairly well off[2]; and having set before us in the Acts the community of goods as the ideal of church life, he would have been only too ready to place his purse, as well as his person, at the service of the apostle. Such a service of private affection S. Paul would have accepted.

The appeal to Caesar shews the vast strides Christianity has made. In thirty years it takes us from the Galilean company in the upper chamber to the imperial palace at Rome. From the highest court at Jerusalem its representative appeals to the highest tribunal in the empire—the judgement-seat of Caesar. The *Caesar* to whom S. Paul appealed—such is the irony of history—was Nero. Nero Claudius Caesar Drusus Germanicus was the son of Cnaeus Domitius Ahenobarbus and Agrippina; and when the latter became the wife of the emperor Claudius, her son passed with her into the imperial household. On the death of his step-father, October 13, A.D. 54, Nero succeeded him, when only 17 years old. The years covered by these chapters fall it is true in the first five years or 'golden quinquennium' of Nero's reign, when under the administration of the philosopher Seneca and Burrhus the praetorian prefect the empire enjoyed peace and prosperity. But

---

[1] *Paul the Traveller* pp. 310–3. [2] Failing S. Luke, some other member of the apostle's 'company' may have been a man of means: e.g. Aristarchus, who shared the voyage and captivity at Rome.

Nero's poisoning of his step-brother Britannicus within a year of his accession was an ominous sign of what was to come.

On the death of king Agrippa I in 44 Judaea had again been reduced to a Roman province. It was governed by a procurator, who, though subordinate to the legate of Syria, was appointed by the emperor and acted as his immediate representative. In 51 or 52 *Antonius Felix* had been appointed to this office. Felix and his brother Pallas were Greeks and had been slaves of Antonia, the mother of the emperor Claudius. Antonia gave them their freedom, and Pallas managed to acquire great influence over Claudius: he became his chief minister and amassed enormous wealth. Through Pallas' advancement a career was opened for his brother Felix; and we find him holding a military command in Samaria under the procurator Ventidius Cumanus. In this position he became involved in some desperate reprisals between Samaritans and Jews, in which the latter came into conflict with the Roman soldiers. After many executions and crucifixions the Jews appealed to Rome and through influence at court won their cause. Cumanus was banished; but the lucky (*felix*) brother of Pallas, instead of sharing his fall, stepped into his place. After this, by the aid of Simon, a Jewish magician of Cyprus, he succeeded in seducing the Jewess *Drusilla* (xxiv 24), sister of Agrippa II, away from her husband Azizus, king of Emesa, and by marrying her connected himself with royal blood.

Felix began well by suppressing the brigands who infested Judaea, but his rule was disastrous to the Jews. It is best described in the cutting epigram of Tacitus[1]: 'he revelled in cruelty and lust, and wielded the power of a king with the mind of a slave.' His conduct was such as to exasperate the Jews. For a long time they had been bearing the Roman yoke with ill-concealed impatience. The Samaritan incident was only one among many similar collisions, and the Roman measures of repression only intensified the national feeling. The nationalists consolidated themselves into a definite party known as the Zealots, and made the rejection of the Roman rule a matter of religious faith and duty. An epoch in this growth of feeling was marked by the assassination of the high-priest Jonathan in the temple in broad daylight. This was perpetrated at the instigation of Felix by the *Sicarii*, whom we find mentioned for the first time in Acts xxi 38. The Sicarii were the extreme partisans among the Zealots, who aimed at carrying out their policy by the assassination of their political opponents, mainly the rich and aristocratic Jews whose interests lay on the side of peace with the Romans (Jn xi 48). These murders were committed with the utmost effrontery; and the name of Sicarii came from the *sica* or dagger which the assassins carried in their girdles. Meanwhile the mass of the people were the prey of 'magi' and false prophets. Thus a 'prophet,' who came out of Egypt (xxi 38), had led an enormous crowd—of 30,000 men, according to Josephus[2]—to the summit of the

---

[1] *Hist.* v 9.   [2] *B. J.* II 13. 5, *Ant.* xx 8. 6.

Mount of Olives on the pretence that at his word the walls of Jerusalem would fall flat like those of Jericho. But instead of the walls falling down, a detachment of soldiers surprised the mob and slew some hundreds while the pretender made his escape. Such an incident shews the excitable and restless spirit of the whole nation. At the root of it lay a genuine, if fanatical, zeal for God; and from this the Jews drew the astonishing strength which they shewed in their struggle against the power of Rome. Now, if we realize the feelings of intense religious hatred for the Gentiles which then inspired the Jews, we can form a more adequate conception of their fury against an apostate Jew who taught the equality of the Gentile with Israel in the sight of God. Into such a whirlpool of religious passion S. Paul is now to be cast. And in his fortunes we shall trace—his relations to the church (xxi 15-26); to the Jews (xxi 27-xxiii); to the Roman procurators (xxiv-xxv); and lastly, to the public at large (xxvi), which completes the apostle's 'Defence' to the world.

SECTION II A (= Ch. 21. 15—26)

Paul and the church at Jerusalem

In verse 15 begins the actual going up of the pilgrims to the holy city[1]. Some years have elapsed since our last view of the church in Jerusalem which was at the time of the council of ch. xv[2]; and the present history seems a repetition of the same scenes on a smaller scale. We have a similar reception by the church (xv 4) and a renewal of the concordat between Jewish and Gentile Christians[3]. By this time all of the Twelve had left the city. S. Peter, last heard of at Antioch (p. 259), is possibly working his way along the northern road in Asia Minor through Cappadocia, North Galatia, Pontus, and Bithynia,—a road which will lead him also to Rome[4]. In place of the Twelve we find *James*, the Lord's brother, *and the presbyters*—an early and unmistakeable exemplar of the later 'bishop' and his clergy. The church at Jerusalem has grown in numbers. The 5000 of iv 4 have become several *myriads*. In this number S. James may be reckoning the Christians *among the Jews* in all countries, i.e. the distinctively Hebrew Christians (vi 1), great numbers of whom would be coming up for the feast, like S. Paul himself. Otherwise it would be an instance of hyperbole or exaggeration, which marks other passages in these chapters[5]. In its doctrine the Jewish church had made no advance.

---

[1] Cp. Lk xviii 31, xix 28. [2] The mention of the church in xviii 22 is so brief that it may be left out of account. [3] Even the language recalls ch. xv: cp. *which have believed* (perfect tense xv 5), *brother* (xv 7), *rehearse what God had wrought* (xv 12, 4), *judge, wrote, Moses* (xv 19-21). [4] If indeed he is not there already (p. 362). [5] Cp. xxv 24, xxvi 10, 11, 20. *Myriads* may be simply the expression for a great multitude (Lk xii 1). The Bezan text limits the numbers to Judaea.

From the first, the Hebrew Christians, as Jews, had continued to frequent the temple and *keep the law*. Such observance was almost second nature, and, we might say, unconscious. But the preaching of S. Paul had made it conscious. The question of the observance of the law by the Gentiles had been discussed, and a relaxation allowed to them, at the council of Jerusalem (verse 25). But the Hebrew Christians continued to keep the law, and it was becoming more and more a matter of principle with them; *all* of these *myriads* were *zealous for the law*[1]. This zeal won for them toleration, if not sympathy, among the Jews. We hear no more of persecution. On the contrary, S. James enjoyed a great reputation among all the people for the austerity of his life. Acceptance of Jesus as the Messiah, as long as it caused no radical interference with the Judaic *customs* of life, was merely regarded as a foolish eccentricity. Further, this general zeal on the part of the Hebrew Christians was specially intensified in that party of Judaizers which had arisen in the church and whose animating spirit, as we have seen (p. 258), was that of violent antagonism to S. Paul. Although S. Luke makes no direct mention of them at this crisis, there is plain evidence of their work in a systematic misrepresentation of S. Paul According to the reports sent home by their emissaries from the Galatian and other churches, the Christians of Jerusalem had been *instructed*[2] that S. Paul was deliberately *teaching apostasy from Moses*, viz.—what was in fact untrue—that he was teaching the Jewish Christians of the Dispersion *not to circumcise their children or* observe *the customs* of the law. Other rumours must have come to Jerusalem concerning the positive teaching of the apostle. It was only a few months, or rather weeks, since he had published his Epistle to the Romans, and a copy of it had probably reached the mother church. In any case, S. Paul's doctrine of justification by faith had become notorious; it was a doctrine very easy to be misunderstood, and—as the Epistle itself shews (iii 8)—it had already been misinterpreted. In some circles S. Paul was painted as a preacher of apostasy, not merely from the law of Moses, but from the moral law itself; and S. James felt bound to notice the doctrine and write against antinomian ideas of faith[3]. We cannot, however, suppose that the whole church of Jerusalem shared these prejudices against S. Paul. S. James was president of the church; and there must have still been in it descendants of the school of Stephen and Philip, such as Mnason for instance,—not to speak of Agabus. But there was sufficient ground to justify S. Paul's apprehensions as to the manner in which 'the saints' would receive the offerings of the Gentiles (Rom xv 31).

15 'And after these days we [4]took up our baggage, and went

---

[1] as the Jews were *zealous for God* (xxii 3).   [2] The word is that used in Lk i 4 and early Christian phraseology for *instruction* in the faith.   [3] Jas ii 14–26. His epistle must have been written in this decade, as he was martyred in 61 or 62.   [4] Bezan reads *And after certain days we took our leave [and went up ...Caesarea] and these brought us to those with whom we should lodge. And we came to a certain village and were (lodged) with [Mnason of Cyprus an early disciple], and departing thence we came [to Jerusalem.*   [5] Marg *made ready.*

16 up to Jerusalem. And there went with us also *certain* of the disciples from Cæsarea, bringing *with them* one Mnason of Cyprus, an early disciple, with whom we should lodge.

17 And when we were come to Jerusalem, the brethren
18 received us gladly. And the day following Paul went in
19 with us unto James; and all the [1] elders were present. And when he had saluted them, he rehearsed one by one the things which God had wrought among the Gentiles by his
20 ministry. And they, when they heard it, glorified God; and they said unto him, Thou seest, brother, how many [2] thousands there are [3] among the Jews of them which have believed;
21 and they are all zealous for the law: and they have been [4] informed concerning thee, that thou teachest all the Jews which are among the Gentiles [5] to forsake Moses, telling them not to circumcise their children, neither to walk after the
22 customs. What is it therefore? [6] they will certainly hear
23 that thou art come. Do therefore this that we say to thee:
24 We have four men which have a vow on them; these take, and purify thyself with them, and be at charges for them, that they may shave their heads: and all shall know that [7] there is no truth in the things whereof they have been [4] informed concerning thee; but that thou thyself also walkest
25 orderly, keeping the law. But as touching the Gentiles which have believed,[8] we [9] wrote, giving judgement that [10] they should keep themselves from things sacrificed to idols, and from blood, [10] and from what is strangled, and from fornication.
26 Then Paul took the men, and the next day purifying himself with them went into the temple, declaring the fulfilment of the days of purification, [11] until the offering was offered for every one of them.

15 *After these days* of the journey and preparation[12], on the

---

[1] Gk *presbyters*.   [2] Gk *myriads*, i.e. *tens of thousands*.   [3] Bezan *in Judaea*, AV *of Jews which believe*.   [4] or *instructed*, Gk *catechized* (so verse 24).   [5] Gk *apostasy from Moses*.   [6] Bezan and AV insert *the multitude must needs come together, for* [*they will hear*.   [7] more literally, as AV, *those things whereof they were informed concerning thee, are nothing*.   [8] Bezan inserts *they have nothing to say against thee for* [*we wrote*.   [9] Marg *enjoined* (xv 20): BD read *sent* (xv 27).   [10] Bezan and AV insert *they observe no such thing save only that* [*they keep*. Bezan omits *and from what is strangled* as in xv 20, 29.   [11] Bezan reads *in order that the offering might be* [*offered*.   [12] They were actually at Caesarea about a week; but *after these days* marks a fresh start in the narrative.

Wednesday or Thursday before Pentecost, Paul and his company of Greek delegates *packed up their baggage* and laded their beasts[1]—they were a large party and carrying treasure—and started *for Jerusalem*. There would be large crowds of other pilgrims
16 from the west journeying along the same road; and *some of the* Christian *disciples of Caesarea went with* S. Paul's company. These would also find hospitality for them on the way. The Greek construction in verse 16 is rather compressed, so that it is possible to translate either *bringing with them Mnason* or *bringing us to Mnason*. The difficulty is cleared up by the Bezan text. The distance to Jerusalem was between 60 and 70 miles, more than one day's journey[2]: accordingly they spent a night *at a certain village* where Mnason lived, and were lodged by him. Mnason was one of the *original*[3] disciples, i.e. probably one of the 120 of ch. i 15 upon whom the Holy Ghost descended at the first Pentecost. He was *of Cyprus*, which suggests some connexion with S. Paul; he may have been a friend of S. Barnabas (iv 36), or one of the forerunners of the Pauline gospel, the earliest preachers to the
17 Greeks, of xi 20. Next day they entered *Jerusalem* and S. Paul's apprehensions were in part relieved, for the various hosts, to whom they were conducted by the Caesarean brethren, gave them a *glad welcome*, and behaved like *brothers*[4].

The feast of Pentecost was kept on the morrow after the Sabbath, that is, on Sunday. The Christian Jews would probably attend the festival sacrifices in the temple; their own special celebration of the feast would consist in the breaking of bread at home. On the first day of the week, then,—i.e. after sunset on Saturday evening,—they gathered together in their various 'upper chambers' for their celebration of the Agape, which would close with the Holy Eucharist. The reading of scripture, preaching, and singing of psalms, probably lasted throughout the night; and after partaking of the Eucharist in the hours of dawn, the congregation would proceed to the temple for the Jewish sacrifices[5]. As the day before Pentecost was a Sabbath, S. Paul's party must have arrived at Jerusalem on the Friday[6]—
18 an earlier day is excluded by xxiv 11. On *the next day*, viz. the Sabbath, took place their official reception by the church. S. James had no doubt heard of his proposed visit and had consulted his presbyters, for there was ground for apprehension on their side as well as S. Paul's. And now that the apostle had come, *James*, in

---

[1] *Carriage* in the AV means what one carries, i.e. baggage. The Greek verb in the active voice is used for the *lading* of horses, etc.: so the middle voice here may denote their *procuring for themselves* beasts of burden (cp. xxiii 24). A more common meaning is that of *repairing* or *restoring* ruined buildings, etc.: so in the OT it is used of the restoration of the temple. Perhaps here it has a metaphorical meaning —*when we had restored* or *refreshed ourselves*. [2] Cp. xxiii 31-3. [3] lit. disciples *of the beginning*: cp. xi 15. [4] The sentence concludes with this emphatic word. [5] In Silvia's time (see p. 379) Pentecost was preceded by a vigil which began at the first cockcrow. [6] S. Paul would not, without cause, have broken the Jewish limit of the 'sabbath day's journey' (i 12).

order to receive him, summoned the whole body of his *presbyters*, and S. Paul *came in*[1], accompanied by the delegates, who brought the alms of the Gentile churches (p. 374).

19 They *saluted* one another with the brotherly kiss; the delegates delivered up the alms of the Gentile churches[2]; and then S. Paul gave a detailed account of what *God had wrought by his ministry among the Gentiles*[3]. This the presbyters accepted as the divine
20 confirmation of his office, and they *glorified* God. Paul himself they received as a *brother*, and they ratified again the concessions made to the Gentile believers. At the same time they put before him the danger of the situation, arising from the prejudices which had been instilled into the minds of *the believing Jews*. Because of this danger S. James had summoned to the reception not the whole church, as in xv 4,
22 but only the presbyters. But the meetings of the church cannot be deferred or prevented, and the news of Paul's arrival will bring together, as we should say, a crowded congregation[4]. The safest course would be for S. Paul, having delivered the alms, simply to attend the festival service and then leave the city as he had done on his last visit (xviii 24). But S. Paul had come for the very purpose of disarming prejudices and cementing the unity between both sides
23 of the church (Eph ii 14). Accordingly S. James put forward a proposal, which had been suggested by the presbyters. Deeds are
24 the best refutation of slanders, and the sight of S. Paul performing some ritual act would be the most convincing proof that he did not teach *apostasy from Moses* but himself *walked orderly*. This, as we have seen (p. 332), was quite true. When principle was not at stake S. Paul lived normally as a Jew, *keeping the law*; and if as a rule 'to the Jews he became as a Jew,' how much more readily would he do so at Jerusalem! Indeed the proposal itself was probably suggested by his own conduct. For on his last visit to Jerusalem he had fulfilled the vow of a Nazirite (xviii 18, p. 333): and as he speaks of himself (in xxiv 17) as having come 'to make offerings,' it is not unlikely that he was bound on this occasion also under some vow of thanksgiving[5].

To take the vow of a Nazirite was a very popular form of devotion among the Jews, but it was an expensive one. When the Nazirite came to fulfil the vow by shaving his head and burning the hair at the door of the temple (p. 333), he had to offer two lambs and a ram, a loaf and cakes, with meal and drink offerings. Hence it frequently happened that poor men from lack of means were unable to *shave their heads* and free themselves from their vow; and it was a work of piety for rich Jews to pay the expenses of their poorer brethren. Thus when king Agrippa I came to Jerusalem in 41 to give thanks

---

[1] The uncommon form of this verb in the Greek marks the solemnity of the occasion: so verse 26. [2] xxiv 17. S. Luke does not mention the fact here— a silent sign of his modesty, for he was himself one of the bearers. [3] So xv 12, and Rom xv 18-9. [4] Cp. ii 6, v 16. [5] Dr Hort makes a similar suggestion in *Judaistic Christianity* pp. 109-10.

for his accession, he commanded very many of the Nazirites to shave themselves,—that is to say, he paid for their sacrifices¹. Now among the Christians there were *four* Nazirites in this predicament, and the Christian community was a poor one : so the presbyters advised Paul to *pay their expenses*. Our knowledge of the ritual which this procedure involved is very imperfect. But it is very natural to suppose that such a benefactor of poor Nazirites would have to identify himself with them, by taking the vow in some sense, in order that his sacrifices might avail for them. This at least 26 seems to have been the case on the present occasion. For *Paul took the men*, and *the next day* associated himself *with them* by *purifying himself*, viz. by placing himself under the vow². Then he *entered* with them *into the temple*, in order to offer the offerings for them ; and the act of offering was in itself a public notification to the Jews that these men (S. Paul included) had been under the vow of a Nazirite *the days of* which vow were now completed³. It is not necessary to assume that the vows of all the four Nazirites expired on the same day; S. Paul apparently had to go through the ceremony more than once. And, until the last vow had been fulfilled, i.e. *until the offering had been offered for each one of them*, S. Paul would not have been released from his vow (xxiv 18). It seems very likely that he *went into the temple* four days—one day for each one of them⁴. In any case the offering for the last one fell on a day which completed a week since his arrival in Jerusalem⁵; and on that day a fatal incident happened. If, as we have seen, the Christians were prejudiced against S. Paul, what must have been the feelings of the Jews? There can have been no redeeming features in the reports sent home by the Jews who had fought with him at Corinth and Ephesus ; and there was no tie of a common faith in the Christ or fellowship in the Holy Ghost to counteract the passions of party spirit. And now, on the seventh day, the last of *the seven days*,—that fatal week,—the Jews discover the 'apostate' in the temple.

---

¹ Jos. *Ant.* xix 6. 1. Cp. *B. J.* ii 15. 1. For the rites see Num vi 13-20.
² This is the technical meaning of *purifying*; as *purified* in xxiv 18 denotes the condition of one under a vow.   ³ It would be natural to interpret *declaring* as *giving notice* to the priests; but there seems to be a reference to verse 24. S. Paul's action was meant to be a public declaration of his loyalty to the national customs. See also the next note.   ⁴ This passage is a difficult one, and the above is only one possible interpretation. If S. Paul had come up to Jerusalem himself under a vow, or with the intention of making a special thank-offering (xxiv 17), the course of events would be much easier to understand. The language reminds us of Lk ii 22 (*when the days of their purification were fulfilled*); and we cannot help feeling that S. Luke has that presentation or dedication of the child Jesus in his mind, and that he regards this offering as, in some sense, a solemn dedication by S. Paul of the Gentile churches in the temple. Certainly this idea of himself, as a priest offering up the Gentiles in sacrifice to God, was in S. Paul's mind at this time (Rom xv 16).   ⁵ If we compare the *seven days* at Troas and Tyre (xx 6, xxi 4) and the *twelve days* of xxiv 11, which =7+5 (xxiv 1), this seems to be the natural meaning of '*the*' *seven days* here (verse 27). If we pressed the grammar, they would refer to *the days of purification* of verse 26 ; but why these should have been seven in number we do not know.

SECTION II B (= Ch. 21. 27—23)

Paul and the Jews at Jerusalem

§ 1 *The riot in the temple and Paul's arrest*

The subject of this section is the treatment of the apostle by the people of the Jews. They reject him, and cause him to make his first appeal to Rome, viz. to his Roman citizenship. But their rejection of Paul, like their choice of Barabbas (iii 14), was their own condemnation. We have witnessed popular tumults at Philippi and Thessalonica, and one on a greater scale at Ephesus: but the riot at Jerusalem exceeds them all. The chosen people of God exhibit themselves as a maddened crowd, thirsting for blood in the very temple of their God, in 'the house of prayer.'

So we return to the Temple. This has been already described (pp. 46-7), but it may be well to recall the chief features connected with the riot. *The temple* in verses 27, 28, etc., is not the building or house; it stands for the whole of the inner court which lay within the great outer enclosure called the Court of the Gentiles. This outer court was open to all comers, and was the scene of the attempted murder of the apostle (vv. 31-4). From this the inner court, the Court of Israel, was separated by 'the middle wall of partition[1].' There was first a barrier, upon which pillars stood at intervals with inscriptions in Greek and Latin, forbidding any stranger to pass within on pain of death[2], for within the ground was 'holy': S. Paul was supposed to have *polluted the temple*, i.e. made it *common* ground, by having introduced Trophimus within this barrier (verse 29, xxiv 6). Inside the barrier was a high wall, which surrounded the inner court; and it was *the doors* in this wall which *were straightway shut* (verse 30). The western part of the court was occupied by the Temple proper, or the House; the eastern part formed the Court of the Women. A colonnade ran round the Court of the Women, and in its angles were chambers. That at the south-east corner was the House of the Nazirites, where the Nazirites boiled their peace offerings, shaved their heads, and burnt the hair: and it must have been here that the Ephesian Jews discovered Paul with his vow upon him (verse 27, xxiv 18).

The outer Court of the Gentiles was also surrounded by colonnades, which formed great cloisters with spacious roofs. At the north-west corner these cloisters communicated by a flight of *stairs* with *the Castle*, i.e. the fortress of Antonia. This fortress was built upon a crag of rock which had been made still more precipitous by artificial means, and

---

[1] Eph ii 14.   [2] The inscription on the pillar discovered by M. Clermont Ganneau runs thus: *No alien to pass within the fence and enclosure round the temple. Whosoever shall be taken shall be responsible to himself alone for the death which will ensue.* This illustrates the tact which the Romans shewed in their concessions to local customs; and it confirms the accuracy of the Acts and Josephus (cp. B. J. v 5. 2, Ant. xv 11. 5).

thus commanded the temple, and through the temple the city. The Asmonaean princes had first fortified it; Herod the Great rebuilt it and made it a palace as well as a fortress, giving it, after his patron Antony, the name of Antonia. It was now the head-quarters of the Roman garrison or *cohort*. The procurator, when at Jerusalem, resided in Herod's palace at the west end of the city: in his absence, his place was taken by the commandant of the garrison, who was *the tribune of the cohort*. A Roman legion was nominally divided into six cohorts of 1000 men each, and each cohort was commanded by a tribune,—in the Greek, *chiliarch* (captain of a thousand): a cohort was composed of ten centuries, each under a centurion. The tribune at this moment was *Claudius Lysias*. His Greek name *Lysias* tells us that he was not a Roman by birth, while his adopted Latin name *Claudius* shews that he had received—really, as he tells us himself, purchased—the citizenship from (or in the reign of) Claudius.

Within the temple order was maintained by the Jews themselves. There was a guard of Levites under the *Captain of the temple*. His office was one of high rank: at this moment it was filled by Ananus, son of the high-priest Ananias. But at the time of great festivals, such as Passover or Pentecost, when the courts were thronged by thousands of pilgrims, Roman soldiers came down from Antonia and kept watch on the roofs of the northern and western cloisters. For popular disturbances were of frequent occurrence, and their usual result was the shedding of blood. Pilate had mingled the blood of Galileans with their sacrifices[1]. And only a few years before this, when Cumanus was procurator, an insult offered by one of the soldiers had roused the Jews to such fury that they pelted the guard with stones, and Cumanus had to march his full force down into the temple courts: at the sight of the troops a panic seized the multitude and they fled, and in the flight 20,000 (according to Josephus[2]) were trodden under foot. Such incidents enable us to form a better idea of the present outbreak.

This scene, in its turn, serves to illustrate the 'stirring' of the city of Jerusalem on the final entry of the Lord on Palm Sunday (Mt xxi 10), the powerlessness of the Jewish authorities to molest him when the crowd was on his side, and also the behaviour of the multitude when they turned against him. The language especially recalls the scene in Lk xxiii 13-25, when the people cried *Away with this man*, and Pilate *spake unto them* and the people *shouted against him*[3]. We should also compare the tumultuous stoning of Stephen in vii 57-60. In the OT we read of two tragedies enacted in the temple. In one the blood of Zachariah was shed 'in the court of the Lord's house' (II Chron xxiv 21); in the other Athaliah was led out of the court and slain in the entry (II Kings xi 4-16).

27 And when the seven days were almost completed, the

---

[1] Lk xiii 1. [2] *Ant.* xx 5. 3. [3] Lk xxiii 20, 21: the same Greek words recur in Acts xxi 40, xxii 2 and xxi 34, xxii 24 respectively.

Jews from Asia, when they saw him in the temple, ¹stirred
up all the ²multitude, and laid hands on him, crying out,
28 Men of Israel, help: This is the man, that teacheth all men
everywhere against the people, and the law, and this place:
and moreover he brought Greeks also into the temple, and
29 hath ³defiled this holy place. For they had before seen with
him in the city Trophimus the Ephesian, whom they supposed
30 that Paul had brought into the temple. And all the city was
moved, and the people ran together: and they laid hold on
Paul, and dragged him out of the temple: and straightway
31 the doors were shut. And as they were seeking to kill him,
tidings came up to the ⁴chief captain of the ⁵band, that all
32 Jerusalem was in confusion⁶. And forthwith he took soldiers
and centurions, and ran down upon them: and they, when
they saw the chief captain and the soldiers, left off beating
33 Paul. Then the chief captain came near, and laid hold on
him, and commanded him to be bound with two chains; and
34 inquired who he was, and what he had done. And some
shouted one thing, some another, among the crowd: and
when he could not know the certainty for the uproar, he
35 commanded him to be brought into the castle. And when
he came upon the stairs, so it was, that he was borne of the
36 soldiers for the violence of the crowd; for the multitude of
the people followed after, crying out, ⁷Away with him.
37 And as Paul was about to be brought into the castle, he
saith unto the chief captain, May I say something unto thee?
38 And he said, Dost thou know Greek? Art thou not then the
Egyptian, which before these days stirred up to sedition and
led out into the wilderness the four thousand men of the
39 ⁸Assassins? But Paul said, ⁹I am a Jew, of Tarsus in Cilicia,
a citizen of no mean city: and I beseech thee, give me leave
40 to speak unto the people. And when he had given him
leave, Paul, standing on the stairs, beckoned with the hand

---

¹ or *confounded*: so verse 31 *is confounded*. ² i.e. *crowd*, as in vv. 34, 35.
³ literally *made common* (x 15). ⁴ Marg *military tribune*, Gk *chiliarch*.
⁵ Gk *cohort*. ⁶ Bezan adds *See* (or *Take heed*) *therefore that they make not
insurrection*. ⁷ Bezan reads *that he* (or *our enemy*) *be put to death*.
⁸ Gk *Sicarii*. ⁹ literally *I am a man a Jew*, or *as a man I am a Jew*; cp. AV
I am a man which am a Jew: Bezan continues *but born in Tarsus of Cilicia*.

unto the people; and when there was made a great silence, he spake unto them in the Hebrew language, saying,

22 Brethren and fathers, hear ye the defence which I now make unto you.

2 And when they heard that he spake unto them in the Hebrew language, they were the more quiet.

27 Notorious as the name of Paul was among the Jews, he was probably known by sight to but a few at Jerusalem. It was more than twenty years since he had lived there among the aristocracy. Since then his visits had been few and brief, and he might well have escaped notice this time also. But he was known only too well to *the Jews* of Ephesus, and some of the pilgrims *from Asia had seen him* in the streets with *Trophimus* their fellow-citizen. This however gave them no handle and they bided their time. *And now when the seven days*—the week which would have sufficed for his stay at Jerusalem[1]—were drawing to a close, on the seventh day, they *caught sight of him in the temple*. He was making the offerings for the fourth and last Nazirite. The Ephesians however at once assumed that his Greeks were with him, and they had got their opportunity— *he had defiled* the temple. Straightway they *seized hold of him* and
28 shouted for *help*. They appealed to the bystanders by the name which would stir their religious patriotism—*Men of Israel*[2], and the charge was one well calculated to arouse their fanaticism: '*this man is the teacher* of treason *against the people, the law, and this holy place,*' the temple[3]. The news that the temple had been *polluted* (AV) by the presence of *Greeks* within *the holy place* at once *stirred*
30 *into motion the whole city*. The expression is hardly an exaggeration: an eastern city, even a Hellenic city like Ephesus, was liable to be convulsed by a sudden commotion of the people, which would shake it like an earthquake[4]. *The people ran together*, as when Peter healed the lame man (iii 11), but with very different feelings. What exactly had happened, or who the guilty person was, they knew not[5]; but no punishment was too great for the man who had defiled the temple. To avoid further pollution they *dragged him out of the* holy place, the inner court, and the Levite guards *at*
31 *once shut the doors*. Stoning was the penalty for an act of blasphemy; but the mob was too impatient to 'cast him out of the city' and so stone him (vii 58): they *sought to kill him* then and there by blows and *beating*—so perhaps they thought to avoid the pollution of the temple precincts by the actual shedding of blood. Paul

---

[1] as at Troas and Tyre (xx 6, xxi 4), and at Puteoli (xxviii 14). Cp. ii 1, Lk ix 51.
[2] ii 22, iii 12, xiii 16. [3] This was the charge which had aroused the popular enmity against Stephen (vi 11–4), and Saul the Pharisee was consenting to it: now the retribution has come. [4] Mt xxi 10. Cp. verse 31 and xix 29. [5] Cp. xix 32.

32 however was saved just in time. The mob found themselves surprised by a strong force of soldiers, and *they left off beating Paul*. The Roman guard had been keeping watch on the cloister roof, and news of the gravity of the disturbance had brought down from
33 Antonia *the commandant* Lysias in person. Paul was given up to him, and promptly *chained* by each arm to a soldier[1]. Lysias thought he was lucky enough to have got hold of *the Egyptian*
34 impostor, whose escapade has been described above[2]. The noise and confusion *of the tumult*, however, prevented his ascertaining *who* the prisoner *might be, and what he had done*; and so *he commanded him*
35 *to be taken* up to Antonia. *But when they had come to the* first flight of *stairs*, leading up to the roof of the cloisters, the mob, realizing that their prey was being snatched from them, with wild cries for his murder, flung themselves *violently* on the soldiers like a great wave of the sea[3]; and Paul had to be hoisted up out of their reach over *the soldiers'* heads. This mode of conveyance was as undignified for an eastern as being let down from the wall in a basket[4]; and the sight of his master thus *carried* away made a deep impression on the eye of S. Luke.
37 Thus was S. Paul at last 'delivered into the hands of the Gentiles' and into 'the bondage' which will last for five years[5] But he would make one attempt to conciliate his countrymen. When the soldiers had reached the second flight of stairs, leading from the cloisters up to Antonia, and *he was on the point of being carried into the fortress*, having recovered himself somewhat, he spoke to the commandant. Hearing him speak *in Greek*, Lysias
38 was disappointed to find that he had not got *the Egyptian* after all, and his exclamation roused in S. Paul the sense of human dignity. The apostle had not wholly lost the patriotic pride of the Greek citizen nor the human satisfaction in good birth. By descent[6]
39 he was *of the Jewish race*, by birth *a Tarsian* of the province of *Cilicia*, and so politically *a citizen of no mean* (or *undistinguished*) *city*. For the present, however, this was of no consequence; what he wanted was *leave to speak to the people*[7]. S. Paul's spirit was indeed unquenchable, his courage invincible. At Ephesus he had 'fought with wild beasts,' and was ready to face the raging Dēmos: and now, although he had just been beaten almost to death, he

---

[1] like S. Peter (xii 6): for the *chains* cp. xxviii 20, Eph vi 20, II Tim i 16.
[2] pp. 409-10. S. Luke does not mention the march to Olivet, nor Josephus the *4000 Sicarii* of verse 38. But in Josephus *leading into the wilderness* was evidently a preparatory step to the march to Olivet; and the *4000 Sicarii* were probably the nucleus of the multitude of 30,000 who, according to Josephus, gathered round the false prophet in his march. [3] Cp. *the violence* of the waves in xxvii 41.
[4] II Cor xi 33. [5] i.e. from the spring of 55 to the spring of 60. Cp. xx 23, xxi 11; xxvi 29, Eph iii 1, iv 1, Phil i 13, Col iv 3, 18, Philem 1. [6] In verse 38 the Greek word for *man* is that which denotes man simply as a human being: in xxii 3 a more honourable term is used, denoting man as a member of society etc. (but S. Paul himself spoke in Aramaic). [7] This may represent the apparent contrast in the Greek particles μὲν and δέ: the Bezan text makes the contrast lie between the Jewish race and the city of Tarsus.

wants to speak to the fanatical mob which is still yelling for his execution. The reason was that his heart yearned for them
40 as for his brothers¹. *Leave being granted*, he chose a spot *on the stairs* which commanded the temple court, and *beckoned* for *silence*.
22 When it was obtained, he made an effort² and began *his present defence* (or *apology*). His first words reveal his ready tact. In spite of his recent treatment he addresses the crowd as his *brethren and fathers*; and also, as was indeed natural, he spoke to them *in*
2 *the* national *Hebrew*, i.e. Aramaic, *tongue*. This made a favourable impression, and a yet greater *stillness* prevailed.

§ 2 *S. Paul's defence to the people of the Jews*

S. Luke was no doubt among the audience, and understood enough Aramaic to follow. Certainly the speech, as it stands, is most true to life, exactly to the point, and full of S. Paul's tact. It corresponds to S. Peter's great sermon in the temple at the first Pentecost, but differs in being autobiographical. It is all about Paul himself; his personality is the hinge of the controversy, and the speech is characteristically marked by an emphatic *I* at the beginning of each division (verses 3, 6 and 17). As a defence it is perfectly clear. S. Paul's history was unknown to the mass of the Jews, and so he begins by giving an account of himself. 1. The charge he had to answer was that of 'teaching against the people, the law, and the temple'; but it could be expressed under a single head. He had taught the equality of the Gentile with the Jew in the kingdom of God. The crying scandal was that this doctrine should have been taught by a Jew. Paul was an apostate, a renegade. S. Paul's answer is to shew that he was a Jew and a thorough Jew. If we, as well as his hearers, could be convinced of this, we should obtain a much more vivid grasp of the following history. In our minds, Paul the Christian apostle is separated by a wide gulf from his countrymen: but he remained a Jew at heart, and to the Jews he pleads the intensity of his patriotism. II. If he was then in heart an intense Jew, how could he have been guilty of such 'apostasy'? There must have been some adequate cause, and there was. 'The word of the LORD' had come to him. He had been acting in obedience to a divine command. III. This command came through Jesus of Nazareth; and the validity of his mission and his preaching, of his life's work and his own change of heart, all depended on the vision he saw on the way to Damascus. To narrate that vision—that was his simple defence.

And he saith,
3   I am ³a Jew, born in Tarsus of Cilicia, but brought up in this city, at the feet of Gamaliel, instructed according to the strict manner of the law of our fathers, being zealous for God,

---

¹ Rom ix 1-3, x 1.   ² It required an effort of the voice, he *called to them* (Lk xxiii 20).   ³ AV *I am verily a man which am a Jew.*

S

4 even as ye all are this day: and I persecuted this Way unto the death, binding and delivering into prisons both men and
5 women. As also the high priest doth bear me witness, and all ¹the estate of the elders: from whom also I received letters unto the brethren, and journeyed to Damascus, to bring them also which were there unto Jerusalem in bonds, for to be punished.
6 And it came to pass, that, as I made my journey, and drew nigh unto Damascus, about noon, suddenly there shone
7 from heaven a great light round about me. And I fell unto the ground, and heard a voice saying unto me, Saul, Saul,
8 why persecutest thou me? And I answered, Who art thou, Lord? And he said unto me, I am Jesus of Nazareth, whom
9 thou persecutest. And they that were with me beheld indeed the light², but they heard not the voice of him that
10 spake to me. And I said, What shall I do, Lord? And the Lord said unto me, Arise, and go into Damascus; and there it shall be told thee of all things which are appointed for
11 thee to do. And when I could not see for the glory of that light, being led by the hand of them that were with me,
12 I came into Damascus. And one Ananias, a devout man according to the law, well reported of by all the Jews that
13 dwelt there, came unto me, and standing by me said unto me, Brother Saul, receive thy sight. And in that very hour I
14 ³looked up on him. And he said, The God of our fathers hath appointed thee to know his will, and to see the Righteous
15 One, and to hear a voice from his mouth. For thou shalt be a witness for him unto all men of what thou hast seen and
16 heard. And now why tarriest thou? arise, and be baptized, and wash away thy sins, calling on his name.
17 And it came to pass, that, when I had returned to Jerusalem, and while I prayed in the temple, ⁴I fell into a
18 trance, and saw him saying unto me, Make haste, and get thee quickly out of Jerusalem: because they will not receive
19 of thee testimony concerning me. And I said, Lord, they

---

¹ Gk *the presbytery*.   ² AV and Bezan add *and were afraid*.   ³ Marg *received my sight* and looked *upon him*: the Greek words translated *receive-sight* and *look-up* are from the same verb.   ⁴ lit. *I became in an ecstasy.*

themselves know that I imprisoned and beat in every
20 synagogue them that believed on thee: and when the blood
of Stephen thy ¹witness was shed, I also was standing by
and consenting, and keeping the garments of them that slew
21 him. And he said unto me, Depart: for I will send thee
forth far hence unto the Gentiles.

3   I. As in ch. xxvi 4-5, Gal i 14, II Cor xi 22, Phil iii 4-7, S. Paul recounts his Jewish 'advantages' to prove that he was *a true Jew*. Though (1) *born* outside the holy land, yet (2) he had been *educated* at the centre of their national religion, Jerusalem, and in the school of the eminent Pharisee *Gamaliel*, 'a doctor of the law, had in honour of all the people².' (3) In this school he had been *trained*³ in the principles of the most *punctilious* and scrupulous observance of *the law* and the traditions,—i.e. in the principles of the Pharisees, in 'the strictest sect of their religion⁴'; and he was a ready pupil. (4) Naturally of a *zealous* temperament, he was filled with zeal *for God, even as ye all are this day*. S. Paul's courtesy and magnanimity are unsurpassable. The fanatical frenzy which had a moment ago been seeking to kill him, he acknowledges as a zeal for God. This jealousy for God S. Paul always grants to the Jews; but unfortunately it had manifested itself too much in zeal for the traditions *of the fathers*⁵. Here again in speaking of *the fathers' law*⁶ he identifies himself with his hearers, claiming their fathers for his own and thereby vindicating the continuity of his doctrine. (5) The reality of his zeal he had proved in deed. Like his hearers
4 at this moment, he too had *persecuted* the first depreciators of the law, Stephen and the Nazarenes. He calls them by the Jewish term of *the way* (p. 76), and so avoids any irritating party names.
5 For *testimony* to his persecuting, even *unto death*, he appeals to *the high priest and the Sanhedrin*. Possibly members of the high-priestly party were present in the crowd, as in that which had chosen Barabbas and cried out 'Crucify him.' But there would not be many survivors of the Sanhedrin of 23 years ago; Caiaphas the high priest was probably dead; and S. Paul is really appealing to their records.

    II. The sincerity of his persecuting zeal was demonstrated by his pursuit of the Nazarenes even outside the holy land—a typical foreshadowing of his future relation to Judaism. But on the way
6 occurred the crisis of his life. It came in a vision: and the reality of visions the Pharisees at least would not gainsay. The circumstances have already been described at length (ix 3-7, pp. 130-1) and we

---

¹ Gk *martyr*.   ² v 34. The teacher sat on an elevated seat and his disciples on the ground *at his feet*: hence the metaphorical use of the phrase in iv 35, 37, v 2.
³ So Moses *was trained* in all the wisdom of Egypt (vii 22).   ⁴ xxvi 5.
⁵ Rom x 2: Gal i 14.   ⁶ Cp. verse 14, xxviii 17, II Tim i 3 *from my forefathers*. S. Peter and S. Stephen made the same claim (iii 13, v 30: vii 32).

need only note the special points brought out by the present occasion. (1) The brilliance of *the flood of light*, which *flashed around* him at high *noon*, outshining the sun[1], shewed that it was supernatural. It was in fact the light of the divine *glory*[2], and testified to a real divine epiphany. (2) The addition *of Nazareth* identifies the speaker with the *Jesus* whom the Jews called in contempt 'the Nazarene.' (3) The Jewish character of *Ananias* is made very clear: he was *pious*[3], shewing his piety in a blameless observance of the law, and he was in high favour with *all the Jews* of Damascus. These Jews, we also note, are spoken of as *the brethren*[4]. (4) The dominant idea is *the will of God*. In verse 10 *what things have been ordained for thee to do* takes the place of *what thou must do* in ix 6. Nothing in this matter was of S. Paul's own choice: all was of God. The vision was the manifestation to Saul of the divine will for him, and the purpose for which it was made was God's also. By it *the God* of Israel—who had chosen *the fathers* Abraham, Isaac, and Jacob, and called the prophets—had *appointed*[5] Paul also for his work, which was simply to bear *witness* to what he had *seen and heard*, viz. to testify to the Lord Jesus as thus revealed to eye and ear[6]. To avoid unnecessary points of controversy Paul says nothing of 'the Christ'; but we notice that (i) it is in the revelation of Jesus that *the will of God* is made known. (ii) Jesus himself is *the Righteous*. This is eminently the Jewish conception, which appears in the early days of the church, and denotes the one who fulfilled the Jewish ideal and all the aspirations of the Jew after righteousness, in a word the one who fulfilled the law[7]. (iii) The commission to S. Paul will be given from his lips. (iv) The result of the vision is S. Paul's *baptism*, in which the apostle's part was to *call upon his name* in prayer, as upon that of JEHOVAH[8].

III. S. Paul's commission extended *to all men*. The full significance of this was brought out in a second commission, to which S. Paul passes at once. Again it was given in a vision. *An ecstasy* fell upon S. Paul[9] *in* this very *temple*, whither he had come up like a faithful Jew to *pray* (Lk xviii 10): in this ecstasy he again *saw him*[10] and heard his voice. The Lord bade him leave *Jerusalem* with all *haste and speed*, for they would not *receive witness* from him. S. Paul's answer should have convinced his hearers of the sincerity of his affection for his race. For he was extremely reluctant to leave the city, and began to make excuse[11].

---

[1] xxvi 13. [2] verse 11: cp. vii 2, 55, and p. 102. [3] as was Simeon (Lk ii 25: cp. i 6). The Greek word distinguishes the *pious* Jew (ii 5, viii 2) from the *devout* Gentile (x 2, 7). [4] verse 5 (cp. xxviii 21): they were still his *kinsmen after the flesh* (Rom ix 3). [5] xiii 17, iii 13: iii 20, x 41, xxvi 16, ix 15 *the vessel of choice* and p. 134. [6] In the church this was to be an 'apostle': see i 8, iv 26 and p. 7. [7] See iii 14, and pp. 52, 135. [8] ix 14, 21 and pp. 76, 135. [9] as upon S. Peter at Caesarea (x 10). [10] No name is given; but to the Christian *he* could have but one meaning. [11] This hesitation of the apostle, with his repeated commissions, might have reminded his audience of the history of the prophet Jonah.

But his excuse was not for himself, but for the Jews. How could they believe the word of one whom they had seen *beating* the
20 Christians, and presiding over *Stephen's* execution[1]? He seems to be pleading for a little delay (Lk xiii 8). But the answer is
21 peremptory: *Go thy way, for to the Gentiles afar off* (Eph ii 13) *will I send thee forth.* The *I* is emphatic, and from the Christian point of view these last words made S. Paul the apostle of the Gentiles[2]. His defence was unanswerable,—granted the truth of his visions: but neither reason nor protestation was of any avail with his fanatical audience. With a great strain on their patience they had listened up till now, but at the fatal word
22 *Gentiles*, their pent-up fury burst forth and they shouted *Away with such a fellow from off the earth*[3]: *it is not fit that* such a renegade *should live.*

Paul's appeal to his Roman citizenship

22 And they [4]gave him audience unto this word; and they lifted up their voice, and said, Away with such a fellow from the earth: for it is not fit that he should live.

23 And as they cried out, and [5]threw off their garments,
24 and cast dust into the air, the chief captain commanded him to be brought into the castle, bidding that he should be examined by scourging, that he might know for what cause
25 they so shouted against him. And when they had tied him up [6]with the thongs, Paul said unto the centurion that stood by, Is it lawful for you to scourge a man that is a Roman,
26 and uncondemned? And when the centurion heard it, he went to the chief captain, and told him, saying, [7]What art
27 thou about to do? for this man is a Roman. And the chief captain came, and said unto him, Tell me, art thou a Roman?
28 And he said, Yea. And the chief captain answered, [8]With a great sum obtained I this citizenship. And Paul said, But
29 I am *a Roman* born. They then which were about to [9]examine him straightway departed from him: and the chief captain also was afraid, when he knew that he was a Roman, and because he had bound him[10].

---

[1] With his usual tact S. Paul does not say, like the bold S. Peter, *whom ye slew* (iii 14, iv 10, v 30), but *when his blood was being shed*; cp. Lk xi 50. [2] Cp. Jn xx 21 *so send I you.* [3] Cp. viii 33. [4] i.e. *heard* or *were listening.* [5] or *cast about*: AV *cast off.* [6] Marg *for.* [7] AV and Bezan read *See,* i.e. *Take heed, [what thou art about to do.* [8] Bezan reads *I know for how great [a sum I obtained*: some authorities insert before this *Dost thou so easily say that thou art a Roman citizen? Why, I know etc.* [9] AV marg *torture.* [10] Some Bezan texts add *and straightway he loosed him.*

In his Gospel S. Luke does not record the scourging of the Lord, which forms so prominent a feature in the passion of the other Gospels[1]. Here however the corresponding incident is circumstantially narrated, because it was the immediate occasion of S. Paul's claiming his Roman citizenship, and for the sake of Jewish readers it was expedient to make the reason for such apparent disloyalty to his nation quite clear.

23 The tumult continued, and *the commandant*, who had been unable to follow the Aramaic, saw only a sea of waving *garments* and a cloud of *dust thrown into the air*—the ordinary oriental symptoms of excitement[2].
24 Hopeless of obtaining any information from the Jews, he decided to have recourse to 'the *question*'—the cruel and useless method of extracting the truth by torture, which prevailed universally down to quite modern times. Augustus had indeed put some limitations upon its use; he had for instance forbidden scourging except in the case of slaves. But the conduct of Lysias is only an example of the arbitrary treatment of provincials by a Roman official.
25 A *centurion* led away Paul to the chamber in Antonia which served for such purposes[3]. But a new surprise was in store for the bewildered commandant. The servants had already stripped the apostle and *tied him for the lashes*[4], when Paul declared that he was *a Roman* citizen and disputed the legality of the action.
26 *The centurion went and told the commandant.*
27 Lysias *came* at once and incredulously questioned the apostle.
28 After receiving an affirmative reply, he was still hardly convinced; he expressed his surprise that a poor Jew, so bedraggled as Paul must have been after his treatment in the temple, should be *a Roman*, by reflecting aloud, as it were, on the *great sum* it had cost him to *purchase* that privilege for himself. Under Claudius the venality of the court favourites who openly sold the citizenship was notorious. With quiet dignity Paul, the Jew but Roman by birth, asserts his superiority to the Greek, his parvenu fellow-citizen; *but I am in fact* a Roman *by birth*. Of course the examination was at an end.
29 Lysias indeed, like the magistrates at Philippi, *was alarmed* for himself: for though he had not scourged Paul, yet to have bound him to the scourging post was illegal[5]. At

---

[1] He alludes to it in Pilate's threats in Lk xxiii 16, 22. [2] They were *shaking their garments*, not throwing them off: cp. the use made of them at the entry to Jerusalem (Lk xix 36). *Casting dust* on the head or *into the air* was a mode of expressing abhorrence (II Sam xvi 13) or grief (Job ii 12, Rev xviii 19). [3] Probably not the same chamber in which the Lord had been scourged. The scene of that scourging would have been in the palace of Herod (the Praetorium). [4] i.e. *the lashes* of the scourge. The exact translation of the Greek is uncertain. It may be *tied with the thongs to the post*. Dr Field (*Notes on Trans.* etc.) gives some reason for thinking it denotes being *strung up with thongs*. [5] The actual enactments of the law about the privileges of the citizenship are not definitely known. The same point is introduced here as at Philippi, the fact of being *uncondemned* (? or *unheard*). Cp. the account of the scourging and assertion of the citizenship at Philippi in ch. xvi (pp. 290-1).

once the apostle was *loosed*, but not from his bonds altogether: he was still kept in custody, chained to a soldier[1].

Thus the rejection of S. Paul by the Jewish people led to an appeal to Rome. They cast him out of their citizenship or synagogue[2]; and in answer the apostle claimed his other citizenship. So afterwards, when the rulers of his people condemned him, he was constrained to make the final appeal to Caesar. Henceforth, however much against his will, S. Paul is to the Jews no more a Jew, but a Roman. This is no doubt the significance of the present incident. The claim to the Roman citizenship was the first step in the separation: though why it was made at this particular moment is not obvious. For S. Paul made it deliberately, having allowed himself first to be tied up. It was not that he shrank from pain: he was beaten at Philippi before he declared his citizenship. Probably he saw that the appeal to Roman justice had become inevitable, and to undergo needless suffering is not a Christian principle[3], while the illegality to which he had already been subjected afforded him some hold over Lysias and protection against arbitrary treatment at his hands.

§ 3 *Paul and the Sanhedrin*

For the fifth time the Sanhedrin, the supreme court of the Jews, has to adjudicate upon the claims of the new kingdom of God. After Jesus himself, S. Peter and S. John, the Twelve, and S. Stephen[4], S. Paul now stands before them. The case of the Lord was unique. When struck he had given a very different answer from that of S. Paul, and except when adjured he had kept silence, for indeed he was subject to no earthly jurisdiction. Peter and the Twelve appeared to the Sanhedrin as men 'unlearned,' men of the people, and they addressed their judges as *Rulers and Elders*. Stephen, on a higher level, spoke to them as *Brethren and Fathers*. Paul, as their equal in birth and learning, calls them *Brethren*. He had indeed occupied a seat, either upon the bench or among the 'disciples of the learned' (p. 58), when Stephen was brought in to be judged, and now he was experiencing an exact retribution for the past.

The trial opens a new phase in S. Paul's case, which has its exact parallel in the history of the Lord and of the early church. It brings him into collision with *the Sadducees* or the high-priestly party, and it was this which in each case brought about the decisive conclusion. As we have seen in Part I (p. 44), the policy of the Sadducean aristocracy was purely that of expediency. To preserve their own position they were extremely jealous of any disturbance which might

---

[1] It is evident from verse 30 that he was not altogether freed. The binding for the scourge was illegal because it was part of an illegal punishment; but though a citizen Paul continued to wear a chain, as he does to the end of the Acts—see the references on p. 420. This distinction in the bindings may explain the Bezan reading which appears to anticipate verse 30.   [2] Cp. Jn ix 34, xii 42.   [3] Cp. Col ii 23. Besides, after his beating by the Jews, a Roman scourging might well have proved fatal.   [4] Lk xxii 66–71, Acts iv 5–22, v 21–40, vi 12–vii 58.

cause the intervention of the Romans. And now Paul had caused a riot in the temple and brought into it the Roman soldiery. However indifferent they might be to his teaching, he was a fanatic and must be suppressed. The power of the Sadducees however was held in check by the opposition of *the Pharisees*, who enjoyed the support of the mass of the people. Hence as long as the church stood well with the Pharisees and the people, the Sadducees were powerless. Their opportunity came when the church lost its 'favour with all the people' (ii 47) and provoked the jealousy of the Pharisees. In the case of the Lord, the people had been alienated from him by priestly craft; in the history of the early church, it was the teaching of Stephen which had opened the eyes of the Pharisees to the full significance of the faith in Christ, and excited the patriotic instincts of the people to open hostility. And now history is repeating itself. The zeal for the law in the church at Jerusalem had once more, it would appear, conciliated the Pharisees and gained the favour of the people, when the arrival of Paul, bringing with him Stephen's doctrine fully developed and carried out to its logical consequences, again broke up the peace. First the people were roused to fury; and this at once drew upon the apostle the bitter animosity of the high-priestly faction. But S. Paul's doctrine was no less obnoxious to the Pharisees, and he was only saved from instant condemnation by a momentary outburst of party spirit among the Jews themselves. The party jealousy of the Pharisees was awakened. For the moment even Paul was not so hateful as their political opponents; as Gamaliel had once shielded the Twelve (v 34-40), so now the Pharisees espoused S. Paul's cause, and it was left to the high-priest to press forward the prosecution (cp. xxiv 1). This may account for the attitude of the Jews at Rome towards S. Paul later on: they had received no information against him (xxviii 21).

The overbearing conduct of Ananias in commanding Paul to be struck on the mouth is typical of the Sadducean priesthood. According to Josephus[1], their predominant characteristics at this time were cruelty and avarice. They were 'cruel above all the Jews in their judgements.' The high-priests surrounded themselves with armed retainers and acted like lawless tyrants. To enrich themselves, they robbed the inferior priests of their share of the tithes, even sending their servants to take the grain from the threshing floors by force. Pre-eminent among these tyrants was the present high-priest, *Ananias* the son of Nebedaeus, who by such violent means had acquired enormous wealth. As high-priest, he had been sent to Rome in A.D. 52, together with his son Ananus the captain of the Temple (p. 56) and other leading Jews, to answer for the Samaritan affair (p. 409). He was acquitted, however, and now was at the height of his power. But in 58 or 59 he was deposed to make room for Ishmael ben Phabi; and on the breaking out of the Jewish war, Ananias, like other Sadducean leaders, was assassinated by the popular zealots.

---

[1] *Ant.* xx 9. 1, and 8. 8.

The animosity of the Sadducees to S. Paul however was not based on political grounds alone. When he came before the Sanhedrin, they soon discovered him to be a 'fanatical' champion of the distinctive doctrines of their opponents, the Pharisees. The main points of dispute between the rival sects were (1) *the existence of spirits*[1], and (2) *the resurrection of the dead*. Both of these were denied by the Sadducees, who represented the rationalist type of thought among the Jews; and it is striking that they first came into collision with the Lord, in the closing week of his ministry, on this very point of the resurrection of the dead[2]. But if these theological differences placed them in an attitude of hostility towards S. Paul, the feeling was cordially reciprocated by the apostle.

For we must remember that he had been brought up as a Pharisee of the Pharisees, and therefore in ardent antagonism to the Sadducees. This mutual relation, then, helps to explain S. Paul's conduct. His behaviour in the Sanhedrin was certainly very different from that on the previous day in the temple. He shews no tact, nor even any desire to be conciliatory[3]. He had indeed little cause to trust the Sanhedrin as an impartial tribunal. And when he stood before the Saducean high-priest in the chamber where he had once sat on the opposition benches, all the old nature, the party spirit of the Pharisee, came to life again. He was in fact so carried away by these feelings that three out of his four utterances may be thought to lay him open to criticism.

(1) He begins without waiting for any formal question, with a somewhat defiant declaration of his own righteousness. This was certainly lacking in tact; and the utterance itself seems to clash with S. Paul's actual history, e.g. his persecution of the church, and with his own humble confession that he is 'less than the least of all saints' and 'the chiefest of sinners[4].' No doubt both forms of statement are entirely compatible. The confession of sin is the self-condemnation of a penitent spirit in the sight of God. The protestation of innocence, which has many parallels in the Epistles, refers to his external relations to men[5]. Even when he had been a persecutor, he had been acting with a *good conscience*. It was his conscience which had been at fault: it was unenlightened—'I did it ignorantly[6].' But, however literally justifiable, the present utterance savours rather of the self-righteousness of Saul the Pharisee than of the humble-mindedness (xx 19) of Paul the servant of Jesus Christ.

(2) The smiting on the mouth provoked a very sharp retort. This was, it is true, a perfectly justifiable outburst of righteous indignation. But it was not a strict imitation of the meekness and gentleness of the Christ: the Lord had made a different protest when

---

[1] whether human or angelic.   [2] Lk xx 27–38 : Mt xxii 23–32, Mk xii 18–27, the very words *which say that there is no resurrection* occur in the Gospels.   [3] We notice that while he addresses the Sanhedrin as *Brethren*, to the multitude he said *Brethren and Fathers*.   [4] I Tim i 13–5, Eph iii 8, I Cor xv 9.   [5] I Cor iv 4, II Cor i 12, iv 2, v 11, II Tim i 3, iv 7.   [6] I Tim i 13.

he had suffered the same indignity in the same place[1]. (3) This retort led to an utterance which has proved a great difficulty to commentators: *I knew not that he is the high-priest.* S. Paul must have known who the high-priest was, at least from the fact of his presiding; and so the apostle appears not to be speaking the truth. Various explanations have been offered[2]. The most plausible is that the acting high-priest need not necessarily have been the president of the Sanhedrin. At that epoch there were a number of ex-high-priests, who retained the title, and very often the actual power, of 'high-priest.' Annas, for instance, retained the first place in the governing body long after his actual period of office[3], and he was known as 'the high-priest.' Such a 'high-priest' may well have occupied the seat of president. This explanation however will not suffice. Not to mention S. Paul's familiarity with the customs of the Sanhedrin, it is quite evident from his speech that he knew who Ananias was; and in any case Ananias was one of the judges, to all of whom reverence was equally due. The difficulty really arises from our taking the word *know* in its literal matter-of-fact sense. But among the Jews *to know* had several meanings. Thus (*a*) it denoted the recognition or acknowledgment of persons, as when the apostle asks the Thessalonians *to know those that labour among them*, or when the Lord shall say *I know you not, I never knew you*. Again (*b*) it is used of the deeper or more real understanding of events, as when the Lord's murderers *knew not what they were doing*, or Peter *knew not that it was true which was done by the angel*[4]. So here in S. Paul's utterance we have a confession of error. That 'good conscience' of his quickly reminded him of the Lord's example and the words of scripture: he had again kicked against the goad and it pricked him. He had spoken with his usual warmth of heart, but the same warmth moved him to repentance, and he confessed that he had not reflected that it was the high-priest: for the moment he had forgotten his office and not 'known' or acknowledged him with that reverence which the scripture commanded.

(4) S. Paul's last utterance is open to the charge of being based on policy and not on principle. This was a charge which before now the apostle had had indignantly to refute[5]. Certainly after reading the Epistles to the Romans and Galatians, it is startling to hear S. Paul, when set for the defence of the gospel, exclaim *I am a Pharisee, a son of Pharisees*, and declare that it is the doctrines of Pharisaism which are at stake,—*the hope and resurrection of the dead*. But the charge will fall to the ground when we realize the persons and the situation. Paul was, as he has himself striven to convince us (p. 421), a genuine Jew, and he was also a Pharisee. The name of Pharisee had not yet

---

[1] Jn xviii 23: II Cor x 1. His own words may have been in the apostle's mind when he afterwards wrote Phil ii 1–11. [2] e.g. that the apostle was shortsighted. [3] iv 6, Lk iii 2, Jn xviii 13, 15, 19. For a plurality of 'high-priests' see ver. 30 and p. 44. [4] (*a*) I Thess v 12, Lk xiii 25, 27, Mt xxv 12, vii 23. (*b*) Lk xxiii 34, Acts xii 9. S. Peter said of the Lord *I know him not, I know not what thou sayest* (Lk xxii 57, 60). [5] Cp. II Cor i 12 foll., Gal i 10 *pleasing men*.

become a synonym for hypocrite. That identification has come about through long familiarity with the Lord's denunciations of them in the Gospels. But as yet the Gospels had not been published abroad; and in Jerusalem the name of Pharisee still stood for what was best in Judaism, that of which the Jews were most proud. If the Pharisees had made themselves worthy of the Lord's denunciation, it was because *corruptio optimi pessima*. And in fact, if the majority of the Pharisees were as our Lord painted them, yet among them were good men; certainly the sympathies of 'the pious' among the Jews,—of such persons as Simeon, Elisabeth and Zachariah, Nicodemus and Joseph of Arimathea—would have been on their side. If then it was any 'gain' to S. Paul to have been a Jew, he would still more pride himself on having been a Pharisee and not a Sadducee: in fact, in the Ep. to the Philippians, which was written subsequently to this, he still describes himself as 'a Hebrew of Hebrews; as touching the law, a Pharisee[1].' Accordingly, as yesterday before the people he had vindicated his true Judaism, so today before the Sanhedrin he vindicates his true Pharisaism. He was on the side of the party of faith and hope, not on that of cynicism and scepticism. Nay more, he and the Christians—and they alone—had realized the ideal of the Pharisees: they had found *the hope* of Israel, they had discovered the secret of righteousness, and they possessed the proof of the *resurrection of the dead*.

30 But on the morrow, desiring to know the certainty, wherefore he was accused of the Jews, he loosed him, and commanded the [2]chief priests and all the council to come together, and brought Paul down, and set him before them.

23 And Paul, looking stedfastly on the council, said, Brethren, I have lived before God in all good conscience until this day. 2 And the high priest Ananias commanded them that stood by 3 him to smite him on the mouth. Then said Paul unto him, God [3]shall smite thee, thou whited wall: and sittest thou to judge me according to the law, and commandest me to be 4 smitten contrary to the law? And they that stood by said, 5 Revilest thou God's high priest? And Paul said, I wist not, brethren, that he was [4]high priest: for it is written, [5]Thou 6 shalt not speak evil of a ruler of thy people. But when Paul perceived that the one part were Sadducees, and the other Pharisees, he cried out in the council, Brethren, I am a Pharisee, a son of [6]Pharisees: touching the hope and

---

[1] xxvi 5: Phil iii 5 (cp. verse 7 *gains*). [2] Gk *high-priests*. [3] Gk *is about to* or *intends to smite*. [4] or *the high-priest* (AV). [5] Exod xxii 28. [6] AV reads *a Pharisee*.

7 resurrection of the dead I am ¹called in question. And when he had so said, there arose a dissension between the Pharisees and Sadducees: and ²the assembly was divided.
8 For the Sadducees say that there is no resurrection, neither
9 angel, nor spirit: but the Pharisees confess both. And there arose a great clamour: and some of the scribes of the Pharisees' part stood up, and strove³, saying, We find no evil in this man: ⁴and what if a spirit hath spoken to him, or an
10 angel? And when there arose a great dissension, the chief captain, fearing lest Paul should be torn in pieces by them, commanded the soldiers to go down and take him by force from among them, and bring him into the castle.

30   The natural course for Lysias was to submit Paul's case to the Jewish courts; and, as he represented the Procurator, *the next day* he summoned a meeting of *the Sanhedrin*. Then *he set Paul free* from the soldier to whom he was chained, *brought him down* to the council chamber on the west side of the Temple hill, and *set*
23 *him* at the bar of the Sanhedrin for examination. Paul however
1 refused to stand before them as a criminal. He *looked stedfastly at the council*⁵; and, before the formal proceedings had begun, with his accustomed boldness of speech he protested his innocence. *Brethren, with all good conscience have I lived towards God until this day*⁶. (1) He uses a noticeable word, which means *to live as a citizen*: he had lived as God's citizen, as a member of God's commonwealth. The idea of citizenship was Greek and not Jewish: the Jews thought of God's people or God's inheritance, rather than of God's city. But the idea of citizenship becomes prominent in these chapters⁷, and it corresponds with the actual crossing over of the apostle from his Jewish heritage to his Roman citizenship (p. 427). Certainly the idea recurs in the epistles which he wrote subsequently to this: e.g. in Phil i 27, iii 20; and in Eph ii 12 he applies the idea to Israel, which he calls God's 'polity,' or 'commonwealth.' (2) The continuous loyalty of S. Paul's citizen life was testified by his *conscience*. The Greek word for the conscience (like the English word itself) means literally *knowing-with*; and its action is exactly expressed by S. Paul's saying, *I know nothing against* (literally *with*) *myself* in I Cor iv 4. The conscience is a consciousness which bears testimony with, or to, our personality within; and the subject-matter of the testimony is the moral value of actions,

---

¹ literally *being judged*.   ² Gk *multitude*.   ³ i.e. *contended* or *fought-together* (a strong word).   ⁴ AV reads *and if a spirit or an angel hath spoken to him, let us not fight against God* (v 39).   ⁵ Cp. vi 15, vii 55.   ⁶ The emphatic *I* comes first in the Greek.   ⁷ Cp. xxi 39, xxii 28. This may be due to the hand of S. Luke: the word *citizen* occurs in S. Luke's writings alone in the NT.

the testimony itself being a pronouncement whether they are right or wrong[1]. A *good conscience*[2] gives a good verdict, and this it can only do if the faculty of judgement is itself clear. Accordingly, to possess an honest or unperverted conscience in *all* matters had been the aim of S. Paul's life, and in this aim he had succeeded[3].

2 Ananias however, provoked by this self-assertion, *ordered the attendants to smite him on his mouth*. At once S. Paul's fiery
3 spirit flashed out. Like a prophet of the OT[4], he exclaimed *Smite thee—that is what God is about to do, thou whited wall*: and his prophecy was fulfilled at the outbreak of the Jewish rebellion (p. 428). The high-priest should have been a wall of defence to the people, but Ananias was only plastered over to look white and fair; underneath the surface there was a breach which would 'swell out' suddenly[5]. The Lord had called the Pharisees 'whited sepulchres,' and the Sadducees were daubed with the same plaster of hypocrisy. Long before this S. Paul had discovered the inconsistency of the Jews, and indeed of all human judges[6]. But at this fresh instance he could not contain himself. *What, dost thou sit in judgement on me to try my observance of the law, while thou breakest it by such a*
4 *command?* At these words the attendants made a protest, and at once S. Paul recollected himself. His humble-mindedness recovered
5 itself, and calling the attendants his *brothers*, he confessed his fault. In his indignation against the man he had forgotten his office, and this in spite of the warning voice of the law. By quoting scripture Paul at the same time testified to his own loyalty to the law.
6 This overbearing conduct of the Sadducean high-priest may have given his critics among the Pharisees an opportunity of protest, of which S. Paul would take advantage. But it seems unlikely that one more utterance on his part would have sufficed to bring matters to a crisis. We may assume that the examination was formally opened, and S. Paul accused of having defiled the temple[7]. If so, then, in answer to the president's question—*Are these things so?* Paul made his defence, and told once more the story of the vision on the way to Damascus (as would appear from verse 9). *The Sadducees* received his words with ostentatious scepticism and ridicule: this provoked counter-expressions of sympathy and credulity among *the Pharisees*. Paul's keen eye *perceived* that he had thrown an apple of discord into the assembly, viz. the question as to the existence of spirits; and he completed his work by throwing another. He boldly identified himself with the Pharisees and the other distinctive article of their creed. *Brethren*, he

---

[1] See Rom ii 15, ix 1, II Cor i 12: Rom xiii 5, I Cor viii 7–12, x 25–9, II Cor iv 2, v 11.   [2] Elsewhere in S. Paul this phrase is found only in the Pastoral Epistles (I Tim i 5, 19; cp. iii 9, II Tim i 3 *a pure conscience*).   [3] xxiv 16, Phil iii 6.
[4] Both Micaiah, the son of Imlah, and Jeremiah had been thus smitten, and they had made stern answers (I K xxii 24–5, Jer xx 2–3).   [5] I Sam xxv 16: Ezek xiii 10–6; Isai xxx 13.   [6] Cp. Rom ii 1, 3, 21–3.   [7] From xxiii 30 we learn that there were accusers.

cried out, *I am a* thorough *Pharisee*, born and bred a Pharisee[1]: what is really at stake is the Pharisees' faith in *the hope* (of Israel) *and the resurrection of the dead.* (1) *The hope* was the Messianic hope. To this the Pharisees, as the idealists of Judaism, clung, while the Sadducees had virtually abandoned it or rather had never risen to it. This expectation is found at the beginning of the Gospel[2]; it was then answered by the coming of the Messiah; and that coming, together with his second coming in glory, was the subject of the first preaching of the Twelve. But since those early days nearly thirty years had elapsed; and still 'the seasons of refreshing and of the restitution of all things,' 'the time of the restoration of the kingdom to Israel[3],' had not arrived. Thus for the Christians also the coming of the Messiah still remained an object of hope: and in these chapters the faith in the Messiah is expressed in this form, viz. as a hope[4]. His second coming would coincide with (2) *the resurrection of the dead*; and of this resurrection that of the Messiah was the proof and pledge. S. Paul's
7 utterance had its effect. It called up all the latent party spirit and created *a dissension* or *faction* in the Sanhedrin. The phraseology takes us back to a similar dissension in the church[5]. But here there was no Peter nor James—we might say, no Holy Spirit (xv 28)—to heal the division; and *the multitude*—the whole body of the Sanhedrin, with the attendants and the 'disciples of the
9 learned' (p. 58)—*was torn* into two contending parties. *There was a great outcry*; the grave and reverend presbyters of Israel began to shout out like a frantic mob[6]. Carried away by partisanship *some members of the Pharisees' party* entirely took Paul's side. *They stood up* as if to give their verdict[7], which was that he was innocent; '*and if a spirit has spoken to him or an angel,*'—their conclusion was interrupted by hostile cries, but it would have been that of Gamaliel in v 39 'let us not fight against God[8].' This action
10 precipitated matters, the shouting gave place to blows and Paul ran serious risk of being *torn in pieces*. Lysias, whose respect for the Jews can hardly have been enhanced, had to send a message to Antonia for the whole force of the garrison to *come down*[9]; and even so Paul was only extricated with difficulty (verse 29 Bezan).

This stormy scene is our last sight of the supreme court of the Jews, the elders of Israel. It left Lysias no more enlightened than before, except as to the personal importance of the apostle. But to

---

[1] He lays stress on the strong Hebrew traditions of his family in Phil iii 5, II Tim i 3.   [2] Lk ii 25, 38; cp. xxiv 21.   [3] Acts i 6, iii 20.   [4] xxiv 15, xxvi 6, 7, xxviii 20.   [5] xv 2, 7, 12.   [6] We might think that S. Luke was using the word *multitude* in contempt: cp. xxi 36, and xxii 23 *crying*. But it is not the word for *crowd* in Greek, and it is used of the Christian council in xv 12; cp. Lk xxiii 1.   [7] Cp. v 34, xv 7, Mt xxvi 62, Mk xiv 60.   [8] which is added in the AV. For a similar aposiopesis see Lk xiii 9.   [9] The words in the Greek, *go down* and *bring*, seem to imply that Lysias was in the castle; but they probably indicate that S. Luke was there, and that he is writing from the point of view of the castle.

the public for whom S. Luke was writing it gave the first sentence of acquittal of S. Paul, pronounced by his own nation : *We find no evil in this man*[1].

The vision of the Lord

After these two exciting days S. Paul must have been terribly dejected. Not to speak of the physical effect of his beating in the temple and of the bodily violence in the Sanhedrin, there was the apparent failure of his plans at the last moment, the hopeless and obdurate hatred of his fellow-countrymen, his pain of heart at the hardness of God's chosen people, the questionings of his own conscience: all these must have combined to bring on one of S. Paul's attacks of spiritual depression. Far more than at Ephesus he must have 'had the answer of death in himself[2].' Doubtless he besought the Lord; and an answer came, proportionate to the need[3]. It was yet another vision. That *night*—not an angel (as in xii 7) but—*the Lord* Jesus himself *came upon him* and strengthened him. (1) He encouraged him with the word *Be of good cheer*, which is found in the mouth of the Lord alone in the NT. (2) He calmed all the questionings of conscience by his approval of what Paul had done : he had *borne* good *witness* to the people and Sanhedrin, and so fulfilled his ministry to the Jews[4]. (3) He gave assurance for the future : the apostle's ambition to *bear witness at Rome* would be fulfilled *also*. There still remained the divine necessity which 'cannot be shaken' (*must* xix 21).

11   And the night following the Lord stood by him, and said, Be of good cheer[5]: for as thou hast testified concerning me at Jerusalem, so must thou bear witness also at Rome.

The appearances of the Lord to S. Paul are not recorded at haphazard. They all mark great crises in his life. First there came the conversion and his mission to the Gentiles: then visions of encouragement follow, both at Corinth and Jerusalem[6]. The two latter are evidently recorded with the intention of shewing the divine sanction which rested upon S. Paul's action. The need for this was especially pressing at this moment. The appeal to the Roman citizenship was bad enough, but the coming appeal to Caesar would be to the Jews the extremest act of apostasy : it would be equivalent to 'accusing their nation' (xxviii 19). Even a Christian might have felt doubtful at the introduction of the alien, worldly, authority of Rome. But in this vision the Lord gives his sanction to the one appeal, and by the mention of Rome directs the mind of S. Paul to the other. All critics then, whether Jewish or Christian, must 'hold their peace' (xi 18, xxi 14).

---

[1] Cp. xxv 25, xxvi 31; and in the case of the Lord Lk xxiii 4, 14, 22.
[2] II Cor i 9.   [3] II Cor xii 8–9.   [4] xx 24; cp. ix 15, xxii 15, xxvi 20.
[5] AV adds *Paul*.   [6] xxii 7–10, 18–21 ; xviii 9–10 and here.

§ 4 *The conspiracy against Paul and his delivery into the hands of the Gentiles*

Lysias' further course of action was decided for him by events. While the Jewish government betrayed indecision, the people took the matter into their own hands. If some of the Pharisees were inclined to favour Paul as an ally against the Sadducees, the Zealots would have no such compromise, and forty of them made a plot to assassinate the apostle. Such a plot faithfully reflects the state of the Jews as pictured by Josephus. The fanatical party were now manifesting their patriotism by murdering those of their countrymen who were on the side of peace. He tells us that after the murder of the high-priest Jonathan (p. 409), which passed unavenged, the robbers (i.e. the Sicarii) came up to the feasts with daggers concealed on their persons and mingling with the crowds assassinated their enemies—some to gratify personal enmity, others for hire,—and this in the very temple[1]. In Cumanus' days the brigands had gone so far as to molest an imperial postman on his way to Caesarea and so brought about one of the periodical and disastrous collisions with the Roman arms. This incident shews the need for the excessive precautions taken to secure Paul's safe delivery at Caesarea. This delivery was the immediate result of the plot; and S. Luke tells the story, with the most circumstantial detail, in order to prove to the world, and to the Jews in particular, that it was their own doing. For (1) in fact S. Paul's innocence is, for the second time, expressly declared by the Roman commandant (verse 29). And (2) the action of the 40 conspirators was but a symbol of that of the whole nation; just as S. Luke writes in verse 12 *the Jews*. When the Lord was crucified they had cried 'His blood be upon us and our children,' and now they again bring God's *curse* upon them, so that his 'wrath should come upon them to the uttermost[2].'

S. Luke is able to write in such detail because he was an eye-witness. The vividness with which he describes the interview in the castle shews that he was there: cp. also verse 11. He may have been admitted as a friend, or even a servant of S Paul. Very likely the physical condition of the apostle demanded medical attendance, and S. Luke may have seized the opportunity; or again, S. Luke—as Aristarchus also—may have been involved in the charge of polluting the temple, as to which, with his usual self-effacement, he keeps silence. They may have been seen with S. Paul in the outer court, and S. Luke may have been arrested on the charge of having been the Gentile trespasser[3]. In any case the order to provide *beasts* (in the plural, verse 24) seems to imply that S. Paul was not alone.

12   And when it was day, the Jews banded together, and bound themselves under a curse, saying that they would

---

[1] *Ant.* xx 8. 5.   [2] Mt xxvii 25; 1 Thess ii 16.   [3] See below on xxvii 1.

13 neither eat nor drink till they had killed Paul. And they
14 were more than forty which made this conspiracy. And they came to the ¹chief priests and the ²elders, and said, We have ³bound ourselves under a great curse, to taste nothing until
15 we have killed Paul. Now therefore ⁴do ye with the council signify to the chief captain that he bring him down unto you⁵, as though ye would judge of his case more exactly: and we, or ever he come near, are ready to slay him⁶.
16 But Paul's sister's son heard of their lying in wait, ⁷and he
17 came and entered into the castle, and told Paul. And Paul called unto him one of the centurions, and said, Bring this young man unto the chief captain: for he hath something
18 to tell him. So he took him, and brought him to the chief captain, and saith, Paul the prisoner called me unto him, and asked me to bring this young man unto thee, who hath
19 something to say to thee. And the chief captain took him by the hand, and going aside asked him privately, What is
20 that thou hast to tell me? And he said, The Jews have agreed to ask thee to bring down Paul to-morrow unto the council, as though ⁸thou wouldest inquire somewhat more
21 exactly concerning him. Do not thou therefore yield unto them: for there lie in wait for him of them more than forty men, which have bound themselves under a curse, neither to eat nor to drink till they have slain him: and now are they
22 ready, looking for the promise from thee. So the chief captain let the young man go, charging him, Tell no man that thou hast signified these things to me.
23 And he called unto him two of the centurions, and said, Make ready two hundred soldiers to go as far as Cæsarea, and horsemen ⁹threescore and ten, and spearmen two hundred,
24 at the third hour of the night: and *he bade them* provide beasts, that they might set Paul thereon, and bring him safe
25 unto Felix the governor¹⁰. And he wrote a letter after this

---

¹ Gk *high-priests*. ² Gk *presbyters*. ³ literally *cursed with a curse* or *devoted with a vow* (a Hebraism). ⁴ Bezan reads *we ask you to do this for us: when ye have summoned* [*the council, signify*. ⁵ AV adds *to-morrow*. ⁶ Bezan adds *if need be, even to die*. ⁷ Marg *having come in* upon them, *and he entered*. ⁸ AV reads *they would*. ⁹ Bezan reads *a hundred*. ¹⁰ Bezan adds *for he was afraid lest the Jews should seize and slay him* (i.e. Paul), *and he afterwards be accused of having taken money* (i.e. *a bribe*).

26 form: *Claudius Lysias unto the most excellent governor*
27 *Felix, greeting. This man was seized by the Jews, and was about to be slain of them, when I came upon them with the soldiers, and rescued him, ¹having learned that he was*
28 *a Roman. And desiring to know the cause wherefore they*
29 *accused him, ²I brought him down unto their council: whom I found to be accused about questions of ³their law, but to have nothing laid to his charge worthy of death or of bonds⁴.*
30 *And when it was shewn to me that there would be a plot against the man, I sent him to thee forthwith, charging his accusers also to speak against him before thee⁵.*
31 So the soldiers, as it was commanded them, took Paul,
32 and brought him by night to Antipatris. But on the morrow they left the horsemen to go with him, and returned to the
33 castle: and they, when they came to Cæsarea, and delivered the letter to the governor, presented Paul also before him.
34 And when he had ⁶read it, he asked of what province he was;
35 and when he understood that he was of Cilicia, I will hear thy cause, said he, when thine accusers also are come: and he commanded him to be kept in Herod's ⁷palace.

12 Like Judas (Lk xxii 4), the *forty* men *went to the high-priests.* They had *devoted themselves* or *placed themselves under an anathema,* which meant that if they failed to keep their pledge, they would become '*anathema,*' i.e. devoted (to destruction), under God's ban⁸.
15 The Bezan text makes clear—what is indeed to be gathered from the narrative—that *the Sanhedrin* was first to meet on the morrow and then send a formal message to Lysias. But they were anti-
16 cipated by *Paul's nephew.* This mention of S. Paul's relative is one of those touches which make the whole world kin. It reminds us of another family picture, of 'the house of Mary the mother of John Mark,' who was cousin of Barnabas (xii 12). From it we may infer that some at least of S. Paul's family were reconciled to

---

¹ or *and learned.* ² Marg with B omits *I brought him down into their council.* ³ Bezan reads *the law of Moses and one Jesus.* ⁴ Bezan adds *and I scarcely brought him forth by force.* ⁵ Marg and AV add *Farewell.*
⁶ Bezan has *read*] *the letter and asked Of what province art thou? he said Cilicia* (or *I am a Cilician*), *and when he had learned* (or *made enquiry*) *he said I will hear thee [when.* ⁷ Gk *praetorium.* ⁸ The Greek verb is literally *to make anathema,* i.e. *to devote* to God. This meant in practice *to utterly-destroy,* as the corresponding Hebrew verb in the OT is translated, and as is shewn by the fate of Jericho and the Amalekites (Josh vi 17-21, I Sam xv 3). The *anathema* was 'the thing devoted' to God and therefore to be utterly destroyed: hence it came to denote the curse which lay upon the thing. Cp. Levit xxvii 28-9, and I Cor xvi 22 *let him be anathema.*

him; and that they occupied an influential position, within reach of information about the secret policy of the high-priests. S. Paul was in 'free custody,' chained to a soldier but otherwise at liberty, and so his nephew had easy access to him. S. Luke also was by his side; and his sudden fear for the apostle when he heard about the plot impressed the scene indelibly on his memory. As he writes,
19 he still sees before him Lysias kindly *taking the young man by the hand* and leading him aside out of earshot, and makes us share his own anxiety about the result.
20 The RV reading in verse 20 *as though thou wouldest enquire* is in itself more probable than the AV *they*. The Sanhedrin wanted to *judge* or *decide* (verse 15) about S. Paul: it was Lysias who would be anxious to *enquire* or *learn* about him.

But Lysias' anxiety was different now. He had got entangled in a difficult case. Though the murder of a Jew in a religious dispute might be a matter of little consequence to a Roman, yet Paul was a Roman citizen, and Lysias wanted to get rid of the responsibility. The obvious course was to send him at once to the
23 procurator Felix at Caesarea. Accordingly he ordered an escort to be *made ready*—of *two centurions* with their centuries, viz. *200 soldiers*, and in addition *70 horse and 200* footmen from the
24 irregular forces[1]. The centurions were *to provide horses* for *Paul* and his companions[2], for after his ill-treatment in the temple and Sanhedrin the apostle would have hardly been equal to a long and rapid march. The preparations had to be made with speed, for as soon as night had fully fallen, i.e. at about nine o'clock, they were to start. The sudden despatch *by night* was to avoid any plot, the large escort to prevent any forcible seizure of S. Paul. The reason for Lysias' extreme precautions is well given by the addition in the Bezan text—if an attack was made and Paul killed, Lysias *might be accused of having been bribed* to allow it. This was the very charge for which Cumanus had been banished, viz. of having accepted
25 bribes from the Samaritans (p. 409). In sending a prisoner to a higher court it was necessary to send a written statement of the case, called an 'elogium.' S. Luke now gives S. Paul's 'elogium.' It is written in S. Luke's own style; the original would have been in Latin, and he only professes to give the *form* or tenour of it. But it would not have been difficult to ascertain its contents at Caesarea, and it bears the stamp of truth. For the version of the affair which it presents puts Lysias' action in the most favourable light: for instance, it makes no mention of his order to scourge
27 the prisoner. According to the RV translation (*having learned*), Lysias even went so far as to distort the facts and convey the impression that it was the fact that S. Paul *was a Roman* which prompted Lysias to rescue him, instead of its being an after-discovery.

---

[1] The word for these *spearmen* is a rare one; elsewhere it is found only in late Byzantine writers. [2] viz. S. Luke and Aristarchus, who were certainly with him at Caesarea (xxvii 1-2).

But if our interpretation of S. Luke's use of participles be correct[1], the proper translation should be *I rescued him and learned that he was a Roman*. In any case some ambiguity remains, which is exactly what Lysias would desire, in order that he might gain the credit of zeal for the citizenship. From the letter we learn that Lysias told Paul's *accusers* to carry their complaint to the procurator's court. What happened to the forty 'devoted' conspirators we are not told: but in that age of legal subtlety, patriotic 'doctors of the law' would have no difficulty in finding some valid excuse for declaring the vow null and void.

31, 32 The escort and their prisoner marched all *night to Antipatris*, a distance of about 35 miles. At Antipatris they halted; and, the immediate danger being passed, the foot *soldiers returned* thence to Jerusalem, *leaving the horsemen* to conduct Paul the remaining 27

33 miles *to Caesarea*[2], where they probably arrived on the following day. So within a fortnight Paul was back at Caesarea, and the apprehensions of the disciples there were fulfilled. The arrival of the apostle was probably their first intimation of what had happened.

34 The soldiers took him to the procurator's court. Felix *read* the elogium and *asked* Paul *of what province he was*[3]. This was perhaps to make sure that Paul's case fell under his jurisdiction: possibly the question was part of the formal verification of his Roman citizenship. *Cilicia* indeed was at that time as closely attached to the province of Syria as was Judaea. After ascertaining the

35 necessary information, Felix determined to *hear the case* when the *accusers should arrive*. Meanwhile Paul was to be confined in free custody in *Herod's palace*, now the residence of the Roman governor and therefore called by the Romans the *Praetorium*[4].

Though S. Paul had been first bound by Lysias in the temple (xxi 33), this was his real 'delivery up into the hands of the Gentiles.' His own nation had rejected him, and delivered him up to Felix, as they had delivered up the Lord to Pilate[5]. S. Paul has now left Jerusalem for ever. Like the Lord he had gone 'without the gate'; and they both went forth in weakness—the Master unable to carry his cross, the disciple carried by a beast.

Note on the diary of xxi 17–xxiv 1

It is not easy to be certain about the diary of these events. We should at first sight take xxiv 1 to mean that Ananias came down to Caesarea *five days after* S. Paul's arrival there. But the day of his arrival is not given: the

---

[1] viz. that their order denotes the order of the actions in time (p. 184). [2] The exact site of Antipatris is still uncertain, and the figures above are only a rough estimate of the relative distances. [3] The Greek interrogative properly asks *what kind of* province it was. Was it, e.g., imperial or senatorial? or again was it a 'province' or a dependent state? Pilate referred the case of the Lord to Herod, because he was of Galilee (Lk xxiii 6, 7): but S. Paul was at all events a Roman citizen. This form of the interrogative however was often used as an equivalent for the simple *what?* [4] Mt xxvii 27, Mk xv 16. [5] xxi 11; Lk xviii 32, xxiii 1, 14, Mt xxvii 2.

morrow of xxiii 32 is the date of the departure of the foot-soldiers for Jerusalem; and it is not likely that S. Paul would have reached Caesarea the same day, for in that case he would have travelled 62 miles in 24 hours (or at the most 27). Again it would be incompatible with xxiv 11, where S. Paul states that it was *not more than twelve days* since his coming up to Jerusalem, and by the time he reached Caesarea at least 10 days must have elapsed. Now S. Paul was arrested on the seventh day (xxi 27 *when the seven days were on the point of being completed*); and *seven* plus *five* = *twelve*. Hence the *five days* of xxiv 1 probably look back to xxi 27 (the last chronological statement), and begin with the meeting of the Sanhedrin on the morning of the eighth day, when *the seven days were* now *completed*.

The 40 conspirators expected Paul to be brought down to the Sanhedrin on the day after their vow. This would hardly have been a Sabbath; and so by working backwards we can fix S. Paul's arrival on the Friday before Pentecost.

The diary then will stand somewhat as follows, continuing that given on pp. 402-3.

Day			
1 Friday			Arrival at Jerusalem
2 Sat	**Sabbath**		Reception by James
3 Sun	**Pentecost**		Paul takes the Nazirites
4 Mon			Offerings for the Nazirites
5 Tues			,, ,,
6 Wed			,, ,,
7 Thurs			,, ,,
8 Fri			Riot in the temple, and arrest of Paul
			Paul before the Sanhedrin
			Vision of the Lord in the night
9 Sat	**Sabbath**		Conspiracy of the forty Jews
			9 p.m. Paul sent to Caesarea
10 Sun	**Trinity Sunday**		Arrival at Antipatris
11 Mon			Paul arrives at Caesarea
12 Tues			Ananias arrives at Caesarea
13 Wed			Trial before Felix

SECTION II C (= Ch. 24—26)

Paul and the Romans at Caesarea

§ 1 *The trial before Felix*

24 Paul having been delivered up to Felix, it depended on the Jews whether the case was to go forward. They indeed were not behindhand, and the whole nation became his accusers. Of the hostility of the multitude and the Zealots there was no question: and now after the scene in the Sanhedrin, the Sadducees were ready to take the 1 lead. *The high-priest Ananias*, transformed into a bitter personal enemy, *came down* to Caesarea in person, together with a deputation from the Sanhedrin, and to ensure success they had brought a professional *advocate* with them. They had lost no time: for *on the fifth day* after the beginning of the affair with the riot in the temple, the party arrived at Caesarea. They would probably have reached the city in the evening; and next morning, on the opening of the procurator's court, the Jewish embassy formally *indicted Paul before Felix*[1]. Paul was then *cited* by the crier of the court, and when he had responded to his name, the counsel for the Jews opened the case for the prosecution[2]. His name *Tertullus*, a diminutive form of Tertius[3], seems to shew that he was a Roman, and his speech certainly reads like a translation from the Latin[4]. Tertullus would be familiar with Roman law, and like a Roman is brief and to the point (verse 4): S. Luke however is obliged still further to compress his concise statement, and this has caused some confusion in verses 6–8.

Speech for the prosecution

24 And after five days the high priest Ananias came down with certain [5]elders, and *with* an orator, one Tertullus; and
2 they informed the governor against Paul. And when he was called, Tertullus began to accuse him, saying,

Seeing that by thee we enjoy much peace, and that by
3 thy providence [6]evils are corrected for this nation, we accept it in all ways and in all places, most excellent Felix, with all
4 thankfulness. But, that I be not further tedious unto thee,
5 I intreat thee to hear us of thy clemency a few words. For we have found this man a pestilent fellow, and a mover of insurrections among all the Jews throughout the world, and
6 a ringleader of the sect of the Nazarenes: who moreover assayed to profane the temple: on whom also we laid hold[7]:
8 from whom thou wilt be able, by examining him thyself, to take knowledge of all these things, whereof we accuse him.
9 And the Jews also [8]joined in the charge, affirming that these things were so.

2 Tertullus begins with the usual *captatio benevolentiae* or endeavour to win the judge's good will by the way of personal compliment or flattery. It was true that Felix had secured some *peace* for the country by his suppression of the brigands on his entry into office, but what the *reforms* were we do not know. The

---

[1] Cp. xxv 6. [2] For the legal forms, see *Oxyrhynchus papyri* II p. 162 line 19. [3] Rom xvi 22. [4] Thus the phrases *by thy providence, of thy clemency, a pestilent fellow, to profane* have a Latin ring. [5] Gk *presbyters*. [6] literally *reforms are being carried out*: for *reforms* AV reads *very worthy deeds* (Gk *successes*). [7] Marg with AV and Bezan inserts *and we would have judged him according to our law.* 7 *But the chief captain Lysias came, and with great violence took him away out of our hands,* 8 *commanding his accusers to come before thee.* [8] AV reads *assented.*

worthy deeds of the AV would include the capture of Eleazar the chief of the brigands, and the suppression of the Egyptian impostor (pp. 409-10).

3   In any case the gratitude of the Jews is expressed with the exaggeration customary to orators (*all...all...all*). The words *thankfulness* and *providence*[1]—the latter especially, being chiefly used of the action of the gods—indicate the flattery of the speaker and the general attitude of the provincials to their rulers. *Most excellent*, however, is nothing more than the recognized conventional epithet.
5 Tertullus then proceeds to the charge. (1) The defendant was, as we should say, a public *nuisance*—literally, a *pest*: for he excited *dissensions*[2], or *seditions, among the Jews throughout the empire*. By so doing he was guilty of 'laesa majestas' or treason against Caesar, who represented the Roman people. (2) He was moreover *a ringleader of the sect of the Nazarenes*, a body which had no legal status, being a Jewish sect and yet violating the law of the Jews. The description of the Christians as *Nazarenes* shews that we have returned to Jewish soil and ideas[3]. We also note that the preeminence of Paul in the church is no exaggeration of S. Luke's: his enemies, taking a figure from the army, acknowledge him to
6 be *a front rank man* or head of the file. (3) In particular, he had *actually attempted*—for the Jews had now discovered that the cry raised in the temple (xxi 28) was false—*to profane the temple*, by taking Gentiles within the barrier. In the actual speech no doubt Tertullus had to give some account of the origin of the present case with the Jewish version of the action of Lysias, whose evidence would be the most important element in the trial (verse 22). This is represented in the AV and the Bezan text, where Lysias is the
8 antecedent of the relative pronoun in verse 8 (*from whom*). This passage may have been original, but afterwards cut out by S. Luke, in his desire for compression. The result is that Paul becomes the antecedent to the pronoun, instead of Lysias, and is to be the subject of the judge's own *examination*[4]. At the conclusion of the
9 speech the accusers, the Jewish deputation, made themselves parties to the indictment by emphatic assertions of the truth of Tertullus' statement[5].

The indictment of S. Paul, then, contained three counts: one political (*A*), one religious (*B*), and a particular breach of the law (*C*). These correspond to S. Paul's summary in xxv 8 : *neither against the law of the Jews* (*B*), *nor against the temple* (*C*), *nor against Caesar* (*A*) *have I sinned at all*. (*A*) The first charge, viz. of disturbing the public peace, had been brought against him at Philippi and Thessalonica. And, although S. Paul himself was perfectly innocent of any

---

[1] in the Greek—*eucharistia, pronoia* (=Lat. *providentia*).   [2] xv 2, xxiii 7.
[3] vi 14, cp. ii 22, iii 6, iv 10: so also *the way* in verse 14.   [4] But even in the AV and Bezan texts the *from whom* of verse 8 probably looks back to S. Paul: for *examining* is a word much more applicable to Paul the prisoner than to a witness of the rank of Lysias.   [5] Cp. vii 1.

seditious intentions, his preaching had certainly been attended by public disturbances, which were very distasteful to the Roman authorities. This then was the most dangerous charge, suggestive of conspiracy against the imperial government. The mention of Caesar had terrified the provincial magistrates at Thessalonica; and at Jerusalem it had finally overcome Pilate's reluctance to condemn the Lord. It is significant that Tertullus does not actually speak of Caesar, and the reason was no doubt the same as at Corinth (p. 330): S. Paul had been very careful in his utterances about the kingdom, and the question of loyalty to Caesar was a dangerous weapon for the Jews to handle. (*B*) The religious charge had been brought forward at Corinth, but it was peculiarly irksome and tedious to the Romans. It concerned the Jewish law which the Romans did not attempt or desire to understand. Such questions they left to the Jews to be settled among themselves. But if the Jews repudiated the Nazarene sect, it was thereby rendered an 'unlawful religion,' having received as yet no independent official recognition from the state. By the strange irony of events, at Philippi Paul had been attacked by the Gentiles for spreading Jewish customs. (*C*) The third charge, if proved, would have been fatal. Even a Roman was liable to the penalty of death for trespassing beyond the barrier in the temple. But there were no witnesses to prove the trespass (verse 19); nor could the actual trespasser, the Gentile in question, be produced,—unless indeed S. Luke was accused on this ground and stood with S. Paul at the bar; but, except for xxvii 1, the narrative is silent as to S. Luke's share in the proceedings.

It is possible to make a similar distinction in the various accusations brought against the Lord himself. There too was (*A*) a political charge—he was a mover of insurrections among the people, and had actually made himself a 'king' as against Caesar: (*B*) a religious charge—he was guilty of blasphemy, an offence against the Jewish law: and (*C*) a particular charge—he had spoken against the temple[1].

S. Paul's defence to the Roman governor

After hearing the case for the prosecution, Felix with a gesture called on the prisoner for the defence; and for the third time Paul stands up to speak before a Roman governor. But the Greek freedman, who after all was but a procurator, was a very different person from the aristocratic proconsuls Gallio and Sergius Paulus (pp. 200, 329). Paul conforms to usage in beginning with a *captatio benevolentiae*, and then answers the charges. The first (*A*) he denies: the second (*B*) he admits in a sense: against the third (*C*) he indignantly protests, giving his version of the affair. Brief as this summary is, we can yet detect the customary lines of S. Paul's thought in the mention of *faith* and *hope*, in conjunction with his example of charity; and the indignant conclusion, which breaks up the grammatical construction in verses 18–20, is characteristic of his usual vehemence.

---

[1] (*A*) Lk xxiii 2, 5, Mt xxvii 11, Mk xv 2, Jn xviii 33. (*B*) Lk xxiii 66–71, Mt xxvi 65, Mk xiv 64, Jn xix 7. (*C*) Mt xxvi 61, Mk xiv 58.

10   And when the governor had beckoned unto him to speak, Paul answered,

Forasmuch as I know that thou hast been of many years a judge unto this nation, I do ¹cheerfully make my defence:
11 seeing that thou canst take knowledge, that it is not more than twelve days since I went up to worship at Jerusalem:
12 and neither in the temple did they find me disputing with any man or ²stirring up a crowd, nor in the synagogues,
13 nor in the city. Neither can they prove to thee the things
14 whereof they now accuse me. But this I confess unto thee, that after the Way which they call ³a sect, so ⁴serve I the God of our fathers, believing all things which are ⁵according
15 to the law, and which are written in the prophets: having hope toward God, which these also themselves ⁶look for, that there shall be a resurrection both of the just and unjust.
16 Herein do I also exercise myself to have a conscience void
17 of offence toward God and men alway. Now after many years I came to bring alms to my nation, and offerings:
18 ⁷amidst which they found me purified in the temple, with no crowd, nor yet with tumult: but *there were* certain Jews
19 from Asia—who ought to have been here before thee, and to
20 make accusation, if they had aught against me. Or else let these men themselves say what wrong-doing they found, when
21 I stood before the council, except it be for this one voice, that I cried standing among them, Touching the resurrection of the dead I am ⁸called in question before you this day.

Though S. Paul's lips were apparently unable to frame the words *most excellent Felix* however conventional, yet he still finds cause for congratulation. Felix had been *a judge* for the Jews *several years*, viz. as procurator since 51 or 52 and before that as a prefect in Samaria. This continuance in office, in itself an advantage to a province, gave to Felix an acquaintance with Jewish customs,—and in particular with the history of the Nazarenes (verse 22),—which in its turn gave S Paul more heart for his defence. Felix
11 *would be able to* understand not only the reason of Paul's visit to Jerusalem, but his loyalty to his nation. Paul had *come up* as a

---

¹ AV reads *the more cheerfully*.   ² AV reads *raising up the people*.   ³ Gk *heresy*.   ⁴ or *worship*.   ⁵ AV reads *written in the law and the prophets*.   ⁶ Marg *accept*, AV *allow*.   ⁷ Marg *in* presenting *which*: AV reads *whereupon certain Jews from Asia found me...with tumult: [who ought*.   ⁸ Gk *being judged*.

pilgrim to take part in the great national festival of Pentecost: and he had come, not only *to worship* with his fellow-countrymen, but also *to bring* them *aims*.

(*A*) *Twelve days* had elapsed since his arrival—it could be verified by the date of the festival. And in that short space of time (which was itself preceded by an absence of *many years*), so 12 far from 'moving an insurrection,' nowhere—neither *in temple, synagogue*, nor *street*,—had he been guilty of *causing a crowd to collect* (verse 18)[1]. Nor had he even *reasoned* or discussed with individuals on any provocative topic, such as 'the sect of the Nazarenes.' It is evident that in Jerusalem Paul had abstained from any evangelistic work: since the compact made with the other apostles at the council of Jerusalem (p. 246), he no longer reckoned that city as lying within his province[2].

14 But (*B*) he admitted that he belonged to the so-called '*sect* of the Nazarenes.' The word *sect* (Gk *heresy*), which means 'choice' and so was used for a 'choice' of opinions, i.e. a school of thought, is evidently acquiring the bad sense of a self-willed 'choice' or 'heresy[3].' But S. Paul will not allow the faith in Jesus to be so definitely a *sect* among the Jews as the *sects* of the Pharisees and Sadducees[4]. It was only *a way*, or manner of living. In that *way* (i) he *worshipped* the same God as the rest of the Jews; and to *serve the ancestral God* was as sacred a tradition among the Gentiles as among the Jews[5]. Further, in this service he had the same 15 entire *faith* in the Jewish scriptures[6], and the same *hope in God*, as his accusers here present. But when S. Paul goes on to define this hope as the expectation of *a resurrection* of the dead, the Sadducees would part company with him; and, when he further adds *both of the just and the unjust*, or *the righteous and the wicked*, it is doubtful how far he would carry all the Pharisees with him. Daniel xii 2 certainly taught the resurrection of the wicked, but whether this extended to the Gentiles—and it was evidently the thought of his Roman judge which prompted Paul's remark, verse 25—was a matter of discussion among the doctors. (ii) Further, apart from 16 the doctrinal aspect of the Way, its moral requirements were such as to make S. Paul more than ever anxious, even at the cost of diligent *self-discipline*, to avoid giving *offence to God or man at*

---

[1] There is no exact parallel to the phrase in the Greek, the literal translation of which is *making a stopping of a crowd*. The noun (ἐπίστασις) is used for the *halting* of soldiers, and for a *stoppage* in medical language. S. Paul had not *stopped* the passers by and so collected a *crowd*. As used in II Macc vi 3 and II Cor xi 28, the word has a more active sense, viz. of the *pressure* of anxiety or the *onset* of misfortune; and so here it might denote the *pressure* exercised by the crowd upon the authorities. But S. Paul is instancing the least, and not the greatest, causes of offence. Indeed, a passage in Polybius (XL 4) might make us ask whether the phrase could not mean *attracting the attention of the crowd*. [2] as he had done before, ix 29: cp. II Cor x 14–6, Rom xv 20. [3] as in I Cor xi 19, Gal vi 21: see p. 44. [4] xxvi 5, v 17. [5] Cp. I Pet i 18. [6] Taken strictly the RV denotes faith in (1) the customs, ritual, observance of the law (with its fulfilment in Christ), and (2) the scriptures of the prophets.

*any time*¹. Certainly his *conscience* acquitted him of having caused
17 any offence to his countrymen. Indeed, life in the Way had called
out into more active exercise his charity towards them. For he had
come up to Jerusalem *to bring alms to his nation*. As he had
denied the Nazarenes to be a *sect*, so the apostle refuses to acknowledge that those of the Way, to whom he had brought the alms,
viz. the Christian poor, are a whit less Jews than his accusers.
S. Paul adds that he had also come up *to make offerings*. The next
clause seems to identify these *offerings* with the sacrifices for the
Nazirites (xxi 26), which had not in fact formed part of the object
of S. Paul's visit. But, bearing in mind that this is only a compressed report of S. Paul's actual speech, we can readily understand
that the word *offerings* is simply an abbreviation for S. Paul's fuller
account of the events of xxi 26-7, which S. Luke considers it unnecessary to repeat. If, however, we still wish to press the literal
meaning of the phrase *to bring offerings*, it will imply that, as has
been suggested above (p. 414), S. Paul came up to Jerusalem with
the additional intention of fulfilling a vow of his own, or of making
some thank-offering in the temple.

18 (*C*) So far from profaning *the temple*, the Jews *had found him*
duly observing their national customs therein, as described above,
p. 419. But at the recollection of the riot S. Paul's indignation
at the utter falsity of the charge causes him to break off suddenly²
20 and turn round on his accusers. Even they, the Sanhedrin, had
been unable to pronounce him guilty, when *standing before them*;
and now he challenges them to say *what crime they found* in him,
21 unless indeed they reckoned as such his faith in the *resurrection*, of
which the Pharisees themselves were ardent supporters (verse 15).

Felix adjourns the case

22 But Felix, having more exact knowledge concerning the
Way, deferred them, saying, When Lysias the chief captain
23 shall come down, I will determine your matter. And he gave
order to the centurion that he should be kept in charge, and
should have indulgence; and not to forbid any of ³his friends
to minister⁴ unto him.

22 To S. Paul's indignant question his accusers could give no
answer: there was no evidence whatever against him. His real
crime was simply that he was a consistent Christian. *Felix*, owing
to his residence in Palestine, had for a Roman *a very accurate
knowledge* of this new *Way*, and he perceived this. He knew also

---

¹ The whole of life falls under the interrogation of conscience, because God is *alway* present (ii 25). Cp. xxiii 1, p. 432. ² *There were* (RV) is not in the Greek, and the sentence is left unfinished: cp. xxiii 9. ³ literally *his own* (Jn i 11). ⁴ AV adds *or come*.

that this was no real crime; the other Christians were left unmolested even by the Jews, and Paul ought to have been set free. Nevertheless he *adjourned* the case. He had already had difficulties with the Jews; an influential deputation had now come down, which represented the whole nation, and he did not want to offend them. There was a good excuse: the accusers and accused contradicted one another, and the obvious course was to wait for the evidence of *Lysias*. Accordingly Felix pronounced the word 'Amplius,' and
23 the case was adjourned. Meanwhile Paul was to *be kept in charge*, viz. in 'free custody.' He was probably chained by the arm to a soldier, and placed under the surveillance of a *centurion*; but otherwise he enjoyed his 'liberty' (AV), and *his friends* had free access to him[1].

Lysias however did not come. Nor did Felix seem in a hurry to sit for the second hearing. The Jews would not press for it. They knew that they had a bad case; and their relations with Felix were becoming more and more strained. Accordingly, although unconvicted, Paul was kept in confinement. S. Luke however avenges the injustice. In one of his vivid pictures he portrays, and so condemns, the character of Felix, like that of another unjust judge—Agrippa I (xii 20-23).

Paul and Felix

24 But after certain days, Felix came with Drusilla, ²his wife, which was a Jewess³, and sent for Paul, and heard him
25 concerning the faith in Christ Jesus. And as he reasoned of righteousness, and ⁴temperance, and the judgement to come, Felix was ⁵terrified, and answered, Go thy way for this time; and when I have a convenient season, I will call thee unto
26 me. He hoped withal that money would be given him of Paul⁶: wherefore also he sent for him the oftener, and communed with him.

27 But when two years were fulfilled, Felix was succeeded by Porcius Festus; ⁷and desiring to gain favour with the Jews, Felix left Paul in bonds.

24 The recent events at Jerusalem, as well as the rapid growth of Christianity, had aroused much curiosity as to S. Paul—among others in the governor's *wife*. His present wife *Drusilla* (for Felix

---

[1] This *indulgence* may be illustrated by Josephus' description of the confinement of Agrippa I who was imprisoned by Tiberius for uttering some rash words (*Ant.* xviii 6. 7). After his liberation by Caligula he dedicated a chain of gold in the temple. ² Gk *his own wife*. ³ Bezan adds *who asked to see Paul and hear the word. Being willing therefore to satisfy her, he* [*sent*. ⁴ Marg *self-control*. ⁵ or *alarmed*. ⁶ AV adds *that he might loose him*. ⁷ Bezan reads *but Paul he left in ward for the sake of Drusilla*.

was thrice married) *was a Jewess*. Drusilla was the daughter of the Herod (Agrippa I) who slew James and would have slain Peter, and the sister of the Agrippa (II) of ch. xxvi. Her brother had given her in marriage to Azizus king of Emesa, who had for her sake submitted to circumcision. But, as we have seen (p. 409), Drusilla abandoned Azizus for Felix, out of jealousy (it was alleged) of her sister Berenice, a rival beauty. At the death of her father in 44 Drusilla was 6 years old, so she would now be about 17 or 18. According to the very probable version of some Bezan authorities, it was in order to gratify her curiosity that Felix *sent for Paul*[1] to give account of his *faith*. This was probably to be given in the audience chamber; and the scene was an anticipation, on a smaller scale, of that described in ch. xxvi[2]. Felix however was a man of
25 a different moral fibre to Festus. Paul read his character well; he would also know that Drusilla was another man's wife. Therefore, instead of delivering an oratorical 'apologia,' S. Paul, like another John the Baptist[3], *reasoned* concerning the first principles of the Christ, viz. *righteousness, continence, and the judgement to come*[4]. The first two chapters of the Epistle to the Romans shew us how the apostle could treat the subject. *Felix was alarmed* (as he had reason to be) and broke off the audience saying that when he *found*
26 another *opportunity* he would *summon* him again for a (public) audience. For in private Felix had frequent conversations with him. Felix' conscience had not been very deeply stirred, and he *hoped* that Paul would purchase his liberty by a bribe. In this expectation S. Luke gives us his estimate of Felix' administration of justice[5]. We cannot help being surprised at the little effect produced upon Felix by his intercourse with S. Paul. The case had been very different with the governor of Cyprus. But in the servile character of this Greek adventurer there was not any depth of soil in which the word could germinate.

Work at Caesarea

S. Paul remained in confinement at Caesarea, waiting for the second hearing, *two full years*. This note of time marks an epoch. After Antioch, Corinth, and Ephesus, Caesarea now in its turn becomes S. Paul's head-quarters. As a capital Caesarea was not equal to the other cities: but as the scene of the reception of Cornelius into the church by S. Peter (ch. x), it could be considered as the mother-city of the Gentile churches; and, having S. Philip the Evangelist for an intermediary, it forms a link between the two 'front-rank' apostles.

---

[1] from his place of confinement, which need not have been in the Praetorium. [2] Cp. also xiii 7. [3] who told Herod Antipas that he might not have his brother Philip's wife (Lk iii 19). The emphasis in the words *his own wife* may therefore be an instance of irony, unless they are meant to convey a reproach to the *Jewess* Drusilla for marrying the Gentile Felix. [4] Cp. Hebr vi 1. [5] Similarly, when Albinus, the successor of Festus, left the province, 'only he who did not give was left in prison as a criminal' (Josephus *B. J.* II 14. 11).

S. Paul's confinement was not harsh. It was the 'custodia libera' described above; and very likely, as afterwards at Rome, he lived in a lodging of his own[1]. He would enjoy the society of S. Philip and the Christians of Caesarea, and his own disciples would quickly gather round. S. Luke and Aristarchus were at his side, sharing in some way his captivity[2]. Further, communication with his churches of Macedonia, Achaia, and Asia, would be reopened. Indeed there is some ground for supposing that the Epistles to the Ephesians, Colossians, and Philemon, were written from the apostle's prison—not at Rome but—at Caesarea. It is almost certain that he must have written during this period to the churches 'in Asia'—and who so fitting a messenger as Tychicus, who had come up with him to Jerusalem[3]? He must also have been counting on restoration to liberty as soon as Felix would hear his case[4]. Nevertheless, though some circumstances would suit Caesarea very well, the general situation implied in the letters, together with their style and theology, has decided most critics in favour of the Roman imprisonment.

Other literary works however, we may be confident, were in progress. Precluded from active work by his attendance on S. Paul, the mind of S. Luke must have turned to literary occupations, for which he was so well fitted. The development of affairs and the contact with governors and Roman personages shewed that the Roman world was ready for a literary presentation of Christianity. Besides, there were pressing needs at home within the church. The churches of Asia, Achaia, and Macedonia, now deprived of their founder, stood in sore need of some authentic account of the word he preached. His own literary instincts must have convinced S. Luke of the necessity of some permanent record of 'the matters which had been fulfilled among' the passing generation, if they were not to be wholly lost. In fact there had already been a number of attempts at such records. But these had been fragmentary, and not wholly successful. Indeed they could hardly have been otherwise, until sufficient time had elapsed to enable the eye to take in the past as a whole. Now however the moment had come to draw up an orderly narrative 'of all things from the first[5].' For carrying out such a work the evangelist had unrivalled opportunities at Caesarea. The apostolic cycle of oral teaching must have assumed a more or less fixed form some years earlier, before the Twelve had left Jerusalem: this form would correspond to the groundwork of S. Mark's Gospel, and so much may have already been committed to writing. At any rate in Palestine S. Luke would have access to the apostolic tradition in its purest form; as also to many of the original authorities, who had been 'eye-witnesses and ministers of the word from the beginning.' If not the Blessed Virgin herself, there were members of the Lord's family still living: such was James the Lord's brother. There were also 'early disciples,' like Mnason, who could recollect incidents of the Lord's ministry, and

---
[1] xxviii 30. [2] xxvii 1-2: Col iv 10 *Aristarchus my fellow-prisoner.*
[3] xx 4, Eph vi 21-2, Col iv 7-9. [4] Philem 22. [5] Lk i 1-4.

give an account of the early growth of the church. Preeminent among these would rank Philip the Evangelist; and from him S. Luke might have obtained most of his information for the early part of the Acts. Besides this, S. Luke had his own notes of S. Paul's work on the shores of the Aegean and of the recent journey and the trials: these could now be written out at leisure. The Acts of course could not have been completed as yet; but there seems no adequate reason why the Gospel may not have been substantially compiled (if not actually published and sent to Theophilus) in the course of these two years.

All this however is matter of conjecture. From Josephus we can learn something of the political events that were taking place outside S. Paul's prison. Caesarea was originally a Syrian city; but after it had been refounded and rebuilt by Herod the Great, Jews and Syrians enjoyed equal rights of citizenship. This led to constant friction and disturbance. The Jews formed the wealthier and more influential class of citizens; but the Syrian populace was supported by the Roman garrison, which was largely recruited from the Syrian inhabitants. While Paul was at Caesarea, the party jealousies at last broke out in an open fight between Jews and Gentiles in the market-place. Felix ordered the Jews to return home; and when they refused to go, he let loose his soldiery, who slew many of them and pillaged their houses. This resulted in appeals to Rome, and Felix himself was recalled to answer for the riot. The Jewish deputation at Rome then accused Felix of misgovernment, and it would have gone badly with him but for the influence of his brother Pallas (p. 409).

27   When he left Caesarea, having now good reason *to conciliate the Jews, Felix left Paul in bonds*[1]. The Bezan text informs us that he did so at the special request of Drusilla, who can have borne no greater love for Paul than Herodias for John the Baptist. Felix' *successor* was *Porcius Festus*, of whom we know little. In comparison with his predecessor Felix and his successor Albinus, he seems to have been a just and good governor. His name has a genuine Roman sound; Roman ideals of justice were his guiding principles (xxv 16); and S. Paul treats him with evident respect (xxvi 25). Unfortunately for the Jews he died after a short term of office.

§ 2   *The trial before Festus and appeal to Caesar*

One of the first duties of a new governor would be to settle all causes left undecided by his predecessor. The Jews too were quick to seize their opportunity with a new and inexperienced governor: no doubt the presence of the apostle at Caesarea had proved a great source of strength to the 'sect of the Nazarenes,' and so inflamed their hostility.

---

[1] Cp. xii 3. Albinus, having similar reasons to curry favour with the Jews when he left Judaea, executed the most guilty of his prisoners, but set free those accused of lighter charges (Josephus *Ant.* xx 9. 5). For the exact meaning of the phrase translated *to gain favour*, see on xxv 9, p. 455.

Accordingly they at once lodged a fresh indictment against S. Paul. Festus on his side displayed the qualities of a just judge. He appealed to the Roman traditions of justice; he made no delay; and there is no suggestion of bribery. But he was evidently perplexed by these questions about Jewish law, which were entirely new to him. The unanimous feeling of the Jewish nation must have had great weight with him, and their Sanhedrin was obviously the natural court to settle such matters. His attitude decided S. Paul's course of action. S. Paul had waited two years for the hearing of his case; and now with a good governor, who admitted his innocence from the point of view of a Roman judge, he finds that all that he can expect is to have his case sent back to the Sanhedrin. What their sentence would be he knew very well, viz. *that he ought not to live any longer* (verse 24). There was but one alternative left, and this he adopted; it was an appeal unto Caesar.

This appeal was originally to the Roman people, but since the days of Augustus, the Caesar had stepped into their place. This change made the power of appeal one of the most valuable privileges of a citizen of the empire. For the Caesar's jealousy for his own power made him very scrupulous to protect this right of appeal to himself. There were certain restrictions to prevent abuse of the privilege, as, for instance, in the case of brigandage or sedition when prompt measures were necessary. But otherwise, the moment the appellant uttered the words *Caesarem appello*, all proceedings in the provincial court were stayed and his case was remitted to Rome. Till he was heard there, he was treated as uncondemned, and protected from any violent treatment by the severest penalties. Thus by uttering two words S. Paul was able to deliver himself altogether out of the power of the Jews. This utterance (in verse 11) is the critical moment in the whole process. The final issue was probably still uncertain when S. Luke was penning this narrative[1]; but for the present the apostle was secured against all attacks of the Jews, and transferred to another arena.

For this very reason, however, it was with great reluctance that S. Paul made his appeal. It was the final and complete assertion of his Roman citizenship and acceptance of Caesar as his king: to the Jews it meant repudiation of the theocracy and apostasy from Moses. But the apostle in the past two years must have thoroughly weighed the question. The Lord himself in the vision at Jerusalem (xxiii 11) might almost be said to have suggested it; for it seemed at the time the only possible method of reaching Rome. And lastly, the Jews were quite accustomed to making appeals themselves. This very year deputations had gone to Rome from Caesarea: the difficulties, which arose out of the Samaritan disturbance mentioned above, had been settled at Rome by Claudius: before that the Jews had been obliged to appeal against their procurators Cuspius Fadus and Pontius Pilate: and we have the famous account of the embassy of Alexandrine Jews to Caligula written

---

[1] See Introd. ch. iii § 5.

by Philo, himself one of the delegates. But all these appeals were against the Roman officials or Gentile violence. The Jews had not appealed against one another on matters of their own law. Therefore S. Luke endeavours to make it clear, by an accurate narrative of the facts, that in this matter of the appeal Paul was acting under the same compulsion as the Jews themselves, viz. the compulsion of injustice: *I was constrained to appeal unto Caesar*, says the apostle at Rome[1].

25 Festus therefore, having ²come into the province, after
2 three days went up to Jerusalem from Cæsarea. And the ³chief priests and the ⁴principal men of the Jews informed
3 him against Paul; and they besought him, asking favour against him, that he would send for him to Jerusalem;
4 laying wait to kill him on the way. Howbeit Festus answered, that Paul was kept in charge at Cæsarea, and that he himself
5 was about to depart *thither* shortly. Let them therefore, saith he, which are ⁵of power among you, go down with me, and if there is anything amiss in the man, let them accuse him.
6 And when he had tarried among them ⁶not more than eight or ten days, he went down unto Cæsarea; and on the morrow he sat on the ⁷judgement-seat, and commanded Paul
7 to be brought. And when he was come, the Jews which had come down from Jerusalem stood round about him, bringing against him many and ⁸grievous charges, which they could
8 not prove; while Paul said in his defence, Neither against the law of the Jews, nor against the temple, nor against
9 Cæsar, have I sinned at all. But Festus, desiring to gain favour with the Jews, answered Paul, and said, Wilt thou go up to Jerusalem, and there be judged of these things before
10 me? But Paul said, I am standing before Cæsar's ⁷judgement-seat, where I ought to be judged: to the Jews have
11 I done no wrong, as thou also very well knowest. If then I am a wrong-doer, and have committed anything worthy of death, I refuse not to die: but ⁹if none of those things is *true*,

---

[1] xxviii 19. See also pp. 405–6. ² Marg *entered upon his province*.
³ Gk *high-priests*: AV reads *high-priest*. ⁴ Gk *first*. ⁵ AV *able*. ⁶ AV omits *not* and *eight or*; but AV marg agrees with our text. ⁷ Gk *bēma*.
⁸ Gk *heavy*. ⁹ AV translates the Gk literally *if there be none of these things* (omitting *is true*).

T

whereof these accuse me, no man can ¹give me up unto them.
12 I appeal unto Cæsar. Then Festus, when he had conferred with the council, answered, ²Thou hast appealed unto Cæsar: unto Cæsar shalt thou go.

1 *Festus* probably landed at Caesarea in the early summer of 57; and after a day's rest³, *went up*, like an active and conscientious governor, *to Jerusalem*, the real capital of the country. At Jerusalem there was a new high-priest, Ishmael ben Phabi having taken the
2 place of Ananias, but the change meant no change of policy. For *the high-priests and the first men of the Jews*, i.e. the Sadducean faction and the leaders of the Sanhedrin⁴, at once *lodged an indictment against Paul*. This was endorsed by *the whole people*, who in a tumultuous throng demanded his death (verse 24). Festus refused to condemn him without a proper trial and hearing his
3 defence⁵. Then the Jewish authorities *asked* as a *favour* that he might be *brought to Jerusalem* for trial before the Sanhedrin, their object being to procure his assassination on the way. This would be no difficult matter in the unsettled state of the country⁶: and two years ago forty men had taken a vow to kill Paul (xxiii 12).
4 *Festus replied that*, as the prisoner was *at Caesarea*, and he himself was returning thither (to receive Agrippa and the other magnates
5 of the province), the trial should take place there; and an *influential*⁷ body of the Jews should *come down and accuse him, if* he had done anything *amiss*.
6 Festus only stayed at Jerusalem *eight or ten days*⁸; and after his return to Caesarea he held his court *without delay* (verse 17),
7 and *Paul was brought in* for trial. The prosecutors *from Jerusalem surrounded him* and made up for their want of evidence by the violence of their *outcries*, declaring that *he was unfit to live*⁹. Festus was surprised to find that the *grievous* misdemeanours of which he was accused were not of a criminal character, but *concerned their religion*¹⁰, their *temple* and *law*, and in particular *one Jesus who was dead* and whose claims were
8 supposed to affect the position of *Caesar*. Paul denied the charges but *affirmed* more than once *that this Jesus was alive*. Festus, not having Felix' acquaintance with 'the way,' was completely bewildered;

---

¹ Gk *grant me by favour*. ² or, as AV, *Hast thou appealed unto Caesar?* ³ *after three days* = *on the third day*; cp. xxviii 17. ⁴ For the 'First Ten' see p. 222 n. ⁵. On a later occasion Festus allowed Ishmael and 'the first ten' of the Jews to go on a deputation to Rome (Joseph. *Ant.* xx 8. 11). Here, as in xiii 50 and xvii 4, we see *the first* becoming a general term for the leading men of a place. ⁵ We have Festus' account of the proceedings in vv. 14-21, 24-5. ⁶ Festus' first occupation was to try and clear Judaea of the *sicarii* and brigands (Joseph. *Ant.* xx 8. 10). ⁷ The Greek word (lit. *powerful*) is regularly used in Josephus for the 'influential': as also in I Cor i 26 *mighty*. ⁸ The expression shews S. Luke's care to be accurate, and that we can depend upon his figures elsewhere. ⁹ Cp. Lk xxiii 10 *stood, vehemently accusing him*. ¹⁰ verse 19 · for this word see on xvii 22, p. 308.

and the obvious solution was to refer the matter, as the Jews had
9 requested, to the Sanhedrin. Besides, he was not indisposed to seize
the opportunity of *gaining popularity with the Jews*[1], while his own
presence at the sitting of the Sanhedrin would be a guarantee
against injustice. But Paul was a Roman citizen and his case
could not be submitted to a provincial tribunal without his own
10 consent. This he refused to give. He was already *in Caesar's
court*, for the procurator was Caesar's representative, and in that
court *judgement ought to be* pronounced. Festus could very clearly
perceive, in fact he had admitted, *that he was guilty of no crime
11 against the Jews*. If it could be proved that he had been guilty of
any specific injury, he was ready to be punished : but he refused, as
a confessedly innocent man, *to be made a present of* to the Jews[2].
This he once for all made *impossible* by uttering the two words
12 *Caesarem appello, I appeal unto Caesar*. Festus first *conferred
with his council*, the officials and legal advisers who formed a
Roman governor's 'court,' and then declared that the appeal was
allowed. '*To Caesar thou hast appealed*[3]. *To Caesar thou shalt go*.'
By these solemn and decisive words the Jews, who had been
thronging Paul like hungry wolves, were balked of their prey.
Festus' difficulty however was not at an end. With the prisoner
he would have to send 'letters dimissory' containing a statement
of the case (verse 26), and how was he to present this affair in a
Roman dress? Circumstances solved the difficulty by the introduction of a new personage.

§ 3 *Paul and Agrippa*

On the arrival of a new governor the dependent princes of the
neighbourhood and other magnates would hasten to pay him their
respects, and accordingly *Agrippa the king and Berenice*[4] *came down to
Caesarea*. This Agrippa (II) was the son of the Herod Agrippa who
had been king of Judaea and died in 44 (ch. xii). At the time of
his father's death Agrippa II was at Rome, where he was being brought
up at the court of Claudius. As he was then only 17 years old, Claudius
did not give him his father's kingdom, but kept him still at Rome.
About eight years later, Herod king of Chalcis[5], who was Agrippa's
uncle and had married his sister Berenice, died, and Claudius gave
Chalcis to Agrippa. At the same time he gave him the prerogative of

---

[1] The literal sense of the Greek is *lay up favour as a deposit*, i.e. lay the Jews under an obligation.   [2] as had been the case with the Lord (iii 14).
[3] The verb may be affirmative or interrogative. The order of the words in the Greek is in favour of the former alternative; I Cor vii 18, 21, 27 of the latter. The interrogative translation rather detracts from the solemnity of the sentence and gives it a ring of annoyance, as if Festus was not pleased with being appealed against in his first trial. In I Cor i 13 there is a similar uncertainty.   [4] The *Bernice* of the text is a popular abbreviation of *Berenice*, which is the Macedonian form of the Greek *Pherenice* (=*carrying off the victory*). Veronica is another form of the same name.   [5] Chalcis was a principality of Coele Syria in Mt Lebanon, NW of Damascus.

appointing the high-priests of the Jews, together with the supervision of the temple. In 53 Claudius gave him, in exchange for Chalcis, some principalities in Northern Palestine with the title of *king*. This was the cause of Agrippa's leaving Rome, and he returned to Palestine, where we now find him at the age of thirty. Besides this son, Agrippa I had also left behind him three daughters—Berenice, Mariamne and Drusilla. Drusilla's fortunes we have traced. Berenice, on the death of her uncle and first husband Herod, had joined her brother Agrippa at Rome. When scandalous reports began to be circulated in Roman society as to their mutual relations, Berenice left the city to marry Polemo, a Cilician potentate. It was not long, however, before she deserted him, and returned to her brother, in whose company she was now visiting Caesarea.

The arrival of Agrippa was a godsend for Festus. On the one side he was a real Jew and held an authoritative position in the Jewish religious polity. He was therefore fully conversant with Jewish customs and theology. When at Rome, he had on two occasions used his influence with Claudius on behalf of his countrymen with success. Against one governor, Cuspius Fadus, he had secured for the Jews the custody of the high-priest's vestments; he also procured for them the condemnation of another governor, Cumanus. On the other side, like all the Herods and their partisans the Herodians, he was thoroughly Roman in tastes and sympathies. He had been educated at Rome and before his accession had hardly seen Judaea. On his coins he calls himself PHILOCAESAR and PHILOROMAIOS. Further, at the present moment he was not on good terms with the high-priestly party. He had deposed Ananias from the high-priesthood[1], and an open rupture was imminent. In his palace at Jerusalem Agrippa was building a tower which overlooked the temple courts; to cut off his view the high-priests raised a counter-wall; and the quarrel which ensued had to be settled at Rome. When the Jewish rebellion was on the point of breaking out in 66, Herod did his utmost to avert it; as did Berenice, who at the time of the outbreak was in Jerusalem in fulfilment of a Nazirite vow. But when the war actually broke out, Herod sided with the Romans and remained loyal to them to the end.

This double character of Agrippa made Paul also the more ready to make his defence before him. Agrippa would thoroughly understand the points at issue, and at the same time was no bigot; rather, his actual relations to the high-priests would dispose him to give Paul an impartial hearing. Accordingly the apostle made a great effort and delivered the speech which is evidently intended by S. Luke to form a climax in his work. The solemnity of the occasion is marked by its elaborate setting, and the repetitions which it involves[2]. Three times over we read the account of Festus' dealings with the Jews; and thereby three times is the apostle's innocence insinuated[3]. For the

---

[1] So in later years he deposed Ananus after his illegal murder of S. James.
[2] There is similar repetition in chapters x-xi, which also centre round Caesarea.
[3] vv. 10, 18, 25.

third time we hear the story of S. Paul's conversion. That famous episode is now told by the apostle in a scene of pomp and before a distinguished audience of Jewish and Gentile magnates, before a Roman governor and a Jewish king,—in a word *before the Gentiles and kings and the children of Israel* (ix 15).

The emphasis lies on the word *king* (v. 13)[1]. Christianity is the religion of glad tidings to the poor, and it began with them[2]. But as it affects all human life, sooner or later it reaches the highest ranks and royalty itself. Since the Incarnation all kings and ruling powers within the sphere of Christian influence have had to make their reckoning with the church. They cannot avoid it, for the life of the church is intimately connected with the welfare of their subjects; and because of their public character and the widespread consequences of their actions, the attitude of rulers towards Christianity is at once most conspicuous and most pregnant with results for good or evil. Thus with good reason S. Luke, whose sympathies on the side of poverty are most evident, is careful to sketch for us the appeal which the gospel makes to the great and noble of the earth. We have already noticed some aristocratic leanings[3]; and this scene shews us the catholic character of his interests, which can take in all, both great and small (xxvi 22). In the political world indeed Agrippa was only a petty potentate, but socially he represented a great influence. The Herodian family stand out conspicuous for their intimate connexion with the family of the Caesars, which gave them a leading position in Roman society. Herod the Great had been a favourite both of Antony and Augustus. His grandson Agrippa I was educated in the imperial household, and it was his intimate friendship with the young Gaius Caesar, afterwards the Emperor Caligula, which brought him under the displeasure of Tiberius (p. 173). His son, again, Agrippa II, was brought up at the court of Claudius. Even when the Julian line was displaced by the family of the Flavians the connexion still continued. For Berenice attracted the attention of Vespasian, and became the mistress of his son Titus. She accompanied Titus to Rome, but when he succeeded his father, the scandal became too great and Berenice had to leave the city.

And now Paul the apostle is brought into contact with this worldly and philo-roman family of the Herods. It is striking how the fortunes of that family were bound up with the origins of the church, but it was an ill-starred connexion for the Herods. Their founder, Herod the Great, had tried to destroy the infant Jesus. His son Antipas, the tetrarch of Galilee, beheaded John the Baptist, and won from the Lord the title of 'fox.' His grandson Agrippa I slew James the son of Zebedee with the sword. Now we see Paul brought before Agrippa's son. As the Lord before Herod Antipas, so Paul stands before Herod Agrippa II; and on each occasion the trial served to cement the friend-

---

[1] It occurs in these chapters 11 times, elsewhere in the Acts only 9 times altogether: cp. also *the Augustus* in vv. 21, 25 and *the lord* (= *dominus*) in 26.
[2] Cp. Lk iv 18, vi 20, vii 22.   [3] See p. 292.

ship between the Herodian prince and the Roman governor. S. Peter also had the honour of being arrested by a Herod: and the pomp of this scene is an evident counterpicture to the ostentatious display made at Caesarea by the first Agrippa[1]. Of all these Herods, Agrippa II comes out the best. The Lord would not open his lips before Antipas; nor would Paul give an exposition of his faith before Drusilla. But before Agrippa II the apostle makes his most elaborate 'apologia pro vitâ suâ'; he bears witness to the king's Jewish faith; he had even hopes of winning him to Christianity. It is true that Agrippa somewhat cynically warded off S. Paul's advances, but had he been as morally worthless as the other Herods, we feel sure that the apostle would have adopted a different tone[2].

Agrippa's visit to Festus

13 Now when certain days were passed, Agrippa the king
14 and Bernice arrived at Caesarea, [3]and saluted Festus. And as they tarried there many days, Festus laid Paul's case before the king, saying, There is a certain man left a prisoner
15 by Felix: about whom, when I was at Jerusalem, [4]the chief priests and the elders of the Jews informed me, asking for
16 sentence against him. To whom I answered, that it is not the custom of the Romans to give up any man[5], before that the accused have the accusers face to face, and have had opportunity to make his defence concerning the matter laid
17 against him. When therefore they were come together here, I made no delay, but on the next day sat down on the [6]judgement-seat, and commanded the man to be brought.
18 Concerning whom, when the accusers stood up, they brought
19 no charge of such evil things as I supposed; but had certain questions against him of their own [7]religion, and of one Jesus,
20 who was dead, whom Paul affirmed to be alive. And I, being perplexed how to inquire concerning these things, asked whether he would go to Jerusalem, and there be judged of
21 these matters. But when Paul had appealed to be kept for

---

[1] xii 20-3. For the Herods see Mt ii, Lk iii 19-20, ix 9 (Mt xiv 1-12), xiii 32, xxiii 7-12, Acts iv 27, xii, xiii 1.   [2] Agrippa was also a friend and patron of Josephus; and, in order to give employment to the workmen thrown out of work at the completion of the temple, he paved the city of Jerusalem.   [3] Marg *having saluted*: AV with the later MSS reads *to salute*.   [4] Gk *the high-priests and the presbyters*.   [5] AV and Bezan add *to die* (lit. *to destruction* viii 20).   [6] Gk *béma*.   [7] Marg *superstition* (p. 308).

the decision of ¹the emperor, I commanded him to be kept
22 till I should send him to Cæsar. And Agrippa *said* unto
Festus, I also ²could wish to hear the man myself. To-morrow,
saith he, thou shalt hear him.
23   So on the morrow, when Agrippa was come, and Bernice,
with great pomp, and they were entered into the place of
hearing, with the chief captains, and the principal men³ of
the city, at the command of Festus Paul was brought in.
24 And Festus saith, King Agrippa, and all men which are here
present with us, ye behold this man, about whom all the
multitude of the Jews made suit to me, both at Jerusalem
25 and here⁴, crying that he ought not to live any longer. But
I found that he had committed nothing worthy of death:
and as he himself appealed to ¹the emperor I determined to
26 send him. Of whom I have no certain thing to write unto
⁵my lord. Wherefore I have brought him forth before you,
and specially before thee, king Agrippa, that, after examination
27 had, I may have somewhat to write. For it seemeth to me
unreasonable, in sending a prisoner, not withal to signify the
charges against him.

13   *After some days Agrippa and Berenice came down to Caesarea*
from their territory in Northern Palestine⁶, *and paid Festus a
ceremonial visit.* The past participle (translated in the margin
having saluted) early proved a difficulty, and most copyists altered
it into the future—*to salute* (AV); but the translation in the text
14 *and saluted* seems to be in accordance with S. Luke's usage⁷. *They
made a stay of some days* at Caesarea, *and Festus seized the opportunity of referring Paul's case to Agrippa.* How S. Luke ascertained

---

¹ Gk *the Sebastos* (Lat. *Augustus*).   ² Marg *was wishing*.   ³ A Bezan authority
has *who had come down from the province*.   ⁴ Bezan reads *that I should deliver
him up to them for torture* [or *death*] *without any defence. But I could not deliver
him up because of the orders which we have from the Augustus. But if any one was
willing to accuse him, I said that he should follow me to Caesarea where he was in
custody. And when they had come, they cried out that his life should be taken away.*
25 *But when I had heard both sides, I found that in no respect was he worthy of
death. But when I said Wilt thou be judged with them in Jerusalem? he appealed
to Caesar.* [26 *Of whom etc.*   ⁵ Gk *the lord*.   ⁶ Had they been at their
palace in Jerusalem, they would probably have saluted Festus there.   ⁷ For
S. Luke's treatment of participles see pp. 183–4. In this part of the Acts we have
the following instances, where the words in italics stand for past participles which
come after the finite verb: xxii 24 'commanded him to be brought into the castle
and bade,' xxiii 23–5 'and he called...*and said*...*and wrote* a letter,' xxiv 22–3 'Felix
...deferred them *and said*...*and commanded.*'

what transpired between them is not obvious; Festus' communication may have been made at some public interview; at any rate the
16 account before us has every mark of truthfulness. The proud boast of *the custom of the Romans* is very characteristic of an honest Roman judge, contrasting Roman and oriental ideas of justice. The Romans do not sell their verdicts for money or for popularity[1]; nor do they condemn a man unheard. Justice was one of the virtues of the early Romans; and even in later days, compared with the corrupt administration of eastern countries, 'the Roman custom' must have seemed ideal[2]. But Roman virtue had not been proof against the temptations of power and avarice, and the oppression of the provinces with the repeated trials of their governors proves that the actual practice had fallen far below the theory. The Acts itself affords a somewhat ironical commentary on this boast. Pilate 'made a present of' Jesus to the Jews: Felix expected a bribe from S. Paul and left him in prison in order to curry favour with the Jews: Festus himself, though convinced of the apostle's innocence, kept him in prison, also to please the Jews—a motive which he naturally suppresses in the account he gives Agrippa[3].
19 Festus' words *one Jesus who was dead whom Paul affirmed to be alive* exactly represent the idea which a Roman would have about
21 the Lord. Further, in addressing a native king, he uses instead of 'Caesar' the more imposing title *the Augustus*. This word was not originally a personal name, but a Latin adjective applied in religious usage to things venerable or sacred. In B.C. 27 Octavian Caesar, having made himself master of the Roman state, adopted it as a surname. This was a device for securing a regal position in the imagination of the populace, without adopting any title which would arouse popular prejudices because of its despotic associations. As his successors likewise adopted the title, *Augustus* (like *Caesar* which was originally a private family name) became the official designation of the supreme ruler of the empire. In its Greek equivalent *Sebastos* the religious conception was still more evident. It was derived from the word for *worship*, which is used in the Acts for *the worshippers of God* or devout proselytes[4]; and being akin to *sebasma* (*an object of worship*, xvii 25), it would help on the worship of the emperor and pave the way for another title which occurs below (*Lord*). Paul having *appealed to the Augustus*, Festus had nothing to do but to wait until police and postal arrangements admitted of Paul's despatch to Rome. He was however at a loss to describe the case and applied to Agrippa for assistance.
22 This application entirely fell in with Agrippa's own desire. Like his sister Drusilla, he also had been curious to see Paul and *had*

---

[1] verse 16 *give as a favour or present*: so in verse 11 and iii 14; cp. also vv. 3, 9, and xxiv 27.   [2] Cp. Jn vii 51.   [3] See Lysias' letter for a similar suppression (xxiii 27-30).   [4] in xiii 43, 50, xvi 14, xvii 4, 17, xviii 7: the verb also occurs in xix 27. Cp. the *cohors Augusta* (Gk *Sebastē*) of xxvii 1. When Herod rebuilt Samaria he gave it the name of *Sebastē*.

XXV 22-26   IN THE AUDIENCE CHAMBER

intended[1] to ask Festus for an opportunity of *hearing the man*—a somewhat contemptuous expression when compared with the more polite word (for *man*) used by Festus in verses 5 and 14.

Agrippa's wish was gratified. Festus decided to make Paul's 'hearing' an occasion for a compliment to the king. In compensation for their loss of liberty and real power, the dependent princes and wealthy provincials found scope for their ambition in the outward show of dress and ceremonial, of decorations and grand titles. So Festus gave the young Herodian prince the opportunity of making a public display with the semblance of power; for he conceded to him (it would seem) the judge's seat, Agrippa permits Paul to speak, takes precedence of the governor in rising from his seat, and pronounces the final verdict. The scene was to be in the Palace (p. 440); not in its Basilica or hall of justice, but in the Auditorium or hall of hearing. This would be the hall devoted to matters of public ceremonial, oratorical displays, and similar shows, so corresponding to the 'schools' and 'porches' in the public gymnasia[2].

23 *Agrippa* and *Berenice* accordingly *came* to the palace in royal state, *with much splendour* of apparel[3] and escort; and then, *together with the procurator* and *the chief captains* of the Roman garrison[4], *the chief men of the city*, both Jews and Syrians, and the notables who had accompanied them from the province, they *entered the Audience-chamber* and took their seats. Then *Paul was brought*
24 *in*, still wearing his chain[5], *and Festus* presented him to the king and assembled magnates.

Festus' speech is given with fuller detail in the Bezan text; its
26 conclusion was that he had no *safe* or reliable information about Paul to *write to the lord*, viz. the emperor. The Greek word *kyrios* is here the translation of the Latin *dominus*; and the significance of both words is the same. *Dominus* denoted the master of the house (*domus*); and as the authority of the Roman paterfamilias over his household or 'family' of sons and slaves alike was well-nigh absolute, an idea of absolutism attached itself to *dominus*, which made it a term especially appropriate to the deity. Hence both Augustus and Tiberius refused the title when pressed upon them: the latter sharply rebuked those who spoke of his work as 'divine' and styled him 'lord[6].' But the ready adulation of their subjects prevailed, and after Tiberius' reign *dominus*, i.e. *the lord*, became the regular designation of the emperor. Similarly the Greek *kyrios* denoted mastership or ownership (as in xvi 19); and while on the one hand

---

[1] In comparison with the different expression for a wish in xxvi 29, the Greek verb must be taken literally, as in the margin, *I was wishing*, i.e. it had been his mind or intention. If it is simply the expression of a present wish, the form in the text should properly denote a wish which was incapable of fulfilment, as in Rom ix 3. Cp. the curiosity of Herod Antipas in Lk xxiii 8.   [2] See p. 351.
[3] not so splendid however as Agrippa I's *royal apparel* of silver (xii 21).   [4] This consisted of 5 cohorts, each of which was under a *military tribune* or *chiliarch*, of the same rank as Lysias.   [5] In verse 29 Paul uses the more dramatic and oratorical expression *these bonds*.   [6] Tacitus *Ann*. II 87.

it was used in polite conversation as equivalent to *Sir* (xvi 30, Jn xx 15), on the other *kyrios* most fitly designated the master of all things. Thus in the Greek OT *Kyrios* is JEHOVAH, while in the NT the title is shared with JEHOVAH by Jesus of Nazareth, who was to his disciples *the Lord*[1]. Festus, then, in order to solve his difficulty,
26 submits Paul to the *examination* of *king Agrippa*, who thereupon gave Paul *permission to speak on his own behalf.* Strictly speaking there was no need for S. Paul to make any defence. Having appealed to Caesar, his civil position remained unimpaired (his 'status' was 'integer'); and this preliminary examination was not a legal, but an informal, hearing. The apostle however was only too ready to accept the opportunity of bearing witness before such an assembly and would not insist upon his technical rights. The scene was one well calculated to call out his characteristic *courage*[2] and boldness of speech; and inspired by *the comfort of the Holy Ghost, he stretched forth* his arm, with the chain hanging from it,— as it were to call God to witness[3]—and *began his 'apologia.'*

Paul's defence to the world, and 'apologia pro vitâ suâ'

This speech marks the supreme effort both of the speaker and of his reporter. It is one of the most finished passages in the Acts[4], adorned with rare words[5] and with an elaboration of style, not to say grandiloquence. However much of this may be due to S. Luke's editing, the voice of S. Paul makes itself heard throughout the speech. We recognize his tact in the polite but strictly truthful compliment with which he wins the king to a patient hearing. More evident than his tact is his emotion—as in the frequent personal appeals to Agrippa (2, 13, 19, 27), and in the rush of feeling which, as in his epistles, carries him away into parentheses and digressions. Even at the beginning he turns on his audience with a direct question (8); and towards the end three times his zeal draws him from his narrative into making a statement of his gospel. Similarly the suppression of links in the argument shews the same rapidity of thought which we find in the Epistles: and the harping upon a word is a Pauline trait, e.g. *all*

---

[1] The disciples called him *Master* and *Lord*, *Magister* and *Dominus* (Jn xiii 13). Cp. ii 36 'made him *Lord.*' In many places in the Acts it is impossible to distinguish whether *Lord* stands for JEHOVAH or the Christ: see Introd. p. lxxii.
[2] This and the following mention of the Spirit are from the Bezan text. They are very characteristic and appropriate. For the former cp. xxvi 26 *speak-freely*; for the latter cp. iv 8 and the solemn word in xxvi 25 *speak-forth*, which was used in ii 14 for *utterance* inspired by the Spirit. [3] Like the Christ before Pilate, he 'witnesses the good confession' before Festus and Agrippa; and also in the sight of God and Christ—the only Potentate (I Tim vi 13-5). [4] There is hardly any variation here between the Bezan and RV text. Still in one or two places there remains an unevenness, e.g. in vv. 3, 20, 22. [5] There are 13 words which are found here alone in the NT, viz. *expert, patiently, manner of life, twelve-tribes, earnestness, being mad against, commission, brightness, kick, help, must-suffer, turn, madness.* We also notice the *if* for *that* in vv. 8, 23, and several rare forms in the Greek.

(2–4), *many* (9–11). The order of the words in the Greek makes clear the frequent rhetorical emphasis—'I lived...*a Pharisee!*' 'I am accused...*by Jews, O king!*' 'I saw, O king, from heaven...flashing round me *a light!*' 'I am Jesus...for this cause I appeared unto thee ...by the faith which is *in me!*' 'me...they endeavoured *to slay!*' (5, 7, 13, 18, 21). The last sentence, as also verse 7, is marked by barely suppressed irony—'for these things Jews(!) endeavoured to slay me.' Yet again the speaker's ardour seems to betray him into an orator's license of exaggeration, e.g. (several) *being put to death, all the synagogues, foreign cities, all the country of Judaea.*

The clearest evidence that the speech is S. Paul's is given by the way in which he adapts his witness for the gospel *both to the People* (i.e. the Jews) *and the Gentiles* (ver. 23); and these concluding words are the keynote of the whole speech. Ostensibly it is a defence to the Jews, addressed to a Jewish king, and the argument is the same as before. The apostle shews his thorough Judaism in blood, in education, and in feeling. As a patriot he bears witness to the Jews' zealous service of God, and he takes his own firm stand upon the national hope. It was by the very God of the Jews that he was converted; and his mission, which has aroused their hatred, was undertaken solely in obedience to the divine command.

But when he reaches his commission S. Paul discloses its content, which was a gospel for all nations; and his enthusiasm altogether carries him beyond the task of vindicating his conduct to the Jews. To the recent events which had led to the present hearing he only makes a momentary allusion (21), because any personal injustice to himself is of no account in comparison with the glory of the gospel. For the same reason probably he is silent about his blindness[1]. So also, having in mind the Gentiles, Festus and his court, he says nothing of his baptism—a Jewish ceremony,—and he uses familiar Greek sayings such as *kicking against the goad* and *doing things in a corner*. He speaks of God simply as *God*, not as 'the God of our fathers'; nor does he use the Jewish name of LORD (i.e. JEHOVAH). In the latter half of the speech the dominating thought is that of *Light* (13, 18, 23)—an idea familiar to all men, and, as 'darkness' was the condition of the Gentiles, specially associated with their conversion in scripture[2]. In correspondence with this, the Jews are regarded not as a nation (*the Jews*) but in their religious aspect. In contrast to the Gentiles they had been the *people* of God (23): and S. Paul has in view the whole 'Israel of God,' *the twelve tribes* (7). When he does use the word *Jew* it is as denoting a type of character—not *the Jews*, but *Jews*[3].

Like the speech, the 'gospel' with which it ends, is the climax of all former utterances. At Antioch we had S. Paul's gospel to the Jews, at Ephesus to the Christians. To the Lycaonians and Athenians he had preached the elements of natural religion in preparation for Christianity. Now we have a dogmatic gospel for all the world, Jews and Gentiles

---

[1] except for a possible allusion in verse 18. xlii 6, xlix 6, lx 1–3; Eph iv 18, v 8; cp. Jn i 4–9. [2] xiii 47, Lk ii 32, Isai ix 1–2, [3] as in Rom iii 9, 29.

alike. It is indeed the same gospel that the Twelve preached, but now unfolded in S. Paul's manner; and in this brief summary are comprised all the characteristic ideas of his teaching. (1) The foundation of the gospel is *faith* in *Jesus*, verse 18. This foundation is laid—such was S. Paul's personal experience—in a turning or *conversion*. On man's side conversion means a turning of the will or *repentance*, which is sealed by admission into the new life of holiness or *sanctification* in the church. (2) On the divine side, this repentance can be made acceptable, and the gift of a new life made possible, only through the passion and resurrection of Jesus, who is *the Christ*: and on the latter fact, or *the resurrection of the dead*, the whole fabric hangs. (3) From it issues the specially Pauline doctrine which crowns the speech, viz. the catholic character of the gospel which is offered to all men alike. For the resurrection demonstrated the catholic character of the person of *the Christ*, who as the Son of God and Son of Man stands in an equal relation to all mankind. Thus the doctrine of verse 23 is but the outcome of the message S. Paul had first proclaimed to the Jews at Damascus, viz. that *this* (Jesus) *is the Christ*, and *this* (Jesus) *is the Son of God*. That *Jesus is the Christ* he had also preached at Thessalonica and at Corinth[1]. And now the name of *the Christ*, which is not found in his earlier sermon (xiii) or his defence (xxii) to the Jews, comes in to crown his last speech[2]. In chapter xiii the apostle had spoken of Abraham, of Samuel, and of David: here as *the Christ*, Jesus stands over against *Moses*. To the Gentile world it was Moses who was the founder and patron of Judaism: and now, like a second Moses, the Christ is set forth as the head of a new body, the society of Christians. S. Paul began his defence by asserting his identity with the true Israel, but as the contemporary Jews had rejected the hope of Israel, so S. Paul rejects them: and the recurrence of this word *Christian*[3] will help to make clear to the Roman world the distinction between the real apostates from Moses, the Jews, and the true followers of the Christ, the Christians.

Besides the style and doctrine, there is an unmistakeable stamp of genuineness in the personality of the speaker, what we may venture to call his egotism. It is on his own personality that he stakes the whole issue. His defence begins with *my manner of life*; the crisis of the argument is his own conversion, marked with the emphatic *I* (vv. 9, 15); the gospel is the message which he bore; and at the end we are left with the picture of Paul *standing* as it were 'contra mundum.' Incidentally, for Christian readers, the authority of the apostle, which had been so severely questioned, is vindicated. His vision of the Christ (16), the words *from the beginning* (4), and the title of the office he received, *minister and witness* (16), raise him to the first rank of Christian authorities, viz. those *who from the beginning were eye-witnesses and ministers of the word* (Lk i 2). Lastly, it is not without interest

---

[1] ix 22, 20, xvii 3, xviii 5. [2] verse 32; as also in the last verse of the whole book. [3] which thus marks the close of the 2nd as of the 1st part of the Acts (xi 26).

that we again discover, as in the speech before Felix, the triad of theological virtues—Hope (verse 6), Faith (18) and Charity (in spirit, 29; cp. Rom ix 3).

26 And Agrippa said unto Paul, Thou art permitted to speak for thyself. Then Paul¹ stretched forth his hand, and made his defence:

2 I think myself ²happy, king Agrippa, that I am to make my defence before thee this day touching all the things
3 whereof I am accused by ³the Jews: ⁴especially because thou art expert in all customs and questions which are among ³the Jews: wherefore I beseech thee to hear me patiently.
4 My manner of life then from my youth up, which was from the beginning among mine own nation, and at Jerusalem,
5 know all ³the Jews; having knowledge of me from the first, if they be willing to testify, how that after the straitest sect
6 of our religion I lived a Pharisee. And now I stand *here* to be judged for the hope of the promise made of God unto our
7 fathers; unto which *promise* our twelve tribes, earnestly ⁵serving *God* night and day, hope to attain. And concerning
8 this hope I am accused by ³the Jews, O king! Why is it judged incredible with you, if God doth raise the dead?
9 I verily thought with myself, that I ought to do many things
10 contrary to the name of Jesus of Nazareth. And this I also did in Jerusalem: and I both shut up many of the saints in prisons, having received authority from the ⁶chief priests, and when they were put to death, I gave my vote against them.
11 And punishing them oftentimes in all the synagogues, I ⁷strove to make them blaspheme; and being exceedingly mad against them, I persecuted them even unto ⁸foreign cities.
12 Whereupon as I journeyed to Damascus with the authority
13 and commission of the ⁶chief priests, at midday, O king, I saw on the way a light from heaven, above the brightness of the sun, shining round about me and them that journeyed

---

¹ Bezan inserts *taking courage and receiving comfort* (i.e. *paraclêsis*) *in the Holy Spirit*. ² Gk *blessed*. ³ There is no *the* in the Greek. ⁴ Marg *because thou art especially expert*. ⁵ or *worshipping*. ⁶ Gk *high-priests*.
⁷ or *compelled* (AV), or *was trying to compel*. ⁸ Gk *outside*.

14 with me. And when we were all fallen to the earth[1], I heard a voice saying unto me in the Hebrew language, Saul, Saul, why persecutest thou me? it is hard for thee to kick against
15 the [2]goad. And I said, Who art thou, Lord? And the Lord
16 said, I am Jesus whom thou persecutest. But arise, and stand upon thy feet: for to this end have I appeared unto thee, to appoint thee a minister and a witness both of the things [3]wherein thou hast seen me, and of the things wherein
17 I will appear unto thee; delivering thee from the people,
18 and from the Gentiles, unto whom I send thee, to open their eyes, [4]that they may turn from darkness to light, and from the [5]power of Satan unto God, that they may receive remission of sins and [6]an inheritance among them that are sanctified by faith in me.
19 Wherefore, O king Agrippa, I was not disobedient unto
20 the heavenly vision: but declared both to them of Damascus first, and at Jerusalem, and throughout all the country of Judæa, and also to the Gentiles, that they should repent and
21 turn to God, doing works worthy of repentance. For this cause [7]the Jews seized me in the temple, and assayed to kill
22 me. Having therefore obtained the help that is from God, I stand unto this day testifying both to small and great, saying nothing but what the prophets and Moses did say
23 should come; [8]how that the Christ [9]must suffer, *and* [8]how that he first by the resurrection of the dead should proclaim light both to the people and to the Gentiles.

2   I. S. Paul begins his *captatio benevolentiae* with words *concerning all* the charges brought against him. (1) This word *all* is a hint of the completeness of his gospel which is to be the main ground of his defence. (2) In being able to lay this *before king Agrippa* the apostle, in spite of his bonds and station at the bar, *esteems himself blessed*[10]. To proclaim the gospel to such an audience is all the happiness that he can desire: and, by so congratulating
3 himself, he pays a most delicate compliment to the king. For (3) the *special* ground for his self-congratulation was the king's

---

[1] Bezan inserts *for fear, I alone* [*heard*.   [2] Gk *goads* (AV *pricks*).   [3] Marg with AV reads *which thou hast seen*.   [4] Marg with AV *to turn them*.   [5] Gk *authority*.   [6] Gk *a lot*.   [7] There is no *the* in the Greek.   [8] Gk *if*.
[9] Marg *is subject to suffering*.   [10] For a similar 'beatitude' or estimate of happiness see Phil iii 7-8, and cp. xx 35.

acquaintance with *Jewish* life and thought, which will enable him to appreciate the apostle's answer to *Jewish* accusations.

4 II. S. Paul then vindicates his own Judaism by an appeal to his early life, education, and devotion to the observances of *religion*[1], *at Jerusalem*—matters notorious to *all Jews*, unwilling as they were to admit his loyalty to their nation. The evidence of this has been already recounted, to the Jews in the temple (xxii 3); the special emphasis here is laid on the long range backwards of his appeal—*from my youth up, from the beginning, knowing-(me)-before from the first*: an emphasis which may be due to the motive suggested above, viz. the importance of original witness in the
6 church[2]. From the beginning S. Paul passes on to the present, thus shewing the continuity of his religious faith. For his faith is still grounded, and at the bar he takes his *stand, upon the hope of the promise made unto our fathers*, i.e. the promise of the regenera-
7 tion of Israel, which was the aim and object of the unceasing *worship* and eager *expectation* (not of Judah only but) of *the twelve-tribes*[3], the whole Israel of God. In Romans viii the apostle draws a picture of the expectation of Nature, stretching out her head for very eagerness; so here we see Israel stretching forward in the *intense* expectation of its worship, *intense* like the prayer in Gethsemane and the prayer of the church for S. Peter[4]. Such worship found a symbol in the prophetess Anna of the tribe of Asher, who never left the temple but worshipped God with fasting and prayer *night and day*, and spake of the Christ to all who were expecting the redemption of Israel[5]. And now *concerning this* very *hope*, by a strange irony, he is being *accused by Jews*! For 'the promise made unto the fathers, God hath fulfilled the same by raising up Jesus' (xiii 32). The regeneration of Israel is bound up with the resurrection of Jesus, which the Jews denied. This is the link in the argument which leads to the abrupt question which
8 follows. S. Paul recollects that he is addressing an audience largely Gentile; and to the Gentiles, as he had learnt at Athens (xvii 32), the idea of the resurrection of the dead was not merely *incredible*, it was absurd. But if there was any disposition to levity in the present audience, it was crushed at once by an appeal to the
9 almighty power of *God*. From this sudden digression the apostle returns to the final and convincing proof of his Jewish patriotism. That proof was his persecution of *Jesus* in the persons of the Nazarenes—a course of action[6] which he had felt to be a religious
10 *duty*. He gives here the severest picture of that persecution; and his self-accusing conscience may have led to some exaggeration, if by *the cities outside* (the holy land) is meant Damascus alone, and

---

[1] The Greek word here used for *religion* refers rather to the external cult, than the inner faith.   [2] Cp. p. 4 for references to *the beginning*.   [3] Jas i 1.
[4] Lk xxii 44, Acts xii 5.   [5] Lk ii 36–8.   [6] There is the same distinction between habitual practice (verse 9) and actual deeds (verse 10) as in Rom i 32, vii 17–21; so in verse 20 *doing* (=*practising*).

by *their being put to death* the martyrdom of S. Stephen. Taken literally, however, this account will better explain the complete dispersal of the church in viii 1–4, and give special point to his pleading, before the Roman governor, *the authority and commission of the high-priests* as the excuse for his illegal conduct. In any case the persecution would make it obvious to his hearers, both Jew and Gentile, that to arrest such a career of frenzied zeal required a very real and adequate cause. To that he now passes, viz. to

12   III. His conversion. The cause was nothing less than a divine epiphany. It is the same story as before, only delivered in a more oratorical form. It begins with a long sentence which reaches its
13 climax in the word *light*:...*at midday on the way I saw, O king, from heaven, above the bright-shining of the sun, shining around me—a light*: then as an afterthought he adds *and those that journeyed with me*. The comparison with the brilliance of the sun would suggest to his audience, both Jews and Gentiles, the divine character of the light, which *flashed around him* like lightning; just as the glory of the Lord had once flashed upon the shepherds of Bethlehem[1]. In the Acts the use of the word *light* is almost confined to the light of the divine glory (vii 2) and of the spiritual glory of Jesus—'the light to lighten the Gentiles[2]'; and when S. Paul writes to the Corinthians[3] that 'it is God, that said Light shall shine out of darkness, who shined in our hearts to give the light of the knowledge of the glory of God in the face of Jesus Christ,' he is in spirit
14 still contemplating this shining. For his Gentile hearers he adds an explanatory note—*in the Hebrew tongue*; as also the illustration, in the Lord's saying, of the ox *kicking against the spiked goad* with which it is driven and so wounding itself. This proverb was a very familiar one, and is found both in Greek and Latin literature[4]. It supplies an apt figure for resistance to God; and here it conveys an important intimation that Saul's zeal for Judaism had not been according to knowledge, but rather against the driving of the divine will. Now however when the divine goad has, as it were, even
16 felled him to the earth, he is bidden to *arise and stand upon his feet*[5]. This was in order to receive the divine message; but the expression is symbolical of the spiritual meaning of his sudden 'apprehension,' which was to issue in resurrection to a new life, and to give him that new and firm foundation upon which he still continued to *stand* (vv. 6, 22).

Whether it is due to S. Luke's compression or to the rush of S. Paul's enthusiasm, the utterance of the Lord, which the apostle now reports, sums up the whole meaning of the office to which he had been appointed[6] by the divine will: although in fact

---

[1] Lk ii 9, xvii 24.   [2] Lk ii 32.   [3] II Cor iv 6. See Acts ix 3, xxii 6, 9, 11, xxvi 13; metaphorically xxvi 18, 23, xiii 47; and elsewhere, xii 7 *a light shined*.
[4] e.g. in Aeschylus *Agam.* 1624, Euripides *Bacch.* 795, Terence *Phorm.* I 2. 27.
[5] like Ezekiel (ii 1–3).   [6] iii 20, x 41, xxii 44, and p. 134.

the full extent of his commission was only gradually unfolded to him. His office, then, was to be (1) *a minister* of the word[1]—which denotes the humble, personal service, in which Paul rejoiced to labour as 'the slave of the Lord'; and (2) *a witness*—by which he was raised to the level of the Twelve[2]. For the witness which constituted an apostle, and which S. Paul was to bear, was witness to the resurrection of the Lord, whom he had now *seen* in the vision, and *was to see* again. In his epistles[3] S. Paul speaks of the great visions and revelations of the Lord which he had seen, and of the unspeakable words which he had heard; but the context here indicates that he had specially in view the vision in the temple when the Lord gave him his definite mission to *the Gentiles* (xxii 17-21).

17 The witness, however, which S. Paul had to bear would not always be acceptable to men, whether Jews or Gentiles. Indeed in his prophetic office Paul greatly resembled Jeremiah[4]. Each of them was appointed a prophet to the nations as well as to the Jews; and each of them was destined to meet with opposition and strife. But to each was given a promise of *deliverance*. The Lord repeated to the apostle the words spoken to the prophet—'I am with thee to deliver thee'; and having thus prepared and strengthened him, he gives him his special commission, viz. to be (3) the Apostle of the Gentiles—*to whom I send thee*[5]. And the final end of his appointment was the conversion of the Gentiles (xv 3).

18 The *conversion* of the Gentiles was the result of *opening their eyes* to see the Lord; and the spiritual experience which this denotes was symbolized by S. Paul's own bodily experience, when sight was restored to his blinded eyes and he passed from the *authority* of the high-priests to that of Jesus of Nazareth. *Conversion* means the *turning* of the whole life to God, and so it is the external counterpart of the inner change of mind or repentance which S. Paul adds below in verse 20—*repent and turn*[6]. To be converted, then, is to be taken out of one sphere of life into another; and the two spheres are here characterized by two antitheses. (1) They are the spheres of *Light and Darkness*[7]. Here the primary thought is that of mental light and darkness, or of knowledge and ignorance. But mental darkness is closely associated with moral darkness; and in Rom i the apostle shews that it is the 'senselessness of the heart' or will that originates the darkness of the mind, which in its turn issues in yet deeper abysses of moral darkness. So the Gentiles who 'had been dark-

---

[1] Lk i 2. The word denotes humbler service than that of the *deacon*: cp. Acts v 22, 26, xiii 5; and also xx 19.   [2] Cp. p. 7.   [3] II Cor xii 1-4.   [4] See Jer i 5 (Gal i 15); xv 10; i 8, 19: and above p. 128.   [5] Jn xx 21.   [6] so in iii 19. *Conversion* is used of the turning of the Gentiles to the true God in xiv 15, xv 19, I Thess i 9: cp. ix 35, xi 21. The verb is usually intransitive, as in verse 20: but in verse 18 the parallel *to open the eyes* and the aorist tense are in favour of a transitive sense (as in AV).   [7] This antithesis is found in S. Paul— I Thess v 4-8, Rom xiii 12, II Cor iv 6, vi 14, Eph v 8-14: S. Peter—I ii 9: S. John —i 4-9 and throughout: cp. Rom ii 19.

ened in their understanding' had fallen under the dominion of idols[1]. For (2) these spheres are two kingdoms, under the *authority of God and Satan* respectively. At the head of the kingdom of darkness stands a personal ruler, whom S. Paul calls by his Jewish name of *Satan*, and who has his hierarchy of 'authorities and world-rulers of this darkness[2].' Ultimately of course all authority is derived from God; but so long as Satan's power is economically permitted, he can say that 'all the authority of the world is committed unto him.' S. Paul also agrees with S. John that the antithesis is absolute; outside of the kingdom of God 'the world lies in the evil one,' of whose kingdom the Roman empire afterwards appeared in the eyes of the persecuted Christians to be the visible embodiment[3]. Over against the kingdom of darkness is the kingdom of light or of *God*. At its head is the Son of God, and its citizens are those who have been consecrated to God, the *saints* or *sanctified*: in other words, it is the church. Conversion is then the translation from one kingdom to the other, as S. Paul has expressed it in Col i 12: the FATHER *made us sufficient for the portion of the lot of the saints in the light, who delivered us out of the authority of the darkness and translated us into the kingdom of the Son of his love*[4].

Such a translation must have a visible expression in time and in outward act; and this 'visible sign' is the sacrament of baptism, in which the baptized is *sanctified* or consecrated to God, and so made a *saint* or 'holy.' This brings us to the divine side of conversion. For at baptism are *received* the divine gifts which make this translation possible and a reality, viz. (1) *the forgiveness of sins*, i.e. deliverance from the authority of darkness; and (2) *the lot or portion among the sanctified*, i.e. the promised inheritance or gift of the Spirit which enables the baptized to walk in holiness and newness of life. Below, in verse 20, S. Paul describes this new life as *doing works worthy of repentance*[5], and this phrase introduces another familiar antithesis, viz. that between Faith and Works. But there is no real contradiction between them. *Doing works* is the outward expression of the inward life or character; the works are not the cause, but the fruit of this new life. And the principle of this inward life is *faith in (Jesus)*; faith being that secret and inward surrender of the will which places the life of the believer in the sphere of the life of Jesus[6]. Thus these last words of the Lord give us the instrumental cause of the whole spiritual process: the opening of the eye, the turning of the life, the transference from Satan to God, the gift of forgiveness and of the inheritance in the church—all these are *by the faith which is in me*.

IV. From this doctrinal digression S. Paul returns to *the heavenly vision* and describes his subsequent life. It had been a

---

[1] Cp. Rom i; Eph iv 17-9; I Thess i 9.   [2] Eph vi 12, Col ii 15.   [3] Rom xiii 1-2; Lk iv 6; I Jn v 19.   [4] Cp. also xx 32 and p. 395.   [5] Cp. xiii 24, Lk iii 8.   [6] The Greek preposition (*in*) properly means *into*.

life of *obedience* to the divine command[1], spent in fulfilling his
20 mission. In his account of his preaching there appears to be some
exaggeration, when we compare ix 26–30 and Gal i 22. But just as
the Acts contains the potential fulfilment of the apostolic mission
to bear witness 'unto the uttermost part of the earth' (i 8), so
S. Paul had potentially and in effect preached *to all* the Jews *and*
21 *to the Gentiles*[2]. This preaching, or rather the jealousy of the
Gentiles which it excited, was the cause of the continuous *attempts*
22 made by *Jews* to *murder*[3] him. So determined were their efforts,
that it was only by *the succour of God* that S. Paul had been
delivered; but by the grace of God he was at this moment still
standing[4], and able to deliver his *witness* (potentially) to all the
world, *both to small and great*.

The witness which he now delivers discloses (1) the source of the
divine gifts mentioned above,—how the forgiveness of sins and the
heritage of the new life were won for man: and (2) the ground of
'the faith in Christ.' For the witness is indeed 'the gospel' itself,
which is the declaration of the facts of the death and resurrection
of the Christ. First, however, the apostle preserves the unity of
his speech, and vindicates the continuity of the divine purpose or
plan of salvation, by shewing that this gospel is not inconsistent
with Judaism. On the contrary it is the fulfilment of the whole
Jewish dispensation; both of the utterances of *the prophets*, i.e.
the scriptures, and of the whole system of law and worship which
was represented by the name of *Moses*[5]. (1) Both of these had fore-
23 shewn—what was the scandal to the Jews—that[6] *the Christ* (himself
the hope of Israel) *should suffer*. The expression in the Greek,
literally *is possible*, would in later theology mean *capable of suffering*,
i.e. as man, in distinction from the impassibility of the divine nature.
Here however the apostle is not dealing with the theological problem
as to the union of the divine and human natures in Christ, but
meeting the difficulties of the Jewish mind. For, in spite of such
prophecies as Isai liii, the idea that *the Christ should suffer* was to
the Jews inconceivable. (2) Death however is the necessary prelude
to resurrection; and by 'raising up Jesus God fulfilled the promise
he had made unto the fathers.' According to this promise the Christ
was to be the *first*—like a second Adam—*to proclaim light to* all
mankind, Jew and Gentile alike, *by the resurrection of the dead*.
We should have expected *by his resurrection from the dead*: but
the expression shews how S. Paul identified in his own mind the

---

[1] Contrast the *disobedient* Jews in xiv 2, xix 9. [2] The construction in the Greek is somewhat irregular: we should have expected him to say—*both at Damascus first and at Jerusalem and then in every country, both to Jews and Gentiles*. [3] The word, which is also used in v 30, is a strong one and emphatic in its position at the end of the sentence. [4] I Cor xv 10, x 12. [5] For the parallel between Moses and the Christ, cp. iii 22, vii 20–40, esp. 37. [6] The *if* in the Greek is either (*a*) a softening of dogmatic abruptness, characteristic of the refinement of Greek speech, or (*b*) the protasis to the preceding sentence *I say nothing... if I do say that...* So in verse 8.

resurrection of Christ, the firstfruits, with the resurrection of 'them that are his[1].' His resurrection was not only the first instance, but the pledge, of the resurrection of the dead. The same connexion had also been taught by the Twelve (iv 2), but the phrase *the resurrection of the dead* is characteristic of S. Paul[2]. The resurrection brought *light*, because it brought (as we have already learned[3]) the gift of the Spirit, the power of faith, the forgiveness of sins, and the resurrection of the dead. But to S. Paul the greatest *light* was the proof it afforded of the divine sonship of Jesus (Rom i 4); for the gospel which the apostle *proclaimed* to the Gentiles was 'Jesus' himself, the Light of the World, the Light to lighten the Gentiles—Christ in them the hope of glory[4].

The verdict of 'not guilty'

S. Paul had thus laid a good foundation, but his gospel was by no means complete. Nothing had been said (except inferentially) of the gift of the Spirit and the practical confession of the name of Jesus in baptism, when, at this point, he was interrupted[5] by a *loud exclamation*.

24 And as he thus made his defence, Festus saith with a loud voice, Paul, thou art mad; thy much learning doth
25 turn thee to madness. But Paul saith, I am not mad, most excellent Festus; but speak forth [6]words of truth and
26 soberness. For the king knoweth of these things, unto whom also I speak freely: for I am persuaded that none of these things is hidden from him; for this hath not been done in a
27 corner. King Agrippa, believest thou the prophets? I know
28 that thou believest. And Agrippa *said* unto Paul, [7]With but little persuasion thou wouldest fain make me a Christian.
29 And Paul *said*, I would to God, that whether [8]with little or with much, not thou only, but also all that hear me this day, might become such as [9]I am, except these bonds.
30 And[10] the king rose up, and the governor, and Bernice,

---

[1] See pp. 319, 407 and I Cor xv 20-3. So in xvii 31-2 *raising him from the dead* passes into *the raising of the dead*.   [2] xvii 32, xxiii 6, xxiv 21, Rom i 4, I Cor xv 12, 13, 21: so Heb vi 2.   [3] in ii 33; iii 16, iv 10; iii 26, v 31, xiii 38; iv 2. Cp. II Tim i 10.   [4] Cp. xvii 3, 18, Phil i 18; Col i 27.   [5] So Peter's preaching was cut short on two occasions iv 1, x 44.   [6] A Hebraism for *matters*.
[7] literally *In a little thou persuadest me to make a Christian*: AV *Almost thou persuadest me to be a Christian*. A reads *thou-persuadest-thyself* (*art-confident*): later MSS, followed by AV, have *to become* for *to make*.   [8] literally *in little and in great*: for *great* (RV Gk text) AV and most later MSS read *much*: AV translates *were both almost and altogether such as I am*.   [9] Gk *even I*.   [10] AV and Bezan add *when he had thus spoken*.

31 and they that sat with them: and when they had withdrawn, they spake one to another, saying, This man doeth nothing
32 worthy of death or of bonds. And Agrippa said unto Festus, This man might have been set at liberty, if he had not appealed unto Cæsar.

24 *Festus* had not been able to follow much of S. Paul's speech, but he was startled by his enthusiasm. That enthusiasm for the 'persuasion¹' or conversion of men had before now laid the apostle open to the charge of being 'beside himself²'; and now Festus cries out *Paul, thou art mad*. The charge of madness is one to which enthusiasts have been liable in all ages; the Lord himself was not excepted³. But we must also remember that in the ancient world madness was closely associated with inspiration: a madman was supposed to be possessed by some supernatural power and was looked upon with awe⁴. Festus must have had some such feeling. The mention of Moses and the prophets suggested to him that through excessive study of Jewish lore the apostle had become
25 possessed of a religious *frenzy*. But of his sanity the apostle's courteous and ready response gave decisive proof. He admits that he is making an inspired *utterance*⁵, but, not in Festus' sense; for it is about serious matters of fact: *soberness* or sound-minded-
26 ness being the exact opposite of ecstasy⁶. For support he turns to Agrippa, but again his enthusiasm carries him into his characteristic *boldness of speech*⁷. He was *convinced* that his story appeared perfectly sane to the king; for the facts of the crucifixion and the growth of the church had not happened *in an* obscure *corner*, but in broad daylight before all the Jews at Jerusalem; and his theology was taken out of the Jewish scriptures. At this personal address Agrippa probably shewed some sign of discomfort. S. Paul, whose charity believed and hoped all things, may have taken it for the
27 dawning of faith; and he drove the charge home by a direct appeal. Agrippa must assent, for he believed the scriptures. *King Agrippa, believest thou the prophets? I know that thou believest.* This was too much. As it was, the young king had no doubt found the practice of Judaism irksome enough in the scoffing society of Rome, and it was too much to expose him to the astonishment of the Roman governor and the distinguished audience by extorting from him the patronage, if not the profession, of this new faith. His courtly breeding was equal to the occasion, and he passed it off by a piece
28 of raillery: *A little more persuasion and you will make me too a Christian*. Agrippa uses the term by which the followers of 'the

---

¹ Paul's characteristic *persuasion* (see p. 220) reappears (verse 28).   ² II Cor v 11, 13.   ³ Both his own family and the Jews esteemed him mad (Mk iii 21, Jn x 20).   ⁴ See the quotation from Plato on p. 20. The Jews said of the Lord 'He hath a devil and is mad.' In verse 11 S. Paul says he was *exceeding mad*.
⁵ *speak-forth* is used in ii 4 of the result of being filled with the Spirit.   ⁶ II Cor v 13.   ⁷ *freely* represents the Greek participle translated *preaching boldly* in ix 28.

Christ' (verse 23) were known to the Gentile world¹. At once
29 S. Paul falls back into his soberness, but with intense earnestness
he takes up the king's word: *I would to God that, whether with little
persuasion or with great*², *not only thou but even all who are listening
to me to-day might become just such as even I Paul—except for these
bonds.*

The general sense of the two utterances is quite clear, but
Agrippa's saying is a well-known crux. It is certainly not to be
taken in a serious sense, as in the AV; for nowhere else is *almost*
the equivalent of the Greek words used here—*in a little*. This
phrase usually means *in a little time*; but if it is so taken here, the
correspondence in S. Paul's answer—*in little and in great* (which
cannot apply to time)—will be less exact. Probably it takes its
complexion from the verb, as in the RV,—*with but little persuasion*
or *effort*. Besides this difficulty, the rest of the sentence is not easy
to explain. Taken literally, it runs : *me thou-persuadest—to make
a Christian*. Here we should have expected *to become a Christian*,
as the AV reads; but that is too much like a later correction. One
early MS reads *thou-persuadest-thyself*, i.e. *art-confident*: this involves a change of only one or two letters, and corresponds to
S. Paul's *I-am-persuaded* in verse 26. Even then the sentence
does not run naturally in the Greek: *me thou art confident to make
a Christian*. The same must be said of a similar suggestion of
Dr Hort, which by a slight change alters *me thou-persuadest* into
one word *thou-art-confident*. We must be content to leave the
problem to wait for further light.

30   This incident broke up the hearing. Agrippa and Festus had
alike had enough: Paul was getting into too close quarters, as he
had done with Felix and Drusilla. So together with their 'council'
31 and *Berenice*, they *withdrew* for private consultation. All agreed
that S. Paul's *doings*, i.e. his manner of life, made him in no way
liable to punishment, not even to detention. Then they return to the
32 auditorium, and to give a formal close to the proceedings *Agrippa
makes a public answer to Festus'* enquiry: *This man*³ *might have
been dismissed, had he not appealed to Caesar.* Thus, however
grudgingly conceded, the whole process of two years and more, at
Jerusalem and Caesarea, ended in a public and decisive acquittal
of S. Paul. Claudius Lysias, Festus, and Agrippa, had each declared
him innocent; three times was it publicly announced of the apostle,
as of the Lord, that he had *done nothing worthy of death*⁴.

---

¹ See xi 26 and pp. 169-70.   ² Cp. the *small and great* above (verse 22).
³ See on xxv 22 and cp. Lk xxiii 4, 14. Perhaps it is the translation of the Latin,
cp. Mk xv 39, Lk xxiii 47.   ⁴ xxiii 29 xxv 25 (10, 18), xxvi 32: Lk xxiii 4, 14, 22.

SECTION III A (= Ch. 27—28. 10)

The going down into the deep

The modern joy and delight in the sea was a sentiment almost unknown to the peoples of antiquity. One Greek poet, Aeschylus, could write of 'the many-twinkling smile of ocean,' but to the ancients generally the sea only inspired emotions of dislike and dread. The incommodious ships and the possibilities of long delays owing to contrary winds made a voyage anything but a pleasure: the lack of nautical instruments and the imperfect knowledge of navigation made the perils of the sea ten times worse than they are to-day. Hence the allusions to the sea in classical literature are generally prompted by the violence of storms and the horrors of shipwreck, or (in private correspondence) by the tediousness of a voyage or the unexpected good luck of a quick passage. During the winter months the sea was practically closed for navigation; and the present narrative is an illustration of what a traveller who ventured too near that season might expect. The party start from Palestine in August or September and do not reach Rome till the following March, having in the meanwhile lost their ship with all their belongings.

If the sea had perils and drawbacks even for born sailors such as the Greeks and Phenicians, to the agricultural Israelites the Mediterranean which formed their western boundary must have indeed been an object of awe. This aspect of the sea was part of their most ancient heritage. In Babylonian mythology, before the earth was created there had existed chaos, a waste of waters, the realm of disorder and confusion. From this the earth or kingdom of order had been won, and the existing ocean was a remnant of the original waste, and therefore it was the symbol and the sphere of evil both physical and spiritual[1]. These ideas we find reflected in the OT. There was the primeval chaos when 'darkness was upon the face of the deep and the wind of God was brooding upon the face of the waters.' In prophecy and apocalypse the raging waves were the symbol, as of confusion in general, so of the restless and tumultuous surging of the nations. The passage of the Red Sea made the sea the established type of the greatest peril through which man must pass on his way to the promised land,—the peril of death. Lastly, as the home of evil, the ocean represented the pit: it was the abyss, and the swallowing up of shipwrecked men in its cruel billows was the fittest picture of man's going down into the deep. Turning to the NT, it is true that in the Gospels the sea of Tiberias casts a halo of beauty over the Galilean ministry. Yet it was but a lake, and to the apostles was chiefly associated with

---

[1] Cp. Dr Smythe Palmer's *Babylonian Influence on the Bible* (Nutt) for an account of the sea in early cosmology.

nights of fruitless toil, with storms and sudden squalls. S. Paul's experience of the sea was similar: some years before now he could write that he had 'three times suffered shipwreck and been a night and a day in the deep' (II Cor xi 25). In the Revelation one condition of the ideal heaven and earth is that 'there shall be no more sea.'

It comes upon us, then, somewhat as a surprise to find in the Acts full and picturesque accounts of two voyages. This is indeed an illustration of the all-embracing sympathies of Christianity, which extend to those also 'who go down to the sea in ships and occupy themselves in great waters.' The narratives seem specially written for sea-faring and sea-loving nations like our own: it is said that Nelson was reading this 27th chapter on the morning of the battle of Copenhagen. If S. Luke was a Greek, the fulness of the narrative might be put down to his national instincts: but, as we shall see, such a hypothesis is not needed. In these voyages the chief interest, as is natural, centres on the shipwreck. The story is told with such a wealth of detail that in all classical literature there is no passage which gives us so much information about the working of an ancient ship. Accurate as it is, nautical critics tell us that it is the account not of a sailor, but of a landsman—of a landsman, however, familiar with the sea and with a faculty of careful observation, who must have been himself on board. This being so, the terrible experience he went through must have indelibly impressed the details on his memory. To have been not one day but fourteen days in the deep, driven by a tempest along an unknown course, without light of sun or stars, unable to take food and expecting at any moment to founder—such an experience in itself is sufficient to prompt the pen of a ready writer.

But we shall strangely fail to understand S. Luke, if we suppose that the vividness of the picture is simply due to the traveller's impulse to tell over his adventures to the public. We cannot but see how the whole narrative, the very desperateness of the situation, throws into the strongest relief the personality of S. Paul. At the moment of utter despair, he rises up in the midst and is found to be a rock on which all can trust, the inspirer of hope and the master-mind which is able to direct and command as the crisis requires—in a word their saviour. Nowhere in the Acts is there a finer display of sympathy and strength. Thus the very passages which glorify the apostle—and are for that reason suspected by some critics—are those which contain S. Luke's motive for relating the history of the voyage, and the multitude of details supply the necessary background. S. Paul is the main subject throughout. The narrative begins with his own physical weakness. Then he appears as a counsellor and a prophet, with his warnings and foresight of danger. In the crisis, like the rest he too falls into the deep of despair (though for others rather than himself), but as an intercessor he has recourse to prayer. Strengthened by a heavenly vision, he rises up to inspire his companions with courage. In the hour of danger he commands like a captain, like a priest he offers thanks to God, and like a deliverer brings them into a haven of safety.

The Maltese, in the words which conclude the history, unconsciously express its true lesson—*they said that he was a god*[1].

Besides the personal element, there is the inner spiritual meaning. There is one scene in the OT of which this is the most obvious counterpart—the shipwreck of Jonah. If S. Paul in some respects resembled Jeremiah, the parallel between the NT prophet and Jonah is still more striking,—all the more so because of the equally obvious contrast in character. Jonah is the prophet in the OT who more than any other might, like S. Paul, be called 'the prophet of the Gentiles.' Jonah indeed received his mission in a very different way: he fled from the presence of the Lord and took ship for Tarshish. But in their voyages the experience of the prophets coincided. Both suffered shipwreck; and although Jonah, unlike S. Paul, brought the storm upon his vessel, yet in each case the prophet won the salvation of his company,—Jonah by the sacrifice of himself. Finally both alike experienced deliverance, Jonah from the deep, Paul from the peril of death; and after this they fulfil their respective missions to the great cities of Nineveh and Rome.

Jonah, however, was above all the sign of one greater than either[2], viz. of the Lord, who afforded the supreme example of the law that suffering goes before victory, going down to the deep before deliverance or resurrection. This experience had been realized by S. Peter in chapter xii. Now in S. Paul we have here another and a conspicuous instance. For if in the scheme of the Acts the last chapters correspond to the last chapters of the Gospel, this chapter forms the parallel (as is fairly evident) to the crucifixion or Lk xxii–xxiii. Of this a hint is given by one of the incidents of the shipwreck, viz. the breaking of bread on the last morning of the wreck before they committed themselves to the sea. No doubt S. Luke's medical experience made him appreciate S. Paul's sagacity in insisting on the partaking of food[3]. But the very words with which he describes the apostle's action recall at once the picture of the Lord breaking bread before his apostles on his last evening (Lk xxii 19). It is difficult to believe that this meal was what we should call a celebration of the Holy Eucharist; yet we cannot but feel that S. Luke wishes to remind his readers of the Last Supper. Without, however, insisting upon this or noticing many resemblances which might be pointed out in details, we can draw attention to the parallelism in the general scheme. The storm and darkness correspond to the spiritual storm and darkness on Calvary, as the actual wreck and plunging into the deep to the death upon the cross (Lk xxiii 26–49, Acts xxvii 14–44). The rest and peace of the three winter months at Malta, when the apostle was entirely cut off from the outside world and his old life, is like the rest of the three days in the grave (Lk xxiii 50–6, Acts xxviii 1–10). The voyage to Rome in the spring, which was to the apostle

---

[1] Cp. the similar conclusion of the storm on the Sea of Galilee—*Who is this that he commandeth even the winds and the water, and they obey him?* (Lk viii 25).
[2] Lk xi 29–32; Mt xii 39–41. [3] Cp. pp. xx, 37 n. 8.

the entrance into a new life, will correspond to the joyful period after the resurrection (Lk xxiv 1-49, Acts xxviii 11-28); and lastly the picture of quiet and expectant work at Rome is like that of the praying and waiting church at Jerusalem (Lk xxiv 52-3, Acts xxviii 30-1).

But the application of this law is universal and not confined to S. Paul. The keynote to the interpretation is given in verse 34 in the word *salvation*. This and cognate words occur altogether 7 times: *hope to be saved, ye cannot be saved, to be completely-saved* (RV *escape*)[1]. While the contrary fate is no less richly depicted—*injury, loss, throwing away* (22), *perish, kill,* and *to be cast away*[2]. The history, then, is a parable of the great salvation, by which man is brought through death to life. It is the companion to the picture in chapters iii-iv[3]; and in iv 12 S. Peter has already given the means by which the salvation is won.

Of all the narratives in the Acts this chapter bears the most indisputable marks of authenticity. In one passage (verses 9-12) there is some obscurity due to editing or revision, but the attempt of some critics to remove as interpolations those passages which bring out the spiritual power of S. Paul (e.g. verses 21-6, 31-2 or 31-6) is as impossible as it is to eliminate the miraculous element from the Gospels; for, as we have seen, it was S. Paul's action which inspired the writer to pen the narrative. Historical research and inscriptions have confirmed S. Luke's facts, while the accuracy of his nautical observations is shewn by the great help he has given to our understanding of ancient seamanship. None have impugned the correctness of his phrases; on the contrary, from his description contained in a few sentences, the scene of the wreck has been identified. Its traditional identification with S. Paul's Bay has been tested and, we may say, satisfactorily proved by Mr James Smith, of Jordanhill, who also thoroughly examined the whole narrative from the seaman's point of view[4]. Into such nautical investigations we need not enter, but it is quite easy for an ordinary landsman to follow the general course of the voyage, which we will proceed to do.

§ 1 *The voyage. Caesarea to Fair Havens*

S. Paul's appeal to Caesar having been allowed, the matter now rested with the imperial police. Recent researches of Prof. Mommsen and others have thrown great light on this branch of the imperial administration and so upon the Acts[5]. As the empire extended, the commissariat of the legions, which were generally stationed in distant provinces, necessitated regular communication with the capital; and the

---

[1] vv. 20: 31: 43, 44, xxviii 1, 4. The Bezan addition in verse 29 and the reading of B in ver. 39 will make 9 times. [2] This word occurs four times, vv. 17, 26, 29, 32: cp. Rom ix 6, xi 11. [3] in which salvation is the leading thought, see p. 49. [4] in his *Voyage and Shipwreck of S. Paul*, 1848 (4th ed. 1880, Longmans). See also Breusing *Die Nautik der Alten*, Bremen, 1886. [5] See Mommsen *Sitzungsberichte der Berlin. Akad.* 1895, pp. 495-503: Ramsay *Paul the Traveller* pp. 314-5, 347-8: Rendall *Acts* p. 340: Hastings *Bible Dict.* under Julius.

business was entrusted to a body of legionaries who had a camp at Rome on the Caelian hill. These soldiers were called *Frumentarii* ('corn-men'), or, as they were generally recruited from legions on distant service, *Peregrini* ('foreigners'). Such a body in constant movement to and from the provinces was evidently suited for other services; and as the emperors preferred as a rule to adapt existing institutions for the new requirements of the imperial system, they made use of these *Frumentarii* both as special service messengers for carrying out a system of espionage in the provinces, and also as imperial police for conveying political prisoners to and from Rome. We must admit that our present information does not enable us to carry back the fully developed system before the time of Hadrian (117-138 A.D.); but it calls for no unreasonable stretch of the imagination to ascribe the first beginnings of the system to the early emperors or even, with Prof. Mommsen, to Augustus himself. Certainly the office performed by *Julius* is exactly that of a *centurion* of the Peregrini. If then this was the body to whom S. Paul was entrusted, the *captain of the camp* (*stratopedarch*, xxviii 16) to whom he was handed over at Rome was the *captain*—not of the Praetorian guard, but—of the Peregrini, the 'Princeps Peregrinorum[1]'; and *the camp* was their station on the Caelian hill. The *Augustan cohort* (xxvii 1) may well have been—if not the official, yet—a popular title of this corps or one of its divisions. Otherwise it has not as yet been identified. The epithet *Augustan* was used for a complimentary title very much as *royal* is now. The cohorts of the legions however did not receive distinctive titles; and so if this cohort was not a division of the Peregrini, it may have been either one of the auxiliary cohorts of the garrison of Caesarea, or more probably one of the 'Italian cohorts of citizen volunteers[2]' (see p. 146).

27 'And when it was determined that we should sail for Italy, they delivered Paul and certain other prisoners to a
2 centurion named Julius, of the Augustan [4]band. And embarking in a ship of Adramyttium, [5]which was about to sail unto the places on the coast of Asia, we put to sea, Aristarchus, a Macedonian of Thessalonica, being with us.

---

[1] This title is given in a late Bezan text (Gigas). It is said that there is no evidence for its use before the time of Severus c. A.D. 250. But if the name was new, that does not prevent the previous existence of a *Captain of the camp*. [2] An Augustan cohort is mentioned in an interesting inscription from Berytus in Syria (*CIL* III no. 6687), in which Q. Aemilius Secundus, who 'took the census of the city of Apamea at the command of Quirinius' (Lk ii 2), states that he had been 'PRAEFECT. COH. AVG. I (prefect of the First Augustan Cohort).' Dr Mommsen however finds the inscription full of difficulties and mistakes, among which he would include this title.
[3] Bezan reads *So then the governor determined that he should be sent to Caesar and on the morrow he summoned a certain centurion of the Augustan cohort named Julius and delivered to him Paul with the rest of the prisoners.* [4] Gk *cohort*.
[5] In AV, and Blass' Bezan text, this clause belongs to the subject of the sentence—*we launched, meaning to sail by the coasts of Asia.*

3 And the next day we touched at Sidon: and Julius treated Paul kindly, and ¹gave him leave to go unto his friends and
4 ²refresh himself. And putting to sea from thence, we sailed under the lee of Cyprus, because the winds were contrary.
5 And when we had sailed across the sea which is off Cilicia
6 and Pamphylia³, we came to Myra, *a city* of Lycia. And there the centurion found a ship of Alexandria sailing for
7 Italy; and he put us therein. And when we had sailed slowly many days, and were come with difficulty over against Cnidus, the wind not further suffering us, we sailed under
8 the lee of Crete, over against Salmone; and with difficulty coasting along it we came unto a certain place called Fair Havens; nigh whereunto was the city of ⁴Lasea.

1   After the hearing before Agrippa Festus at once⁵ *handed over Paul and the other prisoners* bound for Rome to the custody of *Julius*. The word for *other* should properly imply a different class⁶; and *the other prisoners* were probably not appellants but criminals, condemned it may be to suffer their penalty in the games of the amphitheatre. S. Paul however was not alone in his 'bonds,' for the first person *we* shews that S. Luke was with him, and S. Luke adds that *Aristarchus of Thessalonica was with us*, i.e. was one of their party⁷. We have not had the first person since xxi 18, when both Luke and Aristarchus went in with S. Paul to James. Now they are despatched with S. Paul to Rome. The obvious inference is that they had been sharing his captivity in the interval, and we have had reason to suspect S. Luke's presence more than once⁸. In the Epistle to the Colossians, which was written from Rome, the apostle calls Aristarchus his 'fellow-prisoner' (iv 10). There is no reason why this should not be taken literally. Aristarchus was a Jew. Perhaps he was with S. Paul in the Nazirites' chamber on that memorable day of the riot and was involved in the consequent charge. S. Luke was a Gentile. The Ephesian Jews had no doubt seen him also close to S. Paul in the city, and they may have substituted him for Trophimus as the Gentile who had actually polluted the temple⁹. In Col iv 14, however, S. Paul does not call S. Luke his fellow-prisoner but 'the beloved physician'; and it is very likely that S. Luke may have accompanied him as an attendant in that

---

¹ A Bezan text has *gave leave to his friends who came to him to take care of him.*
² Gk *receive attention.*   ³ Bezan adds *in fifteen days.*   ⁴ ℵ with most MSS has *Lasaia* (ℵ* *Lassaia*), B *Lasea*, A *Alassa*: we have also *Laissa* (ℵᶜ), and in the Vulgate *Thalassa*.   ⁵ So in the Bezan text.   ⁶ as in Lk xxiii 32 *two others, malefactors, were led with him.* The word for *prisoner* is peculiar to this passage in the NT. S. Paul was *in bonds* but not a (convicted) *prisoner.*
⁷ This is shewn by the word for *with*, which is different from the *with* of verse 24.
⁸ p. 403.   ⁹ See pp. 419: 420–1, 434, 436.

capacity. As S. Paul was evidently suffering from ill health, Julius would have been glad of the services of a doctor. What is certain is that Julius would not have taken Luke and Aristarchus simply as passengers. If not 'in bonds,' they could only have been taken with Paul, as Prof. Ramsay points out[1], as his personal attendants (i.e. slaves): but S. Luke's language here, taken in its natural sense, would suggest that he as well as S. Paul was a subject of Festus' decision.

2   It was the end of August or beginning of September before Julius was ready to start; the sailing season was far advanced and there was no ship in port sailing direct for Rome. So he put his prisoners with their guard of soldiers on board *a ship of Adramyttium* (a Mysian town near Assos, xx 13) which was making the return voyage to the coast of Asia Minor. The vessel would be certain to touch at Ephesus, where Julius would find a vessel crossing to Corinth; or going on to Adramyttium, he could quickly march from there to Troas, and crossing to Philippi traverse Macedonia along the Egnatian Road. This was the route along which fifty years later S. Ignatius, bishop of Antioch, was taken by his guard of ten soldiers, when he was sent to Rome to be thrown to the wild
3 beasts in the Coliseum. Julius' party started with a favourable wind, for *the next day they put in at Sidon,*—a run of about 70 miles. Here the centurion had an opportunity of doing Paul an act of *kindness* or *humanity*. The centurions of the NT strike us generally as a class of men of a high stamp of character, and Julius is no exception. He makes a worthy match to that other centurion of Caesarea, Cornelius. We do not know whether he became a Christian, but it is evident that S. Paul made a great impression upon him and even won his personal affection. The apostle was now suffering from depression or illness, and Julius *permitted him to visit his friends and obtain* the requisite rest and *attention*. The Greek word implies that these were personal *friends* or relatives rather
4 than simply 'brethren' in the faith. When they started again from Sidon, the Etesian winds had already begun to blow. These are westerly winds which blow regularly in the Levant in the late summer or autumn. They were consequently prevented from crossing the open sea, as Paul had done in coming to Caesarea (xxi 3); and after *sailing under the lee,* i.e. to the east, *of Cyprus*, they had to work their way, with the aid of currents and land breezes, along
5 the coast of Asia Minor, off *Cilicia and Pamphylia*. It took them fifteen days to reach *Myra*, whose harbour—for the city itself was some way up the river—was the great port for Egyptian and Syrian
6 traffic. Here they were fortunate enough to *find* in port *a ship of Alexandria* bound *for Italy*. By this time the vast city of Rome had become almost entirely dependent upon foreign cornfields for its bread. Egypt was the chief source of supply and

---

[1] *Paul the Traveller* (pp. 315–6).

every year an enormous quantity of grain was shipped at Alexandria for Puteoli or Ostia. The vessels which carried it were of a specially large build[1], and the Alexandrian corn-fleet was the most striking feature in the commerce of the eastern Mediterranean. As any delay in the arrival of the fleet was the source of great anxiety at Rome, so it was hailed at Puteoli with great rejoicings. Signalmen were on the look-out to announce its approach, and they were able to recognize it by the privilege these vessels possessed of entering the bay of Naples with their topsails set. One of these ships now lay in the harbour of Myra. It had started late, and the same Etesian winds which had delayed Julius, had driven it across the Mediterranean, perhaps to Phenicia whence it would have coasted along like the Adramyttian. *The centurion* thought it a veritable godsend and at once *put* his detachment *on board*, which raised the
7 complement to 276 souls in all[2]. The greater commodiousness of the vessel however was not matched by an improvement in the weather. The wind continued to blow from the NW, and it took them *many days*, probably another fortnight, to reach *Cnidus*, the SE point of Asia Minor. From Cnidus they ought to have crossed the open sea to Greece, in order to round Cape Matapan, but when they lost the shelter of the land *the wind would not allow them to go any further* in its face. So turning southwards to *Crete*,—of which island Cape *Salmone* was the NE point—*they sailed under its lee*, i.e. along its southern side, being partially sheltered from the
8 wind by the mountains. Even then they had *difficulty* in getting so far as the roadstead, which still bears its ancient name of *Fair Havens*[3]. Two leagues beyond Fair Havens lay Cape Matala, where the coast makes a sharp turn to the north, which would again expose them to the full force of the gale. So they gave up further attempts and waited for a change of wind.

The storm. Fair Havens to Malta

9 As *a long time passed* and the wind did not drop, it became necessary to take counsel as to their course of action. S. Luke has so compressed the account of what happened as to cause some obscurity[4], but the Bezan text again helps us. There were two questions before them: (1) the question of continuing the voyage to Italy. They were now in the *dangerous* season for navigation, for *the Fast* (of the Atonement) was passed. This day might fall towards the end of September or in the beginning of October: in

---

[1] A dialogue of Lucian's (*Navigium seu vota*) gives an amusing account of the astonishment caused at Athens by the arrival of one of these vast ships, driven thither by stress of weather. [2] See however below on verse 37. [3] *Kalous Limionas*, according to Captain Spratt, R.N. (*Travels and Researches in Crete*, 1865). Mr Tennent in 1856 writes *Calolimiounas* (in Smith *Voyage etc.* p. 251). Capt. Spratt, who surveyed Crete in 1853, identified Phoenix with Lutro and claims to have discovered the site of Lasea. [4] Thus the *voyage* in verse 10 we should naturally take to be the voyage to Italy, but from vv. 12-3 it would appear to be the voyage to Phoenix. It probably covers both voyages.

A.D. 57 its date was September 27. The autumnal equinox was generally reckoned to put an end to navigation, but one writer[1] gives as a definite date Nov. 11, adding that from Sept. 14 to Nov. 11 was 'dangerous.' (2) If the voyage to Italy was given up, they would have to settle on their winter quarters. Fair Havens, however fair as a haven, was a very unsuitable place to winter in: it was an open roadstead, there was no town there, and the great variety in the spelling of the name of the nearest city, Lasea, shews that it was but a small place. Further along the coast however, past Cape Matala, there was a good harbour at Phoenix[2]; and this city, which was no doubt familiar to the Alexandrian sailors[3], was much more suitable for winter quarters.

Julius as a Roman officer would be the chief authority on board and accordingly he held a council. To this he summoned *Paul*; for besides his evident spiritual and prophetic power, the apostle had had great experience of the sea. When admitted to the council, S. Paul's personality at once brought him to the front;
10 and speaking with prophetic wisdom, he strongly dissuaded them from any idea of continuing the voyage to Italy. To this all
12 agreed. Then, passing to the question of winter quarters, the officers of the ship advised that they should make for *Phoenix*, though they were not very sanguine as to their *being able to reach*
11 *it*. These officers were *the helmsman*, who was captain of the crew, and *the owner of the ship*, or his agent; and their opinions naturally had most weight with *the centurion*. Even this attempt, however, Paul strongly resisted, but he was out-voted, with what consequences we shall see.

The Fast was that of the great Day of Atonement[4]. Its use by S. Luke as a mark of time is striking. It is hardly likely that Christians would have retained the Jewish system of fast and festival simply as marks of time without any other observance. Besides, we should rather have expected mention of the Feast of Tabernacles which occurred five days after the Day of Atonement and was reckoned by the Jews to close the sailing season[5]. S. Luke's expression then may indicate a date which fell between the Fast and the Feast. But a very natural explanation would be that S. Paul's company did fast at Fair Havens and that S. Luke recollects the circumstance. If this was the case, we have another sign of S. Paul's normal observance of the Law, on which see p. 332.

---

[1] Vegetius. See the references in Wetstein. [2] S. Luke says *the harbour looked against the SW and NW (winds)*. But the harbour of the modern Lutro, which is identified with Phoenix, looks NE and SE. We must then, either translate with the margin *looking down* (i.e. *along*) *the SW and NW winds*; or with Dr Field suppose that S. Luke is speaking from the point of view of the harbour, facing landwards. [3] At Lutro there has been found a dedication to Jupiter, Sarapis, and all the gods, 'erected under the supervision of Dionysius an Alexandrian and *captain* of the ship *whose sign was* Isopharia' (*CIL* III 1, no. 3). The italicized words occur in the Acts (verse 11 and xxviii 11). [4] Levit xvi. [5] Schoettgen *Horae Hebr.* 1 p. 482.

9 And when much time was spent, and the voyage was now dangerous, because the Fast was now already gone by, Paul
10 admonished them, and said unto them, Sirs, I perceive that the voyage will be with injury and much loss, not only of the
11 lading and the ship, but also of our lives. ¹But the centurion gave more heed to the master and to the owner of the ship,
12 than to those things which were spoken by Paul. And because the haven was not commodious to winter in, the more part advised to put to sea from thence, if by any means they could reach Phœnix, and winter *there*; *which is* a
13 haven of Crete, ²looking north-east and south-east. And when the south wind blew softly, supposing that they had obtained their purpose, they weighed anchor and sailed along
14 Crete, close in shore. But after no long time there ³beat down from it a tempestuous wind, which is called ⁴Euraquilo:
15 and when the ship was caught, and could not face the wind,
16 we gave way ⁵*to it*, and were driven. And running under the lee of a small island called ⁶Cauda, we were able, with
17 difficulty, to secure the boat: and when they had hoisted it up, they used helps, under-girding the ship; and, fearing lest they should be cast upon the Syrtis, they lowered ⁷the
18 gear, and so were driven. And as we laboured exceedingly with the storm, the next day they began to throw *the freight*
19 overboard; and the third day ⁸they cast out with their own
20 hands the ⁹tackling of the ship. And when neither sun nor stars shone upon *us* for many days, and no small tempest lay on *us*, all hope that we should be saved was now taken away.
21 And when they had been long without food, then Paul stood forth in the midst of them, and said, Sirs, ye should have hearkened unto me, and not have set sail from Crete,
22 and have gotten this injury and loss. And now I exhort you

---

¹ A Bezan text has *But*] *the master and the owner of the ship counselled to sail, if by any means they could reach Phoenix a harbour of Crete, (and) the centurion gave more heed to them than to the things which were spoken by Paul. And when the S wind blew softly they weighed anchor and with speed [began to sail along.*
² Gk *looking against the SW wind* (Gk *Libs*, Lat. *Africus*) *and against the NW wind* (Gk *Chôrus*, Lat. *Caurus*): so marg with *down* instead of *against*. ³ AV *arose against it*. ⁴ AV with late MSS reads *Euroclydon*. ⁵ Bezan inserts *to the wind and reefing the sails* [*were driven*. ⁶ Marg with AV reads *Clauda*.
⁷ A Bezan text has *a certain weight to drag*. ⁸ AV reads *we cast out*; Bezan adds *into the sea*. ⁹ Marg *furniture*.

to be of good cheer: for there shall be no loss of life among
23 you, but *only* of the ship. For there stood by me this night
24 an angel of the God whose I am, whom also I [1]serve, saying,
Fear not, Paul; thou must stand before Cæsar: and lo, God
25 hath granted thee all them that sail with thee. Wherefore,
sirs, be of good cheer: for I believe God, that it shall be
26 even so as it hath been spoken unto me. Howbeit we must
be cast upon a certain island.

13   Soon after the council had been held the wind changed, and a
gentle breeze sprang up from the *south* which seemed to justify the
proposal of the ship's officers. *They began to coast along, close in
shore* (because the wind blew from the south). But when they
14 reached Cape Matala, S. Paul's warnings came true. A sudden
gale or *hurricane*, known as the *Euraquilo*[2], burst upon them from
the NE. It blew *down from*[3] the mountains of Crete and, so to
15 speak, *caught hold of the ship*, which was quite unable to continue
its course to Phoenix (NW) or *look the wind in the face*. So, *giving
way* to it and reefing the sails, they had to let the ship be *driven*.
16 When they reached the island of *Cauda* or *Clauda*, now Gaudo,
they got some shelter *under its lee* and were able to make some
necessary preparations. (1) *The ship's boat* had been towed behind.
This they could now *hoist* on board; but it was a difficult matter,
and the passengers, or at least S. Luke, gave a helping hand, which
17 no doubt accounts for the reminiscence here. (2) Then they had
to *use helps* to prevent the ship's timbers from starting under the
strain. The method was one which has been put in practice even
as late as last century[4], viz. that of *undergirding* or 'frapping' *the
ship* by passing coils of cable round the hull. In this operation
only the sailors could take part. (3) The great danger was lest
the wind should drive them *on the Syrtis*, the great stretch of
sand-banks off the coast of Tunis and Tripoli, for which it was
blowing direct. Accordingly *they lowered the* great main *sail*[5],

---

[1] or *worship*.   [2] *Eurus* is the SE wind, *Aquilo* the N; so strictly speaking *Euraquilo* is the ENE. Neither *Euraquilo* nor *Euroclydon* is found elsewhere: nor is the form of either word grammatically defensible. Whichever of them may be the correct reading, it is probably a sailor's or local name for a particular 'tempestuous wind.'   [3] Cp. Lk viii 23. *It* in ver. 14 can hardly be *the ship*, which word last occurred in ver. 11 and is of a different gender.   [4] For instances see Smith *Voyage etc.* pp. 108—9.   [5] The Greek word (σκεῦος) is used for the great sheet in S. Peter's vision (x 11). Its usual meaning is a vessel of some kind, or piece of furniture; and here it may denote *the gear* or the main yard-arm. Dr Breusing (*op. cit.*) however has suggested a more probable interpretation than either this or that given above. He has shewn that it was the custom for the ancients in a storm to lower cables, with weights or anchors attached, into the sea, in order to retard the vessel (Plut. *Moral.* 507 a): and σκεῦος is used of such a weight or anchor, only to be used in the last extremity (Plut. *Moral.* 812 d). To retard the vessel was the present need: and this is how the Bezan text (in Gigas), to which Bede bears witness, understands it—*they lowered a weight to drag*. The sails would have been reefed before now as the Bezan text in fact states in verse 15.

and let the vessel drift *so*, under as little canvas as possible. (4) This phrase—*lowering the sail* (or *gear*)—probably covers another operation. They must have put the ship's helm as close to the wind as possible and set some storm sail, in order to steady the vessel and enable them to make some points against the wind. The effect of this would be to change the ship's course from SW
18 to W or WNW. When they had drifted past Cauda, once more they felt the full force of *the gale* which continued to increase, so *next day* to lighten the ship they had to throw the cargo overboard. The Greek tense shews that this was not completely done; for indeed, as we are reminded in verse 38, they had to keep some of the grain for
19 their own wants. Next day *they threw* overboard *the tackling*[1], i.e.
20 all the ship's furniture that was not absolutely necessary. They had now done all that was possible and nothing remained but to wait. *The storm* lasted day after day; and, being unable to see the stars, they could not tell where they were. A cloud of despair settled down upon them, and *all hope of being saved was taken away*[2]. Further, even had they had any appetite for food, the state of the vessel prevented its preparation, and so to their misery of
21 mind was added *fasting* of the body.

In this situation their first need was encouragement, and S. Paul, the great apostle of 'comfort[3],' was enabled to encourage them, as he had so often encouraged the disciples. But first he had himself to experience the depression and fear[4]. It was small satisfaction for his prediction to have been verified, if this was to be the end of all—instead of Rome, a watery grave. He had indeed the Lord's promise (xxiii 11) but depression leads to doubt; and knowing that the fulfilment of the divine promises is not absolute but conditioned, he prayed for the confirmation of his faith. But more than for himself he was anxious for the safety of his fellow-shipmates; and as a great intercessor he prayed for them also[5]
23 His prayer was heard. As in other moments of desperation, he was strengthened by a heavenly vision. An *angel* appeared and
24 took away his *fear*, by assuring him that the Lord's promise would stand and that *God had granted him*, or made him a present of, the lives of all for whom he had prayed[6]. Next day accordingly
21 *he stood up in the midst* to encourage the men and to bear witness to his *God*[7]. It was the God to whom they all belonged, but whom

---

[1] According to the AV (*we*) the passengers again assisted in this work—but landsmen would hardly know what they might throw overboard. Cp. Jonah i 5.
[2] In xiv 9 (xv 11) we had *faith to be saved*. Here the hopelessness is balanced by faith in verse 25. [3] i.e. *paraclēsis*. [4] Notice the word *us* not *them* in verse 20. For this condition of the power of 'comfort,' cp. II Cor i 4–7. [5] Cp. the intercession of Christ for his own (Jn xvii) and his enemies (Lk xxiii 34); and the call of Jonah to prayer (Jonah i 6). [6] The same word as in xxv 11, 16. For the *angel* cp. xii 7, and p. 71 n.[4]; and Lk xxii 43. [7] So Jonah's shipwreck calls out faith in God (i 6, 9, 16). For the distinction between the divine lordship over man, and man's recognition of God, cp. Dan v 23 and vi 20: of the latter verse this is almost a quotation. The words also recall S. Paul's witness to the true God in the midst of the Areopagus (xvii 22).

Paul alone recognized by conscious *worship*. First he reminds them of the truth of his prediction and rebukes them for their disobedience, through which they had *gained*—he adds with some irony—*this loss*[1]. This trait of true human nature, always so quick to prove itself in the right, is a sign of S. Luke's faithfulness: he
22 does not forget the man in the apostle. Then S. Paul assures them of their safety,—only, as it were in punishment, they must suffer
25 *loss of their ship*. Therefore he exhorts them to *take heart* and be like *men*: and this because effort will be required on their part. There are conditions on which the fulfilment of the divine promise depends: and God requires on man's part co-operation or correspondence to his will. Of such necessary conditions or essential means we shall find three instances.

The wreck. S. Paul's Bay

27 All this time, they *were being driven across*[2] *the sea of Adria*. This term was not always confined (as now) to the Adriatic; at one period it was also used of the 'Sicilian' or 'Ionian Sea,' viz. the part of the Mediterranean which lay between Sicily and Greece[3]. It is interesting to learn that seven years later (A.D. 64) the same sea was the scene of the shipwreck of Josephus the Jewish historian, likewise on his way to Rome. His ship did actually founder and, after a night in the deep, he with 80 others—the sole survivors out of a total of 600—was picked up by a ship of Cyrene.

27 But when the fourteenth night was come, as we were driven ⁴to and fro in the *sea of* Adria, about midnight the sailors surmised that ⁵they were drawing near to some
28 country; and they sounded, and found twenty fathoms: and after a little space, they sounded again, and found fifteen
29 fathoms. And fearing lest haply we should be cast ashore on rocky ground, they let go four anchors from the stern,
30 and ⁶wished for the day⁷. And as the sailors were seeking to flee out of the ship, and had lowered the boat into the sea, under colour as though they would lay out anchors from the
31 foreship⁸, Paul said to the centurion and to the soldiers,

---

[1] The Greek words however may be translated *Ye should have hearkened and so saved* (i.e. *avoided*) *this loss*. [2] The arrival at Malta postulates the ship's having held a straight course under the gale. There is no need to translate, as AV and RV, *up and down* or *to and fro*. [3] Strabo (flor. B.C. 24) definitely restricts *the Adriatic* to its present limits: by Ptolemy (flor. A.D. 139) the term is as definitely used in its extended sense. The period of the Acts falls exactly in the middle between these two geographers. [4] or *across*. [5] B reads *some country was resounding* (with the noise of the breakers). [6] Marg *prayed*. [7] A Bezan text adds *that they might know if we can be saved*, and [8] *to make the ship ride more securely*.

32 Except these abide in the ship, ye cannot be saved. Then the soldiers cut away the ropes of the boat, and let her fall off.
33 And while the day was coming on, Paul besought them all to take some food, saying, This day is the fourteenth day that ye wait and continue fasting, having taken nothing.
34 Wherefore I beseech you to take some food: for this is for your ¹safety: for there shall not a hair ²perish from the head
35 of any of you. And when he had said this, and had taken bread, he gave thanks to God in the presence of all: and he
36 brake it, and began to eat³. Then were they all of good cheer,
37 and themselves also took food. And we were in all in the
38 ship ⁴two hundred threescore and sixteen souls. And when they had eaten enough, they lightened the ship, throwing out the wheat into the sea.
39 And when it was day, ⁵they knew not the land: but they perceived a certain bay with a beach, and they took counsel
40 whether they could ⁶drive the ship upon it. And casting off the anchors, they left them in the sea, at the same time loosing the bands of the rudders; and hoisting up the foresail to the
41 wind, they made for the beach But lighting upon a place where two seas met, they ran the vessel aground; and the foreship struck and remained unmoveable, but the stern began
42 to break up by the violence *of the waves*. And the soldiers' counsel was to kill the prisoners, lest any *of them* should
43 swim out, and escape. But the centurion, desiring to save Paul, stayed them from their purpose; and commanded that they which could swim should cast themselves overboard,
44 and get first to the land: and the rest, some on planks, and some on *other* things from the ship. And so it came to pass, that they all escaped safe to the land.

27 On *the fourteenth night* the practised ears of *the sailors* detected the sound of breakers, and they concluded that they were *nearing*
28 *land*⁷. This was proved by *soundings*; and so, to prevent *being cast*
29 *on rocks*, they anchored the ship. *Four anchors* were lowered—not

---
¹ or *salvation*. ² AV reads *fall*. ³ Bezan adds *and gave also unto us*.
⁴ Marg with B reads *about threescore and sixteen*. ⁵ Bezan *the sailors*.
⁶ Marg with B reads *bring the ship safe to shore* (lit. *save-out-of*—the sea).
⁷ S. Luke really says *some land was nearing us*, as a seaman would.

from the usual place, the prow of the vessel, but—*from the stern*. This was to prevent the ship swinging round to the wind and to keep her facing shorewards, ready to be run aground in the morning. Before they could anchor from the stern, they had first to take up and lash the two great paddles which served the ancients for *rudders* (verse 40). This done they remained *longing for day*[1]. Dawn would shew them their fate, for they had no idea where they were. The land was in fact the island of Malta[2] and the noise came from the breakers off Koura Point, the western promontory of S. Paul's Bay. It has been calculated from the averages of modern vessels that a ship drifting like this would in fourteen days just cover the 480 miles which lie between Gaudo and Malta, and the first bay it would reach, coming from that direction, would be that of S. Paul. Further details correspond so that there is no reasonable doubt that this is the scene of the apostle's shipwreck[3].

30 The fulfilment of the divine will, however, depended upon the proper co-operation on man's part. Thus the crew of the ship had not the same confidence in S. Paul as the centurion; possibly there was a feeling of irritation or jealousy at the interference of a landsman. In any case they hoped to make sure of their own escape by selfishly making off with the boat instead of waiting for the dawn. So while it was still dark, *they lowered the boat* (verse 17) *into the sea under the pretence of stretching out anchors from the*
31 *prow* to keep the ship steadier. *Paul*, however, saw through the flimsy pretext and warned Julius. The sailors would be wanted next morning to run the ship aground, and without them the soldiers would be helpless. So the apostle uttered a warning which has ever since formed a text for maintaining at all costs the unity of the church: *unless these* (sailors) *abide in the ship, ye* (soldiers)
32 *cannot be saved*. The *soldiers* shewed their faith in S. Paul by *cutting the ropes* and sacrificing *the boat*; and by so doing they may have saved the lives of the sailors in spite of themselves.

33 A second condition needful *for their safety* was *to take some food*. The work of getting to shore would require all their strength and nerve, but *for fourteen days* they had been in a state of *fasting*. S. Paul then again assumed the office of comforter and commander: as he had prayed for them, so now he sustains them; and his attitude is very much like that of the Lord feeding the Five Thousand. Just before the point of dawn all the ship's company were assembled (perhaps for a roll-call) and *Paul exhorted*
34 *them to partake of food*. By urging them to eat he declared his

---

[1] The Greek word primarily means *praying*: here it must denote the ardent longing for the dawn, which they could hardly have hoped to accelerate by prayer.
[2] The Greek form *Melita* caused it once to be identified with the isle of Meleda in the Adriatic. This idea cannot now-a-days be considered seriously. [3] For this calculation see Smith *Voyage etc.* pp. 125–8. In the particular creek which Mr Smith identifies with the point of appulse there is no sandy *beach* (p. 142, Acts xxvii 39). Dr Field however shews that the Greek word is not necessarily limited to a *sandy beach*.

belief that their condition was not hopeless: he was convinced that if they did their part, *not a hair of their head would perish*. He uses a proverbial saying familiar to the Jews[1]. Then, in order to set an
35 example, *he took a loaf* and said grace over it, i.e. *he gave thanks to God*. And so *in the presence of* and in behalf of them *all* he offered an act of worship to the God whom he served (verse 23). Then *breaking the loaf he* first ate of it himself and then gave also to Aristarchus and Luke his fellow-disciples[2]. We have already noticed the correspondence with the Last Supper, but we need not conclude that this was technically a celebration of the Holy Eucharist. It is not likely that S. Paul would have celebrated the holy mysteries before a company of unbelievers; nor is the condition of a ship tossing in a heavy sea favourable for the solemnities of religious worship. The similarity is due, not so much to the fact that the Holy Eucharist is a meal, as that every meal has a sacred character and food 'is sanctified by the word of God and prayer.' Thus S. Paul offered thanks to God; and this meal, like those after the resurrection at Emmaus and on the shore of
36 the lake of Galilee, is a pattern of the Christian meal[3]. The effect was proportionate. The rest were *encouraged and took their food*.
37 In some way, as in the case of the Five Thousand, the meal was connected with a numbering of the people. *In all* they came to *276 souls*. Here our desire for a perfect picture is baffled by a discrepancy in our authorities: the Vatican MS has *about 76*. The vessels of the ancients were as a rule smaller than ours: but if we remember the large size of the Alexandrian corn-ships and the 600 souls on board Josephus' ship, 276 will not be too many
38 When they had eaten as much as they would, *they threw into the sea* the rest of *the wheat* for which they had no further need and so completed the operation begun in verse 18.
39 By this time *it was* full *day*, but the sailors *did not recognize the coast*. Most of them had probably been at Malta before, but they would have visited the harbour of Valetta, like the other Alexandrian ship of xxviii 11. *They discovered however a bay* (S. Paul's Bay) *with a beach*, and therefore a possible place to run the ship aground. Accordingly after a final *council*, they
40 decided to make the attempt. *The anchors* were cast loose, *the rudder paddles* unlashed, the small *foresail* raised up (for the gale was still *blowing*) and they steered straight *for the beach*. But they
41 had 'reckoned without their host.' There is an island cut off from the northern promontory of the bay by a narrow channel, and the current through this channel meeting the tide in the bay causes sand-banks to form. On one of these the ship *stuck fast*, and the heavy sea at once began *to break up its stern part*. At
42 this final and fatal moment S. Paul had the narrowest escape of all.

---

[1] It occurs in the OT (1 Sam xiv 45, II xiv 11, I K i 52) with *fall*, as in the margin; but, as in the text, in Lk xxi 18. Cp. Mt x 30, Lk xii 7. [2] Bezan.
[3] See pp. 37, 40: and cp. I Tim iv 5; Lk xxiv 30, Jn xxi 13.

He was on the point of losing his life not by the sea but by the sword[1], and the sword not of the lawful executioner but of selfish murderers. Human selfishness made another attempt to frustrate the divine purpose. Before, it was the sailors; now, it is *the soldiers*. These were responsible for *the prisoners* with their lives[2]; and as the latter had now a good opportunity to make their escape, 43 the simplest *plan was to kill* them at once. But Julius, however indifferent he might be to the fate of the rest, felt a real gratitude if not affection towards the apostle, and forbade his men to carry out the proposal. Instead, *he ordered* all to make their way *to the land* 44 as best they could, and in the end *all were saved completely*[3]. Like Israel they found dry land in the midst of the sea, and like Jonah they were cast out of the deep on to the shore.

After the wreck

After the wreck the shipwrecked company found not merely safety but comfort and hospitality; and an incident occurred which completed the exaltation of the apostle. With this incident we must compare similar conduct on the part of the other 'barbarians' of the Acts, the Lycaonians, in xiv 8–19.

28 And when we were escaped, then we knew that the island
2 was called 'Melita. And the barbarians shewed us no common kindness: for they kindled a fire, and received us all, because
3 of the present rain, and because of the cold. But when Paul had gathered a bundle of sticks, and laid them on the fire, a viper came out by reason of the heat, and fastened on his
4 hand. And when the barbarians saw the beast hanging from his hand, they said one to another, No doubt this man is a murderer, whom, though he hath escaped from the sea, yet
5 Justice hath not suffered to live. Howbeit he shook off the
6 beast into the fire, and took no harm. But they expected that he would have swollen, or fallen down dead suddenly: but when they were long in expectation, and beheld nothing amiss come to him, they changed their minds, and said that he was a god.

1 The Maltese were mainly of Phenician extraction, and S. Luke shews his Greek feeling[5] by calling them *barbarians*; for that was the summary title given by the Greeks to all non-Greek-speaking

---

[1] like S. Peter in ch. xii. [2] Cp. xii 19, xvi 27. [3] or *got safe through*. The use of the same verb in the Greek in vv. 43, 44 may be intentional—because the centurion *saved* Paul, they were all *saved*. [4] Marg with B reads *Melitene*.
[5] not that he was necessarily a Greek: S. Paul also uses the word in Rom i 14, I Cor xiv 11, Col iii 11.

peoples. There were colonies of Syrians and Phenicians in most of the great commercial cities, and so their dialect would have been intelligible to some of the sailors—possibly to S. Luke himself, who had visited Syria and Phenicia; for when the shipwrecked party got on shore, they found some of the natives waiting for them, and
2 S. Luke heard them say, *The island is called Malta*. Though *barbarians* in speech, they were not such in conduct. Instead of acting like wreckers, they treated the party with *unusual kindness*[1]. As it was *cold*—it was now autumn—and *raining* hard, *they lighted a fire and received us all*, even the prisoners, like
3 brothers[2]. S. Paul's energy was again conspicuous[3]; in spite of the exhaustion of getting to shore, he set about *collecting* fuel with such zeal as to attract the notice of the Maltese, who observed (probably from the chain on his wrist) that he was a prisoner. *As he threw his faggot on the fire, the heat* made *a viper*
4 *dart out and fasten on his hand*. When they saw it, the simple *barbarians* concluded that *this man* must have committed some great crime[4], and that, although he had escaped one death, *Justice* would *not suffer him to live*. They speak of *Justice* as a goddess. There is no evidence of the actual worship of *Diké* at Malta[5]. But it was the tendency not only of the barbarian, but of the 'religious' Athenian, mind to personify and deify qualities and attributes: thus the Athenians took 'the resurrection' for a deity, and as we speak of 'Providence,' so the Maltese spoke of 'Justice[6].' S. Paul
6 however did not *drop down dead*, nor did even any *inflammation* ensue; so when they had stared for a long time and nothing happened, they exclaimed *that he was a god*. There was the same credulity in the Lycaonians, who were equally quick in altering their judgement—only in the reverse direction, from good to bad.

An objection is made to the story on the ground that no poisonous snakes are to be found in Malta to-day; but it would be much more astonishing, if any such had managed to survive after so many centuries in that populous island[7]. It is of course possible that the snake was not poisonous, or that S. Luke misunderstood what was taking place in the barbarian mind. But the impression conveyed by the text is certainly that of an extraordinary preservation, as at Lystra. And we cannot help thinking that this incident was in the mind of the writer of Mk xvi 18—*They shall take up serpents...and it shall not hurt them*. The teaching is the same. The whole history of the voyage had shewn that there was a divine Justice watching over S. Paul; and the character to which it had

---

[1] Thus Julius' *kindness* (xxvii 3) was rewarded. *No common* occurs in xix 11.
[2] The Greek word implies receiving into fellowship: cp. Rom xiv 1, 3, and Acts xvii 5.
[3] Cp. xiv 19–20. [4] Cp. Lk xiii 1–5, Jn ix 1–2. [5] Apparently there was a temple to Justice (Gk *Diké*) in the Megarid (*CIG* 1080). [6] The personification of the '*Diké*' of Zeus was common in the Greek poets. In mythology she was reckoned as a goddess, being the daughter of Zeus and Themis (Hesiod). [7] Wolves were to be found in England centuries after this viper at Malta, but are now extinct.

borne witness was so prophetic and inspired, that the simple-minded Maltese could only describe it in the words that he was divine or 'a god.' These last words contain the real lesson of the narrative, and they resemble the similar verdict of the centurion in Lk xxiii 47 : *Certainly this was a righteous man.*

§ 2   *The winter in Malta*

Malta, or Melita as the ancients called it, was an important centre in the navigation of the Mediterranean. The Phenicians had first colonized the island ; Greeks followed ; then Carthage annexed it ; and finally it passed from the dominion of Carthage to that of Rome, and was assigned to the province of Sicily. Since 1800 it has been a British possession; and so, while the traditions of S. Paul's having visited England are worthless, it is some gratification to our patriotism to know that S. Paul did set foot on British soil. The governor of Sicily would have some representative in the island; otherwise it retained its local self-government, which was constituted after the Greek model with a Senate, Archons, and Dêmos (People). Under the empire we find a procurator in Malta[1]. Whether he was merely the steward of the imperial revenues or the actual governor we do not know[2]. Besides the procurator there was a 'First of the Maltese.' This title has been found on inscriptions[3]; but again we do not know whether this was a title of office or of compliment. At the present moment it was borne by one *Publius*. This is a Roman name; but as it is only a praenomen[4] and no other name is given, we should rather infer that Publius was not of Roman blood.

The three winter months spent at Malta were for S. Paul a time of rest and recovery and freedom from controversy. The 'barbarians' were conspicuous for their hospitality and gratitude. They justified the statement of Vergil that 'Justice when she forsook the earth left her last footsteps among the simple country-folk[5].' And the apostle repaid them—not with silver and gold (iii 6) but—with gifts of healing, which take us back to the early chapters and especially remind us of the healing of Aeneas and of the multitude from the cities round about Jerusalem (ix 32–5, v 16).

7   Now in the neighbourhood of that place were lands belonging to the [6]chief man of the island, named Publius ; who received us, and entertained us three days courteously. 8 And it was so, that the father of Publius lay sick of fever and

---

[1] On one inscription (*CIL* x no. 7494) we find the name of *Chrestion*, a freedman of *Augustus*, procurator *of the islands of Melita and Gaulos* (Gozzo).
[2] Mommsen is in favour of the latter alternative (on *CIL* x no. 6785).   [3] In *CIL* x no. 7495 we read MEL(*itensium*) PRIMUS OMNI(*um*)—*first of all the Maltese* (but this inscription has disappeared); and in a Greek inscription (*CIG* no. 5754) *Prudens a Roman knight, first of the Maltese.*   For the title cp. xiii 50, xxv 2.
[4] corresponding to our 'Christian name.'   [5] *Georg.* II 473–4.   [6] Gk *first.*

dysentery : unto whom Paul entered in, and prayed, and laying
9 his hands on him healed him. And when this was done, the
rest also which had diseases in the island came, and were
10 cured : who also honoured us with many honours ; and when
we sailed, they put on board such things as we needed.

7   *Publius had estates* near S. Paul's Bay ; and while the centurion
was securing quarters for the winter he offered hospitality to
the prisoners and their guards. This is the third instance of
kindness or *courtesy* which S. Luke marks on this journey[1]. He
would call the attention of the Roman public to the courteous
treatment S. Paul received at the hands of all save his own country-
8 men. S. Paul shewed his gratitude to Publius by *healing* his
father[2]. The means he employed were those in normal use
among the Christians, viz. *prayer* and *imposition of hands* by the
presbyters of the church[3]. And accordingly we can look upon this
healing not as something extraordinary, like the healing of the
lame man at Lystra ; or marvellous, like the cures through cloths
and napkins at Ephesus; but as the ordinary exercise of the 'gift
9 of healing[4].' Similarly in the description of the cures which were
wrought during the winter we can recognize, besides this spiritual
method, the use of medical *treatment*. S. Luke was a doctor,
10 and the *us* of verse 10 shews that he too had contributed to the
healing of the sick. The Maltese shewed their gratitude by
honouring the apostolic company *with many honours*. The usual
way of 'honouring' a benefactor at that time was to erect a statue
of him or at least a complimentary inscription. The honours of
the Maltese may have taken a form more profitable to the recipients.
The word is generally used in the Acts for *price* or *value*[5]; and when
the travellers resumed their voyage, as they had lost all their
belongings in the shipwreck, the Maltese *laded them*[6] with *such
things as they needed*.

SECTION III B (=Ch. 28. 11—31)

ROME

In the next spring after his shipwreck S. Paul came to the end
of his journey; and thus the divine will that he should 'bear witness
at Rome' was, in spite of the resistance of the elements and of human

---

[1] xxviii 2 and xxvii 3.   [2] His ailment is described with medical accuracy by
S. Luke; cp. Lk iv 38.   [3] Jas v 14, where oil is also specified (as in Mk vi 13).
Laying on of hands and prayer was the medium for conveyance of blessings both
spiritual and material, cp. p. 85.   [4] I Cor xii 9, 30.   [5] iv 34, v 2–3, vii 16,
xix 19. Cp. Ecclus xxxviii 1 : '*Honour* a physician *according to thy need* of him
with the honours due unto him' (the words in italics stand for Greek words, which
occur here).   [6] The word may mean *put-on them* or *put-on board*.

perversity, at last fulfilled. Its fulfilment was also the triumph of the apostle, who had ever striven to identify his own with the Lord's will. A long while ago he had prayed for a prosperous journey to Rome (Rom i 10); and though events had fallen out very differently from his expectation, yet the prayer had been answered. The chain of circumstances is made complete by the addition of the last link: the meeting with Aquila and Priscilla at Corinth, the plan formed at Ephesus, the letter written from Corinth, the vision of the Lord at Jerusalem, the delivery up to the Romans at Caesarea, the appeal to Caesar, are now fulfilled by the arrival of the apostle himself at Rome[1].

On his entry into the city, S. Paul would find himself confronted with three 'nations' or divisions of mankind.

(i) *The Gentiles.* As the centre of the world, the vast city of Rome represented, and contained representatives of, all nations: potentially it answers to 'the uttermost part of the earth' (i 8). The rest of 'the nations' had been subdued by the Romans: accordingly, as the centre of power, the city of Rome was the visible embodiment of 'the kingdom of the world,' with the Caesar at its head.

(ii) *The Jews.* The history of the Jewish colony at Rome has been briefly sketched above (p. 23). Claudius had expelled them from the city (p. 324). But his edict soon became a dead letter; and the Jews at Rome were now as numerous as ever, swarming especially in their quarter across the Tiber, the modern Trastevere. They were so numerous as to have several synagogues. Inscriptions have made us acquainted with the synagogues 'of the Augustesians,' 'of the Agrippesians,' and 'of Volumnius,' called after their patrons; 'of the Campesians' in the Campus Martis, 'of the Siburesians' in the Subura; also 'of the Hebrews,' 'of the Rhodians,' and 'of the olive[2].' Though Jewish beggars abounded, there were also Jews among the wealthy. By means of proselytism among Roman ladies, the Jews exercised a great influence upon society: and in the society of Rome the Herodian family, who were Jews, held a leading position. Even in the emperor's palace the Jews were well represented by slaves, freedmen, and others, who secured for them considerable interest with Nero: Haliturus, his favourite actor, was a Jew, and his mistress Poppaea a Jewish proselyte.

(iii) *The Christians.* The origins of the church at Rome are wrapt in obscurity. As every movement in the empire was reflected at the capital which was the place of universal resort from all quarters, as again there was close communication between the Jews of Rome and of Palestine, we should expect the news of Christianity to find its way to Rome as soon as anywhere. Possibly the first seeds of the truth were carried home by some of the 'Romans' from the first Pentecost[3]. Certainly in the reign of Claudius Christianity had made some progress, for the tumults it occasioned among the Jews led to their banishment

---

[1] See xvi 37, xviii 2, xix 21, xxii 25, xxiii 11, xxv 11. [2] For full information see Schürer, especially his *Gemeindeverfassung der Juden im Rom.* [3] ii 10: cp. xviii 2.

from the city: this progress is at least confirmed by the traditions which speak of visits of Simon Magus and of S. Peter to the city in Claudius' days. At the beginning of Nero's reign (A.D. 54) the Roman Christians were so important a body that S. Paul, although personally a stranger, addressed to them his great doctrinal epistle. From this Epistle to the Romans we can draw one or two inferences. (1) The Christians were so fully established in the faith that S. Paul does not claim to come to them as more than a visitor, and he almost apologizes for admonishing them[1]. (2) The Gentile element predominated among them. This is confirmed by the evidence of the Acts. The speech of the Jews in verses 21-22 shews that a great separation had already taken place between the Synagogue and the Ecclesia. Claudius' edict of banishment would fully account for such a divorce. If Jewish Christians had to leave the city, the Gentile Christians would have remained behind: again, when the Jews returned, Jews and Christians would now form independent bodies. (3) And yet the Roman Christians do not appear to be fully organized into one body or church. The salutations at the end of the epistle shew them to be grouped round various centres[2]. This is exactly what we should expect in a great city. In Rome, as at Ephesus, Christianity would spring up in various groups, in various localities, and from various sources[3]: and this is borne out by the history of S. Paul's relation to the church when he arrives This state of affairs would be perfectly natural if Christianity at Rome had not been planted by one great founder or apostle. Nevertheless, it does not exclude a previous visit of S. Peter: he may have visited the city, and yet been prevented by the need of secrecy, or other limitations, from organizing the Christians into one united church[4].

Now, however, we are to trace the journey and arrival of S. Paul, about which there is no doubt. On the opening of the sailing season of A.D. 58 he starts upon what may be called his third voyage. It takes about a week; and its diary is carefully marked like that of the eventful voyage up to Jerusalem in 55, just three years ago.

§ 1 *Journey to Rome. Paul and the Christians*

11 And after three months we set sail in a ship of Alexandria, which had wintered in the island, whose sign was [5]The Twin
12 Brothers. And touching at Syracuse, we tarried there three
13 days. And from thence we [6]made a circuit, and arrived at Rhegium: and after one day a south wind sprang up, and on
14 the second day we came to Puteoli: where we found brethren,

---

[1] See Rom i 11-2, xv 14-6, 24, 28. [2] S. Paul does not write to 'the church' at Rome; and his allusion to ministries in xii 6-8 agrees with a very democratic feeling in the church, on which see p. 510. [3] Compare the growth of the church at Ephesus, p. 348. [4] See pp. 179-80, 362. [5] Gk *Dioscuri*. [6] Marg with ℵB reads *cast loose*, i.e. *weighed anchor* (xxvii 40).

and ¹were intreated to tarry with them seven days: and so we came to Rome.

15 And from thence the brethren, when they heard of us, came to meet us as far as ²The Market of Appius, and The Three Taverns: whom when Paul saw, he thanked God, and took courage.

11 Like the ill-fated vessel of Julius, another *Alexandrian ship* had been prevented from reaching Rome and *had wintered* at Malta. It was the *Dioscuri*: that was the name of the twin gods, Castor and Pollux, who were the patrons of sailors and whose figures adorned the vessel's prow. As soon as the sea was again 'open' for navigation, viz. at the beginning of March³, this vessel prepared to
12 start and Julius impressed it to carry his company. They first called at *Syracuse* in Sicily. Here they were kept *three days*,
13 probably through adverse winds. For when they did start they had to tack or *fetch a compass* (AV) in order to get to *Rhegium* in the straits of Messina. After another day's delay, *a south wind sprang up* and carried them straight *to Puteoli*, 180 miles distant, which they reached the next day⁴. Puteoli, now Pozzuoli, in the bay of Naples, although 140 miles distant from the city was yet the port of Rome. For the harbour of Ostia at the mouth of the Tiber suffered from the silting of the river. Claudius had done a great deal to improve it; but Ostia could never be a rival of Puteoli. As the port of Rome, the harbour of Puteoli would be crowded with shipping from all quarters, and its streets with men of all nationalities. Among these would be a large proportion of orientals, for here 'the Syrian Orontes first disgorged its crowds on the way to
14 the Roman Tiber⁵.' There was a large Jewish quarter, and quite naturally a body of Christians, i.e. *brethren*. The apostolic company were entertained by them for a week, and *were* much *comforted* and encouraged⁶. *And so*, i.e. with a good courage and in a spirit of thankfulness (as will be further explained in the following verse)⁷,

---

¹ Bezan reads *were comforted, tarrying [with them.* ² i.e. *Appii Forum* and *Tres Tabernae.* ³ or even earlier. According to Vegetius (see p. 483) the sea was 'shut' from Nov. 11 to March 5; and the festival of 'the sailing of Isis' on March 5 was the formal opening of the navigation season. But there was another reckoning. Pliny (*Nat. Hist.* II 47) says that the advent of spring, i.e. Feb. 7 or 8, 'opened the sea to sailors.' Pf. C. Erbes (from whom I have borrowed this information) even dates the departure from Malta on Jan. 26, and the arrival at Rome on Feb. 12 (*die Todestage der Apostel Paulus u. Petrus*, in *Texte u. Untersuch.* n. f. IV i, pp. 47–9). ⁴ This was the usual course for travellers. Titus, when hurrying to Rome after the destruction of Jerusalem, sailed from Alexandria in a merchant vessel, touched at Rhegium and landed at Puteoli (Suetonius *Titus* 5). ⁵ Juvenal *Sat.* III 62. ⁶ The Bezan text is more natural than the RV. The Greek verb, which corresponds to *paraclēsis*, may be translated *beseech* or *encourage*: but Julius rather than S. Paul was the person *to be intreated*, and the idea of *encouragement* suits the context best. ⁷ S. Luke may simply mean 'by the usual land route': but for his significant use of *so*, cp. xvii 33, xix 20, xx 11.

we came to Rome—*the Rome* (so the Greek has it) which had been so long the apostle's goal and ambition.

But now when he had at last come within sight of the goal, the apostle was overcome once more by depression. Wonderfully preserved as he had been by the divine Justice from the perils of the sea and the plots of the Jews, his own spirit was now cast down. No doubt all the sufferings he had gone through were beginning to tell on his physical frame. But the real burden was mental anxiety—not so much for his own safety, as on behalf of the gospel. It would be a critical moment when he should stand before the Caesar, and the powers that be would have to decide upon the quarrel between Judaism and Christianity. Then his kinsmen, the Jews—would they still reject his offer? and yet again, his brethren of the church—how would they receive his gospel? It is quite evident from the Epistle to the Romans that S. Paul had considered their attitude toward his gospel to be of the greatest importance: and now, how would they receive him in person? Aquila and Priscilla, his faithful fellow-workers, were Roman Christians, and he had many friends in the city. But to the majority he was unknown. In his letter to them he had shewn the greatest care to avoid any assumption of authority. It was now over three years since he had written that letter; what response he had received we do not know, but we can quite imagine the state of anxiety in which he left Puteoli, under the escort of Julius and his soldiers.

15 At Capua they would join the famous Appian Way which ran from Brindisi to Rome, and a hundred miles from Puteoli they came to *Appii Forum*. This station is familiar to us from allusions in Roman writers. Horace in particular, recounting a journey to Brindisi, describes it as 'crowded with boatmen and inn-keepers,—and rogues[1].' But a joyful surprise awaited S. Paul. Here they met a body of Christian *brethren* who had come to welcome them to Rome. At the next stage, *Tres Tabernae*, 10 miles further on, another body met them. Josephus relates that, when an impostor claiming to be Alexander a son of Herod the Great visited Rome, the whole nation of the Jews came to meet and escort him to the city[2]. The Roman Christians determined to pay the apostle the same honour. As soon as he arrived at Puteoli, news had been sent off, but the time had not allowed them to get further than the 40 miles to Appii Forum. They came in two bodies, which may have represented the two sides of the church, Gentile and Jewish, respectively: or possibly the want of a central organization had led to independent action. However that may be, *when S. Paul saw them*, at this sign of loyalty and tribute of honour, his depression vanished, *he thanked God[3], and took courage[4]*.

---

[1] *Sat.* I 5. 4. [2] *Ant.* XVII 12. 1. [3] as in the storm, xxvii 35. [4] The courage was the gift of the Lord, who had said 'be of good *courage*' (xxiii 11, p. 435).

§ 2 *Entry into Rome. Paul and the Jews*

After leaving Tres Tabernae, the Appian Way (which can still be trodden by those who wish to follow in the apostle's footsteps) led the party for thirty miles straight across the Campagna to the city; and passing under the Porta Capena, S. Paul, together with Luke and Aristarchus, at last *entered into Rome*. The pronoun *we*, which meets us for the last time, is an indication that S. Luke shared the feelings with which the apostle for the first time trod the streets and viewed the buildings of the Eternal City, the Mistress of the World, the Babylon on the Seven Hills.

16 And when we entered into Rome, [1] Paul was suffered to abide by himself [2] with the soldier that guarded him.

17 And it came to pass, that after three days he called together [3] those that were the [4] chief of the Jews: and when they were come together, he said unto them, I, brethren, though I had done nothing against the people, or the customs of our fathers, yet was delivered prisoner from Jerusalem

18 into the hands of the Romans: who, when they had examined me, desired to set me at liberty, because there was no cause

19 of death in me. But when the Jews spake against it [5], I was constrained to appeal unto Cæsar; not that I had aught to

20 accuse my nation of [5]. For this cause therefore did I [6] intreat you to see and to speak with *me*: for because of the hope

21 of Israel I am bound with this chain. And they said unto him, We neither received letters from Judæa concerning thee, nor did any of the brethren come hither and report or speak

22 any harm of thee. But we desire to hear of thee what thou thinkest: for as concerning this sect, it is known to us that everywhere it is spoken against.

16 On entering the city, Julius' first care was to march to his head-quarters—the *Castra Peregrinorum*, i.e. the Camp of the Peregrini on the Caelian Hill (p. 479)—and there *hand over the prisoners to* his official superior, *the Captain of the Camp*, or

---

[1] Marg with AV and Bezan inserts *the centurion delivered the prisoners to the captain of the praetorian guard, but* [*Paul.* The Gk word is *captain-of-the-camp*: AV translates *captain of the guard*, a Bezan Latin text (Gigas, p. xxiv) *princeps peregrinorum.* [2] Bezan adds *without the camp* (Hebr xiii 11). [3] Marg *those that were of the Jews first.* [4] Gk *first.* [5] Bezan inserts *and cried out Away with our enemy*: and at the end of the verse *but that I might deliver* (lit. *redeem*) *my soul from death.* [6] Marg with AV *call for you, to see and to speak with* you.

'Chief of the Peregrini,' as he was subsequently called[1]. This is no doubt the officer meant: the usual reference to the Praetorian guard, as in the margin, naturally originated in days when the existence of the Peregrini had been forgotten. But the Praetorians did not act as imperial police; it is true that important political offenders, dangerous to the Caesar, were committed to the custody of the Prefect of the Praetorian guard, but hardly ordinary appellants like these Jews. The Captain of the Peregrini, on receiving Paul, would read his 'elogium' (p. 439), from which he would learn his freedom from guilt in the eyes of a Roman, while the body of Christians who escorted him would testify to his personal importance. Accordingly he *allowed him* to live in a house of his own *outside* the precincts of *the camp*, *with* (of course) *the soldier* to whom he was chained (verse 20) as his *warder*.

S. Paul's anxiety as to the Christians had been set at rest. There remained the Jews. There was constant communication between Jerusalem and Rome, and no doubt the Jewish authorities would have sent messengers—'apostles' they were called at a later date—or written letters to secure the interest of their Roman brethren in promoting active measures against Paul. Accordingly it was important for him to ascertain the attitude they would adopt, and to disarm their prejudices by assuring them of his loyalty to his nation. But though S. Paul begins his address to them with his emphatic *I*, his personal prospects would not be his chief motive for approaching them. The apostle had come with a readiness or zeal 'to preach the gospel to them also who were at Rome'; and his rule was 'to the Jew first, then to the Greek[2].'

17 Accordingly after a day's rest, in which he could realize his new surroundings, S. Paul *invited* to his lodging *those who were the first of the Jews*[3], i.e. no doubt the rulers and archisynagogi of the various synagogues. They *came in a body*[4], and S. Paul made his final defence to the Jews, to explain his present position. (1) He denied that he had been guilty of any act of disloyalty to *the People* (of Israel) *or the customs of the fathers*, although he had been *delivered into the hands of the Romans*[5] and had come from
18 Jerusalem (as they saw) *in bonds*. The Romans themselves had pronounced him guiltless and *their intention had been to let him*
19 *go free*, but the Jews had *spoken against it*[6]. This compelled Paul *to appeal to Caesar—not to impeach his nation* but—to save
20 himself from death. His hearers however, to whom no doubt the apostle's name was known, were aware that S. Paul's real offence was his profession of Christianity, and would argue that there must

---

[1] i.e. in the time of Septimius Severus, but the title may have been older, as the office certainly was. [2] Rom i 15-6. This is in favour of the marginal rendering of ver. 17: but the Greek construction, which is the same as in v 17, xiii 1, is against it. [3] Cp. xiii 50, xxv 2, xxviii 7. [4] The words recall the *coming together* of 'the first' of the Christians in i 6. [5] See above p. 401. [6] Cp. the *gainsaying* of Heb xii 3.

be some great heresy in his teaching to account for this otherwise inexplicable opposition. To this then S. Paul at once passes. (2) Lifting up his arm with its *chain,* S. Paul testifies before God[1] that it is *the hope of Israel* which is in question, and for which he is 'an ambassador in chains[2]'; and it was in order to *expound* this hope to them that he had *besought* them to grant him this interview.

21 The Jews assumed an impartial attitude. By their emphatic *we* (corresponding to S. Paul's *I*) they distinguish themselves from the Jews of Jerusalem. They assert that they had received no official *letter* or messenger about S. Paul, nor had any private person 22 brought an evil report of him from Judaea. On the other hand they were aware that *this sect* of the Nazarenes *was everywhere spoken against* in the Jewish world. Still they did not wish to be prejudiced and so asked S. Paul to give an exposition of *his views*[3]. It was difficult for outsiders, in the absence of an authoritative teacher, to ascertain the real doctrines of the sect, especially the advanced views which were most offensive to the Jews. But S. Paul, as they knew, was 'a ringleader of the Nazarenes' (xxiv 5): hence there was a great opportunity of obtaining information from the teacher himself[4]. Accordingly a day was *fixed* for a discussion, and they departed.

This short speech presents two difficulties. (1) It seems surprising that the high-priests should not have written to Rome. It is possible that they had done so, and that their messenger had been detained by the same storm as S. Paul himself. Or the Jews at Jerusalem may have felt their case to be too weak to be vigorously followed up at Rome, especially after the favourable verdicts of Festus and Agrippa. Or they may have been too fully occupied with anxieties at home (2) We should have thought that the Roman Jews could have obtained some information about 'this sect' at Rome. But in this speech they entirely ignore the Roman Christians. There seems to be a deep gulf between the Synagogue and the Ecclesia in Rome, such as was not the case in other cities, in Corinth or Ephesus. But, as has been suggested above, the edict of Claudius may solve the difficulty. The expulsion of the Jews would have caused the Gentile element in the church to predominate, and resulted in a complete divorce from the synagogue. After the edict the Christians would have begun to meet for worship in their own houses, as is evident from the Epistle to the Romans. When the Jews returned, the tie of common worship having once been broken, there would be no reason for the renewal of intercourse. And in a vast city like Rome the separated bodies would soon lose sight of each other.

---

[1] See xxvi 1, p. 462. xii 3, 16, xiv 6, xv 5. p. 334.
[2] Eph vi 20, Col iv 3.
[3] Cp. Rom viii 5,
[4] Cp. the interest of the Ephesian Jews in xviii 20,

Conclusion of the Acts

The day appointed—by God[1], as well as by the Jews—has arrived. The goal is reached. *The kingdom of God* has grown like the mustard seed. From its cradle in the upper chamber at Jerusalem it has reached the capital of the world; and its herald is on the eve of bearing his witness before the king of this world. The task of the historian also is finished. His main purpose had been to describe the extension of the church from Jerusalem 'to the uttermost part of the earth' (i 8); and now that Rome is reached, he concludes the Acts with two pictures which bring before us the chief subjects of the history. (1) The scenes at Antioch in Pisidia, at Corinth and Ephesus[2], are re-presented in a final scene at Rome where *the Jews* reject the Messiah, and the gospel of salvation is offered to *the Gentiles*. (2) The series of notices which recorded from time to time the steady growth of the church[3] are concluded with a picture, in which we see *Paul* at work in Rome, in the undisturbed exercise of his apostolate, as a herald and teacher[4], testifying *the kingdom of God*[5]. This conclusion of the Acts corresponds to that of the Gospel. There (1) the Lord expounds the message of the 'salvation of God,' which is to 'be preached unto all the nations, beginning from Jerusalem.' And (2) the Gospel ends with a picture of the disciples, engaged in uninterrupted worship and waiting in quiet expectation for the future[6].

§ 3 *The rejection of the Jews: the mission to the Gentiles*

At the end of the Gospel the Lord 'opened the mind' of the disciples to understand what had been to them the supreme stumbling-block, viz. the fact that the Christ had been crucified and that by 'his own[7].' At the end of the Acts we are brought face to face with the same difficulty, in a later stage of development. The coming of Jesus had been followed by the coming of the Spirit and the establishment of the church. But as the Jews had crucified the Messiah, so they would have none of his kingdom: consequently, as they rejected the kingdom of God, so God rejected his people from their inheritance. This, then, was the intellectual and spiritual problem of the early church—the utter failure of God's chosen people to recognize their calling, and consequently the seeming failure of God's promises to them. At this moment the problem was weighing heavily on S. Paul's mind and heart: and in his Epistle to the Romans he had made the most determined attempt to grapple with it[8]. The difficulty was also felt by S. John, and by the Evangelists,—indeed by the whole church. But the Lord had answered it, giving the answer which the church could then receive: and that answer, which is contained in the words 'it is written,' is here repeated. Both the crucifixion and the unbelief were

---

[1] Cp. xvii 31.   [2] xiii 44–8, xviii 6, xix 9.   [3] i 13–4, ii 41–7, iv 31–3, v 42, vi 7, ix 31, xii 24, xvi 5, xix 20.   [4] xi 26, xiv 7, xv 35, xviii 11, xix 8.   [5] i 3, viii 12, xix 8.   [6] Lk xxiv 44–9: 52–3.   [7] Lk xxiv 46.   [8] Rom ix–xi.

recognized in the divine plan, as revealed in scripture: and the passage of Isaiah which the Lord quoted is recorded by all the Synoptists, and again by S. Luke in the Acts, by S. Paul in the Ep. to the Romans, and at the close of the century by S. John, who concludes the strife between belief and unbelief (in which form he presents to us the Lord's ministry) with the same divine judgment[1].

23 And when they had appointed him a day, they came to him into his lodging in great number; to whom he expounded *the matter*, testifying the kingdom of God, and persuading them concerning Jesus, both from the law of Moses and from
24 the prophets, from morning till evening. And some believed
25 the things which were spoken, and some disbelieved. And when they agreed not among themselves, they departed, after that Paul had spoken one word, Well spake the Holy Ghost
26 by Isaiah the prophet unto your fathers, saying,

'Go thou unto this people, and say,
By hearing ye shall hear, and shall in no wise understand;
And seeing ye shall see, and shall in no wise perceive:
27   For this people's heart is waxed gross,
And their ears are dull of hearing,
And their eyes they have closed;
Lest haply they should perceive with their eyes,
And hear with their ears,
And understand with their heart, and should turn again,
And I should heal them.
28 Be it known therefore unto you, that this salvation of God is sent unto the Gentiles: they will also hear[2].

23   On the *appointed day* the Jews *came to his lodging in great numbers*, and Paul made a great *exposition* of his faith, which lasted *from* early *morning till the afternoon* and reminds us of his day's work at Ephesus[4]. He spoke as an apostle, fulfilling the apostolic office of *testifying*[5]: and also as a brother, with his special power and manner of *persuading*[6]. (1) The subject of his testimony was *the kingdom of God*, which he fitly proclaimed in the capital of the world. The Messiah was king of this kingdom; and Jesus was the Messiah. (2) So *Jesus* was the object of his

---

[1] Isai vi 9-10: Mt xiii 14-5, Mk iv 12, Lk viii 10: Acts xxviii 26-7, Rom xi 8: Jn xii 39-40.   [2] Isai vi 9-10.   [3] Marg with AV and Bezan adds *And when he had said these words the Jews departed, having much disputing among themselves.*
[4] xix 9 (Bezan): our *afternoon* (3 to 5 p.m.) best represents the ancient *evening*.
[5] Lk xxiv 48, Acts i 8, xxii 15: ii 40, viii 25, x 42, xviii 5, xx 21, 24, xxiii 11.
[6] xiii 43, xviii 4, xix 8, 26, xxvi 28, II Cor v 11, Gal i 10.

persuasion—Jesus who inspired both his personal devotion and his public preaching[1]. What S. Paul persuaded *concerning* him is contained in Lk xxiv 46[2]—viz. that 'the Christ should suffer and rise again from the dead the third day.' (3) The kingdom of the Christ is the fulfilment of all that was contained in *the law of Moses and the prophets*, i.e. the old covenant: it was in fact *the hope of Israel* (verse 20)[3].

24 This exposition caused a division among the Jews. *Some were persuaded, others disbelieved*; so—to keep up the metaphor con-
25 tained in the Greek word for *agreed-not-among-themselves*—there was a discord or *breach of harmony* between them[4]. This was a sign of the fall of the kingdom of the old covenant; for a kingdom divided against itself cannot stand. This division relieved *Paul* from the necessity of further 'reasoning.' He was raised from the position of advocate to that of arbitrator, who declares the award of God in a divine *word*. He had proclaimed the kingdom of God in Christ Jesus; now through him speaks the living voice of the Spirit. The event of the day has given S. Paul a still deeper insight into the truth and meaning of the Spirit's utterances in the prophets of old, and he exclaims *Well spake the Holy Ghost*. As the spectator in the amphitheatre, at the sight of a great victory of strength and skill, exclaims 'Well done'; so in the arena of the world's history the apostle, overcome by the wonderful progress of the divine truth, exclaims 'It was well spoken.'

26-7 In repeating the divine utterance (1) S. Paul, like Isaiah, another messenger of God *unto this people*, pronounces the divine judgement upon them. Again, in so doing he resembles S. James who pronounced judgement at the council at Jerusalem in another divine word. But that word foretold the calling of the Gentiles, this word the rejection of the Jews; and from the unbelieving Jews S. Paul now finally dissociates himself—he says *your*, no longer 'our,' *fathers*. (2) In his Epistle to the Romans the apostle, in seeking to vindicate the ways of God to man, takes a wide outlook over the history of the world: he sees how good is brought out of evil, how it is the divine method to work for the many through the few, and how the rejection of the Jews led to the conversion of the Gentiles. But these thoughts are no explanation of the ultimate mystery— why does one individual believe and another disbelieve? If we answer that the one believes through the grace of God, this only drives the problem further back—why is divine grace given to one and not to another? This question must remain insoluble to finite intelligences: as Dante perceived, it is so hidden 'in the abyss of the eternal law' that it is 'cut off from all created sight[5].' But the

---

[1] xx 19, 24, xxi 13: ix 20, xvii 3, 18, cp. iv 2.   [2] Cp. Acts xvii 3, xxvi 23.
[3] ii 16, iii 18 f., x 43, xiii 27, 32 f., xv 15, xxiv 14, xxvi 22, 27: hope xxiii 6, xxiv 15, xxvi 6, 7.   [4] The corresponding noun (=*symphony*) occurs in its literal sense in Lk xv 25: the use of the verb in Acts xv 15 suggests that the new kingdom is in true harmony with the old.   [5] *Paradiso* xxi 91-6, xix 61-3.

believing Jew could find satisfaction for his intellect and peace for his heart, in the thought that the unbelief was foreseen by God: 'known to the Lord were these things from the beginning' (xv 18). This knowledge God had revealed to man in the scriptures; and the fulfilment of the scriptures in the crucifixion of the Messiah and the rejection of the Jews only disclosed the fulness of the foreknowledge and of the forbearance of God. (3) Further, their rejection was a moral judgement on the Jews. Difficulty is caused to modern thought by the form in which the prophecy is clothed in the original (and repeated in S. John): *Make the heart of this people fat...lest they see....* This suggests a Calvinistic interpretation as if men's hearts were deliberately hardened by the divine will; but this idea is due to a misunderstanding of the Hebraic idiom. The Hebrew form of expression is really the prophetical (or poetical) description of the result of disobedience; and the Greek translation in the LXX, which is given here, is a fair equivalent: *This people's heart is waxed gross.* Where there is the power of choice, there the presentation of new light or truth, if it is rejected, becomes a judgement. Before the coming of the light or truth, the darkness is not felt, the sin is dormant: when the light and truth come and are rejected, then the sin becomes alive, the darkness conscious. Accordingly, the effect of the preaching of the gospel is to harden the hearts of those who will not receive it: and this hardening is not to be thought of as a fate predestined for certain individuals, but as a judgement allowed by, and in fact the expression of, the divine law. Thus S. Paul's preaching was for life or death; wherever he went, he divided the Jews into two: they had either to believe or disbelieve[1].

28 But the divine will must ultimately prevail, although the wilfulness of man may make its path crooked. The will is that men should be saved; and if the Jews reject God's counsel for them, the *salvation of God* will be *sent to the Gentiles*. This too was written down in one of the Psalms (lxvii 2) which S. Paul here quotes. This salvation is the gift of the Holy Spirit[2]. The news of it the Gentiles *shall indeed hear*, and they will receive it with joy[3]. So through the fall of the Jews came the salvation of the Gentiles. Nor were all of the Jews rejected, *some of them believed*: Paul was himself a Jew. For the rest, S. Luke pictures them here as saying their 'Nunc Dimittis' (i.e. 'Now art thou dismissing'), but it is very different from the canticle of faithful Simeon; for they wilfully *dismissed themselves*[4], refusing to see *the salvation of God*, and so fulfilled *the word* of the Lord[5].

---

[1] II Cor ii 16: cp. xiv 1-2, xvii 4-5, 12-3, xix 9. [2] Cp. ii 17, x 45, etc.; and xiii 26. [3] as in xiii 48. [4] a more literal translation of the word for *they departed* in ver. 25. [5] Cp. Lk ii 29-32.

§ 4 *Paul the apostle: the kingdom of God*

From Jews and Gentiles we turn to those who believed. The Acts began with *the kingdom of God* (i 3) and with the kingdom of God it ends. The Lord has answered the question of the Twelve (i 6), *Dost thou at this time restore the kingdom to Israel?* The kingdom has been 'restored,' but in a manner very different from their expectations. Rejected by Israel, it has been given to the Gentiles (Lk xx 16),—proclaimed first in Sebaste the capital of the Samaritans, then in Ephesus a capital of Hellenism, and now in Rome the capital of the world[1].

30 And ²he abode two whole years in his own hired dwelling,
31 and received all that went in unto him³, preaching the kingdom of God, and teaching the things concerning the Lord Jesus Christ with all boldness, none forbidding him⁴.

30 The work of the living church is represented in the work of a person, and he is S. Paul. The note of time, *two whole years*, links on his work at Rome to that at Antioch, Corinth, Ephesus and Caesarea[5]. At Rome he 'fulfils his ministry,' which was 'to be a herald and an apostle and a teacher[6]': S. Luke represents him as *proclaiming* and *teaching*, and these functions together form the work of an 'apostle.' His method retains its catholic character: *he receives all who enter in unto him*[7], both Jews and Greeks[8]. In xix 21 he had fulfilled his ministry to the churches of the Gentiles: now he fulfils his ministry to all the world (ix 15).
31 To those without he *proclaims the kingdom*: to those within he *teaches the things concerning the Lord Jesus.* This preaching comprehends the whole message of the Gospel and Acts which was to record 'all that Jesus began both to do and to teach' (i 1). So the apostle's life-work ends in triumph (II Cor ii 14). In spite of the hatred and opposition of the Jews, he continues to proclaim his full catholic 'gospel' *with all* his characteristic *boldness* and plainness of utterance[9]; and among the Gentiles, the Romans and the powers that be, none is found to *prevent* or *hinder him.*

This triumph of the apostle is a figure of the victory of the church[10]. Her message of the kingdom has been proclaimed 'with all boldness' from the first[11]; her faith in Jesus still burns unquenched within; and no obstacles without can impede her progress. It is true that S. Paul

---

[1] viii 12, xix 8, xx 25, xxviii 23.   [2] AV and Bezan *Paul*.   [3] Bezan adds *both Jews and Greeks*.   [4] Some Bezan texts add *saying that this is Christ Jesus* (or *this Jesus is the Christ*), *the Son of God, through whom the whole world is about to be judged*.   [5] xi 26, xviii 11, xix 10, xxiv 27.   [6] II Tim iv 5, i 11.
[7] i 8, ii 39, xi 43, xiii 39, xv 17.   [8] This is Bezan and very characteristic: cp. xiv 1, xviii 4, xix 10, 17, xx 21.   [9] ix 27, 29, xiii 46, xiv 3, xix 8, xxvi 26.
[10] Cp. the conclusion of the work at Ephesus in xix 20, p. 356.   [11] ii 29, iv 13, 29, 31.

is bound; and so the church is girded about with afflictions. But 'the word of God is not bound'; and the afflictions are but the threshold to the further advance of the kingdom[1]. Each persecution has been followed by a time of peace, which in its turn was a time of preparation for a step forward[2]. So, finally, this peace at Rome is but a preparation for a fresh development. This is one reason why the Acts does not end in some great act, a dramatic scene before the emperor or the martyrdom of the apostle. For there is no end, or rather the end is but a beginning; the whole history of the church is a succession of beginnings[3]; and as such the end of the Acts resembles the end of the Gospel, where we also find added the characteristic note of joy[4].

That S. Luke intended this paragraph to form the conclusion of his book is evident from the care with which he has composed it, and from the existence of more than one 'attempt' or draft in its composition, which is supplied by the Bezan texts. From them we can restore a clause which would also form an appropriate conclusion— *saying that this Jesus is the Christ, the Son of God, through whom the whole world shall be judged.* This clause gives the full doctrine of the person of *Jesus*: to the Jews he is *the Christ*, to the Gentiles *the Son of God*, and to all men their *Judge*[5]. Then it adds the doctrine of the judgement which brings all things to an end. The day of judgement is the 'time' which will finally close the 'season' of the church's work on earth: it will bring in the restitution of all things and the complete restoration of the kingdom to Israel[6].

Epilogue

S. Luke's brief summary of the two years' work at Rome makes a fitting close to the Acts, but it does not satisfy our desire for information as to the subsequent fate of the apostle and the history of the Roman church. We are not indeed without authorities: there are the remaining epistles of S. Paul, the first epistle of S. Peter (written from Rome), the statements in Tacitus and Suetonius about the persecution of the Christians, and the traditions reported in Christian writers. Unfortunately the more light we get, the more difficult does it become to restore the exact history of events.

We have seen that the trial of S. Paul, or at least the final sentence, was delayed for two whole years, i.e. till March A.D. 60. The delay may have been due to Jewish influence, or to the indifference of the emperor, or to the simple pressure of judicial business. All this time S. Paul was living, chained to a soldier, *in his own hired dwelling*[7]. The emphasis on *his own* implies that the apostle paid the rent. It

---

[1] II Tim ii 9; Acts xiv 22.   [2] Cp. p. 223 note[1].   [3] i 1, p. 4 note[2].
[4] Lk xxiv 52; the *sitting (tarry)* of verse 49 corresponds to the *abiding* here.
[5] (*a*) ii 36, v 42, viii 5, ix 22, xvii 3, xviii 28, xxvi 23: (*b*) ix 20, xiii 33: (*c*) x 42, xvii 31.   [6] i 7, iii 21, i 6.   [7] This was probably a more permanent residence than the *lodging* (xxviii 23, cp. Philem 22) where he found hospitality for the first few days. For the bonds cp. Eph iii 1, 13, iv 1, Col i 24, iv 3, Philem 1, 9.

is true that during his confinement he received a contribution from the Philippians, but his acknowledgment of it implies that, although not 'abounding,' yet he had sufficient for his needs (Phil iv 10–19).

When the news of S. Paul's arrival had spread to the provinces, his intimate disciples gathered round him once more and correspondence was reopened with his churches. Of this correspondence we have four letters surviving, which shew that 'the care of all the churches' still pressed upon the apostle. These are the Epistles to the Ephesians, the Colossians, and Philemon, and the Epistle to the Philippians. The first three were despatched together by the same messenger Tychicus, who was accompanied by Onesimus. Their style and matter shew a great development when compared with his earlier epistles and (we may add) with Philippians; Bishop Lightfoot accordingly dated them at the end of the two years, and English opinion has generally followed him. Certainly the apostle was expecting a speedy release[1], when they were written. On the other hand, although the Ep. to the Philippians has more in common with the subject-matter of S. Paul's earlier epistles than these, its language is much more definite and clearly implies that the crisis is at hand. S. Paul has already appeared before the Praetorium, i.e. the imperial court; and there is a tone of anxiety which hangs over the epistle[2]. This may refer, however, to a preliminary examination soon after his arrival, and S. Paul's expectation of a speedy decision may have been disappointed. Still the intercourse with Philippi, implied in Phil ii 25–30, will require an interval of some months at least since his arrival at Rome.

Taken together, these four epistles give us a picture of S. Paul's company—'the brethren who were with him' (Phil iv 21), and who added another group to the church in Rome. From the Asian Epistles we learn that Timothy is with him, and he is joined with the apostle in the inscription of the Epistles. Besides Timothy there were three Jews who were 'a comfort' to S. Paul: Aristarchus who had shared the voyage and is called a 'fellow-prisoner,' Jesus Justus, and Mark the cousin of Barnabas. The breach opened at Antioch (xv 39) is now healed and S. Mark forgiven. Mark had gone with Barnabas to Cyprus. Cyprus was in close communication with Egypt, and as tradition makes S. Mark the founder of the Alexandrian episcopate it is not improbable that he had crossed over to Alexandria. Between Alexandria and Rome there was the closest intercourse; and at Rome we now find him. From among the Gentiles S. Paul had two 'fellow-workers,' Demas and Luke. S. Luke is now 'the beloved physician,' which reads like a grateful recognition of services received at his hands. It is evident that S. Paul's years at Rome, as elsewhere, were marked with sickness and suffering. Besides these S. Paul had other visitors—Tychicus, whom he employed as his messenger: Epaphras, who had brought him news of Colossae and for some reason is entitled his 'fellow-prisoner': Epaphroditus, who brought him the contribution from Philippi and fell

---

[1] Philem 22. For Tychicus Eph v 21, 22, Col iv 7–9; and Onesimus Philem 12.
[2] Phil i 12–26.

dangerously ill at Rome[1]. It may have been now also that Onesiphorus of Ephesus sought out S. Paul and was not ashamed of his chain (II Tim i 17). Lastly, among those who were drawn under S. Paul's attraction, who came to his lodging and were converted, was a runaway slave belonging to Philemon, a Christian of Colossae. His name was Onesimus and S. Paul sent him back to his master.

The Epistle to the Philippians is our chief source of information as to S. Paul's relations to the Roman Christians, and these relations are difficult to estimate. He speaks of 'all the saints, and especially they of Caesar's household' (iv 22), but there are no personal allusions; not one of the names in Rom xvi is mentioned again. S. Paul's bold witness to the gospel before the court had greatly encouraged the majority of the brethren to speak the word of God more boldly: and yet some of the preachers preached Christ out of envy, thinking to cause affliction to the imprisoned apostle (i 12-17). So the Roman church was not wholly at one with him. Later on in the epistle we find that his own company was somewhat broken up, for he complains that besides Timothy he has 'no one like-minded' who will really care for the Philippians (ii 20)[2]. There are hardly any signs of such a predominant position of the apostle in the Roman church, and of such an affectionate intimacy between him and the Roman Christians, as we should have expected. (1) This may be accounted for by his confinement. He could not attend the public worship and meetings of the church: he could only receive those who came to his house: and his missionary work lay among the public with whom he was most thrown in contact, viz. 'the praetorium,' which would denote the officials and servants of the court of appeal, together with the imperial 'household' of slaves and freedmen[3]. The uncertainty of the issue of the trial would also have been a bar to S. Paul's taking an active part in the administration of the church. (2) Again, the situation would be very intelligible, if another apostle had organized the different groups of Roman Christians into a unity; and in fact the tradition of the Roman church has always looked to S. Peter rather than S. Paul as its founder. Tradition makes S. Peter visit Rome very early, in the reign of Claudius, and a previous visit of Peter would explain S. Paul's evident hesitation in his Epistle to the Romans and his intention of visiting them as a guest rather than as an apostle or ruler. Indeed S. Peter may have been in Rome at this very time. On the other hand against these suppositions is to be balanced the silence of S. Paul and S. Luke. S. Paul's silence may be due to his extreme tact and delicacy. But if S. Peter was in Rome in 60, the union of the two 'chiefest' apostles in common work at Rome would have supplied S. Luke with a very appropriate conclusion for his book[4]. (3) A more probable explanation is to be found in the independent character of the Roman church. Christianity was, as we might say,

---

[1] See Col iv 10-4, Philem 23-4, Phil ii 25-30. [2] S. Luke must have been absent on a temporary mission. [3] i 13, iv 22. [4] Had S. Peter been at Rome, John Mark would more likely have been with him than with S. Paul.

'self-sown' at Rome. It sprang up almost spontaneously; and there was no one 'father in Christ' (I Cor iv 15) to whom the Christians were under a special obligation of obedience. At Antioch (under somewhat similar circumstances) we observed a democratic independence and freedom of spirit, and how much more may we look for the same among the Christians of Rome who would enjoy the prestige of the capital and with the spirit of Romans would tend to look down upon visitors from the provinces as 'foreigners.' The Ep. to the Romans in itself bears witness to an independence of spirit and organization[1]; and such freedom S. Paul would cordially respect. Besides, his imprisonment would have hindered the assumption of any active authority over the church. This character of the Roman church lasted on for many years. In epistolary correspondence with Rome we read of 'the church' of Rome, rather than the bishop. Bishops there were, but the capital lent the weight of its authority to the church as a whole rather than to its bishop[2].

As the result of his trial S. Paul was, in answer to his expectation, set at liberty[3]; for there was no real case against him. This fact we infer from the Pastoral Epistles, which are much later in style than those of the imprisonment, and can nowhere be fitted into the apostle's previous life. These letters shew that, after all the activity and suffering of his previous life, the apostle had passed the prime of his powers; and if S. Luke was his amanuensis (as the style suggests), he still continued at the apostle's side. Tradition, as recorded by S. Clement of Rome and the author of the Muratorian Canon, makes it probable that S. Paul at first carried out his project of visiting Spain[4]. Later, we find from I Timothy and Titus that he also returned to Greece. He visited Crete—the payment of a debt contracted at Fair Havens—and Ephesus. From Ephesus he went on to Macedonia, passing through Troas; and he was intending to spend a winter at Nicopolis in Epirus[5]. But in that—or the following—summer, the sky became suddenly overcast, his plans were once more broken and he was hurried off to Rome. On July 19, A.D. 64, the great fire of Rome burst out. When it had destroyed the greater part of the city, in order to avert the suspicion and fury of the populace from himself, Nero made the Christians his scapegoats. They were accused of having set the city on fire, and multitudes of them were put to death with most barbarous tortures. The chief scene of execution was the emperor's gardens on the Vatican hill, where the Christians were burnt as torches to illuminate games and festivities. Naturally the emperor would remember and send for 'the ringleader of the Nazarenes'

---

[1] See p. 496 note [2].   [2] This position is illustrated by Ignatius' letter to the Romans in 115. There is no mention of any bishop or rulers, and the bishop of Antioch writes to the church with great respect and humility: 'Not as Peter and Paul do I command you: they were apostles, I am one condemned.'   [3] Cp. Philem 20, Phil i 25.   [4] Rom xv 28. The Muratorian Canon speaks of his *setting forth from the city for Spain*, S. Clement says that he reached *the boundary of the west*.   [5] I Tim i 3, Tit i 5, iii 12, II Tim iv 13.

who had stood before him in 60. The blow surprised the apostle in 'Asia,' possibly at Miletus or Ephesus. Consternation fell upon the Ephesian Christians, who dared not stand by him[1]—except indeed Priscilla and Aquila, who were now at Ephesus,—and his own company of followers were dispersed. Demas apparently went to Thessalonica, Crescens to Galatia, Titus to Dalmatia. This left Luke and Erastus, Tychicus and Trophimus. But Trophimus fell sick and remained at Miletus, Erastus stayed behind at Corinth his own city, Tychicus was sent back to Ephesus with some message[2]. So only S. Luke was left with the apostle when he reached Rome. The leading Roman Christians (whose names are new to us), Eubulus, Pudens, Linus (whom tradition makes the first bishop of Rome after the apostles), and Claudia, welcomed him, but none dared appear at his first examination. It was an ordeal, like entering 'the lion's mouth.' But S. Paul was delivered. He had no difficulty probably in proving his absence from Rome. Facts however would be of little avail, and he wrote off a passionate appeal to Timothy to come to Rome before winter and to bring Mark with him[3]. The apostle knows that the end is at hand, and he is conscious that he is writing his last words (II Timothy). His apprehensions were fulfilled. Whether Timothy arrived in time we do not know, but S. Paul was condemned to death, and one day in the winter of A.D. 64–65 he was led out on the Ostian Way and there beheaded. Tradition marks the spot at the Abbey of Tre Fontane, three miles from the city gate; and his body was laid where now stands the church of S. Paolo Fuori le Mura (without-the-walls).

The same persecution was fatal to S. Peter. This apostle, after evangelizing the remaining provinces of Asia Minor,—Cappadocia, North Galatia, Pontus and Bithynia,—may have come to Rome after S. Paul's liberation in A.D. 60, and then organized the Christians into an apostolic church. He may have been in Rome when the persecution broke out, and the tradition that he was crucified on the Vatican suggests that he was one of the first victims. Against this however we have to set S. Peter's first epistle, which he wrote from Rome and sent to the Christians of Asia Minor by the hands of Silvanus,— probably the same as S. Paul's old companion, Silas. When this was written, the Christians of Asia Minor were suffering persecution, and we should naturally assume that their persecution followed after the outbreak of persecution at Rome[4]. S. Peter, then, was probably lying hid in Rome; and if by so doing he was able to cherish the fragments of the broken church[5] and to build it up again and appoint an apostolic successor, we shall better understand the position which S. Peter won in tradition of being the founder of the church of Rome. Ultimately, however, he was discovered by the authorities; and, not being a Roman

---

[1] II Tim i 15.   [2] possibly, from Rome, with the 2nd Ep. to Timothy (II Tim iv 12).   [3] See II Tim iv 9–21.   [4] Besides, S. Mark, who was away from Rome when S. Paul wrote II Timothy, had had time to reach Rome, and was with the apostle (I Pet v 13).   [5] The Roman church must have experienced a 'scattering abroad' as thorough as that of the church of Jerusalem in viii 1.

citizen, he was put to death by crucifixion in the Vatican gardens beyond the Tiber. If this happened in 67 or early in 68, it would account for the date assigned to the martyrdom of both apostles by Eusebius[1].

So the two protagonists of the church, the apostle of the circumcision and the apostle of the uncircumcision, were united in death. Their martyrdom seems pictured for us in that of the Two Witnesses in the Revelation of S. John: and it filled up the cup of Rome's iniquity, the city 'drunken with the blood of the saints and of the martyrs of Jesus[2].' These passages in the Revelation reveal the impression which their deaths made upon the Christian imagination, and not least upon that of S. John—the sole survivor of the 'pillar apostles'; for S. James was martyred by the Jews in the interval between the death of Festus and the arrival of the new governor Albinus (about A.D. 61). But if Rome triumphed over S. Peter and S. Paul, their deaths presaged the downfall of the heathen city, and their tombs were to become the glory of the Christian city. The possession of the bodies of the chief apostles was one—and not the least—cause of the future greatness of the church of Rome. In a persecution of the third century, the bodies were transferred for safety's sake to the catacombs; and the date of the translation, June 29, was henceforth observed as the Festival of the Apostles Peter and Paul[3]. Subsequently the bodies were restored to their original resting-places on the Vatican Hill and by the Ostian Way, where they now repose under the gorgeous basilicas of S. Peter's on the Vatican and S. Paul's Without-the-walls. The early calendar of A.D. 336 which marked June 29 as 'the deposition of the apostles,' marked also Feb. 22 as the accession of S. Peter to 'the (episcopal) chair[4].' Yet one more day celebrates the name of S. Peter—Lammas

---

[1] Of course this reconstruction is only conjectural. The difficulty of the subject will be seen from the various dates given by our authorities and scholars. Eusebius puts the martyrdoms of both apostles in the 13th year of Nero, i.e. about 67–68. But this is the date which he also assigns (wrongly) for the Fire of Rome. The Liberian Catalogue of A.D. 354 gives A.D. 55, some other MS authorities 57. Till recent years English writers in the main (e.g. Farrar, Conybeare and Howson) inclined to 68 (i.e. before Nero's death in June): Lewin gave 65–66 for S. Peter's martyrdom, followed by that of S. Paul in 66: Lightfoot made S. Peter die in 64, S. Paul later in (?) 67. More recently, Harnack places both deaths in 64; Turner (in Hastings' *Bible Dict.*) with a similar scheme prefers a year later, 64–65; Ramsay gives 65 for S. Paul, and 80 (!) for S. Peter: lastly Erbes (in *die Todestage etc.*, *Texte u. Untersuchungen* n. f. IV 1) maintains that S. Paul was beheaded on Feb. 22, A.D. 63, and that S. Peter suffered later, perhaps in 65. [2] Rev xi 3–13, xvii 6, xviii 20, 24. In his Gospel (xxi 18) S. John alludes to the death of S. Peter, in Rev xi 7, 8 (possibly) to that of S. Paul. [3] Unfortunately in our calendar the name of S. Paul has dropped out altogether from June 29. In the middle ages as a compensation for his memory being overshadowed by S. Peter, June 30 was marked as the commemoration of S. Paul. [4] Another date, Jan. 18, was also connected with S. Peter's chair; and in order to remove the confusion, Jan. 18 was made to celebrate his episcopate at Rome, Feb. 22 at Antioch. Erbes thinks Feb. 22 marks the date of S. Paul's execution.

Day or S. Peter's Chains, on August 1. This date perhaps marks the day of the dedication, in the 5th century, of the Church of the Apostles on the Esquiline Hill, in which church were preserved among other relics 'the chains of S. Peter.' The memory of S. Paul did not receive so much attention. In an early French martyrology, Jan. 25 is marked as 'the translation of S. Paul[1]'; and the Gothic Missal has a mass for his 'conversion.' Ultimately, by the twelfth century, Jan. 25 came to be observed as the feast of S. Paul's Conversion[2]. But if in the memories of the church of the south S. Peter stands before S. Paul, the balance has been redressed in the church of the north. For while S. Paul's of London and S. Peter's of Westminster stand like brothers side by side, S. Paul's is the cathedral church of the metropolis of England[3].

The position of the two apostles in the Roman tradition was assured from the first. About the year 95 S. Clement, the bishop of Rome and their own disciple, when writing an earnest appeal to the Corinthian Christians to heal their factions and divisions, holds up the two apostles in the forefront of the Roman martyrs as a splendid example. As this is the earliest reference to them outside the NT, the passage will form a fitting close to S. Luke's Acts of the Apostles[4].

'But,...let us come to those champions who lived very near to our time. Let us set before us the noble examples which belong to our generation. By reason of jealousy and envy the greatest and most righteous pillars of the church were persecuted, and contended even unto death. Let us set before our eyes the good apostles. There was Peter who by reason of unrighteous jealousy endured not one nor two but many labours, and thus having borne his testimony went to his appointed place of glory. By reason of jealousy and strife Paul by his example pointed out the prize of patient endurance. After that he had been seven times in bonds, had been driven into exile, had been stoned, had preached in the East and in the West, he won the noble renown which was the reward of his faith, having taught righteousness unto the whole world and having reached the farthest bounds of the West; and when he had borne his testimony before the rulers, so he departed from the world and went unto the holy place, having been found a notable pattern of patient endurance.'

DEO GRATIAS

---

[1] The meaning of this is not explained. [2] For the information given above I am mainly indebted to Duchesne's *Origines* p. 265 f. It must be remembered that the explanation of the data mainly rests upon the inferences of scholars, who do not agree on all points (e.g. as to the meaning of 'the deposition' on June 29). [3] The cathedral church of York is dedicated to S. Peter. [4] Clem. *ad Cor.* 5 (Bp Lightfoot's trans.).

INDEX

Abraham lxxiii, 49, 55, 93, 99–100, 102, 130 n, 211–4, 317 n, 395
Achaia lviii, 301: lxiv, 22, 196–7, 272–3, 296, 301–33, 335, 361, 372 n, 450
Acts xl–xli: xlviii, lxii–iv, 4, 171, 186, 342;— of Peter 3, 141;— of Paul 124, 187;— of Stephen 81;— of Philip 112;— of the Hellenists 163; — of Apollos 341
Acts of Paul and Thecla 198 n, 226–7
Africa lviii, 23, 40, 189, 337–8
Agabus xcv–vi, 172, 400–1, 411
agapé 37–40, 43, 135, 290, 377–9, 413
agora 309: 287, 297, 307–11, 330; *agoraioi* 297
Agrippa, *see* Herod
Alexander, — the Great 121, 276, 337; — the Asmonean 121;— the priest 58;— of Ephesus 368;— the pretender 498
Alexandria xxviii, 129, 342, 348, 481–2, 508; Jews of — lxi, 23, 142, 165, 240; philosophy of — 88, 101, 105, 341
Alexandrian, — synagogue 89–90; — ship 482, 497
almsgiving 148, 172–3, 183, 188: *see* collection
Ananias and Sapphira 64–7: 12, 42, 111, 118, 354
— of Damascus lxxxiii, 117 n, 129, 133–5, 424
— the high-priest 428, 430, 433, 441, 454
Angel, the — *of the* LORD 71–2, 101–2, 104, 121, 123, 177–9, 181–2
angels 91, 101–2, 149, 178–9, 486
Annas 44, 56, 58, 430
Antioch lviii, 165: xxix–xxx, lxiii, 22, 81, 84, 117, 129, 162, 179, 183–4, 237–8, 256–61, 271, 332–6; church of — lxxxiii–iv, 79–80, 164–70, 171–3, 186–93, 243–5, 255–6, 259, 268, 357, 377

Antioch of Pisidia 205–6: xxx–xxxii, 195–8, 204–22, 225, 226, 230, 235–6 274–5, 333–4
Apocalypse of Baruch 7 n, 53, 61 n
Apollos xli, lxi, lxiv, lxxxv, 23, 340–4, 348–9, 359
apologia lxiv, 92, 239, 371, 383, 404, 421, 462: *see* defence
apostasy 203, 221, 350 n, 411, 414, 421, 435, 452
Apostles, the — xli, 4–5, 7; *see* Twelve, the; lxxix–lxxxii, lxxxix, xc–xciii qualification of — 7, 12, 131, 135, 192, 469; appointment 4, 12–4, 134, 192, 424–5, 468–9; authority 12, 66–7, 83, 117, 160, 192, 223, 372;— and the council 244, 249, 254, 263, 267–9
functions of —, *bear witness* 31, 62, 73, 107, 120, 158, 215, 503; *speak the word* 60, 72, 83; *pray* 60–1, 83–4; *lay on hands* 84–5, 116–8, 237, 346, — conveying the Spirit lxxxiii, xci; *preside* 39, 42, 65; *work signs* 41, 68, 223, 327, 353; *judge* 66–7, 118–9, 201; cp. 63, 143, 383
— the foundation of the church 10, 14, 356; *fellowship of* — 83, 187; *doctrine of* — 33–4, 187, 267
apostolic college 60, 61, 68; extension of apostolate 63, 118, 131, 139, 193 (*see* Paul); *pillar apostle* 48, 246; *apostle of the Gentiles* 193, 425 =messenger 245, 255, 500
Apostles' Creed, the — xliv, lxix–lxxi, lxxvi, 24
appeal to Caesar lvii, lxv, 406, 427, 435, 452–5
appearances and visions of the Lord 5, 6, 107, 130–1, 134, 139, 322, 327, 423–5, 435, 468–9; divine epiphanies 16, 18, 61, 102
Aquila, *see* Priscilla
Arabia 24, 136, 138, 141

INDEX

archisynagôgos 207–8, 228, 326, 331, 334, 500
Areopagus 272, 302, 309–20
Aretas lxviii, 24, 138
Aristarchus xvi, xlii, 196, 295, 350, 367–9, 374–5, 436, 450, 480, 499, 508
aristocracy 222, 292, 299, 320, 444; *see* Luke
army, Roman — lvii, cxvi, 146–7, 417, 479, 499–500
Artemis 338–9, 348, 351, 364–9, 386, 395–6
ascension, the — lxx, 5, 6, 8, 18, 24, 30, 73, 107
Asia, province of — lviii, 337 : lxiv, 22, 90, 195–7, 204, 272, 274–7, 332–70, 375–97; church of — 377
asiarch 363 : 340, 352, 368, 383, 396
Assumption of Moses 53, 54, 94, 99 n, 211 n
Athens 301–3 : xxix, lix, lxiv, cxvi, 272–3, 300–20, 467
atonement, doctrine of — lxxiv, 104, 122–3, 383, 392–3
attendant cv, 199, 469
Augustus 24, 126, 146, 195, 200, 205, 230, 276, 280, 426, 452, 479
Augustus, the — 280 n, 288, 459 n, 460; *see* Caesar
Augustan cohort xlv, 479

Baptism, sacrament of holy — lxxi, lxxvi : 17, 30, 32–3, 34 n, 115–8, 123, 133–5, 159, 167, 193, 199, 202, 220, 283, 290, 326, 346, 424, 470, 472; — of John 5, 10, 13, 30, 157, 340–6; — *in the name* 32–3
barbarians lx, 224, 229, 230, 491–2
Barjesus xcvi, 65, 113, 198–203, 223
Barnabas, *see* Joseph
Barsabbas, *see* Joseph
beginning, the — xxxviii, xli, 4, 13, 52, 157–9, 248, 252, 413, 464, 467
believe lxxvii, 56, 68, 115, 121 n, 146, 167, 201, 218, 221, 290, 300, 320, 326, 344, 356, 414; *believers* lxxvi, 77; *see* faith
Bernice (Berenice) xxxiii, 449, 455–6, 459, 461, 474
Beroea 298 : 292, 298–300, 372
Bezan text xxiii–vi; readings of — 4, 47 n, 58, 60, 86, 99 n, 123, 142 n, 154, 162, 169 n, 172 n, 178, 186 n, 192 n, 198, 199 n, 218, 220, 228, 229, 243–4–5, 249, 256, 263, 266, 289, 290–1, 300–1, 321, 326 n, 331, 343–5–6, 351. 355, 367, 375 n, 381 n, 413, 420 n, 438–9, 443, 449, 451, 462, 479, 480, 482, 485 n, 497, 499–500, 506–7

bishops lxxxix, civ, 143, 180, 190, 234, 383, 387, 410, 510; see *episcopus*
Bithynia 274, 276, 379, 410
blasphemy 90–1, 94, 108, 127, 220, 288 n, 325, 419
blood 12; 264, 266, 269; 316; 326, 391; — of Christ 72, 392–3, 396
boldness 29, 59, 73, 139, 220, 229, 343, 389, 432, 473, 506
bonds or *chains* 374, 390–1, 401, 420, 426–7, 462, 466, 474, 501
breaking of bread, the — 10, 35–40, 43, 135, 188–90, 290, 377–9, 477, 490
Brethren, the — 9, 12, 77, 135, 189, 160, 179–80, 188, 214, 217, 244, 413–4 ; — *of the Lord* lxxix, xciii, 10 ; false — 246 ; — of Jews lx, 77, 255, 424, 501; spirit of brotherhood xxxiii–iv, lxxix
burial 29, 67, 100, 103, 110; — of the Lord lxx, 215

Caesar, the — 136, 297, 330, 405–6, 408, 443–4, 452, 457, 460, 479; *see* appeal, *Augustus*
Caesarea 146 : lxii, lxv, 124, 139, 146–60, 164, 179–82, 334, 399–401, 413, 439–80, 449
Caligula lvi, 23, 142, 173, 452, 457
captain, — of the temple 56, 72, 417; — of the camp xlv, 479; chief — (*chiliarch*) 147, 417, 461; — *of life* 52
catechize, etc. xxxvii, xliii, xliv, xcviii, 34, 342, 411
catholic character, — of the person of Christ lxx–lxxiii, 157, 319, 464; — of the gospel (*for all*) xxxviii, 15, 19, 31, 55, 125, 155, 158, 217, 240, 316, 318, 349, 390–1, 424, 471; realized in the history lxii–lxiv, 8, 112, 125, 141–2, 149–63, 166–9, 218–21, 238–70
Cenchreae 321, 328, 332–3, 373
census, the — of Quirinius xlv, 74, 479 n
centurions lvii, 147, 426, 439, 448, 479
charges brought against, — the Twelve 72 ; Stephen 90–3 ; 176; Paul 222, 229, 235, 288, 297, 310–1, 330, 362, 367–9, 419, 421, 443–4, 454
chief men xcix, 255
Chrestus 169–70, 297 (23)
CHRIST, the — lxxii, 30, 31, 49, 51, 58, 61, 75, 76, 93, 157, 169, 295, 325, 424, 464, 471–2, 507; *see* Messiah
Christian lxiii, cxvi, 76–7, 169–70, 186, 464, 473–4

chronology of the Acts lxv-ix, cxii-v: xliv, 172, 180, 183, 301, 329, 369, 405; 512; notes of time 169, 321, 327, 352, 389, 449, 506; *see* diary
church, the — 67, 75–80; baptism of — 14–5; history of — xxxviii–xl, 9, 110–1, 143, 164, 177–8, 187, 271–2, 326–7, 339–40, 347–50, 356, 383, 502, 506–7; — in council 266–270; life in — 31–43, 62, 273; doctrine of — lxx, lxxi, lxxvi, 66, 349, 392–3, 395, 470; marks of — 32–40, 187–8, 377; *see* catholic, *ecclesia*, kingdom
Cilicia lviii, 90, 126, 139–40, 195, 255, 256 n, 261, 306, 334, 420, 440
circumcision 102, 162, 242–6, 252, 411; — party 160, 242; — of Titus 245–6; — of Timothy 261–3
citizenship 281, 420, 432; Roman — xxviii, lv, lviii, 125–6, 147, 202–3, 255, 280, 288, 290–1, 417, 426–7, 452, 511–2
Claudius, lxviii, 23, 119, 172–3, 179, 181, 225, 291, 301, 324, 329, 408–9, 426, 455, 497
cleave stedfastly 10, 33, 43, 114 n, 148
Clement, — of Alexandria xiv, xvi, 176; — of Philippi 284; — of Rome xv, 13, 396, 513; the Clementines xl, xciii, 119
collection for the church of Jerusalem, the — 42, 171, 246–7, 335–6, 371–2, 374, 414, 447
'collegia' (guilds) 34, 36, 280
colonies, Roman — lvii, 205–6, 230, 276, 280–1, 321
Colossae 275, 337, 345, 352, 508–9
Colossians, Ep. to the —, see *Ephesians*
common 150, 152–3; 'the common (council)' 299, 363
communion, the — of the church (common life) xxxiii, 34–5, 41–2 (common goods), 62, 171–2, 187; — of the apostles 33, 377; — of saints lxxi, 35; *see* breaking of bread
community of goods, *see* communion
confirm 236, 257, 261, 334–6
confirmation, rite of — 117, 346; *see* laying-on of hands
conscience 429, 432–3, 447
conversion (*turning*) lxxvi, 53, 145, 167, 233, 469–70; — of Saul 127–8, 133; — of the Gentiles 194, 245
Corinth 321: lix, lxiv, 269, 271–3, 301, 321–333, 336, 343–4, 359, 362, 372–6, 378
I, II Corinthians, I Cor 359, II Cor 371: lxxxvi, xci–ii, cvi, 19–21, 38–40, 261, 264–5, 320, 322, 328, 340, 359–60, 371–2, 400
Cornelius lvii, lxii, 117, 120, 142, 147–59, 162–3, 241, 252, 283, 481
council at Jerusalem, the — 247–256, 262–4, 266–70, 410, 414
covetousness, *see* money
creation, doctrine of — lxx, 61, 152, 233, 315
Crete 24, 482–5, 510
crucifixion, the — 28, 52–3, 58, 73, 94, 106, 157, 214–5, 477, 502: see *suffer*
Cyprus lix, lxviii, 23, 63, 81, 139, 164–5, 198–203, 261, 398, 409, 413, 481, 508
Cyrene 10, 23, 81, 88–90, 165, 189

Damascus 129: lxii, lxvii, 81, 101, 129–39, 181, 467
Daniel liii, 72, 150, 179, 312
David lxxiii, 11, 29, 105, 191, 209, 212–7, 253
day, the — *of the* LORD 27; — *of* judgement 318–9; 502
deacons civ–vi, 42, 86, 199, 284, 350, 362
defence, the — of the church xxxix, 404–5; — of Stephen 92–106; — of Paul lxiv–v, 382–96, 406–7, 421–5, 444–7, 462–74, 500–1; see *apologia*
Derbe 195, 235–6, 262, 375
devout (Jews) 16, 110, 424; (Gentiles) 147, 219, 295
Diana, *see* Artemis
diary of journeys 376, 381, 402–3, 413, 415 n, 440–1, 482–3, 497
Didaché xcii, xcv n, xcvi, cii, cv, 82, 120, 190, 255 n, 399
Dionysius the Areopagite 292 n, 320
Disciples, the — xxxii–iii, 77, 83, 87, 138, 145, 164, 221, 223, 236, 262, 334, 345, 350, 413; Paul's — 188
discrepancies, etc. 12; 74, 420; 128, 132–3; 239–40
Dispersion, the — 22–4, 111; *see* Jews
divisions in the church xxxiv, xl; murmuring 83, contention 160, controversy 238–57, provocation 261
Dorcas xxxiii, cvi, 144–5, 283
Drusilla xxxiii, 409, 448–9, 451, 456

Earnest (intense) 177, 467
Easter 177, 191, 376–7
eating xx, 5, 36–7, 43, 135, 158, 290, 378, 477, 489–90; — unclean and idol-meats 150, 152, 240, 256, 264–6; — with Gentiles 162, 259
ecclesia 77–80, 103–4, 236–7, 327, 348, 350, 392; (assembly) 249, 257, 268; (Greek) 297, 363, 367–9· *see* church

ecstasy 139, 151, 277, 424
edify 143, 395
Egypt xciv, xcix, 23, 29, 40, 53, 99-100, 103-4, 211, 213, 481
Egyptian, the — 409, 420
election and appointment of officers 13, 83-4, 237, 262, 386; — of delegates 116, 168, 173, 244, 255, 374; the divine choice 4, 134, 211; — of S. Paul 134, 193-4, 424
Elijah (and Elisha) xlviii, 16, 53-4, 112, 121, 136, 144-5, 380, 381, 397
Ephesian, — presbyters 382-97; Jews 416, 419; magic 339, 353
Ephesians, Ep. to the — 450, 508: lxxxvii, xci, xcvii-viii, 347, 349, 356 n, 361, 384, 389-96
Ephesus 338, 363: lviii, lxiv, 197, 204-5, 271-3, 332-4, 337-57, 362-71, 381-2, 385-6, 510-1
episcopus cii-iv: lxxxvii-ix, 12, 190, 284, 351, 386; *see* bishop
Erastus xvi, xlii, 328, 350, 362, 511
Essenes 42, 75-6, 189
eucharist, *see* breaking of bread; *eucharistia* 443
Eunice 230, 235, 262, 283
eunuch, the Ethiopian — 33, 112, 120-3, 241
evangelists xcviii-ix: 112, 164, 278, 391, 399; *evangelize* 75, 111, 124, 166, 215, 233, 236, 257, 277, 310
Ezekiel 16, 72, 127, 152, 468 n

Faith lxxvii, 48-9, 52, 77, 123, 126, 155, 158, 218, 231, 237, 248, 253, 264, 313, 319, 390, 464, 470; *see believe*; —, hope, and charity 444, 465; the — lxxvi, 77, 87, 236, 264
fasting 17, 27, 131, 135, 148, 151, 189-91, 237, 378 n; the Fast 483
FATHER, GOD THE — lxx-lxxvi, 5, 7, 8, 32, 136, 216, 277, 392-3; the fatherhood of God lxx, 211, 317
Felix 409: lxvi, lxviii, 439-51, 460
fellowship, the — 34-5, *see* communion
Festus lxvi, 451-74, 480
First, the — 222, 280-1, 295, 454, 493
forgiveness of sins lxxi, lxxvi, 30, 32, 53, 135, 158, 209, 217, 470, 472
free, — *city* 293, 302, 338, 363; — *custody* 448, 450, 500, 507; *freedman* xxviii, 88, 125, 323, 409
fulfil 17, 212, 215, 237, 356, 358, 361, 385, 506

Gaius, — of Derbe 236, 374; — of Macedonia 350, 367-9; — of Corinth 325, 328, 372; — Caesar 457, *see* Caligula

Galatia 195-6: lviii, 203-237, 511; *the Phrygian and Galatian region* 222, 274-5, 334; the churches of — lxiv, 195-8, 258, 261-4, 334-6, 372
Galatians, Ep. to the — 334-6, 360: liii, lxv-vi, xcviii, 136, 138, 140, 188, 197-8, 204, 206, 211-8, 221-2, 236, 238-40, 245-7, 259
Galilee 6, 9, 75, 129, 143, 157; *Galilaeans* lxiii, 8, 25, 76
Gallio lxviii, 200 n, 329-31, 406 n
Gamaliel 45, 69, 73-4, 125-6, 423, 428
gather-together (synaxis) 61, 79, 169, 188, 237, 249, 257, 377
Gentiles, the — lix, 30, 95, 166, 213, 229, 242, 252-4, 362, 401, 414, 440, 495, 505; gospel for — 233-4, 312-9; admitted to the church 142, 148-63, 237; turning to — 167, 218-21, 296, 322, 326, 350, 504-5; conversion of — 194, 245, 469; *see* catholic, Greeks, Jews
Paul's mission to — 134, 140, 246, 258, 425, 469; apostle of — 125, 193, 194, 469
Gentile Christians 242, 245-6, 254-5, 259, 410; — churches 167, 222, 258, 272, 376-7
GHOST, GOD THE HOLY —, *see* SPIRIT
glory of God, the — lxx, 102, 106-7, 424; Jesus glorified 8, 107, 131-2; xliii, 51
God-fearing 147, 166, 211, 214, 231; see *devout*, Greeks, proselytes
gospel, the — lxx, lxxi, 25, 123, 157-8, 208-9, 214-5, 273, 283, 290, 295, 383-4, 399-91, 464-6, 471, 503-6; see *evangelize*; Gospel and Acts 4, 342
Gospel of S. Luke xxxii, 450-1; — and Acts xlvii, li, 14, 207, 358, 373, 383, 401-2, 403-4, 440, 477-8, 502
Gospels, Synoptic —, *see* oral tradition
grace lxxvii, 43, 62, 168, 213, 220, 229, 237, 253, 344, 391, 395
great 113, 339, 364, 367
Greece 372; Grecian 83, 166; *see* Hellenist
Greek civilization, *see* Hellenism; Greeks and barbarians lx, 312, 316, 461
Greeks lx, lxii, 166-9, 245, 419; *Jews and Greeks* 169, 228, 295, 324, 348, 389, 500, 506

Hand, the — of the LORD 29, 61, 167, 201
Hebraic style xvii, xix, xlvi, 11, 13, 49, 124, 128, 248, 347

Hebrew language 130, 208, 248, 421, 426, 468
Hebrews xix, 83, 125–6, 166, 240, 431, 495; Hebrew Christians 81, 83, 139, 241–2, 255, 259, 410–1; — church 167
Hebrews, Ep. to the — lxxxvii, xcix, cvii, 92–3, 102
Hellenism lx, 87, 126, 165, 206, 272, 279, 292, 302–7, 309, 321, 337–9, 341, 351
Hellenists lxi, lxii, 88–90, 95, 124, 139, 166, 240, 312, 362; Christian — 81, 83, 87–8, 110, 160, 163–8, 241–2, 255, 399; Hellenist church 167, 188
heresy, see sect
Herod the Great 46, 114, 146, 165, 189, 303, 417
— Antipas 24, 61, 138, 189, 404, 449 n
— Agrippa I 173: lxvi, 147, 172–82, 414, 448
— Agrippa II 455–6 : 134, 170, 454, 455–74
Herodian, the — family xlii, 189, 457–8; — party 76, 173
high-priest, see priests
holy, see saint; the Holy One lxxiii, 51–2, 216
hope 444, 446, 465, 486; the hope lxxiii, 406–7, 434, 467, 501

Iconium 225: 83, 195–8, 225–9, 235–6, 262–3
Ignatius, S. xv, xcvi, cii, cvi, 13, 165, 382 n, 393 n, 481
ignorance, excuse of — 53, 215, 429; times of — 233, 318
imprisonment 56, 71, 111, 174–9, 288–91; S. Paul's — 440, 448–51, 479–80, 491, 499–500, 507–10
incarnation, doctrine of the — lxxii, 152, 393, 471
inheritance 53–4, 213–4, 395
inscriptions xxxi n, xlv, xciv n, xcix n, cii n, 206 n, 280 n, 287, 293, 308, 364, 369 n, 479, 483, 493
Irenaeus, S. xiv, xvi, xxiv, xxxiii, 8, 99 n, 249 n, 278 n, 357, 382 n
Isaiah ciii, 106, 122–3, 127, 191, 216, 221, 254, 471, 503–5
Israel 25, 30, 75–9, 93, 211–3, 216, 253, 327, 395, 419, 467, 501
Italy 323, 481; Italian cohort xlv, 146–7

James, son of Alphaeus 10
— son of Zebedee 10, 174–6
— the brother of the Lord xlii,
li, lxxxiv, xciii, 10, 13, 110 n, 131, 139, 179–80, 242, 246–54, 259, 269, 410–4, 450, 512
James, Ep. of S. liv, lxxxvii, 79, 411, 494 n
jealousy (zeal) 71, 220, 222, 297; 411, 423
Jeremiah 128, 184, 172, 284, 327, 401, 433 n, 469, 477
Jerusalem lix: li–ii, lxii, 6, 9–111, 25, 57, 116, 120, 125–6, 138–41, 162, 171, 173–80, 183–4, 203, 244–56, 259, 270, 333–6, 361, 373–4, 401, 413–40, 454, 500–1; church of — 79, 110, 162–3, 168, 241–2, 244–56, 334, 410–5
JESUS 4, 9, 19, 25, 51–2, 55, 56, 59, 61, 73, 107–8, 130–1, 214–6, 276–7, 325, 341–4, 355, 460, 503–4, 507; name of — 59, 61, 75; preach — 75, 122, 138, 166, 295, 310; see Nazareth
JESUS CHRIST 145, 157, 192 (448);
name of — 30, 32, 48, 58, 159
the Lord JESUS 135, 166, 253, 290, 391, 396; name of — 346, 355, 401
the Lord JESUS CHRIST 351, 506;
name of — 256
Jews, the — and Judaism xxxix, lix–lx, 125–6, 142, 146, 280, 288, 330, 341, 344, 355, 406, 409, 436, 463, 467, 497; — of the Dispersion lx–lxi, cxvi, 22–4, 129, 165, 198, 206–8, 230, 281–2, 292–3, 299, 307, 323–4, 334, 495; — and Gentiles xl, lix–lxi, 142, 149–50, 240, 264–6, 331, 368, 374, 390–1, 407, 410, 421, 451, 463; — and S. Paul 138, 228–9, 235, 297, 300, 325, 330–1, 349–50, 352, 374, 375, 389, 416–40, 451–2, 454–5, 467, 471, 501–5; gospel for — 25–31, 48–55, 208–218, 503; brotherhood of — lx, 25, 30, 77, 214, 422, 424, 499
John, the baptist xciv, 5, 10, 30, 38, 54, 157, 176, 201, 212, 340–6, 354, 449, 457
— the apostle 9, 48, 56–60, 107, 116–7, 132, 174, 246, 340, 357, 470, 512; Gospel and Epp. of — lxxxi, lxxxviii, xci n, xcvi, 79, 108, 158, 346, 394, 470; style of — xliii, 5, 50, 56 n, 220, 221 n, 347
— Mark xlii, cv, 10, 63, 174, 178–9, 183, 197, 199, 203–5, 260–1, 278, 508, 511
— the priest 58 ; — Hyrcanus 303
Jonah 127, 134, 150, 424 n, 477
Joppa 124, 142, 145–6, 148–53
Joseph, the patriarch 93, 100, 103, 327
— of Arimathaea 10, 45, 69

Joseph Barnabas lxxxi, lxxxiv, xcv, 10, 23, 63-4, 139, 168-9, 173, 182-4, 187-94, 194-238 (203, 208, 232), 244-61 (245, 247, 256, 259, 260-1), 413
— Barsabbas 10, 13, 255
— Caiaphas 44, 56, 58, 91, 423
Josephus xviii, lxviii, 45, 57, 74, 99-103, 110 n, 126 n, 129, 146, 182, 183, 189, 282 n, 303 n, 334, 409, 415 n, 417, 420 n, 428, 436, 449 n, 451, 454 n, 458 n, 487, 498
joy and gladness xxix, xxxvi, 9, 43, 75, 115, 123, 168, 172, 221, 223, 234, 257, 284, 290, 305 n
Judaea lviii, 22, 25, 44, 74, 79, 143, 146, 173, 243, 400, 409, 440, 501
Judaizers 242, 258, 263, 292, 335-6, 372, 411
Judas, the apostle lxxviii, 10-3, 65-6, 438
— Barsabbas xcix, 255-7; — of Gamala 74-5
judgement, doctrine of — lxxi, 27, 34 n, 181-2, 218, 313, 318-9, 449, 505, 507; Jesus the judge lxxiii, 31, 155, 158, 319
Julius, — Caesar 23, 126, 277, 321; — the centurion 478-99
justification lxxvii, 155-6, 209, 217-8

King 134, 457; Jesus the—lxxiii, 209, 212-3, 297
kingdom of God, the—xxxviii, 4, 7, 34, 77, 79, 112, 214, 236, 296, 330, 342, 348-9, 391-2, 444, 470, 503, 506; *see* Messiah

Law, the — of Moses lxxvii, 87, 93-5, 104-5, 127, 149-50, 212-3, 217-8, 240-4, 254, 263, 264-6, 411, 424, 433, 471; Roman and other law 108, 111, 130, 288, 290-1, 369, 416 n, 426, 440, 444, 452, 455, 462; 'lawful religion' 288, 310, 330, 406, 444; *see* Paul
laying-on of hands 85: cii, 33, 34 n, 41, 116-8, 135, 191-3, 237, 263, 343, 346, 386, 494
life lxxi, lxxvi, 29, 52, 72, 77, 104, 144, 162, 220-1 (*eternal*)
light 130, 177, 201, 221, 379, 424, 463, 468-9, 471-2
liturgy 189-90
LORD, the — (=JEHOVAH) lxxii-iii, 49, 71, 76, 101-2, 122, 128, 136, 179, 401, 424, 462-3; Jesus the LORD 13, 30, 76, 128, 130, 137, 155, 157: 134, 229, 327, 435; lord 286 n, 289, 461

Lucius of Cyrene xlii, 23, 166, 188-9
Luke, S. xv-xvii, xxvii-xxxii: 171-2, 197-8, 204, 245, 274, 278, 281, 284, 291, 371, 376, 399-400, 414 n, 420, 436, 439, 444, 450-1, 480-1, 492, 494, 499, 508, 510; his character xxxii-xxxvi; medical knowledge xx, xxviii, xlv, 367 n, 477, 494; aristocratic sympathies xxxi, 222, 292, 299, 457
his sources xli-iv, 22, 56, 124, 189, 273, 347-8, 385, 407, 439, 459-60; honesty and fidelity xliv-vii, 13, 163, 247-9, 260, 462, 487; accuracy 200, 293, 329, 478, 493; — and Josephus xviii, 74, 182, 420 n; — and S. Paul xix-xx, 140-1, 238-40
his motives and method xxxvii-xli, xlvii-l, 56, 124, 136, 163-4, 170, 173-4, 186-7, 194, 261, 271-2, 339-40, 348, 358-9, 373, 377, 401, 403-5, 415 n, 435-6, 462-4, 476-8, 502, 507
his style 5, 31, 77, 80, 183-4, 248, 384, 432 n, 440, 459; summaries 43, 75, 263, 271, 356; notes 11-12, 68, 271; pictures 9, 32, 62, 283, 448, 476; typical pictures 1, 84, 117, 143, 207-8, 218, 249, 272; artistic sense xlvi-vii, 63, 120, 181, 292, 358, 375, 403-4, 477: compression 123, 228, 442-3, 447, 468
Lydia xxiii, cvi, 282-3, 286, 291
Lysias, Claudius 126, 417, 420, 426, 432-4, 439-40, 443, 474
Lystra 230: 195-8, 224, 229-37, 262-3

Macedonia lviii, 279: xxx-xxxi, lxiv, 196-7, 271-3, 277-301, 335, 361-2, 371-2, 374-6, 510
madness 20, 320, 473
magus 113, 200, 409; magic xxviii, xxxix, 339, 353-6
Malta 493: 489-97
Manaen xlii, 189
Mark, S., *see* John
Mark, Gospel of S. liv, 174, 450, 492
Mary, the mother of Jesus lxxiv, lxxix, cvi, 9, 14, 450
— the mother of John Mark 9, 10, 178, 183, 438
— of Bethany cvii, 10, 145 n, 283
Master xcvii, 33, 76, 137, 462 n; 61
Matthew, Gospel of S. liii-iv, lxxx, 12, 32, 72, 79 n, 174
Matthias, S. xci, 10-11, 13, 134
Messiah, the—xxxix, 25, 28-30, 45, 49-54, 58-9, 61, 73, 114, 129-30, 136-8, 158, 208, 212-5, 325, 340-4,

407, 411, 503; the Messianic kingdom, 7, 49, 53–4, 75–6, 114, 176, 502–4;—expectations 113, 155, 215, 434, 467
Miletus 237, 338, 381–2
ministry, ministration 42, 82–3, 183, 391; *minister* lxxxv, civ–vi, 42, 86, 159 n, 262, 284, 350, 362; *to minister* (of the liturgy) 189–90; see *attendant*, deacon
miracles 15–6, 19–20, 28, 41, 48, 51, 67–9, 89, 104, 114–5, 143–4, 223–5, 229, 230–1, 289, 353–5, 380–1, 494
missionary journeys lxiii, 194, 271
Mnason xlii, 10, 411, 413, 450
money, love of — etc. xxxiv, 65, 118, 166, 284, 287, 356, 362, 367, 394, 396, 449
Moses 53–4, 85, 90–1, 93–4, 100, 103–6, 127, 134, 136, 212–3, 216, 254, 327, 383, 397, 411, 464, 471, 503
multitude, the — lxxxi–ii, 9, 83–4, 188, 228–9, 237, 249, 257, 268, 350, 434

Name, the — lxxiii, 32, 49, 52, 53, 58, 76, 101, 128, 134, 253, 353; see JESUS
names xxvii–viii, xxxvii, 9, 63, 101, 113 n, 126, 170, 199, 202–3, 255, 282, 338, 341, 417, 442, 451, 455 n, 456, 460
Nazareth 57, 76, 103, 207; Jesus of— 28, 48, 58, 91, 424; Nazarenes 76, 170, 424, 443
Nazirite vow 332–3, 414–5, 416, 419, 447, 456
neôkoros 363: 293, 299
Nero 408: lii, lxvi, lxviii, 206, 405, 510
Nicodemus 10, 45, 69, 73 n, 431
Nicolas of Antioch 84, 142, 241
numbers 9, 32, 56, 87, 167, 264, 327, 347, 356, 410, 439, 490

Oral tradition, the — xliii–iv, 34, 180, 342, 396, 450–1
ordain (= *determine*) 28, 158, 173, 316; (= *marshal*) 221; cp. 7, 386
ordination or appointment 13, 63, 83–5, 191–3, 237, 263, 386

Paraclêsis xxxiii, 63, 143, 168, 208, 234, 257, 277, 291, 372, 381, 421, 462, 497
parties, — among the Jews 44–5, 75, 173, 409, 428, 433–4, 436, 441;—in the church 83, 160, 242, 258, 335, 410–1
Passover, the— 38–9, 177, 376

Pastoral Epistles, the — xvi, liii, lxvi-vii, lxxxviii, ci–ii, civ, 384, 390, 394, 433 n, 510–1
Paul, S., acts of — xlviii, lxiii–v, 124–41, 171, 186, 358–9
his origin and early life 125–7, 420, 423–4, 429, 467; appearance 227; means 408; Roman citizenship 288, 291, 426
Saul and Stephen 88, 91–2, 95;— persecutes 108–11, 467–8; his conversion 127–41, 423–4, 468–9;— visits Jerusalem 138–9, and 173, 183–4, 239, 244–56, 334, 410–5;—at Antioch 169
his ordination 188–193; and apostolate lxxxv, xcii, 134, 140, 194, 246, 424, 469–72, 506; *see* Apostles
work in Galatia 194–238, 261–3; change of name 202–3; separation from Barnabas 260–1
controversy with the circumcision party 119, 244–7, 258–9, 262–4, 335–6, 373, 411; observance of the law 332–3, 376, 414–5, 483; *see* Jews, Judaizers
mission work 272;—in Macedonia 274–301,—Achaia 301–334,— Asia 345–57; manual labour 296, 324, 351, 396; Paul and Rome 202–3, 322–4, 361–2, 372–3, 427, 435; last year's work 359–60, 367–8, 370–3; journey to Jerusalem 373–402
his process 404–507; Paul bound 420;—and the Jews at Jerusalem 419–440;— Romans at Caesarea 441–74;—appeals to Caesar 452–5; journey to Rome 479–98;—at Rome 499–507; his martyrdom 511
his sermons and speeches 208–18, 233–4, 312–9: 382–97: 421–5, 444–7: 462–72: 500–1, 503–5; doctrine and gospel 95, 136, 212–3, 217, 295, 310, 313, 349, 351, 449, 460, 463–4
miraculous power 41, 223, 231, 327, 353, 380–1, 494; visions of the Lord 130–1, 139, 327, 424, 435, 468 (cp. 486)
depression and infirmity 204, 206, 298, 300–1, 324, 360, 370, 435, 498; sufferings 134, 138, 235, 287–9, 352, 401, 419
his style 80, 92, 248, 384, 462–3; see *boldness, persuade, reason*
S. Paul and S. Peter xxxiv, xli, xlvii–ix, xciii, 56, 69, 88, 125, 144, 215, 353, 356, 380, 404, 427, 449, 477–8, 493, 512–3
Paulus, *see* Sergius
peace 79, 142, 182, 229, 256–7; 157

INDEX

Pentecost lxii, 14–9, 61, 116–8, 133, 142, 159, 345; 333, 376, 381, 413, 446
People, the — 43, 45, 48, 68, 71–3, 90, 109, 416, 428; — of God (= *láos*) 75, 79, 158, 211, 253, 327, 419, 436, 463, 500; — (= *démos*) 293, 297, 363, 367–9
Perga 203–4, 237
persecutions lii, 109–11, 173–7, 222, 229, 236, 296–8, 327–8, 405, 510–1; see peace
persuade 220, 235, 295, 324, 401, 473–4, 503
Peter, S., acts of — lxii–iii, 171; — and the Twelve xcii–iii, 9; speaks for the Twelve 12–3, 18, 60, 73; preaches 24–31, 48–55, 154–8; works miracles 48, 68–9, 145; before the Sanhedrin 56–60, 73; judges 66–7, 118–9; in Samaria 116–20; receives Saul 139, and Cornelius 141–63; delivered from Herod 174–9; — and Mark 183; circumcision controversy 242, 246–53, 258–9; subsequent history 276, 410; — and Rome 119, 179–80, 362, 496, 509; his martyrdom 511 his style etc. 24, 49–50, 60, 92 n, 247
Peter, Epp. of S. 511: lxxxvii, xci, ciii–iv, 170, 386, 394
Pharisees and Sadducees 44–5, 59, 69, 73–5, 109, 130, 305, 427–34, 436, 446; Pharisees 90; Christian — 160, 243, 245; Saul the — 125, 423, 429
Phenicia 164, 181, 245, 397–8
Philip, the apostle cxvi, 83, 399
— the evangelist xlii, lxii, lxxxii, xcv, xcviii, 84, 86, 112–5, 120–4, 142, 145, 148, 159, 241, 399–400, 449–51
Philippi, Philippians 279–80: xxix–xxxii, 196, 273, 276, 278–92, 297, 325, 371, 376, 508
Philippians, Ep. to the — 508: xvi, ciii, 189, 284, 291–2, 408, 509
Philo lxi, 23, 99–100, 103 n, 303, 341, 453
Phrygia 22, 195, 206, 225, 274
Pilate, Pontius — 44, 50, 61, 108, 115 n, 404, 417, 440 n, 444, 452, 460
Pisidia 195, 205, 237
politarch xlv, 293, 297–8
Polycarp, S. xv, xcvi, 13, 357, 370, 446
power 7, 62, 89, 138, 157, 356; 'the Power' 113, 119; powers 28, 41, 114 n, 224, 353; see miracles
praetorium 440, 449 n, 509; praetorian guard 479, 500

prayer xxxv–vi, 10, 13, 83–4, 131, 139, 148–9, 151, 177, 191, 282, 289, 396, 399, 424; prayers 13, 60–1, 108–9, 401; *the prayers* 40–1, 188, 377
predestination lxxviii, 28, 43, 221–2, 283, 504–5
presbyters, Jewish — 44, 207, xcix–c; Christian — xcix–cii: lxxxiv–vi, 67, 86, 172–3, 180, 236–7, 244–5, 249, 268, 284, 296, 328, 351, 382–3, 385–7, 410, 413–4
priests (*and* high-priests), Jewish — 44, 57–8, 87, 355, 428, 430; pagan — 232, 286, 338, 365; Christian — cvii, 189–90
Priscilla and Aquila xvi, lxviii, cvi, 323–4, 333, 343–5, 347–8, 350–1, 370, 511
proconsul xlv, lvii, 200, 329, 338, 362, 369
procurator lvii, 44, 74, 409, 439, 444–5, 451–2, 493
promise, the — 5, 30, 212, 215–6, 467
prophecy xciv–vi: OT — 16, 93; Christian — 19, 27, 257, 277, 296, 346, 390–1, 400–1
prophets xciv–vi: OT — 27–8, 29, 54–5, 99, 100–1, 106, 121, 158, 207, 212, 215, 471, 473, 504; Christian — 63, 112, 120, 172, 188–9, 191, 255, 374, 390, 400; false — 113, 115 n, 200–1, 409, 420; *the Prophet* lxxiii, 54, 104
proselytes xxix, lx, 23, 83–4, 147, 162, 166, 207, 219, 240, 495; see *devout*, *God-fearing*, *Greeks*
Psalms, The — 12, 29, 61, 78, 210 n, 212 n, 216, 392
Psalms of Solomon 8 n, 53
Publius 144, 493

Rabbis lxxxi, xcvii, 33–4, 62, 73, 76–7, 99–100, 126, 208, 343
Ramsay, Prof. xxix–xxx, xlv n, liii, lv, lxviii, 125 n, 204, 226, 229 n, 238–9, 281, 288 n, 298, 334, 345, 512 n
reason 294, 309, 324, 378, 446, 449
redeemer lxxiii, 104: redemption 392
religion 454; religious 307–8, 314; *religio licita* 288, 310–1, 330, 443–4, 446
repentance lxxvi–vii, 30, 32, 34 n, 53, 118, 143–4, 162, 212, 217, 312–3, 318, 351, 354–5, 464, 469–70
resurrection, — of the Lord lxx, 7, 29, 52, 58, 62, 73, 131, 158, 215–6, 295, 313, 319, 454, 471–2; — of the dead lxxi, 34 n, 55, 158, 310, 319, 407, 429, 434, 446, 467, 471–2; raise up 55, 216; raising the dead 145, 380

INDEX

Revelation of S. John xlviii, lii, lvi, lxxxi, lxxxviii–ix, xci, xcv, cvii, 10, 79, 107, 404, 476, 512
righteousness 52, 127, 155–6, 217, 313, 319, 429, 449; *the Righteous* lxxiii, 51, 92 n, 95, 106, 135, 424; cp. 229
roads and routes lvii–viii, 204–5, 225, 275–6, 300, 338, 345, 481
Rome and the Romans lv–lix, lxiv–v, 8, 23, 88, 119–20, 173, 202–3, 276–7, 322–4, 331, 339, 359, 361–2, 404–5, 427, 442, 444, 480, 494–513; the Roman government and provinces lviii, 195, 272, 275–6, 279, 301, 337–8, 362–3, 369, 452, 460, 478–9, 493; Rome and the Jews 44, 74–5, 146, 330, 409–10, 417, 436, 451–2; the Jews at Rome 23, 173, 323–4, 456–7, 495, 500–1; the Roman Christians 348, 495–6, 509–11; *see* army, *Augustus*, Caesar, citizenship, colonies, law, Paul, Peter
Romans, Ep. to the — 373: lxxxvi, 179, 233–4, 258, 313, 318 n, 319 n, 361–2, 411, 449
rulers of the synagogue, see *archisynagôgos*

Sadducees, *see* Pharisees; 55–6, 71, 105, 441
saint lxx–lxxi, 77, 128–9, 142, 465; *sanctify* lxxvi, 135 n, 395, 464, 470
Samaria 8, 103, 112–120, 143, 173, 245, 445; the Samaritans 112, 114–6, 120, 344, 353, 409, 428, 439
Samuel 54, 127, 130 n, 134, 212 n, 383
Sanhedrin, the — 44–5, 56–61, 69–75, 85, 90–108, 111, 125, 130, 404, 423, 427–34, 447, 454–5
Sapphira, *see* Ananias
Satan 66, 79, 201, 277, 298, 301, 470
Saul, the son of Kish 11, 127, 212–3
— the Pharisee 125–7, *see* Paul
save 31, 43, 52, 58, 77, 161, 231, 243–4, 252, 289, 478, 491; *salvation* 49–55, 59, 77, 214, 221, 232, 287, 478; doctrine of — lxxvi–vii; *saviour* 287; *the Saviour* lxxiii, 73, 103, 209, 214
scriptures, the — of the OT lxxviii, 34, 92–4, 99–102, 158, 214–5, 248, 295, 300, 344, 346, 386, 392, 394, 433, 446, 471, 473, 477, 502, 504
— quoted 11, 25–6, 50–1, 60, 95–99, 121, 209–11, 219, 250–1, 431, 503
sect 44, 71, 76, 243, 443, 446

separate 191, 350
Sergius Paulus lxviii, 200–203, 444
Servant, the — of the LORD lxxiii, lxxiv, 51, 55, 61, 122–3
serve, service, see *ministry*
Seven, the — lxxxii, xciii, 81–6, 112, 117, 180, 375, 399; cv, lxxxvii
Seventy, the — c, 10, 81, 86, 134 n; xcix
signs 28, 41, 48, 57 n, 61, 223, *see* miracles; prophetic — 172, 401
Silas lxxxv, 10, 255–7, 261, 274–5, 284–91, 297–301, 325, 334 n, 343; Silvanus 280
Simon, the Cananean 10, 75
— of Cyprus 409, 200
— of Cyrene 10, 23
— Magus xcvi, 51, 65, 112-120, 200, 353
— Niger (Symeon) 166, 189
— Peter, 130 n, 149, (Symeon) 248; *see* Peter
— the tanner 145–6, 149
sin in the church xxxiv, xxxix, 62, 64–6, 115, 118–9; *see* divisions
soldiers 177, 179, 439, 489, 491, 500, 507
Solomon 105, 122, 355; —'s Porch lxxxi, 43, 46: 18, 48, 68, 71
SON, GOD THE — lxxii–iii, 7–8, 32; the Son of God 123, 136–8, 209, 216; Son of Man 107–8; sonship 134, 211, 213
Sopater xlii, 299, 375–6
speaking with tongues 17, 19–21, 159, 346
SPIRIT, doctrine of the HOLY — lxxiv–vi: personality of — 152, 191, 276, 503; divine 401, *see* TRINITY; *the Spirit of the* LORD 66, 123; — *of Jesus* 276–7; Jesus anointed by — 157, 15; Acts the gospel of — xxxvii, 4, 342
descent of — 16–19, 27–8; the gift of — xxxviii, lxxv, 5, 29–30, 33, 115–7, 135, 156, 159, 167, 216, 252, 343, 346
— in the church xxxviii, lxx, 14–5, 24–5, 35, 66, 73, 393; — and the ministry 84–5, 262, 386
spiritual gifts xc, xciv–v, 19–21, 41, 223, 296, 328; prophecy 112, 172, 390, 398; power 7, 89, 157; *paraclesis* 143, 168; joy 223; *full of the Spirit* 83, 90–1, 107, 168
inspires prophets of the OT xciv, 60, 503; and NT (*filled with the Spirit*) 58, 62, 201, 390, 401; can be resisted 106
— guides the church xxxviii, 122–3,

INDEX

152, 191; the council 254-5, 256, 269; S. Paul 274, 276, 345, 361, 374, 375 n
Stephen, S. 88: lxii, lxxxii, 81-111, 124, 139, 163, 208-9, 222, 235, 315, 419 n, 425, 427, 468
Stoics and Epicureans 303-6, 315-7
stoning 108, 176, 235, 419; *the Stone* lxxiii, 58
suffer 50-1, 295, 471; suffering xlix, 75, 134, 236, 477
Symeon, *see* Simon
synagogue, name of — 78-9; service in the — 207-8; 40-1, 43, 89-90, 111, 130, 138, 199, 228, 240, 292, 294-5, 299-300, 307, 324-6, 334, 350, 446, 495
Syria lviii, 22, 74, 140, 146, 255-6, 261, 269, 333, 374, 440, 451

Tarsus xxix, xxxi, 125-6, 140, 169, 262, 306, 420
teach lxxxi, 75, 169, 208, 257, 295, 327, 343, 506; *the teaching* xcvii, 33-4, 187, 267, *see* oral tradition; teachers xcvi-viii, 33, 68, 188-9, 191-2
Temple, the — of Jerusalem 46-7, 416-7: 17-31, 46-56, 68, 72, 75, 91-2, 94-5, 105, 415-421, 424, 443, 446-7; Christians worship in — 10, 40, 43, 47, 413
temples 105, 315; pagan — 146, 232; T. of Artemis 338-9, 363-5, 367; *temple-robbery* 369
tempt 66, 252, 276; *temptation* 256, 389, 397
testify 31, 120, 325, 389, 391, 435, 503
Theophilus xv, xxiv, xxxvii, cxvi, 342, 451
Thessalonica 293: 196, 292-8, 300, 307, 325, 371
I, II *Thessalonians* 325: lxxxvi, xcvi, 7, 21, 288 n, 289 n, 295 n, 296-7, 301, 322, 325-6
Theudas xviii, 74
Tiberius 23, 173, 301, 324, 329, 461
times and seasons 7, 53; 233-4, 316, 318
Timothy and Titus xvi, xlii, lxxxviii-ix, cii, 198, 350, 510

Timothy cv, 191, 230, 235, 262-3, 274, 284, 291, 300-1, 307, 323-5, 340, 362, 371-2, 374-5, 508, 511; see *Pastoral Epp.*
Titus 227, 245-6, 371, 511
— Justus 326
Tobit 149 n, 179, 266 n
Trinity, doctrine of the Holy — lxxi, 32, 35, 163, 277, 393
Troas 276-8: xxx, 40, 352, 371, 375-81
Twelve, the — lxxix, xci, xciii, 3-9, 11-13, 18, 27, 37, 41, 60-2, 69-75, 83-4, 110, 116, 138-9, 160, 174, 180, 183, 450
Tychicus and Trophimus xvi, xlii, 350, 374-5, 511; 450, 508; 416, 419
Tyre (and Sidon) 164, 181, 398-9

Unanimity xxxiii, 17-8, 35, 41, 43, 60, 62, 67, 169, 254-5, 270
upper chamber 6, 9-10, 17, 60, 144, (151), 379

Virgins cvii, 400
visions, *see* appearances
vows 438; *see* Nazirite

Way, the lxxvi, 76-7, 129-31, 340-3, 347, 423, 446
we passages xvi-xvii, xxvii, 171-2, 278, 376, 414 n, 480, 499
widows cvi, 82, 145
will, the — of God lxxviii, 28, 61, 135, 212, 221, 295, 316, 361, 389-91, 401, 424
wisdom 88, 100, 103, 312, 320, 341
witness, — of apostles 7, 12, 27, 57, 62, 73, 158, 215, 424, 435, 469, 471; divine — 73, 212, 229, 252; 233
women xxxii-iii, lxxix, cvi-vii, 9-10, 111, 222, 227, 279, 282, 295, 300, 320, 399, 400
word 4, 372; *words* 31, 72; *the word* 61, 120, 157, 214, 290, 325, 328
worship 154, 234, 315, 320, 446, 460, 467, 487; Christian — 36-41, 43, 189-90, 289, 377-9

Zealots lx, 10, 75, 409, 436, 441

www.ingramcontent.com/pod-product-compliance
Lightning Source LLC
Chambersburg PA
CBHW052040290426
44111CB00011B/1566